The Insider Guide to Policy Experts 2003

The 2003 edition of *Policy Experts* was prepared by the
Heritage Foundation's Coalition Relations Department in collaboration
with Publishing Services.

Director of Coalition Relations
Bridgett G. Wagner

Deputy Director
John E. Hilboldt

Project Coordinator
Kelli B. Fulton

Staff of Publishing Services

Director: *Jonathan Larsen*

Production Editor: *Daryl Malloy*

Sr. Graphic Designer: *Brian Cobb*

Sr. Desktop Publisher: *Michelle Smith*

Production Coordinator: *Therese Pennefather*

Jr. Designer: *Suzanne Kesler*

Composition Services by Port City Press

Programmer: *Elmer Barnes*

Compositor: *Judy Krause*

THE INSIDER
GUIDE TO
POLICY EXPERTS

2003

The Definitive Directory of the
Conservative Public Policy Community

16th Edition

Edited by
Bridgett Wagner, John Hilboldt,
and Kelli Fulton

The Heritage Foundation

The Heritage Foundation, Washington, DC 20002
Copyright © 2003 by The Heritage Foundation
All rights reserved
First edition published in 1982
Sixteenth edition 2003

Published in the United States of America

Library of Congress Control Number 2002116551
International Standard Serial Number 1542-6173

ISBN 0-89195-109-1

Cover design by Suzanne Kesler
Book design by Brian Cobb and Daryl Malloy

Preface

With a demonstrated belief in the power of ideas and a firm conviction that ideas have conse-quences, the 2003 edition of *The Insider Guide to Policy Experts* is envisioned as the single-source reference to "the best and the brightest" thinkers and policy organizations throughout the United States and around the world. While uniformity of opinion is not sought, the persons listed in *Policy Experts 2003* can fairly be said to represent broadly the "conservative" or "classical liberal" point of view. By giving a voice in the policy-making process to this commonsense perspective, *Policy Experts 2003* merits a special place on the desks of journalists, congressional staff, government officials, librarians, academics, as well as the inquisitive general reader. *Policy Experts 2003* is intended to help users quickly locate leading authorities and organizations, which are actively engaged in a broad range of public policy issues, both foreign and domestic. This essential directory of the conservative public policy community represents the sixteenth such edition produced by The Heritage Foundation.

Many thanks to the many individuals who contributed to the production of this edition and its accompanying online directory, including Online Communications' Ryan Zempel and Melissa Kaiser; Coalition Relations interns Todd Baldwin, Corey Brooks, Catherine Graham, Matthew Holt, Jane Kembabazi, and Danielle Wright; and Eric Korsvall, Heritage's director of Administration.

— *The Editors*

Significant features found in this edition:

·   An Index of more than 2,200 U.S. policy experts, including complete contact information and areas of expertise.

·   An alphabetical listing of over 420 public policy organizations in the United States detailing their mission statement, priority issues, tax status, and contact information.

·   A 14-part Subject Index, featuring 161 different categories of expertise, under which the U.S. experts are classified.

·   An asterisk (*) notation identifying 970 individuals who have testified before state or federal legislative committees.

·   A separate listing of 250 international policy experts and 150 international organizations.

·   A set of printed page-edge tabs located on the first page and on the back cover for quick resource identification and location.

·   Indexes for cross-referencing experts and organizations by location, subject area, or issue, as well as a list of 112 periodicals produced throughout the public policy community.

For additional information and recent updates, visit the online edition of Policy Experts at
www.policyexperts.org

Contents

Indexes

HERITAGE MISSION

Founded in 1973, The Heritage Foundation is a research and educational institute—a think tank—whose mission is to formulate and promote conservative public policies based on the principles of free enterprise, limited government, individual freedom, traditional American values, and a strong national defense.

Heritage's staff pursues this mission by performing timely and accurate research addressing key policy issues and effectively marketing these findings to its primary audiences: members of Congress, key congressional staff members, policymakers in the executive branch, the nation's news media, and the academic and policy communities. Heritage's products include publications, articles, lectures, conferences, and meetings.

Governed by an independent Board of Trustees, The Heritage Foundation is a non-partisan, tax-exempt institution. Heritage relies on the private financial support of the general public—individuals, foundations, and corporations—for its income, and accepts no government funds and performs no contract work. More than 200,000 contributors make it the most broadly supported public policy organization in America.

Heritage Foundation Experts
and Board of Trustees

Frederick "Tripp" Baird
Director, U.S. Senate Relations

As Director of U.S. Senate Relations, Baird is responsible for educating senators and their staff about Heritage's mission and latest policy research. Before coming to Heritage, Baird worked on Capitol Hill for Senate Majority Leader Trent Lott (R–MS) for four years. Prior to that, he interned for Sen. Connie Mack (R–FL). Baird is a graduate of Florida A & M University with a bachelor's degree in political science and public administration.

William Beach
John M. Olin Senior Fellow in Economics
Director, Center for Data Analysis

Beach has developed a computer model for Heritage that estimates in detail the probable impact of such tax reform proposals as the flat tax on families and businesses. From 1981 to 1985, he served as an economist for the state of Missouri, where he designed and managed the state's econometric model and advised the governor on revenue and economic issues. A graduate of Washburn University in Topeka, Kansas, Beach earned a master's degree in history and economics from the University of Missouri–Columbia.

William J. Bennett
Distinguished Fellow, Cultural Policy Studies

Bennett holds a bachelor of arts degree in philosophy from Williams College, a Ph.D. in political philosophy from the University of Texas, and a law degree from Harvard University. Known for his advocacy of bold education reform, Bennett serves as co-director of Empower America and chairman of K12. He served as Secretary of Education and chairman of the National Endowment for the Humanities under President Ronald Reagan and director of the Office of National Drug Control Policy under President George H.W. Bush.

Herb B. Berkowitz
Senior Communications Fellow

An award-winning public relations executive and former Vice President for Communications at Heritage, Berkowitz has played a key role in making the Foundation America's best-known public policy organization. He is a former magazine writer and editor who holds a degree in journalism from George Washington University. Berkowitz writes and lectures on the U.S. news media. In 1985, under his direction, the Heritage public relations program was awarded the public relations industry's highest honor, the Silver Anvil Award from the Public Relations Society of America.

Peter Brookes
Senior Fellow for National Security Affairs
and Director, Asian Studies Center

Brookes, a former Navy aviator, CIA officer, State Department official and Capitol Hill staff member, oversees Heritage's work on economic, diplomatic, and security relations between the United States and Asia. He additionally serves as a member of the Heritage team of experts monitoring and providing ideas for the new Department of Homeland Security. Prior to joining the Foundation, Brookes served as Deputy Assistant Secretary of Defense for Asia and Pacific Affairs at the Pentagon.

Stuart M. Butler
Vice President, Domestic and Economic Policy Studies

A nationally recognized specialist on social and economic issues, Butler has co-authored *The Heritage Consumer Choice Health Plan* and *Out of the Poverty Trap: A Conservative Strategy for Welfare Reform.* He also wrote *Enterprise Zones: Greenlining the Inner Cities* and *Privatizing Federal Spending.* Dr. Butler earned a B.A. in physics and mathematics, an M.A. in economics, and a Ph.D. in American economic history from St. Andrews University in Scotland.

Ariel Cohen
Research Fellow
Kathryn and Shelby Cullom Davis Institute for International Studies

As one of Washington's leading authorities on Russian and former Soviet politics, economics, and law, Cohen often testifies before the U.S. Congress and provides media commentary on political and economic developments in Russia and Eurasia. A former member of the Board of Directors of the California–Russia Trade Association, Cohen has managed media research projects for Radio Liberty's then-Soviet audience. He earned his Ph.D. at the Fletcher School of Law and Diplomacy at Tufts University and his L.L.B. at Bar Ilan University Law School in Israel.

Charlene "Charli" Coon
Senior Policy Analyst, Energy and Environment
Thomas A. Roe Institute for Economic Policy Studies

Coon researches and writes on all aspects of energy and environmental policy. Before coming to Heritage, Coon worked for House Speaker Dennis Hastert (R–IL), the House Commerce Committee and the House Civil Service Subcommittee. Coon received her law degree from Loyola University in Chicago and a master's degree in public administration from the University of Illinois–Springfield. She holds a bachelor's degree from Arizona State University. Currently, Coon is working on a master's degree in environmental law at George Washington University.

Ambassador Henry F. Cooper, Jr.
Visiting Fellow

Ambassador Cooper served as Chairman of The Heritage Foundation's Commission on Missile Defense which prepared a comprehensive plan for building a cost-efficient, layered missile defense system. Cooper is the former director of the Strategic Defense Initiative Organization and was chief negotiator for the Defense and Space Group at the Nuclear and Space Arms Talks with the then-Soviet Union. He also has served as assistant director of the U.S. Arms Control and Disarmament Agency and as Deputy Assistant Secretary of the Air Force. A graduate of Clemson University, Cooper earned his Ph.D. from New York University.

Wendell Cox
Visiting Fellow

Cox is a noted expert on urban sprawl, smart growth and transportation issues. As principal of Wendell Cox Consultancy, an international public policy firm, he has provided consulting assistance to the U.S. Department of Transportation and public transit authorities in 49 states as well as governments in Canada, Asia, Africa, Australia, and New Zealand. He has also authored scores of monographs and book chapters addressing urban sprawl, mass transit, congestion, smart growth, transportation, and demographic trends.

Helle C. Dale
Deputy Director
Kathryn and Shelby Cullom Davis Institute for International Studies

Dale manages the Institute's research and educational programs which address national defense and homeland security matters as well as a wide range of international economic, diplomatic, and political issues. Prior to joining Heritage, she wrote extensively on U.S. foreign policy and security affairs for *The Washington Times*, ultimately serving as editorial page editor. Dale holds a degree in English Studies from Oxford University and an M.A. in English and American Studies from the University of Copenhagen. She is also a media fellow at the Hoover Institution and a board member at Georgetown University's Institute on Political Journalism.

Dana Robert Dillon
Senior Policy Analyst, Asian Studies Center

A former U.S. Army specialist on Southeast Asia, Dillon is a recognized expert on Southeast Asia policy. After graduating from Nebraska's Kearney State College with a bachelor's degree in political science, Dillon served 20 years in the U.S. Army, the last 12 as a foreign area officer specializing in Southeast Asia political and military events. Dillon also graduated from the Indonesian Language–Defense Language Institute, was a Visiting Fellow at the Institute of Southeast Asian Studies in Singapore, and attended the National University of Singapore. He earned his master's degree in Southeast Asian Studies from the University of Wisconsin.

Danielle Doane
Director, U.S. House Relations

As Director of U.S. House Relations, Doane is responsible for educating House members and their staff about Heritage's mission and latest policy research. She previously served as Director of Government Affairs for Citizens for a Sound Economy and as legislative director and ultimately chief of staff for Rep. Dan Miller (R–FL). Doane began her Washington career in Heritage's Asian Studies Center and served as assistant to the Vice President for Domestic and Economic Policy Studies. She holds a master's degree in International Management from the University of Maryland and a bachelor's degree in International Relations from Rollins College.

Becky Norton Dunlop
Vice President, External Relations

Dunlop directs the foundation's strategic outreach to conservative public policy institutions and other leadership organizations; international, state and local government officials; business leaders and grassroots policy activists. Before joining Heritage, she was the Secretary of Natural Resources for the Commonwealth of Virginia. During the 1980s, Dunlop served in the Reagan Administration as Deputy Assistant to the President with responsibility for Presidential Personnel and administration of the President's Cabinet, Senior Special Assistant to Attorney General Edwin Meese, and Assistant Secretary of the Interior. Dunlop earned her bachelor's degree from Miami University in Oxford, Ohio.

Lee Edwards
Distinguished Fellow, Center for American Studies

As a Distinguished Fellow, Lee Edwards has chronicled the definitive history of The Heritage Foundation, *The Power of Ideas: The Heritage Foundation at Twenty-Five Years.* An accomplished journalist, Edwards serves as senior editor of the *World & I* magazine and has been published in many leading magazines and newspapers. He also serves as an adjunct professor of politics at The Catholic University of America in Washington, D.C. He is president of the Victims of Communism Memorial Foundation, an organization founded to design, construct and operate an international memorial and museum in our nation's capital to the more than 100 million victims of communism. Edwards holds a bachelor's degree in English from Duke University and a doctorate in world politics from The Catholic University of America.

Ana Eiras
Latin America Policy Analyst,
Center for International Trade and Economics

Eiras specializes in Latin America and economic development as a policy analyst at Heritage. A native of Argentina, Eiras previously worked in her home country as a marketing analyst for multinational corporations such as Shell Oil and American Express. She also worked for SIBLEY International, a United States Agency for International Development (USAID) contractor, which brought her to Latin America and the former Soviet Union. Eiras holds a bachelor's degree in economics from George Mason University and is pursuing a master's degree in economics at Johns Hopkins University.

Patrick Fagan
William H.G. FitzGerald Research Fellow in Family and Cultural Issues

A former Deputy Assistant Secretary of Health and Human Services during the Bush Administration, Fagan examines the relationship between family, community, and social problems. He also studies the breakdown of the family in America, crime, the practice of religion, and cultural issues. He has served as a legislative analyst for Senator Dan Coats (R–IN) and, before becoming involved in public policy, was a family therapist, sociologist, and psychologist in the inner city and elsewhere. Fagan, a native of Ireland, earned his master's degree in psychology at University College Dublin and has pursued doctoral studies at The American University.

Megan Farnsworth
Education Fellow

Farnsworth explores the effect of Heritage's "No Excuses" Schools Project— showcasing schools with low-income students and high academic results—on education policy. Previously, she was a curriculum specialist at Walt Disney Elementary, a high-poverty school in Burbank, California. She was a bilingual third-grade and fifth-grade teacher at the Burbank Unified School District in California and a school evaluator for the Massachusetts Department of Education. Farnsworth received a bachelor's degree in classical studies from Occidental College in Los Angeles, a master's degree in education and teaching credentials at University of California, Los Angeles, and also graduated from Harvard's Graduate School of Education.

Ambassador Harvey Feldman
Senior Fellow in China Policy

A former U.S. Ambassador to Papua New Guinea and the Solomon Islands, Feldman examines U.S. policy toward the People's Republic of China and the Republic of China on Taiwan. In a foreign service career which spanned more than three decades and three continents, Feldman also served as Director of Republic of China Affairs in the State Department, where he created the American Institute in Taiwan, which handles the responsibilities of the former U.S. embassy. As an Alternate U.S. Representative to the United Nations, he served as a delegate to five General Assemblies as well as representing the United States on several Commissions.

Edwin J. Feulner, Ph.D.
President

A veteran of the national political scene, Feulner most recently served on the Congressional Commission on International Financial Institutions. A leading conservative strategist and thinker on issues from American foreign policy in the post–Cold War era to how Washington works, Feulner is a former Director of the House Republican Study Committee. Feulner also serves on the boards of several foundations and research institutes, is on the Board of Visitors at George Mason University, and is a trustee of the Acton Institute and the International Republican Institute. He also served as a consultant to President Reagan on domestic policy issues. Feulner holds a bachelor's degree from Regis University, an M.B.A. from the Wharton School, and a Ph.D. from the University of Edinburgh.

Sara Fitzgerald
Trade Policy Analyst, Center for International Trade and Economics

As trade policy analyst at the Foundation's Center for International Trade and Economics, Fitzgerald explores the link between free-trade policies and economic growth. Previously, Fitzgerald worked as lectures manager for nearly four years at Heritage. She holds a bachelor's degree in government and politics and earned a master's degree in international commerce and policy from George Mason University. Prior to joining Heritage, Fitzgerald served as project manager at Americans for Tax Reform, a Washington-based watchdog group.

Michael G. Franc
Vice President, Government Relations

A long-time veteran of Washington policymaking, Franc oversees Heritage's outreach to members of the U.S. House and Senate and their staffs. From 1993 to 1996, he served as Heritage's director of Congressional Relations. In 1996, he served as director of communications for House Majority Leader Richard Armey of Texas. Before joining Heritage, he served in the Office of National Drug Control Policy and as legislative counsel for former Rep. William Dannemeyer of California. A graduate of Yale University, Franc earned his J.D. from Georgetown University Law Center.

Barbara Hackman Franklin
Chairman, Asian Studies Center Advisory Council

Franklin utilizes her expertise on international trade policy issues to promote free trade's growth around the world. When she served as the 29th U.S. Secretary of Commerce, Franklin achieved a major goal—increasing American exports—with emphasis on market-opening initiatives in China, Russia, Japan, and Mexico. She has served four terms on the Advisory Committee for Trade Policy and Negotiations, and as an Alternative Representative and Public Delegate to the United Nations General Assembly. Currently, Franklin is president and CEO of Barbara Franklin Enterprises, an international trade consulting and investment firm.

Nile Gardiner
Visiting Fellow
Kathryn and Shelby Cullom Davis Institute for International Studies

Before joining Heritage, Gardiner did research for two years as a foreign policy analyst for Lady Margaret Thatcher in her private office in London. He is a graduate of Oxford University, where he received his Bachelor of Arts degree in Modern History. Gardiner earned both his master's and Ph.D. degree in History from Yale University, where he was awarded several academic fellowships for his doctoral research. Born in Miyazaki, Kyushu, Japan, he grew up in Harare, Zimbabwe and Oxford, England.

Jennifer Garrett
Research Associate

As a research associate, Garrett specializes in education reform and school choice. She is one of the contributors to *School Choice: What's Happening in the States*, published annually by The Heritage Foundation. She also conducts research in welfare, social policy issues, and crime. Garrett holds a bachelor's degree in social ecology from the University of California, Irvine and a master's degree in Public Administration and Policy from the University of Southern California. She studied additionally in Cambridge, England and is currently pursuing a law degree at George Mason University.

Jonathan Garthwaite
Director, Online Communications

Garthwaite oversees online projects, including the Heritage website and TownHall.com, which bring Foundation publications and events to online visitors 24 hours a day. Town Hall, launched in 1995 as the first online conservative community, combines its own issues-oriented content with that of 90 other public policy organizations and periodicals to create a unique resource for Capitol Hill staff and grassroots activists. Garthwaite, who received his B.S. degree from Colorado State University, also served as an aide to Colorado State Representative Mark Paschall, concentrating on legislation on the EPA and mandated automobile emissions testing.

James Gattuso
Research Fellow in Regulatory Policy
Thomas A. Roe Institute for Economic Policy Studies

Gattuso addresses a broad range of regulatory issues. Prior to his return to Heritage in 2002, he served as Vice President for Policy at the Competitive Enterprise Institute. Previously he has served as Vice President for Policy Development with Citizens for a Sound Economy; as Deputy Chief of the Office of Plans and Policy at the Federal Communications Commission; and as Associate Director of the President's Council on Competitiveness in the Office of Vice President Dan Quayle. Gattuso earned his undergraduate degree from the University of Southern California and received his J.D. degree from the University of California at Los Angeles.

Todd Gaziano
Senior Fellow in Legal Studies
Director, Center for Legal and Judicial Studies

Gaziano focuses on legal and judicial reform and such constitutional issues as ensuring that all citizens are accorded equal treatment under the law and the separation of powers. Before joining Heritage, Gaziano was chief counsel to the House Subcommittee on National Economic Growth, Natural Resources, and Regulatory Affairs. He also served in the Office of Legal Counsel in the U.S. Justice Department and as a judicial law clerk to Judge Edith H. Jones of the Fifth Circuit Court of Appeals. Gaziano received his J.D. from the University of Chicago Law School, where he was selected as a John M. Olin Fellow in Law and Economics.

James S. Gilmore
Distinguished Fellow

Gilmore, who served as Governor of Virginia from 1997 through 2001, focuses on developing policies to improve homeland security and to shape the growing debate on Internet taxation. He chairs the Congressional Advisory Panel to Assess Domestic Response Capabilities for Terrorism Involving Weapons of Mass Destruction, established by Congress in 1999. Gilmore also chaired the Advisory Commission on Electronic Commerce, appointed to advise Congress on the Internet taxation issue.

Alfredo Goyburu
Policy Analyst, Center for Data Analysis

As a CDA policy analyst, Goyburu focuses on Social Security and budget-related issues. He previously worked as a regional and energy economist for WEFA, a leader in economic information and forecasting. While at WEFA, he analyzed state economies and created models to forecast sales of electricity and natural gas. Before that, he worked as an economist for the New York State Legislature, studying the impact of tax policy. Goyburu holds a bachelor's degree in economics from Cornell and an advanced economics degree from the University of Albany.

Rebecca Hagelin
Vice President for Communications and Marketing

Hagelin oversees the Foundation's public relations and media outreach efforts. Prior to joining Heritage, she served as Vice President for Communications with WorldNetDaily.com. In addition to being an independent public affairs/marketing consultant, she previously was Director of Communications for Concerned Women for America and Director of Public Relations for the Center for Judicial Studies. Her articles have been featured in numerous publications, and she has appeared frequently on local and national television and radio programs. She received her B.S. in Broadcast Journalism *cum laude* from Troy State University.

Gina Marie Hatheway
Deputy Director, Government Relations

Hatheway works to advance Heritage's policy recommendations on a range of foreign policy and defense issues among decision makers in the executive branch. Before coming to Heritage, she was the senior foreign policy adviser to Sen. Mike DeWine (R–OH) and a professional staff member of the Senate Foreign Relations Committee. She also worked at the U.S. Information Agency and the State Department. Hatheway received her master's degree in public policy from Harvard University's John F. Kennedy School of Government and bachelor's degrees in political science and Spanish at the University of California, Irvine.

Rea Hederman, Jr.
Manager of Operations, Center for Data Analysis

Hederman's responsibilities include management of the Center's legislative evaluation activities and related functions. He works closely with the Center's Research & Development Project Manager to make certain that the CDA's evaluation work for the administration, Congress, the media, other think tanks, and state organizations proceeds on schedule and on budget. In addition, Hederman provides statistical analysis and econometric modeling for many key Heritage policy initiatives ranging from taxes to welfare. He is a graduate of the University of Virginia with bachelor's degrees in history and foreign affairs.

Thomas Hinton
Director, State Relations

Hinton is responsible for working with the nation's governors, state legislators, and other key state and community officials to advance Heritage's strategic outreach and communication at the state and local government levels. Prior to joining Heritage, he was a senior vice president of T-3/Family Companies, where he directed the firm's governmental affairs and customer relations efforts. Hinton was also Administrative Director of the United States Fireworks Safety Council. He served as an adviser for numerous Indiana state and local political campaigns and spoke frequently on issues affecting the family. He holds a bachelor's degree from Indiana Wesleyan University.

John Hulsman
Research Fellow, European Affairs
Kathryn and Shelby Cullom Davis Institute for International Studies

In his position as Research Fellow, Hulsman examines European security and NATO affairs, the European Union, European politics and economics, and U.S.–European trade and economic relations. He also serves as a frequent commentator on all aspects of the transatlantic relationship and global geopolitics. Prior to joining Heritage, Hulsman was a fellow in European studies at the Center for Strategic and International Studies in Washington. He also taught world politics and U.S. foreign policy at the University of St. Andrews, Scotland, where he earned his master's and doctorate degrees in modern history and international relations.

Balbina Hwang
Policy Analyst, Northeast Asia, Asian Studies Center

A native of Korea, Hwang is completing her doctoral dissertation at Georgetown University, where she also lectures. She went to South Korea as a Fulbright Scholar in 1998–99 to conduct dissertation field research and has received several writing awards, including ones from the International Studies Association and the National Capital Area Political Science Association. She earned a master's degree in international affairs from Columbia University, an MBA from the University of Virginia, and a bachelor's degree in philosophy and government from Smith College.

David John
Research Fellow, Thomas A. Roe Institute for Economic Policy Studies

John serves as Heritage's lead analyst on issues relating to Social Security reform. He previously served as administrative assistant and legislative director for Rep. Mark Sanford of South Carolina, where he developed legislation, including a Social Security reform plan. Before that, he served as a Director of Legislative Affairs at the National Association of Federal Credit Unions, as a special assistant to Rep. Matthew Rinaldo of New Jersey, and as a vice president for public policy and corporate issues at Chase Manhattan Bank. He holds a bachelor's degree in journalism and master's degrees in finance and economics from the University of Georgia.

Daniel "Stormy" Johnson, M.D.
Visiting Fellow in Health Policy

A former president of the American Medical Association, Johnson works with Heritage to promote free-market solutions to America's health care problems and keeps the medical community informed of developments to promote patient choice and health care market competition. He is a clinical professor of Radiology and Otolaryngology at Tulane University. He was co-founder and president of the American Society of Head and Neck Radiology and is a past president and chairman of the board of the New Orleans Radiology Society. Johnson earned his medical degree from the University of Texas at Galveston.

Stephen Johnson
Policy Analyst, Latin America
Kathryn and Shelby Cullom Davis Institute for International Studies

A former State Department officer, Johnson serves as the Latin America Policy Analyst for Heritage's Kathryn and Shelby Cullom Davis Institute for International Studies. During his time at the State Department, he was a writer and researcher, serving as Director of the Central American Staff Working Group and as the head of the Editorial Division of the Public Affairs Bureau. Johnson, who has lived in El Salvador, Honduras and Uruguay, earned a bachelor's degree in communications from the University of Wyoming and a master's degree in International Relations from Georgetown University.

Krista Kafer
Senior Policy Analyst, Education

As Senior Policy Analyst in Education at The Heritage Foundation, Kafer researches and writes on all aspects of education policy, including school choice, standardized testing and character education. Before coming to Heritage, Kafer was legislative director for Rep. Dave McIntosh (R–IN). She has also served as a legislative assistant for Rep. Bob Schaffer (R–CO). Kafer, a native of Littleton, Colorado, graduated from the University of Colorado at Denver with a bachelor's degree in history.

Ann C. Klucsarits
Director of Development

As Director of Development, Klucsarits assists The Heritage Foundation in fundraising. Prior to assuming her current position, she was the Director of Publishing Services, where she worked with other Heritage departments to coordinate production of the think tank's research products as well as the sales of all Heritage publications. Klucsarits previously served as Director of Marketing for the pre-eminent conservative website, Town Hall, formerly a joint venture between Heritage and *National Review* magazine, and now part of Heritage's Online Communications department. She is a graduate of The Catholic University of America.

Joe Loconte
William E. Simon Fellow in Religion and a Free Society

Loconte writes and researches under the auspices of Heritage's Center for American Studies. A regular commentator on religion, politics, and culture for National Public Radio's "All Things Considered," his articles have appeared in several major newspapers. He is the author of *God, Government and the Good Samaritan* and *Seducing the Samaritan: How Government Contracts Are Reshaping Social Services.* He earned his bachelor's degree in journalism from the University of Illinois-Urbana and is completing his master's degree in Christian history and theology from Wheaton College, Wheaton, Illinois.

Bernard T. Lomas
Counselor

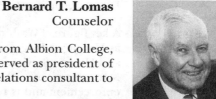

Counselor to Heritage since 1984, Lomas holds degrees from Albion College, Oberlin College, and Vanderbilt University. He previously served as president of Albion College in Michigan and as personnel and human relations consultant to American and foreign businesses and industries.

Edwin Meese III
Ronald Reagan Distinguished Fellow in Public Policy
Chairman, Center for Legal and Judicial Studies

Former U.S. Attorney General Edwin Meese was among President Reagan's most important advisors, playing a key role as Chairman of the Domestic Policy Council and the National Drug Policy Board and as a member of the National Security Council. During the 1970s, he was Director of the Center for Criminal Justice Policy and Management and a law professor at the University of San Diego and served as Chief of Staff for then-Governor Reagan. Meese is a Distinguished Visiting Fellow at the Hoover Institution and a Distinguished Senior Fellow at the Institute of United States Studies, University of London. He earned his B.A. from Yale University and his J.D. from the University of California, Berkeley.

Norbert Michel
Policy Analyst, Center for Data Analysis

Michel specializes in analyzing how public policy changes affect the U. S. economy, and he is active in the construction of the CDA's U.S. macroeconomic model. He holds a B.B.A. in finance and economics *magna cum laude* from Loyola University, New Orleans and has completed his course work toward his Ph.D. Prior to joining Heritage, Michel served as a research associate at the National Ports and Waterways Institute in Washington, D.C.

Daniel J. Mitchell
McKenna Senior Fellow in Political Economy

Mitchell is chief expert on tax policy and related economic issues at Heritage and argues for fundamental tax reform, economic growth and Social Security privatization. He also is the nation's leading opponent of tax harmonization schemes developed by the Brussels-based European Union, the Paris-based Organization for Economic Cooperation and Development (OECD), and the United Nations. Additionally, he has served as a staff economist for the National Commission on Economic Growth and Tax Reform and was a member of the Joint Committee on Taxation's Revenue Estimating Advisory Board. He holds a Ph.D. in economics from George Mason University and master's and bachelor's degrees in economics from the University of Georgia.

Robert E. Moffit
Director, Domestic Policy Studies

A key figure of Washington policymaking for more than two decades, Moffit serves as Heritage's Director for Domestic Policy. A former U.S. Department of Health and Human Services Deputy Assistant Secretary and a senior Office of Personnel Management official, he also specializes in health care policy, civil service, and law enforcement and is responsible for coordinating Heritage's research on poverty, welfare, crime, education, and family issues. Moffit earned his B.A. from LaSalle University in Philadelphia and his M.A. and Ph.D. from the University of Arizona.

Ted Morgan
Director, Information Systems

As Director of Information Systems, Morgan manages Heritage's computer and network systems, telephony infrastructure, and computer training programs. He previously served as a project manager at Heritage, overseeing database implementation and website development. Morgan received his B.S. in Computer and Information Science from the University of Maryland and is currently completing his MBA at Johns Hopkins University.

David Muhlhausen
Policy Analyst, Center for Data Analysis

As a CDA policy analyst, Muhlhausen works on domestic policy issues, focusing on criminal justice policy and evaluating the performance of government programs. Previously, he was employed at the U.S. Senate Committee on the Judiciary, where he specialized in crime and juvenile justice policy. Before coming to Washington, D.C., he was a manager at a juvenile correctional facility in Baltimore, Maryland. Muhlhausen holds a master's degree in policy sciences from the University of Maryland, Baltimore County, where he is currently pursuing a doctoral degree in policy sciences.

Lauren Noyes
Director of Research Projects

Noyes manages the Foundation's efforts to advance welfare and family policy issues. Previously, she served as Heritage's Director of U.S. House Relations. Before coming to the Foundation, Noyes was legislative director for Rep. Joseph Pitts (R–PA) and a legislative correspondent for Rep. John Shadegg (R–AZ). Prior to working on Capitol Hill, she taught high school-level English at Westminster Academy in Fort Lauderdale, Florida. Noyes graduated from Wake Forest University with a bachelor's degree in English.

Scott O'Connell
Director of Planned Giving

O'Connell is responsible for communicating Heritage's mission and goals to the think tank's members nationwide. He formerly served as Heritage's director of development, specializing in estate planning and charitable giving and played a major role in Heritage's two-year, $105 million "Leadership for America" campaign. O'Connell has worked at both the U.S. Department of Commerce and the U.S. Chamber of Commerce. He has a bachelor's degree in economics from Pennsylvania State University.

Nina Owcharenko
Policy Analyst, Health Care

Owcharenko researches and writes on all aspects of health care policy, from the debate over the "Patients' Bill of Rights" to Medicare reform. Before coming to Heritage, Owcharenko served as the legislative director for Rep. Jim DeMint (R–SC) and Rep. Sue Myrick (R–NC). She also worked for Sen. Jesse Helms (R–NC). Owcharenko received her bachelor's degree in political science from the University of North Carolina at Chapel Hill.

The Heritage Foundation

Robert Rector
Senior Research Fellow in Domestic and Economic Policy Studies

One of the leading authorities on families, poverty, and the U.S. welfare system, Rector examines the range of issues surrounding welfare reform, family breakdown, and how to rectify America's social ills. He played a major role in crafting the national welfare reform legislation passed in 1996 and has conducted extensive research on both the economic costs of welfare and welfare's role in undermining families. An expert on the political process, he also is co-editor of *Steering the Elephant: How Washington Works*. Rector holds a B.A. from the College of William and Mary and an M.A. in political science from Johns Hopkins University.

Brian Riedl
Grover M. Hermann Fellow in Federal Budgetary Affairs
Thomas A. Roe Institute for Economic Policy Studies

Riedl, who joined Heritage in 2001, received his master's degree in public affairs from Princeton University's Woodrow Wilson School of Public and International Affairs after earning his bachelor's degree at the University of Wisconsin at Madison. In addition to his academic work, Riedl worked as a field coordinator for Congressman Mark Green (R–WI), as a policy analyst for Governor Tommy Thompson, and as Deputy Policy Director for the Speaker of the Wisconsin Assembly.

Aldona Robbins
Visiting Fellow in Social Security Analysis

Robbins works with Heritage policy analysts in estimating the fiscal and economic effects of proposed reforms to Social Security's flagship program, Old-Age and Survivors Insurance. Robbins is vice president of Fiscal Associates, an expert in Social Security and other retirement programs, and has written on a wide range of issues including the retirement earnings test, the taxation of benefits, bias in the Consumer Price Index, and health care spending by the elderly. Her previous experience includes eleven years as senior economist in the Office of the Assistant Secretary for Economic Policy at the U.S. Treasury Department.

Gary Robbins
Visiting Fellow in Tax Analysis

Working with Heritage's CDA staff, Robbins is involved in efforts to institute reality based scoring by the Congress and in the construction of the CDA's second U.S. macroeconomic model. Among the handful of the nation's leading macroeconomists, he has been a major player in federal tax reform over the past twenty years and is president of Fiscal Associates. Robbins served for sixteen years in the U.S. Treasury Department, where among other acomplishments, he was one of the developers of the Treasury Tax Model, which is still the basis for revenue estimates done by the Treasury and the Joint Committee on Taxation.

Paul Rosenzweig
Senior Legal Research Fellow, Center for Legal and Judicial Studies

Before joining Heritage, Rosenzweig was in private legal practice. His prior experience includes serving as the Investigative Counsel for the House Committee on Transportation as well as Senior Litigation Counsel in the Office of the Independent Counsel. He earned a Bachelor of Arts degree in Chemistry from Haverford College and a Master of Science degree in Chemical Oceanography from the Scripps Institution of Oceanography at the University of California in San Diego. Rosenzweig received his law degree from the University of Chicago.

Robert E. Russell, Jr.
Counselor to the President

Russell has been affiliated with The Heritage Foundation since 1982, and was named Counselor in 1986. The President of Robert Russell & Associates Inc., Geneva, Illinois, Russell is a former director of the Philanthropy Roundtable. He previously served as counselor and Vice President of Marketing for Hillsdale College in Hillsdale, Michigan. Russell holds a degree from Wabash College and attended the Wharton School of Finance.

Michael Scardaville
Policy Analyst, Homeland Defense
Kathryn and Shelby Cullom Davis Institute for International Studies

Scardaville is primarily responsible for analyzing American homeland defense policy. During his time at Heritage, he has also done research on the United Nations and the Balkans, including the UN and NATO peacekeeping missions in Kosovo and Bosnia, and served as a research assistant in the Asian Studies Center. Scardaville holds a bachelor's degree in international relations from Boston University.

Brett D. Schaefer
Senior Policy Analyst, Center for International Trade and Economics
and Jay Kingham Fellow in International Regulatory Affairs

Schaefer examines such issues as international economics, international treaties, foreign assistance, and the proper role of such international institutions as the United Nations, the International Monetary Fund, and the World Bank, as well as their relationship with the United States. Schaefer earned his master's degree in international development and economics from The American University.

Kenneth E. Sheffer, Jr.
Counselor to the President

An expert in international business, Sheffer serves as counselor to the Foundation's President Edwin Feulner. For nine years, he was president of ASIA, EUROPE, AMERICA (AEA), an international trade and management consultancy based in Seoul, South Korea. Sheffer also served as staff assistant to Richard V. Allen, President Reagan's first National Security Advisor, and as a Heritage Asian Studies Center analyst.

Matthew Spalding
Director, B. Kenneth Simon Center for American Studies

An expert on the American Founding, constitutionalism, religious liberty, civil rights, and government reform and civic renewal, Spalding oversees Heritage's Center for American Studies. He is currently a visiting assistant professor of government with Claremont McKenna College. Spalding is the author of *A Sacred Union of Citizens: George Washington's Farewell Address and the American Character* and co-editor of *Patriot Sage: George Washington and the American Political Tradition*. He holds a Ph.D. in government from the Claremont Graduate School.

Jack Spencer
Policy Analyst, Defense and National Security
Kathryn and Shelby Cullom Davis Institute for International Studies

Spencer works on issues involving military readiness, force structure, roles and missions, information warfare, policies related to the revolution in military affairs, and missile defense. He holds a bachelor's degree in international politics from Frostburg State University and a master's degree in international studies from the University of Limerick. Spencer joined the Heritage Foundation in 1998 as a research assistant and authored the *Ballistic Missile Threat Handbook*.

Michael Spiller
Vice President, Information Technology

Spiller manages Heritage's team of IT professionals that includes PC support and training, network management, Internet outreach and database applications. He oversees the technology and Internet infrastructure of the Foundation. Prior to joining the Heritage staff, Spiller served as Manager of Policy Information Systems for the U.S. Chamber of Commerce. He received his Masters of Science degree in Information Technology for Business from Johns Hopkins University and his B.S. in Information Systems from the University of South Florida.

H. Baker Spring
F. M. Kirby Research Fellow in National Security Policy
Kathryn and Shelby Cullom Davis Institute for International Studies

Spring examines the threat of ballistic missiles from Third World countries and U.S. national security issues. Previously, he served as a defense and foreign policy expert in the offices of two U.S. Senators. A graduate of Washington and Lee University, Spring received his M.A. in national security studies from Georgetown University.

Mark Tapscott
Director, Center for Media and Public Policy
Marilyn and Fred Guardabassi Fellow

A veteran Washington journalist, Tapscott oversees the Media Visitor's Center, works to establish domestic and international fact-finding tours for journalists, and forges links between Heritage's Center for Data Analysis and the nation's top practitioners of computer-assisted reporting. He also organizes issues seminars that allow national and international journalists and top policy analysts to discuss how critical stories are developing. Tapscott has been a newspaper editor and reporter since 1985. Before that he was a Capitol Hill press secretary and manager of one of the Reagan Administration's most successful agency public relations programs.

Virginia L. Thomas
Director, Executive Branch Relations

As Director of Executive Branch Relations, Thomas works to advance Heritage's policy recommendations on a range of foreign and domestic issues among decision-makers in the executive branch. Previously, Thomas served as Heritage's senior fellow in government studies. Her work helped guide the implementation of the Government Performance and Results Act, which requires government agencies to define their missions and set performance goals so Congress can better carry out its oversight responsibilities. She holds a graduate and an undergraduate degree from Creighton University.

John J. Tkacik, Jr.
Research Fellow in China Policy, Asian Studies Center

Tkacik studies policies and events concerning China, Taiwan, Hong Kong, and Macao. Prior to joining Heritage, he served as the head of China Business Intelligence, a consulting firm, and as publisher of the newsletter, *Taiwan Weekly Business Bulletin*. He also was a foreign service officer in the State Department from 1971 to 1994, stationed in China, Hong Kong, and Taiwan. From 1996 to 1997, Tkacik was Vice President for External Relations for Asia at R.J. Reynolds Tobacco International. He received his bachelor's degree in international relations from Georgetown University and a master's degree in public administration from Harvard.

Phillip N. Truluck
Executive Vice President

Truluck is Heritage's chief operating officer, responsible for overseeing all day-to-day operations. During 1982 and 1983, he served on the Executive Committee of the President's Private Sector Survey on Cost Control, more commonly known as the Grace Commission. Before joining Heritage in 1977, he was on the staffs of Sen. Strom Thurmond (R–SC) and Rep. Ben Blackburn (R–GA) and served as Deputy Director of the Republican Study Committee. He is a founding director of the Board of Directors of the Center for International Private Enterprise, an affiliate of the National Endowment for Democracy, where he served from 1983 to 1991.

Jason Turner
Visiting Fellow

Before his association with Heritage, Turner served from 1998–2001 as New York Mayor Giuliani's Welfare Commissioner, creating the largest work program in the country and implementing the Mayor's Healthstat initiatives. Prior to this, he was one of the chief architects of the Wisconsin welfare-to-work program under former Governor Tommy Thompson and leader of the policy group that designed "Wisconsin Works." Turner also worked as Director of Family Assistance at the U.S. Department of Health and Human Services during the first Bush Administration.

Ronald Utt
Herbert and Joyce Morgan Senior Research Fellow
Thomas A. Roe Institute for Economic Policy Studies

Utt conducts research on housing, transportation, federal budgetary matters and privatization issues. He has served as staff director for a subcommittee of the Senate Committee on Government Affairs; vice president of the National Chamber Foundation, where he created and edited the *Journal of Economic Growth* and the *Journal of Regulation and Social Costs*; and president of Potomac Renovations. In 1987, President Reagan appointed him to be the first director of privatization at the U.S. Office of Management and Budget. Utt earned his doctorate from Indiana University and his bachelor's degree from Pennsylvania State University.

Yevgeny Volk
Moscow Office Coordinator

A native of Russia, Volk is an international security and economics expert who heads Heritage's Moscow Office. He serves as a liaison between Heritage and Russian reformers struggling to make their country a more democratic, free-market society. Volk is former deputy director of the Russian Institute for Strategic Studies and previously was advisor to the Supreme Soviet of the Russian Federation. He is a graduate of the Moscow State Institute of International Relations.

Visit our regularly updated web site www.policyexperts.org

John Von Kannon
Vice President and Treasurer

As Vice President and Treasurer, Von Kannon oversees Heritage's development operations. He is a former publisher of *The American Spectator*. Von Kannon previously served as vice president of the Pacific Legal Foundation in Sacramento, CA, and as president of Russell & Von Kannon, a Chicago-based marketing and consulting firm. A graduate of Indiana University, Von Kannon is a Senior Fellow at the Foundation for Research on Economics and the Environment in Bozeman, Montana.

Bridgett G. Wagner
Director, Coalition Relations

As Director of Coalition Relations, Wagner serves as Heritage's liaison to conservative policy organizations and experts at the state, national and international levels, and she advises state think tanks on ways to build support for their policy prescriptions. She is a member of the President's Advisory Council of the State Policy Network and a trustee of the International Policy Network. Wagner edits the *policyexperts.org* online directory and its accompanying biennial publication, and she oversees the work of the Heritage Job Bank, Intern Program, and Speaker's Bureau. She earned her bachelor's degree in economics from the University of Dallas.

Malcolm Wallop
Chung Ju-Yung Fellow for Policy Studies

In this position, Senator Wallop focuses on U.S. trade and security policy toward Asia, with a special emphasis on the future of the Korean Peninsula. He analyzes relations between North and South Korea and produces policy studies on the eventual reunification of the two. He also promotes enhanced two-way trade between Asia and the United States, producing studies that identify barriers to such trade and developing policies to remove them. Elected to the U.S. Senate in 1976, he held his seat for 18 years, retiring in 1994. He holds a bachelor's degree from Yale University.

Dana White
International Communications Associate
and Director of the Washington Roundtable for the Asia–Pacific Press

Dana White joined Heritage after working as a publicist at the Fox News Channel. Previously, she served as East Asian Affairs legislative aide and then as deputy press secretary for the House Republican Conference. White received her bachelor's degree in East Asian Languages and Civilizations from the University of Chicago in 1998. Proficient in Mandarin Chinese, White also studied at Capital University of Business and Economics in Beijing and did post-graduate work at Hankuk University for Foreign Studies in Seoul, South Korea.

Walter E. Williams
Distinguished Scholar

Williams, the John M. Olin Distinguished Professor of Economics at George Mason University, is a nationally syndicated columnist, lecturer, social critic, and author of over 60 publications. He holds a B.A. degree in economics from California State University and an M.A. and a Ph.D. in economics from the University of California, Los Angeles. In addition, he holds a Doctor of Humane Letters degree from Virginia Union University.

Larry M. Wortzel
Vice President and Director
Kathryn and Shelby Cullom Davis Institute for International Studies

Wortzel is the senior managing officer in charge of Heritage's foreign and defense policy research, including the Asian Studies Center, the Center for International Trade and Economics, and Heritage's Moscow Office. Previously, he was Director of the Foundation's Asian Studies Center for three years. A retired U.S. Army Colonel who served in military and diplomatic posts throughout Asia, Wortzel was Director of the Strategic Studies College in Carlisle, Pennsylvania. He is a graduate of the Armed Forces Staff College, the U.S. Army War College, and attended the National University of Singapore. He earned his B.A. from Columbus College, Georgia, and his M.A. and Ph.D. from the University of Hawaii.

Heritage has flown the flag for conservatism over this last quarter-century with pride and distinction. I've always considered America fortunate in having an apparently inexhaustible supply of conservative thinkers prepared to challenge the fashionable liberal consensus.

– Baroness Margaret Thatcher

The Heritage Foundation

List of Subject Headings and Topics

List of Subject Headings and Topics

U.S. Experts

*Abraham, Dr. Henry J.
James Hart Professor, Emeritus
906 Fendall Terrace
Charlottesville, VA 22903-1617
804-924-3958   fax 804-924-3359
Issues: Church-state relations; Civil rights/racial preferences; Constitutional law; Free Speech; Immigration; Judicial activism/judicial reform; Religious freedom

Abraham, Jane
President
Susan B. Anthony List
1800 Diagonal Road, Suite 285
Alexandria, VA 22314-5404
703-683-5558   fax 703-549-5588
info@sba-list.org
Issues: Family and children

Abram, Theodore David
Executive Director
American Institute for Full Employment
2636 Biehn Street
Klamath Falls, OR 97601
800-562-7752   fax 541-885-7454
teda@jeld-wen.com
Issues: Job training/welfare to work; Poverty and dependency; Social Security and retirement; Unemployment insurance; Welfare/welfare reform

*Achilles, Dr. Charles M.
Professor, Education Leadership, College of Education
Eastern Michigan University
Ypsilanti, MI 48197
734-487-0255   fax 734-487-4608
plato9936@yahoo.com
Issues: Federal education policy; Higher education; Public school finance and administration

Adams, Rev. David L.
Associate Professor
Concordia Seminary
801 DeMun Street
St. Louis, MO 63105
314-505-7654   fax 314-505-7001
Issues: Church-state relations; Family and children; Religion and public life; School choice

Adams, Dr. Jefferson
Professor, Department of History
Sarah Lawrence College
One Meadway
Bronxville, NY 10708
914-395-2446   fax 914-395-2663
jadams@mail.slc.edu
Issues: Central and Eastern Europe; Intelligence gathering and covert operations; Western Europe

*Adams, Stephen
Executive Director
Pioneer Institute for Public Policy Research
85 Devonshire Street, 8th Floor
Boston, MA 02190
617-723-2277   fax 617-723-1880
sadams@pioneerinstitute.org
Issues: Economic forecasting; The Economy; Energy; Entrepreneurship/free enterprise; Government debt; Government waste; Infrastructure; Job training/welfare to work; State and local public finance; Taxation/tax reform; Transportation; Urban sprawl/livable cities

Addison, Dr. John T.
Professor of Economics, Department of Economics
University of South Carolina
Darla Moore School of Business
Columbia, SC 29208
803-777-4608   fax 803-777-6876
ecceaddi@moore.sc.edu
Issues: Job training/welfare to work; Labor and employment; Minimum wage; Unemployment insurance; Unions

Adelman, Carol
Senior Fellow
Hudson Institute
1015 18th Street, N.W., Suite 300
Washington, DC 20036
202-223-7770   fax 202-223-8537
info@hudsondc.org
Issues: Economic development/foreign aid; Trade

---

* Has testified before a state or federal legislative committee

Adelman, Dr. Ken L.
Defense Host
TechCentralStation
P. O. Box 33705
Washington, DC 20033
800-619-5258   fax 202-530-0255
Issues: American diplomacy/foreign policy;
Arms control; Intelligence gathering and
covert operations; Missile defense; Readiness
and manpower; Terrorism and international
crime; United Nations

*Adie, Dr. Douglas K.
Professor of Economics
Ohio University
P. O. Box 500
Athens, OH 45701
740-593-2040   fax 740-593-0181
adie@ohio.edu
Issues: The American Founding; Minimum
wage; Privatization/Contracting-out;
Regulatory reform

Adkinson, William F.
Senior Policy Counsel
Progress & Freedom Foundation
1401 H Street, N.W., Suite 1075
Washington, DC 20005
202-289-8928   fax 202-289-6079
mail@pff.org
Issues: Anti-trust; Intellectual property;
Regulatory reform

*Adler, Jonathan H.
Assistant Professor of Law, School of Law
Case Western Reserve University
11075 Euclid Avenue
Cleveland, OH 44106-7148
216-368-2535   fax 216-368-2086
jhadler@earthlink.net
Issues: Advocacy and nonprofit public funding;
Air; Climate change; Constitutional law; Costs
and benefits of regulation; Environmental
education; Environmental regulation;
Federalism; Free-market environmentalism;
Land use; Non-governmental organizations;
Property rights; Regulatory budgeting;
Regulatory reform; Stewardship; Unfunded
mandates; Urban sprawl/livable cities; Waste
management; Water; Wildlife management/
endangered species

*Agee, Mary Cunningham
Executive Director
The Nurturing Network
P. O. Box 1489
White Salmon, WA 98672
800-866-4666   fax 509-493-4027
mcagee@msn.com
Issues: Abstinence and out-of-wedlock births;
Adoption, foster care, & child care services;
Ethics; Faith-based and volunteer initiatives;
Family and children; Home schooling; Media
and popular culture; Philanthropy; Political
correctness and multiculturalism; Religion and
public life

*Agresto, Dr. John
John Agresto and Associates
609 Old Taos Highway
Santa Fe, NM 87501
505-983-9625
Issues: American history/political tradition;
Arts, humanities and historic resources;
Conservative thought; Higher education;
Philanthropy; Political correctness and
multiculturalism; Political philosophy;
Standards, curriculum, and testing

*Aguirre, Robert
1017 North Main Avenue, Suite 222
San Antonio, TX 78212-4721
210-299-1171   fax 210-299-4076
rba@onr.com
Issues: School choice

Ahiakpor, Dr. James C. W.
Professor and Chairman, Department of
Economics
California State University, Hayward
Hayward, CA 94542-3068
510-885-3137   fax 510-885-4796
jahiakpo@csuhayward.edu
Issues: Africa; Economic development/foreign
aid; Economic theory

*Ahmad, Dr. I. Dean
President
Minaret of Freedom Institute
4323 Rosedale Avenue
Bethesda, MD 20814
301-907-0947   fax 301-656-4714
ahmad@minaret.org
Issues: Adoption, foster care, & child care services; Church-state relations; Citizenship and civil society; Comparative government; Constitutional law; Economic development/ foreign aid; Electoral reform/voting rights; Ethics; Family and children; Free-market environmentalism; Human rights; Land use; Middle East; Promoting democracy/public diplomacy; Property rights; Religion and public life; Religious freedom; School choice; State and local government; Terrorism and international crime

*Aldridge, M. Gene
President and CEO
New Mexico Independence Research Institute
2401 Nieve Lane
Las Cruces, NM 88005
505-523-8700   fax 505-523-8800
gsaldridge@zianet.com
Issues: Aging/elder care; American diplomacy/ foreign policy; The American Founding; China; Economic development/foreign aid; Economic education; Health care reform; Higher education; Homeland security/civil defense; Immigration; Latin America; Media and popular culture; Mexico; School choice; Southeast Asia (including Burma, Cambodia, Laos, Vietnam, Singapore, Malaysia, Indonesia, the Philippines, Australia, and New Zealand); State and local government; Taxation/tax reform; Terrorism and international crime; Trade; Western Europe

Alexander, Dr. Benjamin
Professor, English Department
Franciscan University of Steubenville
100 Franciscan
Steubenville, OH 43952
740-283-6261   fax 740-283-6401
bbeben@aol.com
Issues: Abstinence and out-of-wedlock births; Arts, humanities and historic resources; Citizenship and civil society; Faith-based and volunteer initiatives; Federal education policy; Higher education; Media and popular culture; Political correctness and multiculturalism; School choice; Standards, curriculum, and testing

Alexander, Dr. Donald L.
Professor, Economics Department
Western Michigan University
1903 West Michigan Avenue
Kalamazoo, MI 49008-5023
269-387-5526   fax 269-387-5637
donald.alexander@wmich.edu
Issues: Anti-trust; Costs and benefits of regulation; Telecommunications and the Internet

*Alexander, Dr. Lawrence
Professor of Law
University of San Diego School of Law
5998 Alcala Park
San Diego, CA 92110
619-260-2317   fax 619-260-4728
larrya@acusd.edu
Issues: Church-state relations; Civil rights/racial preferences; Constitutional law; Criminal law and procedure; Electoral reform/voting rights; Federalism; Free Speech; Political correctness and multiculturalism; Religious freedom

Alger, Judy
President
Center for Market-Based Education, Inc.
P. O. Box 373
Rumney, NH 03266-0373
603-786-9562   fax 603-786-9463
choiceforchildren@juno.com
Issues: Home schooling; School choice

Allen, Jeanne
President
Center for Education Reform
1001 Connecticut Avenue, N.W., Suite 204
Washington, DC 20036
202-822-9000   fax 202-822-5077
cer@edreform.com
Issues: Business and education partnerships; Charter schools; Education unions and interest groups; Public school finance and administration; School choice; Standards, curriculum, and testing

Allen, Richard V.
1615 L Street, N.W., Suite 900
Washington, DC 20036
202-737-2824   fax 202-783-0228
Issues: American diplomacy/foreign policy; Northeast Asia

---

*Allen, Dr. William
Professor, Department of Political Science
Michigan State University
307 South Kedzie Hall
East Lansing, MI 48824-1032
517-432-9967   fax 517-432-1091
allenwi@pilot.msu.edu
Issues: American history/political tradition;
Arts, humanities and historic resources;
Citizenship and civil society; Civil rights/racial
preferences; Congress; Conservative thought;
Constitutional law; Electoral reform/voting
rights; Ethics; Executive Branch/The
Presidency; Federalism; Higher education;
Judiciary; Political correctness and
multiculturalism; Political philosophy; The
Reagan legacy; Religion and public life; School
choice; Standards, curriculum, and testing;
State and local government

Almasi, David W.
Executive Director, Project 21
National Center for Public Policy Research
777 North Capitol Street, N.E., Suite 803
Washington, DC 20002
202-371-1400   fax 202-408-7773
project21@nationalcenter.org
Issues: Civil rights/racial preferences; Costs and
benefits of regulation; Environmental
education; Environmental regulation; Free-
market environmentalism; Media and popular
culture; Property rights; Right to work; Urban
sprawl/livable cities

*Alpert, Dr. William T.
Associate Professor, Department of
Economics
University of Connecticut
One University Place
Stamford, CT 06901-2315
203-251-8413   fax 203-384-0564
alpert@uconn.edu
Issues: Davis-Bacon Act; Economic education;
Family and medical leave; Minimum wage;
Philanthropy; Unions

Alston, Dr. Lee J.
Professor of Economics, and Director,
Program on Environment and Behavior,
Institute of Behavioral Sciences
University of Colorado-Boulder
483 UCB
Boulder, CO 80309-0483
303-492-4257   lee.alston@colorado.edu
Issues: Agriculture; American history/political
tradition; Comparative government; Economic
development/foreign aid; Latin America;
Property rights

*Amacher, Dr. Ryan C.
Professor of Economics and Public Affairs
University of Texas, Arlington
Box 19479
Arlington, TX 76019
817-272-3888   fax 817-468-2972
amacher@rmi.net
Issues: Comparative economics; Higher
education; State and local public finance

Ames, Dr. Bruce N.
Professor, Children's Hospital Oakland
Research Institute
University of California, Berkeley
401 Barker Hall, Number 3202
Berkeley, CA 94720-3202
510-450-7625   fax 510-597-7128
bnames@uclink4.berkeley.edu
Issues: Agriculture; Air; Government health
programs; Regulatory reform; Sound science;
Waste management; Water

Andelson, Dr. Robert V.
Distinguished Research Fellow
American Institute for Economic Research
534 Cary Drive
Auburn, AL 36830
334-887-5957   fax 334-887-6461
rvandelson@mindspring.com
Issues: Ethics; Political philosophy; Property
rights; Taxation/tax reform; Urban sprawl/
livable cities

Andereggen, Dr. Anton
Professor
Lewis and Clark College
0615 S.W. Palatine Hill Road
Portland, OR 97219
503-557-2314   fax 503-557-2314
andereggen@attbi.com
Issues: Africa; Bilingual education; Western
Europe

Anderson, Dr. Annelise

Senior Research Fellow
Hoover Institution
Stanford University
Stanford, CA 94305
650-723-3139　　fax 650-723-1687
andrsn@hoover.stanford.edu
Issues: The Reagan legacy

Anderson, Barbara

Executive Director
Citizens for Limited Taxation and
Government
P. O. Box 408
Peabody, MA 01960
508-384-0100　　cltg@cltg.org
Issues: Federal budget; International tax
policy/tax competition; Taxation/tax reform

Anderson, Dr. Brian C.

Senior Editor, *City Journal*
Manhattan Institute for Policy Research
52 Vanderbilt Avenue
New York, NY 10017
212-599-7000　　fax 212-599-0371
banderson@city-journal.org
Issues: The American Founding; Church-state
relations; Citizenship and civil society; Civil
rights/racial preferences; Conservative
thought; Constitutional law; Ethics; Faith-based
and volunteer initiatives; Family and children;
Judiciary; Marriage and divorce; Police;
Political correctness and multiculturalism;
Political philosophy; Religion and public life

*Anderson, Hon. Carl A.

Supreme Knight
Knights of Columbus
One Columbus Plaza
New Haven, CT 06510
203-772-2130　　fax 203-865-2310
carl.anderson@kofc-supreme.com
Issues: Church-state relations; Faith-based and
volunteer initiatives; Family and children;
Marriage and divorce; The Reagan legacy;
Religion and public life; Religious freedom

*Anderson, Edward C.

National Arbitration Forum
P. O. Box 50191
Minneapolis, MN 55405
651-631-1105　　fax 651-631-0802
eanderson@arb-forum.com
Issues: Judicial activism/judicial reform; Tort
and liability reform

Anderson, Eloise

Director, Program for the American Family
Claremont Institute
1127 11th Street, Suite 206
Sacramento, CA 95814
916-446-7924　　fax 916-446-7990
eloisea@msn.com
Issues: Abstinence and out-of-wedlock births;
Adoption, foster care, & child care services;
Aging/elder care; Family and children; Job
training/welfare to work; Labor and
employment; Marriage and divorce; Poverty
and dependency; State and local government;
Substance abuse; Welfare/welfare reform

Anderson, Ford A., II

Senior Advisor
State Policy Network
5736 Still Forest Drive
Dallas, TX 75252
972-931-6408　　drewa50@aol.com
Issues: Arts, humanities and historic resources;
Citizenship and civil society; Faith-based and
volunteer initiatives; Non-governmental
organizations; Philanthropy; Promoting
democracy/public diplomacy

Anderson, Martin

Keith and Jan Hurlbut Senior Fellow
Hoover Institution
Stanford University
Stanford, CA 94305
650-723-4742　　fax 650-723-0309
mca@hoover.stanford.edu
Issues: The Economy; Higher education; Missile
defense; The Reagan legacy; Regulatory
reform; Trade; Welfare/welfare reform

Anderson, Terry L.

Executive Director
PERC – The Center for Free Market
Environmentalism
502 South 19th Avenue, Suite 211
Bozeman, MT 59718-6827
406-587-9591　　fax 406-586-7555
tla@perc.org
Issues: Environmental regulation; Free-market
environmentalism; Property rights;
Stewardship; Wildlife management/
endangered species

*Andrews, Lewis
Executive Director
Yankee Institute for Public Policy Studies
Trinity College, P. O. Box 260660
Hartford, CT 06126
860-297-4271   fax 860-987-6218
info@yankeeinstitute.org
Issues: Bilingual education; Business and
education partnerships; Charter schools;
Education unions and interest groups; Federal
education policy; Free-market
environmentalism; Higher education; Home
schooling; Public school finance and
administration; School choice; School-to-work;
Standards, curriculum, and testing; Urban
sprawl/livable cities

*Angell, Martin
Director
A Choice for Every Child Foundation
9805 Walnut Street, Suite C206
Dallas, TX 75243
972-699-3446
mtylerangell@earthlink.net
Issues: Public school finance and
administration; School choice

Annunziata, Dr. Frank
Chairman, Department of History
Rochester Institute of Technology
92 Lomb Memorial Drive
Rochester, NY 14623
585-475-6981   fax 585-475-7120
fxagsh@rit.edu
Issues: American history/political tradition;
Conservative thought; Faith-based and
volunteer initiatives; Philanthropy; Political
correctness and multiculturalism; Political
philosophy; The Reagan legacy; Religion and
public life

Ansell, Damon
Vice President of Policy
Americans for Tax Reform
1920 L Street, N.W., Suite 200
Washington, DC 20036
202-785-0266   fax 202-785-0261
dansell@atr.org
Issues: Africa; American history/political
tradition; Campaign finance reform;
Comparative economics; Comparative
government; Congress; Conservative thought;
Economic theory; Elections/polling;
Entrepreneurship/free enterprise; Federal
budget; International tax policy/tax
competition; The Reagan legacy; Regulation
through litigation; State and local public
finance; Taxation/tax reform; Transportation;
Transportation deregulation; Unfunded
mandates; Wealth creation/financial
empowerment

*Anthony, Prof. Robert A.
Foundation Professor of Law
George Mason University School of Law
3301 North Fairfax Drive
Arlington, VA 22201-4426
703-993-8046   fax 703-993-8088
ranthony@gmu.edu
Issues: Regulatory reform

Antonucci, Michael
Director
Education Intelligence Agency
P. O. Box 580007
Elk Grove, CA 95758
916-422-4373   fax 916-392-1482
educationintel@aol.com
Issues: Education unions and interest groups

*Antos, Joseph
Resident Scholar
American Enterprise Institute
1150 17th Street, N.W.
Washington, DC 20036
202-862-5938   fax 202-862-7177
jantos@aei.org
Issues: Government health programs; Health
care reform; Medicare

Applegate, David L.
Olson & Hierl, LTD
20 North Wacker Drive, Floor 36
Chicago, IL 60606
312-580-1180   fax 312-580-1189
dapp993@aol.com
Issues: Intellectual property; Privacy;
Telecommunications and the Internet

*Appling, Julaine K.
Executive Director
Family Research Institute of Wisconsin
222 South Hamilton Street, Suite 23
Madison, WI 53701
608-256-3228   fax 608-256-3370
fri@fri-wi.org
Issues: Abstinence and out-of-wedlock births;
Adoption, foster care, & child care services;
Aging/elder care; American history/political
tradition; Charter schools; Church-state
relations; Citizenship and civil society; Ethics;
Family and children; Free Speech; Home
schooling; Judicial activism/judicial reform;
Marriage and divorce; Privacy; Religious
freedom; School choice; Second Amendment;
Standards, curriculum, and testing; State and
local public finance; State-sponsored gambling

*Aquila, Prof. Dominic A.
Ave Maria University
300 West Forest Avenue
Ypsilanti, MI 48197
734-283-6343   daquila@franuniv.edu
Issues: Abstinence and out-of-wedlock births;
American history/political tradition; Arts,
humanities and historic resources; Citizenship
and civil society; Conservative thought; Family
and children; Federalism; Home schooling;
Media and popular culture; Philanthropy;
Political philosophy; Religion and public life

Arkes, Dr. Hadley
Edward N. Ney Professor of American
Institutes, Political Science Department
Amherst College
206 Converse Hall
Amherst, MA 01002
413-542-2293   fax 413-542-2264
hparkes@amherst.edu
Issues: Constitutional law; Ethics; Judiciary;
Political philosophy; Religion and public life

*Armentano, Dr. Dominick T.
Professor Emeritus
University of Hartford
200 Bloomfield Avenue
West Hartford, CT 06115
772-234-3793   armentad@irene.net
Issues: Anti-trust

*Armor, Dr. David J.
Professor of Public Policy, School of Public
Policy
George Mason University
Finley 201B
Fairfax, VA 22030
540-987-9712   fax 540-987-9031
darmor@gmu.edu
Issues: Civil rights/racial preferences; Family
and children; Readiness and manpower;
School choice; Standards, curriculum, and
testing; Substance abuse

*Armstrong, Dr. Frank H.
Associate Professor Emeritus
University of Vermont
7 Deborah Drive
Burlington, VT 05403-7816
802-658-2042   fax 802-658-2042
farmst1037@aol.com
Issues: Forestry and national parks; Higher
education; State and local government

Arnn, Dr. Larry P.
President
Hillsdale College
33 East College Street
Hillsdale, MI 49242
517-437-7341   fax 517-437-3923
Issues: The American Founding; American
history/political tradition; Citizenship and civil
society; Higher education; Religion and public
life; Standards, curriculum, and testing

Arnold, Dr. N. Scott
Professor of Philosophy
University of Alabama, Birmingham
407D Humanities Building, 900 13th Street
Birmingham, AL 35294-1260
205-934-8292   fax 205-975-6639
sarnold@uab.edu
Issues: Ethics; Political philosophy

Arnold, Ron
Executive Vice President
Center for the Defense of Free Enterprise
12500 N.E. 10th Place
Bellevue, WA 98005
425-455-5038   fax 425-451-3959
Issues: Agriculture; Air; Economic education;
Energy; Forestry and national parks; Property
rights; Waste management; Water; Wildlife
management/endangered species

*Aron, Dr. Leon
Resident Scholar
American Enterprise Institute
1150 17th Street, N.W.
Washington, DC 20036
202-862-5898   fax 202-862-7177
laron@aei.org
Issues: Russia and Eurasia

Aronoff, Dr. Craig E.
Dinos Eminent Scholar of Private Enterprise
Kennesaw State College
1000 Chastain Road
Kennesaw, GA 30144
770-423-6045   fax 770-423-6721
Issues: Business and education partnerships;
The Economy; Entrepreneurship/free
enterprise; Family and children; Taxation/tax
reform

*Arrison, Sonia
Director, Center for Technology Studies
Pacific Research Institute
755 Sansome Street, Suite 450
San Francisco, CA 94111
415-989-0833   fax 415-989-2411
Issues: The Economy; Entrepreneurship/free
enterprise; Intellectual property; Political
philosophy; Privacy; State-sponsored gambling;
Telecommunications and the Internet

Ashford, Dr. Nigel
Senior Program Officer
Institute for Humane Studies at George
Mason University
3301 North Fairfax Drive, Suite 440
Arlington, VA 22201
703-993-4913   fax 703-993-4890
nashford@gmu.edu
Issues: Comparative government; Conservative
thought; Political philosophy; The Reagan
legacy; Western Europe

Asmus, Dr. Barry
Senior Economist
National Center for Policy Analysis
8777 East Via de Ventura, Suite 175
Scottsdale, AZ 85258
480-596-3442   fax 480-596-4051
barryasmus@aol.com
Issues: Economic education; Political
philosophy

*Aswad, Charles N., M.D.
Executive Vice President
Medical Society of the State of New York
420 Lakeville Road
Lake Success, NY 11042
516-488-6100   fax 516-488-6136
caswad@mssny.org
Issues: Health care reform

*Atkins, Chris
Director, Tax and Fiscal Policy Task Force
American Legislative Exchange Council
1129 20th Street, N.W., Suite 500
Washington, DC 20036
202-466-3800   fax 202-466-3801
catkins@alec.org
Issues: State and local public finance; Taxation/
tax reform

*Atwood, Thomas C.
President
National Council For Adoption
225 North Washington Street
Alexandria, VA 22314
703-299-6633   fax 703-299-6004
tatwood@adoptioncouncil.org
Issues: Abstinence and out-of-wedlock births;
Adoption, foster care, & child care services;
Citizenship and civil society; Conservative
thought; Faith-based and volunteer initiatives;
Family and children; Federalism; Marriage and
divorce; Religion and public life; Taxation/tax
reform; Unfunded mandates

Auchterlonie, Bryan
Vice President and Executive Director,
Collegiate Network
Intercollegiate Studies Institute
3901 Centerville Road, P. O. Box 4431
Wilmington, DE 19807-0431
800-225-2862   fax 302-652-1760
bauchterlonie@isi.org
Issues: Higher education

Avery, Alex
Director of Research and Education, Center
for Global Food Issues
Hudson Institute
742 Opie Street
Staunton, VA 22401
540-337-6354   fax 540-337-8593
cgfi@rica.net
Issues: Agriculture; Climate change; Forestry
and national parks; Sound science; Waste
management; Water; Wildlife management/
endangered species

*Avery, Dennis T.
Director, Center for Global Food Issues
Hudson Institute
P. O. Box 202
Churchville, VA 24421
540-337-6354   fax 540-337-8593
cgfi@rica.net
Issues: Agriculture; Climate change; The
Economy; Environmental education;
Environmental regulation; Forestry and
national parks; Sound science; Trade; Wildlife
management/endangered species

*Ayittey, Dr. George
Associate Professor, Department of
Economics
American University
4400 Massachusetts Avenue, N.W.
Washington, DC 20016
202-885-3779   fax 202-885-3790
ayittey@american.edu
Issues: Africa; International finance and
multilateral banks; Promoting democracy/
public diplomacy

*Azis, Prof. Iwan
Professor
Cornell University
7 Lowell Place
Ithaca, NY 14853
607-257-8341   fax 607-255-6681
ija1@cornell.edu
Issues: Comparative economics; Economic
forecasting; The Economy; Money and
financial services; Trade

Bacevich, Prof. Andrew J.
Professor, Department of International
Relations
Boston University
152 Bay State Road
Boston, MA 02215
617-358-0194   fax 617-358-0190
bacevich@bu.edu
Issues: American diplomacy/foreign policy;
Military strategy; Readiness and manpower

Backstrom, Brian
Vice President
Empire Foundation for Policy Research
Four Chelsea Place, Second Floor
Clifton Park, NY 12065
518-383-2877   fax 518-383-2841
empire@capital.net
Issues: Charter schools; The Economy;
Education unions and interest groups; Higher
education; Public school finance and
administration; School choice; Standards,
curriculum, and testing; State and local public
finance; Taxation/tax reform; Term limits;
Unfunded mandates; Welfare/welfare reform

Baden, Dr. John
Chairman
Foundation for Research on Economics and
the Environment
945 Technology Boulevard, Suite 101F
Bozeman, MT 59715
406-585-1776   fax 406-585-3000
jbaden@free-eco.org
Issues: Forestry and national parks; Land use;
Property rights; Sound science; Wildlife
management/endangered species

Bader, Lawson R.
Director of Economic Education
Mercatus Center at George Mason University
3301 North Fairfax Drive, Suite 450
Arlington, VA 22201-4433
703-993-4940   fax 703-993-4935
lbader@gmu.edu
Issues: Economic education; Economic
forecasting

Baer, Dr. Richard A., Jr.
Professor of Natural Resources
Cornell University
Fernow Hall
Ithaca, NY 14853
607-255-7797   fax 607-255-0349
Issues: Church-state relations; Environmental
education; Ethics; Higher education; Land use;
Political philosophy; Religion and public life;
Religious freedom; School choice

Bailey, Karen
State Projects Manager
Americans for Tax Reform
1920 L Street, N.W., Suite 200
Washington, DC 20036
202-785-0266   fax 202-785-0261
kbailey@atr.org
Issues: Initiative and referendum; State and
local government; Taxation/tax reform

Bainbridge, Stephen M.
Professor of Law, School of Law
University of California at Los Angeles
405 Hilgard Avenue, Box 951476
Los Angeles, CA 90095-1476
310-206-1599   fax 310-825-6023
bainbrid@law.ucla.edu
Issues: Economic theory; Entrepreneurship/
free enterprise; Federalism

*Baird, Dr. Charles W.
Director, Smith Center for Private Enterprise
Studies
California State University, Hayward
25800 Carlos Bee Boulevard, MB 2597
Hayward, CA 94542-3095
510-885-3275   fax 510-885-4222
cbaird@csuhayward.edu
Issues: Davis-Bacon Act; Entrepreneurship/free
enterprise; Minimum wage; Right to work;
School choice; Taxation/tax reform; Unions

Baird, Tripp
Director, U.S. Senate Relations
The Heritage Foundation
214 Massachusetts Avenue, N.E.
Washington, DC 20002
202-608-6070   fax 202-675-1778
tripp.baird@heritage.org
Issues: Congress

Baker, Brent
Vice President
Media Research Center
325 South Patrick Street
Alexandria, VA 22314
703-683-9733   fax 703-683-9736
bbaker@mediaresearch.org
Issues: Media and popular culture;
Telecommunications and the Internet

Baker, Hunter
Director of Public Policy
Georgia Family Council
5380 Peachtree Industrial Boulevard, Suite
100
Norcross, GA 30071-1565
770-242-0001   fax 770-242-0501
hunter@gafam.org
Issues: Abstinence and out-of-wedlock births;
Adoption, foster care, & child care services;
Church-state relations; Citizenship and civil
society; Constitutional law; Family and
children; Marriage and divorce; Religion and
public life; Religious freedom; School choice;
State-sponsored gambling; Welfare/welfare
reform

*Baker, Dr. John S., Jr.
Professor of Law, Paul M. Hebert Law Center
Louisiana State University
Dalrymple and Highland Streets
Baton Rouge, LA 70803
225-578-8846   fax 225-578-5935
jbaker@lsu.edu
Issues: American history/political tradition;
Church-state relations; Citizenship and civil
society; Civil rights/racial preferences;
Congress; Conservative thought;
Constitutional law; Criminal law and
procedure; Ethics; Executive Branch/The
Presidency; Federalism; Free Speech; Higher
education; Home schooling; Homeland
security/civil defense; Judicial activism/
judicial reform; Judiciary; Public interest law;
The Reagan legacy; Religious freedom; School
choice; Tort and liability reform

Baker, Joshua K.
Staff Attorney
The Marriage Law Project
3600 John MacCormack Road, N.E.
Washington, DC 20064
202-319-6755   fax 202-319-4459
jbaker@marriagewatch.org
Issues: Constitutional law; Family and children;
Marriage and divorce

*Baker, Dr. Keith G.
Senior Vice President
Florida TaxWatch Research Institute, Inc.
106 North Bronough Street
Tallahassee, FL 32302-2209
850-222-5052   fax 850-222-7476
kbaker@floridataxwatch.org
Issues: Business and education partnerships;
Congress; Costs and benefits of regulation; The
Economy; Entrepreneurship/free enterprise;
Federalism; Government waste; Higher
education; Infrastructure; Privatization/
Contracting-out; Standards, curriculum, and
testing; State and local government; State and
local public finance; Taxation/tax reform;
Telecommunications and the Internet;
Transportation; Unfunded mandates

*Baker, M. Miller
McDermott, Will & Emery
600 13th Street, N.W.
Washington, DC 20005
202-756-8233   fax 202-756-8087
mbaker@mwe.com
Issues: Constitutional law; Elections/polling;
Electoral reform/voting rights; Executive
Branch/The Presidency; Homeland security/
civil defense; Judicial activism/judicial reform;
Judiciary

Balch, Dr. Stephen H.
President
National Association of Scholars
221 Witherspoon Street, 2nd Floor
Princeton, NJ 08542-3215
609-683-7878   fax 609-683-0316
balch@nas.org
Issues: Higher education; Standards,
curriculum, and testing

Baldacchino, Joseph
President
National Humanities Institute
P. O. Box 1387
Bowie, MD 20718-1387
301-464-4277   fax 301-464-4277
jb@nhinet.org
Issues: Arts, humanities and historic resources;
Church-state relations; Constitutional law;
Ethics; Federalism; Political philosophy

Baldwin, Steve
10329-A Democracy Lane
Fairfax, VA 22030
703-890-0113   fax 703-890-0121
baldwins@adelphia.net
Issues: Family and children

*Baliunas, Sallie
Staff Astrophysicist
Harvard University
M.S. 15, 60 Garden Street
Cambridge, MA 02138
617-495-7415   fax 617-495-7049
baliunas@cfa.harvard.edu
Issues: Climate change; Energy; Environmental
education; Research funding; Sound science

Ball, Carlos
Editor
Agencia Interamericana de Prensa
Economica
7172 Montrico Drive
Boca Raton, FL 33433
561-393-0592   fax 561-393-0594
ball.aipe@worldnet.att.net
Issues: American diplomacy/foreign policy;
Economic development/foreign aid;
Immigration; Latin America; Promoting
democracy/public diplomacy

Ball, Dr. David S.
Associate Professor, Department of
Economics
North Carolina State University
4148 Nelson Hall, Box 8110
Raleigh, NC 27695
919-515-3275   fax 919-515-7873
david_ball@ncsu.edu
Issues: Economic education; Political
philosophy; Trade

Ball, Whitney L.
Executive Director
DonorsTrust
111 North Henry Street
Alexandria, VA 22314
703-535-3563   fax 703-535-3564
wball@donorstrust.org
Issues: Citizenship and civil society; Faith-based
and volunteer initiatives; Philanthropy

Ball, Dr. William
Associate Professor, Department of Political
Science
Northern Michigan University
252 Magers Hall
Marquette, MI 49855
906-227-1821   fax 906-227-1819
wball@nmu.edu
Issues: Economic development/foreign aid;
Southeast Asia (including Burma, Cambodia,
Laos, Vietnam, Singapore, Malaysia, Indonesia,
the Philippines, Australia, and New Zealand)

*Ballard, Charles A.
Founder and Chief Executive Officer
Institute for Responsible Fatherhood and
Family Revitalization
9500 Arena Drive, Suite 400
Largo, MD 20774-3716
301-773-2044   fax 301-773-4298
irffr@hotmail.com
Issues: Civil rights/racial preferences;
Corrections and sentencing; Crime/crime
statistics; Family and children; Marriage and
divorce; Welfare/welfare reform

*Balling, Dr. Robert C.
Director, Office of Climatology
Arizona State University
Tempe, AZ 85287
480-965-6265   fax 480-965-1473
robert.balling@asu.edu
Issues: Climate change

Ballou, Dr. Dale
Associate Professor, Department of
Economics
University of Massachusetts
Thompson Hall
Amherst, MA 01003
413-545-6358   fax 413-545-2921
Issues: Education unions and interest groups;
Standards, curriculum, and testing

*Balogh, Dr. Bela A.
Professor of Psychology
University of Mary
7500 University Drive, South Campus
Bismarck, ND 58501
701-255-7500   fax 701-255-7687
babalogh@umary.edu
Issues: Juvenile justice; Substance abuse

*Balogh, Dr. Sandor
Professor Emeritus
Hudson Valley Community College
7 Greenbush Avenue
East Greenbush, NY 12061
518-477-5476   fax 518-477-8647
Issues: American diplomacy/foreign policy;
Central and Eastern Europe; Conservative
thought; Constitutional law; Faith-based and
volunteer initiatives; Family and children;
Federalism; Human rights; International
organizations (European Union, OECD, etc.);
Judicial activism/judicial reform; Promoting
democracy/public diplomacy; Religious
freedom; United Nations

*Bandow, Doug
Senior Fellow
Cato Institute
1000 Massachusetts Avenue, N.W.
Washington, DC 20001
202-842-0200   fax 202-842-3490
dbandow@cato.org
Issues: Adoption, foster care, & child care
services; American diplomacy/foreign policy;
Campaign finance reform; Defense budget;
Economic development/foreign aid;
Emerging threats/threat assessment; Faith-
based and volunteer initiatives; Federal budget;
Free-market environmentalism; Health care
reform; International finance and multilateral
banks; Japan; Korea; Military strategy; NATO
and other alliances; Northeast Asia;
Peacekeeping; Southeast Asia (including
Burma, Cambodia, Laos, Vietnam, Singapore,
Malaysia, Indonesia, the Philippines, Australia,
and New Zealand); Term limits; Terrorism and
international crime

*Barfield, Claude E.
Resident Scholar
American Enterprise Institute
1150 17th Street, N.W.
Washington, DC 20036
202-862-5879   fax 202-862-7177
cbarfield@aei.org
Issues: American history/political tradition;
China; Entrepreneurship/free enterprise;
Executive Branch/The Presidency; Federalism;
Intellectual property; International finance
and multilateral banks; Japan; Korea; Latin
America; Regulatory reform; Southeast Asia
(including Burma, Cambodia, Laos, Vietnam,
Singapore, Malaysia, Indonesia, the
Philippines, Australia, and New Zealand);
Trade; Western Europe

Bark, Dr. Dennis L.
Senior Fellow
Hoover Institution
Stanford University
Stanford, CA 94305
650-723-2216   fax 650-723-1687
bark@hoover.stanford.edu
Issues: American diplomacy/foreign policy;
International organizations (European Union,
OECD, etc.); NATO and other alliances;
Peacekeeping; Telecommunications and the
Internet; Western Europe

Barkey, Michael B.
President
Center for the Study of Compassionate
Conservatism
521 Bayberry Point Drive, N.W., Suite A
Grand Rapids, MI 49544
616-453-2019
mbarkey@compassionateconservative.cc
Issues: Citizenship and civil society;
Conservative thought; Faith-based and
volunteer initiatives; Political philosophy;
Poverty and dependency; Stewardship;
Welfare/welfare reform

*Barnett, Prof. Randy
Austin B. Fletcher Professor
Boston University School of Law
765 Commonwealth Avenue
Boston, MA 02215
617-353-3099   fax 617-353-3077
rbarnett@bu.edu
Issues: The American Founding; American
history/political tradition; Constitutional law;
Crime/crime statistics; Criminal law and
procedure; Federalism; Free Speech; Initiative
and referendum; Judicial activism/judicial
reform; Judiciary; Police; Political philosophy;
Second Amendment; Term limits

*Barr, Dr. Saul Z.
Professor Emeritus of Economics
University of Tennessee
325 West 8th Street, Suite B
Gulf Shores, AL 36542
334-948-6583
Issues: Defense budget; Homeland security/
civil defense; International finance and
multilateral banks; Military strategy; Money
and financial services; NATO and other
alliances; Readiness and manpower; Trade

Barrett, John
Research Economist
Beacon Hill Institute
Suffolk University, 8 Ashburn Place
Boston, MA 02108
617-573-8750   fax 617-720-4272
jbarrett@beaconhill.org
Issues: Government waste; Health care reform;
State and local public finance; Taxation/tax
reform

Barro, Dr. Robert J.
Robert C. Waggoner Professor of Economics
Harvard University
Littauer Center 218
Cambridge, MA 02138
617-495-3203   fax 617-496-8629
barro@husc3.harvard.edu
Issues: The Economy; Entrepreneurship/free
enterprise; Money and financial services;
Regulatory reform; Trade

*Barry, John S.
Director of Research and Chief Economist
Tax Foundation
1900 M Street, N.W., Suite 550
Washington, DC 20036
202-464-6200   fax 202-464-6201
barry@taxfoundation.org
Issues: Discretionary spending; Economic
forecasting; Economic theory; The Economy;
Entitlement spending; Entrepreneurship/free
enterprise; Federal budget; Government debt;
Government waste; Higher education;
International tax policy/tax competition;
Money and financial services; Philanthropy;
State and local public finance; Taxation/tax
reform

*Bartlett, Bruce R.
Senior Fellow
National Center for Policy Analysis
439 Seneca Road
Great Falls, VA 22066-1113
703-421-7784   fax 703-421-7785
73440.3456@compuserve.com
Issues: Agriculture; American history/political
tradition; Comparative economics;
Discretionary spending; Economic education;
Economic forecasting; Economic theory; The
Economy; Entitlement spending; Ethics;
Federal budget; Government debt;
Infrastructure; International tax policy/tax
competition; Money and financial services;
Privatization/Contracting-out; The Reagan
legacy; State and local public finance;
Taxation/tax reform; Trade; Transportation;
Unfunded mandates

*Barton, David
President and Founder
WallBuilders, Inc.
P. O. Box 397
Aledo, TX 76008
817-441-6044   fax 817-441-6866
info@wallbuilders.com
Issues: The American Founding; American
history/political tradition

Basham, Dr. Patrick

Senior Fellow, Center for Representative
Government
Cato Institute
1000 Massachusetts Avenue, N.W.
Washington, DC 20001-5403
202-842-0200   fax 202-842-3490
pbasham@cato.org

Issues: Campaign finance reform; Elections/
polling; Electoral reform/voting rights; Term
limits

*Bast, Joseph L.

President and CEO
Heartland Institute
19 South LaSalle, Suite 903
Chicago, IL 60603
312-377-4000   fax 312-377-5000
jbast@heartland.org

Issues: Free-market environmentalism; School
choice

Basu, Dr. Sammy

Associate Professor, Department of Politics
Willamette University
900 State Street, Smullin 322
Salem, OR 97301
503-370-6264   fax 503-370-6720
sbasu@willamette.edu

Issues: Ethics; Political philosophy; Property
rights

Bate, Roger

Director
International Policy Network
1001 Connecticut Avenue, N.W., Suite 1250
Washington, DC 20036
202-431-5635   fax 202-331-0640
roger@policynetwork.net

Issues: Africa; Climate change; Economic
development/foreign aid; Free-market
environmentalism; Property rights; South Asia
(including India and Pakistan); Trade; Water

Batemarco, Robert J.

935 Parkway Place
Peekskill, NY 10566-1823
914-739-9655   fax 914-734-2139
rbate@advinc.com

Issues: Economic theory; The Economy;
Entrepreneurship/free enterprise; Money and
financial services; Trade

*Bauer, Gary L.

Chairman
Campaign for Working Families
2800 Shirlington Road, Suite 605
Arlington, VA 22206
703-671-8800   fax 703-671-8899
info@mail.cwfpac.com

Issues: China; Elections/polling; Executive
Branch/The Presidency; Faith-based and
volunteer initiatives; Family and children;
Home schooling; Immigration; Middle East;
Political correctness and multiculturalism;
Religion and public life; Religious freedom;
School choice; State-sponsored gambling

*Bauman, Naomi Lopez

2227 South Conway Road, Apartment 1212
Orlando, FL 32812
321-235-0196   fax 413-556-4258
naomi_lopez_bauman@yahoo.com

Issues: Adoption, foster care, & child care
services; Aging/elder care; Arms control; Costs
and benefits of regulation; Davis-Bacon Act;
Entitlement spending; Entrepreneurship/free
enterprise; Faith-based and volunteer
initiatives; Family and children; Family and
medical leave; Government health programs;
Health care reform; Housing and
homelessness; Intellectual property; Labor and
employment; Medicaid; Medicare; Poverty and
dependency; Privatization/Contracting-out;
Social Security and retirement; Unemployment
insurance; Wealth creation/financial
empowerment; Welfare/welfare reform

Baylor, Gregory S.

Director
Center for Law and Religious Freedom
4208 Evergreen Lane, Suite 222
Annandale, VA 22003
703-642-1070   fax 703-642-1075
clrf@clsnet.org

Issues: Faith-based and volunteer initiatives;
Public interest law; Religious freedom

*Beach, William W.
John M. Olin Senior Fellow in Economics
and Director, Center for Data Analysis
The Heritage Foundation
214 Massachusetts Avenue, N.E.
Washington, DC 20002
202-608-6206   fax 202-675-1772
bill.beach@heritage.org
Issues: Agriculture; Anti-trust; Comparative
economics; Costs and benefits of regulation;
Economic forecasting; Economic theory; The
Economy; Energy; Entitlement spending;
Federal budget; Government debt;
International finance and multilateral banks;
Medicaid; Money and financial services; Social
Security and retirement; State and local public
finance; Taxation/tax reform;
Telecommunications and the Internet; Wealth
creation/financial empowerment

*Beales, Janet
Kids One
10 Auer Court, Suite 120
East Brunswick, NJ 08816
732-390-0303   fax 732-390-5577
Issues: Business and education partnerships;
Charter schools; School choice

Bean, Dr. Jonathan James
Associate Professor, Department of History
Southern Illinois University
Carbondale, IL 62901-4519
618-453-7872   fax 618-453-5440
jonbean@siu.edu
Issues: American history/political tradition;
Anti-trust; Civil rights/racial preferences;
Entrepreneurship/free enterprise

*Beck, Dr. John H.
Associate Professor of Economics, School of
Business Administration
Gonzaga University
502 East Boone, AD Box 9
Spokane, WA 99258
509-323-3429   fax 509-323-5811
beck@gem.gonzaga.edu
Issues: State and local public finance; Taxation/
tax reform

Becker, Bill
Executive Director
Maine Policy Center
P. O. Box 7829
Portland, ME 04112
207-831-4674   info@mainepolicy.org
Issues: Health care reform; School choice;
Taxation/tax reform

Becker, Dr. Gary
Department of Economics
University of Chicago
1126 East 59th Street
Chicago, IL 60637
773-702-8168   fax 773-702-8490
gbecker@midway.uchicago.edu
Issues: Civil rights/racial preferences; Crime/
crime statistics; Economic education;
Economic theory; Labor and employment

*Beckner, Gary
Executive Director
Association of American Educators
25201 Paseo de Alicia, Suite 104
Laguna Hills, CA 92653
800-704-7799   fax 949-595-7970
info@aaeteachers.org
Issues: Education unions and interest groups;
Federal education policy; School-to-work;
Standards, curriculum, and testing; Unions

Beckner, Paul
President
Citizens for a Sound Economy
1900 M Street, N.W., Suite 500
Washington, DC 20036
202-783-3870   fax 202-783-4687
pbeckner@cse.org
Issues: Congress; Costs and benefits of
regulation; Economic theory; The Economy;
Entrepreneurship/free enterprise; Executive
Branch/The Presidency; Government waste;
Judiciary; Regulatory reform; School choice;
Taxation/tax reform; Tort and liability reform;
Trade

*Becks, Gary D.
President
Rescue Task Force
P. O. Box 12701
El Cajon, CA 92022
619-424-7415   fax 619-424-9393
gary@rescuetaskforce.org
Issues: Latin America

Beehler, Alex A.

Program Officer, Environment
Charles G. Koch Charitable Foundation
655 15th Street, N.W., Suite 445
Washington, DC 20005
202-737-8361   fax 202-737-8111
beehlera@kochind.com

Issues: Air; Climate change; Energy;
Environmental education; Environmental
regulation; Forestry and national parks; Free-
market environmentalism; Land use; Property
rights; Research funding; Sound science;
Stewardship; Urban sprawl/livable cities; Waste
management; Water; Wildlife management/
endangered species

Beers, Rev. John M.

Annecy Institute for the Study of Virtue and
Liberty
429 North Street S.W., Suite 109 South
Washington, DC 20024
202-863-0756   fax 202-863-0756
jmbeers@earthlink.com

Issues: Environmental education; Ethics; Free-
market environmentalism; Religion and public
life; Stewardship

*Behrens, Mark A.

Shook, Hardy & Bacon, L.L.P.
Hamilton Square, 600 14th Street, N.W.,
Suite 800
Washington, DC 20005
202-639-5621   fax 202-783-4211
mbehrens@shb.com

Issues: Health care reform; Judicial activism/
judicial reform; Judiciary; Tort and liability
reform

Beichman, Dr. Arnold

Research Fellow
Hoover Institution
Stanford University
Stanford, CA 94305
650-723-1754   fax 650-723-1687
beichman@hoover.stanford.edu

Issues: Africa; American diplomacy/foreign
policy; Canada; Human rights; Intelligence
gathering and covert operations; Middle East;
Southeast Asia (including Burma, Cambodia,
Laos, Vietnam, Singapore, Malaysia, Indonesia,
the Philippines, Australia, and New Zealand);
Terrorism and international crime

Beiting, Dr. Christopher

Senior Tutor in History
Ave Maria College
300 West Forest Avenue
Ypsilanti, MI 48197
734-337-4603   fax 734-337-4187
cjbeiting@aol.com

Issues: Arts, humanities and historic resources;
Church-state relations; Conservative thought;
Higher education; Religion and public life

Beito, Dr. David

Associate Professor, Department of History
University of Alabama
Box 870212
Tuscaloosa, AL 35487
205-348-1870   fax 205-348-0670

Issues: Civil rights/racial preferences; Higher
education; Philanthropy; Poverty and
dependency

Belgrad, Dr. Eric A.

Professor, Political Science Department
Towson State University
8000 York Road
Towson, MD 21252
410-704-2149   fax 410-704-2960
ebelgrad@towson.edu

Issues: Middle East; NATO and other alliances;
Peacekeeping; Political philosophy

*Bell, Charles H., Jr.

Bell, McAndrews, Hiltachk & Davidian
455 Capitol Mall, Suite 801
Sacramento, CA 95814
916-442-7757   fax 916-442-7759
cbell@bmhlaw.com

Issues: Campaign finance reform; Electoral
reform/voting rights; Initiative and
referendum

Bell, Mariam

Director for National Policy
The Wilburforce Forum
Prison Fellowship Ministries
P. O. Box 17500
Washington, DC 20041
703-478-0100   fax 703-904-7301
mbell@pfm.org

Issues: Church-state relations; Faith-based and
volunteer initiatives; Religion and public life

*Bell, Prof. Tom W.
Associate Professor, School of Law
Chapman University
One University Drive
Orange, CA 92866
714-628-2503   fax 714-628-2576
tbell@chapman.edu
Issues: Free Speech; Intellectual property;
Privacy; Telecommunications and the Internet

Bellante, Dr. Donald
Professor of Economics, Department of
Economics
University of South Florida
4202 East Flower Avenue
Tampa, FL 33620
813-974-4252   fax 813-974-6510
Issues: Labor and employment; Minimum wage;
Unions

*Belz, Dr. Herman
Professor, Department of History
University of Maryland
2137 Francis Scott Key Hall
College Park, MD 20742
301-405-4287   fax 301-314-9399
redbelz@aol.com
Issues: The American Founding; American
history/political tradition; Civil rights/racial
preferences; Congress; Conservative thought;
Constitutional law; Federalism; Judiciary; The
Reagan legacy

Belz, Joel
Publisher and CEO
World Magazine
P. O. Box 2230
Asheville, NC 28802
828-253-8063   fax 828-253-1556
worldmag@palmcoastd.com
Issues: Higher education; Marriage and divorce;
Media and popular culture; Political
correctness and multiculturalism; Religion and
public life

*Belzer, Richard B., Ph.D.
President
Regulatory Checkbook
819 7th Street, N.W., Suite 305
Washington, DC 20001
202-898-2050   fax 202-478-1626
belzer@regulatorycheckbook.org
Issues: Air; Costs and benefits of regulation;
Environmental regulation; Executive Branch/
The Presidency; OSHA; Regulatory budgeting;
Regulatory reform; Risk assessment; Unfunded
mandates; Waste management

BenDaniel, Dr. David J.
Berens Professor of Entrepreneurship,
Johnson Graduate School of Management
Cornell University
341 Sage Hall
Ithaca, NY 14853-6201
607-255-4220   fax 607-254-4590
Issues: Entrepreneurship/free enterprise

*Benedetto, Kathy
Program Director
National Wilderness Institute
Georgetown Station, P. O. Box 25766
Washington, DC 20027
703-836-7404   fax 703-836-7405
kmb@nwi.org
Issues: Free-market environmentalism; Land
use; Property rights

*Benigno, Pamela
Education Policy Center Director
Independence Institute
14142 Denver West Parkway, Suite 185
Golden, CO 80401
303-279-6536   fax 303-279-4176
pam@i2i.org
Issues: Charter schools; Education unions and
interest groups; Home schooling; School
choice; Standards, curriculum, and testing

*Benn, LeAnna
National Director
Teen Aid
723 East Jackson
Spokane, WA 99207
509-482-2868   fax 509-482-7994
teenaid@teen-aid.org
Issues: Abstinence and out-of-wedlock births

*Bennett, Elayne
President and Founder
Best Friends Foundation
4455 Connecticut Avenue, N.W., Suite 310
Washington, DC 20008
202-237-8156   fax 202-237-2776
Issues: Abstinence and out-of-wedlock births

*Bennett, Dr. James T.
Professor of Economics
George Mason University
4400 University Drive, MSN 3G4
Fairfax, VA 22030
703-993-1155   fax 703-993-1133
jbennett@osf1.gmu.edu
Issues: Advocacy and nonprofit public funding;
Government debt; Government waste;
Privatization/Contracting-out

*Bennett, Dr. William J.
Distinguished Fellow, Cultural Policy
Studies, The Heritage Foundation
and Co-Director,
Empower America
1801 K Street, N.W., Suite 410
Washington, DC 20006
202-452-8200   fax 202-833-0388
bennett@empower.org
Issues: Arts, humanities and historic resources;
Bilingual education; Business and education
partnerships; Charter schools; Church-state
relations; Citizenship and civil society; Civil
rights/racial preferences; Corrections and
sentencing; Crime/crime statistics; Education
unions and interest groups; Family and
children; Higher education; Home schooling;
Media and popular culture; Philanthropy;
Political correctness and multiculturalism;
Public school finance and administration;
Religion and public life; School choice;
Standards, curriculum, and testing

Benston, Dr. George J.
John H. Harland Professor of Finance,
Accounting and Economics, Goizueta
Business School
Emory University
Atlanta, GA 30322
404-727-7831   fax 404-727-5238
george_benston@bus.emory.edu
Issues: Anti-trust; Money and financial services;
Second Amendment

Berkowitz, Herbert B.
Senior Communications Fellow
The Heritage Foundation
1501 Market Street
Wilimington, NC 28401
910-362-0319
herb.berkowitz@heritage.org
Issues: Media and popular culture; Political
correctness and multiculturalism

*Berliner, Dana
Staff Attorney
Institute for Justice
1717 Pennsylvania Avenue, N.W., Suite 200
Washington, DC 20006
202-955-1300   fax 202-955-1329
dberliner@ij.org
Issues: Transportation deregulation

Berman, Ilan
Vice President for Policy
American Foreign Policy Council
1521 16th Street, N.W
Washington, DC 20036
202-462-6055   fax 202-462-6045
berman@afpc.org
Issues: Arms control; Emerging threats/threat
assessment; Middle East; Military strategy;
Missile defense; NATO and other alliances;
Promoting democracy/public diplomacy;
Russia and Eurasia; Terrorism and
international crime

Berns, Dr. Walter
Resident Scholar
American Enterprise Institute
1150 17th Street, N.W.
Washington, DC 20036
202-862-5859   fax 202-862-7178
wberns@aei.org
Issues: Constitutional law; Judiciary; Political
philosophy

Bernstein, Jonas
Editor, *Russia Reform Monitor*
American Foreign Policy Council
1521 16th Street, N.W.
Washington, DC 20036
202-462-6055   fax 202-462-6045
bernstein@afpc.org
Issues: Russia and Eurasia

Bernstein, Dr. Lisa E.
Professor of Law
University of Chicago Law School
1111 East 60th Street
Chicago, IL 60637
773-834-2881   fax 773-702-0730
lisa_bernstein@law.uchicago.edu
Issues: Costs and benefits of regulation; Judicial
activism/judicial reform; Privatization/
Contracting-out; Transportation deregulation

*Berry, Saundra
Director
Cleveland Scholarship and Tutoring
Program
615 West Superior, Suite 535
Cleveland, OH 44113
216-787-5;680   fax 216-787-5679
cst_berry@ode.state.oh.us
Issues: School choice; Standards, curriculum, and testing

*Berthoud, John E.
President
National Taxpayers Union
108 North Alfred Street
Alexandria, VA 22314
703-683-5700   fax 703-683-5722
jberthoud@ntu.org
Issues: American history/political tradition; Conservative thought; Defense budget; Discretionary spending; Economic theory; Entitlement spending; Federal budget; Federal education policy; Government debt; Government waste; Privatization/Contracting-out; School choice; State and local government; State and local public finance; Taxation/tax reform; Term limits; Unfunded mandates

*Bertsch, Jason
Corporate Relations Director
American Enterprise Institute
1150 17th Street, N.W.
Washington, DC 20036
202-862-5873   fax 202-862-7171
jbertsch@aei.org
Issues: The American Founding; American history/political tradition; Business and education partnerships; Charter schools; Citizenship and civil society; Conservative thought; Home schooling; Media and popular culture; Political philosophy; School choice; Standards, curriculum, and testing

Besharov, Douglas
Joseph J. and Violet Jacobs Scholar in Social Welfare Studies
American Enterprise Institute
1150 17th Street, N.W.
Washington, DC 20036
202-862-5904   fax 202-862-5802
dbesharov@aei.org
Issues: Abstinence and out-of-wedlock births; Adoption, foster care, & child care services; Aging/elder care; Economic theory; Family and children; Health care reform; Job training/welfare to work; Juvenile justice; Marriage and divorce; Medicaid; Medicare; Poverty and dependency; School choice; School-to-work; Social Security and retirement; Substance abuse; Welfare/welfare reform

*Bessette, Dr. Joseph
Alice Tweed Tuohy Professor of Government and Ethics
Claremont McKenna College
850 Columbia Avenue
Claremont, CA 91711
909-607-3989   fax 909-621-8416
jbessette@mckenna.edu
Issues: Corrections and sentencing; Crime/crime statistics

*Best, Dr. Judith A.
Distinguished Teaching Professor, Political Science Department
State University of New York, Cortland
217-B Old Main
Cortland, NY 13045
607-753-4801   fax 607-753-5979
bestj@snycorva.cortland.edu
Issues: The American Founding; American history/political tradition; Elections/polling; Electoral reform/voting rights; Executive Branch/The Presidency

*Best, Robert K.
President
Pacific Legal Foundation
10360 Old Placerville Road, Suite 100
Sacramento, CA 95827
916-362-2833   fax 916-362-2932
rkb@pacificlegal.org
Issues: Civil rights/racial preferences; Constitutional law; Federalism; Free Speech; Land use; Privatization/Contracting-out; Property rights; Public interest law; Regulation through litigation; Regulatory reform; Sound science; Term limits; Tort and liability reform; Urban sprawl/livable cities; Water

Bethune, Dr. John J.
Kennedy Chair in Economics, School of Business
Barton College
P. O. Box 5000
Wilson, NC 27893
252-399-6422   fax 252-399-6571
jbethune@barton.edu
Issues: Economic education; Entrepreneurship/free enterprisc; Intellectual property

*Bevan, Fran
President
Eagle Forum of Pennsylvania
640 Stonebridge Drive
North Huntingdon, PA 15642
724-864-5989   fax 724-864-6125
fran@eagleforumpa.org
Issues: Business and education partnerships; Health care reform; Political correctness and multiculturalism; Religion and public life; School choice; School-to-work; Sound science; Standards, curriculum, and testing; State-sponsored gambling

*BeVier, Lillian
Doherty Charitable Foundation
Professor of Law, School of Law
University of Virginia
580 Massie Road
Charlottesville, VA 22903
804-924-3132   fax 804-924-7536
lrb5s@virginia.edu
Issues: Campaign finance reform; Constitutional law; Forestry and national parks; Intellectual property; Judiciary; Privacy; Property rights; Tort and liability reform

Bibby, Dr. John F.
Professor of Political Science
University of Wisconsin, Milwaukee
5507 North Kent Avenue
Milwaukee, WI 53217
414-964-5376   fax 414-229-5021
jfbibby@csd.uwm.edu
Issues: Campaign finance reform; Congress; Elections/polling; Executive Branch/The Presidency; Federalism

Biggs, Andrew
Social Security Analyst and Assistant Director, Project on Social Security Choice
Cato Institute
1000 Massachusetts Avenue, N.W.
Washington, DC 20001-5403
202-842-0200   fax 202-842-3490
abiggs@cato.org
Issues: Social Security and retirement

Binning, Dr. William C.
Chairman of Political Science
Youngstown State University
One University Plaza
Youngstown, OH 44555
330-941-3435   fax 330-941-3439
fr025701@ysub.ysu.edu
Issues: Electoral reform/voting rights; Federalism; Government health programs; Health care reform; Initiative and referendum; State and local government

*Bishirjian, Dick
President
YorktownUniversity.com
P. O. Box 41211
Norfolk, VA 23541
757-325-1000   fax 253-540-8843
president@yorktownuniversity.com
Issues: Federal education policy; Higher education; Political philosophy; The Reagan legacy

*Bishop, Col. Wayman R., USMC (Ret.)
Executive Director
The Family Foundation of Virginia
One Capitol Square, 830 East Main Street, Suite 1201
Richmond, VA 23219
804-343-0010   fax 804-343-0050
wayman@familyfoundation.org
Issues: Abstinence and out-of-wedlock births; The American Founding; American history/political tradition; Charter schools; Church-state relations; Citizenship and civil society; Family and children; Home schooling; Judicial activism/judicial reform; Marriage and divorce; Political philosophy; Public school finance and administration; Religion and public life; Religious freedom; School choice; Standards, curriculum, and testing; State and local government; State and local public finance; State-sponsored gambling; Taxation/tax reform

Bjornseth, Richard
Professor, Art Department
Valdosta State University
909 Ridgewood Drive
Valdosta, GA 31601
229-293-0358   fax 229-245-3799
dlbjorns@valdosta.edu
Issues: Arts, humanities and historic resources;
Higher education; Land use; Philanthropy;
Urban sprawl/livable cities

Black, Amy E.
Assistant Professor, Department of Political
Science
Wheaton College
501 College Avenue
Wheaton, IL 60187-5593
630-752-5980   fax 630-752-7037
amy.e.black@wheaton.edu
Issues: Citizenship and civil society; Congress;
Elections/polling; Executive Branch/The
Presidency; Faith-based and volunteer
initiatives; Media and popular culture; Religion
and public life; Religious freedom

Blackman, Paul H., Ph.D.
Research Coordinator
NRA Institute for Legislative Action
11250 Waplcs Mill Road
Fairfax, VA 22030
703-267-1226   fax 703-267-3973
pblackman@nrahq.org
Issues: Crime/crime statistics; Second
Amendment

Blackwell, Morton
President
Leadership Institute
1101 North Highland Street
Arlington, VA 22201
703-247-2000   fax 703-247-2001
morton.blackwell@leadershipinstitute.org
Issues: Africa; Campaign finance reform;
Central and Eastern Europe; Congress;
Conservative thought; Elections/polling;
Electoral reform/voting rights; Executive
Branch/The Presidency; Higher education;
Media and popular culture; Non-governmental
organizations; Philanthropy; Political
correctness and multiculturalism; Promoting
democracy/public diplomacy; The Reagan
legacy; Religion and public life; Russia and
Eurasia

*Blank, Dr. Stephen J.
Professor, Department of the Army
U. S. Army War College
122 Forbes Avenue
Carlisle, PA 17013
717-245-4085   fax 717-245-3820
Issues: Arms control; Central and Eastern
Europe; Emerging threats/threat assessment;
Export controls/military transfers; Middle
East; Military strategy; Missile defense; NATO
and other alliances; Russia and Eurasia

*Blankenhorn, David
President
Institute for American Values
1841 Broadway, Suite 211
New York, NY 10023
212-246-3942   fax 212-541-6665
iav@worldnet.att.net
Issues: Family and children; Marriage and
divorce

Blankenship, Greg
Director
Illinois Policy Institute
718 South 7th Street, Suite 305
Springfield, IL 62703
217-544-4759
info@illinoispolicyinstitute.org
Issues: Electoral reform/voting rights; Health
care reform; School choice; Taxation/tax
reform; Telecommunications and the Internet

*Blevins, Sue A.
President
Institute for Health Freedom
1825 Eye Street, N.W., Suite 400
Washington, DC 20006
202-429-6610   fax 202-861-1973
sblevins@forhealthfreedom.org
Issues: Government health programs; Health
care reform; Medicare; Privacy

*Blitz, Dr. Mark
Fletcher-Jones Professor of Political
Philosophy
Claremont McKenna College
850 Columbia Avenue
Claremont, CA 91711
909-607-3232   fax 909-621-8419
Issues: American diplomacy/foreign policy;
The American Founding; American history/
political tradition; Arts, humanities and
historic resources; Citizenship and civil society;
Conservative thought; Ethics; Faith-based and
volunteer initiatives; Higher education;
Human rights; Philanthropy; Political
correctness and multiculturalism; Political
philosophy; Promoting democracy/public
diplomacy; The Reagan legacy; School choice

Block, Michael K., Ph.D.
President, Goldwater Institute, and Professor
of Economics
University of Arizona
401 McClelland Hall, P. O. Box 210108
Tucson, AZ 85721-0108
520-621-2854   MKBlock@aol.com
Issues: Corrections and sentencing; Economic
education; Economic theory; Electricity
deregulation; Regulatory reform

Block, Dr. Walter
Wirth Eminent Scholar Endowed Chair in
Economics, College of Business
Administration
Loyola University New Orleans
6363 St. Charles Avenue, Box 15, Miller 321
New Orleans, LA 70118
504-864-7934   fax 504-864-7970
wblock@loyno.edu
Issues: Anti-trust; Comparative economics;
Davis-Bacon Act; The Economy;
Entrepreneurship/free enterprise;
Environmental education; Free-market
environmentalism; Health care reform;
Immigration; Infrastructure; Intellectual
property; Labor and employment; Minimum
wage; OSHA; Property rights; Social Security
and retirement; Trade; Transportation;
Transportation deregulation; Unions; Urban
sprawl/livable cities; Welfare/welfare reform

*Bloomfield, Mark A.
President
American Council for Capital Formation
1750 K Street, N.W., Suite 400
Washington, DC 20006
202-293-5811   fax 202-785-8165
mbloomfield@accf.org
Issues: Central and Eastern Europe; Climate
change; Comparative government; Congress;
The Economy; Elections/polling;
Entrepreneurship/free enterprise; Federal
budget; International tax policy/tax
competition; Political philosophy; Taxation/
tax reform

Blowe, Felita
Legislative Coordinator
Concerned Women for America
1015 15th Street, N.W., Suite 1100
Washington, DC 20005
202-488-7000   fax 202-488-0806
fblowe@cwfa.org
Issues: School choice; School-to-work;
Standards, curriculum, and testing

*Boarman, Dr. Patrick M.
Professor Emeritus of Economics
National University San Diego
6421 Caminito Estrellado
San Diego, CA 92120
619-286-2453   fax 619-286-2431
patboarman@hotmail.com
Issues: Anti-trust; Campaign finance reform;
Comparative economics; Comparative
government; Costs and benefits of regulation;
Economic development/foreign aid;
Economic theory; The Economy;
Environmental regulation; Ethics; Federal
budget; Government debt; International
finance and multilateral banks; International
tax policy/tax competition; Money and
financial services; Regulatory reform; Religion
and public life; Taxation/tax reform; Western
Europe

*Boaz, David
Executive Vice President
Cato Institute
1000 Massachusetts Avenue, N.W.
Washington, DC 20001
202-842-0200   fax 202-842-3490
dboaz@cato.org
Issues: American history/political tradition;
Arts, humanities and historic resources;
Conservative thought; Marriage and divorce;
Political philosophy; The Reagan legacy;
School choice; Substance abuse

Bobb, David J.
Director, Hoogland Center for Teacher
Excellence
Hillsdale College
33 East College Street
Hillsdale, MI 49242
517-607-2628   fax 517-437-4347
david.bobb@hillsdale.edu
Issues: The American Founding; American
history/political tradition; Citizenship and civil
society; Political philosophy; Religion and
public life; Standards, curriculum, and testing

*Boehm, Kenneth
Chairman
National Legal and Policy Center
107 Park Washington Court
Falls Church, VA 22046-4237
703-237-1970   fax 703-237-2090
kboehm@nlpc.org
Issues: Advocacy and nonprofit public funding;
Campaign finance reform; Ethics; Public
interest law; Unions

Boettke, Dr. Peter J.
Deputy Director
James M. Buchanan Center for Political
Economy
George Mason University, 4400 University
Drive, 324 Enterprise Hall
Fairfax, VA 22030
703-993-1149   fax 703-993-1133
pboettke@gmu.edu
Issues: Central and Eastern Europe; China;
Comparative economics; Economic
development/foreign aid; Economic theory;
Entrepreneurship/free enterprise; Federalism;
Northeast Asia; Political philosophy; Russia and
Eurasia

Boeyink, Jeffrey R.
Executive Vice President
Iowans for Tax Relief
2610 Park Avenue, P. O. Box 747
Muscatine, IA 52761
563-264-8080   fax 563-264-2413
jboeyink@taxrelief.org
Issues: Elections/polling; State and local
government; State and local public finance;
Taxation/tax reform

Bohanon, Dr. Cecil E.
Professor of Economics, Department of
Economics
Ball State University
McKinley Avenue
Muncie, IN 47306
765-289-1241   fax 765-285-8024
cbohanon@bsu.edu
Issues: Elections/polling; Energy; Housing and
homelessness; Immigration; Property rights;
State and local public finance

*Bolick, Clint
Vice President and Director of Litigation
Institute for Justice
111 West Monroe Street
Phoenix, AZ 85003
602-324-5440   fax 602-324-5441
cbolick@ij.org
Issues: Constitutional law; Public interest law;
School choice

*Bolin, Richard L.
Director and Trustee
The Flagstaff Institute
P. O. Box 986
Flagstaff, AZ 86002-0986
928-779-0052   fax 928-774-8589
bolinflag@aol.com
Issues: Economic development/foreign aid;
International finance and multilateral banks;
International organizations (European Union,
OECD, etc.)

Bom, Dr. Philip
Professor of Government, Robertson School
of Government
Regent University
9629 162nd Avenue, N.E.
Redmond, WA 98052
757-226-4746   philbom@regent.edu
Issues: American diplomacy/foreign policy;
Canada; Human rights; United Nations

Bond, Dr. James E.
Professor, School of Law
Seattle University
900 Broadway
Seattle, WA 98122-4338
206-398-4309   jbond@seattleu.edu
Issues: Civil rights/racial preferences;
Constitutional law; Criminal law and
procedure; Federalism; Judicial activism/
judicial reform; Judiciary; Term limits

Bonicelli, Dr. Paul J.
Dean of Academic Affairs and Associate
Professor of Government
Patrick Henry College
One Patrick Henry Circle
Purcellville, VA 20132
540-338-8733   fax 540-338-8705
pjbonicelli@phc.edu
Issues: American diplomacy/foreign policy;
Economic development/foreign aid; Higher
education; Home schooling; Human rights;
International organizations (European Union,
OECD, etc.); Latin America; Mexico; NATO
and other alliances; Peacekeeping; Promoting
democracy/public diplomacy; Terrorism and
international crime; United Nations; Western
Europe

*Booth, Dr. Donald R.
Professor of Economics, School of Business
and Economics
Chapman University
One University Drive
Orange, CA 92866
714-997-6804   fax 714-532-6081
booth@chapman.edu
Issues: China; Conservative thought; Economic
development/foreign aid; Economic
education; Economic theory

*Bopp, James, Jr.
General Counsel
James Madison Center for Free Speech
1747 Pennsylvania Avenue, N.W., Suite 1000
Washington, DC 20006
812-232-2434   fax 812-235-3685
jboppjr@bopplaw.com
Issues: Campaign finance reform;
Constitutional law; Free Speech; Judicial
activism/judicial reform; Judiciary; Non-
governmental organizations; Public interest
law; Religious freedom

Borcherding, Dr. Thomas E.
Professor of Economics and Politics,
Department of Economics
Claremont Graduate University
160 East 10th Street
Claremont, CA 91711-6165
909-621-8783   fax 909-621-8460
thomas.borcherding@cgu.edu
Issues: Government waste; Privatization/
Contracting-out; Regulatory budgeting; Social
Security and retirement; Taxation/tax reform

Borders, Harry
Program Director
Kentucky League for Educational
Alternatives
1042 Burlington Lane
Frankfort, KY 40601
502-875-8010   fax 502-875-2841
Issues: School choice

Bork, Ellen
Senior Fellow
Project for the New American Century
1150 17th Street, N.W.
Washington, DC 20036
202-293-4983   fax 202-293-4572
Issues: Southeast Asia (including Burma,
Cambodia, Laos, Vietnam, Singapore,
Malaysia, Indonesia, the Philippines, Australia,
and New Zealand)

*Bork, Hon. Robert H.
Senior Fellow
American Enterprise Institute
1150 17th Street, N.W.
Washington, DC 20036
202-862-5851   fax 202-862-7178
rbork@aei.org
Issues: Constitutional law; Federalism; Judiciary

Boskin, Dr. Michael J.
Senior Fellow
Hoover Institution
Stanford University
Stanford, CA 94305-6010
650-723-6482   fax 650-723-6494
boskin@hoover.stanford.edu
Issues: Comparative economics; Costs and
benefits of regulation; Economic education;
Economic forecasting; The Economy;
Executive Branch/The Presidency; Federal
budget; Government debt; Regulatory reform;
Taxation/tax reform

Bostaph, Dr. Samuel
Associate Professor, Department of
Economics
University of Dallas
1845 East Northgate Drive
Irving, TX 75062
972-721-5159   fax 972-721-4034
bostaph@acad.udallas.edu
Issues: Comparative economics; Political
philosophy; Trade

Botkin, Dr. Daniel B.
President and Founder
Center for the Study of the Environment
P. O. Box 30700
Santa Barbara, CA 93130
805-452-3988   fax 805-569-9170
info@naturestudy.org
Issues: Environmental education;
Environmental regulation; Forestry and
national parks; Land use; Sound science;
Urban sprawl/livable cities; Wildlife
management/endangered species

*Boudreaux, Donald J.
Chairman, Department of Economics
George Mason University
4400 University Drive, 339 Enterprise Hall
Fairfax, VA 22030-4444
703-993-1157   fax 703-993-1133
dboudrea@gmu.edu
Issues: Anti-trust; Economic education; Trade

Boudreaux, Karol
Assistant Dean and Director, Juris Master
Program
George Mason University School of Law
3301 North Fairafx Drive
Arlington, VA 22201-4498
703-993-8050   fax 703-993-8124
kboudrea@gmu.edu
Issues: Economic education; Free-market
environmentalism; Property rights; United
Nations; Wildlife management/endangered
species

*Bourne, Sandy Liddy
Director, Energy, Environment, Natural
Resources and Agriculture Task Force
American Legislative Exchange Council
1129 20th Street, N.W., Suite 500
Washington, DC 20006
202-466-3800   fax 202-466-3801
abourne@alec.org
Issues: Air; Climate change; Electricity
deregulation; Energy; Environmental
education; Environmental regulation; Forestry
and national parks; Free-market
environmentalism; Homeland security/civil
defense; Land use; Property rights; Regulatory
reform; Research funding; Risk assessment;
Sound science; Stewardship; Urban sprawl/
livable cities; Waste management; Water;
Wildlife management/endangered species

Boutros, Theodore
Attorney
Gibson, Dunn & Crutcher LLP
1050 Connecticut Avenue, N.W., Suite 900
Washington, DC 20036
202-955-8500   fax 202-467-0539
tboutrous@gdclaw.com
Issues: Constitutional law; Tort and liability
reform

Bovard, James
1345 Templeton Place
Rockville, MD 20852
301-309-6817   fax 301-309-6738
jbovard@his.com
Issues: Agriculture; Second Amendment; Trade

Bowman, James
Resident Scholar
Ethics and Public Policy Center
1015 15th Street, N.W., Suite 900
Washington, DC 20005
202-216-0855   fax 202-408-0632
Issues: Media and popular culture

Bowman, Karlyn Keene
Resident Fellow
American Enterprise Institute
1150 17th Street, N.W.
Washington, DC 20036
202-862-5910   fax 202-862-7178
kbowman@aei.org
Issues: Elections/polling; Media and popular
culture

*Bowyer, Jim L.
Professor, Department of Wood and Paper
Science
University of Minnesota
2004 Folwell Avenue
St. Paul, MN 55108
612-624-4292   fax 612-625-6286
jbowyer@umn.edu
Issues: Environmental education;
Environmental regulation; Forestry and
national parks

Boyle, Brian
O'Melveny & Myers LLP
555 13th Street, N.W., Suite 500 West
Washington, DC 20004
202-383-5300   fax 202-383-5414
bboyle@omm.com
Issues: Government health programs; Health
care reform; Regulation through litigation;
Tort and liability reform

Bozell, L. Brent, III

Founder and President
Media Research Center
325 South Patrick Street
Alexandria, VA 22314
703-683-9733   fax 703-683-9736
bbozell@9733.org
Issues: American history/political tradition;
Arts, humanities and historic resources;
Campaign finance reform; Citizenship and civil
society; Conservative thought; Family and
children; Media and popular culture; The
Reagan legacy

Braceras, Jennifer C.

Senior Fellow for Legal Policy
Independent Women's Forum
P. O. Box 3058
Arlington, VA 22203-0058
703-558-4991   fax 703-558-4994
jbraceras@iwf.org
Issues: Civil rights/racial preferences;
Constitutional law; Federalism; Judicial
activism/judicial reform; Judiciary; Labor and
employment; Political correctness and
multiculturalism; Standards, curriculum, and
testing

Brach, Philip L.

Executive Director
Midtown Educational Foundation
718 South Loomis Street
Chicago, IL 60607
312-738-8301   fax 312-738-8306
pbrach@midtown-metro.org
Issues: Abstinence and out-of-wedlock births;
Business and education partnerships;
Entrepreneurship/free enterprise; Faith-based
and volunteer initiatives; Family and children;
Marriage and divorce; Philanthropy

*Bradburn, Pat

President
Virginians for Property Rights
12750 Chatter Brook Drive
Catharpin, VA 20143-1031
703-754-7900   fax 703-753-3005
pbradburn@erols.com
Issues: Land use; Property rights; Right to work;
Urban sprawl/livable cities

Bradford, Dr. David F.

Professor, Woodrow Wilson School of Public
and International Affairs
Princeton University
408 Robertson Hall
Princeton, NJ 08544
609-258-1856   fax 609-258-2809
bradford@princeton.edu
Issues: Air; Climate change; Government debt;
State and local public finance; Taxation/tax
reform; Unfunded mandates

Bradley, Anthony

Acton Institute for the Study of Religion and
Liberty
161 Ottawa Avenue, N.W., Suite 301
Grand Rapids, MI 49503
616-454-3080   fax 616-454-9454
Issues: Civil rights/racial preferences;
Conservative thought; Ethics; Job training/
welfare to work; Political correctness and
multiculturalism; Political philosophy; Poverty
and dependency; Religious freedom; School
choice; Wealth creation/financial
empowerment; Welfare/welfare reform

*Bradley, Gerard V.

Professor of Law
Notre Dame Law School
Notre Dame, IN 46556
219-631-8385   fax 219-631-4197
gerard.v.bradley.16@nd.edu
Issues: The American Founding; American
history/political tradition; Church-state
relations; Constitutional law; Criminal law and
procedure; Judicial activism/judicial reform;
Religious freedom; School choice

*Bradley, Dr. Robert L., Jr.

President
Institute for Energy Research
6219 Olympia Drive
Houston, TX 77057
713-974-1918   fax 713-974-1918
iertx@hern.org
Issues: Climate change; Energy

Brady, Demian

Policy Analyst
National Taxpayers Union Foundation
108 North Alfred Street
Alexandria, VA 22314
703-683-5700   fax 703-683-5722
Issues: Congress; Taxation/tax reform

Brady, Dr. Gordon L.
Senior Research Fellow
Center for the Study of Public Choice
George Mason University, Mail Stop 1D3
Fairfax, VA 22030
703-993-2321   fax 703-993-2323
gbrady@gmu.edu
Issues: Air; Comparative government;
Conservative thought; Economic education;
Economic theory; Environmental education;
Environmental regulation; Political
philosophy; Property rights; Research funding;
Telecommunications and the Internet;
Wildlife management/endangered species

*Brakel, S. Jan
Vice President
Isaac Ray Center, Inc.
1720 West Polk Street
Chicago, IL 60612
312-942-4462   fax 312-942-2224
Issues: Corrections and sentencing; Judicial
activism/judicial reform; Tort and liability
reform

*Brase, Twila, R.N.
President
Citizens' Council on Health Care
1954 University Avenue, West, No. 8
Box 40065
St. Paul, MN 55104
651-646-8935   fax 651-646-0100
twila@cchc-mn.org
Issues: Government health programs; Health
care reform; Privacy

Brasor, Gary Crosby
Associate Director
National Association of Scholars
221 Witherspoon Street, 2nd Floor
Princeton, NJ 08542-3215
609-683-1437   fax 609-683-0316
brasor@nas.org
Issues: Higher education; Political correctness
and multiculturalism; Standards, curriculum,
and testing

*Braunlich, Christian N.
Vice President
Thomas Jefferson Institute for Public Policy
7011 Dreams Way Court
Alexandria, VA 22315
703-922-4145   fax 703-922-8137
c.braunlich@att.net
Issues: Charter schools; Education unions and
interest groups; Public school finance and
administration; School choice; Standards,
curriculum, and testing

Breeden, Dr. Charles H.
Associate Professor, Department of
Economics
Marquette University
P. O. Box 1881
Milwaukee, WI 53201-1881
414-288-3370   fax 414-288-5757
charles.breeden@marquette.edu
Issues: State and local public finance; Tort and
liability reform

*Breger, Marshall J.
Professor, Columbus School of Law
Catholic University of America
3600 John MacCormack Road, N.E.
Washington, DC 20064
202-319-5140   fax 202-319-4459
breger@cua.edu
Issues: Church-state relations; Citizenship and
civil society; Constitutional law; Costs and
benefits of regulation; Executive Branch/The
Presidency; Faith-based and volunteer
initiatives; Federalism; Homeland security/
civil defense; Immigration; Judiciary; Middle
East; Regulation through litigation; Regulatory
budgeting; Regulatory reform; Religion and
public life; Religious freedom; Risk assessment;
School choice; Terrorism and international
crime

Breit, Dr. William
Taylor Distinguished Professor of Economics
Trinity University
715 Stadium Drive
San Antonio, TX 78212-7200
210-999-8492   fax 210-999-7255
wbreit@trinity.edu
Issues: Comparative economics; Government
debt; Regulatory reform

Brennan, David
White Hat Management
159 South Main Street, Suite 210
Akron, OH 44308-1317
330-535-6868   fax 330-535-5055
david.brennan@whitehatmg.com
Issues: Business and education partnerships;
Charter schools; School choice

Breslint, Dr. Thomas A.
Vice President, Department of Research and
Graduate Studies
Florida International University
University Park, MARC 462
Miami, FL 33199
305-348-2494   fax 305-348-4117
breslint@fiu.edu
Issues: American diplomacy/foreign policy;
China

*Brickman, Lester
Professor of Law
Cardozo School of Law
55 Fifth Avenue
New York, NY 10003
212-790-0327   fax 212-790-0205
brickman@ymail.yu.edu
Issues: Judicial activism/judicial reform;
Judiciary; Tort and liability reform

*Brickner, Mychele
Program Officer
Clare Boothe Luce Policy Institute
112 Elden Street, Suite P
Herndon, VA 20170
703-318-0730   fax 703-318-8867
cblpi@erols.com
Issues: Standards, curriculum, and testing

Briggs, Dedrick
Executive Director
Charter School Resource Center of
Tennessee
22 North Front Street, 2nd Floor
Memphis, TN 38103
901-543-3567   tncharters@aol.com
Issues: Business and education partnerships;
Charter schools; Federal education policy;
School choice; Standards, curriculum, and
testing

Brigham, Adrian
Executive Director
Citizens for Educational Freedom of Illinois
129 Red Cedar Drive
Streamwood, IL 60107
630-550-5052   fax 630-213-1882
abrigham@educational-freedom.org
Issues: School choice

Brinker, Gregory Paul
Chief Financial Officer
Marion County Justice Agency
200 East Washington Street, Room 1901
Indianapolis, IN 46204
317-327-3111   fax 317-327-3143
gbrinker@indygov.org
Issues: Corrections and sentencing; Crime/
crime statistics; Juvenile justice; Police

*Brookes, Peter
Senior Fellow for National Security Affairs
and Director, Asian Studies Center
The Heritage Foundation
214 Massachusetts Avenue, N.E.
Washington, DC 20002
202-608-6097   fax 202-675-1758
peter.brookes@heritage.org
Issues: Afghanistan; American diplomacy/
foreign policy; Arms control; China; Defense
budget; Economic development/foreign aid;
Emerging threats/threat assessment; Export
controls/military transfers; Homeland
security/civil defense; Human rights;
Intelligence gathering and covert operations;
Japan; Korea; Military strategy; Missile defense;
NATO and other alliances; Northeast Asia;
Peacekeeping; Promoting democracy/public
diplomacy; Readiness and manpower; South
Asia (including India and Pakistan); Southeast
Asia (including Burma, Cambodia, Laos,
Vietnam, Singapore, Malaysia, Indonesia, the
Philippines, Australia, and New Zealand);
Terrorism and international crime

Brooks, Dr. Arthur C.
Associate Professor of Public Administration,
Maxwell School of Public Affairs
Syracuse University
Syracuse, NY 13244
315-443-3719   fax 315-443-1081
acbrooks@maxwell.syr.edu
Issues: Arts, humanities and historic resources;
Media and popular culture; Military strategy;
Philanthropy; Religion and public life;
Telecommunications and the Internet

Brooks, B. Jason
Senior Research Associate
Empire Foundation for Policy Research
Four Chelsea Place, Second Floor
Clifton Park, NY 12065
518-383-2877   fax 518-383-2841
bjbrooks@nycap.rr.com
Issues: Charter schools; Higher education;
School choice; Standards, curriculum, and
testing; State and local government; State and
local public finance; Taxation/tax reform

*Brooks, Bill
President
North Carolina Family Policy Council
P. O. Box 20607
Raleigh, NC 27619
919-807-0800   fax 919-807-0900
ncfpc@aol.com
Issues: Abstinence and out-of-wedlock births;
Charter schools; Marriage and divorce; School
choice; State and local government; State-
sponsored gambling; Taxation/tax reform

Brooks, Brian P.
O'Melveny & Myers LLP
555 13th Street, N.W., Suite 500 West
Washington, DC 20004
202-383-5127   fax 202-383-5414
bbrooks@omm.com
Issues: Judicial activism/judicial reform;
Judiciary; Regulation through litigation; Tort
and liability reform

Brooks, Charles
Washington Director
The Strategy Group
16 South Manchester Street
Arlington, VA 22204
703-998-5800   fax 703-998-5800
chetz18@aol.com
Issues: Congress; Economic development/
foreign aid; Elections/polling; Emerging
threats/threat assessment; Export controls/
military transfers; Homeland security/civil
defense; International finance and multilateral
banks; International organizations (European
Union, OECD, etc.); Middle East; Military
strategy; Promoting democracy/public
diplomacy; The Reagan legacy; Russia and
Eurasia; South Asia (including India and
Pakistan); Terrorism and international crime;
Trade; Western Europe

*Brooks, Kay
Founder
TnHomeEd.com
3929 Ivy Drive
Nashville, TN 37216
615-226-6139   fax 775-205-1468
Kay@TnHomeEd.com
Issues: Home schooling

Brooks, Matthew
Executive Director
Jewish Policy Center
50 F Street, N.W., Suite 100
Washington, DC 20001
202-638-2411   fax 202-638-6694
Issues: Elections/polling; Middle East

*Brough, Dr. Wayne T.
Chief Economist
Citizens for a Sound Economy
1900 M Street, N.W., Suite 500
Washington, DC 20036
202-942-7627   fax 202-783-4687
wbrough@cse.org
Issues: Air; Anti-trust; Climate change; Costs
and benefits of regulation; Economic theory;
The Economy; Electricity deregulation;
Energy; Entrepreneurship/free enterprise;
Environmental education; Environmental
regulation; Regulatory reform; Risk
assessment; Tort and liability reform;
Transportation

*Brouillette, Matthew J.
President
The Commonwealth Foundation
225 State Street, Suite 302
Harrisburg, PA 17101
717-671-1901   fax 717-671-1905
brouillette@commonwealthfoundation.org
Issues: The American Founding; American
history/political tradition; Charter schools;
Conservative thought; Economic education;
Education unions and interest groups;
Entrepreneurship/free enterprise; Free-
market environmentalism; Home schooling;
Labor and employment; Minimum wage;
Political philosophy; Property rights; Public
school finance and administration; Right to
work; School choice; Second Amendment;
Standards, curriculum, and testing; State and
local government; Taxation/tax reform;
Unions; Urban sprawl/livable cities

Broussard, James H.
Chairman
Citizens Against Higher Taxes
P. O. Box 343
Hershey, PA 17033
717-867-5491   fax 717-867-6124
caht@aol.com
Issues: Government waste; State and local
public finance; Taxation/tax reform

*Brown, Brian
Executive Director
Family Institute of Connecticut
77 Buckingham Street
Hartford, CT 06106
860-548-0066   fax 860-548-9545
bbrown@ctfamily.org
Issues: Abstinence and out-of-wedlock births;
Family and children; Marriage and divorce;
Religion and public life

*Brown, Floyd G.
Executive Director
Young America's Foundation Reagan Ranch
Project
217 State Street
Santa Barbara, CA 93101
805-957-1980   fax 805-957-9152
floydb@reaganranch.org
Issues: Arts, humanities and historic resources;
Charter schools; Federal education policy;
Media and popular culture; Philanthropy; The
Reagan legacy; School choice; Standards,
curriculum, and testing

*Brown, Dr. Harold O. J.
Professor of Theology and Philosophy
Reformed Theological Seminary
2101 Carmel Road
Charlotte, NC 28226
704-366-5066   fax 704-366-9295
hbrown@rts.edu
Issues: Abstinence and out-of-wedlock births;
Adoption, foster care, & child care services;
Arts, humanities and historic resources;
Church-state relations; Civil rights/racial
preferences; Ethics; Faith-based and volunteer
initiatives; Federal education policy; Health
care reform; Higher education; Home
schooling; Human rights; Media and popular
culture; Political correctness and
multiculturalism; Political philosophy;
Promoting democracy/public diplomacy;
Religion and public life; School choice

*Brown, Kenneth M., Ph.D.
Director of Research
Rio Grande Foundation
5800 Valerian Place, NE
Albuquerque, NM 87111
505-797-2324   fax 505-286-2422
kmbbrown23@aol.com
Issues: Conservative thought; Economic theory;
Government waste; Intelligence gathering and
covert operations; Medicaid; Political
correctness and multiculturalism; The Reagan
legacy; Research funding; School choice; State
and local public finance; Taxation/tax reform

Brown, Linda
Director Charter School Resource Center
Pioneer Institute for Public Policy Research
85 Devonshire Street, 8th Floor
Boston, MA 02109-3504
617-723-2277   fax 617-723-1880
lbrown@pioneerinstitute.org
Issues: Charter schools

*Brown, Martin D.
6706 Irongate Drive
Richmond, VA 23234
804-275-7050   fax 804-275-6706
mdb@comcast.net
Issues: Abstinence and out-of-wedlock births;
Adoption, foster care, & child care services;
Faith-based and volunteer initiatives; Family
and children; Marriage and divorce; Poverty
and dependency; Religion and public life;
School choice; Welfare/welfare reform

Brown, Morgan
Senior Fellow for Education Policy
Center of the American Experiment
12 South 6th Street, Suite 1024
Minneapolis, MN 55402
612-338-3605   fax 612-338-3621
morgan@amexp.org
Issues: Federal education policy; School choice

*Browne, Sharon
Attorney
Pacific Legal Foundation
10360 Old Placerville Road, Suite 100
Sacramento, CA 95827
916-362-2833   fax 916-362-2932
Issues: Bilingual education; Charter schools;
Civil rights/racial preferences; Constitutional
law; School choice

*Browne, Dr. William P.
Professor, Department of Political Science
Central Michigan University
ANSPA 313C
Mount Pleasant, MI 48859
989-774-3442   fax 989-774-1136
brown1wp@cmich.edu
Issues: Agriculture; Urban sprawl/livable cities

Browning, Dr. Don S.
Professor Emeritus, The Divinity School
University of Chicago
1025 East 58th Street, 401 Swift Hall
Chicago, IL 60637
773-702-8275   fax 773-702-8223
dsbrowni@midway.uchicago.edu
Issues: Family and children; Marriage and divorce; Religion and public life

Brownlee, David, III
Executive Vice President
Family First
101 East Kennedy Boulevard, Suite 1070
Tampa, FL 33602
813-222-8300   fax 813-222-8301
chris@thefamilyfirst.org
Issues: Aging/elder care; Family and children; Juvenile justice; Marriage and divorce; Media and popular culture; Religion and public life

Bruner, James, Esq.
Executive Director
New York Family Policy Council
3 E-Comm Square, Suite 16
Albany, NY 12207
518-432-8756   fax 518-426-4351
jbruner@nyfpc.org
Issues: Abstinence and out-of-wedlock births; Adoption, foster care, & child care services; Family and children; Government health programs; Marriage and divorce

*Bruno, Dr. Harry
Division Chairman, School of Justice Studies
Thomas University
1501 Mill Pond Road
Thomasville, GA 31792
800-538-9784   fax 912-226-1653
hbruno@thomasu.edu
Issues: Homeland security/civil defense; Intelligence gathering and covert operations; Juvenile justice; Police; Terrorism and international crime

*Brzeski, Dr. Andrzej
Professor of Economics Emeritus
University of California
Department of Economics
Davis, CA 95616
530-756-0665   fax 530-756-0694
abrzeski@ucdavis.edu
Issues: Central and Eastern Europe; Comparative economics; Russia and Eurasia

*Buchanan, Dr. Allen
Professor of Philosophy, Department of Philosophy
University of Arizona
Tucson, AZ 85721-0027
520-621-3120   fax 520-621-9559
allen@u.arizona.edu
Issues: Canada; Ethics; Health care reform; Human rights; Political philosophy; United Nations

Buchanan, Dr. James M.
Advisory General Director
Center for the Study of Public Choice
George Mason University, Buchanan House 1E6
Fairfax, VA 22030
703-993-2327   fax 703-993-2334
Issues: Advocacy and nonprofit public funding; Comparative economics; Comparative government; Congress; Economic education; Economic forecasting; Economic theory; Executive Branch/The Presidency; Federal budget; Federalism; Health care reform; International tax policy/tax competition; Non-governmental organizations; Political philosophy; Poverty and dependency; Privatization/Contracting-out; Social Security and retirement; State and local government; State and local public finance; Taxation/tax reform; Wealth creation/financial empowerment; Welfare/welfare reform

Buckley, Francis H.
Professor of Law and Director, Law and Economics Center
George Mason University School of Law
3301 North Fairfax Drive
Arlington, VA 22201
703-993-8028   fax 703-993-8088
fbuckley@gmu.edu
Issues: Canada; Charter schools; Church-state relations; Comparative government; Conservative thought; Federalism; Immigration; Marriage and divorce; Political philosophy; Tort and liability reform

*Buckstein, Steve
President
Cascade Policy Institute
813 S.W. Alder Street, Suite 450
Portland, OR 97205
503-242-0900   fax 503-242-3822
steve@cascadepolicy.org
Issues: Privatization/Contracting-out; School choice; Social Security and retirement

Bullert, Dr. Gary
Professor of Political Science
Columbia Basin College
2600 North 20th Street
Pasco, WA 99301
509-547-0511   fax 509-546-0401
gbullert@ctc.edu
Issues: American diplomacy/foreign policy; Church-state relations; Political philosophy; Religion and public life; Religious freedom

*Bullock, Scott
Senior Attorney
Institute for Justice
1717 Pennsylvania Avenue, N.W., Suite 200
Washington, DC 20006
202-955-1300   fax 202-955-1329
sbullock@ij.org
Issues: Campaign finance reform; Constitutional law; Federalism; Privacy; Property rights; Public interest law

*Bunce, Victoria Craig
Director of Research and Policy
Council for Affordable Health Insurance
10778 Alison Way
Inver Grove Heights, MN 55077-5459
651-688-6518   fax 651-905-4982
torybunce@cahi.org
Issues: Aging/elder care; Costs and benefits of regulation; Entitlement spending; Federal budget; Government health programs; Health care reform; Medicare; Privacy; Taxation/tax reform; Unfunded mandates

Burd, Dr. Frank A.
President
Baltimore Council on Foreign Affairs
World Trade Center, 401 East Pratt Street, Suite 1611
Baltimore, MD 21202
410-727-2150   fax 410-727-2174
bcfaprograms@aol.com
Issues: American diplomacy/foreign policy

Burke, Dr. T. Patrick
St. Joseph's University
104 Haverford Road
Wynnewood, PA 19096-3817
610-642-2563   fax 610-642-2654
ptburke@astro.temple.edu
Issues: Civil rights/racial preferences; Conservative thought; Ethics; Health care reform; Higher education; Political correctness and multiculturalism; Political philosophy; Southeast Asia (including Burma, Cambodia, Laos, Vietnam, Singapore, Malaysia, Indonesia, the Philippines, Australia, and New Zealand); Tort and liability reform

Burkhardt, Shane
Research Fellow
Hudson Institute
Herman Kahn Center, 5395 Emerson Way
Indianapolis, IN 46226
317-545-1000   fax 317-545-9639
info@hudson.org
Issues: Urban sprawl/livable cities

*Burling, James
Principal, Property Rights Practice Group
Pacific Legal Foundation
10360 Old Placerville Road, Suite 100
Sacramento, CA 95827
916-362-2833   fax 916-362-2932
jsb@pacificlegal.org
Issues: Constitutional law; Land use; Property rights

*Burnett, Dr. H. Sterling
Senior Fellow
National Center for Policy Analysis
12655 North Central Expressway, Suite 720
Dallas, TX 75243
972-386-6272   fax 972-386-0924
hsburnett@ncpa.org
Issues: Agriculture; Climate change; Costs and benefits of regulation; Electricity deregulation; Energy; Ethics; Forestry and national parks; Free-market environmentalism; Land use; Political philosophy; Property rights; Regulation through litigation; Risk assessment; Second Amendment; Stewardship; Tort and liability reform; Urban sprawl/livable cities; Wildlife management/endangered species

*Burnham, Dr. James B.
Murrin Professor of Global Competitiveness,
Donahue Graduate School of Business
Duquesne University
600 Forbes Avenue
Pittsburgh, PA 15282-3016
412-396-5118   fax 412-396-1797
burnham@duq.edu
Issues: Economic development/foreign aid;
International finance and multilateral banks;
Money and financial services; Trade

Burstion-Donbraye, Deborah
Managing Director
American Multimedia Inc. of Nigeria
19808 Longbrook Road
Cleveland, OH 44128-2767
216-295-2556   fax 216-295-2186
d.burstion-donbraye@worldnet.att.net
Issues: Abstinence and out-of-wedlock births;
Africa; Civil rights/racial preferences; Media
and popular culture; Political correctness and
multiculturalism; Religion and public life

*Burton, David
Partner
Argus Group
333 North Fairfax Drive, Suite 302
Alexandria, VA 22314
703-548-5868   fax 703-548-5869
drbargus@aol.com
Issues: Advocacy and nonprofit public funding;
The American Founding; Central and Eastern
Europe; Church-state relations; Conservative
thought; Constitutional law; Economic
development/foreign aid; Economic theory;
Entitlement spending; Federal budget;
International finance and multilateral banks;
International organizations (European Union,
OECD, etc.); International tax policy/tax
competition; Political philosophy; Privacy;
Religious freedom; State and local public
finance; Taxation/tax reform

Busch, Dr. Andrew E.
Assistant Professor, Political Science
Department
University of Denver
2199 South University Boulevard
Denver, CO 80208
303-871-2133   fax 303-871-2045
abusch@du.edu
Issues: Congress; Elections/polling; Executive
Branch/The Presidency; Political philosophy;
The Reagan legacy

*Butler, Dr. Henry N.
James Farley Professor of Economics,
Argyros School of Business & Economics
Chapman University
One University Drive
Orange, CA 92866
714-997-6576   fax 714-532-6081
hbutler@chapman.edu
Issues: Anti-trust; Federalism; Health care
reform; Judicial activism/judicial reform;
Regulation through litigation; Tort and liability
reform

Butler, Dr. John S.
Chairman and Professor, Management
Department
University of Texas
Burdine Hall 356
Austin, TX 78712
512-232-6328   fax 512-471-1748
john.butler@bus.utexas.edu
Issues: Citizenship and civil society; The
Economy

*Butler, Dr. Stuart
Vice President, Domestic and Economic
Policy Studies
The Heritage Foundation
214 Massachusetts Avenue, N.E.
Washington, DC 20002
202-546-4400   fax 202-544-5421
info@heritage.org
Issues: Aging/elder care; American history/
political tradition; Citizenship and civil society;
Comparative government; Entitlement
spending; Federalism; Government health
programs; Health care reform; Medicare;
Privatization/Contracting-out; The Reagan
legacy; School choice; Social Security and
retirement; Taxation/tax reform; Wealth
creation/financial empowerment

Butt, Dr. Mahmood
Professor and Chairman, Secondary
Education Department
Eastern Illinois University
213 Buzzard Building
Charleston, IL 61920
217-581-5931   fax 217-581-7147
cfmhb@eiu.edu
Issues: Middle East; South Asia (including India
and Pakistan); Standards, curriculum, and
testing

Butterworth, Dr. Charles E.
Professor, Department of Government and Politics
University of Maryland
3140 Tydings Hall
College Park, MD 20742-7215
301-405-4110   fax 301-314-9690
cebworth@gvpt.umd.edu
Issues: Political philosophy

*Byfield, Dan
President
American Land Foundation
P. O. Box 1033
Taylor, TX 76574
512-708-8083   fax 512-708-8298
dbliberty@aol.com
Issues: Land use; Property rights; Urban sprawl/ livable cities; Water; Wildlife management/ endangered species

Cahill, George F., CAE
Proprietor
The "Pride in America" Company
176 Warwick Drive
Pittsburgh, PA 15241
412-833-1717
Issues: The American Founding; American history/political tradition

Caine, Priscilla
President
Children First Tennessee
102 Walnut Street
Chattanooga, TN 37403
423-756-0410   fax 423-756-8250
priscilla@childrenfirsttn.org
Issues: School choice

*Caire, Kaleem
American Education Reform Council
4101 Woodrow Lane
Bowie, MD 20715
301-809-9761   fax 301-809-9762
kaleemc@aol.com
Issues: Business and education partnerships; Charter schools; School choice; Standards, curriculum, and testing

Calabresi, Steven
Professor of Law
Northwestern University School of Law
357 East Chicago Avenue
Chicago, IL 60611
312-503-7012   fax 312-503-2035
s-calabresi@nwu.edu
Issues: Constitutional law; Federalism; Judiciary; Public interest law

*Calabro, Dominic M.
President and CEO
Florida TaxWatch Research Institute, Inc.
106 North Bronough Street
Tallahassee, FL 32302-2209
850-222-5052   fax 850-222-7476
dcalabro@floridataxwatch.org
Issues: The American Founding; Comparative economics; Comparative government; The Economy; Government waste; Health care reform; Infrastructure; Initiative and referendum; Privatization/Contracting-out; Public school finance and administration; School choice; Social Security and retirement; Standards, curriculum, and testing; State and local government; State and local public finance; Taxation/tax reform; Tort and liability reform; Trade; Transportation; Unfunded mandates; Welfare/welfare reform

*Caldara, Jon Charles
President
Independence Institute
14142 Denver West Parkway, Suite 185
Golden, CO 80401
303-279-6536   fax 303-279-4176
jon@i2i.org
Issues: Advocacy and nonprofit public funding; Comparative economics; Conservative thought; Economic education; Education unions and interest groups; Health care reform; Privatization/Contracting-out; School choice; Taxation/tax reform; Transportation; Transportation deregulation; Unfunded mandates; Unions

*Calfee, Dr. John
Resident Scholar
American Enterprise Institute
1150 17th Street, N.W.
Washington, DC 20036
202-862-7175   fax 202-862-7177
calfeej@aei.org
Issues: Government health programs; Medicare; Regulation through litigation; Risk assessment; Substance abuse; Tort and liability reform

Calingaert, Daniel
Regional Program Director, Asia
International Republican Institute
1225 Eye Street, N.W., Suite 700
Washington, DC 20005
202-408-9450   fax 202-408-9462
asia@iri.org
Issues: China; Japan; Korea; Northeast Asia;
South Asia (including India and Pakistan);
Southeast Asia (including Burma, Cambodia,
Laos, Vietnam, Singapore, Malaysia, Indonesia,
the Philippines, Australia, and New Zealand)

*Callahan, F. Patricia
President
American Association of Small Property
Owners
4200 Cathedral Avenue, N.W., Suite 515
Washington, DC 20016
202-244-6277   fax 202-363-3669
president@aaspo.org
Issues: Congress; Constitutional law;
Entrepreneurship/free enterprise;
Environmental regulation; Federalism;
Initiative and referendum; Judicial activism/
judicial reform; Judiciary; Land use; Money and
financial services; Property rights; Public
interest law; State and local government;
Taxation/tax reform; Urban sprawl/livable
cities

Calomiris, Charles
Visiting Scholar
American Enterprise Institute
1150 17th Street, N.W.
Washington, DC 20036
202-862-5800   fax 212-316-9219
Issues: Costs and benefits of regulation; The
Economy; International finance and
multilateral banks; Latin America; Risk
assessment

Cameron, Bruce N.
Staff Attorney
National Right to Work Legal Defense
Foundation
8001 Braddock Road, Suite 600
Springfield, VA 22160
703-321-8510   fax 703-321-9319
bnc@nrtw.org
Issues: Constitutional law; Religious freedom;
Right to work

Cameron, Nigel M. de S.
Senior Program Officer
Institute for Humane Studies at George
Mason University
3301 North Fairfax Drive, Suite 440
Arlington, VA 22201
703-993-4880   fax 703-993-4890
nashford@gmu.edu
Issues: Ethics; Sound science

Campaigne, Jameson, Jr.
Publisher
Jameson Books, Inc.
722 Columbus Street, P. O. Box 738
Ottawa, IL 61350
815-434-7905   fax 815-434-7907
jamesonbooks@yahoo.com
Issues: The American Founding; Church-state
relations; Conservative thought; Higher
education; Intellectual property; Intelligence
gathering and covert operations; Political
philosophy; Property rights; Religion and
public life; Second Amendment; Social
Security and retirement; Wildlife
management/endangered species

Campbell, Kurt
Senior Vice President and Director,
International Security Program
Center for Strategic and International
Studies
1800 K Street, N.W., Suite 400
Washington, DC 20006
202-877-0200   fax 202-775-3199
kcampbel@csis.org
Issues: Arms control; China; Emerging threats/
threat assessment; Homeland security/civil
defense; Japan; Korea; Military strategy;
Northeast Asia; Promoting democracy/public
diplomacy; Russia and Eurasia; Southeast Asia
(including Burma, Cambodia, Laos, Vietnam,
Singapore, Malaysia, Indonesia, the
Philippines, Australia, and New Zealand)

Campbell, Dr. William F.
Secretary
The Philadelphia Society
3914 Broussard Street
Baton Rouge, LA 70808
225-927-2042   fax 225-924-4727
campbellw1@prodigy.net
Issues: Arts, humanities and historic resources;
Conservative thought; Latin America; Political
philosophy; Religion and public life

*Canfield, Ken R., Ph.D.
President
National Center for Fathering
P. O. Box 413888
Kansas City, MO 64141
913-384-4661   fax 913-384-4665
kencanfield@fathers.com
Issues: Family and children; Marriage and divorce

Capaldi, Dr. Nicholas
Legendre-Soule Distinguished Chair in Business Ethics, College of Business Administration
Loyola University New Orleans
6363 St. Charles Avenue, Campus Box 15
New Orleans, LA 70118
504-864-7957   fax 504-864-7970
capaldi@loyno.edu
Issues: Entrepreneurship/free enterprise; Ethics; Higher education; Immigration; Political philosophy; School choice

*Caprara, David
President
The Empowerment Network
17 Rosewood Drive
Fredericksburg, VA 22408
540-220-8841   fax 540-891-4624
davidcap@aol.com
Issues: Citizenship and civil society; Conservative thought; Faith-based and volunteer initiatives; Family and children; Marriage and divorce; Poverty and dependency; Wealth creation/financial empowerment

Carbone, Leslie
3303 Cannongate Road, Suite 204
Fairfax, VA 22031
703-206-9679   lesliecarbone@yahoo.com
Issues: Family and children; Free Speech; Higher education; Marriage and divorce; Political correctness and multiculturalism; Taxation/tax reform; Welfare/welfare reform

*Cardle, James B.
Texas Citizen Action Network
104 Racebrook Court
Austin, TX 78734
512-608-0083   fax 512-476-5906
lessgovt@austin.rr.com
Issues: Charter schools; Citizenship and civil society; Conservative thought; The Economy; Electricity deregulation; Entrepreneurship/free enterprise; Family and children; Government waste; Health care reform; Job training/welfare to work; Poverty and dependency; Property rights; Public school finance and administration; Religion and public life; School choice; Social Security and retirement; Standards, curriculum, and testing; State and local public finance; State-sponsored gambling; Taxation/tax reform

*Carey, John E.
International Defense Consultants, Inc.
1801 Crystal Drive, Suite 1109
Arlington, VA 22202
703-920-2789
Issues: Afghanistan; American diplomacy/foreign policy; American history/political tradition; Arms control; Central and Eastern Europe; China; Conservative thought; Defense budget; Emerging threats/threat assessment; Ethics; Export controls/military transfers; Higher education; Homeland security/civil defense; Intelligence gathering and covert operations; International organizations (European Union, OECD, etc.); Japan; Korea; Middle East; Military strategy; Missile defense; NATO and other alliances; Northeast Asia; Promoting democracy/public diplomacy; Russia and Eurasia; South Asia (including India and Pakistan); Southeast Asia (including Burma, Cambodia, Laos, Vietnam, Singapore, Malaysia, Indonesia, the Philippines, Australia, and New Zealand); Terrorism and international crime; Western Europe

Carey, Merrick
Chief Executive Officer
Lexington Institute
1600 Wilson Boulevard, Suite 900
Arlington, VA 22209
703-522-5828   fax 703-522-5837
carey@lexingtoninstitute.org
Issues: Bilingual education; Charter schools;
Defense budget; Emerging threats/threat
assessment; Environmental regulation; Federal
education policy; Homeland security/civil
defense; Military strategy; Missile defense;
Readiness and manpower; School choice;
Standards, curriculum, and testing; Taxation/
tax reform; Terrorism and international crime

*Carleson, Robert
Chairman/CEO
American Civil Rights Union
3213 Duke Street, Number 625
Alexandria, VA 22314
703-566-2696   fax 703-566-2322
rcarleson@aol.com
Issues: The American Founding; American
history/political tradition; Church-state
relations; Citizenship and civil society; Civil
rights/racial preferences; Comparative
government; Conservative thought;
Constitutional law; Ethics; Executive Branch/
The Presidency; Federalism; Free Speech; Job
training/welfare to work; Judicial activism/
judicial reform; Land use; Political philosophy;
Property rights; Public interest law; The Reagan
legacy; Regulatory reform; Religious freedom;
Second Amendment; State and local
government; Tort and liability reform;
Welfare/welfare reform

Carlisle, John K.
Research Associate and Editor, *Organization
Trends* and *Foundation Watch*
Capital Research Center
1513 16th Street, N.W.
Washington, DC 20036
202-483-6900   fax 202-483-6902
Issues: Climate change; Environmental
regulation; Federal education policy; Health
care reform; Land use; Property rights; Urban
sprawl/livable cities

*Carlson, Dr. Allan C.
Distinguished Fellow for Family Policy
Studies, Family Research Council, and
President
Howard Center for Family, Religion and
Society
934 North Main Street
Rockford, IL 61103
815-964-5819   fax 815-965-1826
allan@profam.org
Issues: Abstinence and out-of-wedlock births;
Adoption, foster care, & child care services;
Agriculture; American history/political
tradition; Church-state relations; Family and
children; Home schooling; Marriage and
divorce; Religion and public life; School
choice; Taxation/tax reform; Welfare/welfare
reform

*Carlson, John
Board Member
Washington Policy Center
c/o KVI Radio-Tower Boulevard
1809 7th Avenue, Suite 200
Seattle, WA 98101
206-223-5700   fax 425-635-1181
johnc@fisherradio.com
Issues: Criminal law and procedure; Initiative
and referendum; Police; Political correctness
and multiculturalism; The Reagan legacy; State
and local public finance

*Carozza, Michael
Vice President, Federal Government Affairs
Bristol-Myers Squibb
655 15th Street, N.W., Suite 300
Washington, DC 20005
202-783-0900   fax 202-783-2308
michael.carozza@bms.com
Issues: Entitlement spending; Federal budget;
Medicaid; Medicare; Social Security and
retirement

Carpenter, Brian
Director of Leadership Development
Mackinac Center for Public Policy
140 West Main Street, P. O. Box 568
Midland, MI 48640
989-631-0900   fax 989-631-0964
carpenter@mackinac.org
Issues: Public school finance and
administration; School choice; Standards,
curriculum, and testing

Carpenter, Dr. Ted Galen
Vice President for Defense and Foreign
Policy Studies
Cato Institute
1000 Massachusetts Avenue, N.W.
Washington, DC 20001-5403
202-842-0200   fax 202-842-3490
tcarpent@cato.org
Issues: American diplomacy/foreign policy;
Central and Eastern Europe; International
organizations (European Union, OECD, etc.);
Middle East; NATO and other alliances; South
Asia (including India and Pakistan); Southeast
Asia (including Burma, Cambodia, Laos,
Vietnam, Singapore, Malaysia, Indonesia, the
Philippines, Australia, and New Zealand);
United Nations; Western Europe

Carr, Chris
Vice President and General Counsel
Georgia Public Policy Foundation
6100 Lake Forest Drive, N.W., Suite 110
Atlanta, GA 30328
404-256-4050   fax 404-256-9909
ccarr@gppf.org
Issues: Charter schools; Congress; Defense
budget; Military strategy

Carrington, Don
Vice President
John Locke Foundation
200 West Morgan Street, Suite 200
Raleigh, NC 27601
919-828-3876   fax 919-821-5117
carrington@johnlocke.org
Issues: Entrepreneurship/free enterprise;
Ethics; State and local government;
Unemployment insurance

*Carroll, Thomas
President
Empire Foundation for Policy Research
Four Chelsea Place, Second Floor
Clifton Park, NY 12065
518-383-2877   fax 518-383-2380
empire@capital.net
Issues: Charter schools; Higher education;
School choice

*Carter, Samuel Casey
Director of Research
Acade Metrics, LLC
5345 Chevy Chase Parkway, N.W., Suite 300
Washington, DC 20015
202-487-7902   caseycarter@earthlink.net
Issues: Business and education partnerships;
Charter schools; Citizenship and civil society;
Conservative thought; Ethics; Federal
education policy; Home schooling; Political
philosophy; Religion and public life; School
choice; Standards, curriculum, and testing;
Telecommunications and the Internet

*Carvin, Michael A.
Jones, Day, Reavis & Pogue
51 Louisiana Avenue, N.W.
Washington, DC 20001-2113
202-879-7643   fax 202-626-1700
mcarvin@jonesday.com
Issues: Civil rights/racial preferences;
Constitutional law; Electoral reform/voting
rights; Electricity deregulation; Free Speech;
Judicial activism/judicial reform

Casale, Ralph L.
Senior Associate Counsel
Center for Individual Rights
1233 20th Street, N.W., Suite 300
Washington, DC 20036
202-833-8400   fax 202-833-8410

*Casey, Samuel
Executive Director
Christian Legal Society
4208 Evergreen Lane, Suite 222
Annandale, VA 22003
703-642-1070   fax 703-642-1075
sbcasey@clsnet.org
Issues: Church-state relations; Faith-based and
volunteer initiatives; Religion and public life;
Religious freedom

Caslin, Michael John, III
CEO and Executive Director
National Foundation for Teaching
Entrepreneurship
120 Wall Street, 29th Floor
New York, NY 10005
212-232-3333   fax 212-232-2244
nfte@nfte.org
Issues: Entrepreneurship/free enterprise

*Caso, Anthony T.
Senior Vice President and General Counsel
Pacific Legal Foundation
10360 Old Placerville Road, Suite 100
Sacramento, CA 95827
916-362-2833   fax 916-362-2932
atc@pacificlegal.org
Issues: Civil rights/racial preferences;
Constitutional law; Federalism; Free Speech;
Initiative and referendum; Public interest law;
Right to work; State and local government

*Cass, Dr. Ronald
Dean
Boston University School of Law
765 Commonwealth Avenue
Boston, MA 02115
617-353-3112   fax 617-353-7400
roncass@bu.edu
Issues: Anti-trust; Free Speech; International
law; Judiciary; Trade

*Cassell, Paul
Professor, College of Law
University of Utah
332 South 1400 East Front
Salt Lake City, UT 84112
801-585-5202   fax 801-581-6897
cassellp@law.utah.edu
Issues: Corrections and sentencing; Crime/
crime statistics; Criminal law and procedure;
Police

Chafuen, Dr. Alejandro A.
President and CEO
Atlas Economic Research Foundation
4084 University Drive, Suite 103
Fairfax, VA 22030
703-934-6969   fax 703-352-7530
alex.chafuen@atlasusa.org
Issues: Economic development/foreign aid;
Ethics; Latin America; Philanthropy; Property
rights; Religion and public life; Stewardship;
Trade

Chang, Dr. Cecilia
Vice President for International Relations
and Dean, Center of Asian Studies
St. John's University
8000 Utopia Parkway
Jamaica, NY 11439
718-990-6581   fax 718-990-2088
Issues: China; Japan; Northeast Asia

*Chapman, Bruce K.
President
Discovery Institute
1402 Third Avenue, Suite 400
Seattle, WA 98101
206-292-0401   fax 206-682-5320
bchapman@discovery.org
Issues: Conservative thought; The Economy;
Ethics; Federal civil service; Federalism; Trade;
Transportation

*Chapman, James
Executive Director
Rocky Mountain Family Council
P. O. Box 13619
Denver, CO 80201
303-292-1800   fax 303-796-7848
rmfc@aol.com
Issues: Abstinence and out-of-wedlock births;
Citizenship and civil society; Family and
children; Marriage and divorce; Religion and
public life

*Chappell, Milton L.
Staff Attorney
National Right to Work Legal Defense
Foundation
8001 Braddock Road, Suite 600
Springfield, VA 22160
703-321-8510   fax 703-321-9319
mlc@nrtw.org
Issues: Constitutional law; Education unions
and interest groups; Free Speech; Labor and
employment; Right to work; Unions

Charles, Dr. J. Daryl
Associate Professor, Department of Religion
and Philosophy
Taylor University
236 West Reade Avenue
Upland, IN 46989
765-998-5223   fax 765-998-4930
drcharles@tayloru.edu
Issues: Civil rights/racial preferences; Crime/
crime statistics; Higher education; Religion
and public life

*Charles, John A.
Environmental Policy Director
Cascade Policy Institute
813 S.W. Alder Street, Suite 450
Portland, OR 97205
503-242-0900   fax 503-242-3822
john@cascadepolicy.org
Issues: Free-market environmentalism; Land
use; Property rights; Transportation
deregulation; Urban sprawl/livable cities

Chauhan, Dr. Pradyumna S.
Chairman, Department of English
Arcadia University
240 Berkley Road
Glenside, PA 19038
215-572-2106   fax 215-572-2126
Issues: Arts, humanities and historic resources;
Bilingual education; Higher education; Media
and popular culture; South Asia (including
India and Pakistan); United Nations

*Chavez, Linda
President
Center for Equal Opportunity
14 Pidgeon Hill Drive, Suite 500
Sterling, VA 20165
703-421-5443   fax 703-421-6401
lchavez@ceousa.org
Issues: Abstinence and out-of-wedlock births;
Bilingual education; Campaign finance
reform; Civil rights/racial preferences;
Education unions and interest groups; Federal
education policy; Higher education;
Immigration; Labor and employment; Latin
America; Minimum wage; Political correctness
and multiculturalism; The Reagan legacy;
Standards, curriculum, and testing; Unions

*Cheney, Hon. Lynne V.
Senior Fellow
American Enterprise Institute
1150 17th Street, N.W.
Washington, DC 20036
202-862-5918   fax 202-862-7177
lcheney@aei.org
Issues: Arts, humanities and historic resources;
Federal education policy; Higher education;
Media and popular culture; Political
correctness and multiculturalism; Standards,
curriculum, and testing

Chickering, Lawrence A.
President
Educate Girls Globally
P. O. Box 29090
San Francisco, CA 94118
415-561-2260   lac@educategirls.org
Issues: Religion and public life

*Chieppo, Charles
Director, Shamie Center for Restructuring
Government
Pioneer Institute for Public Policy Research
85 Devonshire Street, 8th Floor
Boston, MA 02109
617-723-2277   fax 617-723-1880
cchieppo@pioneerinstitute.org
Issues: Privatization/Contracting-out;
Transportation

*Chilton, Kenneth W., Ph.D.
Associate Professor of Management and
Director
Institute for Study of Economics and the
Environment
Lindenwood University, 209 South
Kingshighway
St. Charles, MO 63301-1695
636-949-4742   fax 636-949-4992
kchilton@lindenwood.edu
Issues: Air; Costs and benefits of regulation;
Energy; Environmental regulation; Regulatory
reform; Risk assessment; Sound science; Waste
management

*Chiswick, Dr. Barry R.
UIC Distinguished Professor, Department of
Economics
University of Illinois, Chicago
601 South Morgan Street, M/C 144
Chicago, IL 60607-7121
312-996-2683   fax 312-996-3344
brchis@uic.edu
Issues: Economic education; Economic theory;
Immigration; Labor and employment;
Minimum wage

Chitester, Robert
President
Palmer R. Chitester Fund
1502 Powell Avenue
Erie, PA 16505
814-464-9066   fax 814-464-9069
Issues: Arts, humanities and historic resources;
Economic education; Forestry and national
parks; Intellectual property; Property rights;
Telecommunications and the Internet

*Chiu, Dr. Hungdah
Director, East Asian Legal Studies
University of Maryland School of Law
500 West Baltimore Street
Baltimore, MD 21201-1700
410-706-3870   fax 410-706-1516
Issues: China; Comparative government;
Immigration; International law; Peacekeeping;
Terrorism and international crime

Christainsen, Dr. Gregory B.
Professor of Economics
California State University, Hayward
25800 Carlos Bee Boulevard
Hayward, CA 94542
510-885-3301   fax 510-885-4339
gchrista@csuhayward.edu
Issues: Comparative economics; Free-market
environmentalism; Southeast Asia (including
Burma, Cambodia, Laos, Vietnam, Singapore,
Malaysia, Indonesia, the Philippines, Australia,
and New Zealand)

*Christensen, Bryce J.
Instructor, Department of English
Southern Utah University
Multipurpose Center
Cedar City, UT 84720
435-865-8048   fax 435-865-8169
christensenb@suu.edu
Issues: Family and children; Marriage and
divorce

Christmas, Dr. Barbara
Executive Director
Professional Association of Georgia
Educators
2971 Flowers Road South
Chamblee, GA 30341
770-216-8555   fax 770-216-8589
Issues: Education unions and interest groups

*Chubb, John
Chief Education Officer
Edison Schools, Inc.
521 Fifth Avenue, 11th Floor
New York, NY 10175
212-419-1600   fax 212-419-1604
jchubb@newyork.edisonproject.com
Issues: Business and education partnerships;
Charter schools; Education unions and interest
groups; Federal education policy; Public school
finance and administration; School choice;
Standards, curriculum, and testing

*Ciamarra, Michael A.
Vice President
Alabama Policy Institute
402 Office Park Drive, Suite 300
Birmingham, AL 35223
205-870-9900   fax 205-870-4407
michaelc@alabamapolicy.org
Issues: Aging/elder care; American history/
political tradition; Business and education
partnerships; Campaign finance reform;
Corrections and sentencing; Economic
education; Electoral reform/voting rights;
Entrepreneurship/free enterprise; Ethics;
Faith-based and volunteer initiatives; Family
and children; Intellectual property; Judicial
activism/judicial reform; Marriage and
divorce; Media and popular culture; Medicaid;
Privacy; School choice; Standards, curriculum,
and testing; State and local government; State
and local public finance; Taxation/tax reform;
Telecommunications and the Internet; Tort
and liability reform; Welfare/welfare reform

*Cihak, Robert, M.D.
Health Policy Analyst
Evergreen Freedom Foundation
405 Slater Street South
Kirkland, WA 98033
425-828-0444   r.cihak@verizon.net
Issues: Government health programs; Health
care reform; Medicaid; Medicare

Clair, Richard J.
Corporate Counsel
National Right to Work Legal Defense
Foundation
8001 Braddock Road, Suite 600
Springfield, VA 22160
703-321-8510   fax 703-321-0528
rjc@nrtw.org
Issues: Right to work; Unions

Clark, Dr. Henry C., III
Professor of History
Canisius College
2001 Main Street
Buffalo, NY 14208
716-888-2682   fax 716-888-2525
clark@canisius.edu
Issues: Higher education

*Clark, Dr. J. R.
Probasco Chair of Free Enterprise
University of Tennessee, Chattanooga
Fletcher Hall, Dept. 6106, 615 McCallie
Avenue, Suite 313
Chattanooga, TN 37403
423-425-4118   fax 423-425-5218
j-clark@utc.edu
Issues: Economic education; Environmental
education; Free-market environmentalism;
Poverty and dependency; School choice; Social
Security and retirement; State and local public
finance; Taxation/tax reform

Clark, John
Senior Fellow and Director, Center for
Central European and Eurasian Studies
Hudson Institute
Herman Kahn Center, 5395 Emerson Way
Indianapolis, IN 46226
317-549-4159   fax 317-545-9639
johnc@hudson.org
Issues: American history/political tradition;
Central and Eastern Europe; Citizenship and
civil society; International organizations
(European Union, OECD, etc.); NATO and
other alliances; Russia and Eurasia; Welfare/
welfare reform

*Clark, Micah
Executive Director
American Family Association
P. O. Box 26208
Indianapolis, IN 46226
317-541-9287   fax 317-541-9707
micah@netusa1.net
Issues: Abstinence and out-of-wedlock births;
Charter schools; Citizenship and civil society;
Family and children; Home schooling;
Marriage and divorce; Media and popular
culture; Religion and public life; Religious
freedom; School choice; State-sponsored
gambling

*Clark, Michele A.
Co-Director, The Protection Project
Johns Hopkins University School of
Advanced International Studies
1717 Massachusetts Avenue, N.W., Suite 515
Washington, DC 20036
202-663-5892   fax 202-663-5899
mclark23@jhu.edu
Issues: Human rights

Clarke, Jody Manley
Vice President, Communications
Competitive Enterprise Institute
1001 Connecticut Avenue, N.W., Suite 1250
Washington, DC 20036
202-331-1010   fax 202-331-0640
jclarke@cei.org
Issues: Media and popular culture

Clarke, Jonathan
Research Fellow in Foreign Policy Studies
Cato Institute
1000 Massachusetts Avenue, N.W.
Washington, DC 20001-5403
202-842-0200   fax 202-842-3490
Issues: Africa; American diplomacy/foreign
policy; Central and Eastern Europe; Northeast
Asia; Southeast Asia (including Burma,
Cambodia, Laos, Vietnam, Singapore,
Malaysia, Indonesia, the Philippines, Australia,
and New Zealand); Western Europe

Clarkson, Dr. Kenneth W.
Director, Law and Economics Center
University of Miami
1509 Garcia Avenue
Coral Gables, FL 33146-1029
305-284-6174   fax 305-662-9159
k.clarkson@miami.edu
Issues: Adoption, foster care, & child care
services; Economic education; The Economy;
Entitlement spending; Government waste;
Health care reform; Poverty and dependency;
Privatization/Contracting-out; Property rights;
Social Security and retirement; State and local
public finance; Telecommunications and the
Internet; Trade

Cleary, Peter
Deputy Director and Director of CPAC
American Conservative Union
1007 Cameron Street
Alexandria, VA 22314
703-836-8602   fax 703-836-8606
pcleary@conservative.org
Issues: Campaign finance reform; Federal
budget; Government waste; Taxation/tax
reform; Unions; Urban sprawl/livable cities

*Clegg, Roger
General Counsel
Center for Equal Opportunity
14 Pidgeon Hill Drive, Suite 500
Sterling, VA 20165
703-421-5443   fax 703-421-6401
rclegg@ceousa.org
Issues: Bilingual education; Civil rights/racial
preferences; Constitutional law; Higher
education; Judicial activism/judicial reform;
Labor and employment; Political correctness
and multiculturalism

*Cleland, Bartlett D.
Director, Center for Technology Freedom
Institute for Policy Innovation
250 South Stemmons, Suite 215
Lewisville, TX 75067
972-874-5139   fax 972-874-5144
bcleland@ipi.org
Issues: Intellectual property; Privacy;
Telecommunications and the Internet

Clements, Elisa
Executive Director
Education Excellence Utah
4897 Lake Park Boulevard, Suite 100
Salt Lake City, UT 84120
801-415-2813   fax 801-415-2810
elisa@edexutah.org
Issues: School choice

Cleveland, Paul A., Ph.D.
Associate Professor of Economics
Birmingham Southern College
Box 549023
Birmingham, AL 35254
205-226-4817   fax 205-226-3080
pclevela@bsc.edu
Issues: Comparative economics; Costs and
benefits of regulation; Entrepreneurship/free
enterprise

*Climer, Jerome F.
President
The Congressional Institute
401 Wythe Street, Suite 103
Alexandria, VA 22314
703-837-8817   fax 703-837-8812
change_leader@congInst.org
Issues: Campaign finance reform; Congress;
Elections/polling; Electoral reform/voting
rights; Executive Branch/The Presidency;
Federal civil service; Health care reform;
Homeland security/civil defense; Social
Security and retirement; State and local
government

*Clinton, Robert L.
Professor, Department of Political Science
Southern Illinois University
Carbondale, IL 62901-4501
618-453-3198   fax 618-453-3163
rclinton@siu.edu
Issues: Constitutional law; Judicial activism/
judicial reform; Judiciary; Religion and public
life; Religious freedom

Clor, Dr. Harry M.
Professor Emeritus, Department of Political
Science
Kenyon College
Horwitz House 4
Gambier, OH 43022
740-427-5309   clor@kenyon.edu
Issues: Constitutional law; Ethics; Political
philosophy

*Clowes, George
Editor, *School Reform News*
Heartland Institute
19 South LaSalle, Suite 903
Chicago, IL 60603
312-377-4000   fax 312-377-5000
clowesga@aol.com
Issues: School choice

Cobane, Craig T.
Assistant Professor, Department of History
and Political Science
Culver-Stockton College
One College Hill
Canton, MO 63435
217-231-6395   fax 217-231-6611
ccobane@culver.edu
Issues: NATO and other alliances; Political
correctness and multiculturalism; Terrorism
and international crime

Cobin, Dr. John
Investment Advisor
Montauk Financial Group
P. O. Box 25686
Greenville, SC 29616
864-444-3728   fax 413-622-9441
jcobin@policyofliberty.net
Issues: Bilingual education; Costs and benefits
of regulation; Family and children; Home
schooling; Land use; Latin America;
Privatization/Contracting-out; Property rights;
Public interest law; Standards, curriculum, and
testing; Transportation; Transportation
deregulation

Cochran, Dr. Howard, Jr.
Professor of Economics and Management
Belmont University
1900 Belmont Boulevard
Nashville, TN 37212
615-460-6784   fax 615-460-6487
cochranh@mail.belmont.edu
Issues: The Economy; Faith-based and
volunteer initiatives; Higher education;
Standards, curriculum, and testing

Codevilla, Dr. Angelo M.
Professor, International Relations,
Department of International Relations
Boston University
156 Bay State Road
Boston, MA 02215
617-353-6417   fax 617-353-5350
acodevil@bu.edu
Issues: Arms control; Comparative government;
Intelligence gathering and covert operations;
Latin America; Military strategy; Missile
defense; NATO and other alliances; Political
philosophy; Readiness and manpower; Western
Europe

*Coffey, Dr. Joseph I.
Distinguished Service Professor Emeritus
89 Castle Howard Court
Princeton, NJ 08540
609-497-2882   fax 609-683-9691
Issues: American diplomacy/foreign policy;
Arms control; Emerging threats/threat
assessment; International organizations
(European Union, OECD, etc.); Military
strategy; Missile defense; NATO and other
alliances; Peacekeeping; Western Europe

Cogan, Dr. John F.
Leonard and Shirley Ely Senior Fellow
Hoover Institution
Stanford University
Stanford, CA 94305
650-723-2585   fax 650-723-1687
cogan@hoover.stanford.edu
Issues: Discretionary spending; Entitlement
spending; Federalism; Government debt;
Government health programs; Health care
reform; Medicaid; Medicare; Poverty and
dependency; Social Security and retirement;
Unfunded mandates; Welfare/welfare reform

Cohen, Andrew I.
Assistant Professor of Philosophy,
Department of Philosophy
University of Oklahoma
455 West Lindsey, Room 605 DaHT
Norman, OK 73019-2006
405-325-6433   aicohen@ou.edu
Issues: Arts, humanities and historic resources;
Citizenship and civil society; Ethics; Free-
market environmentalism; Intellectual
property; Political philosophy; Privacy;
Property rights

*Cohen, Dr. Ariel
Research Fellow, Kathryn and Shelby Cullom
Davis Institute for International Studies
The Heritage Foundation
214 Massachusetts Avenue, N.E.
Washington, DC 20002
202-546-4400   fax 202-675-1758
ariel.cohen@heritage.org
Issues: Afghanistan; American diplomacy/
foreign policy; Central and Eastern Europe;
Economic development/foreign aid; Human
rights; International finance and multilateral
banks; Middle East; Promoting democracy/
public diplomacy; Russia and Eurasia; Western
Europe

*Cohen, Dr. Bernard L.
Professor, Department of Physics
University of Pittsburgh
3941 O'Hara Street, 100 Allen Hall
Pittsburgh, PA 15260
412-624-9245   fax 412-624-9163
blc@pitt.edu
Issues: Energy; Sound science; Waste
management

Cohen, Dr. Bonner R.
Senior Fellow
Lexington Institute
1600 Wilson Boulevard, Suite 900
Arlington, VA 22209
703-522-9643   fax 703-522-5837
cohen@lexingtoninstitute.org
Issues: Environmental regulation; Forestry and
national parks; Free-market environmentalism;
Land use; Property rights; Regulatory reform;
Risk assessment; Sound science; Wildlife
management/endangered species

Cohen, Dr. Eliot A.
Professor and Director of Strategic Studies
The Paul H. Nitze School of Advanced
International Studies
Johns Hopkins University, 1740
Massachusetts Avenue, N.W.
Washington, DC 20036
202-663-5781   fax 202-663-5656
Issues: Defense budget; NATO and other
alliances; Readiness and manpower

Cohen, Eric
Resident Scholar
Ethics and Public Policy Center
1015 15th Street, N.W.
Washington, DC 20005
202-862-0855   fax 202-408-0632
ecohen@eppc.org
Issues: American diplomacy/foreign policy;
American history/political tradition;
Citizenship and civil society; Conservative
thought; Ethics; Higher education; Political
philosophy

*Cohen, Laurence
Senior Fellow
Yankee Institute for Public Policy Studies
117 New London Tournpike
Glastonbury, CT 06033
860-633-8188   fax 860-657-9444
104415.1625@compuserve.com
Issues: Health care reform; School choice; State
and local government; Urban sprawl/livable
cities

*Colarelli, Dr. Stephen M.
Professor, Department of Psychology
Central Michigan University
235 Sloan
Mount Pleasant, MI 48859
989-774-6483   fax 989-774-2553
Issues: Job training/welfare to work; School-
to-work

Colburn, Dr. Brooks
Interim President
Foundation for Economic Education
30 South Broadway
Irvington-on-Hudson, NY 10533
914-591-7230   fax 914-591-8910
fee@fee.org
Issues: Ethics; Political philosophy

*Cole, Dr. Stephen
Professor, Department of Sociology
State University of New York
Stony Brook University
Stony Brook, NY 11794-0001
631-632-7732   fax 631-632-8203
stephen.cole@sunysb.edu
Issues: Civil rights/racial preferences; Crime/
crime statistics; Environmental regulation;
Health care reform; Higher education;
Political correctness and multiculturalism;
Research funding

*Colgan, Dr. Richard T.
Professor of Psychology
Bridgewater State College
24 Seneca Street
Warwick, RI 02886
508-531-2247   fax 508-531-4247
rcolgan@bridgew.edu
Issues: Aging/elder care; Family and children;
Higher education; Home schooling; Standards,
curriculum, and testing; Taxation/tax reform

Collier, Dr. Boyd D.
Professor, College of Business
Administration
Tarleton State University
P. O. Box 0505-T
Stephenville, TX 76402
254-968-9354   fax 254-968-9920
collier@tarleton.edu
Issues: Comparative economics; Conservative
thought; Economic education; Economic
theory; Ethics; Free-market environmentalism;
Minimum wage; Water

Collier, Peter
Vice President
Center for the Study of Popular Culture
9911 West Pico Boulevard, Suite 1290
Los Angeles, CA 90035
323-556-2550   baseball@telis.org
Issues: Civil rights/racial preferences; Media
and popular culture; Political correctness and
multiculturalism

Collins, Richard H.
Founder and Chairman
Children's Education Fund
P. O. Box 225748
Dallas, TX 75222-5748
972-298-1811   fax 972-572-1515
rhcoll@yahoo.com
Issues: School choice

*Colson, Charles
Chairman
Prison Fellowship Ministries
P. O. Box 17500
Washington, DC 20041
703-478-0100   fax 703-904-7324
nniemayer@pfm.org
Issues: Church-state relations; Constitutional law; Corrections and sentencing; Crime/crime statistics; Criminal law and procedure; Judicial activism/judicial reform; Juvenile justice; Religious freedom

Colwell, Dr. Peter F.
Professor of Finance
University of Illinois
304B David Kinley Hall, 1407 West Gregory Drive
Urbana, IL 61801
217-333-1185   fax 217-244-9867
Issues: Federal budget; Land use; Property rights; State and local public finance; Stewardship; Taxation/tax reform; Urban sprawl/livable cities

Colyandro, John
Executive Director
Texas Conservative Coalition
P. O. Box 2659
Austin, TX 78768
512-474-1798   fax 512-482-8355
mike.price@txcc.org
Issues: Elections/polling; Social Security and retirement; State and local government; Telecommunications and the Internet

Combs, Dr. J. Paul
Director
Appalachian Regional Development Institute
Appalachian State University, University Hall
Boone, NC 28608
828-262-6161   fax 828-265-8673
combsjp@appstate.edu
Issues: Entrepreneurship/free enterprise; State and local public finance

Combs, Roberta
President
Christian Coalition of America
499 South Capitol Street, S.W., Suite 615
Washington, DC 20003
202-479-6900   fax 202-479-4260
coalition@cc.org
Issues: Abstinence and out-of-wedlock births; Adoption, foster care, & child care services; Citizenship and civil society; Faith-based and volunteer initiatives; Family and children; Marriage and divorce; Religion and public life

Conant, Dr. John L.
Professor and Chairman, Department of Economics
Indiana State University
Holmstedt Hall 273
Terre Haute, IN 47809
812-237-2163   fax 812-237-4349
jconant@indstate.edu
Issues: Economic education

*Conerly, Dr. William
Conerly Consulting
7145 S.W. Varns Street
Portland, OR 97223-8018
503-598-2096   fax 503-598-2093
bill@conerlyconsulting.com
Issues: Economic education; Economic forecasting; The Economy; Family and medical leave; Labor and employment; Unemployment insurance

Congdon, Dr. Lee
Professor of History
James Madison University
800 South Main Street
Harrisonburg, VA 22807
540-568-6187   fax 540-568-6556
congdolw@jmu.edu
Issues: Central and Eastern Europe; Higher education; Political philosophy; Religion and public life

Conko, Gregory
Director of Food Safety Policy
Competitive Enterprise Institute
1001 Connecticut Avenue, N.W., Suite 1250
Washington, DC 20036
202-331-1010   fax 202-331-0640
gconko@cei.org
Issues: Agriculture; Costs and benefits of regulation; Non-governmental organizations; Sound science; Trade

Connelly, William
Professor of Politics
Washington and Lee University
Williams School
Lexington, VA 24450
540-463-8627   fax 540-463-8639
connellyw@wlu.edu
Issues: The American Founding; Congress

*Connerly, Ward
Chairman
American Civil Rights Institute
P. O. Box 188350
Sacramento, CA 95818
916-444-2278   fax 916-444-2279
Issues: Charter schools; Civil rights/racial
preferences; Higher education; Immigration;
Initiative and referendum; Land use; Political
correctness and multiculturalism; The Reagan
legacy; School choice; Standards, curriculum,
and testing

*Connor, Kenneth L.
President
Family Research Council
801 G Street, N.W.
Washington, DC 20001
202-393-2100   fax 202-393-2134
Issues: Abstinence and out-of-wedlock births;
Adoption, foster care, & child care services;
Aging/elder care; Faith-based and volunteer
initiatives; Family and children; Federal
education policy; Judicial activism/judicial
reform; Marriage and divorce; Religion and
public life; Religious freedom; School choice;
Tort and liability reform

Conquest, Dr. Robert
Senior Research Fellow
Hoover Institution
Stanford University
Stanford, CA 94305
650-493-5152   fax 650-723-1687
conquest@hoover.stanford.edu
Issues: Central and Eastern Europe; Russia and
Eurasia; Western Europe

Constantine, William
Board Member/Treasurer
Centre for New Black Leadership
2400 Earlesgates Court
Reston, VA 20191
703-264-2024   fax 703-264-2084
bill@constantinefinancial.com
Issues: Advocacy and nonprofit public funding;
Elections/polling; Electoral reform/voting
rights; Federal budget; State and local public
finance; Taxation/tax reform

Conway, Kellyanne
President and CEO
the polling company/WomanTrend
1220 Connecticut Avenue, N.W.
Washington, DC 20036
202-667-6557   fax 202-467-6551
kellyanne@pollingcompany.com
Issues: Congress; Conservative thought;
Elections/polling; Entrepreneurship/free
enterprise; Free Speech; Health care reform;
Home schooling; Media and popular culture;
Political correctness and multiculturalism;
Political philosophy; Property rights; The
Reagan legacy; Research funding; Social
Security and retirement; Sound science;
Taxation/tax reform

Cook, Douglas H.
Professor and Associate Dean for Academic
Affairs, School of Law
Regent University
1000 Regent University Drive
Virginia Beach, VA 23464
757-226-4331   fax 757-226-4329
dougcoo@regent.edu
Issues: Advocacy and nonprofit public funding;
Church-state relations; Home schooling;
Judiciary; Philanthropy; Religious freedom;
Tort and liability reform

Coon, Charli
Senior Policy Analyst, Energy and
Environment, Thomas A. Roe Institute for
Economic Policy Studies
The Heritage Foundation
214 Massachusetts Avenue, N.E.
Washington, DC 20002
202-608-6139   fax 202-544-5421
charli.coon@heritage.org
Issues: Air; Climate change; Electricity
deregulation; Energy; Environmental
education; Environmental regulation; Forestry
and national parks; Free-market
environmentalism; Property rights; Regulation
through litigation; Sound science; Stewardship;
Water; Wildlife management/endangered
species

Coonradt, John
Director of Advancement
Mackinac Center for Public Policy
140 West Main Street, P. O. Box 568
Midland, MI 48640
989-631-0900   fax 989-631-0964
coonradt@mackinac.org
Issues: Philanthropy

*Coons, Dr. John E.
Professor of Law Emeritus, School of Law
University of California at Berkeley
Boalt Hall
Berkeley, CA 94720
510-642-0880   fax 510-642-3728
Issues: Bilingual education; Business and
education partnerships; Charter schools;
Church-state relations; Education unions and
interest groups; Ethics; Faith-based and
volunteer initiatives; Family and children;
Federal education policy; Federalism; Higher
education; Home schooling; Human rights;
Initiative and referendum; Political correctness
and multiculturalism; Political philosophy;
Poverty and dependency; Privatization/
Contracting-out; Public school finance and
administration; Religion and public life; School
choice; School-to-work; Standards, curriculum,
and testing; State and local public finance

*Cooper, Charles J.
Partner
Cooper & Kirk, PLLC
1500 K Street, N.W., Suite 200
Washington, DC 20005
202-220-9600   fax 202-220-9601
ccooper@cooperkirk.com
Issues: Campaign finance reform; Church-state
relations; Civil rights/racial preferences;
Constitutional law; Electoral reform/voting
rights; Executive Branch/The Presidency;
Federalism; Free Speech; Judicial activism/
judicial reform; Judiciary; Religious freedom;
Second Amendment

Cooper, Amb. Henry F.
Visiting Fellow, The Heritage Foundation,
and Director
High Frontier
2800 Shirlington Road, Suite 405
Arlington, VA 22206
703-671-4111   fax 703-931-6432
high.frontier@verizon.net
Issues: Arms control; Emerging threats/threat
assessment; Export controls/military transfers;
Intelligence gathering and covert operations;
Military strategy; Missile defense

Cope, Prof. Kevin L.
Professor of English and Comparative
Literature, Department of English
Louisiana State University
Baton Rouge, LA 70803
225-766-2719   fax 225-578-4129
Issues: The American Founding; Arts,
humanities and historic resources; Ethics;
Religion and public life

Copeland, Lois J., M.D.
47 Central Avenue
Hillsdale, NJ 07642
201-664-1212   fax 201-666-7433
loisjcope@aol.com
Issues: Medicare

*Copper, Dr. John F.
Stanley J. Buckman Distinguished Professor,
Department of International Studies
Rhodes College
2000 North Parkway
Memphis, TN 38112
901-843-3741   fax 901-843-3371
copper@rhodes.edu
Issues: American diplomacy/foreign policy;
China; Comparative government; Economic
development/foreign aid; Emerging threats/
threat assessment; Higher education; Human
rights; Northeast Asia; Political correctness and
multiculturalism

Copulos, Milton R.
President
National Defense Council Foundation
1220 King Street, Suite 1
Alexandria, VA 22314
703-836-3443   fax 703-836-5402
Issues: Defense budget; Energy; Military
strategy; Readiness and manpower; Sound
science

Cordato, Dr. Roy E.
Vice President for Research
John Locke Foundation
200 West Morgan Street, Suite 200
Raleigh, NC 27601
919-828-3876   fax 919-821-5117
Issues: Air; Climate change; Economic
education; Economic theory; The Economy;
Environmental education; Environmental
regulation; Free-market environmentalism;
Home schooling; State and local public
finance; Taxation/tax reform

*Cordia, Louis J.
President and CEO
Cordia Companies
122 South Royal Street
Alexandria, VA 22314-3328
703-838-0373   fax 703-684-8959
lou@cordia.com
Issues: Business and education partnerships;
Congress; Conservative thought; Elections/
polling; Energy; Executive Branch/The
Presidency; Federal budget; Federalism; Free-
market environmentalism; Health care reform;
Homeland security/civil defense; Missile
defense; Property rights; The Reagan legacy;
Regulatory reform; Social Security and
retirement; State and local government;
Taxation/tax reform; Telecommunications
and the Internet; Trade; Urban sprawl/livable
cities; Wealth creation/financial
empowerment

Corkins, Bob
Executive Director
Kansas Legislative Education and Research
827 S.W. Topeka Boulevard, 2nd Floor
Topeka, KS 66612
785-233-8765   fax 520-244-3262
ks-klear@swbell.net
Issues: Aging/elder care; Agriculture; Business
and education partnerships; The Economy;
Entrepreneurship/free enterprise; Federal
budget; Government health programs; Health
care reform; Privatization/Contracting-out;
Public school finance and administration;
School choice; Social Security and retirement;
State and local public finance; Taxation/tax
reform; Trade

*Cors, Al
Vice President, Government Affairs
National Taxpayers Union and Foundation
108 North Alfred Street
Alexandria, VA 22314
703-683-5700   fax 703-683-5722
Issues: Advocacy and nonprofit public funding;
Congress; Health care reform

*Cossa, Ralph A.
President
Pacific Forum CSIS
1001 Bishop Street, Suite 1150
Honolulu, HI 96813
808-521-6745   fax 808-599-8690
pacforum@hawaii.rr.com
Issues: Arms control; China; Emerging threats/
threat assessment; International organizations
(European Union, OECD, etc.); Japan; Korea;
Military strategy; Missile defense; Northeast
Asia; Russia and Eurasia; South Asia (including
India and Pakistan); Southeast Asia (including
Burma, Cambodia, Laos, Vietnam, Singapore,
Malaysia, Indonesia, the Philippines, Australia,
and New Zealand); Terrorism and
international crime

Costello, Robert
President
Social Security Choice.org
1300 Pennsylvania Avenue, N.W., Suite 700
Washington, DC 20004
202-204-3040   fax 202-789-7349
info@socialsecuritychoice.org
Issues: Social Security and retirement; Wealth
creation/financial empowerment

Couch, Dr. Jim F.
Associate Professor of Economics,
Department of Economics and Finance
University of North Alabama
Box 5141
Florence, AL 35632-0001
256-765-4412   fax 256-765-4930
jcouch@unanov.una.edu
Issues: American history/political tradition;
Home schooling; Immigration; School choice

Coulson, Andrew
Senior Fellow in Education Policy
Mackinac Center for Public Policy
PMB 354, 19689 7th Avenue, NE
Poulsbo, WA 98370
360-981-4730   fax 360-394-9517
andrewjcoulson@attbi.com
Issues: School choice

*Coupal, Jon
President
Howard Jarvis Taxpayers Association
921 11th Street, Suite 1201
Sacramento, CA 95814
916-444-9950   fax 916-444-9823
jon@hjta.org
Issues: Government waste; Political philosophy;
Privatization/Contracting-out; Public school
finance and administration; School choice;
State and local public finance; Taxation/tax
reform; Unfunded mandates

Courter, Hon. James
Chairman
Lexington Institute
1600 Wilson Boulevard, Suite 900
Arlington, VA 22209
703-522-5828   fax 703-522-5837
Issues: Defense budget; Emerging threats/
threat assessment; Military strategy; Missile
defense; NATO and other alliances; Readiness
and manpower

*Courtney, John W.
Senior Fellow
American Institute for Full Employment
2636 Biehn Street
Klamath Falls, OR 97601
800-562-7752   fax 541-273-6496
johnc@jeld-wen.com
Issues: Job training/welfare to work;
Unemployment insurance

Cowen, Tyler
General Director, James Buchanan Center
and the Mercatus Center
George Mason University
MSN 1D3, Carow Hall
Fairfax, VA 22030
703-993-2312   fax 703-993-2323
tcowen@gmu.edu
Issues: Economic education

*Cowles, Dr. C. W.
Associate Professor of Administration
Central Michigan University
3011 Vistapoint Road
Midlothian, VA 23113-3928
804-327-9330   fax 804-327-9332
Issues: Advocacy and nonprofit public funding;
Costs and benefits of regulation; Defense
budget; Discretionary spending; Entitlement
spending; Ethics; Federal budget; Government
debt; Government waste; Higher education;
Regulation through litigation; Regulatory
budgeting; Regulatory reform; State and local
public finance; Taxation/tax reform

*Cox, Douglas
Partner
Gibson, Dunn & Crutcher LLP
1050 Connecticut Avenue, N.W., Suite 900
Washington, DC 20036
202-955-8500   fax 202-467-0539
dcox@gibsondunn.com
Issues: Civil rights/racial preferences;
Congress; Constitutional law; Executive
Branch/The Presidency; Federalism; Judiciary;
Regulatory reform

*Cox, Jerry
Executive Director
Arkansas Family Council
414 South Pulaski, Suite 2
Little Rock, AR 72201
501-375-7000   fax 501-375-7040
info@familycouncil.org
Issues: Abstinence and out-of-wedlock births;
Government health programs; School choice

*Cox, Matt
Policy Fellow, Center for School Reform
Pacific Research Institute
1414 K Street, Suite 200
Sacramento, CA 95814
916-448-1926   mcox@pacificresearch.org
Issues: Higher education; School choice;
Standards, curriculum, and testing

Cox, Dr. Stephen D.
Professor, Humanities Department
University of California, San Diego
9500 Gilman Drive
La Jolla, CA 92093-0306
858-534-4721   sdcox@ucsd.edu
Issues: American history/political tradition;
Higher education; Religion and public life

*Cox, Wendell
Principal
Wendell Cox Consultancy
P. O. Box 841
Belleville, IL 62222
618-632-8507   fax 810-821-8136
aa@publicpurpose.com
Issues: Comparative economics; Comparative
government; Economic theory; Federalism;
Government waste; Labor and employment;
Privatization/Contracting-out; Property rights;
State and local government; Transportation;
Transportation deregulation; Urban sprawl/
livable cities

Coyle, Dr. Dennis
Associate Professor, Department of Politics
Catholic University of America
620 Michigan Avenue, N.E.
Washington, DC 20064
202-319-5813   fax 202-319-6289
coyle@cua.edu
Issues: The American Founding; American
history/political tradition; Church-state
relations; Conservative thought; Constitutional
law; Economic theory; Environmental
regulation; Free Speech; Free-market
environmentalism; Higher education; Judicial
activism/judicial reform; Judiciary; Land use;
Political correctness and multiculturalism;
Political philosophy; Property rights; Religion
and public life; Religious freedom

Coyne, Hon. James K.
President
National Air Transportation Association
4226 King Street
Alexandria, VA 22302
703-845-9000   fax 703-845-8176
Issues: Congress; Regulatory reform;
Transportation

*Crafton, Dr. Christine G.
Vice President and Director, Broadband
Policy
Motorola, Inc.
1350 Eye Street, N.W., Suite 400
Washington, DC 20005
202-371-6900   fax 202-842-3578
chris.crafton@motorola.com
Issues: Costs and benefits of regulation;
Regulatory reform; Telecommunications and
the Internet

Craig, Dr. Mickey
Ross Alexander Professor of Political
Science, Department of Political Science
Hillsdale College
33 East College Street
Hillsdale, MI 49242
517-607-2367   fax 517-607-2208
mickey.craig@hillsdale.edu
Issues: The American Founding; American
history/political tradition; Campaign finance
reform; Congress; Conservative thought;
Elections/polling; Electoral reform/voting
rights; Political philosophy; The Reagan legacy

Crain, Dr. W. Mark
Professor of Economics and Director, Center
for Economic Education
George Mason University
Mail Stop 1D3
Fairfax, VA 22030
703-993-2325   fax 703-993-1133
mcrain@gmu.edu
Issues: Economic education

Craiutu, Aurelian
Assistant Professor, Department of Political
Science
Indiana University
Woodburn Hall 210, 1100 East Seventh St.
Bloomington, IN 47405-7110
812-855-2027   fax 812-855-2027
acraiutu@indiana.edu
Issues: Central and Eastern Europe;
Comparative government; Conservative
thought; Political philosophy

*Cramton, Prof. Roger C.
Cornell Law School
Myron Taylor Hall
Ithaca, NY 14853-4901
607-255-3379   fax 607-255-7193
rcc10@cornell.edu
Issues: Judicial activism/judicial reform;
Judiciary; Regulation through litigation;
Regulatory reform; Tort and liability reform

*Cranberg, Dr. Lawrence
Consulting Physicist
1205 Constant Springs Drive
Austin, TX 78746
512-327-1794   fax 512-329-6306
info@lawrencecranberg.org
Issues: Aging/elder care; Energy; Government
health programs; Police; Tort and liability
reform

Crandall, Robert
Senior Fellow, Economic Studies
Brookings Institution
1775 Massachusetts Avenue, N.W.
Washington, DC 20036
202-797-6000   fax 202-797-6181
rcrandall@brook.edu
Issues: Air; Anti-trust; Costs and benefits of
regulation; Regulatory reform;
Telecommunications and the Internet

Crane, Edward H.
President
Cato Institute
1000 Massachusetts Avenue, N.W.
Washington, DC 20001
202-842-0200   fax 202-842-3490
Issues: Campaign finance reform; Discretionary
spending; Entitlement spending; Federalism;
Judicial activism/judicial reform; Political
philosophy; School choice; Social Security and
retirement; Taxation/tax reform; Term limits

Crawford, Kay
Research Fellow, Crime Control Policy
Center
Hudson Institute
Herman Kahn Center, 5395 Emerson Way
Indianapolis, IN 46226
317-549-4112   fax 317-545-9639
kayc@hudson.org
Issues: Crime/crime statistics; Criminal law and
procedure; Juvenile justice

*Crew, Dr. Michael A.
Director, Center for Research and Regulated
Industries, Rutgers Business School
Rutgers University
180 University Avenue
Newark, NJ 07102
973-353-5049   fax 973-353-1348
mcrew@andromeda.rutgers.edu
Issues: Costs and benefits of regulation; Energy;
Environmental regulation; Regulatory reform;
Telecommunications and the Internet; Waste
management; Water

*Crews, Clyde Wayne
Director of Technology Policy
Cato Institute
1000 Massachusetts Avenue, N.W.
Washington, DC 20001
202-218-4602   fax 202-842-3490
wcrews@cato.org
Issues: Anti-trust; Costs and benefits of
regulation; Electricity deregulation; Free
Speech; Infrastructure; Intellectual property;
Privacy; Regulatory budgeting; Regulatory
reform; Telecommunications and the Internet

*Crews, Dr. Ron
President
Massachusetts Family Institute
381 Elliot Street, Suite 130L
Newton Upper Falls, MA 02464-1156
617-928-0800   fax 617-928-1515
ron@mafamily.org
Issues: Abstinence and out-of-wedlock births;
Adoption, foster care, & child care services;
The American Founding; American history/
political tradition; Church-state relations;
Citizenship and civil society; Conservative
thought; Ethics; Faith-based and volunteer
initiatives; Family and children; Home
schooling; Marriage and divorce; Media and
popular culture; Religion and public life;
School choice; State-sponsored gambling

Cribb, T. Kenneth, Jr.
President
Intercollegiate Studies Institute
3901 Centerville Road, P. O. Box 4431
Wilmington, DE 19807
302-652-4600   fax 302-652-1760
bkrauss@isi.org
Issues: Conservative thought; Higher
education; Judicial activism/judicial reform;
Political correctness and multiculturalism; The
Reagan legacy

Crippen, Alan R., II
Rector, The Witherspoon Fellowship and
Vice President for Academic Affairs
Family Research Council
801 G Street, N.W.
Washington, DC 20001
202-393-2100   fax 202-393-2134
arc@frc.org
Issues: The American Founding; American
history/political tradition; Citizenship and civil
society; Ethics; Political philosophy; Religion
and public life

Crispo, Dr. Neil S.
Professor, Reubin O'D Askew School
Florida State University
629 Bellamy Building, MC 2250
Tallahassee, FL 32306
850-645-3525   fax 850-644-7617
ncrispo@garnet.acns.fsu.edu
Issues: Campaign finance reform; Comparative
government; Costs and benefits of regulation;
Economic education; The Economy;
Education unions and interest groups;
Entrepreneurship/free enterprise; Federalism;
Higher education; Medicare; Political
correctness and multiculturalism;
Privatization/Contracting-out; Regulatory
reform; School choice; Social Security and
retirement; Standards, curriculum, and testing;
State and local government; State and local
public finance; Welfare/welfare reform

Croan, Dr. Melvin
Professor Emeritus, Department of Political
Science
University of Wisconsin
4137 Hawatha Drive
Madison, WI 53711
608-263-2414   fax 608-265-2663
croan@polisci.wisc.edu
Issues: American diplomacy/foreign policy;
American history/political tradition; Central
and Eastern Europe; Comparative economics;
Comparative government; Conservative
thought; Military strategy; NATO and other
alliances; Peacekeeping; Political philosophy;
Russia and Eurasia; Western Europe

Cromartie, Michael
Vice President
Ethics and Public Policy Center
1015 15th Street, N.W., Suite 900
Washington, DC 20005
202-216-0855   fax 202-408-0632
crom@eppc.org
Issues: Religion and public life

*Crouch, John
Executive Director
Americans for Divorce Reform
1300 North Utah Street
Arlington, VA 22201
703-528-6700   fax 703-522-9107
crouch@patriot.net
Issues: Family and children; Marriage and
divorce

*Crouse, Dr. Janice Shaw
Executive Director and Senior Fellow,
Beverly LaHaye Institute
Concerned Women for America
1015 15th Street, N.W., Suite 1100
Washington, DC 20005
202-488-7000   fax 202-488-0806
jcrouse@cwfa.org
Issues: Abstinence and out-of-wedlock births;
Arts, humanities and historic resources;
Executive Branch/The Presidency; Family and
children; Higher education; Marriage and
divorce; Political correctness and
multiculturalism; Religion and public life;
Welfare/welfare reform

*Cunningham, Charles H.
Director of Federal Affairs
National Rifle Association
410 First Street, S.E., 2nd Floor
Washington, DC 20003
202-651-2570   fax 202-651-2587
chuckc@visi.net
Issues: Campaign finance reform; Church-state
relations; Congress; Crime/crime statistics;
Elections/polling; Family and children; Higher
education; Home schooling; Initiative and
referendum; Juvenile justice; Political
correctness and multiculturalism; Religion and
public life; Right to work; Second Amendment;
State and local government; State-sponsored
gambling; Tort and liability reform; Wildlife
management/endangered species

*Curran, Dr. Ward S.
George M. Ferris Professor of Corporate
Finance and Investments
Trinity College
300 Summit Street
Hartford, CT 06106
860-247-2489   fax 860-297-2163
Issues: Costs and benefits of regulation;
Electricity deregulation; Higher education;
Regulation through litigation; Regulatory
budgeting; Regulatory reform; Risk assessment

Currier, Elizabeth
President
Committee for Monetary Research and
Education, Inc.
10004 Greenwood Court
Charlotte, NC 28215
704-598-3717   fax 704-599-7036
Issues: Economic education; Money and
financial services

*Cushman, Charles
Executive Director
American Land Rights Association
30218 N.E. 82nd Avenue, P. O. Box 400
Battle Ground, WA 98604
360-687-3087   fax 360-687-2973
ccushman@pacifier.com
Issues: Environmental regulation; Forestry and
national parks; Land use; Property rights;
Wildlife management/endangered species

*Cynkar, Robert J.
Partner
Cooper & Kirk, PLLC
1500 K Street, N.W., Suite 200
Washington, DC 20005
202-220-9655   fax 202-220-9601
rcynkar@coopercarvin.com
Issues: Church-state relations; Constitutional
law; Costs and benefits of regulation; Electricity
deregulation; Executive Branch/The
Presidency; Federalism; Medicaid; Medicare;
Property rights; Regulation through litigation;
Regulatory reform; State and local government

D'Souza, Dinesh
Robert and Karen Rishwain Research Fellow
Hoover Institution
Stanford University
Stanford, CA 94305
650-723-1754   fax 650-723-1687
Issues: Citizenship and civil society; Civil rights/
racial preferences; The Economy; Higher
education; The Reagan legacy

*Dacus, Brad W., Esq.
President
Pacific Justice Institute
P. O. Box 4366
Citrus Heights, CA 95611
916-857-6900   fax 916-857-6902
braddacus@pacificjustice.org
Issues: Abstinence and out-of-wedlock births;
Adoption, foster care, & child care services;
The American Founding; American history/
political tradition; Charter schools; Church-
state relations; Constitutional law; Education
unions and interest groups; Faith-based and
volunteer initiatives; Free Speech; Home
schooling; Judicial activism/judicial reform;
Juvenile justice; Public interest law; Public
school finance and administration; Religious
freedom; Right to work; School choice;
Standards, curriculum, and testing; Unions

Dailey, Timothy J.
Senior Writer/Analyst
Family Research Council
801 G Street, N.W.
Washington, DC 20001
202-393-2100   fax 202-393-2134
tjd@frc.org
Issues: Family and children; Religion and public life

Dale, Helle C.
Deputy Director, Kathryn and Shelby Cullom
Davis Institute for International Studies
The Heritage Foundation
214 Massachusetts Avenue, N.E.
Washington, DC 20002
202-546-4400   fax 202-675-1758
helle.dale@heritage.org
Issues: Afghanistan; American diplomacy/foreign policy; Central and Eastern Europe; Economic development/foreign aid; Emerging threats/threat assessment; Homeland security/civil defense; International organizations (European Union, OECD, etc.); Korea; Middle East; NATO and other alliances; Peacekeeping; Promoting democracy/public diplomacy; Russia and Eurasia; Terrorism and international crime; United Nations; Western Europe

Dalton, Derrick Allen
Professor of Economics
Boise State University
736 High Point Lane
Boise, ID 83712
208-426-3465   fax 208-426-2071
dalton@micron.net
Issues: Economic education

Danford, Dr. John W.
Professor, Department of Political Science
Loyola University Chicago
Damen Hall, Ninth Floor, 6525 North
Sheridan Road
Chicago, IL 60626
773-508-3069   fax 773-508-3131
jdanfor@luc.edu
Issues: Ethics; Political philosophy

*Daniels, Matt
President
Alliance for Marriage
P. O. Box 1305
Springfield, VA 22151-0305
703-425-9060   fax 703-425-9061
afm1@allianceformarriage.org
Issues: Abstinence and out-of-wedlock births; Adoption, foster care, & child care services; Faith-based and volunteer initiatives; Family and children; Judicial activism/judicial reform; Judiciary; Marriage and divorce; Media and popular culture; Religion and public life; School choice; State-sponsored gambling; Taxation/tax reform

Dannenfelser, Marjorie
Chairman of the Board
Susan B. Anthony List
1511 North Harrison Street
Arlington, VA 22205
703-534-3830   fax 703-534-3896
marjoried@erols.com
Issues: Family and children

Dannhauser, Dr. Werner J.
Visiting Professor, Political Philosophy,
Department of Political Science
Michigan State University
331 South Kedzie Hall
East Lansing, MI 48824
517-353-7970   fax 517-432-1091
Issues: Executive Branch/The Presidency; Middle East; Political philosophy

Danzon, Dr. Patricia M.
Celia Moh Professor, The Wharton School,
Health Care Department
University of Pennsylvania
3641 Locust Walk
Philadelphia, PA 19104
215-898-6861   fax 215-573-2157
danzon@wharton.upenn.edu
Issues: Health care reform

*Darby, Dr. Michael R.
Warren C. Cordner Professor of Money and
Financial Markets, Anderson Graduate
School of Management
University of California at Los Angeles
Box 951481
Los Angeles, CA 90095
310-825-4180   fax 310-454-2748
darby@ucla.edu
Issues: Economic forecasting; The Economy;
Entrepreneurship/free enterprise; Higher
education; International finance and
multilateral banks; Money and financial
services; The Reagan legacy; Research funding

Davis, Richard S.
President
Washington Research Council
108 South Washington Street, Suite 406
Seattle, WA 98104
206-467-7088   fax 206-467-6957
rsdavis@researchcouncil.org
Issues: Charter schools; Discretionary spending;
Poverty and dependency; Privatization/
Contracting-out; Public school finance and
administration; School choice; State and local
public finance; Taxation/tax reform; Welfare/
welfare reform

*De Alessi, Michael
Director of Natural Resources Policy
Reason Foundation
3415 South Sepulveda Boulevard, Suite 400
Los Angeles, CA 90034
310-391-2245   fax 310-391-4395
michael.dealessi@reason.org
Issues: Air; Climate change; Costs and benefits
of regulation; Energy; Environmental
education; Environmental regulation; Forestry
and national parks; Free-market
environmentalism; Infrastructure; Land use;
Property rights; Regulatory reform; Risk
assessment; Sound science; Stewardship;
Urban sprawl/livable cities; Waste
management; Water; Wildlife management/
endangered species

de Alvarez, Prof. Leo Paul S.
Professor of Politics
University of Dallas
1845 East Northgate Drive
Irving, TX 75062
972-721-5344   fax 972-721-4007
alvarez@udallas.edu
Issues: Political philosophy

*de Bettencourt, Kathleen B., Ph.D.
Executive Director
Environmental Literacy Council
1625 K Street, N.W., Suite 1020
Washington, DC 20006
202-296-0390   fax 202-822-0991
debett@enviroliteracy.org
Issues: Air; Business and education
partnerships; Climate change; Energy;
Environmental education; Environmental
regulation; Federal education policy; Forestry
and national parks; Public interest law;
Standards, curriculum, and testing

*de Borchgrave, Arnaud
Director, Transnational Threats Initiative
Center for Strategic and International
Studies
1800 K Street, N.W., Suite 400
Washington, DC 20006
202-775-3282   fax 202-785-1688
adeborchgrave@csis.org
Issues: Afghanistan; American diplomacy/
foreign policy; China; Defense budget;
Emerging threats/threat assessment;
Intelligence gathering and covert operations;
Middle East; Military strategy; Missile defense;
NATO and other alliances; Peacekeeping;
Russia and Eurasia; South Asia (including India
and Pakistan); Terrorism and international
crime; Western Europe

*de Graffenreid, Dr. Kenneth E.
Faculty Member in Intelligence Studies
Institute of World Politics
1521 16th Street, N.W.
Washington, DC 20036
202-462-2101   fax 202-462-7031
kdeg@nsc-inc.net
Issues: Emerging threats/threat assessment;
Export controls/military transfers; Intelligence
gathering and covert operations; Military
strategy; Missile defense; Promoting
democracy/public diplomacy; Terrorism and
international crime

de Krnjevic-Miskovic, Damjan
Assistant Managing Editor
The National Interest
1615 L Street, N.W., Suite 1230
Washington, DC 20036
202-467-4884   fax 202-467-0006
dvkm@nationalinterest.org
Issues: American diplomacy/foreign policy;
The American Founding; American history/
political tradition; Canada; Central and Eastern
Europe; Comparative government; Ethics;
Executive Branch/The Presidency; NATO and
other alliances; Peacekeeping; Political
philosophy; Terrorism and international
crime; Western Europe

de Posada, Robert G.
President
The Latino Coalition
725 Massachusetts Avenue, N.E.
Washington, DC 20002
202-546-0008   fax 202-546-0807
info@thelatinocoalition.com
Issues: Bilingual education; Health care reform;
School choice; Social Security and retirement

*De Rosa, Dr. Marshall L.
Professor, Department of Political Science
Florida Atlantic University
2912 College Avenue
Davie, FL 33314
954-236-1131   fax 954-236-1150
de_rosa@bellsouth.net
Issues: The American Founding; American
history/political tradition; Constitutional law;
Federalism; Free Speech; Higher education;
Judicial activism/judicial reform; Judiciary;
Political correctness and multiculturalism;
Second Amendment

de Rugy, Dr. Veronique
Fiscal Policy Analyst
Cato Institute
1000 Massachusetts Avenue, N.W.
Washington, DC 20001-5403
202-218-4601   fax 202-842-3490
Issues: Federal budget; International tax
policy/tax competition; State and local public
finance; Taxation/tax reform

de Russy, Candace
Trustee
State University of New York
50 Hampshire Road
Bronxville, NY 10708
914-779-9607   fax 914-698-0699
Issues: Bilingual education; Charter schools;
Citizenship and civil society; Education unions
and interest groups; Family and children;
Federal education policy; Higher education;
Media and popular culture; Political
correctness and multiculturalism; Public
school finance and administration; Religion
and public life; School choice; School-to-work;
Standards, curriculum, and testing

de Solenni, Pia
Fellow for Human Life Studies
Family Research Council
801 G Street, N.W.
Washington, DC 20001
202-393-2100   fax 202-393-2134
Issues: Abstinence and out-of-wedlock births;
Adoption, foster care, & child care services;
Family and children; Marriage and divorce;
Religion and public life

De Young, Mark
Regional Director North America
World Youth Alliance
847A Second Avenue Box 502
New York, NY 10017
646-796-3458   fax 646-796-3478
mark@wya.net
Issues: Abstinence and out-of-wedlock births;
International organizations (European Union,
OECD, etc.); United Nations

Dean, Brian
Regional Program Director, Latin America
and Caribbean
International Republican Institute
1225 Eye Street, N.W., Suite 700
Washington, DC 20005
202-408-9450   fax 202-408-9462
lac@iri.org
Issues: Latin America

---

*Dean, Lisa
Vice President for Policy
Free Congress Foundation
717 Second Street, N.E.
Washington, DC 20002
202-546-3000   fax 202-543-5605
Issues: Constitutional law; Criminal law and procedure; Free Speech; Government health programs; Immigration; International law; Money and financial services; Privacy; Second Amendment; State-sponsored gambling; Telecommunications and the Internet

DeBow, Michael E.
Professor, Cumberland School of Law
Samford University
800 Lakeshore Drive
Birmingham, AL 35229
205-726-2434   fax 205-726-2587
medebow@samford.edu
Issues: Anti-trust; Conservative thought; Judiciary; Regulation through litigation; Tort and liability reform

DeBreaux-Watts, Buffy
Director of Marketing and Outreach
American Board for Certification of Teacher Excellence
1225 19th Street, N.W., Suite 400
Washington, DC 20036
202-261-2637   fax 202-261-2638
bdebreaux-watts@abcte.org
Issues: Advocacy and nonprofit public funding; Arts, humanities and historic resources; Business and education partnerships; Corrections and sentencing; Criminal law and procedure; Faith-based and volunteer initiatives; Federal education policy; Juvenile justice; Non-governmental organizations; Political correctness and multiculturalism; Religion and public life; School-to-work; State and local government; State and local public finance

*Decker, Dr. Fred W.
President
Mount Hood Society
827 N.W. 31st Street
Corvallis, OR 97330
541-753-7271   fax 541-752-2349
deckerf@ucs.orst.edu
Issues: Climate change; Environmental education; Federal education policy; Higher education

*Decter, Midge
120 East 81st Street, Number 7H
New York, NY 10028-1432
212-861-0286   fax 212-861-9029
midgedecter@hotmail.com
Issues: American diplomacy/foreign policy; Arms control; Arts, humanities and historic resources; Central and Eastern Europe; Citizenship and civil society; Economic development/foreign aid; Emerging threats/ threat assessment; Faith-based and volunteer initiatives; Family and children; Homeland security/civil defense; Human rights; Intelligence gathering and covert operations; International organizations (European Union, OECD, etc.); Japan; Korea; Media and popular culture; Middle East; Military strategy; Missile defense; NATO and other alliances; Philanthropy; Political correctness and multiculturalism; Promoting democracy/ public diplomacy; Religion and public life; Russia and Eurasia; South Asia (including India and Pakistan); Terrorism and international crime; United Nations; Western Europe

Delattre, Dr. Edwin J.
Professor of Education, School of Education, and Professor of Philosophy, College of Arts and Sciences
Boston University
621 Commonwealth Avenue
Boston, MA 02215
617-353-5480   fax 617-358-1476
ejd@bu.edu
Issues: Ethics; Higher education; Police; Standards, curriculum, and testing

*Delgaudio, Eugene
Executive Director
Public Advocate
5613 Leesburg Pike, Suite 17
Falls Church, VA 22041
703-845-1808   fax 703-845-1990
eugenedelgaudio@erols.com
Issues: Citizenship and civil society; Federal education policy; Government debt; Government waste; Religion and public life

*Delk, Glenn
President
Georgia Charter Schools
1355 Peachtree Street, N.E., Suite 1150
Atlanta, GA 30309
404-876-3335   fax 404-876-3338
glenndelk@mindspring.com
Issues: Charter schools; Church-state relations;
Education unions and interest groups; Public
interest law; Public school finance and
administration; School choice

*DeLong, James
Senior Fellow and Director, Center for the
Study of Digital Property
Progress & Freedom Foundation
1401 H Street, N.W., Suite 1075
Washington, DC 20005
202-289-8928   fax 202-289-6079
mail@pff.org
Issues: Campaign finance reform; Intellectual
property; Property rights; Regulation through
litigation; Regulatory reform;
Telecommunications and the Internet

Delorme, Dr. Charles, Jr.
Emeritus Professor of Economics
University of Georgia
Brooks Hall
Athens, GA 30602
706-542-3682   fax 706-542-3376
delorme@terry.uga.edu
Issues: The Economy; Money and financial
services

DeLuca, Peter
Vice President for Finance and
Administration
Thomas Aquinas College
10000 North Ojai Road
Santa Paula, CA 93060
805-525-4417   fax 805-525-9342
pdeluca@thomasaquinas.edu
Issues: Higher education

*DeMaio, Carl
Director of Government Redesign
Reason Foundation
3415 South Sepulveda Boulevard, Suite 400
Los Angeles, CA 90034
310-391-2245   fax 310-391-4395
carldemaio@aol.com
Issues: Congress; Discretionary spending;
Entitlement spending; Executive Branch/The
Presidency; Federal budget; Federal civil
service; Federalism; Government debt;
Government waste; Labor and employment;
Privatization/Contracting-out; Regulatory
budgeting; Regulatory reform; State and local
government

DeMuth, Christopher
President
American Enterprise Institute
1150 17th Street, N.W.
Washington, DC 20036
202-862-5895   fax 202-862-5921
cdemuth@aei.org
Issues: Environmental regulation; Free-market
environmentalism; Regulatory reform

*Denholm, David
President
Public Service Research Foundation
320-D Maple Avenue East
Vienna, VA 22180
703-242-3575   fax 703-242-3579
info@psrf.org
Issues: Davis-Bacon Act; Education unions and
interest groups; Federal civil service; Labor and
employment; Minimum wage; Privatization/
Contracting-out; Right to work; State and local
government; Unions

Denney, Helene
Executive Director
Nevada Policy Research Insitute
2073 East Sahara Avenue, Suite B
Las Vegas, NV 89104
702-222-0642   fax 702-227-0927
hd@npri.org
Issues: Labor and employment; School choice;
Taxation/tax reform

Dennis, Kimberly
Executive Director
D & D Foundation
1150 17th Street, N.W., 11th Floor
Washington, DC 20036-4670
202-862-5830   fax 425-963-4234
dennisko@aol.com
Issues: Citizenship and civil society; Faith-based and volunteer initiatives; Philanthropy

Dennis, Dr. William C.
Dennis Consulting
1044 Douglas Drive
MacLean, VA 22101
703-288-0680   denniswilliamc@aol.com
Issues: American history/political tradition; Conservative thought; Free-market environmentalism; Philanthropy; Stewardship

*Dennis, William J.
Senior Research Fellow
National Federation of Independent Business Research Foundation
1201 F Street, N.W., Suite 200
Washington, DC 20004
202-554-9000   fax 202-554-5572
denny.dennis@nfib.org
Issues: Costs and benefits of regulation; The Economy; Entrepreneurship/free enterprise; Health care reform; Labor and employment

*Denton, James S.
315 C Street, N.E.
Washington, DC 20002
202-546-6929   fax 202-546-6929
dentonjs@aol.com
Issues: American diplomacy/foreign policy; Central and Eastern Europe; Economic development/foreign aid; Human rights; Promoting democracy/public diplomacy; Russia and Eurasia

*Deo, Len
Executive Director
New Jersey Family Policy Council
P. O. Box 6011
Parsippany, NJ 07054
973-263-5258   fax 888-453-6346
len@njfpc.org
Issues: Abstinence and out-of-wedlock births; The American Founding; Church-state relations; Citizenship and civil society; Conservative thought; Entrepreneurship/free enterprise; Faith-based and volunteer initiatives; Family and children; Family and medical leave; Marriage and divorce; Media and popular culture; Political correctness and multiculturalism; Political philosophy; Religion and public life; Religious freedom; School choice; Standards, curriculum, and testing; State and local government; Substance abuse; Welfare/welfare reform

Derham, Richard
Member of the Board
Washington Policy Center
4025 Delridge Way, S.W., Suite 210
Seattle, WA 98106
206-937-9691   fax 206-938-6313
wpc@washingtonpolicy.org
Issues: Campaign finance reform; Economic development/foreign aid; Elections/polling; Initiative and referendum; Judiciary; Privatization/Contracting-out

Desser, John
Executive Director
Coalition for Affordable Health Coverage
1615 L Street, N.W., Suite 650
Washington, DC 20036
202-626-8545   fax 202-626-8593
jdesser@jeffersongr.com
Issues: Health care reform

*Destro, Dr. Robert
Professor of Law, Columbus School of Law
Catholic University of America
620 Michigan Avenue, N.E.
Washington, DC 20064
202-319-5139   fax 202-319-4459
destro@law.cua.edu
Issues: Advocacy and nonprofit public funding;
Church-state relations; Citizenship and civil
society; Civil rights/racial preferences;
Constitutional law; Education unions and
interest groups; Electoral reform/voting rights;
Federalism; Free Speech; International law;
Judicial activism/judicial reform; Judiciary;
Non-governmental organizations; Privacy;
Public school finance and administration;
Religion and public life; Religious freedom;
School choice

*Devine, Dr. Donald J.
Adjunct Scholar, The Heritage Foundation,
and Director
Center for American Values
4805 Idlewilde Road
Shady Side, MD 20764-9768
703-683-6833   fax 703-684-7642
devined@conservative.org
Issues: The American Founding; Citizenship
and civil society; Comparative government;
Congress; Conservative thought; Economic
education; Economic theory; Executive
Branch/The Presidency; Federal civil service;
Federalism; Political philosophy; Readiness
and manpower; The Reagan legacy; Unfunded
mandates; Welfare/welfare reform

*Devlin, William T.
Founder
Urban Family Council
P. O. Box 11415
Philadelphia, PA 19111
215-663-9494   fax 215-663-9444
devlin@urbanfamily.org
Issues: Abstinence and out-of-wedlock births;
Adoption, foster care, & child care services;
Church-state relations; Citizenship and civil
society; Ethics; Faith-based and volunteer
initiatives; Family and children; Free Speech;
Human rights; Marriage and divorce; Media
and popular culture; Religion and public life;
Religious freedom; School choice; State-
sponsored gambling

*DeVous, Phillip
Public Policy Manager
Acton Institute for the Study of Religion and
Liberty
161 Ottawa Avenue, N.W., Suite 301
Grand Rapids, MI 49503
616-454-3080   fax 616-454-9454
pdevous@acton.org
Issues: Economic education; Education unions
and interest groups; Electricity deregulation;
Environmental education; Environmental
regulation; Faith-based and volunteer
initiatives; Federal education policy; Free-
market environmentalism; Labor and
employment; Property rights; Religion and
public life; Right to work; School choice;
Stewardship; Trade; Unions; Welfare/welfare
reform

*DeWeese, Thomas
President
American Policy Center
98 Alexandria Pike, Suite 43
Warrenton, VA 20186-2849
540-341-8911   fax 540-341-8917
tadcc@aol.com
Issues: Environmental education; Federal
education policy; Free-market
environmentalism; Home schooling; Privacy;
Property rights; School-to-work; Sound science;
Standards, curriculum, and testing; United
Nations; Urban sprawl/livable cities

Dewey, Douglas Dean
Executive Vice President
Children's Scholarship Fund
8 West 38th Street, 9th Floor
New York, NY 10018-6229
212-515-7104   fax 425-969-3172
ddewey@scholarshipfund.org
Issues: Federal education policy; Home
schooling; School choice

Dezenhall, Eric
President
Nichols Dezenhall Management Group
1130 Connecticut Avenue, N.W., Suite 600
Washington, DC 20036
202-296-0263   fax 202-452-9370
mail@ndez.com
Issues: Media and popular culture; Sound
science

Di Napoli, Stephanie M.

Director of Government Affairs
Family Research Council
801 G Street, N.W.
Washington, DC 20001
202-393-2100   fax 202-393-2134
Issues: Congress; Family and children

Diamond, Dr. Arthur M., Jr.

Noddle Professor of Business
Administration, Department of Economics
University of Nebraska, Omaha
RH 512E
Omaha, NE 68182-0048
402-554-3657   fax 402-554-2853
mail@unomaha.edu
Issues: Economic education;
Entrepreneurship/free enterprise; Political
philosophy; Research funding; Sound science;
Telecommunications and the Internet

Diaz, Miguel

Director, South America Project
Center for Strategic and International
Studies
1800 K Street, N.W., Suite 400
Washington, DC 20006
202-775-3273   fax 202-466-4739
mdiaz@csis.org
Issues: Latin America

*Dickinson, Gerry

Vice President, Policy
South Carolina Policy Council
1323 Pendleton Street
Columbia, SC 29201
803-779-5022   fax 803-779-4953
gpd@scpolicycouncil.com
Issues: Free-market environmentalism; Land
use; Medicaid; Property rights; Right to work;
School choice; State-sponsored gambling;
Transportation

Diffine, Dr. D. P.

Professor of Economics
Harding University
900 East Center Street
Searcy, AR 72149
501-279-4470   fax 501-279-4195
ddiffine@harding.edu
Issues: American history/political tradition;
Arts, humanities and historic resources;
Comparative economics; Economic education;
Economic forecasting; Economic theory; The
Economy; Entitlement spending;
Entrepreneurship/free enterprise; Faith-based
and volunteer initiatives; Family and children;
Federal budget; Government debt;
Government waste; International tax policy/
tax competition; Marriage and divorce; Media
and popular culture; Money and financial
services; Religion and public life; Taxation/tax
reform

*Diggs, John R., Jr., M.D.

Two Burnett Avenue
South Hadley, MA 01075
413-535-3321   fax 413-535-3321
diggsthis@aol.com
Issues: Abstinence and out-of-wedlock births;
Ethics; Home schooling; Marriage and divorce;
Media and popular culture; Political
correctness and multiculturalism

DiIulio, Dr. John J., Jr.

Frederic Fox Leadership Professor of Policy,
Religion and Civil Society
University of Pennsylvania
3814 Walnut Street, Leadership Hall
Philadelphia, PA 19104
215-746-7100   fax 215-746-7101
sheriaC1@sas.upenn.edu
Issues: Citizenship and civil society; Corrections
and sentencing; Crime/crime statistics; Faith-
based and volunteer initiatives; Juvenile justice;
Religion and public life

Dillon, Dana
Senior Policy Analyst, Asian Studies Center
The Heritage Foundation
214 Massachusetts Avenue, N.E.
Washington, DC 20002
202-608-6133   fax 202-675-1779
dana.dillon@heritage.org
Issues: Afghanistan; Emerging threats/threat
assessment; Homeland security/civil defense;
Military strategy; Promoting democracy/public
diplomacy; South Asia (including India and
Pakistan); Southeast Asia (including Burma,
Cambodia, Laos, Vietnam, Singapore,
Malaysia, Indonesia, the Philippines, Australia,
and New Zealand); Terrorism and
international crime

Dillon, Dr. Thomas
President
Thomas Aquinas College
10000 North Ojai Road
Santa Paula, CA 93060
805-525-4417   fax 805-525-0620
Issues: Federal education policy; Higher
education; Standards, curriculum, and testing

*DiLorenzo, Dr. Thomas J.
Professor of Economics
Loyola College
6473 Haviland Mill Road
Clarksville, MD 21029
410-617-2755   fax 410-617-2118
tdilorenzo@loyola.edu
Issues: Advocacy and nonprofit public funding;
Anti-trust; Costs and benefits of regulation;
Economic theory; Entrepreneurship/free
enterprise; Federal budget; Federalism;
Government waste; Labor and employment;
Regulation through litigation; State and local
public finance; Unfunded mandates

*DioGuardi, Hon. Joseph
President
Albanian American Civic League
P. O. Box 70
Ossining, NY 10562
914-762-5530   fax 914-762-5102
jjd@aacl.com
Issues: American diplomacy/foreign policy;
Central and Eastern Europe; Human rights;
Promoting democracy/public diplomacy

Doane, Danielle
Director, U.S. House Relations
The Heritage Foundation
214 Massachusetts Avenue, N.E.
Washington, DC 20002
202-546-4400   fax 202-675-1778
danielle.doane@heritage.org
Issues: Congress; Discretionary spending

Dobson, Dr. James C.
President
Focus on the Family
8605 Explorer Drive
Colorado Springs, CO 80920
719-531-3400   fax 719-531-3385
Issues: Abstinence and out-of-wedlock births;
Adoption, foster care, & child care services;
Family and children; Home schooling; Juvenile
justice; Marriage and divorce; Media and
popular culture; Political correctness and
multiculturalism; Religion and public life;
School choice; State-sponsored gambling

Dodd, John
President
Jesse Helms Center
P. O. Box 247, 3918 U.S. Highway 74E
Wingate, NC 28174
704-233-1776   fax 704-233-1787
johndodd@wingate.edu
Issues: Business and education partnerships

Doherty, Dr. Thomas
Chairman, Film Studies Program
Brandeis University
P. O. Box 9110
Waltham, MA 02254
617-736-3032   fax 617-736-3040
doherty@brandeis.edu
Issues: Arts, humanities and historic resources;
Media and popular culture

Dolan, Marie
Legislative Chairman
New York State Federation of Catholic
School Parents
149-56 Delaware Avenue
Flushing, NY 11355
212-575-7698   fax 212-575-7669
Issues: Abstinence and out-of-wedlock births;
Adoption, foster care, & child care services;
Aging/elder care; Business and education
partnerships; Federal education policy; Home
schooling; School choice

*Donnelly, Elaine
President
Center for Military Readiness
P. O. Box 51600
Livonia, MI 48151
734-464-9430   fax 734-464-6678
emdcmr@bignet.net
Issues: Family and children; Readiness and manpower

Donnelly, Thomas
Research Fellow, Defense Policy
American Enterprise Institute
1150 17th Street, N.W.
Washington, DC 20036
202-293-4983   fax 202-293-4572
Issues: American diplomacy/foreign policy; Defense budget; Military strategy

*Donohue, Dr. William A.
President
Catholic League for Religious and Civil Rights
450 7th Avenue
New York, NY 10123
212-371-3191   fax 212-371-3394
cl@catholicleague.org
Issues: Media and popular culture; Religion and public life

*Dorn, Dr. James A.
Vice President for Academic Affairs
Cato Institute
1000 Massachusetts Avenue, N.W.
Washington, DC 20001
202-842-0200   fax 202-842-3490
jdorn@cato.org
Issues: The American Founding; China; Comparative economics; Economic development/foreign aid; Human rights; Money and financial services; Trade

Doudney, Douglas S.
Executive Director
Coalition for Property Rights
824 North Highland Avenue
Orlando, FL 32803
407-481-2283   fax 407-648-8901
ddoudney@yahoo.com
Issues: Environmental education; Land use; Property rights; Urban sprawl/livable cities; Water; Wildlife management/endangered species

Dougherty, Daniel J.
Executive Director
Pennsylvania Federation-Citizens for Educational Freedom
1625 Oregon Avenue
Philadelphia, PA 19145
215-462-8970   fax 215-462-3106
Issues: Federal education policy; School choice

*Dougherty, Dr. Jude P.
Professor of Philosophy and Dean Emeritus, School of Philosophy
Catholic University of America
620 Michigan Avenue, N.E.
Washington, DC 20064
202-319-5589   fax 202-319-4731
dougherj@cua.edu
Issues: Church-state relations; Constitutional law; Higher education; Religious freedom

Dougherty, Dr. Richard J.
Associate Professor, Department of Politics
University of Dallas
1845 East Northgate Drive
Irving, TX 75062
972-721-5043   fax 972-721-4007
dough4@udallas.edu
Issues: The American Founding; American history/political tradition; Church-state relations; Citizenship and civil society; Constitutional law; Executive Branch/The Presidency; Family and children; Home schooling; Judiciary; Political philosophy

*Douglas, John
Alston & Bird
1201 West Peachtree Street
Atlanta, GA 30309
404-881-7880   fax 404-881-7777
jdouglas@alston.com
Issues: Money and financial services

Douglass, Dr. John Jay
Professor of Law
University of Houston Law Center
100 Law Center
Houston, TX 77204-6060
713-743-1831   fax 713-743-2223
jdouglass@central.uh.edu
Issues: Campaign finance reform; Corrections and sentencing; Criminal law and procedure; Electoral reform/voting rights; Judicial activism/judicial reform; State and local government

*Douglass, Dr. Joseph D., Jr.
Director
The Redwood Institute
203 Garden Court
Falls Church, VA 22046-3415
703-533-9452   fax 703-532-8685
j.d.douglass@worldnet.att.net
Issues: Arms control; Central and Eastern
Europe; Emerging threats/threat assessment;
Intelligence gathering and covert operations;
Military strategy; Missile defense; NATO and
other alliances; Promoting democracy/public
diplomacy; Russia and Eurasia; Substance
abuse; Terrorism and international crime

Dowd, Dr. Bryan
Professor, Division of Health Services
Research and Policy
University of Minnesota
420 Delaware Street, S.E., Box 729
Minneapolis, MN 55455
612-624-5468   fax 612-624-2196
Issues: Government health programs; Health
care reform; Medicare

Downing, Jeff
Chairman
Family First
645 M Street, Suite 21
Lincoln, NE 68508
402-435-3210   fax 402-435-3280
nebfirst@familyfirst.org
Issues: Abstinence and out-of-wedlock births;
Adoption, foster care, & child care services;
Arts, humanities and historic resources;
Citizenship and civil society; Faith-based and
volunteer initiatives; Family and children;
Marriage and divorce; Media and popular
culture; Philanthropy; Political correctness and
multiculturalism; Religion and public life;
State-sponsored gambling

*Dowty, Dr. Alan
Professor
University of Notre Dame
0313 Hesburgh Center
Notre Dame, IN 46556
574-631-5098   fax 574-631-6973
dowty.1@nd.edu
Issues: Arms control; Middle East

Doyle, Denis
President
Doyle Associates
110 Summerfield Road
Chevy Chase, MD 20815
301-986-9350   fax 301-907-4959
denis@schoolnet.com
Issues: Business and education partnerships;
Charter schools; Education unions and interest
groups; Federal education policy; Public school
finance and administration; School choice;
Standards, curriculum, and testing

Dphrepaulezz, Diallo
Fellow, *The Doyle Report*
New York, NY 10018
212-626-7600   fax 212-626-7455
diallo@schoolnet.com
Issues: Business and education partnerships;
Charter schools; Federal education policy;
Home schooling; Political correctness and
multiculturalism; School choice

*Dreyer, Dr. June Teufel
Professor and Chairman, Department of
Political Science
University of Miami
P. O. Box 248047
Coral Gables, FL 33124
305-284-2403   fax 305-284-3636
jdreyer@miami.edu
Issues: China

*Driessen, Paul K., Esq.
Senior Fellow
Committee for a Constructive Tomorrow
8760 Copeland Pond Court
Fairfax, VA 22031
703-698-6171   fax 703-698-6172
pdriessen@cox.net
Issues: Climate change; Energy; Forestry and
national parks; Risk assessment; Sound science;
Stewardship; Waste management; Wealth
creation/financial empowerment

du Pont, Hon. Pete
Policy Chairman
National Center for Policy Analysis
P. O. Box 551
Wilmington, DE 19899
302-651-7728   fax 302-658-6548
Issues: Agriculture; Campaign finance reform;
Charter schools; Conservative thought;
Economic education; School choice; Social
Security and retirement; Taxation/tax reform;
Trade

*Dudley, Susan E.
Senior Research Fellow
Mercatus Center at George Mason University
3301 North Fairfax Drive, Suite 450
Arlington, VA 22201
703-993-4934   fax 703-995-4835
sdudley@gmu.edu
Issues: Air; Costs and benefits of regulation;
Electricity deregulation; Energy;
Environmental education; Environmental
regulation; Federalism; Forestry and national
parks; Free-market environmentalism; OSHA;
Property rights; Regulatory budgeting;
Regulatory reform; Risk assessment; Sound
science; Waste management; Water

*Duesterberg, Dr. Thomas
President and CEO
Manufacturers Alliance
1525 Wilson Boulevard, Suite 900
Arlington, VA 22209
703-841-9000   fax 703-841-9514
Issues: China; The Economy;
Entrepreneurship/free enterprise;
Telecommunications and the Internet; Trade;
Western Europe

*Duggan, Mae
National President
Citizens for Educational Freedom
12571 Northwinds Drive
St. Louis, MO 63146
314-434-4171   fax 314-434-6995
citedfree@aol.com
Issues: Federal education policy; Religion and
public life; School choice

Duggan, Martin
Educational Freedom Foundation
12571 Northwinds Drive
St. Louis, MO 63146
314-434-4171   fax 314-434-6995
martinduggan2@aol.com
Issues: Free Speech; Initiative and referendum;
Media and popular culture; The Reagan legacy;
Religion and public life; Religious freedom;
School choice

Duignan, Dr. Peter J.
Lillick Curator-Senior Fellow
Hoover Institution
Stanford University
Stanford, CA 94305
650-725-3596   fax 650-723-9852
Issues: Afghanistan; Africa; American
diplomacy/foreign policy; American history/
political tradition; Bilingual education;
Canada; Central and Eastern Europe; China;
Comparative government; Conservative
thought; Defense budget; Emerging threats/
threat assessment; Ethics; Executive Branch/
The Presidency; Federal education policy;
Homeland security/civil defense; Immigration;
Intelligence gathering and covert operations;
International organizations (European Union,
OECD, etc.); Mexico; Middle East; Military
strategy; NATO and other alliances;
Peacekeeping; Political correctness and
multiculturalism; Terrorism and international
crime; Western Europe

Dujarric, Robert
Senior Fellow, National Security Studies
Hudson Institute
1015 18th Street, N.W., Suite 300
Washington, DC 20036
202-944-2764   fax 202-223-8595
rdujarric@aol.com
Issues: American diplomacy/foreign policy;
Emerging threats/threat assessment; Japan;
Korea; Northeast Asia; Readiness and
manpower; Western Europe

*Duncan, Dr. Richard
Professor of Law, College of Law
University of Nebraska
Lincoln, NE 68583
402-472-6044   fax 402-472-5185
conlawprof@yahoo.com
Issues: Church-state relations; Civil rights/racial
preferences; Constitutional law; Faith-based
and volunteer initiatives; Family and children;
Free Speech; Home schooling; Judicial
activism/judicial reform; Marriage and
divorce; Public interest law; Religion and
public life; Religious freedom; School choice

*Duncan, William C.
Acting Director
The Marriage Law Project
3600 John MacCormack Road, N.E.
Washington, DC 20064
202-319-6215   fax 202-319-4459
duncanw@law.edu
Issues: Family and children; Marriage and divorce

*Dunkelberg, Dr. William C.
Chief Economist
National Federation of Independent Business
515 Sabine Circle
Wynnewood, PA 19096
610-642-6473   fax 610-642-6473
wdunk@aol.com
Issues: Costs and benefits of regulation; The Economy; Entitlement spending; Entrepreneurship/free enterprise; Federal budget; Government debt; Higher education; Money and financial services; Privatization/ Contracting-out; Taxation/tax reform; Unfunded mandates

*Dunlop, Becky Norton
Vice President, External Relations
The Heritage Foundation
214 Massachusetts Avenue, N.E.
Washington, DC 20002
202-546-4400   fax 202-675-1753
bndunlop@heritage.org
Issues: Air; Arts, humanities and historic resources; Climate change; Energy; Environmental education; Environmental regulation; Executive Branch/The Presidency; Faith-based and volunteer initiatives; Federal civil service; Federalism; Forestry and national parks; Free-market environmentalism; Land use; Property rights; The Reagan legacy; Research funding; Second Amendment; Sound science; State and local government; Stewardship; Urban sprawl/livable cities; Waste management; Water; Wildlife management/ endangered species

*Dunn, David
Research and Project Director
Oklahoma Family Policy Council
3908 North Peniel Avenue, Suite 100
Bethany, OK 73008-3458
405-787-7744   fax 405-787-3900
okfamilypc@aol.com
Issues: Abstinence and out-of-wedlock births; The American Founding; Faith-based and volunteer initiatives; Family and children; Federal education policy; Home schooling; Marriage and divorce; Media and popular culture; Political correctness and multiculturalism; Religion and public life; School-to-work; State-sponsored gambling

Dunn, Dr. Dennis J.
Professor of History and Director of International Studies
Southwest Texas State University
Flowers 324
San Marcos, TX 78666
512-245-2339   fax 512-245-2301
Issues: Central and Eastern Europe; Russia and Eurasia; Western Europe

*Dunn, Dr. Paul
Director, Entrepreneurship Studies Center
University of Louisiana, Monroe
Monroe, LA 71209
318-342-1224   fax 318-342-1209
Issues: Business and education partnerships; Economic forecasting; Entrepreneurship/free enterprise; Ethics; Free-market environmentalism; Higher education; Poverty and dependency; Property rights; Urban sprawl/livable cities; Waste management; Water; Wealth creation/financial empowerment

Duran, Dr. Khalid
Editor
TransIslam Magazine
7420 Lakeview Drive, Apt. 302
Bethesda, MD 20817
301-767-1740   fax 301-767-1741
Issues: Africa; Emerging threats/threat assessment; Middle East; Political correctness and multiculturalism; Religion and public life; South Asia (including India and Pakistan); Terrorism and international crime

*Durant, Clark
New Common School Foundation
6861 East Nevada
Detroit, MI 48234
313-368-8580
cdurant@newcommonschool.org
Issues: The American Founding; Charter schools; Citizenship and civil society; Faith-based and volunteer initiatives; Philanthropy; Political philosophy; The Reagan legacy; Religion and public life; School choice

Dutcher, Brandon
Research Director
Oklahoma Council of Public Affairs
100 West Wilshire Boulevard, Suite C-3
Oklahoma City, OK 73116
405-843-9212   fax 405-843-9436
brandondutcher@yahoo.com
Issues: Education unions and interest groups; Home schooling; Media and popular culture; School choice

Dutcher, Valle Simms
General Counsel
Southeastern Legal Foundation
3340 Peachtree Road, N.E., Suite 2515
Atlanta, GA 30326
404-365-8500   fax 404-365-0017
vsdutcher@southeasternlegal.org
Issues: Campaign finance reform; Civil rights/racial preferences; Constitutional law; Free Speech

Dwyer, Prof. Gerald P., Jr.
Vice President
Federal Reserve Bank of Atlanta
1000 Peachtree Street, N.E.
Atlanta, GA 30309
404-614-7095   gerald.p.dwyer@atl.frb.org
Issues: Federal budget; Government debt; Intellectual property; Privacy; Social Security and retirement; Taxation/tax reform

Dye, Dr. Thomas R.
Professor
Florida State University
633 Bellamy Building, MC 2230
Tallahassee, FL 32306
850-644-3848   tomrdye@aol.com
Issues: Federalism; State and local government; State and local public finance; Taxation/tax reform

Dzierba, Dr. Timothy R.
Professor, Social Sciences
Medaille College
18 Agassiz Circle
Buffalo, NY 14214
716-884-3411   fax 716-884-0291
tdzierba@medaille.edu
Issues: Higher education; Unions

*Eagle, Steven J.
Professor of Law
George Mason University School of Law
3301 North Fairfax Drive
Arlington, VA 22201
703-993-8054   fax 703-993-8124
seagle@gmu.edu
Issues: The American Founding; Environmental regulation; Land use; Property rights; Urban sprawl/livable cities

Ealy, Lenore T., Ph.D.
Emergent Enterprises
10 Shady Lane
Carmel, IN 46032
317-581-0914   fax 317-582-0355
lenoree@att.net
Issues: Arts, humanities and historic resources; Business and education partnerships; Philanthropy

Ealy, Steven D.
Senior Fellow
Liberty Fund, Inc.
8335 Allison Pointe Trail, Suite 300
Indianapolis, IN 46250
317-842-0880   fax 317-577-9067
sealy@libertyfund.org
Issues: The American Founding; Church-state relations; Congress; Ethics; Political philosophy

Earley, Hon. Mark L.
President and Chief Executive Officer
Prison Fellowship Ministries
P. O. Box 17500
Washington, DC 20041
703-478-0100   fax 703-834-3658
mark_earley@pfm.org
Issues: Citizenship and civil society; Corrections and sentencing; Criminal law and procedure; Religion and public life; Religious freedom

*Earll, Carrie Gordon
Bioethics Policy Analyst, Social Research and
Cultural Affairs
Focus on the Family
8605 Explorer Drive
Colorado Springs, CO 80920
719-548-5819   fax 719-531-3385
earllcg@fotf.org
Issues: Aging/elder care; Family and children

*Easley, Paula
Senior Policy Analyst
Resource Development Council for Alaska
2134 Crataegus Avenue
Anchorage, AK 99508
907-274-6800   fax 907-277-2844
peasley@gci.net
Issues: Energy; Environmental regulation;
Federalism; Forestry and national parks; Free-
market environmentalism; Land use; Property
rights; Regulatory reform; Unfunded
mandates; Urban sprawl/livable cities; Wildlife
management/endangered species

*Eastman, Prof. John C.
Associate Professor and Director, Center for
Constitutional Jurisprudence
Chapman University School of Law
One University Drive
Orange, CA 92866
714-628-2587   fax 603-908-7774
jeastman@chapman.edu
Issues: The American Founding; American
history/political tradition; Campaign finance
reform; Church-state relations; Citizenship and
civil society; Civil rights/racial preferences;
Congress; Conservative thought;
Constitutional law; Electoral reform/voting
rights; Executive Branch/The Presidency;
Federal education policy; Federalism; Free
Speech; International law; Judicial activism/
judicial reform; Judiciary; Land use; Political
philosophy; Property rights; Public interest law;
The Reagan legacy; Religion and public life;
Religious freedom; School choice; Second
Amendment; State and local government;
Term limits; Unfunded mandates

*Easton, Michelle
President
Clare Boothe Luce Policy Institute
112 Elden Street, Suite P
Herndon, VA 20170
703-318-0730   fax 703-318-8867
cblpi@erols.com
Issues: American history/political tradition;
Charter schools; Church-state relations; Civil
rights/racial preferences; Conservative
thought; Education unions and interest
groups; Family and children; Federal
education policy; Home schooling; Juvenile
justice; Marriage and divorce; Political
correctness and multiculturalism; Public
school finance and administration; The
Reagan legacy; Religion and public life; School
choice; Standards, curriculum, and testing

*Eaton, Fran
Eagle Forum of Illinois
P. O. Box 233
Oak Forest, IL 60452
708-687-4264   fax 708-401-0379
ileagles@ileagles.net
Issues: Family and children; Government health
programs; Home schooling

Ebeling, Richard M.
Ludwig von Mises Professor of Economics
Hillsdale College
33 East College Street
Hillsdale, MI 49242
517-437-7341   fax 517-437-3923
richard.ebeling@hillsdale.edu
Issues: American diplomacy/foreign policy;
Central and Eastern Europe; Comparative
economics; Economic education; Economic
theory; The Economy; Entrepreneurship/free
enterprise; International organizations
(European Union, OECD, etc.); Money and
financial services; Political philosophy; Russia
and Eurasia; Trade

---

* Has testified before a state or federal legislative committee

*Ebell, Myron
Director, Global Warming and International Environmental Policy
Competitive Enterprise Institute
1001 Connecticut Avenue, N.W., Suite 1250
Washington, DC 20036
202-331-1010   fax 202-331-2192
mebell@cei.org
Issues: American history/political tradition; Climate change; Conservative thought; Costs and benefits of regulation; Energy; Ethics; Forestry and national parks; International organizations (European Union, OECD, etc.); Land use; Non-governmental organizations; Political philosophy; Property rights; Trade; Wildlife management/endangered species

Eberstadt, Mary
Consulting Editor
Policy Review
818 Connecticut Avenue, N.W., Suite 601
Washington, DC 20006
202-466-6730   fax 202-466-6733
polrev@hoover.standford.edu
Issues: Congress; Elections/polling; Executive Branch/The Presidency

*Eberstadt, Dr. Nicholas Nash
Henry Wendt Scholar in Political Economy
American Enterprise Institute
1150 17th Street, N.W.
Washington, DC 20036
202-862-5825   fax 202-862-7177
eberstadt@aei.org
Issues: Economic development/foreign aid; Korea; Northeast Asia; Poverty and dependency; Russia and Eurasia

*Ebzery, Evelyn
Chairman
Memorial Hospital of Sheridan County
P. O. Box 6387
Sheridan, WY 82801
307-672-6206   eebzery@attbi.com
Issues: Agriculture; Citizenship and civil society; Conservative thought; Environmental regulation; Forestry and national parks; Free-market environmentalism; Government health programs; Health care reform; Land use; Medicare; Non-governmental organizations; Property rights; Public interest law; State and local government; Stewardship; Wildlife management/endangered species

Echols, Tim G.
President
TeenPact Teen Leadership School
P. O. Box 9
Jefferson, GA 30549
706-367-1334   fax 706-367-2502
tim@teenpact.com
Issues: Citizenship and civil society; Family and children; Home schooling; Religion and public life

*Eckerly, Susan
Director Government Relations-Senate
National Federation of Independent Business
1201 F Street, N.W., Suite 200
Washington, DC 20004
202-554-9000   fax 202-484-1566
susan.eckerly@nfib.org
Issues: Costs and benefits of regulation; Davis-Bacon Act; Electricity deregulation; Family and medical leave; Job training/welfare to work; Labor and employment; Minimum wage; OSHA; Regulation through litigation; Regulatory budgeting; Regulatory reform; Right to work; Risk assessment; Transportation deregulation; Unemployment insurance; Unions

Eden, Dr. Robert
Professor, Department of Political Science
Hillsdale College
33 East College Street
Hillsdale, MI 49242
517-437-7341   fax 517-437-3923
Issues: The American Founding; American history/political tradition; Executive Branch/The Presidency; Political philosophy

Edgens, Jefferson G., Ph.D.
Director
Morehead State University – Jackson Center
1170 Main Street, P. O. Box 602
Jackson, KY 41339
606-666-2800   fax 606-666-8496
j.edgens@moreheadstate.edu
Issues: Costs and benefits of regulation; Energy; Environmental regulation; Forestry and national parks; Free-market environmentalism; Land use; Property rights; Regulatory reform; Taxation/tax reform; Urban sprawl/livable cities; Water; Wildlife management/endangered species

Edwards, Dr. Bruce L., Jr.
Associate Dean, Distance Learning and
International Education
Bowling Green State University
47 College Park
Bowling Green, OH 43403
419-372-7302   fax 419-372-8667
edwards@bgnet.bgsu.edu
Issues: Africa; Religion and public life

Edwards, Christopher
Director of Fiscal Policy Studies
Cato Institute
1000 Massachusetts Avenue, N.W.
Washington, DC 20001
202-842-0200   fax 202-842-3490
cedwards@cato.org
Issues: Advocacy and nonprofit public funding;
Agriculture; Discretionary spending;
Entitlement spending; Entrepreneurship/free
enterprise; Federal budget; Government debt;
Government waste; International tax policy/
tax competition; Privatization/Contracting-
out; State and local public finance; Taxation/
tax reform

*Edwards, Dr. James R., Jr.
Adjunct Fellow
Hudson Institute
1101 17th Street, N.W., Suite 602
Washington, DC 20036
202-467-8206   fax 202-467-8204
jedwards@olive-edwards.com
Issues: American history/political tradition;
Anti-trust; Citizenship and civil society;
Congress; Conservative thought;
Constitutional law; Health care reform;
Homeland security/civil defense; Immigration;
Intellectual property; Judicial activism/judicial
reform; Media and popular culture; Political
correctness and multiculturalism; Political
philosophy; Religion and public life; Religious
freedom; Terrorism and international crime;
Tort and liability reform

*Edwards, Lee
Distinguished Fellow, Center for American
Studies
The Heritage Foundation
214 Massachusetts Avenue, N.E.
Washington, DC 20002
202-608-6186   fax 202-544-6979
lee.edwards@heritage.org
Issues: American diplomacy/foreign policy;
American history/political tradition;
Conservative thought; Executive Branch/The
Presidency; The Reagan legacy

*Edwards, Mickey
John Quincy Adams Lecturer in Legislative
Politics, John F. Kennedy School of
Government
Harvard University
79 John F. Kennedy Street
Cambridge, MA 02138
617-496-3484   fax 617-496-5960
mickey_edwards@harvard.edu
Issues: Campaign finance reform; China;
Citizenship and civil society; Congress;
Conservative thought; Constitutional law;
Economic development/foreign aid;
Elections/polling; Federal budget; Human
rights; Judicial activism/judicial reform;
Judiciary; Media and popular culture;
Northeast Asia; Political philosophy; Term
limits

Edwards, Dr. Paul
President
Mercatus Center at George Mason University
3301 North Fairfax Drive, Suite 450
Arlington, VA 22201
703-993-4930   fax 703-993-4935
pedward2@gmu.edu
Issues: The American Founding; American
history/political tradition; Campaign finance
reform; Comparative economics;
Constitutional law; Judiciary; Religious
freedom

*Eggers, William
Senior Fellow, Manhattan Institute for Policy
Research, and Director
Deloitte Research-Public Sector
555 12th Street, N.W., Suite 450
Washington, DC 20004-1207
202-220-2994   fax 202-220-2750
weggers@dc.com
Issues: Discretionary spending; Faith-based and
volunteer initiatives; Federal budget; Federal
civil service; Federalism; Government waste;
Privacy; Privatization/Contracting-out; State
and local government; State and local public
finance; Telecommunications and the
Internet; Unfunded mandates

Ehrlich, Dr. Isaac
Distinguished Professor of Economics and
Melvin H. Baker Professor of American
Enterprise
State University of New York, Buffalo
North Campus, 415 Fronczak Hall
Buffalo, NY 14260-1520
716-645-2121   fax 716-645-2127
mgtehrl@buffalo.edu
Issues: Comparative economics; Crime/crime
statistics; Economic development/foreign aid;
Economic education; Entitlement spending;
Middle East; Privatization/Contracting-out;
Social Security and retirement; Taxation/tax
reform; Unfunded mandates

Eiras, Ana
Latin American Policy Analyst, Center for
International Trade and Economics
The Heritage Foundation
214 Massachusetts Avenue, N.E.
Washington, DC 20002
202-608-6125   fax 202-675-1772
ana.eiras@heritage.org
Issues: Costs and benefits of regulation;
Economic development/foreign aid;
International finance and multilateral banks;
Latin America; Mexico; Trade

*Eisenach, Jeffrey A.
Member, Board of Directors
Progress & Freedom Foundation
1401 H Street, N.W., Suite 1075
Washington, DC 20005
202-289-8928   fax 202-289-6079
jeisenach@pff.org
Issues: Costs and benefits of regulation;
Electricity deregulation; Intellectual property;
Privacy; Regulatory reform;
Telecommunications and the Internet

Ekelund, Dr. Robert B.
Lowder Eminent Scholar of Economics
Auburn University
415 West Magnolia Avenue
Auburn, AL 36849
334-844-2929   fax 334-844-4615
Issues: Arts, humanities and historic resources;
Costs and benefits of regulation; Electricity
deregulation; Regulatory reform; Religion and
public life; Transportation deregulation

Ekirch, Dr. A. Roger
Professor, Department of History
Virginia Polytechnic Institute
341 Major Williams Hall
Blacksburg, VA 24061
540-231-8381   fax 540-231-8724
arekirch@vt.edu
Issues: Corrections and sentencing

Elam, Dr. Joyce
Dean, College of Business Administration
Florida International University
University Park - BA310
Miami, FL 33199
305-348-2754   fax 305-348-3278
joyce.elam@fiu.edu
Issues: Entrepreneurship/free enterprise;
Higher education; Telecommunications and
the Internet

Eland, Dr. Ivan
Director of Defense Policy Studies
Cato Institute
1000 Massachusetts Avenue, N.W.
Washington, DC 20001-5403
202-842-0200   fax 202-842-3490
ieland@cato.org
Issues: Arms control; Central and Eastern
Europe; Defense budget; Intelligence
gathering and covert operations; Missile
defense; NATO and other alliances; Northeast
Asia; Readiness and manpower; Southeast Asia
(including Burma, Cambodia, Laos, Vietnam,
Singapore, Malaysia, Indonesia, the
Philippines, Australia, and New Zealand);
Terrorism and international crime; Western
Europe

Elliott, Barbara
President
Center for Renewal
9525 Katy Freeway, Suite 303
Houston, TX 77024
713-984-1343   fax 713-984-0409
belliott@centerforrenewal.org
Issues: American history/political tradition;
Church-state relations; Citizenship and civil
society; Conservative thought; Ethics; Faith-
based and volunteer initiatives; Family and
children; Job training/welfare to work;
Philanthropy; Political philosophy; Poverty and
dependency; Religion and public life; Religious
freedom; Welfare/welfare reform

Elliott, Dr. Mark

Director, The Global Center, Beeson Divinity
School
Samford University
P. O. Box 292268
Birmingham, AL 35229-2268
205-726-2170   fax 205-726-2271
melliott@samford.edu

Issues: Central and Eastern Europe; Human
rights; Russia and Eurasia

Elliott, W. Winston, III

President
Center for the American Idea
9525 Katy Freeway, Suite 303
Houston, TX 77024
713-984-1343   fax 713-984-0409
welliott@americanidea.org

Issues: The American Founding; American
history/political tradition; Citizenship and civil
society; Conservative thought; Economic
education; Entrepreneurship/free enterprise

*Elliott, Dr. Ward

Burnet C. Wohlford Professor of American
Political Institutions
Claremont McKenna College
850 Columbia Avenue
Claremont, CA 91711
909-607-3649   fax 909-621-8419
wardelliot@claremontmckenna.edu

Issues: Air; Civil rights/racial preferences;
Constitutional law; Immigration

*Ellis, Ryan

Director of Congressional Relations
Council for Government Reform
3124 North Tenth Street
Arlington, VA 22201
703-243-7400   fax 703-243-7403
rellis@govreform.org

Issues: Advocacy and nonprofit public funding;
Discretionary spending; The Economy;
Entitlement spending; Federal budget;
Government debt; Medicare; Money and
financial services; Social Security and
retirement; Taxation/tax reform

Ellmers, Glenn

Director of Research
Claremont Institute
250 West First Street, Suite 330
Claremont, CA 91711
909-621-6825   fax 909-626-8724
gellmers@claremont.org

Issues: The American Founding; American
history/political tradition; Campaign finance
reform; Electoral reform/voting rights;
Political philosophy

*Elshtain, Dr. Jean Bethke

Professor of Social and Political Ethics,
Divinity School
University of Chicago
1025 East 58th Street
Chicago, IL 60637
773-702-7252   fax 773-702-8223

Issues: American history/political tradition;
Church-state relations; Civil rights/racial
preferences; Constitutional law; Ethics;
Homeland security/civil defense;
Peacekeeping; Political philosophy; Terrorism
and international crime

*Elson, Charles M.

Edgar S. Woolard, Jr. Professor, Center for
Corporate Governance
University of Delaware
104 MBNA America Hall
Newark, DE 19716-2709
302-831-6157   fax 302-831-3329
elson@be.udel.edu

Issues: The Economy; Entrepreneurship/free
enterprise; Money and financial services

*Ely, Bert

President
Ely & Company, Inc.
P. O. Box 21010
Alexandria, VA 22320
703-836-4101   fax 703-836-1403
bert@ely-co.com

Issues: Agriculture; The Economy; Government
debt; Japan; Money and financial services;
Regulatory reform

Elzinga, Dr. Kenneth G.

Professor of Economics
University of Virginia
114 Rouss Hall
Charlottesville, VA 22903
804-924-6752   fax 804-982-2317
kge8z@virginia.edu

Issues: Anti-trust; Economic education;
Entrepreneurship/free enterprise

Engeman, Dr. Thomas
Associate Professor, Department of Political Science
Loyola University Chicago
6525 North Sheridan Road
Chicago, IL 60626
773-508-3063   fax 773-508-3131
tengema@luc.edu
Issues: American history/political tradition; Church-state relations; Conservative thought; Political philosophy; Religion and public life

*Engen, Dr. Eric M.
Resident Scholar
American Enterprise Institute
1150 17th Street, N.W.
Washington, DC 20036
202-862-5837   fax 202-862-7177
eengen@aei.org
Issues: Entitlement spending; Federal budget; Government debt; Social Security and retirement; Taxation/tax reform

*Enlow, Robert C.
Vice President, Programs and Public Affairs
Milton and Rose Friedman Foundation
One American Square, Suite 1750
Indianapolis, IN 46282
317-681-0745   fax 317-681-0945
rcenlow@friedmanfoundation.org
Issues: Business and education partnerships; Charter schools; Education unions and interest groups; Home schooling; Public school finance and administration; School choice

*Enoff, Louis D.
Principal
Enoff Associates Limited
103 Streaker Road
Sykesville, MD 21784
410-549-0455   fax 410-549-0460
louenoff@erols.com
Issues: Abstinence and out-of-wedlock births; Aging/elder care; Central and Eastern Europe; Comparative economics; Comparative government; Congress; Economic development/foreign aid; Faith-based and volunteer initiatives; Federal budget; Government health programs; Health care reform; Immigration; Privatization/Contracting-out; Religious freedom; Social Security and retirement; Unemployment insurance; Welfare/welfare reform

*Entin, Stephen
President and Executive Director
Institute for Research on the Economics of Taxation
1710 Rhode Island Avenue, N.W., 11th Floor
Washington, DC 20036
202-463-6192   fax 202-463-6199
sentin@iret.org
Issues: Climate change; Comparative economics; Economic forecasting; Economic theory; The Economy; Energy; Entitlement spending; Environmental regulation; Federal budget; Free-market environmentalism; Government debt; International tax policy/tax competition; Medicare; Money and financial services; Privatization/Contracting-out; The Reagan legacy; Social Security and retirement; Taxation/tax reform; Trade; Urban sprawl/livable cities

Epstein, Dr. Richard A.
James Parker Hall Distinguished Service Professor of Law
University of Chicago Law School
1111 East 60th Street
Chicago, IL 60637
773-702-9563   fax 773-702-0730
repstein@law.uchicago.edu
Issues: Civil rights/racial preferences; Constitutional law; Health care reform; Intellectual property; Political philosophy; Property rights; Regulatory reform; Tort and liability reform

*Erickson, Dr. Edward W.
Professor of Economics
North Carolina State University
Box 8110
Raleigh, NC 27695-8110
919-513-2876   fax 919-515-7873
ed_erickson@ncsu.edu
Issues: Electricity deregulation; Energy

*Erler, Dr. Edward J.
Professor, Department of Political Science
California State University, San Bernardino
5500 University Parkway
San Bernardino, CA 92407
909-880-5535   fax 909-880-7018
eerler@csusb.edu
Issues: The American Founding; Campaign finance reform; Civil rights/racial preferences; Constitutional law; Crime/crime statistics; Immigration; Initiative and referendum; Judicial activism/judicial reform; Religious freedom; Second Amendment

Ermarth, Fritz W.
Director of National Security Programs
The Nixon Center
1615 L Street, N.W., Suite 1250
Washington, DC 20036
202-887-1000   fax 202-887-5222
mail@nixoncenter.org
Issues: Arms control; Intelligence gathering and covert operations; Military strategy

*Ernst, Robert
Attorney
Banbury Fund
P. O. Box 487
Salmas, CA 93902
831-753-6125   fax 831-753-1035
bobernst@pacbell.net
Issues: Land use; Philanthropy; Property rights; Religious freedom; Second Amendment; Water; Wildlife management/endangered species

Evans, M. Stanton
Chairman
Education and Research Institute
800 Maryland Avenue, N.E.
Washington, DC 20002
202-546-1710   fax 202-546-3489
Issues: Congress; Elections/polling; Executive Branch/The Presidency; Judiciary; Media and popular culture

*Evers, Dr. Williamson M.
Research Fellow
Hoover Institution
Stanford University
Stanford, CA 94305
650-723-4148   fax 650-723-1687
evers@hoover.stanford.edu
Issues: Bilingual education; Charter schools; Education unions and interest groups; Federal education policy; Home schooling; School choice; Standards, curriculum, and testing

Ewing, Richard Daniel
Research Fellow in Chinese Studies
The Nixon Center
1615 L Street, N.W., Suite 1250
Washington, DC 20036
202-887-1000   fax 202-887-5222
mail@nixoncenter.org
Issues: China

*Fagan, Patrick
William H.G. FitzGerald Research Fellow in Family and Cultural Issues
The Heritage Foundation
214 Massachusetts Avenue, N.E.
Washington, DC 20002
202-546-4400   fax 202-544-5421
info@heritage.org
Issues: Abstinence and out-of-wedlock births; Adoption, foster care, & child care services; Faith-based and volunteer initiatives; Family and children; Marriage and divorce; Religion and public life

*Fagin, Dr. Barry S.
Professor, Department of Computer Science
United States Air Force Academy
2354 Fairchild Drive
USAF Academy, CO 80840-6234
719-333-7377   fax 719-333-3338
barry@faginfamily.net
Issues: Higher education; Intellectual property; Privacy; Russia and Eurasia; Telecommunications and the Internet

Failor, Edward D., Sr.
President
Iowans for Tax Relief
2610 Park Avenue
Muscatine, IA 52761
563-264-8080   fax 563-264-2413
itr@taxrelief.org
Issues: State and local public finance; Taxation/tax reform

*Fairbanks, Dr. Charles H., Jr.
Director, Central Asia Caucasus Institute
The Paul H. Nitze School of Advanced International Studies
Johns Hopkins University, 1740 Massachusetts Avenue, N.W.
Washington, DC 20036
202-663-5777   fax 202-663-5656
Issues: Afghanistan; American diplomacy/foreign policy; Human rights; Peacekeeping; Political philosophy; Russia and Eurasia; Terrorism and international crime

*Fairbanks, Richard
Counselor
Center for Strategic and International
Studies
1800 K Street, N.W., Suite 400
Washington, DC 20006
202-775-3130   fax 202-822-6354
rfairban@csis.org
Issues: China; Energy; Japan; Middle East;
Western Europe

Falcoff, Mark
Resident Scholar
American Enterprise Institute
1150 17th Street, N.W.
Washington, DC 20036
202-862-5902   fax 202-862-7163
mfalcoff@aei.org
Issues: Economic development/foreign aid;
Human rights; Latin America; United Nations

*Falero, Dr. Frank
Consulting Economist
40144 Balch Park Road, P. O. Box 950
Springville, CA 93265
559-539-2705   fax 559-539-5610
ffalero@ocsnet.net
Issues: Economic education; Economic
forecasting; Economic theory; Money and
financial services

*Faller, Dr. Thompson Mason
Professor of Philosophy
University of Portland
5000 North Willamette Boulevard
Portland, OR 97203
503-943-7144   fax 503-943-7802
faller@up.edu
Issues: Abstinence and out-of-wedlock births;
Church-state relations; Faith-based and
volunteer initiatives; Higher education;
Human rights; Religion and public life; School
choice

*Fand, David I.
Professor of Economics
James M. Buchanan Center for Political
Economy
George Mason University, 3301 North
Fairfax Drive
Fairfax, VA 22201
703-993-4915   fax 703-522-4952
dfand@gmu.edu
Issues: Economic theory; The Economy;
Federal budget; Government debt; Money and
financial services; The Reagan legacy; Trade

Faris, Jack
President
National Federation of Independent
Business
1201 F Street, N.W., Suite 200
Washington, DC 20004
202-554-9000   fax 202-554-2470
Issues: Entrepreneurship/free enterprise;
Regulation through litigation; Regulatory
budgeting; Taxation/tax reform

Farnsworth, Megan
Education Fellow
The Heritage Foundation
214 Massachusetts Avenue, N.E.
Washington, DC 20002
202-608-6173   fax 202-608-6087
megan.farnsworth@heritage.org
Issues: Bilingual education; Charter schools;
School choice; Standards, curriculum, and
testing

*Farris, Michael P.
President
Patrick Henry College
One Patrick Henry Circle
Purcellville, VA 20134
540-338-1776   fax 540-338-7611
president@phc.edu
Issues: Abstinence and out-of-wedlock births;
Adoption, foster care, & child care services;
The American Founding; American history/
political tradition; Business and education
partnerships; Charter schools; Church-state
relations; Citizenship and civil society;
Constitutional law; Education unions and
interest groups; Faith-based and volunteer
initiatives; Family and children; Federal
education policy; Federalism; Free Speech;
Higher education; Home schooling; Judicial
activism/judicial reform; Judiciary; Juvenile
justice; Marriage and divorce; Public interest
law; Public school finance and administration;
Religion and public life; Religious freedom;
School-to-work; Second Amendment;
Standards, curriculum, and testing; State-
sponsored gambling

Faulkner, Chip
Associate Director
Citizens for Limited Taxation and
Government
444 Taunton Street
Wentham, MA 02093
508-384-0100   cltg@cltg.org
Issues: Taxation/tax reform

Fauriol, Dr. Georges
Vice President for Strategic Planning
International Republican Institute
1225 Eye Street, NW
Washington, DC 20005
202-572-1529   fax 202-898-0861
gfauriol@iri.org
Issues: Economic development/foreign aid;
Emerging threats/threat assessment; Latin
America; Peacekeeping; Promoting
democracy/public diplomacy; Trade

Feidler, Robert
President
International Legal Projects Institute
2232 South 38th Street
Grand Forks, ND 58201-8843
701-775-7800   fax 701-780-8783
openchamp@aol.com
Issues: Congress; Federalism; Judicial activism/
judicial reform; Judiciary; Promoting
democracy/public diplomacy

*Feigenbaum, Susan K.
Professor, Department of Economics
University of Missouri, St. Louis
8001 Natural Bridge Road
St. Louis, MO 63121
314-516-5554   fax 314-516-5352
Issues: Government health programs; Health
care reform; Medicare; Regulatory reform

*Feldman, Amb. Harvey
Senior Fellow in China Policy
The Heritage Foundation
214 Massachusetts Avenue, N.E.
Washington, DC 20002
703-276-7882   fax 703-276-8849
hjfeldman@earthlink.net
Issues: American diplomacy/foreign policy;
Central and Eastern Europe; China; Emerging
threats/threat assessment; Northeast Asia;
Russia and Eurasia; Terrorism and
international crime; United Nations

*Feldman, Roger
Blue Cross Professor of Health Insurance,
Division of Health Services Research and
Policy
University of Minnesota
Mayo MIC-729, 420 Delaware Street, S.E.
Minneapolis, MN 55455
612-624-5669   fax 614-624-2196
feldm002@umn.edu
Issues: Costs and benefits of regulation;
Government health programs; Health care
reform; Medicare

Feldstein, Dr. Martin
President and CEO
National Bureau of Economic Research
1050 Massachusetts Avenue
Cambridge, MA 02138
617-868-3900   fax 617-868-7194
msfeldst@nber.org
Issues: International finance and multilateral
banks; Money and financial services; Social
Security and retirement

Feldstein, Dr. Paul J.
Professor, Graduate School of Management
University of California, Irvine
Irvine, CA 92697-3125
949-824-8156   fax 949-824-8469
pfeldste@uci.edu
Issues: Government health programs; Health
care reform

Ferrara, Peter
International Center for Law and Economics
Washington, DC
703-582-8466   peterferrara@msn.com
Issues: Civil rights/racial preferences;
Constitutional law; Discretionary spending;
The Economy; Entitlement spending; Federal
budget; Health care reform; Medicare; Poverty
and dependency; Privatization/Contracting-
out; Regulation through litigation; Social
Security and retirement; State and local public
finance; Taxation/tax reform; Welfare/welfare
reform

Ferry, Richard M.
President
Catholic Education Foundation
3424 Wilshire Boulevard
Los Angeles, CA 90010
213-637-7576   fax 213-637-5901
cef@cefdn.org
Issues: Business and education partnerships;
Education unions and interest groups; Federal
education policy; Higher education; Public
school finance and administration; School
choice; School-to-work; Standards, curriculum,
and testing

*Feulner, Dr. Edwin J.
President
The Heritage Foundation
214 Massachusetts Avenue, N.E.
Washington, DC 20002
202-608-6000   fax 202-546-0904
ed.feulner@heritage.org
Issues: Advocacy and nonprofit public funding;
Conservative thought; Entrepreneurship/free
enterprise; International tax policy/tax
competition; Northeast Asia; The Reagan
legacy; Southeast Asia (including Burma,
Cambodia, Laos, Vietnam, Singapore,
Malaysia, Indonesia, the Philippines, Australia,
and New Zealand); Western Europe

*Fey, Marc
Education Policy Analyst, Social Research
and Cultural Affairs
Focus on the Family
8605 Explorer Drive
Colorado Springs, CO 80920
719-548-5826   fax 719-531-3385
carpendm@fotf.org
Issues: Charter schools; Education unions and
interest groups; Federal education policy;
Higher education; Home schooling; Public
school finance and administration; The
Reagan legacy; School choice; Standards,
curriculum, and testing

Fienberg, Howard
Senior Analyst
Statistical Assessment Service
2100 L Street, N.W., Suite 300
Washington, DC 20037
202-223-3193   fax 202-872-4014
hfienberg@stats.org
Issues: Agriculture; Arms control; Canada;
Climate change; Energy; Media and popular
culture; Military strategy; Philanthropy;
Research funding; Risk assessment; Sound
science; Telecommunications and the Internet

*Fike, Robert
Federal Affairs Manager
Americans for Tax Reform
1920 L Street, N.W., Suite 200
Washington, DC 20036
202-785-0266   fax 202-785-0261
rfike@atr.org
Issues: American diplomacy/foreign policy;
American history/political tradition;
Campaign finance reform; Citizenship and civil
society; Comparative government; Congress;
Constitutional law; Costs and benefits of
regulation; Economic development/foreign
aid; The Economy; Education unions and
interest groups; Elections/polling; Energy;
Executive Branch/The Presidency; Federal
civil service; Federalism; Free Speech;
Government health programs; Infrastructure;
International finance and multilateral banks;
International law; International organizations
(European Union, OECD, etc.); International
tax policy/tax competition; Judiciary; Political
correctness and multiculturalism;
Privatization/Contracting-out; Property rights;
Right to work; School choice; Second
Amendment; Social Security and retirement;
State and local government; Taxation/tax
reform; Tort and liability reform; Trade;
Unions; Urban sprawl/livable cities; Western
Europe

Findley, John
Attorney
Pacific Legal Foundation
10360 Old Placerville Road, Suite 100
Sacramento, CA 95827
916-362-2833   fax 916-362-2932
Issues: Bilingual education; Charter schools;
Civil rights/racial preferences; Constitutional
law; Immigration; Initiative and referendum;
Judiciary; Public interest law; School choice;
Tort and liability reform; Welfare/welfare
reform

Finger, Dr. J. Michael
Resident Scholar
American Enterprise Institute
1150 17th Street, N.W.
Washington, DC 20036
202-862-5858   fax 202-862-7178
mfinger@aei.org
Issues: Economic development/foreign aid;
International organizations (European Union,
OECD, etc.); Trade

*Finn, Dr. Chester E., Jr.
President
Thomas B. Fordham Foundation
1627 K Street, N.W., Suite 600
Washington, DC 20006
202-223-5452   fax 202-223-9226
cefinnjr@aol.com
Issues: Business and education partnerships;
Charter schools; Education unions and interest
groups; Federal education policy; School
choice; Standards, curriculum, and testing

Fischel, Dr. William A.
Professor of Economics, Economics
Department
Dartmouth College
6106 Rockefeller Hall
Hanover, NH 03755
603-646-2940   fax 603-646-2122
william.a.fischel@dartmouth.edu
Issues: Initiative and referendum; Land use;
Property rights; Public school finance and
administration; State and local government;
State and local public finance

Fishback, Dr. Price V.
Professor, Department of Economics
University of Arizona
Tucson, AZ 85721
520-621-4421   fishback@u.arizona.edu
Issues: American history/political tradition;
OSHA

Fisher, Dr. Eric
AGIP Professor of international Economics,
Jean Monnet Fellow, Johns Hopkins
University, European University Institute
Ohio State University
via Belmeloro 11
40126 Bologna, ITALY,
011-39-051-2917-811
fax 011-39-015-22-85-05
fisher.244@osu.edu
Issues: Economic development/foreign aid;
Economic education; Economic theory;
International finance and multilateral banks;
Middle East

*Fisher, Gloria Taylor
Chairman
Interstate Commission on the Potomac
River Basin
6223 Arkendale Road
Alexandria, VA 22307
703-329-1725   fax 703-329-1725
glofisher@aol.com
Issues: Central and Eastern Europe;
Environmental education; Environmental
regulation; Free-market environmentalism;
Land use; Non-governmental organizations;
Property rights; Russia and Eurasia; Sound
science; State and local government;
Stewardship; Transportation; Urban sprawl/
livable cities; Water

*Fisher, Susan
President and Executive Director
Citizens for Law and Order
P. O. Box 412
Carlsbad, CA 92018
760-631-2028   fax 760-724-0385
info@doristate.com
Issues: Judicial activism/judicial reform

*Fitschen, Steve
President
National Legal Foundation
2224 Virginia Beach Boulevard, Suite 204
Virginia Beach, VA 23454
757-463-6133   fax 757-463-6055
nlf@nlf.net
Issues: The American Founding; Church-state
relations; Constitutional law; Free Speech;
Judicial activism/judicial reform; Public
interest law; Religion and public life; Religious
freedom

FitzGerald, Mary C.
Research Fellow, National Security Issues
Hudson Institute
1015 18th Street, N.W., Suite 300
Washington, DC 20036
703-823-2230   fax 202-223-8595
mary@hudsondc.org
Issues: Central and Eastern Europe; Emerging
threats/threat assessment; Military strategy;
Readiness and manpower; Russia and Eurasia

Fitzgerald, Sara
Trade Policy Analyst, Center for
International Trade and Economics
The Heritage Foundation
214 Massachusetts Avenue, N.E.
Washington, DC 20002
202-608-6079   fax 202-608-6129
sara.fitzgerald@heritage.org
Issues: Agriculture; Southeast Asia (including
Burma, Cambodia, Laos, Vietnam, Singapore,
Malaysia, Indonesia, the Philippines, Australia,
and New Zealand); Trade; Western Europe

*Fitzsimmons, Dr. Allan
President
Balanced Resource Solutions
3192 Rivanna Court
Woodbridge, VA 22192
703-491-5615   fax 703-491-5615
afitzsimm@aol.com
Issues: Energy; Environmental education;
Environmental regulation; Forestry and
national parks; Free-market environmentalism;
Land use; Property rights; Sound science;
Stewardship; Wildlife management/
endangered species

*Flaherty, Peter
President
National Legal and Policy Center
107 Park Washington Court
Falls Church, VA 22046-4237
703-237-1970   fax 703-237-2090
pflaherty@nlpc.org
Issues: Advocacy and nonprofit public funding;
Campaign finance reform; Civil rights/racial
preferences; Ethics; Free Speech; Public
interest law; Unions

Flannery, Dr. Christopher
Chairman, Department of History and
Political Science
Azusa Pacific University
901 East Alosta Avenue
Azusa, CA 91702
626-815-3843   flannery@apu.edu
Issues: The American Founding; American
history/political tradition; Political philosophy

*Fleischman, Edward H.
Linklaters
1345 6th Avenue, Suite 1900
New York, NY 10105
212-424-9000   fax 212-424-9100
efleisch@linklaters.com
Issues: Costs and benefits of regulation;
Regulation through litigation; Regulatory
reform

Fleming, Thomas
President
Rockford Institute
928 North Main Street
Rockford, IL 61103
815-964-5053   fax 815-964-9403
info@rockfordinstitute.org
Issues: American diplomacy/foreign policy;
Family and children; Federalism

*Fliegel, Seymour
President
Center for Educational Innovation – Public
Education Association
28 West 44th Street
New York, NY 10036
212-302-8800   fax 212-302-0088
sfliegel@ceiintl.org
Issues: Business and education partnerships;
Charter schools; Higher education; School
choice

Flowers, Dr. Marilyn R.
Professor of Economics, Department of
Economics
Ball State University
Muncie, IN 47306
765-285-5361   fax 765-285-8024
mflowers@bsu.edu
Issues: Entitlement spending; Federal budget;
Health care reform; Social Security and
retirement; Taxation/tax reform; Unfunded
mandates

*Flynn, Michael
Director of Legislation and Policy
American Legislative Exchange Council
1129 20th Street, N.W., Suite 500
Washington, DC 20036
202-466-3800   fax 202-466-3801
flynn@alec.org
Issues: The American Founding; Conservative
thought; Constitutional law; Federalism;
Regulation through litigation; State and local
government; State and local public finance;
Taxation/tax reform; Term limits; Tort and
liability reform

Foldvary, Dr. Fred E.

Professor of Economics, Department of
Economics
Santa Clara University
Santa Clara, CA 95053
408-554-6968   fax 408-554-2331
ffoldvary@scu.edu

Issues: Ethics; International tax policy/tax
competition; Political philosophy; State and
local public finance; Taxation/tax reform;
Urban sprawl/livable cities

Folsom, Dr. Burton W., Jr.

Historian in Residence
Center for the American Idea
9525 Katy Freeway, Suite 303
Houston, TX 77024
713-984-1343   fax 713-984-0409
bfolsom@americanidea.org

Issues: American history/political tradition;
Government debt; Taxation/tax reform

*Folsom, George

President
International Republican Institute
1225 Eye Street, N.W., Suite 700
Washington, DC 20005
202-408-9450   fax 202-408-9462
gfolsom@iri.org

Issues: Afghanistan; Africa; American
diplomacy/foreign policy; Central and Eastern
Europe; Comparative economics; Comparative
government; Economic development/foreign
aid; Emerging threats/threat assessment;
Intelligence gathering and covert operations;
International finance and multilateral banks;
Japan; Latin America; Mexico; NATO and
other alliances; Peacekeeping; Promoting
democracy/public diplomacy; Russia and
Eurasia; Western Europe

*Fonte, John, Ph.D.

Senior Fellow and Director, Center for
American Common Culture
Hudson Institute
1015 18th Street, N.W., Suite 300
Washington, DC 20036
202-974-2435   fax 202-223-8595
johnf@hudsondc.org

Issues: The American Founding; American
history/political tradition; Arts, humanities
and historic resources; Citizenship and civil
society; Civil rights/racial preferences;
Conservative thought; Human rights;
Immigration; Non-governmental
organizations; Political correctness and
multiculturalism; Political philosophy; The
Reagan legacy; Standards, curriculum, and
testing

Ford, Dr. William F.

Professor and Weatherford Chair of Finance,
College of Business
Middle Tennessee State University
P. O. Box 27
Murfreesboro, TN 37132
615-898-2889   fax 615-898-5962
wfford@mtsu.edu

Issues: Conservative thought; Economic theory;
Government waste; Health care reform;
Regulatory reform; Social Security and
retirement; State and local public finance;
Taxation/tax reform

*Forte, Dr. David

Professor of Law, Cleveland-Marshall
College of Law
Cleveland State University
1801 Euclid Avenue
Cleveland, OH 44115
216-687-2342   fax 216-687-6881
david.forte@law.csuohio.edu

Issues: Afghanistan; American history/political
tradition; Arms control; Arts, humanities and
historic resources; Church-state relations;
Citizenship and civil society; Civil rights/racial
preferences; Comparative government;
Conservative thought; Constitutional law;
Ethics; Family and children; Federalism; Free
Speech; Home schooling; Human rights;
International law; Judicial activism/judicial
reform; Judiciary; Marriage and divorce; Media
and popular culture; Middle East; NATO and
other alliances; Political correctness and
multiculturalism; Political philosophy; Privacy;
The Reagan legacy; Religion and public life;
Religious freedom; Russia and Eurasia; School
choice; United Nations

Foshee, Dr. Andrew W.
Professor of Economics, College of Business
McNeese State University
P. O. Box 91415
Lake Charles, LA 70609
318-475-5562   fax 318-475-5010
awfoshee@juno.com
Issues: Comparative economics; Waste
management

Fox-Genovese, Elizabeth
Elénore Raoul Professor of History
Emory University
205 Bowden Hall
Atlanta, GA 30322
404-727-4063   fax 404-315-1204
efoxgen@bellsouth.net
Issues: Abstinence and out-of-wedlock births;
American history/political tradition; Arts,
humanities and historic resources; Business
and education partnerships; Church-state
relations; Citizenship and civil society;
Comparative economics; Comparative
government; Congress; Conservative thought;
Economic theory; Education unions and
interest groups; Elections/polling; Ethics;
Executive Branch/The Presidency; Faith-based
and volunteer initiatives; Family and children;
Federal education policy; Federalism; Higher
education; Marriage and divorce; Media and
popular culture; Political correctness and
multiculturalism; Political philosophy;
Religion and public life; Religious freedom;
Standards, curriculum, and testing; Western
Europe

Fradkin, Dr. Hillel
President
Ethics and Public Policy Center
1015 15th Street, N.W.
Washington, DC 20005
202-682-1200   fax 202-408-0632
Issues: The American Founding; American
history/political tradition; Citizenship and civil
society; Conservative thought; Emerging
threats/threat assessment; Ethics; Faith-based
and volunteer initiatives; Human rights;
Middle East; Philanthropy; Political correctness
and multiculturalism; Political philosophy;
Promoting democracy/public diplomacy;
Religion and public life; South Asia (including
India and Pakistan); Terrorism and
international crime

Franc, Michael
Vice President, Government Relations
The Heritage Foundation
214 Massachusetts Avenue, N.E.
Washington, DC 20002
202-546-4400   fax 202-675-1778
info@heritage.org
Issues: Congress; Executive Branch/The
Presidency; Federal education policy; Health
care reform

*Franciosi, Robert
Director, Urban Growth and Economics
Goldwater Institute
500 East Coronado Road
Phoenix, AZ 85004
602-744-9601   fax 602-256-7045
rfrancio@goldwaterinstitute.org
Issues: Anti-trust; Campaign finance reform;
Energy; Environmental regulation;
Infrastructure; Public school finance and
administration; School choice; State and local
government; Transportation; Urban sprawl/
livable cities

*Francis, Walton
5700 Robeys Meadow Lane
Fairfax, VA 22030
703-278-0041   fax 703-278-0042
waltonjf@aol.com
Issues: Costs and benefits of regulation;
Federalism; Health care reform; Medicare;
Regulatory budgeting; Regulatory reform

*Franck, Dr. Matthew J.
Professor of Political Science
Radford University
Box 6945
Radford, VA 24142
540-831-5854   fax 540-831-6075
mfranck@radford.edu
Issues: The American Founding; Constitutional
law; Federalism; Judicial activism/judicial
reform; Judiciary; Political philosophy

Frankel, Dr. Micah Paul
Professor, School of Business and Economics
California State University, Hayward
25800 Carlos Bee Boulevard
Hayward, CA 94542
510-885-3341   fax 510-885-4796
mfrankel@csuhayward.edu
Issues: Entrepreneurship/free enterprise;
Government waste; Taxation/tax reform

*Franklin, Hon. Barbara Hackman
Chairman, Asian Studies Center Advisory
Council, The Heritage Foundation, and
President and CEO
Barbara Franklin Enterprises
2600 Virginia Avenue, N.W., Suite 506
Washington, DC 20037
202-337-9100   fax 202-337-9104
bhfranklin@aol.com
Issues: American diplomacy/foreign policy;
China; Costs and benefits of regulation; The
Economy; Entrepreneurship/free enterprise;
Intellectual property; Japan; Latin America;
Mexico; Money and financial services;
Regulatory reform; Russia and Eurasia; Trade;
Western Europe

Frantz, Amy
Research Analyst
Public Interest Institute
600 North Jackson Street
Mount Pleasant, IA 52641
319-385-3462   fax 319-385-3799
afrantz@limitedgovernment.org
Issues: Charter schools; Congress; Regulatory
reform; School choice

*Franz, Dr. Wanda
President
National Right to Life Committee
512 10th Street, N.W.
Washington, DC 20004
202-626-8800   fax 202-737-9189
nrlc@nrlc.org
Issues: Abstinence and out-of-wedlock births;
Adoption, foster care, & child care services;
Campaign finance reform; Family and
children; Government health programs;
Health care reform; United Nations

Frates, Dr. Steven B.
Senior Fellow, Rose Institute of State and
Local Government
Claremont McKenna College
340 East Ninth Street
Claremont, CA 91711
909-621-8159   fax 909-607-4288
steven.frates@mckenna.edu
Issues: Discretionary spending; Government
debt; Government waste; Public school finance
and administration; State and local public
finance; Unfunded mandates; Waste
management; Water

*Frech, Dr. H. E., III
Professor of Economics, Economics
Department
University of California, Santa Barbara
2171 North Hall
Santa Barbara, CA 93106
805-893-2124   fax 805-893-8830
frech@econ.ucsb.edu
Issues: Anti-trust; Government health
programs; Health care reform; Medicare;
Regulatory reform; Tort and liability reform

Freedman, Robert
Staff Attorney
Institute for Justice
1717 Pennsylvania Avenue, N.W., Suite 200
Washington, DC 20006
202-955-1300   fax 202-955-1329
rfreedman@ij.org
Issues: Public interest law; School choice

*Freedman, Dr. Robert O.
President and Peggy Meyerhoff Pearlstone
Professor of Political Science
Baltimore Hebrew University
5800 Park Heights Avenue
Baltimore, MD 21215
410-484-6851   fax 410-578-6940
freedman@bhu.edu
Issues: Emerging threats/threat assessment;
Middle East; Russia and Eurasia; Southeast Asia
(including Burma, Cambodia, Laos, Vietnam,
Singapore, Malaysia, Indonesia, the
Philippines, Australia, and New Zealand)

Freeman, Neal B.
Chairman
Blackwell Corporation
P. O. Box 2169
Vienna, VA 22183
703-242-6400   fax 703-242-8996
nealfreeman@blackwellcorp.com
Issues: Media and popular culture;
Philanthropy; The Reagan legacy;
Telecommunications and the Internet

Freeman, Richard B.
Program Director, Labor Studies
National Bureau of Economic Research
1050 Massachusetts Avenue
Cambridge, MA 02138
617-868-3900   fax 617-868-2742
Issues: Elections/polling; Labor and
employment; Poverty and dependency

Freund, Chris
Public Policy Analyst
The Family Foundation of Virginia
One Capitol Square, 830 East Main Street,
Suite 1201
Richmond, VA 23219
804-343-0010   fax 804-343-0050
Issues: Family and children

Frieden, Dr. Bernard J.
Ford Professor of Urban Development
Emeritus, Department of Urban Studies
Massachusetts Institute of Technology
77 Massachusetts Avenue, Room 9-641
Cambridge, MA 02139
617-253-2017   fax 617-253-2654
bfrieden@mit.edu
Issues: Environmental regulation; Higher
education; Housing and homelessness; Land
use; Privatization/Contracting-out; Urban
sprawl/livable cities

Friedland, Michael
Knobbe, Martens, Olson & Bear, LLP
2040 Main Street, 14th Floor
Irvine, CA 92614
949-721-6303   fax 949-760-9502
mkf@kmob.com
Issues: Intellectual property

Friedman, Dr. David D.
Professor, School of Law
Santa Clara University
3806 Williams Street
San Jose, CA 95117
408-554-5732   fax 408-544-4426
ddfr@best.com
Issues: Corrections and sentencing; Criminal
law and procedure; Energy; Regulatory reform;
School choice; Telecommunications and the
Internet

Friedman, Dr. George
Chairman
Stratfor.com
700 Lavaca Street, Suite 405
Austin, TX 78701
512-744-4300   fax 512-744-4334
friedman@stratfor.com
Issues: Africa; Arms control; Canada; Central
and Eastern Europe; Defense budget;
Economic development/foreign aid;
Emerging threats/threat assessment; Export
controls/military transfers; Latin America;
Middle East; Military strategy; Missile defense;
NATO and other alliances; Northeast Asia;
Readiness and manpower; Russia and Eurasia;
South Asia (including India and Pakistan);
Southeast Asia (including Burma, Cambodia,
Laos, Vietnam, Singapore, Malaysia, Indonesia,
the Philippines, Australia, and New Zealand);
Western Europe

Friedman, Jeffrey M.
Editor
Critical Review
113 Sayre Drive
Princeton, NJ 08540
609-720-1565
Issues: Political philosophy

*Friedman, Dr. Milton
Senior Research Fellow
Hoover Institution
Stanford University
Stanford, CA 94305
650-723-1755   fax 650-723-1687
Issues: The Economy; International finance and
multilateral banks; Money and financial
services; Promoting democracy/public
diplomacy; School choice

*Friedman, Dr. Murray
Director, Middle Atlantic Region
American Jewish Committee
117 South 17th Street, Suite 1010
Philadelphia, PA 19103
215-665-2300   fax 215-665-8737
murrayfrie@aol.com
Issues: American history/political tradition;
Church-state relations; Civil rights/racial
preferences; Immigration; Philanthropy; The
Reagan legacy; Religion and public life; School
choice

Friedman, Richard E.
President and Chairman
National Strategy Forum
53 West Jackson Boulevard, Suite 516
Chicago, IL 60604
312-697-1286   fax 312-697-1296
nsf@nationalstrategy.com
Issues: Afghanistan; American diplomacy/
foreign policy; Central and Eastern Europe;
Homeland security/civil defense; Terrorism
and international crime

Fritz, Marshall
President
Alliance for the Separation of School & State
4546 East Ashlan, Number 3282
Fresno, CA 93726
559-292-1776   fax 559-292-7582
marshall@sepschool.org
Issues: Charter schools; Family and children;
Federal education policy; Home schooling;
Public school finance and administration;
Religion and public life; Religious freedom;
School choice; School-to-work; Standards,
curriculum, and testing

*Frogue, James
Director, Health and Human Services Task
Force
American Legislative Exchange Council
1129 20th Street, N.W., Suite 500
Washington, DC 20036
202-466-3800   fax 202-466-3801
jfrogue@alec.org
Issues: Aging/elder care; Government health
programs; Health care reform; Medicaid;
Medicare

*Frydenlund, John
Director, Center for International Food and
Agriculture Policy
Citizens Against Government Waste
1301 Connecticut Avenue, N.W., Suite 400
Washington, DC 20036
202-467-5300   fax 202-467-4253
jfrydenlund@cagw.org
Issues: Agriculture; Government waste;
Taxation/tax reform; Trade

Fukuyama, Francis
Bernard Schwartz Professor of International
Political Economy
The Paul H. Nitze School of Advanced
International Studies
Johns Hopkins University, 1740
Massachusetts Avenue, N.W.
Washington, DC 20036-2213
202-663-5765   fax 202-663-5769
fukuyama@jhu.edu
Issues: Comparative government; Political
philosophy

Fuller, Adam
Research Associate
Toward Tradition
P. O. Box 58
Mercer Island, WA 98040
206-236-3046   fax 206-236-3288
afuller@towardtradition.org
Issues: Abstinence and out-of-wedlock births;
Adoption, foster care, & child care services;
Arts, humanities and historic resources;
Church-state relations; Citizenship and civil
society; Faith-based and volunteer initiatives;
Family and children; Marriage and divorce;
Media and popular culture; Middle East;
Political correctness and multiculturalism;
Religion and public life; School choice;
Taxation/tax reform; Terrorism and
international crime

Fuller, Dr. Howard
Distinguished Professor of Education and
Director, Institute for the Transformation of
Learning
Marquette University
School of Education
Milwaukee, WI 53201
414-288-5775   fax 414-288-6199
fullerh@marquette.edu
Issues: Charter schools; Education unions and
interest groups; School choice

Fumento, Michael
Senior Fellow
Hudson Institute
1015 18th Street, N.W., Suite 300
Washington, DC 20036
202-223-7770   fax 202-223-8595
Issues: Air; Climate change; Energy;
Environmental education; Environmental
regulation; Research funding; Sound science

---

* Has testified before a state or federal legislative committee

Fund, John H.
Columnist
OpinionJournal.com
New York, NY 10281
917-510-2847   fax 212-416-2658
john.fund@wsj.com
Issues: Elections/polling; Initiative and
referendum; Media and popular culture;
Privatization/Contracting-out; Term limits

Furchtgott-Roth, Dr. Harold
Visiting Fellow
American Enterprise Institute
1150 17th Street, N.W.
Washington, DC 20036
202-862-5819   fax 202-862-7177
hfr@aei.org
Issues: Costs and benefits of regulation;
Regulatory reform; Telecommunications and
the Internet

Furubotn, Dr. Eirik
Research Fellow, Private Enterprise Research
Center
Texas A&M University
3028 Academic Building West
College Station, TX 77843-4231
979-845-7559   fax 979-845-6636
perc@tamu.edu
Issues: Comparative economics; Economic
theory

*Fyfe, James
Professor, Department of Criminal Justice
Temple University
512 Gladfeiter Hall
Philadelphia, PA 19122
215-204-1670   fax 215-204-3872
james.fyfe@temple.edu
Issues: Civil rights/racial preferences; Crime/
crime statistics; Criminal law and procedure;
Police

Gabbert, Dr. Janice J.
Chairman and Professor of Classics
Wright State University
3640 Colonel Glenn Highway
Dayton, OH 45435
937-775-3062   fax 937-775-2892
jan.gabbert@wright.edu
Issues: Business and education partnerships;
Central and Eastern Europe; Higher
education; Intelligence gathering and covert
operations; Military strategy; Missile defense;
Standards, curriculum, and testing

Gache, Dana R., MPH, J.D.
Alabama Policy Institute
402 Office Park Drive, Suite 300
Birmingham, AL 35223
205-870-9900   fax 205-870-4407
danag@alabamapolicy.org
Issues: Government health programs; Health
care reform; Medicaid; Medicare

*Gaffney, Frank J., Jr.
President and CEO
Center for Security Policy
1920 I Street, N.W., Suite 210
Washington, DC 20036
202-835-9077   fax 202-835-9066
gaffney@security-policy.org
Issues: Afghanistan; American diplomacy/
foreign policy; Arms control; Canada; China;
Defense budget; Emerging threats/threat
assessment; Export controls/military transfers;
Homeland security/civil defense; Human
rights; Intelligence gathering and covert
operations; International organizations
(European Union, OECD, etc.); Korea; Latin
America; Middle East; Military strategy; Missile
defense; NATO and other alliances;
Peacekeeping; Promoting democracy/public
diplomacy; Readiness and manpower; Russia
and Eurasia; South Asia (including India and
Pakistan); Terrorism and international crime;
United Nations; Western Europe

Galandak, John
President
Foundation for Free Enterprise
South 61 Paramus Road, P. O. Box 768
Paramus, NJ 07653-0768
201-368-2100   fax 201-368-3438
jgalandak@fffe.org
Issues: Economic education; Environmental
education; Privatization/Contracting-out;
School-to-work

Gallagher, Maggie
Nationally Syndicated Columnist
53 Cedar Lane
Offining, NY 10562
914-762-7143   fax 914-762-7152
Issues: Family and children

Gallarotti, Dr. Giulio
Associate Professor of Government,
Department of Government
Wesleyan University
Middletown, CT 06457
860-685-2496   fax 860-685-2241
ggallarotti@wesleyan.edu
Issues: Economic development/foreign aid;
Free-market environmentalism; Human rights;
International finance and multilateral banks;
Trade; United Nations

Gallaway, Dr. Lowell E.
Distinguished Professor of Economics,
Department of Economics
Ohio University
Haning Hall 209
Athens, OH 45701-3335
740-593-2036   fax 740-593-0181
Issues: Davis-Bacon Act; Immigration; Labor
and employment; Minimum wage; Poverty and
dependency; Taxation/tax reform

Gardiner, Nile, Ph.D.
Visiting Fellow in Anglo-American Security
Policy, Kathryn and Shelby Cullom Davis
Institute for International Studies
The Heritage Foundation
214 Massachusetts Avenue, N.E.
Washington, DC 20002
202-608-6118   fax 202-675-1758
nile.gardiner@heritage.org
Issues: International organizations (European
Union, OECD, etc.); Middle East; NATO and
other alliances; Western Europe

Gardner, Dr. Bruce L.
Distinguished University Professor,
Department of Agricultural and Resource
Economics
University of Maryland
2212 Symons Hall
College Park, MD 20742
301-405-1271   fax 301-314-9091
bgardner@umd.edu
Issues: Agriculture; Trade

Garnett, Richard W.
Professor
Notre Dame Law School
327 Law School
Notre Dame, IN 46556
574-631-6981   fax 574-631-4197
garnett.4@nd.edu
Issues: Church-state relations; Constitutional
law; Corrections and sentencing; Criminal law
and procedure; Free Speech; Religion and
public life; Religious freedom; School choice

Garrett, Jennifer
Research Associate
The Heritage Foundation
214 Massachusetts Avenue, N.E.
Washington, DC 20002
202-546-4400   fax 202-544-5421
info@heritage.org
Issues: Abstinence and out-of-wedlock births;
Charter schools; Education unions and interest
groups; Marriage and divorce; Political
correctness and multiculturalism; School
choice; Welfare/welfare reform

Garrison, Steven
Research Analyst
Public Interest Institute
600 North Jackson Street
Mount Pleasant, IA 52641
319-385-3462   fax 319-385-3799
garrison@limitedgovernment.org
Issues: Agriculture; Energy; Taxation/tax
reform

Garthwaite, Jonathan
Director, Online Communications
The Heritage Foundation
214 Massachusetts Avenue, N.E.
Washington, DC 20002
202-608-6099   fax 202-544-7330
jon.garthwaite@heritage.org
Issues: Telecommunications and the Internet

Gaston, James R.
Assistant Professor of History
Franciscan University of Steubenville
University Boulevard
Steubenville, OH 43952
740-283-6245   fax 740-283-6401
jgaston@franuniv.edu
Issues: Arts, humanities and historic resources;
Conservative thought; Political philosophy;
Religion and public life

---

*Gatto, John Taylor
Odysseus Group Inc.
295 East 8th Street, Suite 3W
New York, NY 10009
212-874-3631   fax 212-721-6124
info@johntaylorgatto.com
Issues: School choice

*Gattuso, Dana Joel
Adjunct Scholar
Competitive Enterprise Institute
8256 Colling Ridge Court
Alexandria, VA 22308
703-768-7376   fax 703-768-7376
kjgattuso@cei.org
Issues: Air; Environmental regulation; Free-market environmentalism; Privatization/Contracting-out; Sound science; State and local government; State and local public finance; Unfunded mandates; Waste management

*Gattuso, James
Research Fellow, Thomas A. Roe Institute for Economic Policy Studies
The Heritage Foundation
214 Massachusetts Avenue, N.E.
Washington, DC 20002
202-546-4400   fax 202-544-5421
info@heritage.org
Issues: Anti-trust; Costs and benefits of regulation; Regulation through litigation; Regulatory budgeting; Regulatory reform; Telecommunications and the Internet; Tort and liability reform; Transportation; Transportation deregulation

Gavora, Carrie J.
Consultant/Policy Analyst
Strategic Health Solutions
1001 Pennsylvania Avenue, N.W., Suite 700 North
Washington, DC 20004
202-661-7062   fax 202-661-7066
cgavora@strat-health.com
Issues: Government health programs; Health care reform; Medicare

Gay, Prof. David E. R.
Department of Economics, Sam Walton College of Business
University of Arkansas
Fayetteville, AR 72701-1201
479-575-6222   fax 479-575-3241
dgay@walton.uark.edu
Issues: American history/political tradition; Comparative economics; Economic education; Entrepreneurship/free enterprise; Property rights; Taxation/tax reform

*Gayner, Jeffrey B.
Chairman
Americans for Sovereignty
104 North Carolina Avenue, S.E.
Washington, DC 20003
202-546-1119   fax 202-546-3091
jbgayner@hotmail.com
Issues: American diplomacy/foreign policy; American history/political tradition; China; Comparative government; Economic development/foreign aid; Human rights; International organizations (European Union, OECD, etc.); Missile defense; NATO and other alliances; Non-governmental organizations; Peacekeeping; Promoting democracy/public diplomacy; Russia and Eurasia; Southeast Asia (including Burma, Cambodia, Laos, Vietnam, Singapore, Malaysia, Indonesia, the Philippines, Australia, and New Zealand); Terrorism and international crime; United Nations; Western Europe

*Gaziano, Todd
Senior Fellow in Legal Studies and Director, Center for Legal and Judicial Studies
The Heritage Foundation
214 Massachusetts Avenue, N.E.
Washington, DC 20002
202-608-6182   fax 202-547-0641
info@heritage.org
Issues: Campaign finance reform; Civil rights/racial preferences; Constitutional law; Corrections and sentencing; Criminal law and procedure; Electoral reform/voting rights; Executive Branch/The Presidency; Federalism; Free Speech; Judicial activism/judicial reform; Judiciary; Property rights; Public interest law; Regulation through litigation; Regulatory budgeting; Regulatory reform; Religious freedom; Second Amendment; Tort and liability reform

*Geer, Michael
President
Pennsylvania Family Institute
1240 North Mountain Road
Harrisburg, PA 17112
717-545-0600   fax 717-545-8107
mgeer@pafamily.org
Issues: Abstinence and out-of-wedlock births;
Adoption, foster care, & child care services;
Business and education partnerships; Church-
state relations; Faith-based and volunteer
initiatives; Family and children; Home
schooling; Marriage and divorce; Religion and
public life; Religious freedom; School choice;
State-sponsored gambling

*Geimer, William
President
Jamestown Foundation
4516 43rd Street, N.W.
Washington, DC 20016
202-483-8888   fax 202-483-8337
host@jamestown.org
Issues: Russia and Eurasia

Geipel, Gary L.
Vice President and Chief Operating Officer
Hudson Institute
Herman Kahn Center, 5395 Emerson Way
Indianapolis, IN 46226
317-549-4105   fax 317-545-9639
gary@hudson.org
Issues: American diplomacy/foreign policy;
Citizenship and civil society; Elections/polling;
Emerging threats/threat assessment; NATO
and other alliances; State and local
government; Western Europe

*Gelak, Deanna R.
President, Working for the Future LLC, and
Executive Director
Family and Medical Leave Act Technical
Corrections Coalition
7505 Inzer Street
Springfield, VA 22151
703-256-0829   workfuture@aol.com
Issues: Adoption, foster care, & child care
services; Citizenship and civil society; Congress;
Costs and benefits of regulation; Ethics; Family
and children; Family and medical leave; Labor
and employment; Unemployment insurance

*Gellhorn, Dr. Ernest
Professor of Law
George Mason University School of Law
2907 Normanstone Lane, N.W.
Washington, DC 20008
202-319-7104   fax 202-319-7106
egellhor@gmu.edu
Issues: Anti-trust; Costs and benefits of
regulation; Regulatory reform; Risk assessment

*George, Dr. Robert P.
McCormick Professor of Jurisprudence,
Department of Politics
Princeton University
244 Corwin Hall
Princeton, NJ 08544
609-258-3270   fax 609-258-6837
rgeorge@princeton.edu
Issues: Church-state relations; Citizenship and
civil society; Civil rights/racial preferences;
Conservative thought; Constitutional law;
Ethics; Faith-based and volunteer initiatives;
Family and children; Judiciary; Marriage and
divorce; Media and popular culture; Political
correctness and multiculturalism; Political
philosophy; Religion and public life

Georgia, Paul
Enviornmental Policy Analyst
Competitive Enterprise Institute
1001 Connecticut Avenue, N.W., Suite 1250
Washington, DC 20036
202-331-1010   fax 202-331-0640
pgeorgia@cei.org
Issues: Climate change; Costs and benefits of
regulation; Electricity deregulation; Energy;
Environmental regulation; Free-market
environmentalism; Property rights; Regulatory
reform; Risk assessment; Sound science

*Gerard, Dr. Jules B.
Professor of Law Emeritus, School of Law
Washington University
Box 1120
St. Louis, MO 63130
314-935-6427   fax 314-935-5150
jbg51h@aol.com
Issues: Free Speech; Judicial activism/judicial
reform

Gerecht, Reuel Marc
Resident Fellow
American Enterprise Institute
1150 17th Street, N.W.
Washington, DC 20036
202-293-4983   fax 202-293-4572
Issues: American diplomacy/foreign policy;
Intelligence gathering and covert operations;
Middle East; Russia and Eurasia; Terrorism and
international crime

*Gerow, Charlie
Principal
Quantum Communications
224 Pine Street
Harrisburg, PA 17101
717-213-4955   fax 717-730-0514
crgerow@aol.com
Issues: The American Founding; American
history/political tradition; Campaign finance
reform; Elections/polling; Electoral reform/
voting rights; Initiative and referendum; The
Reagan legacy

Gersten, David
Executive Director
Center for Equal Opportunity
1400 Pidgeon Hill Drive, Suite 500
Sterling, VA 20165
703-421-5443   fax 703-421-6401
dgersten@ceousa.org
Issues: Bilingual education; Civil rights/racial
preferences; Immigration; Political correctness
and multiculturalism

*Getchell, Kathy
Board Member
Center for Market-Based Education, Inc.
15 King Henry Drive
Londonderry, NH 03053
603-432-3376   kathygetchell@juno.com
Issues: School choice

*Gifford, Mary F.
Senior Consultant
Field, Sarvas, King and Coleman
3101 North Central Avenue, Suite 1100
Phoenix, AZ 85012
602-241-1200   fax 602-241-0162
mgifford@fskcpa.com
Issues: Business and education partnerships;
Charter schools; Federal education policy;
Higher education; Home schooling; Public
school finance and administration; School
choice; Standards, curriculum, and testing

Gifford, Raymond L.
President
Progress & Freedom Foundation
1401 H Street, N.W., Suite 1075
Washington, DC 20005
202-289-8928   fax 202-289-6079
info@pff.org
Issues: Costs and benefits of regulation;
Electricity deregulation; Intellectual property;
Privacy; Regulatory reform;
Telecommunications and the Internet

Gilbert, Roberta M., M.D.
Director
Center for the Study of Human Systems
313 Park Avenue, Suite 308
Falls Church, VA 22046
703-532-1501   fax 703-532-3823
Issues: Citizenship and civil society; Family and
children; Juvenile justice; Marriage and
divorce; Media and popular culture; Religion
and public life; Religious freedom

Gillespie, Nick
Editor in Chief, *Reason* Magazine
Reason Foundation
3415 South Sepulveda Boulevard, Suite 400
Los Angeles, CA 90034
310-391-2245   fax 310-391-4395
Issues: Criminal law and procedure;
Immigration; Media and popular culture;
Substance abuse

Gilmore, Hon. James S.
Distinguished Fellow
The Heritage Foundation
214 Massachusetts Avenue, N.E.
Washington, DC 20002
202-546-4400   fax 202-675-1758
james.gilmore@heritage.org
Issues: Homeland security/civil defense;
Taxation/tax reform; Telecommunications
and the Internet

Gilroy, Leonard
Research Fellow, Urban Futures Program
Reason Foundation
3415 South Sepulveda Boulevard, Suite 400
Los Angeles, CA 90034
310-391-2245   fax 310-391-4395
leonard.gilroy@reason.org
Issues: Costs and benefits of regulation; The
Economy; Entrepreneurship/free enterprise;
Infrastructure; Land use; Property rights;
Regulatory reform; State and local
government; State and local public finance;
Transportation; Urban sprawl/livable cities

Giorno, Dennis A.
Executive Director
REACH Alliance
P. O. Box 1283
Harrisburg, PA 17108
717-238-1878   fax 717-703-3182
pachoice@aol.com
Issues: School choice

*Giovanetti, Tom
President
Institute for Policy Innovation
250 South Stemmons, Suite 215
Lewisville, TX 75067
972-874-5139   fax 972-874-5144
tomg@ipi.org
Issues: Anti-trust; Economic forecasting;
Economic theory; The Economy; Entitlement
spending; Entrepreneurship/free enterprise;
Ethics; Federal budget; Government debt;
Intellectual property; Minimum wage; Money
and financial services; Privacy; The Reagan
legacy; Social Security and retirement;
Taxation/tax reform; Telecommunications
and the Internet; Unfunded mandates; Wealth
creation/financial empowerment; Welfare/
welfare reform

Glahe, Dr. Fred R.
Professor, Department of Economics
University of Colorado
3870 Cloverleaf Drive
Boulder, CO 80304-1521
303-492-5186   fax 303-492-8960
fred.glahe@colorado.edu
Issues: Economic education; Economic theory;
International finance and multilateral banks;
Money and financial services

*Glassman, James K.
Resident Fellow
American Enterprise Institute
1150 17th Street, N.W.
Washington, DC 20036
202-862-7198   fax 202-862-7177
jglassman@aei.org
Issues: Climate change; Economic education;
Economic theory; The Economy;
Entrepreneurship/free enterprise; Federal
budget; Japan; Money and financial services;
School choice; Telecommunications and the
Internet; Western Europe

Glastris, Paul
Senior Fellow
Western Policy Center
1990 M Street, N.W., Suite 610
Washington, DC 20036
202-530-1425   fax 202-530-0261
info@westernpolicy.org
Issues: Central and Eastern Europe

Gleason, Stefan
Vice President
National Right to Work Legal Defense
Foundation
8001 Braddock Road, Suite 600
Springfield, VA 22160
703-321-8510   fax 703-321-9613
Issues: Campaign finance reform; Education
unions and interest groups; Labor and
employment; Public interest law; Right to work;
Unions

Glendon, Mary Ann
Learned Hand Professor of Law
Harvard Law School
1575 Massachusetts Avenue, Hauser 504
Cambridge, MA 02138
617-495-4769   fax 617-496-4913
Issues: Constitutional law; Federalism; Human
rights

*Glenn, Dr. Charles L.
Professor of Educational Policy and Fellow
of the University Professors Program
Boston University
605 Commonwealth Avenue
Boston, MA 02215
617-353-7108   fax 617-353-8444
glennsed@bu.edu
Issues: Bilingual education; Charter schools;
School choice; Standards, curriculum, and
testing

*Glenn, Gary
President
American Family Association of Michigan
P. O. Box 1904
Midland, MI 48641-1904
989-835-7978   fax 810-222-5109
garyglenn@afamichigan.org
Issues: Education unions and interest groups;
Family and children; Health care reform;
Home schooling; Initiative and referendum;
Land use; Marriage and divorce; Media and
popular culture; Property rights; Religion and
public life; Religious freedom; Right to work;
School choice; State and local government;
Term limits

Glenn, Dr. Norval D.
Stiles Professor in American Studies,
Department of Sociology
University of Texas
Burdine Hall 330
Austin, TX 78712-1088
512-232-6320   fax 512-471-1748
ndglenn@mail.la.utexas.edu
Issues: Abstinence and out-of-wedlock births;
Adoption, foster care, & child care services;
Faith-based and volunteer initiatives; Family
and children; Marriage and divorce; Religion
and public life

*Globerman, Dr. Steven
Ross Distinguished Professor, College of
Business and Economics
Western Washington University
Parks Hall 413
Bellingham, WA 98225
360-650-7288   fax 360-650-4844
steven.globerman@wwu.edu
Issues: Canada; Costs and benefits of regulation;
Government health programs; Health care
reform; Intellectual property; Regulatory
reform; Telecommunications and the Internet

Glover, Kay
Founder
Citizens for Choice in Education
411 Glover Street
Sturgis, SD 57785
605-347-2495   fax 605-347-6390
Issues: School choice

*Godson, Roy
President
National Strategy Information Center
1730 Rhode Island Avenue, N.W., Suite 500
Washington, DC 20036
202-429-0129   fax 202-659-5429
nsic@ix.netcom.com
Issues: Citizenship and civil society; Emerging
threats/threat assessment; Intelligence
gathering and covert operations; International
organizations (European Union, OECD, etc.);
Juvenile justice; Mexico; Promoting
democracy/public diplomacy; Terrorism and
international crime

Golab, Thomas
Vice President of Development
Competitive Enterprise Institute
1001 Connecticut Avenue, N.W., Suite 1250
Washington, DC 20036
202-331-1010   fax 202-331-0640
tgolab@cei.org
Issues: Non-governmental organizations;
Philanthropy; Police; Telecommunications
and the Internet; Terrorism and
international crime

Gold, Dr. Philip
Senior Fellow
Discovery Institute
1402 Third Avenue, Suite 400
Seattle, WA 98101
206-292-0401   fax 206-682-5320
pgold@discovery.org
Issues: Arms control; Arts, humanities and
historic resources; Defense budget; Emerging
threats/threat assessment; Homeland
security/civil defense; Media and popular
culture; Military strategy; NATO and other
alliances

*Goldberg, Robert, Ph.D.
Senior Fellow and Director, Center for
Medical Progress
Manhattan Institute
72 Troy Drive, Apt. A
Springfield, NJ 07081-2063
973-379-4029   fax 973-467-5579
bobgoldberg@yahoo.com
Issues: Aging/elder care; Costs and benefits of
regulation; Government health programs;
Health care reform; Medicaid; Medicare

*Goldberg, Dr. Steven
Chairman, Department of Sociology
City College
138th and Convent Avenue
New York, NY 10031
212-650-5485   fax 212-650-6615
Issues: Corrections and sentencing; Family and
children; Marriage and divorce

Goldhaber, Dr. Daniel J.
Research Associate Professor, Evans School
of Public Affairs
University of Washington
109K Parrington Hall, Box 353060
Seattle, WA 98195-3060
206-685-2214   fax 206-221-7402
dgoldhab@u.washington.edu
Issues: Federal education policy; School choice;
Standards, curriculum, and testing

*Goldsmith, Hon. Stephen

Faculty Director, Innovations in American Government Program, Kennedy School of Government and, Chairman, Center for Civic Innovation
Manhattan Institute for Policy Research
52 Vanderbilt Avenue
New York, NY 10017
212-599-7000   fax 212-599-3494
stephen_goldsmith@harvard.edu

Issues: Abstinence and out-of-wedlock births; Adoption, foster care, & child care services; Church-state relations; Citizenship and civil society; Conservative thought; Faith-based and volunteer initiatives; Family and children; Federalism; Housing and homelessness; Infrastructure; Job training/welfare to work; Marriage and divorce; Media and popular culture; Philanthropy; Poverty and dependency; Privatization/Contracting-out; Religion and public life; State and local government; Telecommunications and the Internet; Transportation; Wealth creation/ financial empowerment; Welfare/welfare reform

Goldwin, Dr. Robert A.

Resident Scholar
American Enterprise Institute
1150 17th Street, N.W.
Washington, DC 20036
202-862-5912   fax 301-961-6611
bobgoldwin@compuserve.com

Issues: The American Founding; American history/political tradition; Human rights; Political philosophy; Second Amendment

Gomory, Dr. Tomi

Assistant Professor, School of Social Work
Florida State University
2410 University Center Building C
Tallahassee, FL 32306-2024
850-644-2328   fax 850-644-9750
tgomory@mailer.fsu.edu

Issues: Citizenship and civil society; Government health programs; Higher education; Housing and homelessness; Poverty and dependency; Sound science; Welfare/ welfare reform

Goodman, Dr. John C.

President
National Center for Policy Analysis
12655 North Central Expressway, Suite 720
Dallas, TX 75243
972-386-6272   fax 972-386-0924
jcgoodman@ncpa.org

Issues: Government health programs; Health care reform; Medicare; School choice; Social Security and retirement

*Goodrick, Stephen O.

Vice President, Communications
National Right to Work Committee
8001 Braddock Road, Suite 500
Springfield, VA 22160
703-321-9820   fax 703-321-7143
sog@nrtw.org

Issues: American history/political tradition; Campaign finance reform; Conservative thought; Davis-Bacon Act; Economic education; The Economy; Education unions and interest groups; Entrepreneurship/free enterprise; Government waste; Labor and employment; Political philosophy; Public interest law; Right to work; Taxation/tax reform; Unions

Gordon, Doris

National Coordinator
Libertarians for Life
13424 Hathaway Drive
Wheaton, MD 20906
301-460-4141   fax 301-871-8552
libertarian@erols.com

Issues: Ethics; Family and children; Political philosophy

*Gordon, Dr. Peter

Professor of Planning and Economics, School of Policy, Planning and Development
University of Southern California
331C Ralph and Goldy Lewis Hall
Los Angeles, CA 90089-0626
213-740-1467   fax 213-740-6170
pgordon@usc.edu

Issues: Land use; Urban sprawl/livable cities

*Gordon, Robert E., Jr.
Executive Director
National Wilderness Institute
Georgetown Station, P. O. Box 25766
Washington, DC 20027
703-836-7404   fax 703-836-7405
rgordon@nwi.org
Issues: Free-market environmentalism;
Property rights; Wildlife management/
endangered species

*Gorman, Linda
Senior Fellow, Economic and Health Care
Policy
Independence Institute
14142 Denver West Parkway, Suite 185
Golden, CO 80401
303-279-6536   fax 303-279-4176
linda@i2i.org
Issues: Comparative economics; Economic
education; The Economy; Entrepreneurship/
free enterprise; Government health programs;
Health care reform; Immigration; Minimum
wage; Money and financial services; Second
Amendment; Trade

*Gottfredson, Dr. Linda S.
Professor, School of Education
University of Delaware
219B Willard Hall Educational Building
Newark, DE 19716-2901
302-831-1650   fax 302-831-6058
gottfred@udel.edu
Issues: Civil rights/racial preferences; Political
correctness and multiculturalism; Standards,
curriculum, and testing

Gottfried, Dr. Paul
Professor of Humanities, Department of
Humanities
Elizabethtown College
One Alpha Drive
Elizabethtown, PA 17022
717-361-1312   fax 717-361-1487
gottfrpe@etown.edu
Issues: Civil rights/racial preferences;
Conservative thought; Immigration; Political
philosophy; Standards, curriculum, and testing

*Gottlieb, Alan
Chairman
Citizens Committee for the Right to Keep
and Bear Arms
12500 N.E. 10th Place
Bellevue, WA 98005
425-454-4911   fax 425-451-3959
akagunnet@aol.com
Issues: Civil rights/racial preferences;
Constitutional law; Crime/crime statistics;
Second Amendment

Gottlieb, Dr. Gidon A.
Leo Spitz Professor of International Law
University of Chicago Law School
1111 East 60th Street
Chicago, IL 60637
773-702-9607   fax 773-702-0730
gidon_gottlieb@law.uchicago.edu
Issues: Africa; Emerging threats/threat
assessment; Human rights; Middle East; NATO
and other alliances; Political philosophy;
United Nations; Western Europe

Gottlieb, Scott, M.D.
Resident Fellow
American Enterprise Institute
1150 17th Street, N.W.
Washington, DC 20036
888-991-7667   fax 202-862-5808
scott.gottlieb@mssm.edu
Issues: Aging/elder care; Health care reform

Gourman, Dr. Jack
Director of Research
National Education Standards
600 Wilshire Boulevard, Suite 1200
Los Angeles, CA 90017
213-426-6569
jackgourman@thegourmanreport.com
Issues: Congress; Executive Branch/The
Presidency; Higher education

Goyburu, Alfredo
Policy Analyst, Center for Data Analysis
The Heritage Foundation
214 Massachusetts Avenue, N.E.
Washington, DC 20002
202-608-6293   fax 202-675-1772
alfredo.goyburu@heritage.org
Issues: Social Security and retirement

*Graglia, Dr. Lino A.
A. Dalton Cross Professor of Law
University of Texas
727 East 26th Street
Austin, TX 78705
512-471-0145   fax 512-471-6988
lgraglia@mail.law.utexas.edu
Issues: Anti-trust; Constitutional law;
Federalism; Free Speech; Initiative and
referendum; Judiciary; Religious freedom

Grainger, Andrew
President
New England Legal Foundation
150 Lincoln Street
Boston, MA 02111
617-695-3660   fax 617-695-3656
argrainger@juno.com
Issues: Constitutional law; Entrepreneurship/
free enterprise; Labor and employment;
Money and financial services; Privacy; Property
rights; Regulation through litigation; Tort and
liability reform

*Gramm, Dr. Wendy Lee
Director, Regulatory Studies Program
Mercatus Center at George Mason University
3301 North Fairfax Drive, Suite 450
Arlington, VA 22201
703-993-4930   fax 703-993-4935
wgramm@gmu.edu
Issues: Costs and benefits of regulation;
Regulation through litigation; Regulatory
budgeting; Regulatory reform; Risk assessment

Green, A. C., Jr.
President
A. C. Green Youth Foundation
P. O. Box 1709
Phoenix, AZ 85001
602-528-0790   fax 602-528-0783
info@acgreen.com
Issues: Abstinence and out-of-wedlock births;
Family and children

Green, Clint W.
Programs Officer
Acton Institute for the Study of Religion and
Liberty
161 Ottawa Avenue, N.W., Suite 301
Grand Rapids, MI 49503
616-454-3080   fax 616-454-9454
cgreen@acton.org
Issues: Charter schools; Education unions and
interest groups; Federal education policy;
Public school finance and administration;
Religion and public life; School choice;
Standards, curriculum, and testing; Unions

Green, Dr. John
Professor of Political Science, Ray C. Bliss
Institute
University of Akron
Akron, OH 44325
330-972-5182   fax 330-972-5479
jgreen@uakron.edu
Issues: Campaign finance reform; Citizenship
and civil society; Congress; Elections/polling;
Electoral reform/voting rights; Faith-based
and volunteer initiatives; Religion and public
life

Greenberg, Reuben
Chief of Police
Charleston Police Department
180 Lockwood Boulevard
Charleston, SC 29403
843-720-2401   fax 843-579-7518
greenbergr@ci.charleston.sc.us
Issues: Civil rights/racial preferences;
Corrections and sentencing; Crime/crime
statistics; Criminal law and procedure; Police

*Greene, Dr. Jay P.
Senior Fellow
Manhattan Institute for Policy Research
4801 South University Drive, Suite 2070
Davie, FL 33328
954-680-8083   fax 954-680-8981
jgreene@manhattan-institute.org
Issues: Charter schools; Education unions and
interest groups; Federal education policy;
Home schooling; Public school finance and
administration; School choice; Standards,
curriculum, and testing

Greene, Leonard M.
President
Institute for SocioEconomic Studies
20 New King Street
White Plains, NY 10604
914-428-7400   fax 914-684-1809
Issues: Economic theory; Taxation/tax reform;
Welfare/welfare reform

Greenwalt, Charles, II
Senior Fellow
Susquehanna Valley Center for Public Policy
P. O. Box 338
Hershey, PA 17033
717-361-8905   fax 717-361-8945
susvalley@aol.com
Issues: Charter schools; Civil rights/racial
preferences; Ethics; Higher education; Juvenile
justice; Political correctness and
multiculturalism; Privatization/Contracting-
out; School choice; Standards, curriculum, and
testing; Taxation/tax reform

Gregg, Dr. Samuel
Director of Research
Acton Institute for the Study of Religion and
Liberty
161 Ottawa Avenue, N.W., Suite 301
Grand Rapids, MI 49503
616-454-3080   fax 616-454-9454
sgregg@acton.org
Issues: Central and Eastern Europe; Church-
state relations; Conservative thought;
Constitutional law; Ethics; Faith-based and
volunteer initiatives; Human rights;
Intellectual property; Political philosophy;
Property rights; Religion and public life;
Religious freedom; Southeast Asia (including
Burma, Cambodia, Laos, Vietnam, Singapore,
Malaysia, Indonesia, the Philippines, Australia,
and New Zealand); United Nations

Gregorsky, Frank
Managing Director
Exacting Editorial Services
8119 Heatherton Lane, Number 103
Vienna, VA 22180
703-849-8068
gregorsky@millennials.com
Issues: Conservative thought; Economic theory;
Family and children; Media and popular
culture; Telecommunications and the Internet

*Greve, Dr. Michael S.
John G. Searle Scholar and Director,
Federalism Project
American Enterprise Institute
1150 17th Street, N.W.
Washington, DC 20036
202-862-4874   fax 202-862-7178
mgreve@aei.org
Issues: The American Founding; Anti-trust; Civil
rights/racial preferences; Constitutional law;
Federalism; International tax policy/tax
competition; Judicial activism/judicial reform;
Regulation through litigation; State and local
government; Tort and liability reform

*Griswold, Daniel T.
Associate Director, Center for Trade Policy
Studies
Cato Institute
1000 Massachusetts Avenue, N.W.
Washington, DC 20001
202-789-5260   fax 202-842-3490
dgriswol@cato.org
Issues: Immigration; Trade

Grosby, Dr. Steven E.
Professor, Department of Philosophy and
Religion
Clemson University
Clemson, SC 29634-0528
864-656-5358   fax 864-656-2858
sgrosby@clemson.edu
Issues: Citizenship and civil society;
Conservative thought; Political correctness and
multiculturalism; Political philosophy;
Religion and public life

Groseclose, Dr. Timothy J.
Associate Professor of Political Economy,
Graduate School of Business
Stanford University
350 Memorial Way
Stanford, CA 94305
650-723-2459   fax 650-725-0468
groseclose_tim@gsb.stanford.edu
Issues: Campaign finance reform; Congress;
Elections/polling

Grossman, Steven A.
President
HPS Group, LLC
13326 Hathaway Drive
Silver Spring, MD 20906
301-460-5500   fax 301-460-9100
sgrossman@hpsgroup.com
Issues: Aging/elder care; Government health programs; Health care reform; Medicaid; Medicare; Substance abuse

Groth, Dr. Alexander J.
Professor Emeritus of Political Science
University of California, Davis
1848 Rushmore Lane
Davis, CA 95616
530-752-0975   ajgroth@ucdavis.edu
Issues: Central and Eastern Europe; Comparative government; Conservative thought; Executive Branch/The Presidency; Political philosophy; Russia and Eurasia; United Nations

Grub, Dr. Phillip D.
Distinguished Executive in Residence
Eastern Washington University
4810 St. Andrews Lane
Spokane, WA 99223
509-448-6875   fax 509-448-5693
drpgrub@hotmail.com
Issues: China; Economic development/foreign aid; The Economy; Higher education; Japan; Korea; Middle East; Northeast Asia; South Asia (including India and Pakistan); Southeast Asia (including Burma, Cambodia, Laos, Vietnam, Singapore, Malaysia, Indonesia, the Philippines, Australia, and New Zealand); Trade

Gryphon, Marie
Education Policy Analyst
Cato Institute
1000 Massachusetts Avenue, N.W.
Washington, DC 20001
202-789-5249   fax 202-842-3490
Issues: Charter schools; Education unions and interest groups; Federal education policy; Higher education; School choice

Guinness, Dr. Os
Senior Fellow
Trinity Forum
7902 Westpark Drive, Suite A
McLean, VA 22102-4202
703-827-8998   fax 703-827-9559
mail@ttf.org
Issues: Religion and public life

*Gulibon, Grant R.
Senior Policy Analyst
The Commonwealth Foundation
225 State Street, Suite 302
Harrisburg, PA 17101
717-671-1901   fax 717-671-1905
gulibon@commonwealthfoundation.org
Issues: Campaign finance reform; Entrepreneurship/free enterprise; Government debt; Government waste; Land use; Minimum wage; Privatization/Contracting-out; Public school finance and administration; State and local public finance; Taxation/tax reform; Transportation; Urban sprawl/livable cities

Gulker, Dr. Virgil
Executive Director
Kids Hope USA
P. O. Box 2517
Holland, MI 49422-2517
616-546-3580   fax 616-546-3586
vgulker@kidshopeusa.org
Issues: Faith-based and volunteer initiatives; Family and children; Juvenile justice; Poverty and dependency; Welfare/welfare reform

*Gunderson, Dr. Gerald A.
Shelby Cullom Davis Professor of American Business and Economic Enterprise
Trinity College
300 Summit Street, Box 702533
Hartford, CT 06106
860-297-2395   fax 860-297-5111
gerald.gunderson@mail.trincoll.edu
Issues: Entrepreneurship/free enterprise; Public school finance and administration; School choice

*Gunnells, Lawrence
Executive Director
CSF Arkansas
P. O. Box 3060
Little Rock, AR 72203
501-907-0044   fax 501-907-0047
Issues: School choice

---

* Has testified before a state or federal legislative committee

*Guppy, Paul
Vice President for Research
Washington Policy Center
4025 Delridge Way, S.W., Suite 210
Seattle, WA 98106
206-937-9691   fax 206-938-6313
pguppy@washingtonpolicy.org
Issues: The American Founding; Civil rights/
racial preferences; Corrections and sentencing;
Government waste; Health care reform;
Initiative and referendum; Land use; Minimum
wage; Political philosophy; Privatization/
Contracting-out; State and local public finance;
Taxation/tax reform; Unfunded mandates

*Gustafson, Erick
Vice President, Federal and State Affairs
Citizens for a Sound Economy
1900 M Street, N.W., Suite 500
Washington, DC 20036
202-942-7641   fax 202-783-4687
egustafson@cse.org
Issues: Aging/elder care; Air; Anti-trust;
Climate change; Congress; Costs and benefits
of regulation; Discretionary spending; The
Economy; Energy; Entitlement spending;
Entrepreneurship/free enterprise;
Environmental education; Environmental
regulation; Federal budget; Forestry and
national parks; Free-market environmentalism;
Government debt; Government health
programs; Government waste; Health care
reform; Housing and homelessness;
Intellectual property; Land use; Medicaid;
Medicare; Money and financial services;
Privacy; Privatization/Contracting-out;
Property rights; Regulation through litigation;
Regulatory reform; Social Security and
retirement; Sound science; State and local
government; State and local public finance;
Taxation/tax reform; Telecommunications
and the Internet; Trade; Unfunded mandates;
Urban sprawl/livable cities

Gvosdev, Nikolas
Executive Editor
The National Interest
1615 L Street N.W., Suite 1230
Washington, DC 20036
202-467-4884   fax 202-467-0006
gvosdev@nationalinterest.org
Issues: American diplomacy/foreign policy;
Central and Eastern Europe; Church-state
relations; NATO and other alliances;
Promoting democracy/public diplomacy;
Religious freedom; Russia and Eurasia;
Terrorism and international crime

*Gwartney, Dr. James D.
Professor of Economics, Department of
Economics
Florida State University
150A Bellamy Building
Tallahassee, FL 32306-2180
850-644-7645   fax 850-644-0581
jdgwart@aol.com
Issues: Comparative economics; Comparative
government; Costs and benefits of regulation;
The Economy; Entrepreneurship/free
enterprise; Government waste; Taxation/tax
reform; Trade

Haakonssen, Dr. Knud
Professor, Department of Philosophy
Boston University
745 Commonwealth Avenue
Boston, MA 02215
617-353-4581   haakon@bu.edu
Issues: Ethics; Political philosophy

*Haar, Charlene
President
Education Policy Institute
4401-A Connecticut Avenue, N.W., PMB 294
Washington, DC 20008-2322
202-537-9285   fax 202-537-9289
sdchar@aol.com
Issues: Business and education partnerships;
Charter schools; Education unions and interest
groups; Federal education policy; Labor and
employment; Public school finance and
administration; School choice; Unions

Hackett, James T.
7473 Neptune Drive
Carlsbad, CA 92009
760-929-9741   fax 760-929-9741
jthackett@adelphia.net
Issues: Arms control; Emerging threats/threat
assessment; Missile defense

Hagelin, Rebecca
Vice President for Communications
The Heritage Foundation
214 Massachusetts Avenue, N.E.
Washington, DC 20002
202-546-4400   fax 202-544-6979
info@heritage.org
Issues: Abstinence and out-of-wedlock births;
Citizenship and civil society; Family and
children; Home schooling; Marriage and
divorce; Media and popular culture; Religion
and public life; School choice; Second
Amendment; Telecommunications and the
Internet

Haggard, Dr. Thomas R.
David W. Robinson Chair, Professor of Law,
School of Law
University of South Carolina
Greene and Main Streets
Columbia, SC 29208
803-777-4790   fax 803-777-2368
tom@law.law.sc.edu
Issues: Labor and employment

*Hahn, Dr. Robert
Resident Scholar
American Enterprise Institute
1150 17th Street, N.W.
Washington, DC 20036
202-862-5909   fax 202-862-7169
rhahn@aei.org
Issues: Anti-trust; Costs and benefits of
regulation; Economic theory; The Economy;
Electricity deregulation; Federalism;
Intellectual property; Regulation through
litigation; Regulatory reform; State and local
government; Tort and liability reform;
Transportation deregulation

*Haislmaier, Edmund F.
President
Strategic Policy Management
777 North Capitol Street, N.E., Suite 803
Washington, DC 20002
202-408-0620   fax 202-543-2518
ed@haislmaier.com
Issues: Government health programs; Health
care reform; Medicaid; Medicare

*Hale, Robert
President
Northwest Legal Foundation
315 South Main, Suite 204
Minot, ND 58701
701-858-0080   fax 701-852-5032
bobhnlf@ndak.net
Issues: Agriculture; American history/political
tradition; Constitutional law;
Entrepreneurship/free enterprise;
Environmental regulation; Free Speech;
Government waste; Home schooling;
Infrastructure; Judicial activism/judicial
reform; Judiciary; Land use; Property rights;
Public interest law; Regulatory reform;
Religion and public life; Religious freedom;
School choice; State and local public finance;
Unfunded mandates

Hales, Daniel B.
President
Americans for Effective Law Enforcement
200 East Randolph Drive, Suite 7300
Chicago, IL 60601
312-946-4236   fax 312-565-0832
danhales@hotmail.com
Issues: Criminal law and procedure; Economic
theory; Police; Political philosophy

*Hall, Joshua
Director, Center for Education Excellence
Buckeye Institute for Public Policy Solutions
4100 North High Street, Suite 200
Columbus, OH 43214
614-262-1593   fax 614-262-1927
hall@buckeyeinstitute.org
Issues: Business and education partnerships;
Charter schools; Education unions and interest
groups; Public school finance and
administration; School choice; Standards,
curriculum, and testing; State and local public
finance

Hall, Dr. Robert
Robert and Carole McNeil Senior Fellow
Hoover Institution
Stanford University
Stanford, CA 94305
650-725-7320   fax 650-723-1687
hall@hoover.stanford.edu
Issues: Comparative economics; The Economy;
Taxation/tax reform; Trade

Halvorssen, Thor L.
Executive Director
The Foundation for Individual Rights in
Education
210 West Washington Square, Suite 303
Philadelphia, PA 19106
215-717-3473   fax 215-717-3440
thor@thefire.org
Issues: Free Speech; Higher education;
Philanthropy; Political correctness and
multiculturalism; Religious freedom

Hamburg, Dr. Roger

Professor Emeritus of Political Science and
Public Affairs
Indiana University South Bend
1800 Mishawaka Avenue
South Bend, IN 46634-7111
574-237-4131   fax 574-237-6514
hamburgr@iusb.edu
Issues: American diplomacy/foreign policy;
American history/political tradition; Church-
state relations; Citizenship and civil society;
Comparative government; Constitutional law;
Defense budget; Emerging threats/threat
assessment; Free Speech; Higher education;
Intelligence gathering and covert operations;
Job training/welfare to work; Marriage and
divorce; Military strategy; Promoting
democracy/public diplomacy; Russia and
Eurasia; School choice; Terrorism and
international crime

Hamilton, James M.

National Director
For Our Grandchildren
10400 Eaton Place, Suite 450
Fairfax, VA 22030
703-621-3880   fax 703-621-3870
james.m.hamilton@att.net
Issues: Social Security and retirement

*Hamilton, Dr. Randy H.

Visiting Scholar, Institute of Governmental
Studies
University of California, Berkeley
109 Moses Hall
Berkeley, CA 94720
510-642-4633   fax 510-642-3020
Issues: Charter schools; Federalism; Juvenile
justice; Police; School choice; State and local
government; State and local public finance;
Unfunded mandates; Urban sprawl/livable
cities

Hammad, Dr. Alam E.

819 South Fairfax Street
Alexandria, VA 22314-4311
703-548-4840   fax 703-836-2890
hammad@gmu.edu
Issues: Economic development/foreign aid;
The Economy; Energy; Entrepreneurship/free
enterprise; Faith-based and volunteer
initiatives; Higher education; Middle East;
Religion and public life; Trade

Hammond, Dr. Paul Y.

Distinguished Service Professor, Graduate
School of Public and International Affairs
University of Pittsburgh
3N23 Forbes Quad
Pittsburgh, PA 15260
412-648-7651   fax 412-648-2605
pyh@pitt.edu
Issues: Economic development/foreign aid;
NATO and other alliances; Northeast Asia;
Peacekeeping; Readiness and manpower;
Western Europe

Hamp, Paige Holland

Executive Director, Maryland Education
Alliance
Maryland Public Policy Institute
P. O. Box 195
Germantown, MD 20876-0195
240-686-3510   fax 240-686-3511
Issues: Federal education policy; School choice

Hancock, Dr. Ralph C.

Professor of Political Science
Brigham Young University
772 SWKT
Provo, UT 84602
801-378-3302   fax 801-378-5730
ralph_hancock@byu.edu
Issues: Political philosophy

Hanke, Dr. Steve H.
Professor of Applied Economics
Johns Hopkins University
34th & Charles Streets
Baltimore, MD 21218
410-516-7183   fax 410-516-8996
hanke@jhu.edu
Issues: Africa; Anti-trust; Canada; Central and
Eastern Europe; China; Comparative
economics; Conservative thought; Costs and
benefits of regulation; Economic
development/foreign aid; Economic
forecasting; Economic theory; The Economy;
Energy; Entrepreneurship/free enterprise;
Federal budget; Forestry and national parks;
International finance and multilateral banks;
International organizations (European Union,
OECD, etc.); International tax policy/tax
competition; Japan; Korea; Latin America;
Mexico; Money and financial services;
Privatization/Contracting-out; Property rights;
The Reagan legacy; Regulatory reform; Risk
assessment; Russia and Eurasia; South Asia
(including India and Pakistan); Southeast Asia
(including Burma, Cambodia, Laos, Vietnam,
Singapore, Malaysia, Indonesia, the
Philippines, Australia, and New Zealand); State
and local public finance; Taxation/tax reform;
Trade; Water; Western Europe

*Hansen, Dr. Ronald
Senior Associate Dean for Faculty and
Research, William E. Simon Graduate School
of Business
University of Rochester
Carol Simon Hall 2-202E
Rochester, NY 14627
585-275-2668   fax 585-275-0095
hansen@simon.rochester.edu
Issues: Costs and benefits of regulation; Health
care reform; Intellectual property; Regulatory
reform; Risk assessment

Hanson, Dr. Bertil L.
Professor of Political Science, Political
Science Department
Oklahoma State University
Stillwater, OK 74078
405-377-6685   fax 405-744-6534
Issues: Economic theory; Religion and public
life

Hanson, Dr. John R., II
Professor, Department of Economics
Texas A&M University
3098 Academic Building West
College Station, TX 77843-4228
979-845-4593   fax 979-847-8757
hanson@econ.tamu.edu
Issues: Economic development/foreign aid;
Economic education; Trade

Hanson, Robin
Assistant Professor of Economics
George Mason University
MSN 1D3, 10 B Carow Hall
Fairfax, VA 22030
703-993-2326   fax 703-993-2323
rhanson@gmu.edu
Issues: Elections/polling; Government health
programs; Health care reform; Initiative and
referendum; Regulatory reform; Research
funding; Risk assessment

Hanus, Jerome J., Ph.D.
Scholar in Resident, Department of
Government
American University
4400 Massachusetts Avenue, N.W.
Washington, DC 20016
202-885-6228   fax 202-885-2967
jhanus@american.edu
Issues: American history/political tradition;
Charter schools; Church-state relations;
Conservative thought; Constitutional law;
Ethics; Federal education policy; Higher
education; Political philosophy; School choice

Hanushek, Dr. Eric
Hanna Senior Fellow on Education Policy
Hoover Institution
Stanford University
Stanford, CA 94305-6010
650-736-0942   fax 650-723-1687
hanushek@hoover.stanford.edu
Issues: Aging/elder care; Bilingual education; Business and education partnerships; Charter schools; Economic education; Education unions and interest groups; Federal education policy; Federalism; Government health programs; Health care reform; Higher education; Home schooling; Housing and homelessness; Medicaid; Medicare; Poverty and dependency; Public school finance and administration; School choice; School-to-work; Social Security and retirement; Standards, curriculum, and testing; State and local government; State and local public finance; Substance abuse; Wealth creation/financial empowerment; Welfare/welfare reform

Harberger, Paul V.
President
Foundation Francisco Marroquin
P. O. Box 1806
Santa Monica, CA 90406-1806
310-395-5047   fax 772-288-0670
pvh@ffmnet.org
Issues: Latin America; Social Security and retirement

*Hardiman, Mike
President
Hardiman Consulting
507 Seward Square, S.E.
Washington, DC 20003
202-251-3473   fax 202-543-7126
mike@hardimanconsulting.com
Issues: Energy; Environmental regulation; Forestry and national parks; Free-market environmentalism; Land use; Property rights; Sound science; Stewardship; Urban sprawl/ livable cities; Wildlife management/ endangered species

Hardin, Charles G.
President
Council for Government Reform
3124 North Tenth Street
Arlington, VA 22201
703-243-7400   fax 703-243-7403
chardin@govreform.org
Issues: Social Security and retirement

*Harmon, Dr. Christopher C.
Professor of International Relations, Command and Staff College
Marine Corps University
2076 South Street
Quantico, VA 22134-5068
703-784-6855   fax 703-784-2628
harmoncc@tecom.usmc.mil
Issues: Terrorism and international crime

Harned, Karen R., Esq.
Executive Director
National Federation of Independent Business Legal Foundation
1201 F Street, N.W., Suite 200
Washington, DC 20004
202-518-6324   fax 202-484-1566
karen.harned@nfib.org
Issues: Costs and benefits of regulation

Harper, Dr. Charles L.
Executive Director and Senior Vice President
John Templeton Foundation
Five Radnor Corporate Center, Suite 100
Radnor, PA 19087
610-687-8942   fax 610-687-8961
harper@templeton.org
Issues: Faith-based and volunteer initiatives; Philanthropy; Religion and public life; Religious freedom; Research funding; Sound science

Harpham, Dr. Edward J.
Associate Professor of Government and Political Economy, School of Social Sciences
University of Texas, Dallas
Box 830688
Richardson, TX 75083
972-883-2044   fax 972-883-2735
harpham@utdallas.edu
Issues: The American Founding; American history/political tradition; Conservative thought; Ethics; Political philosophy

Harrington, Scott E.
Professor of Insurance and Finance, College of Business Administration
University of South Carolina
Darla Moore School of Business
Columbia, SC 29208
803-777-4925   fax 803-777-6876
harrington@moore.sc.edu
Issues: Costs and benefits of regulation; The Economy; Money and financial services; Regulation through litigation; Regulatory reform; Trade

Harrison, John C.
Research Professor in Law, School of Law
University of Virginia
580 Massie Road
Charlottesville, VA 22903
804-924-3093   fax 804-924-7536
jch4v@Virginia.edu
Issues: Constitutional law; Judiciary

Harrison, Robert C.
Director of Public Policy
Defenders of Property Rights
1350 Connecticut Avenue, N.W., Suite 410
Washington, DC 20036
202-822-6770   fax 202-822-6774
robert@yourpropertyrights.org
Issues: Congress; Environmental regulation;
Forestry and national parks; Free-market
environmentalism; Land use; Political
philosophy; Property rights; Urban sprawl/
livable cities; Water; Wildlife management/
endangered species

*Harriss, Dr. C. Lowell
Professor Emeritus of Economics
Columbia University
14 Plateau Circle
Bronxville, NY 10708
914-337-5015   fax 914-337-5015
Issues: Economic education; Federalism;
International tax policy/tax competition;
Political philosophy; State and local public
finance; Taxation/tax reform

*Harsh, Lynn
Senior Researcher and Executive Director
Evergreen Freedom Foundation
P. O. Box 552
Olympia, WA 98507
360-956-3482   fax 360-352-1874
lharsh@effwa.org
Issues: The American Founding; Bilingual
education; Comparative economics; Economic
education; Education unions and interest
groups; Entrepreneurship/free enterprise;
Health care reform; School choice; Standards,
curriculum, and testing; Unions; Welfare/
welfare reform

Hart, Larry
President
Hartco Strategies
8 E Street, S.E.
Washington, DC 20003
202-547-1175   fax 202-547-1174
larry.hart2@att.net
Issues: Afghanistan; Climate change; Congress;
Energy; Environmental education;
Environmental regulation; Risk assessment;
Sound science

Hartgen, Prof. David T.
Professor of Transportation Studies
University of North Carolina, Charlotte
Cameron Center 274, Highway 49
Charlotte, NC 28223
704-687-4308   fax 704-687-3442
Issues: Privatization/Contracting-out; State and
local public finance; Transportation;
Transportation deregulation; Urban sprawl/
livable cities

Hartley, Dr. James E.
Associate Professor of Economics
Mount Holyoke College
126 Skinner Hall
South Hadley, MA 01075
413-538-2566   fax 413-538-2323
jhartley@mhc.mtholyoke.edu
Issues: Economic education; Economic theory;
Higher education

Hartman, David
Chairman
The Lone Star Foundation
10711 Burnett Road, Suite 333
Austin, TX 78758
512-339-9771   fax 512-997-7826
dahartman@hartman-llc.com
Issues: Taxation/tax reform; Welfare/welfare
reform

Hartwig, Mark
Religion and Society Analyst, Social Research
and Cultural Affairs
Focus on the Family
8605 Explorer Drive
Colorado Springs, CO 80920
719-548-5855   fax 719-531-3385
hartwimd@fotf.org
Issues: Religion and public life; Religious
freedom

---

*Hassett, Kevin A.
Resident Scholar
American Enterprise Institute
1150 17th Street, N.W.
Washington, DC 20036
202-862-7157   fax 202-862-7177
khassett@aei.org
Issues: Economic forecasting; The Economy;
Federal budget; International tax policy/tax
competition; Taxation/tax reform

Hasson, Kevin J.
President
The Becket Fund for Religious Liberty
1350 Connecticut Avenue, N.W., Suite 605
Washington, DC 20036
202-955-0095   fax 202-955-0090
bswink@becketfund.org
Issues: Church-state relations; Human rights;
Public interest law; Religion and public life;
Religious freedom

Hatchett, Dr. Ronald L.
Director, Center for International Studies
University of St. Thomas
3800 Montrose Boulevard
Houston, TX 77006
713-525-3534   fax 713-525-3872
rlhatchett@stthom.edu
Issues: Central and Eastern Europe; Middle
East; Russia and Eurasia; Western Europe

Hatheway, Gina Marie
Deputy Director, Government Relations for
Foreign and Defense Policy
The Heritage Foundation
214 Massachusetts Avenue, N.E.
Washington, DC 20002
202-608-6065   fax 202-675-1778
GinaMarie.Hathaway@heritage.org
Issues: American diplomacy/foreign policy;
Economic development/foreign aid;
Homeland security/civil defense; Intelligence
gathering and covert operations; Latin
America; Mexico; Missile defense; Trade

*Haulk, Dr. Jake
President
Allegheny Institute for Public Policy
305 Mt. Lebanon Boulevard, Suite 305
Pittsburgh, PA 15234
412-440-0079   fax 412-440-0085
jake@alleghenyinstitute.org
Issues: Comparative economics; Economic
forecasting; Economic theory; The Economy;
Entrepreneurship/free enterprise; Minimum
wage; Taxation/tax reform

Hauptmann, Dr. Jerzy
Interim Director, Hauptmann School of
Public Affairs
Park University
934 Wyandotte Street
Kansas City, MO 64105
816-421-1125   fax 816-471-1658
Issues: Central and Eastern Europe; Federal
civil service; Federalism; NATO and other
alliances; State and local government

*Havighurst, Dr. Clark C.
William Neal Reynolds Professor of Law
Duke University School of Law
Box 90360
Durham, NC 27708
919-613-7061   fax 919-613-7231
hav@law.duke.edu
Issues: Central and Eastern Europe; Church-
state relations; Immigration; Religion and
public life; Religious freedom; Russia and
Eurasia

Hawkins, Dr. Robert, Jr.
President and CEO
Institute for Contemporary Studies
1611 Telegraph Avenue, Suite 406
Oakland, CA 94612
510-238-5010   fax 510-238-8440
BobHawkins@sbcglobal.net
Issues: Charter schools; Federalism; Political
philosophy; Promoting democracy/public
diplomacy; The Reagan legacy; School choice;
State and local government; Urban sprawl/
livable cities

*Hay, Dr. Joel W.
Associate Professor, Department of
Pharmaceutical Economics
University of Southern California
1540 East Alcazar Street, Number 140
Los Angeles, CA 90089
323-442-3296   fax 323-337-7370
jhay@usc.edu
Issues: Aging/elder care; Government health
programs; Health care reform; Medicaid;
Medicare; Substance abuse

Hay, William Anthony, Ph.D.

Executive Director, Center for the Study of America and the West
Foreign Policy Research Institute
1528 Walnut Street, Suite 610
Philadelphia, PA 19102-3684
215-732-3774   fax 215-732-4401
wh@fpri.org

Issues: American diplomacy/foreign policy; American history/political tradition; Canada; Central and Eastern Europe; Conservative thought; Emerging threats/threat assessment; International organizations (European Union, OECD, etc.); NATO and other alliances; Political philosophy; Russia and Eurasia; Western Europe

*Hayward, Dr. Steven

F. K. Weyerhaeuser Fellow
American Enterprise Institute
1150 17th Street, N.W.
Washington, DC 20036
202-862-5882   fax 202-862-4875
shayward@aei.org

Issues: Air; The American Founding; American history/political tradition; Campaign finance reform; Conservative thought; Costs and benefits of regulation; Energy; Environmental regulation; Executive Branch/The Presidency; Free-market environmentalism; Land use; Political philosophy; The Reagan legacy; Regulation through litigation; Urban sprawl/livable cities

*Haywood, Robert C.

Associate Director, The Flagstaff Institute
Director, WEPZA
28577 Buffalo Park Road, Number 270
Evergreen, CO 80439
303-679-0980   fax 303-679-0985
bobhaywood@aol.com

Issues: Economic development/foreign aid; International organizations (European Union, OECD, etc.); International tax policy/tax competition; Trade

Hazlett, Dr. Thomas

Senior Fellow, Center for the Digital Economy
Manhattan Institute for Policy Research
1615 M Street, N.W., Suite 400
Washington, DC 20036
202-463-6630   fax 202-463-8003
twhazlett@yahoo.com

Issues: Anti-trust; Costs and benefits of regulation; Property rights; Telecommunications and the Internet

Healy, Gene

Senior Editor
Cato Institute
1000 Massachusetts Avenue, N.W.
Washington, DC 20001-5403
202- 842-0200   fax 202-842-3490

Issues: Constitutional law; Crime/crime statistics; Executive Branch/The Presidency; Federalism; Second Amendment

*Hearne, Donna H.

Executive Director
Constitutional Coalition
15820 Clayton Road
St. Louis, MO 63011
314-434-7028   fax 314-878-6294
constitu@mvp.net

Issues: The American Founding; American history/political tradition; Business and education partnerships; Citizenship and civil society; Environmental education; Ethics; Family and children; Federal education policy; Forestry and national parks; Land use; Political philosophy; Property rights; Religion and public life; School-to-work; Standards, curriculum, and testing; Stewardship; Urban sprawl/livable cities; Water; Wildlife management/endangered species

Heath, Dr. Eugene

Associate Professor of Philosophy
State University of New York, New Platz
75 South Manheim Boulevard
New Paltz, NY 12561-2440
845-257-2981   fax 845-257-2735
heathe@newplatz.edu

Issues: Ethics; Political philosophy

Heath, Micheal S.

Executive Director
Christian Civic League of Maine
P. O. Box 5459
Augusta, ME 04332
207-622-7634   fax 207-621-0035
email@cclmaine.org

Issues: Family and children; Religion and public life; School choice; State and local government; Taxation/tax reform

---

Hederman, Rea, Jr.

Manager of Operations, Center for Data Analysis
The Heritage Foundation
214 Massachusetts Avenue, N.E.
Washington, DC 20002
202-608-6296   fax 202-675-1772
rea.hederman@heritage.org
Issues: The American Founding; American history/political tradition; The Economy; Federal budget; Poverty and dependency; Public school finance and administration; State and local public finance; Taxation/tax reform; Welfare/welfare reform

Heet, Justin

Research Fellow
Hudson Institute
Herman Kahn Center, 5395 Emerson Way
Indianapolis, IN 46226
317-549-4108   fax 317-545-9639
justin@hudson.org
Issues: Business and education partnerships; Charter schools; Federal education policy; Labor and employment; School choice

Hein, Jay F.

Director, Welfare Policy Center
Hudson Institute
Herman Kahn Center, 5395 Emerson Way
Indianapolis, IN 46226
317-549-4138   fax 317-545-9639
jay@hudson.org
Issues: Abstinence and out-of-wedlock births; Advocacy and nonprofit public funding; Church-state relations; Citizenship and civil society; Conservative thought; Faith-based and volunteer initiatives; Family and children; Federalism; Government health programs; Health care reform; Job training/welfare to work; Philanthropy; Poverty and dependency; Privatization/Contracting-out; Religion and public life; Wealth creation/financial empowerment; Welfare/welfare reform

Heineke, Dr. John M.

Professor of Economics, Department of Economics
Santa Clara University
500 El Camino Real
Santa Clara, CA 95053
408-554-4346   fax 408-554-2331
jheineke@scu.edu
Issues: Crime/crime statistics; Criminal law and procedure; Economic forecasting; Economic theory

Heineman, Dr. Robert A.

Professor of Political Science, Department of Political Science
Alfred University
P. O. Box 1156
Alfred, NY 14802
607-871-2866   fax 607-871-2114
heineman1@alfred.edu
Issues: American history/political tradition; Congress; Conservative thought; Constitutional law; Federalism; Immigration; Judicial activism/judicial reform; Political philosophy; State and local government

*Heller, Frank J., MPA

Senior Associate
Maine Policy Ronin Network
12 Belmont Street
Brunswick, ME 04011-3004
207-729-6090   fax 207-729-1590
global1@gwi.net
Issues: Federal education policy; Health care reform; School choice

*Helms, Dr. Robert B.

Resident Scholar, Health Policy Studies
American Enterprise Institute
1150 17th Street, N.W.
Washington, DC 20036
202-862-5877   fax 202-862-7177
rhelms@aei.org
Issues: Government health programs; Health care reform; Medicare

Helstrom, Carl

Chairman, State Policy Network, and Associate Executive Director
JM Foundation
60 East 42nd Street, Suite 1651
New York, NY 10165
212-687-7735   fax 212-697-5495
Issues: Philanthropy

*Henderson, Dr. David R.

Research Fellow
Hoover Institution
944 Forest Avenue
Pacific Grove, CA 93950
831-648-1776   fax 831-647-1776
drhend@mbay.net
Issues: Anti-trust; Costs and benefits of regulation; Entrepreneurship/free enterprise; Health care reform; Minimum wage; Taxation/tax reform; Telecommunications and the Internet

*Henderson, James M., Sr.
Senior Counsel
American Center for Law and Justice
205 3rd Street, S.E.
Washington, DC 20003
202-546-8890   fax 202-544-5172
jmhenderson@aclj-dc.org
Issues: The American Founding; Campaign finance reform; Church-state relations; Civil rights/racial preferences; Constitutional law; Free Speech; Judicial activism/judicial reform; Judiciary; Religious freedom

*Henriksen, Dr. Thomas H.
Associate Director and Senior Fellow
Hoover Institution
Stanford University
Stanford, CA 94305-6010
650-723-4255   fax 650-725-5677
henriksen@hoover.stanford.edu
Issues: Afghanistan; Africa; American diplomacy/foreign policy; Korea; Western Europe

Henry, Lowman
Chairman and CEO
Lincoln Institute of Public Opinion Research, Inc.
453 Springlake Road
Harrisburg, PA 17112
717-671-0776   fax 717-671-1176
lhenry@lincolninstitute.org
Issues: Church-state relations; Faith-based and volunteer initiatives; Government waste; Judicial activism/judicial reform; Privatization/Contracting-out; Public school finance and administration; School choice; State and local public finance; Taxation/tax reform

Hensler, Louis W., III
Assistant Professor, School of Law
Regent University
1000 Regent University Drive
Virginia Beach, VA 23464
757-226-4623   fax 757-226-4329
louihen@regent.edu
Issues: Tort and liability reform

Henze, Paul
Rock Mills Farm, Post Office Box 95
Washington, VA 22747
540-937-4311   fax 540-937-3814
pbhenze@erols.com
Issues: Afghanistan; Africa; American diplomacy/foreign policy; Central and Eastern Europe; China; Economic development/foreign aid; Federalism; Human rights; Intelligence gathering and covert operations; Middle East; Military strategy; Peacekeeping; Promoting democracy/public diplomacy; Russia and Eurasia; Terrorism and international crime

Herbster, Dr. Carl
President
American Association of Christian Schools
P. O. Box 1097
Independence, MO 64051-0597
816-252-9900   fax 816-252-6700
national@aacs.org
Issues: Faith-based and volunteer initiatives; Family and children; Marriage and divorce; School choice; School-to-work

Herdlein, Wendy
Staff Attorney
The Marriage Law Project
3600 John MacCormack Road, N.E.
Washington, DC 20064
202-319-6155   fax 202-319-4459
wherdlein@marriagewatch.org
Issues: Constitutional law; Family and children; Marriage and divorce; Public interest law

Herren, Dr. Robert Stanley
Professor, Department of Economics
North Dakota State University
Box 5636
Fargo, ND 58105-5636
701-231-7698   fax 701-231-7400
robert.herren@ndsu.nodak.edu
Issues: Economic theory; Federal budget; Money and financial services; The Reagan legacy; Taxation/tax reform

Herring, Dr. Mark Y.
Dean of Library Services
Winthrop University
Dacus Library, 428 Guilford Road
Rock Hill, SC 29732
803-323-2131   fax 803-323-2215
herringm@exchange.winthrop.edu
Issues: Conservative thought; Higher education; Intellectual property; Privacy

Herschensohn, Bruce

Pepperdine University School of Public
Policy
24255 Pacific Coast Highway
Malibu, CA 90263
310-506-7490   fax 323-851-3499
Issues: Afghanistan; Africa; American
diplomacy/foreign policy; Canada; Central
and Eastern Europe; China; Human rights;
International organizations (European Union,
OECD, etc.); Japan; Korea; Latin America;
Mexico; Middle East; Northeast Asia;
Promoting democracy/public diplomacy;
Russia and Eurasia; South Asia (including India
and Pakistan); Southeast Asia (including
Burma, Cambodia, Laos, Vietnam, Singapore,
Malaysia, Indonesia, the Philippines, Australia,
and New Zealand); United Nations; Western
Europe

*Hershey, Dr. Robert L.

Consulting Engineer
Robert L. Hershey, P.E.
1255 New Hamphsire Avenue, Suite 1033
Washington, DC 20036
202-659-9529   fax 202-429-1835
hershey@cpcug.org
Issues: Air; Central and Eastern Europe;
Climate change; Costs and benefits of
regulation; Electricity deregulation; Energy;
Entrepreneurship/free enterprise;
Environmental education; Environmental
regulation; Federal budget; Free-market
environmentalism; Homeland security/civil
defense; Privacy; Privatization/Contracting-
out; Regulatory reform; Research funding; Risk
assessment; Sound science;
Telecommunications and the Internet; Waste
management

*Herzberg, Dr. Roberta

Director, Institute of Political Economy
Utah State University
0725 Old Main Hill
Logan, UT 84322
435-797-1307   fax 435-797-3751
bobbih@hass.usu.edu
Issues: Entitlement spending; Federalism;
Government health programs; Health care
reform; Privatization/Contracting-out

Herzlinger, Dr. Regina E.

Nancy R. McPherson Professor of Business
Administration
Harvard Business School
Soldiers Field Road, Baker 163
Boston, MA 02163
617-495-6646   fax 617-495-0358
Issues: Health care reform; Medicaid; Medicare;
Poverty and dependency; Social Security and
retirement; Welfare/welfare reform

Hess, Dr. Frederick M.

Resident Scholar
American Enterprise Institute
1150 17th Street, N.W.
Washington, DC 20036
202-828-6030   fax 202-862-7178
rhess@aei.org
Issues: Federal education policy

*Hess, Dr. Karl

President
The Land Center
712 Stagecoach Drive
Las Cruces, NM 88011
505-522-1172   fax 505-522-2782
khess4@aol.com
Issues: Environmental education;
Environmental regulation; Forestry and
national parks; Free-market environmentalism;
Land use; Property rights; Research funding;
Sound science; Stewardship; Urban sprawl/
livable cities; Water; Wildlife management/
endangered species

*Hicks, Randy

President
Georgia Family Council
5380 Peachtree Industrial Boulevard
Suite 100
Norcross, GA 30071
770-242-0001   fax 770-242-0501
randy@gafam.org
Issues: Abstinence and out-of-wedlock births;
Adoption, foster care, & child care services;
Citizenship and civil society; Home schooling;
Marriage and divorce; Media and popular
culture; Religion and public life; School choice;
Welfare/welfare reform

Higgins, Heather
Senior Fellow
Independent Women's Forum
255 East 49th Street, Suite 23C
New York, NY 10017
212-752-7148   fax 212-752-7316
hrh@hrhoffice.org
Issues: Citizenship and civil society; Civil rights/
racial preferences; Media and popular culture;
Philanthropy; Political correctness and
multiculturalism

Higgs, Dr. Robert
Senior Fellow in Political Economy
The Independent Institute
413 West 14th Avenue
Covington, LA 70433
985-867-5385   fax 985-809-7082
rhiggs@independent.org
Issues: American history/political tradition;
Costs and benefits of regulation; Defense
budget; Federal budget

High, Prof. Jack
Professor of Economics, School of Public
Policy
George Mason University
3401 North Fairfax Drive, MS 3B1
Arlington, VA 22201
703-993-1864   fax 703-993-3788
jhigh@gmu.edu
Issues: American history/political tradition;
Anti-trust; Economic development/foreign
aid; Economic theory; Government debt

*Hill, Dr. John R.
Director of Research
Alabama Policy Institute
402 Office Park Drive, Suite 300
Birmingham, AL 35223
205-870-9900   fax 205-870-4407
johnh@alabamapolicy.org
Issues: Air; Charter schools; Climate change;
Crime/crime statistics; Marriage and divorce;
Media and popular culture; Privatization/
Contracting-out; State-sponsored gambling

Hill, Jonathan
Director
North Carolina Citizens for a Sound
Economy
115 1/2 West Morgan Street
Raleigh, NC 27601
919-807-0100   fax 919-807-0400
Issues: Entrepreneurship/free enterprise;
Government waste; State and local
government; State and local public finance;
Taxation/tax reform

*Hill, Dr. Paul T.
Director, Center on Reinventing Public
Education
University of Washington
Box 353060
Seattle, WA 98195-3060
206-685-2214   fax 206-616-5769
crpe@u.washington.edu
Issues: Charter schools; Federal education
policy; Public school finance and
administration; School choice; Standards,
curriculum, and testing

Hill, Dr. Peter J.
Senior Associate, PERC – The Center for
Free Market Environmentalism, and,
Professor of Economics
Wheaton College
501 College Avenue
Wheaton, IL 60187-5593
630-752-5033   fax 630-752-7037
p.j.hill@wheaton.edu
Issues: The American Founding; American
history/political tradition; Comparative
government; Ethics; Property rights

*Hillen, Dr. John
Senior Fellow
Foreign Policy Research Institute
1528 Walnut Street, Suite 610
Philadephia, PA 19102
212-231-5000   jhillen@island.com
Issues: Afghanistan; American diplomacy/
foreign policy; Conservative thought; Defense
budget; Emerging threats/threat assessment;
Homeland security/civil defense; Intelligence
gathering and covert operations; Military
strategy; NATO and other alliances;
Peacekeeping; Political philosophy; Readiness
and manpower; The Reagan legacy; Terrorism
and international crime; United Nations

Hills, Chad
Research Associate
Focus on the Family
8605 Explorer Drive
Colorado Springs, CO 80920
719-548-4531   fax 719-531-3385
pardotr@fotf.org
Issues: Arts, humanities and historic resources; Education unions and interest groups; State-sponsored gambling

*Himelson, Dr. Alfred N.
Professor of Sociology Emeritus
22811 Mulholland Drive
Woodland Hills, CA 91364
818-591-1259   ahimelson@csun.edu
Issues: Corrections and sentencing; Substance abuse

Hinish, James E., Jr.
Adjunct Professor of Government
Regent University
114 The Green, Kingsmill on the James
Williamsburg, VA 23185-8252
757-226-4535   fax 757-226-4735
jehinish@widomaker.com
Issues: Citizenship and civil society; Congress; Immigration; Regulatory reform; Religion and public life; Standards, curriculum, and testing; State and local government

*Hinton, Thomas
Director, State Relations
The Heritage Foundation
214 Massachusetts Avenue, N.E.
Washington, DC 20002
202-608-6045   fax 202-675-1753
tom.hinton@heritage.org
Issues: The American Founding; Business and education partnerships; Church-state relations; Conservative thought; Family and children; Federalism; Home schooling; Religion and public life; Religious freedom; School choice; State and local government

Hipple, Natalie K.
Research Fellow and Assistant Director,
Crime Control Policy Center
Hudson Institute
Herman Kahn Center, 5395 Emerson Way
Indianapolis, IN 46226
317-545-1000   fax 317-545-9639
info@hudson.org
Issues: Crime/crime statistics; Juvenile justice

Hirsch, Dr. E. D., Jr.
Chairman of the Board
Core Knowledge Foundation
801 East High Street
Charlottesville, VA 22902
434-977-7550   fax 434-977-0021
Issues: Standards, curriculum, and testing

Hirschmann, David
Executive Vice President
National Chamber Foundation
1615 H Street, N.W.
Washington, DC 20062
202-463-5500   fax 202-463-3129
Issues: Latin America

Hisrich, Dr. Robert D.
A. Malachi Mixon III Professor of Entrepreneurial Studies, Weatherhead School of Management
Case Western Reserve University
10900 Euclid Avenue
Cleveland, OH 44106
216-368-5354   fax 216-368-4785
rdh7@po.cwru.edu
Issues: Business and education partnerships; Economic education; The Economy; Entrepreneurship/free enterprise; Higher education; Infrastructure; Standards, curriculum, and testing; Trade

Hitchcock, Dr. James
Professor, Department of History
St. Louis University
221 North Grand Boulevard
St. Louis, MO 63103
314-863-1654   fax 314-863-5858
hitchcpj@slu.edu
Issues: Church-state relations; Religion and public life; Religious freedom; Standards, curriculum, and testing

*Hodel, Hon. Don
P. O. Box 23099
Silverthorne, CO 80498
970-468-0730   fax 970-468-0737
dphodel@vail.net
Issues: Electricity deregulation; Energy; Forestry and national parks; Property rights; Stewardship

*Hodge, Scott
Executive Director
Tax Foundation
1900 M Street, N.W., Suite 550
Washington, DC 20036
202-464-6200   fax 202-464-6201
shodge@taxfoundation.org
Issues: Advocacy and nonprofit public funding;
Discretionary spending; Entitlement spending;
Federal budget; Government debt;
Government waste; International tax policy/
tax competition; Privatization/Contracting-
out; State and local public finance; Taxation/
tax reform; Unfunded mandates

Hogberg, David
Research Analyst
Public Interest Institute
600 North Jackson Street
Mount Pleasant, IA 52641
319-385-3462   fax 319-385-3799
hogberg@limitedgovernment.org
Issues: Higher education; School choice;
Taxation/tax reform; Welfare/welfare reform

Hogenson, Scott
Executive Editor
CNSNews.com
325 South Patrick Street
Alexandria, VA 22314-3580
703-683-9733   fax 703-683-7045
shogenson@cnsnews.com
Issues: Conservative thought; Elections/
polling; Media and popular culture; Political
correctness and multiculturalism; Political
philosophy

Hoke, Candice
Associate Professor of Law, Cleveland-
Marshall College of Law
Cleveland State University
1801 Euclid Avenue
Cleveland, OH 44115
216-687-2344   fax 216-687-6881
Issues: Federalism; Political philosophy;
Unfunded mandates

*Holcombe, Dr. Randall G.
Professor of Economics, Department of
Economics
Florida State University
P. O. Box 2180
Tallahassee, FL 32306
850-644-7095   fax 850-644-4535
holcombe@coss.fsu.edu
Issues: Land use; State and local public finance;
Taxation/tax reform; Urban sprawl/livable
cities

*Holden, Fred
Phoenix Enterprises
P. O. Box 1900
Arvada, CO 80001
303-421-7619   fax 303-423-3180
fredholden@aol.com
Issues: Business and education partnerships;
Citizenship and civil society; Constitutional law;
Economic education; Entrepreneurship/free
enterprise; Federal budget; Government debt;
Health care reform; Initiative and referendum;
Public school finance and administration; State
and local government; State and local public
finance; State-sponsored gambling; Taxation/
tax reform; Wealth creation/financial
empowerment

*Holland, Dr. Kenneth M.
Professor, Department of Political Science
University of Memphis
437 Clement Hall
Memphis, TN 38152
901-678-3320   fax 901-678-5596
kholland@memphis.edu
Issues: Civil rights/racial preferences;
Constitutional law; Federalism; Judicial
activism/judicial reform; Judiciary

*Holland, Robert
Senior Fellow
Lexington Institute
1600 Wilson Boulevard, Suite 900
Arlington, VA 22209
703-522-5828   fax 703-522-5837
holland@lexingtoninstitute.org
Issues: Charter schools; Education unions and
interest groups; Home schooling; School
choice; Standards, curriculum, and testing

*Hollerman, Dr. Leon
Professor, Peter F. Drucker Graduate School
of Management
Claremont Graduate University
4239 Via Padova
Claremont, CA 91711
909-624-3876   fax 909-624-0771
Issues: Economic development/foreign aid;
The Economy; Japan; Money and financial
services; Trade

Hollins, Susan D., Ph.D.
Director, New Hampshire Charter School
Resource Center
The Josiah Bartlett Center for Public Policy
7 South State Street, P. O. Box 897
Concord, NH 03302-0897
603-224-4450   fax 603-224-4329
suefromnh@aol.com
Issues: Charter schools

*Holmes, Dr. John C.
Director of Government Affairs
Association of Christian Schools
International
723 2nd Street N.E., Suite 100
Washington, DC 20002-4307
202-546-9390   fax 202-546-9370
acsidc@aol.com
Issues: Church-state relations; Federal
education policy; Higher education; Religious
freedom; School choice; Standards,
curriculum, and testing

*Hood, John MacDonald
President
John Locke Foundation
200 West Morgan Street, Suite 200
Raleigh, NC 27601
919-828-3876   fax 919-821-5117
jhood@johnlocke.org
Issues: Aging/elder care; The American
Founding; American history/political
tradition; Business and education partnerships;
Charter schools; Elections/polling;
Entitlement spending; Entrepreneurship/free
enterprise; Federal education policy;
Federalism; Government health programs;
Health care reform; Higher education;
Infrastructure; Initiative and referendum;
Medicaid; Medicare; Poverty and dependency;
Public school finance and administration;
School choice; Social Security and retirement;
Standards, curriculum, and testing; State and
local government; State and local public
finance; Taxation/tax reform; Term limits;
Transportation; Unemployment insurance;
Urban sprawl/livable cities; Wealth creation/
financial empowerment; Welfare/welfare
reform

Hoover, Dr. Dale M.
Professor Emeritus, Agriculture and
Resource Economics
North Carolina State University
4311 Nelson Hall, Box 8109
Raleigh, NC 27695
919-515-6090   fax 919-515-1824
dale_hoover@ncsu.edu
Issues: Agriculture; The Economy

*Hopkins, Dr. Thomas D.
Dean, College of Business
Rochester Institute of Technology
107 Lomb Memorial Drive
Rochester, NY 14623-5608
585-475-7042   fax 585-475-7055
tdhbbu@rit.edu
Issues: Business and education partnerships;
Costs and benefits of regulation; Higher
education; Regulatory budgeting; Regulatory
reform

Horn, Claudia B.
President
The Alliance Group, LLC
P. O. Box 4218
North Potomac, MD 20885
301-963-5953   fax 209-882-9979
claudia@thealliancegroup.com

*Horn, Dr. Joseph
Professor of Psychology
University of Texas
3311 Big Bend Drive
Austin, TX 78731-5310
512-452-7566   fax 512-471-6175
horn@mail.utexas.edu
Issues: Adoption, foster care, & child care
services; Higher education; Political
correctness and multiculturalism; Standards,
curriculum, and testing

Hornberger, Jacob G.
President
Future of Freedom Foundation
11350 Random Hills Road, Suite 800
Fairfax, VA 22030
703-934-6101   fax 703-352-8678
jhornberger@fff.org
Issues: The American Founding; American
history/political tradition; Civil rights/racial
preferences; Constitutional law; Economic
education; Free Speech; Immigration;
Religious freedom; Second Amendment

Horner, Charles
Senior Fellow
Hudson Institute
1015 18th Street, N.W., Suite 300
Washington, DC 20036
202-223-7770   fax 202-223-8537
charles@hudsondc.org
Issues: China; Human rights; Japan; Korea;
Promoting democracy/public diplomacy;
Russia and Eurasia

*Horner, Chris
Counsel to the Cooler Heads Coalition, and
Senior Fellow,
Competitive Enterprise Institute
1001 Connecticut Avenue, N.W., Suite 1250
Washington, DC 20036
202-331-1010   fax 202-331-0640
chorner@cei.org
Issues: Climate change; Energy; Environmental
regulation; Free-market environmentalism;
Property rights

Horner, Constance
Guest Scholar
Brookings Institution
1775 Massachusetts Avenue, N.W.
Washington, DC 20036
202-797-6000   fax 202-797-6144
chorner@brook.edu
Issues: Federal civil service

Horowitz, David
President
Center for the Study of Popular Culture
9911 West Pico Boulevard, Suite 1290
Los Angeles, CA 90035
323-556-2550   dhorowitz@cspc.org
Issues: American history/political tradition;
Civil rights/racial preferences; Conservative
thought; Higher education; Media and popular
culture; Philanthropy; Political correctness and
multiculturalism; Political philosophy; School
choice

*Horowitz, Michael
Senior Fellow and Director of Project on
Civil Justice Reform
Hudson Institute
1015 18th Street, N.W., Suite 300
Washington, DC 20036
202-223-9200   fax 202-223-8537
devram@aol.com
Issues: Advocacy and nonprofit public funding;
Church-state relations; Citizenship and civil
society; Civil rights/racial preferences; Faith-
based and volunteer initiatives; Federalism;
Government waste; Human rights; Judicial
activism/judicial reform; Korea; Philanthropy;
Promoting democracy/public diplomacy; The
Reagan legacy; Regulation through litigation;
Religion and public life; School choice; Tort
and liability reform; Unfunded mandates

*Horton, Dr. Joseph
Chairman, Department of Economics,
Finance, and Insurance
University of Central Arkansas
201 Donaghey Avenue
Conway, AR 72035-0001
501-450-5310   fax 501-450-5302
jhorton@mail.uca.edu
Issues: Comparative economics; Costs and
benefits of regulation; Economic
development/foreign aid; Economic
education; Economic theory; The Economy;
Entrepreneurship/free enterprise;
International finance and multilateral banks;
Minimum wage; Money and financial services

Horwitz, Dr. Steven
Associate Dean of the First Year and
Professor of Economics
St. Lawrence University
23 Romoda Drive, Whitman Hall
Canton, NY 13617
315-229-5731   fax 315-229-5709
sghorwitz@stlawu.edu
Issues: Comparative economics; Economic
theory; Money and financial services

*Hough, Richard R., III
National Program Director
Children's Scholarship Fund
8 West 38th Street, 9th Floor
New York, NY 10018-6229
212-515-7105   fax 801-720-3574
rhough@scholarshipfund.org
Issues: School choice

Houston, Dr. Douglas A.
Professor, School of Business
University of Kansas
Summerfield Hall
Lawrence, KS 66045
785-864-7564   fax 785-864-5328
dhouston@ku.edu
Issues: Costs and benefits of regulation;
Electricity deregulation; Energy; Regulatory
reform

*Houston, Kerri
National Field Director
American Conservative Union Field Office
3541 Regent Drive
Dallas, TX 75229-5138
214-357-1504   fax 509-277-5861
khouston@conservative.org
Issues: Adoption, foster care, & child care
services; Government health programs; Health
care reform; Social Security and retirement;
Taxation/tax reform

*Howard, John A.
Senior Fellow
Howard Center for Family, Religion and
Society
934 North Main Street
Rockford, IL 61103
815-964-5819   fax 815-965-1826
Issues: Citizenship and civil society; Federal
education policy; Substance abuse

Howard, Dr. William
Professor of English
Chicago State University
1596 Surrey Drive
Wheaton, IL 60187
773-995-2166   w-howard@csu.edu
Issues: Civil rights/racial preferences; Higher
education; Political correctness and
multiculturalism; Standards, curriculum, and
testing

*Howden, Michael
Executive Director
Stronger Families for Oregon
P. O. Box 948
Salem, OR 97308
503-585-9383   fax 503-399-1698
michael@oregonfamily.org
Issues: Abstinence and out-of-wedlock births;
Church-state relations; Citizenship and civil
society; Faith-based and volunteer initiatives;
Family and children; Juvenile justice; Marriage
and divorce; State-sponsored gambling

*Hoxby, Dr. Caroline M.
Professor of Economics, Department of
Economics
Harvard University
Cambridge, MA 02138
617-496-3588   fax 617-495-8570
choxby@harvard.edu
Issues: Bilingual education; Business and
education partnerships; Charter schools;
Economic education; Education unions and
interest groups; Federal education policy;
Federalism; Higher education; Public school
finance and administration; School choice;
School-to-work; Standards, curriculum, and
testing; State and local government; State and
local public finance

*Hoy, Robert L.
Executive Director
Educational CHOICE Charitable Trust
7440 North Woodland Drive
Indianapolis, IN 46278
317-293-7600   fax 317-293-0603
rhoy@choicetrust.org
Issues: School choice

Hoyt, Martin
Director, Government Affairs
American Association of Christian Schools
119 C Street, S.E.
Washington, DC 20003
202-547-2991   fax 202-547-2992
Issues: Church-state relations; Federal
education policy; Home schooling; Religious
freedom; School choice

*Hruby, Olga S.
Executive Director
Research Center for Religious and Human
Rights
475 Riverside Drive, Suite 448
New York, NY 10115
212-870-2481   fax 212-663-6771
rcda1962@msn.com
Issues: Human rights; Promoting democracy/
public diplomacy; Russia and Eurasia

Huber, Peter
Senior Fellow, Center for Legal Policy
Manhattan Institute for Policy Research
52 Vanderbilt Avenue
New York, NY 10017
301-654-0502   fax 301-654-0504
phuber@manhattan-institute.org
Issues: Environmental regulation; Free-market
environmentalism; Sound science;
Telecommunications and the Internet; Tort
and liability reform

*Huberty, Robert
Executive Vice President
Capital Research Center
1513 16th Street, N.W.
Washington, DC 20036
202-483-6900   fax 202-483-6990
rhuberty@capitalresearch.org
Issues: Advocacy and nonprofit public funding;
American history/political tradition;
Conservative thought; Non-governmental
organizations; Philanthropy

Hudgins, Dr. Edward L.
Washington Director
The Objectivist Center
1001 Connecticut Avenue, N.W., Suite 1028
Washington, DC 20036
202-296-7263   fax 202-296-0771
ehudgins@objectivistcenter.org
Issues: Citizenship and civil society; Economic
development/foreign aid; Economic theory;
Entrepreneurship/free enterprise; Ethics;
Political philosophy; Privatization/
Contracting-out; Promoting democracy/
public diplomacy; Regulatory reform; Trade;
Transportation; Western Europe

Hudson, Dr. Deal
Editor and Publisher
Crisis Magazine
1814 1/2 N Street, N.W.
Washington, DC 20005
202-861-7790   fax 202-861-7788
hudson@crisismagazine.com
Issues: Adoption, foster care, & child care
services; Arts, humanities and historic
resources; Ethics; Faith-based and volunteer
initiatives; Media and popular culture; Religion
and public life; Standards, curriculum, and
testing

*Huffman, James
Dean
Lewis and Clark Law School
10015 S.W. Terwilliger
Portland, OR 97219
503-768-6601   fax 503-768-6671
huffman@lclark.edu
Issues: Congress; Environmental regulation;
Federalism; Forestry and national parks; Free-
market environmentalism; Judiciary; Land use;
Property rights; Urban sprawl/livable cities;
Water; Wildlife management/endangered
species

*Huggins, Gary
Executive Director
Education Leaders Action Council
1225 19th Street, N.W., Suite 400
Washington, DC 20036
202-261-2600   fax 202-261-2638
gmh@educationleaders.org
Issues: Business and education partnerships;
Charter schools; Federal education policy;
Public school finance and administration;
School choice; Standards, curriculum, and
testing

Hughes, Donna Rice
President
Enough Is Enough
746 Walker Road, P. O. Box 116
Great Falls, VA 22066
eieca@enough.org
Issues: Family and children; Media and popular culture; Telecommunications and the Internet

Hughes, G. Philip
Senior Director
White House Writer's Group
1030 15th Street, N.W., 11th Floor
Washington, DC 20005
202-783-4600   fax 202-783-4601
phughes@whwg.com
Issues: American diplomacy/foreign policy; Export controls/military transfers; Latin America; Mexico; Promoting democracy/public diplomacy; Trade

*Hughes, Robert
President
The National Association for the Self-Employed
1225 Eye Street, N.W., Suite 500
Washington, DC 20005
202-466-2100   fax 202-466-2123
robert.hughes@nase.org
Issues: Entrepreneurship/free enterprise; Health care reform; Labor and employment; Taxation/tax reform

*Hughes, Victoria
President
Bill of Rights Institute
1001 Connecticut Avenue, N.W., Suite 219
Washington, DC 20036
202-822-4622   fax 202-822-4630
vhughes@billofrightsinstitute.org
Issues: Federal education policy; Standards, curriculum, and testing

Hulsman, John C.
Research Fellow, European Affairs, Kathryn and Shelby Cullom Davis Institute for International Studies
The Heritage Foundation
214 Massachusetts Avenue, N.E.
Washington, DC 20002
202-608-6086   fax 202-675-1779
john.hulsman@heritage.org
Issues: Afghanistan; American diplomacy/foreign policy; The American Founding; American history/political tradition; Arms control; Central and Eastern Europe; Comparative economics; Comparative government; Conservative thought; Economic development/foreign aid; Emerging threats/threat assessment; Human rights; Intelligence gathering and covert operations; International finance and multilateral banks; International organizations (European Union, OECD, etc.); Middle East; Military strategy; NATO and other alliances; Peacekeeping; Political philosophy; Russia and Eurasia; Terrorism and international crime; Trade; Western Europe

Hunter, Dr. James D.
Professor, Sociology Department
University of Virginia
548 Cabell Hall
Charlottesville, VA 22901
434-924-6524   fax 434-924-7028
jdh6c@Virginia.edu
Issues: Citizenship and civil society; Ethics; Media and popular culture; Religion and public life

*Hunter, Lawrence
Chief Economist
Empower America
1801 K Street, N.W., Suite 410
Washington, DC 20006
202-452-8200   fax 202-833-0388
hunterl@empower.org
Issues: Advocacy and nonprofit public funding; Comparative economics; Discretionary spending; Economic education; Economic forecasting; Economic theory; Entitlement spending; Federal budget; Government debt; Government waste; International tax policy/tax competition; Privatization/Contracting-out; State and local public finance; Taxation/tax reform; Unfunded mandates

*Hunter, Robert
Director of Labor Policy
Mackinac Center for Public Policy
140 West Main Street, P. O. Box 568
Midland, MI 48640
989-631-0900   fax 989-631-0964
hunter@mackinac.org
Issues: Civil rights/racial preferences; Davis-
Bacon Act; Education unions and interest
groups; Executive Branch/The Presidency; Job
training/welfare to work; Labor and
employment; Minimum wage; Public interest
law; The Reagan legacy; Religious freedom;
Right to work; School choice; Unemployment
insurance; Unions

Huntington, Dr. Samuel P.
Chairman, Harvard Academy for
International and Area Studies
Harvard University
1033 Massachusetts Avenue, Room 340
Cambridge, MA 02138
617-495-4432   fax 617-495-1384
Issues: Comparative government

*Hurley, Charles D.
President
Iowa Family Policy Center
1100 North Hickory, Suite 105
Pleasant Hill, IA 50327
515-263-3495   fax 515-263-3498
info@iowaprofamily.org
Issues: Abstinence and out-of-wedlock births;
Adoption, foster care, & child care services;
Advocacy and nonprofit public funding;
Church-state relations; Citizenship and civil
society; Constitutional law; Corrections and
sentencing; Faith-based and volunteer
initiatives; Family and children; Home
schooling; Marriage and divorce; Privatization/
Contracting-out; Religion and public life;
Religious freedom; School choice; Welfare/
welfare reform

Husock, Howard
Director, Social Entrepreneurship Iniative
Manhattan Institute for Policy Research
52 Vanderbilt Avenue
New York, NY 10017
212-599-7000
Issues: Housing and homelessness; State and
local government; Urban sprawl/livable cities

*Hutchison, Dr. Harry G.
Professor of Law, School of Law
Wayne State University
471 Palmer
Detroit, MI 48202
313-577-0508
harry.hutchison@wayne.edu
Issues: Charter schools; Labor and
employment; School choice; Trade

Hutchison, Richard P.
Vice President and General Counsel
Landmark Legal Foundation
3100 Broadway, Suite 1110
Kansas City, MO 64111
816-931-5559   fax 816-931-1115
llegal@swbell.net
Issues: Church-state relations; Education
unions and interest groups; Religious freedom;
School choice

Hwang, Balbina
Policy Analyst, Northeast Asia, Asian Studies
Center
The Heritage Foundation
214 Massachusetts Avenue, N.E.
Washington, DC 20002
202-608-6134   fax 202-675-1779
balbina.hwang@heritage.org
Issues: American diplomacy/foreign policy;
Japan; Korea

Hyde, Dr. Thomas
Professor, Department of Political Science
Pfeiffer University
P. O. Box 960
Misenheimer, NC 28109
704-463-1360   fax 704-463-1363
Issues: Congress; Executive Branch/The
Presidency; Political philosophy; Term limits

Iannone, Dr. Carol
310 Riverside Drive, Apartment 1518-19
New York, NY 10025
212-866-7725   fax 212-866-7725
carol.iannone@att.net
Issues: Arts, humanities and historic resources;
Higher education; Immigration; Media and
popular culture; Political correctness and
multiculturalism; Religion and public life

*Ichinaga, Nancy
Member
California State Board of Education
4260 Campbell Drive
Los Angeles, CA 90066
310-391-1583   fax 310-391-1583
fichinaga@aol.com
Issues: Federal education policy; Standards,
curriculum, and testing

Ikeda, Dr. Sanford
Associate Professor of Economics, Purchase
College
State University of New York
735 Anderson Hill Road
Purchase, NY 10577
914-251-6614   fax 914-251-6603
sanford.ikeda@purchase.edu
Issues: Comparative economics; Costs and
benefits of regulation; Economic theory;
Entrepreneurship/free enterprise; Urban
sprawl/livable cities

Ikenson, Daniel J.
Trade Policy Analyst, Center for Trade Policy
Studies
Cato Institute
1000 Massachusetts Avenue, N.W.
Washington, DC 20001
202-842-0200   fax 202-842-3490
dikenson@cato.org
Issues: Trade

*Ikle, Dr. Fred C.
Distinguished Scholar
Center for Strategic and International
Studies
1800 K Street, N.W., Suite 400
Washington, DC 20006
202-775-3155   fax 301-951-0286
iklef@erols.com
Issues: American diplomacy/foreign policy;
Emerging threats/threat assessment;
Homeland security/civil defense; Immigration;
Political philosophy; Promoting democracy/
public diplomacy; United Nations

Imber, Dr. Jonathan
Professor of Sociology, Department of
Sociology
Wellesley College
Wellesley, MA 02481-8203
781-283-2139   fax 781-283-3662
jimber@wellesley.edu
Issues: Conservative thought; Political
correctness and multiculturalism; Religion and
public life; Sound science; State-sponsored
gambling

*Inman, Alan
Welfare To Work National Program Director
Institute for Responsible Fatherhood and
Family Revitalization
9500 Arena Drive, Suite 400
Largo, MD 20774-3716
301-773-2044   fax 301-773-4298
ajinman@responsiblefatherhood.org
Issues: Civil rights/racial preferences; Faith-
based and volunteer initiatives; Family and
children; Marriage and divorce; Poverty and
dependency; Religion and public life; Religious
freedom; Wealth creation/financial
empowerment; Welfare/welfare reform

Innis, Niger Roy
National Spokesman
Congress of Racial Equality
817 Broadway
New York, NY 10003
212-598-4000   fax 212-529-3568
corenyc@aol.com
Issues: Abstinence and out-of-wedlock births;
Africa; American diplomacy/foreign policy;
Bilingual education; Campaign finance
reform; Charter schools; Civil rights/racial
preferences; Congress; Conservative thought;
Crime/crime statistics; Elections/polling;
Executive Branch/The Presidency; Free
Speech; Housing and homelessness; Human
rights; Immigration; International
organizations (European Union, OECD, etc.);
Japan; Job training/welfare to work; Korea;
Media and popular culture; Middle East;
Minimum wage; Poverty and dependency;
Promoting democracy/public diplomacy; The
Reagan legacy; Right to work; School choice;
Second Amendment; Standards, curriculum,
and testing; United Nations; Urban sprawl/
livable cities; Wealth creation/financial
empowerment; Welfare/welfare reform;
Western Europe

Ippolito, Dr. Dennis S.
Eugene McElvaney Professor of Political
Science
Southern Methodist University
221 Carr Collins Hall
Dallas, TX 75275
214-768-2524   fax 214-768-3469
Issues: Defense budget; Entitlement spending;
Social Security and retirement; Taxation/tax
reform

Ireland, Dr. Thomas R.
Professor of Economics
University of Missouri, St. Louis
8001 Natural Bridge Road
St. Louis, MO 63121
314-516-5558   fax 314-516-5352
ireland@umsl.edu
Issues: Family and medical leave; Immigration;
Risk assessment; Tort and liability reform

Irvine, Reed J.
Chairman
Accuracy in Media
4455 Connecticut Avenue, N.W., Suite 330
Washington, DC 20008
202-364-4401   fax 202-364-4098
roger@aim.org
Issues: Conservative thought; Media and
popular culture; Political correctness and
multiculturalism

Irvine, Dr. William B., III
Professor, Department of Philosophy
Wright State University
383 Millett Hall
Dayton, OH 45435
937-775-2610   fax 937-775-3301
william.irvine@wright.edu
Issues: Ethics; Family and children; Political
philosophy

Ivancie, Thomas
President and CEO
America's Future Foundation
1508 21st Street, N.W.
Washington, DC 20036
202-544-7707   fax 202-530-1084
tom@americasfuture.org
Issues: Arts, humanities and historic resources;
Conservative thought; Entitlement spending;
Entrepreneurship/free enterprise; Media and
popular culture; Social Security and
retirement; Taxation/tax reform

*Izumi, Lance T.
Director, Center for School Reform
Pacific Research Institute
1414 K Street, Suite 200
Sacramento, CA 95814
916-448-1926   fax 916-448-3856
izumi58@aol.com
Issues: Charter schools; Education unions and
interest groups; Government waste; Higher
education; Public school finance and
administration; School choice; Standards,
curriculum, and testing; State and local public
finance

Jackson, Bishop Earl W., Sr.
Samaritan Project
P. O. Box 15301
Chesapeake, VA 23328
757-546-8815   fax 757-546-1848
ejmsp@home.com
Issues: Abstinence and out-of-wedlock births;
Civil rights/racial preferences; Conservative
thought; Ethics; Family and children; Media
and popular culture; Political correctness and
multiculturalism; Poverty and dependency;
Religion and public life; School choice

*Jackson, Eve
Founder and Director
The PEERS Project
P. O. Box 1410
Indianapolis, IN 46206-1410
317-592-4015   fax 317-592-4009
ejackson@peersproject.org
Issues: Abstinence and out-of-wedlock births;
Faith-based and volunteer initiatives

*Jacob, Bradley P.
Associate Professor, School of Law
Regent University
1000 Regent University Drive
Virginia Beach, VA 23464-9800
757-226-4523   fax 757-226-4329
bradjac@regent.edu
Issues: Church-state relations; Constitutional
law; Home schooling; Religion and public life;
Religious freedom

*Jacob, Paul
President
Citizens in Charge and Citizens in Charge
Foundation
2617 Pheasant Hunt Road
Woodbridge, VA 22192
703-580-7130   fax 703-897-0726
pj@citizensincharge.org
Issues: Campaign finance reform; Initiative and
referendum; Term limits

*Jacobs, Dr. Harvey M.
Professor, Department of Urban and
Regional Planning
University of Wisconsin
925 Bascom Mall/Old Music Hall
Madison, WI 53706
608-262-0552   fax 608-262-9307
hmjacobs@facstaff.wisc.edu
Issues: Africa; Land use; Promoting
democracy/public diplomacy; Property rights;
Urban sprawl/livable cities

Jacoby, Tamar
Senior Fellow
Manhattan Institute for Policy Research
52 Vanderbilt Avenue
New York, NY 10017
212-599-7000   fax 212-599-3494
Issues: Immigration

Jaffa, Dr. Harry V.
Distinguished Fellow
Claremont Institute
250 West First Street, Suite 330
Claremont, CA 91711
909-621-6825   fax 909-626-8724
Issues: American history/political tradition;
Constitutional law; Political philosophy

James, Louis
President and CEO
Henry Hazlitt Foundation and
Free-Market.Net
401 North Franklin Street, Suite 3E
Chicago, IL 60610
312-494-9433   fax 312-494-9441
ljames@free-market.net
Issues: Entrepreneurship/free enterprise;
Telecommunications and the Internet

*Jarvik, Dr. Laurence
3735 Jocelyn Street, N.W.
Washington, DC 20015
202-363-8415   fax 202-363-8415
Issues: Arts, humanities and historic resources;
Higher education; Media and popular culture;
Philanthropy; Political correctness and
multiculturalism; Privatization/Contracting-
out; Russia and Eurasia; Telecommunications
and the Internet

*Jarvis, Charles W.
Chairman and Chief Executive Officer
United Seniors Association
3900 Jermantown Road, Suite 450
Fairfax, VA 22030
703-359-6500   fax 703-359-6510
skorchnak@unitedseniors.org
Issues: Aging/elder care; American history/
political tradition; Campaign finance reform;
Congress; Conservative thought;
Constitutional law; The Economy; Entitlement
spending; Environmental education; Ethics;
Executive Branch/The Presidency; Faith-based
and volunteer initiatives; Family and children;
Free-market environmentalism; Health care
reform; Immigration; Judicial activism/judicial
reform; Media and popular culture; Medicaid;
Medicare; Political correctness and
multiculturalism; Promoting democracy/
public diplomacy; The Reagan legacy; School
choice; Social Security and retirement;
Taxation/tax reform; Tort and liability reform;
Wealth creation/financial empowerment

Jastrow, Dr. Robert
Chairman
George C. Marshall Institute
1625 K Street, N.W., Suite 1050
Washington, DC 20006
202-296-9655   fax 202-296-9714
info@marshall.org
Issues: Climate change; Defense budget;
Environmental education; Missile defense;
Sound science

Jeffrey, Douglas A.
Vice President for External Affairs
Hillsdale College
33 East College Street
Hillsdale, MI 49242
517-607-2538   fax 517-437-0654
douglas.jeffrey@hillsdale.edu
Issues: The American Founding; American history/political tradition; Conservative thought; Higher education; Media and popular culture; Political correctness and multiculturalism; Political philosophy

*Jennings, Marianne
Professor, College of Business
Arizona State University
P. O. Box 874806
Tempe, AZ 85287-4806
480-965-6044
Issues: Ethics; Family and children; Higher education; Political correctness and multiculturalism

*Jerman, Mike
Vice President
Utah Taxpayers Association
1578 West 1700 South, Suite 201
Salt Lake City, UT 84104
801-972-8814   fax 801-973-2324
Issues: Public school finance and administration; State and local public finance

Jestes, Michael L.
Executive Director
Oklahoma Family Policy Council
3908 North Peniel Avenue, Suite 100
Bethany, OK 73008-3458
405-787-7744   fax 405-787-3900
okfamilypc@aol.com
Issues: Abstinence and out-of-wedlock births; Faith-based and volunteer initiatives; Juvenile justice

Jewell, Walter
Executive Director
Professional Educators of Tennessee
810 Cresent Centre Drive, Suite 130, Four Corporate Center
Franklin, TN 37067
615-778-0803   fax 615-778-0149
walter@teacherspet.com
Issues: Education unions and interest groups

*Jipping, Thomas L.
Senior Fellow in Legal Studies
Concerned Women for America
1015 15th Street, N.W., Suite 1100
Washington, DC 20005
202-488-7000   fax 202-488-0806
tjipping@cwfa.org
Issues: Church-state relations; Civil rights/racial preferences; Constitutional law; Federalism; Judicial activism/judicial reform; Judiciary; Juvenile justice; Media and popular culture; Religion and public life; Religious freedom; School choice

*John, David
Research Fellow, Thomas A. Roe Institute for Economic Policy Studies
The Heritage Foundation
214 Massachusetts Avenue, N.E.
Washington, DC 20002
202-546-4400   fax 202-544-5421
info@heritage.org
Issues: Campaign finance reform; Congress; Money and financial services; Privatization/Contracting-out; Regulatory reform; Social Security and retirement; Wealth creation/financial empowerment

John, Theodore
Director, SIFE Africa
Students In Free Enterprise
1959 East Kerr Street
Springfield, MO 65803-4775
417-831-9505   fax 417-831-6165
sjohn@sife.org
Issues: Africa; Business and education partnerships; Economic education; Entrepreneurship/free enterprise

*Johns, Michael
321 Avalon Court Drive
Melville, NY 11747
631-752-0984   mjohns8@aol.com
Issues: Africa; Aging/elder care; American diplomacy/foreign policy; Economic development/foreign aid; Government health programs; Health care reform; Human rights; International finance and multilateral banks; Medicaid; Medicare; Promoting democracy/public diplomacy

---

*Johnson, Dr. Bruce Alan
Chairman
Bruce Alan Johnson Associates
5138 Thrush Drive
Indianapolis, IN 46224
317-501-1052   fax 317-297-4225
baj.liberty@mindspring.com
Issues: Africa; Economic development/foreign
aid; Economic theory; Sound science; Wealth
creation/financial empowerment

Johnson, Byron
Distinguished Senior Fellow, Center for
Research on Religion and Urban Civil
Society
University of Pennsylvania
3814 Walnut Street, Leadership Hall
Philadelphia, PA 19104-6197
215-746-7121   fax 215-746-7101
byronj@sas.upenn.edu
Issues: Church-state relations; Citizenship and
civil society; Corrections and sentencing;
Crime/crime statistics; Faith-based and
volunteer initiatives; Juvenile justice

*Johnson, Dr. Chalmers
President
Japan Policy Research Institute
2138 Via Tiempo
Cardiff, CA 92007
760-944-3950   fax 760-944-9022
info@jpri.org
Issues: China; Defense budget; Economic
theory; The Economy; Emerging threats/
threat assessment; Intelligence gathering and
covert operations; Japan; Korea; Military
strategy; Missile defense; Northeast Asia;
Southeast Asia (including Burma, Cambodia,
Laos, Vietnam, Singapore, Malaysia, Indonesia,
the Philippines, Australia, and New Zealand)

Johnson, Dr. D. Gale
Professor Emeritus of Economics
University of Chicago
1126 East 59th Street
Chicago, IL 60637
773-702-8251   fax 773-702-8490
dg-johnson@uchicago.edu
Issues: Central and Eastern Europe; China;
Economic development/foreign aid; Higher
education; Russia and Eurasia

*Johnson, Daniel H. "Stormy", Jr., M.D.
Visiting Fellow in Health Policy
The Heritage Foundation
214 Massachusetts Avenue, N.E.
Washington, DC 20002
504-885-4223   fax 504-887-6620
stormyj@aol.com
Issues: Health care reform

*Johnson, Douglas
Legislative Director
National Right to Life Committee
512 10th Street, N.W.
Washington, DC 20004
202-626-8820   fax 202-347-3668
legfederal@aol.com
Issues: Campaign finance reform; Family and
children; Free Speech

Johnson, Dr. Kirk A.
Director of Education Policy
Mackinac Center for Public Policy
140 West Main Street, P. O. Box 568
Midland, MI 48604
989-631-0900   fax 989-631-0964
johnson@mackinac.org
Issues: Charter schools; Education unions and
interest groups; Federal education policy;
Poverty and dependency; Public school finance
and administration; School choice; Standards,
curriculum, and testing; Welfare/welfare
reform

Johnson, Robin
Senior Policy Analyst, Privatization and
Government Reform Center
Reason Public Policy Institute
3415 South Sepulveda Boulevard, Suite 400
Los Angeles, CA 90034
310-391-2245   fax 310-391-4395
robinj@reason.org
Issues: Privatization/Contracting-out; State and
local public finance

Johnson, Steve
Policy Analyst, Latin America, Kathryn and
Shelby Cullom Davis Institute for
International Studies
The Heritage Foundation
214 Massachusetts Avenue, N.E.
Washington, DC 20002
202-546-4400   fax 202-675-1758
info@heritage.org
Issues: Latin America; Mexico; Promoting
democracy/public diplomacy; Terrorism and
international crime; Transportation

Johnston, Jim
Member, Board of Directors
Heartland Institute
2143 Chestnut Avenue
Wilmette, IL 60091
847-256-1294   fax 847-346-7607
jamesljohnston@cs.com
Issues: Air; Costs and benefits of regulation;
Electricity deregulation; Energy;
Environmental regulation; Free-market
environmentalism; Property rights; Regulatory
reform; Risk assessment

Jorgenson, Dr. Dale W.
Frederic E. Abbe Professor of Economics,
Department of Economics
Harvard University
122 Littauer Center
Cambridge, MA 02138
617-495-4661   fax 617-495-4660
Issues: China; Comparative economics; Costs
and benefits of regulation; Economic
education; Economic theory; The Economy;
Energy; Environmental regulation; Taxation/
tax reform

Joyce, Dr. Michael S.
President
Foundation for Community and Faith
Centered Enterprise
6245 North 24th Parkway, Suite 106
Phoenix, AZ 85016
602-840-9066   fax 602-840-9064
information@fcfe.org
Issues: Arts, humanities and historic resources;
Citizenship and civil society; Family and
children; Media and popular culture;
Philanthropy; Political correctness and
multiculturalism; School choice

Joyce, Sherman
President
American Tort Reform Association
1101 Connecticut Avenue, N.W., Suite 400
Washington, DC 20036
202-682-1163   fax 202-682-1022
sjoyce@atra.org
Issues: Tort and liability reform

*Joyner, Dr. Christopher
Professor of Government, Department of
Government
Georgetown University
681 ICC
Washington, DC 20057-1034
202-687-5112   fax 703-280-5292
joynerc@gunet.georgetown.edu
Issues: American diplomacy/foreign policy;
Climate change; Human rights; International
law; International organizations (European
Union, OECD, etc.); Middle East;
Peacekeeping; Promoting democracy/public
diplomacy; Terrorism and international crime;
United Nations

Kaempfer, Dr. William H.
Professor and Associate Vice Chancellor of
Academic Affairs for Budget and Planning,
Department of Economics
University of Colorado
Campus Box 256
Boulder, CO 80309-0256
303-492-6923   fax 303-492-8861
kaempfer@colorado.edu
Issues: Africa; Economic theory; International
finance and multilateral banks; International
organizations (European Union, OECD, etc.);
Trade

*Kafer, Krista
Policy Analyst, Education
The Heritage Foundation
214 Massachusetts Avenue, N.E.
Washington, DC 20002
202-546-4400   fax 202-544-5421
krista.kafer@heritage.org
Issues: Bilingual education; Charter schools;
Education unions and interest groups; Federal
education policy; Home schooling; School
choice; School-to-work; Standards, curriculum,
and testing

Kafoglis, Dr. Milton
George Woodruff Professor of Economics
Emeritus
Emory University
209 East Parlwood Road
Decatur, GA 30030
404-712-9269   fax 404-727-4639
mkafogl@emory.edu
Issues: The Economy; Regulatory reform; State
and local public finance; Telecommunications
and the Internet

*Kagan, Doug
State Chairman
Nebraska Taxpayers for Freedom
P. O. Box 6452
Omaha, NE 68106
402-551-0921   fax 402-551-0921
ncf@phonet.com
Issues: American history/political tradition;
Initiative and referendum; Public school
finance and administration; Taxation/tax
reform

*Kain, John
Professor, School of Social Science, Green
Center for the Study of Science and Society
University of Texas, Dallas
Mail Station GC21, P. O. Box 830688
Richardson, TX 75083
972-883-2554   fax 972-883-2551
jkain@utdallas.edu
Issues: Bilingual education; Charter schools;
Federal education policy; Higher education;
School choice; Standards, curriculum, and
testing; Transportation

Kakadelis, Lindalyn
Director
North Carolina Education Alliance
10828 Copperfield Drive
Pineville, NC 28134
704-373-2378   fax 704-373-1739
kakadelis@bellsouth.net
Issues: Business and education partnerships;
Charter schools; Federal education policy;
Home schooling; Public school finance and
administration; School choice; School-to-work;
Standards, curriculum, and testing

Kamath, Dr. Shyam J.
Professor of International Business and
Economics, Department of Economics
California State University, Hayward
25800 Carlos Bee Boulevard
Hayward, CA 94542-3066
510-885-4275   fax 510-885-2908
skamath@csuhayward.edu
Issues: Comparative economics; Costs and
benefits of regulation; Economic theory;
Entrepreneurship/free enterprise; Northeast
Asia; Privatization/Contracting-out; Russia and
Eurasia; South Asia (including India and
Pakistan); Southeast Asia (including Burma,
Cambodia, Laos, Vietnam, Singapore,
Malaysia, Indonesia, the Philippines, Australia,
and New Zealand); Trade

*Kamenar, Paul
Senior Executive Counsel
Washington Legal Foundation
2009 Massachusetts Avenue, N.W.
Washington, DC 20036
202-588-0302   fax 202-588-0386
pkamenar@wlf.org
Issues: Constitutional law; Costs and benefits of
regulation; Environmental regulation;
Federalism; Judicial activism/judicial reform;
Judiciary; Land use; Property rights; Public
interest law; Terrorism and international
crime; Tort and liability reform

*Kane, Dr. Edward J.
Professor, Department of Finance
Boston College
Fulton Hall 330A
Chestnut Hill, MA 02467
617-552-3986   fax 617-552-0431
Issues: Costs and benefits of regulation;
Regulatory reform; Risk assessment

Kane, Dr. Francis X.
President
Strategy, Technology and Space, Inc.
6 Darby Glen
San Antonio, TX 78257
210-698-0716   fax 210-698-0209
Issues: American diplomacy/foreign policy;
Middle East; Promoting democracy/public
diplomacy; Russia and Eurasia; United Nations;
Western Europe

Kantor, Dr. Shawn
Professor, Department of Economics
University of Arizona
McClelland 401
Tucson, AZ 85721
520-621-6226   fax 520-621-8450
skantor@u.arizona.edu
Issues: Costs and benefits of regulation;
Discretionary spending; Risk assessment;
Unfunded mandates

Kaplar, Richard T.
Vice President
Media Institute
1000 Potomac Street, N.W., Suite 301
Washington, DC 20007
202-298-7512   fax 202-337-7092
kaplar@mediainstitute.org
Issues: Media and popular culture; Regulatory
reform; Telecommunications and the Internet

Kapur, Paul, Ph.D.
Assistant Professor of Government
Claremont McKenna College
Pitzer Hall 207
Claremont, CA 91711
909-607-3382   fax 909-621-8419
Issues: Arms control; Defense budget;
Emerging threats/threat assessment; Export
controls/military transfers; Intelligence
gathering and covert operations; Military
strategy; Missile defense; NATO and other
alliances; Readiness and manpower; Terrorism
and international crime

Karatnycky, Adrian
President
Freedom House
120 Wall Street, 26th Floor
New York, NY 10005
212-514-8040   fax 212-514-8055
fhpres@aol.com
Issues: Central and Eastern Europe; Economic
development/foreign aid; Human rights;
NATO and other alliances; Promoting
democracy/public diplomacy; Russia and
Eurasia; United Nations

Kass, Leon R., M.D.
Hertog Fellow
American Enterprise Institute
1150 17th Street, N.W.
Washington, DC 20036
202-862-5852   fax 202-862-5808
lkass@aei.org
Issues: Ethics; Family and children; Marriage
and divorce; Media and popular culture;
Political philosophy

*Kasun, Dr. Jacqueline
Professor Emeritus, Department of
Economics
Humboldt State University
One Harpst Street
Arcata, CA 95521
707-443-6194   fax 707-443-6194
jacque@northcoast.com
Issues: Advocacy and nonprofit public funding;
Comparative economics; Economic
development/foreign aid; Research funding

Katz, Diane S.
Director of Science, Environment and
Technology Policy
Mackinac Center for Public Policy
140 West Main Street, P. O. Box 568
Midland, MI 48640
989-631-0900   fax 989-631-0964
katz@mackinac.org
Issues: Air; Anti-trust; Climate change; Costs
and benefits of regulation; Electricity
deregulation; Energy; Environmental
education; Environmental regulation; Free-
market environmentalism; Land use; Property
rights; Regulation through litigation;
Regulatory reform; Sound science;
Stewardship; Telecommunications and the
Internet; Unfunded mandates; Urban sprawl/
livable cities; Waste management; Water;
Wildlife management/endangered species

*Katz, Dr. Mark N.
Professor of Government and Politics,
Department of Public and International
Affairs
George Mason University
4400 University Drive, MSN 3F4
Fairfax, VA 22030
703-993-1420   fax 703-255-1473
mkatz@gmu.edu
Issues: Emerging threats/threat assessment;
Middle East; Promoting democracy/public
diplomacy; Russia and Eurasia

Kau, Dr. James B.
The C. Herman and Mary Virginia Terry
Chair in Business Administration, Terry
College of Business
University of Georgia
314 Brooks Hall
Athens, GA 30602-6255
706-542-9110   fax 706-542-4295
jkau@terry.uga.edu
Issues: Money and financial services

Kauffman, Amy
Director, Project on Campaign and Election
Laws, Research Fellow
Hudson Institute
1015 18th Street, N.W., Suite 300
Washington, DC 20036
202-974-6442   fax 202-223-8595
amy@hudsondc.org
Issues: Campaign finance reform; Congress;
Elections/polling; Electoral reform/voting
rights

*Kaufman, Dr. George G.
John F. Smith Professor of Finance and
Economics
Loyola University Chicago
820 North Michigan Avenue
Chicago, IL 60611
312-915-7075   fax 312-915-8508
gkaufma@luc.edu
Issues: Money and financial services

Kaufman, Martin S.
Senior Vice President and General Counsel
Atlantic Legal Foundation
150 East 42nd Street, 2nd Floor
New York, NY 10017
212-573-1960   fax 212-857-3653
Issues: Civil rights/racial preferences;
Constitutional law; Costs and benefits of
regulation; Entrepreneurship/free enterprise;
Environmental regulation; Free Speech;
International law; Property rights; Public
interest law; Regulation through litigation;
Regulatory reform; Risk assessment; School
choice; Tort and liability reform

Kaufman, Dr. Robert G.
Assistant Professor, Department of Political
Science
University of Vermont
536 Old Mill Building
Burlington, VT 05403
802-656-4369   fax 802-656-0758
rgkaufma@zoo.uvm.edu
Issues: Arms control; Constitutional law;
Emerging threats/threat assessment; Human
rights; Military strategy; NATO and other
alliances; Readiness and manpower; United
Nations

*Kaza, Hon. Greg
Executive Director
Arkansas Policy Foundation
111 Center Street, Suite 1610
Little Rock, AR 72201
501-537-0825   fax 501-375-4171
kaza@reformarkansas.org
Issues: Economic forecasting; Intellectual
property; State and local public finance;
Telecommunications and the Internet

*Kazman, Sam
General Counsel
Competitive Enterprise Institute
1001 Connecticut Avenue, N.W., Suite 1250
Washington, DC 20036
202-331-1010   fax 202-331-0640
kazman@cei.org
Issues: Costs and benefits of regulation;
Environmental regulation; Property rights;
Public interest law; Transportation

Keating, Dr. Barry P.
Professor, Department of Finance and
Business Economics
University of Notre Dame
Mendoza College of Business, Room 102
Notre Dame, IN 46556
219-631-9127   fax 219-631-5255
keating.1@nd.edu
Issues: Conservative thought; Economic
education; Economic forecasting;
Philanthropy; Telecommunications and the
Internet

*Keating, David
Senior Counselor
National Taxpayers Union
108 North Alfred Street
Alexandria, VA 22314
703-683-5700   fax 703-683-5722
ntu@ntu.org
Issues: Electricity deregulation; Federal budget;
Government debt; Initiative and referendum;
State and local public finance; Taxation/tax
reform

*Keating, Raymond J.
Chief Economist
Small Business Survival Committee
P. O. Box 576
Manorville, NY 11949
631-878-3109   fax 631-878-3129
rkeat614@aol.com
Issues: Costs and benefits of regulation;
Economic theory; The Economy;
Entrepreneurship/free enterprise; Federal
budget; Health care reform; Minimum wage;
School choice; State and local public finance;
Taxation/tax reform; Trade

*Keegan, Lisa Graham
Chief Executive Officer
Education Leaders Council
1225 19th Street, N.W., Suite 400
Washington, DC 20036
202-261-2600 fax 202-261-2638
info@educationleaders.org
Issues: Bilingual education; Business and
education partnerships; Charter schools;
Education unions and interest groups; Federal
education policy; Public school finance and
administration; School choice; Standards,
curriculum, and testing; Telecommunications
and the Internet

*Keene, Dr. David A.
Chairman
American Conservative Union
c/o The Carmen Group, Inc., 1299
Pennsylvania Avenue, N.W., 8th Floor West
Washington, DC 20004-2400
202-785-0500 fax 202-785-5277
keened@carmengroup.com
Issues: Campaign finance reform; Conservative
thought; Electricity deregulation; Free Speech;
Immigration; Political philosophy; The Reagan
legacy; Second Amendment; Taxation/tax
reform; Trade

Kekes, Dr. John
Professor of Philosophy and Public Policy
2041 Cook Road
Charlton, NY 12019
518-882-6056 fax 518-882-6056
jonkekes@nycap.rr.com
Issues: Ethics; Higher education; Political
philosophy

*Keleher, Patrick J., Jr.
President
TEACH America
Georgetown Square, 522 4th Street
Wilmette, IL 60091
847-256-8476 fax 847-256-8482
pjkjr@mindspring.com
Issues: Business and education partnerships;
Ethics; Higher education; Political correctness
and multiculturalism; School choice

Keller, Dennis J.
Chairman
DeVry Inc.
One Tower Lane
Oakbrook Terrace, IL 60181
630-574-1900 fax 630-574-1903
dkeller@devry.com
Issues: Higher education

Kelley, David
Executive Director
The Objectivist Center
11 Raymond Avenue, Suite 31
Poughkeepsie, NY 12603
845-471-6100 fax 845-471-6195
dkelley@objectivistcenter.org
Issues: Citizenship and civil society; Ethics;
Political correctness and multiculturalism;
Political philosophy

Kelling, George
Professor, School of Criminal Justice
Rutgers University
15 Washington Street
Newark, NJ 07102
973-353-5923 fax 973-353-1229
gkelling@andromeda.rutgers.edu
Issues: Crime/crime statistics; Juvenile justice;
Police

Kellman, Dr. Michael
Professor, Department of Chemistry
University of Oregon
212A Willamette Hall
Eugene, OR 97403-1253
541-346-4196 fax 541-346-4643
kellman@oregon.uoregon.edu
Issues: Environmental education; Higher
education; Research funding; Sound science;
Standards, curriculum, and testing

*Kelly, W. Thomas
President
Savers and Investors League
P. O. Box 210
Mirror Lake, NH 03853
603-569-8283   fax 603-569-1595
t_kelly@conknet.com
Issues: Advocacy and nonprofit public funding;
Aging/elder care; Comparative economics;
Congress; Conservative thought; Costs and
benefits of regulation; Economic forecasting;
Economic theory; The Economy; Entitlement
spending; Federal budget; Government debt;
Health care reform, International tax policy/
tax competition; Money and financial services;
Philanthropy; Political philosophy; Property
rights; The Reagan legacy; Regulatory reform;
School choice; Social Security and retirement;
Taxation/tax reform; Wealth creation/
financial empowerment

Kelman, Maurice
Professor of Law Emeritus
Wayne State University Law School
1177-D Kirts Boulevard
Troy, MI 48084
248-362-0735
Issues: Campaign finance reform;
Constitutional law; Electoral reform/voting
rights; Initiative and referendum; Judiciary

*Kemp, Dr. Geoffrey
Director of Regional Strategic Programs
The Nixon Center
1615 L Street, N.W., Suite 1250
Washington, DC 20036
202-887-5228   fax 202-887-5222
gkemp@nixoncenter.org
Issues: American diplomacy/foreign policy;
Arms control; Emerging threats/threat
assessment; Energy; Middle East; South Asia
(including India and Pakistan); Terrorism and
international crime; Western Europe

*Kemp, Hon. Jack
Co-Director
Empower America
1801 K Street, N.W., Suite 410
Washington, DC 20006
202-452-8200   fax 202-833-0555
jfkemp@empower.org
Issues: Congress; Discretionary spending;
Entitlement spending; Housing and
homelessness; Taxation/tax reform; Urban
sprawl/livable cities

Kemp, Jeff
Executive Director
Families Northwest
P. O. Box 40584
Bellevue, WA 98015
425-869-4001   fax 425-869-4002
info@familiesnorthwest.org
Issues: Citizenship and civil society; Family and
children; Marriage and divorce

Kendrick, David
Director, Organized Labor Accountability
Project
National Legal and Policy Center
107 Park Washington Court
Falls Church, VA 22046
703-237-1970   fax 703-237-2090
dkendrick@nlpc.org
Issues: Labor and employment; Right to work;
Unions

Kengor, Dr. Paul
Professor, Department of Political Science
Grove City College
100 Campus Drive
Grove City, PA 16127
724-488-3394   fax 724-458-2181
Issues: Middle East; The Reagan legacy;
Terrorism and international crime

Kennedy, Brian T.
President
Claremont Institute
250 West First Street, Suite 330
Claremont, CA 91711
909-621-6825   fax 909-626-8724
bkennedy@claremont.org
Issues: American diplomacy/foreign policy;
China; Emerging threats/threat assessment;
Military strategy; Missile defense; Promoting
democracy/public diplomacy; Russia and
Eurasia

Kennedy, Prof. Darlene A.

Senior Fellow and Communications
Consultant
Centre for New Black Leadership
11 South Eutaw Street, Suite 1201
Baltimore, MD 21201
410-493-1250   fax 410-547-3352
Kennedydak@aol.com
Issues: Abstinence and out-of-wedlock births;
Adoption, foster care, & child care services;
Civil rights/racial preferences; Faith-based and
volunteer initiatives; Family and children;
International tax policy/tax competition;
Judicial activism/judicial reform; Media and
popular culture; Minimum wage; Political
correctness and multiculturalism; Poverty and
dependency; School choice; Social Security
and retirement; Taxation/tax reform; Wealth
creation/financial empowerment; Welfare/
welfare reform

Kennedy, Kate

Director, Campus Project
Independent Women's Forum
P. O. Box 3058
Arlington, VA 22203-0058
703-558-4991   fax 703-558-4994
kkennedy@iwf.org
Issues: Media and popular culture

Kent, Phil

President
Southeastern Legal Foundation
3340 Peachtree Road, N.E., Suite 2515
Atlanta, GA 30326
404-365-8500   fax 404-365-0017
phil@southeasternlegal.org
Issues: Campaign finance reform; Church-state
relations; Citizenship and civil society; Civil
rights/racial preferences; Congress;
Constitutional law; Costs and benefits of
regulation; Elections/polling; Electoral
reform/voting rights; Electricity deregulation;
Energy; Environmental regulation; Federal
education policy; Federalism; Free Speech;
Government debt; Government waste;
Immigration; Judicial activism/judicial reform;
Judiciary; Political correctness and
multiculturalism; Poverty and dependency;
Property rights; Regulation through litigation;
Religion and public life; Religious freedom;
Right to work; Second Amendment; Sound
science; Terrorism and international crime;
Tort and liability reform; Welfare/welfare
reform

Kerrigan, Karen

Senior Consultant
the polling company
1220 Connecticut Avenue, N.W.
Washington, DC 20036
202-785-0238   fax 202-467-6551
kkerrigan@att.net
Issues: Climate change; Costs and benefits of
regulation; Davis-Bacon Act;
Entrepreneurship/free enterprise;
Environmental regulation; Family and medical
leave; Health care reform; Minimum wage;
OSHA; The Reagan legacy; Regulation through
litigation; Regulatory budgeting; Regulatory
reform; Risk assessment; Sound science;
Taxation/tax reform; Telecommunications
and the Internet; Trade; Unfunded mandates;
Unions

*Kesari, Dimitri

Special Assistant to the President
Family Research Council
801 G Street, N.W.
Washington, DC 20001
202-393-2100   fax 202-393-2134
dnk@frc.org
Issues: Elections/polling; Marriage and
divorce; Religion and public life; State and
local government; State-sponsored gambling

*Kesler, Dr. Charles R.

Director
Henry Salvatori Center
Claremont McKenna College, Pitzer Hall
114
Claremont, CA 91711
909-621-8201   fax 909-621-8416
ckesler@mckenna.edu
Issues: The American Founding; American
history/political tradition; Conservative
thought; Elections/polling; Ethics; Human
rights; Political correctness and
multiculturalism; Political philosophy;
Promoting democracy/public diplomacy; The
Reagan legacy; Term limits

*Keyes, William A.

Executive Director
The Institute on Political Journalism
1706 New Hampshire Avenue, N.W.
Washington, DC 20009
202-986-0384   fax 202-986-0390
wkeyes@tfas.org
Issues: Citizenship and civil society;
Conservative thought; Davis-Bacon Act; Media
and popular culture; Minimum wage; The
Reagan legacy; School choice

---

* Has testified before a state or federal legislative committee

Keyworth, Dr. George A.
Chairman of the Board and Senior Fellow
Progress & Freedom Foundation
1401 H Street, N.W., Suite 1075
Washington, DC 20005
202-289-8928   fax 202-289-6079
gkeyworth@aol.com
Issues: Privatization/Contracting-out;
Telecommunications and the Internet

Kibbe, Matthew
Executive Vice President
Citizens for a Sound Economy
1900 M Street, N.W., Suite 500
Washington, DC 20036
202-942-7610   fax 202-783-4687
mkibbe@cse.org
Issues: Congress; The Economy; Federalism;
Taxation/tax reform

Kidder, Steven J., Ph.D.
Chairman
New York Family Policy Council
3 E-Comm Square, Suite 16
Albany, NY 12207-2959
518-356-1630   fax 518-356-4989
skidder@nyfpc.org
Issues: Business and education partnerships;
Standards, curriculum, and testing

Kieff, Prof. F. Scott
Washington University
Campus Box 1120, One Brookings Drive
St. Louis, MO 63130
314-935-5052   fax 314-935-5356
fskieff.91@alum.mit.edu
Issues: Anti-trust; Economic development/
foreign aid; Economic theory; Intellectual
property; Property rights; Regulation through
litigation; Research funding; Sound science

*Kiesling, Dr. Lynne
Director of Economic Policy
Reason Public Policy Institute
3415 South Sepulveda Boulevard, Suite 400
Los Angeles, CA 90034
310-391-2245   fax 310-391-4395
lynne.kiesling@reason.org
Issues: Costs and benefits of regulation;
Economic education; Economic forecasting;
Economic theory; The Economy; Electricity
deregulation; Energy; Free-market
environmentalism; Infrastructure; Regulation
through litigation; Regulatory budgeting;
Regulatory reform; State and local public
finance; Telecommunications and the Internet

Kiesner, Dr. Fred
Professor, Department of Management
Loyola Marymount University
One LMU Drive, 371 Hilton
Los Angeles, CA 90045
310-338-4569   fax 310-338-3000
fkiesner@lmu.edu
Issues: Entrepreneurship/free enterprise;
Privatization/Contracting-out; Russia and
Eurasia

Kilgore, Jane
Program Administrator
Austin CEO Foundation
12407 North Mopac Expressway, Suite 100,
PMB 340
Austin, TX 78758
512-472-0153   fax 512-310-1688
austinceo@aol.com
Issues: Charter schools; Federal education
policy; Home schooling; School choice

Kilner, John F.
President
The Center for Bioethics and Human
Dignity
2065 Half Day Road
Bannockburn, IL 60015
847-317-8180   fax 847-317-8153
cbhd@cbhd.org
Issues: Aging/elder care; Ethics; Health care
reform

Kim, Dr. Synja P.
President and Chairman
Institute for Corean-American Studies
965 Clover Court
Blue Bell, PA 19422
610-277-9989   fax 610-277-3289
icas@icasinc.org
Issues: Korea; Northeast Asia

*Kincaid, Dr. John
Director, Meyner Center
Lafayette College
002 Kirby Hall of Civil Rights
Easton, PA 18042-1785
610-330-5598   fax 610-330-5648
meynerc@lafayette.edu
Issues: Federalism; State and local government;
State and local public finance

Kindel, Christina

Executive Director
North Dakota Family Alliance
4007 State Street North
Bismarck, ND 58503
701-223-3575   fax 701-223-1133
ndfa@mindspring.com

Issues: Family and children; Home schooling;
Religion and public life

King, Kent

Executive Director
Missouri State Teachers Association
P. O. Box 458
Columbia, MO 65205
573-442-3127   fax 573-443-5079
msta_mail@mail.msta.org

Issues: American history/political tradition;
Bilingual education; Business and education
partnerships; Charter schools; Education
unions and interest groups; Entitlement
spending; Family and children; Federal
education policy; Federalism; Home schooling;
Labor and employment; Public school finance
and administration; Right to work; School
choice; School-to-work; Social Security and
retirement; Standards, curriculum, and testing;
State and local government; State and local
public finance; Taxation/tax reform; Tort and
liability reform; Unfunded mandates; Unions

Kirby, Owen

Regional Program Director, Middle East and
North Africa
International Republican Institute
1225 Eye Street, N.W., Suite 700
Washington, DC 20005
202-408-9450   fax 202-408-9462
mena@iri.org

Issues: Africa; Middle East

Kirk, Dr. Annette

President
Russell Kirk Center
729 West Main Street, P. O. Box 4
Mecosta, MI 49332
231-972-7655   fax 231-972-8078
rkcenter@centurytel.net

Issues: Arts, humanities and historic resources;
Citizenship and civil society; Family and
children; Religion and public life

*Kirkpatrick, David W.

Editor, *www.schoolreformers.com*
Citizens for Educational Freedom
108 Highland Court
Douglassville, PA 19518
610-689-0633   fax 208-723-5817
kirkdw@aol.com

Issues: Charter schools; Education unions and
interest groups; Federal education policy;
Higher education; Home schooling; Public
school finance and administration; School
choice; State and local government; Unions

Kirkpatrick, Dr. Jeane J.

Senior Fellow
American Enterprise Institute
1150 17th Street, N.W.
Washington, DC 20036
202-862-5814   fax 202-862-7177
jkirkpatrick@aei.org

Issues: Afghanistan; American diplomacy/
foreign policy; The American Founding;
American history/political tradition; Central
and Eastern Europe; China; Comparative
government; Conservative thought; Emerging
threats/threat assessment; Federalism;
Homeland security/civil defense; Human
rights; Japan; Korea; Latin America; Mexico;
Middle East; Military strategy; Missile defense;
NATO and other alliances; Northeast Asia;
Peacekeeping; Political philosophy; Promoting
democracy/public diplomacy; Readiness and
manpower; The Reagan legacy; Russia and
Eurasia; South Asia (including India and
Pakistan); Southeast Asia (including Burma,
Cambodia, Laos, Vietnam, Singapore,
Malaysia, Indonesia, the Philippines, Australia,
and New Zealand); Terrorism and
international crime; United Nations; Western
Europe

Kirschke, Dr. James J.

Professor
Villanova University
SAC 402
Villanova, PA 19085
610-519-7330   fax 610-519-7864
james.kirschke@villanova.edu

Issues: The American Founding; American
history/political tradition; Arts, humanities
and historic resources; Federal education
policy; Higher education

Kirtley, John
President and CEO
Children First America
P. O. Box 330
Bentonville, AR 72712
479-273-6957   fax 479-273-9362
info@childrenfirstamerica.org
Issues: Charter schools; Federal education
policy; Public school finance and
administration; School choice

Kiviat, Dr. Joy
Research Director
Citizens for Educational Freedom
1925 Tower Bridge
St. Louis, MO 63146
314-469-2723   fax 314-469-2736
jefnjoy@swbell.net
Issues: Federal education policy; School choice

*Klausner, Manuel, P.C.
Attorney
Individual Rights Foundation
One Bunker Hill Building, 601 West Fifth
Street, Eighth Floor
Los Angeles, CA 90071
213-617-0414   fax 213-617-1314
mklaus@aol.com
Issues: Civil rights/racial preferences;
Constitutional law; Free Speech; Initiative and
referendum; Public interest law; School choice

Klayman, Larry
Chairman and General Counsel
Judicial Watch
501 School Street, S.W., Suite 500
Washington, DC 20024
202-646-5172   fax 202-646-5199
info@judicialwatch.org
Issues: Campaign finance reform; Church-state
relations; Civil rights/racial preferences;
Criminal law and procedure; Ethics; Executive
Branch/The Presidency; Judicial activism/
judicial reform

*Kleckner, Dean
Truth About Trade and Technology
309 Court Avenue, Suite 214
Des Moines, IA 50309
515-274-0800   fax 240-201-8451
Issues: Agriculture; Trade

Klee, Mary Beth
Board Member
Link Institute
126 Annette Drive
Portsmouth, NH 02871
401-683-7744   fax 603-448-3375
Issues: Charter schools; School choice;
Standards, curriculum, and testing

Klein, Dr. Daniel
Associate Professor of Economics, and
General Director, Civil Society Institute
Santa Clara University
500 El Camino Real
Santa Clara, CA 95053
408-554-6951   fax 408-554-2331
dklein@scu.edu
Issues: Costs and benefits of regulation; Health
care reform; Privacy; Regulatory reform

*Klicka, Christopher J.
Senior Counsel
Home School Legal Defense Association
P. O. Box 3000
Purcellville, VA 20134
540-338-5600   fax 540-338-1952
chris@hslda.org
Issues: Charter schools; Constitutional law;
Federal education policy; Higher education;
Home schooling; Religious freedom; School
choice; School-to-work; Standards, curriculum,
and testing

Klucsarits, Ann C.
Director of Development
The Heritage Foundation
214 Massachusetts Avenue, N.E.
Washington, DC 20002
202-546-4400   fax 202-547-6360
info@heritge.org
Issues: Philanthropy

*Kmiec, Douglas W.
Dean and St. Thomas More Professor of Law,
School of Law
The Catholic University of America
Cardinal Station
Washington, DC 20064
202-319-5139   fax 202-319-5473
dean@law.edu
Issues: The American Founding; Church-state
relations; Civil rights/racial preferences;
Constitutional law; Executive Branch/The
Presidency; Faith-based and volunteer
initiatives; Family and children; Federalism;
Free Speech; Higher education; Judicial
activism/judicial reform; Judiciary; Land use;
Marriage and divorce; Media and popular
culture; Property rights; The Reagan legacy;
Religion and public life; Religious freedom;
School choice; State and local government;
Terrorism and international crime; Urban
sprawl/livable cities

Knauer, Dorothy
Deputy Director
Protestant Community Centers, Inc.
25 James Street
Newark, NJ 07102
973-621-2273   fax 973-621-8120
djknauer@cacofnj.com
Issues: Business and education partnerships;
Faith-based and volunteer initiatives; Family
and children

*Knight, Robert H.
Director, Culture and Family Institute
Concerned Women for America
1015 15th Street, N.W., Suite 1100
Washington, DC 20005
202-488-7000   fax 202-488-0806
rknight@cwfa.org
Issues: Abstinence and out-of-wedlock births;
Adoption, foster care, & child care services;
Arts, humanities and historic resources;
Citizenship and civil society; Education unions
and interest groups; Ethics; Faith-based and
volunteer initiatives; Family and children; Free
Speech; Marriage and divorce; Media and
popular culture; Philanthropy; Political
correctness and multiculturalism; Political
philosophy; Religion and public life; Religious
freedom; State-sponsored gambling

Knippenberg, Dr. Joseph M.
Associate Provost for Student Achievement
and Director, Rich Foundation Urban
Leadership Program
Oglethorpe University
4484 Peachtree Road, N.E.
Atlanta, GA 30319
404-364-8341   fax 404-364-8500
jknippenberg@facstaff.oglethorpe.edu
Issues: The American Founding; American
history/political tradition; Church-state
relations; Citizenship and civil society;
Conservative thought; Constitutional law;
Ethics; Faith-based and volunteer initiatives;
Higher education; Political philosophy;
Religion and public life; Religious freedom

*Knippers, Diane
President
Institute on Religion and Democracy
1110 Vermont Avenue, N.W., Suite 1180
Washington, DC 20005-3544
202-969-8430   fax 202-969-8429
mail@ird.renew.org
Issues: Human rights; Religion and public life;
Religious freedom

Knoeber, Dr. Charles R.
Professor, Department of Economics
North Carolina State University
4166 Nelson Hall, Box 8110
Raleigh, NC 27695
919-513-2874   fax 919-515-7873
charles_knoeber@ncsu.edu
Issues: Economic education; State and local
public finance

Knopp, Dr. Anthony K.
Professor of History, Department of Social
Sciences
University of Texas, Brownsville
80 Fort Brown
Brownsville, TX 78520
956-544-8258   fax 956-983-7072
aknopp@utb.edu
Issues: Latin America; Mexico

Koehler, John L., M.D.
Co-Chairman
Illinois Family Institute
799 West Roosevelt Road, Building 3
Suite 218
Glen Ellyn, IL 60137
630-790-8370   fax 630-790-8390
jkoehler@illinoisfamily.org
Issues: Marriage and divorce; Religion and
public life

---

*Kolassa, Dr. Eugene M.
Associate Professor of Pharmacy
Administration, School of Pharmacy
University of Mississippi
219-B Faser Hall
University, MS 38677
662-915-1020   fax 662-915-5102
mkolassa@olemiss.edu
Issues: Government health programs; Health
care reform; Medicaid; Medicare

Komer, Richard D.
Senior Litigation Attorney
Institute for Justice
1717 Pennsylvania Avenue, N.W., Suite 200
Washington, DC 20006
202-955-1300   fax 202-955-1329
rkomer@ij.org
Issues: School choice

*Koons, Dr. Robert C.
Associate Professor, Department of
Philosophy
University of Texas
Department of Philosophy, C3500
Austin, TX 78712-1180
512-471-5530   fax 512-471-4806
rkoons@mail.utexas.edu
Issues: Arts, humanities and historic resources;
Church-state relations; Conservative thought;
Constitutional law; Ethics; Higher education;
Political philosophy; Religion and public life;
Religious freedom

*Kopel, David B.
Research Director
Independence Institute
14142 Denver West Parkway, Suite 185
Golden, CO 80401
303-279-6536   fax 303-279-4176
david@i2i.org
Issues: Abstinence and out-of-wedlock births;
The American Founding; American history/
political tradition; Anti-trust; Campaign
finance reform; Canada; Congress;
Constitutional law; Corrections and
sentencing; Criminal law and procedure;
Elections/polling; Environmental regulation;
Federalism; Free Speech; Japan; Judiciary;
Middle East; Political correctness and
multiculturalism; Privacy; Regulation through
litigation; Second Amendment; Substance
abuse; Telecommunications and the Internet;
Terrorism and international crime; Tort and
liability reform; United Nations; Waste
management; Welfare/welfare reform

Kopp, Wendy
President
Teach for America
315 West 36th Street, 6th Floor
New York, NY 10018
212-279-2080   fax 212-279-2081
wendy@teachforamerica.org
Issues: Federal education policy

Kors, Dr. Alan Charles
President
The Foundation for Individual Rights in
Education
210 West Washington Square, Suite 303
Philadelphia, PA 19106
215-717-3473   fax 215-717-3440
akors@sas.upenn.edu
Issues: Arts, humanities and historic resources;
Federal education policy; Higher education;
Political correctness and multiculturalism

Korsak, Lisa M.
Associate Director, Government
Accountability
Mercatus Center at George Mason University
3301 North Fairfax Drive, Suite 450
Arlington, VA 22201
703-993-4911   fax 703-783-8390
lkorsak@gmu.edu
Issues: Congress; Executive Branch/The
Presidency; Federal civil service; Government
waste; Privatization/Contracting-out; State and
local government

*Korten, Patrick
Vice President for Communications
The Becket Fund for Religious Liberty
1350 Connecticut Avenue, N.W., Suite 605
Washington, DC 20036
202-955-0095   fax 202-955-0090
pkorten@becketfund.org
Issues: Federal civil service; Media and popular
culture; The Reagan legacy; Religion and
public life

Kosma, Montgomery N.
Jones, Day, Reavis & Pogue
51 Louisiana Avenue, N.W.
Washington, DC 20001-2113
202-879-3939   fax 202-626-1700
mkosma@greenbag.org
Issues: Anti-trust; Federalism; Police; Privacy;
Regulatory reform; State and local
government; Telecommunications and the
Internet; Tort and liability reform

*Kosters, Dr. Marvin H.
Director, Economic Policy Studies
American Enterprise Institute
1150 17th Street, N.W.
Washington, DC 20036
202-862-5846   fax 202-862-7177
mkosters@aei.org
Issues: Costs and benefits of regulation; Davis-Bacon Act; The Economy; Family and medical leave; Federal budget; Federal education policy; Japan; Job training/welfare to work; Labor and employment; Minimum wage; Poverty and dependency; Regulatory budgeting; Regulatory reform; Unemployment insurance; Unions; Welfare/welfare reform; Western Europe

Kostrava, James E.
President
Funding Freedom
2698 North Peterson Drive
Stanford, MI 48657
989-687-6367   fax 989-687-9088
jkostrava@fundingfreedom.com
Issues: Philanthropy

Kotkin, Joel
Senior Research Fellow, Davenport Institute, School of Public Policy
Pepperdine University
24255 Pacific Coast Highway
Malibu, CA 90046
310-506-7466   fax 310-506-4059
jkotkin@worldnet.att.net
Issues: Immigration; Telecommunications and the Internet

Kotlikoff, Dr. Laurence
Chairman, Department of Economics
Boston University
270 Bay State Road
Boston, MA 02215
617-353-4002   fax 617-353-4001
Issues: Aging/elder care; Discretionary spending; Entitlement spending; Federal budget; Government health programs; Health care reform; Medicaid; Medicare; Social Security and retirement; Taxation/tax reform; Welfare/welfare reform

*Kovacs, Dr. Malcolm
Professor of Sociology
Montgomery College
51 Mannakee Street
Rockville, MD 20850
301-251-7480   fax 301-251-7478
mkovacs@mc.cc.md.us
Issues: Marriage and divorce; Middle East; Religion and public life

*Krakowski, Dr. Elie
President
EDK Consulting
3504 Seven Mile Lane
Baltimore, MD 21208
410-764-3980   fax 410-764-6352
eddie1223@msn.com
Issues: Afghanistan; American diplomacy/ foreign policy; Economic development/ foreign aid; Emerging threats/threat assessment; Human rights; Intelligence gathering and covert operations; International law; Peacekeeping; Promoting democracy/ public diplomacy; Russia and Eurasia; South Asia (including India and Pakistan); Southeast Asia (including Burma, Cambodia, Laos, Vietnam, Singapore, Malaysia, Indonesia, the Philippines, Australia, and New Zealand); Terrorism and international crime; United Nations

Kramer, John E.
Vice President for Communications
Institute for Justice
1717 Pennsylvania Avenue, N.W., Suite 200
Washington, DC 20006
202-955-1300   fax 202-955-1329
jkramer@ij.org
Issues: Civil rights/racial preferences; Constitutional law; Davis-Bacon Act; Entrepreneurship/free enterprise; Free Speech; Public interest law; School choice; Transportation deregulation

Krannawitter, Thomas L.
Director of Civic Education
Claremont Institute
250 West First Street, Suite 330
Claremont, CA 91711
909-621-6825   fax 909-626-8724
tkrannawitter@claremont.org
Issues: The American Founding; American history/political tradition; Church-state relations; Civil rights/racial preferences; Constitutional law; Judicial activism/judicial reform; Political philosophy; Religious freedom; Second Amendment

---

Krason, Dr. Stephen
Professor of Political Science and Legal
Studies, Department of Humanities and
Catholic Social Thought
Franciscan University of Steubenville
1235 University Boulevard
Steubenville, OH 43952
740-283-6245   fax 740-283-6401
scss@franuniv.edu
Issues: The American Founding; Church-state
relations; Constitutional law; Family and
children; Free Speech; Political philosophy

*Krauss, Michael
Professor of Law
George Mason University School of Law
3301 North Fairfax Drive
Arlington, VA 22201
703-993-8024   fax 703-993-8124
mkrauss@gmu.edu
Issues: Canada; Civil rights/racial preferences;
Ethics; Political correctness and
multiculturalism; Tort and liability reform

Kravis, Marie-Josee
Board Member and Senior Fellow
Hudson Institute
Herman Kahn Center, 5395 Emerson Way
Indianapolis, IN 46226
317-545-1000   fax 317-545-9639
Issues: Canada; Central and Eastern Europe;
The Economy; Entrepreneurship/free
enterprise; Latin America; Western Europe

Kreep, Gary
Executive Director
United States Justice Foundation
2091 East Valley Parkway, Suite 1-C
Escondido, CA 92027
760-741-8086   fax 760-741-9548
Issues: Church-state relations; Constitutional
law; Free Speech; Home schooling; Privacy;
Property rights; Public interest law; Religious
freedom; School choice

*Krikorian, Mark
Executive Director
Center for Immigration Studies
1522 K Street, N.W., Suite 820
Washington, DC 20005
202-466-8185   fax 202-466-8076
msk@cis.org
Issues: Citizenship and civil society;
Immigration

Krilla, Jeffrey
Regional Program Director, Africa
International Republican Institute
1225 Eye Street, N.W., Suite 700
Washington, DC 20005
202-408-9450   fax 202-408-9462
africa@iri.org
Issues: Africa

Kristol, Irving
Co-Editor
The Public Interest
1112 16th Street, N.W., Suite 140
Washington, DC 20016
202-785-8555   fax 202-785-8441
Issues: Family and children; Media and popular
culture; Religion and public life

Kristol, William
Editor
The Weekly Standard
1150 17th Street, N.W., Suite 505
Washington, DC 20036
202-293-4900   fax 202-293-4901
Issues: American diplomacy/foreign policy;
Citizenship and civil society; Elections/polling;
Judiciary; Political philosophy; Religion and
public life

Krizek, Dr. Raymond J.
Stanley F. Pepper Chair in Civil Engineering
Northwestern University
2145 Sheridan Road
Evanston, IL 60208-3109
847-491-4040   fax 847-491-4011
rjkrizek@nwu.edu
Issues: Business and education partnerships;
Sound science; Waste management

Krol, Dr. Robert
Professor, Department of Economics
California State University, Northridge
18111 Nordhoff Street
Northridge, CA 91330-8374
818-677-2430   fax 818-677-6264
robert.krol@csun.edu
Issues: Economic development/foreign aid;
The Economy; Infrastructure; International
finance and multilateral banks; Money and
financial services; Regulatory reform; Trade

*Kroszner, Dr. Randall
Professor of Economics, Graduate School of Business
University of Chicago
1101 East 58th Street
Chicago, IL 60637
773-702-8779   fax 773-702-0458
randy.kroszner@gsb.uchicago.edu
Issues: American history/political tradition; Anti-trust; Campaign finance reform; Congress; Costs and benefits of regulation; Economic forecasting; Economic theory; The Economy; Entrepreneurship/free enterprise; Government debt; International finance and multilateral banks; Money and financial services; Privatization/Contracting-out; Regulatory reform; Term limits

Krumbhaar, George
USBUDGET.COM
3732 Windom Place, N.W.
Washington, DC 20016
202-364-0108   fax 202-244-0638
georgek@usbudget.com
Issues: Discretionary spending; The Economy; Entitlement spending; Federal budget; Government debt; Government waste; Taxation/tax reform

*Kudlow, Lawrence
CEO
Kudlow & Co., LLC
885 Second Avenue, 26th Floor
New York, NY 10017
212-644-8610   fax 212-588-1636
Issues: Abstinence and out-of-wedlock births; American diplomacy/foreign policy; The American Founding; American history/political tradition; Comparative economics; Conservative thought; Defense budget; Discretionary spending; Economic development/foreign aid; Economic education; Economic forecasting; Economic theory; Emerging threats/threat assessment; Entitlement spending; Faith-based and volunteer initiatives; Federal budget; Government debt; Government waste; Intelligence gathering and covert operations; International finance and multilateral banks; International organizations (European Union, OECD, etc.); International tax policy/tax competition; Media and popular culture; Military strategy; Missile defense; Privatization/Contracting-out; Promoting democracy/public diplomacy; The Reagan legacy; Religion and public life; Russia and Eurasia; State and local public finance; Taxation/tax reform; Terrorism and international crime; Unfunded mandates

Kulbicki, Melvin A., Ph.D.
Professor of Political Science and Chairman, Department of History and Political Science
York College of Pennsylvania
307 Life Sciences Building
York, PA 17405-7199
717-815-1269   fax 717-849-1653
mkulbick@ycp.edu
Issues: The American Founding; American history/political tradition; Campaign finance reform; Citizenship and civil society; Conservative thought; Elections/polling; Higher education; Political correctness and multiculturalism; Political philosophy; The Reagan legacy; Religion and public life; State and local government

Kunreuther, Dr. Howard
Co-Director, Wharton Risk Management and Decision Processes Center
University of Pennsylvania
1326 Steinberg-Dietrich Hall
Philadelphia, PA 19104
215-898-4589   fax 215-573-2130
kunreuth@wharton.upenn.edu
Issues: Risk assessment; Waste management

---

* Has testified before a state or federal legislative committee

Kurzweil, John
President
California Public Policy Foundation
P. O. Box 931
Camarillo, CA 93011-0931
805-445-9183   calprev@cppf.org
Issues: Conservative thought; Judicial activism/
judicial reform; Political philosophy; Religion
and public life; Religious freedom

Kwong, Dr. Jo
Director of Institute Relations
Atlas Economic Research Foundation
1084 University Drive, Suite 103
Fairfax, VA 22030
703-934-6969   fax 703-352-7530
jo.kwong@atlas-fdn.org
Issues: Free-market environmentalism;
Property rights; Urban sprawl/livable cities

Laband, Dr. David N.
Professor, Economics and Policy, School of
Forestry and Wildlife Sciences
Auburn University
205 M. White Smith Hall
Auburn, AL 36849
334-844-1074   fax 334-844-1084
Issues: Economic education; Environmental
education; Environmental regulation; Forestry
and national parks; Land use

LaBarbera, Peter J.
Senior Policy Analyst, Culture and Family
Institute
Concerned Women for America
1015 15th Street, N.W., Suite 1100
Washington, DC 20005
202-488-7000   fax 202-488-0806
plabarbera@cwfa.org
Issues: Abstinence and out-of-wedlock births;
Education unions and interest groups; Faith-
based and volunteer initiatives; Family and
children; Marriage and divorce; Media and
popular culture; Political correctness and
multiculturalism; Religion and public life

*Lacey, Jill Cunningham
Editor, *Compassion and Culture*
Capital Research Center
10523 Santa Anita Terrace
Damascus, MD 20872
301-482-0246   fax 301-414-0245
jlacey@capitalresearch.org
Issues: Faith-based and volunteer initiatives;
Philanthropy; Welfare/welfare reform

Ladd, Stacey
Executive Director
Worth the Wait
P. O. Box 962
Pampa, TX 79066-0962
806-669-6222   fax 806-699-1297
ladd@worthwait.org
Issues: Abstinence and out-of-wedlock births;
Faith-based and volunteer initiatives; Family
and children; Media and popular culture

*Ladner, Matthew, Ph.D.
Director of Communications and Policy
Children First America
4412 Spicewood Springs Road, Suite 201
Austin, TX 78759
512-345-1083   fax 512-345-1280
Issues: Charter schools; Education unions and
interest groups; Home schooling; School
choice

*Ladwig, T. Craig
Editor-in-Chief
Indiana Policy Review Foundation
P. O. Box 12306
Fort Wayne, IN 46863
260-420-9131   fax 260-424-7104
ipr@iquest.net
Issues: Media and popular culture

*LaFaive, Michael D.
Research Project Manager
Mackinac Center for Public Policy
140 West Main Street, P. O. Box 568
Midland, MI 48640
989-631-0900   fax 989-631-0964
lafaive@mackinac.org
Issues: Privatization/Contracting-out;
Taxation/tax reform

LaFetra, Deborah J.
Principal Attorney
Pacific Legal Foundation
10360 Old Placerville Road, Suite 100
Sacramento, CA 95827
916-362-2833   fax 916-362-2932
djl@pacificlegal.org
Issues: Constitutional law; Electoral reform/
voting rights; Entrepreneurship/free
enterprise; Initiative and referendum; Term
limits; Tort and liability reform

Laffer, Dr. Arthur B.
Chairman and CEO
A. B. Laffer Associates
5405 Morehouse Drive, Suite 340
San Diego, CA 92121
858-458-0811   fax 858-458-9856
Issues: Comparative economics; Comparative
government; Conservative thought;
Discretionary spending; Economic education;
Economic forecasting; Economic theory;
Entitlement spending; Federal budget; Free-
market environmentalism; Minimum wage;
Political philosophy; Poverty and dependency;
The Reagan legacy; Social Security and
retirement; State and local public finance;
Taxation/tax reform; Welfare/welfare reform

*Lafferty, Andrea S.
Executive Director
Traditional Values Coalition
139 C Street, S.E.
Washington, DC 20003
202-547-8570   fax 202-546-6403
tvcwashdc@traditionalvalues.org
Issues: Abstinence and out-of-wedlock births;
Adoption, foster care, & child care services;
Africa; American history/political tradition;
Arts, humanities and historic resources; China;
Church-state relations; Faith-based and
volunteer initiatives; Family and children;
Federal education policy; Government health
programs; Judicial activism/judicial reform;
Media and popular culture; Middle East;
Religion and public life; Religious freedom;
School choice; State-sponsored gambling;
Taxation/tax reform; Welfare/welfare reform

*Lafferty, James
Massachusetts Citizens Alliance
1277 Main Street
Waltham, MA 02451
781-647-1942   fax 781-647-1950
jameslafferty@usa.net
Issues: Marriage and divorce; Media and
popular culture; Religion and public life;
Second Amendment

Lagomarsino, Robert J.
Chairman
American Alliance for Tax Equity
1600 Braodway, Suite 2500
Denver, CO 80202
303-831-5000   fax 303-831-5032
Issues: Government waste; Taxation/tax reform

*LaGrasse, Carol W.
President and Founder
Property Rights Foundation of America, Inc.
P. O. Box 75
Stony Creek, NY 12878
518-696-5748   lagrasse@prfamerica.org
Issues: Environmental regulation; Land use;
Non-governmental organizations; Property
rights

LaHaye, Beverly
Chairman
Concerned Women for America
1015 15th Street, N.W., Suite 1100
Washington, DC 20005
202-488-7000   fax 202-488-0806
Issues: Family and children; Marriage and
divorce

*LaJeunesse, Raymond J., Jr.
Vice President and Legal Director
National Right to Work Legal Defense
Foundation
8001 Braddock Road, Suite 600
Springfield, VA 22160
703-321-8510   fax 703-321-8239
rjl@nrtw.org
Issues: Campaign finance reform;
Constitutional law; Education unions and
interest groups; Judiciary; Labor and
employment; Public interest law; Right to work;
Unions

*Lal, Dr. Deepak
Professor, Department of Economics
University of California at Los Angeles
Los Angeles, CA 90095-1477
310-825-4521   fax 310-825-9528
dlal@econ.ucla.edu
Issues: Africa; China; Comparative economics;
Conservative thought; Costs and benefits of
regulation; Economic development/foreign
aid; Economic forecasting; Economic theory;
The Economy; Electricity deregulation;
Entitlement spending; Ethics; Free-market
environmentalism; Higher education;
International finance and multilateral banks;
International organizations (European Union,
OECD, etc.); International tax policy/tax
competition; Latin America; Political
philosophy; South Asia (including India and
Pakistan)

Lamer, Timothy
Deputy Managing Editor
World Magazine
16266 Westwood Business Park Drive
Ellisville, MO 63021
828-253-8063   fax 828-253-1556
worldmag@palmcoastd.com
Issues: Media and popular culture

Lamm, Byron S.
Board Member
State Policy Network
830 Mill Lake Road
Fort Wayne, IN 46845-6400
219-637-7778   fax 219-637-7779
blamm630@aol.com
Issues: Education unions and interest groups;
Entrepreneurship/free enterprise; Federalism;
Political philosophy; State and local public
finance; Taxation/tax reform

Lammi, Glenn G.
Chief Counsel, Legal Studies Division
Washington Legal Foundation
2009 Massachusetts Avenue, N.W.
Washington, DC 20036
202-588-0302   fax 202-588-0386
glammi@wlf.org
Issues: Constitutional law; Environmental
regulation; Free Speech; Homeland security/
civil defense; Judiciary; Land use; Property
rights; Regulation through litigation;
Terrorism and international crime; Tort and
liability reform

Lampton, David M.
Director of Chinese Studies
The Nixon Center
1615 L Street, N.W., Suite 1250
Washington, DC 20036
202-887-1000   fax 202-887-5222
mail@nixoncenter.org
Issues: China

*Land, Dr. Richard D.
President
Ethics and Religious Liberty Commission
901 Commerce Street, Suite 550
Nashville, TN 37203
615-244-2495   fax 615-242-0065
rdland@erlc.com
Issues: Church-state relations; Ethics; Family
and children; Media and popular culture;
Religion and public life

Landers, Kristin D.
Communications Director
Alabama Policy Institute
P. O. Box 59468
Birmingham, AL 35259
205-870-9900   fax 205-870-4407
Kristind@alabamapolicyinstitute.org
Issues: Adoption, foster care, & child care
services; Family and children; Religion and
public life

*Landrith, George
Executive Director
Frontiers of Freedom Institute
12011 Lee Jackson Memorial Highway
Suite 310
Fairfax, VA 22033
703-246-0110   fax 703-246-0129
glandrith@ff.org
Issues: American diplomacy/foreign policy;
American history/political tradition; Anti-trust;
Arms control; Campaign finance reform;
Citizenship and civil society; Climate change;
Comparative government; Congress;
Conservative thought; Constitutional law; Costs
and benefits of regulation; The Economy;
Energy; Ethics; Family and children; Federal
budget; Federal education policy; Federalism;
Free Speech; Homeland security/civil defense;
Intellectual property; Judicial activism/judicial
reform; Land use; Minimum wage; Missile
defense; Political correctness and
multiculturalism; Political philosophy;
Property rights; Regulation through litigation;
Religious freedom; School choice; Second
Amendment; Sound science; Standards,
curriculum, and testing; Taxation/tax reform;
Telecommunications and the Internet;
Terrorism and international crime; Tort and
liability reform; Trade; Unions; Urban sprawl/
livable cities

*Langbein, Dr. John H.
Sterling Professor of Law and Legal History
Yale Law School
P. O. Box 208215
New Haven, CT 06520
203-432-7299   fax 203-432-1109
john.langbein@yale.edu
Issues: Labor and employment; Social Security
and retirement

*Langer, Andrew
Manager, Regulatory Policy
National Federation of Independent
Business
1201 F Street, N.W., Suite 200
Washington, DC 20004
202-554-9000   fax 202-554-0496
andrew.langer@nfib.org
Issues: Air; The American Founding; American
history/political tradition; Central and Eastern
Europe; Citizenship and civil society; Civil
rights/racial preferences; Climate change;
Comparative economics; Comparative
government; Conservative thought;
Constitutional law; Costs and benefits of
regulation; Economic education; The
Economy; Energy; Entrepreneurship/free
enterprise; Environmental education;
Environmental regulation; Ethics; Executive
Branch/The Presidency; Family and medical
leave; Federalism; Forestry and national parks;
Free Speech; Free-market environmentalism;
Human rights; Judicial activism/judicial
reform; Judiciary; Land use; Media and popular
culture; Non-governmental organizations;
OSHA; Philanthropy; Political correctness and
multiculturalism; Political philosophy;
Property rights; Public interest law; Regulation
through litigation; Regulatory reform; Risk
assessment; Russia and Eurasia; Sound science;
Stewardship; Unfunded mandates; Urban
sprawl/livable cities; Waste management;
Water; Wildlife management/endangered
species

*Langlois, Dr. Richard
Professor, Department of Economics
University of Connecticut
321 Monteith Building, 341 Mansfield Road
Storrs, CT 06269-1063
860-486-3472   fax 860-486-4463
Issues: American history/political tradition;
Anti-trust; Economic theory;
Entrepreneurship/free enterprise; Intellectual
property; Political philosophy;
Telecommunications and the Internet

*LaPierre, Wayne
Executive Vice President
National Rifle Association
11250 Waples Mill Road
Fairfax, VA 22030
703-267-1000   fax 703-267-3989
Issues: Second Amendment

Lapin, Rabbi Daniel
President
Toward Tradition
P. O. Box 58
Mercer Island, WA 98040
206-236-3046   fax 206-236-3288
rabbilapin@towardtradition.org
Issues: Abstinence and out-of-wedlock births;
The American Founding; Comparative
economics; Economic education; The
Economy; Entrepreneurship/free enterprise;
Ethics; Faith-based and volunteer initiatives;
Family and children; Free-market
environmentalism; Home schooling;
International finance and multilateral banks;
Marriage and divorce; Media and popular
culture; Money and financial services; Property
rights; Religion and public life; School choice;
Telecommunications and the Internet; United
Nations; Wealth creation/financial
empowerment

Lara, Juan
President
Hispanic Council for Reform and
Educational Options
8122 Datapoint Drive, Suite 316
San Antonio, TX 78229
877-888-2736   hcreo@hcreo.org
Issues: School choice

Lark, Dr. James W., III
Assistant Professor, Department of Systems
Engineering
University of Virginia
Olsson Hall, Room 101 B
Charlottesville, VA 22904
804-982-2100   fax 804-982-2972
jwl3s@Virginia.edu
Issues: Risk assessment

*Larsen, Randy
Director
ANSER Institute for Homeland Security
2900 South Quincy Street, Suite 800
Arlington, VA 22206
703-416-3597   fax 703-416-3126
randall.larsen@anser.org
Issues: Homeland security/civil defense;
Military strategy; Terrorism and international
crime

*Larson, Dr. Edward J.
Talmadge Professor of Law and Russell
Professor of History
University of Georgia School of Law
329 Rusk Hall
Athens, GA 30602
706-542-2660   fax 706-542-5001
edlarson@uga.edu
Issues: American history/political tradition;
Ethics; Executive Branch/The Presidency;
Health care reform; Judiciary

Larson, Reed
President
National Right to Work Committee
8001 Braddock Road, Suite 500
Springfield, VA 22160
703-321-9820   fax 703-321-8239
info@nrtw.org
Issues: Education unions and interest groups;
Labor and employment; Right to work; Unions

Lartigue, Casey, Jr.
Education Policy Analyst
Cato Institute
1000 Massachusetts Avenue, N.W.
Washington, DC 20001
202-789-5238   fax 202-842-3490
cjl@cato.org
Issues: Federal education policy; Home
schooling; Korea; School choice; Standards,
curriculum, and testing

*LaRue, Janet
Chief Counsel
Concerned Women for America
1015 15th Street, N.W., Suite 1100
Washington, DC 20005
202-488-7000   fax 202-488-0806
jlarue@cwfa.org
Issues: Church-state relations; Constitutional
law; Criminal law and procedure; Free Speech;
Judicial activism/judicial reform; Media and
popular culture; Religious freedom

*Lassman, Kent
Research Fellow and Director, The Digital
Policy Network
Progress & Freedom Foundation
5 West Hargett Street, Suite 305
Raleigh, NC 27601
919-754-9902   fax 919-754-9909
klassman@pff.org
Issues: The American Founding; Costs and
benefits of regulation; Economic theory;
Federalism; Infrastructure; Intellectual
property; Privacy; State and local government;
Telecommunications and the Internet

Lau, Dr. Lawrence J.
Professor, Department of Economics
Stanford University
340 Landau Economics Building
Stanford, CA 94305-6072
650-723-3708   fax 650-723-7145
ljlau@stanford.edu
Issues: Economic development/foreign aid;
The Economy; Energy; International finance
and multilateral banks; Northeast Asia

Lavery, Jack W.
Lavery Consulting Group, LLC
P. O. Box 26
Washington Crossing, NJ 08560-0026
609-737-7018   fax 609-737-7027
jlavery@laveryconsultinggroup.com
Issues: Economic forecasting; The Economy;
Money and financial services

Lawler, Dr. Peter Augustine
Dana Professor of Government
Berry College
Box 118
Mount Berry, GA 30149-0118
706-233-4085   fax 706-236-2205
plawler@berry.edu
Issues: The American Founding; American
history/political tradition; Church-state
relations; Citizenship and civil society;
Constitutional law; Ethics; Higher education;
Political correctness and multiculturalism;
Political philosophy; Religion and public life;
Religious freedom

Lawler, Phillip F.
Editor
Catholic World Report
P. O. Box 1608
South Lancaster, MA 01561
978-365-6046   fax 978-365-4307
editor@cwnews.com
Issues: Abstinence and out-of-wedlock births;
The American Founding; American history/
political tradition; Conservative thought;
Family and children; Home schooling;
Marriage and divorce; Political correctness and
multiculturalism; Political philosophy;
Religion and public life; School choice

*Lawson, Dr. Robert A.
George H. Moor Chair in Business and
Economics
Capital University
2199 East Main Street, Renner Hall
Columbus, OH 43209-2394
614-236-6138   fax 614-236-6540
rlawson@capital.edu
Issues: Comparative economics;
Entrepreneurship/free enterprise; State and
local public finance

*Lazarus, Stephen
Senior Policy Associate
Center for Public Justice
2444 Solomons Island Road, Suite 201
Annapolis, MD 21401
410-571-6300   fax 410-571-6365
stephen@cpjustice.org
Issues: Citizenship and civil society; Climate
change; Faith-based and volunteer initiatives;
Poverty and dependency; Religion and public
life; Religious freedom; School choice

*Leal, Donald R.
Senior Associate
PERC – The Center for Free Market
Environmentalism
502 South 19th Avenue, Suite 211
Bozeman, MT 59718-6827
406-587-9591   fax 406-586-7555
perc@perc.org
Issues: Forestry and national parks; Free-market
environmentalism; Property rights;
Stewardship; Water; Wildlife management/
endangered species

Ledeen, Dr. Michael A.
Resident Scholar in the Freedom Chair
American Enterprise Institute
1150 17th Street, N.W.
Washington, DC 20036
202-862-5823   fax 202-862-5924
mledeen@aei.org
Issues: Africa; American diplomacy/foreign
policy; Central and Eastern Europe; China;
Export controls/military transfers; Intelligence
gathering and covert operations; Japan;
Northeast Asia; Religion and public life; Russia
and Eurasia; Western Europe

Lee, Dr. Dwight R.
Professor of Economics and Ramsey Chair
of Private Enterprise, Economics
Department
University of Georgia
Brooks Hall, Terry College of Business
Athens, GA 30602-6254
706-542-3970   fax 706-542-3376
dlee@terry.uga.edu
Issues: Economic education; Environmental
education; Free-market environmentalism;
Labor and employment; Minimum wage;
Property rights; Unions

Lee, Patricia H.
Managing Vice President and National
Director of Clinical Programs
Institute for Justice
1717 Pennsylvania Avenue, N.W., Suite 200
Washington, DC 20006
202-955-1300   fax 202-955-1329
Issues: Entrepreneurship/free enterprise;
Regulatory reform

Lee, Dr. Robert G.
Professor of Forestry and Sociology of
Natural Resources
University of Washington
Box 352100
Seattle, WA 98195
206-685-0879   fax 206-685-3091
boblee@u.washington.edu
Issues: Forestry and national parks

---

* Has testified before a state or federal legislative committee

*Lefever, Dr. Ernest W.
7106 Beechwood Drive
Chevy Chase, MD 20815
301-652-3226   fax 301-652-4090
elefever@aol.com
Issues: American diplomacy/foreign policy;
Arms control; Human rights; Intelligence
gathering and covert operations; Promoting
democracy/public diplomacy; Terrorism and
international crime

*LeFevre, Andrew T.
Director, Criminal Justice Task Force and
Education Task Force
American Legislative Exchange Council
1129 20th Street, N.W., Suite 500
Washington, DC 20036
202-466-3800   fax 202-466-3801
alefevre@alec.org
Issues: The American Founding; American
history/political tradition; Business and
education partnerships; Charter schools;
Corrections and sentencing; Crime/crime
statistics; Criminal law and procedure;
Education unions and interest groups; Federal
education policy; Higher education; Juvenile
justice; Police; School choice; Second
Amendment; Standards, curriculum, and
testing

Lehman, Joseph G.
Executive Vice President
Mackinac Center for Public Policy
140 West Main Street, P. O. Box 568
Midland, MI 48640
989-631-0900   fax 989-631-0964
lehman@mackinac.org
Issues: Citizenship and civil society; Education
unions and interest groups; Home schooling;
Privatization/Contracting-out; Right to work;
School choice; State and local government;
Unions

*Lehr, Jay H.
President
Environmental Education Enterprises
6011 Houseman Road
Ostrander, OH 43061
740-368-9393   fax 740-368-9494
e3@e3power.com
Issues: Agriculture; Air; Climate change;
Energy; Environmental education;
Environmental regulation; Free-market
environmentalism; Land use; Property rights;
Research funding; Sound science; Urban
sprawl/livable cities; Water

*Lehrer, Eli
Senior Editor
The American Enterprise
1150 17th Street, N.W.
Washington, DC 20036
202-862-5887   fax 202-862-7178
eli@aei.org
Issues: Citizenship and civil society; Corrections
and sentencing; Crime/crime statistics; Police;
Substance abuse; Urban sprawl/livable cities

Leibsohn, Seth
Director of Policy
Empower America
1801 K Street, N.W., Suite 410
Washington, DC 20006
202-452-8200   fax 202-833-0556
Issues: The American Founding; American
history/political tradition; Church-state
relations; Citizenship and civil society; Civil
rights/racial preferences; Constitutional law;
Faith-based and volunteer initiatives; Federal
education policy; Higher education; Middle
East; Political correctness and
multiculturalism; Religion and public life;
Religious freedom; School choice; Standards,
curriculum, and testing

Lenard, Tom
Vice President for Research and Senior
Fellow
Progress & Freedom Foundation
1401 H Street, N.W., Suite 1075
Washington, DC 20005
202-289-8928   fax 202-289-6079
tlenard@pff.org
Issues: Anti-trust; Costs and benefits of
regulation; The Economy; Electricity
deregulation; Privacy; Privatization/
Contracting-out; Regulatory budgeting;
Regulatory reform; Risk assessment;
Telecommunications and the Internet

*Lenczowski, Dr. John
Director
Institute of World Politics
1521 16th Street, N.W.
Washington, DC 20036
202-462-2101   fax 202-462-7031
johnl@iwp.edu
Issues: Comparative government; Economic
development/foreign aid; Ethics; Higher
education; Human rights; Promoting
democracy/public diplomacy; The Reagan
legacy; Russia and Eurasia

Leo, Leonard A.

Vice President, Lawyers Division
The Federalist Society for Law and Public
Policy Studies
1015 18th Street, N.W., Suite 425
Washington, DC 20036
202-822-8138   fax 202-296-8061
lleo@fed-soc.org

Issues: Anti-trust; Church-state relations; Civil
rights/racial preferences; Congress;
Constitutional law; Criminal law and
procedure; Executive Branch/The Presidency;
Federalism; Judicial activism/judicial reform;
Judiciary; Money and financial services; Public
interest law; Regulation through litigation;
Regulatory reform; Second Amendment;
Telecommunications and the Internet; Tort
and liability reform; Unfunded mandates

Lessner, Dr. Richard

Executive Director
American Renewal
801 G Street, N.W.
Washington, DC 20001
202-624-3011   fax 202-303-2134
rel@frc.org

Issues: The American Founding; American
history/political tradition; Arts, humanities
and historic resources; Church-state relations;
Citizenship and civil society; Immigration;
Media and popular culture; Military strategy;
Missile defense; Political philosophy; Religion
and public life; Religious freedom

Leube, Prof. Kurt R.

Research Fellow
Hoover Institution
Stanford University
Stanford, CA 94305
650-723-2072   fax 650-723-1687
krl@hoover.stanford.edu

Issues: Comparative economics; Economic
theory; Entrepreneurship/free enterprise;
Ethics; Free-market environmentalism;
Political philosophy; Privatization/
Contracting-out; Western Europe

Levey, Curt A.

Director of Legal and Public Affairs
Center for Individual Rights
1233 20th Street, N.W., Suite 300
Washington, DC 20036
202-833-8400   fax 202-833-8410
levey@cir-usa.org

Issues: Church-state relations; Civil rights/racial
preferences; Constitutional law; Federalism;
Free Speech; Judicial activism/judicial reform;
Judiciary; Political correctness and
multiculturalism; Public interest law; Religious
freedom

*Levin, Mark R.

President
Landmark Legal Foundation
445-B Carlisle Drive
Herndon, VA 20170
703-689-2370   fax 703-689-2373
markrlevin@aol.com

Issues: Advocacy and nonprofit public funding;
The American Founding; American history/
political tradition; Business and education
partnerships; Campaign finance reform;
Charter schools; Comparative economics;
Comparative government; Congress;
Conservative thought; Constitutional law; Costs
and benefits of regulation; Economic theory;
Education unions and interest groups;
Elections/polling; Electoral reform/voting
rights; Entrepreneurship/free enterprise;
Environmental education; Environmental
regulation; Ethics; Executive Branch/The
Presidency; Federal civil service; Federal
education policy; Free Speech; Free-market
environmentalism; Government waste; Judicial
activism/judicial reform; Judiciary; Labor and
employment; Non-governmental
organizations; Political correctness and
multiculturalism; Political philosophy;
Property rights; Public interest law; Public
school finance and administration; The
Reagan legacy; Regulatory reform; School
choice; Taxation/tax reform; Unions;
Welfare/welfare reform

Levin, Dr. Martin A.

Professor, Department of Politics
Brandeis University
415 South Street
Waltham, MA 02254
781-736-4791   fax 781-736-2777
Issues: Federalism; Government waste; Police;
State and local public finance; Urban sprawl/
livable cities

Levy, Jacob T., Ph.D.
Assistant Professor, Political Science
Department
University of Chicago
5828 South University Avenue
Chicago, IL 60637
773-702-8052   fax 773-702-1689
jt-levy@uchicago.edu
Issues: Church-state relations; Citizenship and
civil society; Civil rights/racial preferences;
Constitutional law; Ethics; Immigration;
Political correctness and multiculturalism;
Political philosophy

*Levy, Robert A.
Senior Fellow in Constitutional Studies
Cato Institute
1000 Massachusetts Avenue, N.W.
Washington, DC 20001
202-842-0200   fax 202-842-3490
rlevy@cato.org
Issues: Campaign finance reform;
Constitutional law; Federalism; Regulation
through litigation; School choice; Second
Amendment; Tort and liability reform

*Lewis, James Andrew
Senior Fellow and Director, Technology
Policy
Center for Strategic and International
Studies
1800 K Street, N.W., Suite 400
Washington, DC 20006
202-775-3247   fax 202-775-3199
jalewis@csis.org
Issues: American diplomacy/foreign policy;
China; Export controls/military transfers;
Homeland security/civil defense;
Infrastructure; Intellectual property;
Intelligence gathering and covert operations;
Police; Privacy; Regulatory reform; Southeast
Asia (including Burma, Cambodia, Laos,
Vietnam, Singapore, Malaysia, Indonesia, the
Philippines, Australia, and New Zealand);
Telecommunications and the Internet;
Western Europe

Lewis, Dr. Marlo
Senior Fellow
Competitive Enterprise Institute
1001 Connecticut Avenue, N.W., Suite 1250
Washington, DC 20036
202-331-1010   fax 202-331-0640
mlewis@cei.org
Issues: Environmental regulation; Free-market
environmentalism; Political philosophy;
Regulatory reform

Libecap, Dr. Gary
Professor of Economics and Law,
Department of Economics
University of Arizona
Tucson, AZ 85721
520-621-4821   fax 520-626-5269
glibecap@bpa.arizona.edu
Issues: Air; American history/political tradition;
Climate change; Costs and benefits of
regulation; Environmental regulation; Land
use; Property rights; Regulatory reform; Water

Licht, Eric
President
Coalitions for America
717 Second Street, N.E.
Washington, DC 20002
202-546-3000
Issues: Congress

Lichter, Dr. Linda
Vice President
Center for Media and Public Affairs
2100 L Street, N.W., Suite 300
Washington, DC 20037
202-223-2942   fax 202-872-4014
cmpamm@aol.com
Issues: Media and popular culture

*Lichter, Dr. S. Robert
President
Center for Media and Public Affairs
2100 L Street, N.W., Suite 300
Washington, DC 20037
202-223-2942   fax 202-872-4014
srlichter@cmpa.com
Issues: Media and popular culture

*Lieberman, Ben
Senior Policy Analyst
Competitive Enterprise Institute
1001 Connecticut Avenue, N.W., Suite 1250
Washington, DC 20036
202-331-1010   fax 202-331-0640
blieberman@cei.org
Issues: Air; Energy; Environmental regulation

*Lieberman, Myron
President
Education Policy Institute
4401-A Connecticut Avenue, N.W., PMB 294
Washington, DC 20008
202-244-7535   fax 202-244-7584
lieberman@educationpolicy.org
Issues: Business and education partnerships;
Charter schools; Education unions and interest
groups; Federal education policy;
Privatization/Contracting-out; Public school
finance and administration; Right to work;
School choice; State and local government;
Unions

*Liebmann, George
Executive Director
Calvert Institute for Policy Research
8 West Hamilton Street
Baltimore, MD 21201
410-752-5887   fax 410-539-3973
george.liebmann@psinet.com
Issues: Abstinence and out-of-wedlock births;
Adoption, foster care, & child care services;
Business and education partnerships; Charter
schools; Comparative government;
Constitutional law; Education unions and
interest groups; Faith-based and volunteer
initiatives; Federal education policy;
Federalism; Higher education; Judicial
activism/judicial reform; Land use; Middle
East; Public interest law; Public school finance
and administration; State and local
government; Substance abuse; Transportation;
Urban sprawl/livable cities

Liebowitz, Dr. Stanley J.
Professor of Managerial Economics, School
of Management
University of Texas, Dallas
Mail Station JO51
Richardson, TX 75083
972-883-2807   fax 972-883-2818
liebowit@utdallas.edu
Issues: Anti-trust; Intellectual property;
Telecommunications and the Internet

Liggio, Dr. Leonard P.
Executive Vice President
Atlas Economic Research Foundation
4084 University Drive, Suite 103
Fairfax, VA 22030
703-934-6969   fax 703-352-7530
lliggio@gmu.edu
Issues: American history/political tradition;
Central and Eastern Europe; Church-state
relations; Constitutional law; Higher
education; NATO and other alliances;
Philanthropy; Political philosophy; Promoting
democracy/public diplomacy; Religion and
public life; School choice; Western Europe

Lightfoot, Dianna
President
National Physicians Center for Family
Resources
402 Office Park Drive, Suite G-18
Birmingham, AL 35223
205-870-0234   fax 205-870-1890
dl@physicianscenter.org
Issues: Abstinence and out-of-wedlock births;
Adoption, foster care, & child care services;
Family and children; Government health
programs; Health care reform; Welfare/
welfare reform

Lilley, Hon. James R.
Senior Fellow
American Enterprise Institute
1150 17th Street, N.W.
Washington, DC 20036
202-862-5949   fax 202-862-7178
jlilley@aei.org
Issues: China; Korea

Lind, William S.
Director, Center for Cultural Conservatism
Free Congress Foundation
717 Second Street, N.E.
Washington, DC 20002
202-546-3000   fax 202-543-5605
Issues: American diplomacy/foreign policy;
Conservative thought; Defense budget;
Emerging threats/threat assessment;
Homeland security/civil defense; Immigration;
Military strategy; NATO and other alliances;
Police; Political correctness and
multiculturalism; Readiness and manpower;
Russia and Eurasia; Terrorism and
international crime; Transportation

Lindsay, Dr. Cotton M.
Professor of Economics, Economics
Department
Clemson University
222 Sirrine Hall
Clemson, SC 29634
864-656-3955   fax 864-656-4192
Issues: Government health programs; Higher
education; Labor and employment; Taxation/
tax reform

Lindsay, Dr. Thomas K.
Provost and Vice President for Academic
Affairs
University of Dallas
1845 East Northgate Drive
Irving, TX 75062
927-721-5137   fax 927-721-5109
lindsay@audallas.edu
Issues: Citizenship and civil society; Higher
education; Political correctness and
multiculturalism; Religion and public life;
Religious freedom

Lindsey, Brink
Director, Center for Trade Policy Studies
Cato Institute
1000 Massachusetts Avenue, N.W.
Washington, DC 20001-5403
202-842-0200   fax 202-842-3490
blindsey@cato.org
Issues: Trade

Lindsley, Dr. Art
Scholar in Residence
C. S. Lewis Institute
4208 Evergreen Lane
Annandale, VA 22003
703-914-5602   fax 703-642-1075
Issues: Ethics; Religion and public life

Lindzen, Dr. Richard S.
Alfred P. Sloan Professor of Meteorology,
Department of Earth, Atmospheric and
Planetary Sciences
Massachusetts Institute of Technology
Building 54-1720
Cambridge, MA 02139
617-253-2432   fax 617-964-3953
rlindzen@mit.edu
Issues: Air; Climate change; Sound science

*Linneman, Dr. Peter
Professor of Finance and Public Policy
The Wharton School
University of Pennsylvania
Lauder-Fischer Hall
Philadelphia, PA 19104-6330
215-898-4794   fax 215-636-8495
linnemap@wharton.upenn.edu
Issues: Economic theory; The Economy;
Entrepreneurship/free enterprise; Urban
sprawl/livable cities

Linowes, Dr. D. F.
Professor
University of Illinois
308 Lincoln Hall
Urbana, IL 61801
217-333-0670   fax 217-333-5225
dlinowes@staff.uiuc.edu
Issues: Government waste; Privatization/
Contracting-out

Little, Margaret A.
Law Office of Margaret Little
2268 Main Street
Stratford, CT 06615
203-375-2844   fax 203-375-2910
peggy.little@att.net
Issues: Constitutional law; Judicial activism/
judicial reform; Regulation through litigation;
State and local government; Tort and liability
reform

Liu, Dr. Hsien-Tung
Dean, College of Liberal Arts
Bloomsburg University
400 East 2nd Street
Bloomsburg, PA 17815
570-389-4410   fax 570-389-3026
liu@bloomu.edu
Issues: Charter schools; China; Comparative
government; Higher education

Lloyd, Lindsay
Regional Program Direcotr, Central and
Eastern Europe
International Republican Institute
1225 Eye Street, N.W., Suite 700
Washington, DC 20005
202-408-9450   fax 202-408-9462
cee@iri.org
Issues: Central and Eastern Europe

Llumiquinga, Nelson
Executive Director
Arizona School Choice Trust
3737 East Broadway Road
Phoenix, AZ 85040
602-454-1360   fax 602-454-1362
Issues: Business and education partnerships;
School choice

*Loconte, Joseph
William E. Simon Fellow in Religion and a
Free Society
The Heritage Foundation
214 Massachusetts Avenue, N.E.
Washington, DC 20002
202-608-6164   fax 202-608-6136
joe.loconte@heritage.org
Issues: The American Founding; Church-state
relations; Faith-based and volunteer initiatives;
Religion and public life; Religious freedom

*Loewenberg, Robert J.
President
Institute for Advanced Strategic and Political
Studies
1020 16th Street, N.W., Suite 310
Washington, DC 20036
202-833-9716   fax 202-862-4981
iaspsdc@ponet.net
Issues: Comparative economics; Economic
development/foreign aid; Economic theory;
Emerging threats/threat assessment; Middle
East; Missile defense; Political philosophy;
Russia and Eurasia

Logan, Dr. Charles H.
Professor and Associate Head of Sociology,
Department of Sociology
University of Connecticut
U-2068
Storrs, CT 06269-2068
860-486-3477   fax 860-486-6356
logan@uconnvm.uconn.edu
Issues: Corrections and sentencing; Crime/
crime statistics; Privatization/Contracting-out

Logomasini, Angela
Director of Risk and Enviornmental Policy
Competitive Enterprise Institute
1001 Connecticut Avenue, N.W., Suite 1250
Washington, DC 20036
202-331-1010   fax 202-331-0640
alogomasini@cei.org
Issues: Environmental regulation; Free-market
environmentalism; Sound science; Waste
management; Water

*Logue, Dennis E.
Dean, Price College of Business
University of Oklahoma
Adams Hall, Room 207, 307 West Brooks
Norman, OK 73019-4007
405-325-3421   fax 405-325-2096
Issues: The Economy; Entrepreneurship/free
enterprise; Higher education; Money and
financial services; Regulation through
litigation

Lomas, Dr. Bernard T.
Counselor
The Heritage Foundation
218 West Barbee Chapel Road
Chapel Hill, NC 27517
919-945-0699   fax 919-945-0693
info@heritage.org
Issues: Business and education partnerships;
Higher education; Marriage and divorce;
Religion and public life; Standards,
curriculum, and testing

Lomasky, Loren E.
Professor, Philosophy Department
Bowling Green State University
305 Shatzel Hall
Bowling Green, OH 43403
419-372-7213   fax 419-372-8191
llomask@bgnet.bgsu.edu
Issues: Ethics; Health care reform; Political
philosophy

London, Dr. Herbert L.
President
Hudson Institute
Herman Kahn Center, 5395 Emerson Way
Indianapolis, IN 46226
317-545-1000   fax 317-545-9639
Issues: Comparative government; Economic
forecasting; Military strategy; Political
philosophy; School-to-work; Term limits

London, Josh
Policy Director
Jewish Policy Center
50 F Street, N.W., Suite 100
Washington, DC 20001
202-638-2411   fax 202-638-6694
london@jewish-policy.org
Issues: Middle East

*Long, Mike
Author and Speaker
Complete Abstinence Eduation Program
P. O. Box 61863
Durham, NC 27715-1863
919-309-9818   fax 919-309-0306
mikelong@mikelong.com
Issues: Abstinence and out-of-wedlock births;
Faith-based and volunteer initiatives; Family
and children; Federal education policy;
Government health programs; Home
schooling; Marriage and divorce; Media and
popular culture; Political correctness and
multiculturalism; Religion and public life;
Substance abuse; Welfare/welfare reform

*Long, Morgan
Director, Telecommunications and
Information Technology Task Force
American Legislative Exchange Council
1129 20th Street, N.W., Suite 500
Washington, DC 20036
202-466-3800   fax 202-466-3801
mlong@alec.org
Issues: Privacy; Telecommunications and the
Internet

Lopez, Dr. Carlos
Professor of Spanish
Menlo College
1000 El Camino
Atherton, CA 94027
650-543-3847   fax 508-664-1392
Issues: Latin America

Lopez, Dr. Edward J.
Assistant Professor, Department of
Economics
University of North Texas
P. O. Box 311457
Denton, TX 76203-1457
940-369-7005   fax 940-565-4426
elopez@unt.edu
Issues: Anti-trust; Campaign finance reform;
Congress; Economic theory; Initiative and
referendum; Social Security and retirement;
Term limits

Lopez-Cordero, Romulo
Director, Latin American Program
Atlas Economic Research Foundation
4084 University Drive, Suite 103
Fairfax, VA 22030
703-934-6969   fax 703-352-7530
romulo.lopez@atlasusa.org
Issues: Latin America

Lorence, Jordan
Senior Counsel
Alliance Defense Fund
15333 North Pima Drive, Suite 165
Scottsdale, AZ 85260
480-444-0020   fax 480-444-0025
jlorence@alliancedefensefund.org
Issues: Church-state relations; Constitutional
law; Free Speech; Judiciary; Marriage and
divorce; Religion and public life; Religious
freedom

Lott, Dr. John R., Jr.
Resident Scholar
American Enterprise Institute
1150 17th Street, N.W.
Washington, DC 20036
202-862-4884   fax 202-862-7177
jlott@aei.org
Issues: Anti-trust; Campaign finance reform;
Crime/crime statistics; Elections/polling;
Electoral reform/voting rights; Federal
education policy; Second Amendment

*Lovejoy, Dr. Stephen B.
Professor, Department of Agricultural
Economics
Purdue University
1145 Krannert Building, Number 649
West Lafayette, IN 47907
765-494-4245   fax 765-494-9176
lovejoy@purdue.edu
Issues: Agriculture; Climate change;
Environmental education; Environmental
regulation; Free-market environmentalism;
Land use; Property rights; Sound science;
Stewardship; Water

Lovelace, Telly L.
Director of External Affairs
Coalition on Urban Renewal and Education
126 C Street, N.W.
Washington, DC 20001
202-479-2873   fax 202-783-9376
tellylovelace@urbancure.org
Issues: Federal education policy; Social Security
and retirement; Welfare/welfare reform

Lozansky, Dr. Edward D.
President
American University in Moscow
1800 Connecticut Avenue, N.W.
Washington, DC 20009
202-986-6010   fax 202-667-4244
lozansky@aol.com
Issues: Higher education; Missile defense;
NATO and other alliances; Russia and Eurasia

Lucier, James
First Vice President
Prudential Securities
1911 North Fort Myer Drive, Suite 905
Arlington, VA 22202
703-358-2987   fax 703-358-2977
Issues: Anti-trust; China; Costs and benefits of
regulation; Electricity deregulation;
Environmental regulation; Federal budget;
Intellectual property; International tax policy/
tax competition; Japan; Korea; Money and
financial services; Privacy; Taxation/tax
reform; Telecommunications and the Internet;
Transportation deregulation

Ludwikowski, Rett R.
Director, Comparative and International
Law, Columbus School of Law
Catholic University of America
620 Michigan Avenue, N.E.
Washington, DC 20064
202-319-5557   fax 202-319-4459
ludwikowski@law.cua.edu
Issues: Central and Eastern Europe;
Comparative government; Human rights

*Lund, Nelson
Professor of Law
George Mason University School of Law
3301 North Fairfax Drive
Arlington, VA 22201
703-993-8045   fax 703-993-8088
nlund@gmu.edu
Issues: Civil rights/racial preferences;
Constitutional law; Electoral reform/voting
rights; Executive Branch/The Presidency;
Federalism; Political philosophy; Second
Amendment

Luntz, Dr. Frank
President
Luntz Research Companies
1000 Wilson Boulevard, Suite 950
Arlington, VA 22209
703-358-0080   fax 703-358-0089
Issues: Elections/polling; Initiative and
referendum; Media and popular culture

Lutter, Dr. Randall
Resident Scholar
American Enterprise Institute
1150 17th Street, N.W.
Washington, DC 20036
202-862-5885   fax 202-862-7169
rlutter@aei.org
Issues: Air; Climate change; Costs and benefits
of regulation; Environmental regulation;
Regulatory reform

*Luttwak, Edward N.
Senior Fellow
Center for Strategic and International
Studies
1800 K Street, N.W., Suite 400
Washington, DC 20006
301-656-1972   fax 301-907-8164
Issues: Defense budget; Economic theory;
Emerging threats/threat assessment;
Homeland security/civil defense; Latin
America; Middle East; Military strategy; NATO
and other alliances; Terrorism and
international crime

Luxemberg, Alan
Vice President
Foreign Policy Research Institute
1528 Walnut Street, Suite 610
Philadelphia, PA 19102
215-732-3774   fax 215-732-4401
al@fpri.org
Issues: American diplomacy/foreign policy

Lynch, Dr. Frederick R.
Associate Professor of Government
Claremont McKenna College
850 Columbia Avenue
Claremont, CA 91711
909-607-3799   fax 909-621-8249
fred_lynch@mckenna.edu
Issues: Civil rights/racial preferences;
Immigration; Labor and employment; Political
correctness and multiculturalism; Political
philosophy

Lynch, Michael
National Correspondent
Reason Magazine
50 Vista Terrace
New Haven, CT 06520
203-389-6036
Issues: Civil rights/racial preferences; Health
care reform; Right to work; School choice

---

*Lynch, Timothy
Director, Project on Criminal Justice
Cato Institute
1000 Massachusetts Avenue, N.W.
Washington, DC 20001
202-842-0200   fax 202-842-3490
tlynch@cato.org
Issues: Constitutional law; Criminal law and procedure; Police

MacAvoy, Dr. Paul W.
Williams Brothers Professor of Management Studies
Yale School of Management
135 Prospect Street, P. O. Box 208200
New Haven, CT 06511
203-432-6179   fax 203-432-6185
paul.macavoy@yale.edu
Issues: Costs and benefits of regulation; Electricity deregulation; Regulation through litigation; Regulatory budgeting; Regulatory reform; Risk assessment; Transportation deregulation

MacDonald, Glenn M.
Professor, Olin School of Business
Washington University
Campus Box 1133, One Brookings Drive
St. Louis, MO 63130-4899
314-935-7768   fax 314-935-6359
macdonald@olin.wustl.edu
Issues: Economic theory

*MacDonald, Heather
John M. Olin Fellow
Manhattan Institute for Policy Research
52 Vanderbilt Avenue
New York, NY 10017
212-599-7000   fax 212-599-3494
Issues: Abstinence and out-of-wedlock births; Adoption, foster care, & child care services; Bilingual education; Civil rights/racial preferences; Crime/crime statistics; Family and children; Higher education; Homeland security/civil defense; Housing and homelessness; Intelligence gathering and covert operations; Police; Political correctness and multiculturalism; Poverty and dependency; Standards, curriculum, and testing; Substance abuse; Welfare/welfare reform

*Macey, Johnathon R.
J. DuPratt White Professor of Law, School of Law
Cornell University
Myron Taylor Hall
Ithaca, NY 14853
607-255-3469   fax 607-255-7193
jrm29@cornell.edu
Issues: Ethics; Federalism; Judiciary; Money and financial services; Regulatory reform

Machan, Dr. Tibor R.
Professor
Chapman University
28271 Bond Way, P. O. Box 64
Silverado Canyon, CA 92676
714-649-4464   fax 714-649-9225
machan@chapman.edu
Issues: Citizenship and civil society; Civil rights/racial preferences; Comparative government; Costs and benefits of regulation; Ethics; Human rights; Marriage and divorce; Philanthropy; Political philosophy; Privatization/Contracting-out; Regulatory reform; School choice

Mack, Dr. Eric
Professor, Department of Philosophy
Tulane University
105D Newcomb Hall
New Orleans, LA 70118
504-862-3389   fax 504-862-8714
Issues: Ethics; Political correctness and multiculturalism; Political philosophy; Religion and public life

Mackey, Connie
Director of Federal Relations
Family Research Council
801 G Street, N.W.
Washington, DC 20001
202-393-2100   fax 202-737-3604
cgm@frc.org
Issues: Congress; Family and children; Political correctness and multiculturalism

MacLellan, Lisa
Vice President, Public Policy
Pacific Research Institute
755 Sansome Street, Suite 450
San Francisco, CA 94111
415-989-0833   fax 415-989-2411
lmaclellan@pacificresearch.org
Issues: Climate change; Property rights; Trade; Wildlife management/endangered species

Madigan, Dr. Kathleen
Executive Director
National Council on Teacher Quality
1225 19th Street, N.W., Suite 400
Washington, DC 20036-2411
202-261-2622   kmadigan@nctq.org
Issues: Charter schools; Standards, curriculum, and testing

Madsen, Dr. David W.
Director, Honors Program
Seattle University
900 Broadway
Seattle, WA 98122
206-296-5306   fax 206-296-5997
dmadsen@seattleu.edu
Issues: Religion and public life

Magbee, Brett A.
Executive Director
Oklahoma Council of Public Affairs
100 West Wilshire Boulevard, Suite C-3
Oklahoma City, OK 73116
405-843-9212   fax 405-843-9436
bamagbee@yahoo.com
Issues: Entrepreneurship/free enterprise; Home schooling; Property rights; Right to work; State and local government; State-sponsored gambling; Term limits

Magnet, Myron
Editor, *City Journal*
Manhattan Institute for Policy Research
52 Vanderbilt Avenue
New York, NY 10017
212-599-7000   fax 212-599-0371
magnet@city-journal.org
Issues: Citizenship and civil society; Family and children; Philanthropy; Political correctness and multiculturalism; School choice; Welfare/welfare reform

*Maguire, Rita P.
Arizona Center for Public Policy
432 North 44th Street, Suite 360
Phoenix, AZ 85008
602-275-1110   fax 602-275-2592
rpmaguire@thinkaz.org
Issues: Aging/elder care; Agriculture; Bilingual education; Campaign finance reform; Charter schools; Climate change; Comparative economics; Constitutional law; Economic forecasting; Education unions and interest groups; Elections/polling; Electricity deregulation; Energy; Entitlement spending; Environmental regulation; Family and children; Federalism; Forestry and national parks; Health care reform; Immigration; Initiative and referendum; Land use; Mexico; Minimum wage; Property rights; Public school finance and administration; Risk assessment; School choice; Social Security and retirement; Standards, curriculum, and testing; State and local government; State and local public finance; State-sponsored gambling; Stewardship; Telecommunications and the Internet; Term limits; Tort and liability reform; Transportation; Urban sprawl/livable cities; Water; Welfare/welfare reform; Wildlife management/endangered species

Mahaney, Lara
Director of Corporate and Entertainment Affairs
Parents Television Council
707 Wilshire Boulevard, Suited 2075
Los Angeles, CA 90017
213-629-9255   fax 213-629-9254
lmahaney@parentstv.org
Issues: Media and popular culture

Maher, Bridget
Policy Analyst on Marriage and Family
Family Research Council
801 G Street, N.W.
Washington, DC 20001
202-393-2100   fax 202-393-2134
Issues: Family and children; Marriage and divorce

Mahoney, J. J.
Managing Director
Diversified Consultants
1602 Porcher's Bluff
Mount Pleasant, SC 29466
843-884-8654   fax 843-881-1461
jjconsult@mindspring.com
Issues: Church-state relations;
Entrepreneurship/free enterprise; Federalism;
Political correctness and multiculturalism;
Privatization/Contracting-out; Right to work;
School choice

Mahoney, Mary P.
Vice President of Government Relations
United Seniors Association, Inc.
209 Pennsylvania Avenue, S.E.
Washington, DC 20003
202-454-5205   fax 202-454-5296
mmunitedseniors@aol.com
Issues: Aging/elder care; Campaign finance
reform; Congress; Constitutional law;
Discretionary spending; The Economy;
Electoral reform/voting rights; Entitlement
spending; Government health programs;
Health care reform; Homeland security/civil
defense; Immigration; Initiative and
referendum; Judiciary; Medicare; NATO and
other alliances; Non-governmental
organizations; Poverty and dependency;
Privacy; Social Security and retirement; State
and local government; Term limits; Tort and
liability reform

*Maickel, Dr. Roger P.
Professor Emeritus of Pharmacology and
Toxicology
Purdue University
3567 Canterbury Drive
Lafayette, IN 47909-3714
765-474-2855   fax 765-474-3724
Issues: Aging/elder care; Air; Environmental
education; Environmental regulation; Federal
education policy; Government health
programs; Higher education; Medicare;
Standards, curriculum, and testing; Substance
abuse; Water

*Maitre, Dr. H. Joachim
Director
Center for Defense Journalism
Boston University, 152 Bay State Road
Boston, MA 02215
617-353-9390   fax 617-353-9290
Issues: Afghanistan; Africa; Defense budget;
Military strategy; NATO and other alliances;
Terrorism and international crime

*Makin, John H.
Resident Scholar
American Enterprise Institute
1150 17th Street, N.W.
Washington, DC 20036
202-862-5828   fax 202-862-7177
jmakin@caxton.com
Issues: Economic forecasting; Economic theory;
The Economy; Entitlement spending; Federal
budget; Government debt; Japan; Money and
financial services; Northeast Asia; Taxation/tax
reform; Trade

*Malcolm, Dr. Joyce L.
Professor, Department of History
Bentley College
175 Forest Street
Waltham, MA 02452
781-891-3484   fax 781-891-3410
jmalcolm@bentley.edu
Issues: Constitutional law; Second Amendment

Malek, John M.
Founder and President
Polish-American Foundation for Economic
Research and Education
P. O. Box 1475
Torrance, CA 90505
310-316-6888   fax 310-316-6888
pafere@cs.com
Issues: Central and Eastern Europe; Economic
education

Malik, Dr. Hafeez
Professor of Political Science
Villanova University
416 SAC
Villanova, PA 19085
610-519-4738   fax 610-519-6419
hafeez.malik@villanova.edu
Issues: Afghanistan; Arms control; Emerging
threats/threat assessment; Export controls/
military transfers; Middle East; NATO and
other alliances; Promoting democracy/public
diplomacy; Russia and Eurasia; South Asia
(including India and Pakistan); Terrorism and
international crime

*Malloy, Ken
President
Center for the Advancement of Energy
Markets
1050 17th Street, N.W., Suite 600
Washington, DC 20036
202-496-4972   fax 248-928-5040
kmalloy@caem.org
Issues: Costs and benefits of regulation;
Electricity deregulation; Energy; Infrastructure

*Maltsev, Dr. Yuri N.
Professor of Economics
Carthage College
2001 Alford Park Drive
Kenosha, WI 53140
262-551-5880   fax 262-551-6208
yuri@carthage.edu
Issues: Afghanistan; Central and Eastern
Europe; Comparative economics; Economic
development/foreign aid; Economic theory;
The Economy; Health care reform;
Immigration; International organizations
(European Union, OECD, etc.); International
tax policy/tax competition; Poverty and
dependency; Promoting democracy/public
diplomacy; Russia and Eurasia

*Mandel, Dr. Robert
Chairman and Professor, International
Affairs Department
Lewis and Clark College
0615 S.W. Palatine Hill Road
Portland, OR 97219
503-768-7633   fax 503-768-7379
mandel@lclark.edu
Issues: Africa; Arms control; Canada; Central
and Eastern Europe; Economic development/
foreign aid; Emerging threats/threat
assessment; Export controls/military transfers;
Intelligence gathering and covert operations;
Latin America; Middle East; Missile defense;
NATO and other alliances; Northeast Asia;
Promoting democracy/public diplomacy;
Russia and Eurasia; South Asia (including India
and Pakistan); Southeast Asia (including
Burma, Cambodia, Laos, Vietnam, Singapore,
Malaysia, Indonesia, the Philippines, Australia,
and New Zealand); United Nations; Western
Europe

Mandina, Mario
CEO
National Lawyers Association
P. O. Box 1923
Independence, MO 64055
800-471-2994   fax 816-350-0018
Issues: Church-state relations; Constitutional
law; Federalism; Free Speech; Judicial
activism/judicial reform; Judiciary; Religious
freedom; Second Amendment; Tort and
liability reform

Manne, Dr. Henry G.
Visiting Professor
University of Chicago Law School
1111 East 60th Street
Chicago, IL 60637
239-596-7972   henry@themannes.com
Issues: Comparative economics; Costs and
benefits of regulation; Economic education;
Family and children; Higher education;
Philanthropy; Political correctness and
multiculturalism

Manning, Dr. Willard G.
Professor, Department of Health Studies
University of Chicago
5841 South Maryland Avenue, MC 2007
Chicago, IL 60637
773-834-1971   fax 773-702-1979
w-manning@uchicago.edu
Issues: Health care reform

*Mannix, Brian
Senior Research Fellow
Mercatus Center at George Mason University
3301 North Fairfax Drive, Suite 450
Arlington, VA 22201
703-993-4934   fax 703-993-4935
bmannix@gmu.edu
Issues: Air; Climate change; Costs and benefits
of regulation; Energy; Environmental
regulation; Free-market environmentalism;
Regulatory reform; Risk assessment; Water

*Manno, Dr. Bruno V.
Senior Program Associate
The Annie E. Casey Foundation
701 St. Paul Street
Baltimore, MD 21202
410-223-2938   fax 410-223-2983
brunom@aecf.org
Issues: Business and education partnerships;
Charter schools; Federal education policy;
School choice; Standards, curriculum, and
testing

*Mansfield, Dennis
Consultant
8500 Stynbrook
Boise, ID 83704
208-375-8814   fax 208-375-3299
Issues: Abstinence and out-of-wedlock births;
The American Founding; American history/
political tradition; China; Congress;
Conservative thought; Faith-based and
volunteer initiatives; Family and children;
Home schooling; Korea; Land use; Marriage
and divorce; Media and popular culture; Non-
governmental organizations; Political
philosophy; Property rights; Religion and
public life; School choice; State and local
government; State-sponsored gambling;
Telecommunications and the Internet; Term
limits

Mansfield, Dr. Harvey C.
Professor, Department of Government
Harvard University
Littauer Center M-31
Cambridge, MA 02138
617-495-3333   fax 617-495-0438
h_mansfield@harvard.edu
Issues: The American Founding; Conservative
thought; Ethics; Political philosophy

Mantilla, Yuri
Counsel for Hispanic Affairs and Human
Rights
Family Research Council
801 G Street, N.W.
Washington, DC 20001
202-393-2100   fax 202-393-2134
yurim@frc.org
Issues: Civil rights/racial preferences; Human
rights; International law; Latin America;
Religious freedom; Russia and Eurasia; United
Nations

Marion, Dr. David E.
Director, Wilson Center for Leadership in
the Public Interest
Hampden-Sydney College
P. O. Box 94
Hampden-Sydney, VA 23943
434-223-6240   fax 434-223-6045
damarion@hsc.edu
Issues: Constitutional law; Executive Branch/
The Presidency; Federalism; Free Speech;
Judicial activism/judicial reform; Judiciary

Mariotti, Steve
President
National Foundation for Teaching
Entrepreneurship
120 Wall Street, 29th Floor
New York, NY 10005
212-232-3333   fax 212-232-2244
info@nfte.com
Issues: Business and education partnerships;
Economic education; Juvenile justice; Urban
sprawl/livable cities

*Marks, Jeff
Director, Air Quality
National Association of Manufacturers
1331 Pennsylvania Avenue, N.W.
Washington, DC 20004
202-637-3176   fax 202-637-3182
jmarks@nam.org
Issues: Air; Federalism

Marlow, Dr. Michael
Professor of Economics, Department of
Economics
California Polytechnic State University
San Luis Obispo, CA 93407
805-756-1764   fax 815-361-1995
mmarlow@calpoly.edu
Issues: Costs and benefits of regulation;
Federalism; Public school finance and
administration; School choice; Taxation/tax
reform

*Marotz-Baden, Dr. Ramona
Professor of Family and Consumer Sciences,
Department of Health and Human
Development
Montana State University
HK 318
Bozeman, MT 59717
406-994-5017   fax 406-994-2013
ramonam@montana.edu
Issues: Citizenship and civil society; Family and
children; Marriage and divorce

Marquardt, Elizabeth
Affiliate Scholar
Institute for American Values
1841 Broadway, Suite 211
New York, NY 10023
212-246-3942   fax 212-541-6665
Issues: Family and children; Marriage and
divorce

*Marshall, Dr. J. Stanley
Founder
The James Madison Institute
P. O. Box 37460
Tallahassee, FL 32315
850-386-3131   fax 850-386-1807
jmi@jamesmadison.org
Issues: Charter schools; Higher education;
School choice

Marshall, Jennifer
Policy Analyst and Government Relations
Liaison
Empower America
1801 K Street, N.W., Suite 410
Washington, DC 20006
202-452-8200   fax 202-833-0388
Issues: Charter schools; Education unions and
interest groups; Federal education policy;
Home schooling; School choice; School-to-
work; Standards, curriculum, and testing

*Marshner, Connie
President
Raphael Services
804 Rodney Avenue
Front Royal, VA 22630
540-636-7842   fax 540-636-7937
melkite@aol.com
Issues: Abstinence and out-of-wedlock births;
Adoption, foster care, & child care services;
Family and children; Home schooling

Martin, Dr. Deryl W.
Professor of Finance
Tennessee Technological University
P. O. Box 5083
Cookeville, TN 38505
931-372-3871   fax 931-372-6249
dwmartin@tntech.edu
Issues: The Economy; Money and financial
services; Political philosophy; Privatization/
Contracting-out; Trade

*Martin, Jerry L.
President
American Council of Trustees and Alumni
1726 M Street, N.W., Suite 800
Washington, DC 20036
202-467-6787   fax 202-467-6784
info@goacta.org
Issues: American history/political tradition;
Arts, humanities and historic resources;
Business and education partnerships;
Citizenship and civil society; Ethics; Federal
education policy; Higher education;
Philanthropy; Political correctness and
multiculturalism; Political philosophy;
Standards, curriculum, and testing

*Martin, Jim
President
60 Plus Association
1600 Wilson Boulevard, Suite 960
Arlington, VA 22209
703-807-2070   fax 703-807-2073
jmartin@60plus.org
Issues: Advocacy and nonprofit public funding;
Aging/elder care; Electricity deregulation;
Entitlement spending; Faith-based and
volunteer initiatives; Intellectual property;
Medicare; Missile defense; Social Security and
retirement; Taxation/tax reform; Wealth
creation/financial empowerment

Martin, Mary
Chairman of the Board and Executive
Director
The Seniors Coalition
9001 Braddock Road, Suite 200
Springfield, VA 22151
703-239-1960   fax 703-239-1985
tsc@senior.org
Issues: Aging/elder care; Medicare; Regulatory
reform; Social Security and retirement;
Taxation/tax reform

Marty, Dr. William R.
Professor of Political Science
University of Memphis
437 Clement Hall
Memphis, TN 38152
901-678-3348   fax 901-678-2983
wrmarty@memphis.edu
Issues: Church-state relations; Religion and
public life

*Marzulla, Nancie G.
President and Chief Legal Counsel
Defenders of Property Rights
1350 Connecticut Avenue, N.W., Suite 410
Washington, DC 20036
202-822-6770   fax 202-822-6774
nancie@yourpropertyrights.org
Issues: Air; Climate change; Conservative
thought; Constitutional law; Energy;
Environmental education; Environmental
regulation; Federalism; Forestry and national
parks; Free-market environmentalism;
Intellectual property; Judicial activism/judicial
reform; Land use; Property rights; Public
interest law; Regulation through litigation;
Regulatory reform; Sound science;
Stewardship; Urban sprawl/livable cities;
Water; Wildlife management/endangered
species

*Marzulla, Roger J.
General Counsel
Defenders of Property Rights
1350 Connecticut Avenue, N.W., Suite 410
Washington, DC 20036
202-822-6760   fax 202-822-6774
roger@marzulla.com
Issues: Air; Climate change; Conservative
thought; Constitutional law; Costs and benefits
of regulation; Electricity deregulation; Energy;
Environmental education; Environmental
regulation; Federalism; Forestry and national
parks; Free-market environmentalism;
Intellectual property; Judicial activism/judicial
reform; Judiciary; Land use; Property rights;
Public interest law; Regulation through
litigation; Regulatory budgeting; Regulatory
reform; Risk assessment; Sound science; State
and local government; Stewardship; Urban
sprawl/livable cities; Water; Wildlife
management/endangered species

*Masugi, Ken
Director, Center for Local Government
Claremont Institute
250 West First Street, Suite 330
Claremont, CA 91711
909-621-6825   fax 909-626-8724
kmasugi@claremont.org
Issues: The American Founding; American
history/political tradition; Arts, humanities
and historic resources; Citizenship and civil
society; Civil rights/racial preferences;
Conservative thought; Constitutional law;
Ethics; Executive Branch/The Presidency;
Higher education; Immigration; Judiciary;
Political correctness and multiculturalism;
Political philosophy; State and local
government; State and local public finance

Mataxis, Brig. Gen. Theodore C., USA (Ret.)
American Military University
111 Emerson Street, Number 923
Denver, CO 80218
303-282-0110   metaxissr@msn.org
Issues: Afghanistan; Higher education; South
Asia (including India and Pakistan); Southeast
Asia (including Burma, Cambodia, Laos,
Vietnam, Singapore, Malaysia, Indonesia, the
Philippines, Australia, and New Zealand);
United Nations

Mathys, John N.
Associate Professor of Finance
DePaul University
565 South Poplar Avenue
Elmhurst, IL 60126-4017
630-279-2463   fax 312-362-6566
jmathys@wppost.depaul.edu
Issues: Entitlement spending; Environmental
regulation; Free-market environmentalism;
Medicare; Social Security and retirement;
Taxation/tax reform

Matteo, Dr. Anthony M.
Professor, Department of Philosophy
Elizabethtown College
One Alpha Drive
Elizabethtown, PA 17022
717-361-1346   matteoam@etown.edu
Issues: Ethics; Higher education

Matthews, Merrill, Jr., Ph.D.
Visiting Scholar
Institute for Policy Innovation
250 South Stemmons, Suite 215
Lewisville, TX 75067
972-874-5139   fax 972-874-5144
policyguy1@aol.com
Issues: Aging/elder care; American history/
political tradition; Conservative thought;
Ethics; Government health programs; Health
care reform; Intellectual property; Medicaid;
Medicare; Political philosophy; Social Security
and retirement; Telecommunications and the
Internet; Welfare/welfare reform

Mauren, Kris Alan
Executive Director
Acton Institute for the Study of Religion and
Liberty
161 Ottawa Avenue, N.W., Suite 301
Grand Rapids, MI 49503
616-454-3080   fax 616-454-9454
kmauren@acton.org
Issues: Economic education; Ethics; Faith-based
and volunteer initiatives; Religion and public
life

Maurer, Paul
Senior Vice President for Institutional
Advancement
Trinity International University
2065 Half Day Road
Deerfield, IL 60015
847-317-8106   fax 847-317-4050
pmaurer@tiu.edu
Issues: The American Founding; Church-state
relations; Ethics; Executive Branch/The
Presidency; Philanthropy; Political philosophy;
Religion and public life

Max, Derrick A.
Executive Director
Alliance for Worker Retirement Security
1331 Pennsylvania Avenue, N.W., Suite 600
Washington, DC 20004-1290
202-637-3453   fax 202-637-3182
dmax@awrs.org
Issues: Entitlement spending; Federal budget;
Social Security and retirement; Taxation/tax
reform; Unfunded mandates

May, Clifford D.
Executive Director
The Foundation for the Defense of
Democracies
1020 19th Street, N.W., Suite 340
Washington, DC 20036
202-207-0190   fax 202-207-0191
Issues: Afghanistan; Africa; American
diplomacy/foreign policy; Homeland security/
civil defense; Human rights; Immigration;
Intelligence gathering and covert operations;
International law; Middle East; Promoting
democracy/public diplomacy; Russia and
Eurasia; Terrorism and international crime

May, Colby
Senior Counsel
American Center for Law and Justice
1650 Diagonal Road, Suite 500
Alexandria, VA 22314-2857
202-337-2273   fax 202-337-3167
cmmaclj@aol.com
Issues: Church-state relations; Civil rights/racial
preferences; Constitutional law; Free Speech;
Religious freedom

*May, Nina
Publisher
Renaissance Connection.com/RCNetwork.net
205 3rd Street, S.E.
Washington, DC 20005
202-546-4142   fax 703-790-0070
ninaomay@aol.com
Issues: Adoption, foster care, & child care
services; Africa; Arts, humanities and historic
resources; Civil rights/racial preferences;
Constitutional law; Entrepreneurship/free
enterprise; Faith-based and volunteer
initiatives; Family and children; Free Speech;
Home schooling; Homeland security/civil
defense; Human rights; International
organizations (European Union, OECD, etc.);
Korea; Media and popular culture; Missile
defense; Political correctness and
multiculturalism; Promoting democracy/
public diplomacy; Property rights; Religious
freedom; School choice; Second Amendment;
Trade; United Nations

*May, Randolph J.
Senior Fellow and Director of
Communications Policy Studies
Progress & Freedom Foundation
1401 H Street, N.W., Suite 1075
Washington, DC 20005
202-289-8928   fax 202-289-6079
rmay@pff.org
Issues: Constitutional law; Costs and benefits of
regulation; Federalism; Free Speech;
Intellectual property; Privacy; Regulatory
reform; Telecommunications and the Internet

*Mayer, Dr. David N.
Professor of Law and History
Capital University Law School
303 East Broad Street
Columbus, OH 43215-3200
614-236-6561   fax 614-236-6956
dmayer@law.capital.edu
Issues: The American Founding; American
history/political tradition; Anti-trust; Congress;
Constitutional law; Executive Branch/The
Presidency; Federalism; Intellectual property;
Judicial activism/judicial reform; Judiciary;
Political philosophy; Religious freedom;
School choice; Second Amendment; Term
limits

*McCarthy, Jack
Managing Director
AppleTree Institute for Education
Innovation
101 D Street, S.E., 2nd Floor
Washington, DC 20003
202-544-6530   fax 202-544-8678
jackmacapp@aol.com
Issues: Charter schools; Federal education
policy; School choice

*McCarthy, Vern I., Jr.
Director
Mid-America Institute
P. O. Box 5047
Oak Brook, IL 60522
630-971-8500   fax 630-971-8530
vim@smartgate.com
Issues: Citizenship and civil society; Elections/
polling; Political correctness and
multiculturalism; State and local government

*McClaughry, John
President
Ethan Allen Institute
4836 Kirby Mountain Road
Concord, VT 05824
802-695-1448   fax 802-695-1436
eai@ethanallen.org
Issues: Agriculture; Energy; Environmental
regulation; Faith-based and volunteer
initiatives; Federalism; Free-market
environmentalism; Government health
programs; Health care reform; Initiative and
referendum; Land use; Medicaid; Property
rights; Public school finance and
administration; The Reagan legacy; School
choice; State and local government; State and
local public finance; Taxation/tax reform;
Wealth creation/financial empowerment;
Welfare/welfare reform

McClay, Dr. Wilfred M.
SunTrust Chair of Excellence in Humanities
University of Tennessee, Chattanooga
615 McCallie Avenue
Chattanooga, TN 37403
423-755-5202   fax 423-755-5393
mcclay@mindspring.com
Issues: The American Founding; American
history/political tradition; Arts, humanities
and historic resources; Citizenship and civil
society; Conservative thought; Faith-based and
volunteer initiatives; Higher education; Home
schooling; Political correctness and
multiculturalism; Political philosophy;
Religion and public life

*McClusky, Tom
Senior Policy Analyst
National Taxpayers Union Foundation
108 North Alfred Street
Alexandria, VA 22314
703-683-5700   fax 703-683-5722
mcclusky@ntu.org
Issues: Congress; Elections/polling; Executive
Branch/The Presidency; Faith-based and
volunteer initiatives; Federal budget; Federal
education policy; Government waste;
Homeland security/civil defense

*McConnell, Michael W.
Professor of Law, College of Law
University of Utah
322 South, 1400 East, Room 101
Salt Lake City, UT 84112
801-581-6342   fax 801-581-6897
mcconnellm@law.utah.edu
Issues: Church-state relations; Constitutional law; Faith-based and volunteer initiatives; Federalism; Home schooling; Judicial activism/judicial reform; Religion and public life; School choice; State and local government

*McCormack, Hon. Richard T.
Counselor
Center for the Study of the Presidency
1029 19th Street, N.W., Suite 250
Washington, DC 20036
202-872-9800   fax 202-872-9811
Issues: American diplomacy/foreign policy; International finance and multilateral banks; Japan; Latin America

*McCormick, Dr. Bobby
Professor of Economics and BB&T Scholar
Clemson University
222 Sirrine Hall
Clemson, SC 29634-1309
864-656-3441   fax 864-868-5767
sixmile@clemson.edu
Issues: Air; Climate change; Costs and benefits of regulation; Electricity deregulation; Energy; Forestry and national parks; Free-market environmentalism; Property rights; Telecommunications and the Internet; Transportation deregulation

*McCracken, Dr. Paul W.
Edmund Ezra Day Distinguished University Professor Emeritus
University of Michigan Business School
701 Tappan, D3233 Davidson Hall
Ann Arbor, MI 48109
734-764-1581   fax 734-936-0279
Issues: Economic forecasting; The Economy; Entrepreneurship/free enterprise; Money and financial services

McCulloch, Dr. J. Huston
Professor, Economics and Finance
Ohio State University
1945 North High Street
Columbus, OH 43210
614-292-0382   fax 614-292-3906
mcculloch.2@osu.edu
Issues: Government debt; Money and financial services; Social Security and retirement

*McCulloch, Dr. Rachel
Rosen Family Professor of International Finance, Graduate School of International Economics and Finance
Brandeis University
Sachar 124, Mailstop 021
Waltham, MA 02454
781-736-2245   fax 781-736-2269
mcculloch@brandeis.edu
Issues: Economic development/foreign aid; International finance and multilateral banks; Trade

McCulloch, Dr. Wendell H., Jr.
Director of International Business Programs
California State University, Long Beach
1250 Bellflower Boulevard
Long Beach, CA 90840
562-985-4565   fax 562-985-5543
Issues: American diplomacy/foreign policy; Export controls/military transfers; Intelligence gathering and covert operations; International finance and multilateral banks; International law; International organizations (European Union, OECD, etc.); Privatization/Contracting-out; The Reagan legacy; Religion and public life; Trade; Unions

*McCutchen, Kelly
Executive Vice President
Georgia Public Policy Foundation
6100 Lake Forest Drive, N.W., Suite 110
Atlanta, GA 30328
404-256-4050   fax 404-256-9909
kmccutchen@gppf.org
Issues: Free-market environmentalism; Privatization/Contracting-out; Taxation/tax reform; Urban sprawl/livable cities

McDaniel, Capt. Eugene "Red", USN (Ret.)
President
American Defense Institute
1055 North Fairfax Street, Suite 200
Alexandria, VA 22314
703-519-7000   fax 703-519-8627
Issues: Arms control; Central and Eastern Europe; Defense budget; Emerging threats/threat assessment; Export controls/military transfers; Latin America; Middle East; Military strategy; Missile defense; NATO and other alliances; Northeast Asia; Readiness and manpower; South Asia (including India and Pakistan); United Nations; Western Europe

*McDonald, Dr. Forrest
Distinguished University Research Professor Emeritus
University of Alabama
P. O. Box 155
Coker, AL 35452
205-339-0317   fax 205-348-0670
Issues: The American Founding; American history/political tradition; Constitutional law; Executive Branch/The Presidency; Federalism; Higher education; Political philosophy

McDonald, Olivia M., Ph.D.
Associate Professor of Public Policy and Director, Center for Applied Domestic and International Policy Studies
Regent University
1000 Regent University Drive
Virginia Beach, VA 23464-9800
757-226-4305   fax 757-226-4735
olivmcd@regent.edu
Issues: Economic development/foreign aid; Emerging threats/threat assessment; Federal civil service; Federalism; Government health programs; Homeland security/civil defense; Housing and homelessness; Human rights; Latin America; Mexico; Non-governmental organizations; Peacekeeping; Poverty and dependency; Readiness and manpower; Terrorism and international crime

McDonald, Prof. W. Wesley
Associate Professor of Political Science and Chairman, Department of Political Science
Elizabethtown College
One Alpha Drive, Nicarry 247
Elizabethtown, PA 17022
717-361-1306   fax 717-361-3688
mcdonaldw@etown.edu
Issues: American history/political tradition; Arts, humanities and historic resources; Conservative thought; Higher education; Political correctness and multiculturalism; Political philosophy

McDuffie, Dr. Jerome Anthony
Professor of History (retired)
University of North Carolina, Pembroke
P. O. Box 1636
Lumberton, NC 28359-1186
910-738-5187   fax 910-738-7071
jmcd_2@msn.com
Issues: Charter schools; Higher education; Korea; South Asia (including India and Pakistan); Southeast Asia (including Burma, Cambodia, Laos, Vietnam, Singapore, Malaysia, Indonesia, the Philippines, Australia, and New Zealand); Standards, curriculum, and testing

McGarrell, Edmund
Senior Fellow and Director, Crime Control Policy Center
Hudson Institute
Herman Kahn Center, 5395 Emerson Way
Indianapolis, IN 46226
317-545-1000   fax 317-545-9639
edmc@hudson.org
Issues: Corrections and sentencing; Crime/crime statistics; Juvenile justice; Police; Substance abuse

McGarry, Kathleen
President
Murray Hill Institute
243 Lexington Avenue
New York, NY 10016
646-742-2845   fax 646-742-2851
kmcgarry@mhplace.org
Issues: Citizenship and civil society; Family and children; Religion and public life

*McGee, Robert W.
Professor, Andreas School of Business
Barry University
11300 Northeast Second Avenue
Miami Shores, FL 33161-6695
305-899-3525   fax 305-892-6412
bob414@hotmail.com
Issues: Central and Eastern Europe; Ethics; International tax policy/tax competition; Political philosophy; Taxation/tax reform; Trade

*McGeein, Hon. Marty
President
McGeein Group
8003 Custer Road
Bethesda, MD 20814-1349
301-907-9495   fax 301-951-8003
mcggroup@erols.com
Issues: Family and children; Government health
programs; Health care reform; Medicaid; Tort
and liability reform

McGinnis, John O.
Professor of Law
Cardozo School of Law
55 Fifth Avenue
New York, NY 10003
212-790-0200   fax 212-790-0205
mcginnis@ymail.yu.edu
Issues: Campaign finance reform; Civil rights/
racial preferences; Conservative thought;
Constitutional law; Costs and benefits of
regulation; Entitlement spending; Executive
Branch/The Presidency; Federal budget;
Federalism; Judicial activism/judicial reform;
Judiciary; Political correctness and
multiculturalism; Political philosophy; The
Reagan legacy; Regulatory budgeting;
Regulatory reform; Risk assessment; School
choice; Taxation/tax reform; Trade

McGroarty, Daniel
Senior Director
White House Writer's Group
6817 Brookville Road
Chevy Chase, MD 20815-3249
301-951-7005   fax 301-951-7006
mackhan@aol.com
Issues: Education unions and interest groups;
Elections/polling; Executive Branch/The
Presidency; School choice

McHugh, Joseph P.
Reed Smith LLP
435 6th Avenue
Pittsburgh, PA 15219
412-288-7236   fax 412-288-3063
jmchugh@reedsmith.com
Issues: Labor and employment

*McIlheney, Joe S., Jr., M.D.
President
Medical Institute for Sexual Health
P. O. Box 162306
Austin, TX 78716
512-328-6268   fax 512-328-6269
jmcilhaney@medinstitute.org
Issues: Abstinence and out-of-wedlock births

McIntyre, Dave
Deputy Director for Research
ANSER Institute for Homeland Security
2900 South Quincy Street, Suite 800
Arlington, VA 22206
703-416-4748   fax 703-416-1306
dave.mcintyre@anser.org
Issues: American diplomacy/foreign policy;
Arts, humanities and historic resources;
Emerging threats/threat assessment; Higher
education; Homeland security/civil defense;
Military strategy; Terrorism and international
crime

McKenzie, Dr. Richard B.
Professor, Graduate School of Management
University of California, Irvine
430 Graduate School of Management
Irvine, CA 92697-3125
949-824-2604   fax 949-725-2819
mckenzie@uci.edu
Issues: The Economy; Labor and employment;
Political philosophy

McKigney, Darrell
President
Small Business Survival Committee
1920 L Street, N.W., Suite 200
Washington, DC 20036
202-785-0238   fax 202-822-8118
darrell@sbsc.org
Issues: Entrepreneurship/free enterprise;
Regulatory reform; Taxation/tax reform;
Telecommunications and the Internet; Trade

McMahon, Edmund J.
Senior Fellow, Center for Civic Innovation
Manhattan Institute for Policy Innovation
52 Vanderbilt Avenue
New York, NY 10017
212-599-7000   fax 212-599-3494
Issues: State and local government; State and
local public finance; Taxation/tax reform

---

*McManus, Michael J.
President
Marriage Savers
9311 Harrington Drive
Potomac, MD 20854-4510
301-469-5870   fax 301-469-5871
michaeljmcmanus@cs.com
Issues: Abstinence and out-of-wedlock births;
Adoption, foster care, & child care services;
The American Founding; American history/
political tradition; Church-state relations;
Citizenship and civil society; Conservative
thought; Corrections and sentencing; Ethics;
Faith-based and volunteer initiatives; Family
and children; Human rights; Marriage and
divorce; Media and popular culture; Middle
East; Philanthropy; Political correctness and
multiculturalism; Poverty and dependency;
Religion and public life; Religious freedom;
School choice; State-sponsored gambling;
Substance abuse; Welfare/welfare reform

McMullen, Edward T., Jr., Ph.D.
President
South Carolina Policy Council
1323 Pendleton Street
Columbia, SC 29201
803-779-5022   fax 803-779-4953
etm@scpolicycouncil.com
Issues: Charter schools; Federalism; Higher
education; Job training/welfare to work;
Philanthropy; Privatization/Contracting-out;
Promoting democracy/public diplomacy;
Standards, curriculum, and testing; State and
local government; Taxation/tax reform;
Western Europe

McQuillan, Dr. Lawrence J.
Director, Center for Entrepreneurship
Pacific Research Institute
755 Sansome Street, Suite 450
San Francisco, CA 94111-1709
415-955-6104   fax 415-989-2411
lmcquillan@pacificresearch.org
Issues: Bilingual education; Comparative
economics; Congress; Costs and benefits of
regulation; Crime/crime statistics; Defense
budget; Economic development/foreign aid;
Economic theory; The Economy; Entitlement
spending; Entrepreneurship/free enterprise;
Environmental regulation; Executive Branch/
The Presidency; Federal budget; Federalism;
Free-market environmentalism; Government
health programs; Health care reform; Human
rights; International finance and multilateral
banks; International organizations (European
Union, OECD, etc.); Judicial activism/judicial
reform; Judiciary; Labor and employment;
Police; Promoting democracy/public
diplomacy; Property rights; Regulation
through litigation; Regulatory reform;
Research funding; School choice; Sound
science; State and local public finance;
Stewardship; Taxation/tax reform; Terrorism
and international crime; Tort and liability
reform; Trade; Transportation; Unions;
Wealth creation/financial empowerment;
Welfare/welfare reform

*McTigue, Hon. Maurice
Distinguished Visiting Scholar
Mercatus Center at George Mason University
3301 North Fairfax Drive, Suite 450
Arlington, VA 22201-4433
703-993-4930   fax 703-993-4935
mmctigue@gmu.edu
Issues: Federal civil service; International
organizations (European Union, OECD, etc.);
Labor and employment; Poverty and
dependency; Privatization/Contracting-out;
School choice; Southeast Asia (including
Burma, Cambodia, Laos, Vietnam, Singapore,
Malaysia, Indonesia, the Philippines, Australia,
and New Zealand); Taxation/tax reform;
Transportation

McVaugh, Jack
President Emeritus
Arizona School Choice Trust
7877 East Shooting Star Way
Scottsdale, AZ 85262
480-575-1582   fax 480-575-1586
jemasct@mindspring.com
Issues: Environmental education; Faith-based
and volunteer initiatives; Philanthropy;
Property rights; School choice

*Mead, Lawrence
Professor of Politics, Department of Politics
New York University
715 Broadway
New York, NY 10003
212-998-8540   fax 212-995-4184
Issues: Citizenship and civil society; Family and
children; Federal budget; Job training/welfare
to work; Political philosophy; Poverty and
dependency; Welfare/welfare reform

Mead, Thomas
Maine Policy Center
P. O. Box 7829
Portland, ME 04112
207-967-8996   fax 207-967-8999
info@mainepolicy.org
Issues: Health care reform; Missile defense;
Taxation/tax reform; Unfunded mandates

Mead, Dr. Walter J.
Professor Emeritus of Economics
University of California, Santa Barbara
990 Camino Medio
Santa Barbara, CA 93110
805-893-3670
Issues: Energy; Forestry and national parks

*Mead Smith, Daniel
President
Washington Policy Center
4025 Delridge Way, S.W., Suite 210
Seattle, WA 98106
206-937-9691   fax 206-938-6313
dmeadsmith@washingtonpolicy.org
Issues: Costs and benefits of regulation;
Entrepreneurship/free enterprise;
Government waste; Health care reform;
Privatization/Contracting-out; Regulatory
reform; State and local public finance;
Taxation/tax reform; Transportation

*Meeks, Annette Thompson
Director of Government Affairs and Public
Programs
Center of the American Experiment
12 South 6th Street, Suite 1024
Minneapolis, MN 55402
612-338-3605   fax 612-338-3621
meeks@amexp.org
Issues: Campaign finance reform; Elections/
polling

*Meese, Edwin, III
Ronald Reagan Distinguished Fellow in
Public Policy and Chairman, Center for
Legal and Judicial Studies
The Heritage Foundation
214 Massachusetts Avenue, N.E.
Washington, DC 20002
202-608-6180   fax 202-547-0641
info@heritage.org
Issues: Church-state relations; Citizenship and
civil society; Civil rights/racial preferences;
Conservative thought; Constitutional law;
Corrections and sentencing; Crime/crime
statistics; Criminal law and procedure;
Executive Branch/The Presidency; Federalism;
Homeland security/civil defense; Judicial
activism/judicial reform; Judiciary; Military
strategy; Police; Property rights; Public interest
law; The Reagan legacy; State and local
government; Terrorism and international
crime; Tort and liability reform

*Meier, Conrad F.
Senior Fellow in Health Policy, and
Managing Editor, *Health Care News*
Heartland Institute
19 South LaSalle, Suite 903
Chicago, IL 60603
312-377-4000   fax 312-377-5000
meier@heartland.org
Issues: Aging/elder care; Costs and benefits of
regulation; Government health programs;
Health care reform; Medicaid; Medicare;
Regulatory reform

*Meiners, Dr. Roger E.
Professor of Law and Economics
University of Texas, Arlington
Box 19479
Arlington, TX 76019
817-272-3116   fax 817-468-2972
meiners@uta.edu
Issues: Entrepreneurship/free enterprise;
Federalism; Higher education; Intellectual
property

*Mellor, William H.
President and General Counsel
Institute for Justice
1717 Pennsylvania Avenue, N.W., Suite 200
Washington, DC 20006
202-955-1300   fax 202-955-1329
wmellor@ij.org
Issues: Campaign finance reform;
Constitutional law; Entrepreneurship/free
enterprise; Federalism; Property rights; Public
interest law

*Meltzer, Dr. Allan H.
University Professor of Political Economy,
Graduate School of Industrial
Administration
Carnegie Mellon University
Schenley Park
Pittsburgh, PA 15213
412-268-2282   fax 412-268-6830
Issues: Economic development/foreign aid;
The Economy; Federal budget; Government
debt; International finance and multilateral
banks; International organizations (European
Union, OECD, etc.); Japan; Latin America;
Money and financial services

Menefee, Dr. Samuel P.
Professor of Law, School of Law
Regent University
1000 Regent University Drive
Virginia Beach, VA 23464
757-226-4566   fax 757-226-4329
samumen@regent.edu
Issues: Arts, humanities and historic resources;
Human rights; Intelligence gathering and
covert operations; International law; Media
and popular culture; Promoting democracy/
public diplomacy; Terrorism and international
crime; Western Europe; Wildlife
management/endangered species

*Menges, Dr. Constantine C.
Senior Fellow
Hudson Institute
1015 18th Street, N.W., Suite 300
Washington, DC 20036
202-974-2410   fax 202-223-8537
menges@hudsondc.org
Issues: American diplomacy/foreign policy;
China; Human rights; Intelligence gathering
and covert operations; Japan; Korea; Latin
America; Mexico; Northeast Asia;
Peacekeeping; Promoting democracy/public
diplomacy; The Reagan legacy; Terrorism and
international crime; Western Europe

Merikoski, Ingrid
Director of Program
Earhart Foundation
2200 Green Road, Suite H
Ann Arbor, MI 48105
734-761-8592   fax 734-761-2722
Issues: Conservative thought; Higher
education; Philanthropy; Political philosophy

Mero, Paul T.
President
The Sutherland Institute
111 East 5600 South, Suite 202
Salt Lake City, UT 84107
801-281-2081   fax 801-281-2414
pmero@sutherlandinstitute.org
Issues: Citizenship and civil society;
Conservative thought; Family and children;
Home schooling; Poverty and dependency;
Privatization/Contracting-out; Religion and
public life; School choice; State and local
government

*Merrifield, Dr. John
Professor of Economics
University of Texas, San Antonio
501 West Durango Boulevard
San Antonio, TX 78207
210-458-2519   fax 210-458-2515
jmerrifield@utsa.edu
Issues: Air; Charter schools; Free-market
environmentalism; School choice; State and
local public finance; Taxation/tax reform;
Water; Wildlife management/endangered
species

Merrill, Mark
President
Family First
101 East Kennedy Boulevard, Suite 1070
Tampa, FL 33602
813-222-8300   fax 813-222-8301
mark@familyfirst.net
Issues: Family and children; Marriage and
divorce

Merry, E. Wayne
Senior Associate
American Foreign Policy Council
1521 16th Street, N.W.
Washington, DC 20036
202-462-6055   fax 202-462-6045
merry@afpc.org
Issues: Central and Eastern Europe; Russia and
Eurasia; Western Europe

Messenheimer, Harry, Ph.D.
President
Rio Grande Foundation
P. O. Box 2015
Tijeras, NM 87059
505-286-2030   fax 505-286-2422
hmessen@nmia.com
Issues: The American Founding; Campaign
finance reform; Charter schools; Economic
education; Economic theory; Education unions
and interest groups; Entitlement spending;
Government health programs; Government
waste; Health care reform; Home schooling;
Medicaid; Medicare; Property rights; School
choice; Standards, curriculum, and testing;
State and local government; State and local
public finance; Taxation/tax reform; Welfare/
welfare reform

*Messing, Major F. Andy, Jr., USAR (Ret.)
Executive Director
National Defense Council Foundation
1220 King Street, Suite 1
Alexandria, VA 22314
703-836-3443   fax 703-836-5402
ndfc@erols.com
Issues: Afghanistan; Africa; American
diplomacy/foreign policy; China; Latin
America; Mexico; Middle East; Northeast Asia;
South Asia (including India and Pakistan);
Southeast Asia (including Burma, Cambodia,
Laos, Vietnam, Singapore, Malaysia, Indonesia,
the Philippines, Australia, and New Zealand)

*Metz, Steven
Director of Research and Chairman,
Regional Strategy and Planning Department
U. S. Army War College Strategic Studies
Institute
Carlisle Barracks, PA 17013-5244
717-245-3822   fax 717-245-3820
steven.metz@carlisle.army.mil
Issues: Africa; American diplomacy/foreign
policy; Emerging threats/threat assessment;
Military strategy

Meyer, Eugene B.
Executive Director
The Federalist Society for Law and Public
Policy Studies
1015 18th Street, N.W., Suite 425
Washington, DC 20036
202-822-8138   fax 202-296-8061
ebmeyer@fed-soc.org
Issues: Civil rights/racial preferences;
Constitutional law; Corrections and
sentencing; Crime/crime statistics; Criminal
law and procedure; Free Speech; Immigration;
International law; Judicial activism/judicial
reform; Juvenile justice; Police; Public interest
law; Religious freedom; Second Amendment;
Tort and liability reform

Meyer, Herbert E.
Chairman
Real-World Intelligence, Inc.
P. O. Box 2089
Friday Harbor, WA 98250
360-378-3908   fax 360-378-3912
hmeyer@lookoutpoint.com
Issues: Intelligence gathering and covert
operations; Political philosophy

Meyerson, Adam
President
The Philanthropy Roundtable
1150 17th Street, N.W., Suite 503
Washington, DC 20036
202-822-8333   fax 202-822-8325
ameyerson@philanthropyroundtable.org
Issues: Philanthropy

*Michaels, Dr. Patrick
Research Professor and State Climatologist,
Department of Environmental Sciences
University of Virginia
Clark Hall
Charlottesville, VA 22903
804-924-0549   fax 804-982-2137
pjm8x@virginia.edu
Issues: Agriculture; Air; Climate change;
Energy; Environmental education;
Environmental regulation; Free-market
environmentalism; Research funding; Sound
science

*Michaels, Dr. Robert J.
Professor, Department of Economics
California State University, Fullerton
P. O. Box 6850
Fullerton, CA 92634
714-278-2588   fax 714-278-1258
rmichaels@fullerton.edu
Issues: Electricity deregulation; Energy;
Regulatory reform

Michel, Norbert
Policy Analyst, Center for Data Analysis
The Heritage Foundation
214 Massachusetts Avenue, N.E.
Washington, DC 20002
202-608-6218   fax 202-675-1772
norbert.michel@heritage.org
Issues: Anti-trust; The Economy; Intellectual
property; Property rights; School choice; Social
Security and retirement; Taxation/tax reform

Michelson, Dr. Paul E.
Distinguished Professor of History
Huntington College
2303 College Avenue
Huntington, IN 46750
260-359-4242   fax 260-359-4086
pmichelson@huntington.edu
Issues: Central and Eastern Europe; Citizenship
and civil society; Economic development/
foreign aid; Free-market environmentalism;
NATO and other alliances; Political correctness
and multiculturalism; Political philosophy;
Religion and public life; Russia and Eurasia

*Michener, Roger
P. O. Box 400
Placitas, NM 87043-0400
505-771-1708   fax 505-771-1020
michener@redthistle.com
Issues: The American Founding; American
history/political tradition; Citizenship and civil
society; Comparative government;
Conservative thought; Constitutional law;
Ethics; Higher education; International law;
Political philosophy; The Reagan legacy

Michta, Dr. Andrew A.
Professor, International Studies Department
Rhodes College
2000 North Parkway
Memphis, TN 38112
901-843-3823   fax 901-843-3371
michta@rhodes.edu
Issues: Central and Eastern Europe; NATO and
other alliances; Peacekeeping; Promoting
democracy/public diplomacy; Russia and
Eurasia

Middleton, Christopher
Senior Health and Tax Policy Analyst
Pacific Research Institute
755 Sansome Street, Suite 450
San Francisco, CA 94111
415-989-0833   fax 415-989-2411
cmiddleton@pacificresearch.org
Issues: Government health programs; Health
care reform; Medicaid; Medicare; Taxation/
tax reform

*Miller, Dr. Abraham H.
Professor of Political Science
208 Shady Glen Road
Walnut Creek, CA 94596
925-280-8834   fax 925-280-8836
amill727@sbcglobal.net
Issues: Intelligence gathering and covert
operations; Political correctness and
multiculturalism; Terrorism and
international crime

Miller, Dr. Dennis D.
Associate Professor, Department of
Economics
Baldwin-Wallace College
275 Eastland Road
Berea, OH 44017
440-826-2002   fax 440-826-3835
dmiller@bw.edu
Issues: Central and Eastern Europe; Economic
development/foreign aid; Energy; Free-market
environmentalism; Middle East

Miller, Dr. Fred D., Jr.
Executive Director, Social Philosophy and
Policy Center
Bowling Green State University
225 Troupe Street
Bowling Green, OH 43403
419-372-2536   fax 419-372-8738
Issues: Conservative thought; Ethics; Higher
education; Political philosophy

*Miller, Henry I., M.D.
Senior Fellow
Hoover Institution
Stanford University
Stanford, CA 94305-6010
650-725-0185   fax 650-723-0576
miller@hoover.stanford.edu
Issues: Costs and benefits of regulation;
Environmental regulation; Risk assessment;
Sound science; Terrorism and international
crime

Miller, Dr. James Arnold
President
Interaction Systems Incorporated
1501 Trombone Court
Vienna, VA 22182-1646
703-938-1774   fax 703-938-1727
isinc@mindspring.com
Issues: Emerging threats/threat assessment;
Homeland security/civil defense; Intelligence
gathering and covert operations; Terrorism
and international crime

*Miller, James H.
President
Wisconsin Policy Research Institute
11516 North Port Washington Road, Suite
103
Mequon, WI 53092
262-241-0514   fax 262-241-0774
wpri@execpc.com
Issues: Higher education; School choice;
School-to-work; Standards, curriculum, and
testing; State-sponsored gambling; Welfare/
welfare reform

*Miller, Thomas P.
Director of Health Policy Studies
Cato Institute
1000 Massachusetts Avenue, N.W.
Washington, DC 20001
202-789-5247   fax 202-842-3490
tmiller@cato.org
Issues: Entitlement spending; Government
health programs; Health care reform;
Medicaid; Medicare; Privacy; Social Security
and retirement

Milloy, Steven J.
Founder and Publisher
junkscience.com
1155 Connecticut Avenue, N.W., Suite 300
Washington, DC 20036
202-467-8586   fax 202-467-0768
Issues: Risk assessment; Sound science

*Mills, Dr. Edwin S.
Professor Emeritus of Real Estate and
Finance, Kellogg Graduate School of
Management
Northwestern University
2001 Sheridan Road
Evanston, IL 60208
847-491-8340   fax 847-491-5719
e_mills@nwu.edu
Issues: Costs and benefits of regulation; Land
use; Property rights; Regulation through
litigation; Regulatory reform; Urban sprawl/
livable cities

Mills, Rev. Gene
Executive Director
Louisiana Family Forum
655 Saint Ferdinand Street
Baton Rouge, LA 70802
225-344-8533   fax 225-344-9006
info@lafamilyforum.org
Issues: Abstinence and out-of-wedlock births;
Family and children; Marriage and divorce;
Religion and public life

Milyo, Dr. Jeffrey D.
Assistant Professor, Harris Graduate School
of Public Policy Studies
University of Chicago
1155 East 60th Street
Chicago, IL 60637
773-834-7746   fax 773-702-0926
jdmilyo@uchicago.edu
Issues: Campaign finance reform; Congress;
Elections/polling; Term limits

Minnery, Tom

Vice President, Public Policy
Focus on the Family
8605 Explorer Drive
Colorado Springs, CO 80920
719-531-3400   fax 719-548-4525
minnerta@fotf.org

Issues: Abstinence and out-of-wedlock births;
Adoption, foster care, & child care services;
Advocacy and nonprofit public funding; The
American Founding; American history/
political tradition; Arts, humanities and
historic resources; Charter schools; Church-
state relations, Citizenship and civil society;
Conservative thought; Constitutional law;
Ethics; Faith-based and volunteer initiatives;
Family and children; Free Speech; Marriage
and divorce; Media and popular culture;
Political correctness and multiculturalism;
Political philosophy; Religion and public life;
Religious freedom; School choice; Standards,
curriculum, and testing; State-sponsored
gambling

Mische, Elizabeth

Executive Director
Partnership for Choice in Education
46 East 4th Street, Suite 224 Minnesota
Building
St. Paul, MN 55101-1113
651-293-9196   fax 651-293-9285
pcemail@pcemn.org

Issues: Business and education partnerships;
Charter schools; Education unions and interest
groups; Federal education policy; Higher
education; Home schooling; Public school
finance and administration; School choice

*Mitchell, C. Ben, Ph.D.

Associate Professor of Bioethics and
Contemporary Culture
Trinity International University
2065 Half Day Road
Deerfield, IL 60015
875-317-8022   fax 847-317-8141
bmitchell@tiu.edu

Issues: Citizenship and civil society; Ethics;
Political philosophy; Religion and public life;
Religious freedom

*Mitchell, Cleta Deatherage

Attorney
Foley & Lardner
3000 K Street, N.W.
Washington, DC 20007
202-295-4081   fax 202-672-5399
cmitchell@foleylaw.com

Issues: Campaign finance reform; Elections/
polling; Electoral reform/voting rights;
Federalism; Initiative and referendum;
Judiciary; Non-governmental organizations;
Term limits

*Mitchell, Dan

McKenna Senior Fellow in Political
Economy, Thomas A. Roe Institute for
Economic Policy Studies
The Heritage Foundation
214 Massachusetts Avenue, N.E.
Washington, DC 20002
202-546-4400   fax 202-544-5421
dan.mitchell@heritage.org

Issues: Anti-trust; Comparative economics;
Economic theory; The Economy; Entitlement
spending; Entrepreneurship/free enterprise;
Federal budget; Government debt;
Government waste; International organizations
(European Union, OECD, etc.); International
tax policy/tax competition; The Reagan legacy;
Second Amendment; Taxation/tax reform

Mitchell, Prof. Mark E.

Professor, School of Justice Studies
Thomas University
1501 Mill Pond Road
Thomasville, GA 81792
800-538-9784   fax 229-226-1653
mmitchell@thomasu.edu

Issues: American history/political tradition;
Constitutional law; Corrections and
sentencing; Criminal law and procedure; Free
Speech; Judicial activism/judicial reform;
Judiciary; Juvenile justice; Police; Tort and
liability reform

*Mitchell, Susan

President
The American Education Reform
Foundation
2025 North Summit, Suite 103
Milwaukee, WI 53202
414-319-9160   fax 414-765-0220
mitchell@parentchoice.org

Issues: School choice

*Mittler, Brant S., M.D., J.D.
Senior Fellow, Health Care
Texas Public Policy Foundation
4319 Medical Drive, Suite 131, PMB 363
San Antonio, TX 78229
210-561-5550   fax 210-561-5551
bsmitt@aol.com
Issues: Aging/elder care; Government health
programs; Health care reform; Media and
popular culture; Medicaid; Medicare

*Mix, Mark A.
Senior Vice President
National Right to Work Committee
8001 Braddock Road, Suite 500
Springfield, VA 22160
703-321-9820   fax 703-321-7342
mam@nrtw.org
Issues: Campaign finance reform; Labor and
employment; Right to work; Unions

Moe, Dr. Terry M.
Senior Fellow
Hoover Institution
Stanford University
Stanford, CA 94305
650-725-8212   fax 650-723-1687
moe@hoover.stanford.edu
Issues: Bilingual education; Business and
education partnerships; Charter schools;
Education unions and interest groups; Federal
education policy; Higher education; Home
schooling; Public school finance and
administration; School choice; School-to-work;
Standards, curriculum, and testing

*Moffit, Dr. Robert
Director, Domestic Policy Studies
The Heritage Foundation
214 Massachusetts Avenue, N.E.
Washington, DC 20002
202-546-4400   fax 202-544-5421
robert.moffit@heritage.org
Issues: Aging/elder care; American history/
political tradition; Crime/crime statistics;
Federal civil service; Government health
programs; Health care reform; Medicare;
Police; Political philosophy; The Reagan
legacy; Social Security and retirement

*Moghissi, Dr. A. Alan
President
Institute for Regulatory Science
P. O. Box 7166
Alexandria, VA 22307
703-765-3546   fax 703-765-3143
moghissi@nrsi.org
Issues: Air; Climate change; Environmental
education; Environmental regulation; Free-
market environmentalism; Risk assessment;
Sound science; Waste management

Mohler, Dr. R. Albert, Jr.
President
The Southern Baptist Theological Seminary
2825 Lexington Road
Louisville, KY 40280
502-897-4121   fax 502-899-1770
mohler@sbts.edu
Issues: Abstinence and out-of-wedlock births;
Church-state relations; Conservative thought;
Ethics; Faith-based and volunteer initiatives;
Family and children; Higher education;
Marriage and divorce; Media and popular
culture; Religion and public life; Religious
freedom

Mokhtari, Fariborz L., Ph.D.
Professor of Political Science, Near East
South Asia Center for Strategic Studies
National Defense University
Washington, DC 20319-5066
202-685-2574   fax 202-685-4997
mokhtarif@ndu.edu
Issues: Comparative government; Ethics;
Homeland security/civil defense; Middle East;
Missile defense; Peacekeeping; Political
philosophy; South Asia (including India and
Pakistan); Southeast Asia (including Burma,
Cambodia, Laos, Vietnam, Singapore,
Malaysia, Indonesia, the Philippines, Australia,
and New Zealand); Terrorism and
international crime

*Monaghan, Thomas Patrick
Senior Counsel
American Center for Law and Justice
6375 New Hope Road
New Hope, KY 40052
502-549-7020   fax 502-549-5252
tpmonaghan@aol.com
Issues: Constitutional law; Judicial activism/
judicial reform; Public interest law

Mone, Lawrence
President
Manhattan Institute for Policy Research
52 Vanderbilt Avenue
New York, NY 10017
212-599-7000   fax 212-599-3494
lmone@manhattan-institute.org
Issues: The Economy; Privatization/
Contracting-out

Monsma, Dr. Stephen
Professor of Political Science
Pepperdine University
24255 Pacific Coast Highway
Malibu, CA 90265
310-456-4200   fax 310-317-7271
smonsma@pepperdine.edu
Issues: Faith-based and volunteer initiatives;
Religion and public life; Religious freedom;
Welfare/welfare reform

Moody, Dr. Carlisle E.
Chairman, Department of Economics
College of William and Mary
Williamsburg, VA 23187-8795
757-221-2373   fax 757-221-2390
cemood@wm.edu
Issues: Corrections and sentencing; Crime/
crime statistics

*Moody, J. Scott
Economist
Tax Foundation
1900 M Street, N.W., Suite 550
Washington, DC 20036
202-464-6200   fax 202-464-6201
jsmoody@taxfoundation.org
Issues: State and local public finance; Taxation/
tax reform

*Moore, Adrian T.
Vice President, Research
Reason Foundation
3415 South Sepulveda Boulevard, Suite 400
Los Angeles, CA 90034
310-391-2245   fax 310-391-4395
adrian.moore@reason.org
Issues: Corrections and sentencing; Costs and
benefits of regulation; Davis-Bacon Act;
Discretionary spending; Economic education;
Economic theory; The Economy; Electricity
deregulation; Federal budget; Federal civil
service; Federalism; Government debt;
Government waste; Infrastructure;
Privatization/Contracting-out; Regulatory
budgeting; Regulatory reform; State and local
government; State and local public finance;
Transportation; Transportation deregulation;
Unions; Waste management; Water

Moore, Dr. Cassandra Chrones
Adjunct Scholar
Cato Institute
1000 Massachusetts Avenue, N.W.
Washington, DC 20001
650-493-7358   fax 650-493-8609
ccmassoc@aol.com
Issues: Business and education partnerships;
Charter schools; Costs and benefits of
regulation; Education unions and interest
groups; Federal education policy; Public school
finance and administration; Regulation
through litigation; Regulatory reform; Risk
assessment; School choice; Transportation;
Transportation deregulation

*Moore, Dr. James Elliott, II
Professor of Civil Engineering and Professor
of Public Policy and Management
University of Southern California
KAP 210, MC 2531
Los Angeles, CA 90089-2531
213-740-0595   fax 213-744-1426
jmoore@usc.edu
Issues: Costs and benefits of regulation;
Economic theory; Free-market
environmentalism; Land use; Property rights;
Transportation; Transportation deregulation;
Urban sprawl/livable cities

*Moore, Dr. John H.
President
Grove City College
100 Campus Drive
Grove City, PA 16127
724-458-2500   fax 724-458-2190
jhmoore@gcc.edu
Issues: Central and Eastern Europe;
Comparative economics; Higher education;
Philanthropy; Research funding; Russia and
Eurasia

Moore, Matt
Policy Analyst
National Center for Policy Analysis
12655 North Central Expressway, Suite 720
Dallas, TX 75243
972-386-6272   fax 972-386-0924
mmoore@ncpa.org
Issues: School choice; Social Security and
retirement

Moore, Stephen J.
President
Club for Growth
1776 K Street, NW, Suite 300
Washington, DC 20006
202-955-5500   fax 202-955-9466
smoore@clubforgrowth.org
Issues: Advocacy and nonprofit public funding;
The American Founding; Discretionary
spending; The Economy; Entitlement
spending; Executive Branch/The Presidency;
Federal budget; Government debt;
Government waste; State and local public
finance; Taxation/tax reform

Moore, Suzanne C.
Executive Director
Delaware Public Policy Institute
1201 North Orange Street
Wilmington, DE 19899
302-576-6561   fax 302-655-7220
smoore@dscc.com
Issues: Air; American history/political tradition;
Business and education partnerships; Charter
schools; Costs and benefits of regulation; Davis-
Bacon Act; The Economy; Environmental
education; Environmental regulation; Family
and medical leave; Health care reform; Higher
education; Infrastructure; Job training/welfare
to work; Labor and employment; Land use;
Minimum wage; School choice; School-to-
work; Standards, curriculum, and testing; State
and local government; Taxation/tax reform;
Term limits; Tort and liability reform; Urban
sprawl/livable cities

*Moore, Dr. Thomas Gale
Senior Fellow
Hoover Institution
Stanford University
Stanford, CA 94305-6010
650-723-1411   fax 650-723-1687
moore@hoover.stanford.edu
Issues: Climate change; Costs and benefits of
regulation; Regulatory reform; Transportation
deregulation

*Morgan, Dr. Richard E.
Professor of Government
Bowdoin College
Hubbard Hall
Brunswick, ME 04011
207-725-3296   fax 207-725-3168
Issues: Church-state relations; Civil rights/racial
preferences; Constitutional law; Free Speech;
Judicial activism/judicial reform; Religious
freedom; Second Amendment

Morgan, Ted
Director, Information Systems
The Heritage Foundation
214 Massachusetts Avenue, N.E.
Washington, DC 20002
202-546-4400   fax 202-546-8328
info@heritage.org
Issues: Telecommunications and the Internet

Moriarty, Kevin P.
Executive Director
Scholarship Fund for Inner-City Children
P. O. Box 9500
Newark, NJ 07104
973-497-4279   fax 973-497-4282
Issues: School choice

Morreim, Dr. E. Haavi
Professor, College of Medicine
University of Tennessee, Memphis
956 Court Avenue, Box 11, Suite B-328
Memphis, TN 38163
901-448-5725   fax 901-448-1291
hmorreim@utmem.edu
Issues: Government health programs; Health
care reform; Tort and liability reform

Morris, Christopher
Research Associate and Editor, *Patterns of Corporate Philanthropy*
Capital Research Center
1513 16th Street, N.W.
Washington, DC 20036
202-483-6900   fax 202-483-6990
cmorris@capitalresearch.org
Issues: Advocacy and nonprofit public funding; Philanthropy

*Morris, Joseph A.
President and General Counsel
Lincoln Legal Foundation
100 West Monroe Street, Suite 2101
Chicago, IL 60603
312-606-0876   fax 312-606-0879
mdlrchicago@aol.com
Issues: The American Founding; Arts, humanities and historic resources; Church-state relations; Civil rights/racial preferences; Comparative government; Conservative thought; Constitutional law; Criminal law and procedure; Executive Branch/The Presidency; Federal civil service; Free Speech; Homeland security/civil defense; Human rights; Intellectual property; International law; International organizations (European Union, OECD, etc.); Judicial activism/judicial reform; Middle East; Non-governmental organizations; Privacy; Promoting democracy/public diplomacy; Public interest law; The Reagan legacy; Regulation through litigation; Religion and public life; Religious freedom; State and local government; State and local public finance; Terrorism and international crime; Tort and liability reform; United Nations

*Morrisey, Dr. Michael A.
Director, Lister Hill Center for Health Policy
University of Alabama, Birmingham
1665 University Boulevard
Birmingham, AL 35294-0022
205-975-8966   fax 205-934-3347
morrisey@uab.edu
Issues: Aging/elder care; Costs and benefits of regulation; Government health programs; Health care reform; Labor and employment; Medicaid; Medicare; Regulatory reform; Unfunded mandates

*Morrison, James
President
Morrison Associates
35056 North 80th Way
Scottsdale, AZ 85262-1026
480-515-2859   fax 480-342-8085
Issues: Federal civil service; Government health programs; Health care reform

Morrow, Dr. Laurie
Radio Talk Show Host
15 Deerfield Drive
Montpelier, VT 05602
802-229-9208   lpmorrow@aol.com
Issues: Arts, humanities and historic resources; Higher education; Media and popular culture; Political correctness and multiculturalism; Standards, curriculum, and testing

Morse, Jennifer Roback
Research Fellow
Hoover Institution
935 Parkwood Avenue
Vista, CA 92083
760-295-4929   j-morse@cox.net
Issues: Abstinence and out-of-wedlock births; Adoption, foster care, & child care services; The American Founding; American history/ political tradition; Citizenship and civil society; Conservative thought; Economic education; Ethics; Faith-based and volunteer initiatives; Family and children; Marriage and divorce; Political correctness and multiculturalism; Political philosophy; Religion and public life

Moser, Joe
Policy Analyst
Galen Institute
P. O. Box 19080
Alexandria, VA 22320-0080
703-299-9204   fax 703-299-0721
joe@galen.org
Issues: Government health programs; Health care reform; Medicaid; Medicare

Moses, Stephen
President
Center for Long-Term Care Financing
2212 Queen Anne Avenue North, Suite 110
Seattle, WA 98109
206-283-7036   fax 206-283-6536
david@centerltc.org
Issues: Government health programs; Health care reform; Medicaid

*Mosher, Steven W.
President
Population Research Institute
P. O. Box 1559
Front Royal, VA 22630
540-622-5240   fax 540-622-2728
steve@pop.org
Issues: Abstinence and out-of-wedlock births;
Adoption, foster care, & child care services;
Aging/elder care; American diplomacy/
foreign policy; China; Church-state relations;
Economic development/foreign aid;
Emerging threats/threat assessment; Faith-
based and volunteer initiatives; Family and
children; Government health programs;
Health care reform; Home schooling; Human
rights; Immigration; Intelligence gathering
and covert operations; International law;
International organizations (European Union,
OECD, etc.); International tax policy/tax
competition; Japan; Korea; Marriage and
divorce; Media and popular culture; Missile
defense; Northeast Asia; Philanthropy; Poverty
and dependency; Promoting democracy/
public diplomacy; Religion and public life;
Religious freedom; Social Security and
retirement; South Asia (including India and
Pakistan); Southeast Asia (including Burma,
Cambodia, Laos, Vietnam, Singapore,
Malaysia, Indonesia, the Philippines, Australia,
and New Zealand); Terrorism and
international crime; Wealth creation/financial
empowerment; Welfare/welfare reform

*Moshofsky, William
President
Oregonians in Action Legal Center
P. O. Box 230637
Tigard, OR 97281
503-620-0258   fax 503-639-6891
bill@oia.org
Issues: Land use; Property rights; Urban sprawl/
livable cities; Wildlife management/
endangered species

*Moss, Dr. Laurence S.
Professor, Economics Division
Babson College
Mustard Hall
Babson Park, MA 02457
781-239-4313   fax 781-239-4947
lmos@aol.com
Issues: Criminal law and procedure; Economic
theory; Ethics; Land use; Political philosophy

Mottice, Robert
Executive Director
Mercatus Center at George Mason University
3301 North Fairfax Drive, Suite 450
Arlington, VA 22201
703-993-4941   fax 703-658-0089
rmottice@gmu.edu
Issues: Economic education

*Mueller, Dr. Milton L.
Associate Professor, School of Information
Studies
Syracuse University
4-285 Center for Science and Technology
Syracuse, NY 13244-4100
315-443-5616   fax 315-443-5806
mueller@syr.edu
Issues: Intellectual property;
Telecommunications and the Internet

*Muhlhausen, David B.
Policy Analyst, Center for Data Analysis
The Heritage Foundation
214 Massachusetts Avenue, N.E.
Washington, DC 20002
202-608-6209   fax 202-675-1772
david.muhlhausen@heritage.org
Issues: Corrections and sentencing; Crime/
crime statistics; Government waste;
Immigration; Job training/welfare to work;
Juvenile justice; Police; Second Amendment

Mujica, Mauro E.
Chairman and CEO
U. S. English, Inc.
1747 Pennsylvania Avenue, N.W., Suite 1050
Washington, DC 20006
202-833-0100   fax 202-833-0108
info@us-english.org
Issues: Bilingual education; Immigration

Muller, Dr. James W.
Professor, Department of Political Science
University of Alaska
3211 Providence Drive
Anchorage, AK 99508
907-786-4740   fax 907-786-4647
afjwm@uaa.alaska.edu
Issues: The American Founding; American
history/political tradition; Political philosophy

---

*Munro, Dr. Ross H.
Director of Asian Studies
Center for Security Studies
1521 16th Street, N.W.
Washington, DC 20036
202-265-3715   fax 202-265-3716
ross@munrolink.com
Issues: China; Emerging threats/threat
assessment; Energy; Intelligence gathering and
covert operations; Military strategy; Northeast
Asia; South Asia (including India and
Pakistan); Southeast Asia (including Burma,
Cambodia, Laos, Vietnam, Singapore,
Malaysia, Indonesia, the Philippines, Australia,
and New Zealand)

*Munsil, Len
President and General Counsel
Center for Arizona Policy
11000 North Scottsdale Road, Suite 120
Scottsdale, AZ 85254
480-922-3101   fax 480-922-9785
len@azpolicy.org
Issues: Abstinence and out-of-wedlock births;
The American Founding; Church-state
relations; Citizenship and civil society;
Conservative thought; Constitutional law;
Faith-based and volunteer initiatives; Family
and children; Federalism; Free Speech; Home
schooling; Judicial activism/judicial reform;
Marriage and divorce; Media and popular
culture; Religion and public life; Religious
freedom; School choice; State-sponsored
gambling

*Muravchik, Joshua, Ph.D.
Resident Scholar
American Enterprise Institute
1150 17th Street, N.W.
Washington, DC 20036
202-862-5942   fax 202-862-7163
jmuravchik@aei.org
Issues: American diplomacy/foreign policy;
Human rights; NATO and other alliances;
Peacekeeping; Promoting democracy/public
diplomacy; United Nations

Murchison, William
Professor, Department of Journalism
Baylor University
P. O. Box 97353
Waco, TX 76798-7353
254-710-3261   fax 254-710-3363
william_murchison@baylor.edu
Issues: Church-state relations; Free Speech;
Media and popular culture; Religious freedom

*Murdock, Deroy
Senior Fellow
Atlas Economic Research Foundation
127 Fourth Avenue, Fifth Floor
New York, NY 10003
212-995-1536   fax 212-979-6011
murdock2000@attglobal.net
Issues: American diplomacy/foreign policy;
The American Founding; Campaign finance
reform; Civil rights/racial preferences; Climate
change; Discretionary spending; The
Economy; Entitlement spending; Federal
budget; Free-market environmentalism;
Government waste; Latin America; Media and
popular culture; The Reagan legacy; School
choice; Social Security and retirement; Trade;
Wealth creation/financial empowerment

Murray, Dr. Charles
Bradley Fellow
American Enterprise Institute
1150 17th Street, N.W.
Washington, DC 20036
202-862-5812   fax 202-862-7178
chasmurray@earthlink.net
Issues: Crime/crime statistics; Executive
Branch/The Presidency; Federal civil service;
Poverty and dependency; Welfare/welfare
reform

Murray, Iain
Director of Research
Statistical Assessment Service
2100 L Street, N.W., Suite 300
Washington, DC 20037
202-223-3193   fax 202-872-4014
iain@stats.org
Issues: Climate change; Crime/crime statistics;
Juvenile justice; Media and popular culture;
Second Amendment; Sound science;
Transportation deregulation; Western Europe

Murray, William J.
Chairman
Religious Freedom Coalition
717 Second Street, N.E., Suite 100
P. O. Box 77511
Washington, DC 20013
202-543-0300   fax 202-543-8447
wjmurray@rfcnet.org
Issues: Citizenship and civil society; Faith-based
and volunteer initiatives; Political correctness
and multiculturalism; Religion and public life

Muth, Chuck
Executive Director
American Conservative Union
1007 Cameron Street
Alexandria, VA 22314
703-836-8602   fax 703-836-8606
cmuth@conservative.org
Issues: Adoption, foster care, & child care
services; Campaign finance reform; Civil
rights/racial preferences; Conservative
thought; Costs and benefits of regulation;
Education unions and interest groups;
Entrepreneurship/free enterprise; Free
Speech; Immigration; Labor and employment;
Minimum wage; Privatization/Contracting-
out; Regulation through litigation; Regulatory
reform; Right to work; School choice; Second
Amendment; Social Security and retirement;
Taxation/tax reform; Tort and liability reform;
Unions

Muth, Dr. Richard F.
Fuller E. Callaway Professor of Economics
Emeritus, Department of Economics
Emory University
Rich Building 319
Atlanta, GA 30322
404-727-0328   fax 404-727-4639
rmuth@emory.edu
Issues: The Economy; Transportation; Urban
sprawl/livable cities

Myers, Dr. Henry
Professor of History
James Madison University
800 South Main Street
Harrisonburg, VA 22807
540-568-3992   fax 540-568-6556
myersha@jmu.edu
Issues: Africa; American history/political
tradition; Church-state relations; Comparative
government; Conservative thought; Higher
education; NATO and other alliances; Political
correctness and multiculturalism; Political
philosophy

Myers, Phyllis Berry
Executive Director
Centre for New Black Leadership
202 G Street, N.E.
Washington, DC 20002
202-546-9505   fax 202-546-9506
cnbl@aol.com
Issues: Civil rights/racial preferences;
Congress; Elections/polling; Electoral reform/
voting rights; Entrepreneurship/free
enterprise; Faith-based and volunteer
initiatives; Health care reform; School choice;
Wealth creation/financial empowerment

Myers, Dr. Ramon H.
Senior Fellow and Curator, East Asian
Collection
Hoover Institution
Stanford University
Stanford, CA 94305
650-725-3443   fax 650-723-1687
myers@hoover.stanford.edu
Issues: China; Japan; Korea

Nasby, Bruce A.
Senior Vice President, Global
Students In Free Enterprise
1959 East Kerr Street
Springfield, MO 65803-4775
417-831-9505   fax 417-831-6165
bnasby@sife.org
Issues: Business and education partnerships;
Economic education

Nash, Dr. George H.
P. O. Box 415
South Hadley, MA 01075-0415
413-533-2617
Issues: American history/political tradition;
Conservative thought; Political philosophy

Nash, Dr. Ronald
Professor of Theology and Philosophy
Reformed Theological Seminary
1231 Reformation Drive
Oviedo, FL 32765-7197
407-366-9493   fax 407-366-9425
Issues: Afghanistan; Aging/elder care;
American history/political tradition; Church-
state relations; Comparative economics;
Conservative thought; Economic education;
Economic forecasting; Economic theory; The
Economy; Entrepreneurship/free enterprise;
Ethics; Executive Branch/The Presidency;
Faith-based and volunteer initiatives;
Government health programs; Higher
education; Home schooling; Homeland
security/civil defense; Medicare; Military
strategy; Minimum wage; Political correctness
and multiculturalism; Political philosophy; The
Reagan legacy; Religion and public life;
Religious freedom; Russia and Eurasia; School
choice; Second Amendment; Social Security
and retirement; State-sponsored gambling

Natelson, Robert G.
1113 Lincolnwood
Missoula, MT 59802
406-721-2266   fax 406-728-2803
natelson@montana.com
Issues: Constitutional law; Initiative and
referendum; Property rights; School choice

Nathan, Joe
Director
Center for School Change
301 19th Avenue South, Room 234
Minneapolis, MN 55455
612-626-1834   fax 612-625-0104
Issues: Charter schools; Federal education
policy

Nau, Dr. Henry R.
Professor of Political Science and
International Affairs
George Washington University
2013 G Street, N.W., Stuart 202C
Washington, DC 20052
202-994-3167   fax 202-994-9537
nau@gwu.edu
Issues: American diplomacy/foreign policy;
Economic development/foreign aid;
International finance and multilateral banks;
International organizations (European Union,
OECD, etc.); Japan; Promoting democracy/
public diplomacy; Western Europe

Navarro da Costa, Mario
Director, Washington Bureau
American Society for the Defense of
Tradition, Family and Property
1344 Merrie Ridge Road
McLean, VA 22101
703-243-2104   fax 703-243-2105
cpnoell@pobox.com
Issues: Arts, humanities and historic resources;
Latin America; Media and popular culture;
Political philosophy; Property rights; Religion
and public life; Western Europe

*Neal, Anne D.
Executive Director
American Council of Trustees and Alumni
1726 M Street, N.W., Suite 800
Washington, DC 20036
202-467-6787   fax 202-467-6784
info@goacta.org
Issues: The American Founding; American
history/political tradition; Arts, humanities
and historic resources; Citizenship and civil
society; Comparative economics; Comparative
government; Conservative thought; Economic
education; Economic forecasting; Economic
theory; Ethics; Free Speech; Higher education;
Philanthropy; Political correctness and
multiculturalism; Political philosophy; The
Reagan legacy

Nechyba, Dr. Thomas
Associate Professor, Department of
Economics
Duke University
Box 90097
Durham, NC 27708-0097
919-660-1841   fax 919-684-8974
nechyba@duke.edu
Issues: Abstinence and out-of-wedlock births;
Charter schools; Family and children;
Federalism; Public school finance and
administration; School choice; State and local
government; State and local public finance

Neff, Julie N.
Legislative Coordinator
Concerned Women for America
1015 15th Street, N.W., Suite 1100
Washington, DC 20005
202-488-7000   fax 202-488-0806
jneff@cwfa.org
Issues: Religious freedom; United Nations

Negbenebor, Anthony I., Ph.D.
Professor of Economics and Director,
Graduate School of Business
Gardner-Webb University
Box 7272
Boiling Springs, NC 28017
704-406-4622   fax 704-406-3895
anegbenebor@gardner-webb.edu
Issues: Africa; Business and education
partnerships; Conservative thought; Economic
education; Economic theory; The Economy;
Entrepreneurship/free enterprise; Faith-based
and volunteer initiatives; Trade

*Nehring, Ronald
Senior Consultant
Americans for Tax Reform
12730 High Bluff Drive, Suite 250
San Diego, CA 92130
858-794-2338   fax 858-794-2348
rnehring@atr-dc.org
Issues: Advocacy and nonprofit public funding;
Campaign finance reform; Davis-Bacon Act;
Elections/polling; Electoral reform/voting
rights; Government waste; Labor and
employment; Right to work; State and local
government; Taxation/tax reform; Term
limits; Unions; Western Europe

Neily, Clark
Senior Attorney
Institute for Justice
1717 Pennsylvania Avenue, N.W., Suite 200
Washington, DC 20006
202-955-1300   fax 202-955-1329
cneily@ij.org
Issues: Constitutional law; Federalism; Free
Speech; Judicial activism/judicial reform;
Judiciary; Public interest law; School choice;
Second Amendment

Nelson, Jeff
Vice President, Publications
Intercollegiate Studies Institute
3901 Centerville Road, P. O. Box 4331
Wilmington, DE 19807
302-652-4600   fax 302-652-1760
jnelson@isi.org
Issues: The American Founding; American
history/political tradition; Arts, humanities
and historic resources; Citizenship and civil
society; Conservative thought; Economic
education; Ethics; Higher education; Political
correctness and multiculturalism; Political
philosophy; The Reagan legacy; School choice;
Standards, curriculum, and testing

Nelson, Dr. Michael A.
Professor and Chairman, Department of
Economics
University of Akron
Olin Hall 235C
Akron, OH 44325-1908
330-972-7939   fax 330-972-5356
manelson@uakron.edu
Issues: Federalism; Government waste;
Privatization/Contracting-out; Public school
finance and administration; State and local
public finance; Taxation/tax reform

Nelson, Dr. Richard Alan
Editor, *Journal of Promotion Management,* and
Professor of Mass Communication & Public
Affairs, Manship School of Mass
Communication
Louisiana State University
216 Hatcher Hall
Baton Rouge, LA 70803-7202
225-578-6686   fax 225-578-2125
rnelson@lsu.edu
Issues: Ethics; Free Speech; Higher education;
Intelligence gathering and covert operations;
Media and popular culture; Middle East;
Promoting democracy/public diplomacy;
Telecommunications and the Internet;
Terrorism and international crime

Nelson, Robert H., Ph.D.
Professor, School of Public Affairs
University of Maryland
3131 Van Munching Hall
College Park, MD 20742-1821
301-405-6345   fax 301-403-4675
rn29@umail.umd.edu
Issues: Agriculture; Climate change; The
Economy; Energy; Entrepreneurship/free
enterprise; Environmental regulation; Forestry
and national parks; Free-market
environmentalism; Land use; Money and
financial services; Privatization/Contracting-
out; Sound science

Nesterczuk, George
Nesterczuk and Associates
2013 Westwood Forest Drive
Vienna, VA 22182
703-242-6208   gnesterczuk@cox.net
Issues: Federal civil service; Government health
programs; Health care reform; Homeland
security/civil defense; Transportation; Unions

Neth, Dr. Michael J.

Associate Professor, Department of English
Middle Tennessee State University
MTSU Box X052
Murfreesboro, TN 37132-0001
615-898-2588   fax 615-898-5098
mneth@mtsu.edu

Issues: Higher education; Political correctness
and multiculturalism; Standards, curriculum,
and testing

*Neuhaus, Rev. Richard John

President
Institute on Religion and Public Life
156 Fifth Avenue, Suite 400
New York, NY 10010
212-627-2288   fax 212-627-2184
ft@firstthings.com

Issues: Charter schools; Church-state relations;
Civil rights/racial preferences; Conservative
thought; Constitutional law; Ethics; Family and
children; Human rights; Judiciary; Marriage
and divorce; Political philosophy; Poverty and
dependency; Religion and public life; School
choice

Neumann, Dr. George R.

Professor of Economics
University of Iowa
West 388 Pappa John Building
Iowa City, IA 52242
319-335-0850   fax 319-335-1956
george-neumann@uiowa.edu

Issues: Costs and benefits of regulation;
Economic education; Economic forecasting;
Economic theory; Elections/polling; Higher
education; Labor and employment; Minimum
wage; Privatization/Contracting-out; Right to
work; School-to-work; Telecommunications
and the Internet; Unemployment insurance;
Unions

Neumann, Tom

Executive Director
Jewish Institute for National Security Affairs
1717 K Street, N.W., Suite 800
Washington, DC 20036
202-833-0020   fax 202-296-6452
jinsa2@aol.com

Issues: American diplomacy/foreign policy;
Emerging threats/threat assessment; Export
controls/military transfers; Homeland
security/civil defense; Middle East; Missile
defense; NATO and other alliances; Readiness
and manpower; South Asia (including India
and Pakistan); Terrorism and international
crime

*Neuschler, Edward

Senior Program Officer
Institute for Health Policy Solutions
1444 Eye Street., N.W., Suite 900
Washington, DC 20005
202-789-1491   fax 202-789-1879
eneuschler@ihps.org

Issues: Government health programs; Health
care reform; Medicaid

Neusner, Prof. Jacob

Research Professor of Religion and Theology
Bard College
39 Kalina Drive
Rhinebeck, NY 12572-1022
845-876-7320

Issues: Arts, humanities and historic resources;
Higher education; Political correctness and
multiculturalism; Religion and public life

Nice, Dr. David Charles

Professor of Political Science
Washington State University
P. O. Box 644880
Pullman, WA 99164-4880
509-335-8320   fax 509-335-7990
dnice@wsu.edu

Issues: Citizenship and civil society; Congress;
Discretionary spending; Entitlement spending;
Executive Branch/The Presidency; Federal
budget; Federalism; Government debt; State
and local government; State and local public
finance; Transportation

Nichols, Dr. Thomas M.

Professor and Chairman, Department of
Strategy and Policy
U. S. Naval War College
Newport, RI 02842
401-841-7507   fax 401-841-6418
nicholst@nwc.navy.mil

Issues: Arms control; Military strategy; NATO
and other alliances; Russia and Eurasia

*Nickerson, Dr. Charles C.

Professor of English and Director of College
Honors Program
Bridgewater College
Honors Center
Bridgewater, MA 02325
508-531-1378   fax 508-531-1336
cnickerson@bridgew.edu

Issues: Higher education

*Nims, Frank
President
Oregonians in Action
8255 S.W. Hunziker Road, Suite 200
Tigard, OR 97281
503-620-0258   fax 503-639-6891
oiaec@oia.org
Issues: Forestry and national parks; Land use;
Property rights; Urban sprawl/livable cities;
Wildlife management/endangered species

*Niskanen, Dr. William A.
Chairman
Cato Institute
1000 Massachusetts Avenue, N.W.
Washington, DC 20001
202-789-5236   fax 202-842-3490
wniskan@cato.org
Issues: Comparative government; Federal
budget; Federalism; The Reagan legacy;
Regulatory reform; Taxation/tax reform;
Trade

Nix, Stephen
Regional Program Director, Eurasia
International Republican Institute
1225 Eye Street, N.W., Suite 700
Washington, DC 20005
202-408-9450   fax 202-408-9462
eurasia@iri.org
Issues: Russia and Eurasia

Noell, C. Preston, III
President
Tradition, Family, Property, Inc.
1344 Merrie Ridge Road
McLean, VA 22101
703-243-2104   fax 703-243-2105
cpnoell@pobox.com
Issues: Arts, humanities and historic resources;
Emerging threats/threat assessment; Judicial
activism/judicial reform; Media and popular
culture; Missile defense; Religion and public
life

*Nolan, Pat
President
Justice Fellowship
1856 Old Reston Avenue
Reston, VA 20190
703-904-7313   fax 703-904-7307
pnolan@justicefellowship.org
Issues: Church-state relations; Corrections and
sentencing; Crime/crime statistics; Criminal
law and procedure; Juvenile justice; Religious
freedom

Nolan, Stuart W., Jr.
Attorney
8489 Kitchener Drive
Springfield, VA 22153
703-644-2964   stu@legalworks.com
Issues: Advocacy and nonprofit public funding;
The American Founding; American history/
political tradition; Campaign finance reform;
Church-state relations; Conservative thought;
Constitutional law; Faith-based and volunteer
initiatives; Family and children; Free Speech;
Judicial activism/judicial reform;
Philanthropy; Political philosophy; Religion
and public life; Religious freedom;
Telecommunications and the Internet

Noll, Dr. Mark
McManis Chair of Christian Thought,
Department of History
Wheaton College
501 College Avenue
Wheaton, IL 60187
630-752-5865   fax 630-752-5294
Mark.Noll@wheaton.edu
Issues: Religion and public life

Noonan, Michael
Deputy Director, Program on National
Security
Foreign Policy Research Institute
1528 Walnut Street, Suite 610
Philadelphia, PA 19102
215-732-3774   fax 215-732-4401
fpri@fpri.org
Issues: Emerging threats/threat assessment;
Homeland security/civil defense; Military
strategy; Readiness and manpower; Terrorism
and international crime

*Norquist, Grover
President
Americans for Tax Reform
1920 L Street, N.W., Suite 200
Washington, DC 20036
202-785-0266   fax 202-785-0261
gnorquist@atr.org
Issues: Government waste; Immigration; The
Reagan legacy; Second Amendment;
Taxation/tax reform

---

*Northrup, Dr. Herbert R.
Professor Emeritus of Management, The Wharton School
University of Pennsylvania
205 Avon Road
Haverford, PA 19041
610-642-1293　　fax 610-642-1576
Issues: Davis-Bacon Act; Family and medical leave; Free Speech; Job training/welfare to work; Labor and employment; Minimum wage; OSHA; The Reagan legacy; Right to work; Transportation deregulation; Unemployment insurance; Unions

Norton, Seth W.
Aldeen Professor of Business
Wheaton College
501 College Avenue, Blanchard 116
Wheaton, IL 60187-5593
630-752-5310　　fax 630-752-7037
seth.norton@wheaton.edu
Issues: Anti-trust; Comparative economics; Entrepreneurship/free enterprise; Infrastructure; Poverty and dependency; Religion and public life; Telecommunications and the Internet

*Norton, Col. Stephen R., USA (Ret.)
Senior Policy Advisor
Western Policy Center
1990 M Street, N.W., Suite 610
Washington, DC 20036
202-530-1425　　fax 202-530-0261
stephen@westernpolicy.org
Issues: Intelligence gathering and covert operations; Middle East; Military strategy; NATO and other alliances; Peacekeeping; Western Europe

Nott, David C.
President
Reason Foundation
3415 South Sepulveda Boulevard, Suite 400
Los Angeles, CA 90034
310-391-2245　　fax 310-391-4395
david.nott@reason.org
Issues: Costs and benefits of regulation; Executive Branch/The Presidency; Federal budget; Federal civil service; Federalism; Government waste; Privatization/Contracting-out; Regulatory budgeting; Regulatory reform

Novak, Michael J., Jr.
George Frederick Jewett Chair in Religion and Public Policy
American Enterprise Institute
1150 17th Street, N.W.
Washington, DC 20036
202-862-5839　　fax 202-862-7177
mnovak@aei.org
Issues: The American Founding; American history/political tradition; Church-state relations; Citizenship and civil society; Conservative thought; Economic theory; Ethics; Human rights; International organizations (European Union, OECD, etc.); Philanthropy; Political philosophy; Poverty and dependency; Promoting democracy/public diplomacy; Religion and public life; Religious freedom; Wealth creation/financial empowerment

Novotny, Dr. Erie J.
11649 Havenner Road
Fairfax Station, VA 22039
703-425-4973　　fax 703-425-4974
novotnyej@hotmail.com
Issues: Central and Eastern Europe; Export controls/military transfers; Intelligence gathering and covert operations; International organizations (European Union, OECD, etc.); Privacy; Telecommunications and the Internet; Terrorism and international crime

Nowacki, John
Director for Legal Policy
Free Congress Foundation
717 Second Street, N.E.
Washington, DC 20002
202-546-3000　　fax 202-543-5605
jnowacki@freecongress.org
Issues: The American Founding; Constitutional law; Judicial activism/judicial reform; Judiciary

*Noyes, James H.
Research Fellow
Hoover Institution
Stanford University
Stanford, CA 94305
415-309-2466　　fax 415-345-9834
noyes@hoover.stanford.edu
Issues: Afghanistan; Middle East; South Asia (including India and Pakistan)

Noyes, Lauren
Director of Research Projects
The Heritage Foundation
214 Massachusetts Avenue, N.E.
Washington, DC 20002
202-546-4400   fax 202-544-5421
lauren.noyes@heritage.org
Issues: Abstinence and out-of-wedlock births;
Congress; Family and children; Marriage and
divorce; Welfare/welfare reform

Nuechterlein, James
Editor
First Things
156 Fifth Avenue, Suite 400
New York, NY 10010
212-627-2288   fax 212-627-2184
jn@firstthings.com
Issues: Church-state relations; Civil rights/racial
preferences; Conservative thought; The
Reagan legacy; Religion and public life;
Religious freedom

Nutter, David
Director of Special Programs
Mercatus Center at George Mason University
3301 North Fairfax Drive, Suite 450
Arlington, VA 22201
703-993-4952   fax 703-993-4935
dnutter@gmu.edu
Issues: Congress; Environmental education;
Stewardship

Nuttle, R. Marc
Attorney-at-Law
900 36th Avenue, N.W., Suite 202
Norman, OK 73072
405-364-5946   fax 405-329-9143
rmnuttle@nuttle.com
Issues: Campaign finance reform; Congress;
Elections/polling; Executive Branch/The
Presidency; Right to work; State and local
government; Trade

O'Beirne, Kate
Washington Editor
National Review
219 Pennsylvania Avenue, S.E., Suite 300
Washington, DC 20003
202-543-9226   fax 202-543-9341
Issues: Congress; Executive Branch/The
Presidency; Poverty and dependency; Welfare/
welfare reform

O'Brien, Lisa Coldwell
President
New York Charter Schools Association
49 Turner Lane
Loudonville, NY 12211
518-433-0505   fax 518-433-7065
lobrien@nycsa.org
Issues: Charter schools

O'Connell, Scott
Director of Planned Giving
The Heritage Foundation
214 Massachusetts Avenue, N.E.
Washington, DC 20002
Issues: Philanthropy

*O'Dea, Michael
Christus Medicus Foundation
3707 West Maple
Bloomfield Hills, MI 48301
248-594-8664   fax 248-594-8663
mikeodea@christusmedicus.com
Issues: Adoption, foster care, & child care
services; Church-state relations; Faith-based
and volunteer initiatives; Government health
programs; Health care reform; Medicaid;
Religious freedom

*O'Driscoll, Gerald P., Jr.
Senior Fellow
Cato Institute
2313 Highland Avenue
Falls Church, VA 22046
703-237-3483   fax 703-237-3485
gpo@ix.netcom.com
Issues: Comparative economics; Economic
development/foreign aid; The Economy; Latin
America; Money and financial services; Trade

*O'Keefe, William
President
George C. Marshall Institute
1625 K Street, N.W., Suite 1050
Washington, DC 20006
202-296-9655   fax 202-296-9714
info@marshall.org
Issues: Emerging threats/threat assessment;
Federalism; Homeland security/civil defense;
Military strategy; Missile defense; Terrorism
and international crime

---

* Has testified before a state or federal legislative committee

O'Keeffe, Jeremiah
4212 Donnington Drive
Plano, TX 75093
972-998-9222   fax 972-867-3461 (call
first)   okeeffe_global_advisors@msn.com
Issues: China; Electricity deregulation;
Emerging threats/threat assessment;
Homeland security/civil defense; Intelligence
gathering and covert operations; Latin
America; Middle East; Military strategy;
Northeast Asia; Risk assessment; Russia and
Eurasia; South Asia (including India and
Pakistan); Southeast Asia (including Burma,
Cambodia, Laos, Vietnam, Singapore,
Malaysia, Indonesia, the Philippines, Australia,
and New Zealand); Terrorism and
international crime; Trade; Western Europe

O'Leary, Dr. James P.
Associate Professor, Department of Politics
Catholic University of America
620 Michigan Avenue, N.E.
Washington, DC 20064
202-319-6227   fax 202-319-6289
Issues: China; Conservative thought; South Asia
(including India and Pakistan)

*O'Malley, Dr. Charles J.
Private Education Consultant
Charles J. O'Malley & Associates, Inc.
442 Cranes Roost Court
Annapolis, MD 21401
410-349-0139   fax 410-349-0140
cjoainc@mindspring.com
Issues: Church-state relations; Federal
education policy; Higher education; Home
schooling; School choice

*O'Neill, Prof. Michael
Associate Professor of Law
George Mason University School of Law
3301 North Fairfax Drive
Arlington, VA 22201
703-993-8035   fax 703-993-8088
moneill3@gmu.edu
Issues: The American Founding; American
history/political tradition; Church-state
relations; Constitutional law; Corrections and
sentencing; Crime/crime statistics; Criminal
law and procedure; Free Speech; Judiciary;
Juvenile justice; Religious freedom

O'Neill, Mike
Barbara Olson Legal Fellow
Landmark Legal Foundation
445-B Carlisle Drive
Herndon, VA 20170
703-689-2370   fax 703-689-2373
mikelandmark@earthlink.net
Issues: Constitutional law; Education unions
and interest groups; Government waste;
Judicial activism/judicial reform; Judiciary;
School choice; Taxation/tax reform; Unions

*O'Neill, Patsy
Executive Director
Charter School Resource Center of Texas
40 N.E. Loop 410, Suite 408
San Antonio, TX 78216
210-348-7890   fax 210-348-7899
Issues: Charter schools; School choice

O'Rourke, Dr. Timothy G.
Theresa M. Fischer Professor of Citizenship
Education
University of Missouri, St. Louis
357 Marillac Hall, 8001 Natural Bridge Road
St. Louis, MO 63121
314-516-6853   fax 314-516-5227
tg_orourke@umsl.edu
Issues: Civil rights/racial preferences; State and
local government

O'Shea, M. Lester
1912 Highridge Court
Walnut Creek, CA 94596
925-939-4950   fax 925-939-5687
loscha@aol.com
Issues: Civil rights/racial preferences

O'Toole, Randal
Senior Economist
Thoreau Institute
P. O. Box 1590
Bandon, OR 97411
541-347-1517   fax 305-422-0379
rot@ti.org
Issues: Forestry and national parks; Free-market
environmentalism; Land use; Transportation
deregulation; Urban sprawl/livable cities;
Wildlife management/endangered species

Oaxaca, Dr. Ronald L.
McClelland Professor, Department of
Economics
University of Arizona
McClelland Hall
Tucson, AZ 85721
602-621-4135   fax 520-621-8450
rlo@u.arizona.edu
Issues: Labor and employment; Unemployment
insurance

Odom, Lt. Gen. William E.
Senior Fellow
Hudson Institute
1015 18th Street, N.W., Suite 300
Washington, DC 20036
202-223-7770   fax 202-223-8537
Issues: American diplomacy/foreign policy;
Central and Eastern Europe; Defense budget;
Emerging threats/threat assessment;
Homeland security/civil defense; Intelligence
gathering and covert operations; Military
strategy; Missile defense; NATO and other
alliances; Northeast Asia; Readiness and
manpower; Russia and Eurasia; Western
Europe

Ohlert, Edward J.
Vice President, Strategic and Intelligence
Programs
JAYCOR
1410 Spring Hill Road, Suite 300
McLean, VA 22102
703-847-4137   fax 703-847-4096
Issues: Afghanistan; American diplomacy/
foreign policy; Arms control; Campaign
finance reform; China; Defense budget;
Emerging threats/threat assessment; Ethics;
Export controls/military transfers; Homeland
security/civil defense; Intellectual property;
Intelligence gathering and covert operations;
Military strategy; Missile defense; NATO and
other alliances; Peacekeeping; Police;
Terrorism and international crime

*Oladeinde, Fred O.
President
The Foundation for Democracy in Africa
1900 L Street, N.W.
Washington, DC 20036
202-331-1333   fax 202-331-8547
comments@democracy-africa.org
Issues: Africa; Entrepreneurship/free
enterprise; Non-governmental organizations;
Promoting democracy/public diplomacy;
Wealth creation/financial empowerment

*Olasky, Dr. Marvin
Professor
University of Texas
4106 Firstview Drive
Austin, TX 78731
512-451-6278   fax 512-451-6580
molasky@aol.com
Issues: Adoption, foster care, & child care
services; The American Founding; American
history/political tradition; Church-state
relations; Citizenship and civil society; Faith-
based and volunteer initiatives; Media and
popular culture; Philanthropy; Poverty and
dependency; Religion and public life; Religious
freedom; Welfare/welfare reform

*Olcott, Dr. Martha
Carnegie Endowment for International
Peace
1779 Massachusetts Avenue, N.W.
Washington, DC 20036
202-483-9266   fax 202-483-1840
molcott@ceip.org
Issues: Afghanistan; Russia and Eurasia

*Olivastro, Richard
President
People Dynamics
9 Cypress Trail
Farmington, CT 06032
860-677-4776   fax 860-677-6632
richolivastro@peopledynamics.net
Issues: American diplomacy/foreign policy;
Business and education partnerships;
Citizenship and civil society; Conservative
thought; Economic development/foreign aid;
Emerging threats/threat assessment; Energy;
Entrepreneurship/free enterprise;
Environmental education; Ethics; Family and
children; Federalism; Free Speech; Health care
reform; Higher education; Home schooling;
Homeland security/civil defense; Immigration;
Judicial activism/judicial reform; Political
philosophy; Promoting democracy/public
diplomacy; Property rights; Public school
finance and administration; Readiness and
manpower; The Reagan legacy; School choice;
School-to-work; Second Amendment; Social
Security and retirement; Standards,
curriculum, and testing; State and local
government; Stewardship; Taxation/tax
reform; Term limits; Unfunded mandates;
United Nations

*Oliver, Hon. Daniel
Chairman
Pacific Research Institute
3105 Woodley Road, N.W.
Washington, DC 20008
202-986-2888   fax 202-328-6801
doliver@bellatlantic.net
Issues: Anti-trust; Trade

*Olsen, Darcy A.
Executive Director
Goldwater Institute
500 East Coronado Road
Phoenix, AZ 85004
602-462-5000   fax 602-256-7045
dolsen@goldwaterinstitute.org
Issues: Adoption, foster care, & child care
services; Charter schools; Education unions
and interest groups; Entrepreneurship/free
enterprise; Family and children; Federal
education policy; Higher education; Home
schooling; Public school finance and
administration; School choice; Standards,
curriculum, and testing

*Olsen, Dr. Edgar O.
Professor, Department of Economics
University of Virginia
P. O. Box 400182
Charlottesville, VA 22903
804-924-3443   fax 804-924-7659
eoo@cms.mail.virginia.edu
Issues: Housing and homelessness

Olsen, Dr. Edward A.
Professor of National Security
Naval Postgraduate School
Monterey, CA 93943
831-656-3163   fax 831-656-2949
eolsen@nps.navy.mil
Issues: Japan; Korea; Military strategy; Missile
defense; Northeast Asia; South Asia (including
India and Pakistan); Southeast Asia (including
Burma, Cambodia, Laos, Vietnam, Singapore,
Malaysia, Indonesia, the Philippines, Australia,
and New Zealand)

*Olsen, Henry, III
Executive Director, Center for Civic
Innovation
Manhattan Institute for Policy Research
52 Vanderbilt Avenue
New York, NY 10017
212-599-7000   fax 212-599-3494
holsen@manhattan-institute.org
Issues: Elections/polling; State and local public
finance

*Olson, Walter K.
Senior Fellow
Manhattan Institute for Policy Research
875 King Street
Chappaqua, NY 10514
914-747-0447   fax 914-747-1666
wo@walterolson.com
Issues: Judiciary; Regulation through litigation;
Tort and liability reform

Ong, Dr. B. Nelson
Associate Professor, Division of Social
Sciences
College of New Rochelle
29 Castle Place
New Rochelle, NY 10805
914-632-2374   fax 914-576-4960
nelson.ong@verizon.net
Issues: The American Founding; American
history/political tradition; Higher education;
The Reagan legacy

Oppel, Glenn
Executive Director
Rocky Mountain Enterprise Institute
540 O'Malley Drive
Billings, MT 59102
406-861-5730   rmeimt@yahoo.com
Issues: American history/political tradition;
Conservative thought; Economic theory;
Health care reform; Medicare; Political
philosophy; Social Security and retirement

*Orient, Jane M., M.D.
Executive Director
Association of American Physicians and
Surgeons
1601 North Tucson Boulevard, Suite 9
Tucson, AZ 85716
520-327-4885   fax 520-326-3529
71161.1263@compuserve.com
Issues: Government health programs; Health
care reform; Medicare; Privacy; Readiness and
manpower; Risk assessment; Sound science

Ornstein, Dr. Norman J.
Resident Scholar
American Enterprise Institute
1150 17th Street, N.W.
Washington, DC 20036
202-862-5893   fax 202-862-5821
nornstein@aei.org
Issues: Congress; Elections/polling

Osborn, Dr. J. Marshall
Professor, Department of Mathematics
University of Wisconsin
6214 Old Sauk Road
Madison, WI 53705-2509
608-263-4283   fax 608-263-8891
osborn@math.wisc.edu
Issues: Higher education

Osorio, Ivan G.
Research Associate and Editor, *Labor Watch*
Capital Research Center
1513 16th Street, N.W.
Washington, DC 20036
202-483-6900   fax 202-483-6990
iosorio@capitalresearch.org
Issues: Advocacy and nonprofit public funding;
Davis-Bacon Act; Education unions and interest
groups; Labor and employment; Latin
America; OSHA; Right to work; Unions

Ostrander, Kent
Executive Director
The Family Foundation of Kentucky
P. O. Box 22100
Lexington, KY 40522
859-255-5400   fax 859-233-3330
tffky@mis.net
Issues: Citizenship and civil society; Faith-based
and volunteer initiatives; Family and children;
Religion and public life; State-sponsored
gambling

*Otis, William G.
3513 Wentworth Drive
Falls Church, VA 22044
703-916-1847   fax 703-916-8316
lee_otis@msn.com
Issues: Corrections and sentencing; Criminal
law and procedure; Police

*Overton, Joseph P.
Senior Vice President
Mackinac Center for Public Policy
140 West Main Street, P. O. Box 568
Midland, MI 48640
989-631-0900   fax 989-631-0964
overton@mackinac.org
Issues: Charter schools; Education unions and
interest groups; Public school finance and
administration; Right to work; School choice;
Unions

Owcharenko, Nina
Policy Analyst, Health Care
The Heritage Foundation
214 Massachusetts Avenue, N.E.
Washington, DC 20002
202-608-6221   fax 202-544-5421
nina.owcharenko@heritage.org
Issues: Aging/elder care; Government health
programs; Health care reform; Medicaid;
Medicare

*Owens, Dr. Mackubin T.
Associate Dean of Academics for Electives
and Directed Research
U. S. Naval War College
686 Cushing Road
Newport, RI 02841
401-841-2015   fax 401-841-6402
owensm@nwc.navy.mil
Issues: American diplomacy/foreign policy;
The American Founding; American history/
political tradition; Arms control; Defense
budget; Military strategy; Political philosophy

Paige, Sean
Former Warren Brookes Fellow & Editorial
Director
Competitive Enterprise Institute
1001 Connecticut Avenue, N.W., Suite 1250
Washington, DC 20036
202-331-1010   fax 202-331-0640
spaige@cei.org
Issues: Costs and benefits of regulation;
Discretionary spending; Energy;
Environmental education; Environmental
regulation; Federal budget; Forestry and
national parks; Free-market environmentalism;
Government waste; Land use; Property rights;
Regulation through litigation; Sound science;
Stewardship; Unfunded mandates; Urban
sprawl/livable cities; Wildlife management/
endangered species

Palm, Dr. Daniel
Associate Professor of Political Science
Azusa Pacific University
921 East Alosta Avenue
Azusa, CA 91702
626-815-3782   fax 626-815-3868
dpalm@apu.edu
Issues: The American Founding; American
history/political tradition; China; Conservative
thought; Second Amendment

*Palmer, Gary J.

President
Alabama Policy Institute
402 Office Park Drive, Suite 300
Birmingham, AL 35223
205-870-9900   fax 205-870-4407
garyp@alabamapolicy.org
Issues: Energy; Marriage and divorce;
Privatization/Contracting-out; School choice;
State-sponsored gambling; Taxation/tax
reform; Tort and liability reform; Welfare/
welfare reform

Palmer, Dr. Tom G.

Senior Fellow and Director of Cato
University
Cato Institute
1000 Massachusetts Avenue, N.W.
Washington, DC 20001-5403
202-842-0200   fax 202-842-3490
tpalmer@cato.org
Issues: American history/political tradition;
Citizenship and civil society; Federalism;
Political philosophy

*Panyard, Jim

President
Pennsylvania Manufacturer's Association
225 State Street
Harrisburg, PA 17101
717-232-0737   fax 717-232-8623
panyard@pamanufacturers.org
Issues: American history/political tradition;
Conservative thought; Economic theory;
Ethics; Government waste; Minimum wage;
Religion and public life; Right to work; School
choice; State and local government; State and
local public finance; Taxation/tax reform

Paone, Dr. Rocco M.

Professor Emeritus
U. S. Naval Academy
1001 Boom Court
Annapolis, MD 21401
410-224-2753
Issues: American diplomacy/foreign policy;
China; Economic development/foreign aid;
Emerging threats/threat assessment; Ethics;
Homeland security/civil defense; Military
strategy; NATO and other alliances; Political
philosophy; Russia and Eurasia; Western
Europe

*Parde, Duane

Executive Director
American Legislative Exchange Council
1129 20th Street, N.W., Suite 500
Washington, DC 20036
202-466-3800   fax 202-466-3801
dparde@alec.org
Issues: Advocacy and nonprofit public funding;
American history/political tradition;
Federalism; Medicaid; State and local
government; State and local public finance;
Tort and liability reform

*Parker, Allan E., Jr., J.D.

President
Texas Justice Foundation
8122 Datapoint Drive, Suite 812
San Antonio, TX 78229
210-614-7157   fax 210-614-6656
aparker@txjf.org
Issues: Charter schools; Church-state relations;
Citizenship and civil society; Civil rights/racial
preferences; Constitutional law; Education
unions and interest groups; Ethics; Federal
education policy; Free Speech; Home
schooling; Judicial activism/judicial reform;
Political philosophy; Public interest law;
Religious freedom; School choice

*Parker, J. A.

President
Lincoln Institute for Research and
Education
1001 Connecticut Avenue, N.W., Suite 1135
Washington, DC 20036
703-759-4599   fax 703-759-7308
Issues: Africa; Aging/elder care; Campaign
finance reform; Civil rights/racial preferences;
Conservative thought; Costs and benefits of
regulation; Federal education policy; Free
Speech; Government debt; Health care reform;
Home schooling; Homeland security/civil
defense; Housing and homelessness;
Intellectual property; Judiciary; Juvenile
justice; Labor and employment; Medicaid;
Medicare; Non-governmental organizations;
Philanthropy; Political correctness and
multiculturalism; Property rights; Readiness
and manpower; The Reagan legacy; Right to
work; School choice; Second Amendment;
Social Security and retirement; State and local
government; Telecommunications and the
Internet; Term limits; Unions; United Nations

Parker, Kyle
Vice President for Programs
American Foreign Policy Council
1521 16th Street, N.W.
Washington, DC 20036
202-462-6055   fax 202-462-6045
parker@afpc.org
Issues: Russia and Eurasia

Parker, Patrick J.
1993 Orchard Road
Hollister, CA 95023-9420
909-625-1435   fax 831-636-3340
pparker@stl.nps.navy.mil
Issues: Emerging threats/threat assessment;
Military strategy; Readiness and manpower

*Parker, Star
President
Coalition on Urban Renewal and Education
126 C Street, N.W.
Washington, DC 20001
202-479-2873   fax 202-479-2876
policy@urbancure.org
Issues: Abstinence and out-of-wedlock births;
Davis-Bacon Act; Faith-based and volunteer
initiatives; Housing and homelessness; Poverty
and dependency; Religion and public life;
School choice; Social Security and retirement;
Wealth creation/financial empowerment;
Welfare/welfare reform

Parrott, Dr. Bruce
Director, Russian and Eastern European
Studies
The Paul H. Nitze School for Advanced
International Studies
Johns Hopkins University, 1740
Massachusetts Avenue, N.W.
Washington, DC 20036
202-663-5600   fax 202-663-5656
Issues: Russia and Eurasia

Parshall, Janet
Host
Janet Parshall's America
1901 North Moore Street, Suite 201A
Arlington, VA 22209
703-276-8597   fax 703-516-7212
janet@jpamerica.com
Issues: Family and children; Media and popular
culture; School choice

Pasicolan, Paolo
Policy Analyst, Asian Studies Center
The Heritage Foundation
214 Massachusetts Avenue, N.E.
Washington, DC 20002
202-546-4400   fax 202-675-1779
paolo.pasicolan@heritage.org
Issues: Economic development/foreign aid;
Southeast Asia (including Burma, Cambodia,
Laos, Vietnam, Singapore, Malaysia, Indonesia,
the Philippines, Australia, and New Zealand);
Terrorism and international crime

Pasour, Dr. E. C., Jr.
Professor Emeritus
North Carolina State University
4309 Nelson Hall, Box 8109
Raleigh, NC 27695
919-515-6250   fax 919-515-1824
ec_pasour@ncsu.edu
Issues: Agriculture; Costs and benefits of
regulation; Economic theory;
Entrepreneurship/free enterprise;
Environmental regulation; Free-market
environmentalism; Land use; Research
funding

Patray, Bobbie
Eagle Forum of Tennessee
3216 Bluewater Trace
Nashville, TN 37217
fax 615-360-9005   bpatray@aol.com
Issues: Adoption, foster care, & child care
services; State-sponsored gambling

*Patrick, Lawrence C., III
President and CEO
Black Alliance for Educational Options
501 C Street, N.E., Suite 3
Washington, DC 20002
202-544-9870   fax 202-544-7680
lawrence@baeo.org
Issues: Business and education partnerships;
Charter schools; School choice

*Patterson, Christine
Director of Education Research
Texas Public Policy Foundation
P. O. Box 40519
San Antonio, TX 78229
210-614-0080   fax 210-614-2649
chrispat@tppf.org
Issues: Business and education partnerships;
Charter schools; Environmental education;
Federal education policy; Higher education;
Home schooling; Public school finance and
administration; School choice; School-to-work;
Standards, curriculum, and testing

Patterson, Dr. David A.
Bornblum Chair in Judaic Studies
University of Memphis
301 Mitchell Hall
Memphis, TN 38152
901-678-2919   fax 901-678-2777
dapttrsn@memphis.edu
Issues: Higher education; Middle East;
Standards, curriculum, and testing

*Patton, Dr. Judd W.
Associate Professor of Economics,
Entrepreneurial Leadership Center
Bellevue University
1000 Galvin Road, South
Bellevue, NE 68005
402-293-3743   fax 402-293-3819
jpatton@bellevue.edu
Issues: The American Founding; Comparative
economics; Economic education; Economic
theory; Ethics

Paul, Dr. Ellen F.
Deputy Director, Social Philosophy and
Policy Center
Bowling Green State University
225 Troupe Street
Bowling Green, OH 43403
419-372-2536   fax 419-372-8738
ellenfp@bgnet.bgsu.edu
Issues: Civil rights/racial preferences; Free
Speech; Land use; Political philosophy;
Property rights; Russia and Eurasia

Paul, Dr. Jeffrey E.
Professor and Associate Director, Social
Philosophy and Policy Center
Bowling Green State University
Bowling Green, OH 43403
419-372-2536   fax 419-372-8738
Issues: Political philosophy

*Paulk, John
Homosexuality and Gender Analyst, Social
Research and Cultural Affairs
Focus on the Family
8605 Explorer Drive
Colorado Springs, CO 80920
719-548-4565   fax 719-268-4804
paulkjt@fotf.org
Issues: Media and popular culture; Political
correctness and multiculturalism; Religion and
public life

*Paulson, Dr. Darryl
Professor of Government
University of South Florida
140 Seventh Avenue South
St. Petersburg, FL 33701
727-553-1582   fax 727-553-1526
dpaulson@stpt.usf.edu
Issues: Campaign finance reform; Civil rights/
racial preferences; Congress; Elections/
polling; Electoral reform/voting rights;
Initiative and referendum; State and local
government; Term limits; Urban sprawl/livable
cities; Welfare/welfare reform

*Paulton, John
Director, Family Policy Councils
Focus on the Family
8605 Explorer Drive
Colorado Springs, CO 80920
719-531-3471   fax 719-531-3385
paultojh@fotf.org
Issues: Church-state relations; Religion and
public life; Right to work; State-sponsored
gambling

*Pauly, Mark V., Ph.D.
Bendheim Professor of Health Care Systems,
The Wharton School
University of Pennsylvania
3641 Locust Walk
Philadelphia, PA 19104
215-898-5411   fax 215-573-2157
pauly@wharton.upenn.edu
Issues: Government health programs; Health
care reform; Medicare

Paust, Jordan
Law Foundation Professor of Law
University of Houston Law Center
4800 Calhoun Road
Houston, TX 77204
713-743-2177   fax 713-743-2238
JPaust@central.UH.edu
Issues: Human rights; United Nations

Peacock, Dr. Anthony A.
Assistant Professor, Department of Political
Science
Utah State University
0725 Old Main Hill
Logan, UT 84322-0725
435-797-1314   fax 435-797-3751
apeacock@wpo.hass.usu.edu
Issues: The American Founding; Civil rights/
racial preferences; Constitutional law; Electoral
reform/voting rights; Federalism; Judiciary;
Political philosophy

*Pearlstein, Mitchell B., Ph.D.
President
Center of the American Experiment
12 South 6th Street, Suite 1024
Minneapolis, MN 55402
612-338-3605   fax 612-338-3621
mitch@amexp.org
Issues: Abstinence and out-of-wedlock births;
Adoption, foster care, & child care services;
Church-state relations; Civil rights/racial
preferences; Higher education; Marriage and
divorce; Political correctness and
multiculturalism; Religion and public life;
School choice

*Pearson, Ronald W.
President
Pearson & Pipkin, Inc.
104 North Carolina Avenue, S.E.
Washington, DC 20003
202-547-7177   fax 202-546-3091
public.policy@verizon.net
Issues: Africa; Campaign finance reform; China;
Congress; Conservative thought; Elections/
polling; Immigration; The Reagan legacy;
United Nations

Pearson, Dr. Sidney A., Jr.
Professor of Political Science
Radford University
Box 6945
Radford, VA 24142
540-831-5370   fax 540-831-6075
sapearso@runet.edu
Issues: The American Founding; American
history/political tradition; Conservative
thought; Elections/polling; Executive Branch/
The Presidency; Political correctness and
multiculturalism; Political philosophy;
Religion and public life; Religious freedom

*Pech, Valery J.
3625 Hill Circle
Colorado Springs, CO 80904
719-330-1220   fax 719-634-1219
valerypech@aol.com
Issues: Civil rights/racial preferences;
Property rights

*Peirce, Prof. William S.
Professor of Economics, Weatherhead
School of Management
Case Western Reserve University
10900 Euclid Avenue
Cleveland, OH 44106
216-368-4131   fax 216-368-5039
wsp@po.cwru.edu
Issues: Anti-trust; Energy; Federal civil service;
Federalism; International organizations
(European Union, OECD, etc.); Privatization/
Contracting-out; State and local public finance

*Pejovich, Dr. Svetozar
Professor Emeritus, Department of
Economics
Texas A&M University
6959 Joyce Way
Dallas, TX 75225
214-363-4691   fax 214-696-5081
s-pejovich@tamu.edu
Issues: Comparative economics; Costs and
benefits of regulation; Economic
development/foreign aid; Economic
education; The Reagan legacy; Russia and
Eurasia

Pell, Terence J.
Chief Executive Officer
Center for Individual Rights
1233 20th Street, N.W., Suite 300
Washington, DC 20036
202-833-8400   fax 202-833-8410
pell@cir-usa.org
Issues: Church-state relations; Civil rights/racial
preferences; Constitutional law; Ethics;
Federalism; Free Speech; Judicial activism/
judicial reform; Political correctness and
multiculturalism; Political philosophy; Public
interest law; Regulation through litigation;
Religion and public life; Religious freedom;
School choice

---

*Peltzman, Sam
Ralph and Dorothy Keller Distinguished
Service Professor of Economics
University of Chicago Graduate School of
Business
1101 East 58th Street
Chicago, IL 60637
773-702-7457   fax 773-702-0458
sam.peltzman@gsb.uchicago.edu
Issues: Anti-trust; Costs and benefits of
regulation; The Economy; Electricity
deregulation; Entrepreneurship/free
enterprise; Environmental regulation; Free-
market environmentalism; Infrastructure;
Public school finance and administration;
Regulation through litigation; Regulatory
reform; School choice; Transportation;
Transportation deregulation

Pemberton, Laura
Manager, Legislative Affairs-Senate
National Federation of Independent
Business
1201 F Street, N.W., Suite 200
Washington, DC 20004
202-314-2092   fax 202-484-1566
laura.pemberton@nfib.org
Issues: Health care reform; Privacy; Social
Security and retirement; Telecommunications
and the Internet

Pena, Charles V.
Senior Defense Policy Analyst
Cato Institute
1000 Massachusetts Avenue, N.W.
Washington, DC 20001-5403
202-842-0200   fax 202-842-3490
cpena@cato.org
Issues: Arms control; Defense budget; Missile
defense; Readiness and manpower; Terrorism
and international crime

Pendell, Judyth
475 Simsbury Road
Bloomfield, CT 06002
860-242-4727   pendelljudyth@msn.com
Issues: Judicial activism/judicial reform; Tort
and liability reform

*Pendley, William Perry
President and Chief Legal Officer
Mountain States Legal Foundation
2596 South Lewis Way
Lakewood, CO 80227
303-292-2021   fax 303-292-1980
pendley@mountainstateslegal.org
Issues: Air; Civil rights/racial preferences;
Constitutional law; Energy; Environmental
education; Environmental regulation;
Federalism; Forestry and national parks; Free
Speech; Land use; Property rights; Public
interest law; Sound science; Stewardship;
Water; Wildlife management/endangered
species

Perelli, Sam
President
United Taxpayers of New Jersey
P. O. Box 103
Cedar Grove, NJ 07009
973-857-2530   fax 973-857-2534
Issues: Taxation/tax reform

*Perla, Steve
Executive Director
Parent's Alliance for Catholic Education
124 Summer Street
Fitchburg, MA 01420
978-665-9890   fax 978-665-9885
sperla@paaog.net
Issues: Federal education policy; School choice

*Perle, Richard
Resident Scholar
American Enterprise Institute
1150 17th Street, N.W.
Washington, DC 20036
202-862-5849   fax 202-862-5924
richard@perle.org
Issues: Arms control; Defense budget;
Emerging threats/threat assessment; Export
controls/military transfers; Intelligence
gathering and covert operations; Military
strategy; Missile defense; NATO and other
alliances; Peacekeeping; Readiness and
manpower; Terrorism and international crime

Perry, Dr. Charles M.
Vice President and Director of Studies
Institute for Foreign Policy Analysis
675 Massachusetts Avenue, 10th Floor
Cambridge, MA 02139
617-492-2116   fax 617-492-8242
cperry@ifpa.org
Issues: American diplomacy/foreign policy;
Arms control; Central and Eastern Europe;
Defense budget; Emerging threats/threat
assessment; Export controls/military transfers;
Homeland security/civil defense; Japan; Korea;
Middle East; Military strategy; Missile defense;
NATO and other alliances; Northeast Asia;
Peacekeeping; Western Europe

Perry, Dr. Mark J.
Assistant Professor of Economics,
Department of Economics
University of Michigan, Flint
350 French Hall
Flint, MI 48502
810-762-3191   fax 810-762-3687
mjperry@umich.edu
Issues: Economic theory; Money and financial
services

Perry, William
President
William Perry & Associates
33302 Falconwood Road
Agua Dulce, CA 91350
661-268-8044   fax 661-268-8102
perry@calawfirm.com
Issues: Latin America

Perusse, Dr. Roland I.
Director
Inter-American Institute
2475 Virginia Avenue, N.W., Suite 607
Washington, DC 20037-2639
202-342-7238   fax 202-452-7820
Issues: Latin America

Peter, Val
Executive Director
Boys Town
14100 Crawford
Boys Town, NE 68010
402-498-1000   fax 402-498-1010
Issues: Faith-based and volunteer initiatives;
Family and children; Marriage and divorce;
Media and popular culture; Philanthropy;
Religion and public life

*Peterjohn, Karl
Executive Director
Kansas Taxpayers Network
P. O. Box 20050
Wichita, KS 67208
316-684-0082   fax 316-684-7527
kpeterjohn@prodigy.net
Issues: Entrepreneurship/free enterprise;
Government waste; State and local public
finance; Taxation/tax reform

*Peters, Lovett C.
Founding Chairman
Pioneer Institute for Public Policy Research
85 Devonshire Street, 8th Floor
Boston, MA 02109
617-723-2277   fax 617-723-1880
lpeters@pioneerinstitute.org
Issues: Charter schools; Economic education;
Education unions and interest groups;
Entrepreneurship/free enterprise; Health care
reform; Philanthropy; Public school finance
and administration; School choice; Social
Security and retirement

Peters, Philip
Vice President
Lexington Institute
1600 Wilson Boulevard, Suite 900
Arlington, VA 22209
703-522-9639   fax 703-522-5837
peters@dgs.net
Issues: Immigration; Latin America; United
Nations

Peterson, Laura Bennett, Esq.
700 New Hampshire Avenue, N.W., Suite 520
Washington, DC 20037
202-298-5608   fax 202-298-8788
laurabpeterson@cs.com
Issues: Anti-trust; Costs and benefits of
regulation; The Economy; Intellectual
property; Judicial activism/judicial reform;
Judiciary; Regulation through litigation;
Regulatory reform; Telecommunications and
the Internet; Tort and liability reform

Peterson, Dr. Paul C.
Professor, Department of Politics
Coastal Carolina University
P. O. Box 261954
Conway, SC 29528-6054
843-349-2627   fax 843-349-2943
peterson@coastal.edu
Issues: The American Founding; American history/political tradition; Citizenship and civil society; Conservative thought; Executive Branch/The Presidency; Judicial activism/judicial reform; Judiciary; Media and popular culture; Political correctness and multiculturalism; Political philosophy; The Reagan legacy

*Peterson, Dr. William H.
700 New Hampshire Avenue, N.W.,
Apartment 617
Washington, DC 20037
202-337-2986   whpeterson@aol.com
Issues: Anti-trust; Comparative economics; Comparative government; Conservative thought; Economic education; The Economy; Electricity deregulation; Entrepreneurship/free enterprise; Executive Branch/The Presidency; Political philosophy; Privacy; Privatization/Contracting-out; The Reagan legacy; Regulatory reform; Trade

*Pfaltzgraff, Dr. Robert, Jr.
President
Institute for Foreign Policy Analysis
675 Massachusetts Avenue, 10th Floor
Cambridge, MA 02139
617-492-2116   fax 617-492-8242
rlp@ifpa.org
Issues: American diplomacy/foreign policy; Arms control; Central and Eastern Europe; China; Emerging threats/threat assessment; Homeland security/civil defense; Military strategy; Missile defense; NATO and other alliances; Northeast Asia; Peacekeeping; Russia and Eurasia; Western Europe

Pfiffner, Penn
Senior Fellow in Legislative Affairs
Independence Institute
14142 Denver West Parkway, Suite 185
Golden, CO 80401
303-279-6536   fax 303-279-4176
constecon@hotmail.com
Issues: Economic education; Economic forecasting; Economic theory; Privatization/Contracting-out; State and local public finance; Taxation/tax reform; Transportation; Transportation deregulation

*Pfotenhauer, Nancy M.
President
Independent Women's Forum
P. O. Box 3058, 4141 North Henderson Road
Arlington, VA 22203
703-558-4991   fax 703-558-4994
nmf@iwf.org
Issues: Charter schools; Citizenship and civil society; Costs and benefits of regulation; Discretionary spending; Economic theory; The Economy; Education unions and interest groups; Energy; Entitlement spending; Entrepreneurship/free enterprise; Environmental regulation; Family and children; Family and medical leave; Home schooling; Job training/welfare to work; Regulatory reform; Risk assessment; School choice; Second Amendment; Social Security and retirement; Taxation/tax reform; Trade; Transportation; Welfare/welfare reform

*Phillips, Bruce
Senior Fellow, Regulatory Studies
National Federation of Independent Business
1201 F Street, N.W., Suite 200
Washington, DC 20024
202-554-9000   fax 202-554-5572
bruce.phillips@nfib.org
Issues: Costs and benefits of regulation; Entrepreneurship/free enterprise; Family and medical leave; Health care reform; Minimum wage; Regulation through litigation; Telecommunications and the Internet

*Phillips, Howard
Chairman
The Conservative Caucus, Inc.
450 Maple Avenue, East
Vienna, VA 22180
703-893-2777   fax 703-281-4108
Issues: Advocacy and nonprofit public funding; Africa; American history/political tradition; China; Conservative thought; Constitutional law; Executive Branch/The Presidency; Faith-based and volunteer initiatives; Home schooling; Judiciary; NATO and other alliances; Second Amendment; Taxation/tax reform; Trade; United Nations

*Phillips, James
Research Fellow, Kathryn and Shelby Cullom
Davis Institute for International Studies
The Heritage Foundation
214 Massachusetts Avenue, N.E.
Washington, DC 20002
202-546-4400   fax 202-675-1758
jim.phillips@heritage.org
Issues: Afghanistan; American diplomacy/
foreign policy; Emerging threats/threat
assessment; Energy; Intelligence gathering and
covert operations; Middle East; The Reagan
legacy; South Asia (including India and
Pakistan); Terrorism and international crime

Piasecki, Dr. Bruce
President and Founder
AHC Group
4 Franklin Square, Suite B
Saratoga Springs, NY 12866
518-583-9619   fax 518-583-9726
bruce@ahcgroup.com
Issues: Air; Business and education
partnerships; Climate change; Comparative
government; Costs and benefits of regulation;
Economic theory; Energy; Entrepreneurship/
free enterprise; Free-market
environmentalism; Political philosophy;
Property rights; Regulatory reform; Standards,
curriculum, and testing; Stewardship;
Taxation/tax reform; Waste management;
Water

Piedra, Dr. Albert M.
Professor of Economics, Department of
Business and Economics
Catholic University of America
620 Michigan Avenue, N.E.
Washington, DC 20064
202-319-5235   fax 202-319-4426
piedra@cua.edu
Issues: Comparative economics; Economic
development/foreign aid; The Economy

Piereson, James
Executive Director
John M. Olin Foundation, Inc.
330 Madison Avenue, 22nd Floor
New York, NY 10017
212-661-2670   fax 212-661-5917
jpiereson@jmof.org
Issues: Advocacy and nonprofit public funding;
The American Founding; American history/
political tradition; Conservative thought;
Elections/polling; Higher education;
Judiciary; Political correctness and
multiculturalism; The Reagan legacy; School
choice

Pilon, Dr. Juliana Geran
Associate Director, Center for Democracy
and Election Management
American University
4400 Massachusetts Avenue, N.W.
Washington, DC 20016
202-885-1524   juliana@american.edu
Issues: American diplomacy/foreign policy;
Central and Eastern Europe; Economic
development/foreign aid; Human rights;
International organizations (European Union,
OECD, etc.); Promoting democracy/public
diplomacy; Russia and Eurasia; United Nations

*Pilon, Roger, Ph.D.
Vice President for Legal Affairs
Cato Institute
1000 Massachusetts Avenue, N.W.
Washington, DC 20001
202-789-5233   fax 202-842-3490
rpilon@cato.org
Issues: The American Founding; American
history/political tradition; Campaign finance
reform; Church-state relations; Civil rights/
racial preferences; Constitutional law; Ethics;
Federalism; Free Speech; Judicial activism/
judicial reform; Judiciary; Land use; Political
philosophy; Promoting democracy/public
diplomacy; Property rights; Term limits

Pinera, Dr. Jose
Co-Chairman, Project on Social Security
Choice
Cato Institute
1000 Massachusetts Avenue, N.W.
Washington, DC 20001-5403
202-842-0200   fax 202-842-3490
jose@cato.org
Issues: Social Security and retirement

*Pinkus, David R.
President
Small Business United of Texas
1011 West 11th Street, Suite A
Austin, TX 78703
512-476-1707   fax 512-477-9697
sbutx@att.net
Issues: Entrepreneurship/free enterprise;
Health care reform; Labor and employment;
Minimum wage

Pinsker, Dr. Sanford
Arthur and Katherine Shadek Humanities
Professor, Department of English
Franklin and Marshall College
P. O. Box 3003
Lancaster, PA 17604-3003
717-291-4050   fax 717-291-4156
Issues: Arts, humanities and historic resources;
Higher education

*Pipes, Dr. Daniel
Director
Middle East Forum
1500 Walnut Street, Suite 1050
Philadelphia, PA 19102
215-546-5406   fax 215-546-5409
meqmef@aol.com
Issues: Homeland security/civil defense;
Middle East; Terrorism and international
crime

*Pipes, Dr. Richard
Baird Research Professor in History,
Emeritus
17 Berkeley Street
Cambridge, MA 02138
617-492-0727   fax 617-661-4580
rpipes23@aol.com
Issues: American diplomacy/foreign policy;
Emerging threats/threat assessment;
Intelligence gathering and covert operations;
Russia and Eurasia

*Pipes, Sally C.
President and CEO
Pacific Research Institute
755 Sansome Street, Suite 450
San Francisco, CA 94111
415-955-6100   fax 415-989-2411
spipes@pacificresearch.org
Issues: Bilingual education; Civil rights/racial
preferences; Entrepreneurship/free
enterprise; Health care reform; Medicaid;
Medicare; School choice

Pirchner, Herman, Jr.
President
American Foreign Policy Council
1521 16th Street, N.W.
Washington, DC 20036
202-462-6055   fax 202-462-6045
pirchner@afpc.org
Issues: Russia and Eurasia

Pitney, Dr. John J., Jr.
Professor of Government
Claremont McKenna College
850 Columbia Avenue
Claremont, CA 91711-6420
909-607-4224   fax 909-621-8419
jpitney@mckenna.edu
Issues: Congress; Elections/polling; Executive
Branch/The Presidency; The Reagan legacy

Platt, Dr. Rorin Morse
Assistant Professor of History, Department
of Government, History and Justice
Campbell University
P. O. Box 356
Buies Creek, NC 27506
910-893-1474   fax 910-814-4311
platt@mailcenter.campbell.edu
Issues: American diplomacy/foreign policy;
Intelligence gathering and covert operations

Pletka, Danielle
Vice President, Foreign and Defense Policy
American Enterprise Institute
1150 17th Street, N.W.
Washington, DC 20036
202-862-5943   fax 202-862-7178
dpletka@aei.org
Issues: Afghanistan; Middle East; South Asia
(including India and Pakistan); Terrorism and
international crime

Plosser, Dr. Charles I.
Dean, William E. Simon Graduate School of
Business
University of Rochester
Carol Simon Hall 2-202
Rochester, NY 14627
716-275-3316   fax 716-275-0095
Issues: Business and education partnerships;
Economic education; Economic forecasting;
Economic theory; The Economy; Federal
budget; Money and financial services;
Taxation/tax reform; Trade

*Plunk, Daryl
Senior Visiting Fellow
The Heritage Foundation
214 Massachusetts Avenue, N.E.
Washington, DC 20002
202-546-4400   fax 202-675-1758
dplunk@columbusgroup.com
Issues: China; Emerging threats/threat
assessment; Japan; Korea; Northeast Asia;
Promoting democracy/public diplomacy

*Podgursky, Dr. Michael
Professor of Economics and Chairman,
Department of Economics
University of Missouri
118 Profesional Building
Columbia, MO 65211
573-882-4574   fax 573-882-2697
podgurskym@missouri.edu
Issues: Charter schools; Costs and benefits of
regulation; Education unions and interest
groups; Federal education policy; Higher
education; Public school finance and
administration; School choice

*Polachek, Dr. Solomon W.
Distinguished Scholar of Economics and
Professor of Political Science
State University of New York, Binghamton
P. O. Box 6000
Binghamton, NY 13902-6000
607-777-6866   fax 607-777-2675
polachek@binghamton.edu
Issues: Health care reform; Higher education;
Job training/welfare to work; Labor and
employment; Minimum wage; Promoting
democracy/public diplomacy

*Polhill, Dennis
Senior Fellow in Public Infrastructure
Independence Institute
14142 Denver West Parkway, Suite 185
Golden, CO 80401
303-279-6536   fax 303-279-4176
dpolhill@aol.com
Issues: Central and Eastern Europe; Electoral
reform/voting rights; Electricity deregulation;
Infrastructure; Initiative and referendum;
Privatization/Contracting-out; Promoting
democracy/public diplomacy; Russia and
Eurasia; State and local government; State and
local public finance; Taxation/tax reform;
Term limits; Transportation; Transportation
deregulation

Pontynen, Arthur
Associate Professor and Chairman,
Department of Art
University of Wisconsin
800 Algoma Boulevard
Oshkosh, WI 54901
920-424-0492   fax 920-424-1738
pontynen@vaxa.cis.uwosh.edu
Issues: Arts, humanities and historic resources;
Higher education; Political correctness and
multiculturalism; Religion and public life

*Poole, Robert W., Jr.
Director of Transportation Studies
Reason Foundation
3415 South Sepulveda Boulevard, Suite 400
Los Angeles, CA 90034
310-391-2245   fax 310-391-4395
bob.poole@reason.org
Issues: Infrastructure; Privatization/
Contracting-out; State and local public finance;
Transportation; Transportation deregulation

Pooley, Gale L., Ph.D.
5713 North Hill Haven Place
Star, ID 83669
208-286-0777   fax 208-286-7590
gpooley@spro.net
Issues: Comparative economics; Economic
education; Environmental education; Property
rights; School choice

*Popenoe, Dr. David
Professor of Sociology and Co-Director of
The National Marriage Project
Rutgers University
54 Joyce Kilmer Avenue, Lucy Stone A347
New Brunswick, NJ 08901-1181
732-445-7922   fax 732-445-6110
marriage@rci.rutgers.edu
Issues: Family and children; Marriage and
divorce

---

* Has testified before a state or federal legislative committee

*Popeo, Daniel J.
Chairman and General Counsel
Washington Legal Foundation
2009 Massachusetts Avenue, N.W.
Washington, DC 20036
202-588-0302   fax 202-588-0386
dpopeo@wlf.org
Issues: Advocacy and nonprofit public funding;
The American Founding; Citizenship and civil
society; Comparative government;
Constitutional law; Corrections and
sentencing; Costs and benefits of regulation;
Entrepreneurship/free enterprise;
Environmental regulation; Ethics; Free
Speech; Government waste; Homeland
security/civil defense; Intellectual property;
Judicial activism/judicial reform; Judiciary;
Land use; OSHA; Philanthropy; Property
rights; Public interest law; Regulation through
litigation; Regulatory reform; Risk assessment;
Stewardship; Terrorism and international
crime; Tort and liability reform; Wildlife
management/endangered species

Porlier, Victor
Executive Director
Center for Civic Renewal, Inc.
159 Delaware Avenue, Suite 301
Delmar, NY 12054
518-872-9230   fax 518-872-9290
vporlier@aol.com
Issues: Agriculture; Education unions and
interest groups; Environmental education;
Home schooling; Media and popular culture;
Religion and public life; School choice

Porter, Dr. Philip K.
Professor, Department of Economics
University of South Florida
4202 East Fowler Avenue, DFN 3401
Tampa, FL 33620-8000
813-974-6539   fax 813-974-6510
pporter@coba.usf.edu
Issues: Government waste; Privatization/
Contracting-out; School choice

*Porter, Rosalie
READ Institute
1400 Pidgeon Hill Drive, Suite 500
Sterling, VA 20165
703-421-5443   fax 703-421-6401
comment@erols.com
Issues: Bilingual education; Standards,
curriculum, and testing

Portney, Paul
President
Resources for the Future
1616 P Street, N.W.
Washington, DC 20036
202-328-5103   fax 202-939-3460
portney@rff.org
Issues: Air; Costs and benefits of regulation;
Energy; Forestry and national parks;
Regulatory reform; Risk assessment; Waste
management; Water

*Post, David G.
Associate Professor
Temple University School of Law
1719 North Broad Street
Philadelphia, PA 19122
215-204-4539   fax 215-204-1185
dpost@vm.temple.edu
Issues: Intellectual property;
Telecommunications and the Internet

*Potter, Edward
President
Employment Policy Foundation
1015 15th Street, N.W., Suite 1200
Washington, DC 20005
202-789-8618   fax 202-789-8684
epotter@epf.org
Issues: Costs and benefits of regulation; Davis-
Bacon Act; Entrepreneurship/free enterprise;
Family and medical leave; Health care reform;
Human rights; Job training/welfare to work;
Labor and employment; Minimum wage;
OSHA; Promoting democracy/public
diplomacy; Regulatory reform; Right to work;
Social Security and retirement; Standards,
curriculum, and testing; Unemployment
insurance; Unions; United Nations; Urban
sprawl/livable cities; Welfare/welfare reform

*Potter, Dr. William C.
Director, Center for Russian and Eurasian
Studies
Monterey Institute of International Studies
425 Van Buren Street
Monterey, CA 93940
408-647-4154   fax 408-647-3519
wpotter@miis.edu
Issues: Arms control; Export controls/military
transfers; Russia and Eurasia; Terrorism and
international crime

Poulson, Barry W.

Professor of Economics
University of Colorado
Campus Box 256
Boulder, CO 80309
303-492-7414   fax 303-492-8960
poulson@colorado.edu

Issues: Africa; The American Founding;
American history/political tradition; Canada;
Central and Eastern Europe; Comparative
economics; Comparative government;
Conservative thought; Discretionary spending;
Economic development/foreign aid;
Economic education; The Economy;
Entitlement spending; Executive Branch/The
Presidency; Federal budget; Government debt;
Government waste; International finance and
multilateral banks; International tax policy/tax
competition; Latin America; Middle East;
Northeast Asia; Political philosophy;
Privatization/Contracting-out; The Reagan
legacy; Russia and Eurasia; South Asia
(including India and Pakistan); Southeast Asia
(including Burma, Cambodia, Laos, Vietnam,
Singapore, Malaysia, Indonesia, the
Philippines, Australia, and New Zealand); State
and local public finance; Taxation/tax reform;
Unfunded mandates; Western Europe

*Powell, John

Chief Executive Officer
The Seniors Coalition
9001 Braddock Road, Suite 200
Springfield, VA 22151
703-239-1960   fax 703-239-1985
jpowell@senior.org

Issues: Aging/elder care; Government health
programs; Health care reform; Medicaid;
Medicare; Social Security and retirement

Prager, Dennis

President
The Prager Perspective
15531 Lanark Street
Van Nuys, CA 91406-1412
800-225-8584   fax 818-376-8376
tpp@dennisprager.com

Issues: Citizenship and civil society; Ethics;
Family and children; Media and popular
culture; Religion and public life

*Preeg, Ernest

Senior Fellow
Manufacturers Alliance
1525 Wilson Boulevard, Suite 900
Arlington, VA 22209
703-841-9000   fax 703-841-9514

Issues: American diplomacy/foreign policy;
Economic development/foreign aid; The
Economy; International finance and
multilateral banks; International organizations
(European Union, OECD, etc.); Japan; Korea;
Latin America; Trade; Western Europe

*Premack, Eric

Co-Director, Charter Schools Development
Center
California State University Institute for
Education Reform
6000 J Street
Sacramento, CA 95819-6018
916-278-4600   fax 916-278-4094

Issues: Charter schools; Education unions and
interest groups; Home schooling;
Privatization/Contracting-out; Public school
finance and administration; School choice;
Standards, curriculum, and testing

*Prendergast, James

Executive Director
Americans for Technology Leadership
1413 K Street, N.W., 12th Floor
Washington, DC 20005
202-835-2030   fax 202-318-7803
info@techleadership.org

Issues: Anti-trust; Intellectual property; Privacy;
Telecommunications and the Internet

---

*Presser, Stephen
Raoul Berger Professor of Legal History
Northwestern University School of Law
357 East Chicago Avenue
Chicago, IL 60611
312-503-8371   fax 312-503-3440
s-presser@nwu.edu
Issues: Adoption, foster care, & child care
services; The American Founding; American
history/political tradition; Arts, humanities
and historic resources; Church-state relations;
Civil rights/racial preferences; Conservative
thought; Constitutional law; Costs and benefits
of regulation; Executive Branch/The
Presidency; Family and children; Federalism;
Homeland security/civil defense; Human
rights; Judicial activism/judicial reform;
Judiciary; Media and popular culture; Political
correctness and multiculturalism; Political
philosophy; Regulation through litigation;
Regulatory reform; Religion and public life;
Religious freedom; Tort and liability reform

*Pressnell, Dr. Claude
President
Tennessee Independent Colleges and
Universities
2409 21st Avenue South, Suite 202
Nashville, TN 37212-5317
615-242-6400   fax 615-242-8033
pressnell@ticua.edu
Issues: Business and education partnerships;
Federal education policy; Higher education;
Religion and public life

Price, Dr. Terry L.
Assistant Professor, Jepson School of
Leadership Studies
University of Richmond
Richmond, VA 23173
804-287-6088   fax 804-287-6062
tprice@richmond.edu
Issues: Ethics; Political philosophy

*Prichard, Thomas
President
Minnesota Family Council
2855 Anthony Lane South, Suite 150
Minneapolis, MN 55418
612-789-8811   fax 612-789-8858
tom@mfc.org
Issues: Abstinence and out-of-wedlock births;
Church-state relations; Family and children;
Free Speech; Home schooling; Judicial
activism/judicial reform; Marriage and
divorce; Religion and public life; School
choice; Standards, curriculum, and testing;
State-sponsored gambling

Priest, George
John M. Olin Professor of Law and
Economics
Yale Law School
P. O. Box 208215
New Haven, CT 06520
203-624-8331   fax 203-432-7225
george.priest@yale.edu
Issues: Anti-trust; Campaign finance reform;
Economic development/foreign aid;
Federalism; Judiciary; Privatization/
Contracting-out; Tort and liability reform

Prinzinger, Dr. Joseph M.
Professor, School of Business and Economics
Lynchburg College
1501 Lakeside Drive
Lynchburg, VA 24501
804-544-8329   fax 804-544-8639
Issues: Conservative thought; Economic theory

Pritchard, Dr. Adam
Assistant Professor
Georgetown University Law Center
600 New Jersey Avenue, N.W.
Washington, DC 20001
202-662-9936   fax 202-662-9680
acplaw@umich.edu
Issues: Money and financial services

*Proctor, Dr. William L.
Chancellor
Flagler College
P. O. Box 1027
St. Augustine, FL 32085
904-829-6481   fax 904-824-6017
proctorw@flagler.edu
Issues: Advocacy and nonprofit public funding;
Higher education; Public school finance and
administration; Standards, curriculum, and
testing; Unfunded mandates

*Prybyla, Dr. Jan S.
Professor Emeritus of Economics
Pennsylvania State University
5197 North Spring Pointe Place
Tucson, AZ 85749-7119
520-749-4982   fax 520-760-1733
jprybyla@prodigy.net
Issues: China; Comparative economics;
Economic development/foreign aid; Korea

*Przystup, Jim
Senior Fellow
Institute for National Strategic Studies
300 5th Avenue, S.W., Room 314B
Washington, DC 20319
202-685-2359   przystupj@ndu.edu
Issues: American diplomacy/foreign policy;
China; Japan; Korea; Northeast Asia; Southeast
Asia (including Burma, Cambodia, Laos,
Vietnam, Singapore, Malaysia, Indonesia, the
Philippines, Australia, and New Zealand)

Puddington, Arch
Vice President, Research
Freedom House
120 Wall Street, 26th Floor
New York, NY 10005
212-514-8040   fax 212-514-8055
puddington@freedomhouse.org
Issues: American diplomacy/foreign policy;
Citizenship and civil society; Civil rights/racial
preferences; Human rights; Political
correctness and multiculturalism; Promoting
democracy/public diplomacy; Unions; United
Nations

*Pullen, Hon. Penny
President
Life Advocacy Resource Project, Inc.
2004 East Sherwood road
Arlington Heights, IL 60004
847-392-4858   lifeadvocacy@aol.com
Issues: Religion and public life

*Pulliam, Mark S.
Partner
Latham & Watkins
701 B Street, Suite 2100
San Diego, CA 92101
619-236-1234   fax 619-696-7419
mark.pulliam@lw.com
Issues: Judicial activism/judicial reform;
Judiciary; Labor and employment; Public
interest law; Tort and liability reform

*Pullins, Scott
Chairman
Ohio Taxpayers Association and OTA
Foundation
P. O. Box 163339
Columbus, OH 43216-3339
614-224-2785   fax 614-471-0273
scottpullins@ohiotaxpayers.com
Issues: Advocacy and nonprofit public funding;
Anti-trust; Charter schools; Discretionary
spending; The Economy; Education unions
and interest groups; Electricity deregulation;
Energy; Entitlement spending;
Entrepreneurship/free enterprise; Intellectual
property; Medicaid; Privacy; Privatization/
Contracting-out; Property rights; Public
interest law; Regulation through litigation;
Regulatory reform; State and local
government; State and local public finance;
Taxation/tax reform; Telecommunications
and the Internet; Term limits; Tort and liability
reform; Unfunded mandates; Welfare/welfare
reform

*Purcell, Dr. Susan Kaufman
Vice President
Americas Society/Council of the Americas
680 Park Avenue
New York, NY 10021
212-249-8950   fax 212-517-6247
spurcell@as-coa.org
Issues: American diplomacy/foreign policy;
Latin America; Mexico

*Quinlan, Andrew F.
President
Center for Freedom and Prosperity
P. O. Box 10882
Alexandria, VA 22310-9998
202-285-0244   fax 208-728-9639
quinlan@freedomandprosperity.org
Issues: Costs and benefits of regulation; Privacy;
Promoting democracy/public diplomacy;
Taxation/tax reform; Trade

Quinlivan, Dr. Gary M.
Executive Director
Center for Economic and Policy Education
Saint Vincent College, 300 Fraser Purchase
Road
Latrobe, PA 15650
724-537-4597   fax 724-537-4599
gq@stvincent.edu
Issues: China; Economic development/
foreign aid

Rabkin, Dr. Jeremy
Associate Professor of Government
Cornell University
M103 McGraw Hall
Ithaca, NY 14853
607-255-4915   fax 607-255-4530
jar11@cornell.edu
Issues: Church-state relations; Civil rights/racial preferences; Comparative government; Constitutional law; Human rights; Public interest law; United Nations

*Rabushka, Dr. Alvin
David and Joan Traitel Senior Fellow
Hoover Institution
Stanford University
Stanford, CA 94305
650-725-5674   fax 650-723-1687
rabushka@hoover.stanford.edu
Issues: Comparative economics; Economic development/foreign aid; State and local public finance; Taxation/tax reform

*Racheter, Dr. Don
President
Public Interest Institute
600 North Jackson Street
Mount Pleasant, IA 52641
319-385-3462   fax 319-385-3799
racheter@limitedgovernment.org
Issues: The American Founding; Congress; Costs and benefits of regulation; Entrepreneurship/free enterprise; Executive Branch/The Presidency; Federalism; Government waste; Higher education; Initiative and referendum; Judicial activism/judicial reform; Judiciary; Regulatory reform; Right to work; Second Amendment; State and local government; Term limits

Radford, R. S.
Director, Program for Judicial Awareness
Pacific Legal Foundation
10360 Old Placerville Road, Suite 100
Sacramento, CA 95827
916-362-2833   fax 916-362-2932
rsr@pacificlegal.org
Issues: Land use; Property rights; Urban sprawl/livable cities

*Radu, Dr. Michael
Chairman, Center on Terrorism and Counter-Terrorism
Foreign Policy Research Institute
1528 Walnut Street, Suite 610
Philadelphia, PA 19102
215-732-3774   fax 215-732-4401
fpri@fpri.org
Issues: Afghanistan; Africa; Central and Eastern Europe; Human rights; Latin America; Terrorism and international crime; Western Europe

*Radvanyi, Dr. Janos
The Radvanyi Chair in International Studies
Mississippi State University
P. O. Box 6261
Mississippi State, MS 39762
662-325-8406   fax 662-325-7291
jri@ra.msstate.edu
Issues: Homeland security/civil defense

Rafalko, Dr. Robert J.
Assistant Professor of Philosophy, Department of Visual and Performing Arts and Philosophy
University of New Haven
119 Campbell Avenue
West Haven, CT 06516
203-932-7179   fax 203-931-6097
rafalko@newhaven.edu
Issues: Ethics; Political philosophy; Terrorism and international crime

Raffety, Rob
Program Director, Capitol Hill Campus
Mercatus Center at George Mason University
3301 North Fairfax Drive, Suite 450
Arlington, VA 22201
703-993-4960   fax 703-993-4935
rraffety@gmu.edu
Issues: Health care reform; Trade; Transportation

Rahe, Paul A.
Jay P. Walker Professor of American History,
Department of History
University of Tulsa
600 South College Avenue
Tulsa, OK 74104
918-631-2115   fax 918-631-2057
paul-rahe@utulsa.edu
Issues: Afghanistan; American diplomacy/
foreign policy; The American Founding;
American history/political tradition; Church-
state relations; Civil rights/racial preferences;
Comparative government; Conservative
thought; Defense budget; Economic theory;
The Economy; Emerging threats/threat
assessment; Judicial activism/judicial reform;
Middle East; Military strategy; Money and
financial services; Political correctness and
multiculturalism; Political philosophy;
Religious freedom; Second Amendment; Term
limits; Terrorism and international crime;
Western Europe

Rahn, Dr. Richard W.
Chairman
NOVECON
333 North Fairfax Street
Alexandria, VA 22314
202-659-3200   fax 202-659-3215
rwrahn@aol.com
Issues: Comparative economics; International
tax policy/tax competition; Money and
financial services; Promoting democracy/
public diplomacy; The Reagan legacy; Russia
and Eurasia; Taxation/tax reform

Raisian, Dr. John
Director
Hoover Institution
Stanford University
Stanford, CA 94305
650-723-1198   fax 650-725-8990
Raisan@Hoover.Stanford.edu
Issues: Labor and employment; Political
correctness and multiculturalism; Poverty and
dependency; School choice; Taxation/tax
reform

Rajapatirana, Dr. Sarath
Visting Scholar
American Enterprise Institute
1150 17th Street, N.W.
Washington, DC 20036
202-862-5927   fax 202-862-7177
sr@aei.org
Issues: Economic development/foreign aid;
Latin America; Trade

*Randolph, R. Sean
President
Bay Area Economic Forum
200 Pine Street, Suite 300
San Francisco, CA 94104
415-981-7117   fax 415-981-6408
sean@bayeconfor.org
Issues: American diplomacy/foreign policy;
China; The Economy; Electricity deregulation;
Entrepreneurship/free enterprise;
Infrastructure; Japan; Mexico; Southeast Asia
(including Burma, Cambodia, Laos, Vietnam,
Singapore, Malaysia, Indonesia, the
Philippines, Australia, and New Zealand);
Trade

Rasmussen, Dr. Douglas B.
Professor of Philosophy
St. John's University
SJH B30
Jamaica, NY 11439
718-990-5437   fax 718-990-1907
dbrlogos@earthlink.net
Issues: Economic theory; Ethics; Political
philosophy

*Ratliff, William
Research Fellow and Curator, Americas
Collection
Hoover Institution
Stanford University
Stanford, CA 94305
650-723-2106   fax 650-723-1687
ratliff@hoover.stanford.edu
Issues: American diplomacy/foreign policy;
China; Economic development/foreign aid;
Latin America; Terrorism and international
crime

*Rauchut, Ed
Executive Director
CEO Omaha
901 Ivy Court
Bellevue, NE 68005
402-571-3614   fax 402-293-2023
erauchut@bellevue.edu
Issues: Business and education partnerships;
Charter schools; Higher education; Home
schooling; Public school finance and
administration; School choice; Standards,
curriculum, and testing

---

*Raul, Hon. Alan C.
Sidley & Austin Brown & Wood, LLP
1501 K Street, N.W., 9th Floor
Washington, DC 20005
202-736-8000   fax 202-736-8711
araul@sidley.com
Issues: Constitutional law; Environmental
regulation; Free Speech; Intellectual property;
Privacy; Regulation through litigation;
Regulatory budgeting; Regulatory reform; Risk
assessment; Sound science;
Telecommunications and the Internet

Ravitch, Dr. Diane
Research Professor of Education
New York University
82 Washington Square East
New York, NY 10003
212-998-5146
Issues: American history/political tradition;
Federal education policy; School choice;
Standards, curriculum, and testing

Ray, Bishop Harold Calvin
Chairman and CEO
National Center for Faith-Based Initiatives
2101 North Australian Avenue
West Palm Beach, FL 33407
561-833-3366   fax 561-832-7844
bishopray@ncfbi.org
Issues: Abstinence and out-of-wedlock births;
Adoption, foster care, & child care services;
Africa; Business and education partnerships;
Charter schools; Church-state relations; Civil
rights/racial preferences; Comparative
economics; Conservative thought;
Constitutional law; Crime/crime statistics;
Economic development/foreign aid;
Economic theory; Ethics; Faith-based and
volunteer initiatives; Family and children;
Family and medical leave; Federal education
policy; Free Speech; Government health
programs; Housing and homelessness; Human
rights; Job training/welfare to work; Latin
America; Marriage and divorce; Philanthropy;
Political philosophy; Poverty and dependency;
Religion and public life; Religious freedom;
School choice; School-to-work; Substance
abuse; Wealth creation/financial
empowerment; Welfare/welfare reform

Ream, Roger
President
The Fund for American Studies
1706 New Hampshire Avenue, N.W.
Washington, DC 20009
202-986-0384   fax 202-986-0390
rream@tfas.org
Issues: Conservative thought; Economic
education; Economic theory

Rector, Ralph
Senior Research Fellow, Center for Data
Analysis
The Heritage Foundation
214 Massachusetts Avenue, N.E.
Washington, DC 20002
202-608-6115   fax 202-675-1772
ralph.rector@heritage.org
Issues: Economic forecasting; Social Security
and retirement; Taxation/tax reform; Wealth
creation/financial empowerment

Rector, Robert
Senior Research Fellow
The Heritage Foundation
214 Massachusetts Avenue, N.E.
Washington, DC 20002
202-608-5213   fax 202-544-5421
info@heritage.org
Issues: Abstinence and out-of-wedlock births;
Family and children; Job training/welfare to
work; Marriage and divorce; Poverty and
dependency; Welfare/welfare reform

*Reed, Lawrence W.
President
Mackinac Center for Public Policy
140 West Main Street, P. O. Box 568
Midland, MI 48640
989-631-0900   fax 989-631-0964
reed@mackinac.org
Issues: American history/political tradition;
Comparative economics; Economic education;
Economic theory; Education unions and
interest groups; Entrepreneurship/free
enterprise; Privatization/Contracting-out;
Right to work; School choice

Reed, Patricia
Director of Programs
Independent Women's Forum
P. O. Box 3058
Arlington, VA 22203-0058
703-558-4991   fax 703-558-4994
preed@iwf.org
Issues: Environmental regulation; Waste
management

*Reed, Dr. W. Robert
Professor, Department of Economics
University of Oklahoma
307 West Brooks, Room 306
Norman, OK 73019
405-325-2358   fax 405-325-5842
breed@ou.edu
Issues: Entrepreneurship/free enterprise;
Marriage and divorce; State and local public
finance; Welfare/welfare reform

Reedy, Dr. Jeremiah
Professor of Classics
Macalester College
1600 Grand Avenue
St. Paul, MN 55105
651-696-6722   fax 651-696-6689
reedy@macalester.edu
Issues: Charter schools; Higher education;
Political correctness and multiculturalism;
Religion and public life; School choice;
Standards, curriculum, and testing

Reid, Dr. Joseph D., Jr.
Associate Professor
George Mason University
4400 University Drive, MSN 3G4
Fairfax, VA 22030
703-993-1159   fax 703-993-1133
jreid@osf1.gmu.edu
Issues: American history/political tradition;
Comparative government; Elections/polling;
Federal civil service; State and local
government; Unions

*Reid, William H., M.D.
P. O. Box 4015
Horseshoe, TX 78657
800-256-6627   fax 830-596-9047
reidw@reidpsychiatry.com
Issues: Central and Eastern Europe;
Corrections and sentencing; Criminal law and
procedure; Emerging threats/threat
assessment; Ethics; Government health
programs; Health care reform; Human rights;
Substance abuse; Terrorism and international
crime; Tort and liability reform

Reilly, Patrick
President and CEO
Cardinal Newman Society
207 Park Avenue, Suite B-2
Falls Church, VA 22046
703-536-9585   fax 703-532-3094
Issues: Advocacy and nonprofit public funding;
Education unions and interest groups;
Entrepreneurship/free enterprise; Faith-based
and volunteer initiatives; Non-governmental
organizations; Philanthropy; Religion and
public life; School choice

Reiser, Martin G.
Vice President, Public Affairs
Citizens for a Sound Economy
1900 M Street, N.W., Suite 500
Washington, DC 20036
202-942-7628   fax 202-942-7679
mreiser@cse.org
Issues: Congress; Entitlement spending;
Federal budget; Tort and liability reform

Reisman, Dr. George
Professor of Economics, The Graziadio
School of Business and Management
Pepperdine University
26881 Rocking Horse Lane
Laguna Hills, CA 92653
949-831-6579   fax 949-831-1783
greisman@capitalism.net
Issues: Anti-trust; Climate change; Comparative
economics; Economic education; Economic
theory; Electricity deregulation; Energy;
Entrepreneurship/free enterprise;
Environmental regulation; Free Speech;
Government debt; Minimum wage; Political
philosophy; Social Security and retirement;
Taxation/tax reform; Unions

Reno, Ron
Senior Research Analyst
Focus on the Family
8605 Explorer Drive
Colorado Springs, CO 80920
719-548-5801   fax 719-531-3385
renora@fotf.org
Issues: State-sponsored gambling

---

*Rettenmaier, Dr. Andrew
Executive Associate Director, Private
Enterprise Research Center
Texas A&M University
3028 Academic Building W, 4231 TAMU
College Station, TX 77843-4231
979-845-7559   fax 979-845-6636
Issues: Government debt; Medicare; Social
Security and retirement

Reynolds, Alan
Senior Fellow
Cato Institute
1000 Massachusetts Avenue, N.W.
Washington, DC 20001-5403
202-842-0200   fax 202-842-3490
areynolds@cato.org
Issues: The Economy; Federal budget;
Government debt; Social Security and
retirement; State and local public finance;
Taxation/tax reform

Rhoads, Dr. Steven
Professor of Government
University of Virginia
244 Cabell Hall
Charlottesville, VA 22901
434-973-4879   fax 434-924-3359
ser6f@Virginia.edu
Issues: Economic education; Marriage and
divorce

*Ricardo-Campbell, Dr. Rita
Senior Fellow, Emerita
Hoover Institution
Stanford University
Stanford, CA 94305
650-723-2074   fax 650-723-1687
ricardo-campbell@hoover.stanford.edu
Issues: Health care reform; Social Security and
retirement

*Rice, Dr. Charles E.
Professor of Law
Notre Dame Law School
Notre Dame, IN 46556
219-631-5667   fax 219-631-4197
Issues: Church-state relations; Civil rights/racial
preferences; Constitutional law; Faith-based
and volunteer initiatives; Family and children;
Free Speech; Higher education; Home
schooling; Privacy; Religion and public life;
Religious freedom; School choice; Second
Amendment

Rice, Dr. William Craig
American Academy for Liberal Education
1710 Rhode Island Avenue, N.W., 4th Floor
Washington, DC 20036
202-452-8611   fax 202-452-8620
wrice@aale.org
Issues: Arts, humanities and historic resources;
Charter schools; Education unions and interest
groups; Federal education policy; Higher
education; Philanthropy; Political correctness
and multiculturalism; School choice;
Standards, curriculum, and testing

*Richardson, Brig. Gen. Robert C.
Deputy Director
High Frontier
2800 Shirlington Road, Suite 405
Arlington, VA 22206
703-671-4111   fax 703-931-6432
Issues: Defense budget; Emerging threats/
threat assessment; Homeland security/civil
defense; Military strategy; Missile defense;
NATO and other alliances

Richardson, Dr. William D.
Director, Farber Center for Civic Leadership
and Director, Department of Political
Science
University of South Dakota
414 East Clark Street
Vermillion, SD 57069
605-677-5702   fax 605-677-6302
wrichard@usd.edu
Issues: Citizenship and civil society; Federalism

Ricketts, Dr. Glenn M.
Public Affairs Director
National Association of Scholars
221 Witherspoon Street, 2nd Floor
Princeton, NJ 08542-3215
609-683-7878   fax 609-683-0316
ricketts@nas.org
Issues: Arts, humanities and historic resources;
Higher education; Political correctness and
multiculturalism; Standards, curriculum, and
testing

*Ridenour, Amy
President
National Center for Public Policy Research
777 North Capitol Street, N.E., Suite 803
Washington, DC 20002
202-371-1400   fax 202-408-7773
aridenour@nationalcenter.org
Issues: Aging/elder care; Arms control; Civil
rights/racial preferences; Congress; Defense
budget; Emerging threats/threat assessment;
Energy; Executive Branch/The Presidency;
Free-market environmentalism; Health care
reform; Homeland security/civil defense;
Human rights; Medicare; Military strategy;
Missile defense; Property rights; Russia and
Eurasia; Social Security and retirement; South
Asia (including India and Pakistan); Southeast
Asia (including Burma, Cambodia, Laos,
Vietnam, Singapore, Malaysia, Indonesia, the
Philippines, Australia, and New Zealand);
Taxation/tax reform; Telecommunications
and the Internet; Terrorism and international
crime; Tort and liability reform; United
Nations; Urban sprawl/livable cities

*Ridenour, David
Vice President
National Center for Public Policy Research
777 North Capitol Street, N.E., Suite 803
Washington, DC 20002
202-371-1400   fax 202-408-7773
dridenour@nationalcenter.org
Issues: Air; Climate change; Energy;
Environmental regulation; Forestry and
national parks; Free-market environmentalism;
Land use; Property rights; Regulatory reform;
Urban sprawl/livable cities; Wildlife
management/endangered species

*Riedl, Brian
Grover M. Herman Fellow in Federal
Budgetary Affairs, Thomas A. Roe Institute
for Economic Policy Studies
The Heritage Foundation
214 Massachusetts Avenue, N.E.
Washington, DC 20002
202-546-4400   fax 202-544-5421
brian.riedl@heritage.org
Issues: Agriculture; Discretionary spending;
Economic theory; The Economy; Entitlement
spending; Federal budget; Federal education
policy; Federalism; Government debt;
Government waste; Job training/welfare to
work; Poverty and dependency; Privatization/
Contracting-out; State and local public finance;
Taxation/tax reform; Welfare/welfare reform

*Riggs, David W.
Executive Director, *Green Watch* and
Education Watch
Capital Research Center
1513 16th Street, N.W.
Washington, DC 20036
202-483-6900   fax 202-483-6902
driggs@capitalresearch.org
Issues: Education unions and interest groups;
Environmental regulation; Forestry and
national parks; Free-market environmentalism;
Land use; Property rights; Research funding;
School choice; Sound science; Stewardship;
Urban sprawl/livable cities; Waste
management; Water; Wildlife management/
endangered species

Riley, Michael
President
Taxpayers Network, Inc.
W67 N222 Evergreen Boulevard, Suite 202
Cedarburg, WI 53012-2645
262-375-4190   fax 262-375-3732
mriley@taxpayersnetwork.org
Issues: Social Security and retirement;
Taxation/tax reform

Rios, Sandy
President
Concerned Women for America
1015 15th Street, N.W., Suite 1100
Washington, DC 20005
202-488-7000   fax 202-488-0806
nodam@cwfa.org
Issues: Abstinence and out-of-wedlock births;
China; Church-state relations; Citizenship and
civil society; Congress; Conservative thought;
Education unions and interest groups;
Elections/polling; Ethics; Family and children;
Free Speech; Judicial activism/judicial reform;
Korea; Marriage and divorce; Media and
popular culture; Political correctness and
multiculturalism; Religion and public life;
Russia and Eurasia; School choice; Standards,
curriculum, and testing; State-sponsored
gambling

Rippel, Barbara
Policy Analyst
Consumer Alert
1001 Connecticut Avenue, N.W., Suite 1128
Washington, DC 20036
202-467-5809
Issues: Agriculture; Trade

---

*Rivett, Robin
Principal, Environmental Law and Director of Regional Offices
Pacific Legal Foundation
10360 Old Placerville Road, Suite 100
Sacramento, CA 95827
916-362-2833   fax 916-362-2932
rlr@pacificlegal.org
Issues: Agriculture; Constitutional law; Environmental regulation; Federalism; Forestry and national parks; Land use; Property rights; Public interest law; Sound science; Water; Wildlife management/endangered species

*Rivkin, David B., Jr.
Baker & Hostetler
1050 Connecticut Avenue, Suite 1100
Washington, DC 20036
202-861-1731   fax 202-861-1783
drivkin@baker-hostetler.com
Issues: Air; American diplomacy/foreign policy; Arms control; Climate change; Constitutional law; Costs and benefits of regulation; Electricity deregulation; Emerging threats/threat assessment; Energy; Environmental regulation; Executive Branch/The Presidency; Federalism; Homeland security/civil defense; International law; International organizations (European Union, OECD, etc.); Military strategy; Missile defense; Peacekeeping; Promoting democracy/public diplomacy; Regulation through litigation; Regulatory reform; Russia and Eurasia; Terrorism and international crime; United Nations; Western Europe

*Robbins, Aldona
Visiting Fellow, The Heritage Foundation, and Vice President
Fiscal Associates
1515 Jefferson Davis Highway
Arlington, VA 22202
703-413-4371   fax 703-413-0280
aerobbins@mindspring.com
Issues: Medicare; Social Security and retirement; Taxation/tax reform

*Robbins, Gary
Visiting Fellow, The Heritage Foundation, and President
Fiscal Associates
1515 Jefferson Davis Highway
Arlington, VA 22202
703-413-4371   fax 703-413-0280
garobbins@mindspring.com
Issues: Federal budget; Health care reform; Taxation/tax reform

*Robbins, Dr. James S.
School for National Security Executive Education
National Defense University
Ft. Lesley J. McNair
Washington, DC 20319
202-685-3877   fax 202-685-3860
robbinsj@ndu.edu
Issues: Afghanistan; American diplomacy/foreign policy; The American Founding; American history/political tradition; Central and Eastern Europe; Conservative thought; Constitutional law; Emerging threats/threat assessment; Homeland security/civil defense; Human rights; Intelligence gathering and covert operations; Middle East; Military strategy; Peacekeeping; Political philosophy; Promoting democracy/public diplomacy; The Reagan legacy; Russia and Eurasia; Terrorism and international crime

Robbins, Dr. John W.
President
Trinity Foundation
P. O. Box 68
Unicoi, TN 37692
423-743-0199   fax 423-743-2005
jrob1517@aol.com
Issues: The American Founding; American history/political tradition; Church-state relations; Comparative economics; Economic theory; Faith-based and volunteer initiatives; Political philosophy; Religion and public life; Religious freedom

*Roberts, Major Gen. J. Milnor
President
High Frontier
2800 Shirlington Road, Suite 405
Arlington, VA 22206
703-671-4111   fax 703-931-6432
hifront@erols.com
Issues: Afghanistan; Emerging threats/threat assessment; Military strategy; Missile defense; NATO and other alliances; United Nations

Roberts, James C.

President
American Studies Center
Radio America, 1030 15th Street, N.W., Suite 700
Washington, DC 20005
202-408-0944   fax 202-408-1087

Issues: American history/political tradition; Comparative government; Conservative thought; Executive Branch/The Presidency; Media and popular culture; Political philosophy; The Reagan legacy

*Roberts, Dr. Paul Craig

Chairman
Institute for Political Economy
169 Pompano Street
Panama City Beach, FL 32413
850-231-1945   fax 850-231-1603
pcr@digitalexp.com

Issues: Civil rights/racial preferences; Comparative economics; Criminal law and procedure; Economic theory; Marriage and divorce; The Reagan legacy; Taxation/tax reform

Roberts, Russell, Ph.D.

John M. Olin Senior Fellow
Weidenbaum Center
Washington University, Campus Box 1027
St. Louis, MO 63130-4899
314-935-4942   fax 314-935-5688
roberts@wc.wustl.edu

Issues: Economic education; The Economy; Entitlement spending; Entrepreneurship/free enterprise; Environmental education; Free-market environmentalism; Minimum wage; Philanthropy; Poverty and dependency; School choice; Social Security and retirement; Taxation/tax reform; Telecommunications and the Internet; Trade; Welfare/welfare reform; Wildlife management/endangered species

Robinson, Holly

Senior Vice President
Georgia Public Policy Foundation
6100 Lake Forest Drive, N.W., Suite 110
Atlanta, GA 30328
404-256-4050   fax 404-256-9909
hrobinson@gppf.org

Issues: American history/political tradition; Business and education partnerships; Charter schools; Education unions and interest groups; Public school finance and administration; School choice; Standards, curriculum, and testing

Robinson, Ron

President
Young America's Foundation
110 Elden Street
Herndon, VA 20170
703-318-9608   fax 703-318-9122
rrobinson@yaf.org

Issues: Conservative thought; Constitutional law; Free Speech; Higher education; Land use; Philanthropy; Political correctness and multiculturalism; Property rights; The Reagan legacy

Rocha, John E., Sr.

Academic Director
Center for the American Idea
9525 Katy Freeway, Suite 303
Houston, TX 77024
713-984-1343   fax 713-984-0409
jrocha@americanidea.org

Issues: Arts, humanities and historic resources; Conservative thought; Home schooling; Political philosophy; Standards, curriculum, and testing

Rockwell, Prof. Llewellyn, Jr.

President
Ludwig von Mises Institute
415 West Magnolia Avenue, Suite 105
Auburn, AL 36849
334-321-2100   fax 334-321-2119
freedom@mises.org

Issues: Discretionary spending; The Economy; Entitlement spending; Government debt; Government waste; Money and financial services; Privatization/Contracting-out; Regulatory reform; Taxation/tax reform; Trade; Unfunded mandates

*Rodriguez, L. Jacobo

Financial Services Analyst
Cato Institute
1000 Massachusetts Avenue, N.W.
Washington, DC 20001-5403
(202) 842-0200   fax 202-842-3490

Issues: Economic development/foreign aid; The Economy; International finance and multilateral banks; Latin America; Mexico; Money and financial services; Regulatory reform; Western Europe

*Rogers, Doug
Executive Director
Association of Texas Professional Educators
305 East Huntland Drive, Suite 300
Austin, TX 78752
512-467-0071   fax 512-467-2203
atpe@atpe.org
Issues: Business and education partnerships;
Charter schools; Education unions and interest
groups; Public school finance and
administration; School choice; Standards,
curriculum, and testing

Rooney, J. Patrick
Chairman Emeritus
Golden Rule Insurance Company
7440 Woodland Drive
Indianapolis, IN 46278
317-290-8100   fax 317-293-0603
wssmith@goldenrule.com
Issues: Health care reform; Home schooling;
School choice; Taxation/tax reform

Root, Dr. Hilton
Senior Fellow
Economy Strategy Institute
1401 H Street, N.W., Suite 560
Washington, DC 20005
202-289-1288   fax 202-289-1319
hroot@econstrat.org
Issues: Africa; China; Comparative economics;
Comparative government; Economic
development/foreign aid; Economic theory;
Federalism; Human rights; International
finance and multilateral banks; Japan; Korea;
Northeast Asia; Promoting democracy/public
diplomacy; Russia and Eurasia; South Asia
(including India and Pakistan); Southeast Asia
(including Burma, Cambodia, Laos, Vietnam,
Singapore, Malaysia, Indonesia, the
Philippines, Australia, and New Zealand)

Rorlich, Dr. Azade-Ayse
Associate Professor, Department of History
University of Southern California
3502 Trousdale Parkway
Los Angeles, CA 90034
213-740-1665   fax 213-740-6999
Issues: Russia and Eurasia

*Rosati, Kelly
Executive Director
Hawaii Family Forum
6301 Pali Highway
Kaneohe, HI 96744-5224
808-230-2100   fax 808-230-2102
hff@pixi.com
Issues: Abstinence and out-of-wedlock births;
Adoption, foster care, & child care services;
Church-state relations; Constitutional law;
Family and children; Marriage and divorce;
Religious freedom; State-sponsored gambling

Rose, Dr. David C.
Professor of Economics
University of Missouri, St. Louis
408 SSB
St. Louis, MO 63121-4499
314-516-5307   fax 314-516-5352
rose@umsl.edu
Issues: China; Economic development/foreign
aid; Economic education; Economic theory;
Ethics; Northeast Asia; School choice

Rose, Dr. Jonathan
Professor of Law, College of Law
Arizona State University
P. O. Box 877906, Armstrong Hall
Tempe, AZ 85287
480-965-6513   fax 480-965-2427
jonathan.rose@asu.edu
Issues: Anti-trust; Regulatory reform; State and
local government

*Rosenzweig, Paul, J.D.
Senior Legal Research Fellow, Center for
Legal and Judicial Studies
The Heritage Foundation
214 Massachusetts Avenue, N.E.
Washington, DC 20002
202-608-6190   fax 202-547-0641
paul.rosenzweig@heritage.org
Issues: Constitutional law; Corrections and
sentencing; Crime/crime statistics; Criminal
law and procedure; Environmental regulation;
Free Speech; Judicial activism/judicial reform;
Judiciary

Rosman, Michael E.
General Counsel
Center for Individual Rights
1233 20th Street, N.W., Suite 300
Washington, DC 20036
202-833-8400   fax 202-833-8410
Issues: Civil rights/racial preferences;
Constitutional law; Public interest law

Rossi, Prof. Peter H.

Professor Emeritus, Social and Demographic
Research Institute
University of Massachusetts
34 Stagecoach Road
Amherst, MA 01002
413-256-0308   fax 413-253-7589
rossi@sadri.umass.edu
Issues: Health care reform; Housing and
homelessness

*Rossum, Dr. Ralph A.

Salvatori Professor of American
Constitutionalism and Director, Rose
Institute for State and Local Government
Claremont McKenna College
850 Columbia Avenue
Claremont, CA 91711
909-607-3392   fax 909-621-1321
rrossum@claremontmckenna.edu
Issues: The American Founding; American
history/political tradition; Constitutional law;
Crime/crime statistics; Criminal law and
procedure; Federalism; Judicial activism/
judicial reform; Judiciary; Juvenile justice; State
and local government

*Roth, Allen H.

Executive Director
New York State Advisory Council on
Privatization
767 Fifth Avenue, Suite 4200
New York, NY 10153
212-572-6954   fax 212-572-4329
roth2@ix.netcom.com
Issues: Central and Eastern Europe; Elections/
polling; Government waste; International tax
policy/tax competition; Middle East; Missile
defense; Privatization/Contracting-out;
Promoting democracy/public diplomacy;
Taxation/tax reform; Terrorism and
international crime; Western Europe

Roth, Gabriel

Privatization Specialist
4815 Falstone Avenue
Chevy Chase, MD 20815
301-656-6094   fax 202-318-2431
roths@earthlink.net
Issues: Economic development/foreign aid;
Entrepreneurship/free enterprise;
Privatization/Contracting-out; Transportation;
Transportation deregulation

*Roth, Dr. Timothy P.

A. B. Templeton Professor and Chairman,
Department of Economics and Finance
University of Texas, El Paso
236 Business Administration Building
El Paso, TX 79968
915-747-8611   fax 915-747-6282
troth@utep.edu
Issues: Conservative thought; Economic theory;
Ethics; Political philosophy

*Rothbard, David

President
Committee for a Constructive Tomorrow
P. O. Box 65722
Washington, DC 20035
202-429-2737   fax 410-838-7223
david@cfact.org
Issues: Air; Climate change; Energy;
Environmental education; Environmental
regulation; Free-market environmentalism;
Property rights; Regulatory reform; Risk
assessment; Sound science; Stewardship

Rothman, Dr. Stanley

Director, Center for the Study of Social and
Political Change
Smith College
Pierce Hall
Northampton, MA 01063
413-585-3546   fax 413-585-7611
srothman@smith.edu
Issues: Media and popular culture

*Rothschild, Kathy

Vice President of Development
The Leadership Institute
1101 North Highland Street
Arlington, VA 22201-2854
703-247-2000   fax 703-247-2001
kathleen.rothschild@leadershipinstitute.org
Issues: Family and children; Philanthropy

*Rotunda, Dr. Ronald D.

George Mason University Foundation
Professor of Law
George Mason University School of Law
3301 North Fairfax Drive
Arlington, VA 22201-4498
703-993-8041   fax 703-993-8124
rrotunda@gmu.edu
Issues: Campaign finance reform; Church-state
relations; Congress; Constitutional law;
Electoral reform/voting rights; Ethics;
Executive Branch/The Presidency; Federalism;
Free Speech; Human rights; Judiciary;
Religious freedom; School choice; Term limits

*Roumasset, Dr. James A.
Professor of Economics
University of Hawaii
2424 Maile Way
Honolulu, HI 96822
808-956-7496   fax 808-956-4347
jimr@hawaii.edu
Issues: Air; Climate change; Energy; Free-
market environmentalism; Government waste;
Political correctness and multiculturalism;
Privatization/Contracting-out; Property rights;
Stewardship; Substance abuse; Wildlife
management/endangered species

Rouse, Dr. Cecilia E.
Professor of Economics and Public Affairs,
Woodrow Wilson School
Princeton University
Firestone Library
Princeton, NJ 08544-1013
609-258-4042   fax 609-258-2907
Issues: School choice

*Rowland, Richard O.
President
Grassroot Institute of Hawaii
P. O. Box 1046
Aiea, HI 96701
808-487-4959   fax 808-484-0117
rowlandr001@hawaii.rr.com
Issues: Aging/elder care; Business and
education partnerships; Citizenship and civil
society; Electoral reform/voting rights;
Entrepreneurship/free enterprise; Free-
market environmentalism; Health care reform;
Media and popular culture; Minimum wage;
Police; School choice; School-to-work;
Standards, curriculum, and testing; State and
local government; Taxation/tax reform;
Transportation; Transportation deregulation;
Unfunded mandates; Urban sprawl/livable
cities; Welfare/welfare reform

*Rowny, Amb. Edward L.
2700 Calvert Street, N.W., Suite 813
Washington, DC 20008
202-986-4752   fax 202-986-4752
Issues: Afghanistan; American diplomacy/
foreign policy; Arms control; Central and
Eastern Europe; China; Defense budget;
Emerging threats/threat assessment;
Homeland security/civil defense; Intelligence
gathering and covert operations; International
organizations (European Union, OECD, etc.);
Japan; Korea; Middle East; Military strategy;
Missile defense; NATO and other alliances;
Northeast Asia; Peacekeeping; Promoting
democracy/public diplomacy; Readiness and
manpower; Russia and Eurasia; South Asia
(including India and Pakistan); Southeast Asia
(including Burma, Cambodia, Laos, Vietnam,
Singapore, Malaysia, Indonesia, the
Philippines, Australia, and New Zealand);
Terrorism and international crime; Western
Europe

Royal, Dr. Robert
President
Faith & Reason Institute
1513 16th Street, N.W.
Washington, DC 20036
202-234-8200   fax 202-234-7702
royal@frinstitute.org
Issues: Arts, humanities and historic resources;
Citizenship and civil society; Environmental
education; Ethics; Faith-based and volunteer
initiatives; Latin America; Political correctness
and multiculturalism; Political philosophy;
Religion and public life; School choice;
Standards, curriculum, and testing; United
Nations; Western Europe

Royce, Shannon
Legal Counsel
Ethics and Religious Liberty Commission
505 2nd Street, N.E.
Washington, DC 20002
202-547-8105   fax 202-547-8165
Issues: Church-state relations; Ethics; School
choice

Rozek, Dr. Edward J.
Professor
University of Northern Colorado
P. O. Box 4654
Boulder, CO 80306
303-351-2058
Issues: Central and Eastern Europe; Russia and
Eurasia

*Rubin, Dr. Alfred P.
Distinguished Professor of International
Law, Fletcher School of Law and Diplomacy
Tufts University
Mugar 242
Medford, MA 02155
617-627-2241   fax 617-627-3712
arubin@tufts.edu
Issues: American diplomacy/foreign policy;
China; Constitutional law; Ethics; International
law; Judiciary; Northeast Asia; Southeast Asia
(including Burma, Cambodia, Laos, Vietnam,
Singapore, Malaysia, Indonesia, the
Philippines, Australia, and New Zealand);
Terrorism and international crime

Rubin, Dr. Charles
Associate Professor of Political Science,
Political Science Department
Duquesne University
College Hall, 600 Forbes Avenue
Pittsburgh, PA 15282
412-396-6485   fax 412-396-5197
rubin@duq.edu
Issues: Citizenship and civil society; Climate
change; Environmental education; Ethics;
Political philosophy; Sound science; Urban
sprawl/livable cities

*Rubin, Paul
Professor of Economics and Law,
Department of Economics
Emory University
Rich Building 324
Atlanta, GA 30322
404-727-6365   fax 630-607-9609
prubin@emory.edu
Issues: Anti-trust; Comparative government;
Congress; Costs and benefits of regulation;
Crime/crime statistics; Criminal law and
procedure; Entrepreneurship/free enterprise;
Federal budget; Free Speech; Judiciary;
Minimum wage; Political correctness and
multiculturalism; Political philosophy; Privacy;
Property rights; Regulation through litigation;
Risk assessment; Tort and liability reform

*Rucker, Craig
Executive Director
Committee for a Constructive Tomorrow
P. O. Box 65722
Washington, DC 20035
202-429-2737   fax 540-955-2481
craig@cfact.org
Issues: Air; Climate change; Energy;
Environmental education; Environmental
regulation; Free-market environmentalism;
Land use; Property rights; Regulatory reform;
Risk assessment; Sound science; Stewardship;
Waste management; Wildlife management/
endangered species

*Ruddy, Amb. Frank
Partner
Ruddy & Muir
5600 Western Avenue
Chevy Chase, MD 20815
202-835-0055   fax 301-654-5237
global@globalltd.com
Issues: Africa; American diplomacy/foreign
policy; Climate change; Constitutional law;
Human rights; International law;
Peacekeeping; Promoting democracy/public
diplomacy; United Nations

*Rufolo, Dr. Anthony
Professor of Urban Studies and Planning
Portland State University
P. O. Box 751
Portland, OR 97207
503-725-4049   fax 503-725-8770
rufoloa@pdx.edu
Issues: Land use; State and local public finance;
Taxation/tax reform; Transportation; Urban
sprawl/livable cities

*Rule, Hon. Charles F.
Fried, Frank, Harris, Shriver & Jacobson
1001 Pennsylvania Avenue, N.W., 9th Floor
Washington, DC 20004-2505
202-639-7300   fax 202-585-6440
rulecf@ffhsj.com
Issues: Anti-trust; Entrepreneurship/free
enterprise; Intellectual property; The Reagan
legacy; Regulation through litigation;
Regulatory reform; Telecommunications and
the Internet; Transportation deregulation

---

*Rumenap, Stacie
Executive Director
U. S. Term Limits
10 G Street, N.E., Suite 410
Washington, DC 20002
202-379-3000   fax 202-379-3010
rumenap@ustermlimits.org
Issues: Congress; Government waste; Initiative and referendum; State and local government; Term limits

*Runbeck, Linda
Executive Vice President
Taxpayers League of Minnesota
One Carlson Parkway, Suite 120
Plymouth, MN 55447
763-249-5950   fax 651-639-5745
Issues: Costs and benefits of regulation; The Economy; International tax policy/tax competition; Privatization/Contracting-out; Risk assessment; State and local public finance; Taxation/tax reform; Trade; Transportation

*Rush, Dr. Mark E.
Professor, Department of Politics
Washington and Lee University
Williams School of Commerce, Economics, and Politics
Lexington, VA 24450
540-458-8904   fax 540-458-8639
rushm@wlu.edu
Issues: Canada; Comparative government; Constitutional law; Electoral reform/voting rights; Western Europe

*Rusher, William A.
Distinguished Fellow
Claremont Institute
850 Powell Street, Apt. 605
San Francisco, CA 94108
415-399-1531   fax 415-399-1531
Issues: American diplomacy/foreign policy; The American Founding; American history/political tradition; China; Conservative thought; Media and popular culture; Northeast Asia; Political philosophy; The Reagan legacy; Terrorism and international crime

Rushford, Michael D.
President
Criminal Justice Legal Foundation
2131 L Street
Sacramento, CA 95816
916-446-0345   fax 916-446-1194
mdr@gps.net
Issues: Crime/crime statistics; Criminal law and procedure; Judicial activism/judicial reform; Public interest law

Russell, Robert E., Jr.
Counselor to the President
The Heritage Foundation
12 South Fifth Street
Geneva, IL 60134
630-208-9700   fax 630-208-1499
rranda@mindspring.com
Issues: American history/political tradition; Conservative thought; Economic education; Economic theory; Ethics; Faith-based and volunteer initiatives; Higher education; Intelligence gathering and covert operations; Non-governmental organizations; Philanthropy; Wealth creation/financial empowerment

*Russo, Frank
State Director
American Family Association of New York
P. O. Box 203
Port Washington, NY 11050
516-767-9179   fax 516-944-3544
Issues: Faith-based and volunteer initiatives; Media and popular culture; Public school finance and administration; Religion and public life; School choice

Ruszkiewicz, John
Professor of Rhetoric and Composition
University of Texas
Parlin 3
Austin, TX 78712
512-471-8764   fax 512-471-4353
ruszkiewicz@mail.utexas.edu
Issues: Higher education

Rutherford, Kristie L.
Director of State and Local Affairs
Family Research Council
801 G Street, N.W.
Washington, DC 20001
202-393-2100   fax 202-393-2134
krl@frc.org
Issues: State and local government

Rutland, Dr. Peter
Professor, Department of Government
Wesleyan University
238 Church Street
Middletown, CT 06459
860-685-2483   fax 860-685-2241
prutland@wesleyan.edu
Issues: Central and Eastern Europe;
Comparative economics; Labor and
employment; Political philosophy;
Privatization/Contracting-out; Russia and
Eurasia; Trade

Ryan, Dr. Edward W.
Bacardi Chair of Economics and Director,
Economic Freedom Institute
Manhattanville College
2900 Purchase Street
Purchase, NY 10577
914-694-3372   fax 914-694-2386
ryane@mville.edu
Issues: Economic education; Economic theory;
Trade

Ryan, Terry
Program Director
Thomas B. Fordham Foundation
1627 K Street, N.W., Suite 600
Washington, DC 20006
202-223-5452   fax 202-223-9226
thourryan@aol.com
Issues: Charter schools; School choice

Ryn, Dr. Claes G.
Professor of Politics
Catholic University of America
620 Michigan Avenue, N.E.
Washington, DC 20064
202-319-6225   fax 202-319-6289
cryn@erols.com
Issues: American diplomacy/foreign policy;
China; Conservative thought; Economic
theory; Ethics; Political philosophy

*Salerno, Dr. Joseph T.
Professor of Economics, Lubin School of
Business
Pace University
One Pace Plaza
New York, NY 10038
212-346-1848   fax 908-756-0659
jsalerno@pace.edu
Issues: Economic theory; Money and financial
services; Trade

Salins, Dr. Peter D.
Senior Fellow, Center for Civic Innovation
Manhattan Institute for Policy Research
52 Vanderbilt Avenue
New York, NY 10017
212-772-5594   fax 212-772-4880
psalins@manhattan-institute.org
Issues: Housing and homelessness;
Immigration; Privatization/Contracting-out;
State and local government; State and local
public finance; Urban sprawl/livable cities

Salisbury, Dallas L.
President and CEO
Employee Benefit Research Institute
2121 K Street, N.W., Suite 600
Washington, DC 20037
202-775-6322   fax 202-775-6312
dallassalisbury@ebri.org
Issues: Entitlement spending; Government
health programs; Health care reform; Labor
and employment; Medicaid; Medicare; Social
Security and retirement; State and local public
finance; Taxation/tax reform; Unemployment
insurance; Unfunded mandates

*Salisbury, David F.
Director of the Center for Educational
Freedom
Cato Institute
1000 Massachusetts Avenue, N.W.
Washington, DC 20001
202-789-5246   fax 202-842-3490
dsalisbury@cato.org
Issues: Business and education partnerships;
Charter schools; Education unions and interest
groups; Federal education policy; Higher
education; Home schooling; School choice;
Standards, curriculum, and testing

*Samp, Richard A.
Chief Counsel
Washington Legal Foundation
2009 Massachusetts Avenue, N.W.
Washington, DC 20036
202-588-0302   fax 202-588-0386
rsamp@wlf.org
Issues: Constitutional law; Free Speech;
Immigration; Judicial activism/judicial reform;
Property rights; Regulation through litigation;
Tort and liability reform

Samples, Dr. John
Director, Center for Representative
Government
Cato Institute
1000 Massachusetts Avenue, N.W.
Washington, DC 20001-5403
202-842-0200   fax 202-842-3490
jsamples@cato.org
Issues: Campaign finance reform; Church-state
relations; Congress; Elections/polling;
Electoral reform/voting rights; Executive
Branch/The Presidency; Federalism; Free
Speech; Term limits

*Samson, Dr. Steven Alan
Professor of Government
Liberty University
1971 University Boulevard
Lynchburg, VA 24502
434-582-2640   fax 434-582-2366
ssamson@liberty.edu
Issues: The American Founding; American
history/political tradition; Arts, humanities
and historic resources; Church-state relations;
Citizenship and civil society; Comparative
government; Conservative thought; Higher
education; Home schooling; Political
philosophy; Religion and public life; Religious
freedom

Samuel, Peter
Editor
Toll Roads Newsletter
102 West Third Street, Unit One
Frederick, MD 21701-5333
301-631-1148   fax 301-631-1248
tollroads@aol.com
Issues: Infrastructure; Transportation; Urban
sprawl/livable cities

Sand, Dr. Gregory W.
Saint Louis College of Pharmacy
4588 Parkview Place
St. Louis, MO 63110-1088
314-367-8700   fax 314-367-2784
gsand@stlcop.edu
Issues: American diplomacy/foreign policy;
American history/political tradition; Ethics;
Higher education; Immigration; Latin
America; Military strategy; Political philosophy;
Terrorism and international crime

Sanders, Ernestine L.
President
Cornerstone Schools
6861 East Nevada
Detroit, MI 48234
313-892-1860   fax 313-892-1861
Issues: Business and education partnerships;
School choice

Sanders, Dr. John T.
Professor, Department of Philosophy
Rochester Institute of Technology
92 Lomb Memorial Drive
Rochester, NY 14623-5604
585-475-2465   fax 585-475-7120
jts@rit.edu
Issues: Ethics; Political philosophy

*Sandoz, Dr. Ellis
Director
Eric Voegelin Institute
Louisiana State University, 240 Stubbs Hall
Baton Rouge, LA 70803
225-578-2552   fax 225-578-4766
esandoz@lsu.edu
Issues: The American Founding; American
history/political tradition; Free Speech;
Higher education; Political philosophy;
Religious freedom

*Sanera, Dr. Michael
Instructor
Basis Charter High School
3825 East 2nd Street
Tucson, AZ 85716
520-326-6367   fax 520-326-6359
BASISinfo@aol.com
Issues: The American Founding; American
history/political tradition; Charter schools;
Economic education; Environmental
education; Political philosophy; School choice;
Sound science

Santoli, Al
Senior Vice President
American Foreign Policy Council
1521 16th Street, N.W.
Washington, DC 20036
202-462-6055   fax 202-462-6045
santoli@afpc.org
Issues: Afghanistan; American diplomacy/
foreign policy; China; Economic
development/foreign aid; Emerging threats/
threat assessment; Human rights; Intelligence
gathering and covert operations; Japan; Korea;
Middle East; Military strategy; Northeast Asia;
Peacekeeping; Promoting democracy/public
diplomacy; Russia and Eurasia; South Asia
(including India and Pakistan); Southeast Asia
(including Burma, Cambodia, Laos, Vietnam,
Singapore, Malaysia, Indonesia, the
Philippines, Australia, and New Zealand);
Terrorism and international crime

Sarkesian, Dr. Sam C.
Professor Emeritus of Political Science
Loyola University Chicago
6525 North Sheridan Road
Chicago, IL 60626
773-508-3058   fax 773-508-3131
ssarkes@wpo.it.luc.edu
Issues: Defense budget; Intelligence gathering
and covert operations; Military strategy;
Peacekeeping

*Sarnoff, Dr. Susan
Assistant Professor and Graduate Chairman,
Department of Social Work
Ohio University
Morton Hall 522
Athens, OH 45701
740-593-7436   fax 740-593-0427
sarnoff@ohio.edu
Issues: Advocacy and nonprofit public funding;
Bilingual education; Civil rights/racial
preferences; Corrections and sentencing; Costs
and benefits of regulation; Crime/crime
statistics; Entitlement spending;
Entrepreneurship/free enterprise;
Government health programs; Health care
reform; Medicaid; Medicare; OSHA; Political
correctness and multiculturalism; Poverty and
dependency; Privatization/Contracting-out;
Regulation through litigation; Substance
abuse; Tort and liability reform; Welfare/
welfare reform

*Satel, Sally, M.D.
W. H. Bradley Fellow
American Enterprise Institute
1150 17th Street, N.W.
Washington, DC 20036
202-862-7154   fax 202-862-7177
ssatel@aei.org
Issues: Health care reform; Housing and
homelessness; Substance abuse

Saunders, Paul J.
Director
The Nixon Center
1615 L Street, N.W., Suite 1250
Washington, DC 20036
202-887-1000   fax 202-887-5222
mail@nixoncenter.org
Issues: American diplomacy/foreign policy;
Russia and Eurasia

Saunders, Dr. Peter J.
Professor of Economics, Economics
Department
Central Washington University
400 East 8th Avenue
Ellensburg, WA 98926
509-963-1266   fax 509-963-1992
saunders@cwu.edu
Issues: Discretionary spending; Federal budget;
Government debt; Taxation/tax reform

Saunders, William L.
Senior Fellow, Life Studies
Family Research Council
801 G Street, N.W.
Washington, DC 20001
202-624-3038   fax 202-393-2134
wls@frc.org
Issues: Ethics; Human rights; International
organizations (European Union, OECD, etc.);
Religious freedom; United Nations

Savas, Dr. E. S.
Professor of Public Policy, Baruch College
City University of New York
17 Lexington Avenue
New York, NY 10010
212-802-5909   fax 212-802-5903
prisect@aol.com
Issues: Government waste; Infrastructure;
Privatization/Contracting-out; The Reagan
legacy; School choice; State and local
government

*Saving, Dr. Thomas R.
Director, Private Enterprise Research Center
Texas A&M University
3028 Academic Building W, 4231 TAMU
College Station, TX 77843-4231
979-845-7559   fax 979-845-6636
t-saving@tamu.edu
Issues: Anti-trust; Costs and benefits of
regulation; Economic forecasting; Economic
theory; The Economy; Electricity deregulation;
Entitlement spending; Federal budget;
Government debt; Government health
programs; Health care reform; Medicare;
Money and financial services; Social Security
and retirement; Tort and liability reform;
Wealth creation/financial empowerment

Saxe, Dr. David W.
Associate Professor of Education
Pennsylvania State University
0144 Chambers Building
University Park, PA 16802
814-863-7409   fax 814-863-7602
dws7@psu.edu
Issues: American history/political tradition;
Charter schools; Citizenship and civil society;
Higher education; Media and popular culture;
Standards, curriculum, and testing

Scalapino, Dr. Robert A.
Robson Research Professor of Government
Emeritus, Institute of East Asian Studies
University of California, Berkeley
2223 Fulton Street
Berkeley, CA 94720
510-643-5540   fax 510-643-7062
Issues: American diplomacy/foreign policy;
China; International organizations (European
Union, OECD, etc.); Japan; Korea; Northeast
Asia; Russia and Eurasia; South Asia (including
India and Pakistan); Southeast Asia (including
Burma, Cambodia, Laos, Vietnam, Singapore,
Malaysia, Indonesia, the Philippines, Australia,
and New Zealand); United Nations

Scalia, John F.
Greenberg Traurig, LLP
1750 Tysons Boulevard, Suite 1200
McLean, VA 22102
703-749-1300   fax 703-749-1301
scaliaj@gtlaw.com
Issues: Family and medical leave; Labor and
employment

Scandlen, Greg
Senior Fellow in Health Policy
National Center for Policy Analysis
655 15th Street, N.W., Suite 375
Washington, DC 20005
202-628-6671   fax 202-628-6474
gmscan@aol.com
Issues: Government health programs; Health
care reform; Medicaid; Medicare

*Scanlon, Terrence M.
President
Capital Research Center
1513 16th Street, N.W.
Washington, DC 20036
202-483-6900   fax 202-483-6990
tscanlon@capitalresearch.org
Issues: Advocacy and nonprofit public funding;
Costs and benefits of regulation; Education
unions and interest groups; Faith-based and
volunteer initiatives; Non-governmental
organizations; Philanthropy; The Reagan
legacy; Regulatory reform; Research funding;
School choice; Unions

Scardaville, Michael
Policy Analyst, Homeland Defense, Kathryn
and Shelby Cullom Davis Institute for
International Studies
The Heritage Foundation
214 Massachusetts Avenue, N.E.
Washington, DC 20002
202-608-6057   fax 202-675-1758
michael.scardaville@heritage.org
Issues: Homeland security/civil defense

Schadler, Robert A.
President
Center for First Principles
2615 O Street, N.W.
Washington, DC 20007
202-338-3239   fax 202-338-3185
cwestciv@yahoo.com
Issues: American diplomacy/foreign policy;
The American Founding; American history/
political tradition; Arts, humanities and
historic resources; Citizenship and civil society;
Conservative thought; Federalism; Political
philosophy; Promoting democracy/public
diplomacy; The Reagan legacy; Religion and
public life

Schaefer, Brett D.

Jay Kingham Fellow in International
Regulatory Affairs and Senior Policy Analyst,
Center for International Trade and
Economics
The Heritage Foundation
214 Massachusetts Avenue, N.E.
Washington, DC 20002
202-546-4400   fax 202-675-1758
info@heritage.org

Issues: Africa; Human rights; International
finance and multilateral banks; International
law; International organizations (European
Union, OECD, etc.); Money and financial
services; Peacekeeping; Trade; United Nations

Schaefer, Dr. David L.

Professor of Political Science
Holy Cross College
P. O. Box 101A
Worcester, MA 01610-0395
508-793-2252   dschaefe@holycross.edu

Issues: The American Founding; American
history/political tradition; Campaign finance
reform; Citizenship and civil society;
Conservative thought; Constitutional law;
Ethics; Executive Branch/The Presidency;
Federal civil service; Free Speech; Higher
education; Judicial activism/judicial reform;
Judiciary; Political correctness and
multiculturalism; Political philosophy;
Religion and public life; Religious freedom

Schaefer, Dr. Roberta Rubel

Executive Director
Worcester Regional Research Bureau
319 Main Street
Worcester, MA 01608
508-799-7169   fax 508-799-4720
rschaefe@wrrb.org

Issues: Charter schools; Standards, curriculum,
and testing; State and local government; State
and local public finance

*Schansberg, D. Eric, Ph.D.

Professor of Economics, School of Business
Indiana University Southeast
4201 Grant Line Road, HH-004
New Albany, IN 47150-6405
812-941-2527   fax 812-941-2672
dschansb@ius.edu

Issues: Ethics; Minimum wage; Political
philosophy; Poverty and dependency; Religion
and public life; School choice; Term limits;
Unions

Schatz, Rick

President
National Coalition for the Protection of
Children and Families
800 Compton Road, Suite 9224
Cincinnati, OH 45231
513-521-6227   fax 513-521-6337
rick@nationalcoalition.org

Issues: Family and children; Media and popular
culture

*Schatz, Thomas A.

President
Citizens Against Government Waste
1301 Connecticut Avenue, N.W., Suite 400
Washington, DC 20036
202-467-5300   fax 202-467-4253
tschatz@cagw.org

Issues: Advocacy and nonprofit public funding;
Agriculture; Anti-trust; Defense budget;
Discretionary spending; Entitlement spending;
Federal budget; Government debt;
Government waste; Health care reform;
Intellectual property; Medicare; Privacy;
Privatization/Contracting-out; Regulation
through litigation; Social Security and
retirement; Taxation/tax reform;
Telecommunications and the Internet

Schaub, Dr. Diana J.

Associate Professor of Political Science
Loyola College
4501 North Charles Street
Baltimore, MD 21210
410-617-2138   fax 410-617-2215
dschaub@loyola.edu

Issues: Political philosophy

*Scheidegger, Kent

Legal Director
Criminal Justice Legal Foundation
2131 L Street
Sacramento, CA 95816
916-446-0345   fax 916-446-1194
cjlf@cjlf.org

Issues: Constitutional law; Corrections and
sentencing; Crime/crime statistics; Criminal
law and procedure; Federalism

---

*Schiller, Bradley R., Ph.D.
Professor, School of Public Affairs
American University
4400 Massachusetts Avenue, N.W.
Washington, DC 20016
202-885-6246
Issues: The Economy; Job training/welfare to
work; Minimum wage; Poverty and
dependency; Social Security and retirement;
Welfare/welfare reform

*Schilling, Bill
President
Wyoming Business Alliance / Wyoming
Heritage Foundation
145 South Durbin Street, Suite 101
Casper, WY 82601
307-577-8000   fax 307-577-8003
wyhf@qwest.net
Issues: Advocacy and nonprofit public funding;
Air; American history/political tradition;
Business and education partnerships; Climate
change; Comparative economics; Economic
education; Economic forecasting; The
Economy; Energy; Entrepreneurship/free
enterprise; Environmental education;
Environmental regulation; Forestry and
national parks; Government debt; Health care
reform; Land use; Privatization/Contracting-
out; School choice; Standards, curriculum, and
testing; State and local public finance;
Taxation/tax reform; Telecommunications
and the Internet; Transportation; Unfunded
mandates

*Schlafly, Phyllis
President
Eagle Forum
7800 Bonhomme
St. Louis, MO 63105
314-721-1213   fax 314-721-3373
phyllis@eagleforum.org
Issues: Arms control; Bilingual education;
Constitutional law; Federal education policy;
Health care reform; Higher education; Home
schooling; Homeland security/civil defense;
Immigration; Intellectual property; Judicial
activism/judicial reform; Military strategy;
Missile defense; Peacekeeping; Political
correctness and multiculturalism; Privacy;
School-to-work; Standards, curriculum, and
testing; United Nations

*Schlicher, John W.
Gray, Cary, Ware & Freidenrich
400 Hamilton Avenue
Palo Alto, CA 94301
650-328-6561   fax 650-320-7401
jschlicher@gcwf.com
Issues: Anti-trust; Intellectual property

*Schlossman, Stuart
Baruj Benacerraf Professor of Medicine,
Dana-Farber Cancer Institute
Harvard Medical School
44 Binney Street, Mayer 557
Boston, MA 02115
617-632-3325   fax 617-632-2690
stuart_schlossman@dfci.harvard.edu
Issues: Research funding; Sound science

Schmidt, LaKay
President Emeritus
Colorado Council on Economic Education
7175 Four Rivers Road
Boulder, CO 80301
303-530-7755   fax 303-530-7755
Issues: Economic education

Schmidtz, Dr. David
Professor of Philosophy and Economics,
Philosophy Department
University of Arizona
Social Science Building, Room 213, P. O.
Box 210027
Tucson, AZ 85721-0027
520-621-3129   fax 520-621-9559
schmidtz@u.arizona.edu
Issues: Poverty and dependency; Property
rights; Wildlife management/endangered
species

Schmitt, Dr. Gary
Executive Director
Project for the New American Century
1150 17th Street, N.W., Suite 510
Washington, DC 20036
202-293-4983   fax 202-293-4572
gschmitt@newamericancentury.org
Issues: Central and Eastern Europe; Defense
budget; Economic development/foreign aid;
Executive Branch/The Presidency;
Intelligence gathering and covert operations;
Middle East; Military strategy; NATO and other
alliances; Western Europe

Schneider, William
Resident Fellow
American Enterprise Institute
1150 17th Street, N.W.
Washington, DC 20036
202-515-2803   fax 202-515-2853
bill.schneider@turner.com
Issues: Elections/polling; Executive Branch/
The Presidency

*Scholte, Suzanne
President
Defense Forum Foundation
3014 Castle Road
Falls Church, VA 22044
703-534-4313   fax 703-538-6149
Issues: Africa; Korea

*Schramm, Dr. Peter W.
Executive Director, Department of Political
Science
John M. Ashbrook Center for Public Affairs
Ashland University, 401 College Avenue
Ashland, OH 44805
419-289-5431   fax 419-289-5425
pschramm@ashbrook.org
Issues: The American Founding; American
history/political tradition; Central and Eastern
Europe; Conservative thought; Higher
education; Homeland security/civil defense;
Immigration; Political philosophy; Promoting
democracy/public diplomacy; The Reagan
legacy; School choice; Standards, curriculum,
and testing; Terrorism and international crime

Schuettinger, Robert
President
Washington International Studies Council
214 Massachusetts Avenue, N.E., Suite 370
Washington, DC 20002
202-547-3275   fax 202-547-1470
Issues: American diplomacy/foreign policy;
Conservative thought; Higher education;
Political philosophy; Promoting democracy/
public diplomacy; The Reagan legacy; Western
Europe

Schuler, Dr. Kurt
Economist
113 South Park Drive
Arlington, VA 22204
703-892-5620   kurrency@erols.com
Issues: International finance and multilateral
banks; Money and financial services

Schuyler, Dr. Michael A.
Senior Economist
Institute for Research on the Economics of
Taxation
1710 Rhode Island Avenue, N.W., 11th Floor
Washington, DC 20036
202-463-1400   fax 202-463-6199
Issues: Taxation/tax reform

*Schwartz, Dr. Anna J.
Research Associate
National Bureau of Economic Research
365 Fifth Avenue, 5th Floor
New York, NY 10016-4309
212-817-7957   fax 212-817-1597
aschwartz@gc.cuny.edu
Issues: Economic development/foreign aid;
International finance and multilateral banks;
Money and financial services

*Schwartz, Dr. Arthur J.
Director, Character Development Programs
John Templeton Foundation
Five Radnor Corporate Center, Suite 100
Radnor, PA 19087
610-687-8942   fax 610-687-8961
schwartz@templeton.org
Issues: Abstinence and out-of-wedlock births;
Business and education partnerships; Church-
state relations; Citizenship and civil society;
Ethics; Faith-based and volunteer initiatives;
Higher education; Juvenile justice;
Philanthropy; Political correctness and
multiculturalism; Religion and public life;
Religious freedom; Standards, curriculum, and
testing

*Schwartz, Michael
Vice President for Government Relations
Concerned Women for America
1015 15th Street, N.W., Suite 1100
Washington, DC 20005
202-488-7000   fax 202-488-0806
mschwartz@cwfa.org
Issues: Abstinence and out-of-wedlock births;
Adoption, foster care, & child care services;
Family and children; Marriage and divorce;
Religion and public life; School choice

*Schwartz, Victor E.
General Counsel
American Tort Reform Association
1850 M Street, N.W., Suite 1095
Washington, DC 20036
202-624-2540   fax 202-628-5116
vschwartz@cromor.com
Issues: Tort and liability reform

Schweikart, Dr. Larry
Professor, Department of History
University of Dayton
300 College Park
Dayton, OH 45469-2265
937-229-2804   fax 937-229-4400
schweikart@erinet.com
Issues: The American Founding; Economic
theory; Media and popular culture; The
Reagan legacy

Schwert, Dr. G. W.
Distinguished University Professor of
Finance & Statistics, William E. Simon
Graduate School of Business
University of Rochester
P. O. Box 270100
Rochester, NY 14627
716-275-2470   fax 716-461-5475
schwert@schwert.ssb.rochester.edu
Issues: Costs and benefits of regulation;
Economic forecasting; Money and financial
services

Scott, Dr. John T.
Professor of Economics, Department of
Economics
Dartmouth College
6106 Rockefeller Hall
Hanover, NH 03755
603-646-2941   fax 603-646-2122
john.scott@dartmouth.edu
Issues: The Economy

Scott, Dr. Robert Haney
Professor, Department of Finance and
Marketing
California State University, Chico
Chico, CA 95929
530-898-6188   fax 530-898-6030
hscott@csuchico.edu
Issues: Economic education; Economic
forecasting; The Economy; Government debt;
Higher education; Intellectual property;
Money and financial services; Property rights

Scully, Dr. Gerald W.
Senior Fellow
National Center for Policy Analysis
27872 Camino del Rio
San Juan Capistrano, CA 92675
949-496-3447
Issues: Taxation/tax reform

*Sears, Alan E.
President
Alliance Defense Fund
15333 North Pima Road, Suite 165
Scottsdale, AZ 85260
480-444-0020   fax 480-444-0025
asears@alliancedefensefund.org
Issues: Abstinence and out-of-wedlock births;
Adoption, foster care, & child care services;
Arts, humanities and historic resources;
Church-state relations; Citizenship and civil
society; Constitutional law; Faith-based and
volunteer initiatives; Family and children; Free
Speech; Judicial activism/judicial reform;
Marriage and divorce; Media and popular
culture; Political correctness and
multiculturalism; Public interest law; Religion
and public life; Religious freedom

Sechrest, Dr. Larry J.
Professor of Economics, Department of
Business Administration
Sul Ross State University
Box C-35
Alpine, TX 79832
915-837-8069   fax 915-837-8003
larrys@sulross.cdu
Issues: American history/political tradition;
Economic theory; Money and financial
services; Political philosophy; Privatization/
Contracting-out

Sedgwick, Dr. Jeffrey Leigh
Associate Professor of Political Science,
Department of Political Science
University of Massachusetts
336 Thompson Hall
Amherst, MA 01003
413-545-6189   fax 413-545-3349
sedgwick@polsci.umass.edu
Issues: American history/political tradition;
Citizenship and civil society; Executive
Branch/The Presidency; Federalism; Political
philosophy; Promoting democracy/public
diplomacy; The Reagan legacy; State and local
government; Term limits

*Segal, Geoffrey F.
Director, Privatization and Government
Reform Policy
Reason Public Policy Institute
3415 South Sepulveda Boulevard, Suite 400
Los Angeles, CA 90034
310-391-2245   fax 310-391-4395
geoffrey.segal@reason.org
Issues: Corrections and sentencing; Costs and
benefits of regulation; Davis-Bacon Act;
Discretionary spending; Entrepreneurship/
free enterprise; Federal budget; Government
debt; Government waste; Infrastructure;
Juvenile justice; Police; Privatization/
Contracting-out; Regulatory reform; State and
local government; State and local public
finance; Unions; Waste management; Welfare/
welfare reform

*Segalman, Dr. Ralph
Professor Emeritus of Sociology
California State University, Northridge
18723 Sunburst Street
Northridge, CA 91324
818-993-5178   fax 818-993-0850
ralph.segalman@csun.edu
Issues: Abstinence and out-of-wedlock births;
Adoption, foster care, & child care services;
Family and children; Government health
programs; Health care reform; Immigration;
Job training/welfare to work; Marriage and
divorce; Philanthropy; Political correctness and
multiculturalism; Poverty and dependency;
School choice; Social Security and retirement;
Welfare/welfare reform; Western Europe

*Segermark, Howard
Segermark Associates, Inc.
904 Massachusetts Avenue, N.E.
Washington, DC 20002
202-547-2222   fax 202-547-7417
howard@segermark.com
Issues: Economic development/foreign aid;
Taxation/tax reform; Telecommunications
and the Internet

*Sekulow, Jay
Chief Counsel
American Center for Law and Justice
P. O. Box 64429
Virginia Beach, VA 23464
757-226-2489   fax 757-226-2836
aclj@aclj.org
Issues: Advocacy and nonprofit public funding;
The American Founding; American history/
political tradition; Campaign finance reform;
Church-state relations; Civil rights/racial
preferences; Constitutional law; Faith-based
and volunteer initiatives; Free Speech;
Homeland security/civil defense; Human
rights; Public interest law; Religion and public
life; Religious freedom; Taxation/tax reform;
Terrorism and international crime

*Self, Jamie
Media and Policy Analyst
Georgia Family Council
5380 Peachtree Industrial Boulevard
Suite 100
Norcross, GA 30071-1565
770-242-0001   fax 770-242-0501
jamie@gafam.org
Issues: Abstinence and out-of-wedlock births;
Adoption, foster care, & child care services;
Church-state relations; Citizenship and civil
society; Constitutional law; Family and
children; Marriage and divorce; Religion and
public life; Religious freedom; School choice;
State-sponsored gambling; Welfare/welfare
reform

*Semmens, John
Economist
Laissez-Faire Institute
828 North Poplar Court
Chandler, AZ 85226
480-940-9824   jsemmens@aol.com
Issues: Economic education; Environmental
education; Initiative and referendum;
Transportation; Transportation deregulation

---

*Senese, Dr. Donald J.
Vice President and Director of Research
60 Plus Association
1600 Wilson Boulevard, Suite 960
Arlington, VA 22209
703-807-2070   fax 703-807-2073
donsenese_60plus@yahoo.com
Issues: American diplomacy/foreign policy;
The American Founding; American history/
political tradition; China; Citizenship and civil
society; Climate change; Congress;
Conservative thought; Education unions and
interest groups; Executive Branch/The
Presidency; Federal education policy;
Federalism; Health care reform; Japan;
Judiciary; Korea; Medicare; The Reagan legacy;
Social Security and retirement; Standards,
curriculum, and testing

*Sennholz, Dr. Hans F.
Professor
Grove City College
200 East Pine Street
Grove City, PA 16127
724-458-8343   fax 724-458-1666
hans@sennholz.com
Issues: Economic education; Economic theory;
Federal budget; Government debt; Labor and
employment; Minimum wage; Money and
financial services; Right to work; Social Security
and retirement; Taxation/tax reform

*Sepp, Pete
Vice President, Communications
National Taxpayers Union
108 North Alfred Street
Alexandria, VA 22314
703-683-5700   fax 703-683-5722
pressguy@ntu.org
Issues: Advocacy and nonprofit public funding;
Anti-trust; Congress; Costs and benefits of
regulation; Discretionary spending;
Entitlement spending; Ethics; Federal budget;
Government health programs; Initiative and
referendum; International tax policy/tax
competition; Privatization/Contracting-out;
Regulation through litigation; Research
funding; State and local government; State and
local public finance; Taxation/tax reform;
Term limits; Transportation deregulation;
Unfunded mandates

*Sewall, Gilbert T.
Director
American Textbook Council
475 Riverside Drive, Suite 448
New York, NY 10115
212-870-2760   fax 212-870-2720
sewall@columbia.edu
Issues: American history/political tradition;
Standards, curriculum, and testing

*Shackelford, Kelly
Executive Director
Free Market Foundation
Nathaniel Barrett Building, 903 East 18th
Street, Suite 230
Plano, TX 75074
972-423-8889   fax 972-423-8899
kelly@freemarket.org
Issues: Church-state relations; Constitutional
law; Free Speech; Judiciary; Religious freedom

Shaffer, David F.
President
Public Policy Institute of New York
152 Washington Avenue
Albany, NY 12210-2289
518-465-7517   fax 518-432-4537
shaffer@bcnys.org
Issues: Taxation/tax reform

Shah, Dr. Timothy Samuel
Resident Scholar
Ethics and Public Policy Center
1015 15th Street, N.W., Suite 900
Washington, DC 20005
202-216-0855   fax 202-408-0632
Issues: Church-state relations; Human rights;
Political philosophy; South Asia (including
India and Pakistan)

Shain, Dr. Barry Alan
Associate Professor, Department of Political
Science
Colgate University
120 Persson Hall
Hamilton, NY 13346
315-228-7965   fax 315-228-7883
bshain@mail.colgate.edu
Issues: American history/political tradition;
Church-state relations; Conservative thought;
Political philosophy

*Shanahan, John
Director, Air Quality
National Mining Association
101 Constitution Avenue, N.W.
Washington, DC 20001
202-463-9793   fax 202-463-3257
jshanahan@nma.org
Issues: Air; Energy; Environmental regulation;
Free-market environmentalism; Property
rights; Regulation through litigation;
Regulatory reform; Risk assessment; Sound
science

Shanmugam, Kannon K.
Associate
Kirkland & Ellis
655 15th Street, N.W., Suite 1200
Washington, DC 20005
202-879-5964   fax 202-654-9520
kannon@kirkland.com
Issues: Constitutional law; Criminal law and
procedure; Federalism; Intellectual property;
Judiciary

*Shapiro, E. Donald
Dean Emeritus
New York Law School
10040 East Happy Valley Road, Desert
Highlands #422
Scottsdale, AZ 85255
480-513-0549   fax 480-419-1602
Issues: Civil rights/racial preferences;
Government health programs; Health care
reform; Judicial activism/judicial reform; Tort
and liability reform

*Sharette, Carolyn
Executive Director
Children First Utah
455 East South Temple
Salt Lake City, UT 84111
801-363-0946   fax 801-524-2374
info@childrenfirstutah.org
Issues: Charter schools; School choice

Sharp, Tracie
President
State Policy Network
6255 Arlington Boulevard
Richmond, CA 94805-1601
510-965-9700   fax 510-965-9701
sharp@spn.org
Issues: Health care reform; School choice

*Shea, Nina
Director, Center for Religious Freedom
Freedom House
1319 18th Street, N.W.
Washington, DC 20036
202-296-5101   fax 202-296-5078
religion@freedomhouse.org
Issues: Africa; China; Human rights; Middle
East; United Nations

*Sheehan, Dr. Colleen
Associate Professor, Department of Political
Science
Villanova University
Villanova, PA 19085-1699
610-519-7421   fax 610-519-4639
Issues: The American Founding; American
history/political tradition; Citizenship and civil
society; Conservative thought; Ethics; Political
philosophy; School choice; Standards,
curriculum, and testing

*Sheffrin, Steven M.
Dean, Division of Social Sciences
University of California, Davis
One Shields Avenue
Davis, CA 95616
530-754-8925   fax 530-752-3490
smsheffrin@ucdavis.edu
Issues: State and local public finance

*Sheldon, Rev. Lou
Chairman
Traditional Values Coalition
139 C Street, S.E.
Washington, DC 20003
202-547-8570   fax 202-546-6403
tvcwashdc@traditionalvalues.org
Issues: Abstinence and out-of-wedlock births;
Adoption, foster care, & child care services;
The American Founding; American history/
political tradition; Arts, humanities and
historic resources; Church-state relations;
Citizenship and civil society; Civil rights/racial
preferences; Congress; Elections/polling;
Electoral reform/voting rights; Ethics;
Executive Branch/The Presidency; Faith-based
and volunteer initiatives; Family and children;
Free Speech; Initiative and referendum;
Judicial activism/judicial reform; Juvenile
justice; Marriage and divorce; Media and
popular culture; Philanthropy; Political
correctness and multiculturalism; Political
philosophy; Religion and public life; Religious
freedom; School choice; State-sponsored
gambling; Unions

Shepherd, Frank A.
Managing Attorney, Atlantic Center
Pacific Legal Foundation
1320 South Dixie Highway
Coral Gables, FL 33146
305-499-9807   fax 305-715-9279
fas@pacificlegal.org
Issues: Property rights; School choice; Sound
science; State and local government; Tort and
liability reform

Sherlock, Dr. Richard
Professor, Languages and Philosophy
Department
Utah State University
0720 Old Main Hill
Logan, UT 84322
435-797-1244   ruffie@cc.usu.edu
Issues: Arts, humanities and historic resources;
Church-state relations; Political philosophy;
Religion and public life

*Sherman, Dr. Amy L.
Senior Fellow, Welfare Policy Center
Hudson Institute
757 King Street
Charlottesville, VA 22923-3442
434-293-5656   fax 434-295-8728
shermana@cstone.net
Issues: Faith-based and volunteer initiatives;
Religion and public life; Welfare/welfare
reform

Sherman, Dr. Lawrence
Director, Fels Center of Government
University of Pennsylvania
3814 Walnut Street, Leadership Hall
Philadelphia, PA 19104-6197
215-898-8216   fax 215-898-0864
lws@sas.upenn.edu
Issues: Crime/crime statistics; Police

*Shockey, Jack
President
Citizens for Property Rights
P. O. Box 70
Hamilton, VA 20159
540-338-7431   fax 540-338-7094
shockeyjointventure@erols.com
Issues: Agriculture; Property rights

Sicherman, Dr. Harvey
President
Foreign Policy Research Institute
1528 Walnut Street, Suite 610
Philadelphia, PA 19102
215-732-3774   fax 215-732-4401
hs@fpri.org
Issues: American diplomacy/foreign policy;
China; Emerging threats/threat assessment;
Middle East; Military strategy; Russia and
Eurasia; Western Europe

Sidak, J. Gregory
Resident Scholar and Director,
Telecommunications Deregulation Project
American Enterprise Institute
1150 17th Street, N.W.
Washington, DC 20036
202-862-5892   fax 202-862-7177
jgsidak@aei.org
Issues: Anti-trust; Constitutional law; Electricity
deregulation; Intellectual property; Regulatory
reform; Telecommunications and the Internet

Siegan, Dr. Bernard
Distinguished Professor of Law
University of San Diego School of Law
5998 Alcala Park
San Diego, CA 92110
619-260-2337   fax 619-260-2218
Issues: Constitutional law

Siegel, Aaron
President and CEO
Freedoms Foundation at Valley Forge
1601 Valley Forge Road, P. O. Box 706
Valley Forge, PA 19482
610-933-8825   fax 610-935-0522
Issues: The American Founding; American
history/political tradition; Citizenship and civil
society; Constitutional law

Sigman, Dr. Betsy Page
Assistant Professor, McDonough School of
Business
Georgetown University
412 Old North
Washington, DC 20057
202-687-7062   bps@georgetown.edu
Issues: Elections/polling; Telecommunications
and the Internet

Sikorski, Radek
Resident Fellow and Executive Director, New Atlantic Initiative
American Enterprise Institute
1150 17th Street, N.W.
Washington, DC 20036
202-862-5800   fax 202-862-7177
rsikorski@aei.org
Issues: Afghanistan; Central and Eastern Europe; Human rights; International organizations (European Union, OECD, etc.); Military strategy; NATO and other alliances; Promoting democracy/public diplomacy; Russia and Eurasia; Western Europe

Silverglate, Harvey
Vice President and Director
The Foundation for Individual Rights in Education
83 Atlantic Avenue
Boston, MA 02110
617-523-5933   fax 617-523-7554
has@world.std.com
Issues: Church-state relations; Constitutional law; Criminal law and procedure; Free Speech; Religious freedom

*Simes, Dimitri
President
The Nixon Center
1615 L Street, N.W., Suite 1250
Washington, DC 20036-5610
202-887-1000   fax 202-887-5222
dsimes@nixoncenter.org
Issues: American diplomacy/foreign policy; Arms control; Emerging threats/threat assessment; NATO and other alliances; Russia and Eurasia; Terrorism and international crime

*Simmons, Dr. Randy T.
Department Head, Political Science Department
Utah State University
0725 Old Main Hill
Logan, UT 84322-0725
435-797-1310   fax 435-797-3751
rsimmons@hass.usu.edu
Issues: Forestry and national parks; Free-market environmentalism; Land use; Privatization/Contracting-out; Property rights; Regulatory reform; State and local public finance; Urban sprawl/livable cities; Wildlife management/endangered species

*Simon, Rita
Professor, School of Public Affairs
American University
4400 Massachusetts Avenue, N.W.
Washington, DC 20016
202-885-2965   fax 202-885-2907
Issues: American history/political tradition; Civil rights/racial preferences; Corrections and sentencing; Crime/crime statistics; Criminal law and procedure; Immigration; Juvenile justice; Marriage and divorce; Media and popular culture; Middle East

*Simon, Dr. Sheldon W.
Professor of Political Science, Department of Political Science
Arizona State University
Tempe, AZ 85287-3902
480-965-1317   fax 480-965-3929
shells@asu.edu
Issues: Arms control; Defense budget; Emerging threats/threat assessment; Southeast Asia (including Burma, Cambodia, Laos, Vietnam, Singapore, Malaysia, Indonesia, the Philippines, Australia, and New Zealand); Terrorism and international crime

*Simpkins, Gregory
Vice President
The Foundation for Democracy in Africa
1900 L Street, N.W.
Washington, DC 20036
202-331-1333   fax 202-331-8547
comments@democracy-africa.org
Issues: Africa; Human rights; Promoting democracy/public diplomacy

*Singer, Dr. S. Fred
President
Science and Environmental Policy Project
1600 South Eads Street, Suite 712-S
Arlington, VA 22202-2907
703-920-2744   fax 815-461-7448
singer@sepp.org
Issues: Air; Climate change; Costs and benefits of regulation; Emerging threats/threat assessment; Energy; Environmental education; Environmental regulation; Higher education; Missile defense; Regulatory reform; Research funding; Risk assessment; Sound science; Water

*Singleton, Solveig
Senior Analyst, Project on Technology and Innovation
Competitive Enterprise Institute
1001 Connecticut Avenue, N.W., Suite 1250
Washington, DC 20036
202-331-1010   fax 202-331-0640
ssingleton@cei.org
Issues: Constitutional law; Costs and benefits of regulation; Elections/polling; Federalism; Intellectual property; Intelligence gathering and covert operations; International tax policy/tax competition; Privacy; Regulation through litigation; Regulatory reform; Telecommunications and the Internet; Terrorism and international crime

*Sirico, Rev. Robert A.
President
Acton Institute for the Study of Religion and Liberty
161 Ottawa Avenue, N.W., Suite 301
Grand Rapids, MI 49503
616-454-3080   fax 616-454-9454
rsirico@acton.org
Issues: Citizenship and civil society; Costs and benefits of regulation; Economic education; Education unions and interest groups; Entrepreneurship/free enterprise; Environmental education; Environmental regulation; Faith-based and volunteer initiatives; Free-market environmentalism; Labor and employment; Political philosophy; Property rights; Religion and public life; Religious freedom; School choice; Sound science; Stewardship; Trade; Unions; Welfare/ welfare reform

*Sitilides, John
Executive Director
Western Policy Center
1990 M Street, N.W., Suite 610
Washington, DC 20036
202-530-1425   fax 202-530-0261
info@westernpolicy.org
Issues: American diplomacy/foreign policy; International organizations (European Union, OECD, etc.); NATO and other alliances; Western Europe

Sjaastad, Larry A.
Professor, Department of Economics
University of Chicago
1126 East 59th Street
Chicago, IL 60637
773-702-8172   fax 773-702-8490
lsjaasta@uchicago.edu
Issues: Economic development/foreign aid; Economic theory; International finance and multilateral banks; Latin America

Skanderup, Mary Jane
Assistant Director of Programs and Development
Pacific Forum CSIS
1001 Bishop Street, Suite 1150
Honolulu, HI 96813
808-521-6745   fax 808-599-8690
pacforum@lava.net
Issues: China; Economic development/foreign aid; International finance and multilateral banks; Japan; Korea; Latin America; Northeast Asia

*Skerry, Dr. Peter
Professor, Department of Government
Claremont McKenna College
850 Columbia Avenue
Claremont, CA 91711
909-607-2811   fax 909-626-3048
pskerry@uia.net
Issues: Bilingual education; Citizenship and civil society; Immigration; Political correctness and multiculturalism

*Skillen, Dr. James
President
Center for Public Justice
2444 Solomons Island Road, Suite 201
Annapolis, MD 21401
410-571-6300   fax 410-571-6365
jim@cpjustice.org
Issues: American diplomacy/foreign policy; The American Founding; Church-state relations; Citizenship and civil society; Electoral reform/voting rights; Ethics; Political philosophy; Religion and public life; School choice; Welfare/welfare reform

Skoble, Dr. Aeon James
Assistant Professor of Philosophy,
Department of Philosophy
Bridgewater State College
Tillinghast Hall
Bridgewater, MA 02325
508-531-2640   fax 508-531-1781
askoble@bridgew.edu
Issues: Arts, humanities and historic resources;
Ethics; Media and popular culture; Political
correctness and multiculturalism; Political
philosophy

Slattery, William H.
President
Atlantic Legal Foundation
150 East 42nd Street, 2nd Floor
New York, NY 10017
212-573-1960   fax 212-857-3653
whslattery@yahoo.com
Issues: Regulation through litigation

Slivinski, Stephen
Director of Tax and Budget Studies
Goldwater Institute
500 East Coronado Road
Phoenix, AZ 85004
602-462-5000   fax 602-256-7056
sslivinski@goldwaterinstitute.org
Issues: Federal budget; Taxation/tax reform

*Sloan, Dr. Stephen
Samuel Roberts Noble Presidential Professor
University of Oklahoma
Department of Political Science
Norman, OK 73019
405-325-5910   fax 405-325-0718
carlos@ou.edu
Issues: Intelligence gathering and covert
operations; Peacekeeping; Terrorism and
international crime

Small, Shaun
Senior Policy Analyst
Empower America
1801 K Street, N.W., Suite 410
Washington, DC 20006
202-452-8200   fax 202-833-0388
Issues: American diplomacy/foreign policy;
International law; International tax policy/tax
competition; Japan; Social Security and
retirement; Taxation/tax reform; Trade;
United Nations

Smith, Anita
Vice President
Institute for Youth Development
P. O. Box 16560
Washington, DC 20041
703-471-8750   fax 703-471-8409
asmith@youthdevelopment.org
Issues: Abstinence and out-of-wedlock births;
Faith-based and volunteer initiatives; Family
and children; Marriage and divorce

*Smith, Baker
Secretary and Treasurer
U. S. Constitutional Rights Legal Defense
Fund, Inc.
3360 East Terrell Branch Court
Marietta, GA 30067
770-980-0921   fax 770-955-0841
atlsmith@msn.com
Issues: Constitutional law; Money and financial
services

*Smith, Christopher
Executive Director
Internet Education Exchange (iEdx)
8655 East Via de Ventura, Suite G-360
Scottsdale, AZ 85258
480-385-1212   fax 480-385-1222
csmith@iedx.org
Issues: Charter schools; Education unions and
interest groups; Federal education policy;
Home schooling; Public school finance and
administration; School choice; Standards,
curriculum, and testing

Smith, Dr. Clifford W.
Epstein Professor of Business
Administration, William E. Simon Graduate
School of Business
University of Rochester
P. O. Box 270100
Rochester, NY 14627
585-275-3217   fax 585-506-1923
smith@simon.rochester.edu
Issues: The Economy; Entrepreneurship/free
enterprise; Labor and employment; Money and
financial services

*Smith, Curt
President
Indiana Family Institute
55 Monument Circle, Suite 322
Indianapolis, IN 46204-5910
317-423-9178   fax 317-423-9421
ifi@hoosierfamily.org
Issues: Abstinence and out-of-wedlock births;
Adoption, foster care, & child care services;
American history/political tradition; Church-
state relations; Citizenship and civil society;
Congress; Elections/polling; Ethics; Faith-
based and volunteer initiatives; Family and
children; Free Speech; Marriage and divorce;
Media and popular culture; Political
philosophy; Religion and public life; Religious
freedom; State-sponsored gambling

Smith, Denison E.
Chairman
For Our Grandchildren
P. O. Box 3539
Washington, DC 20007
800-278-3263
Issues: Social Security and retirement

*Smith, Frances B.
Executive Director
Consumer Alert
1001 Connecticut Avenue, N.W., Suite 1128
Washington, DC 20036
202-467-5809   fax 202-467-5814
Issues: Agriculture; Climate change; Money and
financial services; Privacy; Sound science;
Trade

*Smith, Fred L., Jr.
President
Competitive Enterprise Institute
1001 Connecticut Avenue, N.W., Suite 1250
Washington, DC 20036
202-331-1010   fax 202-331-0640
fsmith@cei.org
Issues: Anti-trust; Costs and benefits of
regulation; Economic development/foreign
aid; Energy; Entrepreneurship/free
enterprise; Environmental education;
Environmental regulation; Free-market
environmentalism; Health care reform;
Intellectual property; International
organizations (European Union, OECD, etc.);
International tax policy/tax competition;
Privacy; Privatization/Contracting-out;
Promoting democracy/public diplomacy;
Property rights; Regulation through litigation;
Regulatory reform; Social Security and
retirement; Stewardship; Trade; United
Nations; Urban sprawl/livable cities; Wealth
creation/financial empowerment

*Smith, Dr. Harvey A.
Professor of Mathematics, Department of
Mathematics
Arizona State University
P. O. Box 871804
Tempe, AZ 85287
480-968-6813   fax 480-968-7780
hsmith@math.la.asu.edu
Issues: Arms control; Economic theory; Energy;
Health care reform; Higher education;
Homeland security/civil defense; Military
strategy; Missile defense; Terrorism and
international crime

Smith, J. Michael, Esq.
President
Home School Legal Defense Association
P. O. Box 3000
Purcellville, VA 20134
540-338-5600   fax 540-338-2733
Issues: Home schooling

Smith, Mark W., Esq.
Kasowitz, Benson, Torres & Friedman, LLP
1633 Broadway
New York, NY 10019
212-506-1722   fax 212-506-1800
msmith@kasowitz.com
Issues: Civil rights/racial preferences; Judicial
activism/judicial reform; Judiciary; Second
Amendment

*Smith, Dr. Oran P.
Executive Director
Palmetto Family Council
P. O. Box 11953
Columbia, SC 29211-1953
803-733-5600   fax 803-733-5601
email@palmettofamily.org
Issues: Business and education partnerships;
Citizenship and civil society; Elections/polling;
Family and children; Higher education;
Religion and public life; State-sponsored
gambling

*Smith, Robert J.
President
Center for Private Conservation
721-R 2nd Street, N.E.
Washington, DC 20002
202-667-0191   fax 202-544-9724
Issues: Economic theory; Energy;
Environmental regulation; Forestry and
national parks; Free-market environmentalism;
Land use; Property rights; Stewardship; Urban
sprawl/livable cities; Water; Wildlife
management/endangered species

*Smith, Steven S.
Director
Weidenbaum Center
Washington University, Campus Box 1027
St. Louis, MO 63130-4899
314-935-5662   fax 314-935-5688
smith@wc.wustl.edu
Issues: Campaign finance reform; Congress;
Elections/polling; Electoral reform/voting
rights; Term limits

Smith, T. Alexander
Professor, Political Science
University of Tennessee, Knoxville
1001 McClung Tower
Knoxville, TN 37996
423-974-7057   fax 423-974-7037
Issues: Comparative government; Conservative
thought; Economic theory; The Economy;
Political correctness and multiculturalism;
Political philosophy

Smith, Dr. Ted J., III
Associate Professor, School of Mass
Communications
Virginia Commonwealth University
Box 842034
Richmond, VA 23284-2034
804-320-0092   fax 804-320-2815
tjsmith@atlas.vcu.edu
Issues: American history/political tradition;
Conservative thought; Elections/polling;
Media and popular culture; Political
correctness and multiculturalism; Sound
science

Smith, Vernon L.
Professor of Economics and Law,
Interdisciplinary Center for Economic
Science
George Mason University
3401 North Fairfax Drive, 400N Truland
Building
Arlington, VA 22201
703-993-4842   fax 703-993-4851
vsmith2@gmu.edu
Issues: Economic education; Economic
forecasting; Economic theory; Electricity
deregulation; Free-market environmentalism

*Smith, W. Shepherd, Jr.
President
Institute for Youth Development
P. O. Box 16560
Washington, DC 20041
703-471-8750   fax 703-471-8409
bbarrett@youthdevelopment.org
Issues: Abstinence and out-of-wedlock births;
Adoption, foster care, & child care services;
Africa; Faith-based and volunteer initiatives;
Family and children; Government health
programs; Marriage and divorce; Substance
abuse; United Nations; Welfare/welfare reform

Snavely, Brad
Executive Director
Michigan Family Forum
P. O. Box 15216
Lansing, MI 48901-5216
517-374-1171   fax 517-374-6112
info@michiganfamily.org
Issues: Church-state relations; Constitutional
law; Health care reform; Judicial activism/
judicial reform; Marriage and divorce;
Regulatory reform; Religion and public life

*Snell, Lisa
Director of Education and Child Welfare
Reason Foundation
3415 South Sepulveda Boulevard, Suite 400
Los Angeles, CA 90034
310-391-2245   fax 310-392-4395
lisa.snell@reason.org
Issues: Adoption, foster care, & child care
services; Bilingual education; Business and
education partnerships; Charter schools;
Education unions and interest groups; Faith-
based and volunteer initiatives; Federal
education policy; Higher education; Home
schooling; Public school finance and
administration; School choice; School-to-work;
Standards, curriculum, and testing; Welfare/
welfare reform

*Snyder, John Michael
Citizens Committee for the Right to Keep
and Bear Arms
1090 Vermont Avenue, N.W., Suite 800
Washington, DC 20005
202-326-5259   fax 202-898-1939
gundean@aol.com
Issues: Police; Political philosophy; Second
Amendment

*Snyder, Dr. Neil H.
Beeton Professor of Free Enterprise,
McIntire School of Commerce, Strategy and
Leadership
University of Virginia
Monroe Hall
Charlottesville, VA 22903
434-924-3218   fax 434-924-7074
nhs8a@virginia.edu
Issues: Church-state relations; The Economy;
Entrepreneurship/free enterprise; Ethics;
Middle East; School choice

Sobel, Dr. Russell S.
Associate Professor, Department of
Economics
West Virginia University
P. O. Box 6025
Morgantown, WV 26506
304-293-7864   fax 304-293-5652
rsobel2@wvu.edu
Issues: State and local public finance; Taxation/
tax reform

*Soifer, Don
Executive Vice President
Lexington Institute
1600 Wilson Boulevard, Suite 900
Arlington, VA 22209
703-522-5809   fax 703-522-5837
soifer@lexingtoninstitute.org
Issues: Bilingual education; Charter schools;
Federal education policy; School choice

*Sokolski, Henry
Executive Director
Non-Proliferation Policy Education Center
1718 M Street, N.W., Suite 244
Washington, DC 20036
202-466-4406   fax 202-659-5429
npec@ix.netcom.com
Issues: Arms control; Export controls/military
transfers; Korea; Missile defense

Soldano, Patricia M.
President
Policy and Taxation Group
3941 South Bristol Street, Unit E, PMB 46
Santa Ana, CA 92704
714-641-6913   fax 714-641-3128
pmsoldano@policyandtaxationgroup.com
Issues: Taxation/tax reform

*Sollee, Diane
Founder and Director
Coalition for Marriage, Family and Couples
Education
5310 Belt Road, N.W.
Washington, DC 20015
202-362-3332   fax 202-362-0973
cmfce@smartmarriages.com
Issues: Family and children; Marriage and
divorce

*Solomon, Amb. Richard H.
President
United States Institute of Peace
1200 17th Street, N.W., Suite 200
Washington, DC 20036
202-457-1700   fax 202-429-6063
usip_requests@usip.org
Issues: Arms control; China; Emerging threats/
threat assessment; Human rights; Korea;
Missile defense; Northeast Asia; Peacekeeping;
Southeast Asia (including Burma, Cambodia,
Laos, Vietnam, Singapore, Malaysia, Indonesia,
the Philippines, Australia, and New Zealand);
Terrorism and international crime

*Sommer, Dr. Jack
President
Political Economy Research Institute
9211 North Tryon Street, Number 4-187
Charlotte, NC 28262-8463
704-779-2824   fax 704-896-0788
jacksommer@aol.com
Issues: Higher education; Privatization/
Contracting-out; Research funding; Sound
science; Urban sprawl/livable cities

Sommers, Dr. Christina Hoff
Resident Scholar
American Enterprise Institute
1150 17th Street, N.W.
Washington, DC 20036
202-862-7180   fax 301-654-0927
sommers22@aol.com
Issues: Citizenship and civil society; Ethics;
Religion and public life

Soper, Dr. John C.
Professor of Economics, Department of
Economics and Finance
John Carroll University
20700 North Park Boulevard
University Heights, OH 44118
216-397-3027   fax 216-397-1728
jsoper@jcu.edu
Issues: American history/political tradition;
Economic education; The Economy;
Environmental education; Free-market
environmentalism; International finance and
multilateral banks; Money and financial
services; School-to-work; Standards,
curriculum, and testing; Western Europe

Sowell, Dr. Thomas
Rose and Milton Friedman Senior Fellow on
Public Policy
Hoover Institution
Stanford University
Stanford, CA 94305
650-723-3303
sowell@hoover.stanford.edu
Issues: Arts, humanities and historic resources;
Citizenship and civil society; Civil rights/racial
preferences; Family and children; Media and
popular culture; Political correctness and
multiculturalism

*Spady, Fawn
Co-Director
Education Excellence Coalition
4426 2nd Avenue NE
Seattle, WA 98105-6191
206-634-0589   fax 206-633-3561
fawnspady@aol.com
Issues: Charter schools; Home schooling;
School choice

*Spady, Jim
Co-Director
Education Excellence Coalition
4426 2nd Avenue NE
Seattle, WA 98105-6191
206-634-0589   fax 206-633-3561
jimspady@aol.com
Issues: Charter schools; Home schooling;
School choice; Standards, curriculum, and
testing

*Spalding, Dr. Matthew
Director, B. Kenneth Simon Center for
American Studies
The Heritage Foundation
214 Massachusetts Avenue, N.E.
Washington, DC 20002
202-608-6171   fax 202-608-6136
info@heritage.org
Issues: The American Founding; American
history/political tradition; Church-state
relations; Citizenship and civil society;
Conservative thought; Executive Branch/The
Presidency; Faith-based and volunteer
initiatives; Higher education; Immigration;
Political philosophy; The Reagan legacy;
Religion and public life; Religious freedom

*Sparks, Dr. John A.
Chairman, Department of Business
Administration
Grove City College
100 Campus Drive
Grove City, PA 16127
724-458-2056   fax 724-458-1552
jasparks@gcc.edu
Issues: Charter schools; Higher education;
Home schooling; Property rights; School
choice; Standards, curriculum, and testing

Spencer, Jack
Policy Analyst, Defense and National
Security, Kathryn and Shelby Cullom Davis
Institute for International Studies
The Heritage Foundation
214 Massachusetts Avenue, N.E.
Washington, DC 20002
202-546-6124   fax 202-675-1758
jack.spencer@heritage.org
Issues: Arms control; Defense budget;
Emerging threats/threat assessment;
Homeland security/civil defense; Military
strategy; Missile defense; Peacekeeping;
Readiness and manpower

Spiller, Michael
Vice President, Information Technology
The Heritage Foundation
214 Massachusetts Avenue, N.E.
Washington, DC 20002
202-608-6280   fax 202-544-7330
info@heritage.org
Issues: Telecommunications and the Internet

*Spillman, Nancy Z.
President
Economic Education Enterprises
7618 Gazette Avenue
Canoga Park, CA 91306-2015
818-347-6087   fax 818-347-6087
Issues: Economic education; The Economy;
Higher education; Money and financial
services

Spreng, Dr. Frank
Professor of Economics, Division of Business
McKendree College
Lebanon, IL 62254
618-537-6902
Issues: Taxation/tax reform

Sprigg, Peter S.
Senior Director of Culture Studies
Family Research Council
801 G Street, N.W.
Washington, DC 20001
202-393-2100   fax 202-393-2134
pss@frc.org
Issues: Abstinence and out-of-wedlock births;
Adoption, foster care, & child care services;
Arts, humanities and historic resources;
Church-state relations; Family and children;
Marriage and divorce; Media and popular
culture; Political correctness and
multiculturalism; Religion and public life;
Religious freedom

*Spring, H. Baker
F. M. Kirby Research Fellow in National
Security Policy, Kathryn and Shelby Cullom
Davis Institute for International Studies
The Heritage Foundation
214 Massachusetts Avenue, N.E.
Washington, DC 20002
202-546-4400   fax 202-675-1758
baker.spring@heritage.org
Issues: Arms control; Defense budget;
Emerging threats/threat assessment; Export
controls/military transfers; Military strategy;
Missile defense

St. Angelo, Gordon
President and CEO
Milton and Rose Friedman Foundation
One American Square, P. O. Box 82078
Indianapolis, IN 46282
317-681-0745   fax 317-681-0945
gordon@friedmanfoundation.org
Issues: American history/political tradition;
Charter schools; Education unions and interest
groups; Federal education policy; Home
schooling; Philanthropy; School choice

*Staar, Dr. Richard F.
Senior Fellow
Hoover Institution
Stanford University
Stanford, CA 94305-6010
650-725-8556   fax 650-723-0576
Issues: Arms control; Central and Eastern
Europe; Emerging threats/threat assessment;
Intelligence gathering and covert operations;
NATO and other alliances; Peacekeeping;
Promoting democracy/public diplomacy;
Russia and Eurasia

Staddon, Dr. John E. R.
Professor of Psychology
Duke University
Experimental Box 90086
Durham, NC 27708
919-660-5724   fax 919-660-5726
staddon@psych.duke.edu
Issues: Higher education; Research funding

*Staley, Dr. Samuel R.
President
Buckeye Institute for Public Policy Solutions
4100 North High Street, Suite 200
Columbus, OH 43214
614-262-1593   fax 614-262-1927
samuelrstaley@aol.com
Issues: Costs and benefits of regulation;
Entrepreneurship/free enterprise; Land use;
Public school finance and administration;
School choice; State and local government;
State and local public finance; Taxation/tax
reform; Urban sprawl/livable cities

*Stanley, David
Chairman
National Taxpayers Union
P. O. Box 209
Muscatine, IA 52761
563-264-8080   fax 563-264-3363
Issues: Government debt; Government waste;
State and local public finance; Taxation/tax
reform; Unfunded mandates

Stanton, Glenn T.
Director and Senior Analyst for Marriage and
Sexuality, Social Research and Cultural
Affairs
Focus on the Family
8605 Explorer Drive
Colorado Springs, CO 80920
719-548-5980   fax 719-531-3385
stantongt@fotf.org
Issues: Abstinence and out-of-wedlock births;
Adoption, foster care, & child care services;
Arts, humanities and historic resources;
Citizenship and civil society; Ethics; Family and
children; Marriage and divorce; Media and
popular culture; Political philosophy; Religion
and public life

*Stavins, Dr. Robert
Albert Pratt Professor of Business and
Government, John F. Kennedy School of
Government
Harvard University
79 John F. Kennedy Street
Cambridge, MA 02138
617-495-1820   fax 617-496-3783
robert_stavins@harvard.edu
Issues: Climate change; Energy; Environmental
education; Environmental regulation; Forestry
and national parks; Land use; Waste
management; Water

Stelzer, Irwin
Director, Regulatory Studies
Hudson Institute
1015 18th Street, N.W., Suite 300
Washington, DC 20036
202-777-3000   fax 202-777-3010
stelzer@aol.com
Issues: Anti-trust; Climate change; Costs and
benefits of regulation; The Economy;
Electricity deregulation; Energy;
Environmental regulation; Free-market
environmentalism; Immigration; Regulatory
reform; Telecommunications and the Internet

*Stergios, James
Research Director
Pioneer Institute for Public Policy Research
85 Devonshire Street, 8th Floor
Boston, MA 02109
617-723-2277   fax 617-723-1880
jstergios@pioneerinstitute.org
Issues: Housing and homelessness;
Infrastructure; Judiciary; Political philosophy;
Privatization/Contracting-out; State and local
government; State and local public finance;
Western Europe

Stetson, Charles P.
Chairman
U. S. Fund for Leadership Training
P. O. Box 58
Southport, CT 06490
203-259-7881   fax 203-254-1039
Issues: Africa; Human rights; Juvenile justice

*Steuerle, C. Eugene
Senior Fellow
Urban Institute
2100 M Street, N.W.
Washington, DC 20037
202-833-7200   fax 202-429-0687
esteuerl@ui.urban.org
Issues: Discretionary spending; Entitlement
spending; Federal budget; Health care reform;
Social Security and retirement; Taxation/tax
reform

*Stevens, Paul Schott
Dechert, Price & Rhoads
1775 Eye Street, N.W.
Washington, DC 20006-2401
202-261-3348   fax 202-261-3333
paul.stevens@dechert.com
Issues: American diplomacy/foreign policy;
Executive Branch/The Presidency; Homeland
security/civil defense; International
organizations (European Union, OECD, etc.);
Japan; Money and financial services; Privacy;
Terrorism and international crime

*Stever, Dr. James A.
Professor of Political Science
University of Cincinnati
720 Elmwood Road
Hamilton, OH 45013
513-556-3305   fax 513-556-2314
Issues: Citizenship and civil society; Federalism;
State and local government

Stiegler, Doug
Executive Director
Association of Maryland Families
3542 Hernwood Road
Woodstock, MD 21163-1030
410-922-1008   fax 410-922-2030
director@mdfamilies.org
Issues: Abstinence and out-of-wedlock births;
Adoption, foster care, & child care services;
Aging/elder care; Charter schools; Church-
state relations; Faith-based and volunteer
initiatives; Family and children; Marriage and
divorce; Media and popular culture; Political
correctness and multiculturalism; Religion and
public life; Religious freedom; School choice;
School-to-work; Standards, curriculum, and
testing; State-sponsored gambling; Unfunded
mandates

Stier, Jeff
Associate Director
American Council on Science and Health
1995 Broadway, 2nd Floor
New York, NY 10023-5860
212-362-7049 ex.225
fax 212-362-4919   stier@acsh.org
Issues: Aging/elder care; Agriculture; Air; Costs
and benefits of regulation; Environmental
education; Environmental regulation; Free-
market environmentalism; Government health
programs; Non-governmental organizations;
Regulation through litigation; Regulatory
reform; Research funding; Risk assessment;
Sound science; Substance abuse; Water

Stilley, Oscar
Chairman
Arkansans for School Choice
Central Mall, Suite 520, 5111 Rogers Avenue
Fort Smith, AR 72903-2041
479-996-4109   fax 479-996-3409
oscar@ostilley.com
Issues: Government waste; Initiative and
referendum; Taxation/tax reform

*Stith, Dr. Richard
Professor of Law
Valpariso University School of Law
Valpariso, IN 46383-6493
219-465-7871   fax 219-465-7872
richard.stith@valpo.edu
Issues: Comparative government; Ethics;
Judicial activism/judicial reform; Judiciary

Stock, Margaret D.
Assistant Professor of Law, Department of
Law
United States Military Academy
West Point, NY 10996
845-938-5818   fax 845-938-5541
em7396@exmail.usma.army.mil
Issues: Citizenship and civil society; Homeland
security/civil defense; Human rights;
Immigration; Terrorism and international
crime

Stockman, Dr. Alan C.
Chairman, Department of Economics
University of Rochester
Harkness Hall, Room 223
Rochester, NY 14627
716-275-7214   fax 716-256-2309
stoc@troi.cc.rochester.edu
Issues: Comparative economics; Economic
education; The Economy; Labor and
employment; Money and financial services;
Trade

*Stolba, Christine
Visiting Scholar
Ethics and Public Policy Center
1015 15th Street, N.W.
Washington, DC 20005
202-216-0855   fax 202-408-0632
stolba@eppc.org
Issues: American history/political tradition;
Arts, humanities and historic resources; Ethics;
Marriage and divorce; Media and popular
culture; Political correctness and
multiculturalism; Religion and public life

*Stone, Dr. J. E.
Principal, Education Consumers
Consultants Network, and Professor, College
of Education
East Tennessee State University
Johnson City, TN 37614
423-282-6832   fax 423-282-6832
professor@education-consumers.com
Issues: Education unions and interest groups;
Federal education policy; Higher education;
School choice; School-to-work; Standards,
curriculum, and testing

Stoner, Dr. James R.
Associate Professor of Political Science,
Department of Political Science
Louisiana State University
208-B Stubbs Hall
Baton Rouge, LA 70803
225-388-2538   fax 225-388-2540
Issues: Constitutional law; Judiciary; Political
philosophy

*Stormo, Jeff
Director of Public Policy Research
Choices for Children
201 Monroe, N.W., Suite 300
Grand Rapids, MI 49503
616-458-3775   fax 616-458-3965
info@choicesforchildren.org
Issues: Campaign finance reform; Charter
schools; Education unions and interest groups;
Public school finance and administration;
School choice

*Streeter, James
Policy Director
National Wilderness Institute
Georgetown Station, P. O. Box 25766
Washington, DC 20007
703-836-7404   fax 703-836-7405
js@nwi.org
Issues: Environmental education;
Environmental regulation; Forestry and
national parks; Free-market environmentalism;
Land use; Property rights; Stewardship; Water;
Wildlife management/endangered species

*Strom, David
Legislative Director
Taxpayers League of Minnesota
One Carlson Parkway, Suite 120
Plymouth, MN 55447
763-249-5950   fax 763-249-5960
dmstrom@taxpayersleague.org
Issues: Advocacy and nonprofit public funding;
The American Founding; Campaign finance
reform; Congress; Conservative thought; Costs
and benefits of regulation; Discretionary
spending; Economic education; Elections/
polling; Electoral reform/voting rights;
Entitlement spending; Entrepreneurship/free
enterprise; Ethics; Federal budget; Federalism;
Government debt; Government waste;
International tax policy/tax competition;
Political correctness and multiculturalism;
Political philosophy; Privatization/
Contracting-out; The Reagan legacy;
Regulation through litigation; State and local
government; State and local public finance;
State-sponsored gambling; Taxation/tax
reform; Term limits; Trade; Transportation;
Unfunded mandates; Wealth creation/
financial empowerment; Welfare/welfare
reform

Stroup, Jane Shaw
Senior Associate
PERC – The Center for Free Market
Environmentalism
502 South 19th Avenue, Suite 211
Bozeman, MT 59718-6827
406-587-9591   fax 406-586-7555
shaw@perc.org
Issues: Environmental education; Free-market
environmentalism

Stroup, Dr. Michael D.
Associate Professor of Economics
Stephen F. Austin State University
Box 13009, SFA Station
Nacogdoches, TX 75962-3009
936-468-1557   fax 936-468-1447
mstroup@sfasu.edu
Issues: Comparative government; Costs and
benefits of regulation; Defense budget;
Discretionary spending; Economic education;
Entitlement spending; Entrepreneurship/free
enterprise; Federal budget; Free-market
environmentalism; Government debt;
Government waste; Infrastructure;
Privatization/Contracting-out; Property rights;
State and local public finance; Taxation/tax
reform

*Stroup, Dr. Richard L.
Professor of Economics, Montana State
University, and Senior Associate
PERC – The Center for Free Market
Environmentalism
9 Arnold Street
Bozeman, MT 59715
406-587-9591   fax 406-586-7555
stroup@perc.org
Issues: Comparative economics; Comparative
government; Economic education;
Environmental regulation; Free-market
environmentalism; Property rights; Risk
assessment; Waste management

Stuart, Dr. Charles
Professor, Department of Economics
University of California, Santa Barbara
Santa Barbara, CA 93106
805-893-4791   fax 805-893-8830
stuart@econ.ucsb.edu
Issues: Comparative economics; Comparative
government; Discretionary spending;
Economic theory; Elections/polling;
Entitlement spending; Federal budget;
Federalism; Government debt; Marriage and
divorce; The Reagan legacy; Social Security and
retirement; State and local public finance;
Taxation/tax reform; Telecommunications
and the Internet; Welfare/welfare reform

*Stubblebine, Dr. William Craig
Professor of Political Economy
Claremont McKenna College
850 Columbia Avenue
Claremont, CA 91711-6420
909-626-2991   fax 909-626-4151
cstubblebine@claremontmckenna.edu
Issues: Economic theory; Electricity
deregulation; Federal budget; Federalism;
Government debt; Health care reform;
Initiative and referendum; Property rights;
Public school finance and administration;
School choice; State and local government;
State and local public finance; Taxation/tax
reform; Tort and liability reform

Subasinghe, Devinda R.
5279 Isla Key Boulevard, Suite 210
St. Petersburg, FL 33715
727-906-8031   fax 727-906-4063
devindas@aol.com
Issues: Afghanistan; Africa; American
diplomacy/foreign policy; Central and Eastern
Europe; China; Economic development/
foreign aid; International finance and
multilateral banks; Latin America; South Asia
(including India and Pakistan); United Nations

*Sulc, Lawrence B.
President
Nathan Hale Institute
24 Harbor River Circle
St. Helena Island, SC 29920
843-838-0191   fax 843-838-0192
sulc@islc.net
Issues: Intelligence gathering and covert
operations; Terrorism and international crime

*Sullivan, John D.
Executive Director
Center for International Private Enterprise
1155 15th Street, N.W., Suite 700
Washington, DC 20005
202-721-9200   fax 202-721-9250
Sullivan@cipe.org
Issues: Central and Eastern Europe;
Comparative government; Economic
development/foreign aid; Economic theory;
International organizations (European Union,
OECD, etc.); Political philosophy; Promoting
democracy/public diplomacy

*Sullivan, Kathleen M.
Director
Project Reality
P. O. Box 97
Golf, IL 60029-0097
847-729-3298   fax 847-729-9744
info@projectreality.org
Issues: Abstinence and out-of-wedlock births;
Advocacy and nonprofit public funding;
Government health programs; Welfare/
welfare reform

Sullivan, Michael
Director of Media and Government
Relations
Texas Public Policy Foundation
101 West 6th Street, Suite 808
Austin, TX 78701
512-472-2700   fax 512-472-2728
msullivan@tppf.org
Issues: Media and popular culture; State and
local government

Sullum, Jacob
Senior Editor
Reason Magazine
4226 Braeburn Drive
Fairfax, VA 22032-1801
703-978-4301   fax 703-978-4302
jsullum@reason.com
Issues: Federal education policy; Free Speech;
Privacy; Religious freedom; Second
Amendment; Substance abuse

Summers, Christopher B.
President
Maryland Public Policy Institute
P. O. Box 195
Germantown, MD 20875-0195
240-686-3510   fax 240-686-3511
csummers@mdpolicy.org
Issues: Crime/crime statistics; Health care
reform; Public school finance and
administration; State and local public finance;
Taxation/tax reform; Telecommunications
and the Internet; Transportation

Sumner, Lt. Gen. Gordon, Jr.
Chairman of the Board
Sumner Association
100 Cienega
Santa Fe, NM 87501
505-984-8041   fax 505-984-3251
102071.3146@compuserve.com
Issues: American diplomacy/foreign policy;
Defense budget; Emerging threats/threat
assessment; Forestry and national parks;
Intelligence gathering and covert operations;
Korea; Latin America; Mexico; Middle East;
Military strategy; Missile defense; Political
philosophy

Surdam, Dr. David G.
Adjunct Associate Professor, Graduate
School of Business
University of Chicago
850 North State Street, Number 6H
Chicago, IL 60610
david.surdam@gsb.uchicago.edu
Issues: American history/political tradition;
Ethics; Health care reform; Social Security and
retirement

Sutherland, Robert
Professor, Department of Politics
Cornell College
600 First Street West
Mount Vernon, IA 52314-1098
319-895-4226   fax 319-895-4284
rsutherland@cornellcollege.edu
Issues: The American Founding; American
history/political tradition; Conservative
thought; Ethics; Political philosophy

Swanson, James
Editor of the *Cato Supreme Court Review*
Cato Institute
1000 Massachusetts Avenue, N.W.
Washington, DC 20001-5403
202-842-0200   fax 202-842-3490
jswanson@cato.org
Issues: Civil rights/racial preferences;
Constitutional law; Executive Branch/The
Presidency; Judiciary

*Swartz, Rebecca
Research Fellow, Welfare Policy Center
Hudson Institute
10 East Doty, Suite 513
Madison, WI 53703
608-251-8162   fax 608-251-8814
rebeccas@hudson.org
Issues: Housing and homelessness; Poverty and
dependency; Wealth creation/financial
empowerment; Welfare/welfare reform

Sweeney, Dr. James L.
Professor, Management Science and
Engineering
Stanford University
Terman Engineering Center 440
Stanford, CA 94305-4026
650-723-2847   fax 650-723-1614
jim.sweeney@soe.stanford.edu
Issues: Climate change; Electricity
deregulation; Energy; Environmental
regulation; Free-market environmentalism

Sweeney, Dr. Jerry K.
Professor and Chairman, Department of
History
South Dakota State University
Box 504
Brookings, SD 57007
605-688-6678   fax 605-688-5977
jerry_sweeney@sdstate.edu
Issues: Western Europe

Sweeney, Dr. Michael P.
Evert McCabe/UPS Endowed Chair in
Economics, Business and Accounting
Hillsdale College
33 East College Street
Hillsdale, MI 49242
517-437-7341   fax 517-437-3923
michael.sweeney@hillsdale.edu
Issues: Higher education; Taxation/tax reform

Sweet, Joy
Executive Director
National Right to Read Foundation
P. O. Box 490
The Plains, VA 20198
540-349-1614   fax 540-349-3065
phonicsman@msn.com
Issues: Federal education policy; Home
schooling; School choice; Standards,
curriculum, and testing

*Swindell, Dr. David
Professor, Department of Political Science
Clemson University
Brackett Hall, Room 230G
Clemson, SC 29634
864-656-3149   fax 864-656-0690
dswinde@clemson.edu
Issues: Citizenship and civil society; Faith-based
and volunteer initiatives; Non-governmental
organizations; Privatization/Contracting-out;
School-to-work; State and local government;
State and local public finance

Sykes, Charles
Senior Fellow
Wisconsin Policy Research Institute
12144 North Ridge Road
Mequon, WI 53092-1025
414-351-3910   fax 414-967-5562
wpri@execpc.com
Issues: Charter schools; Education unions and
interest groups; Higher education; Home
schooling; Political correctness and
multiculturalism; Public school finance and
administration; School choice; Standards,
curriculum, and testing

Szilagyi, Dr. Miklos N.
Professor, Department of Electrical and
Computer Engineering
University of Arizona
Tucson, AZ 85721
520-577-9275   fax 520-626-3144
mns@u.arizona.edu
Issues: Central and Eastern Europe; Citizenship
and civil society; Higher education; Political
philosophy; Research funding

*Tabarrok, Dr. Alexander
Research Affiliate
Mercatus Center at George Mason University
3301 North Fairfax Drive, Suite 450
Arlington, VA 22201-4433
703-993-4930   fax 703-993-4935
atabarrok@mercatus.org
Issues: Business and education partnerships;
Corrections and sentencing; Costs and benefits
of regulation; Crime/crime statistics;
Elections/polling; Electoral reform/voting
rights; Entrepreneurship/free enterprise;
Free-market environmentalism; Government
debt; Health care reform; Intellectual property;
Medicare; Privacy; Privatization/Contracting-
out; Property rights; Regulatory reform; School
choice; Social Security and retirement;
Telecommunications and the Internet; Urban
sprawl/livable cities

Tacker, Dr. Thomas L.
Professor of Business, Department of
Business Administration
Embry-Riddle Aeronautical University
600 South Clyde-Morris Boulevard
Daytona Beach, FL 32114
386-226-6701   fax 386-226-6696
tacker@erau.edu
Issues: Conservative thought; Economic theory;
Privatization/Contracting-out; School choice;
Transportation; Transportation deregulation

*Tambs, Lewis A.
1041 East Sandpiper Drive
Tempe, AZ 85283-2020
602-965-5778
Issues: Latin America; Mexico; Military strategy;
Political correctness and multiculturalism;
Russia and Eurasia; Standards, curriculum, and
testing

*Tanner, Michael
Director of Health and Welfare Studies
Cato Institute
1000 Massachusetts Avenue, N.W.
Washington, DC 20001
202-842-0200   fax 202-842-3490
mtanner@cato.org
Issues: Entitlement spending; Faith-based and volunteer initiatives; Government health programs; Health care reform; Medicare; Philanthropy; Poverty and dependency; Social Security and retirement; Wealth creation/financial empowerment; Welfare/welfare reform

Tapscott, Mark
Director, Center for Media and Public Policy and the Marilyn and Fred Guardabassi Fellow
The Heritage Foundation
214 Massachusetts Avenue, N.E.
Washington, DC 20002
202-608-6155   fax 202-546-8328
mark.tapscott@heritage.org
Issues: Free Speech; Media and popular culture; Political correctness and multiculturalism; Religious freedom

*Taylor, Bruce
President
National Law Center for Children and Families
3819 Plaza Drive
Fairfax, VA 22030-2512
703-691-4626   fax 703-691-4669
brucetaylor@nationallawcenter.org
Issues: Constitutional law; Family and children; Free Speech; Media and popular culture; Telecommunications and the Internet

Taylor, James R. "J.T."
President and CEO
Empower America
1801 K Street, N.W., Suite 410
Washington, DC 20006
202-452-8200   fax 202-833-0388
jt@empower.org
Issues: American diplomacy/foreign policy; American history/political tradition; Citizenship and civil society; Conservative thought; The Economy; Entrepreneurship/free enterprise; Faith-based and volunteer initiatives; Federal education policy; Homeland security/civil defense; Intellectual property; International tax policy/tax competition; Missile defense; Religion and public life; School choice; Social Security and retirement; Standards, curriculum, and testing; Taxation/tax reform; Telecommunications and the Internet; Terrorism and international crime; Wealth creation/financial empowerment

*Taylor, Jerry
Director of Natural Resource Studies
Cato Institute
1000 Massachusetts Avenue, N.W.
Washington, DC 20001
202-789-5240   fax 202-842-3490
jtaylor@cato.org
Issues: Air; Climate change; Electricity deregulation; Energy; Environmental regulation; Forestry and national parks; Free-market environmentalism; Land use; Regulatory reform; Risk assessment; Sound science; Transportation; Urban sprawl/livable cities; Waste management; Water; Wildlife management/endangered species

*Taylor, John
President
Virginia Institute for Public Policy
20461 Tappahannock Place
Potomac Falls, VA 20165-4791
703-421-8635   fax 703-421-8631
jtaylor@virginiainstitute.org
Issues: The American Founding; American history/political tradition; Entrepreneurship/free enterprise; Federalism; Higher education; Political correctness and multiculturalism; Property rights; School choice; Second Amendment; State and local government; State and local public finance; Taxation/tax reform; Urban sprawl/livable cities

*Taylor, Dr. William J., Jr.
President
Taylor Associates, Inc.
6010 Maiden Lane
Bethesda, MD 20817
301-229-9032   fax 301-229-5392
wtaylor@csis.org
Issues: American diplomacy/foreign policy;
Korea; Military strategy; NATO and other
alliances; Northeast Asia; Peacekeeping;
Readiness and manpower

Teasley, Kevin
President
Greater Educational Opportunities
Foundation
302 South Meridian Street, Suite 201
Indianapolis, IN 46225
317-524-3770   fax 317-524-3773
teasleygeo@aol.com
Issues: Bilingual education; Business and
education partnerships; Charter schools;
Education unions and interest groups; Federal
education policy; Higher education; Home
schooling; Public school finance and
administration; School choice; School-to-work;
Standards, curriculum, and testing

*Teller, Dr. Edward
Senior Research Fellow
Hoover Institution
Stanford University
Stanford, CA 94305
650-723-0601   fax 650-723-1687
teller@hoover.stanford.edu
Issues: Arms control; Energy; Export controls/
military transfers; Missile defense; Sound
science

Telser, Dr. Lester G.
Professor of Economics, Department of
Economics
University of Chicago
1126 East 59th Street
Chicago, IL 60637
773-702-8193   fax 773-702-8490
ltelser@midway.uchicago.edu
Issues: Economic theory; Electricity
deregulation

Tengs, Dr. Tammy
Assistant Professor, Urban and Regional
Planning, School of Social Ecology
University of California, Irvine
Irvine, CA 92697-7075
949-824-4630   fax 949-824-8286
tengs@uci.edu
Issues: Costs and benefits of regulation;
Economic theory; Government health
programs; Health care reform; Risk assessment;
Substance abuse; Welfare/welfare reform

*Teske, Richard
President
Strategic Advocacy
2719 North Norwood Street
Arlington, VA 22207
703-465-1878   fax 703-465-1869
rpteske13@comcast.net
Issues: Aging/elder care; American history/
political tradition; Government health
programs; Health care reform; Medicaid;
Medicare; Political philosophy; State and local
government

*Testerman, Karen
Executive Director
Cornerstone Policy Research
Two Eagle Square, Suite 400
Concord, NH 03301
603-672-4735   fax 603-673-4836
nhfamily@earthlink.net
Issues: Abstinence and out-of-wedlock births;
Adoption, foster care, & child care services;
Family and children; Home schooling;
Marriage and divorce; Political correctness and
multiculturalism; Religion and public life;
School choice; State-sponsored gambling

Thacker, Christopher
Executive Director
The Bible Literacy Project
1841 Broadway, 2nd Floor
New York, NY 10023
212-765-8741   fax 212-765-8813
cthacker@aya.yale.edu
Issues: Religion and public life; Standards,
curriculum, and testing

*Thacker, Dr. Rebecca A.
Associate Professor of Human Resource
Management, College of Business
Ohio University
Copeland Hall
Athens, OH 45701
740-593-2087   fax 740-593-9342
thacker@ohio.edu
Issues: Civil rights/racial preferences

Thayer, W. Stephen, III
Director of Legislative & Legal Policy
American Conservative Union
1007 Cameron Street
Alexandria, VA 22314
703-836-8602   fax 703-836-8606
sthayer@conservative.org
Issues: Congress; Constitutional law

*Thernstrom, Dr. Abigail
Senior Fellow
Manhattan Institute for Policy Research
1445 Massachusetts Avenue
Lexington, MA 02420
781-861-7634   fax 781-860-9045
thernstr@fas.harvard.edu
Issues: Civil rights/racial preferences; Political
correctness and multiculturalism; Standards,
curriculum, and testing

*Thernstrom, Stephan
Winthrop Professor of History
Harvard University
1445 Massachusetts Avenue
Lexington, MA 02420
781-861-7634   fax 781-860-9045
thernstr@fas.harvard.edu
Issues: American history/political tradition;
Bilingual education; Civil rights/racial
preferences; Higher education; Immigration;
Standards, curriculum, and testing

*Theroux, David J.
Founder and President
The Independent Institute
100 Swan Way
Oakland, CA 94621-1428
510-632-1366   fax 510-568-6040
dtheroux@independent.org
Issues: The American Founding; Anti-trust;
Arms control; Citizenship and civil society;
Economic education; The Economy;
Entrepreneurship/free enterprise; Family and
children; Free-market environmentalism;
Government waste; Health care reform;
Homeland security/civil defense; Immigration;
Labor and employment; Money and financial
services; Peacekeeping; Political correctness
and multiculturalism; Privatization/
Contracting-out; Property rights; Regulatory
reform; School choice; Second Amendment;
Terrorism and international crime; Tort and
liability reform; Transportation deregulation;
Urban sprawl/livable cities

Theroux, Mary L. G.
Vice President
The Independent Institute
100 Swan Way
Oakland, CA 94621-1428
510-632-1366   fax 510-568-6040
mtheroux@independent.org
Issues: Agriculture; Family and children;
Philanthropy

*Thierer, Adam D.
Director of Telecommunications Studies
Cato Institute
1000 Massachusetts Avenue, N.W.
Washington, DC 20001
202-789-5211   fax 202-842-3490
athierer@cato.org
Issues: Federalism; Intellectual property;
Telecommunications and the Internet

*Thigpen, Forest M.
President
Mississippi Family Council
P. O. Box 13514
Jackson, MS 39236
601-969-1200   fax 601-969-1600
fthigpen@msfamily.org
Issues: Abstinence and out-of-wedlock births;
Adoption, foster care, & child care services;
Charter schools; Church-state relations;
Citizenship and civil society; Crime/crime
statistics; Entitlement spending; Faith-based
and volunteer initiatives; Family and children;
Health care reform; Judicial activism/judicial
reform; Marriage and divorce; Poverty and
dependency; Public school finance and
administration; Religious freedom; Taxation/
tax reform; Tort and liability reform; Welfare/
welfare reform

Thoman, Dr. Roy E.
Professor of Political Science
West Texas A & M University
WT Box 725
Canyon, TX 79016
806-651-2424   fax 806-651-2601
rthoman@mail.wtamu.edu
Issues: China; Comparative government;
Conservative thought; Economic education;
The Economy; Middle East; Missile defense;
Northeast Asia; Peacekeeping; Russia and
Eurasia; United Nations

Thomas, Dr. Chris R.
Associate Professor, Department of
Economics
University of South Florida
4202 East Fowler Avenue
Tampa, FL 33620
813-974-6546   fax 813-974-6510
cthomas@coba.usf.edu
Issues: The Economy

*Thomas, Jason M.
Staff Economist
Citizens for a Sound Economy
1900 M Street, N.W., Suite 500
Washington, DC 20005
202-942-7621   fax 202-783-4687
jthomas@cse.org
Issues: Anti-trust; Costs and benefits of
regulation; Government debt; Intellectual
property; Money and financial services;
Regulatory reform; Telecommunications and
the Internet; Transportation deregulation

Thomas, Stephen R.
Canon Lawyer
North American Canon Law Society
5907 Grand Avenue
Duluth, MN 55807
218-733-0345   fax 218-733-0349
rbsocc@juno.com
Issues: Church-state relations; Constitutional
law

*Thomas, Virginia L.
Director, Executive Branch Relations
The Heritage Foundation
214 Massachusetts Avenue, N.E.
Washington, DC 20002
202-546-4400   fax 202-608-6068
ginni.thomas@heritage.org
Issues: Executive Branch/The Presidency;
Government waste

*Thomasson, Randy
Executive Director
Campaign for California Families
P. O. Box 782
Sacramento, CA 95812
916-443-1410   fax 413-832-2275
mail@savecalifornia.com
Issues: Adoption, foster care, & child care
services; Church-state relations; Family and
children; Marriage and divorce; Media and
popular culture; State-sponsored gambling

Thompson, Edwin R.
President
Personal Retirement Alliance, Ltd.
330 East 38th Street, Suite 55
New York, NY 10016
212-972-9012   ethompson@iOptOut.org
Issues: Social Security and retirement

Thompson, Dr. Ewa M.
Professor of Slavic Studies, Department of
German & Slavic Studies
Rice University
6100 South Main
Houston, TX 77005-1892
713-467-5836   fax 713-467-6348
ethomp@rice.edu
Issues: Arts, humanities and historic resources;
Central and Eastern Europe; Federal education
policy; Higher education; Human rights;
Russia and Eurasia; Standards, curriculum, and
testing; Western Europe

*Thompson, Dr. Loren B.
Chief Operating Officer
Lexington Institute
1600 Wilson Boulevard, Suite 900
Arlington, VA 22209
703-522-9627   fax 703-522-5837
Issues: Defense budget; Emerging threats/
threat assessment; Homeland security/civil
defense; Military strategy; Missile defense

Thompson, Michael W.
President
Thomas Jefferson Institute for Public Policy
9035 Golden Sunset Lane
Springfield, VA 22153
703-440-9447   fax 703-455-1531
mikethompson@erols.com
Issues: Environmental education;
Environmental regulation; Infrastructure;
Privatization/Contracting-out; School choice;
State and local government; State and local
public finance

Thompson, Dr. W. Scott
Associate Professor of International Politics,
Fletcher School of Law and Diplomacy
Tufts University
170 Packard Avenue
Medford, MA 02155
617-627-5066   fax 617-627-3871
wthompso@granite.tufts.edu
Issues: Economic development/foreign aid;
Northeast Asia; South Asia (including India
and Pakistan); United Nations

Thomson, Ann C., J.D.
Policy Analyst
The Commonwealth Foundation
225 State Street, Suite 302
Harrisburg, PA 17101
717-671-1901   fax 717-671-1905
athomson@commonwealthfoundation.org
Issues: Charter schools; Education unions and
interest groups; School choice

Thornburgh, Richard
Counsel
Kirkpatrick & Lockhart, L.L.P.
1800 Massachusetts Avenue, N.W., 2nd Floor
Washington, DC 20036
202-778-9080   fax 202-778-9100
thornbrl@kl.com
Issues: Tort and liability reform

*Thorning, Dr. Margo
Senior Vice President and Chief Economist
American Council for Capital Formation
1750 K Street, N.W., Suite 400
Washington, DC 20006
202-293-5811   fax 202-785-8165
mthorning@accf.org
Issues: Climate change; Energy; Federal budget;
International tax policy/tax competition;
Taxation/tax reform

Thornton, Dr. J. Mills, III
Professor of History, Department of History
University of Michigan
Ann Arbor, MI 48109-1003
734-764-6306   fax 734-647-4881
jmthrntn@umich.edu
Issues: The American Founding; American
history/political tradition; Civil rights/racial
preferences; Constitutional law; Electoral
reform/voting rights; Federalism; Political
philosophy; State and local government; State
and local public finance

*Thornton, Dr. Mark
Professor of Economics
Columbus State University
4225 University Avenue
Columbus, GA 31907
706-562-1662   fax 706-568-2184
mark_thornton@colstate.edu
Issues: Comparative economics; Comparative
government; Costs and benefits of regulation;
Crime/crime statistics; Economic education;
Economic theory; The Economy; Elections/
polling; Electricity deregulation;
Entrepreneurship/free enterprise; Ethics;
Federal budget; Federal education policy;
Government debt; Government waste; Higher
education; Home schooling; Infrastructure;
Judicial activism/judicial reform; Minimum
wage; Money and financial services; Political
philosophy; Privatization/Contracting-out;
Property rights; Public school finance and
administration; Second Amendment; State and
local government; State and local public
finance; Substance abuse; Taxation/tax
reform; Terrorism and international crime;
Tort and liability reform

Thurow, Dr. Glen E.
Provost
University of Dallas
1845 East Northgate Drive
Irving, TX 75062
972-721-5000   provost@acad.udallas.edu
Issues: Constitutional law; Higher education;
Judicial activism/judicial reform; Standards,
curriculum, and testing

*Tierney, Dr. John J., Jr.
Institute of World Politics
1521 16th Street, N.W.
Washington, DC 20036
202-462-2101   fax 202-462-7031
Issues: American diplomacy/foreign policy;
Arms control; Emerging threats/threat
assessment; Human rights; Intelligence
gathering and covert operations; Korea; Latin
America; Promoting democracy/public
diplomacy; Terrorism and international crime;
United Nations; Western Europe

Timberlake, Dr. Richard H., Jr.
Professor Emeritus of Economics
200 Deerfield Road
Bogart, GA 30622
706-546-6731   rightim@earthlink.net
Issues: American history/political tradition;
Climate change; Constitutional law; Economic
forecasting; Economic theory; Energy; Federal
budget; Money and financial services

Timmerman, Kenneth R.
President
Maryland Taxpayers Association
7831 Woodmont Avenue, Suite 396
Bethesda, MD 20814
301-946-2918   president@mdtaxes.org
Issues: Health care reform; Human rights;
Promoting democracy/public diplomacy;
Taxation/tax reform

Tipler, Dr. Frank J.
Professor, Department of Mathematics
Tulane University
305 Gibson Hall
New Orleans, LA 70118
504-862-3449   fax 504-865-5063
frank.tipler@tulane.edu
Issues: Church-state relations; Energy; Higher
education; Intellectual property; Religion and
public life; Sound science

Tismaneanu, Dr. Vladimir
Associate Professor, Department of
Government and Politics
University of Maryland
3140 Tydings Hall
College Park, MD 20742
301-405-4164   fax 301-314-9690
vtismane@umd.edu
Issues: Western Europe

*Titus, Herbert W.
Attorney at Law
5221 Indian River Road
Virginia Beach, VA 23464
757-421-4141   fax 757-421-3644
forecast22@pinn.net
Issues: The American Founding; Campaign
finance reform; Church-state relations;
Constitutional law; Free Speech; Religious
freedom; United Nations

Tkacik, John J., Jr.
Research Fellow in China Policy, Asian
Studies Center
The Heritage Foundation
214 Massachusetts Avenue, N.E.
Washington, DC 20002
202-544-4400   fax 202-675-1779
john.tkacik@heritage.org
Issues: China; Intelligence gathering and covert
operations; Northeast Asia

*Tobin, Jim
Chairman
National Taxpayers United of Illinois
407 South Dearborn, Suite 1170
Chicago, IL 60605
312-427-5128   fax 312-427-5139
ntui@core.com
Issues: Government waste; Public school
finance and administration; State and local
public finance; Taxation/tax reform

Todorov, Dr. Vladislav
Lecturer, Slavic Department
University of Pennsylvania
431 Williams Hall
Philadelphia, PA 19104
215-898-6056   vtodorov@sas.upenn.edu
Issues: Central and Eastern Europe;
Intelligence gathering and covert operations;
Political philosophy; Terrorism and
international crime

Todorovich, Prof. Miro M.

Executive Director
Scientists and Engineers for Secure Energy
410 Riverside Drive, Suite 82A
New York, NY 10025
212-864-0645   fax 212-866-8555
Issues: American diplomacy/foreign policy;
Central and Eastern Europe; Climate change;
Congress; Costs and benefits of regulation;
Electricity deregulation; Emerging threats/
threat assessment; Energy; Environmental
education; Environmental regulation;
Executive Branch/The Presidency; Higher
education; Human rights; Judiciary; Land use;
Media and popular culture; Military strategy;
Missile defense; Non-governmental
organizations; OSHA; Peacekeeping;
Philanthropy; Political correctness and
multiculturalism; Regulation through
litigation; Regulatory budgeting; Risk
assessment; Sound science; Standards,
curriculum, and testing; Stewardship;
Terrorism and international crime; Urban
sprawl/livable cities; Waste management;
Water; Wildlife management/endangered
species

Toft, Dr. Graham S.

Senior Fellow
Hudson Institute
Herman Kahn Center, 5395 Emerson Way
Indianapolis, IN 46226
317-545-1000   fax 317-545-9639
info@hudson.org
Issues: The Economy; Labor and employment

*Tollison, Dr. Robert D.

Robert Hearin Professor of Economics,
Department of Economics
University of Mississippi
University, MS 38677
662-915-5041   fax 662-915-6943
btollison@econ.olemiss.edu
Issues: Campaign finance reform; Comparative
government; Congress; Conservative thought;
Costs and benefits of regulation; Executive
Branch/The Presidency; Federal budget;
Regulatory reform; Taxation/tax reform;
Term limits

Toma, Dr. Eugenia Froedge

Professor and Director, Martin School of
Public Policy and Administration
University of Kentucky
Room 437, P.O.T.
Lexington, KY 40506
606-257-1156   fax 606-323-1937
pub702@pop.uky.edu
Issues: Charter schools; Economic education;
Education unions and interest groups; Federal
education policy; Home schooling; Public
school finance and administration; School
choice; State and local public finance;
Unfunded mandates

Tontz, Dr. Jay L.

Dean, School of Business and Economics
California State University, Hayward
25800 Carlos Bee Boulevard
Hayward, CA 94542
510-885-3291   fax 510-885-4884
jtontz@csuhayward.edu
Issues: Business and education partnerships;
Economic forecasting; The Economy;
Entrepreneurship/free enterprise; Higher
education

*Torrey, Dr. E. Fuller

6204 Ridge Drive
Bethesda, MD 20816
Issues: Housing and homelessness

*Towle, Lex

Managing Director
AppleTree Institute for Education
Innovation
101 D Street, S.E., 2nd Floor
Washington, DC 20003
202-544-8650   fax 202-544-8678
lextowle@aol.com
Issues: Charter schools; Federal education
policy; School choice

Tracy, Brian S.

Chairman and CEO
Brian Tracy International
462 Stevens Avenue, Suite 202
Solana Beach, CA 92075
858-481-2977   fax 858-481-2445
briantracy@briantracy.com
Issues: Citizenship and civil society;
Conservative thought; Economic education;
Entrepreneurship/free enterprise; Political
philosophy; Taxation/tax reform

*Treadwell, Mead
Managing Director
Institute of the North
Alaska Pacific University, P. O. Box 101700
Anchorage, AK 99510
907-342-2444   fax 907-342-2211
meadwell@alaska.net
Issues: Air; Canada; Climate change; Energy;
Environmental regulation; Forestry and
national parks; Missile defense; Northeast Asia;
Research funding; Russia and Eurasia; Sound
science

*Tropea, Dr. Joe
President
International Association for Support of
Privatization
P. O. Box 3617
Washington, DC 20007-0117
202-429-6604   fax 202-466-3439
tropea@gwu.edu
Issues: Corrections and sentencing; Family and
children; Juvenile justice

*Trowbridge, Ron
Maine Policy Center
30 Colonial Drive
Durham, ME 04222
207-353-4219   fax 207-353-4238
ronaldtrowbridge@yahoo.com
Issues: Ethics; School choice

Truluck, Phillip N.
Executive Vice President
The Heritage Foundation
214 Massachusetts Avenue, N.E.
Washington, DC 20002
202-546-4400   fax 202-608-6085
phil.truluck@heritage.org
Issues: Advocacy and nonprofit public funding;
Comparative government; Congress;
Conservative thought; Entrepreneurship/free
enterprise; Non-governmental organizations;
Philanthropy; Promoting democracy/public
diplomacy

*Tryfiates, George
Executive Director
Concerned Women for America
1015 15th Street, N.W., Suite 1100
Washington, DC 20005
202-488-7000   fax 202-488-0806
gtryfiates@cwfa.org
Issues: Bilingual education; Citizenship and
civil society; Federal education policy; Religion
and public life

*Tuerck, Dr. David G.
Executive Director
Beacon Hill Institute
Suffolk University, 8 Ashburton Place
Boston, MA 02108
617-573-8750   fax 617-720-4272
dtuerck@beaconhill.org
Issues: Economic education; Economic theory;
Faith-based and volunteer initiatives;
Standards, curriculum, and testing; State and
local public finance; Taxation/tax reform

*Tullock, Dr. Gordon
Professor of Law and Economics
George Mason University School of Law
3301 North Fairfax Drive
Arlington, VA 22201
703-993-4908   fax 703-993-4935
gtulloc1@gmu.edu
Issues: China; Constitutional law; Economic
theory; Federal budget; Federalism

*Turner, Grace-Marie
President
Galen Institute
P. O. Box 19080
Alexandria, VA 22320-0080
703-299-8900   fax 703-299-0721
gracemarie@galen.org
Issues: Costs and benefits of regulation;
Entitlement spending; Government health
programs; Health care reform; Medicaid;
Medicare; Taxation/tax reform; Wealth
creation/financial empowerment

*Turner, Jason
Visiting Fellow, The Heritage Foundation,
and President
Center for Self-Sufficiency
2425 East Stratford Court
Shorewood, WI 53211
414-906-1600
Issues: Housing and homelessness; Poverty and
dependency; Substance abuse; Welfare/
welfare reform

*Turner, Dr. Robert F.
Associate Director, Center of National
Security Law
University of Virginia School of Law
580 Massie Road
Charlottesville, VA 22903-1789
804-924-4083   fax 804-924-7362
rturner@law5.law.virginia.edu
Issues: American diplomacy/foreign policy;
Arms control; Congress; Executive Branch/
The Presidency; Human rights; Intelligence
gathering and covert operations; International
law; Military strategy; Missile defense; NATO
and other alliances; Peacekeeping; Promoting
democracy/public diplomacy; Second
Amendment; Southeast Asia (including
Burma, Cambodia, Laos, Vietnam, Singapore,
Malaysia, Indonesia, the Philippines, Australia,
and New Zealand); Terrorism and
international crime; United Nations

*Turpen, Forrest L.
Executive Director
Christian Educators Association
International
P. O. Box 41300
Pasadena, CA 91114-8300
626-798-1124   fax 626-798-2346
forrest@ceai.org
Issues: Charter schools; Church-state relations;
Education unions and interest groups; Faith-
based and volunteer initiatives; Federal
education policy; Free Speech; Public school
finance and administration; Religion and
public life; Right to work; Standards,
curriculum, and testing; Unions

Tuskey, John
Assistant Professor, School of Law
Regent University
1000 Regent University Drive
Virginia Beach, VA 23464
757-226-2879   fax 757-226-4139
johntus@regent.edu
Issues: Campaign finance reform;
Constitutional law; Federalism; Free Speech;
Judicial activism/judicial reform; Religious
freedom

*Tuttle, Lil
Education Director
Clare Boothe Luce Policy Institute
112 Elden Street, Suite P
Herndon, VA 20170
703-318-0730   fax 703-318-8867
tuttles@erols.com
Issues: Education unions and interest groups;
School choice; School-to-work; Standards,
curriculum, and testing

Twight, Dr. Charlotte
Department of Economics
Boise State University
1910 University Drive
Boise, ID 83725
208-426-1335   fax 208-426-2071
ctwight@boisestate.edu
Issues: Economic theory; Federal education
policy; Government health programs; Health
care reform; Medicare; Privacy; Social Security
and retirement; Taxation/tax reform

Twitty, Kristina
Education Policy Analyst and Collegians
Director
Eagle Forum
316 Pennsylvania Avenue, S.E., Suite 203
Washington, DC 20003
202-544-0353   fax 202-547-6996
kristina@eagleforum.org
Issues: Federal education policy; Higher
education; Home schooling; School-to-work;
Standards, curriculum, and testing

Tyrrell, R. Emmett
Chairman
The American Alternative Foundation
219 South Alfred Street
Alexandria, VA 22314
Issues: Comparative economics; The Economy;
Poverty and dependency; Telecommunications
and the Internet; Welfare/welfare reform

Ueda, Reed
Professor, Department of History
Tufts University
East Hall
Medford, MA 02155
617-627-2444   fax 617-627-3479
Issues: American history/political tradition;
Bilingual education; Charter schools; Family
and children; Higher education; Immigration;
Standards, curriculum, and testing

*Uhler, Lewis
President
National Tax Limitation Committee
151 North Sunrise Avenue, Suite 901
Roseville, CA 95661
916-786-9400   fax 916-786-8163
lkuhler@earthlink.net
Issues: The American Founding; Federal
budget; Government debt; Government waste;
Initiative and referendum; Political
philosophy; Privatization/Contracting-out;
The Reagan legacy; State and local public
finance; Taxation/tax reform; Term limits;
Unfunded mandates

Uhlmann, Michael M.
Professor of American Government
Claremont Graduate University
170 East 10th Street
Claremont, CA 91711
909-621-8210
Issues: The American Founding; Church-state
relations; Executive Branch/The Presidency;
Judiciary; Religious freedom; School choice

Ulc, Dr. Otto
Professor of Political Science
Binghamton University
P. O. Box 6000
Binghamton, NY 13902
607-777-2455   fax 607-777-2675
ulc@binghamton.edu
Issues: Central and Eastern Europe;
Immigration; International law

Utley, Jon Basil
Robert A. Taft Fellow
Ludwig von Mises Institute
910 17th Street, N.W., Suite 422
Washington, DC 20006
202-298-5514   fax 202-298-3258
jbutley@earthlink.net
Issues: American diplomacy/foreign policy;
Economic development/foreign aid;
Economic education; Emerging threats/threat
assessment; Latin America; Middle East;
Promoting democracy/public diplomacy;
Russia and Eurasia; Terrorism and
international crime; Trade

*Utt, Dr. Ronald
Herbert and Joyce Morgan Senior Research
Fellow, Thomas A. Roe Institute for
Economic Policy Studies
The Heritage Foundation
214 Massachusetts Avenue, N.E.
Washington, DC 20002
202-608-6013   fax 202-544-5421
ron.utt@heritage.org
Issues: Comparative economics; Discretionary
spending; Federal budget; Government waste;
Land use; Privatization/Contracting-out;
Transportation; Urban sprawl/livable cities

Uzzell, Lawrence A.
Director
Keston Institute
510 West Marvin Avenue, Number 208
Waxahachie, TX 75165
972-938-7919   fax 972-938-7919
lauzzell@aol.com
Issues: Arts, humanities and historic resources;
Church-state relations; Elections/polling;
Human rights; International organizations
(European Union, OECD, etc.); NATO and
other alliances; Religion and public life;
Religious freedom

Valis, Wayne
Executive Director
Citizens for Civil Justice Reform
1700 Pennsylvania Avenue, N.W., Suite 950
Washington, DC 20006
202-393-5055   fax 202-393-0120
valis@erols.com
Issues: Tort and liability reform

*Van Allen, Dr. Terry W.
510 Oak Briar Drive
Kemah, TX 77565
281-334-5503
Issues: Civil rights/racial preferences;
Economic development/foreign aid;
Economic education; Economic forecasting;
Economic theory; The Economy;
Entrepreneurship/free enterprise; Faith-based
and volunteer initiatives; Federal civil service;
Federalism; Higher education; Homeland
security/civil defense; Religious freedom;
Research funding; School choice; Taxation/
tax reform; Urban sprawl/livable cities; Wealth
creation/financial empowerment

*Van Cleave, Dr. William R.
University Professor and Department Head,
Department of Defense and Strategic Studies
Southwest Missouri State University
Springfield, MO 65804
417-836-4137   fax 417-836-6667
Issues: American diplomacy/foreign policy;
Arms control; Emerging threats/threat
assessment; Military strategy; Missile defense;
Russia and Eurasia

VanDoren, Peter M.
Editor, *Regulation Magazine*
Cato Institute
1000 Massachusetts Avenue, N.W.
Washington, DC 20001
202-789-5221   fax 202-842-3490
pvandore@cato.org
Issues: Costs and benefits of regulation;
Electricity deregulation; Energy;
Environmental regulation; Land use;
Regulatory reform; Transportation
deregulation

Vasey, Adm. Lloyd R., USN (Ret.)
Founder and Senior Policy Advisor
Pacific Forum CSIS
1001 Bishop Street, Suite 1150
Honolulu, HI 96813
808-521-6745   fax 808-599-8690
pacforum@lava.net
Issues: China; Emerging threats/threat
assessment

*Vasquez, Ian
Director of the Project on Global Economic
Liberty
Cato Institute
1000 Massachusetts Avenue, N.W.
Washington, DC 20001
202-842-0200   fax 202-842-3490
ivasquez@cato.org
Issues: Economic development/foreign aid;
International finance and multilateral banks;
Latin America; Mexico

Vaughn, Dr. Karen I.
Professor of Economics, Department of
Economics
George Mason University
4400 University Drive, 332 Enterprise Hall
Fairfax, VA 22030
703-993-1146   fax 703-993-1133
kvaughn@gmu.edu
Issues: Comparative economics; Economic
education; Economic theory; Political
philosophy

*Vazsonyi, Dr. Balint
Director
Center for the American Founding
1311 Dolley Madison Boulevard, Suite 2A
McLean, VA 22101
703-556-6595   fax 703-556-6875
bv@founding.org
Issues: Bilingual education; Central and Eastern
Europe; Citizenship and civil society; Civil
rights/racial preferences; Constitutional law;
Federal education policy; Federalism; Free
Speech; Higher education; Human rights;
Immigration; International law; Judicial
activism/judicial reform; Middle East; NATO
and other alliances; Political correctness and
multiculturalism; Property rights; Russia and
Eurasia; School-to-work; Second Amendment;
Standards, curriculum, and testing; United
Nations; Western Europe

*Vedder, Richard
Distinguished Professor of Economics
Ohio University
Haning Hall
Athens, OH 45701
740-593-2037   fax 740-593-0181
vedder@ohio.edu
Issues: Davis-Bacon Act; Higher education;
Minimum wage; OSHA; Public school finance
and administration; State and local public
finance; Unions

*Venable, Peggy
Director
Texas Citizens for a Sound Economy
1005 Congress Avenue, Suite 910
Austin, TX 78701
512-476-5905   fax 512-476-5906
pvenable@cse.org
Issues: American history/political tradition;
Conservative thought; Costs and benefits of
regulation; Criminal law and procedure;
Energy; Entitlement spending; Federal budget;
Federal education policy; Free Speech; Free-
market environmentalism; Government waste;
Health care reform; Immigration;
Privatization/Contracting-out; Property rights;
Regulatory reform; Religious freedom; Second
Amendment; Social Security and retirement;
State and local government; State and local
public finance; Taxation/tax reform;
Telecommunications and the Internet; Tort
and liability reform; Unfunded mandates;
Urban sprawl/livable cities; Water; Wealth
creation/financial empowerment

Vickers, Melara Zyla
Senior Fellow for International and
Economic Affairs
Independent Women's Forum
P. O. Box 3058
Arlington, VA 22203-0058
703-558-4991   fax 703-558-4994
mvickers@iwf.org
Issues: American diplomacy/foreign policy;
Economic development/foreign aid

*Vigilante, Kevin, M.D.
8 Holsmith Court
Rumford, RI 02910
kvigilante@aol.com
Issues: Charter schools; Faith-based and
volunteer initiatives; Health care reform;
Human rights; School choice; Substance abuse

*Vinovskis, Dr. Maris A.
A. M. and H. P. Bentley Professor of History
University of Michigan
1029 Tisch Hall
Ann Arbor, MI 48109-1003
734-647-2545   fax 734-663-9967
vinovski@umich.edu
Issues: Abstinence and out-of-wedlock births;
The American Founding; American history/
political tradition; Arts, humanities and
historic resources; Citizenship and civil society;
Executive Branch/The Presidency; Family and
children; Federal education policy; Higher
education; Marriage and divorce; Standards,
curriculum, and testing

*Viscusi, W. Kip
John F. Cogan, Jr. Professor of Law and
Economics
Harvard Law School
1575 Massachusetts Avenue, Hauser 302
Cambridge, MA 02138
617-496-0019   fax 617-495-3010
kip@law.harvard.edu
Issues: Environmental regulation; Regulatory
reform; Risk assessment; Tort and liability
reform

Vitell, Dr. Scott J.
Phil B. Hardin Professor of Marketing,
School of Business Administration
University of Mississippi
University, MS 38677
662-915-5468   fax 662-915-5821
vitell@bus.olemiss.edu
Issues: Ethics

Viteritti, Dr. Joseph P.
Research Professor of Public Policy, Robert
F. Wagner Graduate School of Public Service
New York University
269 Mercer Street, Room 207
New York, NY 10003-6687
212-998-7507   fax 212-995-4165
joseph.viteritti@nyu.edu
Issues: Charter schools; Education unions and
interest groups; Public school finance and
administration; School choice

*Volokh, Prof. Eugene
Professor, School of Law
University of California at Los Angeles
405 North Hilgard Avenue
Los Angeles, CA 90095
310-206-3926   fax 310-206-6489
volokh@law.ucla.edu
Issues: Church-state relations; Civil rights/racial
preferences; Constitutional law; Free Speech;
Intellectual property; Political correctness and
multiculturalism; Privacy; Religion and public
life; Religious freedom; Second Amendment;
Telecommunications and the Internet

Von Kannon, John
Vice President and Treasurer
The Heritage Foundation
214 Massachusetts Avenue, N.E.
Washington, DC 20002
202-546-4400   fax 202-608-6085
info@heritage.org
Issues: Philanthropy

Von Kohorn, Ken
Chairman
Family Institute of Connecticut
77 Buckingham Street
Hartford, CT 06106
860-548-0066   fax 860-548-9545
Issues: Family and children

vonBreichenruchardt, Dane
President
U. S. Bill of Rights Foundation
263 Kentucky Avenue, S.E.
Washington, DC 20003
202-546-7079   fax 202-546-7079
usbor@aol.com
Issues: Advocacy and nonprofit public funding;
The American Founding; Campaign finance
reform; Congress; Constitutional law; Costs and
benefits of regulation; Executive Branch/The
Presidency; Federalism; Free Speech; Judicial
activism/judicial reform; Judiciary; Political
correctness and multiculturalism; Property
rights; Public interest law; Regulation through
litigation; Regulatory reform; School choice;
Second Amendment; Taxation/tax reform;
Unfunded mandates

Vondracek, M. Jon
Vice President
Center for Strategic and International
Studies
1800 K Street, N.W., Suite 400
Washington, DC 20006
202-887-0200   fax 202-775-3199
mjvondracek@csis.org
Issues: American diplomacy/foreign policy

*Wade, T. Rogers
President and CEO
Georgia Public Policy Foundation
6100 Lake Forest Drive, N.W., Suite 110
Atlanta, GA 30328
404-256-4050   fax 404-256-9909
trw@gppf.org
Issues: American diplomacy/foreign policy;
American history/political tradition; Congress;
Defense budget; Intelligence gathering and
covert operations; Military strategy; NATO and
other alliances; Political philosophy; State and
local government; Term limits

Wagner, Bridgett G.
Director, Coalition Relations
The Heritage Foundation
214 Massachusetts Avenue, N.E.
Washington, DC 20002
202-546-4400   fax 202-544-0961
bridgett.wagner@heritage.org
Issues: Advocacy and nonprofit public funding;
Conservative thought; Economic education;
Non-governmental organizations;
Philanthropy

Wagner, Richard
Editor
Carolina Journal/John Locke Foundation
200 West Morgan Street, Suite 200
Raleigh, NC 27601
919-828-3876   fax 919-821-5117
rwagner@johnlocke.org
Issues: Media and popular culture

*Wagner, Dr. Richard E.
Harris Professor of Economics
George Mason University
4400 University Drive, MSN 3G4
Fairfax, VA 22030
703-993-1132   fax 703-993-1133
rwagner@gmu.edu
Issues: Economic theory; The Economy;
Entitlement spending; Entrepreneurship/free
enterprise; Ethics; Federal budget; Federalism;
Government debt; International tax policy/tax
competition; Privatization/Contracting-out;
State and local public finance; Taxation/tax
reform

Waite, Dr. Linda J.
Professor of Sociology and the Social
Sciences, Department of Sociology
University of Chicago
1155 East 60th Street, Number 363
Chicago, IL 60637
773-256-6333   l-waite@uchicago.edu
Issues: Marriage and divorce; Religion and
public life

*Walberg, Dr. Herbert J.
Emeritus Professor
University of Illinois, Chicago
180 East Pearson Street, Apartment 3607
Chicago, IL 60611
312-996-8133   fax 312-996-6400
hwalberg@uic.edu
Issues: Bilingual education; Business and
education partnerships; Charter schools;
Federal education policy; Public school finance
and administration; School choice; Standards,
curriculum, and testing

Waldron, Dr. Arthur
Visiting Scholar and Director of Asian Studies
American Enterprise Institute
1150 17th Street, N.W.
Washington, DC 20036
202-828-6031   fax 202-862-5808
awaldron2@aol.com
Issues: American diplomacy/foreign policy; China; Northeast Asia; Southeast Asia (including Burma, Cambodia, Laos, Vietnam, Singapore, Malaysia, Indonesia, the Philippines, Australia, and New Zealand)

*Waliszewski, Robert
Youth Culture Analyst
Focus on the Family
8605 Explorer Drive
Colorado Springs, CO 80920
719-548-4635   fax 719-531-3385
waliszrs@fotf.org
Issues: Media and popular culture

*Walker, Lee H.
President and CEO
New Coalition for Economic and Social Change
300 South Wacker Drive, Suite 3020
Chicago, IL 60606
312-427-1290   fax 312-427-1291
lwalker@newcoalition.org
Issues: Business and education partnerships; Civil rights/racial preferences; Conservative thought; Entrepreneurship/free enterprise; Ethics; Poverty and dependency; Religion and public life; School choice

*Walker, Dr. Richard L.
Ambassador in Residence, Richard L. Walker Institute of International Studies
University of South Carolina
Gambrell Hall, 4th Floor
Columbia, SC 29208
803-777-8180   fax 803-777-9308
buice@sc.edu
Issues: American diplomacy/foreign policy; China; Higher education; Intelligence gathering and covert operations; Japan; Korea; Northeast Asia; Political philosophy; Readiness and manpower; The Reagan legacy

Walker, Russ
Northwest Director
Citizens for a Sound Economy
7444 Shadowwood Court N.E.
Keizer, OR 97303-3937
503-463-9457   rwalker@cse.org
Issues: Environmental regulation; Free-market environmentalism; Government debt; Government waste; Land use; Privatization/Contracting-out; Property rights; School choice; Social Security and retirement; Sound science; Taxation/tax reform; Telecommunications and the Internet

Waller, William
Venable, Baetjer, Howard & Civiletti, LLP
1201 New York Avenue, N.W., Suite 1000
Washington, DC 20005-3917
202-962-4800   fax 202-962-8300
wcwaller@venable.com
Issues: Free Speech; Health care reform; Regulatory reform

*Wallin, Dr. Jeffrey D.
President
American Academy for Liberal Education
1710 Rhode Island Avenue, N.W., 4th Floor
Washington, DC 20036
202-452-8611   fax 202-452-8620
jwallin@aale.org
Issues: The American Founding; American history/political tradition; Charter schools; Emerging threats/threat assessment; Higher education; Intelligence gathering and covert operations; Missile defense; Political correctness and multiculturalism; Political philosophy; Standards, curriculum, and testing

*Wallis, Ben A., Jr.
President
Institute for Human Rights
800 N.W. Loop 410, Suite 350
San Antonio, TX 78216
210-525-1500   fax 210-525-9323
wallis@txdirect.net
Issues: Agriculture; Constitutional law; Free Speech; Land use; Property rights; Religious freedom; Second Amendment; Water; Wildlife management/endangered species

Wallison, Peter J.
Resident Fellow and Co-Director, Financial
Deregulation Project
American Enterprise Institute
1150 17th Street, N.W.
Washington, DC 20036
202-862-5864   fax 202-862-4875
pwallison@aei.org
Issues: Money and financial services; Regulatory
reform

*Wallop, Hon. Malcolm
Chung Ju-Yung Fellow for Policy Studies, The
Heritage Foundation, and Chairman
Frontiers of Freedom Institute
12011 Lee Jackson Memorial Highway
Suite 310
Fairfax, VA 22033
703-246-0110   fax 703-246-0129
malcolmwallop@ff.org
Issues: Air; American diplomacy/foreign policy;
American history/political tradition;
Comparative government; Congress;
Conservative thought; Costs and benefits of
regulation; Energy; Executive Branch/The
Presidency; Federal budget; Federal education
policy; Federalism; Forestry and national parks;
Free-market environmentalism; Health care
reform; Higher education; Homeland
security/civil defense; Intellectual property;
Intelligence gathering and covert operations;
Judiciary; Military strategy; Missile defense;
Political philosophy; Property rights; The
Reagan legacy; Regulation through litigation;
School choice; Social Security and retirement;
State and local government; Taxation/tax
reform; Telecommunications and the Internet;
Terrorism and international crime; Trade;
Welfare/welfare reform; Wildlife
management/endangered species

Walpin, Gerald
Counsel
Katten Muchin Zavis Rosenman
575 Madison Avenue
New York, NY 10022
212-940-7100   fax 212-940-8743
gerald.walpin@kmzr.com
Issues: Aging/elder care; Church-state
relations; Civil rights/racial preferences;
Constitutional law; Criminal law and
procedure; Free Speech; Judicial activism/
judicial reform; Judiciary; Religious freedom

Walpole, Bob
The Flagstaff Institute
P. O. Box 986
Flagstaff, AZ 86002-0986
928-779-0052   fax 928-774-8589
Issues: Charter schools; China; Japan; Mexico

*Walters, Dr. Stephen J. K.
Professor, Department of Economics
Loyola College
4501 North Charles Street
Baltimore, MD 21210
410-617-2313   fax 410-617-2118
swalters@loyola.edu
Issues: Anti-trust; Costs and benefits of
regulation; Regulation through litigation; State
and local public finance

Walton, Gary M.
President
Foundation for Teaching Economics
260 Russell Boulevard, Suite B
Davis, CA 95616-3839
530-757-4630   fax 530-757-4636
gwalton@fte.org
Issues: The American Founding; American
history/political tradition; Business and
education partnerships; Economic education;
Standards, curriculum, and testing

Wang, William K. S.
Professor
Hastings College of Law
200 McAllister Street
San Francisco, CA 94102
415-565-4666   fax 415-565-4865
wangw@uchastings.edu
Issues: Regulatory reform

Wanniski, Jude
Chairman
Polyconomics
900 Lanidex Plaza, Suite 250
Parsippany, NJ 07054-2707
973-781-1411   fax 973-781-1696
Issues: Central and Eastern Europe;
Comparative economics; Economic
development/foreign aid; Economic
education; The Economy; Health care reform;
Labor and employment; Money and financial
services; Northeast Asia; Poverty and
dependency; Regulatory reform; Russia and
Eurasia; Social Security and retirement; South
Asia (including India and Pakistan); Trade;
Urban sprawl/livable cities; Western Europe

Ward, Robert B.
Director of Research
Public Policy Institute of New York
152 Washington Avenue
Albany, NY 12210
518-654-7511   fax 518-432-4537
wardb@nysnet.net
Issues: Taxation/tax reform

Warder, Michael Y.
Executive Director
Los Angeles Children's Scholarship Fund
1650 Ximeno Avenue, Suite 245
Long Beach, CA 90804
562-961-9250   fax 562-961-0250
mwarder@lacsf.org
Issues: China; Mexico; Missile defense;
Philanthropy; Russia and Eurasia; School
choice

Ware, Prof. Stephen J.
Professor of Law, Cumberland School of Law
Samford University
800 Lakeshore Drive
Birmingham, AL 35229
205-726-2413   fax 205-726-2673
sjware@alumni.uchicago.edu
Issues: Judicial activism/judicial reform;
Judiciary; Tort and liability reform

Warner, Dr. John T.
Professor of Economics, Department of
Economics
Clemson University
222 Sirrine Hall
Clemson, SC 29634-1309
864-656-3967   fax 864-656-4192
jtwarne@clemson.edu
Issues: Economic theory; Labor and
employment; Readiness and manpower

*Warren, Roland
President
National Fatherhood Initiative
101 Lake Forest Boulevard, Suite 360
Gaithersburg, MD 20877
301-948-0599   fax 301-948-4325
r.warren@fatherhood.org
Issues: Family and children; Marriage and
divorce

Washburne, Tom
Director, National Center for Home
Education
Home School Legal Defense Association
P. O. Box 3000
Purcellville, VA 20134
540-338-7600   fax 540-338-8606
nche@hslda.org
Issues: Charter schools; Congress;
Constitutional law; Education unions and
interest groups; Executive Branch/The
Presidency; Family and children; Federal
education policy; Home schooling; Marriage
and divorce; Privacy; Religious freedom;
School choice; School-to-work; Social Security
and retirement; Standards, curriculum, and
testing; State and local government

*Waters, Alan Rufus, Ph.D.
Professor of International Business, Sid
Craig School of Business
California State University, Fresno
5245 North Backer Avenue, M/S PB8
Fresno, CA 93740-8001
559-278-2349   fax 559-278-4911
rufuswaters@earthlink.net
Issues: Africa; Central and Eastern Europe;
Economic development/foreign aid; Latin
America; Privatization/Contracting-out; Russia
and Eurasia; Western Europe

*Waters, Dane
President
Initiative and Referendum Institute
P. O. Box 6306
Leesburg, VA 20178
703-723-9621   fax 703-723-9619
mdanewaters@iandrinstitute.org
Issues: American history/political tradition;
Constitutional law; Elections/polling; Electoral
reform/voting rights; Free Speech; Initiative
and referendum; International law; Political
philosophy; Promoting democracy/public
diplomacy; Taxation/tax reform

*Waters, Lori L.
Executive Director, Washington Office
Eagle Forum
316 Pennsylvania Avenue, S.E., Suite 203
Washington, DC 20003
202-544-0353   fax 202-547-6996
lori@eagleforum.org
Issues: Abstinence and out-of-wedlock births;
Congress; Elections/polling; Family and
children; Privacy

Watson, Dr. Bradley C. S.
Associate Professor of Political Science and
Fellow in Politics and Culture, Center for
Economic and Policy Education
Saint Vincent College
Latrobe, PA 15650
724-532-6600   fax 724-537-4599
bwatson@email.stvincent.edu
Issues: The American Founding; American
history/political tradition; Canada; Church-
state relations; Citizenship and civil society;
Civil rights/racial preferences; Conservative
thought; Constitutional law; Ethics; Free
Speech; Immigration; Judicial activism/
judicial reform; Media and popular culture;
Political correctness and multiculturalism;
Political philosophy; The Reagan legacy;
Religion and public life

*Watson, Donna
Director of Private Initiatives
Children First America
4412 Spicewood Springs Road, Suite 201
Austin, TX 78759
512-345-1083   fax 512-345-1280
dwatson@childrenfirstamerica.org
Issues: Charter schools; School choice;
Standards, curriculum, and testing

*Watson, Michael W.
Executive Vice President
Children First America
4412 Spicewood Springs Road, Suite 201
Austin, TX 78759
512-345-1083   fax 512-345-1280
mwatson@childrenfirstamerica.org
Issues: Federal education policy; Public school
finance and administration; School choice

Watson, Dr. Stanley J.
Professor, Department of Government
Patrick Henry College
One Patrick Henry Circle
Purcellville, VA 20132
540-338-8732   fax 540-338-8707
sjwatson@phc.edu
Issues: Abstinence and out-of-wedlock births;
Adoption, foster care, & child care services;
Campaign finance reform; Church-state
relations; Congress; Constitutional law;
Executive Branch/The Presidency; Faith-based
and volunteer initiatives; Family and children;
Federalism; Higher education; Home
schooling; Immigration; Judicial activism/
judicial reform; Public school finance and
administration; Religion and public life; State
and local government; Tort and liability reform

Wattenberg, Ben J.
Senior Fellow
American Enterprise Institute
1150 17th Street, N.W.
Washington, DC 20036
202-862-5908   fax 202-862-7178
bwattenberg@aei.org
Issues: Citizenship and civil society; Civil rights/
racial preferences; Congress; Elections/
polling; Executive Branch/The Presidency;
Media and popular culture; Political
correctness and multiculturalism; Poverty and
dependency

Watts, Dr. Emily S.
Professor of English, Department of English
University of Illinois at Urbana-Champaign
608 South Wright Street, 208 English
Building
Urbana, IL 61801
217-352-0636   fax 217-356-5753
Issues: Arts, humanities and historic resources;
Higher education; Religion and public life

*Weatherman, Dr. Donald V.
Vice President and Dean of the College
Erskine College
Two Washington Street
Due West, SC 29639-6696
864-379-8873   fax 864-379-2167
weatherman@erskine.edu
Issues: The American Founding; American
history/political tradition; Campaign finance
reform; Citizenship and civil society; Electoral
reform/voting rights; Ethics; Higher
education; Political philosophy

*Weber, Kurt T.
Vice President
Cascade Policy Institute
813 S.W. Alder Street, Suite 450
Portland, OR 97205
503-242-0900   fax 503-242-3822
kurt@cascadepolicy.org
Issues: Advocacy and nonprofit public funding;
Health care reform; Privatization/
Contracting-out

*Weber, Walter M.
Senior Litigation Counsel
American Center for Law and Justice
1650 Diagonal Road, Suite 500
Alexandria, VA 22314
703-740-1450   fax 703-837-8510
wmweber@aclj-dc.org
Issues: Church-state relations; Constitutional
law; Free Speech; Judicial activism/judicial
reform; Religion and public life; Religious
freedom; School choice

Weeks, Dr. David L.
Dean and Professor, College of Liberal Arts
and Sciences
Azusa Pacific University
901 East Alosta Avenue
Azusa, CA 91702
626-969-3434   fax 626-815-3879
dweeks@apu.edu
Issues: Church-state relations; Religion and
public life; Religious freedom

Wegner, Nona
Executive Director
Citizens for Better Medicare
P. O. Box 34337
Washington, DC 20043
202-872-8627   fax 703-560-8821
nona@bettermedicare.org
Issues: Aging/elder care; Health care reform;
Medicare

*Weidenbaum, Dr. Murray
Honorary Chairman
Weidenbaum Center
Washington University, Campus Box 1027
St. Louis, MO 63130
314-935-5662   fax 314-935-5688
Issues: Agriculture; Air; Anti-trust; China;
Climate change; Costs and benefits of
regulation; Davis-Bacon Act; Defense budget;
Discretionary spending; Economic education;
Economic forecasting; The Economy;
Electricity deregulation; Energy;
Entrepreneurship/free enterprise;
Environmental regulation; Executive Branch/
The Presidency; Export controls/military
transfers; Federal budget; Federalism;
Homeland security/civil defense; Japan; Korea;
Labor and employment; Minimum wage;
Money and financial services; OSHA; The
Reagan legacy; Regulatory reform; Risk
assessment; Social Security and retirement;
Southeast Asia (including Burma, Cambodia,
Laos, Vietnam, Singapore, Malaysia, Indonesia,
the Philippines, Australia, and New Zealand);
Taxation/tax reform; Terrorism and
international crime; Trade; Transportation
deregulation; Unions; Western Europe

*Weigel, George
Senior Fellow
Ethics and Public Policy Center
1015 15th Street, N.W., Suite 900
Washington, DC 20005
202-682-1200   fax 202-408-0632
Issues: Church-state relations; Ethics; Human
rights; Political philosophy; Religion and
public life; Religious freedom

*Weil, Dr. Rolf A.
President Emeritus
Roosevelt University
439 South Michigan Avenue
Chicago, IL 60605
312-341-4330   fax 312-341-6487
Issues: Bilingual education; Economic
development/foreign aid; Economic theory;
Federal budget; Higher education; Middle
East; School choice; Social Security and
retirement; Standards, curriculum, and testing;
State and local public finance; Western Europe

*Weinrod, W. Bruce
Managing Director and General Counsel
International Technology and Trade
Associates, Inc.
1330 Connecticut Avenue, N.W., Suite 210
Washington, DC 20036
202-828-2614   fax 202-828-2617
bweinrod@itta.com
Issues: American diplomacy/foreign policy;
Arms control; International organizations
(European Union, OECD, etc.); Japan; Missile
defense; NATO and other alliances; Promoting
democracy/public diplomacy; Western Europe

*Weinstein, Dr. Kenneth
Vice President and Director, Washington
Office
Hudson Institute
1015 18th Street, N.W., Suite 300
Washington, DC 20036
202-974-2404   fax 202-223-8537
ken@hudsondc.org
Issues: Campaign finance reform; Canada;
Elections/polling; Middle East; Political
philosophy; Unions; Western Europe

*Weintraub, Dr. Sidney
William Simon Chair in Political Economy
Center for Strategic and International
Studies
1800 K Street, N.W., Suite 400
Washington, DC 20006
202-775-3292   fax 202-466-4739
sweintraub@csis.org
Issues: Canada; Economic development/
foreign aid; International finance and
multilateral banks; Latin America; Mexico

Weiss, Daniel
Pornography Policy Analyst, Social Research
and Cultural Affairs
Focus on the Family
8605 Explorer Drive
Colorado Springs, CO 80920
719-548-5998   fax 719-531-3385
weissdl@fotf.org
Issues: Media and popular culture; Religion and
public life

Weller, Nick
Education Policy Analyst
Cascade Policy Institute
813 S.W. Alder Street, Suite 450
Portland, OR 97205
503-242-0900   fax 503-242-3822
nick@cascadepolicy.org
Issues: Charter schools; Home schooling; Public
school finance and administration; School
choice; Standards, curriculum, and testing

Wellman, Dr. Christopher Heath
Director, Jean Beer Blumenfeld Center for
Ethics, and Associate Professor, Department
of Philosophy
Georgia State University
P. O. Box 4089
Atlanta, GA 30302-4089
404-651-0718   fax 404-651-1563
cwellman@gsu.edu
Issues: Citizenship and civil society; Ethics;
Immigration; Political philosophy

*Wenzel, Nikolai
Director of Academic Programs
Atlas Economic Research Foundation
4084 University Drive, Suite 103
Fairfax, VA 22030
703-934-6969   fax 703-352-7530
nikolai.wenzel@atlasusa.org
Issues: Higher education; Immigration

Wessels, Dr. Walter J.
Professor
North Carolina State University
4106 Nelson Hall, Box 8110
Raleigh, NC 27695
919-513-2879   fax 919-515-7873
walt_wessels@ncsu.edu
Issues: Minimum wage; Right to work; Unions

West, Dr. John G.
Senior Fellow
Discovery Institute
1402 Third Avenue, Suite 400
Seattle, WA 98101
206-281-2162   fax 206-682-5320
jwest@spu.edu
Issues: Church-state relations; Constitutional
law; Faith-based and volunteer initiatives;
Religion and public life; Religious freedom;
Sound science

West, Dr. Thomas G.
Professor of Politics
University of Dallas
1845 East Northgate Drive
Irving, TX 75062
972-721-5278   fax 972-721-4007
tomwest@acad.udallas.edu
Issues: American history/political tradition;
Campaign finance reform; Citizenship and civil
society; Civil rights/racial preferences;
Constitutional law; Family and children;
Immigration; Marriage and divorce; Political
philosophy; Poverty and dependency; Religion
and public life; Welfare/welfare reform

*Weyrich, Paul
President
Free Congress Foundation
717 Second Street, N.E.
Washington, DC 20002
202-546-3000   fax 202-543-5605
info@freecongress.org
Issues: Advocacy and nonprofit public funding;
American history/political tradition;
Campaign finance reform; Citizenship and civil
society; Congress; Conservative thought;
Elections/polling; Ethics; Executive Branch/
The Presidency; Home schooling; Intellectual
property; Media and popular culture; Political
correctness and multiculturalism; Political
philosophy; Privacy; Promoting democracy/
public diplomacy; The Reagan legacy; Russia
and Eurasia

Whalen, Prof. David M.
Associate Professor of English
Hillsdale College
33 East College Street
Hillsdale, MI 49242
517-437-7341   fax 517-607-2208
david.whalen@hillsdale.edu
Issues: Conservative thought; Higher
education; Religion and public life; Standards,
curriculum, and testing

*Whelan, Dr. Elizabeth M.
President
American Council on Science and Health
1995 Broadway, 2nd Floor
New York, NY 10023
212-362-7044   fax 212-362-4919
whelan@acsh.org
Issues: Environmental education;
Environmental regulation; Free-market
environmentalism; Sound science

Whisker, Dr. James Biser
Professor of Political Science
West Virginia University
Box 6317
Morgantown, WV 26506
304-293-3811   fax 304-293-8644
whisker@wvu.edu
Issues: Comparative government; Conservative
thought; Ethics; Political philosophy; Second
Amendment

White, Dana
International Communications Associate
and Director, Washington Roundtable for
Asia-Pacific Press
The Heritage Foundation
214 Massachusetts Avenue, N.E.
Washington, DC 20002
202-608-6153
Issues: China; Promoting democracy/public
diplomacy

*White, Dr. Lawrence H.
Hayek Chair in Economic History,
Department of Economics
University of Missouri, St. Louis
408 Social Sciences Building
St. Louis, MO 63121-4499
314-516-6129   fax 314-516-5352
lwhite@umsl.edu
Issues: Economic theory; Money and financial
services

Whitehead, Dr. Barbara Dafoe
15 Forest Edge Road
Amherst, MA 01002
413-549-6112   fax 413-549-1835
Issues: Family and children

*Whitehead, John W.
President
The Rutherford Institute
P. O. Box 7482
Charlottesville, VA 22906
434-978-3888   fax 434-978-1789
staff@rutherford.org
Issues: The American Founding; American
history/political tradition; Arts, humanities
and historic resources; Church-state relations;
Civil rights/racial preferences; Constitutional
law; Faith-based and volunteer initiatives; Free
Speech; Homeland security/civil defense;
Intelligence gathering and covert operations;
Judiciary; Media and popular culture; Religion
and public life; Religious freedom

*Whitehurst, Dr. Clinton H., Jr.
Transportation and Defense Studies, Strom
Thurmond Institute
Clemson University
Perimeter Road
Clemson, SC 29634-0125
864-656-4700   fax 864-656-4780
clinton@clemson.edu
Issues: Defense budget; Homeland security/
civil defense; NATO and other alliances;
Transportation; Transportation deregulation

Whitelaw, Dr. Robert
Professor Emeritus, Nuclear and Mechanical
Engineering
Virginia Polytechnic Institute and State
University
111 Alleghany Street
Blacksburg, VA 24060
540-552-2422   fax 540-231-9100
Issues: Air; China; Energy; Environmental
education; Higher education; Missile defense

*Whitley, Joe D., Esq.
Alston & Bird LLP
1201 West Peachtreet Street
Atlanta, GA 30309-3424
404-881-7657   fax 404-881-7777
jwhitley@alston.com
Issues: Corrections and sentencing; Criminal
law and procedure; Immigration

Whitlock, John
President
The Family Foundation of Virginia
3900 Gaskins Road
Richmond, VA 23233
804-330-8331   fax 804-330-8337
vafamily@familyfoundation.org
Issues: Family and children

Whittington, Dr. Keith E.
Associate Professor, Department of Politics
Princeton University
Corwin Hall
Princeton, NJ 08544
609-258-3453   fax 609-258-4772
kewhitt@princeton.edu
Issues: The American Founding; American
history/political tradition; Constitutional law;
Judicial activism/judicial reform; Judiciary

Wielhouwer, Peter W., Ph.D.
Associate Professor, Robertson School of
Government
Regent University
1000 Regent University Drive
Virginia Beach, VA 23464
757-226-4303   fax 757-226-4735
petewie@regent.edu
Issues: Citizenship and civil society; Elections/
polling; Religion and public life

Wildmon, Donald
Executive Director
American Family Association
P. O. Drawer 2440
Tupelo, MS 38803
662-844-5036   fax 662-844-9176
Issues: Family and children; Media and popular
culture; Religion and public life

*Wilensky, Gail
Senior Fellow
Project HOPE
7500 Old Georgetown Road, Suite 600
Bethesda, MD 20814
301-656-7401   fax 301-654-0629
gwilensky@projecthope.org
Issues: Aging/elder care; Government health
programs; Health care reform; Medicaid;
Medicare

Williams, Alvin
President and CEO
Black America's PAC
2029 P Street, N.W., Suite 202
Washington, DC 20036
202-785-9619   fax 202-785-9621
bampac@bampac.org
Issues: Political philosophy; Religious freedom;
School choice; Second Amendment; Social
Security and retirement; Wealth creation/
financial empowerment

---

* Has testified before a state or federal legislative committee

*Williams, Bob
President
Evergreen Freedom Foundation
P. O. Box 552
Olympia, WA 98507
360-956-3482   fax 360-352-1874
effwa@effwa.org
Issues: Campaign finance reform; Davis-Bacon Act; Education unions and interest groups; Government waste; Health care reform; Initiative and referendum; International tax policy/tax competition; Medicaid; Privatization/Contracting-out; Public school finance and administration; Regulation through litigation; Regulatory reform; Right to work; School choice; State and local public finance; Taxation/tax reform; Unemployment insurance; Unfunded mandates; Unions

*Williams, Adm. J. D.
Vice Admiral, USN (Ret.)
Williams Associates International, Inc.
1111 A North Stuart Street
Arlington, VA 22201
703-312-0785   fax 703-312-0785
vadmjdw@aol.com
Issues: Defense budget; Emerging threats/threat assessment; Homeland security/civil defense; Intelligence gathering and covert operations; Military strategy; Missile defense

*Williams, Natalie
Attorney
Robinson, DiLando and Whitaker
7801 Folsom Boulevard, Suite 300
Sacramento, CA 95825
916-386-0743   fax 916-386-0687
nwilliams@rdwlaw.com
Issues: Abstinence and out-of-wedlock births; Adoption, foster care, & child care services; Business and education partnerships; Church-state relations; Constitutional law; Family and children; Home schooling; Privacy; Religion and public life; School-to-work; Standards, curriculum, and testing

Williams, Russell
President
Jefferson Center for Character Education
P. O. Box 4137
Mission Viejo, CA 92690-4137
949-770-7602   fax 949-450-1100
centerjcce@aol.com
Issues: Citizenship and civil society; Family and children

Williams, Dr. Walter E.
John M. Olin Distinguished Professor of Economics
George Mason University
4400 University Drive, MSN 3G4
Fairfax, VA 22030
703-993-1148   fax 703-993-1133
wwilliam@gmu.edu
Issues: The American Founding; Congress; Costs and benefits of regulation; Davis-Bacon Act; Economic theory; The Economy; Labor and employment; Minimum wage

*Williamson, Hon. Edwin D.
Sullivan & Cromwell
1701 Pennsylvania Avenue, N.W., 8th Floor
Washington, DC 20006
202-956-7505   fax 202-956-7651
williamsone@sullcrom.com
Issues: American diplomacy/foreign policy; Executive Branch/The Presidency; International law; International organizations (European Union, OECD, etc.); Money and financial services; Terrorism and international crime; Trade; United Nations

*Williamson, Ron F.
President
Great Plains Public Policy Institute
P. O. Box 88138
Sioux Falls, SD 57109
605-332-2641   fax 605-731-0043
ron.williamson@greatplainsppi.org
Issues: Agriculture; Energy; Forestry and national parks; Higher education; Public school finance and administration; State and local government; State and local public finance; Taxation/tax reform; Trade

*Willke, John C., M.D.
President
Life Issues Institute, Inc.
1821 West Galbraith Road
Cincinnati, OH 45239
513-729-3600   fax 513-729-3636
info@lifeissues.org
Issues: Abstinence and out-of-wedlock births; Adoption, foster care, & child care services; China; Congress; Elections/polling; Electoral reform/voting rights; Faith-based and volunteer initiatives; Family and children; Human rights; Initiative and referendum; International organizations (European Union, OECD, etc.); Marriage and divorce; Media and popular culture; Non-governmental organizations; Religion and public life; United Nations; Western Europe

Willson, Dr. John
Salvatori Professor of History and
Traditional Values
Hillsdale College
33 East College Street
Hillsdale, MI 49242
517-437-7341   fax 517-437-3923
Issues: Family and children

Wilson, Bradford P.
Lecturer in Politics, Princeton University
and Executive Director
National Association of Scholars
221 Witherspoon Street, 2nd Floor
Princeton, NJ 08542-3215
609-683-7878   fax 609-683-0316
wilson@nas.org
Issues: The American Founding; American
history/political tradition; Arts, humanities
and historic resources; Higher education;
Judiciary; Political correctness and
multiculturalism; Political philosophy;
Standards, curriculum, and testing

Wilson, Dr. Clyde N.
Professor of History, Department of History
University of South Carolina
Columbia, SC 29208
803-777-4580   Clyde-Wilson@sc.edu
Issues: Arts, humanities and historic resources;
Federalism; Political philosophy; Religion and
public life

Wilson, Dr. James Q.
Ronald Reagan Professor of Public Policy
Pepperdine University
24255 Pacific Coast Highway
Malibu, CA 90263-7490
310-506-7490   fax 310-506-7494
Issues: Crime/crime statistics; Energy; Ethics;
Executive Branch/The Presidency; Federal
civil service; Police; State and local government

Windels, Catherine
Board Member, Centre for the New Europe
and Director of Policy Communications
Pfizer, Inc.
235 East 42nd Street, 11th Floor
New York, NY 10017
212-573-7437   fax 212-338-1949
catherine.windels@pfizer.com
Issues: Government health programs; Health
care reform; Western Europe

Wirthlin, Richard B.
Chairman
Wirthlin Worldwide
406 West South Jordan Parkway, Suite 550
South Jordan, UT 84095
801-523-2553   fax 801-523-2713
rwirthlin@wirthlin.com
Issues: Economic theory; Faith-based and
volunteer initiatives; Family and children;
Home schooling; Marriage and divorce;
Political correctness and multiculturalism;
Religion and public life; Religious freedom;
School choice

*Witcher, Phyllis H.
President
Protecting Marriage, Inc.
2304 Riddle Avenue
Wilmington, DE 19806
302-655-7764   fax 302-652-4039
phyllaw@conectiv.net
Issues: Family and children; Marriage and
divorce; Public interest law

Witkowsky, Anne A.
Senior Fellow, Technology and Public Policy
Program
Center for Strategic and International
Studies
1800 K Street, N.W., Suite 400
Washington, DC 20006
202-775-3291   fax 202-775-3199
awitkowsky@csis.org
Issues: American diplomacy/foreign policy;
Arms control; Homeland security/civil
defense; Russia and Eurasia; Sound science;
Western Europe

Witt, Dr. James W.
Professor, Department of Government
University of West Florida
11000 University Parkway
Pensacola, FL 32514
850-473-2725   fax 850-473-7001
jwitt@uwf.edu
Issues: Congress; Elections/polling; Initiative
and referendum; Police; Political correctness
and multiculturalism; School choice; Term
limits

---

*Wohl, Dr. Lawrence
Professor of Economics and Management,
Department of Economics
Gustavus Adolphus College
800 West College Avenue
St. Peter, MN 56082
507-933-7453   fax 507-933-6032
law@gac.edu
Issues: Anti-trust; Economic theory; Job
training/welfare to work; Labor and
employment; Minimum wage; School-to-work;
Unemployment insurance

Wohlstetter, John
Senior Fellow
Discovery Institute
700 New Hampshire Avenue, N.W.
Number 604
Washington, DC 200.7
202-965-2857   fax 206-682-5320
wohlstetter@discovery.org
Issues: Telecommunications and the Internet

*Wolf, Dr. Charles, Jr.
Senior Economic Advisor and Corporate
Fellow in International Economics
RAND
1700 Main Street, P. O. Box 2138
Santa Monica, CA 90407-2138
310-451-6926   fax 310-451-6972
wolf@rand.org
Issues: China; Defense budget; Economic
development/foreign aid; Economic
forecasting; Emerging threats/threat
assessment; Japan; Korea; Military strategy;
Northeast Asia; Russia and Eurasia; Southeast
Asia (including Burma, Cambodia, Laos,
Vietnam, Singapore, Malaysia, Indonesia, the
Philippines, Australia, and New Zealand);
Trade; Western Europe

Wolfe, Betty Jean
President
Urban Family Council
P. O. Box 11415
Philadephia, PA 19111
215-663-9494   fax 215-663-9444
bjwolfe@urbanfamily.org
Issues: Abstinence and out-of-wedlock births;
Faith-based and volunteer initiatives; Family
and children; Marriage and divorce; School
choice

*Wolfe, Dr. Christopher
President, American Public Philosophy
Institute
Marquette University
P. O. Box 1881
Milwaukee, WI 53201-1881
414-288-6841   fax 414-288-3360
christopher.wolfe@marquette.edu
Issues: The American Founding; Church-state
relations; Constitutional law; Ethics; Family and
children; Judicial activism/judicial reform;
Judiciary; Marriage and divorce; Political
philosophy; Religion and public life; Religious
freedom

*Wolfram, Dr. Gary
George Munson Professor of Political
Economy
Hillsdale College
33 East College Street
Hillsdale, MI 49242
517-437-7341   fax 517-437-3923
gary.wolfram@hillsdale.edu
Issues: Charter schools; Economic theory;
Higher education; Political philosophy; Public
school finance and administration; Regulatory
reform; School choice; School-to-work; State
and local government; State and local public
finance; Taxation/tax reform

Wolfson, Adam
Executive Editor
The Public Interest
1112 16th Street, N.W., Suite 140
Washington, DC 20036
202-785-8555   fax 202-785-8441
Issues: The American Founding; American
history/political tradition; Church-state
relations; Conservative thought; Political
philosophy; Religious freedom

Wood, Genevieve
Vice President, Communications
Family Research Council
801 G Street, N.W.
Washington, DC 20001
202-393-2100   fax 202-393-2134
gew@frc.org
Issues: Media and popular culture; Political
correctness and multiculturalism

*Wood, Kenneth
Executive Director
The Oklahoma Christian Coalition
4604 N.W. 60th Street
Oklahoma City, OK 73122
405-773-3344   fax 405-773-9798
okcc@tds.net
Issues: Abstinence and out-of-wedlock births;
Adoption, foster care, & child care services;
Faith-based and volunteer initiatives; Family
and children; Marriage and divorce; Religion
and public life; State-sponsored gambling

*Wood, Thomas
President
Americans Against Discrimination and
Preferences
1535 Addison Street, Apartment A
Berkley, CA 94703
510-548-4619   fax 925-934-4917
aadap@aadap.org
Issues: Civil rights/racial preferences; Higher
education; Initiative and referendum

Woodiwiss, Dr. Ashley
Professor, Department of Political Science
Wheaton College
Wheaton, IL 60187
630-752-5878   fax 630-752-7037
Ashley.Woodiwiss@wheaton.edu
Issues: Religion and public life

*Woodson, Robert L., Sr.
President
National Center for Neighborhood
Enterprise
1424 16th Street, N.W., Suite 300
Washington, DC 20036
202-518-6500   fax 202-588-0314
info@ncne.com
Issues: Adoption, foster care, & child care
services; Citizenship and civil society; Davis-
Bacon Act; Faith-based and volunteer
initiatives; Family and children; Housing and
homelessness; Job training/welfare to work;
Juvenile justice; Non-governmental
organizations; Political correctness and
multiculturalism; Poverty and dependency;
Regulatory reform; Religion and public life;
School choice; Social Security and retirement;
Substance abuse; Wealth creation/financial
empowerment; Welfare/welfare reform

Wooster, Martin Morse
President
Northfeld Assocaties
P. O. Box 8093
Silver Spring, MD 20907
301-565-7820   fax 301-565-7820
Issues: Philanthropy

*Worcester, Robert O. C.
Executive Director
Maryland Business for Responsive
Government
10 Light Street, Suite 300-B
Baltimore, MD 21202
410-547-1295   fax 410-539-3126
mbrg@erols.com
Issues: Davis-Bacon Act; Economic education;
Education unions and interest groups; Health
care reform; Right to work; Tort and liability
reform

Wortham, Dr. Anne
Associate Professor, Department of
Sociology
Illinois State University
Campus Box 4660
Normal, IL 61761
309-438-8359   fax 309-438-5378
awortha@ilstu.edu
Issues: The American Founding; American
history/political tradition; Arts, humanities
and historic resources; Citizenship and civil
society; Civil rights/racial preferences;
Conservative thought; Ethics; Family and
children; Higher education; Media and
popular culture; Political correctness and
multiculturalism; Political philosophy; School
choice; Standards, curriculum, and testing

*Wortzel, Dr. Larry
Vice President and Director, Kathryn and
Shelby Cullom Davis Institute for
International Studies
The Heritage Foundation
214 Massachusetts Avenue, N.E.
Washington, DC 20002
202-608-6081   fax 202-675-1779
larry.wortzel@heritage.org
Issues: American diplomacy/foreign policy;
Arms control; China; Comparative
government; Defense budget; Emerging
threats/threat assessment; Export controls/
military transfers; Homeland security/civil
defense; Human rights; Intelligence gathering
and covert operations; Japan; Korea; Military
strategy; Missile defense; NATO and other
alliances; Northeast Asia; Peacekeeping;
Political philosophy; Promoting democracy/
public diplomacy; South Asia (including India
and Pakistan); Southeast Asia (including
Burma, Cambodia, Laos, Vietnam, Singapore,
Malaysia, Indonesia, the Philippines, Australia,
and New Zealand); Terrorism and
international crime; United Nations

Wright, Dr. Frank
Director
Center for Christian Statesmanship
214 Massachusetts Avenue, N.E., Suite 220
Washington, DC 20002
202-547-3052   fax 202-547-3287
wright@statesman.org
Issues: Citizenship and civil society; Religion
and public life

Wright, Jason
Vice President
Frontiers of Freedom Institute
12011 Lee Jackson Memorial Highway, Suite
310
Fairfax, VA 22033
703-246-0110   fax 703-246-0129
jwright@ff.org
Issues: Anti-trust; Campaign finance reform;
Church-state relations; Defense budget;
Economic development/foreign aid;
Elections/polling; Energy; Entrepreneurship/
free enterprise; Family and medical leave;
Federal education policy; Free-market
environmentalism; Government waste;
Homeland security/civil defense; Intellectual
property; Judicial activism/judicial reform;
Minimum wage; Missile defense; Property
rights; Public school finance and
administration; Regulation through litigation;
Religious freedom; Right to work; Second
Amendment; Sound science; State and local
government; Taxation/tax reform;
Telecommunications and the Internet; Urban
sprawl/livable cities; Wildlife management/
endangered species

*Wright, Wendy
Senior Policy Director
Concerned Women for America
1015 15th Street, N.W., Suite 1100
Washington, DC 20005
202-488-7000   fax 202-488-0806
wwright@cwfa.org
Issues: United Nations

Wunder, Dr. Gene C.
Professor, School of Business
Washburn University
1700 S.W. College Avenue
Topeka, KS 66621
785-231-1010   fax 785-231-1063
gcwunder@washburn.edu
Issues: Anti-trust; The Economy; Government
health programs; Health care reform;
Medicare; Money and financial services

Wurmser, Meyrav
Senior Fellow and Director, Center for
Middle East Policy
Hudson Institute
1015 18th Street, N.W., Suite 300
Washington, DC 20036
202-223-7770   fax 202-223-8537
info@hudsondc.org
Issues: Middle East

Wyrick, Dr. Thomas L.
Professor, Department of Economics
Southwest Missouri State University
901 South National Avenue
Springfield, MO 65804
417-836-5060   fax 417-836-8472
twyrick@earthlink.net
Issues: The Economy; Money and financial
services; The Reagan legacy

Yandle, Dr. Bruce
Professor of Economics, Economics
Department
Clemson University
Clemson, SC 29634
864-656-3970   fax 864-656-4192
yandle@clemson.edu
Issues: Air; Costs and benefits of regulation;
Property rights; Regulatory reform; Risk
assessment; Water

Yeager, Dr. Leland
Professor Emeritus of Economics
Auburn University
415 West Magnolia Avenue
Auburn, AL 36849
334-844-4910   fax 334-844-4615
yeagele@auburn.edu
Issues: Trade

*Yelich, Chris
Executive Director
Education Industry Association
104 West Main Street, Suite 101, P. O. Box
348
Watertown, WI 53094-0348
800-252-3280   fax 920-206-1875
cyelich@aepp.org
Issues: Business and education partnerships;
Charter schools; Education unions and interest
groups; School choice

*Yoest, Charmaine Crouse
Author and Mellon, Bradley and Olin Fellow
University of Virginia
1642 Oxford Road
Charlottesville, VA 22903-1330
434-963-7925   fax 434-963-7930
cc62c@virginia.edu
Issues: Abstinence and out-of-wedlock births;
Adoption, foster care, & child care services;
Family and children; Marriage and divorce;
Media and popular culture; Readiness and
manpower; The Reagan legacy; Welfare/
welfare reform

Yoo, John
Professor of Law, Boalt Hall School of Law
University of California, Berkeley
890 Simon Hall
Berkeley, CA 94720
510-643-5089   fax 510-642-3728
yooj@law.berkeley.edu
Issues: American history/political tradition;
Arms control; Civil rights/racial preferences;
Congress; Constitutional law; Executive
Branch/The Presidency; Federalism; Human
rights; Judicial activism/judicial reform;
Judiciary; NATO and other alliances;
Peacekeeping; United Nations

Young, Dr. James V.
629 N.E. Lake Pointe Drive
Lee's Summit, MO 64064-1193
816-478-6539   jimging@hotmail.com
Issues: Church-state relations; Civil rights/racial
preferences; Congress; Constitutional law;
Elections/polling; Executive Branch/The
Presidency; Federal budget; Federalism;
Initiative and referendum; Judicial activism/
judicial reform; Judiciary; State and local
government; State and local public finance;
Term limits

*Young, Dr. Michael K.
Dean and Lobingier Professor of
Comparative Law and Jurisprudence
George Washington University Law School
2000 H Street, N.W., Room L102
Washington, DC 20052
202-994-6288   fax 202-994-5157
myoung@main.nlc.gwu.edu
Issues: Afghanistan; American diplomacy/
foreign policy; Business and education
partnerships; China; Church-state relations;
Comparative government; Economic
development/foreign aid; Environmental
education; Faith-based and volunteer
initiatives; Higher education; Human rights;
International law; International organizations
(European Union, OECD, etc.); Japan;
Judiciary; Korea; Non-governmental
organizations; Northeast Asia; Promoting
democracy/public diplomacy; Religion and
public life; Religious freedom; Terrorism and
international crime; Trade; Western Europe

---

*Young, Todd G.
Research and Communications Director
Southeastern Legal Foundation
3340 Peachtree Road, N.E., Suite 2515
Atlanta, GA 30326
404-365-8500   fax 404-365-0017
todd@dminews.com

Issues: Advocacy and nonprofit public funding;
Constitutional law; Federal budget; Free
Speech; Immigration; Judicial activism/
judicial reform; Media and popular culture;
Public interest law; Religious freedom; Tort
and liability reform

*Young, W. James
Staff Attorney
National Right to Work Legal Defense
Foundation
8001 Braddock Road, Suite 600
Springfield, VA 22160
703-321-8510   fax 703-321-9319
wjy@nrtw.org

Issues: Campaign finance reform;
Constitutional law; Labor and employment;
Right to work; Unions

Younkins, Dr. Edward W.
Professor of Accountancy and Business
Administration, Department of Business and
Technology
Wheeling Jesuit University
316 Washington Avenue
Wheeling, WV 26003
304-243-2255   fax 304-243-8703
younkins@wju.edu

Issues: Anti-trust; Citizenship and civil society;
Costs and benefits of regulation; Economic
education; The Economy; Entrepreneurship/
free enterprise; Ethics; Faith-based and
volunteer initiatives; Free-market
environmentalism; Higher education; Labor
and employment; Media and popular culture;
Political correctness and multiculturalism;
Political philosophy; Privatization/
Contracting-out; Property rights; Religion and
public life; Right to work; Stewardship; Unions

Yu, Dr. George T.
Director, Center for East Asian Studies
University of Illinois
910 South Fifth Street
Champaign, IL 61820
217-333-4850   fax 217-244-5729
g-yu@uiuc.edu

Issues: China; Comparative economics;
Comparative government; Economic
development/foreign aid; International
organizations (European Union, OECD, etc.);
Northeast Asia; Promoting democracy/public
diplomacy; Southeast Asia (including Burma,
Cambodia, Laos, Vietnam, Singapore,
Malaysia, Indonesia, the Philippines, Australia,
and New Zealand)

Zambone, Jennifer
Associate Director, Regulatory Studies
Program
Mercatus Center at George Mason University
3301 North Fairfax Drive, Suite 450
Arlington, VA 22201-4432
703-993-4932   fax 703-993-4935
jzambone@gmu.edu

Issues: Environmental regulation; Regulation
through litigation; Regulatory reform; Risk
assessment; Sound science

Zandstra, Dr. Jerry
Director of Programs
Acton Institute for the Study of Religion and
Liberty
161 Ottawa Avenue, N.W., Suite 301
Grand Rapids, MI 49503
616-454-3080   fax 616-454-9454
jzandstra@acton.org

Issues: Africa; Church-state relations;
Citizenship and civil society;
Entrepreneurship/free enterprise; Faith-based
and volunteer initiatives; Latin America;
Philanthropy; Property rights; Religion and
public life; Religious freedom; Trade

Zanotti, David
President
Ohio Roundtable
11288 Alameda Drive
Strongsville, OH 44149
440-349-3393   fax 440-349-0154
ohroundtab@aol.com

Issues: Business and education partnerships;
Elections/polling; Home schooling; Initiative
and referendum; School choice; Taxation/tax
reform; Term limits

Zeckhauser, Dr. Richard
Frank Plumpton Ramsey Professor of
Political Economy, Kennedy School of
Government
Harvard University
Littauer Center 312
Cambridge, MA 02138
617-495-1174   fax 617-496-3783
Issues: Costs and benefits of regulation; Health
care reform; Risk assessment; Sound science

Zhou, Dr. Kate Xiao
Graduate Faculty
University of Hawaii
2424 Maile Way, 634-A Porteus Hall
Honolulu, HI 96822-2281
808-956-8777   fax 808-956-6877
katezhou@hawaii.edu
Issues: The American Founding; American
history/political tradition; China;
Entrepreneurship/free enterprise; Japan;
School choice

*Zill, Dr. Nicholas
Westat Inc.
1650 Research Boulevard
Rockville, MD 20850
301-294-4448   fax 240-453-2650
zilln1@westat.com
Issues: Family and children; Federal education
policy; Marriage and divorce; Poverty and
dependency; Standards, curriculum, and
testing; Welfare/welfare reform

Zimmerer, Dr. Thomas W.
Dean, School of Business
Saint Leo University
MC 2067, 33701 State Road 52
Saint Leo, FL 33574-6665
352-588-8426   fax 352-588-8912
tom.zimmerer@saintleo.edu
Issues: Entrepreneurship/free enterprise

Zimmerman, Dr. Jerold L.
Alumni Distinguished Professor, William E.
Simon Graduate School of Business
University of Rochester
CS3-160D Carol Simon Hall
Rochester, NY 14627
585-275-3397   fax 585-442-6323
Zimmerman@simon.rochester.edu
Issues: The Economy; Taxation/tax reform

Zimmerman, Malia
Co-Founder
Grassroot Institute of Hawaii
1020-D Aoloa Place, Suite 401B
Kailua, HI 96734
808-388-5088   fax 808-396-1726
maliamz@aol.com
Issues: Media and popular culture

Zinsmeister, Karl
Editor in Chief, *The American Enterprise*
American Enterprise Institute
23 Hurd Street
Cazenovia, NY 13035
315-655-1033   fax 315-655-3893
Issues: Citizenship and civil society; The
Economy; Family and children

*Zuckert, Dr. Catherine
Professor, Department of Government
University of Notre Dame
350 Decio Hall
Notre Dame, IN 46556
219-631-6620   fax 219-631-8209
Issues: American history/political tradition;
Conservative thought; Political philosophy

Zuckert, Dr. Michael
Professor, Department of Government
University of Notre Dame
450 Decio Hall
Notre Dame, IN 46556
574-631-8050   fax 574-631-8209
zuckert.1@nd.edu
Issues: The American Founding; American
history/political tradition; Conservative
thought; Ethics; Higher education; Political
philosophy

Zumbrun, Ronald A.
Managing Attorney
The Zumbrun Law Firm
3800 Watt Avenue, Suite 101
Sacramento, CA 95821
916-486-5900   fax 916-486-5959
zfirm@aol.com

Issues: Advocacy and nonprofit public funding;
Agriculture; Air; Charter schools; Church-state
relations; Civil rights/racial preferences;
Conservative thought; Constitutional law; Costs
and benefits of regulation; Energy;
Environmental regulation; Federalism;
Forestry and national parks; Free Speech; Free-
market environmentalism; Infrastructure;
Judicial activism/judicial reform; Judiciary;
Land use; OSHA; Political correctness and
multiculturalism; Property rights; Public
interest law; The Reagan legacy; Regulation
through litigation; Regulatory reform;
Religious freedom; Right to work; School
choice; State and local government;
Stewardship; Taxation/tax reform; Tort and
liability reform; Transportation; Urban sprawl/
livable cities; Water; Welfare/welfare reform;
Wildlife management/endangered species

Zupan, Marty
President
Institute for Humane Studies at George
Mason University
3301 North Fairfax Drive, Suite 440
Arlington, VA 22201-4432
703-993-4880   fax 703-993-4890
mzupan@gmu.edu
Issues: Media and popular culture

U.S. Experts by Policy Area

Budget and Taxation

ADVOCACY AND NONPROFIT PUBLIC FUNDING

* Has testified before a state or federal legislative committee

ADVOCACY AND NONPROFIT PUBLIC FUNDING (Continued)

Bridgett G. Wagner, The Heritage Foundation, Washington, DC **(p. 286)**
*Kurt T. Weber, Cascade Policy Institute, Portland, OR **(p. 290)**
*Paul Weyrich, Free Congress Foundation, Washington, DC **(p. 293)**
*Todd G. Young, Southeastern Legal Foundation, Atlanta, GA **(p. 301)**
Ronald A. Zumbrun, The Zumbrun Law Firm, Sacramento, CA **(p. 303)**

DISCRETIONARY SPENDING

*John S. Barry, Tax Foundation, Washington, DC **(p. 46)**
*Bruce R. Bartlett, National Center for Policy Analysis, Great Falls, VA **(p. 46)**
*John E. Berthoud, National Taxpayers Union, Alexandria, VA **(p. 52)**
John F. Cogan, Hoover Institution, Stanford, CA **(p. 77)**
*C. W. Cowles, Central Michigan University, Midlothian, VA **(p. 84)**
Edward H. Crane, Cato Institute, Washington, DC **(p. 85)**
Richard S. Davis, Washington Research Council, Seattle, WA **(p. 89)**
*Carl DeMaio, Reason Foundation, Los Angeles, CA **(p. 92)**
Danielle Doane, The Heritage Foundation, Washington, DC **(p. 96)**
Christopher Edwards, Cato Institute, Washington, DC **(p. 104)**
*William Eggers, Deloitte Research-Public Sector, Washington, DC **(p. 104)**
*Ryan Ellis, Council for Government Reform, Arlington, VA **(p. 106)**
Peter Ferrara, International Center for Law and Economics, Washington, DC **(p. 110)**
Steven B. Frates, Claremont McKenna College, Claremont, CA **(p. 116)**
*Erick Gustafson, Citizens for a Sound Economy, Washington, DC **(p. 131)**
*Scott Hodge, Tax Foundation, Washington, DC **(p. 144)**
*Lawrence Hunter, Empower America, Washington, DC **(p. 149)**
Shawn Kantor, University of Arizona, Tucson, AZ **(p. 157)**
*Jack Kemp, Empower America, Washington, DC **(p. 161)**
Laurence Kotlikoff, Boston University, Boston, MA **(p. 168)**
George Krumbhaar, USBUDGET.COM, Washington, DC **(p. 170)**
*Lawrence Kudlow, Kudlow & Co., LLC, New York, NY **(p. 170)**
Arthur B. Laffer, A. B. Laffer Associates, San Diego, CA **(p. 172)**
Mary P. Mahoney, United Seniors Association, Inc., Washington, DC **(p. 187)**
*Adrian T. Moore, Reason Foundation, Los Angeles, CA **(p. 205)**
Stephen J. Moore, Club for Growth, Washington, DC **(p. 206)**
*Deroy Murdock, Atlas Economic Research Foundation, New York, NY **(p. 209)**
David Charles Nice, Washington State University, Pullman, WA **(p. 213)**
Sean Paige, Competitive Enterprise Institute, Washington, DC **(p. 220)**
*Nancy M. Pfotenhauer, Independent Women's Forum, Arlington, VA **(p. 227)**
Barry W. Poulson, University of Colorado, Boulder, CO **(p. 232)**
*Scott Pullins, Ohio Taxpayers Association and OTA Foundation, Columbus, OH **(p. 234)**
*Brian Riedl, The Heritage Foundation, Washington, DC **(p. 240)**
Llewellyn Rockwell, Jr., Ludwig von Mises Institute, Auburn, AL **(p. 242)**
Peter J. Saunders, Central Washington University, Ellensburg, WA **(p. 250)**
*Thomas A. Schatz, Citizens Against Government Waste, Washington, DC **(p. 252)**
*Geoffrey F. Segal, Reason Public Policy Institute, Los Angeles, CA **(p. 256)**
*Pete Sepp, National Taxpayers Union, Alexandria, VA **(p. 257)**
*C. Eugene Steuerle, Urban Institute, Washington, DC **(p. 268)**
*David Strom, Taxpayers League of Minnesota, Plymouth, MN **(p. 270)**
Michael D. Stroup, Stephen F. Austin State University, Nacogdoches, TX **(p. 270)**
Charles Stuart, University of California, Santa Barbara, Santa Barbara, CA **(p. 271)**
*Ronald Utt, The Heritage Foundation, Washington, DC **(p. 283)**
*Murray Weidenbaum, Weidenbaum Center, St. Louis, MO **(p. 291)**

ENTITLEMENT SPENDING

*John S. Barry, Tax Foundation, Washington, DC **(p. 46)**

ENTITLEMENT SPENDING (Continued)

*Bruce R. Bartlett, National Center for Policy Analysis, Great Falls, VA (p. 46)
*Naomi Lopez Bauman, Orlando, FL (p. 47)
*William W. Beach, The Heritage Foundation, Washington, DC (p. 48)
*John E. Berthoud, National Taxpayers Union, Alexandria, VA (p. 52)
*Victoria Craig Bunce, Council for Affordable Health Insurance,
    Inver Grove Heights, MN (p. 65)
*David Burton, Argus Group, Alexandria, VA (p. 66)
*Stuart Butler, The Heritage Foundation, Washington, DC (p. 66)
*Michael Carozza, Bristol-Myers Squibb, Washington, DC (p. 70)
 Kenneth W. Clarkson, University of Miami, Coral Gables, FL (p. 75)
 John F. Cogan, Hoover Institution, Stanford, CA (p. 77)
*C. W. Cowles, Central Michigan University, Midlothian, VA (p. 84)
 Edward H. Crane, Cato Institute, Washington, DC (p. 85)
*Carl DeMaio, Reason Foundation, Los Angeles, CA (p. 92)
 D. P. Diffine, Harding University, Searcy, AR (p. 95)
*William C. Dunkelberg, National Federation of Independent Business,
    Wynnewood, PA (p. 100)
 Christopher Edwards, Cato Institute, Washington, DC (p. 104)
 Isaac Ehrlich, State University of New York, Buffalo, Buffalo, NY (p. 105)
*Ryan Ellis, Council for Government Reform, Arlington, VA (p. 106)
*Eric M. Engen, American Enterprise Institute, Washington, DC (p. 107)
*Stephen Entin, Institute for Research on the Economics of Taxation, Washington, DC (p. 107)
 Peter Ferrara, International Center for Law and Economics, Washington, DC (p. 110)
 Marilyn R. Flowers, Ball State University, Muncie, IN (p. 113)
*Tom Giovanetti, Institute for Policy Innovation, Lewisville, TX (p. 124)
*Erick Gustafson, Citizens for a Sound Economy, Washington, DC (p. 131)
*Roberta Herzberg, Utah State University, Logan, UT (p. 141)
*Scott Hodge, Tax Foundation, Washington, DC (p. 144)
*John MacDonald Hood, John Locke Foundation, Raleigh, NC (p. 145)
*Lawrence Hunter, Empower America, Washington, DC (p. 149)
 Dennis S. Ippolito, Southern Methodist University, Dallas, TX (p. 152)
 Thomas Ivancie, America's Future Foundation, Washington, DC (p. 152)
*Charles W. Jarvis, United Seniors Association, Fairfax, VA (p. 153)
*W. Thomas Kelly, Savers and Investors League, Mirror Lake, NH (p. 161)
*Jack Kemp, Empower America, Washington, DC (p. 161)
 Kent King, Missouri State Teachers Association, Columbia, MO (p. 164)
 Laurence Kotlikoff, Boston University, Boston, MA (p. 168)
 George Krumbhaar, USBUDGET.COM, Washington, DC (p. 170)
*Lawrence Kudlow, Kudlow & Co., LLC, New York, NY (p. 170)
 Arthur B. Laffer, A. B. Laffer Associates, San Diego, CA (p. 172)
*Deepak Lal, University of California at Los Angeles, Los Angeles, CA (p. 172)
*Rita P. Maguire, Arizona Center for Public Policy, Phoenix, AZ (p. 186)
 Mary P. Mahoney, United Seniors Association, Inc., Washington, DC (p. 187)
*John H. Makin, American Enterprise Institute, Washington, DC (p. 187)
*Jim Martin, 60 Plus Association, Arlington, VA (p. 190)
 John N. Mathys, DePaul University, Elmhurst, IL (p. 191)
 Derrick A. Max, Alliance for Worker Retirement Security, Washington, DC (p. 192)
 John O. McGinnis, Cardozo School of Law, New York, NY (p. 196)
 Lawrence J. McQuillan, Pacific Research Institute, San Francisco, CA (p. 197)
 Harry Messenheimer, Rio Grande Foundation, Tijeras, NM (p. 200)
*Thomas P. Miller, Cato Institute, Washington, DC (p. 202)
*Dan Mitchell, The Heritage Foundation, Washington, DC (p. 203)
 Stephen J. Moore, Club for Growth, Washington, DC (p. 206)
*Deroy Murdock, Atlas Economic Research Foundation, New York, NY (p. 209)

---

* Has testified before a state or federal legislative committee

ENTITLEMENT SPENDING (Continued)

David Charles Nice, Washington State University, Pullman, WA (p. 213)
*Nancy M. Pfotenhauer, Independent Women's Forum, Arlington, VA (p. 227)
Barry W. Poulson, University of Colorado, Boulder, CO (p. 232)
*Scott Pullins, Ohio Taxpayers Association and OTA Foundation, Columbus, OH (p. 234)
Martin G. Reiser, Citizens for a Sound Economy, Washington, DC (p. 238)
*Brian Riedl, The Heritage Foundation, Washington, DC (p. 240)
Russell Roberts, Weidenbaum Center, St. Louis, MO (p. 242)
Llewellyn Rockwell, Jr., Ludwig von Mises Institute, Auburn, AL (p. 242)
Dallas L. Salisbury, Employee Benefit Research Institute, Washington, DC (p. 248)
*Susan Sarnoff, Ohio University, Athens, OH (p. 250)
*Thomas R. Saving, Texas A&M University, College Station, TX (p. 251)
*Thomas A. Schatz, Citizens Against Government Waste, Washington, DC (p. 252)
*Pete Sepp, National Taxpayers Union, Alexandria, VA (p. 257)
*C. Eugene Steuerle, Urban Institute, Washington, DC (p. 268)
*David Strom, Taxpayers League of Minnesota, Plymouth, MN (p. 270)
Michael D. Stroup, Stephen F. Austin State University, Nacogdoches, TX (p. 270)
Charles Stuart, University of California, Santa Barbara, Santa Barbara, CA (p. 271)
*Michael Tanner, Cato Institute, Washington, DC (p. 274)
*Forest M. Thigpen, Mississippi Family Council, Jackson, MS (p. 277)
*Grace-Marie Turner, Galen Institute, Alexandria, VA (p. 281)
*Peggy Venable, Texas Citizens for a Sound Economy, Austin, TX (p. 284)
*Richard E. Wagner, George Mason University, Fairfax, VA (p. 286)

FEDERAL BUDGET

Barbara Anderson, Citizens for Limited Taxation and Government, Peabody, MA (p. 38)
Damon Ansell, Americans for Tax Reform, Washington, DC (p. 39)
*Doug Bandow, Cato Institute, Washington, DC (p. 45)
*John S. Barry, Tax Foundation, Washington, DC (p. 46)
*Bruce R. Bartlett, National Center for Policy Analysis, Great Falls, VA (p. 46)
*William W. Beach, The Heritage Foundation, Washington, DC (p. 48)
*John E. Berthoud, National Taxpayers Union, Alexandria, VA (p. 52)
*Mark A. Bloomfield, American Council for Capital Formation, Washington, DC (p. 55)
*Patrick M. Boarman, National University San Diego, San Diego, CA (p. 55)
Michael J. Boskin, Hoover Institution, Stanford, CA (p. 57)
James M. Buchanan, Center for the Study of Public Choice, Fairfax, VA (p. 64)
*Victoria Craig Bunce, Council for Affordable Health Insurance,
    Inver Grove Heights, MN (p. 65)
*David Burton, Argus Group, Alexandria, VA (p. 66)
*Michael Carozza, Bristol-Myers Squibb, Washington, DC (p. 70)
Peter Cleary, American Conservative Union, Alexandria, VA (p. 75)
Peter F. Colwell, University of Illinois, Urbana, IL (p. 79)
William Constantine, Centre for New Black Leadership, Reston, VA (p. 80)
*Louis J. Cordia, Cordia Companies, Alexandria, VA (p. 82)
Bob Corkins, Kansas Legislative Education and Research, Inc., Topeka, KS (p. 82)
*C. W. Cowles, Central Michigan University, Midlothian, VA (p. 84)
Veronique de Rugy, Cato Institute, Washington, DC (p. 90)
*Carl DeMaio, Reason Foundation, Los Angeles, CA (p. 92)
D. P. Diffine, Harding University, Searcy, AR (p. 95)
*Thomas J. DiLorenzo, Loyola College, Clarksville, MD (p. 96)
*William C. Dunkelberg, National Federation of Independent Business,
    Wynnewood, PA (p. 100)
Gerald P. Dwyer, Jr., Federal Reserve Bank of Atlanta, Atlanta, GA (p. 101)
Christopher Edwards, Cato Institute, Washington, DC (p. 104)
*Mickey Edwards, Harvard University, Cambridge, MA (p. 104)

FEDERAL BUDGET (Continued)

*William Eggers, Deloitte Research-Public Sector, Washington, DC (p. 104)
*Ryan Ellis, Council for Government Reform, Arlington, VA (p. 106)
*Eric M. Engen, American Enterprise Institute, Washington, DC (p. 107)
*Louis D. Enoff, Enoff Associates Limited, Sykesville, MD (p. 107)
*Stephen Entin, Institute for Research on the Economics of Taxation, Washington, DC (p. 107)
*David I. Fand, James M. Buchanan Center for Political Economy, Fairfax, VA (p. 109)
 Peter Ferrara, International Center for Law and Economics, Washington, DC (p. 110)
 Marilyn R. Flowers, Ball State University, Muncie, IN (p. 113)
*Tom Giovanetti, Institute for Policy Innovation, Lewisville, TX (p. 124)
*James K. Glassman, American Enterprise Institute, Washington, DC (p. 124)
*Erick Gustafson, Citizens for a Sound Economy, Washington, DC (p. 131)
 Steve H. Hanke, Johns Hopkins University, Baltimore, MD (p. 134)
*Kevin A. Hassett, American Enterprise Institute, Washington, DC (p. 137)
 Rea Hederman, Jr., The Heritage Foundation, Washington, DC (p. 139)
 Robert Stanley Herren, North Dakota State University, Fargo, ND (p. 140)
*Robert L. Hershey, Robert L. Hershey, P.E., Washington, DC (p. 141)
 Robert Higgs, The Independent Institute, Covington, LA (p. 142)
*Scott Hodge, Tax Foundation, Washington, DC (p. 144)
*Fred Holden, Phoenix Enterprises, Arvada, CO (p. 144)
*Lawrence Hunter, Empower America, Washington, DC (p. 149)
*David Keating, National Taxpayers Union, Alexandria, VA (p. 159)
*Raymond J. Keating, Small Business Survival Committee, Manorville, NY (p. 159)
*W. Thomas Kelly, Savers and Investors League, Mirror Lake, NH (p. 161)
*Marvin H. Kosters, American Enterprise Institute, Washington, DC (p. 168)
 Laurence Kotlikoff, Boston University, Boston, MA (p. 168)
 George Krumbhaar, USBUDGET.COM, Washington, DC (p. 170)
*Lawrence Kudlow, Kudlow & Co., LLC, New York, NY (p. 170)
 Arthur B. Laffer, A. B. Laffer Associates, San Diego, CA (p. 172)
*George Landrith, Frontiers of Freedom Institute, Fairfax, VA (p. 173)
 James Lucier, Prudential Securities, Arlington, VA (p. 184)
*John H. Makin, American Enterprise Institute, Washington, DC (p. 187)
 Derrick A. Max, Alliance for Worker Retirement Security, Washington, DC (p. 192)
*Tom McClusky, National Taxpayers Union Foundation, Alexandria, VA (p. 193)
 John O. McGinnis, Cardozo School of Law, New York, NY (p. 196)
 Lawrence J. McQuillan, Pacific Research Institute, San Francisco, CA (p. 197)
*Lawrence Mead, New York University, New York, NY (p. 198)
*Allan H. Meltzer, Carnegie Mellon University, Pittsburgh, PA (p. 199)
*Dan Mitchell, The Heritage Foundation, Washington, DC (p. 203)
*Adrian T. Moore, Reason Foundation, Los Angeles, CA (p. 205)
 Stephen J. Moore, Club for Growth, Washington, DC (p. 206)
*Deroy Murdock, Atlas Economic Research Foundation, New York, NY (p. 209)
 David Charles Nice, Washington State University, Pullman, WA (p. 213)
*William A. Niskanen, Cato Institute, Washington, DC (p. 214)
 David C. Nott, Reason Foundation, Los Angeles, CA (p. 215)
 Sean Paige, Competitive Enterprise Institute, Washington, DC (p. 220)
 Charles I. Plosser, University of Rochester, Rochester, NY (p. 229)
 Barry W. Poulson, University of Colorado, Boulder, CO (p. 232)
 Martin G. Reiser, Citizens for a Sound Economy, Washington, DC (p. 238)
 Alan Reynolds, Cato Institute, Washington, DC (p. 239)
*Brian Riedl, The Heritage Foundation, Washington, DC (p. 240)
*Gary Robbins, Fiscal Associates, Arlington, VA (p. 241)
*Paul Rubin, Emory University, Atlanta, GA (p. 246)
 Peter J. Saunders, Central Washington University, Ellensburg, WA (p. 250)
*Thomas R. Saving, Texas A&M University, College Station, TX (p. 251)

FEDERAL BUDGET (Continued)

*Thomas A. Schatz, Citizens Against Government Waste, Washington, DC (p. 252)
*Geoffrey F. Segal, Reason Public Policy Institute, Los Angeles, CA (p. 256)
*Hans F. Sennholz, Grove City College, Grove City, PA (p. 257)
*Pete Sepp, National Taxpayers Union, Alexandria, VA (p. 257)
Stephen Slivinski, Goldwater Institute, Phoenix, AZ (p. 262)
*C. Eugene Steuerle, Urban Institute, Washington, DC (p. 268)
*David Strom, Taxpayers League of Minnesota, Plymouth, MN (p. 270)
Michael D. Stroup, Stephen F. Austin State University, Nacogdoches, TX (p. 270)
Charles Stuart, University of California, Santa Barbara, Santa Barbara, CA (p. 271)
*William Craig Stubblebine, Claremont McKenna College, Claremont, CA (p. 271)
*Margo Thorning, American Council for Capital Formation, Washington, DC (p. 278)
*Mark Thornton, Columbus State University, Columbus, GA (p. 278)
Richard H. Timberlake, Jr., Bogart, GA (p. 279)
*Robert D. Tollison, University of Mississippi, University, MS (p. 280)
*Gordon Tullock, George Mason University School of Law, Arlington, VA (p. 281)
*Lewis Uhler, National Tax Limitation Committee, Roseville, CA (p. 283)
*Ronald Utt, The Heritage Foundation, Washington, DC (p. 283)
*Peggy Venable, Texas Citizens for a Sound Economy, Austin, TX (p. 284)
*Richard E. Wagner, George Mason University, Fairfax, VA (p. 286)
*Malcolm Wallop, Frontiers of Freedom Institute, Fairfax, VA (p. 288)
*Murray Weidenbaum, Weidenbaum Center, St. Louis, MO (p. 291)
*Rolf A. Weil, Roosevelt University, Chicago, IL (p. 291)
James V. Young, Lee's Summit, MO (p. 300)
*Todd G. Young, Southeastern Legal Foundation, Atlanta, GA (p. 301)

GOVERNMENT DEBT

*Stephen Adams, Pioneer Institute for Public Policy Research, Boston, MA (p. 34)
*John S. Barry, Tax Foundation, Washington, DC (p. 46)
*Bruce R. Bartlett, National Center for Policy Analysis, Great Falls, VA (p. 46)
*William W. Beach, The Heritage Foundation, Washington, DC (p. 48)
*James T. Bennett, George Mason University, Fairfax, VA (p. 51)
*John E. Berthoud, National Taxpayers Union, Alexandria, VA (p. 52)
*Patrick M. Boarman, National University San Diego, San Diego, CA (p. 55)
Michael J. Boskin, Hoover Institution, Stanford, CA (p. 57)
David F. Bradford, Princeton University, Princeton, NJ (p. 59)
William Breit, Trinity University, San Antonio, TX (p. 60)
John F. Cogan, Hoover Institution, Stanford, CA (p. 77)
*C. W. Cowles, Central Michigan University, Midlothian, VA (p. 84)
*Eugene Delgaudio, Public Advocate, Falls Church, VA (p. 91)
*Carl DeMaio, Reason Foundation, Los Angeles, CA (p. 92)
D. P. Diffine, Harding University, Searcy, AR (p. 95)
*William C. Dunkelberg, National Federation of Independent Business, Wynnewood, PA (p. 100)
Gerald P. Dwyer, Jr., Federal Reserve Bank of Atlanta, Atlanta, GA (p. 101)
Christopher Edwards, Cato Institute, Washington, DC (p. 104)
*Ryan Ellis, Council for Government Reform, Arlington, VA (p. 106)
*Bert Ely, Ely & Company, Inc., Alexandria, VA (p. 106)
*Eric M. Engen, American Enterprise Institute, Washington, DC (p. 107)
*Stephen Entin, Institute for Research on the Economics of Taxation, Washington, DC (p. 107)
*David I. Fand, James M. Buchanan Center for Political Economy, Fairfax, VA (p. 109)
Burton W. Folsom, Jr., Center for the American Idea, Houston, TX (p. 114)
Steven B. Frates, Claremont McKenna College, Claremont, CA (p. 116)
*Tom Giovanetti, Institute for Policy Innovation, Lewisville, TX (p. 124)
*Grant R. Gulibon, The Commonwealth Foundation, Harrisburg, PA (p. 130)

GOVERNMENT DEBT (Continued)

*Erick Gustafson, Citizens for a Sound Economy, Washington, DC (p. 131)
Jack High, George Mason University, Arlington, VA (p. 142)
*Scott Hodge, Tax Foundation, Washington, DC (p. 144)
*Fred Holden, Phoenix Enterprises, Arvada, CO (p. 144)
*Lawrence Hunter, Empower America, Washington, DC (p. 149)
*David Keating, National Taxpayers Union, Alexandria, VA (p. 159)
*W. Thomas Kelly, Savers and Investors League, Mirror Lake, NH (p. 161)
Phil Kent, Southeastern Legal Foundation, Atlanta, GA (p. 162)
*Randall Kroszner, University of Chicago, Chicago, IL (p. 170)
George Krumbhaar, USBUDGET.COM, Washington, DC (p. 170)
*Lawrence Kudlow, Kudlow & Co., LLC, New York, NY (p. 170)
*John H. Makin, American Enterprise Institute, Washington, DC (p. 187)
J. Huston McCulloch, Ohio State University, Columbus, OH (p. 194)
*Allan H. Meltzer, Carnegie Mellon University, Pittsburgh, PA (p. 199)
*Dan Mitchell, The Heritage Foundation, Washington, DC (p. 203)
*Adrian T. Moore, Reason Foundation, Los Angeles, CA (p. 205)
Stephen J. Moore, Club for Growth, Washington, DC (p. 206)
David Charles Nice, Washington State University, Pullman, WA (p. 213)
*J. A. Parker, Lincoln Institute for Research and Education, Washington, DC (p. 221)
Barry W. Poulson, University of Colorado, Boulder, CO (p. 232)
George Reisman, Pepperdine University, Laguna Hills, CA (p. 238)
*Andrew Rettenmaier, Texas A&M University, College Station, TX (p. 239)
Alan Reynolds, Cato Institute, Washington, DC (p. 239)
*Brian Riedl, The Heritage Foundation, Washington, DC (p. 240)
Llewellyn Rockwell, Jr., Ludwig von Mises Institute, Auburn, AL (p. 242)
Peter J. Saunders, Central Washington University, Ellensburg, WA (p. 250)
*Thomas R. Saving, Texas A&M University, College Station, TX (p. 251)
*Thomas A. Schatz, Citizens Against Government Waste, Washington, DC (p. 252)
*Bill Schilling, Wyoming Business Alliance / Wyoming Heritage Foundation,
    Casper, WY (p. 253)
Robert Haney Scott, California State University, Chico, Chico, CA (p. 255)
*Geoffrey F. Segal, Reason Public Policy Institute, Los Angeles, CA (p. 256)
*Hans F. Sennholz, Grove City College, Grove City, PA (p. 257)
*David Stanley, National Taxpayers Union, Muscatine, IA (p. 268)
*David Strom, Taxpayers League of Minnesota, Plymouth, MN (p. 270)
Michael D. Stroup, Stephen F. Austin State University, Nacogdoches, TX (p. 270)
Charles Stuart, University of California, Santa Barbara, Santa Barbara, CA (p. 271)
*William Craig Stubblebine, Claremont McKenna College, Claremont, CA (p. 271)
*Alexander Tabarrok, Mercatus Center at George Mason University, Arlington, VA (p. 273)
*Jason M. Thomas, Citizens for a Sound Economy, Washington, DC (p. 277)
*Mark Thornton, Columbus State University, Columbus, GA (p. 278)
*Lewis Uhler, National Tax Limitation Committee, Roseville, CA (p. 283)
*Richard E. Wagner, George Mason University, Fairfax, VA (p. 286)
Russ Walker, Citizens for a Sound Economy, Keizer, OR (p. 287)

GOVERNMENT WASTE

*Stephen Adams, Pioneer Institute for Public Policy Research, Boston, MA (p. 34)
*Keith G. Baker, Florida TaxWatch Research Institute, Inc., Tallahassee, FL (p. 43)
John Barrett, Beacon Hill Institute, Boston, MA (p. 46)
*John S. Barry, Tax Foundation, Washington, DC (p. 46)
Paul Beckner, Citizens for a Sound Economy, Washington, DC (p. 48)
*James T. Bennett, George Mason University, Fairfax, VA (p. 51)
*John E. Berthoud, National Taxpayers Union, Alexandria, VA (p. 52)
Thomas E. Borcherding, Claremont Graduate University, Claremont, CA (p. 57)

GOVERNMENT WASTE (Continued)

James H. Broussard, Citizens Against Higher Taxes, Hershey, PA **(p. 63)**
*****Kenneth Brown,** Rio Grande Foundation, Albuquerque, NM **(p. 63)**
*****Dominic M. Calabro,** Florida TaxWatch Research Institute, Inc., Tallahassee, FL **(p. 67)**
*****James B. Cardle,** Texas Citizen Action Network, Austin, TX **(p. 69)**
Kenneth W. Clarkson, University of Miami, Coral Gables, FL **(p. 75)**
Peter Cleary, American Conservative Union, Alexandria, VA **(p. 75)**
*****Jon Coupal,** Howard Jarvis Taxpayers Association, Sacramento, CA **(p. 83)**
*****C. W. Cowles,** Central Michigan University, Midlothian, VA **(p. 84)**
*****Wendell Cox,** Wendell Cox Consultancy, Belleville, IL **(p. 84)**
*****Eugene Delgaudio,** Public Advocate, Falls Church, VA **(p. 91)**
*****Carl DeMaio,** Reason Foundation, Los Angeles, CA **(p. 92)**
D. P. Diffine, Harding University, Searcy, AR **(p. 95)**
*****Thomas J. DiLorenzo,** Loyola College, Clarksville, MD **(p. 96)**
Christopher Edwards, Cato Institute, Washington, DC **(p. 104)**
*****William Eggers,** Deloitte Research-Public Sector, Washington, DC **(p. 104)**
William F. Ford, Middle Tennessee State University, Murfreesboro, TN **(p. 114)**
Micah Paul Frankel, California State University, Hayward, Hayward, CA **(p. 115)**
Steven B. Frates, Claremont McKenna College, Claremont, CA **(p. 116)**
*****John Frydenlund,** Citizens Against Government Waste, Washington, DC **(p. 118)**
*****Stephen O. Goodrick,** National Right to Work Committee, Springfield, VA **(p. 126)**
*****Grant R. Gulibon,** The Commonwealth Foundation, Harrisburg, PA **(p. 130)**
*****Paul Guppy,** Washington Policy Center, Seattle, WA **(p. 131)**
*****Erick Gustafson,** Citizens for a Sound Economy, Washington, DC **(p. 131)**
*****James D. Gwartney,** Florida State University, Tallahassee, FL **(p. 131)**
*****Robert Hale,** Northwest Legal Foundation, Minot, ND **(p. 132)**
Lowman Henry, Lincoln Institute of Public Opinion Research, Inc., Harrisburg, PA **(p. 140)**
Jonathan Hill, North Carolina Citizens for a Sound Economy, Raleigh, NC **(p. 142)**
*****Scott Hodge,** Tax Foundation, Washington, DC **(p. 144)**
*****Michael Horowitz,** Hudson Institute, Washington, DC **(p. 146)**
*****Lawrence Hunter,** Empower America, Washington, DC **(p. 149)**
*****Lance T. Izumi,** Pacific Research Institute, Sacramento, CA **(p. 152)**
Phil Kent, Southeastern Legal Foundation, Atlanta, GA **(p. 162)**
Lisa M. Korsak, Mercatus Center at George Mason University, Arlington, VA **(p. 167)**
George Krumbhaar, USBUDGET.COM, Washington, DC **(p. 170)**
*****Lawrence Kudlow,** Kudlow & Co., LLC, New York, NY **(p. 170)**
Robert J. Lagomarsino, American Alliance for Tax Equity, Denver, CO **(p. 172)**
*****Mark R. Levin,** Landmark Legal Foundation, Herndon, VA **(p. 178)**
Martin A. Levin, Brandeis University, Waltham, MA **(p. 178)**
D. F. Linowes, University of Illinois, Urbana, IL **(p. 181)**
*****Tom McClusky,** National Taxpayers Union Foundation, Alexandria, VA **(p. 193)**
*****Daniel Mead Smith,** Washington Policy Center, Seattle, WA **(p. 198)**
Harry Messenheimer, Rio Grande Foundation, Tijeras, NM **(p. 200)**
*****Dan Mitchell,** The Heritage Foundation, Washington, DC **(p. 203)**
*****Adrian T. Moore,** Reason Foundation, Los Angeles, CA **(p. 205)**
Stephen J. Moore, Club for Growth, Washington, DC **(p. 206)**
*****David B. Muhlhausen,** The Heritage Foundation, Washington, DC **(p. 208)**
*****Deroy Murdock,** Atlas Economic Research Foundation, New York, NY **(p. 209)**
*****Ronald Nehring,** Americans for Tax Reform, San Diego, CA **(p. 212)**
Michael A. Nelson, University of Akron, Akron, OH **(p. 212)**
*****Grover Norquist,** Americans for Tax Reform, Washington, DC **(p. 214)**
David C. Nott, Reason Foundation, Los Angeles, CA **(p. 215)**
Mike O'Neill, Landmark Legal Foundation, Herndon, VA **(p. 217)**
Sean Paige, Competitive Enterprise Institute, Washington, DC **(p. 220)**
*****Jim Panyard,** Pennsylvania Manufacturer's Association, Harrisburg, PA **(p. 221)**

GOVERNMENT WASTE (Continued)

*Karl Peterjohn, Kansas Taxpayers Network, Wichita, KS (p. 226)

*Daniel J. Popeo, Washington Legal Foundation, Washington, DC (p. 231)

Philip K. Porter, University of South Florida, Tampa, FL (p. 231)

Barry W. Poulson, University of Colorado, Boulder, CO (p. 232)

*Don Racheter, Public Interest Institute, Mount Pleasant, IA (p. 235)

*Brian Riedl, The Heritage Foundation, Washington, DC (p. 240)

Llewellyn Rockwell, Jr., Ludwig von Mises Institute, Auburn, AL (p. 242)

*Allen H. Roth, New York State Advisory Council on Privatization, New York, NY (p. 244)

*James A. Roumasset, University of Hawaii, Honolulu, HI (p. 245)

*Stacie Rumenap, U. S. Term Limits, Washington, DC (p. 247)

E. S. Savas, City University of New York, New York, NY (p. 250)

*Thomas A. Schatz, Citizens Against Government Waste, Washington, DC (p. 252)

*Geoffrey F. Segal, Reason Public Policy Institute, Los Angeles, CA (p. 256)

*David Stanley, National Taxpayers Union, Muscatine, IA (p. 268)

Oscar Stilley, Arkansans for School Choice, Fort Smith, AR (p. 269)

*David Strom, Taxpayers League of Minnesota, Plymouth, MN (p. 270)

Michael D. Stroup, Stephen F. Austin State University, Nacogdoches, TX (p. 270)

*David J. Theroux, The Independent Institute, Oakland, CA (p. 276)

*Virginia L. Thomas, The Heritage Foundation, Washington, DC (p. 277)

*Mark Thornton, Columbus State University, Columbus, GA (p. 278)

*Jim Tobin, National Taxpayers United of Illinois, Chicago, IL (p. 279)

*Lewis Uhler, National Tax Limitation Committee, Roseville, CA (p. 283)

*Ronald Utt, The Heritage Foundation, Washington, DC (p. 283)

*Peggy Venable, Texas Citizens for a Sound Economy, Austin, TX (p. 284)

Russ Walker, Citizens for a Sound Economy, Keizer, OR (p. 287)

*Bob Williams, Evergreen Freedom Foundation, Olympia, WA (p. 295)

Jason Wright, Frontiers of Freedom Institute, Fairfax, VA (p. 299)

INTERNATIONAL TAX POLICY/TAX COMPETITION

Barbara Anderson, Citizens for Limited Taxation and Government, Peabody, MA (p. 38)

Damon Ansell, Americans for Tax Reform, Washington, DC (p. 39)

*John S. Barry, Tax Foundation, Washington, DC (p. 46)

*Bruce R. Bartlett, National Center for Policy Analysis, Great Falls, VA (p. 46)

*Mark A. Bloomfield, American Council for Capital Formation, Washington, DC (p. 55)

*Patrick M. Boarman, National University San Diego, San Diego, CA (p. 55)

James M. Buchanan, Center for the Study of Public Choice, Fairfax, VA (p. 64)

*David Burton, Argus Group, Alexandria, VA (p. 66)

Veronique de Rugy, Cato Institute, Washington, DC (p. 90)

D. P. Diffine, Harding University, Searcy, AR (p. 95)

Christopher Edwards, Cato Institute, Washington, DC (p. 104)

*Stephen Entin, Institute for Research on the Economics of Taxation, Washington, DC (p. 107)

*Edwin J. Feulner, The Heritage Foundation, Washington, DC (p. 111)

*Robert Fike, Americans for Tax Reform, Washington, DC (p. 111)

Fred E. Foldvary, Santa Clara University, Santa Clara, CA (p. 114)

*Michael S. Greve, American Enterprise Institute, Washington, DC (p. 129)

Steve H. Hanke, Johns Hopkins University, Baltimore, MD (p. 134)

*C. Lowell Harriss, Columbia University, Bronxville, NY (p. 136)

*Kevin A. Hassett, American Enterprise Institute, Washington, DC (p. 137)

*Robert C. Haywood, Director, WEPZA, Evergreen, CO (p. 138)

*Scott Hodge, Tax Foundation, Washington, DC (p. 144)

*Lawrence Hunter, Empower America, Washington, DC (p. 149)

*W. Thomas Kelly, Savers and Investors League, Mirror Lake, NH (p. 161)

Darlene A. Kennedy, Centre for New Black Leadership, Baltimore, MD (p. 162)

*Lawrence Kudlow, Kudlow & Co., LLC, New York, NY (p. 170)

INTERNATIONAL TAX POLICY/TAX COMPETITION (Continued)

*Deepak Lal, University of California at Los Angeles, Los Angeles, CA (p. 172)
 James Lucier, Prudential Securities, Arlington, VA (p. 184)
*Yuri N. Maltsev, Carthage College, Kenosha, WI (p. 188)
*Robert W. McGee, Barry University, Miami Shores, FL (p. 195)
*Dan Mitchell, The Heritage Foundation, Washington, DC (p. 203)
*Steven W. Mosher, Population Research Institute, Front Royal, VA (p. 208)
 Barry W. Poulson, University of Colorado, Boulder, CO (p. 232)
 Richard W. Rahn, NOVECON, Alexandria, VA (p. 236)
*Allen H. Roth, New York State Advisory Council on Privatization, New York, NY (p. 244)
*Linda Runbeck, Taxpayers League of Minnesota, Plymouth, MN (p. 247)
*Pete Sepp, National Taxpayers Union, Alexandria, VA (p. 257)
*Solveig Singleton, Competitive Enterprise Institute, Washington, DC (p. 261)
 Shaun Small, Empower America, Washington, DC (p. 262)
*Fred L. Smith, Jr., Competitive Enterprise Institute, Washington, DC (p. 263)
*David Strom, Taxpayers League of Minnesota, Plymouth, MN (p. 270)
 James R. "J.T." Taylor, Empower America, Washington, DC (p. 274)
*Margo Thorning, American Council for Capital Formation, Washington, DC (p. 278)
*Richard E. Wagner, George Mason University, Fairfax, VA (p. 286)
*Bob Williams, Evergreen Freedom Foundation, Olympia, WA (p. 295)

PRIVATIZATION/CONTRACTING-OUT

*Douglas K. Adie, Ohio University, Athens, OH (p. 35)
*Keith G. Baker, Florida TaxWatch Research Institute, Inc., Tallahassee, FL (p. 43)
*Bruce R. Bartlett, National Center for Policy Analysis, Great Falls, VA (p. 46)
*Naomi Lopez Bauman, Orlando, FL (p. 47)
*James T. Bennett, George Mason University, Fairfax, VA (p. 51)
 Lisa E. Bernstein, University of Chicago Law School, Chicago, IL (p. 51)
*John E. Berthoud, National Taxpayers Union, Alexandria, VA (p. 52)
*Robert K. Best, Pacific Legal Foundation, Sacramento, CA (p. 52)
 Thomas E. Borcherding, Claremont Graduate University, Claremont, CA (p. 57)
 James M. Buchanan, Center for the Study of Public Choice, Fairfax, VA (p. 64)
*Steve Buckstein, Cascade Policy Institute, Portland, OR (p. 65)
*Stuart Butler, The Heritage Foundation, Washington, DC (p. 66)
*Dominic M. Calabro, Florida TaxWatch Research Institute, Inc., Tallahassee, FL (p. 67)
*Jon Charles Caldara, Independence Institute, Golden, CO (p. 67)
*Charles Chieppo, Pioneer Institute for Public Policy Research, Boston, MA (p. 73)
 Kenneth W. Clarkson, University of Miami, Coral Gables, FL (p. 75)
 John Cobin, Montauk Financial Group, Greenville, SC (p. 76)
*John E. Coons, University of California at Berkeley, Berkeley, CA (p. 81)
 Bob Corkins, Kansas Legislative Education and Research, Inc., Topeka, KS (p. 82)
*Jon Coupal, Howard Jarvis Taxpayers Association, Sacramento, CA (p. 83)
*Wendell Cox, Wendell Cox Consultancy, Belleville, IL (p. 84)
 Neil S. Crispo, Florida State University, Tallahassee, FL (p. 86)
 Richard S. Davis, Washington Research Council, Seattle, WA (p. 89)
*Carl DeMaio, Reason Foundation, Los Angeles, CA (p. 92)
*David Denholm, Public Service Research Foundation, Vienna, VA (p. 92)
 Richard Derham, Washington Policy Center, Seattle, WA (p. 93)
*William C. Dunkelberg, National Federation of Independent Business,
    Wynnewood, PA (p. 100)
 Christopher Edwards, Cato Institute, Washington, DC (p. 104)
*William Eggers, Deloitte Research-Public Sector, Washington, DC (p. 104)
 Isaac Ehrlich, State University of New York, Buffalo, Buffalo, NY (p. 105)
*Louis D. Enoff, Enoff Associates Limited, Sykesville, MD (p. 107)
*Stephen Entin, Institute for Research on the Economics of Taxation, Washington, DC (p. 107)

PRIVATIZATION/CONTRACTING-OUT (Continued)

Peter Ferrara, International Center for Law and Economics, Washington, DC (p. 110)
*Robert Fike, Americans for Tax Reform, Washington, DC (p. 111)
Bernard J. Frieden, Massachusetts Institute of Technology, Cambridge, MA (p. 117)
John H. Fund, *OpinionJournal.com*, New York, NY (p. 119)
John Galandak, Foundation for Free Enterprise, Paramus, NJ (p. 119)
*Dana Joel Gattuso, Competitive Enterprise Institute, Alexandria, VA (p. 121)
*Stephen Goldsmith, Manhattan Institute for Policy Research, New York, NY (p. 126)
Charles Greenwalt, II, Susquehanna Valley Center for Public Policy, Hershey, PA (p. 129)
*Grant R. Gulibon, The Commonwealth Foundation, Harrisburg, PA (p. 130)
*Paul Guppy, Washington Policy Center, Seattle, WA (p. 131)
*Erick Gustafson, Citizens for a Sound Economy, Washington, DC (p. 131)
Steve H. Hanke, Johns Hopkins University, Baltimore, MD (p. 134)
David T. Hartgen, University of North Carolina, Charlotte, Charlotte, NC (p. 136)
Jay F. Hein, Hudson Institute, Indianapolis, IN (p. 139)
Lowman Henry, Lincoln Institute of Public Opinion Research, Inc., Harrisburg, PA (p. 140)
*Robert L. Hershey, Robert L. Hershey, P.E., Washington, DC (p. 141)
*Roberta Herzberg, Utah State University, Logan, UT (p. 141)
*John R. Hill, Alabama Policy Institute, Birmingham, AL (p. 142)
*Scott Hodge, Tax Foundation, Washington, DC (p. 144)
Edward L. Hudgins, The Objectivist Center, Washington, DC (p. 148)
*Lawrence Hunter, Empower America, Washington, DC (p. 149)
*Charles D. Hurley, Iowa Family Policy Center, Pleasant Hill, IA (p. 150)
*Laurence Jarvik, Washington, DC (p. 153)
*David John, The Heritage Foundation, Washington, DC (p. 154)
Robin Johnson, Reason Public Policy Institute, Los Angeles, CA (p. 155)
Shyam J. Kamath, California State University, Hayward, Hayward, CA (p. 157)
George A. Keyworth, Progress & Freedom Foundation, Washington, DC (p. 163)
Fred Kiesner, Loyola Marymount University, Los Angeles, CA (p. 163)
Lisa M. Korsak, Mercatus Center at George Mason University, Arlington, VA (p. 167)
*Randall Kroszner, University of Chicago, Chicago, IL (p. 170)
*Lawrence Kudlow, Kudlow & Co., LLC, New York, NY (p. 170)
*Michael D. LaFaive, Mackinac Center for Public Policy, Midland, MI (p. 171)
Joseph G. Lehman, Mackinac Center for Public Policy, Midland, MI (p. 177)
Tom Lenard, Progress & Freedom Foundation, Washington, DC (p. 177)
Kurt R. Leube, Hoover Institution, Stanford, CA (p. 178)
*Myron Lieberman, Education Policy Institute, Washington, DC (p. 180)
D. F. Linowes, University of Illinois, Urbana, IL (p. 181)
Charles H. Logan, University of Connecticut, Storrs, CT (p. 182)
Tibor R. Machan, Chapman University, Silverado Canyon, CA (p. 185)
J. J. Mahoney, Diversified Consultants, Mount Pleasant, SC (p. 187)
Deryl W. Martin, Tennessee Technological University, Cookeville, TN (p. 190)
Wendell H. McCulloch, Jr., California State University, Long Beach, Long Beach, CA (p. 194)
*Kelly McCutchen, Georgia Public Policy Foundation, Atlanta, GA (p. 194)
Edward T. McMullen, Jr., South Carolina Policy Council, Columbia, SC (p. 197)
*Maurice McTigue, Mercatus Center at George Mason University, Arlington, VA (p. 197)
*Daniel Mead Smith, Washington Policy Center, Seattle, WA (p. 198)
Paul T. Mero, The Sutherland Institute, Salt Lake City, UT (p. 199)
Lawrence Mone, Manhattan Institute for Policy Research, New York, NY (p. 205)
*Adrian T. Moore, Reason Foundation, Los Angeles, CA (p. 205)
Chuck Muth, American Conservative Union, Alexandria, VA (p. 210)
Michael A. Nelson, University of Akron, Akron, OH (p. 212)
Robert H. Nelson, University of Maryland, College Park, MD (p. 212)
George R. Neumann, University of Iowa, Iowa City, IA (p. 213)
David C. Nott, Reason Foundation, Los Angeles, CA (p. 215)

PRIVATIZATION/CONTRACTING-OUT (Continued)

*Gary J. Palmer, Alabama Policy Institute, Birmingham, AL (p. 221)
*William S. Peirce, Case Western Reserve University, Cleveland, OH (p. 224)
*William H. Peterson, Washington, DC (p. 227)
 Penn Pfiffner, Independence Institute, Golden, CO (p. 227)
*Dennis Polhill, Independence Institute, Golden, CO (p. 230)
*Robert W. Poole, Jr., Reason Foundation, Los Angeles, CA (p. 230)
 Philip K. Porter, University of South Florida, Tampa, FL (p. 231)
 Barry W. Poulson, University of Colorado, Boulder, CO (p. 232)
*Eric Premack, California State University Institute for Education Reform,
    Sacramento, CA (p. 232)
 George Priest, Yale Law School, New Haven, CT (p. 233)
*Scott Pullins, Ohio Taxpayers Association and OTA Foundation, Columbus, OH (p. 234)
*Lawrence W. Reed, Mackinac Center for Public Policy, Midland, MI (p. 237)
*Brian Riedl, The Heritage Foundation, Washington, DC (p. 240)
 Llewellyn Rockwell, Jr., Ludwig von Mises Institute, Auburn, AL (p. 242)
*Allen H. Roth, New York State Advisory Council on Privatization, New York, NY (p. 244)
 Gabriel Roth, Chevy Chase, MD (p. 244)
*James A. Roumasset, University of Hawaii, Honolulu, HI (p. 245)
*Linda Runbeck, Taxpayers League of Minnesota, Plymouth, MN (p. 247)
 Peter Rutland, Wesleyan University, Middletown, CT (p. 248)
 Peter D. Salins, Manhattan Institute for Policy Research, New York, NY (p. 248)
*Susan Sarnoff, Ohio University, Athens, OH (p. 250)
 E. S. Savas, City University of New York, New York, NY (p. 250)
*Thomas A. Schatz, Citizens Against Government Waste, Washington, DC (p. 252)
*Bill Schilling, Wyoming Business Alliance / Wyoming Heritage Foundation,
    Casper, WY (p. 253)
 Larry J. Sechrest, Sul Ross State University, Alpine, TX (p. 255)
*Geoffrey F. Segal, Reason Public Policy Institute, Los Angeles, CA (p. 256)
*Pete Sepp, National Taxpayers Union, Alexandria, VA (p. 257)
*Randy T. Simmons, Utah State University, Logan, UT (p. 260)
*Fred L. Smith, Jr., Competitive Enterprise Institute, Washington, DC (p. 263)
*Jack Sommer, Political Economy Research Institute, Charlotte, NC (p. 266)
*James Stergios, Pioneer Institute for Public Policy Research, Boston, MA (p. 268)
*David Strom, Taxpayers League of Minnesota, Plymouth, MN (p. 270)
 Michael D. Stroup, Stephen F. Austin State University, Nacogdoches, TX (p. 270)
*David Swindell, Clemson University, Clemson, SC (p. 273)
*Alexander Tabarrok, Mercatus Center at George Mason University, Arlington, VA (p. 273)
 Thomas L. Tacker, Embry-Riddle Aeronautical University, Daytona Beach, FL (p. 273)
*David J. Theroux, The Independent Institute, Oakland, CA (p. 276)
 Michael W. Thompson, Thomas Jefferson Institute for Public Policy, Springfield, VA (p. 278)
*Mark Thornton, Columbus State University, Columbus, GA (p. 278)
*Lewis Uhler, National Tax Limitation Committee, Roseville, CA (p. 283)
*Ronald Utt, The Heritage Foundation, Washington, DC (p. 283)
*Peggy Venable, Texas Citizens for a Sound Economy, Austin, TX (p. 284)
*Richard E. Wagner, George Mason University, Fairfax, VA (p. 286)
 Russ Walker, Citizens for a Sound Economy, Keizer, OR (p. 287)
*Alan Rufus Waters, California State University, Fresno, Fresno, CA (p. 289)
*Kurt T. Weber, Cascade Policy Institute, Portland, OR (p. 290)
*Bob Williams, Evergreen Freedom Foundation, Olympia, WA (p. 295)
 Edward W. Younkins, Wheeling Jesuit University, Wheeling, WV (p. 301)

STATE AND LOCAL PUBLIC FINANCE

*Stephen Adams, Pioneer Institute for Public Policy Research, Boston, MA (p. 34)
*Ryan C. Amacher, University of Texas, Arlington, Arlington, TX (p. 37)

STATE AND LOCAL PUBLIC FINANCE (Continued)

Damon Ansell, Americans for Tax Reform, Washington, DC **(p. 39)**
*****Julaine K. Appling,** Family Research Institute of Wisconsin, Madison, WI **(p. 40)**
*****Chris Atkins,** American Legislative Exchange Council, Washington, DC **(p. 41)**
 Brian Backstrom, Empire Foundation for Policy Research, Clifton Park, NY **(p. 42)**
*****Keith G. Baker,** Florida TaxWatch Research Institute, Inc., Tallahassee, FL **(p. 43)**
 John Barrett, Beacon Hill Institute, Boston, MA **(p. 46)**
*****John S. Barry,** Tax Foundation, Washington, DC **(p. 46)**
*****Bruce R. Bartlett,** National Center for Policy Analysis, Great Falls, VA **(p. 46)**
*****William W. Beach,** The Heritage Foundation, Washington, DC **(p. 48)**
*****John H. Beck,** Gonzaga University, Spokane, WA **(p. 48)**
*****John E. Berthoud,** National Taxpayers Union, Alexandria, VA **(p. 52)**
*****Wayman R. Bishop,** The Family Foundation of Virginia, Richmond, VA **(p. 53)**
 Jeffrey R. Boeyink, Iowans for Tax Relief, Muscatine, IA **(p. 56)**
 Cecil E. Bohanon, Ball State University, Muncie, IN **(p. 56)**
 David F. Bradford, Princeton University, Princeton, NJ **(p. 59)**
 Charles H. Breeden, Marquette University, Milwaukee, WI **(p. 60)**
 B. Jason Brooks, Empire Foundation for Policy Research, Clifton Park, NY **(p. 62)**
 James H. Broussard, Citizens Against Higher Taxes, Hershey, PA **(p. 63)**
*****Kenneth Brown,** Rio Grande Foundation, Albuquerque, NM **(p. 63)**
 James M. Buchanan, Center for the Study of Public Choice, Fairfax, VA **(p. 64)**
*****David Burton,** Argus Group, Alexandria, VA **(p. 66)**
*****Dominic M. Calabro,** Florida TaxWatch Research Institute, Inc., Tallahassee, FL **(p. 67)**
*****James B. Cardle,** Texas Citizen Action Network, Austin, TX **(p. 69)**
*****John Carlson,** Washington Policy Center, Seattle, WA **(p. 70)**
*****Michael A. Ciamarra,** Alabama Policy Institute, Birmingham, AL **(p. 74)**
*****J. R. Clark,** University of Tennessee, Chattanooga, Chattanooga, TN **(p. 75)**
 Kenneth W. Clarkson, University of Miami, Coral Gables, FL **(p. 75)**
 Peter F. Colwell, University of Illinois, Urbana, IL **(p. 79)**
 J. Paul Combs, Appalachian Regional Development Institute, Boone, NC **(p. 79)**
 William Constantine, Centre for New Black Leadership, Reston, VA **(p. 80)**
*****John E. Coons,** University of California at Berkeley, Berkeley, CA **(p. 81)**
 Roy E. Cordato, John Locke Foundation, Raleigh, NC **(p. 82)**
 Bob Corkins, Kansas Legislative Education and Research, Inc., Topeka, KS **(p. 82)**
*****Jon Coupal,** Howard Jarvis Taxpayers Association, Sacramento, CA **(p. 83)**
*****C. W. Cowles,** Central Michigan University, Midlothian, VA **(p. 84)**
 Neil S. Crispo, Florida State University, Tallahassee, FL **(p. 86)**
 Richard S. Davis, Washington Research Council, Seattle, WA **(p. 89)**
 Veronique de Rugy, Cato Institute, Washington, DC **(p. 90)**
 Buffy DeBreaux-Watts, American Board for Certification of Teacher Excellence, Washington, DC **(p. 91)**
*****Thomas J. DiLorenzo,** Loyola College, Clarksville, MD **(p. 96)**
 Thomas R. Dye, Florida State University, Tallahassee, FL **(p. 101)**
 Christopher Edwards, Cato Institute, Washington, DC **(p. 104)**
*****William Eggers,** Deloitte Research-Public Sector, Washington, DC **(p. 104)**
 Edward D. Failor, Sr., Iowans for Tax Relief, Muscatine, IA **(p. 108)**
 Peter Ferrara, International Center for Law and Economics, Washington, DC **(p. 110)**
 William A. Fischel, Dartmouth College, Hanover, NH **(p. 112)**
*****Michael Flynn,** American Legislative Exchange Council, Washington, DC **(p. 113)**
 Fred E. Foldvary, Santa Clara University, Santa Clara, CA **(p. 114)**
 William F. Ford, Middle Tennessee State University, Murfreesboro, TN **(p. 114)**
 Steven B. Frates, Claremont McKenna College, Claremont, CA **(p. 116)**
*****Dana Joel Gattuso,** Competitive Enterprise Institute, Alexandria, VA **(p. 121)**
 Leonard Gilroy, Reason Foundation, Los Angeles, CA **(p. 123)**
*****Grant R. Gulibon,** The Commonwealth Foundation, Harrisburg, PA **(p. 130)**

*** Has testified before a state or federal legislative committee**

STATE AND LOCAL PUBLIC FINANCE (Continued)

*Paul Guppy, Washington Policy Center, Seattle, WA (p. 131)
*Erick Gustafson, Citizens for a Sound Economy, Washington, DC (p. 131)
*Robert Hale, Northwest Legal Foundation, Minot, ND (p. 132)
*Joshua Hall, Buckeye Institute for Public Policy Solutions, Columbus, OH (p. 132)
*Randy H. Hamilton, University of California, Berkeley, Berkeley, CA (p. 133)
 Steve H. Hanke, Johns Hopkins University, Baltimore, MD (p. 134)
 Eric Hanushek, Hoover Institution, Stanford, CA (p. 135)
*C. Lowell Harriss, Columbia University, Bronxville, NY (p. 136)
 David T. Hartgen, University of North Carolina, Charlotte, Charlotte, NC (p. 136)
 Rea Hederman, Jr., The Heritage Foundation, Washington, DC (p. 139)
 Lowman Henry, Lincoln Institute of Public Opinion Research, Inc., Harrisburg, PA (p. 140)
 Jonathan Hill, North Carolina Citizens for a Sound Economy, Raleigh, NC (p. 142)
*Scott Hodge, Tax Foundation, Washington, DC (p. 144)
*Randall G. Holcombe, Florida State University, Tallahassee, FL (p. 144)
*Fred Holden, Phoenix Enterprises, Arvada, CO (p. 144)
*John MacDonald Hood, John Locke Foundation, Raleigh, NC (p. 145)
*Caroline M. Hoxby, Harvard University, Cambridge, MA (p. 147)
*Lawrence Hunter, Empower America, Washington, DC (p. 149)
*Lance T. Izumi, Pacific Research Institute, Sacramento, CA (p. 152)
*Mike Jerman, Utah Taxpayers Association, Salt Lake City, UT (p. 154)
 Robin Johnson, Reason Public Policy Institute, Los Angeles, CA (p. 155)
 Milton Kafoglis, Emory University, Decatur, GA (p. 156)
*Greg Kaza, Arkansas Policy Foundation, Little Rock, AR (p. 159)
*David Keating, National Taxpayers Union, Alexandria, VA (p. 159)
*Raymond J. Keating, Small Business Survival Committee, Manorville, NY (p. 159)
*Lynne Kiesling, Reason Public Policy Institute, Los Angeles, CA (p. 163)
*John Kincaid, Lafayette College, Easton, PA (p. 163)
 Kent King, Missouri State Teachers Association, Columbia, MO (p. 164)
 Charles R. Knoeber, North Carolina State University, Raleigh, NC (p. 166)
*Lawrence Kudlow, Kudlow & Co., LLC, New York, NY (p. 170)
 Arthur B. Laffer, A. B. Laffer Associates, San Diego, CA (p. 172)
 Byron S. Lamm, State Policy Network, Fort Wayne, IN (p. 173)
*Robert A. Lawson, Capital University, Columbus, OH (p. 176)
 Martin A. Levin, Brandeis University, Waltham, MA (p. 178)
*Rita P. Maguire, Arizona Center for Public Policy, Phoenix, AZ (p. 186)
*Ken Masugi, Claremont Institute, Claremont, CA (p. 191)
*John McClaughry, Ethan Allen Institute, Concord, VT (p. 193)
 Edmunc J. McMahon, Manhattan Institute for Policy Innovation, New York, NY (p. 196)
 Lawrence J. McQuillan, Pacific Research Institute, San Francisco, CA (p. 197)
*Daniel Mead Smith, Washington Policy Center, Seattle, WA (p. 198)
*John Merrifield, University of Texas, San Antonio, San Antonio, TX (p. 199)
 Harry Messenheimer, Rio Grande Foundation, Tijeras, NM (p. 200)
*J. Scott Moody, Tax Foundation, Washington, DC (p. 205)
*Adrian T. Moore, Reason Foundation, Los Angeles, CA (p. 205)
 Stephen J. Moore, Club for Growth, Washington, DC (p. 206)
*Joseph A. Morris, Lincoln Legal Foundation, Chicago, IL (p. 207)
 Thomas Nechyba, Duke University, Durham, NC (p. 211)
 Michael A. Nelson, University of Akron, Akron, OH (p. 212)
 David Charles Nice, Washington State University, Pullman, WA (p. 213)
*Henry Olsen, III, Manhattan Institute for Policy Research, New York, NY (p. 219)
*Jim Panyard, Pennsylvania Manufacturer's Association, Harrisburg, PA (p. 221)
*Duane Parde, American Legislative Exchange Council, Washington, DC (p. 221)
*William S. Peirce, Case Western Reserve University, Cleveland, OH (p. 224)
*Karl Peterjohn, Kansas Taxpayers Network, Wichita, KS (p. 226)

STATE AND LOCAL PUBLIC FINANCE (Continued)

Penn Pfiffner, Independence Institute, Golden, CO (p. 227)

*Dennis Polhill, Independence Institute, Golden, CO (p. 230)

*Robert W. Poole, Jr., Reason Foundation, Los Angeles, CA (p. 230)

Barry W. Poulson, University of Colorado, Boulder, CO (p. 232)

*Scott Pullins, Ohio Taxpayers Association and OTA Foundation, Columbus, OH (p. 234)

*Alvin Rabushka, Hoover Institution, Stanford, CA (p. 235)

*W. Robert Reed, University of Oklahoma, Norman, OK (p. 238)

Alan Reynolds, Cato Institute, Washington, DC (p. 239)

*Brian Riedl, The Heritage Foundation, Washington, DC (p. 240)

*Anthony Rufolo, Portland State University, Portland, OR (p. 246)

*Linda Runbeck, Taxpayers League of Minnesota, Plymouth, MN (p. 247)

Peter D. Salins, Manhattan Institute for Policy Research, New York, NY (p. 248)

Dallas L. Salisbury, Employee Benefit Research Institute, Washington, DC (p. 248)

Roberta Rubel Schaefer, Worcester Regional Research Bureau, Worcester, MA (p. 252)

*Bill Schilling, Wyoming Business Alliance / Wyoming Heritage Foundation,
    Casper, WY (p. 253)

*Geoffrey F. Segal, Reason Public Policy Institute, Los Angeles, CA (p. 256)

*Pete Sepp, National Taxpayers Union, Alexandria, VA (p. 257)

*Steven M. Sheffrin, University of California, Davis, Davis, CA (p. 258)

*Randy T. Simmons, Utah State University, Logan, UT (p. 260)

Russell S. Sobel, West Virginia University, Morgantown, WV (p. 265)

*Samuel R. Staley, Buckeye Institute for Public Policy Solutions, Columbus, OH (p. 268)

*David Stanley, National Taxpayers Union, Muscatine, IA (p. 268)

*James Stergios, Pioneer Institute for Public Policy Research, Boston, MA (p. 268)

*David Strom, Taxpayers League of Minnesota, Plymouth, MN (p. 270)

Michael D. Stroup, Stephen F. Austin State University, Nacogdoches, TX (p. 270)

Charles Stuart, University of California, Santa Barbara, Santa Barbara, CA (p. 271)

*William Craig Stubblebine, Claremont McKenna College, Claremont, CA (p. 271)

Christopher B. Summers, Maryland Public Policy Institute, Germantown, MD (p. 272)

*David Swindell, Clemson University, Clemson, SC (p. 273)

*John Taylor, Virginia Institute for Public Policy, Potomac Falls, VA (p. 274)

Michael W. Thompson, Thomas Jefferson Institute for Public Policy, Springfield, VA (p. 278)

J. Mills Thornton, III, University of Michigan, Ann Arbor, MI (p. 278)

*Mark Thornton, Columbus State University, Columbus, GA (p. 278)

*Jim Tobin, National Taxpayers United of Illinois, Chicago, IL (p. 279)

Eugenia Froedge Toma, University of Kentucky, Lexington, KY (p. 280)

*David G. Tuerck, Beacon Hill Institute, Boston, MA (p. 281)

*Lewis Uhler, National Tax Limitation Committee, Roseville, CA (p. 283)

*Richard Vedder, Ohio University, Athens, OH (p. 284)

*Peggy Venable, Texas Citizens for a Sound Economy, Austin, TX (p. 284)

*Richard E. Wagner, George Mason University, Fairfax, VA (p. 286)

*Stephen J. K. Walters, Loyola College, Baltimore, MD (p. 288)

*Rolf A. Weil, Roosevelt University, Chicago, IL (p. 291)

*Bob Williams, Evergreen Freedom Foundation, Olympia, WA (p. 295)

*Ron F. Williamson, Great Plains Public Policy Institute, Sioux Falls, SD (p. 295)

*Gary Wolfram, Hillsdale College, Hillsdale, MI (p. 297)

James V. Young, Lee's Summit, MO (p. 300)

TAXATION/TAX REFORM

*Stephen Adams, Pioneer Institute for Public Policy Research, Boston, MA (p. 34)

*M. Gene Aldridge, New Mexico Independence Research Institute, Las Cruces, NM (p. 36)

Robert V. Andelson, American Institute for Economic Research, Auburn, AL (p. 37)

Barbara Anderson, Citizens for Limited Taxation and Government, Peabody, MA (p. 38)

Damon Ansell, Americans for Tax Reform, Washington, DC (p. 39)

---

* Has testified before a state or federal legislative committee

TAXATION/TAX REFORM (Continued)

Craig E. Aronoff, Kennesaw State College, Kennesaw, GA (p. 41)

*Chris Atkins, American Legislative Exchange Council, Washington, DC (p. 41)

*Thomas C. Atwood, National Council For Adoption, Alexandria, VA (p. 41)

Brian Backstrom, Empire Foundation for Policy Research, Clifton Park, NY (p. 42)

Karen Bailey, Americans for Tax Reform, Washington, DC (p. 42)

*Charles W. Baird, California State University, Hayward, Hayward, CA (p. 43)

*Keith G. Baker, Florida TaxWatch Research Institute, Inc., Tallahassee, FL (p. 43)

John Barrett, Beacon Hill Institute, Boston, MA (p. 46)

*John S. Barry, Tax Foundation, Washington, DC (p. 46)

*Bruce R. Bartlett, National Center for Policy Analysis, Great Falls, VA (p. 46)

*William W. Beach, The Heritage Foundation, Washington, DC (p. 48)

*John H. Beck, Gonzaga University, Spokane, WA (p. 48)

Bill Becker, Maine Policy Center, Portland, ME (p. 48)

Paul Beckner, Citizens for a Sound Economy, Washington, DC (p. 48)

*John E. Berthoud, National Taxpayers Union, Alexandria, VA (p. 52)

*Wayman R. Bishop, The Family Foundation of Virginia, Richmond, VA (p. 53)

Greg Blankenship, Illinois Policy Institute, Springfield, IL (p. 54)

*Mark A. Bloomfield, American Council for Capital Formation, Washington, DC (p. 55)

*Patrick M. Boarman, National University San Diego, San Diego, CA (p. 55)

Jeffrey R. Boeyink, Iowans for Tax Relief, Muscatine, IA (p. 56)

Thomas E. Borcherding, Claremont Graduate University, Claremont, CA (p. 57)

Michael J. Boskin, Hoover Institution, Stanford, CA (p. 57)

David F. Bradford, Princeton University, Princeton, NJ (p. 59)

Demian Brady, National Taxpayers Union Foundation, Alexandria, VA (p. 59)

B. Jason Brooks, Empire Foundation for Policy Research, Clifton Park, NY (p. 62)

*Bill Brooks, North Carolina Family Policy Council, Raleigh, NC (p. 62)

*Matthew J. Brouillette, The Commonwealth Foundation, Harrisburg, PA (p. 62)

James H. Broussard, Citizens Against Higher Taxes, Hershey, PA (p. 63)

*Kenneth Brown, Rio Grande Foundation, Albuquerque, NM (p. 63)

James M. Buchanan, Center for the Study of Public Choice, Fairfax, VA (p. 64)

*Victoria Craig Bunce, Council for Affordable Health Insurance,
    Inver Grove Heights, MN (p. 65)

*David Burton, Argus Group, Alexandria, VA (p. 66)

*Stuart Butler, The Heritage Foundation, Washington, DC (p. 66)

*Dominic M. Calabro, Florida TaxWatch Research Institute, Inc., Tallahassee, FL (p. 67)

*Jon Charles Caldara, Independence Institute, Golden, CO (p. 67)

*F. Patricia Callahan, American Association of Small Property Owners, Washington, DC (p. 68)

Leslie Carbone, Fairfax, VA (p. 69)

*James B. Cardle, Texas Citizen Action Network, Austin, TX (p. 69)

Merrick Carey, Lexington Institute, Arlington, VA (p. 70)

*Allan C. Carlson, Howard Center for Family, Religion and Society, Rockford, IL (p. 70)

*Michael A. Ciamarra, Alabama Policy Institute, Birmingham, AL (p. 74)

*J. R. Clark, University of Tennessee, Chattanooga, Chattanooga, TN (p. 75)

Peter Cleary, American Conservative Union, Alexandria, VA (p. 75)

*Richard T. Colgan, Bridgewater State College, Warwick, RI (p. 78)

Peter F. Colwell, University of Illinois, Urbana, IL (p. 79)

William Constantine, Centre for New Black Leadership, Reston, VA (p. 80)

Kellyanne Conway, the polling company/WomanTrend, Washington, DC (p. 80)

Roy E. Cordato, John Locke Foundation, Raleigh, NC (p. 82)

*Louis J. Cordia, Cordia Companies, Alexandria, VA (p. 82)

Bob Corkins, Kansas Legislative Education and Research, Inc., Topeka, KS (p. 82)

*Jon Coupal, Howard Jarvis Taxpayers Association, Sacramento, CA (p. 83)

*C. W. Cowles, Central Michigan University, Midlothian, VA (p. 84)

Edward H. Crane, Cato Institute, Washington, DC (p. 85)

TAXATION/TAX REFORM (Continued)

*Matt Daniels, Alliance for Marriage, Springfield, VA (p. 88)
Richard S. Davis, Washington Research Council, Seattle, WA (p. 89)
Veronique de Rugy, Cato Institute, Washington, DC (p. 90)
Helene Denney, Nevada Policy Research Insitute, Las Vegas, NV (p. 92)
D. P. Diffine, Harding University, Searcy, AR (p. 95)
Pete du Pont, National Center for Policy Analysis, Wilmington, DE (p. 98)
*William C. Dunkelberg, National Federation of Independent Business, Wynnewood, PA (p. 100)
Gerald P. Dwyer, Jr., Federal Reserve Bank of Atlanta, Atlanta, GA (p. 101)
Thomas R. Dye, Florida State University, Tallahassee, FL (p. 101)
Jefferson G. Edgens, Morehead State University – Jackson Center, Jackson, KY (p. 103)
Christopher Edwards, Cato Institute, Washington, DC (p. 104)
Isaac Ehrlich, State University of New York, Buffalo, Buffalo, NY (p. 105)
*Ryan Ellis, Council for Government Reform, Arlington, VA (p. 106)
*Eric M. Engen, American Enterprise Institute, Washington, DC (p. 107)
*Stephen Entin, Institute for Research on the Economics of Taxation, Washington, DC (p. 107)
Edward D. Failor, Sr., Iowans for Tax Relief, Muscatine, IA (p. 108)
Jack Faris, National Federation of Independent Business, Washington, DC (p. 109)
Chip Faulkner, Citizens for Limited Taxation and Government, Wentham, MA (p. 109)
Peter Ferrara, International Center for Law and Economics, Washington, DC (p. 110)
*Robert Fike, Americans for Tax Reform, Washington, DC (p. 111)
Marilyn R. Flowers, Ball State University, Muncie, IN (p. 113)
*Michael Flynn, American Legislative Exchange Council, Washington, DC (p. 113)
Fred E. Foldvary, Santa Clara University, Santa Clara, CA (p. 114)
Burton W. Folsom, Jr., Center for the American Idea, Houston, TX (p. 114)
William F. Ford, Middle Tennessee State University, Murfreesboro, TN (p. 114)
Micah Paul Frankel, California State University, Hayward, Hayward, CA (p. 115)
*John Frydenlund, Citizens Against Government Waste, Washington, DC (p. 118)
Adam Fuller, Toward Tradition, Mercer Island, WA (p. 118)
Lowell E. Gallaway, Ohio University, Athens, OH (p. 120)
Steven Garrison, Public Interest Institute, Mount Pleasant, IA (p. 120)
David E. R. Gay, University of Arkansas, Fayetteville, AR (p. 121)
James S. Gilmore, The Heritage Foundation, Washington, DC (p. 123)
*Tom Giovanetti, Institute for Policy Innovation, Lewisville, TX (p. 124)
*Stephen O. Goodrick, National Right to Work Committee, Springfield, VA (p. 126)
Leonard M. Greene, Institute for SocioEconomic Studies, White Plains, NY (p. 129)
Charles Greenwalt, II, Susquehanna Valley Center for Public Policy, Hershey, PA (p. 129)
*Grant R. Gulibon, The Commonwealth Foundation, Harrisburg, PA (p. 130)
*Paul Guppy, Washington Policy Center, Seattle, WA (p. 131)
*Erick Gustafson, Citizens for a Sound Economy, Washington, DC (p. 131)
*James D. Gwartney, Florida State University, Tallahassee, FL (p. 131)
Robert Hall, Hoover Institution, Stanford, CA (p. 132)
Steve H. Hanke, Johns Hopkins University, Baltimore, MD (p. 134)
*C. Lowell Harriss, Columbia University, Bronxville, NY (p. 136)
David Hartman, The Lone Star Foundation, Austin, TX (p. 136)
*Kevin A. Hassett, American Enterprise Institute, Washington, DC (p. 137)
*Jake Haulk, Allegheny Institute for Public Policy, Pittsburgh, PA (p. 137)
Michael S. Heath, Christian Civic League of Maine, Augusta, ME (p. 138)
Rea Hederman, Jr., The Heritage Foundation, Washington, DC (p. 139)
*David R. Henderson, Hoover Institution, Pacific Grove, CA (p. 139)
Lowman Henry, Lincoln Institute of Public Opinion Research, Inc., Harrisburg, PA (p. 140)
Robert Stanley Herren, North Dakota State University, Fargo, ND (p. 140)
Jonathan Hill, North Carolina Citizens for a Sound Economy, Raleigh, NC (p. 142)
*Scott Hodge, Tax Foundation, Washington, DC (p. 144)

TAXATION/TAX REFORM (Continued)

David Hogberg, Public Interest Institute, Mount Pleasant, IA **(p. 144)**
*****Randall G. Holcombe,** Florida State University, Tallahassee, FL **(p. 144)**
*****Fred Holden,** Phoenix Enterprises, Arvada, CO **(p. 144)**
*****John MacDonald Hood,** John Locke Foundation, Raleigh, NC **(p. 145)**
*****Kerri Houston,** American Conservative Union Field Office, Dallas, TX **(p. 147)**
*****Robert Hughes,** The National Association for the Self-Employed, Washington, DC **(p. 149)**
*****Lawrence Hunter,** Empower America, Washington, DC **(p. 149)**
Dennis S. Ippolito, Southern Methodist University, Dallas, TX **(p. 152)**
Thomas Ivancie, America's Future Foundation, Washington, DC **(p. 152)**
*****Charles W. Jarvis,** United Seniors Association, Fairfax, VA **(p. 153)**
Dale W. Jorgenson, Harvard University, Cambridge, MA **(p. 156)**
*****Doug Kagan,** Nebraska Taxpayers for Freedom, Omaha, NE **(p. 157)**
*****David Keating,** National Taxpayers Union, Alexandria, VA **(p. 159)**
*****Raymond J. Keating,** Small Business Survival Committee, Manorville, NY **(p. 159)**
*****David A. Keene,** American Conservative Union, Washington, DC **(p. 160)**
*****W. Thomas Kelly,** Savers and Investors League, Mirror Lake, NH **(p. 161)**
*****Jack Kemp,** Empower America, Washington, DC **(p. 161)**
Darlene A. Kennedy, Centre for New Black Leadership, Baltimore, MD **(p. 162)**
Karen Kerrigan, the polling company, Washington, DC **(p. 162)**
Matthew Kibbe, Citizens for a Sound Economy, Washington, DC **(p. 163)**
Kent King, Missouri State Teachers Association, Columbia, MO **(p. 164)**
Laurence Kotlikoff, Boston University, Boston, MA **(p. 168)**
George Krumbhaar, USBUDGET.COM, Washington, DC **(p. 170)**
*****Lawrence Kudlow,** Kudlow & Co., LLC, New York, NY **(p. 170)**
*****Michael D. LaFaive,** Mackinac Center for Public Policy, Midland, MI **(p. 171)**
Arthur B. Laffer, A. B. Laffer Associates, San Diego, CA **(p. 172)**
*****Andrea S. Lafferty,** Traditional Values Coalition, Washington, DC **(p. 172)**
Robert J. Lagomarsino, American Alliance for Tax Equity, Denver, CO **(p. 172)**
Byron S. Lamm, State Policy Network, Fort Wayne, IN **(p. 173)**
*****George Landrith,** Frontiers of Freedom Institute, Fairfax, VA **(p. 173)**
*****Mark R. Levin,** Landmark Legal Foundation, Herndon, VA **(p. 178)**
Cotton M. Lindsay, Clemson University, Clemson, SC **(p. 181)**
James Lucier, Prudential Securities, Arlington, VA **(p. 184)**
*****John H. Makin,** American Enterprise Institute, Washington, DC **(p. 187)**
Michael Marlow, California Polytechnic State University, San Luis Obispo, CA **(p. 189)**
*****Jim Martin,** 60 Plus Association, Arlington, VA **(p. 190)**
Mary Martin, The Seniors Coalition, Springfield, VA **(p. 190)**
John N. Mathys, DePaul University, Elmhurst, IL **(p. 191)**
Derrick A. Max, Alliance for Worker Retirement Security, Washington, DC **(p. 192)**
*****John McClaughry,** Ethan Allen Institute, Concord, VT **(p. 193)**
*****Kelly McCutchen,** Georgia Public Policy Foundation, Atlanta, GA **(p. 194)**
*****Robert W. McGee,** Barry University, Miami Shores, FL **(p. 195)**
John O. McGinnis, Cardozo School of Law, New York, NY **(p. 196)**
Darrell McKigney, Small Business Survival Committee, Washington, DC **(p. 196)**
Edmunc J. McMahon, Manhattan Institute for Policy Innovation, New York, NY **(p. 196)**
Edward T. McMullen, Jr., South Carolina Policy Council, Columbia, SC **(p. 197)**
Lawrence J. McQuillan, Pacific Research Institute, San Francisco, CA **(p. 197)**
*****Maurice McTigue,** Mercatus Center at George Mason University, Arlington, VA **(p. 197)**
Thomas Mead, Maine Policy Center, Portland, ME **(p. 198)**
*****Daniel Mead Smith,** Washington Policy Center, Seattle, WA **(p. 198)**
*****John Merrifield,** University of Texas, San Antonio, San Antonio, TX **(p. 199)**
Harry Messenheimer, Rio Grande Foundation, Tijeras, NM **(p. 200)**
Norbert Michel, The Heritage Foundation, Washington, DC **(p. 201)**
Christopher Middleton, Pacific Research Institute, San Francisco, CA **(p. 201)**

TAXATION/TAX REFORM (Continued)

*Dan Mitchell, The Heritage Foundation, Washington, DC (p. 203)
*J. Scott Moody, Tax Foundation, Washington, DC (p. 205)
 Stephen J. Moore, Club for Growth, Washington, DC (p. 206)
 Suzanne C. Moore, Delaware Public Policy Institute, Wilmington, DE (p. 206)
 Chuck Muth, American Conservative Union, Alexandria, VA (p. 210)
*Ronald Nehring, Americans for Tax Reform, San Diego, CA (p. 212)
 Michael A. Nelson, University of Akron, Akron, OH (p. 212)
*William A. Niskanen, Cato Institute, Washington, DC (p. 214)
*Grover Norquist, Americans for Tax Reform, Washington, DC (p. 214)
 Mike O'Neill, Landmark Legal Foundation, Herndon, VA (p. 217)
*Richard Olivastro, People Dynamics, Farmington, CT (p. 218)
*Gary J. Palmer, Alabama Policy Institute, Birmingham, AL (p. 221)
*Jim Panyard, Pennsylvania Manufacturer's Association, Harrisburg, PA (p. 221)
 Sam Perelli, United Taxpayers of New Jersey, Cedar Grove, NJ (p. 225)
*Karl Peterjohn, Kansas Taxpayers Network, Wichita, KS (p. 226)
 Penn Pfiffner, Independence Institute, Golden, CO (p. 227)
*Nancy M. Pfotenhauer, Independent Women's Forum, Arlington, VA (p. 227)
*Howard Phillips, The Conservative Caucus, Inc., Vienna, VA (p. 227)
 Bruce Piasecki, AHC Group, Saratoga Springs, NY (p. 228)
 Charles I. Plosser, University of Rochester, Rochester, NY (p. 229)
*Dennis Polhill, Independence Institute, Golden, CO (p. 230)
 Barry W. Poulson, University of Colorado, Boulder, CO (p. 232)
*Scott Pullins, Ohio Taxpayers Association and OTA Foundation, Columbus, OH (p. 234)
*Andrew F. Quinlan, Center for Freedom and Prosperity, Alexandria, VA (p. 234)
*Alvin Rabushka, Hoover Institution, Stanford, CA (p. 235)
 Richard W. Rahn, NOVECON, Alexandria, VA (p. 236)
 John Raisian, Hoover Institution, Stanford, CA (p. 236)
 Ralph Rector, The Heritage Foundation, Washington, DC (p. 237)
 George Reisman, Pepperdine University, Laguna Hills, CA (p. 238)
 Alan Reynolds, Cato Institute, Washington, DC (p. 239)
*Amy Ridenour, National Center for Public Policy Research, Washington, DC (p. 240)
*Brian Riedl, The Heritage Foundation, Washington, DC (p. 240)
 Michael Riley, Taxpayers Network, Inc., Cedarburg, WI (p. 240)
*Aldona Robbins, Fiscal Associates, Arlington, VA (p. 241)
*Gary Robbins, Fiscal Associates, Arlington, VA (p. 241)
*Paul Craig Roberts, Institute for Political Economy, Panama City Beach, FL (p. 242)
 Russell Roberts, Weidenbaum Center, St. Louis, MO (p. 242)
 Llewellyn Rockwell, Jr., Ludwig von Mises Institute, Auburn, AL (p. 242)
 J. Patrick Rooney, Golden Rule Insurance Company, Indianapolis, IN (p. 243)
*Allen H. Roth, New York State Advisory Council on Privatization, New York, NY (p. 244)
*Richard O. Rowland, Grassroot Institute of Hawaii, Aiea, HI (p. 245)
*Anthony Rufolo, Portland State University, Portland, OR (p. 246)
*Linda Runbeck, Taxpayers League of Minnesota, Plymouth, MN (p. 247)
 Dallas L. Salisbury, Employee Benefit Research Institute, Washington, DC (p. 248)
 Peter J. Saunders, Central Washington University, Ellensburg, WA (p. 250)
*Thomas A. Schatz, Citizens Against Government Waste, Washington, DC (p. 252)
*Bill Schilling, Wyoming Business Alliance / Wyoming Heritage Foundation,
    Casper, WY (p. 253)
 Michael A. Schuyler, Institute for Research on the Economics of Taxation,
    Washington, DC (p. 254)
 Gerald W. Scully, San Juan Capistrano, CA (p. 255)
*Howard Segermark, Segermark Associates, Inc., Washington, DC (p. 256)
*Jay Sekulow, American Center for Law and Justice, Virginia Beach, VA (p. 256)
*Hans F. Sennholz, Grove City College, Grove City, PA (p. 257)

TAXATION/TAX REFORM (Continued)

*Pete Sepp, National Taxpayers Union, Alexandria, VA (p. 257)
  David F. Shaffer, Public Policy Institute of New York, Albany, NY (p. 257)
  Stephen Slivinski, Goldwater Institute, Phoenix, AZ (p. 262)
  Shaun Small, Empower America, Washington, DC (p. 262)
  Russell S. Sobel, West Virginia University, Morgantown, WV (p. 265)
  Patricia M. Soldano, Policy and Taxation Group, Santa Ana, CA (p. 265)
  Frank Spreng, McKendree College, Lebanon, IL (p. 267)
*Samuel R. Staley, Buckeye Institute for Public Policy Solutions, Columbus, OH (p. 268)
*David Stanley, National Taxpayers Union, Muscatine, IA (p. 268)
*C. Eugene Steuerle, Urban Institute, Washington, DC (p. 268)
  Oscar Stilley, Arkansans for School Choice, Fort Smith, AR (p. 269)
*David Strom, Taxpayers League of Minnesota, Plymouth, MN (p. 270)
  Michael D. Stroup, Stephen F. Austin State University, Nacogdoches, TX (p. 270)
  Charles Stuart, University of California, Santa Barbara, Santa Barbara, CA (p. 271)
*William Craig Stubblebine, Claremont McKenna College, Claremont, CA (p. 271)
  Christopher B. Summers, Maryland Public Policy Institute, Germantown, MD (p. 272)
  Michael P. Sweeney, Hillsdale College, Hillsdale, MI (p. 273)
  James R. "J.T." Taylor, Empower America, Washington, DC (p. 274)
*John Taylor, Virginia Institute for Public Policy, Potomac Falls, VA (p. 274)
*Forest M. Thigpen, Mississippi Family Council, Jackson, MS (p. 277)
*Margo Thorning, American Council for Capital Formation, Washington, DC (p. 278)
*Mark Thornton, Columbus State University, Columbus, GA (p. 278)
  Kenneth R. Timmerman, Maryland Taxpayers Association, Bethesda, MD (p. 279)
*Jim Tobin, National Taxpayers United of Illinois, Chicago, IL (p. 279)
*Robert D. Tollison, University of Mississippi, University, MS (p. 280)
  Brian S. Tracy, Brian Tracy International, Solana Beach, CA (p. 280)
*David G. Tuerck, Beacon Hill Institute, Boston, MA (p. 281)
*Grace-Marie Turner, Galen Institute, Alexandria, VA (p. 281)
  Charlotte Twight, Boise State University, Boise, ID (p. 282)
*Lewis Uhler, National Tax Limitation Committee, Roseville, CA (p. 283)
*Terry W. Van Allen, Kemah, TX (p. 283)
*Peggy Venable, Texas Citizens for a Sound Economy, Austin, TX (p. 284)
  Dane vonBreichenruchardt, U. S. Bill of Rights Foundation, Washington, DC (p. 286)
*Richard E. Wagner, George Mason University, Fairfax, VA (p. 286)
  Russ Walker, Citizens for a Sound Economy, Keizer, OR (p. 287)
*Malcolm Wallop, Frontiers of Freedom Institute, Fairfax, VA (p. 288)
  Robert B. Ward, Public Policy Institute of New York, Albany, NY (p. 289)
*Dane Waters, Initiative and Referendum Institute, Leesburg, VA (p. 289)
*Murray Weidenbaum, Weidenbaum Center, St. Louis, MO (p. 291)
*Bob Williams, Evergreen Freedom Foundation, Olympia, WA (p. 295)
*Ron F. Williamson, Great Plains Public Policy Institute, Sioux Falls, SD (p. 295)
*Gary Wolfram, Hillsdale College, Hillsdale, MI (p. 297)
  Jason Wright, Frontiers of Freedom Institute, Fairfax, VA (p. 299)
  David Zanotti, Ohio Roundtable, Strongsville, OH (p. 301)
  Jerold L. Zimmerman, University of Rochester, Rochester, NY (p. 302)
  Ronald A. Zumbrun, The Zumbrun Law Firm, Sacramento, CA (p. 303)

UNFUNDED MANDATES

*Jonathan H. Adler, Case Western Reserve University, Cleveland, OH (p. 35)
  Damon Ansell, Americans for Tax Reform, Washington, DC (p. 39)
*Thomas C. Atwood, National Council For Adoption, Alexandria, VA (p. 41)
  Brian Backstrom, Empire Foundation for Policy Research, Clifton Park, NY (p. 42)
*Keith G. Baker, Florida TaxWatch Research Institute, Inc., Tallahassee, FL (p. 43)
*Bruce R. Bartlett, National Center for Policy Analysis, Great Falls, VA (p. 46)

UNFUNDED MANDATES (Continued)

*Richard B. Belzer, Regulatory Checkbook, Washington, DC (p. 50)
*John E. Berthoud, National Taxpayers Union, Alexandria, VA (p. 52)
 David F. Bradford, Princeton University, Princeton, NJ (p. 59)
*Victoria Craig Bunce, Council for Affordable Health Insurance,
   Inver Grove Heights, MN (p. 65)
*Dominic M. Calabro, Florida TaxWatch Research Institute, Inc., Tallahassee, FL (p. 67)
*Jon Charles Caldara, Independence Institute, Golden, CO (p. 67)
 John F. Cogan, Hoover Institution, Stanford, CA (p. 77)
*Jon Coupal, Howard Jarvis Taxpayers Association, Sacramento, CA (p. 83)
*Donald J. Devine, Center for American Values, Shady Side, MD (p. 94)
*Thomas J. DiLorenzo, Loyola College, Clarksville, MD (p. 96)
*William C. Dunkelberg, National Federation of Independent Business,
   Wynnewood, PA (p. 100)
*Paula Easley, Resource Development Council for Alaska, Anchorage, AK (p. 102)
*John C. Eastman, Chapman University School of Law, Orange, CA (p. 102)
*William Eggers, Deloitte Research-Public Sector, Washington, DC (p. 104)
 Isaac Ehrlich, State University of New York, Buffalo, Buffalo, NY (p. 105)
 Marilyn R. Flowers, Ball State University, Muncie, IN (p. 113)
 Steven B. Frates, Claremont McKenna College, Claremont, CA (p. 116)
*Dana Joel Gattuso, Competitive Enterprise Institute, Alexandria, VA (p. 121)
*Tom Giovanetti, Institute for Policy Innovation, Lewisville, TX (p. 124)
*Paul Guppy, Washington Policy Center, Seattle, WA (p. 131)
*Erick Gustafson, Citizens for a Sound Economy, Washington, DC (p. 131)
*Robert Hale, Northwest Legal Foundation, Minot, ND (p. 132)
*Randy H. Hamilton, University of California, Berkeley, Berkeley, CA (p. 133)
*Scott Hodge, Tax Foundation, Washington, DC (p. 144)
 Candice Hoke, Cleveland State University, Cleveland, OH (p. 144)
*Michael Horowitz, Hudson Institute, Washington, DC (p. 146)
*Lawrence Hunter, Empower America, Washington, DC (p. 149)
 Shawn Kantor, University of Arizona, Tucson, AZ (p. 157)
 Diane S. Katz, Mackinac Center for Public Policy, Midland, MI (p. 158)
 Karen Kerrigan, the polling company, Washington, DC (p. 162)
 Kent King, Missouri State Teachers Association, Columbia, MO (p. 164)
*Lawrence Kudlow, Kudlow & Co., LLC, New York, NY (p. 170)
*Andrew Langer, National Federation of Independent Business, Washington, DC (p. 174)
 Leonard A. Leo, The Federalist Society for Law and Public Policy Studies,
   Washington, DC (p. 178)
 Derrick A. Max, Alliance for Worker Retirement Security, Washington, DC (p. 192)
 Thomas Mead, Maine Policy Center, Portland, ME (p. 198)
*Michael A. Morrisey, University of Alabama, Birmingham, Birmingham, AL (p. 207)
*Richard Olivastro, People Dynamics, Farmington, CT (p. 218)
 Sean Paige, Competitive Enterprise Institute, Washington, DC (p. 220)
 Barry W. Poulson, University of Colorado, Boulder, CO (p. 232)
*William L. Proctor, Flagler College, St. Augustine, FL (p. 233)
*Scott Pullins, Ohio Taxpayers Association and OTA Foundation, Columbus, OH (p. 234)
 Llewellyn Rockwell, Jr., Ludwig von Mises Institute, Auburn, AL (p. 242)
*Richard O. Rowland, Grassroot Institute of Hawaii, Aiea, HI (p. 245)
 Dallas L. Salisbury, Employee Benefit Research Institute, Washington, DC (p. 248)
*Bill Schilling, Wyoming Business Alliance / Wyoming Heritage Foundation,
   Casper, WY (p. 253)
*Pete Sepp, National Taxpayers Union, Alexandria, VA (p. 257)
*David Stanley, National Taxpayers Union, Muscatine, IA (p. 268)
 Doug Stiegler, Association of Maryland Families, Woodstock, MD (p. 269)
*David Strom, Taxpayers League of Minnesota, Plymouth, MN (p. 270)

---

* Has testified before a state or federal legislative committee

UNFUNDED MANDATES (Continued)

Eugenia Froedge Toma, University of Kentucky, Lexington, KY **(p. 280)**
*****Lewis Uhler,** National Tax Limitation Committee, Roseville, CA **(p. 283)**
*****Peggy Venable,** Texas Citizens for a Sound Economy, Austin, TX **(p. 284)**
Dane vonBreichenruchardt, U. S. Bill of Rights Foundation, Washington, DC **(p. 286)**
*****Bob Williams,** Evergreen Freedom Foundation, Olympia, WA **(p. 295)**

Commerce and Infrastructure

AGRICULTURE

Lee J. Alston, University of Colorado-Boulder, Boulder, CO **(p. 37)**
Bruce N. Ames, University of California, Berkeley, Berkeley, CA **(p. 37)**
Ron Arnold, Center for the Defense of Free Enterprise, Bellevue, WA **(p. 40)**
Alex Avery, Hudson Institute, Staunton, VA **(p. 41)**
***Dennis T. Avery,** Hudson Institute, Churchville, VA **(p. 42)**
***Bruce R. Bartlett,** National Center for Policy Analysis, Great Falls, VA **(p. 46)**
***William W. Beach,** The Heritage Foundation, Washington, DC **(p. 48)**
James Bovard, Rockville, MD **(p. 58)**
***William P. Browne,** Central Michigan University, Mount Pleasant, MI **(p. 64)**
***H. Sterling Burnett,** National Center for Policy Analysis, Dallas, TX **(p. 65)**
***Allan C. Carlson,** Howard Center for Family, Religion and Society, Rockford, IL **(p. 70)**
Gregory Conko, Competitive Enterprise Institute, Washington, DC **(p. 79)**
Bob Corkins, Kansas Legislative Education and Research, Inc., Topeka, KS **(p. 82)**
Pete du Pont, National Center for Policy Analysis, Wilmington, DE **(p. 98)**
***Evelyn Ebzery,** Memorial Hospital of Sheridan County, Sheridan, WY **(p. 103)**
Christopher Edwards, Cato Institute, Washington, DC **(p. 104)**
***Bert Ely,** Ely & Company, Inc., Alexandria, VA **(p. 106)**
Howard Fienberg, Statistical Assessment Service, Washington, DC **(p. 111)**
Sara Fitzgerald, The Heritage Foundation, Washington, DC **(p. 113)**
***John Frydenlund,** Citizens Against Government Waste, Washington, DC **(p. 118)**
Bruce L. Gardner, University of Maryland, College Park, MD **(p. 120)**
Steven Garrison, Public Interest Institute, Mount Pleasant, IA **(p. 120)**
***Robert Hale,** Northwest Legal Foundation, Minot, ND **(p. 132)**
Dale M. Hoover, North Carolina State University, Raleigh, NC **(p. 145)**
***Dean Kleckner,** Truth About Trade and Technology, Des Moines, IA **(p. 165)**
***Jay H. Lehr,** Environmental Education Enterprises, Ostrander, OH **(p. 177)**
***Stephen B. Lovejoy,** Purdue University, West Lafayette, IN **(p. 183)**
***Rita P. Maguire,** Arizona Center for Public Policy, Phoenix, AZ **(p. 186)**
***John McClaughry,** Ethan Allen Institute, Concord, VT **(p. 193)**
***Patrick Michaels,** University of Virginia, Charlottesville, VA **(p. 200)**
Robert H. Nelson, University of Maryland, College Park, MD **(p. 212)**
E. C. Pasour, Jr., North Carolina State University, Raleigh, NC **(p. 222)**
Victor Porlier, Center for Civic Renewal, Inc., Delmar, NY **(p. 231)**
***Brian Riedl,** The Heritage Foundation, Washington, DC **(p. 240)**
Barbara Rippel, Consumer Alert, Washington, DC **(p. 240)**
***Robin Rivett,** Pacific Legal Foundation, Sacramento, CA **(p. 241)**
***Thomas A. Schatz,** Citizens Against Government Waste, Washington, DC **(p. 252)**
***Jack Shockey,** Citizens for Property Rights, Hamilton, VA **(p. 259)**
***Frances B. Smith,** Consumer Alert, Washington, DC **(p. 263)**
Jeff Stier, American Council on Science and Health, New York, NY **(p. 269)**
Mary L. G. Theroux, The Independent Institute, Oakland, CA **(p. 276)**
***Ben A. Wallis, Jr.,** Institute for Human Rights, San Antonio, TX **(p. 287)**
***Murray Weidenbaum,** Weidenbaum Center, St. Louis, MO **(p. 291)**
***Ron F. Williamson,** Great Plains Public Policy Institute, Sioux Falls, SD **(p. 295)**
Ronald A. Zumbrun, The Zumbrun Law Firm, Sacramento, CA **(p. 303)**

ANTI-TRUST

William F. Adkinson, Progress & Freedom Foundation, Washington, DC **(p. 35)**
Donald L. Alexander, Western Michigan University, Kalamazoo, MI **(p. 36)**
***Dominick T. Armentano,** University of Hartford, West Hartford, CT **(p. 40)**
***William W. Beach,** The Heritage Foundation, Washington, DC **(p. 48)**
Jonathan James Bean, Southern Illinois University, Carbondale, IL **(p. 48)**

ANTI-TRUST (Continued)

George J. Benston, Emory University, Atlanta, GA (p. 51)

Walter Block, Loyola University New Orleans, New Orleans, LA (p. 55)

*Patrick M. Boarman, National University San Diego, San Diego, CA (p. 55)

*Donald J. Boudreaux, George Mason University, Fairfax, VA (p. 58)

*Wayne T. Brough, Citizens for a Sound Economy, Washington, DC (p. 62)

*Henry N. Butler, Chapman University, Orange, CA (p. 66)

*Ronald Cass, Boston University School of Law, Boston, MA (p. 72)

Robert Crandall, Brookings Institution, Washington, DC (p. 85)

*Clyde Wayne Crews, Jr., Cato Institute, Washington, DC (p. 86)

Michael E. DeBow, Samford University, Birmingham, AL (p. 91)

*Thomas J. DiLorenzo, Loyola College, Clarksville, MD (p. 96)

*James R. Edwards, Jr., Hudson Institute, Washington, DC (p. 104)

Kenneth G. Elzinga, University of Virginia, Charlottesville, VA (p. 106)

*Robert Franciosi, Goldwater Institute, Phoenix, AZ (p. 115)

*H. E. Frech, III, University of California, Santa Barbara, Santa Barbara, CA (p. 116)

*James Gattuso, The Heritage Foundation, Washington, DC (p. 121)

*Ernest Gellhorn, George Mason University School of Law, Washington, DC (p. 122)

*Tom Giovanetti, Institute for Policy Innovation, Lewisville, TX (p. 124)

*Lino A. Graglia, University of Texas, Austin, TX (p. 128)

*Michael S. Greve, American Enterprise Institute, Washington, DC (p. 129)

*Erick Gustafson, Citizens for a Sound Economy, Washington, DC (p. 131)

*Robert Hahn, American Enterprise Institute, Washington, DC (p. 132)

Steve H. Hanke, Johns Hopkins University, Baltimore, MD (p. 134)

Thomas Hazlett, Manhattan Institute for Policy Research, Washington, DC (p. 138)

*David R. Henderson, Hoover Institution, Pacific Grove, CA (p. 139)

Jack High, George Mason University, Arlington, VA (p. 142)

Diane S. Katz, Mackinac Center for Public Policy, Midland, MI (p. 158)

F. Scott Kieff, Washington University, St. Louis, MO (p. 163)

*David B. Kopel, Independence Institute, Golden, CO (p. 167)

Montgomery N. Kosma, Jones, Day, Reavis & Pogue, Washington, DC (p. 167)

*Randall Kroszner, University of Chicago, Chicago, IL (p. 170)

*George Landrith, Frontiers of Freedom Institute, Fairfax, VA (p. 173)

*Richard Langlois, University of Connecticut, Storrs, CT (p. 174)

Tom Lenard, Progress & Freedom Foundation, Washington, DC (p. 177)

Leonard A. Leo, The Federalist Society for Law and Public Policy Studies, Washington, DC (p. 178)

Stanley J. Liebowitz, University of Texas, Dallas, Richardson, TX (p. 180)

Edward J. Lopez, University of North Texas, Denton, TX (p. 183)

John R. Lott, Jr., American Enterprise Institute, Washington, DC (p. 183)

James Lucier, Prudential Securities, Arlington, VA (p. 184)

*David N. Mayer, Capital University Law School, Columbus, OH (p. 193)

Norbert Michel, The Heritage Foundation, Washington, DC (p. 201)

*Dan Mitchell, The Heritage Foundation, Washington, DC (p. 203)

Seth W. Norton, Wheaton College, Wheaton, IL (p. 215)

*Daniel Oliver, Pacific Research Institute, Washington, DC (p. 219)

*William S. Peirce, Case Western Reserve University, Cleveland, OH (p. 224)

*Sam Peltzman, University of Chicago Graduate School of Business, Chicago, IL (p. 225)

Laura Bennett Peterson, Washington, DC (p. 226)

*William H. Peterson, Washington, DC (p. 227)

*James Prendergast, Americans for Technology Leadership, Washington, DC (p. 232)

George Priest, Yale Law School, New Haven, CT (p. 233)

*Scott Pullins, Ohio Taxpayers Association and OTA Foundation, Columbus, OH (p. 234)

George Reisman, Pepperdine University, Laguna Hills, CA (p. 238)

Jonathan Rose, Arizona State University, Tempe, AZ (p. 243)

---

* Has testified before a state or federal legislative committee

ANTI-TRUST (Continued)

*Paul Rubin, Emory University, Atlanta, GA (p. 246)
*Charles F. Rule, Fried, Frank, Harris, Shriver & Jacobson, Washington, DC (p. 246)
*Thomas R. Saving, Texas A&M University, College Station, TX (p. 251)
*Thomas A. Schatz, Citizens Against Government Waste, Washington, DC (p. 252)
*John W. Schlicher, Gray, Cary, Ware & Freidenrich, Palo Alto, CA (p. 253)
*Pete Sepp, National Taxpayers Union, Alexandria, VA (p. 257)
 J. Gregory Sidak, American Enterprise Institute, Washington, DC (p. 259)
*Fred L. Smith, Jr., Competitive Enterprise Institute, Washington, DC (p. 263)
 Irwin Stelzer, Hudson Institute, Washington, DC (p. 268)
*David J. Theroux, The Independent Institute, Oakland, CA (p. 276)
*Jason M. Thomas, Citizens for a Sound Economy, Washington, DC (p. 277)
*Stephen J. K. Walters, Loyola College, Baltimore, MD (p. 288)
*Murray Weidenbaum, Weidenbaum Center, St. Louis, MO (p. 291)
*Lawrence Wohl, Gustavus Adolphus College, St. Peter, MN (p. 297)
 Jason Wright, Frontiers of Freedom Institute, Fairfax, VA (p. 299)
 Gene C. Wunder, Washburn University, Topeka, KS (p. 299)
 Edward W. Younkins, Wheeling Jesuit University, Wheeling, WV (p. 301)

THE ECONOMY

*Stephen Adams, Pioneer Institute for Public Policy Research, Boston, MA (p. 34)
 Martin Anderson, Hoover Institution, Stanford, CA (p. 38)
 Craig E. Aronoff, Kennesaw State College, Kennesaw, GA (p. 41)
*Sonia Arrison, Pacific Research Institute, San Francisco, CA (p. 41)
*Dennis T. Avery, Hudson Institute, Churchville, VA (p. 42)
*Iwan Azis, Cornell University, Ithaca, NY (p. 42)
 Brian Backstrom, Empire Foundation for Policy Research, Clifton Park, NY (p. 42)
*Keith G. Baker, Florida TaxWatch Research Institute, Inc., Tallahassee, FL (p. 43)
 Robert J. Barro, Harvard University, Cambridge, MA (p. 46)
*John S. Barry, Tax Foundation, Washington, DC (p. 46)
*Bruce R. Bartlett, National Center for Policy Analysis, Great Falls, VA (p. 46)
 Robert J. Batemarco, Peekskill, NY (p. 47)
*William W. Beach, The Heritage Foundation, Washington, DC (p. 48)
 Paul Beckner, Citizens for a Sound Economy, Washington, DC (p. 48)
 Walter Block, Loyola University New Orleans, New Orleans, LA (p. 55)
*Mark A. Bloomfield, American Council for Capital Formation, Washington, DC (p. 55)
*Patrick M. Boarman, National University San Diego, San Diego, CA (p. 55)
 Michael J. Boskin, Hoover Institution, Stanford, CA (p. 57)
*Wayne T. Brough, Citizens for a Sound Economy, Washington, DC (p. 62)
 John S. Butler, University of Texas, Austin, TX (p. 66)
*Dominic M. Calabro, Florida TaxWatch Research Institute, Inc., Tallahassee, FL (p. 67)
 Charles Calomiris, American Enterprise Institute, Washington, DC (p. 68)
*James B. Cardle, Texas Citizen Action Network, Austin, TX (p. 69)
*Bruce K. Chapman, Discovery Institute, Seattle, WA (p. 72)
 Kenneth W. Clarkson, University of Miami, Coral Gables, FL (p. 75)
 Howard Cochran, Jr., Belmont University, Nashville, TN (p. 77)
*William Conerly, Conerly Consulting, Portland, OR (p. 79)
 Roy E. Cordato, John Locke Foundation, Raleigh, NC (p. 82)
 Bob Corkins, Kansas Legislative Education and Research, Inc., Topeka, KS (p. 82)
 Neil S. Crispo, Florida State University, Tallahassee, FL (p. 86)
 Dinesh D'Souza, Hoover Institution, Stanford, CA (p. 87)
*Michael R. Darby, University of California at Los Angeles, Los Angeles, CA (p. 89)
 Charles Delorme, Jr., University of Georgia, Athens, GA (p. 92)
*William J. Dennis, National Federation of Independent Business Research Foundation, Washington, DC (p. 93)

THE ECONOMY (Continued)

D. P. Diffine, Harding University, Searcy, AR (p. 95)

*Thomas Duesterberg, Manufacturers Alliance, Arlington, VA (p. 99)

*William C. Dunkelberg, National Federation of Independent Business, Wynnewood, PA (p. 100)

Richard M. Ebeling, Hillsdale College, Hillsdale, MI (p. 102)

*Ryan Ellis, Council for Government Reform, Arlington, VA (p. 106)

*Charles M. Elson, University of Delaware, Newark, DE (p. 106)

*Bert Ely, Ely & Company, Inc., Alexandria, VA (p. 106)

*Stephen Entin, Institute for Research on the Economics of Taxation, Washington, DC (p. 107)

*David I. Fand, James M. Buchanan Center for Political Economy, Fairfax, VA (p. 109)

Peter Ferrara, International Center for Law and Economics, Washington, DC (p. 110)

*Robert Fike, Americans for Tax Reform, Washington, DC (p. 111)

*Barbara Hackman Franklin, Barbara Franklin Enterprises, Washington, DC (p. 116)

*Milton Friedman, Hoover Institution, Stanford, CA (p. 117)

Leonard Gilroy, Reason Foundation, Los Angeles, CA (p. 123)

*Tom Giovanetti, Institute for Policy Innovation, Lewisville, TX (p. 124)

*James K. Glassman, American Enterprise Institute, Washington, DC (p. 124)

*Stephen O. Goodrick, National Right to Work Committee, Springfield, VA (p. 126)

*Linda Gorman, Independence Institute, Golden, CO (p. 127)

Phillip D. Grub, Eastern Washington University, Spokane, WA (p. 130)

*Erick Gustafson, Citizens for a Sound Economy, Washington, DC (p. 131)

*James D. Gwartney, Florida State University, Tallahassee, FL (p. 131)

*Robert Hahn, American Enterprise Institute, Washington, DC (p. 132)

Robert Hall, Hoover Institution, Stanford, CA (p. 132)

Alam E. Hammad, Alexandria, VA (p. 133)

Steve H. Hanke, Johns Hopkins University, Baltimore, MD (p. 134)

Scott E. Harrington, University of South Carolina, Columbia, SC (p. 135)

*Kevin A. Hassett, American Enterprise Institute, Washington, DC (p. 137)

*Jake Haulk, Allegheny Institute for Public Policy, Pittsburgh, PA (p. 137)

Rea Hederman, Jr., The Heritage Foundation, Washington, DC (p. 139)

Robert D. Hisrich, Case Western Reserve University, Cleveland, OH (p. 143)

*Leon Hollerman, Claremont Graduate University, Claremont, CA (p. 145)

Dale M. Hoover, North Carolina State University, Raleigh, NC (p. 145)

*Joseph Horton, University of Central Arkansas, Conway, AR (p. 146)

*Charles W. Jarvis, United Seniors Association, Fairfax, VA (p. 153)

*Chalmers Johnson, Japan Policy Research Institute, Cardiff, CA (p. 155)

Dale W. Jorgenson, Harvard University, Cambridge, MA (p. 156)

Milton Kafoglis, Emory University, Decatur, GA (p. 156)

*Raymond J. Keating, Small Business Survival Committee, Manorville, NY (p. 159)

*W. Thomas Kelly, Savers and Investors League, Mirror Lake, NH (p. 161)

Matthew Kibbe, Citizens for a Sound Economy, Washington, DC (p. 163)

*Lynne Kiesling, Reason Public Policy Institute, Los Angeles, CA (p. 163)

*Marvin H. Kosters, American Enterprise Institute, Washington, DC (p. 168)

Marie-Josee Kravis, Hudson Institute, Indianapolis, IN (p. 169)

Robert Krol, California State University, Northridge, Northridge, CA (p. 169)

*Randall Kroszner, University of Chicago, Chicago, IL (p. 170)

George Krumbhaar, USBUDGET.COM, Washington, DC (p. 170)

*Deepak Lal, University of California at Los Angeles, Los Angeles, CA (p. 172)

*George Landrith, Frontiers of Freedom Institute, Fairfax, VA (p. 173)

*Andrew Langer, National Federation of Independent Business, Washington, DC (p. 174)

Daniel Lapin, Toward Tradition, Mercer Island, WA (p. 174)

Lawrence J. Lau, Stanford University, Stanford, CA (p. 175)

Jack W. Lavery, Lavery Consulting Group, LLC, Washington Crossing, NJ (p. 175)

Tom Lenard, Progress & Freedom Foundation, Washington, DC (p. 177)

THE ECONOMY (Continued)

*Peter Linneman, University of Pennsylvania, Philadelphia, PA (p. 181)
*Dennis E. Logue, University of Oklahoma, Norman, OK (p. 182)
 Mary P. Mahoney, United Seniors Association, Inc., Washington, DC (p. 187)
*John H. Makin, American Enterprise Institute, Washington, DC (p. 187)
*Yuri N. Maltsev, Carthage College, Kenosha, WI (p. 188)
 Deryl W. Martin, Tennessee Technological University, Cookeville, TN (p. 190)
*Paul W. McCracken, University of Michigan Business School, Ann Arbor, MI (p. 194)
 Richard B. McKenzie, University of California, Irvine, Irvine, CA (p. 196)
 Lawrence J. McQuillan, Pacific Research Institute, San Francisco, CA (p. 197)
*Allan H. Meltzer, Carnegie Mellon University, Pittsburgh, PA (p. 199)
 Norbert Michel, The Heritage Foundation, Washington, DC (p. 201)
*Dan Mitchell, The Heritage Foundation, Washington, DC (p. 203)
 Lawrence Mone, Manhattan Institute for Policy Research, New York, NY (p. 205)
*Adrian T. Moore, Reason Foundation, Los Angeles, CA (p. 205)
 Stephen J. Moore, Club for Growth, Washington, DC (p. 206)
 Suzanne C. Moore, Delaware Public Policy Institute, Wilmington, DE (p. 206)
*Deroy Murdock, Atlas Economic Research Foundation, New York, NY (p. 209)
 Richard F. Muth, Emory University, Atlanta, GA (p. 210)
 Ronald Nash, Reformed Theological Seminary, Oviedo, FL (p. 211)
 Anthony I. Negbenebor, Gardner-Webb University, Boiling Springs, NC (p. 212)
 Robert H. Nelson, University of Maryland, College Park, MD (p. 212)
*Gerald P. O'Driscoll, Jr., Cato Institute, Falls Church, VA (p. 216)
*Sam Peltzman, University of Chicago Graduate School of Business, Chicago, IL (p. 225)
 Laura Bennett Peterson, Washington, DC (p. 226)
*William H. Peterson, Washington, DC (p. 227)
*Nancy M. Pfotenhauer, Independent Women's Forum, Arlington, VA (p. 227)
 Albert M. Piedra, Catholic University of America, Washington, DC (p. 228)
 Charles I. Plosser, University of Rochester, Rochester, NY (p. 229)
 Barry W. Poulson, University of Colorado, Boulder, CO (p. 232)
*Ernest Preeg, Manufacturers Alliance, Arlington, VA (p. 232)
*Scott Pullins, Ohio Taxpayers Association and OTA Foundation, Columbus, OH (p. 234)
 Paul A. Rahe, University of Tulsa, Tulsa, OK (p. 236)
*R. Sean Randolph, Bay Area Economic Forum, San Francisco, CA (p. 236)
 Alan Reynolds, Cato Institute, Washington, DC (p. 239)
*Brian Riedl, The Heritage Foundation, Washington, DC (p. 240)
 Russell Roberts, Weidenbaum Center, St. Louis, MO (p. 242)
 Llewellyn Rockwell, Jr., Ludwig von Mises Institute, Auburn, AL (p. 242)
*L. Jacobo Rodriguez, Cato Institute, Washington, DC (p. 242)
*Linda Runbeck, Taxpayers League of Minnesota, Plymouth, MN (p. 247)
*Thomas R. Saving, Texas A&M University, College Station, TX (p. 251)
*Bradley R. Schiller, American University, Washington, DC (p. 253)
*Bill Schilling, Wyoming Business Alliance / Wyoming Heritage Foundation,
   Casper, WY (p. 253)
 John T. Scott, Dartmouth College, Hanover, NH (p. 255)
 Robert Haney Scott, California State University, Chico, Chico, CA (p. 255)
 Clifford W. Smith, University of Rochester, Rochester, NY (p. 262)
 T. Alexander Smith, University of Tennessee, Knoxville, Knoxville, TN (p. 264)
*Neil H. Snyder, University of Virginia, Charlottesville, VA (p. 265)
 John C. Soper, John Carroll University, University Heights, OH (p. 266)
*Nancy Z. Spillman, Economic Education Enterprises, Canoga Park, CA (p. 267)
 Irwin Stelzer, Hudson Institute, Washington, DC (p. 268)
 Alan C. Stockman, University of Rochester, Rochester, NY (p. 269)
 James R. "J.T." Taylor, Empower America, Washington, DC (p. 274)
*David J. Theroux, The Independent Institute, Oakland, CA (p. 276)

THE ECONOMY (Continued)

Roy E. Thoman, West Texas A & M University, Canyon, TX (p. 277)
Chris R. Thomas, University of South Florida, Tampa, FL (p. 277)
*Mark Thornton, Columbus State University, Columbus, GA (p. 278)
Graham S. Toft, Hudson Institute, Indianapolis, IN (p. 280)
Jay L. Tontz, California State University, Hayward, Hayward, CA (p. 280)
R. Emmett Tyrrell, The American Alternative Foundation, Alexandria, VA (p. 282)
*Terry W. Van Allen, Kemah, TX (p. 283)
*Richard E. Wagner, George Mason University, Fairfax, VA (p. 286)
Jude Wanniski, Polyconomics, Parsippany, NJ (p. 288)
*Murray Weidenbaum, Weidenbaum Center, St. Louis, MO (p. 291)
Walter E. Williams, George Mason University, Fairfax, VA (p. 295)
Gene C. Wunder, Washburn University, Topeka, KS (p. 299)
Thomas L. Wyrick, Southwest Missouri State University, Springfield, MO (p. 300)
Edward W. Younkins, Wheeling Jesuit University, Wheeling, WV (p. 301)
Jerold L. Zimmerman, University of Rochester, Rochester, NY (p. 302)
Karl Zinsmeister, American Enterprise Institute, Cazenovia, NY (p. 302)

ENTREPRENEURSHIP/FREE ENTERPRISE

*Stephen Adams, Pioneer Institute for Public Policy Research, Boston, MA (p. 34)
Damon Ansell, Americans for Tax Reform, Washington, DC (p. 39)
Craig E. Aronoff, Kennesaw State College, Kennesaw, GA (p. 41)
*Sonia Arrison, Pacific Research Institute, San Francisco, CA (p. 41)
Stephen M. Bainbridge, University of California at Los Angeles, Los Angeles, CA (p. 43)
*Charles W. Baird, California State University, Hayward, Hayward, CA (p. 43)
*Keith G. Baker, Florida TaxWatch Research Institute, Inc., Tallahassee, FL (p. 43)
*Claude E. Barfield, American Enterprise Institute, Washington, DC (p. 45)
Robert J. Barro, Harvard University, Cambridge, MA (p. 46)
*John S. Barry, Tax Foundation, Washington, DC (p. 46)
Robert J. Batemarco, Peekskill, NY (p. 47)
*Naomi Lopez Bauman, Orlando, FL (p. 47)
Jonathan James Bean, Southern Illinois University, Carbondale, IL (p. 48)
Paul Beckner, Citizens for a Sound Economy, Washington, DC (p. 48)
David J. BenDaniel, Cornell University, Ithaca, NY (p. 50)
John J. Bethune, Barton College, Wilson, NC (p. 53)
Walter Block, Loyola University New Orleans, New Orleans, LA (p. 55)
*Mark A. Bloomfield, American Council for Capital Formation, Washington, DC (p. 55)
Peter J. Boettke, James M. Buchanan Center for Political Economy, Fairfax, VA (p. 56)
Philip L. Brach, Midtown Educational Foundation, Chicago, IL (p. 59)
*Wayne T. Brough, Citizens for a Sound Economy, Washington, DC (p. 62)
*Matthew J. Brouillette, The Commonwealth Foundation, Harrisburg, PA (p. 62)
*F. Patricia Callahan, American Association of Small Property Owners, Washington, DC (p. 68)
Nicholas Capaldi, Loyola University New Orleans, New Orleans, LA (p. 69)
*James B. Cardle, Texas Citizen Action Network, Austin, TX (p. 69)
Don Carrington, John Locke Foundation, Raleigh, NC (p. 71)
Michael John Caslin, III, National Foundation for Teaching Entrepreneurship,
    New York, NY (p. 71)
*Michael A. Ciamarra, Alabama Policy Institute, Birmingham, AL (p. 74)
Paul A. Cleveland, Birmingham Southern College, Birmingham, AL (p. 76)
J. Paul Combs, Appalachian Regional Development Institute, Boone, NC (p. 79)
Kellyanne Conway, the polling company/WomanTrend, Washington, DC (p. 80)
Bob Corkins, Kansas Legislative Education and Research, Inc., Topeka, KS (p. 82)
Neil S. Crispo, Florida State University, Tallahassee, FL (p. 86)
*Michael R. Darby, University of California at Los Angeles, Los Angeles, CA (p. 89)

---

* Has testified before a state or federal legislative committee

ENTREPRENEURSHIP/FREE ENTERPRISE (Continued)

*William J. Dennis, National Federation of Independent Business Research Foundation, Washington, DC **(p. 93)**

*Len Deo, New Jersey Family Policy Council, Parsippany, NJ **(p. 93)**

Arthur M. Diamond, Jr., University of Nebraska, Omaha, Omaha, NE **(p. 95)**

D. P. Diffine, Harding University, Searcy, AR **(p. 95)**

*Thomas J. DiLorenzo, Loyola College, Clarksville, MD **(p. 96)**

*Thomas Duesterberg, Manufacturers Alliance, Arlington, VA **(p. 99)**

*William C. Dunkelberg, National Federation of Independent Business, Wynnewood, PA **(p. 100)**

*Paul Dunn, University of Louisiana, Monroe, Monroe, LA **(p. 100)**

Richard M. Ebeling, Hillsdale College, Hillsdale, MI **(p. 102)**

Christopher Edwards, Cato Institute, Washington, DC **(p. 104)**

Joyce Elam, Florida International University, Miami, FL **(p. 105)**

W. Winston Elliott, III, Center for the American Idea, Houston, TX **(p. 106)**

*Charles M. Elson, University of Delaware, Newark, DE **(p. 106)**

Kenneth G. Elzinga, University of Virginia, Charlottesville, VA **(p. 106)**

Jack Faris, National Federation of Independent Business, Washington, DC **(p. 109)**

*Edwin J. Feulner, The Heritage Foundation, Washington, DC **(p. 111)**

Micah Paul Frankel, California State University, Hayward, Hayward, CA **(p. 115)**

*Barbara Hackman Franklin, Barbara Franklin Enterprises, Washington, DC **(p. 116)**

David E. R. Gay, University of Arkansas, Fayetteville, AR **(p. 121)**

Leonard Gilroy, Reason Foundation, Los Angeles, CA **(p. 123)**

*Tom Giovanetti, Institute for Policy Innovation, Lewisville, TX **(p. 124)**

*James K. Glassman, American Enterprise Institute, Washington, DC **(p. 124)**

*Stephen O. Goodrick, National Right to Work Committee, Springfield, VA **(p. 126)**

*Linda Gorman, Independence Institute, Golden, CO **(p. 127)**

Andrew Grainger, New England Legal Foundation, Boston, MA **(p. 128)**

*Grant R. Gulibon, The Commonwealth Foundation, Harrisburg, PA **(p. 130)**

*Gerald A. Gunderson, Trinity College, Hartford, CT **(p. 130)**

*Erick Gustafson, Citizens for a Sound Economy, Washington, DC **(p. 131)**

*James D. Gwartney, Florida State University, Tallahassee, FL **(p. 131)**

*Robert Hale, Northwest Legal Foundation, Minot, ND **(p. 132)**

Alam E. Hammad, Alexandria, VA **(p. 133)**

Steve H. Hanke, Johns Hopkins University, Baltimore, MD **(p. 134)**

*Lynn Harsh, Evergreen Freedom Foundation, Olympia, WA **(p. 136)**

*Jake Haulk, Allegheny Institute for Public Policy, Pittsburgh, PA **(p. 137)**

*David R. Henderson, Hoover Institution, Pacific Grove, CA **(p. 139)**

*Robert L. Hershey, Robert L. Hershey, P.E., Washington, DC **(p. 141)**

Jonathan Hill, North Carolina Citizens for a Sound Economy, Raleigh, NC **(p. 142)**

Robert D. Hisrich, Case Western Reserve University, Cleveland, OH **(p. 143)**

*Fred Holden, Phoenix Enterprises, Arvada, CO **(p. 144)**

*John MacDonald Hood, John Locke Foundation, Raleigh, NC **(p. 145)**

*Joseph Horton, University of Central Arkansas, Conway, AR **(p. 146)**

Edward L. Hudgins, The Objectivist Center, Washington, DC **(p. 148)**

*Robert Hughes, The National Association for the Self-Employed, Washington, DC **(p. 149)**

Sanford Ikeda, State University of New York, Purchase, NY **(p. 151)**

Thomas Ivancie, America's Future Foundation, Washington, DC **(p. 152)**

Louis James, Henry Hazlitt Foundation and Free-Market.Net, Chicago, IL **(p. 153)**

Theodore "Sylvester" John, Students In Free Enterprise, Springfield, MO **(p. 154)**

Shyam J. Kamath, California State University, Hayward, Hayward, CA **(p. 157)**

Martin S. Kaufman, Atlantic Legal Foundation, New York, NY **(p. 159)**

*Raymond J. Keating, Small Business Survival Committee, Manorville, NY **(p. 159)**

Karen Kerrigan, the polling company, Washington, DC **(p. 162)**

Fred Kiesner, Loyola Marymount University, Los Angeles, CA **(p. 163)**

ENTREPRENEURSHIP/FREE ENTERPRISE (Continued)

John E. Kramer, Institute for Justice, Washington, DC (p. 168)

Marie-Josee Kravis, Hudson Institute, Indianapolis, IN (p. 169)

*Randall Kroszner, University of Chicago, Chicago, IL (p. 170)

Deborah J. LaFetra, Pacific Legal Foundation, Sacramento, CA (p. 171)

Byron S. Lamm, State Policy Network, Fort Wayne, IN (p. 173)

*Andrew Langer, National Federation of Independent Business, Washington, DC (p. 174)

*Richard Langlois, University of Connecticut, Storrs, CT (p. 174)

Daniel Lapin, Toward Tradition, Mercer Island, WA (p. 174)

*Robert A. Lawson, Capital University, Columbus, OH (p. 176)

Patricia H. Lee, Institute for Justice, Washington, DC (p. 176)

Kurt R. Leube, Hoover Institution, Stanford, CA (p. 178)

*Mark R. Levin, Landmark Legal Foundation, Herndon, VA (p. 178)

*Peter Linneman, University of Pennsylvania, Philadelphia, PA (p. 181)

*Dennis E. Logue, University of Oklahoma, Norman, OK (p. 182)

Brett A. Magbee, Oklahoma Council of Public Affairs, Oklahoma City, OK (p. 186)

J. J. Mahoney, Diversified Consultants, Mount Pleasant, SC (p. 187)

*Nina May, *Renaissance Connection.com/RCNetwork.net*, Washington, DC (p. 192)

*Paul W. McCracken, University of Michigan Business School, Ann Arbor, MI (p. 194)

Darrell McKigney, Small Business Survival Committee, Washington, DC (p. 196)

Lawrence J. McQuillan, Pacific Research Institute, San Francisco, CA (p. 197)

*Daniel Mead Smith, Washington Policy Center, Seattle, WA (p. 198)

*Roger E. Meiners, University of Texas, Arlington, Arlington, TX (p. 198)

*William H. Mellor, Institute for Justice, Washington, DC (p. 199)

*Dan Mitchell, The Heritage Foundation, Washington, DC (p. 203)

Chuck Muth, American Conservative Union, Alexandria, VA (p. 210)

Phyllis Berry Myers, Centre for New Black Leadership, Washington, DC (p. 210)

Ronald Nash, Reformed Theological Seminary, Oviedo, FL (p. 211)

Anthony I. Negbenebor, Gardner-Webb University, Boiling Springs, NC (p. 212)

Robert H. Nelson, University of Maryland, College Park, MD (p. 212)

Seth W. Norton, Wheaton College, Wheaton, IL (p. 215)

*Fred O. Oladeinde, The Foundation for Democracy in Africa, Washington, DC (p. 218)

*Richard Olivastro, People Dynamics, Farmington, CT (p. 218)

*Darcy A. Olsen, Goldwater Institute, Phoenix, AZ (p. 219)

E. C. Pasour, Jr., North Carolina State University, Raleigh, NC (p. 222)

*Sam Peltzman, University of Chicago Graduate School of Business, Chicago, IL (p. 225)

*Karl Peterjohn, Kansas Taxpayers Network, Wichita, KS (p. 226)

*Lovett C. Peters, Pioneer Institute for Public Policy Research, Boston, MA (p. 226)

*William H. Peterson, Washington, DC (p. 227)

*Nancy M. Pfotenhauer, Independent Women's Forum, Arlington, VA (p. 227)

*Bruce Phillips, National Federation of Independent Business, Washington, DC (p. 227)

Bruce Piasecki, AHC Group, Saratoga Springs, NY (p. 228)

*David R. Pinkus, Small Business United of Texas, Austin, TX (p. 229)

*Sally C. Pipes, Pacific Research Institute, San Francisco, CA (p. 229)

*Daniel J. Popeo, Washington Legal Foundation, Washington, DC (p. 231)

*Edward Potter, Employment Policy Foundation, Washington, DC (p. 231)

*Scott Pullins, Ohio Taxpayers Association and OTA Foundation, Columbus, OH (p. 234)

*Don Racheter, Public Interest Institute, Mount Pleasant, IA (p. 235)

*R. Sean Randolph, Bay Area Economic Forum, San Francisco, CA (p. 236)

*Lawrence W. Reed, Mackinac Center for Public Policy, Midland, MI (p. 237)

*W. Robert Reed, University of Oklahoma, Norman, OK (p. 238)

Patrick Reilly, Cardinal Newman Society, Falls Church, VA (p. 238)

George Reisman, Pepperdine University, Laguna Hills, CA (p. 238)

Russell Roberts, Weidenbaum Center, St. Louis, MO (p. 242)

Gabriel Roth, Chevy Chase, MD (p. 244)

---

* Has testified before a state or federal legislative committee

ENTREPRENEURSHIP/FREE ENTERPRISE (Continued)

*Richard O. Rowland, Grassroot Institute of Hawaii, Aiea, HI (p. 245)
*Paul Rubin, Emory University, Atlanta, GA (p. 246)
*Charles F. Rule, Fried, Frank, Harris, Shriver & Jacobson, Washington, DC (p. 246)
*Susan Sarnoff, Ohio University, Athens, OH (p. 250)
*Bill Schilling, Wyoming Business Alliance / Wyoming Heritage Foundation, Casper, WY (p. 253)
*Geoffrey F. Segal, Reason Public Policy Institute, Los Angeles, CA (p. 256)
*Robert A. Sirico, Acton Institute for the Study of Religion and Liberty, Grand Rapids, MI (p. 261)
 Clifford W. Smith, University of Rochester, Rochester, NY (p. 262)
*Fred L. Smith, Jr., Competitive Enterprise Institute, Washington, DC (p. 263)
*Neil H. Snyder, University of Virginia, Charlottesville, VA (p. 265)
*Samuel R. Staley, Buckeye Institute for Public Policy Solutions, Columbus, OH (p. 268)
*David Strom, Taxpayers League of Minnesota, Plymouth, MN (p. 270)
 Michael D. Stroup, Stephen F. Austin State University, Nacogdoches, TX (p. 270)
*Alexander Tabarrok, Mercatus Center at George Mason University, Arlington, VA (p. 273)
 James R. "J.T." Taylor, Empower America, Washington, DC (p. 274)
*John Taylor, Virginia Institute for Public Policy, Potomac Falls, VA (p. 274)
*David J. Theroux, The Independent Institute, Oakland, CA (p. 276)
*Mark Thornton, Columbus State University, Columbus, GA (p. 278)
 Jay L. Tontz, California State University, Hayward, Hayward, CA (p. 280)
 Brian S. Tracy, Brian Tracy International, Solana Beach, CA (p. 280)
 Phillip N. Truluck, The Heritage Foundation, Washington, DC (p. 281)
*Terry W. Van Allen, Kemah, TX (p. 283)
*Richard E. Wagner, George Mason University, Fairfax, VA (p. 286)
*Lee H. Walker, New Coalition for Economic and Social Change, Chicago, IL (p. 287)
*Murray Weidenbaum, Weidenbaum Center, St. Louis, MO (p. 291)
 Jason Wright, Frontiers of Freedom Institute, Fairfax, VA (p. 299)
 Edward W. Younkins, Wheeling Jesuit University, Wheeling, WV (p. 301)
 Jerry Zandstra, Acton Institute for the Study of Religion and Liberty, Grand Rapids, MI (p. 301)
 Kate Xiao Zhou, University of Hawaii, Honolulu, HI (p. 302)
 Thomas W. Zimmerer, Saint Leo University, Saint Leo, FL (p. 302)

INFRASTRUCTURE

*Stephen Adams, Pioneer Institute for Public Policy Research, Boston, MA (p. 34)
*Keith G. Baker, Florida TaxWatch Research Institute, Inc., Tallahassee, FL (p. 43)
*Bruce R. Bartlett, National Center for Policy Analysis, Great Falls, VA (p. 46)
 Walter Block, Loyola University New Orleans, New Orleans, LA (p. 55)
*Dominic M. Calabro, Florida TaxWatch Research Institute, Inc., Tallahassee, FL (p. 67)
*Clyde Wayne Crews, Jr., Cato Institute, Washington, DC (p. 86)
*Michael De Alessi, Reason Foundation, Los Angeles, CA (p. 89)
*Robert Fike, Americans for Tax Reform, Washington, DC (p. 111)
*Robert Franciosi, Goldwater Institute, Phoenix, AZ (p. 115)
 Leonard Gilroy, Reason Foundation, Los Angeles, CA (p. 123)
*Stephen Goldsmith, Manhattan Institute for Policy Research, New York, NY (p. 126)
*Robert Hale, Northwest Legal Foundation, Minot, ND (p. 132)
 Robert D. Hisrich, Case Western Reserve University, Cleveland, OH (p. 143)
*John MacDonald Hood, John Locke Foundation, Raleigh, NC (p. 145)
*Lynne Kiesling, Reason Public Policy Institute, Los Angeles, CA (p. 163)
 Robert Krol, California State University, Northridge, Northridge, CA (p. 169)
*Kent Lassman, Progress & Freedom Foundation, Raleigh, NC (p. 175)
*James Andrew Lewis, Center for Strategic and International Studies, Washington, DC (p. 179)
*Ken Malloy, Center for the Advancement of Energy Markets, Washington, DC (p. 188)

INFRASTRUCTURE (Continued)

*Adrian T. Moore, Reason Foundation, Los Angeles, CA (p. 205)
Suzanne C. Moore, Delaware Public Policy Institute, Wilmington, DE (p. 206)
Seth W. Norton, Wheaton College, Wheaton, IL (p. 215)
*Sam Peltzman, University of Chicago Graduate School of Business, Chicago, IL (p. 225)
*Dennis Polhill, Independence Institute, Golden, CO (p. 230)
*Robert W. Poole, Jr., Reason Foundation, Los Angeles, CA (p. 230)
*R. Sean Randolph, Bay Area Economic Forum, San Francisco, CA (p. 236)
Peter Samuel, *Toll Roads Newsletter*, Frederick, MD (p. 249)
E. S. Savas, City University of New York, New York, NY (p. 250)
*Geoffrey F. Segal, Reason Public Policy Institute, Los Angeles, CA (p. 256)
*James Stergios, Pioneer Institute for Public Policy Research, Boston, MA (p. 268)
Michael D. Stroup, Stephen F. Austin State University, Nacogdoches, TX (p. 270)
Michael W. Thompson, Thomas Jefferson Institute for Public Policy, Springfield, VA (p. 278)
*Mark Thornton, Columbus State University, Columbus, GA (p. 278)
Ronald A. Zumbrun, The Zumbrun Law Firm, Sacramento, CA (p. 303)

MONEY AND FINANCIAL SERVICES

*Iwan Azis, Cornell University, Ithaca, NY (p. 42)
*Saul Z. Barr, University of Tennessee, Gulf Shores, AL (p. 46)
Robert J. Barro, Harvard University, Cambridge, MA (p. 46)
*John S. Barry, Tax Foundation, Washington, DC (p. 46)
*Bruce R. Bartlett, National Center for Policy Analysis, Great Falls, VA (p. 46)
Robert J. Batemarco, Peekskill, NY (p. 47)
*William W. Beach, The Heritage Foundation, Washington, DC (p. 48)
George J. Benston, Emory University, Atlanta, GA (p. 51)
*Patrick M. Boarman, National University San Diego, San Diego, CA (p. 55)
*James B. Burnham, Duquesne University, Pittsburgh, PA (p. 66)
*F. Patricia Callahan, American Association of Small Property Owners, Washington, DC (p. 68)
Elizabeth Currier, Committee for Monetary Research and Education, Inc.,
    Charlotte, NC (p. 87)
*Michael R. Darby, University of California at Los Angeles, Los Angeles, CA (p. 89)
*Lisa Dean, Free Congress Foundation, Washington, DC (p. 91)
Charles Delorme, Jr., University of Georgia, Athens, GA (p. 92)
D. P. Diffine, Harding University, Searcy, AR (p. 95)
*James A. Dorn, Cato Institute, Washington, DC (p. 97)
*John Douglas, Alston & Bird, Atlanta, GA (p. 97)
*William C. Dunkelberg, National Federation of Independent Business,
    Wynnewood, PA (p. 100)
Richard M. Ebeling, Hillsdale College, Hillsdale, MI (p. 102)
*Ryan Ellis, Council for Government Reform, Arlington, VA (p. 106)
*Charles M. Elson, University of Delaware, Newark, DE (p. 106)
*Bert Ely, Ely & Company, Inc., Alexandria, VA (p. 106)
*Stephen Entin, Institute for Research on the Economics of Taxation, Washington, DC (p. 107)
*Frank Falero, Springville, CA (p. 109)
*David I. Fand, James M. Buchanan Center for Political Economy, Fairfax, VA (p. 109)
Martin Feldstein, National Bureau of Economic Research, Cambridge, MA (p. 110)
*Barbara Hackman Franklin, Barbara Franklin Enterprises, Washington, DC (p. 116)
*Milton Friedman, Hoover Institution, Stanford, CA (p. 117)
*Tom Giovanetti, Institute for Policy Innovation, Lewisville, TX (p. 124)
Fred R. Glahe, University of Colorado, Boulder, CO (p. 124)
*James K. Glassman, American Enterprise Institute, Washington, DC (p. 124)
*Linda Gorman, Independence Institute, Golden, CO (p. 127)
Andrew Grainger, New England Legal Foundation, Boston, MA (p. 128)
*Erick Gustafson, Citizens for a Sound Economy, Washington, DC (p. 131)

---

* Has testified before a state or federal legislative committee

MONEY AND FINANCIAL SERVICES (Continued)

Steve H. Hanke, Johns Hopkins University, Baltimore, MD (p. 134)

Scott E. Harrington, University of South Carolina, Columbia, SC (p. 135)

Robert Stanley Herren, North Dakota State University, Fargo, ND (p. 140)

*Leon Hollerman, Claremont Graduate University, Claremont, CA (p. 145)

*Joseph Horton, University of Central Arkansas, Conway, AR (p. 146)

Steven Horwitz, St. Lawrence University, Canton, NY (p. 147)

*David John, The Heritage Foundation, Washington, DC (p. 154)

James B. Kau, University of Georgia, Athens, GA (p. 158)

*George G. Kaufman, Loyola University Chicago, Chicago, IL (p. 159)

*W. Thomas Kelly, Savers and Investors League, Mirror Lake, NH (p. 161)

Robert Krol, California State University, Northridge, Northridge, CA (p. 169)

*Randall Kroszner, University of Chicago, Chicago, IL (p. 170)

Daniel Lapin, Toward Tradition, Mercer Island, WA (p. 174)

Jack W. Lavery, Lavery Consulting Group, LLC, Washington Crossing, NJ (p. 175)

Leonard A. Leo, The Federalist Society for Law and Public Policy Studies, Washington, DC (p. 178)

*Dennis E. Logue, University of Oklahoma, Norman, OK (p. 182)

James Lucier, Prudential Securities, Arlington, VA (p. 184)

*Johnathon R. Macey, Cornell University, Ithaca, NY (p. 185)

*John H. Makin, American Enterprise Institute, Washington, DC (p. 187)

Deryl W. Martin, Tennessee Technological University, Cookeville, TN (p. 190)

*Paul W. McCracken, University of Michigan Business School, Ann Arbor, MI (p. 194)

J. Huston McCulloch, Ohio State University, Columbus, OH (p. 194)

*Allan H. Meltzer, Carnegie Mellon University, Pittsburgh, PA (p. 199)

Robert H. Nelson, University of Maryland, College Park, MD (p. 212)

*Gerald P. O'Driscoll, Jr., Cato Institute, Falls Church, VA (p. 216)

Mark J. Perry, University of Michigan, Flint, Flint, MI (p. 226)

Charles I. Plosser, University of Rochester, Rochester, NY (p. 229)

Adam Pritchard, Georgetown University Law Center, Washington, DC (p. 233)

Paul A. Rahe, University of Tulsa, Tulsa, OK (p. 236)

Richard W. Rahn, NOVECON, Alexandria, VA (p. 236)

Llewellyn Rockwell, Jr., Ludwig von Mises Institute, Auburn, AL (p. 242)

*L. Jacobo Rodriguez, Cato Institute, Washington, DC (p. 242)

*Joseph T. Salerno, Pace University, New York, NY (p. 248)

*Thomas R. Saving, Texas A&M University, College Station, TX (p. 251)

Brett D. Schaefer, The Heritage Foundation, Washington, DC (p. 252)

Kurt Schuler, Arlington, VA (p. 254)

*Anna J. Schwartz, National Bureau of Economic Research, New York, NY (p. 254)

G. W. Schwert, University of Rochester, Rochester, NY (p. 255)

Robert Haney Scott, California State University, Chico, Chico, CA (p. 255)

Larry J. Sechrest, Sul Ross State University, Alpine, TX (p. 255)

*Hans F. Sennholz, Grove City College, Grove City, PA (p. 257)

*Baker Smith, U. S. Constitutional Rights Legal Defense Fund, Inc., Marietta, GA (p. 262)

Clifford W. Smith, University of Rochester, Rochester, NY (p. 262)

*Frances B. Smith, Consumer Alert, Washington, DC (p. 263)

John C. Soper, John Carroll University, University Heights, OH (p. 266)

*Nancy Z. Spillman, Economic Education Enterprises, Canoga Park, CA (p. 267)

*Paul Schott Stevens, Dechert, Price & Rhoads, Washington, DC (p. 269)

Alan C. Stockman, University of Rochester, Rochester, NY (p. 269)

*David J. Theroux, The Independent Institute, Oakland, CA (p. 276)

*Jason M. Thomas, Citizens for a Sound Economy, Washington, DC (p. 277)

*Mark Thornton, Columbus State University, Columbus, GA (p. 278)

Richard H. Timberlake, Jr., Bogart, GA (p. 279)

Peter J. Wallison, American Enterprise Institute, Washington, DC (p. 288)

MONEY AND FINANCIAL SERVICES (Continued)

Jude Wanniski, Polyconomics, Parsippany, NJ **(p. 288)**
*Murray Weidenbaum, Weidenbaum Center, St. Louis, MO **(p. 291)**
*Lawrence H. White, University of Missouri, St. Louis, St. Louis, MO **(p. 293)**
*Edwin D. Williamson, Sullivan & Cromwell, Washington, DC **(p. 295)**
Gene C. Wunder, Washburn University, Topeka, KS **(p. 299)**
Thomas L. Wyrick, Southwest Missouri State University, Springfield, MO **(p. 300)**

TRADE

Carol Adelman, Hudson Institute, Washington, DC **(p. 34)**
*M. Gene Aldridge, New Mexico Independence Research Institute, Las Cruces, NM **(p. 36)**
Martin Anderson, Hoover Institution, Stanford, CA **(p. 38)**
*Dennis T. Avery, Hudson Institute, Churchville, VA **(p. 42)**
*Iwan Azis, Cornell University, Ithaca, NY **(p. 42)**
David S. Ball, North Carolina State University, Raleigh, NC **(p. 44)**
*Claude E. Barfield, American Enterprise Institute, Washington, DC **(p. 45)**
*Saul Z. Barr, University of Tennessee, Gulf Shores, AL **(p. 46)**
Robert J. Barro, Harvard University, Cambridge, MA **(p. 46)**
*Bruce R. Bartlett, National Center for Policy Analysis, Great Falls, VA **(p. 46)**
Roger Bate, International Policy Network, Washington, DC **(p. 47)**
Robert J. Batemarco, Peekskill, NY **(p. 47)**
Paul Beckner, Citizens for a Sound Economy, Washington, DC **(p. 48)**
Walter Block, Loyola University New Orleans, New Orleans, LA **(p. 55)**
Samuel Bostaph, University of Dallas, Irving, TX **(p. 57)**
*Donald J. Boudreaux, George Mason University, Fairfax, VA **(p. 58)**
James Bovard, Rockville, MD **(p. 58)**
Charles Brooks, The Strategy Group, Arlington, VA **(p. 62)**
*James B. Burnham, Duquesne University, Pittsburgh, PA **(p. 66)**
*Dominic M. Calabro, Florida TaxWatch Research Institute, Inc., Tallahassee, FL **(p. 67)**
*Ronald Cass, Boston University School of Law, Boston, MA **(p. 72)**
Alejandro A. Chafuen, Atlas Economic Research Foundation, Fairfax, VA **(p. 72)**
*Bruce K. Chapman, Discovery Institute, Seattle, WA **(p. 72)**
Kenneth W. Clarkson, University of Miami, Coral Gables, FL **(p. 75)**
Gregory Conko, Competitive Enterprise Institute, Washington, DC **(p. 79)**
*Louis J. Cordia, Cordia Companies, Alexandria, VA **(p. 82)**
Bob Corkins, Kansas Legislative Education and Research, Inc., Topeka, KS **(p. 82)**
*Phillip DeVous, Acton Institute for the Study of Religion and Liberty, Grand Rapids, MI **(p. 94)**
*James A. Dorn, Cato Institute, Washington, DC **(p. 97)**
Pete du Pont, National Center for Policy Analysis, Wilmington, DE **(p. 98)**
*Thomas Duesterberg, Manufacturers Alliance, Arlington, VA **(p. 99)**
Richard M. Ebeling, Hillsdale College, Hillsdale, MI **(p. 102)**
*Myron Ebell, Competitive Enterprise Institute, Washington, DC **(p. 103)**
Ana Eiras, The Heritage Foundation, Washington, DC **(p. 105)**
*Stephen Entin, Institute for Research on the Economics of Taxation, Washington, DC **(p. 107)**
*David I. Fand, James M. Buchanan Center for Political Economy, Fairfax, VA **(p. 109)**
Georges Fauriol, International Republican Institute, Washington, DC **(p. 110)**
*Robert Fike, Americans for Tax Reform, Washington, DC **(p. 111)**
J. Michael Finger, American Enterprise Institute, Washington, DC **(p. 111)**
Sara Fitzgerald, The Heritage Foundation, Washington, DC **(p. 113)**
*Barbara Hackman Franklin, Barbara Franklin Enterprises, Washington, DC **(p. 116)**
*John Frydenlund, Citizens Against Government Waste, Washington, DC **(p. 118)**
Giulio Gallarotti, Wesleyan University, Middletown, CT **(p. 120)**
Bruce L. Gardner, University of Maryland, College Park, MD **(p. 120)**
*Linda Gorman, Independence Institute, Golden, CO **(p. 127)**
*Daniel T. Griswold, Cato Institute, Washington, DC **(p. 129)**

---

* Has testified before a state or federal legislative committee

TRADE (Continued)

Phillip D. Grub, Eastern Washington University, Spokane, WA (p. 130)
*Erick Gustafson, Citizens for a Sound Economy, Washington, DC (p. 131)
*James D. Gwartney, Florida State University, Tallahassee, FL (p. 131)
Robert Hall, Hoover Institution, Stanford, CA (p. 132)
Alam E. Hammad, Alexandria, VA (p. 133)
Steve H. Hanke, Johns Hopkins University, Baltimore, MD (p. 134)
John R. Hanson, II, Texas A&M University, College Station, TX (p. 134)
Scott E. Harrington, University of South Carolina, Columbia, SC (p. 135)
Gina Marie Hatheway, The Heritage Foundation, Washington, DC (p. 137)
*Robert C. Haywood, Director, WEPZA, Evergreen, CO (p. 138)
Robert D. Hisrich, Case Western Reserve University, Cleveland, OH (p. 143)
*Leon Hollerman, Claremont Graduate University, Claremont, CA (p. 145)
Edward L. Hudgins, The Objectivist Center, Washington, DC (p. 148)
G. Philip Hughes, White House Writer's Group, Washington, DC (p. 149)
John C. Hulsman, The Heritage Foundation, Washington, DC (p. 149)
*Harry G. Hutchison, Wayne State University, Detroit, MI (p. 150)
Daniel J. Ikenson, Cato Institute, Washington, DC (p. 151)
William H. Kaempfer, University of Colorado, Boulder, CO (p. 156)
Shyam J. Kamath, California State University, Hayward, Hayward, CA (p. 157)
*Raymond J. Keating, Small Business Survival Committee, Manorville, NY (p. 159)
*David A. Keene, American Conservative Union, Washington, DC (p. 160)
Karen Kerrigan, the polling company, Washington, DC (p. 162)
*Dean Kleckner, Truth About Trade and Technology, Des Moines, IA (p. 165)
Robert Krol, California State University, Northridge, Northridge, CA (p. 169)
*George Landrith, Frontiers of Freedom Institute, Fairfax, VA (p. 173)
Brink Lindsey, Cato Institute, Washington, DC (p. 181)
Lisa MacLellan, Pacific Research Institute, San Francisco, CA (p. 185)
*John H. Makin, American Enterprise Institute, Washington, DC (p. 187)
Deryl W. Martin, Tennessee Technological University, Cookeville, TN (p. 190)
*Nina May, *Renaissance Connection.com/RCNetwork.net*, Washington, DC (p. 192)
*Rachel McCulloch, Brandeis University, Waltham, MA (p. 194)
Wendell H. McCulloch, Jr., California State University, Long Beach, Long Beach, CA (p. 194)
*Robert W. McGee, Barry University, Miami Shores, FL (p. 195)
John O. McGinnis, Cardozo School of Law, New York, NY (p. 196)
Darrell McKigney, Small Business Survival Committee, Washington, DC (p. 196)
Lawrence J. McQuillan, Pacific Research Institute, San Francisco, CA (p. 197)
*Deroy Murdock, Atlas Economic Research Foundation, New York, NY (p. 209)
Anthony I. Negbenebor, Gardner-Webb University, Boiling Springs, NC (p. 212)
*William A. Niskanen, Cato Institute, Washington, DC (p. 214)
R. Marc Nuttle, Norman, OK (p. 216)
*Gerald P. O'Driscoll, Jr., Cato Institute, Falls Church, VA (p. 216)
Jeremiah O'Keeffe, Plano, TX (p. 217)
*Daniel Oliver, Pacific Research Institute, Washington, DC (p. 219)
*William H. Peterson, Washington, DC (p. 227)
*Nancy M. Pfotenhauer, Independent Women's Forum, Arlington, VA (p. 227)
*Howard Phillips, The Conservative Caucus, Inc., Vienna, VA (p. 227)
Charles I. Plosser, University of Rochester, Rochester, NY (p. 229)
*Ernest Preeg, Manufacturers Alliance, Arlington, VA (p. 232)
*Andrew F. Quinlan, Center for Freedom and Prosperity, Alexandria, VA (p. 234)
Rob Raffety, Mercatus Center at George Mason University, Arlington, VA (p. 235)
Sarath Rajapatirana, American Enterprise Institute, Washington, DC (p. 236)
*R. Sean Randolph, Bay Area Economic Forum, San Francisco, CA (p. 236)
Barbara Rippel, Consumer Alert, Washington, DC (p. 240)
Russell Roberts, Weidenbaum Center, St. Louis, MO (p. 242)

TRADE (Continued)

Llewellyn Rockwell, Jr., Ludwig von Mises Institute, Auburn, AL (p. 242)

*Linda Runbeck, Taxpayers League of Minnesota, Plymouth, MN (p. 247)

Peter Rutland, Wesleyan University, Middletown, CT (p. 248)

Edward W. Ryan, Manhattanville College, Purchase, NY (p. 248)

*Joseph T. Salerno, Pace University, New York, NY (p. 248)

Brett D. Schaefer, The Heritage Foundation, Washington, DC (p. 252)

*Robert A. Sirico, Acton Institute for the Study of Religion and Liberty,
Grand Rapids, MI (p. 261)

Shaun Small, Empower America, Washington, DC (p. 262)

*Frances B. Smith, Consumer Alert, Washington, DC (p. 263)

*Fred L. Smith, Jr., Competitive Enterprise Institute, Washington, DC (p. 263)

Alan C. Stockman, University of Rochester, Rochester, NY (p. 269)

*David Strom, Taxpayers League of Minnesota, Plymouth, MN (p. 270)

Jon Basil Utley, Ludwig von Mises Institute, Washington, DC (p. 283)

*Malcolm Wallop, Frontiers of Freedom Institute, Fairfax, VA (p. 288)

Jude Wanniski, Polyconomics, Parsippany, NJ (p. 288)

*Murray Weidenbaum, Weidenbaum Center, St. Louis, MO (p. 291)

*Edwin D. Williamson, Sullivan & Cromwell, Washington, DC (p. 295)

*Ron F. Williamson, Great Plains Public Policy Institute, Sioux Falls, SD (p. 295)

*Charles Wolf, Jr., RAND, Santa Monica, CA (p. 297)

Leland Yeager, Auburn University, Auburn, AL (p. 300)

*Michael K. Young, George Washington University Law School, Washington, DC (p. 300)

Jerry Zandstra, Acton Institute for the Study of Religion and Liberty,
Grand Rapids, MI (p. 301)

TRANSPORTATION

*Stephen Adams, Pioneer Institute for Public Policy Research, Boston, MA (p. 34)

Damon Ansell, Americans for Tax Reform, Washington, DC (p. 39)

*Keith G. Baker, Florida TaxWatch Research Institute, Inc., Tallahassee, FL (p. 43)

*Bruce R. Bartlett, National Center for Policy Analysis, Great Falls, VA (p. 46)

Walter Block, Loyola University New Orleans, New Orleans, LA (p. 55)

*Wayne T. Brough, Citizens for a Sound Economy, Washington, DC (p. 62)

*Dominic M. Calabro, Florida TaxWatch Research Institute, Inc., Tallahassee, FL (p. 67)

*Jon Charles Caldara, Independence Institute, Golden, CO (p. 67)

*Bruce K. Chapman, Discovery Institute, Seattle, WA (p. 72)

*Charles Chieppo, Pioneer Institute for Public Policy Research, Boston, MA (p. 73)

John Cobin, Montauk Financial Group, Greenville, SC (p. 76)

*Wendell Cox, Wendell Cox Consultancy, Belleville, IL (p. 84)

James K. Coyne, National Air Transportation Association, Alexandria, VA (p. 84)

*Gerry Dickinson, South Carolina Policy Council, Columbia, SC (p. 95)

*Gloria Taylor Fisher, Interstate Commission on the Potomac River Basin,
Alexandria, VA (p. 112)

*Robert Franciosi, Goldwater Institute, Phoenix, AZ (p. 115)

*James Gattuso, The Heritage Foundation, Washington, DC (p. 121)

Leonard Gilroy, Reason Foundation, Los Angeles, CA (p. 123)

*Stephen Goldsmith, Manhattan Institute for Policy Research, New York, NY (p. 126)

*Grant R. Gulibon, The Commonwealth Foundation, Harrisburg, PA (p. 130)

David T. Hartgen, University of North Carolina, Charlotte, Charlotte, NC (p. 136)

*John MacDonald Hood, John Locke Foundation, Raleigh, NC (p. 145)

Edward L. Hudgins, The Objectivist Center, Washington, DC (p. 148)

Steve Johnson, The Heritage Foundation, Washington, DC (p. 155)

*John Kain, University of Texas, Dallas, Richardson, TX (p. 157)

*Sam Kazman, Competitive Enterprise Institute, Washington, DC (p. 159)

*George Liebmann, Calvert Institute for Policy Research, Baltimore, MD (p. 180)

TRANSPORTATION (Continued)

William S. Lind, Free Congress Foundation, Washington, DC **(p. 180)**
*Rita P. Maguire, Arizona Center for Public Policy, Phoenix, AZ **(p. 186)**
Lawrence J. McQuillan, Pacific Research Institute, San Francisco, CA **(p. 197)**
*Maurice McTigue, Mercatus Center at George Mason University, Arlington, VA **(p. 197)**
*Daniel Mead Smith, Washington Policy Center, Seattle, WA **(p. 198)**
*Adrian T. Moore, Reason Foundation, Los Angeles, CA **(p. 205)**
Cassandra Chrones Moore, Cato Institute, Washington, DC **(p. 205)**
*James Elliott Moore, II, University of Southern California, Los Angeles, CA **(p. 205)**
Richard F. Muth, Emory University, Atlanta, GA **(p. 210)**
George Nesterczuk, Nesterczuk and Associates, Vienna, VA **(p. 212)**
David Charles Nice, Washington State University, Pullman, WA **(p. 213)**
*Sam Peltzman, University of Chicago Graduate School of Business, Chicago, IL **(p. 225)**
Penn Pfiffner, Independence Institute, Golden, CO **(p. 227)**
*Nancy M. Pfotenhauer, Independent Women's Forum, Arlington, VA **(p. 227)**
*Dennis Polhill, Independence Institute, Golden, CO **(p. 230)**
*Robert W. Poole, Jr., Reason Foundation, Los Angeles, CA **(p. 230)**
Rob Raffety, Mercatus Center at George Mason University, Arlington, VA **(p. 235)**
Gabriel Roth, Chevy Chase, MD **(p. 244)**
*Richard O. Rowland, Grassroot Institute of Hawaii, Aiea, HI **(p. 245)**
*Anthony Rufolo, Portland State University, Portland, OR **(p. 246)**
*Linda Runbeck, Taxpayers League of Minnesota, Plymouth, MN **(p. 247)**
Peter Samuel, *Toll Roads Newsletter*, Frederick, MD **(p. 249)**
*Bill Schilling, Wyoming Business Alliance / Wyoming Heritage Foundation, Casper, WY **(p. 253)**
*John Semmens, Laissez-Faire Institute, Chandler, AZ **(p. 256)**
*David Strom, Taxpayers League of Minnesota, Plymouth, MN **(p. 270)**
Christopher B. Summers, Maryland Public Policy Institute, Germantown, MD **(p. 272)**
Thomas L. Tacker, Embry-Riddle Aeronautical University, Daytona Beach, FL **(p. 273)**
*Jerry Taylor, Cato Institute, Washington, DC **(p. 274)**
*Ronald Utt, The Heritage Foundation, Washington, DC **(p. 283)**
*Clinton H. Whitehurst, Jr., Clemson University, Clemson, SC **(p. 294)**
Ronald A. Zumbrun, The Zumbrun Law Firm, Sacramento, CA **(p. 303)**

Crime, Justice and the Law

CHURCH-STATE RELATIONS

*Henry J. Abraham, Charlottesville, VA **(p. 34)**
David L. Adams, Concordia Seminary, St. Louis, MO **(p. 34)**
*I. Dean Ahmad, Minaret of Freedom Institute, Bethesda, MD **(p. 36)**
*Lawrence Alexander, University of San Diego School of Law, San Diego, CA **(p. 36)**
Brian C. Anderson, Manhattan Institute for Policy Research, New York, NY **(p. 38)**
*Carl A. Anderson, Knights of Columbus, New Haven, CT **(p. 38)**
*Julaine K. Appling, Family Research Institute of Wisconsin, Madison, WI **(p. 40)**
Richard A. Baer, Jr., Cornell University, Ithaca, NY **(p. 42)**
Hunter Baker, Georgia Family Council, Norcross, GA **(p. 43)**
*John S. Baker, Jr., Louisiana State University, Baton Rouge, LA **(p. 43)**
Joseph Baldacchino, National Humanities Institute, Bowie, MD **(p. 44)**
Christopher Beiting, Ave Maria College, Ypsilanti, MI **(p. 49)**
Mariam Bell, Prison Fellowship Ministries, Washington, DC **(p. 49)**
*William J. Bennett, Empower America, Washington, DC **(p. 51)**
*Wayman R. Bishop, The Family Foundation of Virginia, Richmond, VA **(p. 53)**
*Gerard V. Bradley, Notre Dame Law School, Notre Dame, IN **(p. 59)**
*Marshall J. Breger, Catholic University of America, Washington, DC **(p. 60)**
*Harold O. J. Brown, Reformed Theological Seminary, Charlotte, NC **(p. 63)**
Francis H. Buckley, George Mason University School of Law, Arlington, VA **(p. 64)**
Gary Bullert, Columbia Basin College, Pasco, WA **(p. 65)**
*David Burton, Argus Group, Alexandria, VA **(p. 66)**
Jameson Campaigne, Jr., Jameson Books, Inc., Ottawa, IL **(p. 68)**
*Robert Carleson, American Civil Rights Union, Alexandria, VA **(p. 70)**
*Allan C. Carlson, Howard Center for Family, Religion and Society, Rockford, IL **(p. 70)**
*Samuel Casey, Christian Legal Society, Annandale, VA **(p. 71)**
*Charles Colson, Prison Fellowship Ministries, Washington, DC **(p. 79)**
Douglas H. Cook, Regent University, Virginia Beach, VA **(p. 80)**
*John E. Coons, University of California at Berkeley, Berkeley, CA **(p. 81)**
*Charles J. Cooper, Cooper & Kirk, PLLC, Washington, DC **(p. 81)**
Dennis Coyle, Catholic University of America, Washington, DC **(p. 84)**
*Ron Crews, Massachusetts Family Institute, Newton Upper Falls, MA **(p. 86)**
*Charles H. Cunningham, National Rifle Association, Washington, DC **(p. 87)**
*Robert J. Cynkar, Cooper & Kirk, PLLC, Washington, DC **(p. 87)**
*Brad W. Dacus, Pacific Justice Institute, Citrus Heights, CA **(p. 87)**
*Glenn Delk, Georgia Charter Schools, Atlanta, GA **(p. 92)**
*Len Deo, New Jersey Family Policy Council, Parsippany, NJ **(p. 93)**
*Robert Destro, Catholic University of America, Washington, DC **(p. 94)**
*William T. Devlin, Urban Family Council, Philadelphia, PA **(p. 94)**
*Jude P. Dougherty, Catholic University of America, Washington, DC **(p. 97)**
Richard J. Dougherty, University of Dallas, Irving, TX **(p. 97)**
*Richard Duncan, University of Nebraska, Lincoln, NE **(p. 99)**
Steven D. Ealy, Liberty Fund, Inc., Indianapolis, IN **(p. 101)**
*John C. Eastman, Chapman University School of Law, Orange, CA **(p. 102)**
*Michelle Easton, Clare Boothe Luce Policy Institute, Herndon, VA **(p. 102)**
Barbara Elliott, Center for Renewal, Houston, TX **(p. 105)**
*Jean Bethke Elshtain, University of Chicago, Chicago, IL **(p. 106)**
Thomas Engeman, Loyola University Chicago, Chicago, IL **(p. 107)**
*Thompson Mason Faller, University of Portland, Portland, OR **(p. 109)**
*Michael P. Farris, Patrick Henry College, Purcellville, VA **(p. 109)**
*Steve Fitschen, National Legal Foundation, Virginia Beach, VA **(p. 112)**
*David Forte, Cleveland State University, Cleveland, OH **(p. 114)**
Elizabeth Fox-Genovese, Emory University, Atlanta, GA **(p. 115)**

CHURCH-STATE RELATIONS (Continued)

*Murray Friedman, American Jewish Committee, Philadelphia, PA (p. 117)
 Adam Fuller, Toward Tradition, Mercer Island, WA (p. 118)
 Richard W. Garnett, Notre Dame Law School, Notre Dame, IN (p. 120)
*Michael Geer, Pennsylvania Family Institute, Harrisburg, PA (p. 122)
*Robert P. George, Princeton University, Princeton, NJ (p. 122)
*Stephen Goldsmith, Manhattan Institute for Policy Research, New York, NY (p. 126)
 Samuel Gregg, Acton Institute for the Study of Religion and Liberty, Grand Rapids, MI (p. 129)
 Nikolas Gvosdev, *The National Interest*, Washington, DC (p. 131)
 Roger Hamburg, Indiana University South Bend, South Bend, IN (p. 133)
 Jerome J. Hanus, American University, Washington, DC (p. 134)
 Kevin J. Hasson, The Becket Fund for Religious Liberty, Washington, DC (p. 137)
*Clark C. Havighurst, Duke University School of Law, Durham, NC (p. 137)
 Jay F. Hein, Hudson Institute, Indianapolis, IN (p. 139)
*James M. Henderson, Sr., American Center for Law and Justice, Washington, DC (p. 140)
 Lowman Henry, Lincoln Institute of Public Opinion Research, Inc., Harrisburg, PA (p. 140)
*Thomas Hinton, The Heritage Foundation, Washington, DC (p. 143)
 James Hitchcock, St. Louis University, St. Louis, MO (p. 143)
*John C. Holmes, Association of Christian Schools International, Washington, DC (p. 145)
*Michael Horowitz, Hudson Institute, Washington, DC (p. 146)
*Michael Howden, Stronger Families for Oregon, Salem, OR (p. 147)
 Martin Hoyt, American Association of Christian Schools, Washington, DC (p. 148)
*Charles D. Hurley, Iowa Family Policy Center, Pleasant Hill, IA (p. 150)
 Richard P. Hutchison, Landmark Legal Foundation, Kansas City, MO (p. 150)
*Bradley P. Jacob, Regent University, Virginia Beach, VA (p. 152)
*Thomas L. Jipping, Concerned Women for America, Washington, DC (p. 154)
 Byron Johnson, University of Pennsylvania, Philadelphia, PA (p. 155)
 Phil Kent, Southeastern Legal Foundation, Atlanta, GA (p. 162)
 Larry Klayman, Judicial Watch, Washington, DC (p. 165)
*Douglas W. Kmiec, The Catholic University of America, Washington, DC (p. 166)
 Joseph M. Knippenberg, Oglethorpe University, Atlanta, GA (p. 166)
*Robert C. Koons, University of Texas, Austin, TX (p. 167)
 Thomas L. Krannawitter, Claremont Institute, Claremont, CA (p. 168)
 Stephen Krason, Franciscan University of Steubenville, Steubenville, OH (p. 169)
 Gary Kreep, United States Justice Foundation, Escondido, CA (p. 169)
*Andrea S. Lafferty, Traditional Values Coalition, Washington, DC (p. 172)
*Richard D. Land, Ethics and Religious Liberty Commission, Nashville, TN (p. 173)
*Janet LaRue, Concerned Women for America, Washington, DC (p. 175)
 Peter Augustine Lawler, Berry College, Mount Berry, GA (p. 175)
 Seth Leibsohn, Empower America, Washington, DC (p. 177)
 Leonard A. Leo, The Federalist Society for Law and Public Policy Studies,
    Washington, DC (p. 178)
 Richard Lessner, American Renewal, Washington, DC (p. 178)
 Curt A. Levey, Center for Individual Rights, Washington, DC (p. 178)
 Jacob T. Levy, University of Chicago, Chicago, IL (p. 179)
 Leonard P. Liggio, Atlas Economic Research Foundation, Fairfax, VA (p. 180)
*Joseph Loconte, The Heritage Foundation, Washington, DC (p. 182)
 Jordan Lorence, Alliance Defense Fund, Scottsdale, AZ (p. 183)
 J. J. Mahoney, Diversified Consultants, Mount Pleasant, SC (p. 187)
 Mario Mandina, National Lawyers Association, Independence, MO (p. 188)
 William R. Marty, University of Memphis, Memphis, TN (p. 190)
 Paul Maurer, Trinity International University, Deerfield, IL (p. 192)
 Colby May, American Center for Law and Justice, Alexandria, VA (p. 192)
*Michael W. McConnell, University of Utah, Salt Lake City, UT (p. 194)
*Michael J. McManus, Marriage Savers, Potomac, MD (p. 197)

CHURCH-STATE RELATIONS (Continued)

*Edwin Meese III, The Heritage Foundation, Washington, DC (p. 198)
Tom Minnery, Focus on the Family, Colorado Springs, CO (p. 203)
R. Albert Mohler, Jr., The Southern Baptist Theological Seminary, Louisville, KY (p. 204)
*Richard E. Morgan, Bowdoin College, Brunswick, ME (p. 206)
*Joseph A. Morris, Lincoln Legal Foundation, Chicago, IL (p. 207)
*Steven W. Mosher, Population Research Institute, Front Royal, VA (p. 208)
*Len Munsil, Center for Arizona Policy, Scottsdale, AZ (p. 209)
William Murchison, Baylor University, Waco, TX (p. 209)
Henry Myers, James Madison University, Harrisonburg, VA (p. 210)
Ronald Nash, Reformed Theological Seminary, Oviedo, FL (p. 211)
*Richard John Neuhaus, Institute on Religion and Public Life, New York, NY (p. 213)
*Pat Nolan, Justice Fellowship, Reston, VA (p. 214)
Stuart W. Nolan, Jr., Springfield, VA (p. 214)
Michael J. Novak, Jr., American Enterprise Institute, Washington, DC (p. 215)
James Nuechterlein, *First Things*, New York, NY (p. 216)
*Michael J. O'Dea, Christus Medicus Foundation, Bloomfield Hills, MI (p. 216)
*Charles J. O'Malley, Charles J. O'Malley & Associates, Inc., Annapolis, MD (p. 217)
*Michael O'Neill, George Mason University School of Law, Arlington, VA (p. 217)
*Marvin Olasky, University of Texas, Austin, TX (p. 218)
*Allan E. Parker, Jr., Texas Justice Foundation, San Antonio, TX (p. 221)
*John Paulton, Focus on the Family, Colorado Springs, CO (p. 223)
*Mitchell B. Pearlstein, Center of the American Experiment, Minneapolis, MN (p. 224)
Terence J. Pell, Center for Individual Rights, Washington, DC (p. 224)
*Roger Pilon, Cato Institute, Washington, DC (p. 228)
*Stephen Presser, Northwestern University School of Law, Chicago, IL (p. 233)
*Thomas Prichard, Minnesota Family Council, Minneapolis, MN (p. 233)
Jeremy Rabkin, Cornell University, Ithaca, NY (p. 235)
Paul A. Rahe, University of Tulsa, Tulsa, OK (p. 236)
Harold Calvin Ray, National Center for Faith-Based Initiatives, West Palm Beach, FL (p. 237)
*Charles E. Rice, Notre Dame Law School, Notre Dame, IN (p. 239)
Sandy Rios, Concerned Women for America, Washington, DC (p. 240)
John W. Robbins, Trinity Foundation, Unicoi, TN (p. 241)
*Kelly Rosati, Hawaii Family Forum, Kaneohe, HI (p. 243)
*Ronald D. Rotunda, George Mason University School of Law, Arlington, VA (p. 244)
Shannon Royce, Ethics and Religious Liberty Commission, Washington, DC (p. 245)
John Samples, Cato Institute, Washington, DC (p. 249)
*Steven Alan Samson, Liberty University, Lynchburg, VA (p. 249)
*Arthur J. Schwartz, John Templeton Foundation, Radnor, PA (p. 254)
*Alan E. Sears, Alliance Defense Fund, Scottsdale, AZ (p. 255)
*Jay Sekulow, American Center for Law and Justice, Virginia Beach, VA (p. 256)
*Jamie Self, Georgia Family Council, Norcross, GA (p. 256)
*Kelly Shackelford, Free Market Foundation, Plano, TX (p. 257)
Timothy Samuel Shah, Ethics and Public Policy Center, Washington, DC (p. 257)
Barry Alan Shain, Colgate University, Hamilton, NY (p. 257)
*Lou Sheldon, Traditional Values Coalition, Washington, DC (p. 258)
Richard Sherlock, Utah State University, Logan, UT (p. 259)
Harvey Silverglate, The Foundation for Individual Rights in Education, Boston, MA (p. 260)
*James Skillen, Center for Public Justice, Annapolis, MD (p. 261)
*Curt Smith, Indiana Family Institute, Indianapolis, IN (p. 263)
Brad Snavely, Michigan Family Forum, Lansing, MI (p. 264)
*Neil H. Snyder, University of Virginia, Charlottesville, VA (p. 265)
*Matthew Spalding, The Heritage Foundation, Washington, DC (p. 266)
Peter S. Sprigg, Family Research Council, Washington, DC (p. 267)
Doug Stiegler, Association of Maryland Families, Woodstock, MD (p. 269)

CHURCH-STATE RELATIONS (Continued)

*Forest M. Thigpen, Mississippi Family Council, Jackson, MS (p. 277)
Stephen R. Thomas, North American Canon Law Society, Duluth, MN (p. 277)
*Randy Thomasson, Campaign for California Families, Sacramento, CA (p. 277)
Frank J. Tipler, Tulane University, New Orleans, LA (p. 279)
*Herbert W. Titus, Virginia Beach, VA (p. 279)
*Forrest L. Turpen, Christian Educators Association International, Pasadena, CA (p. 282)
Michael M. Uhlmann, Claremont Graduate University, Claremont, CA (p. 283)
Lawrence A. Uzzell, Keston Institute, Waxahachie, TX (p. 283)
*Eugene Volokh, University of California at Los Angeles, Los Angeles, CA (p. 285)
Gerald Walpin, Katten Muchin Zavis Rosenman, New York, NY (p. 288)
Bradley C. S. Watson, Saint Vincent College, Latrobe, PA (p. 290)
Stanley J. Watson, Patrick Henry College, Purcellville, VA (p. 290)
*Walter M. Weber, American Center for Law and Justice, Alexandria, VA (p. 291)
David L. Weeks, Azusa Pacific University, Azusa, CA (p. 291)
*George Weigel, Ethics and Public Policy Center, Washington, DC (p. 291)
John G. West, Discovery Institute, Seattle, WA (p. 292)
*John W. Whitehead, The Rutherford Institute, Charlottesville, VA (p. 293)
*Natalie Williams, Robinson, DiLando and Whitaker, Sacramento, CA (p. 295)
*Christopher Wolfe, Marquette University, Milwaukee, WI (p. 297)
Adam Wolfson, *The Public Interest*, Washington, DC (p. 297)
Jason Wright, Frontiers of Freedom Institute, Fairfax, VA (p. 299)
James V. Young, Lee's Summit, MO (p. 300)
*Michael K. Young, George Washington University Law School, Washington, DC (p. 300)
Jerry Zandstra, Acton Institute for the Study of Religion and Liberty,
    Grand Rapids, MI (p. 301)
Ronald A. Zumbrun, The Zumbrun Law Firm, Sacramento, CA (p. 303)

CIVIL RIGHTS/RACIAL PREFERENCES

*Henry J. Abraham, Charlottesville, VA (p. 34)
*Lawrence Alexander, University of San Diego School of Law, San Diego, CA (p. 36)
*William Allen, Michigan State University, East Lansing, MI (p. 37)
David W. Almasi, National Center for Public Policy Research, Washington, DC (p. 37)
Brian C. Anderson, Manhattan Institute for Policy Research, New York, NY (p. 38)
*David J. Armor, George Mason University, Fairfax, VA (p. 40)
*John S. Baker, Jr., Louisiana State University, Baton Rouge, LA (p. 43)
*Charles A. Ballard, Institute for Responsible Fatherhood and Family Revitalization,
    Largo, MD (p. 45)
Jonathan James Bean, Southern Illinois University, Carbondale, IL (p. 48)
Gary Becker, University of Chicago, Chicago, IL (p. 48)
David Beito, University of Alabama, Tuscaloosa, AL (p. 49)
*Herman Belz, University of Maryland, College Park, MD (p. 50)
*William J. Bennett, Empower America, Washington, DC (p. 51)
*Robert K. Best, Pacific Legal Foundation, Sacramento, CA (p. 52)
James E. Bond, Seattle University, Seattle, WA (p. 56)
Jennifer C. Braceras, Independent Women's Forum, Arlington, VA (p. 59)
Anthony Bradley, Acton Institute for the Study of Religion and Liberty,
    Grand Rapids, MI (p. 59)
*Harold O. J. Brown, Reformed Theological Seminary, Charlotte, NC (p. 63)
*Sharon Browne, Pacific Legal Foundation, Sacramento, CA (p. 63)
T. Patrick Burke, St. Joseph's University, Wynnewood, PA (p. 65)
Deborah Burstion-Donbraye, American Multimedia Inc. of Nigeria, Cleveland, OH (p. 66)
*Robert Carleson, American Civil Rights Union, Alexandria, VA (p. 70)
*Michael A. Carvin, Jones, Day, Reavis & Pogue, Washington, DC (p. 71)
*Anthony T. Caso, Pacific Legal Foundation, Sacramento, CA (p. 72)

CIVIL RIGHTS/RACIAL PREFERENCES (Continued)

J. Daryl Charles, Taylor University, Upland, IN (p. 72)
*Linda Chavez, Center for Equal Opportunity, Sterling, VA (p. 73)
*Roger Clegg, Center for Equal Opportunity, Sterling, VA (p. 76)
*Stephen Cole, State University of New York, Stony Brook, NY (p. 78)
 Peter Collier, Center for the Study of Popular Culture, Los Angeles, CA (p. 78)
*Ward Connerly, American Civil Rights Institute, Sacramento, CA (p. 80)
*Charles J. Cooper, Cooper & Kirk, PLLC, Washington, DC (p. 81)
*Douglas Cox, Gibson, Dunn & Crutcher LLP, Washington, DC (p. 84)
 Dinesh D'Souza, Hoover Institution, Stanford, CA (p. 87)
*Robert Destro, Catholic University of America, Washington, DC (p. 94)
*Richard Duncan, University of Nebraska, Lincoln, NE (p. 99)
 Valle Simms Dutcher, Southeastern Legal Foundation, Atlanta, GA (p. 101)
*John C. Eastman, Chapman University School of Law, Orange, CA (p. 102)
*Michelle Easton, Clare Boothe Luce Policy Institute, Herndon, VA (p. 102)
*Ward Elliott, Claremont McKenna College, Claremont, CA (p. 106)
*Jean Bethke Elshtain, University of Chicago, Chicago, IL (p. 106)
 Richard A. Epstein, University of Chicago Law School, Chicago, IL (p. 107)
*Edward J. Erler, California State University, San Bernardino, San Bernardino, CA (p. 107)
 Peter Ferrara, International Center for Law and Economics, Washington, DC (p. 110)
 John Findley, Pacific Legal Foundation, Sacramento, CA (p. 111)
*Peter Flaherty, National Legal and Policy Center, Falls Church, VA (p. 113)
*John Fonte, Hudson Institute, Washington, DC (p. 114)
*David Forte, Cleveland State University, Cleveland, OH (p. 114)
*Murray Friedman, American Jewish Committee, Philadelphia, PA (p. 117)
*James Fyfe, Temple University, Philadelphia, PA (p. 119)
*Todd Gaziano, The Heritage Foundation, Washington, DC (p. 121)
*Robert P. George, Princeton University, Princeton, NJ (p. 122)
 David Gersten, Center for Equal Opportunity, Sterling, VA (p. 123)
*Linda S. Gottfredson, University of Delaware, Newark, DE (p. 127)
 Paul Gottfried, Elizabethtown College, Elizabethtown, PA (p. 127)
*Alan Gottlieb, Citizens Committee for the Right to Keep and Bear Arms, Bellevue, WA (p. 127)
 Reuben Greenberg, Charleston Police Department, Charleston, SC (p. 128)
 Charles Greenwalt, II, Susquehanna Valley Center for Public Policy, Hershey, PA (p. 129)
*Michael S. Greve, American Enterprise Institute, Washington, DC (p. 129)
*Paul Guppy, Washington Policy Center, Seattle, WA (p. 131)
*James M. Henderson, Sr., American Center for Law and Justice, Washington, DC (p. 140)
 Heather Higgins, Independent Women's Forum, New York, NY (p. 142)
*Kenneth M. Holland, University of Memphis, Memphis, TN (p. 144)
 Jacob G. Hornberger, Future of Freedom Foundation, Fairfax, VA (p. 146)
 David Horowitz, Center for the Study of Popular Culture, Los Angeles, CA (p. 146)
*Michael Horowitz, Hudson Institute, Washington, DC (p. 146)
 William Howard, Chicago State University, Wheaton, IL (p. 147)
*Robert Hunter, Mackinac Center for Public Policy, Midland, MI (p. 150)
*Alan Inman, Institute for Responsible Fatherhood and Family Revitalization,
    Largo, MD (p. 151)
 Niger Roy Innis, Congress of Racial Equality, New York, NY (p. 151)
 Earl W. Jackson, Sr., Samaritan Project, Chesapeake, VA (p. 152)
*Thomas L. Jipping, Concerned Women for America, Washington, DC (p. 154)
 Martin S. Kaufman, Atlantic Legal Foundation, New York, NY (p. 159)
 Darlene A. Kennedy, Centre for New Black Leadership, Baltimore, MD (p. 162)
 Phil Kent, Southeastern Legal Foundation, Atlanta, GA (p. 162)
*Manuel Klausner, Individual Rights Foundation, Los Angeles, CA (p. 165)
 Larry Klayman, Judicial Watch, Washington, DC (p. 165)
*Douglas W. Kmiec, The Catholic University of America, Washington, DC (p. 166)

CIVIL RIGHTS/RACIAL PREFERENCES (Continued)

John E. Kramer, Institute for Justice, Washington, DC (p. 168)

Thomas L. Krannawitter, Claremont Institute, Claremont, CA (p. 168)

*Michael Krauss, George Mason University School of Law, Arlington, VA (p. 169)

*Andrew Langer, National Federation of Independent Business, Washington, DC (p. 174)

Seth Leibsohn, Empower America, Washington, DC (p. 177)

Leonard A. Leo, The Federalist Society for Law and Public Policy Studies, Washington, DC (p. 178)

Curt A. Levey, Center for Individual Rights, Washington, DC (p. 178)

Jacob T. Levy, University of Chicago, Chicago, IL (p. 179)

*Nelson Lund, George Mason University School of Law, Arlington, VA (p. 184)

Frederick R. Lynch, Claremont McKenna College, Claremont, CA (p. 184)

Michael Lynch, *Reason* Magazine, New Haven, CT (p. 184)

*Heather MacDonald, Manhattan Institute for Policy Research, New York, NY (p. 185)

Tibor R. Machan, Chapman University, Silverado Canyon, CA (p. 185)

Yuri Mantilla, Family Research Council, Washington, DC (p. 189)

*Ken Masugi, Claremont Institute, Claremont, CA (p. 191)

Colby May, American Center for Law and Justice, Alexandria, VA (p. 192)

*Nina May, *Renaissance Connection.com/RCNetwork.net*, Washington, DC (p. 192)

John O. McGinnis, Cardozo School of Law, New York, NY (p. 196)

*Edwin Meese III, The Heritage Foundation, Washington, DC (p. 198)

Eugene B. Meyer, The Federalist Society for Law and Public Policy Studies, Washington, DC (p. 200)

*Richard E. Morgan, Bowdoin College, Brunswick, ME (p. 206)

*Joseph A. Morris, Lincoln Legal Foundation, Chicago, IL (p. 207)

*Deroy Murdock, Atlas Economic Research Foundation, New York, NY (p. 209)

Chuck Muth, American Conservative Union, Alexandria, VA (p. 210)

Phyllis Berry Myers, Centre for New Black Leadership, Washington, DC (p. 210)

*Richard John Neuhaus, Institute on Religion and Public Life, New York, NY (p. 213)

James Nuechterlein, *First Things*, New York, NY (p. 216)

Timothy G. O'Rourke, University of Missouri, St. Louis, St. Louis, MO (p. 217)

M. Lester O'Shea, Walnut Creek, CA (p. 217)

*Allan E. Parker, Jr., Texas Justice Foundation, San Antonio, TX (p. 221)

*J. A. Parker, Lincoln Institute for Research and Education, Washington, DC (p. 221)

Ellen F. Paul, Bowling Green State University, Bowling Green, OH (p. 223)

*Darryl Paulson, University of South Florida, St. Petersburg, FL (p. 223)

Anthony A. Peacock, Utah State University, Logan, UT (p. 224)

*Mitchell B. Pearlstein, Center of the American Experiment, Minneapolis, MN (p. 224)

*Valery J. Pech, Colorado Springs, CO (p. 224)

Terence J. Pell, Center for Individual Rights, Washington, DC (p. 224)

*William Perry Pendley, Mountain States Legal Foundation, Lakewood, CO (p. 225)

*Roger Pilon, Cato Institute, Washington, DC (p. 228)

*Sally C. Pipes, Pacific Research Institute, San Francisco, CA (p. 229)

*Stephen Presser, Northwestern University School of Law, Chicago, IL (p. 233)

Arch Puddington, Freedom House, New York, NY (p. 234)

Jeremy Rabkin, Cornell University, Ithaca, NY (p. 235)

Paul A. Rahe, University of Tulsa, Tulsa, OK (p. 236)

Harold Calvin Ray, National Center for Faith-Based Initiatives, West Palm Beach, FL (p. 237)

*Charles E. Rice, Notre Dame Law School, Notre Dame, IN (p. 239)

*Amy Ridenour, National Center for Public Policy Research, Washington, DC (p. 240)

*Paul Craig Roberts, Institute for Political Economy, Panama City Beach, FL (p. 242)

Michael E. Rosman, Center for Individual Rights, Washington, DC (p. 243)

*Susan Sarnoff, Ohio University, Athens, OH (p. 250)

*Jay Sekulow, American Center for Law and Justice, Virginia Beach, VA (p. 256)

*E. Donald Shapiro, New York Law School, Scottsdale, AZ (p. 258)

CIVIL RIGHTS/RACIAL PREFERENCES (Continued)

*Lou Sheldon, Traditional Values Coalition, Washington, DC (p. 258)
*Rita Simon, American University, Washington, DC (p. 260)
 Mark W. Smith, Kasowitz, Benson, Torres & Friedman, LLP, New York, NY (p. 263)
 Thomas Sowell, Hoover Institution, Stanford, CA (p. 266)
 James Swanson, Cato Institute, Washington, DC (p. 272)
*Rebecca A. Thacker, Ohio University, Athens, OH (p. 276)
*Abigail Thernstrom, Lexington, MA (p. 276)
*Stephan Thernstrom, Lexington, MA (p. 276)
 J. Mills Thornton, III, University of Michigan, Ann Arbor, MI (p. 278)
*Terry W. Van Allen, Kemah, TX (p. 283)
*Balint Vazsonyi, Center for the American Founding, McLean, VA (p. 284)
*Eugene Volokh, University of California at Los Angeles, Los Angeles, CA (p. 285)
*Lee H. Walker, New Coalition for Economic and Social Change, Chicago, IL (p. 287)
 Gerald Walpin, Katten Muchin Zavis Rosenman, New York, NY (p. 288)
 Bradley C. S. Watson, Saint Vincent College, Latrobe, PA (p. 290)
 Ben J. Wattenberg, American Enterprise Institute, Washington, DC (p. 290)
 Thomas G. West, University of Dallas, Irving, TX (p. 293)
*John W. Whitehead, The Rutherford Institute, Charlottesville, VA (p. 293)
*Thomas Wood, Americans Against Discrimination and Preferences, Berkley, CA (p. 298)
 Anne Wortham, Illinois State University, Normal, IL (p. 298)
 John Yoo, University of California, Berkeley, Berkeley, CA (p. 300)
 James V. Young, Lee's Summit, MO (p. 300)
 Ronald A. Zumbrun, The Zumbrun Law Firm, Sacramento, CA (p. 303)

CONSTITUTIONAL LAW

*Henry J. Abraham, Charlottesville, VA (p. 34)
*Jonathan H. Adler, Case Western Reserve University, Cleveland, OH (p. 35)
*I. Dean Ahmad, Minaret of Freedom Institute, Bethesda, MD (p. 36)
*Lawrence Alexander, University of San Diego School of Law, San Diego, CA (p. 36)
*William Allen, Michigan State University, East Lansing, MI (p. 37)
 Brian C. Anderson, Manhattan Institute for Policy Research, New York, NY (p. 38)
 Hadley Arkes, Amherst College, Amherst, MA (p. 40)
 Hunter Baker, Georgia Family Council, Norcross, GA (p. 43)
*John S. Baker, Jr., Louisiana State University, Baton Rouge, LA (p. 43)
 Joshua K. Baker, The Marriage Law Project, Washington, DC (p. 43)
*M. Miller Baker, McDermott, Will & Emery, Washington, DC (p. 44)
 Joseph Baldacchino, National Humanities Institute, Bowie, MD (p. 44)
*Sandor Balogh, Hudson Valley Community College, East Greenbush, NY (p. 45)
*Randy Barnett, Boston University School of Law, Boston, MA (p. 46)
*Herman Belz, University of Maryland, College Park, MD (p. 50)
 Walter Berns, American Enterprise Institute, Washington, DC (p. 51)
*Robert K. Best, Pacific Legal Foundation, Sacramento, CA (p. 52)
*Lillian BeVier, University of Virginia, Charlottesville, VA (p. 53)
*Clint Bolick, Institute for Justice, Phoenix, AZ (p. 56)
 James E. Bond, Seattle University, Seattle, WA (p. 56)
*James Bopp, Jr., James Madison Center for Free Speech, Washington, DC (p. 57)
*Robert H. Bork, American Enterprise Institute, Washington, DC (p. 57)
 Theodore Boutros, Gibson, Dunn & Crutcher LLP, Washington, DC (p. 58)
 Jennifer C. Braceras, Independent Women's Forum, Arlington, VA (p. 59)
*Gerard V. Bradley, Notre Dame Law School, Notre Dame, IN (p. 59)
*Marshall J. Breger, Catholic University of America, Washington, DC (p. 60)
*Sharon Browne, Pacific Legal Foundation, Sacramento, CA (p. 63)
*Scott Bullock, Institute for Justice, Washington, DC (p. 65)
*James Burling, Pacific Legal Foundation, Sacramento, CA (p. 65)

CONSTITUTIONAL LAW (Continued)

*David Burton, Argus Group, Alexandria, VA (p. 66)
Steven Calabresi, Northwestern University School of Law, Chicago, IL (p. 67)
*F. Patricia Callahan, American Association of Small Property Owners, Washington, DC (p. 68)
Bruce N. Cameron, National Right to Work Legal Defense Foundation, Springfield, VA (p. 68)
*Robert Carleson, American Civil Rights Union, Alexandria, VA (p. 70)
*Michael A. Carvin, Jones, Day, Reavis & Pogue, Washington, DC (p. 71)
*Anthony T. Caso, Pacific Legal Foundation, Sacramento, CA (p. 72)
*Milton L. Chappell, National Right to Work Legal Defense Foundation, Springfield, VA (p. 72)
*Roger Clegg, Center for Equal Opportunity, Sterling, VA (p. 76)
*Robert L. Clinton, Southern Illinois University, Carbondale, IL (p. 76)
Harry M. Clor, Kenyon College, Gambier, OH (p. 76)
*Charles Colson, Prison Fellowship Ministries, Washington, DC (p. 79)
*Charles J. Cooper, Cooper & Kirk, PLLC, Washington, DC (p. 81)
*Douglas Cox, Gibson, Dunn & Crutcher LLP, Washington, DC (p. 84)
Dennis Coyle, Catholic University of America, Washington, DC (p. 84)
*Robert J. Cynkar, Cooper & Kirk, PLLC, Washington, DC (p. 87)
*Brad W. Dacus, Pacific Justice Institute, Citrus Heights, CA (p. 87)
*Marshall L. De Rosa, Florida Atlantic University, Davie, FL (p. 90)
*Lisa Dean, Free Congress Foundation, Washington, DC (p. 91)
*Robert Destro, Catholic University of America, Washington, DC (p. 94)
*Jude P. Dougherty, Catholic University of America, Washington, DC (p. 97)
Richard J. Dougherty, University of Dallas, Irving, TX (p. 97)
*Richard Duncan, University of Nebraska, Lincoln, NE (p. 99)
Valle Simms Dutcher, Southeastern Legal Foundation, Atlanta, GA (p. 101)
*John C. Eastman, Chapman University School of Law, Orange, CA (p. 102)
*James R. Edwards, Jr., Hudson Institute, Washington, DC (p. 104)
*Mickey Edwards, Harvard University, Cambridge, MA (p. 104)
Paul Edwards, Mercatus Center at George Mason University, Arlington, VA (p. 104)
*Ward Elliott, Claremont McKenna College, Claremont, CA (p. 106)
*Jean Bethke Elshtain, University of Chicago, Chicago, IL (p. 106)
Richard A. Epstein, University of Chicago Law School, Chicago, IL (p. 107)
*Edward J. Erler, California State University, San Bernardino, San Bernardino, CA (p. 107)
*Michael P. Farris, Patrick Henry College, Purcellville, VA (p. 109)
Peter Ferrara, International Center for Law and Economics, Washington, DC (p. 110)
*Robert Fike, Americans for Tax Reform, Washington, DC (p. 111)
John Findley, Pacific Legal Foundation, Sacramento, CA (p. 111)
*Steve Fitschen, National Legal Foundation, Virginia Beach, VA (p. 112)
*Michael Flynn, American Legislative Exchange Council, Washington, DC (p. 113)
*David Forte, Cleveland State University, Cleveland, OH (p. 114)
*Matthew J. Franck, Radford University, Radford, VA (p. 115)
Richard W. Garnett, Notre Dame Law School, Notre Dame, IN (p. 120)
*Todd Gaziano, The Heritage Foundation, Washington, DC (p. 121)
*Robert P. George, Princeton University, Princeton, NJ (p. 122)
Mary Ann Glendon, Harvard Law School, Cambridge, MA (p. 124)
*Alan Gottlieb, Citizens Committee for the Right to Keep and Bear Arms, Bellevue, WA (p. 127)
*Lino A. Graglia, University of Texas, Austin, TX (p. 128)
Andrew Grainger, New England Legal Foundation, Boston, MA (p. 128)
Samuel Gregg, Acton Institute for the Study of Religion and Liberty, Grand Rapids, MI (p. 129)
*Michael S. Greve, American Enterprise Institute, Washington, DC (p. 129)
*Robert Hale, Northwest Legal Foundation, Minot, ND (p. 132)
Roger Hamburg, Indiana University South Bend, South Bend, IN (p. 133)
Jerome J. Hanus, American University, Washington, DC (p. 134)
John C. Harrison, University of Virginia, Charlottesville, VA (p. 136)
Gene Healy, Cato Institute, Washington, DC (p. 138)

CONSTITUTIONAL LAW (Continued)

Robert A. Heineman, Alfred University, Alfred, NY (p. 139)
*James M. Henderson, Sr., American Center for Law and Justice, Washington, DC (p. 140)
Wendy Herdlein, The Marriage Law Project, Washington, DC (p. 140)
*Fred Holden, Phoenix Enterprises, Arvada, CO (p. 144)
*Kenneth M. Holland, University of Memphis, Memphis, TN (p. 144)
Jacob G. Hornberger, Future of Freedom Foundation, Fairfax, VA (p. 146)
*Charles D. Hurley, Iowa Family Policy Center, Pleasant Hill, IA (p. 150)
*Bradley P. Jacob, Regent University, Virginia Beach, VA (p. 152)
Harry V. Jaffa, Claremont Institute, Claremont, CA (p. 153)
*Charles W. Jarvis, United Seniors Association, Fairfax, VA (p. 153)
*Thomas L. Jipping, Concerned Women for America, Washington, DC (p. 154)
*Paul Kamenar, Washington Legal Foundation, Washington, DC (p. 157)
Martin S. Kaufman, Atlantic Legal Foundation, New York, NY (p. 159)
Robert G. Kaufman, University of Vermont, Burlington, VT (p. 159)
Maurice Kelman, Wayne State University Law School, Troy, MI (p. 161)
Phil Kent, Southeastern Legal Foundation, Atlanta, GA (p. 162)
*Manuel Klausner, Individual Rights Foundation, Los Angeles, CA (p. 165)
*Christopher J. Klicka, Home School Legal Defense Association, Purcellville, VA (p. 165)
*Douglas W. Kmiec, The Catholic University of America, Washington, DC (p. 166)
Joseph M. Knippenberg, Oglethorpe University, Atlanta, GA (p. 166)
*Robert C. Koons, University of Texas, Austin, TX (p. 167)
*David B. Kopel, Independence Institute, Golden, CO (p. 167)
John E. Kramer, Institute for Justice, Washington, DC (p. 168)
Thomas L. Krannawitter, Claremont Institute, Claremont, CA (p. 168)
Stephen Krason, Franciscan University of Steubenville, Steubenville, OH (p. 169)
Gary Kreep, United States Justice Foundation, Escondido, CA (p. 169)
Deborah J. LaFetra, Pacific Legal Foundation, Sacramento, CA (p. 171)
*Raymond J. LaJeunesse, Jr., National Right to Work Legal Defense Foundation, Springfield, VA (p. 172)
Glenn G. Lammi, Washington Legal Foundation, Washington, DC (p. 173)
*George Landrith, Frontiers of Freedom Institute, Fairfax, VA (p. 173)
*Andrew Langer, National Federation of Independent Business, Washington, DC (p. 174)
*Janet LaRue, Concerned Women for America, Washington, DC (p. 175)
Peter Augustine Lawler, Berry College, Mount Berry, GA (p. 175)
Seth Leibsohn, Empower America, Washington, DC (p. 177)
Leonard A. Leo, The Federalist Society for Law and Public Policy Studies, Washington, DC (p. 178)
Curt A. Levey, Center for Individual Rights, Washington, DC (p. 178)
*Mark R. Levin, Landmark Legal Foundation, Herndon, VA (p. 178)
Jacob T. Levy, University of Chicago, Chicago, IL (p. 179)
*Robert A. Levy, Cato Institute, Washington, DC (p. 179)
*George Liebmann, Calvert Institute for Policy Research, Baltimore, MD (p. 180)
Leonard P. Liggio, Atlas Economic Research Foundation, Fairfax, VA (p. 180)
Margaret A. Little, Law Office of Margaret Little, Stratford, CT (p. 181)
Jordan Lorence, Alliance Defense Fund, Scottsdale, AZ (p. 183)
*Nelson Lund, George Mason University School of Law, Arlington, VA (p. 184)
*Timothy Lynch, Cato Institute, Washington, DC (p. 185)
*Rita P. Maguire, Arizona Center for Public Policy, Phoenix, AZ (p. 186)
Mary P. Mahoney, United Seniors Association, Inc., Washington, DC (p. 187)
*Joyce L. Malcolm, Bentley College, Waltham, MA (p. 187)
Mario Mandina, National Lawyers Association, Independence, MO (p. 188)
David E. Marion, Hampden-Sydney College, Hampden-Sydney, VA (p. 189)
*Nancie G. Marzulla, Defenders of Property Rights, Washington, DC (p. 191)
*Roger J. Marzulla, Defenders of Property Rights, Washington, DC (p. 191)

CONSTITUTIONAL LAW (Continued)

*Ken Masugi, Claremont Institute, Claremont, CA (p. 191)
Colby May, American Center for Law and Justice, Alexandria, VA (p. 192)
*Nina May, *Renaissance Connection.com/RCNetwork.net*, Washington, DC (p. 192)
*Randolph J. May, Progress & Freedom Foundation, Washington, DC (p. 193)
*David N. Mayer, Capital University Law School, Columbus, OH (p. 193)
*Michael W. McConnell, University of Utah, Salt Lake City, UT (p. 194)
*Forrest McDonald, University of Alabama, Coker, AL (p. 195)
John O. McGinnis, Cardozo School of Law, New York, NY (p. 196)
*Edwin Meese III, The Heritage Foundation, Washington, DC (p. 198)
*William H. Mellor, Institute for Justice, Washington, DC (p. 199)
Eugene B. Meyer, The Federalist Society for Law and Public Policy Studies, Washington, DC (p. 200)
*Roger Michener, Placitas, NM (p. 201)
Tom Minnery, Focus on the Family, Colorado Springs, CO (p. 203)
Mark E. Mitchell, Thomas University, Thomasville, GA (p. 203)
*Thomas Patrick Monaghan, American Center for Law and Justice, New Hope, KY (p. 204)
*Richard E. Morgan, Bowdoin College, Brunswick, ME (p. 206)
*Joseph A. Morris, Lincoln Legal Foundation, Chicago, IL (p. 207)
*Len Munsil, Center for Arizona Policy, Scottsdale, AZ (p. 209)
Robert G. Natelson, Missoula, MT (p. 211)
Clark Neily, Institute for Justice, Washington, DC (p. 212)
*Richard John Neuhaus, Institute on Religion and Public Life, New York, NY (p. 213)
Stuart W. Nolan, Jr., Springfield, VA (p. 214)
John Nowacki, Free Congress Foundation, Washington, DC (p. 215)
*Michael O'Neill, George Mason University School of Law, Arlington, VA (p. 217)
Mike O'Neill, Landmark Legal Foundation, Herndon, VA (p. 217)
*Allan E. Parker, Jr., Texas Justice Foundation, San Antonio, TX (p. 221)
Anthony A. Peacock, Utah State University, Logan, UT (p. 224)
Terence J. Pell, Center for Individual Rights, Washington, DC (p. 224)
*William Perry Pendley, Mountain States Legal Foundation, Lakewood, CO (p. 225)
*Howard Phillips, The Conservative Caucus, Inc., Vienna, VA (p. 227)
*Roger Pilon, Cato Institute, Washington, DC (p. 228)
*Daniel J. Popeo, Washington Legal Foundation, Washington, DC (p. 231)
*Stephen Presser, Northwestern University School of Law, Chicago, IL (p. 233)
Jeremy Rabkin, Cornell University, Ithaca, NY (p. 235)
*Alan C. Raul, Sidley & Austin Brown & Wood, LLP, Washington, DC (p. 237)
Harold Calvin Ray, National Center for Faith-Based Initiatives, West Palm Beach, FL (p. 237)
*Charles E. Rice, Notre Dame Law School, Notre Dame, IN (p. 239)
*Robin Rivett, Pacific Legal Foundation, Sacramento, CA (p. 241)
*David B. Rivkin, Jr., Baker & Hostetler, Washington, DC (p. 241)
*James S. Robbins, National Defense University, Washington, DC (p. 241)
Ron Robinson, Young America's Foundation, Herndon, VA (p. 242)
*Kelly Rosati, Hawaii Family Forum, Kaneohe, HI (p. 243)
*Paul Rosenzweig, The Heritage Foundation, Washington, DC (p. 243)
Michael E. Rosman, Center for Individual Rights, Washington, DC (p. 243)
*Ralph A. Rossum, Claremont McKenna College, Claremont, CA (p. 244)
*Ronald D. Rotunda, George Mason University School of Law, Arlington, VA (p. 244)
*Alfred P. Rubin, Tufts University, Medford, MA (p. 246)
*Frank Ruddy, Ruddy & Muir, Chevy Chase, MD (p. 246)
*Mark E. Rush, Washington and Lee University, Lexington, VA (p. 247)
*Richard A. Samp, Washington Legal Foundation, Washington, DC (p. 248)
David L. Schaefer, Holy Cross College, Worcester, MA (p. 252)
*Kent Scheidegger, Criminal Justice Legal Foundation, Sacramento, CA (p. 252)
*Phyllis Schlafly, Eagle Forum, St. Louis, MO (p. 253)

---

* Has testified before a state or federal legislative committee

CONSTITUTIONAL LAW (Continued)

*Alan E. Sears, Alliance Defense Fund, Scottsdale, AZ (p. 255)
*Jay Sekulow, American Center for Law and Justice, Virginia Beach, VA (p. 256)
*Jamie Self, Georgia Family Council, Norcross, GA (p. 256)
*Kelly Shackelford, Free Market Foundation, Plano, TX (p. 257)
Kannon K. Shanmugam, Kirkland & Ellis, Washington, DC (p. 258)
J. Gregory Sidak, American Enterprise Institute, Washington, DC (p. 259)
Bernard Siegan, University of San Diego School of Law, San Diego, CA (p. 259)
Aaron Siegel, Freedoms Foundation at Valley Forge, Valley Forge, PA (p. 259)
Harvey Silverglate, The Foundation for Individual Rights in Education, Boston, MA (p. 260)
*Solveig Singleton, Competitive Enterprise Institute, Washington, DC (p. 261)
*Baker Smith, U. S. Constitutional Rights Legal Defense Fund, Inc., Marietta, GA (p. 262)
Brad Snavely, Michigan Family Forum, Lansing, MI (p. 264)
James R. Stoner, Louisiana State University, Baton Rouge, LA (p. 270)
James Swanson, Cato Institute, Washington, DC (p. 272)
*Bruce Taylor, National Law Center for Children and Families, Fairfax, VA (p. 274)
Stephen Thayer, American Conservative Union, Alexandria, VA (p. 276)
Stephen R. Thomas, North American Canon Law Society, Duluth, MN (p. 277)
J. Mills Thornton, III, University of Michigan, Ann Arbor, MI (p. 278)
Glen E. Thurow, University of Dallas, Irving, TX (p. 279)
Richard H. Timberlake, Jr., Bogart, GA (p. 279)
*Herbert W. Titus, Virginia Beach, VA (p. 279)
*Gordon Tullock, George Mason University School of Law, Arlington, VA (p. 281)
John Tuskey, Regent University, Virginia Beach, VA (p. 282)
*Balint Vazsonyi, Center for the American Founding, McLean, VA (p. 284)
*Eugene Volokh, University of California at Los Angeles, Los Angeles, CA (p. 285)
Dane vonBreichenruchardt, U. S. Bill of Rights Foundation, Washington, DC (p. 286)
*Ben A. Wallis, Jr., Institute for Human Rights, San Antonio, TX (p. 287)
Gerald Walpin, Katten Muchin Zavis Rosenman, New York, NY (p. 288)
Tom Washburne, Home School Legal Defense Association, Purcellville, VA (p. 289)
*Dane Waters, Initiative and Referendum Institute, Leesburg, VA (p. 289)
Bradley C. S. Watson, Saint Vincent College, Latrobe, PA (p. 290)
Stanley J. Watson, Patrick Henry College, Purcellville, VA (p. 290)
*Walter M. Weber, American Center for Law and Justice, Alexandria, VA (p. 291)
John G. West, Discovery Institute, Seattle, WA (p. 292)
Thomas G. West, University of Dallas, Irving, TX (p. 293)
*John W. Whitehead, The Rutherford Institute, Charlottesville, VA (p. 293)
Keith E. Whittington, Princeton University, Princeton, NJ (p. 294)
*Natalie Williams, Robinson, DiLando and Whitaker, Sacramento, CA (p. 295)
*Christopher Wolfe, Marquette University, Milwaukee, WI (p. 297)
John Yoo, University of California, Berkeley, Berkeley, CA (p. 300)
James V. Young, Lee's Summit, MO (p. 300)
*Todd G. Young, Southeastern Legal Foundation, Atlanta, GA (p. 301)
*W. James Young, National Right to Work Legal Defense Foundation, Springfield, VA (p. 301)
Ronald A. Zumbrun, The Zumbrun Law Firm, Sacramento, CA (p. 303)

CORRECTIONS AND SENTENCING

*Charles A. Ballard, Institute for Responsible Fatherhood and Family Revitalization, Largo, MD (p. 45)
*William J. Bennett, Empower America, Washington, DC (p. 51)
*Joseph Bessette, Claremont McKenna College, Claremont, CA (p. 52)
Michael K. Block, University of Arizona, Tucson, AZ (p. 55)
*S. Jan Brakel, Isaac Ray Center, Inc., Chicago, IL (p. 60)
Gregory Paul Brinker, Marion County Justice Agency, Indianapolis, IN (p. 61)
*Paul Cassell, University of Utah, Salt Lake City, UT (p. 72)

CORRECTIONS AND SENTENCING (Continued)

*Michael A. Ciamarra, Alabama Policy Institute, Birmingham, AL (p. 74)
*Charles Colson, Prison Fellowship Ministries, Washington, DC (p. 79)
 Buffy DeBreaux-Watts, American Board for Certification of Teacher Excellence, Washington, DC (p. 91)
 John J. DiIulio, Jr., University of Pennsylvania, Philadelphia, PA (p. 95)
 John Jay Douglass, University of Houston Law Center, Houston, TX (p. 97)
 Mark L. Earley, Prison Fellowship Ministries, Washington, DC (p. 101)
 A. Roger Ekirch, Virginia Polytechnic Institute, Blacksburg, VA (p. 105)
 David D. Friedman, Santa Clara University, San Jose, CA (p. 117)
 Richard W. Garnett, Notre Dame Law School, Notre Dame, IN (p. 120)
*Todd Gaziano, The Heritage Foundation, Washington, DC (p. 121)
*Steven Goldberg, City College, New York, NY (p. 125)
 Reuben Greenberg, Charleston Police Department, Charleston, SC (p. 128)
*Paul Guppy, Washington Policy Center, Seattle, WA (p. 131)
*Alfred N. Himelson, Woodland Hills, CA (p. 143)
*Charles D. Hurley, Iowa Family Policy Center, Pleasant Hill, IA (p. 150)
 Byron Johnson, University of Pennsylvania, Philadelphia, PA (p. 155)
*David B. Kopel, Independence Institute, Golden, CO (p. 167)
*Andrew T. LeFevre, American Legislative Exchange Council, Washington, DC (p. 177)
*Eli Lehrer, *The American Enterprise*, Washington, DC (p. 177)
 Charles H. Logan, University of Connecticut, Storrs, CT (p. 182)
 Edmund McGarrell, Hudson Institute, Indianapolis, IN (p. 195)
*Michael J. McManus, Marriage Savers, Potomac, MD (p. 197)
*Edwin Meese III, The Heritage Foundation, Washington, DC (p. 198)
 Eugene B. Meyer, The Federalist Society for Law and Public Policy Studies, Washington, DC (p. 200)
 Mark E. Mitchell, Thomas University, Thomasville, GA (p. 203)
 Carlisle E. Moody, College of William and Mary, Williamsburg, VA (p. 205)
*Adrian T. Moore, Reason Foundation, Los Angeles, CA (p. 205)
*David B. Muhlhausen, The Heritage Foundation, Washington, DC (p. 208)
*Pat Nolan, Justice Fellowship, Reston, VA (p. 214)
*Michael O'Neill, George Mason University School of Law, Arlington, VA (p. 217)
*William G. Otis, Falls Church, VA (p. 220)
*Daniel J. Popeo, Washington Legal Foundation, Washington, DC (p. 231)
*William H. Reid, Horseshoe, TX (p. 238)
*Paul Rosenzweig, The Heritage Foundation, Washington, DC (p. 243)
*Susan Sarnoff, Ohio University, Athens, OH (p. 250)
*Kent Scheidegger, Criminal Justice Legal Foundation, Sacramento, CA (p. 252)
*Geoffrey F. Segal, Reason Public Policy Institute, Los Angeles, CA (p. 256)
*Rita Simon, American University, Washington, DC (p. 260)
*Alexander Tabarrok, Mercatus Center at George Mason University, Arlington, VA (p. 273)
*Joe Tropea, International Association for Support of Privatization, Washington, DC (p. 281)
*Joe D. Whitley, Alston & Bird LLP, Atlanta, GA (p. 294)

CRIME/CRIME STATISTICS

*Charles A. Ballard, Institute for Responsible Fatherhood and Family Revitalization, Largo, MD (p. 45)
*Randy Barnett, Boston University School of Law, Boston, MA (p. 46)
 Gary Becker, University of Chicago, Chicago, IL (p. 48)
*William J. Bennett, Empower America, Washington, DC (p. 51)
*Joseph Bessette, Claremont McKenna College, Claremont, CA (p. 52)
 Paul H. Blackman, NRA Institute for Legislative Action, Fairfax, VA (p. 54)
 Gregory Paul Brinker, Marion County Justice Agency, Indianapolis, IN (p. 61)
*Paul Cassell, University of Utah, Salt Lake City, UT (p. 72)

CRIME/CRIME STATISTICS (Continued)

J. Daryl Charles, Taylor University, Upland, IN **(p. 72)**
*Stephen Cole, State University of New York, Stony Brook, NY **(p. 78)**
*Charles Colson, Prison Fellowship Ministries, Washington, DC **(p. 79)**
Kay Crawford, Hudson Institute, Indianapolis, IN **(p. 85)**
*Charles H. Cunningham, National Rifle Association, Washington, DC **(p. 87)**
John J. DiIulio, Jr., University of Pennsylvania, Philadelphia, PA **(p. 95)**
Isaac Ehrlich, State University of New York, Buffalo, Buffalo, NY **(p. 105)**
*Edward J. Erler, California State University, San Bernardino, San Bernardino, CA **(p. 107)**
*James Fyfe, Temple University, Philadelphia, PA **(p. 119)**
*Alan Gottlieb, Citizens Committee for the Right to Keep and Bear Arms, Bellevue, WA **(p. 127)**
Reuben Greenberg, Charleston Police Department, Charleston, SC **(p. 128)**
Gene Healy, Cato Institute, Washington, DC **(p. 138)**
John M. Heineke, Santa Clara University, Santa Clara, CA **(p. 139)**
*John R. Hill, Alabama Policy Institute, Birmingham, AL **(p. 142)**
Natalie K. Hipple, Hudson Institute, Indianapolis, IN **(p. 143)**
Niger Roy Innis, Congress of Racial Equality, New York, NY **(p. 151)**
Byron Johnson, University of Pennsylvania, Philadelphia, PA **(p. 155)**
George Kelling, Rutgers University, Newark, NJ **(p. 160)**
*Andrew T. LeFevre, American Legislative Exchange Council, Washington, DC **(p. 177)**
*Eli Lehrer, *The American Enterprise,* Washington, DC **(p. 177)**
Charles H. Logan, University of Connecticut, Storrs, CT **(p. 182)**
John R. Lott, Jr., American Enterprise Institute, Washington, DC **(p. 183)**
*Heather MacDonald, Manhattan Institute for Policy Research, New York, NY **(p. 185)**
Edmund McGarrell, Hudson Institute, Indianapolis, IN **(p. 195)**
Lawrence J. McQuillan, Pacific Research Institute, San Francisco, CA **(p. 197)**
*Edwin Meese III, The Heritage Foundation, Washington, DC **(p. 198)**
Eugene B. Meyer, The Federalist Society for Law and Public Policy Studies,
    Washington, DC **(p. 200)**
*Robert Moffit, The Heritage Foundation, Washington, DC **(p. 204)**
Carlisle E. Moody, College of William and Mary, Williamsburg, VA **(p. 205)**
*David B. Muhlhausen, The Heritage Foundation, Washington, DC **(p. 208)**
Charles Murray, American Enterprise Institute, Washington, DC **(p. 209)**
Iain Murray, Statistical Assessment Service, Washington, DC **(p. 209)**
*Pat Nolan, Justice Fellowship, Reston, VA **(p. 214)**
*Michael O'Neill, George Mason University School of Law, Arlington, VA **(p. 217)**
Harold Calvin Ray, National Center for Faith-Based Initiatives, West Palm Beach, FL **(p. 237)**
*Paul Rosenzweig, The Heritage Foundation, Washington, DC **(p. 243)**
*Ralph A. Rossum, Claremont McKenna College, Claremont, CA **(p. 244)**
*Paul Rubin, Emory University, Atlanta, GA **(p. 246)**
Michael D. Rushford, Criminal Justice Legal Foundation, Sacramento, CA **(p. 247)**
*Susan Sarnoff, Ohio University, Athens, OH **(p. 250)**
*Kent Scheidegger, Criminal Justice Legal Foundation, Sacramento, CA **(p. 252)**
Lawrence Sherman, University of Pennsylvania, Philadelphia, PA **(p. 259)**
*Rita Simon, American University, Washington, DC **(p. 260)**
Christopher B. Summers, Maryland Public Policy Institute, Germantown, MD **(p. 272)**
*Alexander Tabarrok, Mercatus Center at George Mason University, Arlington, VA **(p. 273)**
*Forest M. Thigpen, Mississippi Family Council, Jackson, MS **(p. 277)**
*Mark Thornton, Columbus State University, Columbus, GA **(p. 278)**
James Q. Wilson, Pepperdine University, Malibu, CA **(p. 296)**

CRIMINAL LAW AND PROCEDURE

*Lawrence Alexander, University of San Diego School of Law, San Diego, CA **(p. 36)**
*John S. Baker, Jr., Louisiana State University, Baton Rouge, LA **(p. 43)**
*Randy Barnett, Boston University School of Law, Boston, MA **(p. 46)**

CRIMINAL LAW AND PROCEDURE (Continued)

James E. Bond, Seattle University, Seattle, WA (p. 56)
*Gerard V. Bradley, Notre Dame Law School, Notre Dame, IN (p. 59)
*John Carlson, Washington Policy Center, Seattle, WA (p. 70)
*Paul Cassell, University of Utah, Salt Lake City, UT (p. 72)
*Charles Colson, Prison Fellowship Ministries, Washington, DC (p. 79)
Kay Crawford, Hudson Institute, Indianapolis, IN (p. 85)
*Lisa Dean, Free Congress Foundation, Washington, DC (p. 91)
Buffy DeBreaux-Watts, American Board for Certification of Teacher Excellence, Washington, DC (p. 91)
John Jay Douglass, University of Houston Law Center, Houston, TX (p. 97)
Mark L. Earley, Prison Fellowship Ministries, Washington, DC (p. 101)
David D. Friedman, Santa Clara University, San Jose, CA (p. 117)
*James Fyfe, Temple University, Philadelphia, PA (p. 119)
Richard W. Garnett, Notre Dame Law School, Notre Dame, IN (p. 120)
*Todd Gaziano, The Heritage Foundation, Washington, DC (p. 121)
Nick Gillespie, Reason Foundation, Los Angeles, CA (p. 123)
Reuben Greenberg, Charleston Police Department, Charleston, SC (p. 128)
Daniel B. Hales, Americans for Effective Law Enforcement, Chicago, IL (p. 132)
John M. Heineke, Santa Clara University, Santa Clara, CA (p. 139)
Larry Klayman, Judicial Watch, Washington, DC (p. 165)
*David B. Kopel, Independence Institute, Golden, CO (p. 167)
*Janet LaRue, Concerned Women for America, Washington, DC (p. 175)
*Andrew T. LeFevre, American Legislative Exchange Council, Washington, DC (p. 177)
Leonard A. Leo, The Federalist Society for Law and Public Policy Studies, Washington, DC (p. 178)
*Timothy Lynch, Cato Institute, Washington, DC (p. 185)
*Edwin Meese III, The Heritage Foundation, Washington, DC (p. 198)
Eugene B. Meyer, The Federalist Society for Law and Public Policy Studies, Washington, DC (p. 200)
Mark E. Mitchell, Thomas University, Thomasville, GA (p. 203)
*Joseph A. Morris, Lincoln Legal Foundation, Chicago, IL (p. 207)
*Laurence S. Moss, Babson College, Babson Park, MA (p. 208)
*Pat Nolan, Justice Fellowship, Reston, VA (p. 214)
*Michael O'Neill, George Mason University School of Law, Arlington, VA (p. 217)
*William G. Otis, Falls Church, VA (p. 220)
*William H. Reid, Horseshoe, TX (p. 238)
*Paul Craig Roberts, Institute for Political Economy, Panama City Beach, FL (p. 242)
*Paul Rosenzweig, The Heritage Foundation, Washington, DC (p. 243)
*Ralph A. Rossum, Claremont McKenna College, Claremont, CA (p. 244)
*Paul Rubin, Emory University, Atlanta, GA (p. 246)
Michael D. Rushford, Criminal Justice Legal Foundation, Sacramento, CA (p. 247)
*Kent Scheidegger, Criminal Justice Legal Foundation, Sacramento, CA (p. 252)
Kannon K. Shanmugam, Kirkland & Ellis, Washington, DC (p. 258)
Harvey Silverglate, The Foundation for Individual Rights in Education, Boston, MA (p. 260)
*Rita Simon, American University, Washington, DC (p. 260)
*Peggy Venable, Texas Citizens for a Sound Economy, Austin, TX (p. 284)
Gerald Walpin, Katten Muchin Zavis Rosenman, New York, NY (p. 288)
*Joe D. Whitley, Alston & Bird LLP, Atlanta, GA (p. 294)

FREE SPEECH

*Henry J. Abraham, Charlottesville, VA (p. 34)
*Lawrence Alexander, University of San Diego School of Law, San Diego, CA (p. 36)
*Julaine K. Appling, Family Research Institute of Wisconsin, Madison, WI (p. 40)
*John S. Baker, Jr., Louisiana State University, Baton Rouge, LA (p. 43)

---

* Has testified before a state or federal legislative committee

FREE SPEECH (Continued)

*Randy Barnett, Boston University School of Law, Boston, MA (p. 46)
*Tom W. Bell, Chapman University, Orange, CA (p. 50)
*Robert K. Best, Pacific Legal Foundation, Sacramento, CA (p. 52)
*James Bopp, Jr., James Madison Center for Free Speech, Washington, DC (p. 57)
  Leslie Carbone, Fairfax, VA (p. 69)
*Robert Carleson, American Civil Rights Union, Alexandria, VA (p. 70)
*Michael A. Carvin, Jones, Day, Reavis & Pogue, Washington, DC (p. 71)
*Anthony T. Caso, Pacific Legal Foundation, Sacramento, CA (p. 72)
*Ronald Cass, Boston University School of Law, Boston, MA (p. 72)
*Milton L. Chappell, National Right to Work Legal Defense Foundation, Springfield, VA (p. 72)
  Kellyanne Conway, the polling company/WomanTrend, Washington, DC (p. 80)
*Charles J. Cooper, Cooper & Kirk, PLLC, Washington, DC (p. 81)
  Dennis Coyle, Catholic University of America, Washington, DC (p. 84)
*Clyde Wayne Crews, Jr., Cato Institute, Washington, DC (p. 86)
*Brad W. Dacus, Pacific Justice Institute, Citrus Heights, CA (p. 87)
*Marshall L. De Rosa, Florida Atlantic University, Davie, FL (p. 90)
*Lisa Dean, Free Congress Foundation, Washington, DC (p. 91)
*Robert Destro, Catholic University of America, Washington, DC (p. 94)
*William T. Devlin, Urban Family Council, Philadelphia, PA (p. 94)
  Martin Duggan, Educational Freedom Foundation, St. Louis, MO (p. 99)
*Richard Duncan, University of Nebraska, Lincoln, NE (p. 99)
  Valle Simms Dutcher, Southeastern Legal Foundation, Atlanta, GA (p. 101)
*John C. Eastman, Chapman University School of Law, Orange, CA (p. 102)
*Michael P. Farris, Patrick Henry College, Purcellville, VA (p. 109)
*Robert Fike, Americans for Tax Reform, Washington, DC (p. 111)
*Steve Fitschen, National Legal Foundation, Virginia Beach, VA (p. 112)
*Peter Flaherty, National Legal and Policy Center, Falls Church, VA (p. 113)
*David Forte, Cleveland State University, Cleveland, OH (p. 114)
  Richard W. Garnett, Notre Dame Law School, Notre Dame, IN (p. 120)
*Todd Gaziano, The Heritage Foundation, Washington, DC (p. 121)
*Jules B. Gerard, Washington University, St. Louis, MO (p. 122)
*Lino A. Graglia, University of Texas, Austin, TX (p. 128)
*Robert Hale, Northwest Legal Foundation, Minot, ND (p. 132)
  Thor L. Halvorssen, The Foundation for Individual Rights in Education,
    Philadelphia, PA (p. 132)
  Roger Hamburg, Indiana University South Bend, South Bend, IN (p. 133)
*James M. Henderson, Sr., American Center for Law and Justice, Washington, DC (p. 140)
  Jacob G. Hornberger, Future of Freedom Foundation, Fairfax, VA (p. 146)
  Niger Roy Innis, Congress of Racial Equality, New York, NY (p. 151)
*Douglas Johnson, National Right to Life Committee, Washington, DC (p. 155)
  Martin S. Kaufman, Atlantic Legal Foundation, New York, NY (p. 159)
*David A. Keene, American Conservative Union, Washington, DC (p. 160)
  Phil Kent, Southeastern Legal Foundation, Atlanta, GA (p. 162)
*Manuel Klausner, Individual Rights Foundation, Los Angeles, CA (p. 165)
*Douglas W. Kmiec, The Catholic University of America, Washington, DC (p. 166)
*Robert H. Knight, Concerned Women for America, Washington, DC (p. 166)
*David B. Kopel, Independence Institute, Golden, CO (p. 167)
  John E. Kramer, Institute for Justice, Washington, DC (p. 168)
  Stephen Krason, Franciscan University of Steubenville, Steubenville, OH (p. 169)
  Gary Kreep, United States Justice Foundation, Escondido, CA (p. 169)
  Glenn G. Lammi, Washington Legal Foundation, Washington, DC (p. 173)
*George Landrith, Frontiers of Freedom Institute, Fairfax, VA (p. 173)
*Andrew Langer, National Federation of Independent Business, Washington, DC (p. 174)
*Janet LaRue, Concerned Women for America, Washington, DC (p. 175)

FREE SPEECH (Continued)

Curt A. Levey, Center for Individual Rights, Washington, DC (p. 178)

*Mark R. Levin, Landmark Legal Foundation, Herndon, VA (p. 178)

Jordan Lorence, Alliance Defense Fund, Scottsdale, AZ (p. 183)

Mario Mandina, National Lawyers Association, Independence, MO (p. 188)

David E. Marion, Hampden-Sydney College, Hampden-Sydney, VA (p. 189)

Colby May, American Center for Law and Justice, Alexandria, VA (p. 192)

*Nina May, *Renaissance Connection.com/RCNetwork.net*, Washington, DC (p. 192)

*Randolph J. May, Progress & Freedom Foundation, Washington, DC (p. 193)

Eugene B. Meyer, The Federalist Society for Law and Public Policy Studies, Washington, DC (p. 200)

Tom Minnery, Focus on the Family, Colorado Springs, CO (p. 203)

Mark E. Mitchell, Thomas University, Thomasville, GA (p. 203)

*Richard E. Morgan, Bowdoin College, Brunswick, ME (p. 206)

*Joseph A. Morris, Lincoln Legal Foundation, Chicago, IL (p. 207)

*Len Munsil, Center for Arizona Policy, Scottsdale, AZ (p. 209)

William Murchison, Baylor University, Waco, TX (p. 209)

Chuck Muth, American Conservative Union, Alexandria, VA (p. 210)

*Anne D. Neal, American Council of Trustees and Alumni, Washington, DC (p. 211)

Clark Neily, Institute for Justice, Washington, DC (p. 212)

Richard Alan Nelson, Louisiana State University, Baton Rouge, LA (p. 212)

Stuart W. Nolan, Jr., Springfield, VA (p. 214)

*Herbert R. Northrup, University of Pennsylvania, Haverford, PA (p. 215)

*Michael O'Neill, George Mason University School of Law, Arlington, VA (p. 217)

*Richard Olivastro, People Dynamics, Farmington, CT (p. 218)

*Allan E. Parker, Jr., Texas Justice Foundation, San Antonio, TX (p. 221)

*J. A. Parker, Lincoln Institute for Research and Education, Washington, DC (p. 221)

Ellen F. Paul, Bowling Green State University, Bowling Green, OH (p. 223)

Terence J. Pell, Center for Individual Rights, Washington, DC (p. 224)

*William Perry Pendley, Mountain States Legal Foundation, Lakewood, CO (p. 225)

*Roger Pilon, Cato Institute, Washington, DC (p. 228)

*Daniel J. Popeo, Washington Legal Foundation, Washington, DC (p. 231)

*Thomas Prichard, Minnesota Family Council, Minneapolis, MN (p. 233)

*Alan C. Raul, Sidley & Austin Brown & Wood, LLP, Washington, DC (p. 237)

Harold Calvin Ray, National Center for Faith-Based Initiatives, West Palm Beach, FL (p. 237)

George Reisman, Pepperdine University, Laguna Hills, CA (p. 238)

*Charles E. Rice, Notre Dame Law School, Notre Dame, IN (p. 239)

Sandy Rios, Concerned Women for America, Washington, DC (p. 240)

Ron Robinson, Young America's Foundation, Herndon, VA (p. 242)

*Paul Rosenzweig, The Heritage Foundation, Washington, DC (p. 243)

*Ronald D. Rotunda, George Mason University School of Law, Arlington, VA (p. 244)

*Paul Rubin, Emory University, Atlanta, GA (p. 246)

*Richard A. Samp, Washington Legal Foundation, Washington, DC (p. 248)

John Samples, Cato Institute, Washington, DC (p. 249)

*Ellis Sandoz, Eric Voegelin Institute, Baton Rouge, LA (p. 249)

David L. Schaefer, Holy Cross College, Worcester, MA (p. 252)

*Alan E. Sears, Alliance Defense Fund, Scottsdale, AZ (p. 255)

*Jay Sekulow, American Center for Law and Justice, Virginia Beach, VA (p. 256)

*Kelly Shackelford, Free Market Foundation, Plano, TX (p. 257)

*Lou Sheldon, Traditional Values Coalition, Washington, DC (p. 258)

Harvey Silverglate, The Foundation for Individual Rights in Education, Boston, MA (p. 260)

*Curt Smith, Indiana Family Institute, Indianapolis, IN (p. 263)

Jacob Sullum, *Reason* Magazine, Fairfax, VA (p. 272)

Mark Tapscott, The Heritage Foundation, Washington, DC (p. 274)

*Bruce Taylor, National Law Center for Children and Families, Fairfax, VA (p. 274)

FREE SPEECH (Continued)

*Herbert W. Titus, Virginia Beach, VA (p. 279)
*Forrest L. Turpen, Christian Educators Association International, Pasadena, CA (p. 282)
 John Tuskey, Regent University, Virginia Beach, VA (p. 282)
*Balint Vazsonyi, Center for the American Founding, McLean, VA (p. 284)
*Peggy Venable, Texas Citizens for a Sound Economy, Austin, TX (p. 284)
*Eugene Volokh, University of California at Los Angeles, Los Angeles, CA (p. 285)
 Dane vonBreichenruchardt, U. S. Bill of Rights Foundation, Washington, DC (p. 286)
 William Waller, Venable, Baetjer, Howard & Civiletti, LLP, Washington, DC (p. 287)
*Ben A. Wallis, Jr., Institute for Human Rights, San Antonio, TX (p. 287)
 Gerald Walpin, Katten Muchin Zavis Rosenman, New York, NY (p. 288)
*Dane Waters, Initiative and Referendum Institute, Leesburg, VA (p. 289)
 Bradley C. S. Watson, Saint Vincent College, Latrobe, PA (p. 290)
*Walter M. Weber, American Center for Law and Justice, Alexandria, VA (p. 291)
*John W. Whitehead, The Rutherford Institute, Charlottesville, VA (p. 293)
*Todd G. Young, Southeastern Legal Foundation, Atlanta, GA (p. 301)
 Ronald A. Zumbrun, The Zumbrun Law Firm, Sacramento, CA (p. 303)

IMMIGRATION

*Henry J. Abraham, Charlottesville, VA (p. 34)
*M. Gene Aldridge, New Mexico Independence Research Institute, Las Cruces, NM (p. 36)
 Carlos Ball, Agencia Interamericana de Prensa Economica, Boca Raton, FL (p. 44)
*Gary L. Bauer, Campaign for Working Families, Arlington, VA (p. 47)
 Walter Block, Loyola University New Orleans, New Orleans, LA (p. 55)
 Cecil E. Bohanon, Ball State University, Muncie, IN (p. 56)
*Marshall J. Breger, Catholic University of America, Washington, DC (p. 60)
 Francis H. Buckley, George Mason University School of Law, Arlington, VA (p. 64)
 Nicholas Capaldi, Loyola University New Orleans, New Orleans, LA (p. 69)
*Linda Chavez, Center for Equal Opportunity, Sterling, VA (p. 73)
*Barry R. Chiswick, University of Illinois, Chicago, Chicago, IL (p. 73)
*Hungdah Chiu, University of Maryland School of Law, Baltimore, MD (p. 74)
*Ward Connerly, American Civil Rights Institute, Sacramento, CA (p. 80)
 Jim F. Couch, University of North Alabama, Florence, AL (p. 83)
*Lisa Dean, Free Congress Foundation, Washington, DC (p. 91)
 Peter J. Duignan, Hoover Institution, Stanford, CA (p. 99)
*James R. Edwards, Jr., Hudson Institute, Washington, DC (p. 104)
*Ward Elliott, Claremont McKenna College, Claremont, CA (p. 106)
*Louis D. Enoff, Enoff Associates Limited, Sykesville, MD (p. 107)
*Edward J. Erler, California State University, San Bernardino, San Bernardino, CA (p. 107)
 John Findley, Pacific Legal Foundation, Sacramento, CA (p. 111)
*John Fonte, Hudson Institute, Washington, DC (p. 114)
*Murray Friedman, American Jewish Committee, Philadelphia, PA (p. 117)
 Lowell E. Gallaway, Ohio University, Athens, OH (p. 120)
 David Gersten, Center for Equal Opportunity, Sterling, VA (p. 123)
 Nick Gillespie, Reason Foundation, Los Angeles, CA (p. 123)
*Linda Gorman, Independence Institute, Golden, CO (p. 127)
 Paul Gottfried, Elizabethtown College, Elizabethtown, PA (p. 127)
*Daniel T. Griswold, Cato Institute, Washington, DC (p. 129)
*Clark C. Havighurst, Duke University School of Law, Durham, NC (p. 137)
 Robert A. Heineman, Alfred University, Alfred, NY (p. 139)
 James E. Hinish, Jr., Regent University, Williamsburg, VA (p. 143)
 Jacob G. Hornberger, Future of Freedom Foundation, Fairfax, VA (p. 146)
 Carol Iannone, New York, NY (p. 150)
*Fred C. Ikle, Center for Strategic and International Studies, Washington, DC (p. 151)
 Niger Roy Innis, Congress of Racial Equality, New York, NY (p. 151)

IMMIGRATION (Continued)

Thomas R. Ireland, University of Missouri, St. Louis, St. Louis, MO (p. 152)
Tamar Jacoby, Manhattan Institute for Policy Research, New York, NY (p. 153)
*Charles W. Jarvis, United Seniors Association, Fairfax, VA (p. 153)
*David A. Keene, American Conservative Union, Washington, DC (p. 160)
Phil Kent, Southeastern Legal Foundation, Atlanta, GA (p. 162)
Joel Kotkin, Pepperdine University, Malibu, CA (p. 168)
*Mark Krikorian, Center for Immigration Studies, Washington, DC (p. 169)
Richard Lessner, American Renewal, Washington, DC (p. 178)
Jacob T. Levy, University of Chicago, Chicago, IL (p. 179)
William S. Lind, Free Congress Foundation, Washington, DC (p. 180)
Frederick R. Lynch, Claremont McKenna College, Claremont, CA (p. 184)
*Rita P. Maguire, Arizona Center for Public Policy, Phoenix, AZ (p. 186)
Mary P. Mahoney, United Seniors Association, Inc., Washington, DC (p. 187)
*Yuri N. Maltsev, Carthage College, Kenosha, WI (p. 188)
*Ken Masugi, Claremont Institute, Claremont, CA (p. 191)
Clifford D. May, The Foundation for the Defense of Democracies, Washington, DC (p. 192)
Eugene B. Meyer, The Federalist Society for Law and Public Policy Studies,
    Washington, DC (p. 200)
*Steven W. Mosher, Population Research Institute, Front Royal, VA (p. 208)
*David B. Muhlhausen, The Heritage Foundation, Washington, DC (p. 208)
Mauro E. Mujica, U. S. English, Inc., Washington, DC (p. 208)
Chuck Muth, American Conservative Union, Alexandria, VA (p. 210)
*Grover Norquist, Americans for Tax Reform, Washington, DC (p. 214)
*Richard Olivastro, People Dynamics, Farmington, CT (p. 218)
*Ronald W. Pearson, Pearson & Pipkin, Inc., Washington, DC (p. 224)
Philip Peters, Lexington Institute, Arlington, VA (p. 226)
Peter D. Salins, Manhattan Institute for Policy Research, New York, NY (p. 248)
*Richard A. Samp, Washington Legal Foundation, Washington, DC (p. 248)
Gregory W. Sand, Saint Louis College of Pharmacy, St. Louis, MO (p. 249)
*Phyllis Schlafly, Eagle Forum, St. Louis, MO (p. 253)
*Peter W. Schramm, John M. Ashbrook Center for Public Affairs, Ashland, OH (p. 254)
*Ralph Segalman, California State University, Northridge, Northridge, CA (p. 256)
*Rita Simon, American University, Washington, DC (p. 260)
*Peter Skerry, Claremont McKenna College, Claremont, CA (p. 261)
*Matthew Spalding, The Heritage Foundation, Washington, DC (p. 266)
Irwin Stelzer, Hudson Institute, Washington, DC (p. 268)
Margaret D. Stock, United States Military Academy, West Point, NY (p. 269)
*Stephan Thernstrom, Lexington, MA (p. 276)
*David J. Theroux, The Independent Institute, Oakland, CA (p. 276)
Reed Ueda, Tufts University, Medford, MA (p. 282)
Otto Ulc, Binghamton University, Binghamton, NY (p. 283)
*Balint Vazsonyi, Center for the American Founding, McLean, VA (p. 284)
*Peggy Venable, Texas Citizens for a Sound Economy, Austin, TX (p. 284)
Bradley C. S. Watson, Saint Vincent College, Latrobe, PA (p. 290)
Stanley J. Watson, Patrick Henry College, Purcellville, VA (p. 290)
Christopher Heath Wellman, Georgia State University, Atlanta, GA (p. 292)
*Nikolai Wenzel, Atlas Economic Research Foundation, Fairfax, VA (p. 292)
Thomas G. West, University of Dallas, Irving, TX (p. 293)
*Joe D. Whitley, Alston & Bird LLP, Atlanta, GA (p. 294)
*Todd G. Young, Southeastern Legal Foundation, Atlanta, GA (p. 301)

INTERNATIONAL LAW

*Ronald Cass, Boston University School of Law, Boston, MA (p. 72)
*Hungdah Chiu, University of Maryland School of Law, Baltimore, MD (p. 74)

INTERNATIONAL LAW (Continued)

*Lisa Dean, Free Congress Foundation, Washington, DC (p. 91)
*Robert Destro, Catholic University of America, Washington, DC (p. 94)
*John C. Eastman, Chapman University School of Law, Orange, CA (p. 102)
*Robert Fike, Americans for Tax Reform, Washington, DC (p. 111)
*David Forte, Cleveland State University, Cleveland, OH (p. 114)
*Christopher Joyner, Georgetown University, Washington, DC (p. 156)
 Martin S. Kaufman, Atlantic Legal Foundation, New York, NY (p. 159)
*Elie Krakowski, EDK Consulting, Baltimore, MD (p. 168)
 Yuri Mantilla, Family Research Council, Washington, DC (p. 189)
 Clifford D. May, The Foundation for the Defense of Democracies, Washington, DC (p. 192)
 Wendell H. McCulloch, Jr., California State University, Long Beach, Long Beach, CA (p. 194)
 Samuel P. Menefee, Regent University, Virginia Beach, VA (p. 199)
 Eugene B. Meyer, The Federalist Society for Law and Public Policy Studies,
    Washington, DC (p. 200)
*Roger Michener, Placitas, NM (p. 201)
*Joseph A. Morris, Lincoln Legal Foundation, Chicago, IL (p. 207)
*Steven W. Mosher, Population Research Institute, Front Royal, VA (p. 208)
*David B. Rivkin, Jr., Baker & Hostetler, Washington, DC (p. 241)
*Alfred P. Rubin, Tufts University, Medford, MA (p. 246)
*Frank Ruddy, Ruddy & Muir, Chevy Chase, MD (p. 246)
 Brett D. Schaefer, The Heritage Foundation, Washington, DC (p. 252)
 Shaun Small, Empower America, Washington, DC (p. 262)
*Robert F. Turner, University of Virginia School of Law, Charlottesville, VA (p. 282)
 Otto Ulc, Binghamton University, Binghamton, NY (p. 283)
*Balint Vazsonyi, Center for the American Founding, McLean, VA (p. 284)
*Dane Waters, Initiative and Referendum Institute, Leesburg, VA (p. 289)
*Edwin D. Williamson, Sullivan & Cromwell, Washington, DC (p. 295)
*Michael K. Young, George Washington University Law School, Washington, DC (p. 300)

JUDICIAL ACTIVISM/JUDICIAL REFORM

*Henry J. Abraham, Charlottesville, VA (p. 34)
*Edward C. Anderson, National Arbitration Forum, Minneapolis, MN (p. 38)
*Julaine K. Appling, Family Research Institute of Wisconsin, Madison, WI (p. 40)
*John S. Baker, Jr., Louisiana State University, Baton Rouge, LA (p. 43)
*M. Miller Baker, McDermott, Will & Emery, Washington, DC (p. 44)
*Sandor Balogh, Hudson Valley Community College, East Greenbush, NY (p. 45)
*Randy Barnett, Boston University School of Law, Boston, MA (p. 46)
*Mark A. Behrens, Shook, Hardy & Bacon, L.L.P., Washington, DC (p. 49)
 Lisa E. Bernstein, University of Chicago Law School, Chicago, IL (p. 51)
*Wayman R. Bishop, The Family Foundation of Virginia, Richmond, VA (p. 53)
 James E. Bond, Seattle University, Seattle, WA (p. 56)
*James Bopp, Jr., James Madison Center for Free Speech, Washington, DC (p. 57)
 Jennifer C. Braceras, Independent Women's Forum, Arlington, VA (p. 59)
*Gerard V. Bradley, Notre Dame Law School, Notre Dame, IN (p. 59)
*S. Jan Brakel, Isaac Ray Center, Inc., Chicago, IL (p. 60)
*Lester Brickman, Cardozo School of Law, New York, NY (p. 61)
 Brian P. Brooks, O'Melveny & Myers LLP, Washington, DC (p. 62)
*Henry N. Butler, Chapman University, Orange, CA (p. 66)
*F. Patricia Callahan, American Association of Small Property Owners, Washington, DC (p. 68)
*Robert Carleson, American Civil Rights Union, Alexandria, VA (p. 70)
*Michael A. Carvin, Jones, Day, Reavis & Pogue, Washington, DC (p. 71)
*Michael A. Ciamarra, Alabama Policy Institute, Birmingham, AL (p. 74)
*Roger Clegg, Center for Equal Opportunity, Sterling, VA (p. 76)
*Robert L. Clinton, Southern Illinois University, Carbondale, IL (p. 76)

JUDICIAL ACTIVISM/JUDICIAL REFORM (Continued)

*Charles Colson, Prison Fellowship Ministries, Washington, DC (p. 79)
*Kenneth L. Connor, Family Research Council, Washington, DC (p. 80)
*Charles J. Cooper, Cooper & Kirk, PLLC, Washington, DC (p. 81)
 Dennis Coyle, Catholic University of America, Washington, DC (p. 84)
*Roger C. Cramton, Cornell Law School, Ithaca, NY (p. 85)
 Edward H. Crane, Cato Institute, Washington, DC (p. 85)
 T. Kenneth Cribb, Jr., Intercollegiate Studies Institute, Wilmington, DE (p. 86)
*Brad W. Dacus, Pacific Justice Institute, Citrus Heights, CA (p. 87)
*Matt Daniels, Alliance for Marriage, Springfield, VA (p. 88)
*Marshall L. De Rosa, Florida Atlantic University, Davie, FL (p. 90)
*Robert Destro, Catholic University of America, Washington, DC (p. 94)
 John Jay Douglass, University of Houston Law Center, Houston, TX (p. 97)
*Richard Duncan, University of Nebraska, Lincoln, NE (p. 99)
*John C. Eastman, Chapman University School of Law, Orange, CA (p. 102)
*James R. Edwards, Jr., Hudson Institute, Washington, DC (p. 104)
*Mickey Edwards, Harvard University, Cambridge, MA (p. 104)
*Edward J. Erler, California State University, San Bernardino, San Bernardino, CA (p. 107)
*Michael P. Farris, Patrick Henry College, Purcellville, VA (p. 109)
 Robert Feidler, International Legal Projects Institute, Grand Forks, ND (p. 110)
*Susan Fisher, Citizens for Law and Order, Carlsbad, CA (p. 112)
*Steve Fitschen, National Legal Foundation, Virginia Beach, VA (p. 112)
*David Forte, Cleveland State University, Cleveland, OH (p. 114)
*Matthew J. Franck, Radford University, Radford, VA (p. 115)
*Todd Gaziano, The Heritage Foundation, Washington, DC (p. 121)
*Jules B. Gerard, Washington University, St. Louis, MO (p. 122)
*Michael S. Greve, American Enterprise Institute, Washington, DC (p. 129)
*Robert Hale, Northwest Legal Foundation, Minot, ND (p. 132)
 Robert A. Heineman, Alfred University, Alfred, NY (p. 139)
*James M. Henderson, Sr., American Center for Law and Justice, Washington, DC (p. 140)
 Lowman Henry, Lincoln Institute of Public Opinion Research, Inc., Harrisburg, PA (p. 140)
*Kenneth M. Holland, University of Memphis, Memphis, TN (p. 144)
*Michael Horowitz, Hudson Institute, Washington, DC (p. 146)
*Charles W. Jarvis, United Seniors Association, Fairfax, VA (p. 153)
*Thomas L. Jipping, Concerned Women for America, Washington, DC (p. 154)
*Paul Kamenar, Washington Legal Foundation, Washington, DC (p. 157)
 Darlene A. Kennedy, Centre for New Black Leadership, Baltimore, MD (p. 162)
 Phil Kent, Southeastern Legal Foundation, Atlanta, GA (p. 162)
 Larry Klayman, Judicial Watch, Washington, DC (p. 165)
*Douglas W. Kmiec, The Catholic University of America, Washington, DC (p. 166)
 Thomas L. Krannawitter, Claremont Institute, Claremont, CA (p. 168)
 John Kurzweil, California Public Policy Foundation, Camarillo, CA (p. 171)
*Andrea S. Lafferty, Traditional Values Coalition, Washington, DC (p. 172)
*George Landrith, Frontiers of Freedom Institute, Fairfax, VA (p. 173)
*Andrew Langer, National Federation of Independent Business, Washington, DC (p. 174)
*Janet LaRue, Concerned Women for America, Washington, DC (p. 175)
 Leonard A. Leo, The Federalist Society for Law and Public Policy Studies,
    Washington, DC (p. 178)
 Curt A. Levey, Center for Individual Rights, Washington, DC (p. 178)
*Mark R. Levin, Landmark Legal Foundation, Herndon, VA (p. 178)
*George Liebmann, Calvert Institute for Policy Research, Baltimore, MD (p. 180)
 Margaret A. Little, Law Office of Margaret Little, Stratford, CT (p. 181)
 Mario Mandina, National Lawyers Association, Independence, MO (p. 188)
 David E. Marion, Hampden-Sydney College, Hampden-Sydney, VA (p. 189)
*Nancie G. Marzulla, Defenders of Property Rights, Washington, DC (p. 191)

---

* Has testified before a state or federal legislative committee

JUDICIAL ACTIVISM/JUDICIAL REFORM (Continued)

*Roger J. Marzulla, Defenders of Property Rights, Washington, DC (p. 191)
*David N. Mayer, Capital University Law School, Columbus, OH (p. 193)
*Michael W. McConnell, University of Utah, Salt Lake City, UT (p. 194)
 John O. McGinnis, Cardozo School of Law, New York, NY (p. 196)
 Lawrence J. McQuillan, Pacific Research Institute, San Francisco, CA (p. 197)
*Edwin Meese III, The Heritage Foundation, Washington, DC (p. 198)
 Eugene B. Meyer, The Federalist Society for Law and Public Policy Studies,
    Washington, DC (p. 200)
 Mark E. Mitchell, Thomas University, Thomasville, GA (p. 203)
*Thomas Patrick Monaghan, American Center for Law and Justice, New Hope, KY (p. 204)
*Richard E. Morgan, Bowdoin College, Brunswick, ME (p. 206)
*Joseph A. Morris, Lincoln Legal Foundation, Chicago, IL (p. 207)
*Len Munsil, Center for Arizona Policy, Scottsdale, AZ (p. 209)
 Clark Neily, Institute for Justice, Washington, DC (p. 212)
 C. Preston Noell, III, Tradition, Family, Property, Inc., McLean, VA (p. 214)
 Stuart W. Nolan, Jr., Springfield, VA (p. 214)
 John Nowacki, Free Congress Foundation, Washington, DC (p. 215)
 Mike O'Neill, Landmark Legal Foundation, Herndon, VA (p. 217)
*Richard Olivastro, People Dynamics, Farmington, CT (p. 218)
*Allan E. Parker, Jr., Texas Justice Foundation, San Antonio, TX (p. 221)
 Terence J. Pell, Center for Individual Rights, Washington, DC (p. 224)
 Judyth Pendell, Bloomfield, CT (p. 225)
 Laura Bennett Peterson, Washington, DC (p. 226)
 Paul C. Peterson, Coastal Carolina University, Conway, SC (p. 227)
*Roger Pilon, Cato Institute, Washington, DC (p. 228)
*Daniel J. Popeo, Washington Legal Foundation, Washington, DC (p. 231)
*Stephen Presser, Northwestern University School of Law, Chicago, IL (p. 233)
*Thomas Prichard, Minnesota Family Council, Minneapolis, MN (p. 233)
*Mark S. Pulliam, Latham & Watkins, San Diego, CA (p. 234)
*Don Racheter, Public Interest Institute, Mount Pleasant, IA (p. 235)
 Paul A. Rahe, University of Tulsa, Tulsa, OK (p. 236)
 Sandy Rios, Concerned Women for America, Washington, DC (p. 240)
*Paul Rosenzweig, The Heritage Foundation, Washington, DC (p. 243)
*Ralph A. Rossum, Claremont McKenna College, Claremont, CA (p. 244)
 Michael D. Rushford, Criminal Justice Legal Foundation, Sacramento, CA (p. 247)
*Richard A. Samp, Washington Legal Foundation, Washington, DC (p. 248)
 David L. Schaefer, Holy Cross College, Worcester, MA (p. 252)
*Phyllis Schlafly, Eagle Forum, St. Louis, MO (p. 253)
*Alan E. Sears, Alliance Defense Fund, Scottsdale, AZ (p. 255)
*E. Donald Shapiro, New York Law School, Scottsdale, AZ (p. 258)
*Lou Sheldon, Traditional Values Coalition, Washington, DC (p. 258)
 Mark W. Smith, Kasowitz, Benson, Torres & Friedman, LLP, New York, NY (p. 263)
 Brad Snavely, Michigan Family Forum, Lansing, MI (p. 264)
*Richard Stith, Valpariso University School of Law, Valpariso, IN (p. 269)
*Forest M. Thigpen, Mississippi Family Council, Jackson, MS (p. 277)
*Mark Thornton, Columbus State University, Columbus, GA (p. 278)
 Glen E. Thurow, University of Dallas, Irving, TX (p. 279)
 John Tuskey, Regent University, Virginia Beach, VA (p. 282)
*Balint Vazsonyi, Center for the American Founding, McLean, VA (p. 284)
 Dane vonBreichenruchardt, U. S. Bill of Rights Foundation, Washington, DC (p. 286)
 Gerald Walpin, Katten Muchin Zavis Rosenman, New York, NY (p. 288)
 Stephen J. Ware, Samford University, Birmingham, AL (p. 289)
 Bradley C. S. Watson, Saint Vincent College, Latrobe, PA (p. 290)
 Stanley J. Watson, Patrick Henry College, Purcellville, VA (p. 290)

JUDICIAL ACTIVISM/JUDICIAL REFORM (Continued)

*Walter M. Weber, American Center for Law and Justice, Alexandria, VA (p. 291)

Keith E. Whittington, Princeton University, Princeton, NJ (p. 294)

*Christopher Wolfe, Marquette University, Milwaukee, WI (p. 297)

Jason Wright, Frontiers of Freedom Institute, Fairfax, VA (p. 299)

John Yoo, University of California, Berkeley, Berkeley, CA (p. 300)

James V. Young, Lee's Summit, MO (p. 300)

*Todd G. Young, Southeastern Legal Foundation, Atlanta, GA (p. 301)

Ronald A. Zumbrun, The Zumbrun Law Firm, Sacramento, CA (p. 303)

JUVENILE JUSTICE

*Bela A. Balogh, University of Mary, Bismarck, ND (p. 45)

Douglas Besharov, American Enterprise Institute, Washington, DC (p. 52)

Gregory Paul Brinker, Marion County Justice Agency, Indianapolis, IN (p. 61)

David Brownlee, Family First, Tampa, FL (p. 64)

*Harry Bruno, Thomas University, Thomasville, GA (p. 64)

*Charles Colson, Prison Fellowship Ministries, Washington, DC (p. 79)

Kay Crawford, Hudson Institute, Indianapolis, IN (p. 85)

*Charles H. Cunningham, National Rifle Association, Washington, DC (p. 87)

*Brad W. Dacus, Pacific Justice Institute, Citrus Heights, CA (p. 87)

Buffy DeBreaux-Watts, American Board for Certification of Teacher Excellence, Washington, DC (p. 91)

John J. DiIulio, Jr., University of Pennsylvania, Philadelphia, PA (p. 95)

James C. Dobson, Focus on the Family, Colorado Springs, CO (p. 96)

*Michelle Easton, Clare Boothe Luce Policy Institute, Herndon, VA (p. 102)

*Michael P. Farris, Patrick Henry College, Purcellville, VA (p. 109)

Roberta M. Gilbert, Center for the Study of Human Systems, Falls Church, VA (p. 123)

*Roy Godson, National Strategy Information Center, Washington, DC (p. 125)

Charles Greenwalt, II, Susquehanna Valley Center for Public Policy, Hershey, PA (p. 129)

Virgil Gulker, Kids Hope USA, Holland, MI (p. 130)

*Randy H. Hamilton, University of California, Berkeley, Berkeley, CA (p. 133)

Natalie K. Hipple, Hudson Institute, Indianapolis, IN (p. 143)

*Michael Howden, Stronger Families for Oregon, Salem, OR (p. 147)

Michael L. Jestes, Oklahoma Family Policy Council, Bethany, OK (p. 154)

*Thomas L. Jipping, Concerned Women for America, Washington, DC (p. 154)

Byron Johnson, University of Pennsylvania, Philadelphia, PA (p. 155)

George Kelling, Rutgers University, Newark, NJ (p. 160)

*Andrew T. LeFevre, American Legislative Exchange Council, Washington, DC (p. 177)

Steve Mariotti, National Foundation for Teaching Entrepreneurship, New York, NY (p. 189)

Edmund McGarrell, Hudson Institute, Indianapolis, IN (p. 195)

Eugene B. Meyer, The Federalist Society for Law and Public Policy Studies, Washington, DC (p. 200)

Mark E. Mitchell, Thomas University, Thomasville, GA (p. 203)

*David B. Muhlhausen, The Heritage Foundation, Washington, DC (p. 208)

Iain Murray, Statistical Assessment Service, Washington, DC (p. 209)

*Pat Nolan, Justice Fellowship, Reston, VA (p. 214)

*Michael O'Neill, George Mason University School of Law, Arlington, VA (p. 217)

*J. A. Parker, Lincoln Institute for Research and Education, Washington, DC (p. 221)

*Ralph A. Rossum, Claremont McKenna College, Claremont, CA (p. 244)

*Arthur J. Schwartz, John Templeton Foundation, Radnor, PA (p. 254)

*Geoffrey F. Segal, Reason Public Policy Institute, Los Angeles, CA (p. 256)

*Lou Sheldon, Traditional Values Coalition, Washington, DC (p. 258)

*Rita Simon, American University, Washington, DC (p. 260)

Charles P. Stetson, U. S. Fund for Leadership Training, Southport, CT (p. 268)

*Joe Tropea, International Association for Support of Privatization, Washington, DC (p. 281)

---

* Has testified before a state or federal legislative committee

JUVENILE JUSTICE (Continued)

*Robert L. Woodson, Sr., National Center for Neighborhood Enterprise, Washington, DC (p. 298)

POLICE

Brian C. Anderson, Manhattan Institute for Policy Research, New York, NY (p. 38)
*Randy Barnett, Boston University School of Law, Boston, MA (p. 46)
Gregory Paul Brinker, Marion County Justice Agency, Indianapolis, IN (p. 61)
*Harry Bruno, Thomas University, Thomasville, GA (p. 64)
*John Carlson, Washington Policy Center, Seattle, WA (p. 70)
*Paul Cassell, University of Utah, Salt Lake City, UT (p. 72)
*Lawrence Cranberg, Austin, TX (p. 85)
Edwin J. Delattre, Boston University, Boston, MA (p. 91)
*James Fyfe, Temple University, Philadelphia, PA (p. 119)
Thomas Golab, Competitive Enterprise Institute, Washington, DC (p. 125)
Reuben Greenberg, Charleston Police Department, Charleston, SC (p. 128)
Daniel B. Hales, Americans for Effective Law Enforcement, Chicago, IL (p. 132)
*Randy H. Hamilton, University of California, Berkeley, Berkeley, CA (p. 133)
George Kelling, Rutgers University, Newark, NJ (p. 160)
Montgomery N. Kosma, Jones, Day, Reavis & Pogue, Washington, DC (p. 167)
*Andrew T. LeFevre, American Legislative Exchange Council, Washington, DC (p. 177)
*Eli Lehrer, *The American Enterprise*, Washington, DC (p. 177)
Martin A. Levin, Brandeis University, Waltham, MA (p. 178)
*James Andrew Lewis, Center for Strategic and International Studies, Washington, DC (p. 179)
William S. Lind, Free Congress Foundation, Washington, DC (p. 180)
*Timothy Lynch, Cato Institute, Washington, DC (p. 185)
*Heather MacDonald, Manhattan Institute for Policy Research, New York, NY (p. 185)
Edmund McGarrell, Hudson Institute, Indianapolis, IN (p. 195)
Lawrence J. McQuillan, Pacific Research Institute, San Francisco, CA (p. 197)
*Edwin Meese III, The Heritage Foundation, Washington, DC (p. 198)
Eugene B. Meyer, The Federalist Society for Law and Public Policy Studies, Washington, DC (p. 200)
Mark E. Mitchell, Thomas University, Thomasville, GA (p. 203)
*Robert Moffit, The Heritage Foundation, Washington, DC (p. 204)
*David B. Muhlhausen, The Heritage Foundation, Washington, DC (p. 208)
Edward J. Ohlert, JAYCOR, McLean, VA (p. 218)
*William G. Otis, Falls Church, VA (p. 220)
*Richard O. Rowland, Grassroot Institute of Hawaii, Aiea, HI (p. 245)
*Geoffrey F. Segal, Reason Public Policy Institute, Los Angeles, CA (p. 256)
Lawrence Sherman, University of Pennsylvania, Philadelphia, PA (p. 259)
*John Michael Snyder, Citizens Committee for the Right to Keep and Bear Arms, Washington, DC (p. 265)
James Q. Wilson, Pepperdine University, Malibu, CA (p. 296)
James W. Witt, University of West Florida, Pensacola, FL (p. 296)

PUBLIC INTEREST LAW

*John S. Baker, Jr., Louisiana State University, Baton Rouge, LA (p. 43)
Gregory S. Baylor, Center for Law and Religious Freedom, Annandale, VA (p. 47)
*Robert K. Best, Pacific Legal Foundation, Sacramento, CA (p. 52)
*Kenneth Boehm, National Legal and Policy Center, Falls Church, VA (p. 56)
*Clint Bolick, Institute for Justice, Phoenix, AZ (p. 56)
*James Bopp, Jr., James Madison Center for Free Speech, Washington, DC (p. 57)
*Scott Bullock, Institute for Justice, Washington, DC (p. 65)
Steven Calabresi, Northwestern University School of Law, Chicago, IL (p. 67)
*F. Patricia Callahan, American Association of Small Property Owners, Washington, DC (p. 68)

PUBLIC INTEREST LAW (Continued)

*Robert Carleson, American Civil Rights Union, Alexandria, VA (p. 70)
*Anthony T. Caso, Pacific Legal Foundation, Sacramento, CA (p. 72)
 John Cobin, Montauk Financial Group, Greenville, SC (p. 76)
*Brad W. Dacus, Pacific Justice Institute, Citrus Heights, CA (p. 87)
*Kathleen B. de Bettencourt, Environmental Literacy Council, Washington, DC (p. 89)
*Glenn Delk, Georgia Charter Schools, Atlanta, GA (p. 92)
*Richard Duncan, University of Nebraska, Lincoln, NE (p. 99)
*John C. Eastman, Chapman University School of Law, Orange, CA (p. 102)
*Evelyn Ebzery, Memorial Hospital of Sheridan County, Sheridan, WY (p. 103)
*Michael P. Farris, Patrick Henry College, Purcellville, VA (p. 109)
 John Findley, Pacific Legal Foundation, Sacramento, CA (p. 111)
*Steve Fitschen, National Legal Foundation, Virginia Beach, VA (p. 112)
*Peter Flaherty, National Legal and Policy Center, Falls Church, VA (p. 113)
 Robert Freedman, Institute for Justice, Washington, DC (p. 116)
*Todd Gaziano, The Heritage Foundation, Washington, DC (p. 121)
 Stefan Gleason, National Right to Work Legal Defense Foundation, Springfield, VA (p. 124)
*Stephen O. Goodrick, National Right to Work Committee, Springfield, VA (p. 126)
*Robert Hale, Northwest Legal Foundation, Minot, ND (p. 132)
 Kevin J. Hasson, The Becket Fund for Religious Liberty, Washington, DC (p. 137)
 Wendy Herdlein, The Marriage Law Project, Washington, DC (p. 140)
*Robert Hunter, Mackinac Center for Public Policy, Midland, MI (p. 150)
*Paul Kamenar, Washington Legal Foundation, Washington, DC (p. 157)
 Martin S. Kaufman, Atlantic Legal Foundation, New York, NY (p. 159)
*Sam Kazman, Competitive Enterprise Institute, Washington, DC (p. 159)
*Manuel Klausner, Individual Rights Foundation, Los Angeles, CA (p. 165)
 John E. Kramer, Institute for Justice, Washington, DC (p. 168)
 Gary Kreep, United States Justice Foundation, Escondido, CA (p. 169)
*Raymond J. LaJeunesse, Jr., National Right to Work Legal Defense Foundation, Springfield, VA (p. 172)
*Andrew Langer, National Federation of Independent Business, Washington, DC (p. 174)
 Leonard A. Leo, The Federalist Society for Law and Public Policy Studies, Washington, DC (p. 178)
 Curt A. Levey, Center for Individual Rights, Washington, DC (p. 178)
*Mark R. Levin, Landmark Legal Foundation, Herndon, VA (p. 178)
*George Liebmann, Calvert Institute for Policy Research, Baltimore, MD (p. 180)
*Nancie G. Marzulla, Defenders of Property Rights, Washington, DC (p. 191)
*Roger J. Marzulla, Defenders of Property Rights, Washington, DC (p. 191)
*Edwin Meese III, The Heritage Foundation, Washington, DC (p. 198)
*William H. Mellor, Institute for Justice, Washington, DC (p. 199)
 Eugene B. Meyer, The Federalist Society for Law and Public Policy Studies, Washington, DC (p. 200)
*Thomas Patrick Monaghan, American Center for Law and Justice, New Hope, KY (p. 204)
*Joseph A. Morris, Lincoln Legal Foundation, Chicago, IL (p. 207)
 Clark Neily, Institute for Justice, Washington, DC (p. 212)
*Allan E. Parker, Jr., Texas Justice Foundation, San Antonio, TX (p. 221)
 Terence J. Pell, Center for Individual Rights, Washington, DC (p. 224)
*William Perry Pendley, Mountain States Legal Foundation, Lakewood, CO (p. 225)
*Daniel J. Popeo, Washington Legal Foundation, Washington, DC (p. 231)
*Mark S. Pulliam, Latham & Watkins, San Diego, CA (p. 234)
*Scott Pullins, Ohio Taxpayers Association and OTA Foundation, Columbus, OH (p. 234)
 Jeremy Rabkin, Cornell University, Ithaca, NY (p. 235)
*Robin Rivett, Pacific Legal Foundation, Sacramento, CA (p. 241)
 Michael E. Rosman, Center for Individual Rights, Washington, DC (p. 243)
 Michael D. Rushford, Criminal Justice Legal Foundation, Sacramento, CA (p. 247)

PUBLIC INTEREST LAW (Continued)

*Alan E. Sears, Alliance Defense Fund, Scottsdale, AZ (p. 255)
*Jay Sekulow, American Center for Law and Justice, Virginia Beach, VA (p. 256)
 Dane vonBreichenruchardt, U. S. Bill of Rights Foundation, Washington, DC (p. 286)
*Phyllis H. Witcher, Protecting Marriage, Inc., Wilmington, DE (p. 296)
*Todd G. Young, Southeastern Legal Foundation, Atlanta, GA (p. 301)
 Ronald A. Zumbrun, The Zumbrun Law Firm, Sacramento, CA (p. 303)

RELIGIOUS FREEDOM

*Henry J. Abraham, Charlottesville, VA (p. 34)
*I. Dean Ahmad, Minaret of Freedom Institute, Bethesda, MD (p. 36)
*Lawrence Alexander, University of San Diego School of Law, San Diego, CA (p. 36)
*Carl A. Anderson, Knights of Columbus, New Haven, CT (p. 38)
*Julaine K. Appling, Family Research Institute of Wisconsin, Madison, WI (p. 40)
 Richard A. Baer, Jr., Cornell University, Ithaca, NY (p. 42)
 Hunter Baker, Georgia Family Council, Norcross, GA (p. 43)
*John S. Baker, Jr., Louisiana State University, Baton Rouge, LA (p. 43)
*Sandor Balogh, Hudson Valley Community College, East Greenbush, NY (p. 45)
*Gary L. Bauer, Campaign for Working Families, Arlington, VA (p. 47)
 Gregory S. Baylor, Center for Law and Religious Freedom, Annandale, VA (p. 47)
*Wayman R. Bishop, The Family Foundation of Virginia, Richmond, VA (p. 53)
 Amy E. Black, Wheaton College, Wheaton, IL (p. 54)
*James Bopp, Jr., James Madison Center for Free Speech, Washington, DC (p. 57)
 Anthony Bradley, Acton Institute for the Study of Religion and Liberty,
    Grand Rapids, MI (p. 59)
*Gerard V. Bradley, Notre Dame Law School, Notre Dame, IN (p. 59)
*Marshall J. Breger, Catholic University of America, Washington, DC (p. 60)
 Gary Bullert, Columbia Basin College, Pasco, WA (p. 65)
*David Burton, Argus Group, Alexandria, VA (p. 66)
 Bruce N. Cameron, National Right to Work Legal Defense Foundation, Springfield, VA (p. 68)
*Robert Carleson, American Civil Rights Union, Alexandria, VA (p. 70)
*Samuel Casey, Christian Legal Society, Annandale, VA (p. 71)
*Micah Clark, American Family Association, Indianapolis, IN (p. 75)
*Robert L. Clinton, Southern Illinois University, Carbondale, IL (p. 76)
*Charles Colson, Prison Fellowship Ministries, Washington, DC (p. 79)
*Kenneth L. Connor, Family Research Council, Washington, DC (p. 80)
 Douglas H. Cook, Regent University, Virginia Beach, VA (p. 80)
*Charles J. Cooper, Cooper & Kirk, PLLC, Washington, DC (p. 81)
 Dennis Coyle, Catholic University of America, Washington, DC (p. 84)
*Brad W. Dacus, Pacific Justice Institute, Citrus Heights, CA (p. 87)
*Len Deo, New Jersey Family Policy Council, Parsippany, NJ (p. 93)
*Robert Destro, Catholic University of America, Washington, DC (p. 94)
*William T. Devlin, Urban Family Council, Philadelphia, PA (p. 94)
*Jude P. Dougherty, Catholic University of America, Washington, DC (p. 97)
 Martin Duggan, Educational Freedom Foundation, St. Louis, MO (p. 99)
*Richard Duncan, University of Nebraska, Lincoln, NE (p. 99)
 Mark L. Earley, Prison Fellowship Ministries, Washington, DC (p. 101)
*John C. Eastman, Chapman University School of Law, Orange, CA (p. 102)
*James R. Edwards, Jr., Hudson Institute, Washington, DC (p. 104)
 Paul Edwards, Mercatus Center at George Mason University, Arlington, VA (p. 104)
 Barbara Elliott, Center for Renewal, Houston, TX (p. 105)
*Louis D. Enoff, Enoff Associates Limited, Sykesville, MD (p. 107)
*Edward J. Erler, California State University, San Bernardino, San Bernardino, CA (p. 107)
*Robert Ernst, Banbury Fund, Salmas, CA (p. 108)
*Michael P. Farris, Patrick Henry College, Purcellville, VA (p. 109)

RELIGIOUS FREEDOM (Continued)

*Steve Fitschen, National Legal Foundation, Virginia Beach, VA (p. 112)
*David Forte, Cleveland State University, Cleveland, OH (p. 114)
Elizabeth Fox-Genovese, Emory University, Atlanta, GA (p. 115)
Marshall Fritz, Alliance for the Separation of School & State, Fresno, CA (p. 118)
Richard W. Garnett, Notre Dame Law School, Notre Dame, IN (p. 120)
*Todd Gaziano, The Heritage Foundation, Washington, DC (p. 121)
*Michael Geer, Pennsylvania Family Institute, Harrisburg, PA (p. 122)
Roberta M. Gilbert, Center for the Study of Human Systems, Falls Church, VA (p. 123)
*Gary Glenn, American Family Association of Michigan, Midland, MI (p. 124)
*Lino A. Graglia, University of Texas, Austin, TX (p. 128)
Samuel Gregg, Acton Institute for the Study of Religion and Liberty, Grand Rapids, MI (p. 129)
Nikolas Gvosdev, *The National Interest*, Washington, DC (p. 131)
*Robert Hale, Northwest Legal Foundation, Minot, ND (p. 132)
Thor L. Halvorssen, The Foundation for Individual Rights in Education,
   Philadelphia, PA (p. 132)
Charles L. Harper, John Templeton Foundation, Radnor, PA (p. 135)
Mark Hartwig, Focus on the Family, Colorado Springs, CO (p. 136)
Kevin J. Hasson, The Becket Fund for Religious Liberty, Washington, DC (p. 137)
*Clark C. Havighurst, Duke University School of Law, Durham, NC (p. 137)
*James M. Henderson, Sr., American Center for Law and Justice, Washington, DC (p. 140)
*Thomas Hinton, The Heritage Foundation, Washington, DC (p. 143)
James Hitchcock, St. Louis University, St. Louis, MO (p. 143)
*John C. Holmes, Association of Christian Schools International, Washington, DC (p. 145)
Jacob G. Hornberger, Future of Freedom Foundation, Fairfax, VA (p. 146)
Martin Hoyt, American Association of Christian Schools, Washington, DC (p. 148)
*Robert Hunter, Mackinac Center for Public Policy, Midland, MI (p. 150)
*Charles D. Hurley, Iowa Family Policy Center, Pleasant Hill, IA (p. 150)
Richard P. Hutchison, Landmark Legal Foundation, Kansas City, MO (p. 150)
*Alan Inman, Institute for Responsible Fatherhood and Family Revitalization,
   Largo, MD (p. 151)
*Bradley P. Jacob, Regent University, Virginia Beach, VA (p. 152)
*Thomas L. Jipping, Concerned Women for America, Washington, DC (p. 154)
Phil Kent, Southeastern Legal Foundation, Atlanta, GA (p. 162)
*Christopher J. Klicka, Home School Legal Defense Association, Purcellville, VA (p. 165)
*Douglas W. Kmiec, The Catholic University of America, Washington, DC (p. 166)
*Robert H. Knight, Concerned Women for America, Washington, DC (p. 166)
Joseph M. Knippenberg, Oglethorpe University, Atlanta, GA (p. 166)
*Diane Knippers, Institute on Religion and Democracy, Washington, DC (p. 166)
*Robert C. Koons, University of Texas, Austin, TX (p. 167)
Thomas L. Krannawitter, Claremont Institute, Claremont, CA (p. 168)
Gary Kreep, United States Justice Foundation, Escondido, CA (p. 169)
John Kurzweil, California Public Policy Foundation, Camarillo, CA (p. 171)
*Andrea S. Lafferty, Traditional Values Coalition, Washington, DC (p. 172)
*George Landrith, Frontiers of Freedom Institute, Fairfax, VA (p. 173)
*Janet LaRue, Concerned Women for America, Washington, DC (p. 175)
Peter Augustine Lawler, Berry College, Mount Berry, GA (p. 175)
*Stephen Lazarus, Center for Public Justice, Annapolis, MD (p. 176)
Seth Leibsohn, Empower America, Washington, DC (p. 177)
Richard Lessner, American Renewal, Washington, DC (p. 178)
Curt A. Levey, Center for Individual Rights, Washington, DC (p. 178)
Thomas K. Lindsay, University of Dallas, Irving, TX (p. 181)
*Joseph Loconte, The Heritage Foundation, Washington, DC (p. 182)
Jordan Lorence, Alliance Defense Fund, Scottsdale, AZ (p. 183)
Mario Mandina, National Lawyers Association, Independence, MO (p. 188)

---

* Has testified before a state or federal legislative committee

RELIGIOUS FREEDOM (Continued)

Yuri Mantilla, Family Research Council, Washington, DC **(p. 189)**

Colby May, American Center for Law and Justice, Alexandria, VA **(p. 192)**

*****Nina May,** *Renaissance Connection.com/RCNetwork.net,* Washington, DC **(p. 192)**

*****David N. Mayer,** Capital University Law School, Columbus, OH **(p. 193)**

*****Michael J. McManus,** Marriage Savers, Potomac, MD **(p. 197)**

Eugene B. Meyer, The Federalist Society for Law and Public Policy Studies, Washington, DC **(p. 200)**

Tom Minnery, Focus on the Family, Colorado Springs, CO **(p. 203)**

*****C. Ben Mitchell,** Trinity International University, Deerfield, IL **(p. 203)**

R. Albert Mohler, Jr., The Southern Baptist Theological Seminary, Louisville, KY **(p. 204)**

Stephen Monsma, Pepperdine University, Malibu, CA **(p. 205)**

*****Richard E. Morgan,** Bowdoin College, Brunswick, ME **(p. 206)**

*****Joseph A. Morris,** Lincoln Legal Foundation, Chicago, IL **(p. 207)**

*****Steven W. Mosher,** Population Research Institute, Front Royal, VA **(p. 208)**

*****Len Munsil,** Center for Arizona Policy, Scottsdale, AZ **(p. 209)**

William Murchison, Baylor University, Waco, TX **(p. 209)**

Ronald Nash, Reformed Theological Seminary, Oviedo, FL **(p. 211)**

Julie N. Neff, Concerned Women for America, Washington, DC **(p. 211)**

*****Pat Nolan,** Justice Fellowship, Reston, VA **(p. 214)**

Stuart W. Nolan, Jr., Springfield, VA **(p. 214)**

Michael J. Novak, Jr., American Enterprise Institute, Washington, DC **(p. 215)**

James Nuechterlein, *First Things,* New York, NY **(p. 216)**

*****Michael J. O'Dea,** Christus Medicus Foundation, Bloomfield Hills, MI **(p. 216)**

*****Michael O'Neill,** George Mason University School of Law, Arlington, VA **(p. 217)**

*****Marvin Olasky,** University of Texas, Austin, TX **(p. 218)**

*****Allan E. Parker, Jr.,** Texas Justice Foundation, San Antonio, TX **(p. 221)**

Sidney A. Pearson, Jr., Radford University, Radford, VA **(p. 224)**

Terence J. Pell, Center for Individual Rights, Washington, DC **(p. 224)**

*****Stephen Presser,** Northwestern University School of Law, Chicago, IL **(p. 233)**

Paul A. Rahe, University of Tulsa, Tulsa, OK **(p. 236)**

Harold Calvin Ray, National Center for Faith-Based Initiatives, West Palm Beach, FL **(p. 237)**

*****Charles E. Rice,** Notre Dame Law School, Notre Dame, IN **(p. 239)**

John W. Robbins, Trinity Foundation, Unicoi, TN **(p. 241)**

*****Kelly Rosati,** Hawaii Family Forum, Kaneohe, HI **(p. 243)**

*****Ronald D. Rotunda,** George Mason University School of Law, Arlington, VA **(p. 244)**

*****Steven Alan Samson,** Liberty University, Lynchburg, VA **(p. 249)**

*****Ellis Sandoz,** Eric Voegelin Institute, Baton Rouge, LA **(p. 249)**

William L. Saunders, Family Research Council, Washington, DC **(p. 250)**

David L. Schaefer, Holy Cross College, Worcester, MA **(p. 252)**

*****Arthur J. Schwartz,** John Templeton Foundation, Radnor, PA **(p. 254)**

*****Alan E. Sears,** Alliance Defense Fund, Scottsdale, AZ **(p. 255)**

*****Jay Sekulow,** American Center for Law and Justice, Virginia Beach, VA **(p. 256)**

*****Jamie Self,** Georgia Family Council, Norcross, GA **(p. 256)**

*****Kelly Shackelford,** Free Market Foundation, Plano, TX **(p. 257)**

*****Lou Sheldon,** Traditional Values Coalition, Washington, DC **(p. 258)**

Harvey Silverglate, The Foundation for Individual Rights in Education, Boston, MA **(p. 260)**

*****Robert A. Sirico,** Acton Institute for the Study of Religion and Liberty, Grand Rapids, MI **(p. 261)**

*****Curt Smith,** Indiana Family Institute, Indianapolis, IN **(p. 263)**

*****Matthew Spalding,** The Heritage Foundation, Washington, DC **(p. 266)**

Peter S. Sprigg, Family Research Council, Washington, DC **(p. 267)**

Doug Stiegler, Association of Maryland Families, Woodstock, MD **(p. 269)**

Jacob Sullum, *Reason* Magazine, Fairfax, VA **(p. 272)**

Mark Tapscott, The Heritage Foundation, Washington, DC **(p. 274)**

RELIGIOUS FREEDOM (Continued)

*Forest M. Thigpen, Mississippi Family Council, Jackson, MS (p. 277)
*Herbert W. Titus, Virginia Beach, VA (p. 279)
 John Tuskey, Regent University, Virginia Beach, VA (p. 282)
 Michael M. Uhlmann, Claremont Graduate University, Claremont, CA (p. 283)
 Lawrence A. Uzzell, Keston Institute, Waxahachie, TX (p. 283)
*Terry W. Van Allen, Kemah, TX (p. 283)
*Peggy Venable, Texas Citizens for a Sound Economy, Austin, TX (p. 284)
*Eugene Volokh, University of California at Los Angeles, Los Angeles, CA (p. 285)
*Ben A. Wallis, Jr., Institute for Human Rights, San Antonio, TX (p. 287)
 Gerald Walpin, Katten Muchin Zavis Rosenman, New York, NY (p. 288)
 Tom Washburne, Home School Legal Defense Association, Purcellville, VA (p. 289)
*Walter M. Weber, American Center for Law and Justice, Alexandria, VA (p. 291)
 David L. Weeks, Azusa Pacific University, Azusa, CA (p. 291)
*George Weigel, Ethics and Public Policy Center, Washington, DC (p. 291)
 John G. West, Discovery Institute, Seattle, WA (p. 292)
*John W. Whitehead, The Rutherford Institute, Charlottesville, VA (p. 293)
 Alvin Williams, Black America's PAC, Washington, DC (p. 294)
 Richard B. Wirthlin, Wirthlin Worldwide, South Jordan, UT (p. 296)
*Christopher Wolfe, Marquette University, Milwaukee, WI (p. 297)
 Adam Wolfson, *The Public Interest*, Washington, DC (p. 297)
 Jason Wright, Frontiers of Freedom Institute, Fairfax, VA (p. 299)
*Michael K. Young, George Washington University Law School, Washington, DC (p. 300)
*Todd G. Young, Southeastern Legal Foundation, Atlanta, GA (p. 301)
 Jerry Zandstra, Acton Institute for the Study of Religion and Liberty,
    Grand Rapids, MI (p. 301)
 Ronald A. Zumbrun, The Zumbrun Law Firm, Sacramento, CA (p. 303)

SECOND AMENDMENT

*Julaine K. Appling, Family Research Institute of Wisconsin, Madison, WI (p. 40)
*Randy Barnett, Boston University School of Law, Boston, MA (p. 46)
 George J. Benston, Emory University, Atlanta, GA (p. 51)
 Paul H. Blackman, NRA Institute for Legislative Action, Fairfax, VA (p. 54)
 James Bovard, Rockville, MD (p. 58)
*Matthew J. Brouillette, The Commonwealth Foundation, Harrisburg, PA (p. 62)
*H. Sterling Burnett, National Center for Policy Analysis, Dallas, TX (p. 65)
 Jameson Campaigne, Jr., Jameson Books, Inc., Ottawa, IL (p. 68)
*Robert Carleson, American Civil Rights Union, Alexandria, VA (p. 70)
*Charles J. Cooper, Cooper & Kirk, PLLC, Washington, DC (p. 81)
*Charles H. Cunningham, National Rifle Association, Washington, DC (p. 87)
*Marshall L. De Rosa, Florida Atlantic University, Davie, FL (p. 90)
*Lisa Dean, Free Congress Foundation, Washington, DC (p. 91)
*Becky Norton Dunlop, The Heritage Foundation, Washington, DC (p. 100)
*John C. Eastman, Chapman University School of Law, Orange, CA (p. 102)
*Edward J. Erler, California State University, San Bernardino, San Bernardino, CA (p. 107)
*Robert Ernst, Banbury Fund, Salmas, CA (p. 108)
*Michael P. Farris, Patrick Henry College, Purcellville, VA (p. 109)
*Robert Fike, Americans for Tax Reform, Washington, DC (p. 111)
*Todd Gaziano, The Heritage Foundation, Washington, DC (p. 121)
 Robert A. Goldwin, American Enterprise Institute, Washington, DC (p. 126)
*Linda Gorman, Independence Institute, Golden, CO (p. 127)
*Alan Gottlieb, Citizens Committee for the Right to Keep and Bear Arms, Bellevue, WA (p. 127)
 Rebecca Hagelin, The Heritage Foundation, Washington, DC (p. 131)
 Gene Healy, Cato Institute, Washington, DC (p. 138)
 Jacob G. Hornberger, Future of Freedom Foundation, Fairfax, VA (p. 146)

---

* Has testified before a state or federal legislative committee

SECOND AMENDMENT (Continued)

Niger Roy Innis, Congress of Racial Equality, New York, NY **(p. 151)**
*David A. Keene, American Conservative Union, Washington, DC **(p. 160)**
Phil Kent, Southeastern Legal Foundation, Atlanta, GA **(p. 162)**
*David B. Kopel, Independence Institute, Golden, CO **(p. 167)**
Thomas L. Krannawitter, Claremont Institute, Claremont, CA **(p. 168)**
*James Lafferty, Massachusetts Citizens Alliance, Waltham, MA **(p. 172)**
*George Landrith, Frontiers of Freedom Institute, Fairfax, VA **(p. 173)**
*Wayne LaPierre, National Rifle Association, Fairfax, VA **(p. 174)**
*Andrew T. LeFevre, American Legislative Exchange Council, Washington, DC **(p. 177)**
Leonard A. Leo, The Federalist Society for Law and Public Policy Studies, Washington, DC **(p. 178)**
*Robert A. Levy, Cato Institute, Washington, DC **(p. 179)**
John R. Lott, Jr., American Enterprise Institute, Washington, DC **(p. 183)**
*Nelson Lund, George Mason University School of Law, Arlington, VA **(p. 184)**
*Joyce L. Malcolm, Bentley College, Waltham, MA **(p. 187)**
Mario Mandina, National Lawyers Association, Independence, MO **(p. 188)**
*Nina May, *Renaissance Connection.com/RCNetwork.net*, Washington, DC **(p. 192)**
*David N. Mayer, Capital University Law School, Columbus, OH **(p. 193)**
Eugene B. Meyer, The Federalist Society for Law and Public Policy Studies, Washington, DC **(p. 200)**
*Dan Mitchell, The Heritage Foundation, Washington, DC **(p. 203)**
*Richard E. Morgan, Bowdoin College, Brunswick, ME **(p. 206)**
*David B. Muhlhausen, The Heritage Foundation, Washington, DC **(p. 208)**
Iain Murray, Statistical Assessment Service, Washington, DC **(p. 209)**
Chuck Muth, American Conservative Union, Alexandria, VA **(p. 210)**
Ronald Nash, Reformed Theological Seminary, Oviedo, FL **(p. 211)**
Clark Neily, Institute for Justice, Washington, DC **(p. 212)**
*Grover Norquist, Americans for Tax Reform, Washington, DC **(p. 214)**
*Richard Olivastro, People Dynamics, Farmington, CT **(p. 218)**
Daniel Palm, Azusa Pacific University, Azusa, CA **(p. 220)**
*J. A. Parker, Lincoln Institute for Research and Education, Washington, DC **(p. 221)**
*Nancy M. Pfotenhauer, Independent Women's Forum, Arlington, VA **(p. 227)**
*Howard Phillips, The Conservative Caucus, Inc., Vienna, VA **(p. 227)**
*Don Racheter, Public Interest Institute, Mount Pleasant, IA **(p. 235)**
Paul A. Rahe, University of Tulsa, Tulsa, OK **(p. 236)**
*Charles E. Rice, Notre Dame Law School, Notre Dame, IN **(p. 239)**
Mark W. Smith, Kasowitz, Benson, Torres & Friedman, LLP, New York, NY **(p. 263)**
*John Michael Snyder, Citizens Committee for the Right to Keep and Bear Arms, Washington, DC **(p. 265)**
Jacob Sullum, *Reason* Magazine, Fairfax, VA **(p. 272)**
*John Taylor, Virginia Institute for Public Policy, Potomac Falls, VA **(p. 274)**
*David J. Theroux, The Independent Institute, Oakland, CA **(p. 276)**
*Mark Thornton, Columbus State University, Columbus, GA **(p. 278)**
*Robert F. Turner, University of Virginia School of Law, Charlottesville, VA **(p. 282)**
*Balint Vazsonyi, Center for the American Founding, McLean, VA **(p. 284)**
*Peggy Venable, Texas Citizens for a Sound Economy, Austin, TX **(p. 284)**
*Eugene Volokh, University of California at Los Angeles, Los Angeles, CA **(p. 285)**
Dane vonBreichenruchardt, U. S. Bill of Rights Foundation, Washington, DC **(p. 286)**
*Ben A. Wallis, Jr., Institute for Human Rights, San Antonio, TX **(p. 287)**
James Biser Whisker, West Virginia University, Morgantown, WV **(p. 293)**
Alvin Williams, Black America's PAC, Washington, DC **(p. 294)**
Jason Wright, Frontiers of Freedom Institute, Fairfax, VA **(p. 299)**

TORT AND LIABILITY REFORM

*Edward C. Anderson, National Arbitration Forum, Minneapolis, MN (p. 38)

*John S. Baker, Jr., Louisiana State University, Baton Rouge, LA (p. 43)

Paul Beckner, Citizens for a Sound Economy, Washington, DC (p. 48)

*Mark A. Behrens, Shook, Hardy & Bacon, L.L.P., Washington, DC (p. 49)

*Robert K. Best, Pacific Legal Foundation, Sacramento, CA (p. 52)

*Lillian BeVier, University of Virginia, Charlottesville, VA (p. 53)

Theodore Boutros, Gibson, Dunn & Crutcher LLP, Washington, DC (p. 58)

Brian Boyle, O'Melveny & Myers LLP, Washington, DC (p. 58)

*S. Jan Brakel, Isaac Ray Center, Inc., Chicago, IL (p. 60)

Charles H. Breeden, Marquette University, Milwaukee, WI (p. 60)

*Lester Brickman, Cardozo School of Law, New York, NY (p. 61)

Brian P. Brooks, O'Melveny & Myers LLP, Washington, DC (p. 62)

*Wayne T. Brough, Citizens for a Sound Economy, Washington, DC (p. 62)

Francis H. Buckley, George Mason University School of Law, Arlington, VA (p. 64)

T. Patrick Burke, St. Joseph's University, Wynnewood, PA (p. 65)

*H. Sterling Burnett, National Center for Policy Analysis, Dallas, TX (p. 65)

*Henry N. Butler, Chapman University, Orange, CA (p. 66)

*Dominic M. Calabro, Florida TaxWatch Research Institute, Inc., Tallahassee, FL (p. 67)

*John Calfee, American Enterprise Institute, Washington, DC (p. 67)

*Robert Carleson, American Civil Rights Union, Alexandria, VA (p. 70)

*Michael A. Ciamarra, Alabama Policy Institute, Birmingham, AL (p. 74)

*Kenneth L. Connor, Family Research Council, Washington, DC (p. 80)

Douglas H. Cook, Regent University, Virginia Beach, VA (p. 80)

*Roger C. Cramton, Cornell Law School, Ithaca, NY (p. 85)

*Lawrence Cranberg, Austin, TX (p. 85)

*Charles H. Cunningham, National Rifle Association, Washington, DC (p. 87)

Michael E. DeBow, Samford University, Birmingham, AL (p. 91)

*James R. Edwards, Jr., Hudson Institute, Washington, DC (p. 104)

Richard A. Epstein, University of Chicago Law School, Chicago, IL (p. 107)

*Robert Fike, Americans for Tax Reform, Washington, DC (p. 111)

John Findley, Pacific Legal Foundation, Sacramento, CA (p. 111)

*Michael Flynn, American Legislative Exchange Council, Washington, DC (p. 113)

*H. E. Frech, III, University of California, Santa Barbara, Santa Barbara, CA (p. 116)

*James Gattuso, The Heritage Foundation, Washington, DC (p. 121)

*Todd Gaziano, The Heritage Foundation, Washington, DC (p. 121)

Andrew Grainger, New England Legal Foundation, Boston, MA (p. 128)

*Michael S. Greve, American Enterprise Institute, Washington, DC (p. 129)

*Robert Hahn, American Enterprise Institute, Washington, DC (p. 132)

Louis W. Hensler III, Regent University, Virginia Beach, VA (p. 140)

*Michael Horowitz, Hudson Institute, Washington, DC (p. 146)

Peter Huber, Manhattan Institute for Policy Research, New York, NY (p. 148)

Thomas R. Ireland, University of Missouri, St. Louis, St. Louis, MO (p. 152)

*Charles W. Jarvis, United Seniors Association, Fairfax, VA (p. 153)

Sherman Joyce, American Tort Reform Association, Washington, DC (p. 156)

*Paul Kamenar, Washington Legal Foundation, Washington, DC (p. 157)

Martin S. Kaufman, Atlantic Legal Foundation, New York, NY (p. 159)

Phil Kent, Southeastern Legal Foundation, Atlanta, GA (p. 162)

Kent King, Missouri State Teachers Association, Columbia, MO (p. 164)

*David B. Kopel, Independence Institute, Golden, CO (p. 167)

Montgomery N. Kosma, Jones, Day, Reavis & Pogue, Washington, DC (p. 167)

*Michael Krauss, George Mason University School of Law, Arlington, VA (p. 169)

Deborah J. LaFetra, Pacific Legal Foundation, Sacramento, CA (p. 171)

Glenn G. Lammi, Washington Legal Foundation, Washington, DC (p. 173)

*George Landrith, Frontiers of Freedom Institute, Fairfax, VA (p. 173)

---

* Has testified before a state or federal legislative committee

TORT AND LIABILITY REFORM (Continued)

Leonard A. Leo, The Federalist Society for Law and Public Policy Studies, Washington, DC **(p. 178)**

*****Robert A. Levy,** Cato Institute, Washington, DC **(p. 179)**

Margaret A. Little, Law Office of Margaret Little, Stratford, CT **(p. 181)**

*****Rita P. Maguire,** Arizona Center for Public Policy, Phoenix, AZ **(p. 186)**

Mary P. Mahoney, United Seniors Association, Inc., Washington, DC **(p. 187)**

Mario Mandina, National Lawyers Association, Independence, MO **(p. 188)**

*****Marty McGeein,** McGeein Group, Bethesda, MD **(p. 196)**

Lawrence J. McQuillan, Pacific Research Institute, San Francisco, CA **(p. 197)**

*****Edwin Meese III,** The Heritage Foundation, Washington, DC **(p. 198)**

Eugene B. Meyer, The Federalist Society for Law and Public Policy Studies, Washington, DC **(p. 200)**

Mark E. Mitchell, Thomas University, Thomasville, GA **(p. 203)**

Suzanne C. Moore, Delaware Public Policy Institute, Wilmington, DE **(p. 206)**

E. Haavi Morreim, University of Tennessee, Memphis, Memphis, TN **(p. 206)**

*****Joseph A. Morris,** Lincoln Legal Foundation, Chicago, IL **(p. 207)**

Chuck Muth, American Conservative Union, Alexandria, VA **(p. 210)**

*****Walter K. Olson,** Manhattan Institute for Policy Research, Chappaqua, NY **(p. 219)**

*****Gary J. Palmer,** Alabama Policy Institute, Birmingham, AL **(p. 221)**

*****Duane Parde,** American Legislative Exchange Council, Washington, DC **(p. 221)**

Judyth Pendell, Bloomfield, CT **(p. 225)**

Laura Bennett Peterson, Washington, DC **(p. 226)**

*****Daniel J. Popeo,** Washington Legal Foundation, Washington, DC **(p. 231)**

*****Stephen Presser,** Northwestern University School of Law, Chicago, IL **(p. 233)**

George Priest, Yale Law School, New Haven, CT **(p. 233)**

*****Mark S. Pulliam,** Latham & Watkins, San Diego, CA **(p. 234)**

*****Scott Pullins,** Ohio Taxpayers Association and OTA Foundation, Columbus, OH **(p. 234)**

*****William H. Reid,** Horseshoe, TX **(p. 238)**

Martin G. Reiser, Citizens for a Sound Economy, Washington, DC **(p. 238)**

*****Amy Ridenour,** National Center for Public Policy Research, Washington, DC **(p. 240)**

*****Paul Rubin,** Emory University, Atlanta, GA **(p. 246)**

*****Richard A. Samp,** Washington Legal Foundation, Washington, DC **(p. 248)**

*****Susan Sarnoff,** Ohio University, Athens, OH **(p. 250)**

*****Thomas R. Saving,** Texas A&M University, College Station, TX **(p. 251)**

*****Victor E. Schwartz,** American Tort Reform Association, Washington, DC **(p. 254)**

*****E. Donald Shapiro,** New York Law School, Scottsdale, AZ **(p. 258)**

Frank A. Shepherd, Pacific Legal Foundation, Coral Gables, FL **(p. 259)**

*****William Craig Stubblebine,** Claremont McKenna College, Claremont, CA **(p. 271)**

*****David J. Theroux,** The Independent Institute, Oakland, CA **(p. 276)**

*****Forest M. Thigpen,** Mississippi Family Council, Jackson, MS **(p. 277)**

Richard Thornburgh, Kirkpatrick & Lockhart, L.L.P., Washington, DC **(p. 278)**

*****Mark Thornton,** Columbus State University, Columbus, GA **(p. 278)**

Wayne Valis, Citizens for Civil Justice Reform, Washington, DC **(p. 283)**

*****Peggy Venable,** Texas Citizens for a Sound Economy, Austin, TX **(p. 284)**

*****W. Kip Viscusi,** Harvard Law School, Cambridge, MA **(p. 285)**

Stephen J. Ware, Samford University, Birmingham, AL **(p. 289)**

Stanley J. Watson, Patrick Henry College, Purcellville, VA **(p. 290)**

*****Robert O. C. Worcester,** Maryland Business for Responsive Government, Baltimore, MD **(p. 298)**

*****Todd G. Young,** Southeastern Legal Foundation, Atlanta, GA **(p. 301)**

Ronald A. Zumbrun, The Zumbrun Law Firm, Sacramento, CA **(p. 303)**

Economic and Political Thought

THE AMERICAN FOUNDING

*Douglas K. Adie, Ohio University, Athens, OH (p. 35)
*M. Gene Aldridge, New Mexico Independence Research Institute, Las Cruces, NM (p. 36)
 Brian C. Anderson, Manhattan Institute for Policy Research, New York, NY (p. 38)
 Larry P. Arnn, Hillsdale College, Hillsdale, MI (p. 40)
*Randy Barnett, Boston University School of Law, Boston, MA (p. 46)
*David Barton, WallBuilders, Inc., Aledo, TX (p. 46)
*Herman Belz, University of Maryland, College Park, MD (p. 50)
*Jason Bertsch, American Enterprise Institute, Washington, DC (p. 52)
*Judith A. Best, State University of New York, Cortland, Cortland, NY (p. 52)
*Wayman R. Bishop, The Family Foundation of Virginia, Richmond, VA (p. 53)
*Mark Blitz, Claremont McKenna College, Claremont, CA (p. 55)
 David J. Bobb, Hillsdale College, Hillsdale, MI (p. 56)
*Gerard V. Bradley, Notre Dame Law School, Notre Dame, IN (p. 59)
*Matthew J. Brouillette, The Commonwealth Foundation, Harrisburg, PA (p. 62)
*David Burton, Argus Group, Alexandria, VA (p. 66)
 George F. Cahill, The "Pride in America" Company, Pittsburgh, PA (p. 67)
*Dominic M. Calabro, Florida TaxWatch Research Institute, Inc., Tallahassee, FL (p. 67)
 Jameson Campaigne, Jr., Jameson Books, Inc., Ottawa, IL (p. 68)
*Robert Carleson, American Civil Rights Union, Alexandria, VA (p. 70)
 William Connelly, Washington and Lee University, Lexington, VA (p. 80)
 Kevin L. Cope, Louisiana State University, Baton Rouge, LA (p. 81)
 Dennis Coyle, Catholic University of America, Washington, DC (p. 84)
 Mickey Craig, Hillsdale College, Hillsdale, MI (p. 85)
*Ron Crews, Massachusetts Family Institute, Newton Upper Falls, MA (p. 86)
 Alan R. Crippen, II, Family Research Council, Washington, DC (p. 86)
*Brad W. Dacus, Pacific Justice Institute, Citrus Heights, CA (p. 87)
 Damjan de Krnjevic-Miskovic, The National Interest, Washington, DC (p. 90)
*Marshall L. De Rosa, Florida Atlantic University, Davie, FL (p. 90)
*Len Deo, New Jersey Family Policy Council, Parsippany, NJ (p. 93)
*Donald J. Devine, Center for American Values, Shady Side, MD (p. 94)
*James A. Dorn, Cato Institute, Washington, DC (p. 97)
 Richard J. Dougherty, University of Dallas, Irving, TX (p. 97)
*David Dunn, Oklahoma Family Policy Council, Bethany, OK (p. 100)
*Clark Durant, New Common School Foundation, Detroit, MI (p. 101)
*Steven J. Eagle, George Mason University School of Law, Arlington, VA (p. 101)
 Steven D. Ealy, Liberty Fund, Inc., Indianapolis, IN (p. 101)
*John C. Eastman, Chapman University School of Law, Orange, CA (p. 102)
 Robert Eden, Hillsdale College, Hillsdale, MI (p. 103)
 Paul Edwards, Mercatus Center at George Mason University, Arlington, VA (p. 104)
 W. Winston Elliott, III, Center for the American Idea, Houston, TX (p. 106)
 Glenn Ellmers, Claremont Institute, Claremont, CA (p. 106)
*Edward J. Erler, California State University, San Bernardino, San Bernardino, CA (p. 107)
*Michael P. Farris, Patrick Henry College, Purcellville, VA (p. 109)
*Steve Fitschen, National Legal Foundation, Virginia Beach, VA (p. 112)
 Christopher Flannery, Azusa Pacific University, Azusa, CA (p. 113)
*Michael Flynn, American Legislative Exchange Council, Washington, DC (p. 113)
*John Fonte, Hudson Institute, Washington, DC (p. 114)
 Hillel Fradkin, Ethics and Public Policy Center, Washington, DC (p. 115)
*Matthew J. Franck, Radford University, Radford, VA (p. 115)
*Charlie Gerow, Quantum Communications, Harrisburg, PA (p. 123)
 Robert A. Goldwin, American Enterprise Institute, Washington, DC (p. 126)
*Michael S. Greve, American Enterprise Institute, Washington, DC (p. 129)

THE AMERICAN FOUNDING (Continued)

*Paul Guppy, Washington Policy Center, Seattle, WA (p. 131)
Edward J. Harpham, University of Texas, Dallas, Richardson, TX (p. 135)
*Lynn Harsh, Evergreen Freedom Foundation, Olympia, WA (p. 136)
*Steven Hayward, American Enterprise Institute, Washington, DC (p. 138)
*Donna H. Hearne, Constitutional Coalition, St. Louis, MO (p. 138)
Rea Hederman, Jr., The Heritage Foundation, Washington, DC (p. 139)
*James M. Henderson, Sr., American Center for Law and Justice, Washington, DC (p. 140)
Peter J. Hill, Wheaton College, Wheaton, IL (p. 142)
*Thomas Hinton, The Heritage Foundation, Washington, DC (p. 143)
*John MacDonald Hood, John Locke Foundation, Raleigh, NC (p. 145)
Jacob G. Hornberger, Future of Freedom Foundation, Fairfax, VA (p. 146)
John C. Hulsman, The Heritage Foundation, Washington, DC (p. 149)
Douglas A. Jeffrey, Hillsdale College, Hillsdale, MI (p. 154)
*Charles R. Kesler, Henry Salvatori Center, Claremont, CA (p. 162)
Jeane J. Kirkpatrick, American Enterprise Institute, Washington, DC (p. 164)
James J. Kirschke, Villanova University, Villanova, PA (p. 164)
*Douglas W. Kmiec, The Catholic University of America, Washington, DC (p. 166)
Joseph M. Knippenberg, Oglethorpe University, Atlanta, GA (p. 166)
*David B. Kopel, Independence Institute, Golden, CO (p. 167)
Thomas L. Krannawitter, Claremont Institute, Claremont, CA (p. 168)
Stephen Krason, Franciscan University of Steubenville, Steubenville, OH (p. 169)
*Lawrence Kudlow, Kudlow & Co., LLC, New York, NY (p. 170)
Melvin A. Kulbicki, York College of Pennsylvania, York, PA (p. 170)
*Andrew Langer, National Federation of Independent Business, Washington, DC (p. 174)
Daniel Lapin, Toward Tradition, Mercer Island, WA (p. 174)
*Kent Lassman, Progress & Freedom Foundation, Raleigh, NC (p. 175)
Peter Augustine Lawler, Berry College, Mount Berry, GA (p. 175)
Phillip F. Lawler, *Catholic World Report*, South Lancaster, MA (p. 176)
*Andrew T. LeFevre, American Legislative Exchange Council, Washington, DC (p. 177)
Seth Leibsohn, Empower America, Washington, DC (p. 177)
Richard Lessner, American Renewal, Washington, DC (p. 178)
*Mark R. Levin, Landmark Legal Foundation, Herndon, VA (p. 178)
*Joseph Loconte, The Heritage Foundation, Washington, DC (p. 182)
*Dennis Mansfield, Boise, ID (p. 189)
Harvey C. Mansfield, Harvard University, Cambridge, MA (p. 189)
*Ken Masugi, Claremont Institute, Claremont, CA (p. 191)
Paul Maurer, Trinity International University, Deerfield, IL (p. 192)
*David N. Mayer, Capital University Law School, Columbus, OH (p. 193)
Wilfred M. McClay, University of Tennessee, Chattanooga, Chattanooga, TN (p. 193)
*Forrest McDonald, University of Alabama, Coker, AL (p. 195)
*Michael J. McManus, Marriage Savers, Potomac, MD (p. 197)
Harry Messenheimer, Rio Grande Foundation, Tijeras, NM (p. 200)
*Roger Michener, Placitas, NM (p. 201)
Tom Minnery, Focus on the Family, Colorado Springs, CO (p. 203)
Stephen J. Moore, Club for Growth, Washington, DC (p. 206)
*Joseph A. Morris, Lincoln Legal Foundation, Chicago, IL (p. 207)
Jennifer Roback Morse, Hoover Institution, Vista, CA (p. 207)
James W. Muller, University of Alaska, Anchorage, AK (p. 208)
*Len Munsil, Center for Arizona Policy, Scottsdale, AZ (p. 209)
*Deroy Murdock, Atlas Economic Research Foundation, New York, NY (p. 209)
*Anne D. Neal, American Council of Trustees and Alumni, Washington, DC (p. 211)
Jeff Nelson, Intercollegiate Studies Institute, Wilmington, DE (p. 212)
Stuart W. Nolan, Jr., Springfield, VA (p. 214)
Michael J. Novak, Jr., American Enterprise Institute, Washington, DC (p. 215)

THE AMERICAN FOUNDING (Continued)

John Nowacki, Free Congress Foundation, Washington, DC (p. 215)
*Michael O'Neill, George Mason University School of Law, Arlington, VA (p. 217)
*Marvin Olasky, University of Texas, Austin, TX (p. 218)
B. Nelson Ong, College of New Rochelle, New Rochelle, NY (p. 219)
*Mackubin T. Owens, U. S. Naval War College, Newport, RI (p. 220)
Daniel Palm, Azusa Pacific University, Azusa, CA (p. 220)
*Judd W. Patton, Bellevue University, Bellevue, NE (p. 223)
Anthony A. Peacock, Utah State University, Logan, UT (p. 224)
Sidney A. Pearson, Jr., Radford University, Radford, VA (p. 224)
Paul C. Peterson, Coastal Carolina University, Conway, SC (p. 227)
James Piereson, John M. Olin Foundation, Inc., New York, NY (p. 228)
*Roger Pilon, Cato Institute, Washington, DC (p. 228)
*Daniel J. Popeo, Washington Legal Foundation, Washington, DC (p. 231)
Barry W. Poulson, University of Colorado, Boulder, CO (p. 232)
*Stephen Presser, Northwestern University School of Law, Chicago, IL (p. 233)
*Don Racheter, Public Interest Institute, Mount Pleasant, IA (p. 235)
Paul A. Rahe, University of Tulsa, Tulsa, OK (p. 236)
*James S. Robbins, National Defense University, Washington, DC (p. 241)
John W. Robbins, Trinity Foundation, Unicoi, TN (p. 241)
*Ralph A. Rossum, Claremont McKenna College, Claremont, CA (p. 244)
*William A. Rusher, Claremont Institute, San Francisco, CA (p. 247)
*Steven Alan Samson, Liberty University, Lynchburg, VA (p. 249)
*Ellis Sandoz, Eric Voegelin Institute, Baton Rouge, LA (p. 249)
*Michael Sanera, Basis Charter High School, Tucson, AZ (p. 249)
Robert A. Schadler, Center for First Principles, Washington, DC (p. 251)
David L. Schaefer, Holy Cross College, Worcester, MA (p. 252)
*Peter W. Schramm, John M. Ashbrook Center for Public Affairs, Ashland, OH (p. 254)
Larry Schweikart, University of Dayton, Dayton, OH (p. 255)
*Jay Sekulow, American Center for Law and Justice, Virginia Beach, VA (p. 256)
*Donald J. Senese, 60 Plus Association, Arlington, VA (p. 257)
*Colleen Sheehan, Villanova University, Villanova, PA (p. 258)
*Lou Sheldon, Traditional Values Coalition, Washington, DC (p. 258)
Aaron Siegel, Freedoms Foundation at Valley Forge, Valley Forge, PA (p. 259)
*James Skillen, Center for Public Justice, Annapolis, MD (p. 261)
*Matthew Spalding, The Heritage Foundation, Washington, DC (p. 266)
*David Strom, Taxpayers League of Minnesota, Plymouth, MN (p. 270)
Robert Sutherland, Cornell College, Mount Vernon, IA (p. 272)
*John Taylor, Virginia Institute for Public Policy, Potomac Falls, VA (p. 274)
*David J. Theroux, The Independent Institute, Oakland, CA (p. 276)
J. Mills Thornton, III, University of Michigan, Ann Arbor, MI (p. 278)
*Herbert W. Titus, Virginia Beach, VA (p. 279)
*Lewis Uhler, National Tax Limitation Committee, Roseville, CA (p. 283)
Michael M. Uhlmann, Claremont Graduate University, Claremont, CA (p. 283)
*Maris A. Vinovskis, University of Michigan, Ann Arbor, MI (p. 285)
Dane vonBreichenruchardt, U. S. Bill of Rights Foundation, Washington, DC (p. 286)
*Jeffrey D. Wallin, American Academy for Liberal Education, Washington, DC (p. 287)
Gary M. Walton, Foundation for Teaching Economics, Davis, CA (p. 288)
Bradley C. S. Watson, Saint Vincent College, Latrobe, PA (p. 290)
*Donald V. Weatherman, Erskine College, Due West, SC (p. 290)
*John W. Whitehead, The Rutherford Institute, Charlottesville, VA (p. 293)
Keith E. Whittington, Princeton University, Princeton, NJ (p. 294)
Walter E. Williams, George Mason University, Fairfax, VA (p. 295)
Bradford P. Wilson, National Association of Scholars, Princeton, NJ (p. 296)
*Christopher Wolfe, Marquette University, Milwaukee, WI (p. 297)

THE AMERICAN FOUNDING (Continued)

Adam Wolfson, *The Public Interest*, Washington, DC (p. 297)
Anne Wortham, Illinois State University, Normal, IL (p. 298)
Kate Xiao Zhou, University of Hawaii, Honolulu, HI (p. 302)
Michael Zuckert, University of Notre Dame, Notre Dame, IN (p. 302)

AMERICAN HISTORY/POLITICAL TRADITION

*John Agresto, John Agresto and Associates, Santa Fe, NM (p. 35)
*William Allen, Michigan State University, East Lansing, MI (p. 37)
Lee J. Alston, University of Colorado-Boulder, Boulder, CO (p. 37)
Frank Annunziata, Rochester Institute of Technology, Rochester, NY (p. 39)
Damon Ansell, Americans for Tax Reform, Washington, DC (p. 39)
*Julaine K. Appling, Family Research Institute of Wisconsin, Madison, WI (p. 40)
*Dominic A. Aquila, Ave Maria University, Ypsilanti, MI (p. 40)
Larry P. Arnn, Hillsdale College, Hillsdale, MI (p. 40)
*John S. Baker, Jr., Louisiana State University, Baton Rouge, LA (p. 43)
*Claude E. Barfield, American Enterprise Institute, Washington, DC (p. 45)
*Randy Barnett, Boston University School of Law, Boston, MA (p. 46)
*Bruce R. Bartlett, National Center for Policy Analysis, Great Falls, VA (p. 46)
*David Barton, WallBuilders, Inc., Aledo, TX (p. 46)
Jonathan James Bean, Southern Illinois University, Carbondale, IL (p. 48)
*Herman Belz, University of Maryland, College Park, MD (p. 50)
*John E. Berthoud, National Taxpayers Union, Alexandria, VA (p. 52)
*Jason Bertsch, American Enterprise Institute, Washington, DC (p. 52)
*Judith A. Best, State University of New York, Cortland, Cortland, NY (p. 52)
*Wayman R. Bishop, The Family Foundation of Virginia, Richmond, VA (p. 53)
*Mark Blitz, Claremont McKenna College, Claremont, CA (p. 55)
*David Boaz, Cato Institute, Washington, DC (p. 55)
David J. Bobb, Hillsdale College, Hillsdale, MI (p. 56)
L. Brent Bozell, III, Media Research Center, Alexandria, VA (p. 59)
*Gerard V. Bradley, Notre Dame Law School, Notre Dame, IN (p. 59)
*Matthew J. Brouillette, The Commonwealth Foundation, Harrisburg, PA (p. 62)
*Stuart Butler, The Heritage Foundation, Washington, DC (p. 66)
George F. Cahill, The "Pride in America" Company, Pittsburgh, PA (p. 67)
*John E. Carey, International Defense Consultants, Inc., Arlington, VA (p. 69)
*Robert Carleson, American Civil Rights Union, Alexandria, VA (p. 70)
*Allan C. Carlson, Howard Center for Family, Religion and Society, Rockford, IL (p. 70)
*Michael A. Ciamarra, Alabama Policy Institute, Birmingham, AL (p. 74)
John Clark, Hudson Institute, Indianapolis, IN (p. 75)
Eric Cohen, Ethics and Public Policy Center, Washington, DC (p. 78)
Jim F. Couch, University of North Alabama, Florence, AL (p. 83)
Stephen D. Cox, University of California, San Diego, La Jolla, CA (p. 84)
Dennis Coyle, Catholic University of America, Washington, DC (p. 84)
Mickey Craig, Hillsdale College, Hillsdale, MI (p. 85)
*Ron Crews, Massachusetts Family Institute, Newton Upper Falls, MA (p. 86)
Alan R. Crippen, II, Family Research Council, Washington, DC (p. 86)
Melvin Croan, University of Wisconsin, Madison, WI (p. 86)
*Brad W. Dacus, Pacific Justice Institute, Citrus Heights, CA (p. 87)
Damjan de Krnjevic-Miskovic, The National Interest, Washington, DC (p. 90)
*Marshall L. De Rosa, Florida Atlantic University, Davie, FL (p. 90)
William C. Dennis, Dennis Consulting, MacLean, VA (p. 93)
D. P. Diffine, Harding University, Searcy, AR (p. 95)
Richard J. Dougherty, University of Dallas, Irving, TX (p. 97)
Peter J. Duignan, Hoover Institution, Stanford, CA (p. 99)
*John C. Eastman, Chapman University School of Law, Orange, CA (p. 102)

---

* Has testified before a state or federal legislative committee

AMERICAN HISTORY/POLITICAL TRADITION (Continued)

*Michelle Easton, Clare Boothe Luce Policy Institute, Herndon, VA (p. 102)
*Myron Ebell, Competitive Enterprise Institute, Washington, DC (p. 103)
Robert Eden, Hillsdale College, Hillsdale, MI (p. 103)
*James R. Edwards, Jr., Hudson Institute, Washington, DC (p. 104)
*Lee Edwards, The Heritage Foundation, Washington, DC (p. 104)
Paul Edwards, Mercatus Center at George Mason University, Arlington, VA (p. 104)
Barbara Elliott, Center for Renewal, Houston, TX (p. 105)
W. Winston Elliott, III, Center for the American Idea, Houston, TX (p. 106)
Glenn Ellmers, Claremont Institute, Claremont, CA (p. 106)
*Jean Bethke Elshtain, University of Chicago, Chicago, IL (p. 106)
Thomas Engeman, Loyola University Chicago, Chicago, IL (p. 107)
*Michael P. Farris, Patrick Henry College, Purcellville, VA (p. 109)
*Robert Fike, Americans for Tax Reform, Washington, DC (p. 111)
Price V. Fishback, University of Arizona, Tucson, AZ (p. 112)
Christopher Flannery, Azusa Pacific University, Azusa, CA (p. 113)
Burton W. Folsom, Jr., Center for the American Idea, Houston, TX (p. 114)
*John Fonte, Hudson Institute, Washington, DC (p. 114)
*David Forte, Cleveland State University, Cleveland, OH (p. 114)
Elizabeth Fox-Genovese, Emory University, Atlanta, GA (p. 115)
Hillel Fradkin, Ethics and Public Policy Center, Washington, DC (p. 115)
*Murray Friedman, American Jewish Committee, Philadelphia, PA (p. 117)
David E. R. Gay, University of Arkansas, Fayetteville, AR (p. 121)
*Jeffrey B. Gayner, Americans for Sovereignty, Washington, DC (p. 121)
*Charlie Gerow, Quantum Communications, Harrisburg, PA (p. 123)
Robert A. Goldwin, American Enterprise Institute, Washington, DC (p. 126)
*Stephen O. Goodrick, National Right to Work Committee, Springfield, VA (p. 126)
*Robert Hale, Northwest Legal Foundation, Minot, ND (p. 132)
Roger Hamburg, Indiana University South Bend, South Bend, IN (p. 133)
Jerome J. Hanus, American University, Washington, DC (p. 134)
Edward J. Harpham, University of Texas, Dallas, Richardson, TX (p. 135)
William Anthony Hay, Foreign Policy Research Institute, Philadelphia, PA (p. 138)
*Steven Hayward, American Enterprise Institute, Washington, DC (p. 138)
*Donna H. Hearne, Constitutional Coalition, St. Louis, MO (p. 138)
Rea Hederman, Jr., The Heritage Foundation, Washington, DC (p. 139)
Robert A. Heineman, Alfred University, Alfred, NY (p. 139)
Robert Higgs, The Independent Institute, Covington, LA (p. 142)
Jack High, George Mason University, Arlington, VA (p. 142)
Peter J. Hill, Wheaton College, Wheaton, IL (p. 142)
*John MacDonald Hood, John Locke Foundation, Raleigh, NC (p. 145)
Jacob G. Hornberger, Future of Freedom Foundation, Fairfax, VA (p. 146)
David Horowitz, Center for the Study of Popular Culture, Los Angeles, CA (p. 146)
*Robert Huberty, Capital Research Center, Washington, DC (p. 148)
John C. Hulsman, The Heritage Foundation, Washington, DC (p. 149)
Harry V. Jaffa, Claremont Institute, Claremont, CA (p. 153)
*Charles W. Jarvis, United Seniors Association, Fairfax, VA (p. 153)
Douglas A. Jeffrey, Hillsdale College, Hillsdale, MI (p. 154)
*Doug Kagan, Nebraska Taxpayers for Freedom, Omaha, NE (p. 157)
*Charles R. Kesler, Henry Salvatori Center, Claremont, CA (p. 162)
Kent King, Missouri State Teachers Association, Columbia, MO (p. 164)
Jeane J. Kirkpatrick, American Enterprise Institute, Washington, DC (p. 164)
James J. Kirschke, Villanova University, Villanova, PA (p. 164)
Joseph M. Knippenberg, Oglethorpe University, Atlanta, GA (p. 166)
*David B. Kopel, Independence Institute, Golden, CO (p. 167)
Thomas L. Krannawitter, Claremont Institute, Claremont, CA (p. 168)

AMERICAN HISTORY/POLITICAL TRADITION (Continued)

*Randall Kroszner, University of Chicago, Chicago, IL (p. 170)
*Lawrence Kudlow, Kudlow & Co., LLC, New York, NY (p. 170)
 Melvin A. Kulbicki, York College of Pennsylvania, York, PA (p. 170)
*Andrea S. Lafferty, Traditional Values Coalition, Washington, DC (p. 172)
*George Landrith, Frontiers of Freedom Institute, Fairfax, VA (p. 173)
*Andrew Langer, National Federation of Independent Business, Washington, DC (p. 174)
*Richard Langlois, University of Connecticut, Storrs, CT (p. 174)
*Edward J. Larson, University of Georgia School of Law, Athens, GA (p. 175)
 Peter Augustine Lawler, Berry College, Mount Berry, GA (p. 175)
 Phillip F. Lawler, *Catholic World Report*, South Lancaster, MA (p. 176)
*Andrew T. LeFevre, American Legislative Exchange Council, Washington, DC (p. 177)
 Seth Leibsohn, Empower America, Washington, DC (p. 177)
 Richard Lessner, American Renewal, Washington, DC (p. 178)
*Mark R. Levin, Landmark Legal Foundation, Herndon, VA (p. 178)
 Gary Libecap, University of Arizona, Tucson, AZ (p. 179)
 Leonard P. Liggio, Atlas Economic Research Foundation, Fairfax, VA (p. 180)
*Dennis Mansfield, Boise, ID (p. 189)
*Jerry L. Martin, American Council of Trustees and Alumni, Washington, DC (p. 190)
*Ken Masugi, Claremont Institute, Claremont, CA (p. 191)
 Merrill Matthews, Jr., Institute for Policy Innovation, Lewisville, TX (p. 192)
*David N. Mayer, Capital University Law School, Columbus, OH (p. 193)
 Wilfred M. McClay, University of Tennessee, Chattanooga, Chattanooga, TN (p. 193)
*Forrest McDonald, University of Alabama, Coker, AL (p. 195)
 W. Wesley McDonald, Elizabethtown College, Elizabethtown, PA (p. 195)
*Michael J. McManus, Marriage Savers, Potomac, MD (p. 197)
*Roger Michener, Placitas, NM (p. 201)
 Tom Minnery, Focus on the Family, Colorado Springs, CO (p. 203)
 Mark E. Mitchell, Thomas University, Thomasville, GA (p. 203)
*Robert Moffit, The Heritage Foundation, Washington, DC (p. 204)
 Suzanne C. Moore, Delaware Public Policy Institute, Wilmington, DE (p. 206)
 Jennifer Roback Morse, Hoover Institution, Vista, CA (p. 207)
 James W. Muller, University of Alaska, Anchorage, AK (p. 208)
 Henry Myers, James Madison University, Harrisonburg, VA (p. 210)
 George H. Nash, South Hadley, MA (p. 210)
 Ronald Nash, Reformed Theological Seminary, Oviedo, FL (p. 211)
*Anne D. Neal, American Council of Trustees and Alumni, Washington, DC (p. 211)
 Jeff Nelson, Intercollegiate Studies Institute, Wilmington, DE (p. 212)
 Stuart W. Nolan, Jr., Springfield, VA (p. 214)
 Michael J. Novak, Jr., American Enterprise Institute, Washington, DC (p. 215)
*Michael O'Neill, George Mason University School of Law, Arlington, VA (p. 217)
*Marvin Olasky, University of Texas, Austin, TX (p. 218)
 B. Nelson Ong, College of New Rochelle, New Rochelle, NY (p. 219)
 Glenn Oppel, Rocky Mountain Enterprise Institute, Billings, MT (p. 219)
*Mackubin T. Owens, U. S. Naval War College, Newport, RI (p. 220)
 Daniel Palm, Azusa Pacific University, Azusa, CA (p. 220)
 Tom G. Palmer, Cato Institute, Washington, DC (p. 221)
*Jim Panyard, Pennsylvania Manufacturer's Association, Harrisburg, PA (p. 221)
*Duane Parde, American Legislative Exchange Council, Washington, DC (p. 221)
 Sidney A. Pearson, Jr., Radford University, Radford, VA (p. 224)
 Paul C. Peterson, Coastal Carolina University, Conway, SC (p. 227)
*Howard Phillips, The Conservative Caucus, Inc., Vienna, VA (p. 227)
 James Piereson, John M. Olin Foundation, Inc., New York, NY (p. 228)
*Roger Pilon, Cato Institute, Washington, DC (p. 228)
 Barry W. Poulson, University of Colorado, Boulder, CO (p. 232)

---

* Has testified before a state or federal legislative committee

AMERICAN HISTORY/POLITICAL TRADITION (Continued)

*Stephen Presser, Northwestern University School of Law, Chicago, IL (p. 233)
 Paul A. Rahe, University of Tulsa, Tulsa, OK (p. 236)
 Diane Ravitch, New York University, New York, NY (p. 237)
*Lawrence W. Reed, Mackinac Center for Public Policy, Midland, MI (p. 237)
 Joseph D. Reid, Jr., George Mason University, Fairfax, VA (p. 238)
*James S. Robbins, National Defense University, Washington, DC (p. 241)
 John W. Robbins, Trinity Foundation, Unicoi, TN (p. 241)
 James C. Roberts, American Studies Center, Washington, DC (p. 242)
 Holly Robinson, Georgia Public Policy Foundation, Atlanta, GA (p. 242)
*Ralph A. Rossum, Claremont McKenna College, Claremont, CA (p. 244)
*William A. Rusher, Claremont Institute, San Francisco, CA (p. 247)
 Robert E. Russell, Jr., The Heritage Foundation, Geneva, IL (p. 247)
*Steven Alan Samson, Liberty University, Lynchburg, VA (p. 249)
 Gregory W. Sand, Saint Louis College of Pharmacy, St. Louis, MO (p. 249)
*Ellis Sandoz, Eric Voegelin Institute, Baton Rouge, LA (p. 249)
*Michael Sanera, Basis Charter High School, Tucson, AZ (p. 249)
 David W. Saxe, Pennsylvania State University, University Park, PA (p. 251)
 Robert A. Schadler, Center for First Principles, Washington, DC (p. 251)
 David L. Schaefer, Holy Cross College, Worcester, MA (p. 252)
*Bill Schilling, Wyoming Business Alliance / Wyoming Heritage Foundation,
    Casper, WY (p. 253)
*Peter W. Schramm, John M. Ashbrook Center for Public Affairs, Ashland, OH (p. 254)
 Larry J. Sechrest, Sul Ross State University, Alpine, TX (p. 255)
 Jeffrey Leigh Sedgwick, University of Massachusetts, Amherst, MA (p. 255)
*Jay Sekulow, American Center for Law and Justice, Virginia Beach, VA (p. 256)
*Donald J. Senese, 60 Plus Association, Arlington, VA (p. 257)
*Gilbert T. Sewall, American Textbook Council, New York, NY (p. 257)
 Barry Alan Shain, Colgate University, Hamilton, NY (p. 257)
*Colleen Sheehan, Villanova University, Villanova, PA (p. 258)
*Lou Sheldon, Traditional Values Coalition, Washington, DC (p. 258)
 Aaron Siegel, Freedoms Foundation at Valley Forge, Valley Forge, PA (p. 259)
*Rita Simon, American University, Washington, DC (p. 260)
*Curt Smith, Indiana Family Institute, Indianapolis, IN (p. 263)
 Ted J. Smith, III, Virginia Commonwealth University, Richmond, VA (p. 264)
 John C. Soper, John Carroll University, University Heights, OH (p. 266)
*Matthew Spalding, The Heritage Foundation, Washington, DC (p. 266)
 Gordon St. Angelo, Milton and Rose Friedman Foundation, Indianapolis, IN (p. 267)
*Christine Stolba, Ethics and Public Policy Center, Washington, DC (p. 269)
 David G. Surdam, University of Chicago, Chicago, IL (p. 272)
 Robert Sutherland, Cornell College, Mount Vernon, IA (p. 272)
 James R. "J.T." Taylor, Empower America, Washington, DC (p. 274)
*John Taylor, Virginia Institute for Public Policy, Potomac Falls, VA (p. 274)
*Richard Teske, Strategic Advocacy, Arlington, VA (p. 275)
*Stephan Thernstrom, Lexington, MA (p. 276)
 J. Mills Thornton, III, University of Michigan, Ann Arbor, MI (p. 278)
 Richard H. Timberlake, Jr., Bogart, GA (p. 279)
 Reed Ueda, Tufts University, Medford, MA (p. 282)
*Peggy Venable, Texas Citizens for a Sound Economy, Austin, TX (p. 284)
*Maris A. Vinovskis, University of Michigan, Ann Arbor, MI (p. 285)
*T. Rogers Wade, Georgia Public Policy Foundation, Atlanta, GA (p. 286)
*Jeffrey D. Wallin, American Academy for Liberal Education, Washington, DC (p. 287)
*Malcolm Wallop, Frontiers of Freedom Institute, Fairfax, VA (p. 288)
 Gary M. Walton, Foundation for Teaching Economics, Davis, CA (p. 288)
*Dane Waters, Initiative and Referendum Institute, Leesburg, VA (p. 289)

AMERICAN HISTORY/POLITICAL TRADITION (Continued)

COMPARATIVE ECONOMICS

---

* Has testified before a state or federal legislative committee

COMPARATIVE ECONOMICS (Continued)

COMPARATIVE ECONOMICS (Continued)

Jude Wanniski, Polyconomics, Parsippany, NJ **(p. 288)**
George T. Yu, University of Illinois, Champaign, IL **(p. 301)**

COMPARATIVE GOVERNMENT

*__I. Dean Ahmad,__ Minaret of Freedom Institute, Bethesda, MD **(p. 36)**
Lee J. Alston, University of Colorado-Boulder, Boulder, CO **(p. 37)**
Damon Ansell, Americans for Tax Reform, Washington, DC **(p. 39)**
Nigel Ashford, Institute for Humane Studies at George Mason University, Arlington, VA **(p. 41)**
*__Mark A. Bloomfield,__ American Council for Capital Formation, Washington, DC **(p. 55)**
*__Patrick M. Boarman,__ National University San Diego, San Diego, CA **(p. 55)**
Gordon L. Brady, Center for the Study of Public Choice, Fairfax, VA **(p. 60)**
James M. Buchanan, Center for the Study of Public Choice, Fairfax, VA **(p. 64)**
Francis H. Buckley, George Mason University School of Law, Arlington, VA **(p. 64)**
*__Stuart Butler,__ The Heritage Foundation, Washington, DC **(p. 66)**
*__Dominic M. Calabro,__ Florida TaxWatch Research Institute, Inc., Tallahassee, FL **(p. 67)**
*__Robert Carleson,__ American Civil Rights Union, Alexandria, VA **(p. 70)**
*__Hungdah Chiu,__ University of Maryland School of Law, Baltimore, MD **(p. 74)**
Angelo M. Codevilla, Boston University, Boston, MA **(p. 77)**
*__John F. Copper,__ Rhodes College, Memphis, TN **(p. 82)**
*__Wendell Cox,__ Wendell Cox Consultancy, Belleville, IL **(p. 84)**
Aurelian Craiutu, Indiana University, Bloomington, IN **(p. 85)**
Neil S. Crispo, Florida State University, Tallahassee, FL **(p. 86)**
Melvin Croan, University of Wisconsin, Madison, WI **(p. 86)**
Damjan de Krnjevic-Miskovic, The National Interest, Washington, DC **(p. 90)**
*__Donald J. Devine,__ Center for American Values, Shady Side, MD **(p. 94)**
Peter J. Duignan, Hoover Institution, Stanford, CA **(p. 99)**
*__Louis D. Enoff,__ Enoff Associates Limited, Sykesville, MD **(p. 107)**
*__Robert Fike,__ Americans for Tax Reform, Washington, DC **(p. 111)**
*__George Folsom,__ International Republican Institute, Washington, DC **(p. 114)**
*__David Forte,__ Cleveland State University, Cleveland, OH **(p. 114)**
Elizabeth Fox-Genovese, Emory University, Atlanta, GA **(p. 115)**
Francis Fukuyama, The Paul H. Nitze School of Advanced International Studies, Washington, DC **(p. 118)**
*__Jeffrey B. Gayner,__ Americans for Sovereignty, Washington, DC **(p. 121)**
Alexander J. Groth, University of California, Davis, Davis, CA **(p. 130)**
*__James D. Gwartney,__ Florida State University, Tallahassee, FL **(p. 131)**
Roger Hamburg, Indiana University South Bend, South Bend, IN **(p. 133)**
Peter J. Hill, Wheaton College, Wheaton, IL **(p. 142)**
John C. Hulsman, The Heritage Foundation, Washington, DC **(p. 149)**
Samuel P. Huntington, Harvard University, Cambridge, MA **(p. 150)**
Jeane J. Kirkpatrick, American Enterprise Institute, Washington, DC **(p. 164)**
Arthur B. Laffer, A. B. Laffer Associates, San Diego, CA **(p. 172)**
*__George Landrith,__ Frontiers of Freedom Institute, Fairfax, VA **(p. 173)**
*__Andrew Langer,__ National Federation of Independent Business, Washington, DC **(p. 174)**
*__John Lenczowski,__ Institute of World Politics, Washington, DC **(p. 177)**
*__Mark R. Levin,__ Landmark Legal Foundation, Herndon, VA **(p. 178)**
*__George Liebmann,__ Calvert Institute for Policy Research, Baltimore, MD **(p. 180)**
Hsien-Tung Liu, Bloomsburg University, Bloomsburg, PA **(p. 181)**
Herbert L. London, Hudson Institute, Indianapolis, IN **(p. 182)**
Rett R. Ludwikowski, Catholic University of America, Washington, DC **(p. 184)**
Tibor R. Machan, Chapman University, Silverado Canyon, CA **(p. 185)**
*__Roger Michener,__ Placitas, NM **(p. 201)**
Fariborz L. Mokhtari, National Defense University, Washington, DC **(p. 204)**

COMPARATIVE GOVERNMENT (Continued)

*Joseph A. Morris, Lincoln Legal Foundation, Chicago, IL (p. 207)
 Henry Myers, James Madison University, Harrisonburg, VA (p. 210)
*Anne D. Neal, American Council of Trustees and Alumni, Washington, DC (p. 211)
*William A. Niskanen, Cato Institute, Washington, DC (p. 214)
*William H. Peterson, Washington, DC (p. 227)
 Bruce Piasecki, AHC Group, Saratoga Springs, NY (p. 228)
*Daniel J. Popeo, Washington Legal Foundation, Washington, DC (p. 231)
 Barry W. Poulson, University of Colorado, Boulder, CO (p. 232)
 Jeremy Rabkin, Cornell University, Ithaca, NY (p. 235)
 Paul A. Rahe, University of Tulsa, Tulsa, OK (p. 236)
 Joseph D. Reid, Jr., George Mason University, Fairfax, VA (p. 238)
 James C. Roberts, American Studies Center, Washington, DC (p. 242)
 Hilton Root, Economy Strategy Institute, Washington, DC (p. 243)
*Paul Rubin, Emory University, Atlanta, GA (p. 246)
*Mark E. Rush, Washington and Lee University, Lexington, VA (p. 247)
*Steven Alan Samson, Liberty University, Lynchburg, VA (p. 249)
 T. Alexander Smith, University of Tennessee, Knoxville, Knoxville, TN (p. 264)
*Richard Stith, Valpariso University School of Law, Valpariso, IN (p. 269)
 Michael D. Stroup, Stephen F. Austin State University, Nacogdoches, TX (p. 270)
*Richard L. Stroup, PERC – The Center for Free Market Environmentalism,
    Bozeman, MT (p. 271)
 Charles Stuart, University of California, Santa Barbara, Santa Barbara, CA (p. 271)
*John D. Sullivan, Center for International Private Enterprise, Washington, DC (p. 271)
 Roy E. Thoman, West Texas A & M University, Canyon, TX (p. 277)
*Mark Thornton, Columbus State University, Columbus, GA (p. 278)
*Robert D. Tollison, University of Mississippi, University, MS (p. 280)
 Phillip N. Truluck, The Heritage Foundation, Washington, DC (p. 281)
*Malcolm Wallop, Frontiers of Freedom Institute, Fairfax, VA (p. 288)
 James Biser Whisker, West Virginia University, Morgantown, WV (p. 293)
*Larry Wortzel, The Heritage Foundation, Washington, DC (p. 299)
*Michael K. Young, George Washington University Law School, Washington, DC (p. 300)
 George T. Yu, University of Illinois, Champaign, IL (p. 301)

CONSERVATIVE THOUGHT

*John Agresto, John Agresto and Associates, Santa Fe, NM (p. 35)
*William Allen, Michigan State University, East Lansing, MI (p. 37)
 Brian C. Anderson, Manhattan Institute for Policy Research, New York, NY (p. 38)
 Frank Annunziata, Rochester Institute of Technology, Rochester, NY (p. 39)
 Damon Ansell, Americans for Tax Reform, Washington, DC (p. 39)
*Dominic A. Aquila, Ave Maria University, Ypsilanti, MI (p. 40)
 Nigel Ashford, Institute for Humane Studies at George Mason University,
    Arlington, VA (p. 41)
*Thomas C. Atwood, National Council For Adoption, Alexandria, VA (p. 41)
*John S. Baker, Jr., Louisiana State University, Baton Rouge, LA (p. 43)
*Sandor Balogh, Hudson Valley Community College, East Greenbush, NY (p. 45)
 Michael B. Barkey, Center for the Study of Compassionate Conservatism,
    Grand Rapids, MI (p. 46)
 Christopher Beiting, Ave Maria College, Ypsilanti, MI (p. 49)
*Herman Belz, University of Maryland, College Park, MD (p. 50)
*John E. Berthoud, National Taxpayers Union, Alexandria, VA (p. 52)
*Jason Bertsch, American Enterprise Institute, Washington, DC (p. 52)
 Morton Blackwell, Leadership Institute, Arlington, VA (p. 54)
*Mark Blitz, Claremont McKenna College, Claremont, CA (p. 55)
*David Boaz, Cato Institute, Washington, DC (p. 55)

CONSERVATIVE THOUGHT (Continued)

*Donald R. Booth, Chapman University, Orange, CA (p. 57)
L. Brent Bozell, III, Media Research Center, Alexandria, VA (p. 59)
Anthony Bradley, Acton Institute for the Study of Religion and Liberty,
   Grand Rapids, MI (p. 59)
Gordon L. Brady, Center for the Study of Public Choice, Fairfax, VA (p. 60)
*Matthew J. Brouillette, The Commonwealth Foundation, Harrisburg, PA (p. 62)
*Kenneth Brown, Rio Grande Foundation, Albuquerque, NM (p. 63)
Francis H. Buckley, George Mason University School of Law, Arlington, VA (p. 64)
T. Patrick Burke, St. Joseph's University, Wynnewood, PA (p. 65)
*David Burton, Argus Group, Alexandria, VA (p. 66)
*Jon Charles Caldara, Independence Institute, Golden, CO (p. 67)
Jameson Campaigne, Jr., Jameson Books, Inc., Ottawa, IL (p. 68)
William F. Campbell, The Philadelphia Society, Baton Rouge, LA (p. 68)
*David Caprara, The Empowerment Network, Fredericksburg, VA (p. 69)
*James B. Cardle, Texas Citizen Action Network, Austin, TX (p. 69)
*John E. Carey, International Defense Consultants, Inc., Arlington, VA (p. 69)
*Robert Carleson, American Civil Rights Union, Alexandria, VA (p. 70)
*Samuel Casey Carter, Acade Metrics, LLC, Washington, DC (p. 71)
*Bruce K. Chapman, Discovery Institute, Seattle, WA (p. 72)
Eric Cohen, Ethics and Public Policy Center, Washington, DC (p. 78)
Boyd D. Collier, Tarleton State University, Stephenville, TX (p. 78)
Kellyanne Conway, the polling company/WomanTrend, Washington, DC (p. 80)
*Louis J. Cordia, Cordia Companies, Alexandria, VA (p. 82)
Dennis Coyle, Catholic University of America, Washington, DC (p. 84)
Mickey Craig, Hillsdale College, Hillsdale, MI (p. 85)
Aurelian Craiutu, Indiana University, Bloomington, IN (p. 85)
*Ron Crews, Massachusetts Family Institute, Newton Upper Falls, MA (p. 86)
T. Kenneth Cribb, Jr., Intercollegiate Studies Institute, Wilmington, DE (p. 86)
Melvin Croan, University of Wisconsin, Madison, WI (p. 86)
Michael E. DeBow, Samford University, Birmingham, AL (p. 91)
William C. Dennis, Dennis Consulting, MacLean, VA (p. 93)
*Len Deo, New Jersey Family Policy Council, Parsippany, NJ (p. 93)
*Donald J. Devine, Center for American Values, Shady Side, MD (p. 94)
Pete du Pont, National Center for Policy Analysis, Wilmington, DE (p. 98)
Peter J. Duignan, Hoover Institution, Stanford, CA (p. 99)
*John C. Eastman, Chapman University School of Law, Orange, CA (p. 102)
*Michelle Easton, Clare Boothe Luce Policy Institute, Herndon, VA (p. 102)
*Myron Ebell, Competitive Enterprise Institute, Washington, DC (p. 103)
*Evelyn Ebzery, Memorial Hospital of Sheridan County, Sheridan, WY (p. 103)
*James R. Edwards, Jr., Hudson Institute, Washington, DC (p. 104)
*Lee Edwards, The Heritage Foundation, Washington, DC (p. 104)
*Mickey Edwards, Harvard University, Cambridge, MA (p. 104)
Barbara Elliott, Center for Renewal, Houston, TX (p. 105)
W. Winston Elliott, III, Center for the American Idea, Houston, TX (p. 106)
Thomas Engeman, Loyola University Chicago, Chicago, IL (p. 107)
*Edwin J. Feulner, The Heritage Foundation, Washington, DC (p. 111)
*Michael Flynn, American Legislative Exchange Council, Washington, DC (p. 113)
*John Fonte, Hudson Institute, Washington, DC (p. 114)
William F. Ford, Middle Tennessee State University, Murfreesboro, TN (p. 114)
*David Forte, Cleveland State University, Cleveland, OH (p. 114)
Elizabeth Fox-Genovese, Emory University, Atlanta, GA (p. 115)
Hillel Fradkin, Ethics and Public Policy Center, Washington, DC (p. 115)
James R. Gaston, Franciscan University of Steubenville, Steubenville, OH (p. 120)
*Robert P. George, Princeton University, Princeton, NJ (p. 122)

---

* Has testified before a state or federal legislative committee

CONSERVATIVE THOUGHT (Continued)

*Stephen Goldsmith, Manhattan Institute for Policy Research, New York, NY (p. 126)

*Stephen O. Goodrick, National Right to Work Committee, Springfield, VA (p. 126)

Paul Gottfried, Elizabethtown College, Elizabethtown, PA (p. 127)

Samuel Gregg, Acton Institute for the Study of Religion and Liberty, Grand Rapids, MI (p. 129)

Frank Gregorsky, Exacting Editorial Services, Vienna, VA (p. 129)

Steven E. Grosby, Clemson University, Clemson, SC (p. 129)

Alexander J. Groth, University of California, Davis, Davis, CA (p. 130)

Steve H. Hanke, Johns Hopkins University, Baltimore, MD (p. 134)

Jerome J. Hanus, American University, Washington, DC (p. 134)

Edward J. Harpham, University of Texas, Dallas, Richardson, TX (p. 135)

William Anthony Hay, Foreign Policy Research Institute, Philadelphia, PA (p. 138)

*Steven Hayward, American Enterprise Institute, Washington, DC (p. 138)

Jay F. Hein, Hudson Institute, Indianapolis, IN (p. 139)

Robert A. Heineman, Alfred University, Alfred, NY (p. 139)

Mark Y. Herring, Winthrop University, Rock Hill, SC (p. 140)

*John Hillen, Foreign Policy Research Institute, Philadelphia, PA (p. 142)

*Thomas Hinton, The Heritage Foundation, Washington, DC (p. 143)

Scott Hogenson, *CNSNews.com*, Alexandria, VA (p. 144)

David Horowitz, Center for the Study of Popular Culture, Los Angeles, CA (p. 146)

*Robert Huberty, Capital Research Center, Washington, DC (p. 148)

John C. Hulsman, The Heritage Foundation, Washington, DC (p. 149)

Jonathan Imber, Wellesley College, Wellesley, MA (p. 151)

Niger Roy Innis, Congress of Racial Equality, New York, NY (p. 151)

Reed J. Irvine, Accuracy in Media, Washington, DC (p. 152)

Thomas Ivancie, America's Future Foundation, Washington, DC (p. 152)

Earl W. Jackson, Sr., Samaritan Project, Chesapeake, VA (p. 152)

*Charles W. Jarvis, United Seniors Association, Fairfax, VA (p. 153)

Douglas A. Jeffrey, Hillsdale College, Hillsdale, MI (p. 154)

Barry P. Keating, University of Notre Dame, Notre Dame, IN (p. 159)

*David A. Keene, American Conservative Union, Washington, DC (p. 160)

*W. Thomas Kelly, Savers and Investors League, Mirror Lake, NH (p. 161)

*Charles R. Kesler, Henry Salvatori Center, Claremont, CA (p. 162)

*William A. Keyes, The Institute on Political Journalism, Washington, DC (p. 162)

Jeane J. Kirkpatrick, American Enterprise Institute, Washington, DC (p. 164)

Joseph M. Knippenberg, Oglethorpe University, Atlanta, GA (p. 166)

*Robert C. Koons, University of Texas, Austin, TX (p. 167)

*Lawrence Kudlow, Kudlow & Co., LLC, New York, NY (p. 170)

Melvin A. Kulbicki, York College of Pennsylvania, York, PA (p. 170)

John Kurzweil, California Public Policy Foundation, Camarillo, CA (p. 171)

Arthur B. Laffer, A. B. Laffer Associates, San Diego, CA (p. 172)

*Deepak Lal, University of California at Los Angeles, Los Angeles, CA (p. 172)

*George Landrith, Frontiers of Freedom Institute, Fairfax, VA (p. 173)

*Andrew Langer, National Federation of Independent Business, Washington, DC (p. 174)

Phillip F. Lawler, *Catholic World Report*, South Lancaster, MA (p. 176)

*Mark R. Levin, Landmark Legal Foundation, Herndon, VA (p. 178)

William S. Lind, Free Congress Foundation, Washington, DC (p. 180)

*Dennis Mansfield, Boise, ID (p. 189)

Harvey C. Mansfield, Harvard University, Cambridge, MA (p. 189)

*Nancie G. Marzulla, Defenders of Property Rights, Washington, DC (p. 191)

*Roger J. Marzulla, Defenders of Property Rights, Washington, DC (p. 191)

*Ken Masugi, Claremont Institute, Claremont, CA (p. 191)

Merrill Matthews, Jr., Institute for Policy Innovation, Lewisville, TX (p. 192)

Wilfred M. McClay, University of Tennessee, Chattanooga, Chattanooga, TN (p. 193)

W. Wesley McDonald, Elizabethtown College, Elizabethtown, PA (p. 195)

CONSERVATIVE THOUGHT (Continued)

John O. McGinnis, Cardozo School of Law, New York, NY (p. 196)
*Michael J. McManus, Marriage Savers, Potomac, MD (p. 197)
*Edwin Meese III, The Heritage Foundation, Washington, DC (p. 198)
Ingrid Merikoski, Earhart Foundation, Ann Arbor, MI (p. 199)
Paul T. Mero, The Sutherland Institute, Salt Lake City, UT (p. 199)
*Roger Michener, Placitas, NM (p. 201)
Fred D. Miller, Jr., Bowling Green State University, Bowling Green, OH (p. 201)
Tom Minnery, Focus on the Family, Colorado Springs, CO (p. 203)
R. Albert Mohler, Jr., The Southern Baptist Theological Seminary, Louisville, KY (p. 204)
*Joseph A. Morris, Lincoln Legal Foundation, Chicago, IL (p. 207)
Jennifer Roback Morse, Hoover Institution, Vista, CA (p. 207)
*Len Munsil, Center for Arizona Policy, Scottsdale, AZ (p. 209)
Chuck Muth, American Conservative Union, Alexandria, VA (p. 210)
Henry Myers, James Madison University, Harrisonburg, VA (p. 210)
George H. Nash, South Hadley, MA (p. 210)
Ronald Nash, Reformed Theological Seminary, Oviedo, FL (p. 211)
*Anne D. Neal, American Council of Trustees and Alumni, Washington, DC (p. 211)
Anthony I. Negbenebor, Gardner-Webb University, Boiling Springs, NC (p. 212)
Jeff Nelson, Intercollegiate Studies Institute, Wilmington, DE (p. 212)
*Richard John Neuhaus, Institute on Religion and Public Life, New York, NY (p. 213)
Stuart W. Nolan, Jr., Springfield, VA (p. 214)
Michael J. Novak, Jr., American Enterprise Institute, Washington, DC (p. 215)
James Nuechterlein, *First Things*, New York, NY (p. 216)
James P. O'Leary, Catholic University of America, Washington, DC (p. 217)
*Richard Olivastro, People Dynamics, Farmington, CT (p. 218)
Glenn Oppel, Rocky Mountain Enterprise Institute, Billings, MT (p. 219)
Daniel Palm, Azusa Pacific University, Azusa, CA (p. 220)
*Jim Panyard, Pennsylvania Manufacturer's Association, Harrisburg, PA (p. 221)
*J. A. Parker, Lincoln Institute for Research and Education, Washington, DC (p. 221)
*Ronald W. Pearson, Pearson & Pipkin, Inc., Washington, DC (p. 224)
Sidney A. Pearson, Jr., Radford University, Radford, VA (p. 224)
Paul C. Peterson, Coastal Carolina University, Conway, SC (p. 227)
*William H. Peterson, Washington, DC (p. 227)
*Howard Phillips, The Conservative Caucus, Inc., Vienna, VA (p. 227)
James Piereson, John M. Olin Foundation, Inc., New York, NY (p. 228)
Barry W. Poulson, University of Colorado, Boulder, CO (p. 232)
*Stephen Presser, Northwestern University School of Law, Chicago, IL (p. 233)
Joseph M. Prinzinger, Lynchburg College, Lynchburg, VA (p. 233)
Paul A. Rahe, University of Tulsa, Tulsa, OK (p. 236)
Harold Calvin Ray, National Center for Faith-Based Initiatives, West Palm Beach, FL (p. 237)
Roger Ream, The Fund for American Studies, Washington, DC (p. 237)
Sandy Rios, Concerned Women for America, Washington, DC (p. 240)
*James S. Robbins, National Defense University, Washington, DC (p. 241)
James C. Roberts, American Studies Center, Washington, DC (p. 242)
Ron Robinson, Young America's Foundation, Herndon, VA (p. 242)
John E. Rocha, Sr., Center for the American Idea, Houston, TX (p. 242)
*Timothy P. Roth, University of Texas, El Paso, El Paso, TX (p. 244)
*William A. Rusher, Claremont Institute, San Francisco, CA (p. 247)
Robert E. Russell, Jr., The Heritage Foundation, Geneva, IL (p. 247)
Claes G. Ryn, Catholic University of America, Washington, DC (p. 248)
*Steven Alan Samson, Liberty University, Lynchburg, VA (p. 249)
Robert A. Schadler, Center for First Principles, Washington, DC (p. 251)
David L. Schaefer, Holy Cross College, Worcester, MA (p. 252)
*Peter W. Schramm, John M. Ashbrook Center for Public Affairs, Ashland, OH (p. 254)

---

* Has testified before a state or federal legislative committee

CONSERVATIVE THOUGHT (Continued)

Robert Schuettinger, Washington International Studies Council, Washington, DC **(p. 254)**
Donald J. Senese, 60 Plus Association, Arlington, VA **(p. 257)**
Barry Alan Shain, Colgate University, Hamilton, NY **(p. 257)**
Colleen Sheehan, Villanova University, Villanova, PA **(p. 258)**
T. Alexander Smith, University of Tennessee, Knoxville, Knoxville, TN **(p. 264)**
Ted J. Smith, III, Virginia Commonwealth University, Richmond, VA **(p. 264)**
Matthew Spalding, The Heritage Foundation, Washington, DC **(p. 266)**
David Strom, Taxpayers League of Minnesota, Plymouth, MN **(p. 270)**
Robert Sutherland, Cornell College, Mount Vernon, IA **(p. 272)**
Thomas L. Tacker, Embry-Riddle Aeronautical University, Daytona Beach, FL **(p. 273)**
James R. "J.T." Taylor, Empower America, Washington, DC **(p. 274)**
Roy E. Thoman, West Texas A & M University, Canyon, TX **(p. 277)**
Robert D. Tollison, University of Mississippi, University, MS **(p. 280)**
Brian S. Tracy, Brian Tracy International, Solana Beach, CA **(p. 280)**
Phillip N. Truluck, The Heritage Foundation, Washington, DC **(p. 281)**
Peggy Venable, Texas Citizens for a Sound Economy, Austin, TX **(p. 284)**
Bridgett G. Wagner, The Heritage Foundation, Washington, DC **(p. 286)**
Lee H. Walker, New Coalition for Economic and Social Change, Chicago, IL **(p. 287)**
Malcolm Wallop, Frontiers of Freedom Institute, Fairfax, VA **(p. 288)**
Bradley C. S. Watson, Saint Vincent College, Latrobe, PA **(p. 290)**
Paul Weyrich, Free Congress Foundation, Washington, DC **(p. 293)**
David M. Whalen, Hillsdale College, Hillsdale, MI **(p. 293)**
James Biser Whisker, West Virginia University, Morgantown, WV **(p. 293)**
Adam Wolfson, *The Public Interest,* Washington, DC **(p. 297)**
Anne Wortham, Illinois State University, Normal, IL **(p. 298)**
Catherine Zuckert, University of Notre Dame, Notre Dame, IN **(p. 302)**
Michael Zuckert, University of Notre Dame, Notre Dame, IN **(p. 302)**
Ronald A. Zumbrun, The Zumbrun Law Firm, Sacramento, CA **(p. 303)**

ECONOMIC EDUCATION

M. Gene Aldridge, New Mexico Independence Research Institute, Las Cruces, NM **(p. 36)**
William T. Alpert, University of Connecticut, Stamford, CT **(p. 37)**
Ron Arnold, Center for the Defense of Free Enterprise, Bellevue, WA **(p. 40)**
Barry Asmus, National Center for Policy Analysis, Scottsdale, AZ **(p. 41)**
Lawson R. Bader, Mercatus Center at George Mason University, Arlington, VA **(p. 42)**
David S. Ball, North Carolina State University, Raleigh, NC **(p. 44)**
Bruce R. Bartlett, National Center for Policy Analysis, Great Falls, VA **(p. 46)**
Gary Becker, University of Chicago, Chicago, IL **(p. 48)**
John J. Bethune, Barton College, Wilson, NC **(p. 53)**
Michael K. Block, University of Arizona, Tucson, AZ **(p. 55)**
Donald R. Booth, Chapman University, Orange, CA **(p. 57)**
Michael J. Boskin, Hoover Institution, Stanford, CA **(p. 57)**
Donald J. Boudreaux, George Mason University, Fairfax, VA **(p. 58)**
Karol Boudreaux, George Mason University School of Law, Arlington, VA **(p. 58)**
Gordon L. Brady, Center for the Study of Public Choice, Fairfax, VA **(p. 60)**
Matthew J. Brouillette, The Commonwealth Foundation, Harrisburg, PA **(p. 62)**
James M. Buchanan, Center for the Study of Public Choice, Fairfax, VA **(p. 64)**
Jon Charles Caldara, Independence Institute, Golden, CO **(p. 67)**
Barry R. Chiswick, University of Illinois, Chicago, Chicago, IL **(p. 73)**
Robert Chitester, Palmer R. Chitester Fund, Erie, PA **(p. 73)**
Michael A. Ciamarra, Alabama Policy Institute, Birmingham, AL **(p. 74)**
J. R. Clark, University of Tennessee, Chattanooga, Chattanooga, TN **(p. 75)**
Kenneth W. Clarkson, University of Miami, Coral Gables, FL **(p. 75)**
Boyd D. Collier, Tarleton State University, Stephenville, TX **(p. 78)**

ECONOMIC EDUCATION (Continued)

John L. Conant, Indiana State University, Terre Haute, IN **(p. 79)**
*****William Conerly,** Conerly Consulting, Portland, OR **(p. 79)**
Roy E. Cordato, John Locke Foundation, Raleigh, NC **(p. 82)**
Tyler Cowen, George Mason University, Fairfax, VA **(p. 83)**
W. Mark Crain, George Mason University, Fairfax, VA **(p. 85)**
Neil S. Crispo, Florida State University, Tallahassee, FL **(p. 86)**
Elizabeth Currier, Committee for Monetary Research and Education, Inc.,
   Charlotte, NC **(p. 87)**
Derrick Allen Dalton, Boise State University, Boise, ID **(p. 88)**
*****Donald J. Devine,** Center for American Values, Shady Side, MD **(p. 94)**
*****Phillip DeVous,** Acton Institute for the Study of Religion and Liberty, Grand Rapids, MI **(p. 94)**
Arthur M. Diamond, Jr., University of Nebraska, Omaha, Omaha, NE **(p. 95)**
D. P. Diffine, Harding University, Searcy, AR **(p. 95)**
Pete du Pont, National Center for Policy Analysis, Wilmington, DE **(p. 98)**
Richard M. Ebeling, Hillsdale College, Hillsdale, MI **(p. 102)**
Isaac Ehrlich, State University of New York, Buffalo, Buffalo, NY **(p. 105)**
W. Winston Elliott, III, Center for the American Idea, Houston, TX **(p. 106)**
Kenneth G. Elzinga, University of Virginia, Charlottesville, VA **(p. 106)**
*****Frank Falero,** Springville, CA **(p. 109)**
Eric Fisher, Ohio State University, 40126 Bologna, ITALY **(p. 112)**
John Galandak, Foundation for Free Enterprise, Paramus, NJ **(p. 119)**
David E. R. Gay, University of Arkansas, Fayetteville, AR **(p. 121)**
Fred R. Glahe, University of Colorado, Boulder, CO **(p. 124)**
*****James K. Glassman,** American Enterprise Institute, Washington, DC **(p. 124)**
*****Stephen O. Goodrick,** National Right to Work Committee, Springfield, VA **(p. 126)**
*****Linda Gorman,** Independence Institute, Golden, CO **(p. 127)**
John R. Hanson, II, Texas A&M University, College Station, TX **(p. 134)**
Eric Hanushek, Hoover Institution, Stanford, CA **(p. 135)**
*****C. Lowell Harriss,** Columbia University, Bronxville, NY **(p. 136)**
*****Lynn Harsh,** Evergreen Freedom Foundation, Olympia, WA **(p. 136)**
James E. Hartley, Mount Holyoke College, South Hadley, MA **(p. 136)**
Robert D. Hisrich, Case Western Reserve University, Cleveland, OH **(p. 143)**
*****Fred Holden,** Phoenix Enterprises, Arvada, CO **(p. 144)**
Jacob G. Hornberger, Future of Freedom Foundation, Fairfax, VA **(p. 146)**
*****Joseph Horton,** University of Central Arkansas, Conway, AR **(p. 146)**
*****Caroline M. Hoxby,** Harvard University, Cambridge, MA **(p. 147)**
*****Lawrence Hunter,** Empower America, Washington, DC **(p. 149)**
Theodore "Sylvester" John, Students In Free Enterprise, Springfield, MO **(p. 154)**
Dale W. Jorgenson, Harvard University, Cambridge, MA **(p. 156)**
Barry P. Keating, University of Notre Dame, Notre Dame, IN **(p. 159)**
*****Lynne Kiesling,** Reason Public Policy Institute, Los Angeles, CA **(p. 163)**
Charles R. Knoeber, North Carolina State University, Raleigh, NC **(p. 166)**
*****Lawrence Kudlow,** Kudlow & Co., LLC, New York, NY **(p. 170)**
David N. Laband, Auburn University, Auburn, AL **(p. 171)**
Arthur B. Laffer, A. B. Laffer Associates, San Diego, CA **(p. 172)**
*****Andrew Langer,** National Federation of Independent Business, Washington, DC **(p. 174)**
Daniel Lapin, Toward Tradition, Mercer Island, WA **(p. 174)**
Dwight R. Lee, University of Georgia, Athens, GA **(p. 176)**
John M. Malek, Polish-American Foundation for Economic Research and Education,
   Torrance, CA **(p. 187)**
Henry G. Manne, University of Chicago Law School, Chicago, IL **(p. 188)**
Steve Mariotti, National Foundation for Teaching Entrepreneurship, New York, NY **(p. 189)**
Kris Alan Mauren, Acton Institute for the Study of Religion and Liberty,
   Grand Rapids, MI **(p. 192)**

***** Has testified before a state or federal legislative committee**

ECONOMIC EDUCATION (Continued)

Harry Messenheimer, Rio Grande Foundation, Tijeras, NM (p. 200)
*Adrian T. Moore, Reason Foundation, Los Angeles, CA (p. 205)
Jennifer Roback Morse, Hoover Institution, Vista, CA (p. 207)
Robert Mottice, Mercatus Center at George Mason University, Arlington, VA (p. 208)
Bruce A. Nasby, Students In Free Enterprise, Springfield, MO (p. 210)
Ronald Nash, Reformed Theological Seminary, Oviedo, FL (p. 211)
*Anne D. Neal, American Council of Trustees and Alumni, Washington, DC (p. 211)
Anthony I. Negbenebor, Gardner-Webb University, Boiling Springs, NC (p. 212)
Jeff Nelson, Intercollegiate Studies Institute, Wilmington, DE (p. 212)
George R. Neumann, University of Iowa, Iowa City, IA (p. 213)
*Judd W. Patton, Bellevue University, Bellevue, NE (p. 223)
*Svetozar Pejovich, Texas A&M University, Dallas, TX (p. 224)
*Lovett C. Peters, Pioneer Institute for Public Policy Research, Boston, MA (p. 226)
*William H. Peterson, Washington, DC (p. 227)
Penn Pfiffner, Independence Institute, Golden, CO (p. 227)
Charles I. Plosser, University of Rochester, Rochester, NY (p. 229)
Gale L. Pooley, Star, ID (p. 230)
Barry W. Poulson, University of Colorado, Boulder, CO (p. 232)
Roger Ream, The Fund for American Studies, Washington, DC (p. 237)
*Lawrence W. Reed, Mackinac Center for Public Policy, Midland, MI (p. 237)
George Reisman, Pepperdine University, Laguna Hills, CA (p. 238)
Steven Rhoads, University of Virginia, Charlottesville, VA (p. 239)
Russell Roberts, Weidenbaum Center, St. Louis, MO (p. 242)
David C. Rose, University of Missouri, St. Louis, St. Louis, MO (p. 243)
Robert E. Russell, Jr., The Heritage Foundation, Geneva, IL (p. 247)
Edward W. Ryan, Manhattanville College, Purchase, NY (p. 248)
*Michael Sanera, Basis Charter High School, Tucson, AZ (p. 249)
*Bill Schilling, Wyoming Business Alliance / Wyoming Heritage Foundation,
   Casper, WY (p. 253)
LaKay Schmidt, Colorado Council on Economic Education, Boulder, CO (p. 253)
Robert Haney Scott, California State University, Chico, Chico, CA (p. 255)
*John Semmens, Laissez-Faire Institute, Chandler, AZ (p. 256)
*Hans F. Sennholz, Grove City College, Grove City, PA (p. 257)
*Robert A. Sirico, Acton Institute for the Study of Religion and Liberty,
   Grand Rapids, MI (p. 261)
Vernon L. Smith, George Mason University, Arlington, VA (p. 264)
John C. Soper, John Carroll University, University Heights, OH (p. 266)
*Nancy Z. Spillman, Economic Education Enterprises, Canoga Park, CA (p. 267)
Alan C. Stockman, University of Rochester, Rochester, NY (p. 269)
*David Strom, Taxpayers League of Minnesota, Plymouth, MN (p. 270)
Michael D. Stroup, Stephen F. Austin State University, Nacogdoches, TX (p. 270)
*Richard L. Stroup, PERC – The Center for Free Market Environmentalism,
   Bozeman, MT (p. 271)
*David J. Theroux, The Independent Institute, Oakland, CA (p. 276)
Roy E. Thoman, West Texas A & M University, Canyon, TX (p. 277)
*Mark Thornton, Columbus State University, Columbus, GA (p. 278)
Eugenia Froedge Toma, University of Kentucky, Lexington, KY (p. 280)
Brian S. Tracy, Brian Tracy International, Solana Beach, CA (p. 280)
*David G. Tuerck, Beacon Hill Institute, Boston, MA (p. 281)
Jon Basil Utley, Ludwig von Mises Institute, Washington, DC (p. 283)
*Terry W. Van Allen, Kemah, TX (p. 283)
Karen I. Vaughn, George Mason University, Fairfax, VA (p. 284)
Bridgett G. Wagner, The Heritage Foundation, Washington, DC (p. 286)
Gary M. Walton, Foundation for Teaching Economics, Davis, CA (p. 288)

ECONOMIC EDUCATION (Continued)

Jude Wanniski, Polyconomics, Parsippany, NJ (p. 288)
*Murray Weidenbaum, Weidenbaum Center, St. Louis, MO (p. 291)
*Robert O. C. Worcester, Maryland Business for Responsive Government, Baltimore, MD (p. 298)
Edward W. Younkins, Wheeling Jesuit University, Wheeling, WV (p. 301)

ECONOMIC FORECASTING

*Stephen Adams, Pioneer Institute for Public Policy Research, Boston, MA (p. 34)
*Iwan Azis, Cornell University, Ithaca, NY (p. 42)
Lawson R. Bader, Mercatus Center at George Mason University, Arlington, VA (p. 42)
*John S. Barry, Tax Foundation, Washington, DC (p. 46)
*Bruce R. Bartlett, National Center for Policy Analysis, Great Falls, VA (p. 46)
*William W. Beach, The Heritage Foundation, Washington, DC (p. 48)
Michael J. Boskin, Hoover Institution, Stanford, CA (p. 57)
James M. Buchanan, Center for the Study of Public Choice, Fairfax, VA (p. 64)
*William Conerly, Conerly Consulting, Portland, OR (p. 79)
*Michael R. Darby, University of California at Los Angeles, Los Angeles, CA (p. 89)
D. P. Diffine, Harding University, Searcy, AR (p. 95)
*Paul Dunn, University of Louisiana, Monroe, Monroe, LA (p. 100)
*Stephen Entin, Institute for Research on the Economics of Taxation, Washington, DC (p. 107)
*Frank Falero, Springville, CA (p. 109)
*Tom Giovanetti, Institute for Policy Innovation, Lewisville, TX (p. 124)
Steve H. Hanke, Johns Hopkins University, Baltimore, MD (p. 134)
*Kevin A. Hassett, American Enterprise Institute, Washington, DC (p. 137)
*Jake Haulk, Allegheny Institute for Public Policy, Pittsburgh, PA (p. 137)
John M. Heineke, Santa Clara University, Santa Clara, CA (p. 139)
*Lawrence Hunter, Empower America, Washington, DC (p. 149)
*Greg Kaza, Arkansas Policy Foundation, Little Rock, AR (p. 159)
Barry P. Keating, University of Notre Dame, Notre Dame, IN (p. 159)
*W. Thomas Kelly, Savers and Investors League, Mirror Lake, NH (p. 161)
*Lynne Kiesling, Reason Public Policy Institute, Los Angeles, CA (p. 163)
*Randall Kroszner, University of Chicago, Chicago, IL (p. 170)
*Lawrence Kudlow, Kudlow & Co., LLC, New York, NY (p. 170)
Arthur B. Laffer, A. B. Laffer Associates, San Diego, CA (p. 172)
*Deepak Lal, University of California at Los Angeles, Los Angeles, CA (p. 172)
Jack W. Lavery, Lavery Consulting Group, LLC, Washington Crossing, NJ (p. 175)
Herbert L. London, Hudson Institute, Indianapolis, IN (p. 182)
*Rita P. Maguire, Arizona Center for Public Policy, Phoenix, AZ (p. 186)
*John H. Makin, American Enterprise Institute, Washington, DC (p. 187)
*Paul W. McCracken, University of Michigan Business School, Ann Arbor, MI (p. 194)
Ronald Nash, Reformed Theological Seminary, Oviedo, FL (p. 211)
*Anne D. Neal, American Council of Trustees and Alumni, Washington, DC (p. 211)
George R. Neumann, University of Iowa, Iowa City, IA (p. 213)
Penn Pfiffner, Independence Institute, Golden, CO (p. 227)
Charles I. Plosser, University of Rochester, Rochester, NY (p. 229)
Ralph Rector, The Heritage Foundation, Washington, DC (p. 237)
*Thomas R. Saving, Texas A&M University, College Station, TX (p. 251)
*Bill Schilling, Wyoming Business Alliance / Wyoming Heritage Foundation, Casper, WY (p. 253)
G. W. Schwert, University of Rochester, Rochester, NY (p. 255)
Robert Haney Scott, California State University, Chico, Chico, CA (p. 255)
Vernon L. Smith, George Mason University, Arlington, VA (p. 264)
Richard H. Timberlake, Jr., Bogart, GA (p. 279)
Jay L. Tontz, California State University, Hayward, Hayward, CA (p. 280)

ECONOMIC FORECASTING (Continued)

*Terry W. Van Allen, Kemah, TX (p. 283)
*Murray Weidenbaum, Weidenbaum Center, St. Louis, MO (p. 291)
*Charles Wolf, Jr., RAND, Santa Monica, CA (p. 297)

ECONOMIC THEORY

James C. W. Ahiakpor, California State University, Hayward, Hayward, CA (p. 35)
Damon Ansell, Americans for Tax Reform, Washington, DC (p. 39)
Stephen M. Bainbridge, University of California at Los Angeles, Los Angeles, CA (p. 43)
*John S. Barry, Tax Foundation, Washington, DC (p. 46)
*Bruce R. Bartlett, National Center for Policy Analysis, Great Falls, VA (p. 46)
Robert J. Batemarco, Peekskill, NY (p. 47)
*William W. Beach, The Heritage Foundation, Washington, DC (p. 48)
Gary Becker, University of Chicago, Chicago, IL (p. 48)
Paul Beckner, Citizens for a Sound Economy, Washington, DC (p. 48)
*John E. Berthoud, National Taxpayers Union, Alexandria, VA (p. 52)
Douglas Besharov, American Enterprise Institute, Washington, DC (p. 52)
Michael K. Block, University of Arizona, Tucson, AZ (p. 55)
*Patrick M. Boarman, National University San Diego, San Diego, CA (p. 55)
Peter J. Boettke, James M. Buchanan Center for Political Economy, Fairfax, VA (p. 56)
*Donald R. Booth, Chapman University, Orange, CA (p. 57)
Gordon L. Brady, Center for the Study of Public Choice, Fairfax, VA (p. 60)
*Wayne T. Brough, Citizens for a Sound Economy, Washington, DC (p. 62)
*Kenneth Brown, Rio Grande Foundation, Albuquerque, NM (p. 63)
James M. Buchanan, Center for the Study of Public Choice, Fairfax, VA (p. 64)
*David Burton, Argus Group, Alexandria, VA (p. 66)
*Barry R. Chiswick, University of Illinois, Chicago, Chicago, IL (p. 73)
Boyd D. Collier, Tarleton State University, Stephenville, TX (p. 78)
Roy E. Cordato, John Locke Foundation, Raleigh, NC (p. 82)
*Wendell Cox, Wendell Cox Consultancy, Belleville, IL (p. 84)
Dennis Coyle, Catholic University of America, Washington, DC (p. 84)
*Donald J. Devine, Center for American Values, Shady Side, MD (p. 94)
D. P. Diffine, Harding University, Searcy, AR (p. 95)
*Thomas J. DiLorenzo, Loyola College, Clarksville, MD (p. 96)
Richard M. Ebeling, Hillsdale College, Hillsdale, MI (p. 102)
*Stephen Entin, Institute for Research on the Economics of Taxation, Washington, DC (p. 107)
*Frank Falero, Springville, CA (p. 109)
*David I. Fand, James M. Buchanan Center for Political Economy, Fairfax, VA (p. 109)
Eric Fisher, Ohio State University, 40126 Bologna, ITALY (p. 112)
William F. Ford, Middle Tennessee State University, Murfreesboro, TN (p. 114)
Elizabeth Fox-Genovese, Emory University, Atlanta, GA (p. 115)
Eirik Furubotn, Texas A&M University, College Station, TX (p. 119)
*Tom Giovanetti, Institute for Policy Innovation, Lewisville, TX (p. 124)
Fred R. Glahe, University of Colorado, Boulder, CO (p. 124)
*James K. Glassman, American Enterprise Institute, Washington, DC (p. 124)
Leonard M. Greene, Institute for SocioEconomic Studies, White Plains, NY (p. 129)
Frank Gregorsky, Exacting Editorial Services, Vienna, VA (p. 129)
*Robert Hahn, American Enterprise Institute, Washington, DC (p. 132)
Daniel B. Hales, Americans for Effective Law Enforcement, Chicago, IL (p. 132)
Steve H. Hanke, Johns Hopkins University, Baltimore, MD (p. 134)
Bertil L. Hanson, Oklahoma State University, Stillwater, OK (p. 134)
James E. Hartley, Mount Holyoke College, South Hadley, MA (p. 136)
*Jake Haulk, Allegheny Institute for Public Policy, Pittsburgh, PA (p. 137)
John M. Heineke, Santa Clara University, Santa Clara, CA (p. 139)
Robert Stanley Herren, North Dakota State University, Fargo, ND (p. 140)

ECONOMIC THEORY (Continued)

Jack High, George Mason University, Arlington, VA (p. 142)

*Joseph Horton, University of Central Arkansas, Conway, AR (p. 146)

Steven Horwitz, St. Lawrence University, Canton, NY (p. 147)

Edward L. Hudgins, The Objectivist Center, Washington, DC (p. 148)

*Lawrence Hunter, Empower America, Washington, DC (p. 149)

Sanford Ikeda, State University of New York, Purchase, NY (p. 151)

*Bruce Alan Johnson, Bruce Alan Johnson Associates, Indianapolis, IN (p. 155)

*Chalmers Johnson, Japan Policy Research Institute, Cardiff, CA (p. 155)

Dale W. Jorgenson, Harvard University, Cambridge, MA (p. 156)

William H. Kaempfer, University of Colorado, Boulder, CO (p. 156)

Shyam J. Kamath, California State University, Hayward, Hayward, CA (p. 157)

*Raymond J. Keating, Small Business Survival Committee, Manorville, NY (p. 159)

*W. Thomas Kelly, Savers and Investors League, Mirror Lake, NH (p. 161)

F. Scott Kieff, Washington University, St. Louis, MO (p. 163)

*Lynne Kiesling, Reason Public Policy Institute, Los Angeles, CA (p. 163)

*Randall Kroszner, University of Chicago, Chicago, IL (p. 170)

*Lawrence Kudlow, Kudlow & Co., LLC, New York, NY (p. 170)

Arthur B. Laffer, A. B. Laffer Associates, San Diego, CA (p. 172)

*Deepak Lal, University of California at Los Angeles, Los Angeles, CA (p. 172)

*Richard Langlois, University of Connecticut, Storrs, CT (p. 174)

*Kent Lassman, Progress & Freedom Foundation, Raleigh, NC (p. 175)

Kurt R. Leube, Hoover Institution, Stanford, CA (p. 178)

*Mark R. Levin, Landmark Legal Foundation, Herndon, VA (p. 178)

*Peter Linneman, University of Pennsylvania, Philadelphia, PA (p. 181)

*Robert J. Loewenberg, Institute for Advanced Strategic and Political Studies, Washington, DC (p. 182)

Edward J. Lopez, University of North Texas, Denton, TX (p. 183)

*Edward N. Luttwak, Center for Strategic and International Studies, Washington, DC (p. 184)

Glenn M. MacDonald, Washington University, St. Louis, MO (p. 185)

*John H. Makin, American Enterprise Institute, Washington, DC (p. 187)

*Yuri N. Maltsev, Carthage College, Kenosha, WI (p. 188)

Lawrence J. McQuillan, Pacific Research Institute, San Francisco, CA (p. 197)

Harry Messenheimer, Rio Grande Foundation, Tijeras, NM (p. 200)

*Dan Mitchell, The Heritage Foundation, Washington, DC (p. 203)

*Adrian T. Moore, Reason Foundation, Los Angeles, CA (p. 205)

*James Elliott Moore, II, University of Southern California, Los Angeles, CA (p. 205)

*Laurence S. Moss, Babson College, Babson Park, MA (p. 208)

Ronald Nash, Reformed Theological Seminary, Oviedo, FL (p. 211)

*Anne D. Neal, American Council of Trustees and Alumni, Washington, DC (p. 211)

Anthony I. Negbenebor, Gardner-Webb University, Boiling Springs, NC (p. 212)

George R. Neumann, University of Iowa, Iowa City, IA (p. 213)

Michael J. Novak, Jr., American Enterprise Institute, Washington, DC (p. 215)

Glenn Oppel, Rocky Mountain Enterprise Institute, Billings, MT (p. 219)

*Jim Panyard, Pennsylvania Manufacturer's Association, Harrisburg, PA (p. 221)

E. C. Pasour, Jr., North Carolina State University, Raleigh, NC (p. 222)

*Judd W. Patton, Bellevue University, Bellevue, NE (p. 223)

Mark J. Perry, University of Michigan, Flint, Flint, MI (p. 226)

Penn Pfiffner, Independence Institute, Golden, CO (p. 227)

*Nancy M. Pfotenhauer, Independent Women's Forum, Arlington, VA (p. 227)

Bruce Piasecki, AHC Group, Saratoga Springs, NY (p. 228)

Charles I. Plosser, University of Rochester, Rochester, NY (p. 229)

Joseph M. Prinzinger, Lynchburg College, Lynchburg, VA (p. 233)

Paul A. Rahe, University of Tulsa, Tulsa, OK (p. 236)

Douglas B. Rasmussen, St. John's University, Jamaica, NY (p. 236)

ECONOMIC THEORY (Continued)

Harold Calvin Ray, National Center for Faith-Based Initiatives, West Palm Beach, FL (p. 237)

Roger Ream, The Fund for American Studies, Washington, DC (p. 237)

*Lawrence W. Reed, Mackinac Center for Public Policy, Midland, MI (p. 237)

George Reisman, Pepperdine University, Laguna Hills, CA (p. 238)

*Brian Riedl, The Heritage Foundation, Washington, DC (p. 240)

John W. Robbins, Trinity Foundation, Unicoi, TN (p. 241)

*Paul Craig Roberts, Institute for Political Economy, Panama City Beach, FL (p. 242)

Hilton Root, Economy Strategy Institute, Washington, DC (p. 243)

David C. Rose, University of Missouri, St. Louis, St. Louis, MO (p. 243)

*Timothy P. Roth, University of Texas, El Paso, El Paso, TX (p. 244)

Robert E. Russell, Jr., The Heritage Foundation, Geneva, IL (p. 247)

Edward W. Ryan, Manhattanville College, Purchase, NY (p. 248)

Claes G. Ryn, Catholic University of America, Washington, DC (p. 248)

*Joseph T. Salerno, Pace University, New York, NY (p. 248)

*Thomas R. Saving, Texas A&M University, College Station, TX (p. 251)

Larry Schweikart, University of Dayton, Dayton, OH (p. 255)

Larry J. Sechrest, Sul Ross State University, Alpine, TX (p. 255)

*Hans F. Sennholz, Grove City College, Grove City, PA (p. 257)

Larry A. Sjaastad, University of Chicago, Chicago, IL (p. 261)

*Harvey A. Smith, Arizona State University, Tempe, AZ (p. 263)

*Robert J. Smith, Center for Private Conservation, Washington, DC (p. 264)

T. Alexander Smith, University of Tennessee, Knoxville, Knoxville, TN (p. 264)

Vernon L. Smith, George Mason University, Arlington, VA (p. 264)

Charles Stuart, University of California, Santa Barbara, Santa Barbara, CA (p. 271)

*William Craig Stubblebine, Claremont McKenna College, Claremont, CA (p. 271)

*John D. Sullivan, Center for International Private Enterprise, Washington, DC (p. 271)

Thomas L. Tacker, Embry-Riddle Aeronautical University, Daytona Beach, FL (p. 273)

Lester G. Telser, University of Chicago, Chicago, IL (p. 275)

Tammy Tengs, University of California, Irvine, Irvine, CA (p. 275)

*Mark Thornton, Columbus State University, Columbus, GA (p. 278)

Richard H. Timberlake, Jr., Bogart, GA (p. 279)

*David G. Tuerck, Beacon Hill Institute, Boston, MA (p. 281)

*Gordon Tullock, George Mason University School of Law, Arlington, VA (p. 281)

Charlotte Twight, Boise State University, Boise, ID (p. 282)

*Terry W. Van Allen, Kemah, TX (p. 283)

Karen I. Vaughn, George Mason University, Fairfax, VA (p. 284)

*Richard E. Wagner, George Mason University, Fairfax, VA (p. 286)

John T. Warner, Clemson University, Clemson, SC (p. 289)

*Rolf A. Weil, Roosevelt University, Chicago, IL (p. 291)

*Lawrence H. White, University of Missouri, St. Louis, St. Louis, MO (p. 293)

Walter E. Williams, George Mason University, Fairfax, VA (p. 295)

Richard B. Wirthlin, Wirthlin Worldwide, South Jordan, UT (p. 296)

*Lawrence Wohl, Gustavus Adolphus College, St. Peter, MN (p. 297)

*Gary Wolfram, Hillsdale College, Hillsdale, MI (p. 297)

ETHICS

*Mary Cunningham Agee, The Nurturing Network, White Salmon, WA (p. 35)

*I. Dean Ahmad, Minaret of Freedom Institute, Bethesda, MD (p. 36)

*William Allen, Michigan State University, East Lansing, MI (p. 37)

Robert V. Andelson, American Institute for Economic Research, Auburn, AL (p. 37)

Brian C. Anderson, Manhattan Institute for Policy Research, New York, NY (p. 38)

*Julaine K. Appling, Family Research Institute of Wisconsin, Madison, WI (p. 40)

Hadley Arkes, Amherst College, Amherst, MA (p. 40)

N. Scott Arnold, University of Alabama, Birmingham, Birmingham, AL (p. 40)

ETHICS (Continued)

Richard A. Baer, Jr., Cornell University, Ithaca, NY **(p. 42)**
*John S. Baker, Jr., Louisiana State University, Baton Rouge, LA **(p. 43)**
Joseph Baldacchino, National Humanities Institute, Bowie, MD **(p. 44)**
*Bruce R. Bartlett, National Center for Policy Analysis, Great Falls, VA **(p. 46)**
Sammy Basu, Willamette University, Salem, OR **(p. 47)**
John M. Beers, Annecy Institute for the Study of Virtue and Liberty, Washington, DC **(p. 49)**
*Mark Blitz, Claremont McKenna College, Claremont, CA **(p. 55)**
*Patrick M. Boarman, National University San Diego, San Diego, CA **(p. 55)**
*Kenneth Boehm, National Legal and Policy Center, Falls Church, VA **(p. 56)**
Anthony Bradley, Acton Institute for the Study of Religion and Liberty, Grand Rapids, MI **(p. 59)**
*Harold O. J. Brown, Reformed Theological Seminary, Charlotte, NC **(p. 63)**
*Allen Buchanan, University of Arizona, Tucson, AZ **(p. 64)**
T. Patrick Burke, St. Joseph's University, Wynnewood, PA **(p. 65)**
*H. Sterling Burnett, National Center for Policy Analysis, Dallas, TX **(p. 65)**
Nigel M. de S. Cameron, Institute for Humane Studies at George Mason University, Arlington, VA **(p. 68)**
Nicholas Capaldi, Loyola University New Orleans, New Orleans, LA **(p. 69)**
*John E. Carey, International Defense Consultants, Inc., Arlington, VA **(p. 69)**
*Robert Carleson, American Civil Rights Union, Alexandria, VA **(p. 70)**
Don Carrington, John Locke Foundation, Raleigh, NC **(p. 71)**
*Samuel Casey Carter, Acade Metrics, LLC, Washington, DC **(p. 71)**
Alejandro A. Chafuen, Atlas Economic Research Foundation, Fairfax, VA **(p. 72)**
*Bruce K. Chapman, Discovery Institute, Seattle, WA **(p. 72)**
*Michael A. Ciamarra, Alabama Policy Institute, Birmingham, AL **(p. 74)**
Harry M. Clor, Kenyon College, Gambier, OH **(p. 76)**
Andrew I. Cohen, University of Oklahoma, Norman, OK **(p. 77)**
Eric Cohen, Ethics and Public Policy Center, Washington, DC **(p. 78)**
Brooks Colburn, Foundation for Economic Education, Irvington-on-Hudson, NY **(p. 78)**
Boyd D. Collier, Tarleton State University, Stephenville, TX **(p. 78)**
*John E. Coons, University of California at Berkeley, Berkeley, CA **(p. 81)**
Kevin L. Cope, Louisiana State University, Baton Rouge, LA **(p. 81)**
*C. W. Cowles, Central Michigan University, Midlothian, VA **(p. 84)**
*Ron Crews, Massachusetts Family Institute, Newton Upper Falls, MA **(p. 86)**
Alan R. Crippen, II, Family Research Council, Washington, DC **(p. 86)**
John W. Danford, Loyola University Chicago, Chicago, IL **(p. 88)**
Damjan de Krnjevic-Miskovic, The National Interest, Washington, DC **(p. 90)**
Edwin J. Delattre, Boston University, Boston, MA **(p. 91)**
*William T. Devlin, Urban Family Council, Philadelphia, PA **(p. 94)**
*John R. Diggs, Jr., South Hadley, MA **(p. 95)**
Peter J. Duignan, Hoover Institution, Stanford, CA **(p. 99)**
*Paul Dunn, University of Louisiana, Monroe, Monroe, LA **(p. 100)**
Steven D. Ealy, Liberty Fund, Inc., Indianapolis, IN **(p. 101)**
*Myron Ebell, Competitive Enterprise Institute, Washington, DC **(p. 103)**
Barbara Elliott, Center for Renewal, Houston, TX **(p. 105)**
*Jean Bethke Elshtain, University of Chicago, Chicago, IL **(p. 106)**
*Peter Flaherty, National Legal and Policy Center, Falls Church, VA **(p. 113)**
Fred E. Foldvary, Santa Clara University, Santa Clara, CA **(p. 114)**
*David Forte, Cleveland State University, Cleveland, OH **(p. 114)**
Elizabeth Fox-Genovese, Emory University, Atlanta, GA **(p. 115)**
Hillel Fradkin, Ethics and Public Policy Center, Washington, DC **(p. 115)**
*Deanna R. Gelak, Family and Medical Leave Act Technical Corrections Coalition, Springfield, VA **(p. 122)**
*Robert P. George, Princeton University, Princeton, NJ **(p. 122)**

---

* Has testified before a state or federal legislative committee

ETHICS (Continued)

*Tom Giovanetti, Institute for Policy Innovation, Lewisville, TX (p. 124)
Doris Gordon, Libertarians for Life, Wheaton, MD (p. 126)
Charles Greenwalt, II, Susquehanna Valley Center for Public Policy, Hershey, PA (p. 129)
Samuel Gregg, Acton Institute for the Study of Religion and Liberty, Grand Rapids, MI (p. 129)
Knud Haakonssen, Boston University, Boston, MA (p. 131)
Jerome J. Hanus, American University, Washington, DC (p. 134)
Edward J. Harpham, University of Texas, Dallas, Richardson, TX (p. 135)
*Donna H. Hearne, Constitutional Coalition, St. Louis, MO (p. 138)
Eugene Heath, State University of New York, New Platz, New Paltz, NY (p. 138)
Peter J. Hill, Wheaton College, Wheaton, IL (p. 142)
Edward L. Hudgins, The Objectivist Center, Washington, DC (p. 148)
Deal Hudson, *Crisis Magazine*, Washington, DC (p. 148)
James D. Hunter, University of Virginia, Charlottesville, VA (p. 149)
William B. Irvine, III, Wright State University, Dayton, OH (p. 152)
Earl W. Jackson, Sr., Samaritan Project, Chesapeake, VA (p. 152)
*Charles W. Jarvis, United Seniors Association, Fairfax, VA (p. 153)
*Marianne Jennings, Arizona State University, Tempe, AZ (p. 154)
Leon R. Kass, American Enterprise Institute, Washington, DC (p. 158)
John Kekes, Charlton, NY (p. 160)
*Patrick J. Keleher, Jr., TEACH America, Wilmette, IL (p. 160)
David Kelley, The Objectivist Center, Poughkeepsie, NY (p. 160)
*Charles R. Kesler, Henry Salvatori Center, Claremont, CA (p. 162)
John F. Kilner, The Center for Bioethics and Human Dignity, Bannockburn, IL (p. 163)
Larry Klayman, Judicial Watch, Washington, DC (p. 165)
*Robert H. Knight, Concerned Women for America, Washington, DC (p. 166)
Joseph M. Knippenberg, Oglethorpe University, Atlanta, GA (p. 166)
*Robert C. Koons, University of Texas, Austin, TX (p. 167)
*Michael Krauss, George Mason University School of Law, Arlington, VA (p. 169)
*Deepak Lal, University of California at Los Angeles, Los Angeles, CA (p. 172)
*Richard D. Land, Ethics and Religious Liberty Commission, Nashville, TN (p. 173)
*George Landrith, Frontiers of Freedom Institute, Fairfax, VA (p. 173)
*Andrew Langer, National Federation of Independent Business, Washington, DC (p. 174)
Daniel Lapin, Toward Tradition, Mercer Island, WA (p. 174)
*Edward J. Larson, University of Georgia School of Law, Athens, GA (p. 175)
Peter Augustine Lawler, Berry College, Mount Berry, GA (p. 175)
*John Lenczowski, Institute of World Politics, Washington, DC (p. 177)
Kurt R. Leube, Hoover Institution, Stanford, CA (p. 178)
*Mark R. Levin, Landmark Legal Foundation, Herndon, VA (p. 178)
Jacob T. Levy, University of Chicago, Chicago, IL (p. 179)
Art Lindsley, C. S. Lewis Institute, Annandale, VA (p. 181)
Loren E. Lomasky, Bowling Green State University, Bowling Green, OH (p. 182)
*Johnathon R. Macey, Cornell University, Ithaca, NY (p. 185)
Tibor R. Machan, Chapman University, Silverado Canyon, CA (p. 185)
Eric Mack, Tulane University, New Orleans, LA (p. 185)
Harvey C. Mansfield, Harvard University, Cambridge, MA (p. 189)
*Jerry L. Martin, American Council of Trustees and Alumni, Washington, DC (p. 190)
*Ken Masugi, Claremont Institute, Claremont, CA (p. 191)
Anthony M. Matteo, Elizabethtown College, Elizabethtown, PA (p. 191)
Merrill Matthews, Jr., Institute for Policy Innovation, Lewisville, TX (p. 192)
Kris Alan Mauren, Acton Institute for the Study of Religion and Liberty,
   Grand Rapids, MI (p. 192)
Paul Maurer, Trinity International University, Deerfield, IL (p. 192)
*Robert W. McGee, Barry University, Miami Shores, FL (p. 195)
*Michael J. McManus, Marriage Savers, Potomac, MD (p. 197)

ETHICS (Continued)

*Roger Michener, Placitas, NM (p. 201)
 Fred D. Miller, Jr., Bowling Green State University, Bowling Green, OH (p. 201)
 Tom Minnery, Focus on the Family, Colorado Springs, CO (p. 203)
*C. Ben Mitchell, Trinity International University, Deerfield, IL (p. 203)
 R. Albert Mohler, Jr., The Southern Baptist Theological Seminary, Louisville, KY (p. 204)
 Fariborz L. Mokhtari, National Defense University, Washington, DC (p. 204)
 Jennifer Roback Morse, Hoover Institution, Vista, CA (p. 207)
*Laurence S. Moss, Babson College, Babson Park, MA (p. 208)
 Ronald Nash, Reformed Theological Seminary, Oviedo, FL (p. 211)
*Anne D. Neal, American Council of Trustees and Alumni, Washington, DC (p. 211)
 Jeff Nelson, Intercollegiate Studies Institute, Wilmington, DE (p. 212)
 Richard Alan Nelson, Louisiana State University, Baton Rouge, LA (p. 212)
*Richard John Neuhaus, Institute on Religion and Public Life, New York, NY (p. 213)
 Michael J. Novak, Jr., American Enterprise Institute, Washington, DC (p. 215)
 Edward J. Ohlert, JAYCOR, McLean, VA (p. 218)
*Richard Olivastro, People Dynamics, Farmington, CT (p. 218)
*Jim Panyard, Pennsylvania Manufacturer's Association, Harrisburg, PA (p. 221)
 Rocco M. Paone, U. S. Naval Academy, Annapolis, MD (p. 221)
*Allan E. Parker, Jr., Texas Justice Foundation, San Antonio, TX (p. 221)
*Judd W. Patton, Bellevue University, Bellevue, NE (p. 223)
 Terence J. Pell, Center for Individual Rights, Washington, DC (p. 224)
*Roger Pilon, Cato Institute, Washington, DC (p. 228)
*Daniel J. Popeo, Washington Legal Foundation, Washington, DC (p. 231)
 Dennis Prager, The Prager Perspective, Van Nuys, CA (p. 232)
 Terry L. Price, University of Richmond, Richmond, VA (p. 233)
 Robert J. Rafalko, University of New Haven, West Haven, CT (p. 235)
 Douglas B. Rasmussen, St. John's University, Jamaica, NY (p. 236)
 Harold Calvin Ray, National Center for Faith-Based Initiatives, West Palm Beach, FL (p. 237)
*William H. Reid, Horseshoe, TX (p. 238)
 Sandy Rios, Concerned Women for America, Washington, DC (p. 240)
 David C. Rose, University of Missouri, St. Louis, St. Louis, MO (p. 243)
*Timothy P. Roth, University of Texas, El Paso, El Paso, TX (p. 244)
*Ronald D. Rotunda, George Mason University School of Law, Arlington, VA (p. 244)
 Robert Royal, Faith & Reason Institute, Washington, DC (p. 245)
 Shannon Royce, Ethics and Religious Liberty Commission, Washington, DC (p. 245)
*Alfred P. Rubin, Tufts University, Medford, MA (p. 246)
 Charles Rubin, Duquesne University, Pittsburgh, PA (p. 246)
 Robert E. Russell, Jr., The Heritage Foundation, Geneva, IL (p. 247)
 Claes G. Ryn, Catholic University of America, Washington, DC (p. 248)
 Gregory W. Sand, Saint Louis College of Pharmacy, St. Louis, MO (p. 249)
 John T. Sanders, Rochester Institute of Technology, Rochester, NY (p. 249)
 William L. Saunders, Family Research Council, Washington, DC (p. 250)
 David L. Schaefer, Holy Cross College, Worcester, MA (p. 252)
*D. Eric Schansberg, Indiana University Southeast, New Albany, IN (p. 252)
*Arthur J. Schwartz, John Templeton Foundation, Radnor, PA (p. 254)
*Pete Sepp, National Taxpayers Union, Alexandria, VA (p. 257)
*Colleen Sheehan, Villanova University, Villanova, PA (p. 258)
*Lou Sheldon, Traditional Values Coalition, Washington, DC (p. 258)
*James Skillen, Center for Public Justice, Annapolis, MD (p. 261)
 Aeon James Skoble, Bridgewater State College, Bridgewater, MA (p. 262)
*Curt Smith, Indiana Family Institute, Indianapolis, IN (p. 263)
*Neil H. Snyder, University of Virginia, Charlottesville, VA (p. 265)
 Christina Hoff Sommers, American Enterprise Institute, Washington, DC (p. 266)
 Glenn T. Stanton, Focus on the Family, Colorado Springs, CO (p. 268)

---

* Has testified before a state or federal legislative committee

ETHICS (Continued)

*Richard Stith, Valpariso University School of Law, Valpariso, IN (p. 269)
*Christine Stolba, Ethics and Public Policy Center, Washington, DC (p. 269)
*David Strom, Taxpayers League of Minnesota, Plymouth, MN (p. 270)
David G. Surdam, University of Chicago, Chicago, IL (p. 272)
Robert Sutherland, Cornell College, Mount Vernon, IA (p. 272)
*Mark Thornton, Columbus State University, Columbus, GA (p. 278)
*Ron Trowbridge, Maine Policy Center, Durham, ME (p. 281)
Scott J. Vitell, University of Mississippi, University, MS (p. 285)
*Richard E. Wagner, George Mason University, Fairfax, VA (p. 286)
*Lee H. Walker, New Coalition for Economic and Social Change, Chicago, IL (p. 287)
Bradley C. S. Watson, Saint Vincent College, Latrobe, PA (p. 290)
*Donald V. Weatherman, Erskine College, Due West, SC (p. 290)
*George Weigel, Ethics and Public Policy Center, Washington, DC (p. 291)
Christopher Heath Wellman, Georgia State University, Atlanta, GA (p. 292)
*Paul Weyrich, Free Congress Foundation, Washington, DC (p. 293)
James Biser Whisker, West Virginia University, Morgantown, WV (p. 293)
James Q. Wilson, Pepperdine University, Malibu, CA (p. 296)
*Christopher Wolfe, Marquette University, Milwaukee, WI (p. 297)
Anne Wortham, Illinois State University, Normal, IL (p. 298)
Edward W. Younkins, Wheeling Jesuit University, Wheeling, WV (p. 301)
Michael Zuckert, University of Notre Dame, Notre Dame, IN (p. 302)

POLITICAL PHILOSOPHY

*John Agresto, John Agresto and Associates, Santa Fe, NM (p. 35)
*William Allen, Michigan State University, East Lansing, MI (p. 37)
Robert V. Andelson, American Institute for Economic Research, Auburn, AL (p. 37)
Brian C. Anderson, Manhattan Institute for Policy Research, New York, NY (p. 38)
Frank Annunziata, Rochester Institute of Technology, Rochester, NY (p. 39)
*Dominic A. Aquila, Ave Maria University, Ypsilanti, MI (p. 40)
Hadley Arkes, Amherst College, Amherst, MA (p. 40)
N. Scott Arnold, University of Alabama, Birmingham, Birmingham, AL (p. 40)
*Sonia Arrison, Pacific Research Institute, San Francisco, CA (p. 41)
Nigel Ashford, Institute for Humane Studies at George Mason University, Arlington, VA (p. 41)
Barry Asmus, National Center for Policy Analysis, Scottsdale, AZ (p. 41)
Richard A. Baer, Jr., Cornell University, Ithaca, NY (p. 42)
Joseph Baldacchino, National Humanities Institute, Bowie, MD (p. 44)
David S. Ball, North Carolina State University, Raleigh, NC (p. 44)
Michael B. Barkey, Center for the Study of Compassionate Conservatism, Grand Rapids, MI (p. 46)
*Randy Barnett, Boston University School of Law, Boston, MA (p. 46)
Sammy Basu, Willamette University, Salem, OR (p. 47)
Eric A. Belgrad, Towson State University, Towson, MD (p. 49)
Walter Berns, American Enterprise Institute, Washington, DC (p. 51)
*Jason Bertsch, American Enterprise Institute, Washington, DC (p. 52)
*Dick Bishirjian, YorktownUniversity.com, Norfolk, VA (p. 53)
*Wayman R. Bishop, The Family Foundation of Virginia, Richmond, VA (p. 53)
*Mark Blitz, Claremont McKenna College, Claremont, CA (p. 55)
*Mark A. Bloomfield, American Council for Capital Formation, Washington, DC (p. 55)
*David Boaz, Cato Institute, Washington, DC (p. 55)
David J. Bobb, Hillsdale College, Hillsdale, MI (p. 56)
Peter J. Boettke, James M. Buchanan Center for Political Economy, Fairfax, VA (p. 56)
Samuel Bostaph, University of Dallas, Irving, TX (p. 57)

POLITICAL PHILOSOPHY (Continued)

Anthony Bradley, Acton Institute for the Study of Religion and Liberty, Grand Rapids, MI (p. 59)

Gordon L. Brady, Center for the Study of Public Choice, Fairfax, VA (p. 60)

*Matthew J. Brouillette, The Commonwealth Foundation, Harrisburg, PA (p. 62)

*Harold O. J. Brown, Reformed Theological Seminary, Charlotte, NC (p. 63)

*Allen Buchanan, University of Arizona, Tucson, AZ (p. 64)

James M. Buchanan, Center for the Study of Public Choice, Fairfax, VA (p. 64)

Francis H. Buckley, George Mason University School of Law, Arlington, VA (p. 64)

Gary Bullert, Columbia Basin College, Pasco, WA (p. 65)

T. Patrick Burke, St. Joseph's University, Wynnewood, PA (p. 65)

*H. Sterling Burnett, National Center for Policy Analysis, Dallas, TX (p. 65)

*David Burton, Argus Group, Alexandria, VA (p. 66)

Andrew E. Busch, University of Denver, Denver, CO (p. 66)

Charles E. Butterworth, University of Maryland, College Park, MD (p. 67)

Jameson Campaigne, Jr., Jameson Books, Inc., Ottawa, IL (p. 68)

William F. Campbell, The Philadelphia Society, Baton Rouge, LA (p. 68)

Nicholas Capaldi, Loyola University New Orleans, New Orleans, LA (p. 69)

*Robert Carleson, American Civil Rights Union, Alexandria, VA (p. 70)

*Samuel Casey Carter, Acade Metrics, LLC, Washington, DC (p. 71)

Harry M. Clor, Kenyon College, Gambier, OH (p. 76)

Angelo M. Codevilla, Boston University, Boston, MA (p. 77)

Andrew I. Cohen, University of Oklahoma, Norman, OK (p. 77)

Eric Cohen, Ethics and Public Policy Center, Washington, DC (p. 78)

Brooks Colburn, Foundation for Economic Education, Irvington-on-Hudson, NY (p. 78)

Lee Congdon, James Madison University, Harrisonburg, VA (p. 79)

Kellyanne Conway, the polling company/WomanTrend, Washington, DC (p. 80)

*John E. Coons, University of California at Berkeley, Berkeley, CA (p. 81)

*Jon Coupal, Howard Jarvis Taxpayers Association, Sacramento, CA (p. 83)

Dennis Coyle, Catholic University of America, Washington, DC (p. 84)

Mickey Craig, Hillsdale College, Hillsdale, MI (p. 85)

Aurelian Craiutu, Indiana University, Bloomington, IN (p. 85)

Edward H. Crane, Cato Institute, Washington, DC (p. 85)

Alan R. Crippen, II, Family Research Council, Washington, DC (p. 86)

Melvin Croan, University of Wisconsin, Madison, WI (p. 86)

John W. Danford, Loyola University Chicago, Chicago, IL (p. 88)

Werner J. Dannhauser, Michigan State University, East Lansing, MI (p. 88)

Leo Paul S. de Alvarez, University of Dallas, Irving, TX (p. 89)

Damjan de Krnjevic-Miskovic, The National Interest, Washington, DC (p. 90)

*Len Deo, New Jersey Family Policy Council, Parsippany, NJ (p. 93)

*Donald J. Devine, Center for American Values, Shady Side, MD (p. 94)

Arthur M. Diamond, Jr., University of Nebraska, Omaha, Omaha, NE (p. 95)

Richard J. Dougherty, University of Dallas, Irving, TX (p. 97)

*Clark Durant, New Common School Foundation, Detroit, MI (p. 101)

Steven D. Ealy, Liberty Fund, Inc., Indianapolis, IN (p. 101)

*John C. Eastman, Chapman University School of Law, Orange, CA (p. 102)

Richard M. Ebeling, Hillsdale College, Hillsdale, MI (p. 102)

*Myron Ebell, Competitive Enterprise Institute, Washington, DC (p. 103)

Robert Eden, Hillsdale College, Hillsdale, MI (p. 103)

*James R. Edwards, Jr., Hudson Institute, Washington, DC (p. 104)

*Mickey Edwards, Harvard University, Cambridge, MA (p. 104)

Barbara Elliott, Center for Renewal, Houston, TX (p. 105)

Glenn Ellmers, Claremont Institute, Claremont, CA (p. 106)

*Jean Bethke Elshtain, University of Chicago, Chicago, IL (p. 106)

Thomas Engeman, Loyola University Chicago, Chicago, IL (p. 107)

---

* Has testified before a state or federal legislative committee

POLITICAL PHILOSOPHY (Continued)

Richard A. Epstein, University of Chicago Law School, Chicago, IL (p. 107)

*Charles H. Fairbanks, Jr., The Paul H. Nitze School of Advanced International Studies, Washington, DC (p. 108)

Christopher Flannery, Azusa Pacific University, Azusa, CA (p. 113)

Fred E. Foldvary, Santa Clara University, Santa Clara, CA (p. 114)

*John Fonte, Hudson Institute, Washington, DC (p. 114)

*David Forte, Cleveland State University, Cleveland, OH (p. 114)

Elizabeth Fox-Genovese, Emory University, Atlanta, GA (p. 115)

Hillel Fradkin, Ethics and Public Policy Center, Washington, DC (p. 115)

*Matthew J. Franck, Radford University, Radford, VA (p. 115)

Jeffrey M. Friedman, *Critical Review*, Princeton, NJ (p. 117)

Francis Fukuyama, The Paul H. Nitze School of Advanced International Studies, Washington, DC (p. 118)

James R. Gaston, Franciscan University of Steubenville, Steubenville, OH (p. 120)

*Robert P. George, Princeton University, Princeton, NJ (p. 122)

Robert A. Goldwin, American Enterprise Institute, Washington, DC (p. 126)

*Stephen O. Goodrick, National Right to Work Committee, Springfield, VA (p. 126)

Doris Gordon, Libertarians for Life, Wheaton, MD (p. 126)

Paul Gottfried, Elizabethtown College, Elizabethtown, PA (p. 127)

Gidon A. Gottlieb, University of Chicago Law School, Chicago, IL (p. 127)

Samuel Gregg, Acton Institute for the Study of Religion and Liberty, Grand Rapids, MI (p. 129)

Steven E. Grosby, Clemson University, Clemson, SC (p. 129)

Alexander J. Groth, University of California, Davis, Davis, CA (p. 130)

*Paul Guppy, Washington Policy Center, Seattle, WA (p. 131)

Knud Haakonssen, Boston University, Boston, MA (p. 131)

Daniel B. Hales, Americans for Effective Law Enforcement, Chicago, IL (p. 132)

Ralph C. Hancock, Brigham Young University, Provo, UT (p. 133)

Jerome J. Hanus, American University, Washington, DC (p. 134)

Edward J. Harpham, University of Texas, Dallas, Richardson, TX (p. 135)

Robert C. Harrison, Defenders of Property Rights, Washington, DC (p. 136)

*C. Lowell Harriss, Columbia University, Bronxville, NY (p. 136)

Robert Hawkins, Jr., Institute for Contemporary Studies, Oakland, CA (p. 137)

William Anthony Hay, Foreign Policy Research Institute, Philadelphia, PA (p. 138)

*Steven Hayward, American Enterprise Institute, Washington, DC (p. 138)

*Donna H. Hearne, Constitutional Coalition, St. Louis, MO (p. 138)

Eugene Heath, State University of New York, New Platz, New Paltz, NY (p. 138)

Robert A. Heineman, Alfred University, Alfred, NY (p. 139)

*John Hillen, Foreign Policy Research Institute, Philadephia, PA (p. 142)

Scott Hogenson, *CNSNews.com*, Alexandria, VA (p. 144)

Candice Hoke, Cleveland State University, Cleveland, OH (p. 144)

David Horowitz, Center for the Study of Popular Culture, Los Angeles, CA (p. 146)

Edward L. Hudgins, The Objectivist Center, Washington, DC (p. 148)

John C. Hulsman, The Heritage Foundation, Washington, DC (p. 149)

Thomas Hyde, Pfeiffer University, Misenheimer, NC (p. 150)

*Fred C. Ikle, Center for Strategic and International Studies, Washington, DC (p. 151)

William B. Irvine, III, Wright State University, Dayton, OH (p. 152)

Harry V. Jaffa, Claremont Institute, Claremont, CA (p. 153)

Douglas A. Jeffrey, Hillsdale College, Hillsdale, MI (p. 154)

Leon R. Kass, American Enterprise Institute, Washington, DC (p. 158)

*David A. Keene, American Conservative Union, Washington, DC (p. 160)

John Kekes, Charlton, NY (p. 160)

David Kelley, The Objectivist Center, Poughkeepsie, NY (p. 160)

*W. Thomas Kelly, Savers and Investors League, Mirror Lake, NH (p. 161)

*Charles R. Kesler, Henry Salvatori Center, Claremont, CA (p. 162)

POLITICAL PHILOSOPHY (Continued)

Jeane J. Kirkpatrick, American Enterprise Institute, Washington, DC (p. 164)
*Robert H. Knight, Concerned Women for America, Washington, DC (p. 166)
Joseph M. Knippenberg, Oglethorpe University, Atlanta, GA (p. 166)
*Robert C. Koons, University of Texas, Austin, TX (p. 167)
Thomas L. Krannawitter, Claremont Institute, Claremont, CA (p. 168)
Stephen Krason, Franciscan University of Steubenville, Steubenville, OH (p. 169)
William Kristol, *The Weekly Standard*, Washington, DC (p. 169)
Melvin A. Kulbicki, York College of Pennsylvania, York, PA (p. 170)
John Kurzweil, California Public Policy Foundation, Camarillo, CA (p. 171)
Arthur B. Laffer, A. B. Laffer Associates, San Diego, CA (p. 172)
*Deepak Lal, University of California at Los Angeles, Los Angeles, CA (p. 172)
Byron S. Lamm, State Policy Network, Fort Wayne, IN (p. 173)
*George Landrith, Frontiers of Freedom Institute, Fairfax, VA (p. 173)
*Andrew Langer, National Federation of Independent Business, Washington, DC (p. 174)
*Richard Langlois, University of Connecticut, Storrs, CT (p. 174)
Peter Augustine Lawler, Berry College, Mount Berry, GA (p. 175)
Phillip F. Lawler, *Catholic World Report*, South Lancaster, MA (p. 176)
Richard Lessner, American Renewal, Washington, DC (p. 178)
Kurt R. Leube, Hoover Institution, Stanford, CA (p. 178)
*Mark R. Levin, Landmark Legal Foundation, Herndon, VA (p. 178)
Jacob T. Levy, University of Chicago, Chicago, IL (p. 179)
Marlo Lewis, Competitive Enterprise Institute, Washington, DC (p. 179)
Leonard P. Liggio, Atlas Economic Research Foundation, Fairfax, VA (p. 180)
*Robert J. Loewenberg, Institute for Advanced Strategic and Political Studies,
    Washington, DC (p. 182)
Loren E. Lomasky, Bowling Green State University, Bowling Green, OH (p. 182)
Herbert L. London, Hudson Institute, Indianapolis, IN (p. 182)
*Nelson Lund, George Mason University School of Law, Arlington, VA (p. 184)
Frederick R. Lynch, Claremont McKenna College, Claremont, CA (p. 184)
Tibor R. Machan, Chapman University, Silverado Canyon, CA (p. 185)
Eric Mack, Tulane University, New Orleans, LA (p. 185)
*Dennis Mansfield, Boise, ID (p. 189)
Harvey C. Mansfield, Harvard University, Cambridge, MA (p. 189)
Deryl W. Martin, Tennessee Technological University, Cookeville, TN (p. 190)
*Jerry L. Martin, American Council of Trustees and Alumni, Washington, DC (p. 190)
*Ken Masugi, Claremont Institute, Claremont, CA (p. 191)
Merrill Matthews, Jr., Institute for Policy Innovation, Lewisville, TX (p. 192)
Paul Maurer, Trinity International University, Deerfield, IL (p. 192)
*David N. Mayer, Capital University Law School, Columbus, OH (p. 193)
Wilfred M. McClay, University of Tennessee, Chattanooga, Chattanooga, TN (p. 193)
*Forrest McDonald, University of Alabama, Coker, AL (p. 195)
W. Wesley McDonald, Elizabethtown College, Elizabethtown, PA (p. 195)
*Robert W. McGee, Barry University, Miami Shores, FL (p. 195)
John O. McGinnis, Cardozo School of Law, New York, NY (p. 196)
Richard B. McKenzie, University of California, Irvine, Irvine, CA (p. 196)
*Lawrence Mead, New York University, New York, NY (p. 198)
Ingrid Merikoski, Earhart Foundation, Ann Arbor, MI (p. 199)
Herbert E. Meyer, Real-World Intelligence, Inc., Friday Harbor, WA (p. 200)
Paul E. Michelson, Huntington College, Huntington, IN (p. 201)
*Roger Michener, Placitas, NM (p. 201)
Fred D. Miller, Jr., Bowling Green State University, Bowling Green, OH (p. 201)
Tom Minnery, Focus on the Family, Colorado Springs, CO (p. 203)
*C. Ben Mitchell, Trinity International University, Deerfield, IL (p. 203)
*Robert Moffit, The Heritage Foundation, Washington, DC (p. 204)

POLITICAL PHILOSOPHY (Continued)

Fariborz L. Mokhtari, National Defense University, Washington, DC (p. 204)

Jennifer Roback Morse, Hoover Institution, Vista, CA (p. 207)

*Laurence S. Moss, Babson College, Babson Park, MA (p. 208)

James W. Muller, University of Alaska, Anchorage, AK (p. 208)

Henry Myers, James Madison University, Harrisonburg, VA (p. 210)

George H. Nash, South Hadley, MA (p. 210)

Ronald Nash, Reformed Theological Seminary, Oviedo, FL (p. 211)

Mario Navarro da Costa, American Society for the Defense of Tradition, Family and Property, McLean, VA (p. 211)

*Anne D. Neal, American Council of Trustees and Alumni, Washington, DC (p. 211)

Jeff Nelson, Intercollegiate Studies Institute, Wilmington, DE (p. 212)

*Richard John Neuhaus, Institute on Religion and Public Life, New York, NY (p. 213)

Stuart W. Nolan, Jr., Springfield, VA (p. 214)

Michael J. Novak, Jr., American Enterprise Institute, Washington, DC (p. 215)

*Richard Olivastro, People Dynamics, Farmington, CT (p. 218)

Glenn Oppel, Rocky Mountain Enterprise Institute, Billings, MT (p. 219)

*Mackubin T. Owens, U. S. Naval War College, Newport, RI (p. 220)

Tom G. Palmer, Cato Institute, Washington, DC (p. 221)

Rocco M. Paone, U. S. Naval Academy, Annapolis, MD (p. 221)

*Allan E. Parker, Jr., Texas Justice Foundation, San Antonio, TX (p. 221)

Ellen F. Paul, Bowling Green State University, Bowling Green, OH (p. 223)

Jeffrey E. Paul, Bowling Green State University, Bowling Green, OH (p. 223)

Anthony A. Peacock, Utah State University, Logan, UT (p. 224)

Sidney A. Pearson, Jr., Radford University, Radford, VA (p. 224)

Terence J. Pell, Center for Individual Rights, Washington, DC (p. 224)

Paul C. Peterson, Coastal Carolina University, Conway, SC (p. 227)

*William H. Peterson, Washington, DC (p. 227)

Bruce Piasecki, AHC Group, Saratoga Springs, NY (p. 228)

*Roger Pilon, Cato Institute, Washington, DC (p. 228)

Barry W. Poulson, University of Colorado, Boulder, CO (p. 232)

*Stephen Presser, Northwestern University School of Law, Chicago, IL (p. 233)

Terry L. Price, University of Richmond, Richmond, VA (p. 233)

Robert J. Rafalko, University of New Haven, West Haven, CT (p. 235)

Paul A. Rahe, University of Tulsa, Tulsa, OK (p. 236)

Douglas B. Rasmussen, St. John's University, Jamaica, NY (p. 236)

Harold Calvin Ray, National Center for Faith-Based Initiatives, West Palm Beach, FL (p. 237)

George Reisman, Pepperdine University, Laguna Hills, CA (p. 238)

*James S. Robbins, National Defense University, Washington, DC (p. 241)

John W. Robbins, Trinity Foundation, Unicoi, TN (p. 241)

James C. Roberts, American Studies Center, Washington, DC (p. 242)

John E. Rocha, Sr., Center for the American Idea, Houston, TX (p. 242)

*Timothy P. Roth, University of Texas, El Paso, El Paso, TX (p. 244)

Robert Royal, Faith & Reason Institute, Washington, DC (p. 245)

Charles Rubin, Duquesne University, Pittsburgh, PA (p. 246)

*Paul Rubin, Emory University, Atlanta, GA (p. 246)

*William A. Rusher, Claremont Institute, San Francisco, CA (p. 247)

Peter Rutland, Wesleyan University, Middletown, CT (p. 248)

Claes G. Ryn, Catholic University of America, Washington, DC (p. 248)

*Steven Alan Samson, Liberty University, Lynchburg, VA (p. 249)

Gregory W. Sand, Saint Louis College of Pharmacy, St. Louis, MO (p. 249)

John T. Sanders, Rochester Institute of Technology, Rochester, NY (p. 249)

*Ellis Sandoz, Eric Voegelin Institute, Baton Rouge, LA (p. 249)

*Michael Sanera, Basis Charter High School, Tucson, AZ (p. 249)

Robert A. Schadler, Center for First Principles, Washington, DC (p. 251)

POLITICAL PHILOSOPHY (Continued)

David L. Schaefer, Holy Cross College, Worcester, MA (p. 252)
*D. Eric Schansberg, Indiana University Southeast, New Albany, IN (p. 252)
Diana J. Schaub, Loyola College, Baltimore, MD (p. 252)
*Peter W. Schramm, John M. Ashbrook Center for Public Affairs, Ashland, OH (p. 254)
Robert Schuettinger, Washington International Studies Council, Washington, DC (p. 254)
Larry J. Sechrest, Sul Ross State University, Alpine, TX (p. 255)
Jeffrey Leigh Sedgwick, University of Massachusetts, Amherst, MA (p. 255)
Timothy Samuel Shah, Ethics and Public Policy Center, Washington, DC (p. 257)
Barry Alan Shain, Colgate University, Hamilton, NY (p. 257)
*Colleen Sheehan, Villanova University, Villanova, PA (p. 258)
*Lou Sheldon, Traditional Values Coalition, Washington, DC (p. 258)
Richard Sherlock, Utah State University, Logan, UT (p. 259)
*Robert A. Sirico, Acton Institute for the Study of Religion and Liberty, Grand Rapids, MI (p. 261)
*James Skillen, Center for Public Justice, Annapolis, MD (p. 261)
Aeon James Skoble, Bridgewater State College, Bridgewater, MA (p. 262)
*Curt Smith, Indiana Family Institute, Indianapolis, IN (p. 263)
T. Alexander Smith, University of Tennessee, Knoxville, Knoxville, TN (p. 264)
*John Michael Snyder, Citizens Committee for the Right to Keep and Bear Arms, Washington, DC (p. 265)
*Matthew Spalding, The Heritage Foundation, Washington, DC (p. 266)
Glenn T. Stanton, Focus on the Family, Colorado Springs, CO (p. 268)
*James Stergios, Pioneer Institute for Public Policy Research, Boston, MA (p. 268)
James R. Stoner, Louisiana State University, Baton Rouge, LA (p. 270)
*David Strom, Taxpayers League of Minnesota, Plymouth, MN (p. 270)
*John D. Sullivan, Center for International Private Enterprise, Washington, DC (p. 271)
Gordon Sumner, Jr., Sumner Association, Santa Fe, NM (p. 272)
Robert Sutherland, Cornell College, Mount Vernon, IA (p. 272)
Miklos N. Szilagyi, University of Arizona, Tucson, AZ (p. 273)
*Richard Teske, Strategic Advocacy, Arlington, VA (p. 275)
J. Mills Thornton, III, University of Michigan, Ann Arbor, MI (p. 278)
*Mark Thornton, Columbus State University, Columbus, GA (p. 278)
Vladislav Todorov, University of Pennsylvania, Philadelphia, PA (p. 279)
Brian S. Tracy, Brian Tracy International, Solana Beach, CA (p. 280)
*Lewis Uhler, National Tax Limitation Committee, Roseville, CA (p. 283)
Karen I. Vaughn, George Mason University, Fairfax, VA (p. 284)
*T. Rogers Wade, Georgia Public Policy Foundation, Atlanta, GA (p. 286)
*Richard L. Walker, University of South Carolina, Columbia, SC (p. 287)
*Jeffrey D. Wallin, American Academy for Liberal Education, Washington, DC (p. 287)
*Malcolm Wallop, Frontiers of Freedom Institute, Fairfax, VA (p. 288)
*Dane Waters, Initiative and Referendum Institute, Leesburg, VA (p. 289)
Bradley C. S. Watson, Saint Vincent College, Latrobe, PA (p. 290)
*Donald V. Weatherman, Erskine College, Due West, SC (p. 290)
*George Weigel, Ethics and Public Policy Center, Washington, DC (p. 291)
*Kenneth Weinstein, Hudson Institute, Washington, DC (p. 292)
Christopher Heath Wellman, Georgia State University, Atlanta, GA (p. 292)
Thomas G. West, University of Dallas, Irving, TX (p. 293)
*Paul Weyrich, Free Congress Foundation, Washington, DC (p. 293)
James Biser Whisker, West Virginia University, Morgantown, WV (p. 293)
Alvin Williams, Black America's PAC, Washington, DC (p. 294)
Bradford P. Wilson, National Association of Scholars, Princeton, NJ (p. 296)
Clyde N. Wilson, University of South Carolina, Columbia, SC (p. 296)
*Christopher Wolfe, Marquette University, Milwaukee, WI (p. 297)
*Gary Wolfram, Hillsdale College, Hillsdale, MI (p. 297)

---

* Has testified before a state or federal legislative committee

POLITICAL PHILOSOPHY (Continued)

THE REAGAN LEGACY

THE REAGAN LEGACY (Continued)

*Murray Friedman, American Jewish Committee, Philadelphia, PA (p. 117)
*Charlie Gerow, Quantum Communications, Harrisburg, PA (p. 123)
*Tom Giovanetti, Institute for Policy Innovation, Lewisville, TX (p. 124)
 Steve H. Hanke, Johns Hopkins University, Baltimore, MD (p. 134)
 Robert Hawkins, Jr., Institute for Contemporary Studies, Oakland, CA (p. 137)
*Steven Hayward, American Enterprise Institute, Washington, DC (p. 138)
 Robert Stanley Herren, North Dakota State University, Fargo, ND (p. 140)
*John Hillen, Foreign Policy Research Institute, Philadephia, PA (p. 142)
*Michael Horowitz, Hudson Institute, Washington, DC (p. 146)
*Robert Hunter, Mackinac Center for Public Policy, Midland, MI (p. 150)
 Niger Roy Innis, Congress of Racial Equality, New York, NY (p. 151)
*Charles W. Jarvis, United Seniors Association, Fairfax, VA (p. 153)
*David A. Keene, American Conservative Union, Washington, DC (p. 160)
*W. Thomas Kelly, Savers and Investors League, Mirror Lake, NH (p. 161)
 Paul Kengor, Grove City College, Grove City, PA (p. 161)
 Karen Kerrigan, the polling company, Washington, DC (p. 162)
*Charles R. Kesler, Henry Salvatori Center, Claremont, CA (p. 162)
*William A. Keyes, The Institute on Political Journalism, Washington, DC (p. 162)
 Jeane J. Kirkpatrick, American Enterprise Institute, Washington, DC (p. 164)
*Douglas W. Kmiec, The Catholic University of America, Washington, DC (p. 166)
*Patrick Korten, The Becket Fund for Religious Liberty, Washington, DC (p. 167)
*Lawrence Kudlow, Kudlow & Co., LLC, New York, NY (p. 170)
 Melvin A. Kulbicki, York College of Pennsylvania, York, PA (p. 170)
 Arthur B. Laffer, A. B. Laffer Associates, San Diego, CA (p. 172)
*John Lenczowski, Institute of World Politics, Washington, DC (p. 177)
*Mark R. Levin, Landmark Legal Foundation, Herndon, VA (p. 178)
*John McClaughry, Ethan Allen Institute, Concord, VT (p. 193)
 Wendell H. McCulloch, Jr., California State University, Long Beach, Long Beach, CA (p. 194)
 John O. McGinnis, Cardozo School of Law, New York, NY (p. 196)
*Edwin Meese III, The Heritage Foundation, Washington, DC (p. 198)
*Constantine C. Menges, Hudson Institute, Washington, DC (p. 199)
*Roger Michener, Placitas, NM (p. 201)
*Dan Mitchell, The Heritage Foundation, Washington, DC (p. 203)
*Robert Moffit, The Heritage Foundation, Washington, DC (p. 204)
*Joseph A. Morris, Lincoln Legal Foundation, Chicago, IL (p. 207)
*Deroy Murdock, Atlas Economic Research Foundation, New York, NY (p. 209)
 Ronald Nash, Reformed Theological Seminary, Oviedo, FL (p. 211)
*Anne D. Neal, American Council of Trustees and Alumni, Washington, DC (p. 211)
 Jeff Nelson, Intercollegiate Studies Institute, Wilmington, DE (p. 212)
*William A. Niskanen, Cato Institute, Washington, DC (p. 214)
*Grover Norquist, Americans for Tax Reform, Washington, DC (p. 214)
*Herbert R. Northrup, University of Pennsylvania, Haverford, PA (p. 215)
 James Nuechterlein, *First Things*, New York, NY (p. 216)
*Richard Olivastro, People Dynamics, Farmington, CT (p. 218)
 B. Nelson Ong, College of New Rochelle, New Rochelle, NY (p. 219)
*J. A. Parker, Lincoln Institute for Research and Education, Washington, DC (p. 221)
*Ronald W. Pearson, Pearson & Pipkin, Inc., Washington, DC (p. 224)
*Svetozar Pejovich, Texas A&M University, Dallas, TX (p. 224)
 Paul C. Peterson, Coastal Carolina University, Conway, SC (p. 227)
*William H. Peterson, Washington, DC (p. 227)
*James Phillips, The Heritage Foundation, Washington, DC (p. 228)
 James Piereson, John M. Olin Foundation, Inc., New York, NY (p. 228)
 John J. Pitney, Jr., Claremont McKenna College, Claremont, CA (p. 229)
 Barry W. Poulson, University of Colorado, Boulder, CO (p. 232)

THE REAGAN LEGACY (Continued)

Richard W. Rahn, NOVECON, Alexandria, VA (p. 236)

*James S. Robbins, National Defense University, Washington, DC (p. 241)

James C. Roberts, American Studies Center, Washington, DC (p. 242)

*Paul Craig Roberts, Institute for Political Economy, Panama City Beach, FL (p. 242)

Ron Robinson, Young America's Foundation, Herndon, VA (p. 242)

*Charles F. Rule, Fried, Frank, Harris, Shriver & Jacobson, Washington, DC (p. 246)

*William A. Rusher, Claremont Institute, San Francisco, CA (p. 247)

E. S. Savas, City University of New York, New York, NY (p. 250)

*Terrence M. Scanlon, Capital Research Center, Washington, DC (p. 251)

Robert A. Schadler, Center for First Principles, Washington, DC (p. 251)

*Peter W. Schramm, John M. Ashbrook Center for Public Affairs, Ashland, OH (p. 254)

Robert Schuettinger, Washington International Studies Council, Washington, DC (p. 254)

Larry Schweikart, University of Dayton, Dayton, OH (p. 255)

Jeffrey Leigh Sedgwick, University of Massachusetts, Amherst, MA (p. 255)

*Donald J. Senese, 60 Plus Association, Arlington, VA (p. 257)

*Matthew Spalding, The Heritage Foundation, Washington, DC (p. 266)

*David Strom, Taxpayers League of Minnesota, Plymouth, MN (p. 270)

Charles Stuart, University of California, Santa Barbara, Santa Barbara, CA (p. 271)

*Lewis Uhler, National Tax Limitation Committee, Roseville, CA (p. 283)

*Richard L. Walker, University of South Carolina, Columbia, SC (p. 287)

*Malcolm Wallop, Frontiers of Freedom Institute, Fairfax, VA (p. 288)

Bradley C. S. Watson, Saint Vincent College, Latrobe, PA (p. 290)

*Murray Weidenbaum, Weidenbaum Center, St. Louis, MO (p. 291)

*Paul Weyrich, Free Congress Foundation, Washington, DC (p. 293)

Thomas L. Wyrick, Southwest Missouri State University, Springfield, MO (p. 300)

*Charmaine Crouse Yoest, University of Virginia, Charlottesville, VA (p. 300)

Ronald A. Zumbrun, The Zumbrun Law Firm, Sacramento, CA (p. 303)

Education

BILINGUAL EDUCATION

Anton Andereggen, Lewis and Clark College, Portland, OR (p. 37)
*Lewis Andrews, Yankee Institute for Public Policy Studies, Hartford, CT (p. 39)
*William J. Bennett, Empower America, Washington, DC (p. 51)
*Sharon Browne, Pacific Legal Foundation, Sacramento, CA (p. 63)
Merrick Carey, Lexington Institute, Arlington, VA (p. 70)
Pradyumna S. Chauhan, Arcadia University, Glenside, PA (p. 73)
*Linda Chavez, Center for Equal Opportunity, Sterling, VA (p. 73)
*Roger Clegg, Center for Equal Opportunity, Sterling, VA (p. 76)
John Cobin, Montauk Financial Group, Greenville, SC (p. 76)
*John E. Coons, University of California at Berkeley, Berkeley, CA (p. 81)
Robert G. de Posada, The Latino Coalition, Washington, DC (p. 90)
Candace de Russy, State University of New York, Bronxville, NY (p. 90)
Peter J. Duignan, Hoover Institution, Stanford, CA (p. 99)
*Williamson M. Evers, Hoover Institution, Stanford, CA (p. 108)
Megan Farnsworth, The Heritage Foundation, Washington, DC (p. 109)
John Findley, Pacific Legal Foundation, Sacramento, CA (p. 111)
David Gersten, Center for Equal Opportunity, Sterling, VA (p. 123)
*Charles L. Glenn, Boston University, Boston, MA (p. 124)
Eric Hanushek, Hoover Institution, Stanford, CA (p. 135)
*Lynn Harsh, Evergreen Freedom Foundation, Olympia, WA (p. 136)
*Caroline M. Hoxby, Harvard University, Cambridge, MA (p. 147)
Niger Roy Innis, Congress of Racial Equality, New York, NY (p. 151)
*Krista Kafer, The Heritage Foundation, Washington, DC (p. 156)
*John Kain, University of Texas, Dallas, Richardson, TX (p. 157)
*Lisa Graham Keegan, Education Leaders Council, Washington, DC (p. 160)
Kent King, Missouri State Teachers Association, Columbia, MO (p. 164)
*Heather MacDonald, Manhattan Institute for Policy Research, New York, NY (p. 185)
*Rita P. Maguire, Arizona Center for Public Policy, Phoenix, AZ (p. 186)
Lawrence J. McQuillan, Pacific Research Institute, San Francisco, CA (p. 197)
Terry M. Moe, Hoover Institution, Stanford, CA (p. 204)
Mauro E. Mujica, U. S. English, Inc., Washington, DC (p. 208)
*Sally C. Pipes, Pacific Research Institute, San Francisco, CA (p. 229)
*Rosalie Porter, READ Institute, Sterling, VA (p. 231)
*Susan Sarnoff, Ohio University, Athens, OH (p. 250)
*Phyllis Schlafly, Eagle Forum, St. Louis, MO (p. 253)
*Peter Skerry, Claremont McKenna College, Claremont, CA (p. 261)
*Lisa Snell, Reason Foundation, Los Angeles, CA (p. 265)
*Don Soifer, Lexington Institute, Arlington, VA (p. 265)
Kevin Teasley, Greater Educational Opportunities Foundation, Indianapolis, IN (p. 275)
*Stephan Thernstrom, Lexington, MA (p. 276)
*George Tryfiates, Concerned Women for America, Washington, DC (p. 281)
Reed Ueda, Tufts University, Medford, MA (p. 282)
*Balint Vazsonyi, Center for the American Founding, McLean, VA (p. 284)
*Herbert J. Walberg, University of Illinois, Chicago, Chicago, IL (p. 286)
*Rolf A. Weil, Roosevelt University, Chicago, IL (p. 291)

BUSINESS AND EDUCATION PARTNERSHIPS

Jeanne Allen, Center for Education Reform, Washington, DC (p. 36)
*Lewis Andrews, Yankee Institute for Public Policy Studies, Hartford, CT (p. 39)
Craig E. Aronoff, Kennesaw State College, Kennesaw, GA (p. 41)
*Keith G. Baker, Florida TaxWatch Research Institute, Inc., Tallahassee, FL (p. 43)
*Janet Beales, Kids One, East Brunswick, NJ (p. 48)

BUSINESS AND EDUCATION PARTNERSHIPS (Continued)

*William J. Bennett, Empower America, Washington, DC (p. 51)
*Jason Bertsch, American Enterprise Institute, Washington, DC (p. 52)
*Fran Bevan, Eagle Forum of Pennsylvania, North Huntingdon, PA (p. 53)
 Philip L. Brach, Midtown Educational Foundation, Chicago, IL (p. 59)
 David Brennan, White Hat Management, Akron, OH (p. 61)
 Dedrick Briggs, Charter School Resource Center of Tennessee, Memphis, TN (p. 61)
*Kaleem Caire, American Education Reform Council, Bowie, MD (p. 67)
*Samuel Casey Carter, Acade Metrics, LLC, Washington, DC (p. 71)
*John Chubb, Edison Schools, Inc., New York, NY (p. 74)
*Michael A. Ciamarra, Alabama Policy Institute, Birmingham, AL (p. 74)
*John E. Coons, University of California at Berkeley, Berkeley, CA (p. 81)
*Louis J. Cordia, Cordia Companies, Alexandria, VA (p. 82)
 Bob Corkins, Kansas Legislative Education and Research, Inc., Topeka, KS (p. 82)
*Kathleen B. de Bettencourt, Environmental Literacy Council, Washington, DC (p. 89)
 Buffy DeBreaux-Watts, American Board for Certification of Teacher Excellence,
   Washington, DC (p. 91)
 John Dodd, Jesse Helms Center, Wingate, NC (p. 96)
 Marie Dolan, New York State Federation of Catholic School Parents, Flushing, NY (p. 96)
 Denis Doyle, Doyle Associates, Chevy Chase, MD (p. 98)
 Diallo Dphrepaulezz, New York, NY (p. 98)
*Paul Dunn, University of Louisiana, Monroe, Monroe, LA (p. 100)
 Lenore T. Ealy, Emergent Enterprises, Carmel, IN (p. 101)
*Robert C. Enlow, Milton and Rose Friedman Foundation, Indianapolis, IN (p. 107)
*Michael P. Farris, Patrick Henry College, Purcellville, VA (p. 109)
 Richard M. Ferry, Catholic Education Foundation, Los Angeles, CA (p. 111)
*Chester E. Finn, Jr., Thomas B. Fordham Foundation, Washington, DC (p. 112)
*Seymour Fliegel, Center for Educational Innovation – Public Education Association,
   New York, NY (p. 113)
 Elizabeth Fox-Genovese, Emory University, Atlanta, GA (p. 115)
 Janice J. Gabbert, Wright State University, Dayton, OH (p. 119)
*Michael Geer, Pennsylvania Family Institute, Harrisburg, PA (p. 122)
*Mary F. Gifford, Field, Sarvas, King and Coleman, Phoenix, AZ (p. 123)
*Charlene Haar, Education Policy Institute, Washington, DC (p. 131)
*Joshua Hall, Buckeye Institute for Public Policy Solutions, Columbus, OH (p. 132)
 Eric Hanushek, Hoover Institution, Stanford, CA (p. 135)
*Donna H. Hearne, Constitutional Coalition, St. Louis, MO (p. 138)
 Justin Heet, Hudson Institute, Indianapolis, IN (p. 139)
*Thomas Hinton, The Heritage Foundation, Washington, DC (p. 143)
 Robert D. Hisrich, Case Western Reserve University, Cleveland, OH (p. 143)
*Fred Holden, Phoenix Enterprises, Arvada, CO (p. 144)
*John MacDonald Hood, John Locke Foundation, Raleigh, NC (p. 145)
*Thomas D. Hopkins, Rochester Institute of Technology, Rochester, NY (p. 145)
*Caroline M. Hoxby, Harvard University, Cambridge, MA (p. 147)
*Gary Huggins, Education Leaders Action Council, Washington, DC (p. 148)
 Theodore "Sylvester" John, Students In Free Enterprise, Springfield, MO (p. 154)
 Lindalyn Kakadelis, North Carolina Education Alliance, Pineville, NC (p. 157)
*Lisa Graham Keegan, Education Leaders Council, Washington, DC (p. 160)
*Patrick J. Keleher, Jr., TEACH America, Wilmette, IL (p. 160)
 Steven J. Kidder, New York Family Policy Council, Albany, NY (p. 163)
 Kent King, Missouri State Teachers Association, Columbia, MO (p. 164)
 Dorothy Knauer, Protestant Community Centers, Inc., Newark, NJ (p. 166)
 Raymond J. Krizek, Northwestern University, Evanston, IL (p. 169)
*Andrew T. LeFevre, American Legislative Exchange Council, Washington, DC (p. 177)
*Mark R. Levin, Landmark Legal Foundation, Herndon, VA (p. 178)

BUSINESS AND EDUCATION PARTNERSHIPS (Continued)

*Myron Lieberman, Education Policy Institute, Washington, DC (p. 180)
*George Liebmann, Calvert Institute for Policy Research, Baltimore, MD (p. 180)
 Nelson Llumiquinga, Arizona School Choice Trust, Phoenix, AZ (p. 182)
 Bernard T. Lomas, The Heritage Foundation, Chapel Hill, NC (p. 182)
*Bruno V. Manno, The Annie E. Casey Foundation, Baltimore, MD (p. 188)
 Steve Mariotti, National Foundation for Teaching Entrepreneurship, New York, NY (p. 189)
*Jerry L. Martin, American Council of Trustees and Alumni, Washington, DC (p. 190)
 Elizabeth Mische, Partnership for Choice in Education, St. Paul, MN (p. 203)
 Terry M. Moe, Hoover Institution, Stanford, CA (p. 204)
 Cassandra Chrones Moore, Cato Institute, Washington, DC (p. 205)
 Suzanne C. Moore, Delaware Public Policy Institute, Wilmington, DE (p. 206)
 Bruce A. Nasby, Students In Free Enterprise, Springfield, MO (p. 210)
 Anthony I. Negbenebor, Gardner-Webb University, Boiling Springs, NC (p. 212)
*Richard Olivastro, People Dynamics, Farmington, CT (p. 218)
*Lawrence C. Patrick, III, Black Alliance for Educational Options, Washington, DC (p. 222)
*Christine Patterson, Texas Public Policy Foundation, San Antonio, TX (p. 223)
 Bruce Piasecki, AHC Group, Saratoga Springs, NY (p. 228)
 Charles I. Plosser, University of Rochester, Rochester, NY (p. 229)
*Claude Pressnell, Tennessee Independent Colleges and Universities, Nashville, TN (p. 233)
*Ed Rauchut, CEO Omaha, Bellevue, NE (p. 236)
 Harold Calvin Ray, National Center for Faith-Based Initiatives, West Palm Beach, FL (p. 237)
 Holly Robinson, Georgia Public Policy Foundation, Atlanta, GA (p. 242)
*Doug Rogers, Association of Texas Professional Educators, Austin, TX (p. 243)
*Richard O. Rowland, Grassroot Institute of Hawaii, Aiea, HI (p. 245)
*David F. Salisbury, Cato Institute, Washington, DC (p. 248)
 Ernestine L. Sanders, Cornerstone Schools, Detroit, MI (p. 249)
*Bill Schilling, Wyoming Business Alliance / Wyoming Heritage Foundation,
    Casper, WY (p. 253)
*Arthur J. Schwartz, John Templeton Foundation, Radnor, PA (p. 254)
*Oran P. Smith, Palmetto Family Council, Columbia, SC (p. 264)
*Lisa Snell, Reason Foundation, Los Angeles, CA (p. 265)
*Alexander Tabarrok, Mercatus Center at George Mason University, Arlington, VA (p. 273)
 Kevin Teasley, Greater Educational Opportunities Foundation, Indianapolis, IN (p. 275)
 Jay L. Tontz, California State University, Hayward, Hayward, CA (p. 280)
*Herbert J. Walberg, University of Illinois, Chicago, Chicago, IL (p. 286)
*Lee H. Walker, New Coalition for Economic and Social Change, Chicago, IL (p. 287)
 Gary M. Walton, Foundation for Teaching Economics, Davis, CA (p. 288)
*Natalie Williams, Robinson, DiLando and Whitaker, Sacramento, CA (p. 295)
*Chris Yelich, Education Industry Association, Watertown, WI (p. 300)
*Michael K. Young, George Washington University Law School, Washington, DC (p. 300)
 David Zanotti, Ohio Roundtable, Strongsville, OH (p. 301)

CHARTER SCHOOLS

 Jeanne Allen, Center for Education Reform, Washington, DC (p. 36)
*Lewis Andrews, Yankee Institute for Public Policy Studies, Hartford, CT (p. 39)
*Julaine K. Appling, Family Research Institute of Wisconsin, Madison, WI (p. 40)
 Brian Backstrom, Empire Foundation for Policy Research, Clifton Park, NY (p. 42)
*Janet Beales, Kids One, East Brunswick, NJ (p. 48)
*Pamela Benigno, Independence Institute, Golden, CO (p. 50)
*William J. Bennett, Empower America, Washington, DC (p. 51)
*Jason Bertsch, American Enterprise Institute, Washington, DC (p. 52)
*Wayman R. Bishop, The Family Foundation of Virginia, Richmond, VA (p. 53)
*Christian N. Braunlich, Thomas Jefferson Institute for Public Policy, Alexandria, VA (p. 60)
 David Brennan, White Hat Management, Akron, OH (p. 61)

CHARTER SCHOOLS (Continued)

Dedrick Briggs, Charter School Resource Center of Tennessee, Memphis, TN **(p. 61)**

B. Jason Brooks, Empire Foundation for Policy Research, Clifton Park, NY **(p. 62)**

*Bill Brooks, North Carolina Family Policy Council, Raleigh, NC **(p. 62)**

*Matthew J. Brouillette, The Commonwealth Foundation, Harrisburg, PA **(p. 62)**

*Floyd G. Brown, Young America's Foundation Reagan Ranch Project, Santa Barbara, CA **(p. 63)**

Linda Brown, Pioneer Institute for Public Policy Research, Boston, MA **(p. 63)**

*Sharon Browne, Pacific Legal Foundation, Sacramento, CA **(p. 63)**

Francis H. Buckley, George Mason University School of Law, Arlington, VA **(p. 64)**

*Kaleem Caire, American Education Reform Council, Bowie, MD **(p. 67)**

*James B. Cardle, Texas Citizen Action Network, Austin, TX **(p. 69)**

Merrick Carey, Lexington Institute, Arlington, VA **(p. 70)**

Chris Carr, Georgia Public Policy Foundation, Atlanta, GA **(p. 71)**

*Thomas Carroll, Empire Foundation for Policy Research, Clifton Park, NY **(p. 71)**

*Samuel Casey Carter, Acade Metrics, LLC, Washington, DC **(p. 71)**

*John Chubb, Edison Schools, Inc., New York, NY **(p. 74)**

*Micah Clark, American Family Association, Indianapolis, IN **(p. 75)**

*Ward Connerly, American Civil Rights Institute, Sacramento, CA **(p. 80)**

*John E. Coons, University of California at Berkeley, Berkeley, CA **(p. 81)**

*Brad W. Dacus, Pacific Justice Institute, Citrus Heights, CA **(p. 87)**

Richard S. Davis, Washington Research Council, Seattle, WA **(p. 89)**

Candace de Russy, State University of New York, Bronxville, NY **(p. 90)**

*Glenn Delk, Georgia Charter Schools, Atlanta, GA **(p. 92)**

Denis Doyle, Doyle Associates, Chevy Chase, MD **(p. 98)**

Diallo Dphrepaulezz, New York, NY **(p. 98)**

Pete du Pont, National Center for Policy Analysis, Wilmington, DE **(p. 98)**

*Clark Durant, New Common School Foundation, Detroit, MI **(p. 101)**

*Michelle Easton, Clare Boothe Luce Policy Institute, Herndon, VA **(p. 102)**

*Robert C. Enlow, Milton and Rose Friedman Foundation, Indianapolis, IN **(p. 107)**

*Williamson M. Evers, Hoover Institution, Stanford, CA **(p. 108)**

Megan Farnsworth, The Heritage Foundation, Washington, DC **(p. 109)**

*Michael P. Farris, Patrick Henry College, Purcellville, VA **(p. 109)**

*Marc Fey, Focus on the Family, Colorado Springs, CO **(p. 111)**

John Findley, Pacific Legal Foundation, Sacramento, CA **(p. 111)**

*Chester E. Finn, Jr., Thomas B. Fordham Foundation, Washington, DC **(p. 112)**

*Seymour Fliegel, Center for Educational Innovation – Public Education Association, New York, NY **(p. 113)**

Amy Frantz, Public Interest Institute, Mount Pleasant, IA **(p. 116)**

Marshall Fritz, Alliance for the Separation of School & State, Fresno, CA **(p. 118)**

Howard Fuller, Marquette University, Milwaukee, WI **(p. 118)**

Jennifer Garrett, The Heritage Foundation, Washington, DC **(p. 120)**

*Mary F. Gifford, Field, Sarvas, King and Coleman, Phoenix, AZ **(p. 123)**

*Charles L. Glenn, Boston University, Boston, MA **(p. 124)**

Clint W. Green, Acton Institute for the Study of Religion and Liberty, Grand Rapids, MI **(p. 128)**

*Jay P. Greene, Manhattan Institute for Policy Research, Davie, FL **(p. 128)**

Charles Greenwalt, II, Susquehanna Valley Center for Public Policy, Hershey, PA **(p. 129)**

Marie Gryphon, Cato Institute, Washington, DC **(p. 130)**

*Charlene Haar, Education Policy Institute, Washington, DC **(p. 131)**

*Joshua Hall, Buckeye Institute for Public Policy Solutions, Columbus, OH **(p. 132)**

*Randy H. Hamilton, University of California, Berkeley, Berkeley, CA **(p. 133)**

Jerome J. Hanus, American University, Washington, DC **(p. 134)**

Eric Hanushek, Hoover Institution, Stanford, CA **(p. 135)**

Robert Hawkins, Jr., Institute for Contemporary Studies, Oakland, CA **(p. 137)**

CHARTER SCHOOLS (Continued)

Justin Heet, Hudson Institute, Indianapolis, IN (p. 139)

*John R. Hill, Alabama Policy Institute, Birmingham, AL (p. 142)

*Paul T. Hill, University of Washington, Seattle, WA (p. 142)

*Robert Holland, Lexington Institute, Arlington, VA (p. 144)

Susan D. Hollins, The Josiah Bartlett Center for Public Policy, Concord, NH (p. 145)

*John MacDonald Hood, John Locke Foundation, Raleigh, NC (p. 145)

*Caroline M. Hoxby, Harvard University, Cambridge, MA (p. 147)

*Gary Huggins, Education Leaders Action Council, Washington, DC (p. 148)

*Harry G. Hutchison, Wayne State University, Detroit, MI (p. 150)

Niger Roy Innis, Congress of Racial Equality, New York, NY (p. 151)

*Lance T. Izumi, Pacific Research Institute, Sacramento, CA (p. 152)

Kirk A. Johnson, Mackinac Center for Public Policy, Midland, MI (p. 155)

*Krista Kafer, The Heritage Foundation, Washington, DC (p. 156)

*John Kain, University of Texas, Dallas, Richardson, TX (p. 157)

Lindalyn Kakadelis, North Carolina Education Alliance, Pineville, NC (p. 157)

*Lisa Graham Keegan, Education Leaders Council, Washington, DC (p. 160)

Jane Kilgore, Austin CEO Foundation, Austin, TX (p. 163)

Kent King, Missouri State Teachers Association, Columbia, MO (p. 164)

*David W. Kirkpatrick, Citizens for Educational Freedom, Douglassville, PA (p. 164)

John Kirtley, Children First America, Bentonville, AR (p. 165)

Mary Beth Klee, Link Institute, Portsmouth, NH (p. 165)

*Christopher J. Klicka, Home School Legal Defense Association, Purcellville, VA (p. 165)

*Matthew Ladner, Children First America, Austin, TX (p. 171)

*Andrew T. LeFevre, American Legislative Exchange Council, Washington, DC (p. 177)

*Mark R. Levin, Landmark Legal Foundation, Herndon, VA (p. 178)

*Myron Lieberman, Education Policy Institute, Washington, DC (p. 180)

*George Liebmann, Calvert Institute for Policy Research, Baltimore, MD (p. 180)

Hsien-Tung Liu, Bloomsburg University, Bloomsburg, PA (p. 181)

Kathleen Madigan, National Council on Teacher Quality, Washington, DC (p. 186)

*Rita P. Maguire, Arizona Center for Public Policy, Phoenix, AZ (p. 186)

*Bruno V. Manno, The Annie E. Casey Foundation, Baltimore, MD (p. 188)

*J. Stanley Marshall, The James Madison Institute, Tallahassee, FL (p. 190)

Jennifer Marshall, Empower America, Washington, DC (p. 190)

*Jack McCarthy, AppleTree Institute for Education Innovation, Washington, DC (p. 193)

Jerome Anthony McDuffie, University of North Carolina, Pembroke, Lumberton, NC (p. 195)

Edward T. McMullen, Jr., South Carolina Policy Council, Columbia, SC (p. 197)

*John Merrifield, University of Texas, San Antonio, San Antonio, TX (p. 199)

Harry Messenheimer, Rio Grande Foundation, Tijeras, NM (p. 200)

Tom Minnery, Focus on the Family, Colorado Springs, CO (p. 203)

Elizabeth Mische, Partnership for Choice in Education, St. Paul, MN (p. 203)

Terry M. Moe, Hoover Institution, Stanford, CA (p. 204)

Cassandra Chrones Moore, Cato Institute, Washington, DC (p. 205)

Suzanne C. Moore, Delaware Public Policy Institute, Wilmington, DE (p. 206)

Joe Nathan, Center for School Change, Minneapolis, MN (p. 211)

Thomas Nechyba, Duke University, Durham, NC (p. 211)

*Richard John Neuhaus, Institute on Religion and Public Life, New York, NY (p. 213)

Lisa Coldwell O'Brien, New York Charter Schools Association, Loudonville, NY (p. 216)

*Patsy O'Neill, Charter School Resource Center of Texas, San Antonio, TX (p. 217)

*Darcy A. Olsen, Goldwater Institute, Phoenix, AZ (p. 219)

*Joseph P. Overton, Mackinac Center for Public Policy, Midland, MI (p. 220)

*Allan E. Parker, Jr., Texas Justice Foundation, San Antonio, TX (p. 221)

*Lawrence C. Patrick, III, Black Alliance for Educational Options, Washington, DC (p. 222)

*Christine Patterson, Texas Public Policy Foundation, San Antonio, TX (p. 223)

*Lovett C. Peters, Pioneer Institute for Public Policy Research, Boston, MA (p. 226)

CHARTER SCHOOLS (Continued)

*Nancy M. Pfotenhauer, Independent Women's Forum, Arlington, VA **(p. 227)**
*Michael Podgursky, University of Missouri, Columbia, MO **(p. 230)**
*Eric Premack, California State University Institute for Education Reform, Sacramento, CA **(p. 232)**
*Scott Pullins, Ohio Taxpayers Association and OTA Foundation, Columbus, OH **(p. 234)**
*Ed Rauchut, CEO Omaha, Bellevue, NE **(p. 236)**
 Harold Calvin Ray, National Center for Faith-Based Initiatives, West Palm Beach, FL **(p. 237)**
 Jeremiah Reedy, Macalester College, St. Paul, MN **(p. 238)**
 William Craig Rice, American Academy for Liberal Education, Washington, DC **(p. 239)**
 Holly Robinson, Georgia Public Policy Foundation, Atlanta, GA **(p. 242)**
*Doug Rogers, Association of Texas Professional Educators, Austin, TX **(p. 243)**
 Terry Ryan, Thomas B. Fordham Foundation, Washington, DC **(p. 248)**
*David F. Salisbury, Cato Institute, Washington, DC **(p. 248)**
*Michael Sanera, Basis Charter High School, Tucson, AZ **(p. 249)**
 David W. Saxe, Pennsylvania State University, University Park, PA **(p. 251)**
 Roberta Rubel Schaefer, Worcester Regional Research Bureau, Worcester, MA **(p. 252)**
*Carolyn Sharette, Children First Utah, Salt Lake City, UT **(p. 258)**
*Christopher Smith, Internet Education Exchange (iEdx), Scottsdale, AZ **(p. 262)**
*Lisa Snell, Reason Foundation, Los Angeles, CA **(p. 265)**
*Don Soifer, Lexington Institute, Arlington, VA **(p. 265)**
*Fawn Spady, Education Excellence Coalition, Seattle, WA **(p. 266)**
*Jim Spady, Education Excellence Coalition, Seattle, WA **(p. 266)**
*John A. Sparks, Grove City College, Grove City, PA **(p. 266)**
 Gordon St. Angelo, Milton and Rose Friedman Foundation, Indianapolis, IN **(p. 267)**
 Doug Stiegler, Association of Maryland Families, Woodstock, MD **(p. 269)**
*Jeff Stormo, Choices for Children, Grand Rapids, MI **(p. 270)**
 Charles Sykes, Wisconsin Policy Research Institute, Mequon, WI **(p. 273)**
 Kevin Teasley, Greater Educational Opportunities Foundation, Indianapolis, IN **(p. 275)**
*Forest M. Thigpen, Mississippi Family Council, Jackson, MS **(p. 277)**
 Ann C. Thomson, The Commonwealth Foundation, Harrisburg, PA **(p. 278)**
 Eugenia Froedge Toma, University of Kentucky, Lexington, KY **(p. 280)**
*Lex Towle, AppleTree Institute for Education Innovation, Washington, DC **(p. 280)**
*Forrest L. Turpen, Christian Educators Association International, Pasadena, CA **(p. 282)**
 Reed Ueda, Tufts University, Medford, MA **(p. 282)**
*Kevin Vigilante, Rumford, RI **(p. 285)**
 Joseph P. Viteritti, New York University, New York, NY **(p. 285)**
*Herbert J. Walberg, University of Illinois, Chicago, Chicago, IL **(p. 286)**
*Jeffrey D. Wallin, American Academy for Liberal Education, Washington, DC **(p. 287)**
 Bob Walpole, The Flagstaff Institute, Flagstaff, AZ **(p. 288)**
 Tom Washburne, Home School Legal Defense Association, Purcellville, VA **(p. 289)**
*Donna Watson, Children First America, Austin, TX **(p. 290)**
 Nick Weller, Cascade Policy Institute, Portland, OR **(p. 292)**
*Gary Wolfram, Hillsdale College, Hillsdale, MI **(p. 297)**
*Chris Yelich, Education Industry Association, Watertown, WI **(p. 300)**
 Ronald A. Zumbrun, The Zumbrun Law Firm, Sacramento, CA **(p. 303)**

EDUCATION UNIONS AND INTEREST GROUPS

 Jeanne Allen, Center for Education Reform, Washington, DC **(p. 36)**
*Lewis Andrews, Yankee Institute for Public Policy Studies, Hartford, CT **(p. 39)**
 Michael Antonucci, Education Intelligence Agency, Elk Grove, CA **(p. 39)**
 Brian Backstrom, Empire Foundation for Policy Research, Clifton Park, NY **(p. 42)**
 Dale Ballou, University of Massachusetts, Amherst, MA **(p. 45)**
*Gary Beckner, Association of American Educators, Laguna Hills, CA **(p. 48)**
*Pamela Benigno, Independence Institute, Golden, CO **(p. 50)**

---

* Has testified before a state or federal legislative committee

EDUCATION UNIONS AND INTEREST GROUPS (Continued)

*William J. Bennett, Empower America, Washington, DC (p. 51)
*Christian N. Braunlich, Thomas Jefferson Institute for Public Policy, Alexandria, VA (p. 60)
*Matthew J. Brouillette, The Commonwealth Foundation, Harrisburg, PA (p. 62)
*Jon Charles Caldara, Independence Institute, Golden, CO (p. 67)
*Milton L. Chappell, National Right to Work Legal Defense Foundation, Springfield, VA (p. 72)
*Linda Chavez, Center for Equal Opportunity, Sterling, VA (p. 73)
 Barbara Christmas, Professional Association of Georgia Educators, Chamblee, GA (p. 74)
*John Chubb, Edison Schools, Inc., New York, NY (p. 74)
*John E. Coons, University of California at Berkeley, Berkeley, CA (p. 81)
 Neil S. Crispo, Florida State University, Tallahassee, FL (p. 86)
*Brad W. Dacus, Pacific Justice Institute, Citrus Heights, CA (p. 87)
 Candace de Russy, State University of New York, Bronxville, NY (p. 90)
*Glenn Delk, Georgia Charter Schools, Atlanta, GA (p. 92)
*David Denholm, Public Service Research Foundation, Vienna, VA (p. 92)
*Robert Destro, Catholic University of America, Washington, DC (p. 94)
*Phillip DeVous, Acton Institute for the Study of Religion and Liberty, Grand Rapids, MI (p. 94)
 Denis Doyle, Doyle Associates, Chevy Chase, MD (p. 98)
 Brandon Dutcher, Oklahoma Council of Public Affairs, Oklahoma City, OK (p. 101)
*Michelle Easton, Clare Boothe Luce Policy Institute, Herndon, VA (p. 102)
*Robert C. Enlow, Milton and Rose Friedman Foundation, Indianapolis, IN (p. 107)
*Williamson M. Evers, Hoover Institution, Stanford, CA (p. 108)
*Michael P. Farris, Patrick Henry College, Purcellville, VA (p. 109)
 Richard M. Ferry, Catholic Education Foundation, Los Angeles, CA (p. 111)
*Marc Fey, Focus on the Family, Colorado Springs, CO (p. 111)
*Robert Fike, Americans for Tax Reform, Washington, DC (p. 111)
*Chester E. Finn, Jr., Thomas B. Fordham Foundation, Washington, DC (p. 112)
 Elizabeth Fox-Genovese, Emory University, Atlanta, GA (p. 115)
 Howard Fuller, Marquette University, Milwaukee, WI (p. 118)
 Jennifer Garrett, The Heritage Foundation, Washington, DC (p. 120)
 Stefan Gleason, National Right to Work Legal Defense Foundation, Springfield, VA (p. 124)
*Gary Glenn, American Family Association of Michigan, Midland, MI (p. 124)
*Stephen O. Goodrick, National Right to Work Committee, Springfield, VA (p. 126)
 Clint W. Green, Acton Institute for the Study of Religion and Liberty,
   Grand Rapids, MI (p. 128)
*Jay P. Greene, Manhattan Institute for Policy Research, Davie, FL (p. 128)
 Marie Gryphon, Cato Institute, Washington, DC (p. 130)
*Charlene Haar, Education Policy Institute, Washington, DC (p. 131)
*Joshua Hall, Buckeye Institute for Public Policy Solutions, Columbus, OH (p. 132)
 Eric Hanushek, Hoover Institution, Stanford, CA (p. 135)
*Lynn Harsh, Evergreen Freedom Foundation, Olympia, WA (p. 136)
 Chad Hills, Focus on the Family, Colorado Springs, CO (p. 143)
*Robert Holland, Lexington Institute, Arlington, VA (p. 144)
*Caroline M. Hoxby, Harvard University, Cambridge, MA (p. 147)
*Robert Hunter, Mackinac Center for Public Policy, Midland, MI (p. 150)
 Richard P. Hutchison, Landmark Legal Foundation, Kansas City, MO (p. 150)
*Lance T. Izumi, Pacific Research Institute, Sacramento, CA (p. 152)
 Walter Jewell, Professional Educators of Tennessee, Franklin, TN (p. 154)
 Kirk A. Johnson, Mackinac Center for Public Policy, Midland, MI (p. 155)
*Krista Kafer, The Heritage Foundation, Washington, DC (p. 156)
*Lisa Graham Keegan, Education Leaders Council, Washington, DC (p. 160)
 Kent King, Missouri State Teachers Association, Columbia, MO (p. 164)
*David W. Kirkpatrick, Citizens for Educational Freedom, Douglassville, PA (p. 164)
*Robert H. Knight, Concerned Women for America, Washington, DC (p. 166)
 Peter J. LaBarbera, Concerned Women for America, Washington, DC (p. 171)

EDUCATION UNIONS AND INTEREST GROUPS (Continued)

*Matthew Ladner, Children First America, Austin, TX (p. 171)

*Raymond J. LaJeunesse, Jr., National Right to Work Legal Defense Foundation, Springfield, VA (p. 172)

 Byron S. Lamm, State Policy Network, Fort Wayne, IN (p. 173)

 Reed Larson, National Right to Work Committee, Springfield, VA (p. 175)

*Andrew T. LeFevre, American Legislative Exchange Council, Washington, DC (p. 177)

 Joseph G. Lehman, Mackinac Center for Public Policy, Midland, MI (p. 177)

*Mark R. Levin, Landmark Legal Foundation, Herndon, VA (p. 178)

*Myron Lieberman, Education Policy Institute, Washington, DC (p. 180)

*George Liebmann, Calvert Institute for Policy Research, Baltimore, MD (p. 180)

*Rita P. Maguire, Arizona Center for Public Policy, Phoenix, AZ (p. 186)

 Jennifer Marshall, Empower America, Washington, DC (p. 190)

 Daniel McGroarty, White House Writer's Group, Chevy Chase, MD (p. 196)

 Harry Messenheimer, Rio Grande Foundation, Tijeras, NM (p. 200)

 Elizabeth Mische, Partnership for Choice in Education, St. Paul, MN (p. 203)

 Terry M. Moe, Hoover Institution, Stanford, CA (p. 204)

 Cassandra Chrones Moore, Cato Institute, Washington, DC (p. 205)

 Chuck Muth, American Conservative Union, Alexandria, VA (p. 210)

 Mike O'Neill, Landmark Legal Foundation, Herndon, VA (p. 217)

*Darcy A. Olsen, Goldwater Institute, Phoenix, AZ (p. 219)

 Ivan G. Osorio, Capital Research Center, Washington, DC (p. 220)

*Joseph P. Overton, Mackinac Center for Public Policy, Midland, MI (p. 220)

*Allan E. Parker, Jr., Texas Justice Foundation, San Antonio, TX (p. 221)

*Lovett C. Peters, Pioneer Institute for Public Policy Research, Boston, MA (p. 226)

*Nancy M. Pfotenhauer, Independent Women's Forum, Arlington, VA (p. 227)

*Michael Podgursky, University of Missouri, Columbia, MO (p. 230)

 Victor Porlier, Center for Civic Renewal, Inc., Delmar, NY (p. 231)

*Eric Premack, California State University Institute for Education Reform, Sacramento, CA (p. 232)

*Scott Pullins, Ohio Taxpayers Association and OTA Foundation, Columbus, OH (p. 234)

*Lawrence W. Reed, Mackinac Center for Public Policy, Midland, MI (p. 237)

 Patrick Reilly, Cardinal Newman Society, Falls Church, VA (p. 238)

 William Craig Rice, American Academy for Liberal Education, Washington, DC (p. 239)

*David W. Riggs, Capital Research Center, Washington, DC (p. 240)

 Sandy Rios, Concerned Women for America, Washington, DC (p. 240)

 Holly Robinson, Georgia Public Policy Foundation, Atlanta, GA (p. 242)

*Doug Rogers, Association of Texas Professional Educators, Austin, TX (p. 243)

*David F. Salisbury, Cato Institute, Washington, DC (p. 248)

*Terrence M. Scanlon, Capital Research Center, Washington, DC (p. 251)

*Donald J. Senese, 60 Plus Association, Arlington, VA (p. 257)

*Robert A. Sirico, Acton Institute for the Study of Religion and Liberty, Grand Rapids, MI (p. 261)

*Christopher Smith, Internet Education Exchange (iEdx), Scottsdale, AZ (p. 262)

*Lisa Snell, Reason Foundation, Los Angeles, CA (p. 265)

 Gordon St. Angelo, Milton and Rose Friedman Foundation, Indianapolis, IN (p. 267)

*J. E. Stone, East Tennessee State University, Johnson City, TN (p. 270)

*Jeff Stormo, Choices for Children, Grand Rapids, MI (p. 270)

 Charles Sykes, Wisconsin Policy Research Institute, Mequon, WI (p. 273)

 Kevin Teasley, Greater Educational Opportunities Foundation, Indianapolis, IN (p. 275)

 Ann C. Thomson, The Commonwealth Foundation, Harrisburg, PA (p. 278)

 Eugenia Froedge Toma, University of Kentucky, Lexington, KY (p. 280)

*Forrest L. Turpen, Christian Educators Association International, Pasadena, CA (p. 282)

*Lil Tuttle, Clare Boothe Luce Policy Institute, Herndon, VA (p. 282)

 Joseph P. Viteritti, New York University, New York, NY (p. 285)

---

* Has testified before a state or federal legislative committee

EDUCATION UNIONS AND INTEREST GROUPS (Continued)

Tom Washburne, Home School Legal Defense Association, Purcellville, VA **(p. 289)**

Bob Williams, Evergreen Freedom Foundation, Olympia, WA **(p. 295)**

Robert O. C. Worcester, Maryland Business for Responsive Government, Baltimore, MD **(p. 298)**

Chris Yelich, Education Industry Association, Watertown, WI **(p. 300)**

FEDERAL EDUCATION POLICY

Charles M. Achilles, Eastern Michigan University, Ypsilanti, MI **(p. 34)**

Benjamin Alexander, Franciscan University of Steubenville, Steubenville, OH **(p. 36)**

Lewis Andrews, Yankee Institute for Public Policy Studies, Hartford, CT **(p. 39)**

Gary Beckner, Association of American Educators, Laguna Hills, CA **(p. 48)**

John E. Berthoud, National Taxpayers Union, Alexandria, VA **(p. 52)**

Dick Bishirjian, YorktownUniversity.com, Norfolk, VA **(p. 53)**

Dedrick Briggs, Charter School Resource Center of Tennessee, Memphis, TN **(p. 61)**

Floyd G. Brown, Young America's Foundation Reagan Ranch Project, Santa Barbara, CA **(p. 63)**

Harold O. J. Brown, Reformed Theological Seminary, Charlotte, NC **(p. 63)**

Morgan Brown, Center of the American Experiment, Minneapolis, MN **(p. 63)**

Merrick Carey, Lexington Institute, Arlington, VA **(p. 70)**

John K. Carlisle, Capital Research Center, Washington, DC **(p. 70)**

Samuel Casey Carter, Acade Metrics, LLC, Washington, DC **(p. 71)**

Linda Chavez, Center for Equal Opportunity, Sterling, VA **(p. 73)**

Lynne V. Cheney, American Enterprise Institute, Washington, DC **(p. 73)**

John Chubb, Edison Schools, Inc., New York, NY **(p. 74)**

Kenneth L. Connor, Family Research Council, Washington, DC **(p. 80)**

John E. Coons, University of California at Berkeley, Berkeley, CA **(p. 81)**

Kathleen B. de Bettencourt, Environmental Literacy Council, Washington, DC **(p. 89)**

Candace de Russy, State University of New York, Bronxville, NY **(p. 90)**

Buffy DeBreaux-Watts, American Board for Certification of Teacher Excellence, Washington, DC **(p. 91)**

Fred W. Decker, Mount Hood Society, Corvallis, OR **(p. 91)**

Eugene Delgaudio, Public Advocate, Falls Church, VA **(p. 91)**

Phillip DeVous, Acton Institute for the Study of Religion and Liberty, Grand Rapids, MI **(p. 94)**

Thomas DeWeese, American Policy Center, Warrenton, VA **(p. 94)**

Douglas Dean Dewey, Children's Scholarship Fund, New York, NY **(p. 94)**

Thomas Dillon, Thomas Aquinas College, Santa Paula, CA **(p. 96)**

Marie Dolan, New York State Federation of Catholic School Parents, Flushing, NY **(p. 96)**

Daniel J. Dougherty, Pennsylvania Federation-Citizens for Educational Freedom, Philadelphia, PA **(p. 97)**

Denis Doyle, Doyle Associates, Chevy Chase, MD **(p. 98)**

Diallo Dphrepaulezz, New York, NY **(p. 98)**

Mae Duggan, Citizens for Educational Freedom, St. Louis, MO **(p. 99)**

Peter J. Duignan, Hoover Institution, Stanford, CA **(p. 99)**

David Dunn, Oklahoma Family Policy Council, Bethany, OK **(p. 100)**

John C. Eastman, Chapman University School of Law, Orange, CA **(p. 102)**

Michelle Easton, Clare Boothe Luce Policy Institute, Herndon, VA **(p. 102)**

Williamson M. Evers, Hoover Institution, Stanford, CA **(p. 108)**

Michael P. Farris, Patrick Henry College, Purcellville, VA **(p. 109)**

Richard M. Ferry, Catholic Education Foundation, Los Angeles, CA **(p. 111)**

Marc Fey, Focus on the Family, Colorado Springs, CO **(p. 111)**

Chester E. Finn, Jr., Thomas B. Fordham Foundation, Washington, DC **(p. 112)**

Elizabeth Fox-Genovese, Emory University, Atlanta, GA **(p. 115)**

Michael Franc, The Heritage Foundation, Washington, DC **(p. 115)**

Marshall Fritz, Alliance for the Separation of School & State, Fresno, CA **(p. 118)**

FEDERAL EDUCATION POLICY (Continued)

*Mary F. Gifford, Field, Sarvas, King and Coleman, Phoenix, AZ (p. 123)
Daniel J. Goldhaber, University of Washington, Seattle, WA (p. 125)
Clint W. Green, Acton Institute for the Study of Religion and Liberty, Grand Rapids, MI (p. 128)
*Jay P. Greene, Manhattan Institute for Policy Research, Davie, FL (p. 128)
Marie Gryphon, Cato Institute, Washington, DC (p. 130)
*Charlene Haar, Education Policy Institute, Washington, DC (p. 131)
Paige Holland Hamp, Maryland Public Policy Institute, Germantown, MD (p. 133)
Jerome J. Hanus, American University, Washington, DC (p. 134)
Eric Hanushek, Hoover Institution, Stanford, CA (p. 135)
*Donna H. Hearne, Constitutional Coalition, St. Louis, MO (p. 138)
Justin Heet, Hudson Institute, Indianapolis, IN (p. 139)
*Frank J. Heller, Maine Policy Ronin Network, Brunswick, ME (p. 139)
Frederick M. Hess, American Enterprise Institute, Washington, DC (p. 141)
*Paul T. Hill, University of Washington, Seattle, WA (p. 142)
*John C. Holmes, Association of Christian Schools International, Washington, DC (p. 145)
*John MacDonald Hood, John Locke Foundation, Raleigh, NC (p. 145)
*John A. Howard, Howard Center for Family, Religion and Society, Rockford, IL (p. 147)
*Caroline M. Hoxby, Harvard University, Cambridge, MA (p. 147)
Martin Hoyt, American Association of Christian Schools, Washington, DC (p. 148)
*Gary Huggins, Education Leaders Action Council, Washington, DC (p. 148)
*Victoria Hughes, Bill of Rights Institute, Washington, DC (p. 149)
*Nancy Ichinaga, California State Board of Education, Los Angeles, CA (p. 151)
Kirk A. Johnson, Mackinac Center for Public Policy, Midland, MI (p. 155)
*Krista Kafer, The Heritage Foundation, Washington, DC (p. 156)
*John Kain, University of Texas, Dallas, Richardson, TX (p. 157)
Lindalyn Kakadelis, North Carolina Education Alliance, Pineville, NC (p. 157)
*Lisa Graham Keegan, Education Leaders Council, Washington, DC (p. 160)
Phil Kent, Southeastern Legal Foundation, Atlanta, GA (p. 162)
Jane Kilgore, Austin CEO Foundation, Austin, TX (p. 163)
Kent King, Missouri State Teachers Association, Columbia, MO (p. 164)
*David W. Kirkpatrick, Citizens for Educational Freedom, Douglassville, PA (p. 164)
James J. Kirschke, Villanova University, Villanova, PA (p. 164)
John Kirtley, Children First America, Bentonville, AR (p. 165)
Joy Kiviat, Citizens for Educational Freedom, St. Louis, MO (p. 165)
*Christopher J. Klicka, Home School Legal Defense Association, Purcellville, VA (p. 165)
Wendy Kopp, Teach for America, New York, NY (p. 167)
Alan Charles Kors, The Foundation for Individual Rights in Education, Philadelphia, PA (p. 167)
*Marvin H. Kosters, American Enterprise Institute, Washington, DC (p. 168)
*Andrea S. Lafferty, Traditional Values Coalition, Washington, DC (p. 172)
*George Landrith, Frontiers of Freedom Institute, Fairfax, VA (p. 173)
Casey Lartigue, Jr., Cato Institute, Washington, DC (p. 175)
*Andrew T. LeFevre, American Legislative Exchange Council, Washington, DC (p. 177)
Seth Leibsohn, Empower America, Washington, DC (p. 177)
*Mark R. Levin, Landmark Legal Foundation, Herndon, VA (p. 178)
*Myron Lieberman, Education Policy Institute, Washington, DC (p. 180)
*George Liebmann, Calvert Institute for Policy Research, Baltimore, MD (p. 180)
*Mike Long, Complete Abstinence Eduation Program, Durham, NC (p. 183)
John R. Lott, Jr., American Enterprise Institute, Washington, DC (p. 183)
Telly L. Lovelace, Coalition on Urban Renewal and Education, Washington, DC (p. 183)
*Roger P. Maickel, Purdue University, Lafayette, IN (p. 187)
*Bruno V. Manno, The Annie E. Casey Foundation, Baltimore, MD (p. 188)
Jennifer Marshall, Empower America, Washington, DC (p. 190)

---

* Has testified before a state or federal legislative committee

FEDERAL EDUCATION POLICY (Continued)

*Jerry L. Martin, American Council of Trustees and Alumni, Washington, DC (p. 190)
*Jack McCarthy, AppleTree Institute for Education Innovation, Washington, DC (p. 193)
*Tom McClusky, National Taxpayers Union Foundation, Alexandria, VA (p. 193)
 Elizabeth Mische, Partnership for Choice in Education, St. Paul, MN (p. 203)
 Terry M. Moe, Hoover Institution, Stanford, CA (p. 204)
 Cassandra Chrones Moore, Cato Institute, Washington, DC (p. 205)
 Joe Nathan, Center for School Change, Minneapolis, MN (p. 211)
*Charles J. O'Malley, Charles J. O'Malley & Associates, Inc., Annapolis, MD (p. 217)
*Darcy A. Olsen, Goldwater Institute, Phoenix, AZ (p. 219)
*Allan E. Parker, Jr., Texas Justice Foundation, San Antonio, TX (p. 221)
*J. A. Parker, Lincoln Institute for Research and Education, Washington, DC (p. 221)
*Christine Patterson, Texas Public Policy Foundation, San Antonio, TX (p. 223)
*Steve Perla, Parent's Alliance for Catholic Education, Fitchburg, MA (p. 225)
*Michael Podgursky, University of Missouri, Columbia, MO (p. 230)
*Claude Pressnell, Tennessee Independent Colleges and Universities, Nashville, TN (p. 233)
 Diane Ravitch, New York University, New York, NY (p. 237)
 Harold Calvin Ray, National Center for Faith-Based Initiatives, West Palm Beach, FL (p. 237)
 William Craig Rice, American Academy for Liberal Education, Washington, DC (p. 239)
*Brian Riedl, The Heritage Foundation, Washington, DC (p. 240)
*David F. Salisbury, Cato Institute, Washington, DC (p. 248)
*Phyllis Schlafly, Eagle Forum, St. Louis, MO (p. 253)
*Donald J. Senese, 60 Plus Association, Arlington, VA (p. 257)
*Christopher Smith, Internet Education Exchange (iEdx), Scottsdale, AZ (p. 262)
*Lisa Snell, Reason Foundation, Los Angeles, CA (p. 265)
*Don Soifer, Lexington Institute, Arlington, VA (p. 265)
 Gordon St. Angelo, Milton and Rose Friedman Foundation, Indianapolis, IN (p. 267)
*J. E. Stone, East Tennessee State University, Johnson City, TN (p. 270)
 Jacob Sullum, *Reason* Magazine, Fairfax, VA (p. 272)
 Joy Sweet, National Right to Read Foundation, The Plains, VA (p. 273)
 James R. "J.T." Taylor, Empower America, Washington, DC (p. 274)
 Kevin Teasley, Greater Educational Opportunities Foundation, Indianapolis, IN (p. 275)
 Ewa M. Thompson, Rice University, Houston, TX (p. 277)
*Mark Thornton, Columbus State University, Columbus, GA (p. 278)
 Eugenia Froedge Toma, University of Kentucky, Lexington, KY (p. 280)
*Lex Towle, AppleTree Institute for Education Innovation, Washington, DC (p. 280)
*George Tryfiates, Concerned Women for America, Washington, DC (p. 281)
*Forrest L. Turpen, Christian Educators Association International, Pasadena, CA (p. 282)
 Charlotte Twight, Boise State University, Boise, ID (p. 282)
 Kristina Twitty, Eagle Forum, Washington, DC (p. 282)
*Balint Vazsonyi, Center for the American Founding, McLean, VA (p. 284)
*Peggy Venable, Texas Citizens for a Sound Economy, Austin, TX (p. 284)
*Maris A. Vinovskis, University of Michigan, Ann Arbor, MI (p. 285)
*Herbert J. Walberg, University of Illinois, Chicago, Chicago, IL (p. 286)
*Malcolm Wallop, Frontiers of Freedom Institute, Fairfax, VA (p. 288)
 Tom Washburne, Home School Legal Defense Association, Purcellville, VA (p. 289)
*Michael W. Watson, Children First America, Austin, TX (p. 290)
 Jason Wright, Frontiers of Freedom Institute, Fairfax, VA (p. 299)
*Nicholas Zill, Westat Inc., Rockville, MD (p. 302)

HIGHER EDUCATION

*Charles M. Achilles, Eastern Michigan University, Ypsilanti, MI (p. 34)
*John Agresto, John Agresto and Associates, Santa Fe, NM (p. 35)
*M. Gene Aldridge, New Mexico Independence Research Institute, Las Cruces, NM (p. 36)
 Benjamin Alexander, Franciscan University of Steubenville, Steubenville, OH (p. 36)

HIGHER EDUCATION (Continued)

***William Allen,** Michigan State University, East Lansing, MI **(p. 37)**
***Ryan C. Amacher,** University of Texas, Arlington, Arlington, TX **(p. 37)**
  Martin Anderson, Hoover Institution, Stanford, CA **(p. 38)**
***Lewis Andrews,** Yankee Institute for Public Policy Studies, Hartford, CT **(p. 39)**
***Frank H. Armstrong,** University of Vermont, Burlington, VT **(p. 40)**
  Larry P. Arnn, Hillsdale College, Hillsdale, MI **(p. 40)**
  Bryan Auchterlonie, Intercollegiate Studies Institute, Wilmington, DE **(p. 41)**
  Brian Backstrom, Empire Foundation for Policy Research, Clifton Park, NY **(p. 42)**
  Richard A. Baer, Jr., Cornell University, Ithaca, NY **(p. 42)**
***John S. Baker, Jr.,** Louisiana State University, Baton Rouge, LA **(p. 43)**
***Keith G. Baker,** Florida TaxWatch Research Institute, Inc., Tallahassee, FL **(p. 43)**
  Stephen H. Balch, National Association of Scholars, Princeton, NJ **(p. 44)**
***John S. Barry,** Tax Foundation, Washington, DC **(p. 46)**
  Christopher Beiting, Ave Maria College, Ypsilanti, MI **(p. 49)**
  David Beito, University of Alabama, Tuscaloosa, AL **(p. 49)**
  Joel Belz, *World Magazine*, Asheville, NC **(p. 50)**
***William J. Bennett,** Empower America, Washington, DC **(p. 51)**
***Dick Bishirjian,** YorktownUniversity.com, Norfolk, VA **(p. 53)**
  Richard Bjornseth, Valdosta State University, Valdosta, GA **(p. 54)**
  Morton Blackwell, Leadership Institute, Arlington, VA **(p. 54)**
***Mark Blitz,** Claremont McKenna College, Claremont, CA **(p. 55)**
  Paul J. Bonicelli, Patrick Henry College, Purcellville, VA **(p. 57)**
  Gary Crosby Brasor, National Association of Scholars, Princeton, NJ **(p. 60)**
  B. Jason Brooks, Empire Foundation for Policy Research, Clifton Park, NY **(p. 62)**
***Harold O. J. Brown,** Reformed Theological Seminary, Charlotte, NC **(p. 63)**
  T. Patrick Burke, St. Joseph's University, Wynnewood, PA **(p. 65)**
  Jameson Campaigne, Jr., Jameson Books, Inc., Ottawa, IL **(p. 68)**
  Nicholas Capaldi, Loyola University New Orleans, New Orleans, LA **(p. 69)**
  Leslie Carbone, Fairfax, VA **(p. 69)**
***John E. Carey,** International Defense Consultants, Inc., Arlington, VA **(p. 69)**
***Thomas Carroll,** Empire Foundation for Policy Research, Clifton Park, NY **(p. 71)**
  J. Daryl Charles, Taylor University, Upland, IN **(p. 72)**
  Pradyumna S. Chauhan, Arcadia University, Glenside, PA **(p. 73)**
***Linda Chavez,** Center for Equal Opportunity, Sterling, VA **(p. 73)**
***Lynne V. Cheney,** American Enterprise Institute, Washington, DC **(p. 73)**
  Henry C. Clark, III, Canisius College, Buffalo, NY **(p. 74)**
***Roger Clegg,** Center for Equal Opportunity, Sterling, VA **(p. 76)**
  Howard Cochran, Jr., Belmont University, Nashville, TN **(p. 77)**
  Eric Cohen, Ethics and Public Policy Center, Washington, DC **(p. 78)**
***Stephen Cole,** State University of New York, Stony Brook, NY **(p. 78)**
***Richard T. Colgan,** Bridgewater State College, Warwick, RI **(p. 78)**
  Lee Congdon, James Madison University, Harrisonburg, VA **(p. 79)**
***Ward Connerly,** American Civil Rights Institute, Sacramento, CA **(p. 80)**
***John E. Coons,** University of California at Berkeley, Berkeley, CA **(p. 81)**
***John F. Copper,** Rhodes College, Memphis, TN **(p. 82)**
***C. W. Cowles,** Central Michigan University, Midlothian, VA **(p. 84)**
***Matt Cox,** Pacific Research Institute, Sacramento, CA **(p. 84)**
  Stephen D. Cox, University of California, San Diego, La Jolla, CA **(p. 84)**
  Dennis Coyle, Catholic University of America, Washington, DC **(p. 84)**
  T. Kenneth Cribb, Jr., Intercollegiate Studies Institute, Wilmington, DE **(p. 86)**
  Neil S. Crispo, Florida State University, Tallahassee, FL **(p. 86)**
***Janice Shaw Crouse,** Concerned Women for America, Washington, DC **(p. 87)**
***Charles H. Cunningham,** National Rifle Association, Washington, DC **(p. 87)**
***Ward S. Curran,** Trinity College, Hartford, CT **(p. 87)**

---

* Has testified before a state or federal legislative committee

HIGHER EDUCATION (Continued)

Dinesh D'Souza, Hoover Institution, Stanford, CA (p. 87)

*Michael R. Darby, University of California at Los Angeles, Los Angeles, CA (p. 89)

*Marshall L. De Rosa, Florida Atlantic University, Davie, FL (p. 90)

Candace de Russy, State University of New York, Bronxville, NY (p. 90)

*Fred W. Decker, Mount Hood Society, Corvallis, OR (p. 91)

Edwin J. Delattre, Boston University, Boston, MA (p. 91)

Peter DeLuca, Thomas Aquinas College, Santa Paula, CA (p. 92)

Thomas Dillon, Thomas Aquinas College, Santa Paula, CA (p. 96)

*Jude P. Dougherty, Catholic University of America, Washington, DC (p. 97)

*William C. Dunkelberg, National Federation of Independent Business, Wynnewood, PA (p. 100)

*Paul Dunn, University of Louisiana, Monroe, Monroe, LA (p. 100)

Timothy R. Dzierba, Medaille College, Buffalo, NY (p. 101)

Joyce Elam, Florida International University, Miami, FL (p. 105)

*Barry S. Fagin, United States Air Force Academy, USAF Academy, CO (p. 108)

*Thompson Mason Faller, University of Portland, Portland, OR (p. 109)

*Michael P. Farris, Patrick Henry College, Purcellville, VA (p. 109)

Richard M. Ferry, Catholic Education Foundation, Los Angeles, CA (p. 111)

*Marc Fey, Focus on the Family, Colorado Springs, CO (p. 111)

*Seymour Fliegel, Center for Educational Innovation – Public Education Association, New York, NY (p. 113)

Elizabeth Fox-Genovese, Emory University, Atlanta, GA (p. 115)

Bernard J. Frieden, Massachusetts Institute of Technology, Cambridge, MA (p. 117)

Janice J. Gabbert, Wright State University, Dayton, OH (p. 119)

*Mary F. Gifford, Field, Sarvas, King and Coleman, Phoenix, AZ (p. 123)

Tomi Gomory, Florida State University, Tallahassee, FL (p. 126)

Jack Gourman, National Education Standards, Los Angeles, CA (p. 127)

Charles Greenwalt, II, Susquehanna Valley Center for Public Policy, Hershey, PA (p. 129)

Phillip D. Grub, Eastern Washington University, Spokane, WA (p. 130)

Marie Gryphon, Cato Institute, Washington, DC (p. 130)

Thor L. Halvorssen, The Foundation for Individual Rights in Education, Philadelphia, PA (p. 132)

Roger Hamburg, Indiana University South Bend, South Bend, IN (p. 133)

Alam E. Hammad, Alexandria, VA (p. 133)

Jerome J. Hanus, American University, Washington, DC (p. 134)

Eric Hanushek, Hoover Institution, Stanford, CA (p. 135)

James E. Hartley, Mount Holyoke College, South Hadley, MA (p. 136)

Mark Y. Herring, Winthrop University, Rock Hill, SC (p. 140)

Robert D. Hisrich, Case Western Reserve University, Cleveland, OH (p. 143)

David Hogberg, Public Interest Institute, Mount Pleasant, IA (p. 144)

*John C. Holmes, Association of Christian Schools International, Washington, DC (p. 145)

*John MacDonald Hood, John Locke Foundation, Raleigh, NC (p. 145)

*Thomas D. Hopkins, Rochester Institute of Technology, Rochester, NY (p. 145)

*Joseph Horn, University of Texas, Austin, TX (p. 146)

David Horowitz, Center for the Study of Popular Culture, Los Angeles, CA (p. 146)

William Howard, Chicago State University, Wheaton, IL (p. 147)

*Caroline M. Hoxby, Harvard University, Cambridge, MA (p. 147)

Carol Iannone, New York, NY (p. 150)

*Lance T. Izumi, Pacific Research Institute, Sacramento, CA (p. 152)

*Laurence Jarvik, Washington, DC (p. 153)

Douglas A. Jeffrey, Hillsdale College, Hillsdale, MI (p. 154)

*Marianne Jennings, Arizona State University, Tempe, AZ (p. 154)

D. Gale Johnson, University of Chicago, Chicago, IL (p. 155)

*John Kain, University of Texas, Dallas, Richardson, TX (p. 157)

HIGHER EDUCATION (Continued)

John Kekes, Charlton, NY (p. 160)
*Patrick J. Keleher, Jr., TEACH America, Wilmette, IL (p. 160)
Dennis J. Keller, DeVry Inc., Oakbrook Terrace, IL (p. 160)
Michael Kellman, University of Oregon, Eugene, OR (p. 160)
*David W. Kirkpatrick, Citizens for Educational Freedom, Douglassville, PA (p. 164)
James J. Kirschke, Villanova University, Villanova, PA (p. 164)
*Christopher J. Klicka, Home School Legal Defense Association, Purcellville, VA (p. 165)
*Douglas W. Kmiec, The Catholic University of America, Washington, DC (p. 166)
Joseph M. Knippenberg, Oglethorpe University, Atlanta, GA (p. 166)
*Robert C. Koons, University of Texas, Austin, TX (p. 167)
Alan Charles Kors, The Foundation for Individual Rights in Education, Philadelphia, PA (p. 167)
Melvin A. Kulbicki, York College of Pennsylvania, York, PA (p. 170)
*Deepak Lal, University of California at Los Angeles, Los Angeles, CA (p. 172)
Peter Augustine Lawler, Berry College, Mount Berry, GA (p. 175)
*Andrew T. LeFevre, American Legislative Exchange Council, Washington, DC (p. 177)
Seth Leibsohn, Empower America, Washington, DC (p. 177)
*John Lenczowski, Institute of World Politics, Washington, DC (p. 177)
*George Liebmann, Calvert Institute for Policy Research, Baltimore, MD (p. 180)
Leonard P. Liggio, Atlas Economic Research Foundation, Fairfax, VA (p. 180)
Cotton M. Lindsay, Clemson University, Clemson, SC (p. 181)
Thomas K. Lindsay, University of Dallas, Irving, TX (p. 181)
Hsien-Tung Liu, Bloomsburg University, Bloomsburg, PA (p. 181)
*Dennis E. Logue, University of Oklahoma, Norman, OK (p. 182)
Bernard T. Lomas, The Heritage Foundation, Chapel Hill, NC (p. 182)
Edward D. Lozansky, American University in Moscow, Washington, DC (p. 184)
*Heather MacDonald, Manhattan Institute for Policy Research, New York, NY (p. 185)
*Roger P. Maickel, Purdue University, Lafayette, IN (p. 187)
Henry G. Manne, University of Chicago Law School, Chicago, IL (p. 188)
*J. Stanley Marshall, The James Madison Institute, Tallahassee, FL (p. 190)
*Jerry L. Martin, American Council of Trustees and Alumni, Washington, DC (p. 190)
*Ken Masugi, Claremont Institute, Claremont, CA (p. 191)
Theodore C. Mataxis, American Military University, Denver, CO (p. 191)
Anthony M. Matteo, Elizabethtown College, Elizabethtown, PA (p. 191)
Wilfred M. McClay, University of Tennessee, Chattanooga, Chattanooga, TN (p. 193)
*Forrest McDonald, University of Alabama, Coker, AL (p. 195)
W. Wesley McDonald, Elizabethtown College, Elizabethtown, PA (p. 195)
Jerome Anthony McDuffie, University of North Carolina, Pembroke, Lumberton, NC (p. 195)
Dave McIntyre, ANSER Institute for Homeland Security, Arlington, VA (p. 196)
Edward T. McMullen, Jr., South Carolina Policy Council, Columbia, SC (p. 197)
*Roger E. Meiners, University of Texas, Arlington, Arlington, TX (p. 198)
Ingrid Merikoski, Earhart Foundation, Ann Arbor, MI (p. 199)
*Roger Michener, Placitas, NM (p. 201)
Fred D. Miller, Jr., Bowling Green State University, Bowling Green, OH (p. 201)
*James H. Miller, Wisconsin Policy Research Institute, Mequon, WI (p. 202)
Elizabeth Mische, Partnership for Choice in Education, St. Paul, MN (p. 203)
Terry M. Moe, Hoover Institution, Stanford, CA (p. 204)
R. Albert Mohler, Jr., The Southern Baptist Theological Seminary, Louisville, KY (p. 204)
*John H. Moore, Grove City College, Grove City, PA (p. 206)
Suzanne C. Moore, Delaware Public Policy Institute, Wilmington, DE (p. 206)
Laurie Morrow, Montpelier, VT (p. 207)
Henry Myers, James Madison University, Harrisonburg, VA (p. 210)
Ronald Nash, Reformed Theological Seminary, Oviedo, FL (p. 211)
*Anne D. Neal, American Council of Trustees and Alumni, Washington, DC (p. 211)

---

* Has testified before a state or federal legislative committee

HIGHER EDUCATION (Continued)

Jeff Nelson, Intercollegiate Studies Institute, Wilmington, DE (p. 212)
Richard Alan Nelson, Louisiana State University, Baton Rouge, LA (p. 212)
Michael J. Neth, Middle Tennessee State University, Murfreesboro, TN (p. 213)
George R. Neumann, University of Iowa, Iowa City, IA (p. 213)
Jacob Neusner, Bard College, Rhinebeck, NY (p. 213)
*Charles C. Nickerson, Bridgewater College, Bridgewater, MA (p. 213)
*Charles J. O'Malley, Charles J. O'Malley & Associates, Inc., Annapolis, MD (p. 217)
*Richard Olivastro, People Dynamics, Farmington, CT (p. 218)
*Darcy A. Olsen, Goldwater Institute, Phoenix, AZ (p. 219)
B. Nelson Ong, College of New Rochelle, New Rochelle, NY (p. 219)
J. Marshall Osborn, University of Wisconsin, Madison, WI (p. 220)
*Christine Patterson, Texas Public Policy Foundation, San Antonio, TX (p. 223)
David A. Patterson, University of Memphis, Memphis, TN (p. 223)
*Mitchell B. Pearlstein, Center of the American Experiment, Minneapolis, MN (p. 224)
James Piereson, John M. Olin Foundation, Inc., New York, NY (p. 228)
Sanford Pinsker, Franklin and Marshall College, Lancaster, PA (p. 229)
*Michael Podgursky, University of Missouri, Columbia, MO (p. 230)
*Solomon W. Polachek, State University of New York, Binghamton, Binghamton, NY (p. 230)
Arthur Pontynen, University of Wisconsin, Oshkosh, WI (p. 230)
*Claude Pressnell, Tennessee Independent Colleges and Universities, Nashville, TN (p. 233)
*William L. Proctor, Flagler College, St. Augustine, FL (p. 233)
*Don Racheter, Public Interest Institute, Mount Pleasant, IA (p. 235)
*Ed Rauchut, CEO Omaha, Bellevue, NE (p. 236)
Jeremiah Reedy, Macalester College, St. Paul, MN (p. 238)
*Charles E. Rice, Notre Dame Law School, Notre Dame, IN (p. 239)
William Craig Rice, American Academy for Liberal Education, Washington, DC (p. 239)
Glenn M. Ricketts, National Association of Scholars, Princeton, NJ (p. 239)
Ron Robinson, Young America's Foundation, Herndon, VA (p. 242)
Robert E. Russell, Jr., The Heritage Foundation, Geneva, IL (p. 247)
John Ruszkiewicz, University of Texas, Austin, TX (p. 247)
*David F. Salisbury, Cato Institute, Washington, DC (p. 248)
*Steven Alan Samson, Liberty University, Lynchburg, VA (p. 249)
Gregory W. Sand, Saint Louis College of Pharmacy, St. Louis, MO (p. 249)
*Ellis Sandoz, Eric Voegelin Institute, Baton Rouge, LA (p. 249)
David W. Saxe, Pennsylvania State University, University Park, PA (p. 251)
David L. Schaefer, Holy Cross College, Worcester, MA (p. 252)
*Phyllis Schlafly, Eagle Forum, St. Louis, MO (p. 253)
*Peter W. Schramm, John M. Ashbrook Center for Public Affairs, Ashland, OH (p. 254)
Robert Schuettinger, Washington International Studies Council, Washington, DC (p. 254)
*Arthur J. Schwartz, John Templeton Foundation, Radnor, PA (p. 254)
Robert Haney Scott, California State University, Chico, Chico, CA (p. 255)
*S. Fred Singer, Science and Environmental Policy Project, Arlington, VA (p. 260)
*Harvey A. Smith, Arizona State University, Tempe, AZ (p. 263)
*Oran P. Smith, Palmetto Family Council, Columbia, SC (p. 264)
*Lisa Snell, Reason Foundation, Los Angeles, CA (p. 265)
*Jack Sommer, Political Economy Research Institute, Charlotte, NC (p. 266)
*Matthew Spalding, The Heritage Foundation, Washington, DC (p. 266)
*John A. Sparks, Grove City College, Grove City, PA (p. 266)
*Nancy Z. Spillman, Economic Education Enterprises, Canoga Park, CA (p. 267)
John E. R. Staddon, Duke University, Durham, NC (p. 267)
*J. E. Stone, East Tennessee State University, Johnson City, TN (p. 270)
Michael P. Sweeney, Hillsdale College, Hillsdale, MI (p. 273)
Charles Sykes, Wisconsin Policy Research Institute, Mequon, WI (p. 273)
Miklos N. Szilagyi, University of Arizona, Tucson, AZ (p. 273)

HIGHER EDUCATION (Continued)

*John Taylor, Virginia Institute for Public Policy, Potomac Falls, VA (p. 274)
Kevin Teasley, Greater Educational Opportunities Foundation, Indianapolis, IN (p. 275)
*Stephan Thernstrom, Lexington, MA (p. 276)
Ewa M. Thompson, Rice University, Houston, TX (p. 277)
*Mark Thornton, Columbus State University, Columbus, GA (p. 278)
Glen E. Thurow, University of Dallas, Irving, TX (p. 279)
Frank J. Tipler, Tulane University, New Orleans, LA (p. 279)
Miro M. Todorovich, Scientists and Engineers for Secure Energy, New York, NY (p. 280)
Jay L. Tontz, California State University, Hayward, Hayward, CA (p. 280)
Kristina Twitty, Eagle Forum, Washington, DC (p. 282)
Reed Ueda, Tufts University, Medford, MA (p. 282)
*Terry W. Van Allen, Kemah, TX (p. 283)
*Balint Vazsonyi, Center for the American Founding, McLean, VA (p. 284)
*Richard Vedder, Ohio University, Athens, OH (p. 284)
*Maris A. Vinovskis, University of Michigan, Ann Arbor, MI (p. 285)
*Richard L. Walker, University of South Carolina, Columbia, SC (p. 287)
*Jeffrey D. Wallin, American Academy for Liberal Education, Washington, DC (p. 287)
*Malcolm Wallop, Frontiers of Freedom Institute, Fairfax, VA (p. 288)
Stanley J. Watson, Patrick Henry College, Purcellville, VA (p. 290)
Emily S. Watts, University of Illinois at Urbana-Champaign, Urbana, IL (p. 290)
*Donald V. Weatherman, Erskine College, Due West, SC (p. 290)
*Rolf A. Weil, Roosevelt University, Chicago, IL (p. 291)
*Nikolai Wenzel, Atlas Economic Research Foundation, Fairfax, VA (p. 292)
David M. Whalen, Hillsdale College, Hillsdale, MI (p. 293)
Robert Whitelaw, Virginia Polytechnic Institute and State University, Blacksburg, VA (p. 294)
*Ron F. Williamson, Great Plains Public Policy Institute, Sioux Falls, SD (p. 295)
Bradford P. Wilson, National Association of Scholars, Princeton, NJ (p. 296)
*Gary Wolfram, Hillsdale College, Hillsdale, MI (p. 297)
*Thomas Wood, Americans Against Discrimination and Preferences, Berkley, CA (p. 298)
Anne Wortham, Illinois State University, Normal, IL (p. 298)
*Michael K. Young, George Washington University Law School, Washington, DC (p. 300)
Edward W. Younkins, Wheeling Jesuit University, Wheeling, WV (p. 301)
Michael Zuckert, University of Notre Dame, Notre Dame, IN (p. 302)

HOME SCHOOLING

*Mary Cunningham Agee, The Nurturing Network, White Salmon, WA (p. 35)
Judy Alger, Center for Market-Based Education, Inc., Rumney, NH (p. 36)
*Lewis Andrews, Yankee Institute for Public Policy Studies, Hartford, CT (p. 39)
*Julaine K. Appling, Family Research Institute of Wisconsin, Madison, WI (p. 40)
*Dominic A. Aquila, Ave Maria University, Ypsilanti, MI (p. 40)
*John S. Baker, Jr., Louisiana State University, Baton Rouge, LA (p. 43)
*Gary L. Bauer, Campaign for Working Families, Arlington, VA (p. 47)
*Pamela Benigno, Independence Institute, Golden, CO (p. 50)
*William J. Bennett, Empower America, Washington, DC (p. 51)
*Jason Bertsch, American Enterprise Institute, Washington, DC (p. 52)
*Wayman R. Bishop, The Family Foundation of Virginia, Richmond, VA (p. 53)
Paul J. Bonicelli, Patrick Henry College, Purcellville, VA (p. 57)
*Kay Brooks, TnHomeEd.com, Nashville, TN (p. 62)
*Matthew J. Brouillette, The Commonwealth Foundation, Harrisburg, PA (p. 62)
*Harold O. J. Brown, Reformed Theological Seminary, Charlotte, NC (p. 63)
*Allan C. Carlson, Howard Center for Family, Religion and Society, Rockford, IL (p. 70)
*Samuel Casey Carter, Acade Metrics, LLC, Washington, DC (p. 71)
*Micah Clark, American Family Association, Indianapolis, IN (p. 75)
John Cobin, Montauk Financial Group, Greenville, SC (p. 76)

HOME SCHOOLING (Continued)

*__Richard T. Colgan,__ Bridgewater State College, Warwick, RI **(p. 78)**
  __Kellyanne Conway,__ the polling company/WomanTrend, Washington, DC **(p. 80)**
  __Douglas H. Cook,__ Regent University, Virginia Beach, VA **(p. 80)**
*__John E. Coons,__ University of California at Berkeley, Berkeley, CA **(p. 81)**
  __Roy E. Cordato,__ John Locke Foundation, Raleigh, NC **(p. 82)**
  __Jim F. Couch,__ University of North Alabama, Florence, AL **(p. 83)**
*__Ron Crews,__ Massachusetts Family Institute, Newton Upper Falls, MA **(p. 86)**
*__Charles H. Cunningham,__ National Rifle Association, Washington, DC **(p. 87)**
*__Brad W. Dacus,__ Pacific Justice Institute, Citrus Heights, CA **(p. 87)**
*__Thomas DeWeese,__ American Policy Center, Warrenton, VA **(p. 94)**
  __Douglas Dean Dewey,__ Children's Scholarship Fund, New York, NY **(p. 94)**
*__John R. Diggs, Jr.,__ South Hadley, MA **(p. 95)**
  __James C. Dobson,__ Focus on the Family, Colorado Springs, CO **(p. 96)**
  __Marie Dolan,__ New York State Federation of Catholic School Parents, Flushing, NY **(p. 96)**
  __Richard J. Dougherty,__ University of Dallas, Irving, TX **(p. 97)**
  __Diallo Dphrepaulezz,__ New York, NY **(p. 98)**
*__Richard Duncan,__ University of Nebraska, Lincoln, NE **(p. 99)**
*__David Dunn,__ Oklahoma Family Policy Council, Bethany, OK **(p. 100)**
  __Brandon Dutcher,__ Oklahoma Council of Public Affairs, Oklahoma City, OK **(p. 101)**
*__Michelle Easton,__ Clare Boothe Luce Policy Institute, Herndon, VA **(p. 102)**
*__Fran Eaton,__ Eagle Forum of Illinois, Oak Forest, IL **(p. 102)**
  __Tim G. Echols,__ TeenPact Teen Leadership School, Jefferson, GA **(p. 103)**
*__Robert C. Enlow,__ Milton and Rose Friedman Foundation, Indianapolis, IN **(p. 107)**
*__Williamson M. Evers,__ Hoover Institution, Stanford, CA **(p. 108)**
*__Michael P. Farris,__ Patrick Henry College, Purcellville, VA **(p. 109)**
*__Marc Fey,__ Focus on the Family, Colorado Springs, CO **(p. 111)**
*__David Forte,__ Cleveland State University, Cleveland, OH **(p. 114)**
  __Marshall Fritz,__ Alliance for the Separation of School & State, Fresno, CA **(p. 118)**
*__Michael Geer,__ Pennsylvania Family Institute, Harrisburg, PA **(p. 122)**
*__Mary F. Gifford,__ Field, Sarvas, King and Coleman, Phoenix, AZ **(p. 123)**
*__Gary Glenn,__ American Family Association of Michigan, Midland, MI **(p. 124)**
*__Jay P. Greene,__ Manhattan Institute for Policy Research, Davie, FL **(p. 128)**
  __Rebecca Hagelin,__ The Heritage Foundation, Washington, DC **(p. 131)**
*__Robert Hale,__ Northwest Legal Foundation, Minot, ND **(p. 132)**
  __Eric Hanushek,__ Hoover Institution, Stanford, CA **(p. 135)**
*__Randy Hicks,__ Georgia Family Council, Norcross, GA **(p. 141)**
*__Thomas Hinton,__ The Heritage Foundation, Washington, DC **(p. 143)**
*__Robert Holland,__ Lexington Institute, Arlington, VA **(p. 144)**
  __Martin Hoyt,__ American Association of Christian Schools, Washington, DC **(p. 148)**
*__Charles D. Hurley,__ Iowa Family Policy Center, Pleasant Hill, IA **(p. 150)**
*__Bradley P. Jacob,__ Regent University, Virginia Beach, VA **(p. 152)**
*__Krista Kafer,__ The Heritage Foundation, Washington, DC **(p. 156)**
  __Lindalyn Kakadelis,__ North Carolina Education Alliance, Pineville, NC **(p. 157)**
  __Jane Kilgore,__ Austin CEO Foundation, Austin, TX **(p. 163)**
  __Christina Kindel,__ North Dakota Family Alliance, Bismarck, ND **(p. 164)**
  __Kent King,__ Missouri State Teachers Association, Columbia, MO **(p. 164)**
*__David W. Kirkpatrick,__ Citizens for Educational Freedom, Douglassville, PA **(p. 164)**
*__Christopher J. Klicka,__ Home School Legal Defense Association, Purcellville, VA **(p. 165)**
  __Gary Kreep,__ United States Justice Foundation, Escondido, CA **(p. 169)**
*__Matthew Ladner,__ Children First America, Austin, TX **(p. 171)**
  __Daniel Lapin,__ Toward Tradition, Mercer Island, WA **(p. 174)**
  __Casey Lartigue, Jr.,__ Cato Institute, Washington, DC **(p. 175)**
  __Phillip F. Lawler,__ *Catholic World Report,* South Lancaster, MA **(p. 176)**
  __Joseph G. Lehman,__ Mackinac Center for Public Policy, Midland, MI **(p. 177)**

HOME SCHOOLING (Continued)

*Mike Long, Complete Abstinence Eduation Program, Durham, NC (p. 183)

Brett A. Magbee, Oklahoma Council of Public Affairs, Oklahoma City, OK (p. 186)

*Dennis Mansfield, Boise, ID (p. 189)

Jennifer Marshall, Empower America, Washington, DC (p. 190)

*Connie Marshner, Raphael Services, Front Royal, VA (p. 190)

*Nina May, *Renaissance Connection.com/RCNetwork.net*, Washington, DC (p. 192)

Wilfred M. McClay, University of Tennessee, Chattanooga, Chattanooga, TN (p. 193)

*Michael W. McConnell, University of Utah, Salt Lake City, UT (p. 194)

Paul T. Mero, The Sutherland Institute, Salt Lake City, UT (p. 199)

Harry Messenheimer, Rio Grande Foundation, Tijeras, NM (p. 200)

Elizabeth Mische, Partnership for Choice in Education, St. Paul, MN (p. 203)

Terry M. Moe, Hoover Institution, Stanford, CA (p. 204)

*Steven W. Mosher, Population Research Institute, Front Royal, VA (p. 208)

*Len Munsil, Center for Arizona Policy, Scottsdale, AZ (p. 209)

Ronald Nash, Reformed Theological Seminary, Oviedo, FL (p. 211)

*Charles J. O'Malley, Charles J. O'Malley & Associates, Inc., Annapolis, MD (p. 217)

*Richard Olivastro, People Dynamics, Farmington, CT (p. 218)

*Darcy A. Olsen, Goldwater Institute, Phoenix, AZ (p. 219)

*Allan E. Parker, Jr., Texas Justice Foundation, San Antonio, TX (p. 221)

*J. A. Parker, Lincoln Institute for Research and Education, Washington, DC (p. 221)

*Christine Patterson, Texas Public Policy Foundation, San Antonio, TX (p. 223)

*Nancy M. Pfotenhauer, Independent Women's Forum, Arlington, VA (p. 227)

*Howard Phillips, The Conservative Caucus, Inc., Vienna, VA (p. 227)

Victor Porlier, Center for Civic Renewal, Inc., Delmar, NY (p. 231)

*Eric Premack, California State University Institute for Education Reform, Sacramento, CA (p. 232)

*Thomas Prichard, Minnesota Family Council, Minneapolis, MN (p. 233)

*Ed Rauchut, CEO Omaha, Bellevue, NE (p. 236)

*Charles E. Rice, Notre Dame Law School, Notre Dame, IN (p. 239)

John E. Rocha, Sr., Center for the American Idea, Houston, TX (p. 242)

J. Patrick Rooney, Golden Rule Insurance Company, Indianapolis, IN (p. 243)

*David F. Salisbury, Cato Institute, Washington, DC (p. 248)

*Steven Alan Samson, Liberty University, Lynchburg, VA (p. 249)

*Phyllis Schlafly, Eagle Forum, St. Louis, MO (p. 253)

*Christopher Smith, Internet Education Exchange (iEdx), Scottsdale, AZ (p. 262)

J. Michael Smith, Home School Legal Defense Association, Purcellville, VA (p. 263)

*Lisa Snell, Reason Foundation, Los Angeles, CA (p. 265)

*Fawn Spady, Education Excellence Coalition, Seattle, WA (p. 266)

*Jim Spady, Education Excellence Coalition, Seattle, WA (p. 266)

*John A. Sparks, Grove City College, Grove City, PA (p. 266)

Gordon St. Angelo, Milton and Rose Friedman Foundation, Indianapolis, IN (p. 267)

Joy Sweet, National Right to Read Foundation, The Plains, VA (p. 273)

Charles Sykes, Wisconsin Policy Research Institute, Mequon, WI (p. 273)

Kevin Teasley, Greater Educational Opportunities Foundation, Indianapolis, IN (p. 275)

*Karen Testerman, Cornerstone Policy Research, Concord, NH (p. 275)

*Mark Thornton, Columbus State University, Columbus, GA (p. 278)

Eugenia Froedge Toma, University of Kentucky, Lexington, KY (p. 280)

Kristina Twitty, Eagle Forum, Washington, DC (p. 282)

Tom Washburne, Home School Legal Defense Association, Purcellville, VA (p. 289)

Stanley J. Watson, Patrick Henry College, Purcellville, VA (p. 290)

Nick Weller, Cascade Policy Institute, Portland, OR (p. 292)

*Paul Weyrich, Free Congress Foundation, Washington, DC (p. 293)

*Natalie Williams, Robinson, DiLando and Whitaker, Sacramento, CA (p. 295)

Richard B. Wirthlin, Wirthlin Worldwide, South Jordan, UT (p. 296)

HOME SCHOOLING (Continued)

David Zanotti, Ohio Roundtable, Strongsville, OH (p. 301)

PUBLIC SCHOOL FINANCE AND ADMINISTRATION

*Charles M. Achilles, Eastern Michigan University, Ypsilanti, MI (p. 34)
 Jeanne Allen, Center for Education Reform, Washington, DC (p. 36)
*Lewis Andrews, Yankee Institute for Public Policy Studies, Hartford, CT (p. 39)
*Martin Angell, A Choice for Every Child Foundation, Dallas, TX (p. 39)
 Brian Backstrom, Empire Foundation for Policy Research, Clifton Park, NY (p. 42)
*William J. Bennett, Empower America, Washington, DC (p. 51)
*Wayman R. Bishop, The Family Foundation of Virginia, Richmond, VA (p. 53)
*Christian N. Braunlich, Thomas Jefferson Institute for Public Policy, Alexandria, VA (p. 60)
*Matthew J. Brouillette, The Commonwealth Foundation, Harrisburg, PA (p. 62)
*Dominic M. Calabro, Florida TaxWatch Research Institute, Inc., Tallahassee, FL (p. 67)
*James B. Cardle, Texas Citizen Action Network, Austin, TX (p. 69)
 Brian Carpenter, Mackinac Center for Public Policy, Midland, MI (p. 70)
*John Chubb, Edison Schools, Inc., New York, NY (p. 74)
*John E. Coons, University of California at Berkeley, Berkeley, CA (p. 81)
 Bob Corkins, Kansas Legislative Education and Research, Inc., Topeka, KS (p. 82)
*Jon Coupal, Howard Jarvis Taxpayers Association, Sacramento, CA (p. 83)
*Brad W. Dacus, Pacific Justice Institute, Citrus Heights, CA (p. 87)
 Richard S. Davis, Washington Research Council, Seattle, WA (p. 89)
 Candace de Russy, State University of New York, Bronxville, NY (p. 90)
*Glenn Delk, Georgia Charter Schools, Atlanta, GA (p. 92)
*Robert Destro, Catholic University of America, Washington, DC (p. 94)
 Denis Doyle, Doyle Associates, Chevy Chase, MD (p. 98)
*Michelle Easton, Clare Boothe Luce Policy Institute, Herndon, VA (p. 102)
*Robert C. Enlow, Milton and Rose Friedman Foundation, Indianapolis, IN (p. 107)
*Michael P. Farris, Patrick Henry College, Purcellville, VA (p. 109)
 Richard M. Ferry, Catholic Education Foundation, Los Angeles, CA (p. 111)
*Marc Fey, Focus on the Family, Colorado Springs, CO (p. 111)
 William A. Fischel, Dartmouth College, Hanover, NH (p. 112)
*Robert Franciosi, Goldwater Institute, Phoenix, AZ (p. 115)
 Steven B. Frates, Claremont McKenna College, Claremont, CA (p. 116)
 Marshall Fritz, Alliance for the Separation of School & State, Fresno, CA (p. 118)
*Mary F. Gifford, Field, Sarvas, King and Coleman, Phoenix, AZ (p. 123)
 Clint W. Green, Acton Institute for the Study of Religion and Liberty,
    Grand Rapids, MI (p. 128)
*Jay P. Greene, Manhattan Institute for Policy Research, Davie, FL (p. 128)
*Grant R. Gulibon, The Commonwealth Foundation, Harrisburg, PA (p. 130)
*Gerald A. Gunderson, Trinity College, Hartford, CT (p. 130)
*Charlene Haar, Education Policy Institute, Washington, DC (p. 131)
*Joshua Hall, Buckeye Institute for Public Policy Solutions, Columbus, OH (p. 132)
 Eric Hanushek, Hoover Institution, Stanford, CA (p. 135)
 Rea Hederman, Jr., The Heritage Foundation, Washington, DC (p. 139)
 Lowman Henry, Lincoln Institute of Public Opinion Research, Inc., Harrisburg, PA (p. 140)
*Paul T. Hill, University of Washington, Seattle, WA (p. 142)
*Fred Holden, Phoenix Enterprises, Arvada, CO (p. 144)
*John MacDonald Hood, John Locke Foundation, Raleigh, NC (p. 145)
*Caroline M. Hoxby, Harvard University, Cambridge, MA (p. 147)
*Gary Huggins, Education Leaders Action Council, Washington, DC (p. 148)
*Lance T. Izumi, Pacific Research Institute, Sacramento, CA (p. 152)
*Mike Jerman, Utah Taxpayers Association, Salt Lake City, UT (p. 154)
 Kirk A. Johnson, Mackinac Center for Public Policy, Midland, MI (p. 155)
*Doug Kagan, Nebraska Taxpayers for Freedom, Omaha, NE (p. 157)

PUBLIC SCHOOL FINANCE AND ADMINISTRATION (Continued)

Lindalyn Kakadelis, North Carolina Education Alliance, Pineville, NC (p. 157)

*Lisa Graham Keegan, Education Leaders Council, Washington, DC (p. 160)

Kent King, Missouri State Teachers Association, Columbia, MO (p. 164)

*David W. Kirkpatrick, Citizens for Educational Freedom, Douglassville, PA (p. 164)

John Kirtley, Children First America, Bentonville, AR (p. 165)

*Mark R. Levin, Landmark Legal Foundation, Herndon, VA (p. 178)

*Myron Lieberman, Education Policy Institute, Washington, DC (p. 180)

*George Liebmann, Calvert Institute for Policy Research, Baltimore, MD (p. 180)

*Rita P. Maguire, Arizona Center for Public Policy, Phoenix, AZ (p. 186)

Michael Marlow, California Polytechnic State University, San Luis Obispo, CA (p. 189)

*John McClaughry, Ethan Allen Institute, Concord, VT (p. 193)

Elizabeth Mische, Partnership for Choice in Education, St. Paul, MN (p. 203)

Terry M. Moe, Hoover Institution, Stanford, CA (p. 204)

Cassandra Chrones Moore, Cato Institute, Washington, DC (p. 205)

Thomas Nechyba, Duke University, Durham, NC (p. 211)

Michael A. Nelson, University of Akron, Akron, OH (p. 212)

*Richard Olivastro, People Dynamics, Farmington, CT (p. 218)

*Darcy A. Olsen, Goldwater Institute, Phoenix, AZ (p. 219)

*Joseph P. Overton, Mackinac Center for Public Policy, Midland, MI (p. 220)

*Christine Patterson, Texas Public Policy Foundation, San Antonio, TX (p. 223)

*Sam Peltzman, University of Chicago Graduate School of Business, Chicago, IL (p. 225)

*Lovett C. Peters, Pioneer Institute for Public Policy Research, Boston, MA (p. 226)

*Michael Podgursky, University of Missouri, Columbia, MO (p. 230)

*Eric Premack, California State University Institute for Education Reform, Sacramento, CA (p. 232)

*William L. Proctor, Flagler College, St. Augustine, FL (p. 233)

*Ed Rauchut, CEO Omaha, Bellevue, NE (p. 236)

Holly Robinson, Georgia Public Policy Foundation, Atlanta, GA (p. 242)

*Doug Rogers, Association of Texas Professional Educators, Austin, TX (p. 243)

*Frank Russo, American Family Association of New York, Port Washington, NY (p. 247)

*Christopher Smith, Internet Education Exchange (iEdx), Scottsdale, AZ (p. 262)

*Lisa Snell, Reason Foundation, Los Angeles, CA (p. 265)

*Samuel R. Staley, Buckeye Institute for Public Policy Solutions, Columbus, OH (p. 268)

*Jeff Stormo, Choices for Children, Grand Rapids, MI (p. 270)

*William Craig Stubblebine, Claremont McKenna College, Claremont, CA (p. 271)

Christopher B. Summers, Maryland Public Policy Institute, Germantown, MD (p. 272)

Charles Sykes, Wisconsin Policy Research Institute, Mequon, WI (p. 273)

Kevin Teasley, Greater Educational Opportunities Foundation, Indianapolis, IN (p. 275)

*Forest M. Thigpen, Mississippi Family Council, Jackson, MS (p. 277)

*Mark Thornton, Columbus State University, Columbus, GA (p. 278)

*Jim Tobin, National Taxpayers United of Illinois, Chicago, IL (p. 279)

Eugenia Froedge Toma, University of Kentucky, Lexington, KY (p. 280)

*Forrest L. Turpen, Christian Educators Association International, Pasadena, CA (p. 282)

*Richard Vedder, Ohio University, Athens, OH (p. 284)

Joseph P. Viteritti, New York University, New York, NY (p. 285)

*Herbert J. Walberg, University of Illinois, Chicago, Chicago, IL (p. 286)

*Michael W. Watson, Children First America, Austin, TX (p. 290)

Stanley J. Watson, Patrick Henry College, Purcellville, VA (p. 290)

Nick Weller, Cascade Policy Institute, Portland, OR (p. 292)

*Bob Williams, Evergreen Freedom Foundation, Olympia, WA (p. 295)

*Ron F. Williamson, Great Plains Public Policy Institute, Sioux Falls, SD (p. 295)

*Gary Wolfram, Hillsdale College, Hillsdale, MI (p. 297)

Jason Wright, Frontiers of Freedom Institute, Fairfax, VA (p. 299)

---

* Has testified before a state or federal legislative committee

SCHOOL CHOICE

David L. Adams, Concordia Seminary, St. Louis, MO (p. 34)

*Robert Aguirre, San Antonio, TX (p. 35)

*I. Dean Ahmad, Minaret of Freedom Institute, Bethesda, MD (p. 36)

*M. Gene Aldridge, New Mexico Independence Research Institute, Las Cruces, NM (p. 36)

Benjamin Alexander, Franciscan University of Steubenville, Steubenville, OH (p. 36)

Judy Alger, Center for Market-Based Education, Inc., Rumney, NH (p. 36)

Jeanne Allen, Center for Education Reform, Washington, DC (p. 36)

*William Allen, Michigan State University, East Lansing, MI (p. 37)

*Lewis Andrews, Yankee Institute for Public Policy Studies, Hartford, CT (p. 39)

*Martin Angell, A Choice for Every Child Foundation, Dallas, TX (p. 39)

*Julaine K. Appling, Family Research Institute of Wisconsin, Madison, WI (p. 40)

*David J. Armor, George Mason University, Fairfax, VA (p. 40)

Brian Backstrom, Empire Foundation for Policy Research, Clifton Park, NY (p. 42)

Richard A. Baer, Jr., Cornell University, Ithaca, NY (p. 42)

*Charles W. Baird, California State University, Hayward, Hayward, CA (p. 43)

Hunter Baker, Georgia Family Council, Norcross, GA (p. 43)

*John S. Baker, Jr., Louisiana State University, Baton Rouge, LA (p. 43)

*Joseph L. Bast, Heartland Institute, Chicago, IL (p. 47)

*Gary L. Bauer, Campaign for Working Families, Arlington, VA (p. 47)

*Janet Beales, Kids One, East Brunswick, NJ (p. 48)

Bill Becker, Maine Policy Center, Portland, ME (p. 48)

Paul Beckner, Citizens for a Sound Economy, Washington, DC (p. 48)

*Pamela Benigno, Independence Institute, Golden, CO (p. 50)

*William J. Bennett, Empower America, Washington, DC (p. 51)

*Saundra Berry, Cleveland Scholarship and Tutoring Program, Cleveland, OH (p. 52)

*John E. Berthoud, National Taxpayers Union, Alexandria, VA (p. 52)

*Jason Bertsch, American Enterprise Institute, Washington, DC (p. 52)

Douglas Besharov, American Enterprise Institute, Washington, DC (p. 52)

*Fran Bevan, Eagle Forum of Pennsylvania, North Huntingdon, PA (p. 53)

*Wayman R. Bishop, The Family Foundation of Virginia, Richmond, VA (p. 53)

Greg Blankenship, Illinois Policy Institute, Springfield, IL (p. 54)

*Mark Blitz, Claremont McKenna College, Claremont, CA (p. 55)

Felita Blowe, Concerned Women for America, Washington, DC (p. 55)

*David Boaz, Cato Institute, Washington, DC (p. 55)

*Clint Bolick, Institute for Justice, Phoenix, AZ (p. 56)

Harry Borders, Kentucky League for Educational Alternatives, Frankfort, KY (p. 57)

Anthony Bradley, Acton Institute for the Study of Religion and Liberty,
    Grand Rapids, MI (p. 59)

*Gerard V. Bradley, Notre Dame Law School, Notre Dame, IN (p. 59)

*Christian N. Braunlich, Thomas Jefferson Institute for Public Policy, Alexandria, VA (p. 60)

*Marshall J. Breger, Catholic University of America, Washington, DC (p. 60)

David Brennan, White Hat Management, Akron, OH (p. 61)

Dedrick Briggs, Charter School Resource Center of Tennessee, Memphis, TN (p. 61)

Adrian Brigham, Citizens for Educational Freedom of Illinois, Streamwood, IL (p. 61)

B. Jason Brooks, Empire Foundation for Policy Research, Clifton Park, NY (p. 62)

*Bill Brooks, North Carolina Family Policy Council, Raleigh, NC (p. 62)

*Matthew J. Brouillette, The Commonwealth Foundation, Harrisburg, PA (p. 62)

*Floyd G. Brown, Young America's Foundation Reagan Ranch Project,
    Santa Barbara, CA (p. 63)

*Harold O. J. Brown, Reformed Theological Seminary, Charlotte, NC (p. 63)

*Kenneth Brown, Rio Grande Foundation, Albuquerque, NM (p. 63)

*Martin D. Brown, Richmond, VA (p. 63)

Morgan Brown, Center of the American Experiment, Minneapolis, MN (p. 63)

*Sharon Browne, Pacific Legal Foundation, Sacramento, CA (p. 63)

SCHOOL CHOICE (Continued)

*Steve Buckstein, Cascade Policy Institute, Portland, OR (p. 65)
*Stuart Butler, The Heritage Foundation, Washington, DC (p. 66)
 Priscilla Caine, Children First Tennessee, Chattanooga, TN (p. 67)
*Kaleem Caire, American Education Reform Council, Bowie, MD (p. 67)
*Dominic M. Calabro, Florida TaxWatch Research Institute, Inc., Tallahassee, FL (p. 67)
*Jon Charles Caldara, Independence Institute, Golden, CO (p. 67)
 Nicholas Capaldi, Loyola University New Orleans, New Orleans, LA (p. 69)
*James B. Cardle, Texas Citizen Action Network, Austin, TX (p. 69)
 Merrick Carey, Lexington Institute, Arlington, VA (p. 70)
*Allan C. Carlson, Howard Center for Family, Religion and Society, Rockford, IL (p. 70)
 Brian Carpenter, Mackinac Center for Public Policy, Midland, MI (p. 70)
*Thomas Carroll, Empire Foundation for Policy Research, Clifton Park, NY (p. 71)
*Samuel Casey Carter, Acade Metrics, LLC, Washington, DC (p. 71)
*John Chubb, Edison Schools, Inc., New York, NY (p. 74)
*Michael A. Ciamarra, Alabama Policy Institute, Birmingham, AL (p. 74)
*J. R. Clark, University of Tennessee, Chattanooga, Chattanooga, TN (p. 75)
*Micah Clark, American Family Association, Indianapolis, IN (p. 75)
 Elisa Clements, Education Excellence Utah, Salt Lake City, UT (p. 76)
*George Clowes, Heartland Institute, Chicago, IL (p. 76)
*Laurence Cohen, Yankee Institute for Public Policy Studies, Glastonbury, CT (p. 78)
 Richard H. Collins, Children's Education Fund, Dallas, TX (p. 78)
*Ward Connerly, American Civil Rights Institute, Sacramento, CA (p. 80)
*Kenneth L. Connor, Family Research Council, Washington, DC (p. 80)
*John E. Coons, University of California at Berkeley, Berkeley, CA (p. 81)
 Bob Corkins, Kansas Legislative Education and Research, Inc., Topeka, KS (p. 82)
 Jim F. Couch, University of North Alabama, Florence, AL (p. 83)
 Andrew Coulson, Mackinac Center for Public Policy, Poulsbo, WA (p. 83)
*Jon Coupal, Howard Jarvis Taxpayers Association, Sacramento, CA (p. 83)
*Jerry Cox, Arkansas Family Council, Little Rock, AR (p. 84)
*Matt Cox, Pacific Research Institute, Sacramento, CA (p. 84)
 Edward H. Crane, Cato Institute, Washington, DC (p. 85)
*Ron Crews, Massachusetts Family Institute, Newton Upper Falls, MA (p. 86)
 Neil S. Crispo, Florida State University, Tallahassee, FL (p. 86)
*Brad W. Dacus, Pacific Justice Institute, Citrus Heights, CA (p. 87)
*Matt Daniels, Alliance for Marriage, Springfield, VA (p. 88)
 Richard S. Davis, Washington Research Council, Seattle, WA (p. 89)
 Robert G. de Posada, The Latino Coalition, Washington, DC (p. 90)
 Candace de Russy, State University of New York, Bronxville, NY (p. 90)
*Glenn Delk, Georgia Charter Schools, Atlanta, GA (p. 92)
 Helene Denney, Nevada Policy Research Insitute, Las Vegas, NV (p. 92)
*Len Deo, New Jersey Family Policy Council, Parsippany, NJ (p. 93)
*Robert Destro, Catholic University of America, Washington, DC (p. 94)
*William T. Devlin, Urban Family Council, Philadelphia, PA (p. 94)
*Phillip DeVous, Acton Institute for the Study of Religion and Liberty, Grand Rapids, MI (p. 94)
 Douglas Dean Dewey, Children's Scholarship Fund, New York, NY (p. 94)
*Gerry Dickinson, South Carolina Policy Council, Columbia, SC (p. 95)
 James C. Dobson, Focus on the Family, Colorado Springs, CO (p. 96)
 Marie Dolan, New York State Federation of Catholic School Parents, Flushing, NY (p. 96)
 Daniel J. Dougherty, Pennsylvania Federation-Citizens for Educational Freedom,
    Philadelphia, PA (p. 97)
 Denis Doyle, Doyle Associates, Chevy Chase, MD (p. 98)
 Diallo Dphrepaulezz, New York, NY (p. 98)
 Pete du Pont, National Center for Policy Analysis, Wilmington, DE (p. 98)
*Mae Duggan, Citizens for Educational Freedom, St. Louis, MO (p. 99)

---

* Has testified before a state or federal legislative committee

SCHOOL CHOICE (Continued)

Martin Duggan, Educational Freedom Foundation, St. Louis, MO (p. 99)

*Richard Duncan, University of Nebraska, Lincoln, NE (p. 99)

*Clark Durant, New Common School Foundation, Detroit, MI (p. 101)

Brandon Dutcher, Oklahoma Council of Public Affairs, Oklahoma City, OK (p. 101)

*John C. Eastman, Chapman University School of Law, Orange, CA (p. 102)

*Michelle Easton, Clare Boothe Luce Policy Institute, Herndon, VA (p. 102)

*Robert C. Enlow, Milton and Rose Friedman Foundation, Indianapolis, IN (p. 107)

*Williamson M. Evers, Hoover Institution, Stanford, CA (p. 108)

*Thompson Mason Faller, University of Portland, Portland, OR (p. 109)

Megan Farnsworth, The Heritage Foundation, Washington, DC (p. 109)

Richard M. Ferry, Catholic Education Foundation, Los Angeles, CA (p. 111)

*Marc Fey, Focus on the Family, Colorado Springs, CO (p. 111)

*Robert Fike, Americans for Tax Reform, Washington, DC (p. 111)

John Findley, Pacific Legal Foundation, Sacramento, CA (p. 111)

*Chester E. Finn, Jr., Thomas B. Fordham Foundation, Washington, DC (p. 112)

*Seymour Fliegel, Center for Educational Innovation – Public Education Association, New York, NY (p. 113)

*David Forte, Cleveland State University, Cleveland, OH (p. 114)

*Robert Franciosi, Goldwater Institute, Phoenix, AZ (p. 115)

Amy Frantz, Public Interest Institute, Mount Pleasant, IA (p. 116)

Robert Freedman, Institute for Justice, Washington, DC (p. 116)

David D. Friedman, Santa Clara University, San Jose, CA (p. 117)

*Milton Friedman, Hoover Institution, Stanford, CA (p. 117)

*Murray Friedman, American Jewish Committee, Philadelphia, PA (p. 117)

Marshall Fritz, Alliance for the Separation of School & State, Fresno, CA (p. 118)

Adam Fuller, Toward Tradition, Mercer Island, WA (p. 118)

Howard Fuller, Marquette University, Milwaukee, WI (p. 118)

Richard W. Garnett, Notre Dame Law School, Notre Dame, IN (p. 120)

Jennifer Garrett, The Heritage Foundation, Washington, DC (p. 120)

*John Taylor Gatto, Odysseus Group Inc., New York, NY (p. 121)

*Michael Geer, Pennsylvania Family Institute, Harrisburg, PA (p. 122)

*Kathy Getchell, Center for Market-Based Education, Inc., Londonderry, NH (p. 123)

*Mary F. Gifford, Field, Sarvas, King and Coleman, Phoenix, AZ (p. 123)

Dennis A. Giorno, REACH Alliance, Harrisburg, PA (p. 124)

*James K. Glassman, American Enterprise Institute, Washington, DC (p. 124)

*Charles L. Glenn, Boston University, Boston, MA (p. 124)

*Gary Glenn, American Family Association of Michigan, Midland, MI (p. 124)

Kay Glover, Citizens for Choice in Education, Sturgis, SD (p. 125)

Daniel J. Goldhaber, University of Washington, Seattle, WA (p. 125)

John C. Goodman, National Center for Policy Analysis, Dallas, TX (p. 126)

Clint W. Green, Acton Institute for the Study of Religion and Liberty, Grand Rapids, MI (p. 128)

*Jay P. Greene, Manhattan Institute for Policy Research, Davie, FL (p. 128)

Charles Greenwalt, II, Susquehanna Valley Center for Public Policy, Hershey, PA (p. 129)

Marie Gryphon, Cato Institute, Washington, DC (p. 130)

*Gerald A. Gunderson, Trinity College, Hartford, CT (p. 130)

*Lawrence Gunnells, CSF Arkansas, Little Rock, AR (p. 130)

*Charlene Haar, Education Policy Institute, Washington, DC (p. 131)

Rebecca Hagelin, The Heritage Foundation, Washington, DC (p. 131)

*Robert Hale, Northwest Legal Foundation, Minot, ND (p. 132)

*Joshua Hall, Buckeye Institute for Public Policy Solutions, Columbus, OH (p. 132)

Roger Hamburg, Indiana University South Bend, South Bend, IN (p. 133)

*Randy H. Hamilton, University of California, Berkeley, Berkeley, CA (p. 133)

Paige Holland Hamp, Maryland Public Policy Institute, Germantown, MD (p. 133)

SCHOOL CHOICE (Continued)

Jerome J. Hanus, American University, Washington, DC (p. 134)

Eric Hanushek, Hoover Institution, Stanford, CA (p. 135)

*Lynn Harsh, Evergreen Freedom Foundation, Olympia, WA (p. 136)

Robert Hawkins, Jr., Institute for Contemporary Studies, Oakland, CA (p. 137)

Michael S. Heath, Christian Civic League of Maine, Augusta, ME (p. 138)

Justin Heet, Hudson Institute, Indianapolis, IN (p. 139)

*Frank J. Heller, Maine Policy Ronin Network, Brunswick, ME (p. 139)

Lowman Henry, Lincoln Institute of Public Opinion Research, Inc., Harrisburg, PA (p. 140)

Carl Herbster, American Association of Christian Schools, Independence, MO (p. 140)

*Randy Hicks, Georgia Family Council, Norcross, GA (p. 141)

*Paul T. Hill, University of Washington, Seattle, WA (p. 142)

*Thomas Hinton, The Heritage Foundation, Washington, DC (p. 143)

David Hogberg, Public Interest Institute, Mount Pleasant, IA (p. 144)

*Robert Holland, Lexington Institute, Arlington, VA (p. 144)

*John C. Holmes, Association of Christian Schools International, Washington, DC (p. 145)

*John MacDonald Hood, John Locke Foundation, Raleigh, NC (p. 145)

David Horowitz, Center for the Study of Popular Culture, Los Angeles, CA (p. 146)

*Michael Horowitz, Hudson Institute, Washington, DC (p. 146)

*Richard R. Hough, III, Children's Scholarship Fund, New York, NY (p. 147)

*Caroline M. Hoxby, Harvard University, Cambridge, MA (p. 147)

*Robert L. Hoy, Educational CHOICE Charitable Trust, Indianapolis, IN (p. 147)

Martin Hoyt, American Association of Christian Schools, Washington, DC (p. 148)

*Gary Huggins, Education Leaders Action Council, Washington, DC (p. 148)

*Robert Hunter, Mackinac Center for Public Policy, Midland, MI (p. 150)

*Charles D. Hurley, Iowa Family Policy Center, Pleasant Hill, IA (p. 150)

*Harry G. Hutchison, Wayne State University, Detroit, MI (p. 150)

Richard P. Hutchison, Landmark Legal Foundation, Kansas City, MO (p. 150)

Niger Roy Innis, Congress of Racial Equality, New York, NY (p. 151)

*Lance T. Izumi, Pacific Research Institute, Sacramento, CA (p. 152)

Earl W. Jackson, Sr., Samaritan Project, Chesapeake, VA (p. 152)

*Charles W. Jarvis, United Seniors Association, Fairfax, VA (p. 153)

*Thomas L. Jipping, Concerned Women for America, Washington, DC (p. 154)

Kirk A. Johnson, Mackinac Center for Public Policy, Midland, MI (p. 155)

Michael S. Joyce, Foundation for Community and Faith Centered Enterprise, Phoenix, AZ (p. 156)

*Krista Kafer, The Heritage Foundation, Washington, DC (p. 156)

*John Kain, University of Texas, Dallas, Richardson, TX (p. 157)

Lindalyn Kakadelis, North Carolina Education Alliance, Pineville, NC (p. 157)

Martin S. Kaufman, Atlantic Legal Foundation, New York, NY (p. 159)

*Raymond J. Keating, Small Business Survival Committee, Manorville, NY (p. 159)

*Lisa Graham Keegan, Education Leaders Council, Washington, DC (p. 160)

*Patrick J. Keleher, Jr., TEACH America, Wilmette, IL (p. 160)

*W. Thomas Kelly, Savers and Investors League, Mirror Lake, NH (p. 161)

Darlene A. Kennedy, Centre for New Black Leadership, Baltimore, MD (p. 162)

*William A. Keyes, The Institute on Political Journalism, Washington, DC (p. 162)

Jane Kilgore, Austin CEO Foundation, Austin, TX (p. 163)

Kent King, Missouri State Teachers Association, Columbia, MO (p. 164)

*David W. Kirkpatrick, Citizens for Educational Freedom, Douglassville, PA (p. 164)

John Kirtley, Children First America, Bentonville, AR (p. 165)

Joy Kiviat, Citizens for Educational Freedom, St. Louis, MO (p. 165)

*Manuel Klausner, Individual Rights Foundation, Los Angeles, CA (p. 165)

Mary Beth Klee, Link Institute, Portsmouth, NH (p. 165)

*Christopher J. Klicka, Home School Legal Defense Association, Purcellville, VA (p. 165)

*Douglas W. Kmiec, The Catholic University of America, Washington, DC (p. 166)

SCHOOL CHOICE (Continued)

Richard D. Komer, Institute for Justice, Washington, DC (p. 167)

John E. Kramer, Institute for Justice, Washington, DC (p. 168)

Gary Kreep, United States Justice Foundation, Escondido, CA (p. 169)

*Matthew Ladner, Children First America, Austin, TX (p. 171)

*Andrea S. Lafferty, Traditional Values Coalition, Washington, DC (p. 172)

*George Landrith, Frontiers of Freedom Institute, Fairfax, VA (p. 173)

Daniel Lapin, Toward Tradition, Mercer Island, WA (p. 174)

Juan Lara, Hispanic Council for Reform and Educational Options, San Antonio, TX (p. 174)

Casey Lartigue, Jr., Cato Institute, Washington, DC (p. 175)

Phillip F. Lawler, *Catholic World Report*, South Lancaster, MA (p. 176)

*Stephen Lazarus, Center for Public Justice, Annapolis, MD (p. 176)

*Andrew T. LeFevre, American Legislative Exchange Council, Washington, DC (p. 177)

Joseph G. Lehman, Mackinac Center for Public Policy, Midland, MI (p. 177)

Seth Leibsohn, Empower America, Washington, DC (p. 177)

*Mark R. Levin, Landmark Legal Foundation, Herndon, VA (p. 178)

*Robert A. Levy, Cato Institute, Washington, DC (p. 179)

*Myron Lieberman, Education Policy Institute, Washington, DC (p. 180)

Leonard P. Liggio, Atlas Economic Research Foundation, Fairfax, VA (p. 180)

Nelson Llumiquinga, Arizona School Choice Trust, Phoenix, AZ (p. 182)

Michael Lynch, *Reason* Magazine, New Haven, CT (p. 184)

Tibor R. Machan, Chapman University, Silverado Canyon, CA (p. 185)

Myron Magnet, Manhattan Institute for Policy Research, New York, NY (p. 186)

*Rita P. Maguire, Arizona Center for Public Policy, Phoenix, AZ (p. 186)

J. J. Mahoney, Diversified Consultants, Mount Pleasant, SC (p. 187)

*Bruno V. Manno, The Annie E. Casey Foundation, Baltimore, MD (p. 188)

*Dennis Mansfield, Boise, ID (p. 189)

Michael Marlow, California Polytechnic State University, San Luis Obispo, CA (p. 189)

*J. Stanley Marshall, The James Madison Institute, Tallahassee, FL (p. 190)

Jennifer Marshall, Empower America, Washington, DC (p. 190)

*Nina May, *Renaissance Connection.com/RCNetwork.net*, Washington, DC (p. 192)

*David N. Mayer, Capital University Law School, Columbus, OH (p. 193)

*Jack McCarthy, AppleTree Institute for Education Innovation, Washington, DC (p. 193)

*John McClaughry, Ethan Allen Institute, Concord, VT (p. 193)

*Michael W. McConnell, University of Utah, Salt Lake City, UT (p. 194)

John O. McGinnis, Cardozo School of Law, New York, NY (p. 196)

Daniel McGroarty, White House Writer's Group, Chevy Chase, MD (p. 196)

*Michael J. McManus, Marriage Savers, Potomac, MD (p. 197)

Lawrence J. McQuillan, Pacific Research Institute, San Francisco, CA (p. 197)

*Maurice McTigue, Mercatus Center at George Mason University, Arlington, VA (p. 197)

Jack McVaugh, Arizona School Choice Trust, Scottsdale, AZ (p. 198)

Paul T. Mero, The Sutherland Institute, Salt Lake City, UT (p. 199)

*John Merrifield, University of Texas, San Antonio, San Antonio, TX (p. 199)

Harry Messenheimer, Rio Grande Foundation, Tijeras, NM (p. 200)

Norbert Michel, The Heritage Foundation, Washington, DC (p. 201)

*James H. Miller, Wisconsin Policy Research Institute, Mequon, WI (p. 202)

Tom Minnery, Focus on the Family, Colorado Springs, CO (p. 203)

Elizabeth Mische, Partnership for Choice in Education, St. Paul, MN (p. 203)

*Susan Mitchell, The American Education Reform Foundation, Milwaukee, WI (p. 203)

Terry M. Moe, Hoover Institution, Stanford, CA (p. 204)

Cassandra Chrones Moore, Cato Institute, Washington, DC (p. 205)

Matt Moore, National Center for Policy Analysis, Dallas, TX (p. 206)

Suzanne C. Moore, Delaware Public Policy Institute, Wilmington, DE (p. 206)

Kevin P. Moriarty, Scholarship Fund for Inner-City Children, Newark, NJ (p. 206)

*Len Munsil, Center for Arizona Policy, Scottsdale, AZ (p. 209)

SCHOOL CHOICE (Continued)

*Deroy Murdock, Atlas Economic Research Foundation, New York, NY (p. 209)
Chuck Muth, American Conservative Union, Alexandria, VA (p. 210)
Phyllis Berry Myers, Centre for New Black Leadership, Washington, DC (p. 210)
Ronald Nash, Reformed Theological Seminary, Oviedo, FL (p. 211)
Robert G. Natelson, Missoula, MT (p. 211)
Thomas Nechyba, Duke University, Durham, NC (p. 211)
Clark Neily, Institute for Justice, Washington, DC (p. 212)
Jeff Nelson, Intercollegiate Studies Institute, Wilmington, DE (p. 212)
*Richard John Neuhaus, Institute on Religion and Public Life, New York, NY (p. 213)
*Charles J. O'Malley, Charles J. O'Malley & Associates, Inc., Annapolis, MD (p. 217)
Mike O'Neill, Landmark Legal Foundation, Herndon, VA (p. 217)
*Patsy O'Neill, Charter School Resource Center of Texas, San Antonio, TX (p. 217)
*Richard Olivastro, People Dynamics, Farmington, CT (p. 218)
*Darcy A. Olsen, Goldwater Institute, Phoenix, AZ (p. 219)
*Joseph P. Overton, Mackinac Center for Public Policy, Midland, MI (p. 220)
*Gary J. Palmer, Alabama Policy Institute, Birmingham, AL (p. 221)
*Jim Panyard, Pennsylvania Manufacturer's Association, Harrisburg, PA (p. 221)
*Allan E. Parker, Jr., Texas Justice Foundation, San Antonio, TX (p. 221)
*J. A. Parker, Lincoln Institute for Research and Education, Washington, DC (p. 221)
*Star Parker, Coalition on Urban Renewal and Education, Washington, DC (p. 222)
Janet Parshall, Janet Parshall's America, Arlington, VA (p. 222)
*Lawrence C. Patrick, III, Black Alliance for Educational Options, Washington, DC (p. 222)
*Christine Patterson, Texas Public Policy Foundation, San Antonio, TX (p. 223)
*Mitchell B. Pearlstein, Center of the American Experiment, Minneapolis, MN (p. 224)
Terence J. Pell, Center for Individual Rights, Washington, DC (p. 224)
*Sam Peltzman, University of Chicago Graduate School of Business, Chicago, IL (p. 225)
*Steve Perla, Parent's Alliance for Catholic Education, Fitchburg, MA (p. 225)
*Lovett C. Peters, Pioneer Institute for Public Policy Research, Boston, MA (p. 226)
*Nancy M. Pfotenhauer, Independent Women's Forum, Arlington, VA (p. 227)
James Piereson, John M. Olin Foundation, Inc., New York, NY (p. 228)
*Sally C. Pipes, Pacific Research Institute, San Francisco, CA (p. 229)
*Michael Podgursky, University of Missouri, Columbia, MO (p. 230)
Gale L. Pooley, Star, ID (p. 230)
Victor Porlier, Center for Civic Renewal, Inc., Delmar, NY (p. 231)
Philip K. Porter, University of South Florida, Tampa, FL (p. 231)
*Eric Premack, California State University Institute for Education Reform,
    Sacramento, CA (p. 232)
*Thomas Prichard, Minnesota Family Council, Minneapolis, MN (p. 233)
John Raisian, Hoover Institution, Stanford, CA (p. 236)
*Ed Rauchut, CEO Omaha, Bellevue, NE (p. 236)
Diane Ravitch, New York University, New York, NY (p. 237)
Harold Calvin Ray, National Center for Faith-Based Initiatives, West Palm Beach, FL (p. 237)
*Lawrence W. Reed, Mackinac Center for Public Policy, Midland, MI (p. 237)
Jeremiah Reedy, Macalester College, St. Paul, MN (p. 238)
Patrick Reilly, Cardinal Newman Society, Falls Church, VA (p. 238)
*Charles E. Rice, Notre Dame Law School, Notre Dame, IN (p. 239)
William Craig Rice, American Academy for Liberal Education, Washington, DC (p. 239)
*David W. Riggs, Capital Research Center, Washington, DC (p. 240)
Sandy Rios, Concerned Women for America, Washington, DC (p. 240)
Russell Roberts, Weidenbaum Center, St. Louis, MO (p. 242)
Holly Robinson, Georgia Public Policy Foundation, Atlanta, GA (p. 242)
*Doug Rogers, Association of Texas Professional Educators, Austin, TX (p. 243)
J. Patrick Rooney, Golden Rule Insurance Company, Indianapolis, IN (p. 243)
David C. Rose, University of Missouri, St. Louis, St. Louis, MO (p. 243)

---

* Has testified before a state or federal legislative committee

SCHOOL CHOICE (Continued)

*Ronald D. Rotunda, George Mason University School of Law, Arlington, VA (p. 244)

Cecilia E. Rouse, Princeton University, Princeton, NJ (p. 245)

*Richard O. Rowland, Grassroot Institute of Hawaii, Aiea, HI (p. 245)

Robert Royal, Faith & Reason Institute, Washington, DC (p. 245)

Shannon Royce, Ethics and Religious Liberty Commission, Washington, DC (p. 245)

*Frank Russo, American Family Association of New York, Port Washington, NY (p. 247)

Terry Ryan, Thomas B. Fordham Foundation, Washington, DC (p. 248)

*David F. Salisbury, Cato Institute, Washington, DC (p. 248)

Ernestine L. Sanders, Cornerstone Schools, Detroit, MI (p. 249)

*Michael Sanera, Basis Charter High School, Tucson, AZ (p. 249)

E. S. Savas, City University of New York, New York, NY (p. 250)

*Terrence M. Scanlon, Capital Research Center, Washington, DC (p. 251)

*D. Eric Schansberg, Indiana University Southeast, New Albany, IN (p. 252)

*Bill Schilling, Wyoming Business Alliance / Wyoming Heritage Foundation, Casper, WY (p. 253)

*Peter W. Schramm, John M. Ashbrook Center for Public Affairs, Ashland, OH (p. 254)

*Michael Schwartz, Concerned Women for America, Washington, DC (p. 254)

*Ralph Segalman, California State University, Northridge, Northridge, CA (p. 256)

*Jamie Self, Georgia Family Council, Norcross, GA (p. 256)

*Carolyn Sharette, Children First Utah, Salt Lake City, UT (p. 258)

Tracie Sharp, State Policy Network, Richmond, CA (p. 258)

*Colleen Sheehan, Villanova University, Villanova, PA (p. 258)

*Lou Sheldon, Traditional Values Coalition, Washington, DC (p. 258)

Frank A. Shepherd, Pacific Legal Foundation, Coral Gables, FL (p. 259)

*Robert A. Sirico, Acton Institute for the Study of Religion and Liberty, Grand Rapids, MI (p. 261)

*James Skillen, Center for Public Justice, Annapolis, MD (p. 261)

*Christopher Smith, Internet Education Exchange (iEdx), Scottsdale, AZ (p. 262)

*Lisa Snell, Reason Foundation, Los Angeles, CA (p. 265)

*Neil H. Snyder, University of Virginia, Charlottesville, VA (p. 265)

*Don Soifer, Lexington Institute, Arlington, VA (p. 265)

*Fawn Spady, Education Excellence Coalition, Seattle, WA (p. 266)

*Jim Spady, Education Excellence Coalition, Seattle, WA (p. 266)

*John A. Sparks, Grove City College, Grove City, PA (p. 266)

Gordon St. Angelo, Milton and Rose Friedman Foundation, Indianapolis, IN (p. 267)

*Samuel R. Staley, Buckeye Institute for Public Policy Solutions, Columbus, OH (p. 268)

Doug Stiegler, Association of Maryland Families, Woodstock, MD (p. 269)

*J. E. Stone, East Tennessee State University, Johnson City, TN (p. 270)

*Jeff Stormo, Choices for Children, Grand Rapids, MI (p. 270)

*William Craig Stubblebine, Claremont McKenna College, Claremont, CA (p. 271)

Joy Sweet, National Right to Read Foundation, The Plains, VA (p. 273)

Charles Sykes, Wisconsin Policy Research Institute, Mequon, WI (p. 273)

*Alexander Tabarrok, Mercatus Center at George Mason University, Arlington, VA (p. 273)

Thomas L. Tacker, Embry-Riddle Aeronautical University, Daytona Beach, FL (p. 273)

James R. "J.T." Taylor, Empower America, Washington, DC (p. 274)

*John Taylor, Virginia Institute for Public Policy, Potomac Falls, VA (p. 274)

Kevin Teasley, Greater Educational Opportunities Foundation, Indianapolis, IN (p. 275)

*Karen Testerman, Cornerstone Policy Research, Concord, NH (p. 275)

*David J. Theroux, The Independent Institute, Oakland, CA (p. 276)

Michael W. Thompson, Thomas Jefferson Institute for Public Policy, Springfield, VA (p. 278)

Ann C. Thomson, The Commonwealth Foundation, Harrisburg, PA (p. 278)

Eugenia Froedge Toma, University of Kentucky, Lexington, KY (p. 280)

*Lex Towle, AppleTree Institute for Education Innovation, Washington, DC (p. 280)

*Ron Trowbridge, Maine Policy Center, Durham, ME (p. 281)

SCHOOL CHOICE (Continued)

*Lil Tuttle, Clare Boothe Luce Policy Institute, Herndon, VA (p. 282)
 Michael M. Uhlmann, Claremont Graduate University, Claremont, CA (p. 283)
*Terry W. Van Allen, Kemah, TX (p. 283)
*Kevin Vigilante, Rumford, RI (p. 285)
 Joseph P. Viteritti, New York University, New York, NY (p. 285)
 Dane vonBreichenruchardt, U. S. Bill of Rights Foundation, Washington, DC (p. 286)
*Herbert J. Walberg, University of Illinois, Chicago, Chicago, IL (p. 286)
*Lee H. Walker, New Coalition for Economic and Social Change, Chicago, IL (p. 287)
 Russ Walker, Citizens for a Sound Economy, Keizer, OR (p. 287)
*Malcolm Wallop, Frontiers of Freedom Institute, Fairfax, VA (p. 288)
 Michael Y. Warder, Los Angeles Children's Scholarship Fund, Long Beach, CA (p. 289)
 Tom Washburne, Home School Legal Defense Association, Purcellville, VA (p. 289)
*Donna Watson, Children First America, Austin, TX (p. 290)
*Michael W. Watson, Children First America, Austin, TX (p. 290)
*Walter M. Weber, American Center for Law and Justice, Alexandria, VA (p. 291)
*Rolf A. Weil, Roosevelt University, Chicago, IL (p. 291)
 Nick Weller, Cascade Policy Institute, Portland, OR (p. 292)
 Alvin Williams, Black America's PAC, Washington, DC (p. 294)
*Bob Williams, Evergreen Freedom Foundation, Olympia, WA (p. 295)
 Richard B. Wirthlin, Wirthlin Worldwide, South Jordan, UT (p. 296)
 James W. Witt, University of West Florida, Pensacola, FL (p. 296)
 Betty Jean Wolfe, Urban Family Council, Philadephia, PA (p. 297)
*Gary Wolfram, Hillsdale College, Hillsdale, MI (p. 297)
*Robert L. Woodson, Sr., National Center for Neighborhood Enterprise,
    Washington, DC (p. 298)
 Anne Wortham, Illinois State University, Normal, IL (p. 298)
*Chris Yelich, Education Industry Association, Watertown, WI (p. 300)
 David Zanotti, Ohio Roundtable, Strongsville, OH (p. 301)
 Kate Xiao Zhou, University of Hawaii, Honolulu, HI (p. 302)
 Ronald A. Zumbrun, The Zumbrun Law Firm, Sacramento, CA (p. 303)

SCHOOL-TO-WORK

*Lewis Andrews, Yankee Institute for Public Policy Studies, Hartford, CT (p. 39)
*Gary Beckner, Association of American Educators, Laguna Hills, CA (p. 48)
 Douglas Besharov, American Enterprise Institute, Washington, DC (p. 52)
*Fran Bevan, Eagle Forum of Pennsylvania, North Huntingdon, PA (p. 53)
 Felita Blowe, Concerned Women for America, Washington, DC (p. 55)
*Stephen M. Colarelli, Central Michigan University, Mount Pleasant, MI (p. 78)
*John E. Coons, University of California at Berkeley, Berkeley, CA (p. 81)
 Candace de Russy, State University of New York, Bronxville, NY (p. 90)
 Buffy DeBreaux-Watts, American Board for Certification of Teacher Excellence,
    Washington, DC (p. 91)
*Thomas DeWeese, American Policy Center, Warrenton, VA (p. 94)
*David Dunn, Oklahoma Family Policy Council, Bethany, OK (p. 100)
*Michael P. Farris, Patrick Henry College, Purcellville, VA (p. 109)
 Richard M. Ferry, Catholic Education Foundation, Los Angeles, CA (p. 111)
 Marshall Fritz, Alliance for the Separation of School & State, Fresno, CA (p. 118)
 John Galandak, Foundation for Free Enterprise, Paramus, NJ (p. 119)
 Eric Hanushek, Hoover Institution, Stanford, CA (p. 135)
*Donna H. Hearne, Constitutional Coalition, St. Louis, MO (p. 138)
 Carl Herbster, American Association of Christian Schools, Independence, MO (p. 140)
*Caroline M. Hoxby, Harvard University, Cambridge, MA (p. 147)
*Krista Kafer, The Heritage Foundation, Washington, DC (p. 156)
 Lindalyn Kakadelis, North Carolina Education Alliance, Pineville, NC (p. 157)

---

* Has testified before a state or federal legislative committee

SCHOOL-TO-WORK (Continued)

Kent King, Missouri State Teachers Association, Columbia, MO (p. 164)
*Christopher J. Klicka, Home School Legal Defense Association, Purcellville, VA (p. 165)
Herbert L. London, Hudson Institute, Indianapolis, IN (p. 182)
Jennifer Marshall, Empower America, Washington, DC (p. 190)
*James H. Miller, Wisconsin Policy Research Institute, Mequon, WI (p. 202)
Terry M. Moe, Hoover Institution, Stanford, CA (p. 204)
Suzanne C. Moore, Delaware Public Policy Institute, Wilmington, DE (p. 206)
George R. Neumann, University of Iowa, Iowa City, IA (p. 213)
*Richard Olivastro, People Dynamics, Farmington, CT (p. 218)
*Christine Patterson, Texas Public Policy Foundation, San Antonio, TX (p. 223)
Harold Calvin Ray, National Center for Faith-Based Initiatives, West Palm Beach, FL (p. 237)
*Richard O. Rowland, Grassroot Institute of Hawaii, Aiea, HI (p. 245)
*Phyllis Schlafly, Eagle Forum, St. Louis, MO (p. 253)
*Lisa Snell, Reason Foundation, Los Angeles, CA (p. 265)
John C. Soper, John Carroll University, University Heights, OH (p. 266)
Doug Stiegler, Association of Maryland Families, Woodstock, MD (p. 269)
*J. E. Stone, East Tennessee State University, Johnson City, TN (p. 270)
*David Swindell, Clemson University, Clemson, SC (p. 273)
Kevin Teasley, Greater Educational Opportunities Foundation, Indianapolis, IN (p. 275)
*Lil Tuttle, Clare Boothe Luce Policy Institute, Herndon, VA (p. 282)
Kristina Twitty, Eagle Forum, Washington, DC (p. 282)
*Balint Vazsonyi, Center for the American Founding, McLean, VA (p. 284)
Tom Washburne, Home School Legal Defense Association, Purcellville, VA (p. 289)
*Natalie Williams, Robinson, DiLando and Whitaker, Sacramento, CA (p. 295)
*Lawrence Wohl, Gustavus Adolphus College, St. Peter, MN (p. 297)
*Gary Wolfram, Hillsdale College, Hillsdale, MI (p. 297)

STANDARDS, CURRICULUM, AND TESTING

*John Agresto, John Agresto and Associates, Santa Fe, NM (p. 35)
Benjamin Alexander, Franciscan University of Steubenville, Steubenville, OH (p. 36)
Jeanne Allen, Center for Education Reform, Washington, DC (p. 36)
*William Allen, Michigan State University, East Lansing, MI (p. 37)
*Lewis Andrews, Yankee Institute for Public Policy Studies, Hartford, CT (p. 39)
*Julaine K. Appling, Family Research Institute of Wisconsin, Madison, WI (p. 40)
*David J. Armor, George Mason University, Fairfax, VA (p. 40)
Larry P. Arnn, Hillsdale College, Hillsdale, MI (p. 40)
Brian Backstrom, Empire Foundation for Policy Research, Clifton Park, NY (p. 42)
*Keith G. Baker, Florida TaxWatch Research Institute, Inc., Tallahassee, FL (p. 43)
Stephen H. Balch, National Association of Scholars, Princeton, NJ (p. 44)
Dale Ballou, University of Massachusetts, Amherst, MA (p. 45)
*Gary Beckner, Association of American Educators, Laguna Hills, CA (p. 48)
*Pamela Benigno, Independence Institute, Golden, CO (p. 50)
*William J. Bennett, Empower America, Washington, DC (p. 51)
*Saundra Berry, Cleveland Scholarship and Tutoring Program, Cleveland, OH (p. 52)
*Jason Bertsch, American Enterprise Institute, Washington, DC (p. 52)
*Fran Bevan, Eagle Forum of Pennsylvania, North Huntingdon, PA (p. 53)
*Wayman R. Bishop, The Family Foundation of Virginia, Richmond, VA (p. 53)
Felita Blowe, Concerned Women for America, Washington, DC (p. 55)
David J. Bobb, Hillsdale College, Hillsdale, MI (p. 56)
Jennifer C. Braceras, Independent Women's Forum, Arlington, VA (p. 59)
Gary Crosby Brasor, National Association of Scholars, Princeton, NJ (p. 60)
*Christian N. Braunlich, Thomas Jefferson Institute for Public Policy, Alexandria, VA (p. 60)
*Mychele Brickner, Clare Boothe Luce Policy Institute, Herndon, VA (p. 61)
Dedrick Briggs, Charter School Resource Center of Tennessee, Memphis, TN (p. 61)

STANDARDS, CURRICULUM, AND TESTING (Continued)

B. Jason Brooks, Empire Foundation for Policy Research, Clifton Park, NY (p. 62)

*Matthew J. Brouillette, The Commonwealth Foundation, Harrisburg, PA (p. 62)

*Floyd G. Brown, Young America's Foundation Reagan Ranch Project, Santa Barbara, CA (p. 63)

Mahmood Butt, Eastern Illinois University, Charleston, IL (p. 66)

*Kaleem Caire, American Education Reform Council, Bowie, MD (p. 67)

*Dominic M. Calabro, Florida TaxWatch Research Institute, Inc., Tallahassee, FL (p. 67)

*James B. Cardle, Texas Citizen Action Network, Austin, TX (p. 69)

Merrick Carey, Lexington Institute, Arlington, VA (p. 70)

Brian Carpenter, Mackinac Center for Public Policy, Midland, MI (p. 70)

*Samuel Casey Carter, Acade Metrics, LLC, Washington, DC (p. 71)

*Linda Chavez, Center for Equal Opportunity, Sterling, VA (p. 73)

*Lynne V. Cheney, American Enterprise Institute, Washington, DC (p. 73)

*John Chubb, Edison Schools, Inc., New York, NY (p. 74)

*Michael A. Ciamarra, Alabama Policy Institute, Birmingham, AL (p. 74)

John Cobin, Montauk Financial Group, Greenville, SC (p. 76)

Howard Cochran, Jr., Belmont University, Nashville, TN (p. 77)

*Richard T. Colgan, Bridgewater State College, Warwick, RI (p. 78)

*Ward Connerly, American Civil Rights Institute, Sacramento, CA (p. 80)

*John E. Coons, University of California at Berkeley, Berkeley, CA (p. 81)

*Matt Cox, Pacific Research Institute, Sacramento, CA (p. 84)

Neil S. Crispo, Florida State University, Tallahassee, FL (p. 86)

*Brad W. Dacus, Pacific Justice Institute, Citrus Heights, CA (p. 87)

*Kathleen B. de Bettencourt, Environmental Literacy Council, Washington, DC (p. 89)

Candace de Russy, State University of New York, Bronxville, NY (p. 90)

Edwin J. Delattre, Boston University, Boston, MA (p. 91)

*Len Deo, New Jersey Family Policy Council, Parsippany, NJ (p. 93)

*Thomas DeWeese, American Policy Center, Warrenton, VA (p. 94)

Thomas Dillon, Thomas Aquinas College, Santa Paula, CA (p. 96)

Denis Doyle, Doyle Associates, Chevy Chase, MD (p. 98)

*Michelle Easton, Clare Boothe Luce Policy Institute, Herndon, VA (p. 102)

*Williamson M. Evers, Hoover Institution, Stanford, CA (p. 108)

Megan Farnsworth, The Heritage Foundation, Washington, DC (p. 109)

*Michael P. Farris, Patrick Henry College, Purcellville, VA (p. 109)

Richard M. Ferry, Catholic Education Foundation, Los Angeles, CA (p. 111)

*Marc Fey, Focus on the Family, Colorado Springs, CO (p. 111)

*Chester E. Finn, Jr., Thomas B. Fordham Foundation, Washington, DC (p. 112)

*John Fonte, Hudson Institute, Washington, DC (p. 114)

Elizabeth Fox-Genovese, Emory University, Atlanta, GA (p. 115)

Marshall Fritz, Alliance for the Separation of School & State, Fresno, CA (p. 118)

Janice J. Gabbert, Wright State University, Dayton, OH (p. 119)

*Mary F. Gifford, Field, Sarvas, King and Coleman, Phoenix, AZ (p. 123)

*Charles L. Glenn, Boston University, Boston, MA (p. 124)

Daniel J. Goldhaber, University of Washington, Seattle, WA (p. 125)

*Linda S. Gottfredson, University of Delaware, Newark, DE (p. 127)

Paul Gottfried, Elizabethtown College, Elizabethtown, PA (p. 127)

Clint W. Green, Acton Institute for the Study of Religion and Liberty, Grand Rapids, MI (p. 128)

*Jay P. Greene, Manhattan Institute for Policy Research, Davie, FL (p. 128)

Charles Greenwalt, II, Susquehanna Valley Center for Public Policy, Hershey, PA (p. 129)

*Joshua Hall, Buckeye Institute for Public Policy Solutions, Columbus, OH (p. 132)

Eric Hanushek, Hoover Institution, Stanford, CA (p. 135)

*Lynn Harsh, Evergreen Freedom Foundation, Olympia, WA (p. 136)

*Donna H. Hearne, Constitutional Coalition, St. Louis, MO (p. 138)

STANDARDS, CURRICULUM, AND TESTING (Continued)

*Paul T. Hill, University of Washington, Seattle, WA (p. 142)

James E. Hinish, Jr., Regent University, Williamsburg, VA (p. 143)

E. D. Hirsch, Jr., Core Knowledge Foundation, Charlottesville, VA (p. 143)

Robert D. Hisrich, Case Western Reserve University, Cleveland, OH (p. 143)

James Hitchcock, St. Louis University, St. Louis, MO (p. 143)

*Robert Holland, Lexington Institute, Arlington, VA (p. 144)

*John C. Holmes, Association of Christian Schools International, Washington, DC (p. 145)

*John MacDonald Hood, John Locke Foundation, Raleigh, NC (p. 145)

*Joseph Horn, University of Texas, Austin, TX (p. 146)

William Howard, Chicago State University, Wheaton, IL (p. 147)

*Caroline M. Hoxby, Harvard University, Cambridge, MA (p. 147)

Deal Hudson, *Crisis Magazine*, Washington, DC (p. 148)

*Gary Huggins, Education Leaders Action Council, Washington, DC (p. 148)

*Victoria Hughes, Bill of Rights Institute, Washington, DC (p. 149)

*Nancy Ichinaga, California State Board of Education, Los Angeles, CA (p. 151)

Niger Roy Innis, Congress of Racial Equality, New York, NY (p. 151)

*Lance T. Izumi, Pacific Research Institute, Sacramento, CA (p. 152)

Kirk A. Johnson, Mackinac Center for Public Policy, Midland, MI (p. 155)

*Krista Kafer, The Heritage Foundation, Washington, DC (p. 156)

*John Kain, University of Texas, Dallas, Richardson, TX (p. 157)

Lindalyn Kakadelis, North Carolina Education Alliance, Pineville, NC (p. 157)

*Lisa Graham Keegan, Education Leaders Council, Washington, DC (p. 160)

Michael Kellman, University of Oregon, Eugene, OR (p. 160)

Steven J. Kidder, New York Family Policy Council, Albany, NY (p. 163)

Kent King, Missouri State Teachers Association, Columbia, MO (p. 164)

Mary Beth Klee, Link Institute, Portsmouth, NH (p. 165)

*Christopher J. Klicka, Home School Legal Defense Association, Purcellville, VA (p. 165)

*George Landrith, Frontiers of Freedom Institute, Fairfax, VA (p. 173)

Casey Lartigue, Jr., Cato Institute, Washington, DC (p. 175)

*Andrew T. LeFevre, American Legislative Exchange Council, Washington, DC (p. 177)

Seth Leibsohn, Empower America, Washington, DC (p. 177)

Bernard T. Lomas, The Heritage Foundation, Chapel Hill, NC (p. 182)

*Heather MacDonald, Manhattan Institute for Policy Research, New York, NY (p. 185)

Kathleen Madigan, National Council on Teacher Quality, Washington, DC (p. 186)

*Rita P. Maguire, Arizona Center for Public Policy, Phoenix, AZ (p. 186)

*Roger P. Maickel, Purdue University, Lafayette, IN (p. 187)

*Bruno V. Manno, The Annie E. Casey Foundation, Baltimore, MD (p. 188)

Jennifer Marshall, Empower America, Washington, DC (p. 190)

*Jerry L. Martin, American Council of Trustees and Alumni, Washington, DC (p. 190)

Jerome Anthony McDuffie, University of North Carolina, Pembroke, Lumberton, NC (p. 195)

Edward T. McMullen, Jr., South Carolina Policy Council, Columbia, SC (p. 197)

Harry Messenheimer, Rio Grande Foundation, Tijeras, NM (p. 200)

*James H. Miller, Wisconsin Policy Research Institute, Mequon, WI (p. 202)

Tom Minnery, Focus on the Family, Colorado Springs, CO (p. 203)

Terry M. Moe, Hoover Institution, Stanford, CA (p. 204)

Suzanne C. Moore, Delaware Public Policy Institute, Wilmington, DE (p. 206)

Laurie Morrow, Montpelier, VT (p. 207)

Jeff Nelson, Intercollegiate Studies Institute, Wilmington, DE (p. 212)

Michael J. Neth, Middle Tennessee State University, Murfreesboro, TN (p. 213)

*Richard Olivastro, People Dynamics, Farmington, CT (p. 218)

*Darcy A. Olsen, Goldwater Institute, Phoenix, AZ (p. 219)

*Christine Patterson, Texas Public Policy Foundation, San Antonio, TX (p. 223)

David A. Patterson, University of Memphis, Memphis, TN (p. 223)

Bruce Piasecki, AHC Group, Saratoga Springs, NY (p. 228)

STANDARDS, CURRICULUM, AND TESTING (Continued)

*Rosalie Porter, READ Institute, Sterling, VA (p. 231)
*Edward Potter, Employment Policy Foundation, Washington, DC (p. 231)
*Eric Premack, California State University Institute for Education Reform, Sacramento, CA (p. 232)
*Thomas Prichard, Minnesota Family Council, Minneapolis, MN (p. 233)
*William L. Proctor, Flagler College, St. Augustine, FL (p. 233)
*Ed Rauchut, CEO Omaha, Bellevue, NE (p. 236)
 Diane Ravitch, New York University, New York, NY (p. 237)
 Jeremiah Reedy, Macalester College, St. Paul, MN (p. 238)
 William Craig Rice, American Academy for Liberal Education, Washington, DC (p. 239)
 Glenn M. Ricketts, National Association of Scholars, Princeton, NJ (p. 239)
 Sandy Rios, Concerned Women for America, Washington, DC (p. 240)
 Holly Robinson, Georgia Public Policy Foundation, Atlanta, GA (p. 242)
 John E. Rocha, Sr., Center for the American Idea, Houston, TX (p. 242)
*Doug Rogers, Association of Texas Professional Educators, Austin, TX (p. 243)
*Richard O. Rowland, Grassroot Institute of Hawaii, Aiea, HI (p. 245)
 Robert Royal, Faith & Reason Institute, Washington, DC (p. 245)
*David F. Salisbury, Cato Institute, Washington, DC (p. 248)
 David W. Saxe, Pennsylvania State University, University Park, PA (p. 251)
 Roberta Rubel Schaefer, Worcester Regional Research Bureau, Worcester, MA (p. 252)
*Bill Schilling, Wyoming Business Alliance / Wyoming Heritage Foundation, Casper, WY (p. 253)
*Phyllis Schlafly, Eagle Forum, St. Louis, MO (p. 253)
*Peter W. Schramm, John M. Ashbrook Center for Public Affairs, Ashland, OH (p. 254)
*Arthur J. Schwartz, John Templeton Foundation, Radnor, PA (p. 254)
*Donald J. Senese, 60 Plus Association, Arlington, VA (p. 257)
*Gilbert T. Sewall, American Textbook Council, New York, NY (p. 257)
*Colleen Sheehan, Villanova University, Villanova, PA (p. 258)
*Christopher Smith, Internet Education Exchange (iEdx), Scottsdale, AZ (p. 262)
*Lisa Snell, Reason Foundation, Los Angeles, CA (p. 265)
 John C. Soper, John Carroll University, University Heights, OH (p. 266)
*Jim Spady, Education Excellence Coalition, Seattle, WA (p. 266)
*John A. Sparks, Grove City College, Grove City, PA (p. 266)
 Doug Stiegler, Association of Maryland Families, Woodstock, MD (p. 269)
*J. E. Stone, East Tennessee State University, Johnson City, TN (p. 270)
 Joy Sweet, National Right to Read Foundation, The Plains, VA (p. 273)
 Charles Sykes, Wisconsin Policy Research Institute, Mequon, WI (p. 273)
*Lewis A. Tambs, Tempe, AZ (p. 273)
 James R. "J.T." Taylor, Empower America, Washington, DC (p. 274)
 Kevin Teasley, Greater Educational Opportunities Foundation, Indianapolis, IN (p. 275)
 Christopher Thacker, The Bible Literacy Project, New York, NY (p. 275)
*Abigail Thernstrom, Lexington, MA (p. 276)
*Stephan Thernstrom, Lexington, MA (p. 276)
 Ewa M. Thompson, Rice University, Houston, TX (p. 277)
 Glen E. Thurow, University of Dallas, Irving, TX (p. 279)
 Miro M. Todorovich, Scientists and Engineers for Secure Energy, New York, NY (p. 280)
*David G. Tuerck, Beacon Hill Institute, Boston, MA (p. 281)
*Forrest L. Turpen, Christian Educators Association International, Pasadena, CA (p. 282)
*Lil Tuttle, Clare Boothe Luce Policy Institute, Herndon, VA (p. 282)
 Kristina Twitty, Eagle Forum, Washington, DC (p. 282)
 Reed Ueda, Tufts University, Medford, MA (p. 282)
*Balint Vazsonyi, Center for the American Founding, McLean, VA (p. 284)
*Maris A. Vinovskis, University of Michigan, Ann Arbor, MI (p. 285)
*Herbert J. Walberg, University of Illinois, Chicago, Chicago, IL (p. 286)

---

* Has testified before a state or federal legislative committee

STANDARDS, CURRICULUM, AND TESTING (Continued)

*Jeffrey D. Wallin, American Academy for Liberal Education, Washington, DC (p. 287)
 Gary M. Walton, Foundation for Teaching Economics, Davis, CA (p. 288)
 Tom Washburne, Home School Legal Defense Association, Purcellville, VA (p. 289)
*Donna Watson, Children First America, Austin, TX (p. 290)
*Rolf A. Weil, Roosevelt University, Chicago, IL (p. 291)
 Nick Weller, Cascade Policy Institute, Portland, OR (p. 292)
 David M. Whalen, Hillsdale College, Hillsdale, MI (p. 293)
*Natalie Williams, Robinson, DiLando and Whitaker, Sacramento, CA (p. 295)
 Bradford P. Wilson, National Association of Scholars, Princeton, NJ (p. 296)
 Anne Wortham, Illinois State University, Normal, IL (p. 298)
*Nicholas Zill, Westat Inc., Rockville, MD (p. 302)

Family, Culture and Community

ABSTINENCE AND OUT-OF-WEDLOCK BIRTHS

*Mary Cunningham Agee, The Nurturing Network, White Salmon, WA (p. 35)
 Benjamin Alexander, Franciscan University of Steubenville, Steubenville, OH (p. 36)
 Eloise Anderson, Claremont Institute, Sacramento, CA (p. 38)
*Julaine K. Appling, Family Research Institute of Wisconsin, Madison, WI (p. 40)
*Dominic A. Aquila, Ave Maria University, Ypsilanti, MI (p. 40)
*Thomas C. Atwood, National Council For Adoption, Alexandria, VA (p. 41)
 Hunter Baker, Georgia Family Council, Norcross, GA (p. 43)
*LeAnna Benn, Teen Aid, Spokane, WA (p. 50)
*Elayne Bennett, Best Friends Foundation, Washington, DC (p. 50)
 Douglas Besharov, American Enterprise Institute, Washington, DC (p. 52)
*Wayman R. Bishop, The Family Foundation of Virginia, Richmond, VA (p. 53)
 Philip L. Brach, Midtown Educational Foundation, Chicago, IL (p. 59)
*Bill Brooks, North Carolina Family Policy Council, Raleigh, NC (p. 62)
*Brian Brown, Family Institute of Connecticut, Hartford, CT (p. 63)
*Harold O. J. Brown, Reformed Theological Seminary, Charlotte, NC (p. 63)
*Martin D. Brown, Richmond, VA (p. 63)
 James Bruner, New York Family Policy Council, Albany, NY (p. 64)
 Deborah Burstion-Donbraye, American Multimedia Inc. of Nigeria, Cleveland, OH (p. 66)
*Allan C. Carlson, Howard Center for Family, Religion and Society, Rockford, IL (p. 70)
*James Chapman, Rocky Mountain Family Council, Denver, CO (p. 72)
*Linda Chavez, Center for Equal Opportunity, Sterling, VA (p. 73)
*Micah Clark, American Family Association, Indianapolis, IN (p. 75)
 Roberta Combs, Christian Coalition of America, Washington, DC (p. 79)
*Kenneth L. Connor, Family Research Council, Washington, DC (p. 80)
*Jerry Cox, Arkansas Family Council, Little Rock, AR (p. 84)
*Ron Crews, Massachusetts Family Institute, Newton Upper Falls, MA (p. 86)
*Janice Shaw Crouse, Concerned Women for America, Washington, DC (p. 87)
*Brad W. Dacus, Pacific Justice Institute, Citrus Heights, CA (p. 87)
*Matt Daniels, Alliance for Marriage, Springfield, VA (p. 88)
 Pia de Solenni, Family Research Council, Washington, DC (p. 90)
 Mark De Young, World Youth Alliance, New York, NY (p. 90)
*Len Deo, New Jersey Family Policy Council, Parsippany, NJ (p. 93)
*William T. Devlin, Urban Family Council, Philadelphia, PA (p. 94)
*John R. Diggs, Jr., South Hadley, MA (p. 95)
 James C. Dobson, Focus on the Family, Colorado Springs, CO (p. 96)
 Marie Dolan, New York State Federation of Catholic School Parents, Flushing, NY (p. 96)
 Jeff Downing, Family First, Lincoln, NE (p. 98)
*David Dunn, Oklahoma Family Policy Council, Bethany, OK (p. 100)
*Louis D. Enoff, Enoff Associates Limited, Sykesville, MD (p. 107)
*Patrick Fagan, The Heritage Foundation, Washington, DC (p. 108)
*Thompson Mason Faller, University of Portland, Portland, OR (p. 109)
*Michael P. Farris, Patrick Henry College, Purcellville, VA (p. 109)
 Elizabeth Fox-Genovese, Emory University, Atlanta, GA (p. 115)
*Wanda Franz, National Right to Life Committee, Washington, DC (p. 116)
 Adam Fuller, Toward Tradition, Mercer Island, WA (p. 118)
 Jennifer Garrett, The Heritage Foundation, Washington, DC (p. 120)
*Michael Geer, Pennsylvania Family Institute, Harrisburg, PA (p. 122)
 Norval D. Glenn, University of Texas, Austin, TX (p. 125)
*Stephen Goldsmith, Manhattan Institute for Policy Research, New York, NY (p. 126)
 A. C. Green, Jr., A. C. Green Youth Foundation, Phoenix, AZ (p. 128)
 Rebecca Hagelin, The Heritage Foundation, Washington, DC (p. 131)
 Jay F. Hein, Hudson Institute, Indianapolis, IN (p. 139)

ABSTINENCE AND OUT-OF-WEDLOCK BIRTHS (Continued)

*Randy Hicks, Georgia Family Council, Norcross, GA (p. 141)
*Michael Howden, Stronger Families for Oregon, Salem, OR (p. 147)
*Charles D. Hurley, Iowa Family Policy Center, Pleasant Hill, IA (p. 150)
 Niger Roy Innis, Congress of Racial Equality, New York, NY (p. 151)
 Earl W. Jackson, Sr., Samaritan Project, Chesapeake, VA (p. 152)
*Eve Jackson, The PEERS Project, Indianapolis, IN (p. 152)
 Michael L. Jestes, Oklahoma Family Policy Council, Bethany, OK (p. 154)
 Darlene A. Kennedy, Centre for New Black Leadership, Baltimore, MD (p. 162)
*Robert H. Knight, Concerned Women for America, Washington, DC (p. 166)
*David B. Kopel, Independence Institute, Golden, CO (p. 167)
*Lawrence Kudlow, Kudlow & Co., LLC, New York, NY (p. 170)
 Peter J. LaBarbera, Concerned Women for America, Washington, DC (p. 171)
 Stacey Ladd, Worth the Wait, Pampa, TX (p. 171)
*Andrea S. Lafferty, Traditional Values Coalition, Washington, DC (p. 172)
 Daniel Lapin, Toward Tradition, Mercer Island, WA (p. 174)
 Phillip F. Lawler, *Catholic World Report*, South Lancaster, MA (p. 176)
*George Liebmann, Calvert Institute for Policy Research, Baltimore, MD (p. 180)
 Dianna Lightfoot, National Physicians Center for Family Resources, Birmingham, AL (p. 180)
*Mike Long, Complete Abstinence Eduation Program, Durham, NC (p. 183)
*Heather MacDonald, Manhattan Institute for Policy Research, New York, NY (p. 185)
*Dennis Mansfield, Boise, ID (p. 189)
*Connie Marshner, Raphael Services, Front Royal, VA (p. 190)
*Joe S. McIlheney, Jr., Medical Institute for Sexual Health, Austin, TX (p. 196)
*Michael J. McManus, Marriage Savers, Potomac, MD (p. 197)
 Gene Mills, Louisiana Family Forum, Baton Rouge, LA (p. 202)
 Tom Minnery, Focus on the Family, Colorado Springs, CO (p. 203)
 R. Albert Mohler, Jr., The Southern Baptist Theological Seminary, Louisville, KY (p. 204)
 Jennifer Roback Morse, Hoover Institution, Vista, CA (p. 207)
*Steven W. Mosher, Population Research Institute, Front Royal, VA (p. 208)
*Len Munsil, Center for Arizona Policy, Scottsdale, AZ (p. 209)
 Thomas Nechyba, Duke University, Durham, NC (p. 211)
 Lauren Noyes, The Heritage Foundation, Washington, DC (p. 216)
*Star Parker, Coalition on Urban Renewal and Education, Washington, DC (p. 222)
*Mitchell B. Pearlstein, Center of the American Experiment, Minneapolis, MN (p. 224)
*Thomas Prichard, Minnesota Family Council, Minneapolis, MN (p. 233)
 Harold Calvin Ray, National Center for Faith-Based Initiatives, West Palm Beach, FL (p. 237)
 Robert Rector, The Heritage Foundation, Washington, DC (p. 237)
 Sandy Rios, Concerned Women for America, Washington, DC (p. 240)
*Kelly Rosati, Hawaii Family Forum, Kaneohe, HI (p. 243)
*Arthur J. Schwartz, John Templeton Foundation, Radnor, PA (p. 254)
*Michael Schwartz, Concerned Women for America, Washington, DC (p. 254)
*Alan E. Sears, Alliance Defense Fund, Scottsdale, AZ (p. 255)
*Ralph Segalman, California State University, Northridge, Northridge, CA (p. 256)
*Jamie Self, Georgia Family Council, Norcross, GA (p. 256)
*Lou Sheldon, Traditional Values Coalition, Washington, DC (p. 258)
 Anita Smith, Institute for Youth Development, Washington, DC (p. 262)
*Curt Smith, Indiana Family Institute, Indianapolis, IN (p. 263)
*W. Shepherd Smith, Jr., Institute for Youth Development, Washington, DC (p. 264)
 Peter S. Sprigg, Family Research Council, Washington, DC (p. 267)
 Glenn T. Stanton, Focus on the Family, Colorado Springs, CO (p. 268)
 Doug Stiegler, Association of Maryland Families, Woodstock, MD (p. 269)
*Kathleen M. Sullivan, Project Reality, Golf, IL (p. 271)
*Karen Testerman, Cornerstone Policy Research, Concord, NH (p. 275)
*Forest M. Thigpen, Mississippi Family Council, Jackson, MS (p. 277)

ABSTINENCE AND OUT-OF-WEDLOCK BIRTHS (Continued)

*Maris A. Vinovskis, University of Michigan, Ann Arbor, MI (p. 285)
*Lori L. Waters, Eagle Forum, Washington, DC (p. 289)
 Stanley J. Watson, Patrick Henry College, Purcellville, VA (p. 290)
*Natalie Williams, Robinson, DiLando and Whitaker, Sacramento, CA (p. 295)
*John C. Willke, Life Issues Institute, Inc., Cincinnati, OH (p. 295)
 Betty Jean Wolfe, Urban Family Council, Philadephia, PA (p. 297)
*Kenneth Wood, The Oklahoma Christian Coalition, Oklahoma City, OK (p. 298)
*Charmaine Crouse Yoest, University of Virginia, Charlottesville, VA (p. 300)

ADOPTION, FOSTER CARE, & CHILD CARE SERVICES

*Mary Cunningham Agee, The Nurturing Network, White Salmon, WA (p. 35)
*I. Dean Ahmad, Minaret of Freedom Institute, Bethesda, MD (p. 36)
 Eloise Anderson, Claremont Institute, Sacramento, CA (p. 38)
*Julaine K. Appling, Family Research Institute of Wisconsin, Madison, WI (p. 40)
*Thomas C. Atwood, National Council For Adoption, Alexandria, VA (p. 41)
 Hunter Baker, Georgia Family Council, Norcross, GA (p. 43)
*Doug Bandow, Cato Institute, Washington, DC (p. 45)
*Naomi Lopez Bauman, Orlando, FL (p. 47)
 Douglas Besharov, American Enterprise Institute, Washington, DC (p. 52)
*Harold O. J. Brown, Reformed Theological Seminary, Charlotte, NC (p. 63)
*Martin D. Brown, Richmond, VA (p. 63)
 James Bruner, New York Family Policy Council, Albany, NY (p. 64)
*Allan C. Carlson, Howard Center for Family, Religion and Society, Rockford, IL (p. 70)
 Kenneth W. Clarkson, University of Miami, Coral Gables, FL (p. 75)
 Roberta Combs, Christian Coalition of America, Washington, DC (p. 79)
*Kenneth L. Connor, Family Research Council, Washington, DC (p. 80)
*Ron Crews, Massachusetts Family Institute, Newton Upper Falls, MA (p. 86)
*Brad W. Dacus, Pacific Justice Institute, Citrus Heights, CA (p. 87)
*Matt Daniels, Alliance for Marriage, Springfield, VA (p. 88)
 Pia de Solenni, Family Research Council, Washington, DC (p. 90)
*William T. Devlin, Urban Family Council, Philadelphia, PA (p. 94)
 James C. Dobson, Focus on the Family, Colorado Springs, CO (p. 96)
 Marie Dolan, New York State Federation of Catholic School Parents, Flushing, NY (p. 96)
 Jeff Downing, Family First, Lincoln, NE (p. 98)
*Patrick Fagan, The Heritage Foundation, Washington, DC (p. 108)
*Michael P. Farris, Patrick Henry College, Purcellville, VA (p. 109)
*Wanda Franz, National Right to Life Committee, Washington, DC (p. 116)
 Adam Fuller, Toward Tradition, Mercer Island, WA (p. 118)
*Michael Geer, Pennsylvania Family Institute, Harrisburg, PA (p. 122)
*Deanna R. Gelak, Family and Medical Leave Act Technical Corrections Coalition,
   Springfield, VA (p. 122)
 Norval D. Glenn, University of Texas, Austin, TX (p. 125)
*Stephen Goldsmith, Manhattan Institute for Policy Research, New York, NY (p. 126)
*Randy Hicks, Georgia Family Council, Norcross, GA (p. 141)
*Joseph Horn, University of Texas, Austin, TX (p. 146)
*Kerri Houston, American Conservative Union Field Office, Dallas, TX (p. 147)
 Deal Hudson, *Crisis Magazine*, Washington, DC (p. 148)
*Charles D. Hurley, Iowa Family Policy Center, Pleasant Hill, IA (p. 150)
 Darlene A. Kennedy, Centre for New Black Leadership, Baltimore, MD (p. 162)
*Robert H. Knight, Concerned Women for America, Washington, DC (p. 166)
*Andrea S. Lafferty, Traditional Values Coalition, Washington, DC (p. 172)
 Kristin D. Landers, Alabama Policy Institute, Birmingham, AL (p. 173)
*George Liebmann, Calvert Institute for Policy Research, Baltimore, MD (p. 180)
 Dianna Lightfoot, National Physicians Center for Family Resources, Birmingham, AL (p. 180)

ADOPTION, FOSTER CARE, & CHILD CARE SERVICES (Continued)

*Heather MacDonald, Manhattan Institute for Policy Research, New York, NY (p. 185)
*Connie Marshner, Raphael Services, Front Royal, VA (p. 190)
*Nina May, *Renaissance Connection.com/RCNetwork.net*, Washington, DC (p. 192)
*Michael J. McManus, Marriage Savers, Potomac, MD (p. 197)
 Tom Minnery, Focus on the Family, Colorado Springs, CO (p. 203)
 Jennifer Roback Morse, Hoover Institution, Vista, CA (p. 207)
*Steven W. Mosher, Population Research Institute, Front Royal, VA (p. 208)
 Chuck Muth, American Conservative Union, Alexandria, VA (p. 210)
*Michael J. O'Dea, Christus Medicus Foundation, Bloomfield Hills, MI (p. 216)
*Marvin Olasky, University of Texas, Austin, TX (p. 218)
*Darcy A. Olsen, Goldwater Institute, Phoenix, AZ (p. 219)
 Bobbie Patray, Eagle Forum of Tennessee, Nashville, TN (p. 222)
*Mitchell B. Pearlstein, Center of the American Experiment, Minneapolis, MN (p. 224)
*Stephen Presser, Northwestern University School of Law, Chicago, IL (p. 233)
 Harold Calvin Ray, National Center for Faith-Based Initiatives, West Palm Beach, FL (p. 237)
*Kelly Rosati, Hawaii Family Forum, Kaneohe, HI (p. 243)
*Michael Schwartz, Concerned Women for America, Washington, DC (p. 254)
*Alan E. Sears, Alliance Defense Fund, Scottsdale, AZ (p. 255)
*Ralph Segalman, California State University, Northridge, Northridge, CA (p. 256)
*Jamie Self, Georgia Family Council, Norcross, GA (p. 256)
*Lou Sheldon, Traditional Values Coalition, Washington, DC (p. 258)
*Curt Smith, Indiana Family Institute, Indianapolis, IN (p. 263)
*W. Shepherd Smith, Jr., Institute for Youth Development, Washington, DC (p. 264)
*Lisa Snell, Reason Foundation, Los Angeles, CA (p. 265)
 Peter S. Sprigg, Family Research Council, Washington, DC (p. 267)
 Glenn T. Stanton, Focus on the Family, Colorado Springs, CO (p. 268)
 Doug Stiegler, Association of Maryland Families, Woodstock, MD (p. 269)
*Karen Testerman, Cornerstone Policy Research, Concord, NH (p. 275)
*Forest M. Thigpen, Mississippi Family Council, Jackson, MS (p. 277)
*Randy Thomasson, Campaign for California Families, Sacramento, CA (p. 277)
 Stanley J. Watson, Patrick Henry College, Purcellville, VA (p. 290)
*Natalie Williams, Robinson, DiLando and Whitaker, Sacramento, CA (p. 295)
*John C. Willke, Life Issues Institute, Inc., Cincinnati, OH (p. 295)
*Kenneth Wood, The Oklahoma Christian Coalition, Oklahoma City, OK (p. 298)
*Robert L. Woodson, Sr., National Center for Neighborhood Enterprise,
    Washington, DC (p. 298)
*Charmaine Crouse Yoest, University of Virginia, Charlottesville, VA (p. 300)

ARTS, HUMANITIES AND HISTORIC RESOURCES

*John Agresto, John Agresto and Associates, Santa Fe, NM (p. 35)
 Benjamin Alexander, Franciscan University of Steubenville, Steubenville, OH (p. 36)
*William Allen, Michigan State University, East Lansing, MI (p. 37)
 Ford A. Anderson, State Policy Network, Dallas, TX (p. 38)
*Dominic A. Aquila, Ave Maria University, Ypsilanti, MI (p. 40)
 Joseph Baldacchino, National Humanities Institute, Bowie, MD (p. 44)
 Christopher Beiting, Ave Maria College, Ypsilanti, MI (p. 49)
*William J. Bennett, Empower America, Washington, DC (p. 51)
 Richard Bjornseth, Valdosta State University, Valdosta, GA (p. 54)
*Mark Blitz, Claremont McKenna College, Claremont, CA (p. 55)
*David Boaz, Cato Institute, Washington, DC (p. 55)
 L. Brent Bozell, III, Media Research Center, Alexandria, VA (p. 59)
 Arthur C. Brooks, Syracuse University, Syracuse, NY (p. 61)
*Floyd G. Brown, Young America's Foundation Reagan Ranch Project,
    Santa Barbara, CA (p. 63)

ARTS, HUMANITIES AND HISTORIC RESOURCES (Continued)

*Harold O. J. Brown, Reformed Theological Seminary, Charlotte, NC (p. 63)

William F. Campbell, The Philadelphia Society, Baton Rouge, LA (p. 68)

Pradyumna S. Chauhan, Arcadia University, Glenside, PA (p. 73)

*Lynne V. Cheney, American Enterprise Institute, Washington, DC (p. 73)

Robert Chitester, Palmer R. Chitester Fund, Erie, PA (p. 73)

Andrew I. Cohen, University of Oklahoma, Norman, OK (p. 77)

Kevin L. Cope, Louisiana State University, Baton Rouge, LA (p. 81)

*Janice Shaw Crouse, Concerned Women for America, Washington, DC (p. 87)

Buffy DeBreaux-Watts, American Board for Certification of Teacher Excellence, Washington, DC (p. 91)

*Midge Decter, New York, NY (p. 91)

D. P. Diffine, Harding University, Searcy, AR (p. 95)

Thomas Doherty, Brandeis University, Waltham, MA (p. 96)

Jeff Downing, Family First, Lincoln, NE (p. 98)

*Becky Norton Dunlop, The Heritage Foundation, Washington, DC (p. 100)

Lenore T. Ealy, Emergent Enterprises, Carmel, IN (p. 101)

Robert B. Ekelund, Auburn University, Auburn, AL (p. 105)

*John Fonte, Hudson Institute, Washington, DC (p. 114)

*David Forte, Cleveland State University, Cleveland, OH (p. 114)

Elizabeth Fox-Genovese, Emory University, Atlanta, GA (p. 115)

Adam Fuller, Toward Tradition, Mercer Island, WA (p. 118)

James R. Gaston, Franciscan University of Steubenville, Steubenville, OH (p. 120)

Philip Gold, Discovery Institute, Seattle, WA (p. 125)

Chad Hills, Focus on the Family, Colorado Springs, CO (p. 143)

Deal Hudson, *Crisis Magazine*, Washington, DC (p. 148)

Carol Iannone, New York, NY (p. 150)

Thomas Ivancie, America's Future Foundation, Washington, DC (p. 152)

*Laurence Jarvik, Washington, DC (p. 153)

Michael S. Joyce, Foundation for Community and Faith Centered Enterprise, Phoenix, AZ (p. 156)

Annette Kirk, Russell Kirk Center, Mecosta, MI (p. 164)

James J. Kirschke, Villanova University, Villanova, PA (p. 164)

*Robert H. Knight, Concerned Women for America, Washington, DC (p. 166)

*Robert C. Koons, University of Texas, Austin, TX (p. 167)

Alan Charles Kors, The Foundation for Individual Rights in Education, Philadelphia, PA (p. 167)

*Andrea S. Lafferty, Traditional Values Coalition, Washington, DC (p. 172)

Richard Lessner, American Renewal, Washington, DC (p. 178)

*Jerry L. Martin, American Council of Trustees and Alumni, Washington, DC (p. 190)

*Ken Masugi, Claremont Institute, Claremont, CA (p. 191)

*Nina May, *Renaissance Connection.com/RCNetwork.net*, Washington, DC (p. 192)

Wilfred M. McClay, University of Tennessee, Chattanooga, Chattanooga, TN (p. 193)

W. Wesley McDonald, Elizabethtown College, Elizabethtown, PA (p. 195)

Dave McIntyre, ANSER Institute for Homeland Security, Arlington, VA (p. 196)

Samuel P. Menefee, Regent University, Virginia Beach, VA (p. 199)

Tom Minnery, Focus on the Family, Colorado Springs, CO (p. 203)

*Joseph A. Morris, Lincoln Legal Foundation, Chicago, IL (p. 207)

Laurie Morrow, Montpelier, VT (p. 207)

Mario Navarro da Costa, American Society for the Defense of Tradition, Family and Property, McLean, VA (p. 211)

*Anne D. Neal, American Council of Trustees and Alumni, Washington, DC (p. 211)

Jeff Nelson, Intercollegiate Studies Institute, Wilmington, DE (p. 212)

Jacob Neusner, Bard College, Rhinebeck, NY (p. 213)

C. Preston Noell, III, Tradition, Family, Property, Inc., McLean, VA (p. 214)

ARTS, HUMANITIES AND HISTORIC RESOURCES (Continued)

Sanford Pinsker, Franklin and Marshall College, Lancaster, PA (p. 229)
Arthur Pontynen, University of Wisconsin, Oshkosh, WI (p. 230)
*Stephen Presser, Northwestern University School of Law, Chicago, IL (p. 233)
William Craig Rice, American Academy for Liberal Education, Washington, DC (p. 239)
Glenn M. Ricketts, National Association of Scholars, Princeton, NJ (p. 239)
John E. Rocha, Sr., Center for the American Idea, Houston, TX (p. 242)
Robert Royal, Faith & Reason Institute, Washington, DC (p. 245)
*Steven Alan Samson, Liberty University, Lynchburg, VA (p. 249)
Robert A. Schadler, Center for First Principles, Washington, DC (p. 251)
*Alan E. Sears, Alliance Defense Fund, Scottsdale, AZ (p. 255)
*Lou Sheldon, Traditional Values Coalition, Washington, DC (p. 258)
Richard Sherlock, Utah State University, Logan, UT (p. 259)
Aeon James Skoble, Bridgewater State College, Bridgewater, MA (p. 262)
Thomas Sowell, Hoover Institution, Stanford, CA (p. 266)
Peter S. Sprigg, Family Research Council, Washington, DC (p. 267)
Glenn T. Stanton, Focus on the Family, Colorado Springs, CO (p. 268)
*Christine Stolba, Ethics and Public Policy Center, Washington, DC (p. 269)
Ewa M. Thompson, Rice University, Houston, TX (p. 277)
Lawrence A. Uzzell, Keston Institute, Waxahachie, TX (p. 283)
*Maris A. Vinovskis, University of Michigan, Ann Arbor, MI (p. 285)
Emily S. Watts, University of Illinois at Urbana-Champaign, Urbana, IL (p. 290)
*John W. Whitehead, The Rutherford Institute, Charlottesville, VA (p. 293)
Bradford P. Wilson, National Association of Scholars, Princeton, NJ (p. 296)
Clyde N. Wilson, University of South Carolina, Columbia, SC (p. 296)
Anne Wortham, Illinois State University, Normal, IL (p. 298)

CITIZENSHIP AND CIVIL SOCIETY

*I. Dean Ahmad, Minaret of Freedom Institute, Bethesda, MD (p. 36)
Benjamin Alexander, Franciscan University of Steubenville, Steubenville, OH (p. 36)
*William Allen, Michigan State University, East Lansing, MI (p. 37)
Brian C. Anderson, Manhattan Institute for Policy Research, New York, NY (p. 38)
Ford A. Anderson, State Policy Network, Dallas, TX (p. 38)
*Julaine K. Appling, Family Research Institute of Wisconsin, Madison, WI (p. 40)
*Dominic A. Aquila, Ave Maria University, Ypsilanti, MI (p. 40)
Larry P. Arnn, Hillsdale College, Hillsdale, MI (p. 40)
*Thomas C. Atwood, National Council For Adoption, Alexandria, VA (p. 41)
Hunter Baker, Georgia Family Council, Norcross, GA (p. 43)
*John S. Baker, Jr., Louisiana State University, Baton Rouge, LA (p. 43)
Whitney L. Ball, DonorsTrust, Alexandria, VA (p. 44)
Michael B. Barkey, Center for the Study of Compassionate Conservatism, Grand Rapids, MI (p. 46)
*William J. Bennett, Empower America, Washington, DC (p. 51)
*Jason Bertsch, American Enterprise Institute, Washington, DC (p. 52)
*Wayman R. Bishop, The Family Foundation of Virginia, Richmond, VA (p. 53)
Amy E. Black, Wheaton College, Wheaton, IL (p. 54)
*Mark Blitz, Claremont McKenna College, Claremont, CA (p. 55)
David J. Bobb, Hillsdale College, Hillsdale, MI (p. 56)
L. Brent Bozell, III, Media Research Center, Alexandria, VA (p. 59)
*Marshall J. Breger, Catholic University of America, Washington, DC (p. 60)
John S. Butler, University of Texas, Austin, TX (p. 66)
*Stuart Butler, The Heritage Foundation, Washington, DC (p. 66)
*David Caprara, The Empowerment Network, Fredericksburg, VA (p. 69)
*James B. Cardle, Texas Citizen Action Network, Austin, TX (p. 69)
*Robert Carleson, American Civil Rights Union, Alexandria, VA (p. 70)

---

* Has testified before a state or federal legislative committee

CITIZENSHIP AND CIVIL SOCIETY (Continued)

*Samuel Casey Carter, Acade Metrics, LLC, Washington, DC (p. 71)
*James Chapman, Rocky Mountain Family Council, Denver, CO (p. 72)
 John Clark, Hudson Institute, Indianapolis, IN (p. 75)
*Micah Clark, American Family Association, Indianapolis, IN (p. 75)
 Andrew I. Cohen, University of Oklahoma, Norman, OK (p. 77)
 Eric Cohen, Ethics and Public Policy Center, Washington, DC (p. 78)
 Roberta Combs, Christian Coalition of America, Washington, DC (p. 79)
*Ron Crews, Massachusetts Family Institute, Newton Upper Falls, MA (p. 86)
 Alan R. Crippen, II, Family Research Council, Washington, DC (p. 86)
 Dinesh D'Souza, Hoover Institution, Stanford, CA (p. 87)
 Candace de Russy, State University of New York, Bronxville, NY (p. 90)
*Midge Decter, New York, NY (p. 91)
*Eugene Delgaudio, Public Advocate, Falls Church, VA (p. 91)
 Kimberly Dennis, D & D Foundation, Washington, DC (p. 93)
*Len Deo, New Jersey Family Policy Council, Parsippany, NJ (p. 93)
*Robert Destro, Catholic University of America, Washington, DC (p. 94)
*Donald J. Devine, Center for American Values, Shady Side, MD (p. 94)
*William T. Devlin, Urban Family Council, Philadelphia, PA (p. 94)
 John J. DiIulio, Jr., University of Pennsylvania, Philadelphia, PA (p. 95)
 Richard J. Dougherty, University of Dallas, Irving, TX (p. 97)
 Jeff Downing, Family First, Lincoln, NE (p. 98)
*Clark Durant, New Common School Foundation, Detroit, MI (p. 101)
 Mark L. Earley, Prison Fellowship Ministries, Washington, DC (p. 101)
*John C. Eastman, Chapman University School of Law, Orange, CA (p. 102)
*Evelyn Ebzery, Memorial Hospital of Sheridan County, Sheridan, WY (p. 103)
 Tim G. Echols, TeenPact Teen Leadership School, Jefferson, GA (p. 103)
*James R. Edwards, Jr., Hudson Institute, Washington, DC (p. 104)
*Mickey Edwards, Harvard University, Cambridge, MA (p. 104)
 Barbara Elliott, Center for Renewal, Houston, TX (p. 105)
 W. Winston Elliott, III, Center for the American Idea, Houston, TX (p. 106)
*Michael P. Farris, Patrick Henry College, Purcellville, VA (p. 109)
*Robert Fike, Americans for Tax Reform, Washington, DC (p. 111)
*John Fonte, Hudson Institute, Washington, DC (p. 114)
*David Forte, Cleveland State University, Cleveland, OH (p. 114)
 Elizabeth Fox-Genovese, Emory University, Atlanta, GA (p. 115)
 Hillel Fradkin, Ethics and Public Policy Center, Washington, DC (p. 115)
 Adam Fuller, Toward Tradition, Mercer Island, WA (p. 118)
 Gary L. Geipel, Hudson Institute, Indianapolis, IN (p. 122)
*Deanna R. Gelak, Family and Medical Leave Act Technical Corrections Coalition, Springfield, VA (p. 122)
*Robert P. George, Princeton University, Princeton, NJ (p. 122)
 Roberta M. Gilbert, Center for the Study of Human Systems, Falls Church, VA (p. 123)
*Roy Godson, National Strategy Information Center, Washington, DC (p. 125)
*Stephen Goldsmith, Manhattan Institute for Policy Research, New York, NY (p. 126)
 Tomi Gomory, Florida State University, Tallahassee, FL (p. 126)
 John Green, University of Akron, Akron, OH (p. 128)
 Steven E. Grosby, Clemson University, Clemson, SC (p. 129)
 Rebecca Hagelin, The Heritage Foundation, Washington, DC (p. 131)
 Roger Hamburg, Indiana University South Bend, South Bend, IN (p. 133)
*Donna H. Hearne, Constitutional Coalition, St. Louis, MO (p. 138)
 Jay F. Hein, Hudson Institute, Indianapolis, IN (p. 139)
*Randy Hicks, Georgia Family Council, Norcross, GA (p. 141)
 Heather Higgins, Independent Women's Forum, New York, NY (p. 142)
 James E. Hinish, Jr., Regent University, Williamsburg, VA (p. 143)

CITIZENSHIP AND CIVIL SOCIETY (Continued)

*Fred Holden, Phoenix Enterprises, Arvada, CO (p. 144)
*Michael Horowitz, Hudson Institute, Washington, DC (p. 146)
*John A. Howard, Howard Center for Family, Religion and Society, Rockford, IL (p. 147)
*Michael Howden, Stronger Families for Oregon, Salem, OR (p. 147)
 Edward L. Hudgins, The Objectivist Center, Washington, DC (p. 148)
 James D. Hunter, University of Virginia, Charlottesville, VA (p. 149)
*Charles D. Hurley, Iowa Family Policy Center, Pleasant Hill, IA (p. 150)
 Byron Johnson, University of Pennsylvania, Philadelphia, PA (p. 155)
 Michael S. Joyce, Foundation for Community and Faith Centered Enterprise,
     Phoenix, AZ (p. 156)
 David Kelley, The Objectivist Center, Poughkeepsie, NY (p. 160)
 Jeff Kemp, Families Northwest, Bellevue, WA (p. 161)
 Phil Kent, Southeastern Legal Foundation, Atlanta, GA (p. 162)
*William A. Keyes, The Institute on Political Journalism, Washington, DC (p. 162)
 Annette Kirk, Russell Kirk Center, Mecosta, MI (p. 164)
*Robert H. Knight, Concerned Women for America, Washington, DC (p. 166)
 Joseph M. Knippenberg, Oglethorpe University, Atlanta, GA (p. 166)
*Mark Krikorian, Center for Immigration Studies, Washington, DC (p. 169)
 William Kristol, *The Weekly Standard*, Washington, DC (p. 169)
 Melvin A. Kulbicki, York College of Pennsylvania, York, PA (p. 170)
*George Landrith, Frontiers of Freedom Institute, Fairfax, VA (p. 173)
*Andrew Langer, National Federation of Independent Business, Washington, DC (p. 174)
 Peter Augustine Lawler, Berry College, Mount Berry, GA (p. 175)
*Stephen Lazarus, Center for Public Justice, Annapolis, MD (p. 176)
 Joseph G. Lehman, Mackinac Center for Public Policy, Midland, MI (p. 177)
*Eli Lehrer, *The American Enterprise*, Washington, DC (p. 177)
 Seth Leibsohn, Empower America, Washington, DC (p. 177)
 Richard Lessner, American Renewal, Washington, DC (p. 178)
 Jacob T. Levy, University of Chicago, Chicago, IL (p. 179)
 Thomas K. Lindsay, University of Dallas, Irving, TX (p. 181)
 Tibor R. Machan, Chapman University, Silverado Canyon, CA (p. 185)
 Myron Magnet, Manhattan Institute for Policy Research, New York, NY (p. 186)
*Ramona Marotz-Baden, Montana State University, Bozeman, MT (p. 189)
*Jerry L. Martin, American Council of Trustees and Alumni, Washington, DC (p. 190)
*Ken Masugi, Claremont Institute, Claremont, CA (p. 191)
*Vern I. McCarthy, Jr., Mid-America Institute, Oak Brook, IL (p. 193)
 Wilfred M. McClay, University of Tennessee, Chattanooga, Chattanooga, TN (p. 193)
 Kathleen McGarry, Murray Hill Institute, New York, NY (p. 195)
*Michael J. McManus, Marriage Savers, Potomac, MD (p. 197)
*Lawrence Mead, New York University, New York, NY (p. 198)
*Edwin Meese III, The Heritage Foundation, Washington, DC (p. 198)
 Paul T. Mero, The Sutherland Institute, Salt Lake City, UT (p. 199)
 Paul E. Michelson, Huntington College, Huntington, IN (p. 201)
*Roger Michener, Placitas, NM (p. 201)
 Tom Minnery, Focus on the Family, Colorado Springs, CO (p. 203)
*C. Ben Mitchell, Trinity International University, Deerfield, IL (p. 203)
 Jennifer Roback Morse, Hoover Institution, Vista, CA (p. 207)
*Len Munsil, Center for Arizona Policy, Scottsdale, AZ (p. 209)
 William J. Murray, Religious Freedom Coalition, Washington, DC (p. 209)
*Anne D. Neal, American Council of Trustees and Alumni, Washington, DC (p. 211)
 Jeff Nelson, Intercollegiate Studies Institute, Wilmington, DE (p. 212)
 David Charles Nice, Washington State University, Pullman, WA (p. 213)
 Michael J. Novak, Jr., American Enterprise Institute, Washington, DC (p. 215)
*Marvin Olasky, University of Texas, Austin, TX (p. 218)

CITIZENSHIP AND CIVIL SOCIETY (Continued)

*Richard Olivastro, People Dynamics, Farmington, CT (p. 218)
Kent Ostrander, The Family Foundation of Kentucky, Lexington, KY (p. 220)
Tom G. Palmer, Cato Institute, Washington, DC (p. 221)
*Allan E. Parker, Jr., Texas Justice Foundation, San Antonio, TX (p. 221)
Paul C. Peterson, Coastal Carolina University, Conway, SC (p. 227)
*Nancy M. Pfotenhauer, Independent Women's Forum, Arlington, VA (p. 227)
*Daniel J. Popeo, Washington Legal Foundation, Washington, DC (p. 231)
Dennis Prager, The Prager Perspective, Van Nuys, CA (p. 232)
Arch Puddington, Freedom House, New York, NY (p. 234)
William D. Richardson, University of South Dakota, Vermillion, SD (p. 239)
Sandy Rios, Concerned Women for America, Washington, DC (p. 240)
*Richard O. Rowland, Grassroot Institute of Hawaii, Aiea, HI (p. 245)
Robert Royal, Faith & Reason Institute, Washington, DC (p. 245)
Charles Rubin, Duquesne University, Pittsburgh, PA (p. 246)
*Steven Alan Samson, Liberty University, Lynchburg, VA (p. 249)
David W. Saxe, Pennsylvania State University, University Park, PA (p. 251)
Robert A. Schadler, Center for First Principles, Washington, DC (p. 251)
David L. Schaefer, Holy Cross College, Worcester, MA (p. 252)
*Arthur J. Schwartz, John Templeton Foundation, Radnor, PA (p. 254)
*Alan E. Sears, Alliance Defense Fund, Scottsdale, AZ (p. 255)
Jeffrey Leigh Sedgwick, University of Massachusetts, Amherst, MA (p. 255)
*Jamie Self, Georgia Family Council, Norcross, GA (p. 256)
*Donald J. Senese, 60 Plus Association, Arlington, VA (p. 257)
*Colleen Sheehan, Villanova University, Villanova, PA (p. 258)
*Lou Sheldon, Traditional Values Coalition, Washington, DC (p. 258)
Aaron Siegel, Freedoms Foundation at Valley Forge, Valley Forge, PA (p. 259)
*Robert A. Sirico, Acton Institute for the Study of Religion and Liberty,
    Grand Rapids, MI (p. 261)
*Peter Skerry, Claremont McKenna College, Claremont, CA (p. 261)
*James Skillen, Center for Public Justice, Annapolis, MD (p. 261)
*Curt Smith, Indiana Family Institute, Indianapolis, IN (p. 263)
*Oran P. Smith, Palmetto Family Council, Columbia, SC (p. 264)
Christina Hoff Sommers, American Enterprise Institute, Washington, DC (p. 266)
Thomas Sowell, Hoover Institution, Stanford, CA (p. 266)
*Matthew Spalding, The Heritage Foundation, Washington, DC (p. 266)
Glenn T. Stanton, Focus on the Family, Colorado Springs, CO (p. 268)
*James A. Stever, University of Cincinnati, Hamilton, OH (p. 269)
Margaret D. Stock, United States Military Academy, West Point, NY (p. 269)
*David Swindell, Clemson University, Clemson, SC (p. 273)
Miklos N. Szilagyi, University of Arizona, Tucson, AZ (p. 273)
James R. "J.T." Taylor, Empower America, Washington, DC (p. 274)
*David J. Theroux, The Independent Institute, Oakland, CA (p. 276)
*Forest M. Thigpen, Mississippi Family Council, Jackson, MS (p. 277)
Brian S. Tracy, Brian Tracy International, Solana Beach, CA (p. 280)
*George Tryfiates, Concerned Women for America, Washington, DC (p. 281)
*Balint Vazsonyi, Center for the American Founding, McLean, VA (p. 284)
*Maris A. Vinovskis, University of Michigan, Ann Arbor, MI (p. 285)
Bradley C. S. Watson, Saint Vincent College, Latrobe, PA (p. 290)
Ben J. Wattenberg, American Enterprise Institute, Washington, DC (p. 290)
*Donald V. Weatherman, Erskine College, Due West, SC (p. 290)
Christopher Heath Wellman, Georgia State University, Atlanta, GA (p. 292)
Thomas G. West, University of Dallas, Irving, TX (p. 293)
*Paul Weyrich, Free Congress Foundation, Washington, DC (p. 293)
Peter W. Wielhouwer, Regent University, Virginia Beach, VA (p. 294)

CITIZENSHIP AND CIVIL SOCIETY (Continued)

Russell Williams, Jefferson Center for Character Education, Mission Viejo, CA (p. 295)

*Robert L. Woodson, Sr., National Center for Neighborhood Enterprise, Washington, DC (p. 298)

Anne Wortham, Illinois State University, Normal, IL (p. 298)

Frank Wright, Center for Christian Statesmanship, Washington, DC (p. 299)

Edward W. Younkins, Wheeling Jesuit University, Wheeling, WV (p. 301)

Jerry Zandstra, Acton Institute for the Study of Religion and Liberty, Grand Rapids, MI (p. 301)

Karl Zinsmeister, American Enterprise Institute, Cazenovia, NY (p. 302)

FAITH-BASED AND VOLUNTEER INITIATIVES

*Mary Cunningham Agee, The Nurturing Network, White Salmon, WA (p. 35)

Benjamin Alexander, Franciscan University of Steubenville, Steubenville, OH (p. 36)

Brian C. Anderson, Manhattan Institute for Policy Research, New York, NY (p. 38)

*Carl A. Anderson, Knights of Columbus, New Haven, CT (p. 38)

Ford A. Anderson, State Policy Network, Dallas, TX (p. 38)

Frank Annunziata, Rochester Institute of Technology, Rochester, NY (p. 39)

*Thomas C. Atwood, National Council For Adoption, Alexandria, VA (p. 41)

Whitney L. Ball, DonorsTrust, Alexandria, VA (p. 44)

*Sandor Balogh, Hudson Valley Community College, East Greenbush, NY (p. 45)

*Doug Bandow, Cato Institute, Washington, DC (p. 45)

Michael B. Barkey, Center for the Study of Compassionate Conservatism, Grand Rapids, MI (p. 46)

*Gary L. Bauer, Campaign for Working Families, Arlington, VA (p. 47)

*Naomi Lopez Bauman, Orlando, FL (p. 47)

Gregory S. Baylor, Center for Law and Religious Freedom, Annandale, VA (p. 47)

Mariam Bell, Prison Fellowship Ministries, Washington, DC (p. 49)

Amy E. Black, Wheaton College, Wheaton, IL (p. 54)

*Mark Blitz, Claremont McKenna College, Claremont, CA (p. 55)

Philip L. Brach, Midtown Educational Foundation, Chicago, IL (p. 59)

*Marshall J. Breger, Catholic University of America, Washington, DC (p. 60)

*Harold O. J. Brown, Reformed Theological Seminary, Charlotte, NC (p. 63)

*Martin D. Brown, Richmond, VA (p. 63)

*David Caprara, The Empowerment Network, Fredericksburg, VA (p. 69)

*Samuel Casey, Christian Legal Society, Annandale, VA (p. 71)

*Michael A. Ciamarra, Alabama Policy Institute, Birmingham, AL (p. 74)

Howard Cochran, Jr., Belmont University, Nashville, TN (p. 77)

Roberta Combs, Christian Coalition of America, Washington, DC (p. 79)

*Kenneth L. Connor, Family Research Council, Washington, DC (p. 80)

*John E. Coons, University of California at Berkeley, Berkeley, CA (p. 81)

*Ron Crews, Massachusetts Family Institute, Newton Upper Falls, MA (p. 86)

*Brad W. Dacus, Pacific Justice Institute, Citrus Heights, CA (p. 87)

*Matt Daniels, Alliance for Marriage, Springfield, VA (p. 88)

Buffy DeBreaux-Watts, American Board for Certification of Teacher Excellence, Washington, DC (p. 91)

*Midge Decter, New York, NY (p. 91)

Kimberly Dennis, D & D Foundation, Washington, DC (p. 93)

*Len Deo, New Jersey Family Policy Council, Parsippany, NJ (p. 93)

*William T. Devlin, Urban Family Council, Philadelphia, PA (p. 94)

*Phillip DeVous, Acton Institute for the Study of Religion and Liberty, Grand Rapids, MI (p. 94)

D. P. Diffine, Harding University, Searcy, AR (p. 95)

John J. DiIulio, Jr., University of Pennsylvania, Philadelphia, PA (p. 95)

Jeff Downing, Family First, Lincoln, NE (p. 98)

*Richard Duncan, University of Nebraska, Lincoln, NE (p. 99)

FAITH-BASED AND VOLUNTEER INITIATIVES (Continued)

*Becky Norton Dunlop, The Heritage Foundation, Washington, DC (p. 100)
*David Dunn, Oklahoma Family Policy Council, Bethany, OK (p. 100)
*Clark Durant, New Common School Foundation, Detroit, MI (p. 101)
*William Eggers, Deloitte Research-Public Sector, Washington, DC (p. 104)
 Barbara Elliott, Center for Renewal, Houston, TX (p. 105)
*Louis D. Enoff, Enoff Associates Limited, Sykesville, MD (p. 107)
*Patrick Fagan, The Heritage Foundation, Washington, DC (p. 108)
*Thompson Mason Faller, University of Portland, Portland, OR (p. 109)
*Michael P. Farris, Patrick Henry College, Purcellville, VA (p. 109)
 Elizabeth Fox-Genovese, Emory University, Atlanta, GA (p. 115)
 Hillel Fradkin, Ethics and Public Policy Center, Washington, DC (p. 115)
 Adam Fuller, Toward Tradition, Mercer Island, WA (p. 118)
*Michael Geer, Pennsylvania Family Institute, Harrisburg, PA (p. 122)
*Robert P. George, Princeton University, Princeton, NJ (p. 122)
 Norval D. Glenn, University of Texas, Austin, TX (p. 125)
*Stephen Goldsmith, Manhattan Institute for Policy Research, New York, NY (p. 126)
 John Green, University of Akron, Akron, OH (p. 128)
 Samuel Gregg, Acton Institute for the Study of Religion and Liberty, Grand Rapids, MI (p. 129)
 Virgil Gulker, Kids Hope USA, Holland, MI (p. 130)
 Alam E. Hammad, Alexandria, VA (p. 133)
 Charles L. Harper, John Templeton Foundation, Radnor, PA (p. 135)
 Jay F. Hein, Hudson Institute, Indianapolis, IN (p. 139)
 Lowman Henry, Lincoln Institute of Public Opinion Research, Inc., Harrisburg, PA (p. 140)
 Carl Herbster, American Association of Christian Schools, Independence, MO (p. 140)
*Michael Horowitz, Hudson Institute, Washington, DC (p. 146)
*Michael Howden, Stronger Families for Oregon, Salem, OR (p. 147)
 Deal Hudson, Crisis Magazine, Washington, DC (p. 148)
*Charles D. Hurley, Iowa Family Policy Center, Pleasant Hill, IA (p. 150)
*Alan Inman, Institute for Responsible Fatherhood and Family Revitalization, Largo, MD (p. 151)
*Eve Jackson, The PEERS Project, Indianapolis, IN (p. 152)
*Charles W. Jarvis, United Seniors Association, Fairfax, VA (p. 153)
 Michael L. Jestes, Oklahoma Family Policy Council, Bethany, OK (p. 154)
 Byron Johnson, University of Pennsylvania, Philadelphia, PA (p. 155)
 Darlene A. Kennedy, Centre for New Black Leadership, Baltimore, MD (p. 162)
*Douglas W. Kmiec, The Catholic University of America, Washington, DC (p. 166)
 Dorothy Knauer, Protestant Community Centers, Inc., Newark, NJ (p. 166)
*Robert H. Knight, Concerned Women for America, Washington, DC (p. 166)
 Joseph M. Knippenberg, Oglethorpe University, Atlanta, GA (p. 166)
*Lawrence Kudlow, Kudlow & Co., LLC, New York, NY (p. 170)
 Peter J. LaBarbera, Concerned Women for America, Washington, DC (p. 171)
*Jill Cunningham Lacey, Capital Research Center, Damascus, MD (p. 171)
 Stacey Ladd, Worth the Wait, Pampa, TX (p. 171)
*Andrea S. Lafferty, Traditional Values Coalition, Washington, DC (p. 172)
 Daniel Lapin, Toward Tradition, Mercer Island, WA (p. 174)
*Stephen Lazarus, Center for Public Justice, Annapolis, MD (p. 176)
 Seth Leibsohn, Empower America, Washington, DC (p. 177)
*George Liebmann, Calvert Institute for Policy Research, Baltimore, MD (p. 180)
*Joseph Loconte, The Heritage Foundation, Washington, DC (p. 182)
*Mike Long, Complete Abstinence Eduation Program, Durham, NC (p. 183)
*Dennis Mansfield, Boise, ID (p. 189)
*Jim Martin, 60 Plus Association, Arlington, VA (p. 190)
 Kris Alan Mauren, Acton Institute for the Study of Religion and Liberty, Grand Rapids, MI (p. 192)

FAITH-BASED AND VOLUNTEER INITIATIVES (Continued)

*Nina May, *Renaissance Connection.com/RCNetwork.net*, Washington, DC (p. 192)
*John McClaughry, Ethan Allen Institute, Concord, VT (p. 193)
 Wilfred M. McClay, University of Tennessee, Chattanooga, Chattanooga, TN (p. 193)
*Tom McClusky, National Taxpayers Union Foundation, Alexandria, VA (p. 193)
*Michael W. McConnell, University of Utah, Salt Lake City, UT (p. 194)
*Michael J. McManus, Marriage Savers, Potomac, MD (p. 197)
 Jack McVaugh, Arizona School Choice Trust, Scottsdale, AZ (p. 198)
 Tom Minnery, Focus on the Family, Colorado Springs, CO (p. 203)
 R. Albert Mohler, Jr., The Southern Baptist Theological Seminary, Louisville, KY (p. 204)
 Stephen Monsma, Pepperdine University, Malibu, CA (p. 205)
 Jennifer Roback Morse, Hoover Institution, Vista, CA (p. 207)
*Steven W. Mosher, Population Research Institute, Front Royal, VA (p. 208)
*Len Munsil, Center for Arizona Policy, Scottsdale, AZ (p. 209)
 William J. Murray, Religious Freedom Coalition, Washington, DC (p. 209)
 Phyllis Berry Myers, Centre for New Black Leadership, Washington, DC (p. 210)
 Ronald Nash, Reformed Theological Seminary, Oviedo, FL (p. 211)
 Anthony I. Negbenebor, Gardner-Webb University, Boiling Springs, NC (p. 212)
 Stuart W. Nolan, Jr., Springfield, VA (p. 214)
*Michael J. O'Dea, Christus Medicus Foundation, Bloomfield Hills, MI (p. 216)
*Marvin Olasky, University of Texas, Austin, TX (p. 218)
 Kent Ostrander, The Family Foundation of Kentucky, Lexington, KY (p. 220)
*Star Parker, Coalition on Urban Renewal and Education, Washington, DC (p. 222)
 Val Peter, Boys Town, Boys Town, NE (p. 226)
*Howard Phillips, The Conservative Caucus, Inc., Vienna, VA (p. 227)
 Harold Calvin Ray, National Center for Faith-Based Initiatives, West Palm Beach, FL (p. 237)
 Patrick Reilly, Cardinal Newman Society, Falls Church, VA (p. 238)
*Charles E. Rice, Notre Dame Law School, Notre Dame, IN (p. 239)
 John W. Robbins, Trinity Foundation, Unicoi, TN (p. 241)
 Robert Royal, Faith & Reason Institute, Washington, DC (p. 245)
 Robert E. Russell, Jr., The Heritage Foundation, Geneva, IL (p. 247)
*Frank Russo, American Family Association of New York, Port Washington, NY (p. 247)
*Terrence M. Scanlon, Capital Research Center, Washington, DC (p. 251)
*Arthur J. Schwartz, John Templeton Foundation, Radnor, PA (p. 254)
*Alan E. Sears, Alliance Defense Fund, Scottsdale, AZ (p. 255)
*Jay Sekulow, American Center for Law and Justice, Virginia Beach, VA (p. 256)
*Lou Sheldon, Traditional Values Coalition, Washington, DC (p. 258)
*Amy L. Sherman, Hudson Institute, Charlottesville, VA (p. 259)
*Robert A. Sirico, Acton Institute for the Study of Religion and Liberty,
    Grand Rapids, MI (p. 261)
 Anita Smith, Institute for Youth Development, Washington, DC (p. 262)
*Curt Smith, Indiana Family Institute, Indianapolis, IN (p. 263)
*W. Shepherd Smith, Jr., Institute for Youth Development, Washington, DC (p. 264)
*Lisa Snell, Reason Foundation, Los Angeles, CA (p. 265)
*Matthew Spalding, The Heritage Foundation, Washington, DC (p. 266)
 Doug Stiegler, Association of Maryland Families, Woodstock, MD (p. 269)
*David Swindell, Clemson University, Clemson, SC (p. 273)
*Michael Tanner, Cato Institute, Washington, DC (p. 274)
 James R. "J.T." Taylor, Empower America, Washington, DC (p. 274)
*Forest M. Thigpen, Mississippi Family Council, Jackson, MS (p. 277)
*David G. Tuerck, Beacon Hill Institute, Boston, MA (p. 281)
*Forrest L. Turpen, Christian Educators Association International, Pasadena, CA (p. 282)
*Terry W. Van Allen, Kemah, TX (p. 283)
*Kevin Vigilante, Rumford, RI (p. 285)
 Stanley J. Watson, Patrick Henry College, Purcellville, VA (p. 290)

---

* Has testified before a state or federal legislative committee

FAITH-BASED AND VOLUNTEER INITIATIVES (Continued)

John G. West, Discovery Institute, Seattle, WA (p. 292)

*John W. Whitehead, The Rutherford Institute, Charlottesville, VA (p. 293)

*John C. Willke, Life Issues Institute, Inc., Cincinnati, OH (p. 295)

Richard B. Wirthlin, Wirthlin Worldwide, South Jordan, UT (p. 296)

Betty Jean Wolfe, Urban Family Council, Philadephia, PA (p. 297)

*Kenneth Wood, The Oklahoma Christian Coalition, Oklahoma City, OK (p. 298)

*Robert L. Woodson, Sr., National Center for Neighborhood Enterprise, Washington, DC (p. 298)

*Michael K. Young, George Washington University Law School, Washington, DC (p. 300)

Edward W. Younkins, Wheeling Jesuit University, Wheeling, WV (p. 301)

Jerry Zandstra, Acton Institute for the Study of Religion and Liberty, Grand Rapids, MI (p. 301)

FAMILY AND CHILDREN

Jane Abraham, Susan B. Anthony List, Alexandria, VA (p. 34)

David L. Adams, Concordia Seminary, St. Louis, MO (p. 34)

*Mary Cunningham Agee, The Nurturing Network, White Salmon, WA (p. 35)

*I. Dean Ahmad, Minaret of Freedom Institute, Bethesda, MD (p. 36)

Brian C. Anderson, Manhattan Institute for Policy Research, New York, NY (p. 38)

*Carl A. Anderson, Knights of Columbus, New Haven, CT (p. 38)

Eloise Anderson, Claremont Institute, Sacramento, CA (p. 38)

*Julaine K. Appling, Family Research Institute of Wisconsin, Madison, WI (p. 40)

*Dominic A. Aquila, Ave Maria University, Ypsilanti, MI (p. 40)

*David J. Armor, George Mason University, Fairfax, VA (p. 40)

Craig E. Aronoff, Kennesaw State College, Kennesaw, GA (p. 41)

*Thomas C. Atwood, National Council For Adoption, Alexandria, VA (p. 41)

Hunter Baker, Georgia Family Council, Norcross, GA (p. 43)

Joshua K. Baker, The Marriage Law Project, Washington, DC (p. 43)

Steve Baldwin, Fairfax, VA (p. 44)

*Charles A. Ballard, Institute for Responsible Fatherhood and Family Revitalization, Largo, MD (p. 45)

*Sandor Balogh, Hudson Valley Community College, East Greenbush, NY (p. 45)

*Gary L. Bauer, Campaign for Working Families, Arlington, VA (p. 47)

*Naomi Lopez Bauman, Orlando, FL (p. 47)

*William J. Bennett, Empower America, Washington, DC (p. 51)

Douglas Besharov, American Enterprise Institute, Washington, DC (p. 52)

*Wayman R. Bishop, The Family Foundation of Virginia, Richmond, VA (p. 53)

*David Blankenhorn, Institute for American Values, New York, NY (p. 54)

L. Brent Bozell, III, Media Research Center, Alexandria, VA (p. 59)

Philip L. Brach, Midtown Educational Foundation, Chicago, IL (p. 59)

*Brian Brown, Family Institute of Connecticut, Hartford, CT (p. 63)

*Martin D. Brown, Richmond, VA (p. 63)

Don S. Browning, University of Chicago, Chicago, IL (p. 64)

David Brownlee, Family First, Tampa, FL (p. 64)

James Bruner, New York Family Policy Council, Albany, NY (p. 64)

*Ken R. Canfield, National Center for Fathering, Kansas City, MO (p. 69)

*David Caprara, The Empowerment Network, Fredericksburg, VA (p. 69)

Leslie Carbone, Fairfax, VA (p. 69)

*James B. Cardle, Texas Citizen Action Network, Austin, TX (p. 69)

*Allan C. Carlson, Howard Center for Family, Religion and Society, Rockford, IL (p. 70)

*James Chapman, Rocky Mountain Family Council, Denver, CO (p. 72)

*Bryce J. Christensen, Southern Utah University, Cedar City, UT (p. 74)

*Michael A. Ciamarra, Alabama Policy Institute, Birmingham, AL (p. 74)

*Micah Clark, American Family Association, Indianapolis, IN (p. 75)

FAMILY AND CHILDREN (Continued)

John Cobin, Montauk Financial Group, Greenville, SC (p. 76)
*Richard T. Colgan, Bridgewater State College, Warwick, RI (p. 78)
Roberta Combs, Christian Coalition of America, Washington, DC (p. 79)
*Kenneth L. Connor, Family Research Council, Washington, DC (p. 80)
*John E. Coons, University of California at Berkeley, Berkeley, CA (p. 81)
*Ron Crews, Massachusetts Family Institute, Newton Upper Falls, MA (p. 86)
*John Crouch, Americans for Divorce Reform, Arlington, VA (p. 86)
*Janice Shaw Crouse, Concerned Women for America, Washington, DC (p. 87)
*Charles H. Cunningham, National Rifle Association, Washington, DC (p. 87)
Timothy J. Dailey, Family Research Council, Washington, DC (p. 88)
*Matt Daniels, Alliance for Marriage, Springfield, VA (p. 88)
Marjorie Dannenfelser, Susan B. Anthony List, Arlington, VA (p. 88)
Candace de Russy, State University of New York, Bronxville, NY (p. 90)
Pia de Solenni, Family Research Council, Washington, DC (p. 90)
*Midge Decter, New York, NY (p. 91)
*Len Deo, New Jersey Family Policy Council, Parsippany, NJ (p. 93)
*William T. Devlin, Urban Family Council, Philadelphia, PA (p. 94)
Stephanie M. Di Napoli, Family Research Council, Washington, DC (p. 95)
D. P. Diffine, Harding University, Searcy, AR (p. 95)
James C. Dobson, Focus on the Family, Colorado Springs, CO (p. 96)
*Elaine Donnelly, Center for Military Readiness, Livonia, MI (p. 97)
Richard J. Dougherty, University of Dallas, Irving, TX (p. 97)
Jeff Downing, Family First, Lincoln, NE (p. 98)
*Richard Duncan, University of Nebraska, Lincoln, NE (p. 99)
*William C. Duncan, The Marriage Law Project, Washington, DC (p. 100)
*David Dunn, Oklahoma Family Policy Council, Bethany, OK (p. 100)
*Carrie Gordon Earll, Focus on the Family, Colorado Springs, CO (p. 102)
*Michelle Easton, Clare Boothe Luce Policy Institute, Herndon, VA (p. 102)
*Fran Eaton, Eagle Forum of Illinois, Oak Forest, IL (p. 102)
Tim G. Echols, TeenPact Teen Leadership School, Jefferson, GA (p. 103)
Barbara Elliott, Center for Renewal, Houston, TX (p. 105)
*Patrick Fagan, The Heritage Foundation, Washington, DC (p. 108)
*Michael P. Farris, Patrick Henry College, Purcellville, VA (p. 109)
Thomas Fleming, Rockford Institute, Rockford, IL (p. 113)
*David Forte, Cleveland State University, Cleveland, OH (p. 114)
Elizabeth Fox-Genovese, Emory University, Atlanta, GA (p. 115)
*Wanda Franz, National Right to Life Committee, Washington, DC (p. 116)
Chris Freund, The Family Foundation of Virginia, Richmond, VA (p. 117)
Marshall Fritz, Alliance for the Separation of School & State, Fresno, CA (p. 118)
Adam Fuller, Toward Tradition, Mercer Island, WA (p. 118)
Maggie Gallagher, Offining, NY (p. 119)
*Michael Geer, Pennsylvania Family Institute, Harrisburg, PA (p. 122)
*Deanna R. Gelak, Family and Medical Leave Act Technical Corrections Coalition, Springfield, VA (p. 122)
*Robert P. George, Princeton University, Princeton, NJ (p. 122)
Roberta M. Gilbert, Center for the Study of Human Systems, Falls Church, VA (p. 123)
*Gary Glenn, American Family Association of Michigan, Midland, MI (p. 124)
Norval D. Glenn, University of Texas, Austin, TX (p. 125)
*Steven Goldberg, City College, New York, NY (p. 125)
*Stephen Goldsmith, Manhattan Institute for Policy Research, New York, NY (p. 126)
Doris Gordon, Libertarians for Life, Wheaton, MD (p. 126)
A. C. Green, Jr., A. C. Green Youth Foundation, Phoenix, AZ (p. 128)
Frank Gregorsky, Exacting Editorial Services, Vienna, VA (p. 129)
Virgil Gulker, Kids Hope USA, Holland, MI (p. 130)

---

* Has testified before a state or federal legislative committee

FAMILY AND CHILDREN (Continued)

Rebecca Hagelin, The Heritage Foundation, Washington, DC (p. 131)

*Donna H. Hearne, Constitutional Coalition, St. Louis, MO (p. 138)

Michael S. Heath, Christian Civic League of Maine, Augusta, ME (p. 138)

Jay F. Hein, Hudson Institute, Indianapolis, IN (p. 139)

Carl Herbster, American Association of Christian Schools, Independence, MO (p. 140)

Wendy Herdlein, The Marriage Law Project, Washington, DC (p. 140)

*Thomas Hinton, The Heritage Foundation, Washington, DC (p. 143)

*Michael Howden, Stronger Families for Oregon, Salem, OR (p. 147)

Donna Rice Hughes, Enough Is Enough, Great Falls, VA (p. 149)

*Charles D. Hurley, Iowa Family Policy Center, Pleasant Hill, IA (p. 150)

*Alan Inman, Institute for Responsible Fatherhood and Family Revitalization, Largo, MD (p. 151)

William B. Irvine, III, Wright State University, Dayton, OH (p. 152)

Earl W. Jackson, Sr., Samaritan Project, Chesapeake, VA (p. 152)

*Charles W. Jarvis, United Seniors Association, Fairfax, VA (p. 153)

*Marianne Jennings, Arizona State University, Tempe, AZ (p. 154)

*Douglas Johnson, National Right to Life Committee, Washington, DC (p. 155)

Michael S. Joyce, Foundation for Community and Faith Centered Enterprise, Phoenix, AZ (p. 156)

Leon R. Kass, American Enterprise Institute, Washington, DC (p. 158)

Jeff Kemp, Families Northwest, Bellevue, WA (p. 161)

Darlene A. Kennedy, Centre for New Black Leadership, Baltimore, MD (p. 162)

Christina Kindel, North Dakota Family Alliance, Bismarck, ND (p. 164)

Kent King, Missouri State Teachers Association, Columbia, MO (p. 164)

Annette Kirk, Russell Kirk Center, Mecosta, MI (p. 164)

*Douglas W. Kmiec, The Catholic University of America, Washington, DC (p. 166)

Dorothy Knauer, Protestant Community Centers, Inc., Newark, NJ (p. 166)

*Robert H. Knight, Concerned Women for America, Washington, DC (p. 166)

Stephen Krason, Franciscan University of Steubenville, Steubenville, OH (p. 169)

Irving Kristol, The Public Interest, Washington, DC (p. 169)

Peter J. LaBarbera, Concerned Women for America, Washington, DC (p. 171)

Stacey Ladd, Worth the Wait, Pampa, TX (p. 171)

*Andrea S. Lafferty, Traditional Values Coalition, Washington, DC (p. 172)

Beverly LaHaye, Concerned Women for America, Washington, DC (p. 172)

*Richard D. Land, Ethics and Religious Liberty Commission, Nashville, TN (p. 173)

Kristin D. Landers, Alabama Policy Institute, Birmingham, AL (p. 173)

*George Landrith, Frontiers of Freedom Institute, Fairfax, VA (p. 173)

Daniel Lapin, Toward Tradition, Mercer Island, WA (p. 174)

Phillip F. Lawler, *Catholic World Report*, South Lancaster, MA (p. 176)

Dianna Lightfoot, National Physicians Center for Family Resources, Birmingham, AL (p. 180)

*Mike Long, Complete Abstinence Eduation Program, Durham, NC (p. 183)

*Heather MacDonald, Manhattan Institute for Policy Research, New York, NY (p. 185)

Connie Mackey, Family Research Council, Washington, DC (p. 185)

Myron Magnet, Manhattan Institute for Policy Research, New York, NY (p. 186)

*Rita P. Maguire, Arizona Center for Public Policy, Phoenix, AZ (p. 186)

Bridget Maher, Family Research Council, Washington, DC (p. 186)

Henry G. Manne, University of Chicago Law School, Chicago, IL (p. 188)

*Dennis Mansfield, Boise, ID (p. 189)

*Ramona Marotz-Baden, Montana State University, Bozeman, MT (p. 189)

Elizabeth Marquardt, Institute for American Values, New York, NY (p. 189)

*Connie Marshner, Raphael Services, Front Royal, VA (p. 190)

*Nina May, *Renaissance Connection.com/RCNetwork.net*, Washington, DC (p. 192)

Kathleen McGarry, Murray Hill Institute, New York, NY (p. 195)

*Marty McGeein, McGeein Group, Bethesda, MD (p. 196)

FAMILY AND CHILDREN (Continued)

*Michael J. McManus, Marriage Savers, Potomac, MD (p. 197)
*Lawrence Mead, New York University, New York, NY (p. 198)
 Paul T. Mero, The Sutherland Institute, Salt Lake City, UT (p. 199)
 Mark Merrill, Family First, Tampa, FL (p. 199)
 Gene Mills, Louisiana Family Forum, Baton Rouge, LA (p. 202)
 Tom Minnery, Focus on the Family, Colorado Springs, CO (p. 203)
 R. Albert Mohler, Jr., The Southern Baptist Theological Seminary, Louisville, KY (p. 204)
 Jennifer Roback Morse, Hoover Institution, Vista, CA (p. 207)
*Steven W. Mosher, Population Research Institute, Front Royal, VA (p. 208)
*Len Munsil, Center for Arizona Policy, Scottsdale, AZ (p. 209)
 Thomas Nechyba, Duke University, Durham, NC (p. 211)
*Richard John Neuhaus, Institute on Religion and Public Life, New York, NY (p. 213)
 Stuart W. Nolan, Jr., Springfield, VA (p. 214)
 Lauren Noyes, The Heritage Foundation, Washington, DC (p. 216)
*Richard Olivastro, People Dynamics, Farmington, CT (p. 218)
*Darcy A. Olsen, Goldwater Institute, Phoenix, AZ (p. 219)
 Kent Ostrander, The Family Foundation of Kentucky, Lexington, KY (p. 220)
 Janet Parshall, Janet Parshall's America, Arlington, VA (p. 222)
 Val Peter, Boys Town, Boys Town, NE (p. 226)
*Nancy M. Pfotenhauer, Independent Women's Forum, Arlington, VA (p. 227)
*David Popenoe, Rutgers University, New Brunswick, NJ (p. 230)
 Dennis Prager, The Prager Perspective, Van Nuys, CA (p. 232)
*Stephen Presser, Northwestern University School of Law, Chicago, IL (p. 233)
*Thomas Prichard, Minnesota Family Council, Minneapolis, MN (p. 233)
 Harold Calvin Ray, National Center for Faith-Based Initiatives, West Palm Beach, FL (p. 237)
 Robert Rector, The Heritage Foundation, Washington, DC (p. 237)
*Charles E. Rice, Notre Dame Law School, Notre Dame, IN (p. 239)
 Sandy Rios, Concerned Women for America, Washington, DC (p. 240)
*Kelly Rosati, Hawaii Family Forum, Kaneohe, HI (p. 243)
*Kathy Rothschild, The Leadership Institute, Arlington, VA (p. 244)
 Rick Schatz, National Coalition for the Protection of Children and Families,
    Cincinnati, OH (p. 252)
*Michael Schwartz, Concerned Women for America, Washington, DC (p. 254)
*Alan E. Sears, Alliance Defense Fund, Scottsdale, AZ (p. 255)
*Ralph Segalman, California State University, Northridge, Northridge, CA (p. 256)
*Jamie Self, Georgia Family Council, Norcross, GA (p. 256)
*Lou Sheldon, Traditional Values Coalition, Washington, DC (p. 258)
 Anita Smith, Institute for Youth Development, Washington, DC (p. 262)
*Curt Smith, Indiana Family Institute, Indianapolis, IN (p. 263)
*Oran P. Smith, Palmetto Family Council, Columbia, SC (p. 264)
*W. Shepherd Smith, Jr., Institute for Youth Development, Washington, DC (p. 264)
*Diane Sollee, Coalition for Marriage, Family and Couples Education, Washington, DC (p. 265)
 Thomas Sowell, Hoover Institution, Stanford, CA (p. 266)
 Peter S. Sprigg, Family Research Council, Washington, DC (p. 267)
 Glenn T. Stanton, Focus on the Family, Colorado Springs, CO (p. 268)
 Doug Stiegler, Association of Maryland Families, Woodstock, MD (p. 269)
*Bruce Taylor, National Law Center for Children and Families, Fairfax, VA (p. 274)
*Karen Testerman, Cornerstone Policy Research, Concord, NH (p. 275)
*David J. Theroux, The Independent Institute, Oakland, CA (p. 276)
 Mary L. G. Theroux, The Independent Institute, Oakland, CA (p. 276)
*Forest M. Thigpen, Mississippi Family Council, Jackson, MS (p. 277)
*Randy Thomasson, Campaign for California Families, Sacramento, CA (p. 277)
*Joe Tropea, International Association for Support of Privatization, Washington, DC (p. 281)
 Reed Ueda, Tufts University, Medford, MA (p. 282)

---

* Has testified before a state or federal legislative committee

FAMILY AND CHILDREN (Continued)

*Maris A. Vinovskis, University of Michigan, Ann Arbor, MI (p. 285)
Ken Von Kohorn, Family Institute of Connecticut, Hartford, CT (p. 285)
*Roland Warren, National Fatherhood Initiative, Gaithersburg, MD (p. 289)
Tom Washburne, Home School Legal Defense Association, Purcellville, VA (p. 289)
*Lori L. Waters, Eagle Forum, Washington, DC (p. 289)
Stanley J. Watson, Patrick Henry College, Purcellville, VA (p. 290)
Thomas G. West, University of Dallas, Irving, TX (p. 293)
Barbara Dafoe Whitehead, Amherst, MA (p. 293)
John Whitlock, The Family Foundation of Virginia, Richmond, VA (p. 294)
Donald Wildmon, American Family Association, Tupelo, MS (p. 294)
*Natalie Williams, Robinson, DiLando and Whitaker, Sacramento, CA (p. 295)
Russell Williams, Jefferson Center for Character Education, Mission Viejo, CA (p. 295)
*John C. Willke, Life Issues Institute, Inc., Cincinnati, OH (p. 295)
John Willson, Hillsdale College, Hillsdale, MI (p. 296)
Richard B. Wirthlin, Wirthlin Worldwide, South Jordan, UT (p. 296)
*Phyllis H. Witcher, Protecting Marriage, Inc., Wilmington, DE (p. 296)
Betty Jean Wolfe, Urban Family Council, Philadephia, PA (p. 297)
*Christopher Wolfe, Marquette University, Milwaukee, WI (p. 297)
*Kenneth Wood, The Oklahoma Christian Coalition, Oklahoma City, OK (p. 298)
*Robert L. Woodson, Sr., National Center for Neighborhood Enterprise,
    Washington, DC (p. 298)
Anne Wortham, Illinois State University, Normal, IL (p. 298)
*Charmaine Crouse Yoest, University of Virginia, Charlottesville, VA (p. 300)
*Nicholas Zill, Westat Inc., Rockville, MD (p. 302)
Karl Zinsmeister, American Enterprise Institute, Cazenovia, NY (p. 302)

MARRIAGE AND DIVORCE

Brian C. Anderson, Manhattan Institute for Policy Research, New York, NY (p. 38)
*Carl A. Anderson, Knights of Columbus, New Haven, CT (p. 38)
Eloise Anderson, Claremont Institute, Sacramento, CA (p. 38)
*Julaine K. Appling, Family Research Institute of Wisconsin, Madison, WI (p. 40)
*Thomas C. Atwood, National Council For Adoption, Alexandria, VA (p. 41)
Hunter Baker, Georgia Family Council, Norcross, GA (p. 43)
Joshua K. Baker, The Marriage Law Project, Washington, DC (p. 43)
*Charles A. Ballard, Institute for Responsible Fatherhood and Family Revitalization,
    Largo, MD (p. 45)
Joel Belz, World Magazine, Asheville, NC (p. 50)
Douglas Besharov, American Enterprise Institute, Washington, DC (p. 52)
*Wayman R. Bishop, The Family Foundation of Virginia, Richmond, VA (p. 53)
*David Blankenhorn, Institute for American Values, New York, NY (p. 54)
*David Boaz, Cato Institute, Washington, DC (p. 55)
Philip L. Brach, Midtown Educational Foundation, Chicago, IL (p. 59)
*Bill Brooks, North Carolina Family Policy Council, Raleigh, NC (p. 62)
*Brian Brown, Family Institute of Connecticut, Hartford, CT (p. 63)
*Martin D. Brown, Richmond, VA (p. 63)
Don S. Browning, University of Chicago, Chicago, IL (p. 64)
David Brownlee, Family First, Tampa, FL (p. 64)
James Bruner, New York Family Policy Council, Albany, NY (p. 64)
Francis H. Buckley, George Mason University School of Law, Arlington, VA (p. 64)
*Ken R. Canfield, National Center for Fathering, Kansas City, MO (p. 69)
*David Caprara, The Empowerment Network, Fredericksburg, VA (p. 69)
Leslie Carbone, Fairfax, VA (p. 69)
*Allan C. Carlson, Howard Center for Family, Religion and Society, Rockford, IL (p. 70)
*James Chapman, Rocky Mountain Family Council, Denver, CO (p. 72)

MARRIAGE AND DIVORCE (Continued)

*Bryce J. Christensen, Southern Utah University, Cedar City, UT (p. 74)
*Michael A. Ciamarra, Alabama Policy Institute, Birmingham, AL (p. 74)
*Micah Clark, American Family Association, Indianapolis, IN (p. 75)
 Roberta Combs, Christian Coalition of America, Washington, DC (p. 79)
*Kenneth L. Connor, Family Research Council, Washington, DC (p. 80)
*Ron Crews, Massachusetts Family Institute, Newton Upper Falls, MA (p. 86)
*John Crouch, Americans for Divorce Reform, Arlington, VA (p. 86)
*Janice Shaw Crouse, Concerned Women for America, Washington, DC (p. 87)
*Matt Daniels, Alliance for Marriage, Springfield, VA (p. 88)
 Pia de Solenni, Family Research Council, Washington, DC (p. 90)
*Len Deo, New Jersey Family Policy Council, Parsippany, NJ (p. 93)
*William T. Devlin, Urban Family Council, Philadelphia, PA (p. 94)
 D. P. Diffine, Harding University, Searcy, AR (p. 95)
*John R. Diggs, Jr., South Hadley, MA (p. 95)
 James C. Dobson, Focus on the Family, Colorado Springs, CO (p. 96)
 Jeff Downing, Family First, Lincoln, NE (p. 98)
*Richard Duncan, University of Nebraska, Lincoln, NE (p. 99)
*William C. Duncan, The Marriage Law Project, Washington, DC (p. 100)
*David Dunn, Oklahoma Family Policy Council, Bethany, OK (p. 100)
*Michelle Easton, Clare Boothe Luce Policy Institute, Herndon, VA (p. 102)
*Patrick Fagan, The Heritage Foundation, Washington, DC (p. 108)
*Michael P. Farris, Patrick Henry College, Purcellville, VA (p. 109)
*David Forte, Cleveland State University, Cleveland, OH (p. 114)
 Elizabeth Fox-Genovese, Emory University, Atlanta, GA (p. 115)
 Adam Fuller, Toward Tradition, Mercer Island, WA (p. 118)
 Jennifer Garrett, The Heritage Foundation, Washington, DC (p. 120)
*Michael Geer, Pennsylvania Family Institute, Harrisburg, PA (p. 122)
*Robert P. George, Princeton University, Princeton, NJ (p. 122)
 Roberta M. Gilbert, Center for the Study of Human Systems, Falls Church, VA (p. 123)
*Gary Glenn, American Family Association of Michigan, Midland, MI (p. 124)
 Norval D. Glenn, University of Texas, Austin, TX (p. 125)
*Steven Goldberg, City College, New York, NY (p. 125)
*Stephen Goldsmith, Manhattan Institute for Policy Research, New York, NY (p. 126)
 Rebecca Hagelin, The Heritage Foundation, Washington, DC (p. 131)
 Roger Hamburg, Indiana University South Bend, South Bend, IN (p. 133)
 Carl Herbster, American Association of Christian Schools, Independence, MO (p. 140)
 Wendy Herdlein, The Marriage Law Project, Washington, DC (p. 140)
*Randy Hicks, Georgia Family Council, Norcross, GA (p. 141)
*John R. Hill, Alabama Policy Institute, Birmingham, AL (p. 142)
*Michael Howden, Stronger Families for Oregon, Salem, OR (p. 147)
*Charles D. Hurley, Iowa Family Policy Center, Pleasant Hill, IA (p. 150)
*Alan Inman, Institute for Responsible Fatherhood and Family Revitalization,
    Largo, MD (p. 151)
 Leon R. Kass, American Enterprise Institute, Washington, DC (p. 158)
 Jeff Kemp, Families Northwest, Bellevue, WA (p. 161)
*Dimitri Kesari, Family Research Council, Washington, DC (p. 162)
*Douglas W. Kmiec, The Catholic University of America, Washington, DC (p. 166)
*Robert H. Knight, Concerned Women for America, Washington, DC (p. 166)
 John L. Koehler, Illinois Family Institute, Glen Ellyn, IL (p. 166)
*Malcolm Kovacs, Montgomery College, Rockville, MD (p. 168)
 Peter J. LaBarbera, Concerned Women for America, Washington, DC (p. 171)
*James Lafferty, Massachusetts Citizens Alliance, Waltham, MA (p. 172)
 Beverly LaHaye, Concerned Women for America, Washington, DC (p. 172)
 Daniel Lapin, Toward Tradition, Mercer Island, WA (p. 174)

MARRIAGE AND DIVORCE (Continued)

Phillip F. Lawler, *Catholic World Report*, South Lancaster, MA (p. 176)
Bernard T. Lomas, The Heritage Foundation, Chapel Hill, NC (p. 182)
*Mike Long, Complete Abstinence Eduation Program, Durham, NC (p. 183)
Jordan Lorence, Alliance Defense Fund, Scottsdale, AZ (p. 183)
Tibor R. Machan, Chapman University, Silverado Canyon, CA (p. 185)
Bridget Maher, Family Research Council, Washington, DC (p. 186)
*Dennis Mansfield, Boise, ID (p. 189)
*Ramona Marotz-Baden, Montana State University, Bozeman, MT (p. 189)
Elizabeth Marquardt, Institute for American Values, New York, NY (p. 189)
*Michael J. McManus, Marriage Savers, Potomac, MD (p. 197)
Mark Merrill, Family First, Tampa, FL (p. 199)
Gene Mills, Louisiana Family Forum, Baton Rouge, LA (p. 202)
Tom Minnery, Focus on the Family, Colorado Springs, CO (p. 203)
R. Albert Mohler, Jr., The Southern Baptist Theological Seminary, Louisville, KY (p. 204)
Jennifer Roback Morse, Hoover Institution, Vista, CA (p. 207)
*Steven W. Mosher, Population Research Institute, Front Royal, VA (p. 208)
*Len Munsil, Center for Arizona Policy, Scottsdale, AZ (p. 209)
*Richard John Neuhaus, Institute on Religion and Public Life, New York, NY (p. 213)
Lauren Noyes, The Heritage Foundation, Washington, DC (p. 216)
*Gary J. Palmer, Alabama Policy Institute, Birmingham, AL (p. 221)
*Mitchell B. Pearlstein, Center of the American Experiment, Minneapolis, MN (p. 224)
Val Peter, Boys Town, Boys Town, NE (p. 226)
*David Popenoe, Rutgers University, New Brunswick, NJ (p. 230)
*Thomas Prichard, Minnesota Family Council, Minneapolis, MN (p. 233)
Harold Calvin Ray, National Center for Faith-Based Initiatives, West Palm Beach, FL (p. 237)
Robert Rector, The Heritage Foundation, Washington, DC (p. 237)
*W. Robert Reed, University of Oklahoma, Norman, OK (p. 238)
Steven Rhoads, University of Virginia, Charlottesville, VA (p. 239)
Sandy Rios, Concerned Women for America, Washington, DC (p. 240)
*Paul Craig Roberts, Institute for Political Economy, Panama City Beach, FL (p. 242)
*Kelly Rosati, Hawaii Family Forum, Kaneohe, HI (p. 243)
*Michael Schwartz, Concerned Women for America, Washington, DC (p. 254)
*Alan E. Sears, Alliance Defense Fund, Scottsdale, AZ (p. 255)
*Ralph Segalman, California State University, Northridge, Northridge, CA (p. 256)
*Jamie Self, Georgia Family Council, Norcross, GA (p. 256)
*Lou Sheldon, Traditional Values Coalition, Washington, DC (p. 258)
*Rita Simon, American University, Washington, DC (p. 260)
Anita Smith, Institute for Youth Development, Washington, DC (p. 262)
*Curt Smith, Indiana Family Institute, Indianapolis, IN (p. 263)
*W. Shepherd Smith, Jr., Institute for Youth Development, Washington, DC (p. 264)
Brad Snavely, Michigan Family Forum, Lansing, MI (p. 264)
*Diane Sollee, Coalition for Marriage, Family and Couples Education, Washington, DC (p. 265)
Peter S. Sprigg, Family Research Council, Washington, DC (p. 267)
Glenn T. Stanton, Focus on the Family, Colorado Springs, CO (p. 268)
Doug Stiegler, Association of Maryland Families, Woodstock, MD (p. 269)
*Christine Stolba, Ethics and Public Policy Center, Washington, DC (p. 269)
Charles Stuart, University of California, Santa Barbara, Santa Barbara, CA (p. 271)
*Karen Testerman, Cornerstone Policy Research, Concord, NH (p. 275)
*Forest M. Thigpen, Mississippi Family Council, Jackson, MS (p. 277)
*Randy Thomasson, Campaign for California Families, Sacramento, CA (p. 277)
*Maris A. Vinovskis, University of Michigan, Ann Arbor, MI (p. 285)
Linda J. Waite, University of Chicago, Chicago, IL (p. 286)
*Roland Warren, National Fatherhood Initiative, Gaithersburg, MD (p. 289)
Tom Washburne, Home School Legal Defense Association, Purcellville, VA (p. 289)

MARRIAGE AND DIVORCE (Continued)

Thomas G. West, University of Dallas, Irving, TX **(p. 293)**
*John C. Willke, Life Issues Institute, Inc., Cincinnati, OH **(p. 295)**
Richard B. Wirthlin, Wirthlin Worldwide, South Jordan, UT **(p. 296)**
*Phyllis H. Witcher, Protecting Marriage, Inc., Wilmington, DE **(p. 296)**
Betty Jean Wolfe, Urban Family Council, Philadephia, PA **(p. 297)**
*Christopher Wolfe, Marquette University, Milwaukee, WI **(p. 297)**
*Kenneth Wood, The Oklahoma Christian Coalition, Oklahoma City, OK **(p. 298)**
*Charmaine Crouse Yoest, University of Virginia, Charlottesville, VA **(p. 300)**
*Nicholas Zill, Westat Inc., Rockville, MD **(p. 302)**

MEDIA AND POPULAR CULTURE

*Mary Cunningham Agee, The Nurturing Network, White Salmon, WA **(p. 35)**
*M. Gene Aldridge, New Mexico Independence Research Institute, Las Cruces, NM **(p. 36)**
Benjamin Alexander, Franciscan University of Steubenville, Steubenville, OH **(p. 36)**
David W. Almasi, National Center for Public Policy Research, Washington, DC **(p. 37)**
*Dominic A. Aquila, Ave Maria University, Ypsilanti, MI **(p. 40)**
Brent Baker, Media Research Center, Alexandria, VA **(p. 43)**
Joel Belz, *World Magazine*, Asheville, NC **(p. 50)**
*William J. Bennett, Empower America, Washington, DC **(p. 51)**
Herbert B. Berkowitz, The Heritage Foundation, Wilimington, NC **(p. 51)**
*Jason Bertsch, American Enterprise Institute, Washington, DC **(p. 52)**
Amy E. Black, Wheaton College, Wheaton, IL **(p. 54)**
Morton Blackwell, Leadership Institute, Arlington, VA **(p. 54)**
James Bowman, Ethics and Public Policy Center, Washington, DC **(p. 58)**
Karlyn Keene Bowman, American Enterprise Institute, Washington, DC **(p. 58)**
L. Brent Bozell, III, Media Research Center, Alexandria, VA **(p. 59)**
Arthur C. Brooks, Syracuse University, Syracuse, NY **(p. 61)**
*Floyd G. Brown, Young America's Foundation Reagan Ranch Project,
    Santa Barbara, CA **(p. 63)**
*Harold O. J. Brown, Reformed Theological Seminary, Charlotte, NC **(p. 63)**
David Brownlee, Family First, Tampa, FL **(p. 64)**
Deborah Burstion-Donbraye, American Multimedia Inc. of Nigeria, Cleveland, OH **(p. 66)**
Pradyumna S. Chauhan, Arcadia University, Glenside, PA **(p. 73)**
*Lynne V. Cheney, American Enterprise Institute, Washington, DC **(p. 73)**
*Michael A. Ciamarra, Alabama Policy Institute, Birmingham, AL **(p. 74)**
*Micah Clark, American Family Association, Indianapolis, IN **(p. 75)**
Jody Manley Clarke, Competitive Enterprise Institute, Washington, DC **(p. 75)**
Peter Collier, Center for the Study of Popular Culture, Los Angeles, CA **(p. 78)**
Kellyanne Conway, the polling company/WomanTrend, Washington, DC **(p. 80)**
*Ron Crews, Massachusetts Family Institute, Newton Upper Falls, MA **(p. 86)**
*Matt Daniels, Alliance for Marriage, Springfield, VA **(p. 88)**
Candace de Russy, State University of New York, Bronxville, NY **(p. 90)**
*Midge Decter, New York, NY **(p. 91)**
*Len Deo, New Jersey Family Policy Council, Parsippany, NJ **(p. 93)**
*William T. Devlin, Urban Family Council, Philadelphia, PA **(p. 94)**
Eric Dezenhall, Nichols Dezenhall Management Group, Washington, DC **(p. 94)**
D. P. Diffine, Harding University, Searcy, AR **(p. 95)**
*John R. Diggs, Jr., South Hadley, MA **(p. 95)**
James C. Dobson, Focus on the Family, Colorado Springs, CO **(p. 96)**
Thomas Doherty, Brandeis University, Waltham, MA **(p. 96)**
*William A. Donohue, Catholic League for Religious and Civil Rights, New York, NY **(p. 97)**
Jeff Downing, Family First, Lincoln, NE **(p. 98)**
Martin Duggan, Educational Freedom Foundation, St. Louis, MO **(p. 99)**
*David Dunn, Oklahoma Family Policy Council, Bethany, OK **(p. 100)**

MEDIA AND POPULAR CULTURE (Continued)

Brandon Dutcher, Oklahoma Council of Public Affairs, Oklahoma City, OK **(p. 101)**

*James R. Edwards, Jr., Hudson Institute, Washington, DC **(p. 104)**

*Mickey Edwards, Harvard University, Cambridge, MA **(p. 104)**

M. Stanton Evans, Education and Research Institute, Washington, DC **(p. 108)**

Howard Fienberg, Statistical Assessment Service, Washington, DC **(p. 111)**

*David Forte, Cleveland State University, Cleveland, OH **(p. 114)**

Elizabeth Fox-Genovese, Emory University, Atlanta, GA **(p. 115)**

Neal B. Freeman, Blackwell Corporation, Vienna, VA **(p. 116)**

Adam Fuller, Toward Tradition, Mercer Island, WA **(p. 118)**

John H. Fund, *OpinionJournal.com,* New York, NY **(p. 119)**

*Robert P. George, Princeton University, Princeton, NJ **(p. 122)**

Roberta M. Gilbert, Center for the Study of Human Systems, Falls Church, VA **(p. 123)**

Nick Gillespie, Reason Foundation, Los Angeles, CA **(p. 123)**

*Gary Glenn, American Family Association of Michigan, Midland, MI **(p. 124)**

Philip Gold, Discovery Institute, Seattle, WA **(p. 125)**

*Stephen Goldsmith, Manhattan Institute for Policy Research, New York, NY **(p. 126)**

Frank Gregorsky, Exacting Editorial Services, Vienna, VA **(p. 129)**

Rebecca Hagelin, The Heritage Foundation, Washington, DC **(p. 131)**

*Randy Hicks, Georgia Family Council, Norcross, GA **(p. 141)**

Heather Higgins, Independent Women's Forum, New York, NY **(p. 142)**

*John R. Hill, Alabama Policy Institute, Birmingham, AL **(p. 142)**

Scott Hogenson, *CNSNews.com,* Alexandria, VA **(p. 144)**

David Horowitz, Center for the Study of Popular Culture, Los Angeles, CA **(p. 146)**

Deal Hudson, *Crisis Magazine,* Washington, DC **(p. 148)**

Donna Rice Hughes, Enough Is Enough, Great Falls, VA **(p. 149)**

James D. Hunter, University of Virginia, Charlottesville, VA **(p. 149)**

Carol Iannone, New York, NY **(p. 150)**

Niger Roy Innis, Congress of Racial Equality, New York, NY **(p. 151)**

Reed J. Irvine, Accuracy in Media, Washington, DC **(p. 152)**

Thomas Ivancie, America's Future Foundation, Washington, DC **(p. 152)**

Earl W. Jackson, Sr., Samaritan Project, Chesapeake, VA **(p. 152)**

*Laurence Jarvik, Washington, DC **(p. 153)**

*Charles W. Jarvis, United Seniors Association, Fairfax, VA **(p. 153)**

Douglas A. Jeffrey, Hillsdale College, Hillsdale, MI **(p. 154)**

*Thomas L. Jipping, Concerned Women for America, Washington, DC **(p. 154)**

Michael S. Joyce, Foundation for Community and Faith Centered Enterprise, Phoenix, AZ **(p. 156)**

Richard T. Kaplar, Media Institute, Washington, DC **(p. 157)**

Leon R. Kass, American Enterprise Institute, Washington, DC **(p. 158)**

Darlene A. Kennedy, Centre for New Black Leadership, Baltimore, MD **(p. 162)**

Kate Kennedy, Independent Women's Forum, Arlington, VA **(p. 162)**

*William A. Keyes, The Institute on Political Journalism, Washington, DC **(p. 162)**

*Douglas W. Kmiec, The Catholic University of America, Washington, DC **(p. 166)**

*Robert H. Knight, Concerned Women for America, Washington, DC **(p. 166)**

*Patrick Korten, The Becket Fund for Religious Liberty, Washington, DC **(p. 167)**

Irving Kristol, The Public Interest, Washington, DC **(p. 169)**

*Lawrence Kudlow, Kudlow & Co., LLC, New York, NY **(p. 170)**

Peter J. LaBarbera, Concerned Women for America, Washington, DC **(p. 171)**

Stacey Ladd, Worth the Wait, Pampa, TX **(p. 171)**

*T. Craig Ladwig, Indiana Policy Review Foundation, Fort Wayne, IN **(p. 171)**

*Andrea S. Lafferty, Traditional Values Coalition, Washington, DC **(p. 172)**

*James Lafferty, Massachusetts Citizens Alliance, Waltham, MA **(p. 172)**

Timothy Lamer, *World Magazine,* Ellisville, MO **(p. 173)**

*Richard D. Land, Ethics and Religious Liberty Commission, Nashville, TN **(p. 173)**

MEDIA AND POPULAR CULTURE (Continued)

***Andrew Langer,** National Federation of Independent Business, Washington, DC **(p. 174)**
Daniel Lapin, Toward Tradition, Mercer Island, WA **(p. 174)**
***Janet LaRue,** Concerned Women for America, Washington, DC **(p. 175)**
Richard Lessner, American Renewal, Washington, DC **(p. 178)**
Linda Lichter, Center for Media and Public Affairs, Washington, DC **(p. 179)**
***S. Robert Lichter,** Center for Media and Public Affairs, Washington, DC **(p. 179)**
***Mike Long,** Complete Abstinence Eduation Program, Durham, NC **(p. 183)**
Frank Luntz, Luntz Research Companies, Arlington, VA **(p. 184)**
Lara Mahaney, Parents Television Council, Los Angeles, CA **(p. 186)**
***Dennis Mansfield,** Boise, ID **(p. 189)**
***Nina May,** *Renaissance Connection.com/RCNetwork.net*, Washington, DC **(p. 192)**
***Michael J. McManus,** Marriage Savers, Potomac, MD **(p. 197)**
Samuel P. Menefee, Regent University, Virginia Beach, VA **(p. 199)**
Tom Minnery, Focus on the Family, Colorado Springs, CO **(p. 203)**
***Brant S. Mittler,** Texas Public Policy Foundation, San Antonio, TX **(p. 204)**
R. Albert Mohler, Jr., The Southern Baptist Theological Seminary, Louisville, KY **(p. 204)**
Laurie Morrow, Montpelier, VT **(p. 207)**
***Steven W. Mosher,** Population Research Institute, Front Royal, VA **(p. 208)**
***Len Munsil,** Center for Arizona Policy, Scottsdale, AZ **(p. 209)**
William Murchison, Baylor University, Waco, TX **(p. 209)**
***Deroy Murdock,** Atlas Economic Research Foundation, New York, NY **(p. 209)**
Iain Murray, Statistical Assessment Service, Washington, DC **(p. 209)**
Mario Navarro da Costa, American Society for the Defense of Tradition, Family and Property, McLean, VA **(p. 211)**
Richard Alan Nelson, Louisiana State University, Baton Rouge, LA **(p. 212)**
C. Preston Noell, III, Tradition, Family, Property, Inc., McLean, VA **(p. 214)**
***Marvin Olasky,** University of Texas, Austin, TX **(p. 218)**
Janet Parshall, Janet Parshall's America, Arlington, VA **(p. 222)**
***John Paulk,** Focus on the Family, Colorado Springs, CO **(p. 223)**
Val Peter, Boys Town, Boys Town, NE **(p. 226)**
Paul C. Peterson, Coastal Carolina University, Conway, SC **(p. 227)**
Victor Porlier, Center for Civic Renewal, Inc., Delmar, NY **(p. 231)**
Dennis Prager, The Prager Perspective, Van Nuys, CA **(p. 232)**
***Stephen Presser,** Northwestern University School of Law, Chicago, IL **(p. 233)**
Sandy Rios, Concerned Women for America, Washington, DC **(p. 240)**
James C. Roberts, American Studies Center, Washington, DC **(p. 242)**
Stanley Rothman, Smith College, Northampton, MA **(p. 244)**
***Richard O. Rowland,** Grassroot Institute of Hawaii, Aiea, HI **(p. 245)**
***William A. Rusher,** Claremont Institute, San Francisco, CA **(p. 247)**
***Frank Russo,** American Family Association of New York, Port Washington, NY **(p. 247)**
David W. Saxe, Pennsylvania State University, University Park, PA **(p. 251)**
Rick Schatz, National Coalition for the Protection of Children and Families, Cincinnati, OH **(p. 252)**
Larry Schweikart, University of Dayton, Dayton, OH **(p. 255)**
***Alan E. Sears,** Alliance Defense Fund, Scottsdale, AZ **(p. 255)**
***Lou Sheldon,** Traditional Values Coalition, Washington, DC **(p. 258)**
***Rita Simon,** American University, Washington, DC **(p. 260)**
Aeon James Skoble, Bridgewater State College, Bridgewater, MA **(p. 262)**
***Curt Smith,** Indiana Family Institute, Indianapolis, IN **(p. 263)**
Ted J. Smith, III, Virginia Commonwealth University, Richmond, VA **(p. 264)**
Thomas Sowell, Hoover Institution, Stanford, CA **(p. 266)**
Peter S. Sprigg, Family Research Council, Washington, DC **(p. 267)**
Glenn T. Stanton, Focus on the Family, Colorado Springs, CO **(p. 268)**
Doug Stiegler, Association of Maryland Families, Woodstock, MD **(p. 269)**

MEDIA AND POPULAR CULTURE (Continued)

*Christine Stolba, Ethics and Public Policy Center, Washington, DC (p. 269)
 Michael Sullivan, Texas Public Policy Foundation, Austin, TX (p. 272)
 Mark Tapscott, The Heritage Foundation, Washington, DC (p. 274)
*Bruce Taylor, National Law Center for Children and Families, Fairfax, VA (p. 274)
*Randy Thomasson, Campaign for California Families, Sacramento, CA (p. 277)
 Miro M. Todorovich, Scientists and Engineers for Secure Energy, New York, NY (p. 280)
 Richard Wagner, *Carolina Journal*/John Locke Foundation, Raleigh, NC (p. 286)
*Robert Waliszewski, Focus on the Family, Colorado Springs, CO (p. 287)
 Bradley C. S. Watson, Saint Vincent College, Latrobe, PA (p. 290)
 Ben J. Wattenberg, American Enterprise Institute, Washington, DC (p. 290)
 Daniel Weiss, Focus on the Family, Colorado Springs, CO (p. 292)
*Paul Weyrich, Free Congress Foundation, Washington, DC (p. 293)
*John W. Whitehead, The Rutherford Institute, Charlottesville, VA (p. 293)
 Donald Wildmon, American Family Association, Tupelo, MS (p. 294)
*John C. Willke, Life Issues Institute, Inc., Cincinnati, OH (p. 295)
 Genevieve Wood, Family Research Council, Washington, DC (p. 297)
 Anne Wortham, Illinois State University, Normal, IL (p. 298)
*Charmaine Crouse Yoest, University of Virginia, Charlottesville, VA (p. 300)
*Todd G. Young, Southeastern Legal Foundation, Atlanta, GA (p. 301)
 Edward W. Younkins, Wheeling Jesuit University, Wheeling, WV (p. 301)
 Malia Zimmerman, Grassroot Institute of Hawaii, Kailua, HI (p. 302)
 Marty Zupan, Institute for Humane Studies at George Mason University,
  Arlington, VA (p. 303)

PHILANTHROPY

*Mary Cunningham Agee, The Nurturing Network, White Salmon, WA (p. 35)
*John Agresto, John Agresto and Associates, Santa Fe, NM (p. 35)
*William T. Alpert, University of Connecticut, Stamford, CT (p. 37)
 Ford A. Anderson, State Policy Network, Dallas, TX (p. 38)
 Frank Annunziata, Rochester Institute of Technology, Rochester, NY (p. 39)
*Dominic A. Aquila, Ave Maria University, Ypsilanti, MI (p. 40)
 Whitney L. Ball, DonorsTrust, Alexandria, VA (p. 44)
*John S. Barry, Tax Foundation, Washington, DC (p. 46)
 David Beito, University of Alabama, Tuscaloosa, AL (p. 49)
*William J. Bennett, Empower America, Washington, DC (p. 51)
 Richard Bjornseth, Valdosta State University, Valdosta, GA (p. 54)
 Morton Blackwell, Leadership Institute, Arlington, VA (p. 54)
*Mark Blitz, Claremont McKenna College, Claremont, CA (p. 55)
 Philip L. Brach, Midtown Educational Foundation, Chicago, IL (p. 59)
 Arthur C. Brooks, Syracuse University, Syracuse, NY (p. 61)
*Floyd G. Brown, Young America's Foundation Reagan Ranch Project,
  Santa Barbara, CA (p. 63)
 Alejandro A. Chafuen, Atlas Economic Research Foundation, Fairfax, VA (p. 72)
 Douglas H. Cook, Regent University, Virginia Beach, VA (p. 80)
 John Coonradt, Mackinac Center for Public Policy, Midland, MI (p. 81)
*Midge Decter, New York, NY (p. 91)
 Kimberly Dennis, D & D Foundation, Washington, DC (p. 93)
 William C. Dennis, Dennis Consulting, MacLean, VA (p. 93)
 Jeff Downing, Family First, Lincoln, NE (p. 98)
*Clark Durant, New Common School Foundation, Detroit, MI (p. 101)
 Lenore T. Ealy, Emergent Enterprises, Carmel, IN (p. 101)
 Barbara Elliott, Center for Renewal, Houston, TX (p. 105)
*Robert Ernst, Banbury Fund, Salmas, CA (p. 108)
 Howard Fienberg, Statistical Assessment Service, Washington, DC (p. 111)

PHILANTHROPY (Continued)

Hillel Fradkin, Ethics and Public Policy Center, Washington, DC **(p. 115)**
Neal B. Freeman, Blackwell Corporation, Vienna, VA **(p. 116)**
*Murray Friedman, American Jewish Committee, Philadelphia, PA **(p. 117)**
Thomas Golab, Competitive Enterprise Institute, Washington, DC **(p. 125)**
*Stephen Goldsmith, Manhattan Institute for Policy Research, New York, NY **(p. 126)**
Thor L. Halvorssen, The Foundation for Individual Rights in Education,
    Philadelphia, PA **(p. 132)**
Charles L. Harper, John Templeton Foundation, Radnor, PA **(p. 135)**
Jay F. Hein, Hudson Institute, Indianapolis, IN **(p. 139)**
Carl Helstrom, JM Foundation, New York, NY **(p. 139)**
Heather Higgins, Independent Women's Forum, New York, NY **(p. 142)**
David Horowitz, Center for the Study of Popular Culture, Los Angeles, CA **(p. 146)**
*Michael Horowitz, Hudson Institute, Washington, DC **(p. 146)**
*Robert Huberty, Capital Research Center, Washington, DC **(p. 148)**
*Laurence Jarvik, Washington, DC **(p. 153)**
Michael S. Joyce, Foundation for Community and Faith Centered Enterprise,
    Phoenix, AZ **(p. 156)**
Barry P. Keating, University of Notre Dame, Notre Dame, IN **(p. 159)**
*W. Thomas Kelly, Savers and Investors League, Mirror Lake, NH **(p. 161)**
Ann C. Klucsarits, The Heritage Foundation, Washington, DC **(p. 165)**
*Robert H. Knight, Concerned Women for America, Washington, DC **(p. 166)**
James E. Kostrava, Funding Freedom, Stanford, MI **(p. 168)**
*Jill Cunningham Lacey, Capital Research Center, Damascus, MD **(p. 171)**
*Andrew Langer, National Federation of Independent Business, Washington, DC **(p. 174)**
Leonard P. Liggio, Atlas Economic Research Foundation, Fairfax, VA **(p. 180)**
Tibor R. Machan, Chapman University, Silverado Canyon, CA **(p. 185)**
Myron Magnet, Manhattan Institute for Policy Research, New York, NY **(p. 186)**
Henry G. Manne, University of Chicago Law School, Chicago, IL **(p. 188)**
*Jerry L. Martin, American Council of Trustees and Alumni, Washington, DC **(p. 190)**
Paul Maurer, Trinity International University, Deerfield, IL **(p. 192)**
*Michael J. McManus, Marriage Savers, Potomac, MD **(p. 197)**
Edward T. McMullen, Jr., South Carolina Policy Council, Columbia, SC **(p. 197)**
Jack McVaugh, Arizona School Choice Trust, Scottsdale, AZ **(p. 198)**
Ingrid Merikoski, Earhart Foundation, Ann Arbor, MI **(p. 199)**
Adam Meyerson, The Philanthropy Roundtable, Washington, DC **(p. 200)**
*John H. Moore, Grove City College, Grove City, PA **(p. 206)**
Christopher Morris, Capital Research Center, Washington, DC **(p. 207)**
*Steven W. Mosher, Population Research Institute, Front Royal, VA **(p. 208)**
*Anne D. Neal, American Council of Trustees and Alumni, Washington, DC **(p. 211)**
Stuart W. Nolan, Jr., Springfield, VA **(p. 214)**
Michael J. Novak, Jr., American Enterprise Institute, Washington, DC **(p. 215)**
Scott O'Connell, The Heritage Foundation, Washington, DC **(p. 216)**
*Marvin Olasky, University of Texas, Austin, TX **(p. 218)**
*J. A. Parker, Lincoln Institute for Research and Education, Washington, DC **(p. 221)**
Val Peter, Boys Town, Boys Town, NE **(p. 226)**
*Lovett C. Peters, Pioneer Institute for Public Policy Research, Boston, MA **(p. 226)**
*Daniel J. Popeo, Washington Legal Foundation, Washington, DC **(p. 231)**
Harold Calvin Ray, National Center for Faith-Based Initiatives, West Palm Beach, FL **(p. 237)**
Patrick Reilly, Cardinal Newman Society, Falls Church, VA **(p. 238)**
William Craig Rice, American Academy for Liberal Education, Washington, DC **(p. 239)**
Russell Roberts, Weidenbaum Center, St. Louis, MO **(p. 242)**
Ron Robinson, Young America's Foundation, Herndon, VA **(p. 242)**
*Kathy Rothschild, The Leadership Institute, Arlington, VA **(p. 244)**
Robert E. Russell, Jr., The Heritage Foundation, Geneva, IL **(p. 247)**

---

* Has testified before a state or federal legislative committee

PHILANTHROPY (Continued)

*Terrence M. Scanlon, Capital Research Center, Washington, DC (p. 251)
*Arthur J. Schwartz, John Templeton Foundation, Radnor, PA (p. 254)
*Ralph Segalman, California State University, Northridge, Northridge, CA (p. 256)
*Lou Sheldon, Traditional Values Coalition, Washington, DC (p. 258)
 Gordon St. Angelo, Milton and Rose Friedman Foundation, Indianapolis, IN (p. 267)
*Michael Tanner, Cato Institute, Washington, DC (p. 274)
 Mary L. G. Theroux, The Independent Institute, Oakland, CA (p. 276)
 Miro M. Todorovich, Scientists and Engineers for Secure Energy, New York, NY (p. 280)
 Phillip N. Truluck, The Heritage Foundation, Washington, DC (p. 281)
 John Von Kannon, The Heritage Foundation, Washington, DC (p. 285)
 Bridgett G. Wagner, The Heritage Foundation, Washington, DC (p. 286)
 Michael Y. Warder, Los Angeles Children's Scholarship Fund, Long Beach, CA (p. 289)
 Martin Morse Wooster, Northfeld Assocaties, Silver Spring, MD (p. 298)
 Jerry Zandstra, Acton Institute for the Study of Religion and Liberty,
    Grand Rapids, MI (p. 301)

POLITICAL CORRECTNESS AND MULTICULTURALISM

*Mary Cunningham Agee, The Nurturing Network, White Salmon, WA (p. 35)
*John Agresto, John Agresto and Associates, Santa Fe, NM (p. 35)
 Benjamin Alexander, Franciscan University of Steubenville, Steubenville, OH (p. 36)
*Lawrence Alexander, University of San Diego School of Law, San Diego, CA (p. 36)
*William Allen, Michigan State University, East Lansing, MI (p. 37)
 Brian C. Anderson, Manhattan Institute for Policy Research, New York, NY (p. 38)
 Frank Annunziata, Rochester Institute of Technology, Rochester, NY (p. 39)
*Gary L. Bauer, Campaign for Working Families, Arlington, VA (p. 47)
 Joel Belz, World Magazine, Asheville, NC (p. 50)
*William J. Bennett, Empower America, Washington, DC (p. 51)
 Herbert B. Berkowitz, The Heritage Foundation, Wilimington, NC (p. 51)
*Fran Bevan, Eagle Forum of Pennsylvania, North Huntingdon, PA (p. 53)
 Morton Blackwell, Leadership Institute, Arlington, VA (p. 54)
*Mark Blitz, Claremont McKenna College, Claremont, CA (p. 55)
 Jennifer C. Braceras, Independent Women's Forum, Arlington, VA (p. 59)
 Anthony Bradley, Acton Institute for the Study of Religion and Liberty,
    Grand Rapids, MI (p. 59)
 Gary Crosby Brasor, National Association of Scholars, Princeton, NJ (p. 60)
*Harold O. J. Brown, Reformed Theological Seminary, Charlotte, NC (p. 63)
*Kenneth Brown, Rio Grande Foundation, Albuquerque, NM (p. 63)
 T. Patrick Burke, St. Joseph's University, Wynnewood, PA (p. 65)
 Deborah Burstion-Donbraye, American Multimedia Inc. of Nigeria, Cleveland, OH (p. 66)
 Leslie Carbone, Fairfax, VA (p. 69)
*John Carlson, Washington Policy Center, Seattle, WA (p. 70)
*Linda Chavez, Center for Equal Opportunity, Sterling, VA (p. 73)
*Lynne V. Cheney, American Enterprise Institute, Washington, DC (p. 73)
*Roger Clegg, Center for Equal Opportunity, Sterling, VA (p. 76)
 Craig T. Cobane, Culver-Stockton College, Canton, MO (p. 76)
*Stephen Cole, State University of New York, Stony Brook, NY (p. 78)
 Peter Collier, Center for the Study of Popular Culture, Los Angeles, CA (p. 78)
*Ward Connerly, American Civil Rights Institute, Sacramento, CA (p. 80)
 Kellyanne Conway, the polling company/WomanTrend, Washington, DC (p. 80)
*John E. Coons, University of California at Berkeley, Berkeley, CA (p. 81)
*John F. Copper, Rhodes College, Memphis, TN (p. 82)
 Dennis Coyle, Catholic University of America, Washington, DC (p. 84)
 T. Kenneth Cribb, Jr., Intercollegiate Studies Institute, Wilmington, DE (p. 86)
 Neil S. Crispo, Florida State University, Tallahassee, FL (p. 86)

POLITICAL CORRECTNESS AND MULTICULTURALISM (Continued)

*Janice Shaw Crouse, Concerned Women for America, Washington, DC (p. 87)
*Charles H. Cunningham, National Rifle Association, Washington, DC (p. 87)
*Marshall L. De Rosa, Florida Atlantic University, Davie, FL (p. 90)
 Candace de Russy, State University of New York, Bronxville, NY (p. 90)
 Buffy DeBreaux-Watts, American Board for Certification of Teacher Excellence, Washington, DC (p. 91)
*Midge Decter, New York, NY (p. 91)
*Len Deo, New Jersey Family Policy Council, Parsippany, NJ (p. 93)
*John R. Diggs, Jr., South Hadley, MA (p. 95)
 James C. Dobson, Focus on the Family, Colorado Springs, CO (p. 96)
 Jeff Downing, Family First, Lincoln, NE (p. 98)
 Diallo Dphrepaulezz, New York, NY (p. 98)
 Peter J. Duignan, Hoover Institution, Stanford, CA (p. 99)
*David Dunn, Oklahoma Family Policy Council, Bethany, OK (p. 100)
 Khalid Duran, *TransIslam Magazine*, Bethesda, MD (p. 100)
*Michelle Easton, Clare Boothe Luce Policy Institute, Herndon, VA (p. 102)
*James R. Edwards, Jr., Hudson Institute, Washington, DC (p. 104)
*Robert Fike, Americans for Tax Reform, Washington, DC (p. 111)
*John Fonte, Hudson Institute, Washington, DC (p. 114)
*David Forte, Cleveland State University, Cleveland, OH (p. 114)
 Elizabeth Fox-Genovese, Emory University, Atlanta, GA (p. 115)
 Hillel Fradkin, Ethics and Public Policy Center, Washington, DC (p. 115)
 Adam Fuller, Toward Tradition, Mercer Island, WA (p. 118)
 Jennifer Garrett, The Heritage Foundation, Washington, DC (p. 120)
*Robert P. George, Princeton University, Princeton, NJ (p. 122)
 David Gersten, Center for Equal Opportunity, Sterling, VA (p. 123)
*Linda S. Gottfredson, University of Delaware, Newark, DE (p. 127)
 Charles Greenwalt, II, Susquehanna Valley Center for Public Policy, Hershey, PA (p. 129)
 Steven E. Grosby, Clemson University, Clemson, SC (p. 129)
 Thor L. Halvorssen, The Foundation for Individual Rights in Education, Philadelphia, PA (p. 132)
 Heather Higgins, Independent Women's Forum, New York, NY (p. 142)
 Scott Hogenson, *CNSNews.com*, Alexandria, VA (p. 144)
*Joseph Horn, University of Texas, Austin, TX (p. 146)
 David Horowitz, Center for the Study of Popular Culture, Los Angeles, CA (p. 146)
 William Howard, Chicago State University, Wheaton, IL (p. 147)
 Carol Iannone, New York, NY (p. 150)
 Jonathan Imber, Wellesley College, Wellesley, MA (p. 151)
 Reed J. Irvine, Accuracy in Media, Washington, DC (p. 152)
 Earl W. Jackson, Sr., Samaritan Project, Chesapeake, VA (p. 152)
*Laurence Jarvik, Washington, DC (p. 153)
*Charles W. Jarvis, United Seniors Association, Fairfax, VA (p. 153)
 Douglas A. Jeffrey, Hillsdale College, Hillsdale, MI (p. 154)
*Marianne Jennings, Arizona State University, Tempe, AZ (p. 154)
 Michael S. Joyce, Foundation for Community and Faith Centered Enterprise, Phoenix, AZ (p. 156)
*Patrick J. Keleher, Jr., TEACH America, Wilmette, IL (p. 160)
 David Kelley, The Objectivist Center, Poughkeepsie, NY (p. 160)
 Darlene A. Kennedy, Centre for New Black Leadership, Baltimore, MD (p. 162)
 Phil Kent, Southeastern Legal Foundation, Atlanta, GA (p. 162)
*Charles R. Kesler, Henry Salvatori Center, Claremont, CA (p. 162)
*Robert H. Knight, Concerned Women for America, Washington, DC (p. 166)
*David B. Kopel, Independence Institute, Golden, CO (p. 167)

---

* Has testified before a state or federal legislative committee

POLITICAL CORRECTNESS AND MULTICULTURALISM (Continued)

Alan Charles Kors, The Foundation for Individual Rights in Education, Philadelphia, PA **(p. 167)**

*Michael Krauss, George Mason University School of Law, Arlington, VA **(p. 169)**

Melvin A. Kulbicki, York College of Pennsylvania, York, PA **(p. 170)**

Peter J. LaBarbera, Concerned Women for America, Washington, DC **(p. 171)**

*George Landrith, Frontiers of Freedom Institute, Fairfax, VA **(p. 173)**

*Andrew Langer, National Federation of Independent Business, Washington, DC **(p. 174)**

Peter Augustine Lawler, Berry College, Mount Berry, GA **(p. 175)**

Phillip F. Lawler, *Catholic World Report,* South Lancaster, MA **(p. 176)**

Seth Leibsohn, Empower America, Washington, DC **(p. 177)**

Curt A. Levey, Center for Individual Rights, Washington, DC **(p. 178)**

*Mark R. Levin, Landmark Legal Foundation, Herndon, VA **(p. 178)**

Jacob T. Levy, University of Chicago, Chicago, IL **(p. 179)**

William S. Lind, Free Congress Foundation, Washington, DC **(p. 180)**

Thomas K. Lindsay, University of Dallas, Irving, TX **(p. 181)**

*Mike Long, Complete Abstinence Eduation Program, Durham, NC **(p. 183)**

Frederick R. Lynch, Claremont McKenna College, Claremont, CA **(p. 184)**

*Heather MacDonald, Manhattan Institute for Policy Research, New York, NY **(p. 185)**

Eric Mack, Tulane University, New Orleans, LA **(p. 185)**

Connie Mackey, Family Research Council, Washington, DC **(p. 185)**

Myron Magnet, Manhattan Institute for Policy Research, New York, NY **(p. 186)**

J. J. Mahoney, Diversified Consultants, Mount Pleasant, SC **(p. 187)**

Henry G. Manne, University of Chicago Law School, Chicago, IL **(p. 188)**

*Jerry L. Martin, American Council of Trustees and Alumni, Washington, DC **(p. 190)**

*Ken Masugi, Claremont Institute, Claremont, CA **(p. 191)**

*Nina May, *Renaissance Connection.com/RCNetwork.net,* Washington, DC **(p. 192)**

*Vern I. McCarthy, Jr., Mid-America Institute, Oak Brook, IL **(p. 193)**

Wilfred M. McClay, University of Tennessee, Chattanooga, Chattanooga, TN **(p. 193)**

W. Wesley McDonald, Elizabethtown College, Elizabethtown, PA **(p. 195)**

John O. McGinnis, Cardozo School of Law, New York, NY **(p. 196)**

*Michael J. McManus, Marriage Savers, Potomac, MD **(p. 197)**

Paul E. Michelson, Huntington College, Huntington, IN **(p. 201)**

*Abraham H. Miller, Walnut Creek, CA **(p. 201)**

Tom Minnery, Focus on the Family, Colorado Springs, CO **(p. 203)**

Laurie Morrow, Montpelier, VT **(p. 207)**

Jennifer Roback Morse, Hoover Institution, Vista, CA **(p. 207)**

William J. Murray, Religious Freedom Coalition, Washington, DC **(p. 209)**

Henry Myers, James Madison University, Harrisonburg, VA **(p. 210)**

Ronald Nash, Reformed Theological Seminary, Oviedo, FL **(p. 211)**

*Anne D. Neal, American Council of Trustees and Alumni, Washington, DC **(p. 211)**

Jeff Nelson, Intercollegiate Studies Institute, Wilmington, DE **(p. 212)**

Michael J. Neth, Middle Tennessee State University, Murfreesboro, TN **(p. 213)**

Jacob Neusner, Bard College, Rhinebeck, NY **(p. 213)**

*J. A. Parker, Lincoln Institute for Research and Education, Washington, DC **(p. 221)**

*John Paulk, Focus on the Family, Colorado Springs, CO **(p. 223)**

*Mitchell B. Pearlstein, Center of the American Experiment, Minneapolis, MN **(p. 224)**

Sidney A. Pearson, Jr., Radford University, Radford, VA **(p. 224)**

Terence J. Pell, Center for Individual Rights, Washington, DC **(p. 224)**

Paul C. Peterson, Coastal Carolina University, Conway, SC **(p. 227)**

James Piereson, John M. Olin Foundation, Inc., New York, NY **(p. 228)**

Arthur Pontynen, University of Wisconsin, Oshkosh, WI **(p. 230)**

*Stephen Presser, Northwestern University School of Law, Chicago, IL **(p. 233)**

Arch Puddington, Freedom House, New York, NY **(p. 234)**

Paul A. Rahe, University of Tulsa, Tulsa, OK **(p. 236)**

POLITICAL CORRECTNESS AND MULTICULTURALISM (Continued)

John Raisian, Hoover Institution, Stanford, CA **(p. 236)**
Jeremiah Reedy, Macalester College, St. Paul, MN **(p. 238)**
William Craig Rice, American Academy for Liberal Education, Washington, DC **(p. 239)**
Glenn M. Ricketts, National Association of Scholars, Princeton, NJ **(p. 239)**
Sandy Rios, Concerned Women for America, Washington, DC **(p. 240)**
Ron Robinson, Young America's Foundation, Herndon, VA **(p. 242)**
*****James A. Roumasset,** University of Hawaii, Honolulu, HI **(p. 245)**
Robert Royal, Faith & Reason Institute, Washington, DC **(p. 245)**
*****Paul Rubin,** Emory University, Atlanta, GA **(p. 246)**
*****Susan Sarnoff,** Ohio University, Athens, OH **(p. 250)**
David L. Schaefer, Holy Cross College, Worcester, MA **(p. 252)**
*****Phyllis Schlafly,** Eagle Forum, St. Louis, MO **(p. 253)**
*****Arthur J. Schwartz,** John Templeton Foundation, Radnor, PA **(p. 254)**
*****Alan E. Sears,** Alliance Defense Fund, Scottsdale, AZ **(p. 255)**
*****Ralph Segalman,** California State University, Northridge, Northridge, CA **(p. 256)**
*****Lou Sheldon,** Traditional Values Coalition, Washington, DC **(p. 258)**
*****Peter Skerry,** Claremont McKenna College, Claremont, CA **(p. 261)**
Aeon James Skoble, Bridgewater State College, Bridgewater, MA **(p. 262)**
T. Alexander Smith, University of Tennessee, Knoxville, Knoxville, TN **(p. 264)**
Ted J. Smith, III, Virginia Commonwealth University, Richmond, VA **(p. 264)**
Thomas Sowell, Hoover Institution, Stanford, CA **(p. 266)**
Peter S. Sprigg, Family Research Council, Washington, DC **(p. 267)**
Doug Stiegler, Association of Maryland Families, Woodstock, MD **(p. 269)**
*****Christine Stolba,** Ethics and Public Policy Center, Washington, DC **(p. 269)**
*****David Strom,** Taxpayers League of Minnesota, Plymouth, MN **(p. 270)**
Charles Sykes, Wisconsin Policy Research Institute, Mequon, WI **(p. 273)**
*****Lewis A. Tambs,** Tempe, AZ **(p. 273)**
Mark Tapscott, The Heritage Foundation, Washington, DC **(p. 274)**
*****John Taylor,** Virginia Institute for Public Policy, Potomac Falls, VA **(p. 274)**
*****Karen Testerman,** Cornerstone Policy Research, Concord, NH **(p. 275)**
*****Abigail Thernstrom,** Lexington, MA **(p. 276)**
*****David J. Theroux,** The Independent Institute, Oakland, CA **(p. 276)**
Miro M. Todorovich, Scientists and Engineers for Secure Energy, New York, NY **(p. 280)**
*****Balint Vazsonyi,** Center for the American Founding, McLean, VA **(p. 284)**
*****Eugene Volokh,** University of California at Los Angeles, Los Angeles, CA **(p. 285)**
Dane vonBreichenruchardt, U. S. Bill of Rights Foundation, Washington, DC **(p. 286)**
*****Jeffrey D. Wallin,** American Academy for Liberal Education, Washington, DC **(p. 287)**
Bradley C. S. Watson, Saint Vincent College, Latrobe, PA **(p. 290)**
Ben J. Wattenberg, American Enterprise Institute, Washington, DC **(p. 290)**
*****Paul Weyrich,** Free Congress Foundation, Washington, DC **(p. 293)**
Bradford P. Wilson, National Association of Scholars, Princeton, NJ **(p. 296)**
Richard B. Wirthlin, Wirthlin Worldwide, South Jordan, UT **(p. 296)**
James W. Witt, University of West Florida, Pensacola, FL **(p. 296)**
Genevieve Wood, Family Research Council, Washington, DC **(p. 297)**
*****Robert L. Woodson, Sr.,** National Center for Neighborhood Enterprise, Washington, DC **(p. 298)**
Anne Wortham, Illinois State University, Normal, IL **(p. 298)**
Edward W. Younkins, Wheeling Jesuit University, Wheeling, WV **(p. 301)**
Ronald A. Zumbrun, The Zumbrun Law Firm, Sacramento, CA **(p. 303)**

RELIGION AND PUBLIC LIFE

David L. Adams, Concordia Seminary, St. Louis, MO **(p. 34)**
*****Mary Cunningham Agee,** The Nurturing Network, White Salmon, WA **(p. 35)**
*****I. Dean Ahmad,** Minaret of Freedom Institute, Bethesda, MD **(p. 36)**

RELIGION AND PUBLIC LIFE (Continued)

*William Allen, Michigan State University, East Lansing, MI (p. 37)
Brian C. Anderson, Manhattan Institute for Policy Research, New York, NY (p. 38)
*Carl A. Anderson, Knights of Columbus, New Haven, CT (p. 38)
Frank Annunziata, Rochester Institute of Technology, Rochester, NY (p. 39)
*Dominic A. Aquila, Ave Maria University, Ypsilanti, MI (p. 40)
Hadley Arkes, Amherst College, Amherst, MA (p. 40)
Larry P. Arnn, Hillsdale College, Hillsdale, MI (p. 40)
*Thomas C. Atwood, National Council For Adoption, Alexandria, VA (p. 41)
Richard A. Baer, Jr., Cornell University, Ithaca, NY (p. 42)
Hunter Baker, Georgia Family Council, Norcross, GA (p. 43)
*Gary L. Bauer, Campaign for Working Families, Arlington, VA (p. 47)
John M. Beers, Annecy Institute for the Study of Virtue and Liberty, Washington, DC (p. 49)
Christopher Beiting, Ave Maria College, Ypsilanti, MI (p. 49)
Mariam Bell, Prison Fellowship Ministries, Washington, DC (p. 49)
Joel Belz, *World Magazine*, Asheville, NC (p. 50)
*William J. Bennett, Empower America, Washington, DC (p. 51)
*Fran Bevan, Eagle Forum of Pennsylvania, North Huntingdon, PA (p. 53)
*Wayman R. Bishop, The Family Foundation of Virginia, Richmond, VA (p. 53)
Amy E. Black, Wheaton College, Wheaton, IL (p. 54)
Morton Blackwell, Leadership Institute, Arlington, VA (p. 54)
*Patrick M. Boarman, National University San Diego, San Diego, CA (p. 55)
David J. Bobb, Hillsdale College, Hillsdale, MI (p. 56)
*Marshall J. Breger, Catholic University of America, Washington, DC (p. 60)
Arthur C. Brooks, Syracuse University, Syracuse, NY (p. 61)
*Brian Brown, Family Institute of Connecticut, Hartford, CT (p. 63)
*Harold O. J. Brown, Reformed Theological Seminary, Charlotte, NC (p. 63)
*Martin D. Brown, Richmond, VA (p. 63)
Don S. Browning, University of Chicago, Chicago, IL (p. 64)
David Brownlee, Family First, Tampa, FL (p. 64)
Gary Bullert, Columbia Basin College, Pasco, WA (p. 65)
Deborah Burstion-Donbraye, American Multimedia Inc. of Nigeria, Cleveland, OH (p. 66)
Jameson Campaigne, Jr., Jameson Books, Inc., Ottawa, IL (p. 68)
William F. Campbell, The Philadelphia Society, Baton Rouge, LA (p. 68)
*James B. Cardle, Texas Citizen Action Network, Austin, TX (p. 69)
*Allan C. Carlson, Howard Center for Family, Religion and Society, Rockford, IL (p. 70)
*Samuel Casey Carter, Acade Metrics, LLC, Washington, DC (p. 71)
*Samuel Casey, Christian Legal Society, Annandale, VA (p. 71)
Alejandro A. Chafuen, Atlas Economic Research Foundation, Fairfax, VA (p. 72)
*James Chapman, Rocky Mountain Family Council, Denver, CO (p. 72)
J. Daryl Charles, Taylor University, Upland, IN (p. 72)
Lawrence A. Chickering, Educate Girls Globally, San Francisco, CA (p. 73)
*Micah Clark, American Family Association, Indianapolis, IN (p. 75)
*Robert L. Clinton, Southern Illinois University, Carbondale, IL (p. 76)
Roberta Combs, Christian Coalition of America, Washington, DC (p. 79)
Lee Congdon, James Madison University, Harrisonburg, VA (p. 79)
*Kenneth L. Connor, Family Research Council, Washington, DC (p. 80)
*John E. Coons, University of California at Berkeley, Berkeley, CA (p. 81)
Kevin L. Cope, Louisiana State University, Baton Rouge, LA (p. 81)
Stephen D. Cox, University of California, San Diego, La Jolla, CA (p. 84)
Dennis Coyle, Catholic University of America, Washington, DC (p. 84)
*Ron Crews, Massachusetts Family Institute, Newton Upper Falls, MA (p. 86)
Alan R. Crippen, II, Family Research Council, Washington, DC (p. 86)
Michael Cromartie, Ethics and Public Policy Center, Washington, DC (p. 86)
*Janice Shaw Crouse, Concerned Women for America, Washington, DC (p. 87)

RELIGION AND PUBLIC LIFE (Continued)

*Charles H. Cunningham, National Rifle Association, Washington, DC (p. 87)

Timothy J. Dailey, Family Research Council, Washington, DC (p. 88)

*Matt Daniels, Alliance for Marriage, Springfield, VA (p. 88)

Candace de Russy, State University of New York, Bronxville, NY (p. 90)

Pia de Solenni, Family Research Council, Washington, DC (p. 90)

Buffy DeBreaux-Watts, American Board for Certification of Teacher Excellence, Washington, DC (p. 91)

*Midge Decter, New York, NY (p. 91)

*Eugene Delgaudio, Public Advocate, Falls Church, VA (p. 91)

*Len Deo, New Jersey Family Policy Council, Parsippany, NJ (p. 93)

*Robert Destro, Catholic University of America, Washington, DC (p. 94)

*William T. Devlin, Urban Family Council, Philadelphia, PA (p. 94)

*Phillip DeVous, Acton Institute for the Study of Religion and Liberty, Grand Rapids, MI (p. 94)

D. P. Diffine, Harding University, Searcy, AR (p. 95)

John J. DiIulio, Jr., University of Pennsylvania, Philadelphia, PA (p. 95)

James C. Dobson, Focus on the Family, Colorado Springs, CO (p. 96)

*William A. Donohue, Catholic League for Religious and Civil Rights, New York, NY (p. 97)

Jeff Downing, Family First, Lincoln, NE (p. 98)

*Mae Duggan, Citizens for Educational Freedom, St. Louis, MO (p. 99)

Martin Duggan, Educational Freedom Foundation, St. Louis, MO (p. 99)

*Richard Duncan, University of Nebraska, Lincoln, NE (p. 99)

*David Dunn, Oklahoma Family Policy Council, Bethany, OK (p. 100)

Khalid Duran, *TransIslam Magazine*, Bethesda, MD (p. 100)

*Clark Durant, New Common School Foundation, Detroit, MI (p. 101)

Mark L. Earley, Prison Fellowship Ministries, Washington, DC (p. 101)

*John C. Eastman, Chapman University School of Law, Orange, CA (p. 102)

*Michelle Easton, Clare Boothe Luce Policy Institute, Herndon, VA (p. 102)

Tim G. Echols, TeenPact Teen Leadership School, Jefferson, GA (p. 103)

Bruce L. Edwards, Jr., Bowling Green State University, Bowling Green, OH (p. 104)

*James R. Edwards, Jr., Hudson Institute, Washington, DC (p. 104)

Robert B. Ekelund, Auburn University, Auburn, AL (p. 105)

Barbara Elliott, Center for Renewal, Houston, TX (p. 105)

Thomas Engeman, Loyola University Chicago, Chicago, IL (p. 107)

*Patrick Fagan, The Heritage Foundation, Washington, DC (p. 108)

*Thompson Mason Faller, University of Portland, Portland, OR (p. 109)

*Michael P. Farris, Patrick Henry College, Purcellville, VA (p. 109)

*Steve Fitschen, National Legal Foundation, Virginia Beach, VA (p. 112)

*David Forte, Cleveland State University, Cleveland, OH (p. 114)

Elizabeth Fox-Genovese, Emory University, Atlanta, GA (p. 115)

Hillel Fradkin, Ethics and Public Policy Center, Washington, DC (p. 115)

*Murray Friedman, American Jewish Committee, Philadelphia, PA (p. 117)

Marshall Fritz, Alliance for the Separation of School & State, Fresno, CA (p. 118)

Adam Fuller, Toward Tradition, Mercer Island, WA (p. 118)

Richard W. Garnett, Notre Dame Law School, Notre Dame, IN (p. 120)

James R. Gaston, Franciscan University of Steubenville, Steubenville, OH (p. 120)

*Michael Geer, Pennsylvania Family Institute, Harrisburg, PA (p. 122)

*Robert P. George, Princeton University, Princeton, NJ (p. 122)

Roberta M. Gilbert, Center for the Study of Human Systems, Falls Church, VA (p. 123)

*Gary Glenn, American Family Association of Michigan, Midland, MI (p. 124)

Norval D. Glenn, University of Texas, Austin, TX (p. 125)

*Stephen Goldsmith, Manhattan Institute for Policy Research, New York, NY (p. 126)

Clint W. Green, Acton Institute for the Study of Religion and Liberty, Grand Rapids, MI (p. 128)

John Green, University of Akron, Akron, OH (p. 128)

RELIGION AND PUBLIC LIFE (Continued)

Samuel Gregg, Acton Institute for the Study of Religion and Liberty, Grand Rapids, MI **(p. 129)**
Steven E. Grosby, Clemson University, Clemson, SC **(p. 129)**
Os Guinness, Trinity Forum, McLean, VA **(p. 130)**
Rebecca Hagelin, The Heritage Foundation, Washington, DC **(p. 131)**
*****Robert Hale,** Northwest Legal Foundation, Minot, ND **(p. 132)**
Alam E. Hammad, Alexandria, VA **(p. 133)**
Bertil L. Hanson, Oklahoma State University, Stillwater, OK **(p. 134)**
Charles L. Harper, John Templeton Foundation, Radnor, PA **(p. 135)**
Mark Hartwig, Focus on the Family, Colorado Springs, CO **(p. 136)**
Kevin J. Hasson, The Becket Fund for Religious Liberty, Washington, DC **(p. 137)**
*****Clark C. Havighurst,** Duke University School of Law, Durham, NC **(p. 137)**
*****Donna H. Hearne,** Constitutional Coalition, St. Louis, MO **(p. 138)**
Michael S. Heath, Christian Civic League of Maine, Augusta, ME **(p. 138)**
Jay F. Hein, Hudson Institute, Indianapolis, IN **(p. 139)**
*****Randy Hicks,** Georgia Family Council, Norcross, GA **(p. 141)**
James E. Hinish, Jr., Regent University, Williamsburg, VA **(p. 143)**
*****Thomas Hinton,** The Heritage Foundation, Washington, DC **(p. 143)**
James Hitchcock, St. Louis University, St. Louis, MO **(p. 143)**
*****Michael Horowitz,** Hudson Institute, Washington, DC **(p. 146)**
Deal Hudson, *Crisis Magazine*, Washington, DC **(p. 148)**
James D. Hunter, University of Virginia, Charlottesville, VA **(p. 149)**
*****Charles D. Hurley,** Iowa Family Policy Center, Pleasant Hill, IA **(p. 150)**
Carol Iannone, New York, NY **(p. 150)**
Jonathan Imber, Wellesley College, Wellesley, MA **(p. 151)**
*****Alan Inman,** Institute for Responsible Fatherhood and Family Revitalization, Largo, MD **(p. 151)**
Earl W. Jackson, Sr., Samaritan Project, Chesapeake, VA **(p. 152)**
*****Bradley P. Jacob,** Regent University, Virginia Beach, VA **(p. 152)**
*****Thomas L. Jipping,** Concerned Women for America, Washington, DC **(p. 154)**
Phil Kent, Southeastern Legal Foundation, Atlanta, GA **(p. 162)**
*****Dimitri Kesari,** Family Research Council, Washington, DC **(p. 162)**
Christina Kindel, North Dakota Family Alliance, Bismarck, ND **(p. 164)**
Annette Kirk, Russell Kirk Center, Mecosta, MI **(p. 164)**
*****Douglas W. Kmiec,** The Catholic University of America, Washington, DC **(p. 166)**
*****Robert H. Knight,** Concerned Women for America, Washington, DC **(p. 166)**
Joseph M. Knippenberg, Oglethorpe University, Atlanta, GA **(p. 166)**
*****Diane Knippers,** Institute on Religion and Democracy, Washington, DC **(p. 166)**
John L. Koehler, Illinois Family Institute, Glen Ellyn, IL **(p. 166)**
*****Robert C. Koons,** University of Texas, Austin, TX **(p. 167)**
*****Patrick Korten,** The Becket Fund for Religious Liberty, Washington, DC **(p. 167)**
*****Malcolm Kovacs,** Montgomery College, Rockville, MD **(p. 168)**
Irving Kristol, The Public Interest, Washington, DC **(p. 169)**
William Kristol, *The Weekly Standard,* Washington, DC **(p. 169)**
*****Lawrence Kudlow,** Kudlow & Co., LLC, New York, NY **(p. 170)**
Melvin A. Kulbicki, York College of Pennsylvania, York, PA **(p. 170)**
John Kurzweil, California Public Policy Foundation, Camarillo, CA **(p. 171)**
Peter J. LaBarbera, Concerned Women for America, Washington, DC **(p. 171)**
*****Andrea S. Lafferty,** Traditional Values Coalition, Washington, DC **(p. 172)**
*****James Lafferty,** Massachusetts Citizens Alliance, Waltham, MA **(p. 172)**
*****Richard D. Land,** Ethics and Religious Liberty Commission, Nashville, TN **(p. 173)**
Kristin D. Landers, Alabama Policy Institute, Birmingham, AL **(p. 173)**
Daniel Lapin, Toward Tradition, Mercer Island, WA **(p. 174)**
Peter Augustine Lawler, Berry College, Mount Berry, GA **(p. 175)**
Phillip F. Lawler, *Catholic World Report,* South Lancaster, MA **(p. 176)**

RELIGION AND PUBLIC LIFE (Continued)

*Stephen Lazarus, Center for Public Justice, Annapolis, MD (p. 176)
Michael A. Ledeen, American Enterprise Institute, Washington, DC (p. 176)
Seth Leibsohn, Empower America, Washington, DC (p. 177)
Richard Lessner, American Renewal, Washington, DC (p. 178)
Leonard P. Liggio, Atlas Economic Research Foundation, Fairfax, VA (p. 180)
Thomas K. Lindsay, University of Dallas, Irving, TX (p. 181)
Art Lindsley, C. S. Lewis Institute, Annandale, VA (p. 181)
*Joseph Loconte, The Heritage Foundation, Washington, DC (p. 182)
Bernard T. Lomas, The Heritage Foundation, Chapel Hill, NC (p. 182)
*Mike Long, Complete Abstinence Eduation Program, Durham, NC (p. 183)
Jordan Lorence, Alliance Defense Fund, Scottsdale, AZ (p. 183)
Eric Mack, Tulane University, New Orleans, LA (p. 185)
David W. Madsen, Seattle University, Seattle, WA (p. 186)
*Dennis Mansfield, Boise, ID (p. 189)
William R. Marty, University of Memphis, Memphis, TN (p. 190)
Kris Alan Mauren, Acton Institute for the Study of Religion and Liberty,
   Grand Rapids, MI (p. 192)
Paul Maurer, Trinity International University, Deerfield, IL (p. 192)
Wilfred M. McClay, University of Tennessee, Chattanooga, Chattanooga, TN (p. 193)
*Michael W. McConnell, University of Utah, Salt Lake City, UT (p. 194)
Wendell H. McCulloch, Jr., California State University, Long Beach, Long Beach, CA (p. 194)
Kathleen McGarry, Murray Hill Institute, New York, NY (p. 195)
*Michael J. McManus, Marriage Savers, Potomac, MD (p. 197)
Paul T. Mero, The Sutherland Institute, Salt Lake City, UT (p. 199)
Paul E. Michelson, Huntington College, Huntington, IN (p. 201)
Gene Mills, Louisiana Family Forum, Baton Rouge, LA (p. 202)
Tom Minnery, Focus on the Family, Colorado Springs, CO (p. 203)
*C. Ben Mitchell, Trinity International University, Deerfield, IL (p. 203)
R. Albert Mohler, Jr., The Southern Baptist Theological Seminary, Louisville, KY (p. 204)
Stephen Monsma, Pepperdine University, Malibu, CA (p. 205)
*Joseph A. Morris, Lincoln Legal Foundation, Chicago, IL (p. 207)
Jennifer Roback Morse, Hoover Institution, Vista, CA (p. 207)
*Steven W. Mosher, Population Research Institute, Front Royal, VA (p. 208)
*Len Munsil, Center for Arizona Policy, Scottsdale, AZ (p. 209)
William J. Murray, Religious Freedom Coalition, Washington, DC (p. 209)
Ronald Nash, Reformed Theological Seminary, Oviedo, FL (p. 211)
Mario Navarro da Costa, American Society for the Defense of Tradition, Family and Property,
   McLean, VA (p. 211)
*Richard John Neuhaus, Institute on Religion and Public Life, New York, NY (p. 213)
Jacob Neusner, Bard College, Rhinebeck, NY (p. 213)
C. Preston Noell, III, Tradition, Family, Property, Inc., McLean, VA (p. 214)
Stuart W. Nolan, Jr., Springfield, VA (p. 214)
Mark Noll, Wheaton College, Wheaton, IL (p. 214)
Seth W. Norton, Wheaton College, Wheaton, IL (p. 215)
Michael J. Novak, Jr., American Enterprise Institute, Washington, DC (p. 215)
James Nuechterlein, *First Things*, New York, NY (p. 216)
*Marvin Olasky, University of Texas, Austin, TX (p. 218)
Kent Ostrander, The Family Foundation of Kentucky, Lexington, KY (p. 220)
*Jim Panyard, Pennsylvania Manufacturer's Association, Harrisburg, PA (p. 221)
*Star Parker, Coalition on Urban Renewal and Education, Washington, DC (p. 222)
*John Paulk, Focus on the Family, Colorado Springs, CO (p. 223)
*John Paulton, Focus on the Family, Colorado Springs, CO (p. 223)
*Mitchell B. Pearlstein, Center of the American Experiment, Minneapolis, MN (p. 224)
Sidney A. Pearson, Jr., Radford University, Radford, VA (p. 224)

---

* Has testified before a state or federal legislative committee

RELIGION AND PUBLIC LIFE (Continued)

Terence J. Pell, Center for Individual Rights, Washington, DC (p. 224)
Val Peter, Boys Town, Boys Town, NE (p. 226)
Arthur Pontynen, University of Wisconsin, Oshkosh, WI (p. 230)
Victor Porlier, Center for Civic Renewal, Inc., Delmar, NY (p. 231)
Dennis Prager, The Prager Perspective, Van Nuys, CA (p. 232)
*Stephen Presser, Northwestern University School of Law, Chicago, IL (p. 233)
*Claude Pressnell, Tennessee Independent Colleges and Universities, Nashville, TN (p. 233)
*Thomas Prichard, Minnesota Family Council, Minneapolis, MN (p. 233)
*Penny Pullen, Life Advocacy Resource Project, Inc., Arlington Heights, IL (p. 234)
Harold Calvin Ray, National Center for Faith-Based Initiatives, West Palm Beach, FL (p. 237)
Jeremiah Reedy, Macalester College, St. Paul, MN (p. 238)
Patrick Reilly, Cardinal Newman Society, Falls Church, VA (p. 238)
*Charles E. Rice, Notre Dame Law School, Notre Dame, IN (p. 239)
Sandy Rios, Concerned Women for America, Washington, DC (p. 240)
John W. Robbins, Trinity Foundation, Unicoi, TN (p. 241)
Robert Royal, Faith & Reason Institute, Washington, DC (p. 245)
*Frank Russo, American Family Association of New York, Port Washington, NY (p. 247)
*Steven Alan Samson, Liberty University, Lynchburg, VA (p. 249)
Robert A. Schadler, Center for First Principles, Washington, DC (p. 251)
David L. Schaefer, Holy Cross College, Worcester, MA (p. 252)
*D. Eric Schansberg, Indiana University Southeast, New Albany, IN (p. 252)
*Arthur J. Schwartz, John Templeton Foundation, Radnor, PA (p. 254)
*Michael Schwartz, Concerned Women for America, Washington, DC (p. 254)
*Alan E. Sears, Alliance Defense Fund, Scottsdale, AZ (p. 255)
*Jay Sekulow, American Center for Law and Justice, Virginia Beach, VA (p. 256)
*Jamie Self, Georgia Family Council, Norcross, GA (p. 256)
*Lou Sheldon, Traditional Values Coalition, Washington, DC (p. 258)
Richard Sherlock, Utah State University, Logan, UT (p. 259)
*Amy L. Sherman, Hudson Institute, Charlottesville, VA (p. 259)
*Robert A. Sirico, Acton Institute for the Study of Religion and Liberty,
    Grand Rapids, MI (p. 261)
*James Skillen, Center for Public Justice, Annapolis, MD (p. 261)
*Curt Smith, Indiana Family Institute, Indianapolis, IN (p. 263)
*Oran P. Smith, Palmetto Family Council, Columbia, SC (p. 264)
Brad Snavely, Michigan Family Forum, Lansing, MI (p. 264)
Christina Hoff Sommers, American Enterprise Institute, Washington, DC (p. 266)
*Matthew Spalding, The Heritage Foundation, Washington, DC (p. 266)
Peter S. Sprigg, Family Research Council, Washington, DC (p. 267)
Glenn T. Stanton, Focus on the Family, Colorado Springs, CO (p. 268)
Doug Stiegler, Association of Maryland Families, Woodstock, MD (p. 269)
*Christine Stolba, Ethics and Public Policy Center, Washington, DC (p. 269)
James R. "J.T." Taylor, Empower America, Washington, DC (p. 274)
*Karen Testerman, Cornerstone Policy Research, Concord, NH (p. 275)
Christopher Thacker, The Bible Literacy Project, New York, NY (p. 275)
Frank J. Tipler, Tulane University, New Orleans, LA (p. 279)
*George Tryfiates, Concerned Women for America, Washington, DC (p. 281)
*Forrest L. Turpen, Christian Educators Association International, Pasadena, CA (p. 282)
Lawrence A. Uzzell, Keston Institute, Waxahachie, TX (p. 283)
*Eugene Volokh, University of California at Los Angeles, Los Angeles, CA (p. 285)
Linda J. Waite, University of Chicago, Chicago, IL (p. 286)
*Lee H. Walker, New Coalition for Economic and Social Change, Chicago, IL (p. 287)
Bradley C. S. Watson, Saint Vincent College, Latrobe, PA (p. 290)
Stanley J. Watson, Patrick Henry College, Purcellville, VA (p. 290)
Emily S. Watts, University of Illinois at Urbana-Champaign, Urbana, IL (p. 290)

RELIGION AND PUBLIC LIFE (Continued)

*Walter M. Weber, American Center for Law and Justice, Alexandria, VA (p. 291)
David L. Weeks, Azusa Pacific University, Azusa, CA (p. 291)
*George Weigel, Ethics and Public Policy Center, Washington, DC (p. 291)
Daniel Weiss, Focus on the Family, Colorado Springs, CO (p. 292)
John G. West, Discovery Institute, Seattle, WA (p. 292)
Thomas G. West, University of Dallas, Irving, TX (p. 293)
David M. Whalen, Hillsdale College, Hillsdale, MI (p. 293)
*John W. Whitehead, The Rutherford Institute, Charlottesville, VA (p. 293)
Peter W. Wielhouwer, Regent University, Virginia Beach, VA (p. 294)
Donald Wildmon, American Family Association, Tupelo, MS (p. 294)
*Natalie Williams, Robinson, DiLando and Whitaker, Sacramento, CA (p. 295)
*John C. Willke, Life Issues Institute, Inc., Cincinnati, OH (p. 295)
Clyde N. Wilson, University of South Carolina, Columbia, SC (p. 296)
Richard B. Wirthlin, Wirthlin Worldwide, South Jordan, UT (p. 296)
*Christopher Wolfe, Marquette University, Milwaukee, WI (p. 297)
*Kenneth Wood, The Oklahoma Christian Coalition, Oklahoma City, OK (p. 298)
Ashley Woodiwiss, Wheaton College, Wheaton, IL (p. 298)
*Robert L. Woodson, Sr., National Center for Neighborhood Enterprise,
   Washington, DC (p. 298)
Frank Wright, Center for Christian Statesmanship, Washington, DC (p. 299)
*Michael K. Young, George Washington University Law School, Washington, DC (p. 300)
Edward W. Younkins, Wheeling Jesuit University, Wheeling, WV (p. 301)
Jerry Zandstra, Acton Institute for the Study of Religion and Liberty,
   Grand Rapids, MI (p. 301)

STATE-SPONSORED GAMBLING

*Julaine K. Appling, Family Research Institute of Wisconsin, Madison, WI (p. 40)
*Sonia Arrison, Pacific Research Institute, San Francisco, CA (p. 41)
Hunter Baker, Georgia Family Council, Norcross, GA (p. 43)
*Gary L. Bauer, Campaign for Working Families, Arlington, VA (p. 47)
*Fran Bevan, Eagle Forum of Pennsylvania, North Huntingdon, PA (p. 53)
*Wayman R. Bishop, The Family Foundation of Virginia, Richmond, VA (p. 53)
*Bill Brooks, North Carolina Family Policy Council, Raleigh, NC (p. 62)
*James B. Cardle, Texas Citizen Action Network, Austin, TX (p. 69)
*Micah Clark, American Family Association, Indianapolis, IN (p. 75)
*Ron Crews, Massachusetts Family Institute, Newton Upper Falls, MA (p. 86)
*Charles H. Cunningham, National Rifle Association, Washington, DC (p. 87)
*Matt Daniels, Alliance for Marriage, Springfield, VA (p. 88)
*Lisa Dean, Free Congress Foundation, Washington, DC (p. 91)
*William T. Devlin, Urban Family Council, Philadelphia, PA (p. 94)
*Gerry Dickinson, South Carolina Policy Council, Columbia, SC (p. 95)
James C. Dobson, Focus on the Family, Colorado Springs, CO (p. 96)
Jeff Downing, Family First, Lincoln, NE (p. 98)
*David Dunn, Oklahoma Family Policy Council, Bethany, OK (p. 100)
*Michael P. Farris, Patrick Henry College, Purcellville, VA (p. 109)
*Michael Geer, Pennsylvania Family Institute, Harrisburg, PA (p. 122)
*John R. Hill, Alabama Policy Institute, Birmingham, AL (p. 142)
Chad Hills, Focus on the Family, Colorado Springs, CO (p. 143)
*Fred Holden, Phoenix Enterprises, Arvada, CO (p. 144)
*Michael Howden, Stronger Families for Oregon, Salem, OR (p. 147)
Jonathan Imber, Wellesley College, Wellesley, MA (p. 151)
*Dimitri Kesari, Family Research Council, Washington, DC (p. 162)
*Robert H. Knight, Concerned Women for America, Washington, DC (p. 166)
*Andrea S. Lafferty, Traditional Values Coalition, Washington, DC (p. 172)

STATE-SPONSORED GAMBLING (Continued)

Brett A. Magbee, Oklahoma Council of Public Affairs, Oklahoma City, OK **(p. 186)**
*****Rita P. Maguire,** Arizona Center for Public Policy, Phoenix, AZ **(p. 186)**
*****Dennis Mansfield,** Boise, ID **(p. 189)**
*****Michael J. McManus,** Marriage Savers, Potomac, MD **(p. 197)**
*****James H. Miller,** Wisconsin Policy Research Institute, Mequon, WI **(p. 202)**
Tom Minnery, Focus on the Family, Colorado Springs, CO **(p. 203)**
*****Len Munsil,** Center for Arizona Policy, Scottsdale, AZ **(p. 209)**
Ronald Nash, Reformed Theological Seminary, Oviedo, FL **(p. 211)**
Kent Ostrander, The Family Foundation of Kentucky, Lexington, KY **(p. 220)**
*****Gary J. Palmer,** Alabama Policy Institute, Birmingham, AL **(p. 221)**
Bobbie Patray, Eagle Forum of Tennessee, Nashville, TN **(p. 222)**
*****John Paulton,** Focus on the Family, Colorado Springs, CO **(p. 223)**
*****Thomas Prichard,** Minnesota Family Council, Minneapolis, MN **(p. 233)**
Ron Reno, Focus on the Family, Colorado Springs, CO **(p. 238)**
Sandy Rios, Concerned Women for America, Washington, DC **(p. 240)**
*****Kelly Rosati,** Hawaii Family Forum, Kaneohe, HI **(p. 243)**
*****Jamie Self,** Georgia Family Council, Norcross, GA **(p. 256)**
*****Lou Sheldon,** Traditional Values Coalition, Washington, DC **(p. 258)**
*****Curt Smith,** Indiana Family Institute, Indianapolis, IN **(p. 263)**
*****Oran P. Smith,** Palmetto Family Council, Columbia, SC **(p. 264)**
Doug Stiegler, Association of Maryland Families, Woodstock, MD **(p. 269)**
*****David Strom,** Taxpayers League of Minnesota, Plymouth, MN **(p. 270)**
*****Karen Testerman,** Cornerstone Policy Research, Concord, NH **(p. 275)**
*****Randy Thomasson,** Campaign for California Families, Sacramento, CA **(p. 277)**
*****Kenneth Wood,** The Oklahoma Christian Coalition, Oklahoma City, OK **(p. 298)**

Federalism, Governing and Elections

CAMPAIGN FINANCE REFORM

Damon Ansell, Americans for Tax Reform, Washington, DC (**p. 39**)
*__Doug Bandow,__ Cato Institute, Washington, DC (**p. 45**)
Patrick Basham, Cato Institute, Washington, DC (**p. 47**)
*__Charles H. Bell, Jr.,__ Bell, McAndrews, Hiltachk & Davidian, Sacramento, CA (**p. 49**)
*__Lillian BeVier,__ University of Virginia, Charlottesville, VA (**p. 53**)
John F. Bibby, University of Wisconsin, Milwaukee, Milwaukee, WI (**p. 53**)
Morton Blackwell, Leadership Institute, Arlington, VA (**p. 54**)
*__Patrick M. Boarman,__ National University San Diego, San Diego, CA (**p. 55**)
*__Kenneth Boehm,__ National Legal and Policy Center, Falls Church, VA (**p. 56**)
*__James Dopp, Jr.,__ James Madison Center for Free Speech, Washington, DC (**p. 57**)
L. Brent Bozell, III, Media Research Center, Alexandria, VA (**p. 59**)
*__Scott Bullock,__ Institute for Justice, Washington, DC (**p. 65**)
*__Linda Chavez,__ Center for Equal Opportunity, Sterling, VA (**p. 73**)
*__Michael A. Ciamarra,__ Alabama Policy Institute, Birmingham, AL (**p. 74**)
Peter Cleary, American Conservative Union, Alexandria, VA (**p. 75**)
*__Jerome F. Climer,__ The Congressional Institute, Alexandria, VA (**p. 76**)
*__Charles J. Cooper,__ Cooper & Kirk, PLLC, Washington, DC (**p. 81**)
Mickey Craig, Hillsdale College, Hillsdale, MI (**p. 85**)
Edward H. Crane, Cato Institute, Washington, DC (**p. 85**)
Neil S. Crispo, Florida State University, Tallahassee, FL (**p. 86**)
*__Charles H. Cunningham,__ National Rifle Association, Washington, DC (**p. 87**)
*__James DeLong,__ Progress & Freedom Foundation, Washington, DC (**p. 92**)
Richard Derham, Washington Policy Center, Seattle, WA (**p. 93**)
John Jay Douglass, University of Houston Law Center, Houston, TX (**p. 97**)
Pete du Pont, National Center for Policy Analysis, Wilmington, DE (**p. 98**)
Valle Simms Dutcher, Southeastern Legal Foundation, Atlanta, GA (**p. 101**)
*__John C. Eastman,__ Chapman University School of Law, Orange, CA (**p. 102**)
*__Mickey Edwards,__ Harvard University, Cambridge, MA (**p. 104**)
Paul Edwards, Mercatus Center at George Mason University, Arlington, VA (**p. 104**)
Glenn Ellmers, Claremont Institute, Claremont, CA (**p. 106**)
*__Edward J. Erler,__ California State University, San Bernardino, San Bernardino, CA (**p. 107**)
*__Robert Fike,__ Americans for Tax Reform, Washington, DC (**p. 111**)
*__Peter Flaherty,__ National Legal and Policy Center, Falls Church, VA (**p. 113**)
*__Robert Franciosi,__ Goldwater Institute, Phoenix, AZ (**p. 115**)
*__Wanda Franz,__ National Right to Life Committee, Washington, DC (**p. 116**)
*__Todd Gaziano,__ The Heritage Foundation, Washington, DC (**p. 121**)
*__Charlie Gerow,__ Quantum Communications, Harrisburg, PA (**p. 123**)
Stefan Gleason, National Right to Work Legal Defense Foundation, Springfield, VA (**p. 124**)
*__Stephen O. Goodrick,__ National Right to Work Committee, Springfield, VA (**p. 126**)
John Green, University of Akron, Akron, OH (**p. 128**)
Timothy J. Groseclose, Stanford University, Stanford, CA (**p. 129**)
*__Grant R. Gulibon,__ The Commonwealth Foundation, Harrisburg, PA (**p. 130**)
*__Steven Hayward,__ American Enterprise Institute, Washington, DC (**p. 138**)
*__James M. Henderson, Sr.,__ American Center for Law and Justice, Washington, DC (**p. 140**)
Niger Roy Innis, Congress of Racial Equality, New York, NY (**p. 151**)
*__Paul Jacob,__ Citizens in Charge and Citizens in Charge Foundation, Woodbridge, VA (**p. 153**)
*__Charles W. Jarvis,__ United Seniors Association, Fairfax, VA (**p. 153**)
*__David John,__ The Heritage Foundation, Washington, DC (**p. 154**)
*__Douglas Johnson,__ National Right to Life Committee, Washington, DC (**p. 155**)
Amy Kauffman, Hudson Institute, Washington, DC (**p. 158**)
*__David A. Keene,__ American Conservative Union, Washington, DC (**p. 160**)
Maurice Kelman, Wayne State University Law School, Troy, MI (**p. 161**)

CAMPAIGN FINANCE REFORM (Continued)

Phil Kent, Southeastern Legal Foundation, Atlanta, GA (p. 162)
Larry Klayman, Judicial Watch, Washington, DC (p. 165)
*David B. Kopel, Independence Institute, Golden, CO (p. 167)
*Randall Kroszner, University of Chicago, Chicago, IL (p. 170)
Melvin A. Kulbicki, York College of Pennsylvania, York, PA (p. 170)
*Raymond J. LaJeunesse, Jr., National Right to Work Legal Defense Foundation, Springfield, VA (p. 172)
*George Landrith, Frontiers of Freedom Institute, Fairfax, VA (p. 173)
*Mark R. Levin, Landmark Legal Foundation, Herndon, VA (p. 178)
*Robert A. Levy, Cato Institute, Washington, DC (p. 179)
Edward J. Lopez, University of North Texas, Denton, TX (p. 183)
John R. Lott, Jr., American Enterprise Institute, Washington, DC (p. 183)
*Rita P. Maguire, Arizona Center for Public Policy, Phoenix, AZ (p. 186)
Mary P. Mahoney, United Seniors Association, Inc., Washington, DC (p. 187)
John O. McGinnis, Cardozo School of Law, New York, NY (p. 196)
*Annette Thompson Meeks, Center of the American Experiment, Minneapolis, MN (p. 198)
*William H. Mellor, Institute for Justice, Washington, DC (p. 199)
Harry Messenheimer, Rio Grande Foundation, Tijeras, NM (p. 200)
Jeffrey D. Milyo, University of Chicago, Chicago, IL (p. 202)
*Cleta Deatherage Mitchell, Foley & Lardner, Washington, DC (p. 203)
*Mark A. Mix, National Right to Work Committee, Springfield, VA (p. 204)
*Deroy Murdock, Atlas Economic Research Foundation, New York, NY (p. 209)
Chuck Muth, American Conservative Union, Alexandria, VA (p. 210)
*Ronald Nehring, Americans for Tax Reform, San Diego, CA (p. 212)
Stuart W. Nolan, Jr., Springfield, VA (p. 214)
R. Marc Nuttle, Norman, OK (p. 216)
Edward J. Ohlert, JAYCOR, McLean, VA (p. 218)
*J. A. Parker, Lincoln Institute for Research and Education, Washington, DC (p. 221)
*Darryl Paulson, University of South Florida, St. Petersburg, FL (p. 223)
*Ronald W. Pearson, Pearson & Pipkin, Inc., Washington, DC (p. 224)
*Roger Pilon, Cato Institute, Washington, DC (p. 228)
George Priest, Yale Law School, New Haven, CT (p. 233)
*Ronald D. Rotunda, George Mason University School of Law, Arlington, VA (p. 244)
John Samples, Cato Institute, Washington, DC (p. 249)
David L. Schaefer, Holy Cross College, Worcester, MA (p. 252)
*Jay Sekulow, American Center for Law and Justice, Virginia Beach, VA (p. 256)
*Steven S. Smith, Weidenbaum Center, St. Louis, MO (p. 264)
*Jeff Stormo, Choices for Children, Grand Rapids, MI (p. 270)
*David Strom, Taxpayers League of Minnesota, Plymouth, MN (p. 270)
*Herbert W. Titus, Virginia Beach, VA (p. 279)
*Robert D. Tollison, University of Mississippi, University, MS (p. 280)
John Tuskey, Regent University, Virginia Beach, VA (p. 282)
Dane vonBreichenruchardt, U. S. Bill of Rights Foundation, Washington, DC (p. 286)
Stanley J. Watson, Patrick Henry College, Purcellville, VA (p. 290)
*Donald V. Weatherman, Erskine College, Due West, SC (p. 290)
*Kenneth Weinstein, Hudson Institute, Washington, DC (p. 292)
Thomas G. West, University of Dallas, Irving, TX (p. 293)
*Paul Weyrich, Free Congress Foundation, Washington, DC (p. 293)
*Bob Williams, Evergreen Freedom Foundation, Olympia, WA (p. 295)
Jason Wright, Frontiers of Freedom Institute, Fairfax, VA (p. 299)
*W. James Young, National Right to Work Legal Defense Foundation, Springfield, VA (p. 301)

CONGRESS

*William Allen, Michigan State University, East Lansing, MI (p. 37)

---

* Has testified before a state or federal legislative committee

CONGRESS (Continued)

Damon Ansell, Americans for Tax Reform, Washington, DC (p. 39)

Tripp Baird, The Heritage Foundation, Washington, DC (p. 43)

*John S. Baker, Jr., Louisiana State University, Baton Rouge, LA (p. 43)

*Keith G. Baker, Florida TaxWatch Research Institute, Inc., Tallahassee, FL (p. 43)

Paul Beckner, Citizens for a Sound Economy, Washington, DC (p. 48)

*Herman Belz, University of Maryland, College Park, MD (p. 50)

John F. Bibby, University of Wisconsin, Milwaukee, Milwaukee, WI (p. 53)

Amy E. Black, Wheaton College, Wheaton, IL (p. 54)

Morton Blackwell, Leadership Institute, Arlington, VA (p. 54)

*Mark A. Bloomfield, American Council for Capital Formation, Washington, DC (p. 55)

Demian Brady, National Taxpayers Union Foundation, Alexandria, VA (p. 59)

Charles Brooks, The Strategy Group, Arlington, VA (p. 62)

James M. Buchanan, Center for the Study of Public Choice, Fairfax, VA (p. 64)

Andrew E. Busch, University of Denver, Denver, CO (p. 66)

*F. Patricia Callahan, American Association of Small Property Owners, Washington, DC (p. 68)

Chris Carr, Georgia Public Policy Foundation, Atlanta, GA (p. 71)

*Jerome F. Climer, The Congressional Institute, Alexandria, VA (p. 76)

William Connelly, Washington and Lee University, Lexington, VA (p. 80)

Kellyanne Conway, the polling company/WomanTrend, Washington, DC (p. 80)

*Louis J. Cordia, Cordia Companies, Alexandria, VA (p. 82)

*Al Cors, National Taxpayers Union and Foundation, Alexandria, VA (p. 82)

*Douglas Cox, Gibson, Dunn & Crutcher LLP, Washington, DC (p. 84)

James K. Coyne, National Air Transportation Association, Alexandria, VA (p. 84)

Mickey Craig, Hillsdale College, Hillsdale, MI (p. 85)

*Charles H. Cunningham, National Rifle Association, Washington, DC (p. 87)

*Carl DeMaio, Reason Foundation, Los Angeles, CA (p. 92)

*Donald J. Devine, Center for American Values, Shady Side, MD (p. 94)

Stephanie M. Di Napoli, Family Research Council, Washington, DC (p. 95)

Danielle Doane, The Heritage Foundation, Washington, DC (p. 96)

Steven D. Ealy, Liberty Fund, Inc., Indianapolis, IN (p. 101)

*John C. Eastman, Chapman University School of Law, Orange, CA (p. 102)

Mary Eberstadt, *Policy Review*, Washington, DC (p. 103)

*James R. Edwards, Jr., Hudson Institute, Washington, DC (p. 104)

*Mickey Edwards, Harvard University, Cambridge, MA (p. 104)

*Louis D. Enoff, Enoff Associates Limited, Sykesville, MD (p. 107)

M. Stanton Evans, Education and Research Institute, Washington, DC (p. 108)

Robert Feidler, International Legal Projects Institute, Grand Forks, ND (p. 110)

*Robert Fike, Americans for Tax Reform, Washington, DC (p. 111)

Elizabeth Fox-Genovese, Emory University, Atlanta, GA (p. 115)

Michael Franc, The Heritage Foundation, Washington, DC (p. 115)

Amy Frantz, Public Interest Institute, Mount Pleasant, IA (p. 116)

*Deanna R. Gelak, Family and Medical Leave Act Technical Corrections Coalition, Springfield, VA (p. 122)

Jack Gourman, National Education Standards, Los Angeles, CA (p. 127)

John Green, University of Akron, Akron, OH (p. 128)

Timothy J. Groseclose, Stanford University, Stanford, CA (p. 129)

*Erick Gustafson, Citizens for a Sound Economy, Washington, DC (p. 131)

Robert C. Harrison, Defenders of Property Rights, Washington, DC (p. 136)

Larry Hart, Hartco Strategies, Washington, DC (p. 136)

Robert A. Heineman, Alfred University, Alfred, NY (p. 139)

James E. Hinish, Jr., Regent University, Williamsburg, VA (p. 143)

*James Huffman, Lewis and Clark Law School, Portland, OR (p. 148)

Thomas Hyde, Pfeiffer University, Misenheimer, NC (p. 150)

Niger Roy Innis, Congress of Racial Equality, New York, NY (p. 151)

CONGRESS (Continued)

*Charles W. Jarvis, United Seniors Association, Fairfax, VA (p. 153)
*David John, The Heritage Foundation, Washington, DC (p. 154)
 Amy Kauffman, Hudson Institute, Washington, DC (p. 158)
*W. Thomas Kelly, Savers and Investors League, Mirror Lake, NH (p. 161)
*Jack Kemp, Empower America, Washington, DC (p. 161)
 Phil Kent, Southeastern Legal Foundation, Atlanta, GA (p. 162)
 Matthew Kibbe, Citizens for a Sound Economy, Washington, DC (p. 163)
*David B. Kopel, Independence Institute, Golden, CO (p. 167)
 Lisa M. Korsak, Mercatus Center at George Mason University, Arlington, VA (p. 167)
*Randall Kroszner, University of Chicago, Chicago, IL (p. 170)
*George Landrith, Frontiers of Freedom Institute, Fairfax, VA (p. 173)
 Leonard A. Leo, The Federalist Society for Law and Public Policy Studies,
    Washington, DC (p. 178)
*Mark R. Levin, Landmark Legal Foundation, Herndon, VA (p. 178)
 Eric Licht, Coalitions for America, Washington, DC (p. 179)
 Edward J. Lopez, University of North Texas, Denton, TX (p. 183)
 Connie Mackey, Family Research Council, Washington, DC (p. 185)
 Mary P. Mahoney, United Seniors Association, Inc., Washington, DC (p. 187)
*Dennis Mansfield, Boise, ID (p. 189)
*David N. Mayer, Capital University Law School, Columbus, OH (p. 193)
*Tom McClusky, National Taxpayers Union Foundation, Alexandria, VA (p. 193)
 Lawrence J. McQuillan, Pacific Research Institute, San Francisco, CA (p. 197)
 Jeffrey D. Milyo, University of Chicago, Chicago, IL (p. 202)
 Phyllis Berry Myers, Centre for New Black Leadership, Washington, DC (p. 210)
 David Charles Nice, Washington State University, Pullman, WA (p. 213)
 Lauren Noyes, The Heritage Foundation, Washington, DC (p. 216)
 David Nutter, Mercatus Center at George Mason University, Arlington, VA (p. 216)
 R. Marc Nuttle, Norman, OK (p. 216)
 Kate O'Beirne, *National Review*, Washington, DC (p. 216)
 Norman J. Ornstein, American Enterprise Institute, Washington, DC (p. 219)
*Darryl Paulson, University of South Florida, St. Petersburg, FL (p. 223)
*Ronald W. Pearson, Pearson & Pipkin, Inc., Washington, DC (p. 224)
 John J. Pitney, Jr., Claremont McKenna College, Claremont, CA (p. 229)
*Don Racheter, Public Interest Institute, Mount Pleasant, IA (p. 235)
 Martin G. Reiser, Citizens for a Sound Economy, Washington, DC (p. 238)
*Amy Ridenour, National Center for Public Policy Research, Washington, DC (p. 240)
 Sandy Rios, Concerned Women for America, Washington, DC (p. 240)
*Ronald D. Rotunda, George Mason University School of Law, Arlington, VA (p. 244)
*Paul Rubin, Emory University, Atlanta, GA (p. 246)
*Stacie Rumenap, U. S. Term Limits, Washington, DC (p. 247)
 John Samples, Cato Institute, Washington, DC (p. 249)
*Donald J. Senese, 60 Plus Association, Arlington, VA (p. 257)
*Pete Sepp, National Taxpayers Union, Alexandria, VA (p. 257)
*Lou Sheldon, Traditional Values Coalition, Washington, DC (p. 258)
*Curt Smith, Indiana Family Institute, Indianapolis, IN (p. 263)
*Steven S. Smith, Weidenbaum Center, St. Louis, MO (p. 264)
*David Strom, Taxpayers League of Minnesota, Plymouth, MN (p. 270)
 Stephen Thayer, American Conservative Union, Alexandria, VA (p. 276)
 Miro M. Todorovich, Scientists and Engineers for Secure Energy, New York, NY (p. 280)
*Robert D. Tollison, University of Mississippi, University, MS (p. 280)
 Phillip N. Truluck, The Heritage Foundation, Washington, DC (p. 281)
*Robert F. Turner, University of Virginia School of Law, Charlottesville, VA (p. 282)
 Dane vonBreichenruchardt, U. S. Bill of Rights Foundation, Washington, DC (p. 286)
*T. Rogers Wade, Georgia Public Policy Foundation, Atlanta, GA (p. 286)

* Has testified before a state or federal legislative committee

CONGRESS (Continued)

*Malcolm Wallop, Frontiers of Freedom Institute, Fairfax, VA **(p. 288)**
 Tom Washburne, Home School Legal Defense Association, Purcellville, VA **(p. 289)**
*Lori L. Waters, Eagle Forum, Washington, DC **(p. 289)**
 Stanley J. Watson, Patrick Henry College, Purcellville, VA **(p. 290)**
 Ben J. Wattenberg, American Enterprise Institute, Washington, DC **(p. 290)**
*Paul Weyrich, Free Congress Foundation, Washington, DC **(p. 293)**
 Walter E. Williams, George Mason University, Fairfax, VA **(p. 295)**
*John C. Willke, Life Issues Institute, Inc., Cincinnati, OH **(p. 295)**
 James W. Witt, University of West Florida, Pensacola, FL **(p. 296)**
 John Yoo, University of California, Berkeley, Berkeley, CA **(p. 300)**
 James V. Young, Lee's Summit, MO **(p. 300)**

ELECTIONS/POLLING

 Damon Ansell, Americans for Tax Reform, Washington, DC **(p. 39)**
*M. Miller Baker, McDermott, Will & Emery, Washington, DC **(p. 44)**
 Patrick Basham, Cato Institute, Washington, DC **(p. 47)**
*Gary L. Bauer, Campaign for Working Families, Arlington, VA **(p. 47)**
*Judith A. Best, State University of New York, Cortland, Cortland, NY **(p. 52)**
 John F. Bibby, University of Wisconsin, Milwaukee, Milwaukee, WI **(p. 53)**
 Amy E. Black, Wheaton College, Wheaton, IL **(p. 54)**
 Morton Blackwell, Leadership Institute, Arlington, VA **(p. 54)**
*Mark A. Bloomfield, American Council for Capital Formation, Washington, DC **(p. 55)**
 Jeffrey R. Boeyink, Iowans for Tax Relief, Muscatine, IA **(p. 56)**
 Cecil E. Bohanon, Ball State University, Muncie, IN **(p. 56)**
 Karlyn Keene Bowman, American Enterprise Institute, Washington, DC **(p. 58)**
 Charles Brooks, The Strategy Group, Arlington, VA **(p. 62)**
 Matthew Brooks, Jewish Policy Center, Washington, DC **(p. 62)**
 Andrew E. Busch, University of Denver, Denver, CO **(p. 66)**
*Jerome F. Climer, The Congressional Institute, Alexandria, VA **(p. 76)**
 John Colyandro, Texas Conservative Coalition, Austin, TX **(p. 79)**
 William Constantine, Centre for New Black Leadership, Reston, VA **(p. 80)**
 Kellyanne Conway, the polling company/WomanTrend, Washington, DC **(p. 80)**
*Louis J. Cordia, Cordia Companies, Alexandria, VA **(p. 82)**
 Mickey Craig, Hillsdale College, Hillsdale, MI **(p. 85)**
*Charles H. Cunningham, National Rifle Association, Washington, DC **(p. 87)**
 Richard Derham, Washington Policy Center, Seattle, WA **(p. 93)**
 Mary Eberstadt, *Policy Review*, Washington, DC **(p. 103)**
*Mickey Edwards, Harvard University, Cambridge, MA **(p. 104)**
 M. Stanton Evans, Education and Research Institute, Washington, DC **(p. 108)**
*Robert Fike, Americans for Tax Reform, Washington, DC **(p. 111)**
 Elizabeth Fox-Genovese, Emory University, Atlanta, GA **(p. 115)**
 Richard B. Freeman, National Bureau of Economic Research, Cambridge, MA **(p. 116)**
 John H. Fund, *OpinionJournal.com*, New York, NY **(p. 119)**
 Gary L. Geipel, Hudson Institute, Indianapolis, IN **(p. 122)**
*Charlie Gerow, Quantum Communications, Harrisburg, PA **(p. 123)**
 John Green, University of Akron, Akron, OH **(p. 128)**
 Timothy J. Groseclose, Stanford University, Stanford, CA **(p. 129)**
 Robin Hanson, George Mason University, Fairfax, VA **(p. 134)**
 Scott Hogenson, *CNSNews.com*, Alexandria, VA **(p. 144)**
*John MacDonald Hood, John Locke Foundation, Raleigh, NC **(p. 145)**
 Niger Roy Innis, Congress of Racial Equality, New York, NY **(p. 151)**
 Amy Kauffman, Hudson Institute, Washington, DC **(p. 158)**
 Phil Kent, Southeastern Legal Foundation, Atlanta, GA **(p. 162)**
*Dimitri Kesari, Family Research Council, Washington, DC **(p. 162)**

ELECTIONS/POLLING (Continued)

*Charles R. Kesler, Henry Salvatori Center, Claremont, CA (p. 162)
*David B. Kopel, Independence Institute, Golden, CO (p. 167)
 William Kristol, *The Weekly Standard*, Washington, DC (p. 169)
 Melvin A. Kulbicki, York College of Pennsylvania, York, PA (p. 170)
*Mark R. Levin, Landmark Legal Foundation, Herndon, VA (p. 178)
 John R. Lott, Jr., American Enterprise Institute, Washington, DC (p. 183)
 Frank Luntz, Luntz Research Companies, Arlington, VA (p. 184)
*Rita P. Maguire, Arizona Center for Public Policy, Phoenix, AZ (p. 186)
*Vern I. McCarthy, Jr., Mid-America Institute, Oak Brook, IL (p. 193)
*Tom McClusky, National Taxpayers Union Foundation, Alexandria, VA (p. 193)
 Daniel McGroarty, White House Writer's Group, Chevy Chase, MD (p. 196)
*Annette Thompson Meeks, Center of the American Experiment, Minneapolis, MN (p. 198)
 Jeffrey D. Milyo, University of Chicago, Chicago, IL (p. 202)
*Cleta Deatherage Mitchell, Foley & Lardner, Washington, DC (p. 203)
 Phyllis Berry Myers, Centre for New Black Leadership, Washington, DC (p. 210)
*Ronald Nehring, Americans for Tax Reform, San Diego, CA (p. 212)
 George R. Neumann, University of Iowa, Iowa City, IA (p. 213)
 R. Marc Nuttle, Norman, OK (p. 216)
*Henry Olsen, III, Manhattan Institute for Policy Research, New York, NY (p. 219)
 Norman J. Ornstein, American Enterprise Institute, Washington, DC (p. 219)
*Darryl Paulson, University of South Florida, St. Petersburg, FL (p. 223)
*Ronald W. Pearson, Pearson & Pipkin, Inc., Washington, DC (p. 224)
 Sidney A. Pearson, Jr., Radford University, Radford, VA (p. 224)
 James Piereson, John M. Olin Foundation, Inc., New York, NY (p. 228)
 John J. Pitney, Jr., Claremont McKenna College, Claremont, CA (p. 229)
 Joseph D. Reid, Jr., George Mason University, Fairfax, VA (p. 238)
 Sandy Rios, Concerned Women for America, Washington, DC (p. 240)
*Allen H. Roth, New York State Advisory Council on Privatization, New York, NY (p. 244)
 John Samples, Cato Institute, Washington, DC (p. 249)
 William Schneider, American Enterprise Institute, Washington, DC (p. 254)
*Lou Sheldon, Traditional Values Coalition, Washington, DC (p. 258)
 Betsy Page Sigman, Georgetown University, Washington, DC (p. 259)
*Solveig Singleton, Competitive Enterprise Institute, Washington, DC (p. 261)
*Curt Smith, Indiana Family Institute, Indianapolis, IN (p. 263)
*Oran P. Smith, Palmetto Family Council, Columbia, SC (p. 264)
*Steven S. Smith, Weidenbaum Center, St. Louis, MO (p. 264)
 Ted J. Smith, III, Virginia Commonwealth University, Richmond, VA (p. 264)
*David Strom, Taxpayers League of Minnesota, Plymouth, MN (p. 270)
 Charles Stuart, University of California, Santa Barbara, Santa Barbara, CA (p. 271)
*Alexander Tabarrok, Mercatus Center at George Mason University, Arlington, VA (p. 273)
*Mark Thornton, Columbus State University, Columbus, GA (p. 278)
 Lawrence A. Uzzell, Keston Institute, Waxahachie, TX (p. 283)
*Dane Waters, Initiative and Referendum Institute, Leesburg, VA (p. 289)
*Lori L. Waters, Eagle Forum, Washington, DC (p. 289)
 Ben J. Wattenberg, American Enterprise Institute, Washington, DC (p. 290)
*Kenneth Weinstein, Hudson Institute, Washington, DC (p. 292)
*Paul Weyrich, Free Congress Foundation, Washington, DC (p. 293)
 Peter W. Wielhouwer, Regent University, Virginia Beach, VA (p. 294)
*John C. Willke, Life Issues Institute, Inc., Cincinnati, OH (p. 295)
 James W. Witt, University of West Florida, Pensacola, FL (p. 296)
 Jason Wright, Frontiers of Freedom Institute, Fairfax, VA (p. 299)
 James V. Young, Lee's Summit, MO (p. 300)
 David Zanotti, Ohio Roundtable, Strongsville, OH (p. 301)

---

* Has testified before a state or federal legislative committee

ELECTORAL REFORM/VOTING RIGHTS

*I. Dean Ahmad, Minaret of Freedom Institute, Bethesda, MD (p. 36)
*Lawrence Alexander, University of San Diego School of Law, San Diego, CA (p. 36)
*William Allen, Michigan State University, East Lansing, MI (p. 37)
*M. Miller Baker, McDermott, Will & Emery, Washington, DC (p. 44)
 Patrick Basham, Cato Institute, Washington, DC (p. 47)
*Charles H. Bell, Jr., Bell, McAndrews, Hiltachk & Davidian, Sacramento, CA (p. 49)
*Judith A. Best, State University of New York, Cortland, Cortland, NY (p. 52)
 William C. Binning, Youngstown State University, Youngstown, OH (p. 53)
 Morton Blackwell, Leadership Institute, Arlington, VA (p. 54)
 Greg Blankenship, Illinois Policy Institute, Springfield, IL (p. 54)
*Michael A. Carvin, Jones, Day, Reavis & Pogue, Washington, DC (p. 71)
*Michael A. Ciamarra, Alabama Policy Institute, Birmingham, AL (p. 74)
*Jerome F. Climer, The Congressional Institute, Alexandria, VA (p. 76)
 William Constantine, Centre for New Black Leadership, Reston, VA (p. 80)
*Charles J. Cooper, Cooper & Kirk, PLLC, Washington, DC (p. 81)
 Mickey Craig, Hillsdale College, Hillsdale, MI (p. 85)
*Robert Destro, Catholic University of America, Washington, DC (p. 94)
 John Jay Douglass, University of Houston Law Center, Houston, TX (p. 97)
*John C. Eastman, Chapman University School of Law, Orange, CA (p. 102)
 Glenn Ellmers, Claremont Institute, Claremont, CA (p. 106)
*Todd Gaziano, The Heritage Foundation, Washington, DC (p. 121)
*Charlie Gerow, Quantum Communications, Harrisburg, PA (p. 123)
 John Green, University of Akron, Akron, OH (p. 128)
 Amy Kauffman, Hudson Institute, Washington, DC (p. 158)
 Maurice Kelman, Wayne State University Law School, Troy, MI (p. 161)
 Phil Kent, Southeastern Legal Foundation, Atlanta, GA (p. 162)
 Deborah J. LaFetra, Pacific Legal Foundation, Sacramento, CA (p. 171)
*Mark R. Levin, Landmark Legal Foundation, Herndon, VA (p. 178)
 John R. Lott, Jr., American Enterprise Institute, Washington, DC (p. 183)
*Nelson Lund, George Mason University School of Law, Arlington, VA (p. 184)
 Mary P. Mahoney, United Seniors Association, Inc., Washington, DC (p. 187)
*Cleta Deatherage Mitchell, Foley & Lardner, Washington, DC (p. 203)
 Phyllis Berry Myers, Centre for New Black Leadership, Washington, DC (p. 210)
*Ronald Nehring, Americans for Tax Reform, San Diego, CA (p. 212)
*Darryl Paulson, University of South Florida, St. Petersburg, FL (p. 223)
 Anthony A. Peacock, Utah State University, Logan, UT (p. 224)
*Dennis Polhill, Independence Institute, Golden, CO (p. 230)
*Ronald D. Rotunda, George Mason University School of Law, Arlington, VA (p. 244)
*Richard O. Rowland, Grassroot Institute of Hawaii, Aiea, HI (p. 245)
*Mark E. Rush, Washington and Lee University, Lexington, VA (p. 247)
 John Samples, Cato Institute, Washington, DC (p. 249)
*Lou Sheldon, Traditional Values Coalition, Washington, DC (p. 258)
*James Skillen, Center for Public Justice, Annapolis, MD (p. 261)
*Steven S. Smith, Weidenbaum Center, St. Louis, MO (p. 264)
*David Strom, Taxpayers League of Minnesota, Plymouth, MN (p. 270)
*Alexander Tabarrok, Mercatus Center at George Mason University, Arlington, VA (p. 273)
 J. Mills Thornton, III, University of Michigan, Ann Arbor, MI (p. 278)
*Dane Waters, Initiative and Referendum Institute, Leesburg, VA (p. 289)
*Donald V. Weatherman, Erskine College, Due West, SC (p. 290)
*John C. Willke, Life Issues Institute, Inc., Cincinnati, OH (p. 295)

EXECUTIVE BRANCH/THE PRESIDENCY

*William Allen, Michigan State University, East Lansing, MI (p. 37)
*John S. Baker, Jr., Louisiana State University, Baton Rouge, LA (p. 43)

EXECUTIVE BRANCH/THE PRESIDENCY (Continued)

*M. Miller Baker, McDermott, Will & Emery, Washington, DC (p. 44)

*Claude E. Barfield, American Enterprise Institute, Washington, DC (p. 45)

*Gary L. Bauer, Campaign for Working Families, Arlington, VA (p. 47)

Paul Beckner, Citizens for a Sound Economy, Washington, DC (p. 48)

*Richard B. Belzer, Regulatory Checkbook, Washington, DC (p. 50)

*Judith A. Best, State University of New York, Cortland, Cortland, NY (p. 52)

John F. Bibby, University of Wisconsin, Milwaukee, Milwaukee, WI (p. 53)

Amy E. Black, Wheaton College, Wheaton, IL (p. 54)

Morton Blackwell, Leadership Institute, Arlington, VA (p. 54)

Michael J. Boskin, Hoover Institution, Stanford, CA (p. 57)

*Marshall J. Breger, Catholic University of America, Washington, DC (p. 60)

James M. Buchanan, Center for the Study of Public Choice, Fairfax, VA (p. 64)

Andrew E. Busch, University of Denver, Denver, CO (p. 66)

*Robert Carleson, American Civil Rights Union, Alexandria, VA (p. 70)

*Jerome F. Climer, The Congressional Institute, Alexandria, VA (p. 76)

*Charles J. Cooper, Cooper & Kirk, PLLC, Washington, DC (p. 81)

*Louis J. Cordia, Cordia Companies, Alexandria, VA (p. 82)

*Douglas Cox, Gibson, Dunn & Crutcher LLP, Washington, DC (p. 84)

*Janice Shaw Crouse, Concerned Women for America, Washington, DC (p. 87)

*Robert J. Cynkar, Cooper & Kirk, PLLC, Washington, DC (p. 87)

Werner J. Dannhauser, Michigan State University, East Lansing, MI (p. 88)

Damjan de Krnjevic-Miskovic, The National Interest, Washington, DC (p. 90)

*Carl DeMaio, Reason Foundation, Los Angeles, CA (p. 92)

*Donald J. Devine, Center for American Values, Shady Side, MD (p. 94)

Richard J. Dougherty, University of Dallas, Irving, TX (p. 97)

Peter J. Duignan, Hoover Institution, Stanford, CA (p. 99)

*Becky Norton Dunlop, The Heritage Foundation, Washington, DC (p. 100)

*John C. Eastman, Chapman University School of Law, Orange, CA (p. 102)

Mary Eberstadt, *Policy Review*, Washington, DC (p. 103)

Robert Eden, Hillsdale College, Hillsdale, MI (p. 103)

*Lee Edwards, The Heritage Foundation, Washington, DC (p. 104)

M. Stanton Evans, Education and Research Institute, Washington, DC (p. 108)

*Robert Fike, Americans for Tax Reform, Washington, DC (p. 111)

Elizabeth Fox-Genovese, Emory University, Atlanta, GA (p. 115)

Michael Franc, The Heritage Foundation, Washington, DC (p. 115)

*Todd Gaziano, The Heritage Foundation, Washington, DC (p. 121)

Jack Gourman, National Education Standards, Los Angeles, CA (p. 127)

Alexander J. Groth, University of California, Davis, Davis, CA (p. 130)

*Steven Hayward, American Enterprise Institute, Washington, DC (p. 138)

Gene Healy, Cato Institute, Washington, DC (p. 138)

*Robert Hunter, Mackinac Center for Public Policy, Midland, MI (p. 150)

Thomas Hyde, Pfeiffer University, Misenheimer, NC (p. 150)

Niger Roy Innis, Congress of Racial Equality, New York, NY (p. 151)

*Charles W. Jarvis, United Seniors Association, Fairfax, VA (p. 153)

Larry Klayman, Judicial Watch, Washington, DC (p. 165)

*Douglas W. Kmiec, The Catholic University of America, Washington, DC (p. 166)

Lisa M. Korsak, Mercatus Center at George Mason University, Arlington, VA (p. 167)

*Andrew Langer, National Federation of Independent Business, Washington, DC (p. 174)

*Edward J. Larson, University of Georgia School of Law, Athens, GA (p. 175)

Leonard A. Leo, The Federalist Society for Law and Public Policy Studies, Washington, DC (p. 178)

*Mark R. Levin, Landmark Legal Foundation, Herndon, VA (p. 178)

*Nelson Lund, George Mason University School of Law, Arlington, VA (p. 184)

David E. Marion, Hampden-Sydney College, Hampden-Sydney, VA (p. 189)

EXECUTIVE BRANCH/THE PRESIDENCY (Continued)

*Ken Masugi, Claremont Institute, Claremont, CA (p. 191)

Paul Maurer, Trinity International University, Deerfield, IL (p. 192)

*David N. Mayer, Capital University Law School, Columbus, OH (p. 193)

*Tom McClusky, National Taxpayers Union Foundation, Alexandria, VA (p. 193)

*Forrest McDonald, University of Alabama, Coker, AL (p. 195)

John O. McGinnis, Cardozo School of Law, New York, NY (p. 196)

Daniel McGroarty, White House Writer's Group, Chevy Chase, MD (p. 196)

Lawrence J. McQuillan, Pacific Research Institute, San Francisco, CA (p. 197)

*Edwin Meese III, The Heritage Foundation, Washington, DC (p. 198)

Stephen J. Moore, Club for Growth, Washington, DC (p. 206)

*Joseph A. Morris, Lincoln Legal Foundation, Chicago, IL (p. 207)

Charles Murray, American Enterprise Institute, Washington, DC (p. 209)

Ronald Nash, Reformed Theological Seminary, Oviedo, FL (p. 211)

David Charles Nice, Washington State University, Pullman, WA (p. 213)

David C. Nott, Reason Foundation, Los Angeles, CA (p. 215)

R. Marc Nuttle, Norman, OK (p. 216)

Kate O'Beirne, *National Review*, Washington, DC (p. 216)

Sidney A. Pearson, Jr., Radford University, Radford, VA (p. 224)

Paul C. Peterson, Coastal Carolina University, Conway, SC (p. 227)

*William H. Peterson, Washington, DC (p. 227)

*Howard Phillips, The Conservative Caucus, Inc., Vienna, VA (p. 227)

John J. Pitney, Jr., Claremont McKenna College, Claremont, CA (p. 229)

Barry W. Poulson, University of Colorado, Boulder, CO (p. 232)

*Stephen Presser, Northwestern University School of Law, Chicago, IL (p. 233)

*Don Racheter, Public Interest Institute, Mount Pleasant, IA (p. 235)

*Amy Ridenour, National Center for Public Policy Research, Washington, DC (p. 240)

*David B. Rivkin, Jr., Baker & Hostetler, Washington, DC (p. 241)

James C. Roberts, American Studies Center, Washington, DC (p. 242)

*Ronald D. Rotunda, George Mason University School of Law, Arlington, VA (p. 244)

John Samples, Cato Institute, Washington, DC (p. 249)

David L. Schaefer, Holy Cross College, Worcester, MA (p. 252)

Gary Schmitt, Project for the New American Century, Washington, DC (p. 253)

William Schneider, American Enterprise Institute, Washington, DC (p. 254)

Jeffrey Leigh Sedgwick, University of Massachusetts, Amherst, MA (p. 255)

*Donald J. Senese, 60 Plus Association, Arlington, VA (p. 257)

*Lou Sheldon, Traditional Values Coalition, Washington, DC (p. 258)

*Matthew Spalding, The Heritage Foundation, Washington, DC (p. 266)

*Paul Schott Stevens, Dechert, Price & Rhoads, Washington, DC (p. 269)

James Swanson, Cato Institute, Washington, DC (p. 272)

*Virginia L. Thomas, The Heritage Foundation, Washington, DC (p. 277)

Miro M. Todorovich, Scientists and Engineers for Secure Energy, New York, NY (p. 280)

*Robert D. Tollison, University of Mississippi, University, MS (p. 280)

*Robert F. Turner, University of Virginia School of Law, Charlottesville, VA (p. 282)

Michael M. Uhlmann, Claremont Graduate University, Claremont, CA (p. 283)

*Maris A. Vinovskis, University of Michigan, Ann Arbor, MI (p. 285)

Dane vonBreichenruchardt, U. S. Bill of Rights Foundation, Washington, DC (p. 286)

*Malcolm Wallop, Frontiers of Freedom Institute, Fairfax, VA (p. 288)

Tom Washburne, Home School Legal Defense Association, Purcellville, VA (p. 289)

Stanley J. Watson, Patrick Henry College, Purcellville, VA (p. 290)

Ben J. Wattenberg, American Enterprise Institute, Washington, DC (p. 290)

*Murray Weidenbaum, Weidenbaum Center, St. Louis, MO (p. 291)

*Paul Weyrich, Free Congress Foundation, Washington, DC (p. 293)

*Edwin D. Williamson, Sullivan & Cromwell, Washington, DC (p. 295)

James Q. Wilson, Pepperdine University, Malibu, CA (p. 296)

EXECUTIVE BRANCH/THE PRESIDENCY (Continued)

John Yoo, University of California, Berkeley, Berkeley, CA (p. 300)
James V. Young, Lee's Summit, MO (p. 300)

FEDERAL CIVIL SERVICE

*Bruce K. Chapman, Discovery Institute, Seattle, WA (p. 72)
*Jerome F. Climer, The Congressional Institute, Alexandria, VA (p. 76)
*Carl DeMaio, Reason Foundation, Los Angeles, CA (p. 92)
*David Denholm, Public Service Research Foundation, Vienna, VA (p. 92)
*Donald J. Devine, Center for American Values, Shady Side, MD (p. 94)
*Becky Norton Dunlop, The Heritage Foundation, Washington, DC (p. 100)
*William Eggers, Deloitte Research-Public Sector, Washington, DC (p. 104)
*Robert Fike, Americans for Tax Reform, Washington, DC (p. 111)
 Jerzy Hauptmann, Park University, Kansas City, MO (p. 137)
 Constance Horner, Brookings Institution, Washington, DC (p. 146)
 Lisa M. Korsak, Mercatus Center at George Mason University, Arlington, VA (p. 167)
*Patrick Korten, The Becket Fund for Religious Liberty, Washington, DC (p. 167)
*Mark R. Levin, Landmark Legal Foundation, Herndon, VA (p. 178)
 Olivia M. McDonald, Regent University, Virginia Beach, VA (p. 195)
*Maurice McTigue, Mercatus Center at George Mason University, Arlington, VA (p. 197)
*Robert Moffit, The Heritage Foundation, Washington, DC (p. 204)
*Adrian T. Moore, Reason Foundation, Los Angeles, CA (p. 205)
*Joseph A. Morris, Lincoln Legal Foundation, Chicago, IL (p. 207)
*James Morrison, Morrison Associates, Scottsdale, AZ (p. 207)
 Charles Murray, American Enterprise Institute, Washington, DC (p. 209)
 George Nesterczuk, Nesterczuk and Associates, Vienna, VA (p. 212)
 David C. Nott, Reason Foundation, Los Angeles, CA (p. 215)
*William S. Peirce, Case Western Reserve University, Cleveland, OH (p. 224)
 Joseph D. Reid, Jr., George Mason University, Fairfax, VA (p. 238)
 David L. Schaefer, Holy Cross College, Worcester, MA (p. 252)
*Terry W. Van Allen, Kemah, TX (p. 283)
 James Q. Wilson, Pepperdine University, Malibu, CA (p. 296)

FEDERALISM

*Jonathan H. Adler, Case Western Reserve University, Cleveland, OH (p. 35)
*Lawrence Alexander, University of San Diego School of Law, San Diego, CA (p. 36)
*William Allen, Michigan State University, East Lansing, MI (p. 37)
*Dominic A. Aquila, Ave Maria University, Ypsilanti, MI (p. 40)
*Thomas C. Atwood, National Council For Adoption, Alexandria, VA (p. 41)
 Stephen M. Bainbridge, University of California at Los Angeles, Los Angeles, CA (p. 43)
*John S. Baker, Jr., Louisiana State University, Baton Rouge, LA (p. 43)
*Keith G. Baker, Florida TaxWatch Research Institute, Inc., Tallahassee, FL (p. 43)
 Joseph Baldacchino, National Humanities Institute, Bowie, MD (p. 44)
*Sandor Balogh, Hudson Valley Community College, East Greenbush, NY (p. 45)
*Claude E. Barfield, American Enterprise Institute, Washington, DC (p. 45)
*Randy Barnett, Boston University School of Law, Boston, MA (p. 46)
*Herman Belz, University of Maryland, College Park, MD (p. 50)
*Robert K. Best, Pacific Legal Foundation, Sacramento, CA (p. 52)
 John F. Bibby, University of Wisconsin, Milwaukee, Milwaukee, WI (p. 53)
 William C. Binning, Youngstown State University, Youngstown, OH (p. 53)
 Peter J. Boettke, James M. Buchanan Center for Political Economy, Fairfax, VA (p. 56)
 James E. Bond, Seattle University, Seattle, WA (p. 56)
*Robert H. Bork, American Enterprise Institute, Washington, DC (p. 57)
 Jennifer C. Braceras, Independent Women's Forum, Arlington, VA (p. 59)
*Marshall J. Breger, Catholic University of America, Washington, DC (p. 60)

FEDERALISM (Continued)

James M. Buchanan, Center for the Study of Public Choice, Fairfax, VA (p. 64)

Francis H. Buckley, George Mason University School of Law, Arlington, VA (p. 64)

*Scott Bullock, Institute for Justice, Washington, DC (p. 65)

*Henry N. Butler, Chapman University, Orange, CA (p. 66)

*Stuart Butler, The Heritage Foundation, Washington, DC (p. 66)

Steven Calabresi, Northwestern University School of Law, Chicago, IL (p. 67)

*F. Patricia Callahan, American Association of Small Property Owners, Washington, DC (p. 68)

*Robert Carleson, American Civil Rights Union, Alexandria, VA (p. 70)

*Anthony T. Caso, Pacific Legal Foundation, Sacramento, CA (p. 72)

*Bruce K. Chapman, Discovery Institute, Seattle, WA (p. 72)

John F. Cogan, Hoover Institution, Stanford, CA (p. 77)

*John E. Coons, University of California at Berkeley, Berkeley, CA (p. 81)

*Charles J. Cooper, Cooper & Kirk, PLLC, Washington, DC (p. 81)

*Louis J. Cordia, Cordia Companies, Alexandria, VA (p. 82)

*Douglas Cox, Gibson, Dunn & Crutcher LLP, Washington, DC (p. 84)

*Wendell Cox, Wendell Cox Consultancy, Belleville, IL (p. 84)

Edward H. Crane, Cato Institute, Washington, DC (p. 85)

Neil S. Crispo, Florida State University, Tallahassee, FL (p. 86)

*Robert J. Cynkar, Cooper & Kirk, PLLC, Washington, DC (p. 87)

*Marshall L. De Rosa, Florida Atlantic University, Davie, FL (p. 90)

*Carl DeMaio, Reason Foundation, Los Angeles, CA (p. 92)

*Robert Destro, Catholic University of America, Washington, DC (p. 94)

*Donald J. Devine, Center for American Values, Shady Side, MD (p. 94)

*Thomas J. DiLorenzo, Loyola College, Clarksville, MD (p. 96)

*Susan E. Dudley, Mercatus Center at George Mason University, Arlington, VA (p. 99)

*Becky Norton Dunlop, The Heritage Foundation, Washington, DC (p. 100)

Thomas R. Dye, Florida State University, Tallahassee, FL (p. 101)

*Paula Easley, Resource Development Council for Alaska, Anchorage, AK (p. 102)

*John C. Eastman, Chapman University School of Law, Orange, CA (p. 102)

*William Eggers, Deloitte Research-Public Sector, Washington, DC (p. 104)

*Michael P. Farris, Patrick Henry College, Purcellville, VA (p. 109)

Robert Feidler, International Legal Projects Institute, Grand Forks, ND (p. 110)

*Robert Fike, Americans for Tax Reform, Washington, DC (p. 111)

Thomas Fleming, Rockford Institute, Rockford, IL (p. 113)

*Michael Flynn, American Legislative Exchange Council, Washington, DC (p. 113)

*David Forte, Cleveland State University, Cleveland, OH (p. 114)

Elizabeth Fox-Genovese, Emory University, Atlanta, GA (p. 115)

*Walton Francis, Fairfax, VA (p. 115)

*Matthew J. Franck, Radford University, Radford, VA (p. 115)

*Todd Gaziano, The Heritage Foundation, Washington, DC (p. 121)

Mary Ann Glendon, Harvard Law School, Cambridge, MA (p. 124)

*Stephen Goldsmith, Manhattan Institute for Policy Research, New York, NY (p. 126)

*Lino A. Graglia, University of Texas, Austin, TX (p. 128)

*Michael S. Greve, American Enterprise Institute, Washington, DC (p. 129)

*Robert Hahn, American Enterprise Institute, Washington, DC (p. 132)

*Randy H. Hamilton, University of California, Berkeley, Berkeley, CA (p. 133)

Eric Hanushek, Hoover Institution, Stanford, CA (p. 135)

*C. Lowell Harriss, Columbia University, Bronxville, NY (p. 136)

Jerzy Hauptmann, Park University, Kansas City, MO (p. 137)

Robert Hawkins, Jr., Institute for Contemporary Studies, Oakland, CA (p. 137)

Gene Healy, Cato Institute, Washington, DC (p. 138)

Jay F. Hein, Hudson Institute, Indianapolis, IN (p. 139)

Robert A. Heineman, Alfred University, Alfred, NY (p. 139)

Paul Henze, Washington, VA (p. 140)

FEDERALISM (Continued)

*Roberta Herzberg, Utah State University, Logan, UT (p. 141)
*Thomas Hinton, The Heritage Foundation, Washington, DC (p. 143)
 Candice Hoke, Cleveland State University, Cleveland, OH (p. 144)
*Kenneth M. Holland, University of Memphis, Memphis, TN (p. 144)
*John MacDonald Hood, John Locke Foundation, Raleigh, NC (p. 145)
*Michael Horowitz, Hudson Institute, Washington, DC (p. 146)
*Caroline M. Hoxby, Harvard University, Cambridge, MA (p. 147)
*James Huffman, Lewis and Clark Law School, Portland, OR (p. 148)
*Thomas L. Jipping, Concerned Women for America, Washington, DC (p. 154)
*Paul Kamenar, Washington Legal Foundation, Washington, DC (p. 157)
 Phil Kent, Southeastern Legal Foundation, Atlanta, GA (p. 162)
 Matthew Kibbe, Citizens for a Sound Economy, Washington, DC (p. 163)
*John Kincaid, Lafayette College, Easton, PA (p. 163)
 Kent King, Missouri State Teachers Association, Columbia, MO (p. 164)
 Jeane J. Kirkpatrick, American Enterprise Institute, Washington, DC (p. 164)
*Douglas W. Kmiec, The Catholic University of America, Washington, DC (p. 166)
*David B. Kopel, Independence Institute, Golden, CO (p. 167)
 Montgomery N. Kosma, Jones, Day, Reavis & Pogue, Washington, DC (p. 167)
 Byron S. Lamm, State Policy Network, Fort Wayne, IN (p. 173)
*George Landrith, Frontiers of Freedom Institute, Fairfax, VA (p. 173)
*Andrew Langer, National Federation of Independent Business, Washington, DC (p. 174)
*Kent Lassman, Progress & Freedom Foundation, Raleigh, NC (p. 175)
 Leonard A. Leo, The Federalist Society for Law and Public Policy Studies,
    Washington, DC (p. 178)
 Curt A. Levey, Center for Individual Rights, Washington, DC (p. 178)
 Martin A. Levin, Brandeis University, Waltham, MA (p. 178)
*Robert A. Levy, Cato Institute, Washington, DC (p. 179)
*George Liebmann, Calvert Institute for Policy Research, Baltimore, MD (p. 180)
*Nelson Lund, George Mason University School of Law, Arlington, VA (p. 184)
*Johnathon R. Macey, Cornell University, Ithaca, NY (p. 185)
*Rita P. Maguire, Arizona Center for Public Policy, Phoenix, AZ (p. 186)
 J. J. Mahoney, Diversified Consultants, Mount Pleasant, SC (p. 187)
 Mario Mandina, National Lawyers Association, Independence, MO (p. 188)
 David E. Marion, Hampden-Sydney College, Hampden-Sydney, VA (p. 189)
*Jeff Marks, National Association of Manufacturers, Washington, DC (p. 189)
 Michael Marlow, California Polytechnic State University, San Luis Obispo, CA (p. 189)
*Nancie G. Marzulla, Defenders of Property Rights, Washington, DC (p. 191)
*Roger J. Marzulla, Defenders of Property Rights, Washington, DC (p. 191)
*Randolph J. May, Progress & Freedom Foundation, Washington, DC (p. 193)
*David N. Mayer, Capital University Law School, Columbus, OH (p. 193)
*John McClaughry, Ethan Allen Institute, Concord, VT (p. 193)
*Michael W. McConnell, University of Utah, Salt Lake City, UT (p. 194)
*Forrest McDonald, University of Alabama, Coker, AL (p. 195)
 Olivia M. McDonald, Regent University, Virginia Beach, VA (p. 195)
 John O. McGinnis, Cardozo School of Law, New York, NY (p. 196)
 Edward T. McMullen, Jr., South Carolina Policy Council, Columbia, SC (p. 197)
 Lawrence J. McQuillan, Pacific Research Institute, San Francisco, CA (p. 197)
*Edwin Meese III, The Heritage Foundation, Washington, DC (p. 198)
*Roger E. Meiners, University of Texas, Arlington, Arlington, TX (p. 198)
*William H. Mellor, Institute for Justice, Washington, DC (p. 199)
*Cleta Deatherage Mitchell, Foley & Lardner, Washington, DC (p. 203)
*Adrian T. Moore, Reason Foundation, Los Angeles, CA (p. 205)
*Len Munsil, Center for Arizona Policy, Scottsdale, AZ (p. 209)
 Thomas Nechyba, Duke University, Durham, NC (p. 211)

FEDERALISM (Continued)

Clark Neily, Institute for Justice, Washington, DC (p. 212)

Michael A. Nelson, University of Akron, Akron, OH (p. 212)

David Charles Nice, Washington State University, Pullman, WA (p. 213)

*William A. Niskanen, Cato Institute, Washington, DC (p. 214)

David C. Nott, Reason Foundation, Los Angeles, CA (p. 215)

*William O'Keefe, George C. Marshall Institute, Washington, DC (p. 216)

*Richard Olivastro, People Dynamics, Farmington, CT (p. 218)

Tom G. Palmer, Cato Institute, Washington, DC (p. 221)

*Duane Parde, American Legislative Exchange Council, Washington, DC (p. 221)

Anthony A. Peacock, Utah State University, Logan, UT (p. 224)

*William S. Peirce, Case Western Reserve University, Cleveland, OH (p. 224)

Terence J. Pell, Center for Individual Rights, Washington, DC (p. 224)

*William Perry Pendley, Mountain States Legal Foundation, Lakewood, CO (p. 225)

*Roger Pilon, Cato Institute, Washington, DC (p. 228)

*Stephen Presser, Northwestern University School of Law, Chicago, IL (p. 233)

George Priest, Yale Law School, New Haven, CT (p. 233)

*Don Racheter, Public Interest Institute, Mount Pleasant, IA (p. 235)

William D. Richardson, University of South Dakota, Vermillion, SD (p. 239)

*Brian Riedl, The Heritage Foundation, Washington, DC (p. 240)

*Robin Rivett, Pacific Legal Foundation, Sacramento, CA (p. 241)

*David B. Rivkin, Jr., Baker & Hostetler, Washington, DC (p. 241)

Hilton Root, Economy Strategy Institute, Washington, DC (p. 243)

*Ralph A. Rossum, Claremont McKenna College, Claremont, CA (p. 244)

*Ronald D. Rotunda, George Mason University School of Law, Arlington, VA (p. 244)

John Samples, Cato Institute, Washington, DC (p. 249)

Robert A. Schadler, Center for First Principles, Washington, DC (p. 251)

*Kent Scheidegger, Criminal Justice Legal Foundation, Sacramento, CA (p. 252)

Jeffrey Leigh Sedgwick, University of Massachusetts, Amherst, MA (p. 255)

*Donald J. Senese, 60 Plus Association, Arlington, VA (p. 257)

Kannon K. Shanmugam, Kirkland & Ellis, Washington, DC (p. 258)

*Solveig Singleton, Competitive Enterprise Institute, Washington, DC (p. 261)

*James A. Stever, University of Cincinnati, Hamilton, OH (p. 269)

*David Strom, Taxpayers League of Minnesota, Plymouth, MN (p. 270)

Charles Stuart, University of California, Santa Barbara, Santa Barbara, CA (p. 271)

*William Craig Stubblebine, Claremont McKenna College, Claremont, CA (p. 271)

*John Taylor, Virginia Institute for Public Policy, Potomac Falls, VA (p. 274)

*Adam D. Thierer, Cato Institute, Washington, DC (p. 276)

J. Mills Thornton, III, University of Michigan, Ann Arbor, MI (p. 278)

*Gordon Tullock, George Mason University School of Law, Arlington, VA (p. 281)

John Tuskey, Regent University, Virginia Beach, VA (p. 282)

*Terry W. Van Allen, Kemah, TX (p. 283)

*Balint Vazsonyi, Center for the American Founding, McLean, VA (p. 284)

Dane vonBreichenruchardt, U. S. Bill of Rights Foundation, Washington, DC (p. 286)

*Richard E. Wagner, George Mason University, Fairfax, VA (p. 286)

*Malcolm Wallop, Frontiers of Freedom Institute, Fairfax, VA (p. 288)

Stanley J. Watson, Patrick Henry College, Purcellville, VA (p. 290)

*Murray Weidenbaum, Weidenbaum Center, St. Louis, MO (p. 291)

Clyde N. Wilson, University of South Carolina, Columbia, SC (p. 296)

John Yoo, University of California, Berkeley, Berkeley, CA (p. 300)

James V. Young, Lee's Summit, MO (p. 300)

Ronald A. Zumbrun, The Zumbrun Law Firm, Sacramento, CA (p. 303)

INITIATIVE AND REFERENDUM

Karen Bailey, Americans for Tax Reform, Washington, DC (p. 42)

INITIATIVE AND REFERENDUM (Continued)

*Randy Barnett, Boston University School of Law, Boston, MA (p. 46)

*Charles H. Bell, Jr., Bell, McAndrews, Hiltachk & Davidian, Sacramento, CA (p. 49)

William C. Binning, Youngstown State University, Youngstown, OH (p. 53)

*Dominic M. Calabro, Florida TaxWatch Research Institute, Inc., Tallahassee, FL (p. 67)

*F. Patricia Callahan, American Association of Small Property Owners, Washington, DC (p. 68)

*John Carlson, Washington Policy Center, Seattle, WA (p. 70)

*Anthony T. Caso, Pacific Legal Foundation, Sacramento, CA (p. 72)

*Ward Connerly, American Civil Rights Institute, Sacramento, CA (p. 80)

*John E. Coons, University of California at Berkeley, Berkeley, CA (p. 81)

*Charles H. Cunningham, National Rifle Association, Washington, DC (p. 87)

Richard Derham, Washington Policy Center, Seattle, WA (p. 93)

Martin Duggan, Educational Freedom Foundation, St. Louis, MO (p. 99)

*Edward J. Erler, California State University, San Bernardino, San Bernardino, CA (p. 107)

John Findley, Pacific Legal Foundation, Sacramento, CA (p. 111)

William A. Fischel, Dartmouth College, Hanover, NH (p. 112)

John H. Fund, *OpinionJournal.com*, New York, NY (p. 119)

*Charlie Gerow, Quantum Communications, Harrisburg, PA (p. 123)

*Gary Glenn, American Family Association of Michigan, Midland, MI (p. 124)

*Lino A. Graglia, University of Texas, Austin, TX (p. 128)

*Paul Guppy, Washington Policy Center, Seattle, WA (p. 131)

Robin Hanson, George Mason University, Fairfax, VA (p. 134)

*Fred Holden, Phoenix Enterprises, Arvada, CO (p. 144)

*John MacDonald Hood, John Locke Foundation, Raleigh, NC (p. 145)

*Paul Jacob, Citizens in Charge and Citizens in Charge Foundation, Woodbridge, VA (p. 153)

*Doug Kagan, Nebraska Taxpayers for Freedom, Omaha, NE (p. 157)

*David Keating, National Taxpayers Union, Alexandria, VA (p. 159)

Maurice Kelman, Wayne State University Law School, Troy, MI (p. 161)

*Manuel Klausner, Individual Rights Foundation, Los Angeles, CA (p. 165)

Deborah J. LaFetra, Pacific Legal Foundation, Sacramento, CA (p. 171)

Edward J. Lopez, University of North Texas, Denton, TX (p. 183)

Frank Luntz, Luntz Research Companies, Arlington, VA (p. 184)

*Rita P. Maguire, Arizona Center for Public Policy, Phoenix, AZ (p. 186)

Mary P. Mahoney, United Seniors Association, Inc., Washington, DC (p. 187)

*John McClaughry, Ethan Allen Institute, Concord, VT (p. 193)

*Cleta Deatherage Mitchell, Foley & Lardner, Washington, DC (p. 203)

Robert G. Natelson, Missoula, MT (p. 211)

*Darryl Paulson, University of South Florida, St. Petersburg, FL (p. 223)

*Dennis Polhill, Independence Institute, Golden, CO (p. 230)

*Don Racheter, Public Interest Institute, Mount Pleasant, IA (p. 235)

*Stacie Rumenap, U. S. Term Limits, Washington, DC (p. 247)

*John Semmens, Laissez-Faire Institute, Chandler, AZ (p. 256)

*Pete Sepp, National Taxpayers Union, Alexandria, VA (p. 257)

*Lou Sheldon, Traditional Values Coalition, Washington, DC (p. 258)

Oscar Stilley, Arkansans for School Choice, Fort Smith, AR (p. 269)

*William Craig Stubblebine, Claremont McKenna College, Claremont, CA (p. 271)

*Lewis Uhler, National Tax Limitation Committee, Roseville, CA (p. 283)

*Dane Waters, Initiative and Referendum Institute, Leesburg, VA (p. 289)

*Bob Williams, Evergreen Freedom Foundation, Olympia, WA (p. 295)

*John C. Willke, Life Issues Institute, Inc., Cincinnati, OH (p. 295)

James W. Witt, University of West Florida, Pensacola, FL (p. 296)

*Thomas Wood, Americans Against Discrimination and Preferences, Berkley, CA (p. 298)

James V. Young, Lee's Summit, MO (p. 300)

David Zanotti, Ohio Roundtable, Strongsville, OH (p. 301)

---

* Has testified before a state or federal legislative committee

JUDICIARY

*William Allen, Michigan State University, East Lansing, MI (p. 37)
 Brian C. Anderson, Manhattan Institute for Policy Research, New York, NY (p. 38)
 Hadley Arkes, Amherst College, Amherst, MA (p. 40)
*John S. Baker, Jr., Louisiana State University, Baton Rouge, LA (p. 43)
*M. Miller Baker, McDermott, Will & Emery, Washington, DC (p. 44)
*Randy Barnett, Boston University School of Law, Boston, MA (p. 46)
 Paul Beckner, Citizens for a Sound Economy, Washington, DC (p. 48)
*Mark A. Behrens, Shook, Hardy & Bacon, L.L.P., Washington, DC (p. 49)
*Herman Belz, University of Maryland, College Park, MD (p. 50)
 Walter Berns, American Enterprise Institute, Washington, DC (p. 51)
*Lillian BeVier, University of Virginia, Charlottesville, VA (p. 53)
 James E. Bond, Seattle University, Seattle, WA (p. 56)
*James Bopp, Jr., James Madison Center for Free Speech, Washington, DC (p. 57)
*Robert H. Bork, American Enterprise Institute, Washington, DC (p. 57)
 Jennifer C. Braceras, Independent Women's Forum, Arlington, VA (p. 59)
*Marshall J. Breger, Catholic University of America, Washington, DC (p. 60)
*Lester Brickman, Cardozo School of Law, New York, NY (p. 61)
 Brian P. Brooks, O'Melveny & Myers LLP, Washington, DC (p. 62)
 Steven Calabresi, Northwestern University School of Law, Chicago, IL (p. 67)
*F. Patricia Callahan, American Association of Small Property Owners, Washington, DC (p. 68)
*Ronald Cass, Boston University School of Law, Boston, MA (p. 72)
*Robert L. Clinton, Southern Illinois University, Carbondale, IL (p. 76)
 Douglas H. Cook, Regent University, Virginia Beach, VA (p. 80)
*Charles J. Cooper, Cooper & Kirk, PLLC, Washington, DC (p. 81)
*Douglas Cox, Gibson, Dunn & Crutcher LLP, Washington, DC (p. 84)
 Dennis Coyle, Catholic University of America, Washington, DC (p. 84)
*Roger C. Cramton, Cornell Law School, Ithaca, NY (p. 85)
*Matt Daniels, Alliance for Marriage, Springfield, VA (p. 88)
*Marshall L. De Rosa, Florida Atlantic University, Davie, FL (p. 90)
 Michael E. DeBow, Samford University, Birmingham, AL (p. 91)
 Richard Derham, Washington Policy Center, Seattle, WA (p. 93)
*Robert Destro, Catholic University of America, Washington, DC (p. 94)
 Richard J. Dougherty, University of Dallas, Irving, TX (p. 97)
*John C. Eastman, Chapman University School of Law, Orange, CA (p. 102)
*Mickey Edwards, Harvard University, Cambridge, MA (p. 104)
 Paul Edwards, Mercatus Center at George Mason University, Arlington, VA (p. 104)
 M. Stanton Evans, Education and Research Institute, Washington, DC (p. 108)
*Michael P. Farris, Patrick Henry College, Purcellville, VA (p. 109)
 Robert Feidler, International Legal Projects Institute, Grand Forks, ND (p. 110)
*Robert Fike, Americans for Tax Reform, Washington, DC (p. 111)
 John Findley, Pacific Legal Foundation, Sacramento, CA (p. 111)
*David Forte, Cleveland State University, Cleveland, OH (p. 114)
*Matthew J. Franck, Radford University, Radford, VA (p. 115)
*Todd Gaziano, The Heritage Foundation, Washington, DC (p. 121)
*Robert P. George, Princeton University, Princeton, NJ (p. 122)
*Lino A. Graglia, University of Texas, Austin, TX (p. 128)
*Robert Hale, Northwest Legal Foundation, Minot, ND (p. 132)
 John C. Harrison, University of Virginia, Charlottesville, VA (p. 136)
*James M. Henderson, Sr., American Center for Law and Justice, Washington, DC (p. 140)
*Kenneth M. Holland, University of Memphis, Memphis, TN (p. 144)
*James Huffman, Lewis and Clark Law School, Portland, OR (p. 148)
*Thomas L. Jipping, Concerned Women for America, Washington, DC (p. 154)
*Paul Kamenar, Washington Legal Foundation, Washington, DC (p. 157)
 Maurice Kelman, Wayne State University Law School, Troy, MI (p. 161)

JUDICIARY (Continued)

Phil Kent, Southeastern Legal Foundation, Atlanta, GA **(p. 162)**

*Douglas W. Kmiec, The Catholic University of America, Washington, DC **(p. 166)**

*David B. Kopel, Independence Institute, Golden, CO **(p. 167)**

William Kristol, *The Weekly Standard,* Washington, DC **(p. 169)**

*Raymond J. LaJeunesse, Jr., National Right to Work Legal Defense Foundation, Springfield, VA **(p. 172)**

Glenn G. Lammi, Washington Legal Foundation, Washington, DC **(p. 173)**

*Andrew Langer, National Federation of Independent Business, Washington, DC **(p. 174)**

*Edward J. Larson, University of Georgia School of Law, Athens, GA **(p. 175)**

Leonard A. Leo, The Federalist Society for Law and Public Policy Studies, Washington, DC **(p. 178)**

Curt A. Levey, Center for Individual Rights, Washington, DC **(p. 178)**

*Mark R. Levin, Landmark Legal Foundation, Herndon, VA **(p. 178)**

Jordan Lorence, Alliance Defense Fund, Scottsdale, AZ **(p. 183)**

*Johnathon R. Macey, Cornell University, Ithaca, NY **(p. 185)**

Mary P. Mahoney, United Seniors Association, Inc., Washington, DC **(p. 187)**

Mario Mandina, National Lawyers Association, Independence, MO **(p. 188)**

David E. Marion, Hampden-Sydney College, Hampden-Sydney, VA **(p. 189)**

*Roger J. Marzulla, Defenders of Property Rights, Washington, DC **(p. 191)**

*Ken Masugi, Claremont Institute, Claremont, CA **(p. 191)**

*David N. Mayer, Capital University Law School, Columbus, OH **(p. 193)**

John O. McGinnis, Cardozo School of Law, New York, NY **(p. 196)**

Lawrence J. McQuillan, Pacific Research Institute, San Francisco, CA **(p. 197)**

*Edwin Meese III, The Heritage Foundation, Washington, DC **(p. 198)**

*Cleta Deatherage Mitchell, Foley & Lardner, Washington, DC **(p. 203)**

Mark E. Mitchell, Thomas University, Thomasville, GA **(p. 203)**

Clark Neily, Institute for Justice, Washington, DC **(p. 212)**

*Richard John Neuhaus, Institute on Religion and Public Life, New York, NY **(p. 213)**

John Nowacki, Free Congress Foundation, Washington, DC **(p. 215)**

*Michael O'Neill, George Mason University School of Law, Arlington, VA **(p. 217)**

Mike O'Neill, Landmark Legal Foundation, Herndon, VA **(p. 217)**

*Walter K. Olson, Manhattan Institute for Policy Research, Chappaqua, NY **(p. 219)**

*J. A. Parker, Lincoln Institute for Research and Education, Washington, DC **(p. 221)**

Anthony A. Peacock, Utah State University, Logan, UT **(p. 224)**

Laura Bennett Peterson, Washington, DC **(p. 226)**

Paul C. Peterson, Coastal Carolina University, Conway, SC **(p. 227)**

*Howard Phillips, The Conservative Caucus, Inc., Vienna, VA **(p. 227)**

James Piereson, John M. Olin Foundation, Inc., New York, NY **(p. 228)**

*Roger Pilon, Cato Institute, Washington, DC **(p. 228)**

*Daniel J. Popeo, Washington Legal Foundation, Washington, DC **(p. 231)**

*Stephen Presser, Northwestern University School of Law, Chicago, IL **(p. 233)**

George Priest, Yale Law School, New Haven, CT **(p. 233)**

*Mark S. Pulliam, Latham & Watkins, San Diego, CA **(p. 234)**

*Don Racheter, Public Interest Institute, Mount Pleasant, IA **(p. 235)**

*Paul Rosenzweig, The Heritage Foundation, Washington, DC **(p. 243)**

*Ralph A. Rossum, Claremont McKenna College, Claremont, CA **(p. 244)**

*Ronald D. Rotunda, George Mason University School of Law, Arlington, VA **(p. 244)**

*Alfred P. Rubin, Tufts University, Medford, MA **(p. 246)**

*Paul Rubin, Emory University, Atlanta, GA **(p. 246)**

David L. Schaefer, Holy Cross College, Worcester, MA **(p. 252)**

*Donald J. Senese, 60 Plus Association, Arlington, VA **(p. 257)**

*Kelly Shackelford, Free Market Foundation, Plano, TX **(p. 257)**

Kannon K. Shanmugam, Kirkland & Ellis, Washington, DC **(p. 258)**

Mark W. Smith, Kasowitz, Benson, Torres & Friedman, LLP, New York, NY **(p. 263)**

---

* Has testified before a state or federal legislative committee

JUDICIARY (Continued)

*James Stergios, Pioneer Institute for Public Policy Research, Boston, MA (p. 268)

*Richard Stith, Valpariso University School of Law, Valpariso, IN (p. 269)

James R. Stoner, Louisiana State University, Baton Rouge, LA (p. 270)

James Swanson, Cato Institute, Washington, DC (p. 272)

Miro M. Todorovich, Scientists and Engineers for Secure Energy, New York, NY (p. 280)

Michael M. Uhlmann, Claremont Graduate University, Claremont, CA (p. 283)

Dane vonBreichenruchardt, U. S. Bill of Rights Foundation, Washington, DC (p. 286)

*Malcolm Wallop, Frontiers of Freedom Institute, Fairfax, VA (p. 288)

Gerald Walpin, Katten Muchin Zavis Rosenman, New York, NY (p. 288)

Stephen J. Ware, Samford University, Birmingham, AL (p. 289)

*John W. Whitehead, The Rutherford Institute, Charlottesville, VA (p. 293)

Keith E. Whittington, Princeton University, Princeton, NJ (p. 294)

Bradford P. Wilson, National Association of Scholars, Princeton, NJ (p. 296)

*Christopher Wolfe, Marquette University, Milwaukee, WI (p. 297)

John Yoo, University of California, Berkeley, Berkeley, CA (p. 300)

James V. Young, Lee's Summit, MO (p. 300)

*Michael K. Young, George Washington University Law School, Washington, DC (p. 300)

Ronald A. Zumbrun, The Zumbrun Law Firm, Sacramento, CA (p. 303)

NON-GOVERNMENTAL ORGANIZATIONS

*Jonathan H. Adler, Case Western Reserve University, Cleveland, OH (p. 35)

Ford A. Anderson, State Policy Network, Dallas, TX (p. 38)

Morton Blackwell, Leadership Institute, Arlington, VA (p. 54)

*James Bopp, Jr., James Madison Center for Free Speech, Washington, DC (p. 57)

James M. Buchanan, Center for the Study of Public Choice, Fairfax, VA (p. 64)

Gregory Conko, Competitive Enterprise Institute, Washington, DC (p. 79)

Buffy DeBreaux-Watts, American Board for Certification of Teacher Excellence, Washington, DC (p. 91)

*Robert Destro, Catholic University of America, Washington, DC (p. 94)

*Myron Ebell, Competitive Enterprise Institute, Washington, DC (p. 103)

*Evelyn Ebzery, Memorial Hospital of Sheridan County, Sheridan, WY (p. 103)

*Gloria Taylor Fisher, Interstate Commission on the Potomac River Basin, Alexandria, VA (p. 112)

*John Fonte, Hudson Institute, Washington, DC (p. 114)

*Jeffrey B. Gayner, Americans for Sovereignty, Washington, DC (p. 121)

Thomas Golab, Competitive Enterprise Institute, Washington, DC (p. 125)

*Robert Huberty, Capital Research Center, Washington, DC (p. 148)

*Carol W. LaGrasse, Property Rights Foundation of America, Inc., Stony Creek, NY (p. 172)

*Andrew Langer, National Federation of Independent Business, Washington, DC (p. 174)

*Mark R. Levin, Landmark Legal Foundation, Herndon, VA (p. 178)

Mary P. Mahoney, United Seniors Association, Inc., Washington, DC (p. 187)

*Dennis Mansfield, Boise, ID (p. 189)

Olivia M. McDonald, Regent University, Virginia Beach, VA (p. 195)

*Cleta Deatherage Mitchell, Foley & Lardner, Washington, DC (p. 203)

*Joseph A. Morris, Lincoln Legal Foundation, Chicago, IL (p. 207)

*Fred O. Oladeinde, The Foundation for Democracy in Africa, Washington, DC (p. 218)

*J. A. Parker, Lincoln Institute for Research and Education, Washington, DC (p. 221)

Patrick Reilly, Cardinal Newman Society, Falls Church, VA (p. 238)

Robert E. Russell, Jr., The Heritage Foundation, Geneva, IL (p. 247)

*Terrence M. Scanlon, Capital Research Center, Washington, DC (p. 251)

Jeff Stier, American Council on Science and Health, New York, NY (p. 269)

*David Swindell, Clemson University, Clemson, SC (p. 273)

Miro M. Todorovich, Scientists and Engineers for Secure Energy, New York, NY (p. 280)

Phillip N. Truluck, The Heritage Foundation, Washington, DC (p. 281)

NON-GOVERNMENTAL ORGANIZATIONS (Continued)

Bridgett G. Wagner, The Heritage Foundation, Washington, DC **(p. 286)**

*John C. Willke,** Life Issues Institute, Inc., Cincinnati, OH **(p. 295)**

*Robert L. Woodson, Sr.,** National Center for Neighborhood Enterprise, Washington, DC **(p. 298)**

*Michael K. Young,** George Washington University Law School, Washington, DC **(p. 300)**

STATE AND LOCAL GOVERNMENT

*I. Dean Ahmad,** Minaret of Freedom Institute, Bethesda, MD **(p. 36)**

*M. Gene Aldridge,** New Mexico Independence Research Institute, Las Cruces, NM **(p. 36)**

*William Allen,** Michigan State University, East Lansing, MI **(p. 37)**

Eloise Anderson, Claremont Institute, Sacramento, CA **(p. 38)**

*Frank H. Armstrong,** University of Vermont, Burlington, VT **(p. 40)**

Karen Bailey, Americans for Tax Reform, Washington, DC **(p. 42)**

*Keith G. Baker,** Florida TaxWatch Research Institute, Inc., Tallahassee, FL **(p. 43)**

*John E. Berthoud,** National Taxpayers Union, Alexandria, VA **(p. 52)**

William C. Binning, Youngstown State University, Youngstown, OH **(p. 53)**

*Wayman R. Bishop,** The Family Foundation of Virginia, Richmond, VA **(p. 53)**

Jeffrey R. Boeyink, Iowans for Tax Relief, Muscatine, IA **(p. 56)**

B. Jason Brooks, Empire Foundation for Policy Research, Clifton Park, NY **(p. 62)**

*Bill Brooks,** North Carolina Family Policy Council, Raleigh, NC **(p. 62)**

*Matthew J. Brouillette,** The Commonwealth Foundation, Harrisburg, PA **(p. 62)**

James M. Buchanan, Center for the Study of Public Choice, Fairfax, VA **(p. 64)**

*Dominic M. Calabro,** Florida TaxWatch Research Institute, Inc., Tallahassee, FL **(p. 67)**

*F. Patricia Callahan,** American Association of Small Property Owners, Washington, DC **(p. 68)**

*Robert Carleson,** American Civil Rights Union, Alexandria, VA **(p. 70)**

Don Carrington, John Locke Foundation, Raleigh, NC **(p. 71)**

*Anthony T. Caso,** Pacific Legal Foundation, Sacramento, CA **(p. 72)**

*Michael A. Ciamarra,** Alabama Policy Institute, Birmingham, AL **(p. 74)**

*Jerome F. Climer,** The Congressional Institute, Alexandria, VA **(p. 76)**

*Laurence Cohen,** Yankee Institute for Public Policy Studies, Glastonbury, CT **(p. 78)**

John Colyandro, Texas Conservative Coalition, Austin, TX **(p. 79)**

*Louis J. Cordia,** Cordia Companies, Alexandria, VA **(p. 82)**

*Wendell Cox,** Wendell Cox Consultancy, Belleville, IL **(p. 84)**

Neil S. Crispo, Florida State University, Tallahassee, FL **(p. 86)**

*Charles H. Cunningham,** National Rifle Association, Washington, DC **(p. 87)**

*Robert J. Cynkar,** Cooper & Kirk, PLLC, Washington, DC **(p. 87)**

Buffy DeBreaux-Watts, American Board for Certification of Teacher Excellence, Washington, DC **(p. 91)**

*Carl DeMaio,** Reason Foundation, Los Angeles, CA **(p. 92)**

*David Denholm,** Public Service Research Foundation, Vienna, VA **(p. 92)**

*Len Deo,** New Jersey Family Policy Council, Parsippany, NJ **(p. 93)**

John Jay Douglass, University of Houston Law Center, Houston, TX **(p. 97)**

*Becky Norton Dunlop,** The Heritage Foundation, Washington, DC **(p. 100)**

Thomas R. Dye, Florida State University, Tallahassee, FL **(p. 101)**

*John C. Eastman,** Chapman University School of Law, Orange, CA **(p. 102)**

*Evelyn Ebzery,** Memorial Hospital of Sheridan County, Sheridan, WY **(p. 103)**

*William Eggers,** Deloitte Research-Public Sector, Washington, DC **(p. 104)**

*Robert Fike,** Americans for Tax Reform, Washington, DC **(p. 111)**

William A. Fischel, Dartmouth College, Hanover, NH **(p. 112)**

*Gloria Taylor Fisher,** Interstate Commission on the Potomac River Basin, Alexandria, VA **(p. 112)**

*Michael Flynn,** American Legislative Exchange Council, Washington, DC **(p. 113)**

*Robert Franciosi,** Goldwater Institute, Phoenix, AZ **(p. 115)**

*Dana Joel Gattuso,** Competitive Enterprise Institute, Alexandria, VA **(p. 121)**

---

* Has testified before a state or federal legislative committee

STATE AND LOCAL GOVERNMENT (Continued)

Gary L. Geipel, Hudson Institute, Indianapolis, IN (p. 122)

Leonard Gilroy, Reason Foundation, Los Angeles, CA (p. 123)

*Gary Glenn, American Family Association of Michigan, Midland, MI (p. 124)

*Stephen Goldsmith, Manhattan Institute for Policy Research, New York, NY (p. 126)

*Michael S. Greve, American Enterprise Institute, Washington, DC (p. 129)

*Erick Gustafson, Citizens for a Sound Economy, Washington, DC (p. 131)

*Robert Hahn, American Enterprise Institute, Washington, DC (p. 132)

*Randy H. Hamilton, University of California, Berkeley, Berkeley, CA (p. 133)

Eric Hanushek, Hoover Institution, Stanford, CA (p. 135)

Jerzy Hauptmann, Park University, Kansas City, MO (p. 137)

Robert Hawkins, Jr., Institute for Contemporary Studies, Oakland, CA (p. 137)

Michael S. Heath, Christian Civic League of Maine, Augusta, ME (p. 138)

Robert A. Heineman, Alfred University, Alfred, NY (p. 139)

Jonathan Hill, North Carolina Citizens for a Sound Economy, Raleigh, NC (p. 142)

James E. Hinish, Jr., Regent University, Williamsburg, VA (p. 143)

*Thomas Hinton, The Heritage Foundation, Washington, DC (p. 143)

*Fred Holden, Phoenix Enterprises, Arvada, CO (p. 144)

*John MacDonald Hood, John Locke Foundation, Raleigh, NC (p. 145)

*Caroline M. Hoxby, Harvard University, Cambridge, MA (p. 147)

Howard Husock, Manhattan Institute for Policy Research, New York, NY (p. 150)

*Dimitri Kesari, Family Research Council, Washington, DC (p. 162)

*John Kincaid, Lafayette College, Easton, PA (p. 163)

Kent King, Missouri State Teachers Association, Columbia, MO (p. 164)

*David W. Kirkpatrick, Citizens for Educational Freedom, Douglassville, PA (p. 164)

*Douglas W. Kmiec, The Catholic University of America, Washington, DC (p. 166)

Lisa M. Korsak, Mercatus Center at George Mason University, Arlington, VA (p. 167)

Montgomery N. Kosma, Jones, Day, Reavis & Pogue, Washington, DC (p. 167)

Melvin A. Kulbicki, York College of Pennsylvania, York, PA (p. 170)

*Kent Lassman, Progress & Freedom Foundation, Raleigh, NC (p. 175)

Joseph G. Lehman, Mackinac Center for Public Policy, Midland, MI (p. 177)

*Myron Lieberman, Education Policy Institute, Washington, DC (p. 180)

*George Liebmann, Calvert Institute for Policy Research, Baltimore, MD (p. 180)

Margaret A. Little, Law Office of Margaret Little, Stratford, CT (p. 181)

Brett A. Magbee, Oklahoma Council of Public Affairs, Oklahoma City, OK (p. 186)

*Rita P. Maguire, Arizona Center for Public Policy, Phoenix, AZ (p. 186)

Mary P. Mahoney, United Seniors Association, Inc., Washington, DC (p. 187)

*Dennis Mansfield, Boise, ID (p. 189)

*Roger J. Marzulla, Defenders of Property Rights, Washington, DC (p. 191)

*Ken Masugi, Claremont Institute, Claremont, CA (p. 191)

*Vern I. McCarthy, Jr., Mid-America Institute, Oak Brook, IL (p. 193)

*John McClaughry, Ethan Allen Institute, Concord, VT (p. 193)

*Michael W. McConnell, University of Utah, Salt Lake City, UT (p. 194)

Edmunc J. McMahon, Manhattan Institute for Policy Innovation, New York, NY (p. 196)

Edward T. McMullen, Jr., South Carolina Policy Council, Columbia, SC (p. 197)

*Edwin Meese III, The Heritage Foundation, Washington, DC (p. 198)

Paul T. Mero, The Sutherland Institute, Salt Lake City, UT (p. 199)

Harry Messenheimer, Rio Grande Foundation, Tijeras, NM (p. 200)

*Adrian T. Moore, Reason Foundation, Los Angeles, CA (p. 205)

Suzanne C. Moore, Delaware Public Policy Institute, Wilmington, DE (p. 206)

*Joseph A. Morris, Lincoln Legal Foundation, Chicago, IL (p. 207)

Thomas Nechyba, Duke University, Durham, NC (p. 211)

*Ronald Nehring, Americans for Tax Reform, San Diego, CA (p. 212)

David Charles Nice, Washington State University, Pullman, WA (p. 213)

R. Marc Nuttle, Norman, OK (p. 216)

STATE AND LOCAL GOVERNMENT (Continued)

Timothy G. O'Rourke, University of Missouri, St. Louis, St. Louis, MO (p. 217)
*Richard Olivastro, People Dynamics, Farmington, CT (p. 218)
*Jim Panyard, Pennsylvania Manufacturer's Association, Harrisburg, PA (p. 221)
*Duane Parde, American Legislative Exchange Council, Washington, DC (p. 221)
*J. A. Parker, Lincoln Institute for Research and Education, Washington, DC (p. 221)
*Darryl Paulson, University of South Florida, St. Petersburg, FL (p. 223)
*Dennis Polhill, Independence Institute, Golden, CO (p. 230)
*Scott Pullins, Ohio Taxpayers Association and OTA Foundation, Columbus, OH (p. 234)
*Don Racheter, Public Interest Institute, Mount Pleasant, IA (p. 235)
 Joseph D. Reid, Jr., George Mason University, Fairfax, VA (p. 238)
 Jonathan Rose, Arizona State University, Tempe, AZ (p. 243)
*Ralph A. Rossum, Claremont McKenna College, Claremont, CA (p. 244)
*Richard O. Rowland, Grassroot Institute of Hawaii, Aiea, HI (p. 245)
*Stacie Rumenap, U. S. Term Limits, Washington, DC (p. 247)
 Kristie L. Rutherford, Family Research Council, Washington, DC (p. 247)
 Peter D. Salins, Manhattan Institute for Policy Research, New York, NY (p. 248)
 E. S. Savas, City University of New York, New York, NY (p. 250)
 Roberta Rubel Schaefer, Worcester Regional Research Bureau, Worcester, MA (p. 252)
 Jeffrey Leigh Sedgwick, University of Massachusetts, Amherst, MA (p. 255)
*Geoffrey F. Segal, Reason Public Policy Institute, Los Angeles, CA (p. 256)
*Pete Sepp, National Taxpayers Union, Alexandria, VA (p. 257)
 Frank A. Shepherd, Pacific Legal Foundation, Coral Gables, FL (p. 259)
*Samuel R. Staley, Buckeye Institute for Public Policy Solutions, Columbus, OH (p. 268)
*James Stergios, Pioneer Institute for Public Policy Research, Boston, MA (p. 268)
*James A. Stever, University of Cincinnati, Hamilton, OH (p. 269)
*David Strom, Taxpayers League of Minnesota, Plymouth, MN (p. 270)
*William Craig Stubblebine, Claremont McKenna College, Claremont, CA (p. 271)
 Michael Sullivan, Texas Public Policy Foundation, Austin, TX (p. 272)
*David Swindell, Clemson University, Clemson, SC (p. 273)
*John Taylor, Virginia Institute for Public Policy, Potomac Falls, VA (p. 274)
*Richard Teske, Strategic Advocacy, Arlington, VA (p. 275)
 Michael W. Thompson, Thomas Jefferson Institute for Public Policy, Springfield, VA (p. 278)
 J. Mills Thornton, III, University of Michigan, Ann Arbor, MI (p. 278)
*Mark Thornton, Columbus State University, Columbus, GA (p. 278)
*Peggy Venable, Texas Citizens for a Sound Economy, Austin, TX (p. 284)
*T. Rogers Wade, Georgia Public Policy Foundation, Atlanta, GA (p. 286)
*Malcolm Wallop, Frontiers of Freedom Institute, Fairfax, VA (p. 288)
 Tom Washburne, Home School Legal Defense Association, Purcellville, VA (p. 289)
 Stanley J. Watson, Patrick Henry College, Purcellville, VA (p. 290)
*Ron F. Williamson, Great Plains Public Policy Institute, Sioux Falls, SD (p. 295)
 James Q. Wilson, Pepperdine University, Malibu, CA (p. 296)
*Gary Wolfram, Hillsdale College, Hillsdale, MI (p. 297)
 Jason Wright, Frontiers of Freedom Institute, Fairfax, VA (p. 299)
 James V. Young, Lee's Summit, MO (p. 300)
 Ronald A. Zumbrun, The Zumbrun Law Firm, Sacramento, CA (p. 303)

TERM LIMITS

 Brian Backstrom, Empire Foundation for Policy Research, Clifton Park, NY (p. 42)
*Doug Bandow, Cato Institute, Washington, DC (p. 45)
*Randy Barnett, Boston University School of Law, Boston, MA (p. 46)
 Patrick Basham, Cato Institute, Washington, DC (p. 47)
*John E. Berthoud, National Taxpayers Union, Alexandria, VA (p. 52)
*Robert K. Best, Pacific Legal Foundation, Sacramento, CA (p. 52)
 James E. Bond, Seattle University, Seattle, WA (p. 56)

TERM LIMITS (Continued)

Edward H. Crane, Cato Institute, Washington, DC (p. 85)

*John C. Eastman, Chapman University School of Law, Orange, CA (p. 102)

*Mickey Edwards, Harvard University, Cambridge, MA (p. 104)

*Michael Flynn, American Legislative Exchange Council, Washington, DC (p. 113)

John H. Fund, *OpinionJournal.com*, New York, NY (p. 119)

*Gary Glenn, American Family Association of Michigan, Midland, MI (p. 124)

*John MacDonald Hood, John Locke Foundation, Raleigh, NC (p. 145)

Thomas Hyde, Pfeiffer University, Misenheimer, NC (p. 150)

*Paul Jacob, Citizens in Charge and Citizens in Charge Foundation, Woodbridge, VA (p. 153)

*Charles R. Kesler, Henry Salvatori Center, Claremont, CA (p. 162)

*Randall Kroszner, University of Chicago, Chicago, IL (p. 170)

Deborah J. LaFetra, Pacific Legal Foundation, Sacramento, CA (p. 171)

Herbert L. London, Hudson Institute, Indianapolis, IN (p. 182)

Edward J. Lopez, University of North Texas, Denton, TX (p. 183)

Brett A. Magbee, Oklahoma Council of Public Affairs, Oklahoma City, OK (p. 186)

*Rita P. Maguire, Arizona Center for Public Policy, Phoenix, AZ (p. 186)

Mary P. Mahoney, United Seniors Association, Inc., Washington, DC (p. 187)

*Dennis Mansfield, Boise, ID (p. 189)

*David N. Mayer, Capital University Law School, Columbus, OH (p. 193)

Jeffrey D. Milyo, University of Chicago, Chicago, IL (p. 202)

*Cleta Deatherage Mitchell, Foley & Lardner, Washington, DC (p. 203)

Suzanne C. Moore, Delaware Public Policy Institute, Wilmington, DE (p. 206)

*Ronald Nehring, Americans for Tax Reform, San Diego, CA (p. 212)

*Richard Olivastro, People Dynamics, Farmington, CT (p. 218)

*J. A. Parker, Lincoln Institute for Research and Education, Washington, DC (p. 221)

*Darryl Paulson, University of South Florida, St. Petersburg, FL (p. 223)

*Roger Pilon, Cato Institute, Washington, DC (p. 228)

*Dennis Polhill, Independence Institute, Golden, CO (p. 230)

*Scott Pullins, Ohio Taxpayers Association and OTA Foundation, Columbus, OH (p. 234)

*Don Racheter, Public Interest Institute, Mount Pleasant, IA (p. 235)

Paul A. Rahe, University of Tulsa, Tulsa, OK (p. 236)

*Ronald D. Rotunda, George Mason University School of Law, Arlington, VA (p. 244)

*Stacie Rumenap, U. S. Term Limits, Washington, DC (p. 247)

John Samples, Cato Institute, Washington, DC (p. 249)

*D. Eric Schansberg, Indiana University Southeast, New Albany, IN (p. 252)

Jeffrey Leigh Sedgwick, University of Massachusetts, Amherst, MA (p. 255)

*Pete Sepp, National Taxpayers Union, Alexandria, VA (p. 257)

*Steven S. Smith, Weidenbaum Center, St. Louis, MO (p. 264)

*David Strom, Taxpayers League of Minnesota, Plymouth, MN (p. 270)

*Robert D. Tollison, University of Mississippi, University, MS (p. 280)

*Lewis Uhler, National Tax Limitation Committee, Roseville, CA (p. 283)

*T. Rogers Wade, Georgia Public Policy Foundation, Atlanta, GA (p. 286)

James W. Witt, University of West Florida, Pensacola, FL (p. 296)

James V. Young, Lee's Summit, MO (p. 300)

David Zanotti, Ohio Roundtable, Strongsville, OH (p. 301)

Foreign Policy and International Relations

AFGHANISTAN

*Peter Brookes, The Heritage Foundation, Washington, DC (p. 61)
*John E. Carey, International Defense Consultants, Inc., Arlington, VA (p. 69)
*Ariel Cohen, The Heritage Foundation, Washington, DC (p. 77)
  Helle C. Dale, The Heritage Foundation, Washington, DC (p. 88)
*Arnaud de Borchgrave, Center for Strategic and International Studies, Washington, DC (p. 89)
  Dana Dillon, The Heritage Foundation, Washington, DC (p. 96)
  Peter J. Duignan, Hoover Institution, Stanford, CA (p. 99)
*Charles H. Fairbanks, Jr., The Paul H. Nitze School of Advanced International Studies, Washington, DC (p. 108)
*George Folsom, International Republican Institute, Washington, DC (p. 114)
*David Forte, Cleveland State University, Cleveland, OH (p. 114)
  Richard E. Friedman, National Strategy Forum, Chicago, IL (p. 118)
*Frank J. Gaffney, Jr., Center for Security Policy, Washington, DC (p. 119)
  Larry Hart, Hartco Strategies, Washington, DC (p. 136)
*Thomas H. Henriksen, Hoover Institution, Stanford, CA (p. 140)
  Paul Henze, Washington, VA (p. 140)
  Bruce Herschensohn, Pepperdine University School of Public Policy, Malibu, CA (p. 141)
*John Hillen, Foreign Policy Research Institute, Philadephia, PA (p. 142)
  John C. Hulsman, The Heritage Foundation, Washington, DC (p. 149)
  Jeane J. Kirkpatrick, American Enterprise Institute, Washington, DC (p. 164)
*Elie Krakowski, EDK Consulting, Baltimore, MD (p. 168)
*H. Joachim Maitre, Center for Defense Journalism, Boston, MA (p. 187)
  Hafeez Malik, Villanova University, Villanova, PA (p. 187)
*Yuri N. Maltsev, Carthage College, Kenosha, WI (p. 188)
  Theodore C. Mataxis, American Military University, Denver, CO (p. 191)
  Clifford D. May, The Foundation for the Defense of Democracies, Washington, DC (p. 192)
*F. Andy Messing, Jr., National Defense Council Foundation, Alexandria, VA (p. 200)
  Ronald Nash, Reformed Theological Seminary, Oviedo, FL (p. 211)
*James H. Noyes, Hoover Institution, Stanford, CA (p. 215)
  Edward J. Ohlert, JAYCOR, McLean, VA (p. 218)
*Martha Brill Olcott, Carnegie Endowment for International Peace, Washington, DC (p. 218)
*James Phillips, The Heritage Foundation, Washington, DC (p. 228)
  Danielle Pletka, American Enterprise Institute, Washington, DC (p. 229)
*Michael Radu, Foreign Policy Research Institute, Philadelphia, PA (p. 235)
  Paul A. Rahe, University of Tulsa, Tulsa, OK (p. 236)
*James S. Robbins, National Defense University, Washington, DC (p. 241)
*J. Milnor Roberts, High Frontier, Arlington, VA (p. 241)
*Edward L. Rowny, Washington, DC (p. 245)
  Al Santoli, American Foreign Policy Council, Washington, DC (p. 250)
  Radek Sikorski, American Enterprise Institute, Washington, DC (p. 260)
  Devinda R. Subasinghe, St. Petersburg, FL (p. 271)
*Michael K. Young, George Washington University Law School, Washington, DC (p. 300)

AFRICA

  James C. W. Ahiakpor, California State University, Hayward, Hayward, CA (p. 35)
  Anton Andereggen, Lewis and Clark College, Portland, OR (p. 37)
  Damon Ansell, Americans for Tax Reform, Washington, DC (p. 39)
*George Ayittey, American University, Washington, DC (p. 42)
  Roger Bate, International Policy Network, Washington, DC (p. 47)
  Arnold Beichman, Hoover Institution, Stanford, CA (p. 49)
  Morton Blackwell, Leadership Institute, Arlington, VA (p. 54)
  Deborah Burstion-Donbraye, American Multimedia Inc. of Nigeria, Cleveland, OH (p. 66)

AFRICA (Continued)

Jonathan Clarke, Cato Institute, Washington, DC (p. 75)
Peter J. Duignan, Hoover Institution, Stanford, CA (p. 99)
Khalid Duran, *TransIslam Magazine*, Bethesda, MD (p. 100)
Bruce L. Edwards, Jr., Bowling Green State University, Bowling Green, OH (p. 104)
*George Folsom, International Republican Institute, Washington, DC (p. 114)
George Friedman, Stratfor.com, Austin, TX (p. 117)
Gidon A. Gottlieb, University of Chicago Law School, Chicago, IL (p. 127)
Steve H. Hanke, Johns Hopkins University, Baltimore, MD (p. 134)
*Thomas H. Henriksen, Hoover Institution, Stanford, CA (p. 140)
Paul Henze, Washington, VA (p. 140)
Bruce Herschensohn, Pepperdine University School of Public Policy, Malibu, CA (p. 141)
Niger Roy Innis, Congress of Racial Equality, New York, NY (p. 151)
*Harvey M. Jacobs, University of Wisconsin, Madison, WI (p. 153)
Theodore "Sylvester" John, Students In Free Enterprise, Springfield, MO (p. 154)
*Michael Johns, Melville, NY (p. 154)
*Bruce Alan Johnson, Bruce Alan Johnson Associates, Indianapolis, IN (p. 155)
William H. Kaempfer, University of Colorado, Boulder, CO (p. 156)
Owen Kirby, International Republican Institute, Washington, DC (p. 164)
Jeffrey Krilla, International Republican Institute, Washington, DC (p. 169)
*Andrea S. Lafferty, Traditional Values Coalition, Washington, DC (p. 172)
*Deepak Lal, University of California at Los Angeles, Los Angeles, CA (p. 172)
Michael A. Ledeen, American Enterprise Institute, Washington, DC (p. 176)
*H. Joachim Maitre, Center for Defense Journalism, Boston, MA (p. 187)
*Robert Mandel, Lewis and Clark College, Portland, OR (p. 188)
Clifford D. May, The Foundation for the Defense of Democracies, Washington, DC (p. 192)
*Nina May, *Renaissance Connection.com/RCNetwork.net*, Washington, DC (p. 192)
*F. Andy Messing, Jr., National Defense Council Foundation, Alexandria, VA (p. 200)
*Steven Metz, U. S. Army War College Strategic Studies Institute, Carlisle Barracks, PA (p. 200)
Henry Myers, James Madison University, Harrisonburg, VA (p. 210)
Anthony I. Negbenebor, Gardner-Webb University, Boiling Springs, NC (p. 212)
*Fred O. Oladeinde, The Foundation for Democracy in Africa, Washington, DC (p. 218)
*J. A. Parker, Lincoln Institute for Research and Education, Washington, DC (p. 221)
*Ronald W. Pearson, Pearson & Pipkin, Inc., Washington, DC (p. 224)
*Howard Phillips, The Conservative Caucus, Inc., Vienna, VA (p. 227)
Barry W. Poulson, University of Colorado, Boulder, CO (p. 232)
*Michael Radu, Foreign Policy Research Institute, Philadelphia, PA (p. 235)
Harold Calvin Ray, National Center for Faith-Based Initiatives, West Palm Beach, FL (p. 237)
Hilton Root, Economy Strategy Institute, Washington, DC (p. 243)
*Frank Ruddy, Ruddy & Muir, Chevy Chase, MD (p. 246)
Brett D. Schaefer, The Heritage Foundation, Washington, DC (p. 252)
*Suzanne Scholte, Defense Forum Foundation, Falls Church, VA (p. 254)
*Nina Shea, Freedom House, Washington, DC (p. 258)
*Gregory Simpkins, The Foundation for Democracy in Africa, Washington, DC (p. 260)
*W. Shepherd Smith, Jr., Institute for Youth Development, Washington, DC (p. 264)
Charles P. Stetson, U. S. Fund for Leadership Training, Southport, CT (p. 268)
Devinda R. Subasinghe, St. Petersburg, FL (p. 271)
*Alan Rufus Waters, California State University, Fresno, Fresno, CA (p. 289)
Jerry Zandstra, Acton Institute for the Study of Religion and Liberty,
    Grand Rapids, MI (p. 301)

AMERICAN DIPLOMACY/FOREIGN POLICY

Ken L. Adelman, TechCentralStation, Washington, DC (p. 35)
*M. Gene Aldridge, New Mexico Independence Research Institute, Las Cruces, NM (p. 36)
Richard V. Allen, Washington, DC (p. 36)

AMERICAN DIPLOMACY/FOREIGN POLICY (Continued)

Andrew J. Bacevich, Boston University, Boston, MA (p. 42)

Carlos Ball, Agencia Interamericana de Prensa Economica, Boca Raton, FL (p. 44)

*Sandor Balogh, Hudson Valley Community College, East Greenbush, NY (p. 45)

*Doug Bandow, Cato Institute, Washington, DC (p. 45)

Dennis L. Bark, Hoover Institution, Stanford, CA (p. 45)

Arnold Beichman, Hoover Institution, Stanford, CA (p. 49)

*Mark Blitz, Claremont McKenna College, Claremont, CA (p. 55)

Philip Bom, Regent University, Redmond, WA (p. 56)

Paul J. Bonicelli, Patrick Henry College, Purcellville, VA (p. 57)

Thomas A. Breslint, Florida International University, Miami, FL (p. 61)

*Peter Brookes, The Heritage Foundation, Washington, DC (p. 61)

Gary Bullert, Columbia Basin College, Pasco, WA (p. 65)

Frank A. Burd, Baltimore Council on Foreign Affairs, Baltimore, MD (p. 65)

*John E. Carey, International Defense Consultants, Inc., Arlington, VA (p. 69)

Ted Galen Carpenter, Cato Institute, Washington, DC (p. 71)

Jonathan Clarke, Cato Institute, Washington, DC (p. 75)

*Joseph I. Coffey, Princeton, NJ (p. 77)

*Ariel Cohen, The Heritage Foundation, Washington, DC (p. 77)

Eric Cohen, Ethics and Public Policy Center, Washington, DC (p. 78)

*John F. Copper, Rhodes College, Memphis, TN (p. 82)

Melvin Croan, University of Wisconsin, Madison, WI (p. 86)

Helle C. Dale, The Heritage Foundation, Washington, DC (p. 88)

*Arnaud de Borchgrave, Center for Strategic and International Studies, Washington, DC (p. 89)

Damjan de Krnjevic-Miskovic, The National Interest, Washington, DC (p. 90)

*Midge Decter, New York, NY (p. 91)

*James S. Denton, Washington, DC (p. 93)

*Joseph DioGuardi, Albanian American Civic League, Ossining, NY (p. 96)

Thomas Donnelly, American Enterprise Institute, Washington, DC (p. 97)

Peter J. Duignan, Hoover Institution, Stanford, CA (p. 99)

Robert Dujarric, Hudson Institute, Washington, DC (p. 99)

Richard M. Ebeling, Hillsdale College, Hillsdale, MI (p. 102)

*Lee Edwards, The Heritage Foundation, Washington, DC (p. 104)

*Charles H. Fairbanks, Jr., The Paul H. Nitze School of Advanced International Studies, Washington, DC (p. 108)

*Harvey Feldman, The Heritage Foundation, Washington, DC (p. 110)

*Robert Fike, Americans for Tax Reform, Washington, DC (p. 111)

Thomas Fleming, Rockford Institute, Rockford, IL (p. 113)

*George Folsom, International Republican Institute, Washington, DC (p. 114)

*Barbara Hackman Franklin, Barbara Franklin Enterprises, Washington, DC (p. 116)

Richard E. Friedman, National Strategy Forum, Chicago, IL (p. 118)

*Frank J. Gaffney, Jr., Center for Security Policy, Washington, DC (p. 119)

*Jeffrey B. Gayner, Americans for Sovereignty, Washington, DC (p. 121)

Gary L. Geipel, Hudson Institute, Indianapolis, IN (p. 122)

Reuel Marc Gerecht, American Enterprise Institute, Washington, DC (p. 123)

Nikolas Gvosdev, *The National Interest*, Washington, DC (p. 131)

Roger Hamburg, Indiana University South Bend, South Bend, IN (p. 133)

Gina Marie Hatheway, The Heritage Foundation, Washington, DC (p. 137)

William Anthony Hay, Foreign Policy Research Institute, Philadelphia, PA (p. 138)

*Thomas H. Henriksen, Hoover Institution, Stanford, CA (p. 140)

Paul Henze, Washington, VA (p. 140)

Bruce Herschensohn, Pepperdine University School of Public Policy, Malibu, CA (p. 141)

*John Hillen, Foreign Policy Research Institute, Philadephia, PA (p. 142)

G. Philip Hughes, White House Writer's Group, Washington, DC (p. 149)

John C. Hulsman, The Heritage Foundation, Washington, DC (p. 149)

AMERICAN DIPLOMACY/FOREIGN POLICY (Continued)

Balbina Hwang, The Heritage Foundation, Washington, DC (p. 150)
*Fred C. Ikle, Center for Strategic and International Studies, Washington, DC (p. 151)
Niger Roy Innis, Congress of Racial Equality, New York, NY (p. 151)
*Michael Johns, Melville, NY (p. 154)
*Christopher Joyner, Georgetown University, Washington, DC (p. 156)
Francis X. Kane, Strategy, Technology and Space, Inc., San Antonio, TX (p. 157)
*Geoffrey Kemp, The Nixon Center, Washington, DC (p. 161)
Brian T. Kennedy, Claremont Institute, Claremont, CA (p. 161)
Jeane J. Kirkpatrick, American Enterprise Institute, Washington, DC (p. 164)
*Elie Krakowski, EDK Consulting, Baltimore, MD (p. 168)
William Kristol, *The Weekly Standard*, Washington, DC (p. 169)
*Lawrence Kudlow, Kudlow & Co., LLC, New York, NY (p. 170)
*George Landrith, Frontiers of Freedom Institute, Fairfax, VA (p. 173)
Michael A. Ledeen, American Enterprise Institute, Washington, DC (p. 176)
*Ernest W. Lefever, Chevy Chase, MD (p. 177)
*James Andrew Lewis, Center for Strategic and International Studies, Washington, DC (p. 179)
William S. Lind, Free Congress Foundation, Washington, DC (p. 180)
Alan Luxemberg, Foreign Policy Research Institute, Philadelphia, PA (p. 184)
Clifford D. May, The Foundation for the Defense of Democracies, Washington, DC (p. 192)
*Richard T. McCormack, Center for the Study of the Presidency, Washington, DC (p. 194)
Wendell H. McCulloch, Jr., California State University, Long Beach, Long Beach, CA (p. 194)
Dave McIntyre, ANSER Institute for Homeland Security, Arlington, VA (p. 196)
*Constantine C. Menges, Hudson Institute, Washington, DC (p. 199)
*F. Andy Messing, Jr., National Defense Council Foundation, Alexandria, VA (p. 200)
*Steven Metz, U. S. Army War College Strategic Studies Institute, Carlisle Barracks, PA (p. 200)
*Steven W. Mosher, Population Research Institute, Front Royal, VA (p. 208)
*Joshua Muravchik, American Enterprise Institute, Washington, DC (p. 209)
*Deroy Murdock, Atlas Economic Research Foundation, New York, NY (p. 209)
Henry R. Nau, George Washington University, Washington, DC (p. 211)
Tom Neumann, Jewish Institute for National Security Affairs, Washington, DC (p. 213)
William E. Odom, Hudson Institute, Washington, DC (p. 218)
Edward J. Ohlert, JAYCOR, McLean, VA (p. 218)
*Richard Olivastro, People Dynamics, Farmington, CT (p. 218)
*Mackubin T. Owens, U. S. Naval War College, Newport, RI (p. 220)
Rocco M. Paone, U. S. Naval Academy, Annapolis, MD (p. 221)
Charles M. Perry, Institute for Foreign Policy Analysis, Cambridge, MA (p. 226)
*Robert Pfaltzgraff, Jr., Institute for Foreign Policy Analysis, Cambridge, MA (p. 227)
*James Phillips, The Heritage Foundation, Washington, DC (p. 228)
Juliana Geran Pilon, American University, Washington, DC (p. 228)
*Richard Pipes, Cambridge, MA (p. 229)
Rorin Morse Platt, Campbell University, Buies Creek, NC (p. 229)
*Ernest Preeg, Manufacturers Alliance, Arlington, VA (p. 232)
*Jim Przystup, Institute for National Strategic Studies, Washington, DC (p. 234)
Arch Puddington, Freedom House, New York, NY (p. 234)
*Susan Kaufman Purcell, Americas Society/Council of the Americas, New York, NY (p. 234)
Paul A. Rahe, University of Tulsa, Tulsa, OK (p. 236)
*R. Sean Randolph, Bay Area Economic Forum, San Francisco, CA (p. 236)
*William Ratliff, Hoover Institution, Stanford, CA (p. 236)
*David B. Rivkin, Jr., Baker & Hostetler, Washington, DC (p. 241)
*James S. Robbins, National Defense University, Washington, DC (p. 241)
*Edward L. Rowny, Washington, DC (p. 245)
*Alfred P. Rubin, Tufts University, Medford, MA (p. 246)
*Frank Ruddy, Ruddy & Muir, Chevy Chase, MD (p. 246)
*William A. Rusher, Claremont Institute, San Francisco, CA (p. 247)

---

* Has testified before a state or federal legislative committee

AMERICAN DIPLOMACY/FOREIGN POLICY (Continued)

Claes G. Ryn, Catholic University of America, Washington, DC (p. 248)
Gregory W. Sand, Saint Louis College of Pharmacy, St. Louis, MO (p. 249)
Al Santoli, American Foreign Policy Council, Washington, DC (p. 250)
Paul J. Saunders, The Nixon Center, Washington, DC (p. 250)
Robert A. Scalapino, University of California, Berkeley, Berkeley, CA (p. 251)
Robert A. Schadler, Center for First Principles, Washington, DC (p. 251)
Robert Schuettinger, Washington International Studies Council, Washington, DC (p. 254)
*Donald J. Senese, 60 Plus Association, Arlington, VA (p. 257)
Harvey Sicherman, Foreign Policy Research Institute, Philadelphia, PA (p. 259)
*Dimitri Simes, The Nixon Center, Washington, DC (p. 260)
*John Sitilides, Western Policy Center, Washington, DC (p. 261)
*James Skillen, Center for Public Justice, Annapolis, MD (p. 261)
Shaun Small, Empower America, Washington, DC (p. 262)
*Paul Schott Stevens, Dechert, Price & Rhoads, Washington, DC (p. 269)
Devinda R. Subasinghe, St. Petersburg, FL (p. 271)
Gordon Sumner, Jr., Sumner Association, Santa Fe, NM (p. 272)
James R. "J.T." Taylor, Empower America, Washington, DC (p. 274)
*William J. Taylor, Jr., Taylor Associates, Inc., Bethesda, MD (p. 275)
*John J. Tierney, Jr., Institute of World Politics, Washington, DC (p. 279)
Miro M. Todorovich, Scientists and Engineers for Secure Energy, New York, NY (p. 280)
*Robert F. Turner, University of Virginia School of Law, Charlottesville, VA (p. 282)
Jon Basil Utley, Ludwig von Mises Institute, Washington, DC (p. 283)
*William R. Van Cleave, Southwest Missouri State University, Springfield, MO (p. 284)
Melara Zyla Vickers, Independent Women's Forum, Arlington, VA (p. 285)
M. Jon Vondracek, Center for Strategic and International Studies, Washington, DC (p. 286)
*T. Rogers Wade, Georgia Public Policy Foundation, Atlanta, GA (p. 286)
Arthur Waldron, American Enterprise Institute, Washington, DC (p. 287)
*Richard L. Walker, University of South Carolina, Columbia, SC (p. 287)
*Malcolm Wallop, Frontiers of Freedom Institute, Fairfax, VA (p. 288)
*W. Bruce Weinrod, International Technology and Trade Associates, Inc.,
    Washington, DC (p. 292)
*Edwin D. Williamson, Sullivan & Cromwell, Washington, DC (p. 295)
Anne A. Witkowsky, Center for Strategic and International Studies, Washington, DC (p. 296)
*Larry Wortzel, The Heritage Foundation, Washington, DC (p. 299)
*Michael K. Young, George Washington University Law School, Washington, DC (p. 300)

CANADA

Arnold Beichman, Hoover Institution, Stanford, CA (p. 49)
Philip Bom, Regent University, Redmond, WA (p. 56)
*Allen Buchanan, University of Arizona, Tucson, AZ (p. 64)
Francis H. Buckley, George Mason University School of Law, Arlington, VA (p. 64)
Damjan de Krnjevic-Miskovic, The National Interest, Washington, DC (p. 90)
Peter J. Duignan, Hoover Institution, Stanford, CA (p. 99)
Howard Fienberg, Statistical Assessment Service, Washington, DC (p. 111)
George Friedman, Stratfor.com, Austin, TX (p. 117)
*Frank J. Gaffney, Jr., Center for Security Policy, Washington, DC (p. 119)
*Steven Globerman, Western Washington University, Bellingham, WA (p. 125)
Steve H. Hanke, Johns Hopkins University, Baltimore, MD (p. 134)
William Anthony Hay, Foreign Policy Research Institute, Philadelphia, PA (p. 138)
Bruce Herschensohn, Pepperdine University School of Public Policy, Malibu, CA (p. 141)
*David B. Kopel, Independence Institute, Golden, CO (p. 167)
*Michael Krauss, George Mason University School of Law, Arlington, VA (p. 169)
Marie-Josee Kravis, Hudson Institute, Indianapolis, IN (p. 169)
*Robert Mandel, Lewis and Clark College, Portland, OR (p. 188)

CANADA (Continued)

Barry W. Poulson, University of Colorado, Boulder, CO (p. 232)
*Mark E. Rush, Washington and Lee University, Lexington, VA (p. 247)
*Mead Treadwell, Institute of the North, Anchorage, AK (p. 281)
Bradley C. S. Watson, Saint Vincent College, Latrobe, PA (p. 290)
*Kenneth Weinstein, Hudson Institute, Washington, DC (p. 292)
*Sidney Weintraub, Center for Strategic and International Studies, Washington, DC (p. 292)

CENTRAL AND EASTERN EUROPE

Jefferson Adams, Sarah Lawrence College, Bronxville, NY (p. 34)
*Sandor Balogh, Hudson Valley Community College, East Greenbush, NY (p. 45)
Morton Blackwell, Leadership Institute, Arlington, VA (p. 54)
*Stephen J. Blank, U. S. Army War College, Carlisle, PA (p. 54)
*Mark A. Bloomfield, American Council for Capital Formation, Washington, DC (p. 55)
Peter J. Boettke, James M. Buchanan Center for Political Economy, Fairfax, VA (p. 56)
*Andrzej Brzeski, University of California, Davis, CA (p. 64)
*David Burton, Argus Group, Alexandria, VA (p. 66)
*John E. Carey, International Defense Consultants, Inc., Arlington, VA (p. 69)
Ted Galen Carpenter, Cato Institute, Washington, DC (p. 71)
John Clark, Hudson Institute, Indianapolis, IN (p. 75)
Jonathan Clarke, Cato Institute, Washington, DC (p. 75)
*Ariel Cohen, The Heritage Foundation, Washington, DC (p. 77)
Lee Congdon, James Madison University, Harrisonburg, VA (p. 79)
Robert Conquest, Hoover Institution, Stanford, CA (p. 80)
Aurelian Craiutu, Indiana University, Bloomington, IN (p. 85)
Melvin Croan, University of Wisconsin, Madison, WI (p. 86)
Helle C. Dale, The Heritage Foundation, Washington, DC (p. 88)
Damjan de Krnjevic-Miskovic, The National Interest, Washington, DC (p. 90)
*Midge Decter, New York, NY (p. 91)
*James S. Denton, Washington, DC (p. 93)
*Joseph DioGuardi, Albanian American Civic League, Ossining, NY (p. 96)
*Joseph D. Douglass, Jr., The Redwood Institute, Falls Church, VA (p. 98)
Peter J. Duignan, Hoover Institution, Stanford, CA (p. 99)
Dennis J. Dunn, Southwest Texas State University, San Marcos, TX (p. 100)
Richard M. Ebeling, Hillsdale College, Hillsdale, MI (p. 102)
Ivan Eland, Cato Institute, Washington, DC (p. 105)
Mark Elliott, Samford University, Birmingham, AL (p. 106)
*Louis D. Enoff, Enoff Associates Limited, Sykesville, MD (p. 107)
*Harvey Feldman, The Heritage Foundation, Washington, DC (p. 110)
*Gloria Taylor Fisher, Interstate Commission on the Potomac River Basin, Alexandria, VA (p. 112)
Mary C. FitzGerald, Hudson Institute, Washington, DC (p. 112)
*George Folsom, International Republican Institute, Washington, DC (p. 114)
George Friedman, Stratfor.com, Austin, TX (p. 117)
Richard E. Friedman, National Strategy Forum, Chicago, IL (p. 118)
Janice J. Gabbert, Wright State University, Dayton, OH (p. 119)
Paul Glastris, Western Policy Center, Washington, DC (p. 124)
Samuel Gregg, Acton Institute for the Study of Religion and Liberty, Grand Rapids, MI (p. 129)
Alexander J. Groth, University of California, Davis, Davis, CA (p. 130)
Nikolas Gvosdev, *The National Interest*, Washington, DC (p. 131)
Steve H. Hanke, Johns Hopkins University, Baltimore, MD (p. 134)
Ronald L. Hatchett, University of St. Thomas, Houston, TX (p. 137)
Jerzy Hauptmann, Park University, Kansas City, MO (p. 137)
*Clark C. Havighurst, Duke University School of Law, Durham, NC (p. 137)
William Anthony Hay, Foreign Policy Research Institute, Philadelphia, PA (p. 138)

---

* Has testified before a state or federal legislative committee

CENTRAL AND EASTERN EUROPE (Continued)

Paul Henze, Washington, VA **(p. 140)**
Bruce Herschensohn, Pepperdine University School of Public Policy, Malibu, CA **(p. 141)**
*Robert L. Hershey, Robert L. Hershey, P.E., Washington, DC **(p. 141)**
John C. Hulsman, The Heritage Foundation, Washington, DC **(p. 149)**
D. Gale Johnson, University of Chicago, Chicago, IL **(p. 155)**
Adrian Karatnycky, Freedom House, New York, NY **(p. 158)**
Jeane J. Kirkpatrick, American Enterprise Institute, Washington, DC **(p. 164)**
Marie-Josee Kravis, Hudson Institute, Indianapolis, IN **(p. 169)**
*Andrew Langer, National Federation of Independent Business, Washington, DC **(p. 174)**
Michael A. Ledeen, American Enterprise Institute, Washington, DC **(p. 176)**
Leonard P. Liggio, Atlas Economic Research Foundation, Fairfax, VA **(p. 180)**
Lindsay Lloyd, International Republican Institute, Washington, DC **(p. 181)**
Rett R. Ludwikowski, Catholic University of America, Washington, DC **(p. 184)**
John M. Malek, Polish-American Foundation for Economic Research and Education, Torrance, CA **(p. 187)**
*Yuri N. Maltsev, Carthage College, Kenosha, WI **(p. 188)**
*Robert Mandel, Lewis and Clark College, Portland, OR **(p. 188)**
Eugene "Red" McDaniel, American Defense Institute, Alexandria, VA **(p. 194)**
*Robert W. McGee, Barry University, Miami Shores, FL **(p. 195)**
E. Wayne Merry, American Foreign Policy Council, Washington, DC **(p. 199)**
Paul E. Michelson, Huntington College, Huntington, IN **(p. 201)**
Andrew A. Michta, Rhodes College, Memphis, TN **(p. 201)**
Dennis D. Miller, Baldwin-Wallace College, Berea, OH **(p. 201)**
*John H. Moore, Grove City College, Grove City, PA **(p. 206)**
Erie J. Novotny, Fairfax Station, VA **(p. 215)**
William E. Odom, Hudson Institute, Washington, DC **(p. 218)**
Charles M. Perry, Institute for Foreign Policy Analysis, Cambridge, MA **(p. 226)**
*Robert Pfaltzgraff, Jr., Institute for Foreign Policy Analysis, Cambridge, MA **(p. 227)**
Juliana Geran Pilon, American University, Washington, DC **(p. 228)**
*Dennis Polhill, Independence Institute, Golden, CO **(p. 230)**
Barry W. Poulson, University of Colorado, Boulder, CO **(p. 232)**
*Michael Radu, Foreign Policy Research Institute, Philadelphia, PA **(p. 235)**
*William H. Reid, Horseshoe, TX **(p. 238)**
*James S. Robbins, National Defense University, Washington, DC **(p. 241)**
*Allen H. Roth, New York State Advisory Council on Privatization, New York, NY **(p. 244)**
*Edward L. Rowny, Washington, DC **(p. 245)**
Edward J. Rozek, University of Northern Colorado, Boulder, CO **(p. 245)**
Peter Rutland, Wesleyan University, Middletown, CT **(p. 248)**
Gary Schmitt, Project for the New American Century, Washington, DC **(p. 253)**
*Peter W. Schramm, John M. Ashbrook Center for Public Affairs, Ashland, OH **(p. 254)**
Radek Sikorski, American Enterprise Institute, Washington, DC **(p. 260)**
*Richard F. Staar, Hoover Institution, Stanford, CA **(p. 267)**
Devinda R. Subasinghe, St. Petersburg, FL **(p. 271)**
*John D. Sullivan, Center for International Private Enterprise, Washington, DC **(p. 271)**
Miklos N. Szilagyi, University of Arizona, Tucson, AZ **(p. 273)**
Ewa M. Thompson, Rice University, Houston, TX **(p. 277)**
Vladislav Todorov, University of Pennsylvania, Philadelphia, PA **(p. 279)**
Miro M. Todorovich, Scientists and Engineers for Secure Energy, New York, NY **(p. 280)**
Otto Ulc, Binghamton University, Binghamton, NY **(p. 283)**
*Balint Vazsonyi, Center for the American Founding, McLean, VA **(p. 284)**
Jude Wanniski, Polyconomics, Parsippany, NJ **(p. 288)**
*Alan Rufus Waters, California State University, Fresno, Fresno, CA **(p. 289)**

CHINA

*M. Gene Aldridge, New Mexico Independence Research Institute, Las Cruces, NM (p. 36)
*Claude E. Barfield, American Enterprise Institute, Washington, DC (p. 45)
*Gary L. Bauer, Campaign for Working Families, Arlington, VA (p. 47)
 Peter J. Boettke, James M. Buchanan Center for Political Economy, Fairfax, VA (p. 56)
*Donald R. Booth, Chapman University, Orange, CA (p. 57)
 Thomas A. Breslint, Florida International University, Miami, FL (p. 61)
*Peter Brookes, The Heritage Foundation, Washington, DC (p. 61)
 Daniel Claingaert, International Republican Institute, Washington, DC (p. 68)
 Kurt Campbell, Center for Strategic and International Studies, Washington, DC (p. 68)
*John E. Carey, International Defense Consultants, Inc., Arlington, VA (p. 69)
 Cecilia Chang, St. John's University, Jamaica, NY (p. 72)
*Hungdah Chiu, University of Maryland School of Law, Baltimore, MD (p. 74)
*John F. Copper, Rhodes College, Memphis, TN (p. 82)
*Ralph A. Cossa, Pacific Forum CSIS, Honolulu, HI (p. 83)
*Arnaud de Borchgrave, Center for Strategic and International Studies, Washington, DC (p. 89)
*James A. Dorn, Cato Institute, Washington, DC (p. 97)
*June Teufel Dreyer, University of Miami, Coral Gables, FL (p. 98)
*Thomas Duesterberg, Manufacturers Alliance, Arlington, VA (p. 99)
 Peter J. Duignan, Hoover Institution, Stanford, CA (p. 99)
*Mickey Edwards, Harvard University, Cambridge, MA (p. 104)
 Richard Daniel Ewing, The Nixon Center, Washington, DC (p. 108)
*Richard Fairbanks, Center for Strategic and International Studies, Washington, DC (p. 109)
*Harvey Feldman, The Heritage Foundation, Washington, DC (p. 110)
*Barbara Hackman Franklin, Barbara Franklin Enterprises, Washington, DC (p. 116)
*Frank J. Gaffney, Jr., Center for Security Policy, Washington, DC (p. 119)
*Jeffrey B. Gayner, Americans for Sovereignty, Washington, DC (p. 121)
 Phillip D. Grub, Eastern Washington University, Spokane, WA (p. 130)
 Steve H. Hanke, Johns Hopkins University, Baltimore, MD (p. 134)
 Paul Henze, Washington, VA (p. 140)
 Bruce Herschensohn, Pepperdine University School of Public Policy, Malibu, CA (p. 141)
 Charles Horner, Hudson Institute, Washington, DC (p. 146)
*Chalmers Johnson, Japan Policy Research Institute, Cardiff, CA (p. 155)
 D. Gale Johnson, University of Chicago, Chicago, IL (p. 155)
 Dale W. Jorgenson, Harvard University, Cambridge, MA (p. 156)
 Brian T. Kennedy, Claremont Institute, Claremont, CA (p. 161)
 Jeane J. Kirkpatrick, American Enterprise Institute, Washington, DC (p. 164)
*Andrea S. Lafferty, Traditional Values Coalition, Washington, DC (p. 172)
*Deepak Lal, University of California at Los Angeles, Los Angeles, CA (p. 172)
 David M. Lampton, The Nixon Center, Washington, DC (p. 173)
 Michael A. Ledeen, American Enterprise Institute, Washington, DC (p. 176)
*James Andrew Lewis, Center for Strategic and International Studies, Washington, DC (p. 179)
 James R. Lilley, American Enterprise Institute, Washington, DC (p. 180)
 Hsien-Tung Liu, Bloomsburg University, Bloomsburg, PA (p. 181)
 James Lucier, Prudential Securities, Arlington, VA (p. 184)
*Dennis Mansfield, Boise, ID (p. 189)
*Constantine C. Menges, Hudson Institute, Washington, DC (p. 199)
*F. Andy Messing, Jr., National Defense Council Foundation, Alexandria, VA (p. 200)
*Steven W. Mosher, Population Research Institute, Front Royal, VA (p. 208)
*Ross H. Munro, Center for Security Studies, Washington, DC (p. 209)
 Ramon H. Myers, Hoover Institution, Stanford, CA (p. 210)
 Jeremiah O'Keeffe, Plano, TX (p. 217)
 James P. O'Leary, Catholic University of America, Washington, DC (p. 217)
 Edward J. Ohlert, JAYCOR, McLean, VA (p. 218)
 Daniel Palm, Azusa Pacific University, Azusa, CA (p. 220)

---

* Has testified before a state or federal legislative committee

CHINA (Continued)

Rocco M. Paone, U. S. Naval Academy, Annapolis, MD (p. 221)
*Ronald W. Pearson, Pearson & Pipkin, Inc., Washington, DC (p. 224)
*Robert Pfaltzgraff, Jr., Institute for Foreign Policy Analysis, Cambridge, MA (p. 227)
*Howard Phillips, The Conservative Caucus, Inc., Vienna, VA (p. 227)
*Daryl Plunk, The Heritage Foundation, Washington, DC (p. 230)
*Jan S. Prybyla, Pennsylvania State University, Tucson, AZ (p. 234)
*Jim Przystup, Institute for National Strategic Studies, Washington, DC (p. 234)
Gary M. Quinlivan, Center for Economic and Policy Education, Latrobe, PA (p. 234)
*R. Sean Randolph, Bay Area Economic Forum, San Francisco, CA (p. 236)
*William Ratliff, Hoover Institution, Stanford, CA (p. 236)
Sandy Rios, Concerned Women for America, Washington, DC (p. 240)
Hilton Root, Economy Strategy Institute, Washington, DC (p. 243)
David C. Rose, University of Missouri, St. Louis, St. Louis, MO (p. 243)
*Edward L. Rowny, Washington, DC (p. 245)
*Alfred P. Rubin, Tufts University, Medford, MA (p. 246)
*William A. Rusher, Claremont Institute, San Francisco, CA (p. 247)
Claes G. Ryn, Catholic University of America, Washington, DC (p. 248)
Al Santoli, American Foreign Policy Council, Washington, DC (p. 250)
Robert A. Scalapino, University of California, Berkeley, Berkeley, CA (p. 251)
*Donald J. Senese, 60 Plus Association, Arlington, VA (p. 257)
*Nina Shea, Freedom House, Washington, DC (p. 258)
Harvey Sicherman, Foreign Policy Research Institute, Philadelphia, PA (p. 259)
Mary Jane Skanderup, Pacific Forum CSIS, Honolulu, HI (p. 261)
*Richard H. Solomon, United States Institute of Peace, Washington, DC (p. 265)
Devinda R. Subasinghe, St. Petersburg, FL (p. 271)
Roy E. Thoman, West Texas A & M University, Canyon, TX (p. 277)
John J. Tkacik, The Heritage Foundation, Washington, DC (p. 279)
*Gordon Tullock, George Mason University School of Law, Arlington, VA (p. 281)
Lloyd R. Vasey, Pacific Forum CSIS, Honolulu, HI (p. 284)
Arthur Waldron, American Enterprise Institute, Washington, DC (p. 287)
*Richard L. Walker, University of South Carolina, Columbia, SC (p. 287)
Bob Walpole, The Flagstaff Institute, Flagstaff, AZ (p. 288)
Michael Y. Warder, Los Angeles Children's Scholarship Fund, Long Beach, CA (p. 289)
*Murray Weidenbaum, Weidenbaum Center, St. Louis, MO (p. 291)
Dana White, The Heritage Foundation, Washington, DC (p. 293)
Robert Whitelaw, Virginia Polytechnic Institute and State University, Blacksburg, VA (p. 294)
*John C. Willke, Life Issues Institute, Inc., Cincinnati, OH (p. 295)
*Charles Wolf, Jr., RAND, Santa Monica, CA (p. 297)
*Larry Wortzel, The Heritage Foundation, Washington, DC (p. 299)
*Michael K. Young, George Washington University Law School, Washington, DC (p. 300)
George T. Yu, University of Illinois, Champaign, IL (p. 301)
Kate Xiao Zhou, University of Hawaii, Honolulu, HI (p. 302)

ECONOMIC DEVELOPMENT/FOREIGN AID

Carol Adelman, Hudson Institute, Washington, DC (p. 34)
James C. W. Ahiakpor, California State University, Hayward, Hayward, CA (p. 35)
*I. Dean Ahmad, Minaret of Freedom Institute, Bethesda, MD (p. 36)
*M. Gene Aldridge, New Mexico Independence Research Institute, Las Cruces, NM (p. 36)
Lee J. Alston, University of Colorado-Boulder, Boulder, CO (p. 37)
Carlos Ball, Agencia Interamericana de Prensa Economica, Boca Raton, FL (p. 44)
William Ball, Northern Michigan University, Marquette, MI (p. 44)
*Doug Bandow, Cato Institute, Washington, DC (p. 45)
Roger Bate, International Policy Network, Washington, DC (p. 47)
*Patrick M. Boarman, National University San Diego, San Diego, CA (p. 55)

ECONOMIC DEVELOPMENT/FOREIGN AID (Continued)

    Peter J. Boettke, James M. Buchanan Center for Political Economy, Fairfax, VA (p. 56)
*Richard L. Bolin, The Flagstaff Institute, Flagstaff, AZ (p. 56)
    Paul J. Bonicelli, Patrick Henry College, Purcellville, VA (p. 57)
*Donald R. Booth, Chapman University, Orange, CA (p. 57)
*Peter Brookes, The Heritage Foundation, Washington, DC (p. 61)
    Charles Brooks, The Strategy Group, Arlington, VA (p. 62)
*James B. Burnham, Duquesne University, Pittsburgh, PA (p. 66)
*David Burton, Argus Group, Alexandria, VA (p. 66)
    Alejandro A. Chafuen, Atlas Economic Research Foundation, Fairfax, VA (p. 72)
*Ariel Cohen, The Heritage Foundation, Washington, DC (p. 77)
*John F. Copper, Rhodes College, Memphis, TN (p. 82)
    Helle C. Dale, The Heritage Foundation, Washington, DC (p. 88)
*Midge Decter, New York, NY (p. 91)
*James S. Denton, Washington, DC (p. 93)
    Richard Derham, Washington Policy Center, Seattle, WA (p. 93)
*James A. Dorn, Cato Institute, Washington, DC (p. 97)
*Nicholas Nash Eberstadt, American Enterprise Institute, Washington, DC (p. 103)
*Mickey Edwards, Harvard University, Cambridge, MA (p. 104)
    Isaac Ehrlich, State University of New York, Buffalo, Buffalo, NY (p. 105)
    Ana Eiras, The Heritage Foundation, Washington, DC (p. 105)
*Louis D. Enoff, Enoff Associates Limited, Sykesville, MD (p. 107)
    Mark Falcoff, American Enterprise Institute, Washington, DC (p. 109)
    Georges Fauriol, International Republican Institute, Washington, DC (p. 110)
*Robert Fike, Americans for Tax Reform, Washington, DC (p. 111)
    J. Michael Finger, American Enterprise Institute, Washington, DC (p. 111)
    Eric Fisher, Ohio State University, 40126 Bologna, ITALY (p. 112)
*George Folsom, International Republican Institute, Washington, DC (p. 114)
    George Friedman, Stratfor.com, Austin, TX (p. 117)
    Giulio Gallarotti, Wesleyan University, Middletown, CT (p. 120)
*Jeffrey B. Gayner, Americans for Sovereignty, Washington, DC (p. 121)
    Phillip D. Grub, Eastern Washington University, Spokane, WA (p. 130)
    Alam E. Hammad, Alexandria, VA (p. 133)
    Paul Y. Hammond, University of Pittsburgh, Pittsburgh, PA (p. 133)
    Steve H. Hanke, Johns Hopkins University, Baltimore, MD (p. 134)
    John R. Hanson, II, Texas A&M University, College Station, TX (p. 134)
    Gina Marie Hatheway, The Heritage Foundation, Washington, DC (p. 137)
*Robert C. Haywood, Director, WEPZA, Evergreen, CO (p. 138)
    Paul Henze, Washington, VA (p. 140)
    Jack High, George Mason University, Arlington, VA (p. 142)
*Leon Hollerman, Claremont Graduate University, Claremont, CA (p. 145)
*Joseph Horton, University of Central Arkansas, Conway, AR (p. 146)
    Edward L. Hudgins, The Objectivist Center, Washington, DC (p. 148)
    John C. Hulsman, The Heritage Foundation, Washington, DC (p. 149)
*Michael Johns, Melville, NY (p. 154)
*Bruce Alan Johnson, Bruce Alan Johnson Associates, Indianapolis, IN (p. 155)
    D. Gale Johnson, University of Chicago, Chicago, IL (p. 155)
    Adrian Karatnycky, Freedom House, New York, NY (p. 158)
*Jacqueline Kasun, Humboldt State University, Arcata, CA (p. 158)
    F. Scott Kieff, Washington University, St. Louis, MO (p. 163)
*Elie Krakowski, EDK Consulting, Baltimore, MD (p. 168)
    Robert Krol, California State University, Northridge, Northridge, CA (p. 169)
*Lawrence Kudlow, Kudlow & Co., LLC, New York, NY (p. 170)
*Deepak Lal, University of California at Los Angeles, Los Angeles, CA (p. 172)
    Lawrence J. Lau, Stanford University, Stanford, CA (p. 175)

ECONOMIC DEVELOPMENT/FOREIGN AID (Continued)

*John Lenczowski, Institute of World Politics, Washington, DC (p. 177)
*Robert J. Loewenberg, Institute for Advanced Strategic and Political Studies, Washington, DC (p. 182)
*Yuri N. Maltsev, Carthage College, Kenosha, WI (p. 188)
*Robert Mandel, Lewis and Clark College, Portland, OR (p. 188)
*Rachel McCulloch, Brandeis University, Waltham, MA (p. 194)
 Olivia M. McDonald, Regent University, Virginia Beach, VA (p. 195)
 Lawrence J. McQuillan, Pacific Research Institute, San Francisco, CA (p. 197)
*Allan H. Meltzer, Carnegie Mellon University, Pittsburgh, PA (p. 199)
 Paul E. Michelson, Huntington College, Huntington, IN (p. 201)
 Dennis D. Miller, Baldwin-Wallace College, Berea, OH (p. 201)
*Steven W. Mosher, Population Research Institute, Front Royal, VA (p. 208)
 Henry R. Nau, George Washington University, Washington, DC (p. 211)
*Gerald P. O'Driscoll, Jr., Cato Institute, Falls Church, VA (p. 216)
*Richard Olivastro, People Dynamics, Farmington, CT (p. 218)
 Rocco M. Paone, U. S. Naval Academy, Annapolis, MD (p. 221)
 Paolo Pasicolan, The Heritage Foundation, Washington, DC (p. 222)
*Svetozar Pejovich, Texas A&M University, Dallas, TX (p. 224)
 Albert M. Piedra, Catholic University of America, Washington, DC (p. 228)
 Juliana Geran Pilon, American University, Washington, DC (p. 228)
 Barry W. Poulson, University of Colorado, Boulder, CO (p. 232)
*Ernest Preeg, Manufacturers Alliance, Arlington, VA (p. 232)
 George Priest, Yale Law School, New Haven, CT (p. 233)
*Jan S. Prybyla, Pennsylvania State University, Tucson, AZ (p. 234)
 Gary M. Quinlivan, Center for Economic and Policy Education, Latrobe, PA (p. 234)
*Alvin Rabushka, Hoover Institution, Stanford, CA (p. 235)
 Sarath Rajapatirana, American Enterprise Institute, Washington, DC (p. 236)
*William Ratliff, Hoover Institution, Stanford, CA (p. 236)
 Harold Calvin Ray, National Center for Faith-Based Initiatives, West Palm Beach, FL (p. 237)
*L. Jacobo Rodriguez, Cato Institute, Washington, DC (p. 242)
 Hilton Root, Economy Strategy Institute, Washington, DC (p. 243)
 David C. Rose, University of Missouri, St. Louis, St. Louis, MO (p. 243)
 Gabriel Roth, Chevy Chase, MD (p. 244)
 Al Santoli, American Foreign Policy Council, Washington, DC (p. 250)
 Gary Schmitt, Project for the New American Century, Washington, DC (p. 253)
*Anna J. Schwartz, National Bureau of Economic Research, New York, NY (p. 254)
*Howard Segermark, Segermark Associates, Inc., Washington, DC (p. 256)
 Larry A. Sjaastad, University of Chicago, Chicago, IL (p. 261)
 Mary Jane Skanderup, Pacific Forum CSIS, Honolulu, HI (p. 261)
*Fred L. Smith, Jr., Competitive Enterprise Institute, Washington, DC (p. 263)
 Devinda R. Subasinghe, St. Petersburg, FL (p. 271)
*John D. Sullivan, Center for International Private Enterprise, Washington, DC (p. 271)
 W. Scott Thompson, Tufts University, Medford, MA (p. 278)
 Jon Basil Utley, Ludwig von Mises Institute, Washington, DC (p. 283)
*Terry W. Van Allen, Kemah, TX (p. 283)
*Ian Vasquez, Cato Institute, Washington, DC (p. 284)
 Melara Zyla Vickers, Independent Women's Forum, Arlington, VA (p. 285)
 Jude Wanniski, Polyconomics, Parsippany, NJ (p. 288)
*Alan Rufus Waters, California State University, Fresno, Fresno, CA (p. 289)
*Rolf A. Weil, Roosevelt University, Chicago, IL (p. 291)
*Sidney Weintraub, Center for Strategic and International Studies, Washington, DC (p. 292)
*Charles Wolf, Jr., RAND, Santa Monica, CA (p. 297)
 Jason Wright, Frontiers of Freedom Institute, Fairfax, VA (p. 299)
*Michael K. Young, George Washington University Law School, Washington, DC (p. 300)

ECONOMIC DEVELOPMENT/FOREIGN AID (Continued)

George T. Yu, University of Illinois, Champaign, IL (p. 301)

HUMAN RIGHTS

*I. Dean Ahmad, Minaret of Freedom Institute, Bethesda, MD (p. 36)

*Sandor Balogh, Hudson Valley Community College, East Greenbush, NY (p. 45)

Arnold Beichman, Hoover Institution, Stanford, CA (p. 49)

*Mark Blitz, Claremont McKenna College, Claremont, CA (p. 55)

Philip Bom, Regent University, Redmond, WA (p. 56)

Paul J. Bonicelli, Patrick Henry College, Purcellville, VA (p. 57)

*Peter Brookes, The Heritage Foundation, Washington, DC (p. 61)

*Harold O. J. Brown, Reformed Theological Seminary, Charlotte, NC (p. 63)

*Allen Buchanan, University of Arizona, Tucson, AZ (p. 64)

*Michele A. Clark, Johns Hopkins University School of Advanced International Studies, Washington, DC (p. 75)

*Ariel Cohen, The Heritage Foundation, Washington, DC (p. 77)

*John E. Coons, University of California at Berkeley, Berkeley, CA (p. 81)

*John F. Copper, Rhodes College, Memphis, TN (p. 82)

*Midge Decter, New York, NY (p. 91)

*James S. Denton, Washington, DC (p. 93)

*William T. Devlin, Urban Family Council, Philadelphia, PA (p. 94)

*Joseph DioGuardi, Albanian American Civic League, Ossining, NY (p. 96)

*James A. Dorn, Cato Institute, Washington, DC (p. 97)

*Mickey Edwards, Harvard University, Cambridge, MA (p. 104)

Mark Elliott, Samford University, Birmingham, AL (p. 106)

*Charles H. Fairbanks, Jr., The Paul H. Nitze School of Advanced International Studies, Washington, DC (p. 108)

Mark Falcoff, American Enterprise Institute, Washington, DC (p. 109)

*Thompson Mason Faller, University of Portland, Portland, OR (p. 109)

*John Fonte, Hudson Institute, Washington, DC (p. 114)

*David Forte, Cleveland State University, Cleveland, OH (p. 114)

Hillel Fradkin, Ethics and Public Policy Center, Washington, DC (p. 115)

*Frank J. Gaffney, Jr., Center for Security Policy, Washington, DC (p. 119)

Giulio Gallarotti, Wesleyan University, Middletown, CT (p. 120)

*Jeffrey B. Gayner, Americans for Sovereignty, Washington, DC (p. 121)

Mary Ann Glendon, Harvard Law School, Cambridge, MA (p. 124)

Robert A. Goldwin, American Enterprise Institute, Washington, DC (p. 126)

Gidon A. Gottlieb, University of Chicago Law School, Chicago, IL (p. 127)

Samuel Gregg, Acton Institute for the Study of Religion and Liberty, Grand Rapids, MI (p. 129)

Kevin J. Hasson, The Becket Fund for Religious Liberty, Washington, DC (p. 137)

Paul Henze, Washington, VA (p. 140)

Bruce Herschensohn, Pepperdine University School of Public Policy, Malibu, CA (p. 141)

Charles Horner, Hudson Institute, Washington, DC (p. 146)

*Michael Horowitz, Hudson Institute, Washington, DC (p. 146)

*Olga S. Hruby, Research Center for Religious and Human Rights, New York, NY (p. 148)

John C. Hulsman, The Heritage Foundation, Washington, DC (p. 149)

Niger Roy Innis, Congress of Racial Equality, New York, NY (p. 151)

*Michael Johns, Melville, NY (p. 154)

*Christopher Joyner, Georgetown University, Washington, DC (p. 156)

Adrian Karatnycky, Freedom House, New York, NY (p. 158)

Robert G. Kaufman, University of Vermont, Burlington, VT (p. 159)

*Charles R. Kesler, Henry Salvatori Center, Claremont, CA (p. 162)

Jeane J. Kirkpatrick, American Enterprise Institute, Washington, DC (p. 164)

*Diane Knippers, Institute on Religion and Democracy, Washington, DC (p. 166)

*Elie Krakowski, EDK Consulting, Baltimore, MD (p. 168)

HUMAN RIGHTS (Continued)

*Andrew Langer, National Federation of Independent Business, Washington, DC (p. 174)

*Ernest W. Lefever, Chevy Chase, MD (p. 177)

*John Lenczowski, Institute of World Politics, Washington, DC (p. 177)

Rett R. Ludwikowski, Catholic University of America, Washington, DC (p. 184)

Tibor R. Machan, Chapman University, Silverado Canyon, CA (p. 185)

Yuri Mantilla, Family Research Council, Washington, DC (p. 189)

Clifford D. May, The Foundation for the Defense of Democracies, Washington, DC (p. 192)

*Nina May, *Renaissance Connection.com/RCNetwork.net*, Washington, DC (p. 192)

Olivia M. McDonald, Regent University, Virginia Beach, VA (p. 195)

*Michael J. McManus, Marriage Savers, Potomac, MD (p. 197)

Lawrence J. McQuillan, Pacific Research Institute, San Francisco, CA (p. 197)

Samuel P. Menefee, Regent University, Virginia Beach, VA (p. 199)

*Constantine C. Menges, Hudson Institute, Washington, DC (p. 199)

*Joseph A. Morris, Lincoln Legal Foundation, Chicago, IL (p. 207)

*Steven W. Mosher, Population Research Institute, Front Royal, VA (p. 208)

*Joshua Muravchik, American Enterprise Institute, Washington, DC (p. 209)

*Richard John Neuhaus, Institute on Religion and Public Life, New York, NY (p. 213)

Michael J. Novak, Jr., American Enterprise Institute, Washington, DC (p. 215)

Jordan Paust, University of Houston Law Center, Houston, TX (p. 223)

Juliana Geran Pilon, American University, Washington, DC (p. 228)

*Edward Potter, Employment Policy Foundation, Washington, DC (p. 231)

*Stephen Presser, Northwestern University School of Law, Chicago, IL (p. 233)

Arch Puddington, Freedom House, New York, NY (p. 234)

Jeremy Rabkin, Cornell University, Ithaca, NY (p. 235)

*Michael Radu, Foreign Policy Research Institute, Philadelphia, PA (p. 235)

Harold Calvin Ray, National Center for Faith-Based Initiatives, West Palm Beach, FL (p. 237)

*William H. Reid, Horseshoe, TX (p. 238)

*Amy Ridenour, National Center for Public Policy Research, Washington, DC (p. 240)

*James S. Robbins, National Defense University, Washington, DC (p. 241)

Hilton Root, Economy Strategy Institute, Washington, DC (p. 243)

*Ronald D. Rotunda, George Mason University School of Law, Arlington, VA (p. 244)

*Frank Ruddy, Ruddy & Muir, Chevy Chase, MD (p. 246)

Al Santoli, American Foreign Policy Council, Washington, DC (p. 250)

William L. Saunders, Family Research Council, Washington, DC (p. 250)

Brett D. Schaefer, The Heritage Foundation, Washington, DC (p. 252)

*Jay Sekulow, American Center for Law and Justice, Virginia Beach, VA (p. 256)

Timothy Samuel Shah, Ethics and Public Policy Center, Washington, DC (p. 257)

*Nina Shea, Freedom House, Washington, DC (p. 258)

Radek Sikorski, American Enterprise Institute, Washington, DC (p. 260)

*Gregory Simpkins, The Foundation for Democracy in Africa, Washington, DC (p. 260)

*Richard H. Solomon, United States Institute of Peace, Washington, DC (p. 265)

Charles P. Stetson, U. S. Fund for Leadership Training, Southport, CT (p. 268)

Margaret D. Stock, United States Military Academy, West Point, NY (p. 269)

Ewa M. Thompson, Rice University, Houston, TX (p. 277)

*John J. Tierney, Jr., Institute of World Politics, Washington, DC (p. 279)

Kenneth R. Timmerman, Maryland Taxpayers Association, Bethesda, MD (p. 279)

Miro M. Todorovich, Scientists and Engineers for Secure Energy, New York, NY (p. 280)

*Robert F. Turner, University of Virginia School of Law, Charlottesville, VA (p. 282)

Lawrence A. Uzzell, Keston Institute, Waxahachie, TX (p. 283)

*Balint Vazsonyi, Center for the American Founding, McLean, VA (p. 284)

*Kevin Vigilante, Rumford, RI (p. 285)

*George Weigel, Ethics and Public Policy Center, Washington, DC (p. 291)

*John C. Willke, Life Issues Institute, Inc., Cincinnati, OH (p. 295)

*Larry Wortzel, The Heritage Foundation, Washington, DC (p. 299)

HUMAN RIGHTS (Continued)

John Yoo, University of California, Berkeley, Berkeley, CA **(p. 300)**
*****Michael K. Young,** George Washington University Law School, Washington, DC **(p. 300)**

INTERNATIONAL FINANCE AND MULTILATERAL BANKS

*****George Ayittey,** American University, Washington, DC **(p. 42)**
*****Doug Bandow,** Cato Institute, Washington, DC **(p. 45)**
*****Claude E. Barfield,** American Enterprise Institute, Washington, DC **(p. 45)**
*****Saul Z. Barr,** University of Tennessee, Gulf Shores, AL **(p. 46)**
*****William W. Beach,** The Heritage Foundation, Washington, DC **(p. 48)**
*****Patrick M. Boarman,** National University San Diego, San Diego, CA **(p. 55)**
*****Richard L. Bolin,** The Flagstaff Institute, Flagstaff, AZ **(p. 56)**
 Charles Brooks, The Strategy Group, Arlington, VA **(p. 62)**
*****James B. Burnham,** Duquesne University, Pittsburgh, PA **(p. 66)**
*****David Burton,** Argus Group, Alexandria, VA **(p. 66)**
 Charles Calomiris, American Enterprise Institute, Washington, DC **(p. 68)**
*****Ariel Cohen,** The Heritage Foundation, Washington, DC **(p. 77)**
*****Michael R. Darby,** University of California at Los Angeles, Los Angeles, CA **(p. 89)**
 Ana Eiras, The Heritage Foundation, Washington, DC **(p. 105)**
 Martin Feldstein, National Bureau of Economic Research, Cambridge, MA **(p. 110)**
*****Robert Fike,** Americans for Tax Reform, Washington, DC **(p. 111)**
 Eric Fisher, Ohio State University, 40126 Bologna, ITALY **(p. 112)**
*****George Folsom,** International Republican Institute, Washington, DC **(p. 114)**
*****Milton Friedman,** Hoover Institution, Stanford, CA **(p. 117)**
 Giulio Gallarotti, Wesleyan University, Middletown, CT **(p. 120)**
 Fred R. Glahe, University of Colorado, Boulder, CO **(p. 124)**
 Steve H. Hanke, Johns Hopkins University, Baltimore, MD **(p. 134)**
*****Joseph Horton,** University of Central Arkansas, Conway, AR **(p. 146)**
 John C. Hulsman, The Heritage Foundation, Washington, DC **(p. 149)**
*****Michael Johns,** Melville, NY **(p. 154)**
 William H. Kaempfer, University of Colorado, Boulder, CO **(p. 156)**
 Robert Krol, California State University, Northridge, Northridge, CA **(p. 169)**
*****Randall Kroszner,** University of Chicago, Chicago, IL **(p. 170)**
*****Lawrence Kudlow,** Kudlow & Co., LLC, New York, NY **(p. 170)**
*****Deepak Lal,** University of California at Los Angeles, Los Angeles, CA **(p. 172)**
 Daniel Lapin, Toward Tradition, Mercer Island, WA **(p. 174)**
 Lawrence J. Lau, Stanford University, Stanford, CA **(p. 175)**
*****Richard T. McCormack,** Center for the Study of the Presidency, Washington, DC **(p. 194)**
*****Rachel McCulloch,** Brandeis University, Waltham, MA **(p. 194)**
 Wendell H. McCulloch, Jr., California State University, Long Beach, Long Beach, CA **(p. 194)**
 Lawrence J. McQuillan, Pacific Research Institute, San Francisco, CA **(p. 197)**
*****Allan H. Meltzer,** Carnegie Mellon University, Pittsburgh, PA **(p. 199)**
 Henry R. Nau, George Washington University, Washington, DC **(p. 211)**
 Barry W. Poulson, University of Colorado, Boulder, CO **(p. 232)**
*****Ernest Preeg,** Manufacturers Alliance, Arlington, VA **(p. 232)**
*****L. Jacobo Rodriguez,** Cato Institute, Washington, DC **(p. 242)**
 Hilton Root, Economy Strategy Institute, Washington, DC **(p. 243)**
 Brett D. Schaefer, The Heritage Foundation, Washington, DC **(p. 252)**
 Kurt Schuler, Arlington, VA **(p. 254)**
*****Anna J. Schwartz,** National Bureau of Economic Research, New York, NY **(p. 254)**
 Larry A. Sjaastad, University of Chicago, Chicago, IL **(p. 261)**
 Mary Jane Skanderup, Pacific Forum CSIS, Honolulu, HI **(p. 261)**
 John C. Soper, John Carroll University, University Heights, OH **(p. 266)**
 Devinda R. Subasinghe, St. Petersburg, FL **(p. 271)**
*****Ian Vasquez,** Cato Institute, Washington, DC **(p. 284)**

***** Has testified before a state or federal legislative committee**

INTERNATIONAL FINANCE AND MULTILATERAL BANKS (Continued)

*Sidney Weintraub, Center for Strategic and International Studies, Washington, DC **(p. 292)**

INTERNATIONAL ORGANIZATIONS (European Union, OECD, etc.)

*Sandor Balogh, Hudson Valley Community College, East Greenbush, NY **(p. 45)**
 Dennis L. Bark, Hoover Institution, Stanford, CA **(p. 45)**
*Richard L. Bolin, The Flagstaff Institute, Flagstaff, AZ **(p. 56)**
 Paul J. Bonicelli, Patrick Henry College, Purcellville, VA **(p. 57)**
 Charles Brooks, The Strategy Group, Arlington, VA **(p. 62)**
*David Burton, Argus Group, Alexandria, VA **(p. 66)**
*John E. Carey, International Defense Consultants, Inc., Arlington, VA **(p. 69)**
 Ted Galen Carpenter, Cato Institute, Washington, DC **(p. 71)**
 John Clark, Hudson Institute, Indianapolis, IN **(p. 75)**
*Joseph I. Coffey, Princeton, NJ **(p. 77)**
*Ralph A. Cossa, Pacific Forum CSIS, Honolulu, HI **(p. 83)**
 Helle C. Dale, The Heritage Foundation, Washington, DC **(p. 88)**
 Mark De Young, World Youth Alliance, New York, NY **(p. 90)**
*Midge Decter, New York, NY **(p. 91)**
 Peter J. Duignan, Hoover Institution, Stanford, CA **(p. 99)**
 Richard M. Ebeling, Hillsdale College, Hillsdale, MI **(p. 102)**
*Myron Ebell, Competitive Enterprise Institute, Washington, DC **(p. 103)**
*Robert Fike, Americans for Tax Reform, Washington, DC **(p. 111)**
 J. Michael Finger, American Enterprise Institute, Washington, DC **(p. 111)**
*Frank J. Gaffney, Jr., Center for Security Policy, Washington, DC **(p. 119)**
 Nile Gardiner, The Heritage Foundation, Washington, DC **(p. 120)**
*Jeffrey B. Gayner, Americans for Sovereignty, Washington, DC **(p. 121)**
*Roy Godson, National Strategy Information Center, Washington, DC **(p. 125)**
 Steve H. Hanke, Johns Hopkins University, Baltimore, MD **(p. 134)**
 William Anthony Hay, Foreign Policy Research Institute, Philadelphia, PA **(p. 138)**
*Robert C. Haywood, Director, WEPZA, Evergreen, CO **(p. 138)**
 Bruce Herschensohn, Pepperdine University School of Public Policy, Malibu, CA **(p. 141)**
 John C. Hulsman, The Heritage Foundation, Washington, DC **(p. 149)**
 Niger Roy Innis, Congress of Racial Equality, New York, NY **(p. 151)**
*Christopher Joyner, Georgetown University, Washington, DC **(p. 156)**
 William H. Kaempfer, University of Colorado, Boulder, CO **(p. 156)**
*Lawrence Kudlow, Kudlow & Co., LLC, New York, NY **(p. 170)**
*Deepak Lal, University of California at Los Angeles, Los Angeles, CA **(p. 172)**
*Yuri N. Maltsev, Carthage College, Kenosha, WI **(p. 188)**
*Nina May, *Renaissance Connection.com/RCNetwork.net*, Washington, DC **(p. 192)**
 Wendell H. McCulloch, Jr., California State University, Long Beach, Long Beach, CA **(p. 194)**
 Lawrence J. McQuillan, Pacific Research Institute, San Francisco, CA **(p. 197)**
*Maurice McTigue, Mercatus Center at George Mason University, Arlington, VA **(p. 197)**
*Allan H. Meltzer, Carnegie Mellon University, Pittsburgh, PA **(p. 199)**
*Dan Mitchell, The Heritage Foundation, Washington, DC **(p. 203)**
*Joseph A. Morris, Lincoln Legal Foundation, Chicago, IL **(p. 207)**
*Steven W. Mosher, Population Research Institute, Front Royal, VA **(p. 208)**
 Henry R. Nau, George Washington University, Washington, DC **(p. 211)**
 Michael J. Novak, Jr., American Enterprise Institute, Washington, DC **(p. 215)**
 Erie J. Novotny, Fairfax Station, VA **(p. 215)**
*William S. Peirce, Case Western Reserve University, Cleveland, OH **(p. 224)**
 Juliana Geran Pilon, American University, Washington, DC **(p. 228)**
*Ernest Preeg, Manufacturers Alliance, Arlington, VA **(p. 232)**
*David B. Rivkin, Jr., Baker & Hostetler, Washington, DC **(p. 241)**
*Edward L. Rowny, Washington, DC **(p. 245)**
 William L. Saunders, Family Research Council, Washington, DC **(p. 250)**

INTERNATIONAL ORGANIZATIONS (Continued)

Robert A. Scalapino, University of California, Berkeley, Berkeley, CA (p. 251)
Brett D. Schaefer, The Heritage Foundation, Washington, DC (p. 252)
Radek Sikorski, American Enterprise Institute, Washington, DC (p. 260)
*John Sitilides, Western Policy Center, Washington, DC (p. 261)
*Fred L. Smith, Jr., Competitive Enterprise Institute, Washington, DC (p. 263)
*Paul Schott Stevens, Dechert, Price & Rhoads, Washington, DC (p. 269)
*John D. Sullivan, Center for International Private Enterprise, Washington, DC (p. 271)
Lawrence A. Uzzell, Keston Institute, Waxahachie, TX (p. 283)
*W. Bruce Weinrod, International Technology and Trade Associates, Inc., Washington, DC (p. 292)
*Edwin D. Williamson, Sullivan & Cromwell, Washington, DC (p. 295)
*John C. Willke, Life Issues Institute, Inc., Cincinnati, OH (p. 295)
*Michael K. Young, George Washington University Law School, Washington, DC (p. 300)
George T. Yu, University of Illinois, Champaign, IL (p. 301)

JAPAN

*Doug Bandow, Cato Institute, Washington, DC (p. 45)
*Claude E. Barfield, American Enterprise Institute, Washington, DC (p. 45)
*Peter Brookes, The Heritage Foundation, Washington, DC (p. 61)
Daniel Claingaert, International Republican Institute, Washington, DC (p. 68)
Kurt Campbell, Center for Strategic and International Studies, Washington, DC (p. 68)
*John E. Carey, International Defense Consultants, Inc., Arlington, VA (p. 69)
Cecilia Chang, St. John's University, Jamaica, NY (p. 72)
*Ralph A. Cossa, Pacific Forum CSIS, Honolulu, HI (p. 83)
*Midge Decter, New York, NY (p. 91)
Robert Dujarric, Hudson Institute, Washington, DC (p. 99)
*Bert Ely, Ely & Company, Inc., Alexandria, VA (p. 106)
*Richard Fairbanks, Center for Strategic and International Studies, Washington, DC (p. 109)
*George Folsom, International Republican Institute, Washington, DC (p. 114)
*Barbara Hackman Franklin, Barbara Franklin Enterprises, Washington, DC (p. 116)
*James K. Glassman, American Enterprise Institute, Washington, DC (p. 124)
Phillip D. Grub, Eastern Washington University, Spokane, WA (p. 130)
Steve H. Hanke, Johns Hopkins University, Baltimore, MD (p. 134)
Bruce Herschensohn, Pepperdine University School of Public Policy, Malibu, CA (p. 141)
*Leon Hollerman, Claremont Graduate University, Claremont, CA (p. 145)
Charles Horner, Hudson Institute, Washington, DC (p. 146)
Balbina Hwang, The Heritage Foundation, Washington, DC (p. 150)
Niger Roy Innis, Congress of Racial Equality, New York, NY (p. 151)
*Chalmers Johnson, Japan Policy Research Institute, Cardiff, CA (p. 155)
Jeane J. Kirkpatrick, American Enterprise Institute, Washington, DC (p. 164)
*David B. Kopel, Independence Institute, Golden, CO (p. 167)
*Marvin H. Kosters, American Enterprise Institute, Washington, DC (p. 168)
Michael A. Ledeen, American Enterprise Institute, Washington, DC (p. 176)
James Lucier, Prudential Securities, Arlington, VA (p. 184)
*John H. Makin, American Enterprise Institute, Washington, DC (p. 187)
*Richard T. McCormack, Center for the Study of the Presidency, Washington, DC (p. 194)
*Allan H. Meltzer, Carnegie Mellon University, Pittsburgh, PA (p. 199)
*Constantine C. Menges, Hudson Institute, Washington, DC (p. 199)
*Steven W. Mosher, Population Research Institute, Front Royal, VA (p. 208)
Ramon H. Myers, Hoover Institution, Stanford, CA (p. 210)
Henry R. Nau, George Washington University, Washington, DC (p. 211)
Edward A. Olsen, Naval Postgraduate School, Monterey, CA (p. 219)
Charles M. Perry, Institute for Foreign Policy Analysis, Cambridge, MA (p. 226)
*Daryl Plunk, The Heritage Foundation, Washington, DC (p. 230)

JAPAN (Continued)

*Ernest Preeg,** Manufacturers Alliance, Arlington, VA **(p. 232)**
*Jim Przystup,** Institute for National Strategic Studies, Washington, DC **(p. 234)**
*R. Sean Randolph,** Bay Area Economic Forum, San Francisco, CA **(p. 236)**
 Hilton Root, Economy Strategy Institute, Washington, DC **(p. 243)**
*Edward L. Rowny,** Washington, DC **(p. 245)**
 Al Santoli, American Foreign Policy Council, Washington, DC **(p. 250)**
 Robert A. Scalapino, University of California, Berkeley, Berkeley, CA **(p. 251)**
*Donald J. Senese,** 60 Plus Association, Arlington, VA **(p. 257)**
 Mary Jane Skanderup, Pacific Forum CSIS, Honolulu, HI **(p. 261)**
 Shaun Small, Empower America, Washington, DC **(p. 262)**
*Paul Schott Stevens,** Dechert, Price & Rhoads, Washington, DC **(p. 269)**
*Richard L. Walker,** University of South Carolina, Columbia, SC **(p. 287)**
 Bob Walpole, The Flagstaff Institute, Flagstaff, AZ **(p. 288)**
*Murray Weidenbaum,** Weidenbaum Center, St. Louis, MO **(p. 291)**
*W. Bruce Weinrod,** International Technology and Trade Associates, Inc.,
    Washington, DC **(p. 292)**
*Charles Wolf, Jr.,** RAND, Santa Monica, CA **(p. 297)**
*Larry Wortzel,** The Heritage Foundation, Washington, DC **(p. 299)**
*Michael K. Young,** George Washington University Law School, Washington, DC **(p. 300)**
 Kate Xiao Zhou, University of Hawaii, Honolulu, HI **(p. 302)**

KOREA

*Doug Bandow,** Cato Institute, Washington, DC **(p. 45)**
*Claude E. Barfield,** American Enterprise Institute, Washington, DC **(p. 45)**
*Peter Brookes,** The Heritage Foundation, Washington, DC **(p. 61)**
 Daniel Claingaert, International Republican Institute, Washington, DC **(p. 68)**
 Kurt Campbell, Center for Strategic and International Studies, Washington, DC **(p. 68)**
*John E. Carey,** International Defense Consultants, Inc., Arlington, VA **(p. 69)**
*Ralph A. Cossa,** Pacific Forum CSIS, Honolulu, HI **(p. 83)**
 Helle C. Dale, The Heritage Foundation, Washington, DC **(p. 88)**
*Midge Decter,** New York, NY **(p. 91)**
 Robert Dujarric, Hudson Institute, Washington, DC **(p. 99)**
*Nicholas Nash Eberstadt,** American Enterprise Institute, Washington, DC **(p. 103)**
*Frank J. Gaffney, Jr.,** Center for Security Policy, Washington, DC **(p. 119)**
 Phillip D. Grub, Eastern Washington University, Spokane, WA **(p. 130)**
 Steve H. Hanke, Johns Hopkins University, Baltimore, MD **(p. 134)**
*Thomas H. Henriksen,** Hoover Institution, Stanford, CA **(p. 140)**
 Bruce Herschensohn, Pepperdine University School of Public Policy, Malibu, CA **(p. 141)**
 Charles Horner, Hudson Institute, Washington, DC **(p. 146)**
*Michael Horowitz,** Hudson Institute, Washington, DC **(p. 146)**
 Balbina Hwang, The Heritage Foundation, Washington, DC **(p. 150)**
 Niger Roy Innis, Congress of Racial Equality, New York, NY **(p. 151)**
*Chalmers Johnson,** Japan Policy Research Institute, Cardiff, CA **(p. 155)**
 Synja P. Kim, Institute for Corean-American Studies, Blue Bell, PA **(p. 163)**
 Jeane J. Kirkpatrick, American Enterprise Institute, Washington, DC **(p. 164)**
 Casey Lartigue, Jr., Cato Institute, Washington, DC **(p. 175)**
 James R. Lilley, American Enterprise Institute, Washington, DC **(p. 180)**
 James Lucier, Prudential Securities, Arlington, VA **(p. 184)**
*Dennis Mansfield,** Boise, ID **(p. 189)**
*Nina May,** *Renaissance Connection.com/RCNetwork.net,* Washington, DC **(p. 192)**
 Jerome Anthony McDuffie, University of North Carolina, Pembroke, Lumberton, NC **(p. 195)**
*Constantine C. Menges,** Hudson Institute, Washington, DC **(p. 199)**
*Steven W. Mosher,** Population Research Institute, Front Royal, VA **(p. 208)**
 Ramon H. Myers, Hoover Institution, Stanford, CA **(p. 210)**

KOREA (Continued)

Edward A. Olsen, Naval Postgraduate School, Monterey, CA (p. 219)
Charles M. Perry, Institute for Foreign Policy Analysis, Cambridge, MA (p. 226)
*Daryl Plunk, The Heritage Foundation, Washington, DC (p. 230)
*Ernest Preeg, Manufacturers Alliance, Arlington, VA (p. 232)
*Jan S. Prybyla, Pennsylvania State University, Tucson, AZ (p. 234)
*Jim Przystup, Institute for National Strategic Studies, Washington, DC (p. 234)
Sandy Rios, Concerned Women for America, Washington, DC (p. 240)
Hilton Root, Economy Strategy Institute, Washington, DC (p. 243)
*Edward L. Rowny, Washington, DC (p. 245)
Al Santoli, American Foreign Policy Council, Washington, DC (p. 250)
Robert A. Scalapino, University of California, Berkeley, Berkeley, CA (p. 251)
*Suzanne Scholte, Defense Forum Foundation, Falls Church, VA (p. 254)
*Donald J. Senese, 60 Plus Association, Arlington, VA (p. 257)
Mary Jane Skanderup, Pacific Forum CSIS, Honolulu, HI (p. 261)
*Henry Sokolski, Non-Proliferation Policy Education Center, Washington, DC (p. 265)
*Richard H. Solomon, United States Institute of Peace, Washington, DC (p. 265)
Gordon Sumner, Jr., Sumner Association, Santa Fe, NM (p. 272)
*William J. Taylor, Jr., Taylor Associates, Inc., Bethesda, MD (p. 275)
*John J. Tierney, Jr., Institute of World Politics, Washington, DC (p. 279)
*Richard L. Walker, University of South Carolina, Columbia, SC (p. 287)
*Murray Weidenbaum, Weidenbaum Center, St. Louis, MO (p. 291)
*Charles Wolf, Jr., RAND, Santa Monica, CA (p. 297)
*Larry Wortzel, The Heritage Foundation, Washington, DC (p. 299)
*Michael K. Young, George Washington University Law School, Washington, DC (p. 300)

LATIN AMERICA

*M. Gene Aldridge, New Mexico Independence Research Institute, Las Cruces, NM (p. 36)
Lee J. Alston, University of Colorado-Boulder, Boulder, CO (p. 37)
Carlos Ball, Agencia Interamericana de Prensa Economica, Boca Raton, FL (p. 44)
*Claude E. Barfield, American Enterprise Institute, Washington, DC (p. 45)
*Gary D. Becks, Rescue Task Force, El Cajon, CA (p. 48)
Paul J. Bonicelli, Patrick Henry College, Purcellville, VA (p. 57)
Charles Calomiris, American Enterprise Institute, Washington, DC (p. 68)
William F. Campbell, The Philadelphia Society, Baton Rouge, LA (p. 68)
Alejandro A. Chafuen, Atlas Economic Research Foundation, Fairfax, VA (p. 72)
*Linda Chavez, Center for Equal Opportunity, Sterling, VA (p. 73)
John Cobin, Montauk Financial Group, Greenville, SC (p. 76)
Angelo M. Codevilla, Boston University, Boston, MA (p. 77)
Brian Dean, International Republican Institute, Washington, DC (p. 90)
Miguel Diaz, Center for Strategic and International Studies, Washington, DC (p. 95)
Ana Eiras, The Heritage Foundation, Washington, DC (p. 105)
Mark Falcoff, American Enterprise Institute, Washington, DC (p. 109)
Georges Fauriol, International Republican Institute, Washington, DC (p. 110)
*George Folsom, International Republican Institute, Washington, DC (p. 114)
*Barbara Hackman Franklin, Barbara Franklin Enterprises, Washington, DC (p. 116)
George Friedman, Stratfor.com, Austin, TX (p. 117)
*Frank J. Gaffney, Jr., Center for Security Policy, Washington, DC (p. 119)
Steve H. Hanke, Johns Hopkins University, Baltimore, MD (p. 134)
Paul V. Harberger, Foundation Francisco Marroquin, Santa Monica, CA (p. 135)
Gina Marie Hatheway, The Heritage Foundation, Washington, DC (p. 137)
Bruce Herschensohn, Pepperdine University School of Public Policy, Malibu, CA (p. 141)
David Hirschmann, National Chamber Foundation, Washington, DC (p. 143)
G. Philip Hughes, White House Writer's Group, Washington, DC (p. 149)
Steve Johnson, The Heritage Foundation, Washington, DC (p. 155)

LATIN AMERICA (Continued)

Jeane J. Kirkpatrick, American Enterprise Institute, Washington, DC (p. 164)
Anthony K. Knopp, University of Texas, Brownsville, Brownsville, TX (p. 166)
Marie-Josee Kravis, Hudson Institute, Indianapolis, IN (p. 169)
*Deepak Lal, University of California at Los Angeles, Los Angeles, CA (p. 172)
Carlos Lopez, Menlo College, Atherton, CA (p. 183)
Romulo Lopez-Cordero, Atlas Economic Research Foundation, Fairfax, VA (p. 183)
*Edward N. Luttwak, Center for Strategic and International Studies, Washington, DC (p. 184)
*Robert Mandel, Lewis and Clark College, Portland, OR (p. 188)
Yuri Mantilla, Family Research Council, Washington, DC (p. 189)
*Richard T. McCormack, Center for the Study of the Presidency, Washington, DC (p. 194)
Eugene "Red" McDaniel, American Defense Institute, Alexandria, VA (p. 194)
Olivia M. McDonald, Regent University, Virginia Beach, VA (p. 195)
*Allan H. Meltzer, Carnegie Mellon University, Pittsburgh, PA (p. 199)
*Constantine C. Menges, Hudson Institute, Washington, DC (p. 199)
*F. Andy Messing, Jr., National Defense Council Foundation, Alexandria, VA (p. 200)
*Deroy Murdock, Atlas Economic Research Foundation, New York, NY (p. 209)
Mario Navarro da Costa, American Society for the Defense of Tradition, Family and Property, McLean, VA (p. 211)
*Gerald P. O'Driscoll, Jr., Cato Institute, Falls Church, VA (p. 216)
Jeremiah O'Keeffe, Plano, TX (p. 217)
Ivan G. Osorio, Capital Research Center, Washington, DC (p. 220)
William Perry, William Perry & Associates, Agua Dulce, CA (p. 226)
Roland I. Perusse, Inter-American Institute, Washington, DC (p. 226)
Philip Peters, Lexington Institute, Arlington, VA (p. 226)
Barry W. Poulson, University of Colorado, Boulder, CO (p. 232)
*Ernest Preeg, Manufacturers Alliance, Arlington, VA (p. 232)
*Susan Kaufman Purcell, Americas Society/Council of the Americas, New York, NY (p. 234)
*Michael Radu, Foreign Policy Research Institute, Philadelphia, PA (p. 235)
Sarath Rajapatirana, American Enterprise Institute, Washington, DC (p. 236)
*William Ratliff, Hoover Institution, Stanford, CA (p. 236)
Harold Calvin Ray, National Center for Faith-Based Initiatives, West Palm Beach, FL (p. 237)
*L. Jacobo Rodriguez, Cato Institute, Washington, DC (p. 242)
Robert Royal, Faith & Reason Institute, Washington, DC (p. 245)
Gregory W. Sand, Saint Louis College of Pharmacy, St. Louis, MO (p. 249)
Larry A. Sjaastad, University of Chicago, Chicago, IL (p. 261)
Mary Jane Skanderup, Pacific Forum CSIS, Honolulu, HI (p. 261)
Devinda R. Subasinghe, St. Petersburg, FL (p. 271)
Gordon Sumner, Jr., Sumner Association, Santa Fe, NM (p. 272)
*Lewis A. Tambs, Tempe, AZ (p. 273)
*John J. Tierney, Jr., Institute of World Politics, Washington, DC (p. 279)
Jon Basil Utley, Ludwig von Mises Institute, Washington, DC (p. 283)
*Ian Vasquez, Cato Institute, Washington, DC (p. 284)
*Alan Rufus Waters, California State University, Fresno, Fresno, CA (p. 289)
*Sidney Weintraub, Center for Strategic and International Studies, Washington, DC (p. 292)
Jerry Zandstra, Acton Institute for the Study of Religion and Liberty, Grand Rapids, MI (p. 301)

MEXICO

*M. Gene Aldridge, New Mexico Independence Research Institute, Las Cruces, NM (p. 36)
Paul J. Bonicelli, Patrick Henry College, Purcellville, VA (p. 57)
Peter J. Duignan, Hoover Institution, Stanford, CA (p. 99)
Ana Eiras, The Heritage Foundation, Washington, DC (p. 105)
*George Folsom, International Republican Institute, Washington, DC (p. 114)
*Barbara Hackman Franklin, Barbara Franklin Enterprises, Washington, DC (p. 116)

MEXICO (Continued)

*Roy Godson, National Strategy Information Center, Washington, DC (p. 125)
Steve H. Hanke, Johns Hopkins University, Baltimore, MD (p. 134)
Gina Marie Hatheway, The Heritage Foundation, Washington, DC (p. 137)
Bruce Herschensohn, Pepperdine University School of Public Policy, Malibu, CA (p. 141)
G. Philip Hughes, White House Writer's Group, Washington, DC (p. 149)
Steve Johnson, The Heritage Foundation, Washington, DC (p. 155)
Jeane J. Kirkpatrick, American Enterprise Institute, Washington, DC (p. 164)
Anthony K. Knopp, University of Texas, Brownsville, Brownsville, TX (p. 166)
*Rita P. Maguire, Arizona Center for Public Policy, Phoenix, AZ (p. 186)
Olivia M. McDonald, Regent University, Virginia Beach, VA (p. 195)
*Constantine C. Menges, Hudson Institute, Washington, DC (p. 199)
*F. Andy Messing, Jr., National Defense Council Foundation, Alexandria, VA (p. 200)
*Susan Kaufman Purcell, Americas Society/Council of the Americas, New York, NY (p. 234)
*R. Sean Randolph, Bay Area Economic Forum, San Francisco, CA (p. 236)
*L. Jacobo Rodriguez, Cato Institute, Washington, DC (p. 242)
Gordon Sumner, Jr., Sumner Association, Santa Fe, NM (p. 272)
*Lewis A. Tambs, Tempe, AZ (p. 273)
*Ian Vasquez, Cato Institute, Washington, DC (p. 284)
Bob Walpole, The Flagstaff Institute, Flagstaff, AZ (p. 288)
Michael Y. Warder, Los Angeles Children's Scholarship Fund, Long Beach, CA (p. 289)
*Sidney Weintraub, Center for Strategic and International Studies, Washington, DC (p. 292)

MIDDLE EAST

*I. Dean Ahmad, Minaret of Freedom Institute, Bethesda, MD (p. 36)
*Gary L. Bauer, Campaign for Working Families, Arlington, VA (p. 47)
Arnold Beichman, Hoover Institution, Stanford, CA (p. 49)
Eric A. Belgrad, Towson State University, Towson, MD (p. 49)
Ilan Berman, American Foreign Policy Council, Washington, DC (p. 51)
*Stephen J. Blank, U. S. Army War College, Carlisle, PA (p. 54)
*Marshall J. Breger, Catholic University of America, Washington, DC (p. 60)
Charles Brooks, The Strategy Group, Arlington, VA (p. 62)
Matthew Brooks, Jewish Policy Center, Washington, DC (p. 62)
Mahmood Butt, Eastern Illinois University, Charleston, IL (p. 66)
*John E. Carey, International Defense Consultants, Inc., Arlington, VA (p. 69)
Ted Galen Carpenter, Cato Institute, Washington, DC (p. 71)
*Ariel Cohen, The Heritage Foundation, Washington, DC (p. 77)
Helle C. Dale, The Heritage Foundation, Washington, DC (p. 88)
Werner J. Dannhauser, Michigan State University, East Lansing, MI (p. 88)
*Arnaud de Borchgrave, Center for Strategic and International Studies, Washington, DC (p. 89)
*Midge Decter, New York, NY (p. 91)
*Alan Dowty, University of Notre Dame, Notre Dame, IN (p. 98)
Peter J. Duignan, Hoover Institution, Stanford, CA (p. 99)
Khalid Duran, *TransIslam Magazine*, Bethesda, MD (p. 100)
Isaac Ehrlich, State University of New York, Buffalo, Buffalo, NY (p. 105)
*Richard Fairbanks, Center for Strategic and International Studies, Washington, DC (p. 109)
Eric Fisher, Ohio State University, 40126 Bologna, ITALY (p. 112)
*David Forte, Cleveland State University, Cleveland, OH (p. 114)
Hillel Fradkin, Ethics and Public Policy Center, Washington, DC (p. 115)
*Robert O. Freedman, Baltimore Hebrew University, Baltimore, MD (p. 116)
George Friedman, Stratfor.com, Austin, TX (p. 117)
Adam Fuller, Toward Tradition, Mercer Island, WA (p. 118)
*Frank J. Gaffney, Jr., Center for Security Policy, Washington, DC (p. 119)
Nile Gardiner, The Heritage Foundation, Washington, DC (p. 120)
Reuel Marc Gerecht, American Enterprise Institute, Washington, DC (p. 123)

MIDDLE EAST (Continued)

Gidon A. Gottlieb, University of Chicago Law School, Chicago, IL **(p. 127)**

Phillip D. Grub, Eastern Washington University, Spokane, WA **(p. 130)**

Alam E. Hammad, Alexandria, VA **(p. 133)**

Ronald L. Hatchett, University of St. Thomas, Houston, TX **(p. 137)**

Paul Henze, Washington, VA **(p. 140)**

Bruce Herschensohn, Pepperdine University School of Public Policy, Malibu, CA **(p. 141)**

John C. Hulsman, The Heritage Foundation, Washington, DC **(p. 149)**

Niger Roy Innis, Congress of Racial Equality, New York, NY **(p. 151)**

***Christopher Joyner,** Georgetown University, Washington, DC **(p. 156)**

Francis X. Kane, Strategy, Technology and Space, Inc., San Antonio, TX **(p. 157)**

***Mark N. Katz,** George Mason University, Fairfax, VA **(p. 158)**

***Geoffrey Kemp,** The Nixon Center, Washington, DC **(p. 161)**

Paul Kengor, Grove City College, Grove City, PA **(p. 161)**

Owen Kirby, International Republican Institute, Washington, DC **(p. 164)**

Jeane J. Kirkpatrick, American Enterprise Institute, Washington, DC **(p. 164)**

***David B. Kopel,** Independence Institute, Golden, CO **(p. 167)**

***Malcolm Kovacs,** Montgomery College, Rockville, MD **(p. 168)**

***Andrea S. Lafferty,** Traditional Values Coalition, Washington, DC **(p. 172)**

Seth Leibsohn, Empower America, Washington, DC **(p. 177)**

***George Liebmann,** Calvert Institute for Policy Research, Baltimore, MD **(p. 180)**

***Robert J. Loewenberg,** Institute for Advanced Strategic and Political Studies, Washington, DC **(p. 182)**

Josh London, Jewish Policy Center, Washington, DC **(p. 182)**

***Edward N. Luttwak,** Center for Strategic and International Studics, Washington, DC **(p. 184)**

Hafeez Malik, Villanova University, Villanova, PA **(p. 187)**

***Robert Mandel,** Lewis and Clark College, Portland, OR **(p. 188)**

Clifford D. May, The Foundation for the Defense of Democracies, Washington, DC **(p. 192)**

Eugene "Red" McDaniel, American Defense Institute, Alexandria, VA **(p. 194)**

***Michael J. McManus,** Marriage Savers, Potomac, MD **(p. 197)**

***F. Andy Messing, Jr.,** National Defense Council Foundation, Alexandria, VA **(p. 200)**

Dennis D. Miller, Baldwin-Wallace College, Berea, OH **(p. 201)**

Fariborz L. Mokhtari, National Defense University, Washington, DC **(p. 204)**

***Joseph A. Morris,** Lincoln Legal Foundation, Chicago, IL **(p. 207)**

Richard Alan Nelson, Louisiana State University, Baton Rouge, LA **(p. 212)**

Tom Neumann, Jewish Institute for National Security Affairs, Washington, DC **(p. 213)**

***Stephen R. Norton,** Western Policy Center, Washington, DC **(p. 215)**

***James H. Noyes,** Hoover Institution, Stanford, CA **(p. 215)**

Jeremiah O'Keeffe, Plano, TX **(p. 217)**

David A. Patterson, University of Memphis, Memphis, TN **(p. 223)**

Charles M. Perry, Institute for Foreign Policy Analysis, Cambridge, MA **(p. 226)**

***James Phillips,** The Heritage Foundation, Washington, DC **(p. 228)**

***Daniel Pipes,** Middle East Forum, Philadelphia, PA **(p. 229)**

Danielle Pletka, American Enterprise Institute, Washington, DC **(p. 229)**

Barry W. Poulson, University of Colorado, Boulder, CO **(p. 232)**

Paul A. Rahe, University of Tulsa, Tulsa, OK **(p. 236)**

***James S. Robbins,** National Defense University, Washington, DC **(p. 241)**

***Allen H. Roth,** New York State Advisory Council on Privatization, New York, NY **(p. 244)**

***Edward L. Rowny,** Washington, DC **(p. 245)**

Al Santoli, American Foreign Policy Council, Washington, DC **(p. 250)**

Gary Schmitt, Project for the New American Century, Washington, DC **(p. 253)**

***Nina Shea,** Freedom House, Washington, DC **(p. 258)**

Harvey Sicherman, Foreign Policy Research Institute, Philadelphia, PA **(p. 259)**

***Rita Simon,** American University, Washington, DC **(p. 260)**

***Neil H. Snyder,** University of Virginia, Charlottesville, VA **(p. 265)**

MIDDLE EAST (Continued)

Gordon Sumner, Jr., Sumner Association, Santa Fe, NM (p. 272)
Roy E. Thoman, West Texas A & M University, Canyon, TX (p. 277)
Jon Basil Utley, Ludwig von Mises Institute, Washington, DC (p. 283)
*Balint Vazsonyi, Center for the American Founding, McLean, VA (p. 284)
*Rolf A. Weil, Roosevelt University, Chicago, IL (p. 291)
*Kenneth Weinstein, Hudson Institute, Washington, DC (p. 292)
Meyrav Wurmser, Hudson Institute, Washington, DC (p. 299)

NORTHEAST ASIA

Richard V. Allen, Washington, DC (p. 36)
*Doug Bandow, Cato Institute, Washington, DC (p. 45)
Peter J. Boettke, James M. Buchanan Center for Political Economy, Fairfax, VA (p. 56)
*Peter Brookes, The Heritage Foundation, Washington, DC (p. 61)
Daniel Claingaert, International Republican Institute, Washington, DC (p. 68)
Kurt Campbell, Center for Strategic and International Studies, Washington, DC (p. 68)
*John E. Carey, International Defense Consultants, Inc., Arlington, VA (p. 69)
Cecilia Chang, St. John's University, Jamaica, NY (p. 72)
Jonathan Clarke, Cato Institute, Washington, DC (p. 75)
*John F. Copper, Rhodes College, Memphis, TN (p. 82)
*Ralph A. Cossa, Pacific Forum CSIS, Honolulu, HI (p. 83)
Robert Dujarric, Hudson Institute, Washington, DC (p. 99)
*Nicholas Nash Eberstadt, American Enterprise Institute, Washington, DC (p. 103)
*Mickey Edwards, Harvard University, Cambridge, MA (p. 104)
Ivan Eland, Cato Institute, Washington, DC (p. 105)
*Harvey Feldman, The Heritage Foundation, Washington, DC (p. 110)
*Edwin J. Feulner, The Heritage Foundation, Washington, DC (p. 111)
George Friedman, Stratfor.com, Austin, TX (p. 117)
Phillip D. Grub, Eastern Washington University, Spokane, WA (p. 130)
Paul Y. Hammond, University of Pittsburgh, Pittsburgh, PA (p. 133)
Bruce Herschensohn, Pepperdine University School of Public Policy, Malibu, CA (p. 141)
*Chalmers Johnson, Japan Policy Research Institute, Cardiff, CA (p. 155)
Shyam J. Kamath, California State University, Hayward, Hayward, CA (p. 157)
Synja P. Kim, Institute for Corean-American Studies, Blue Bell, PA (p. 163)
Jeane J. Kirkpatrick, American Enterprise Institute, Washington, DC (p. 164)
Lawrence J. Lau, Stanford University, Stanford, CA (p. 175)
Michael A. Ledeen, American Enterprise Institute, Washington, DC (p. 176)
*John H. Makin, American Enterprise Institute, Washington, DC (p. 187)
*Robert Mandel, Lewis and Clark College, Portland, OR (p. 188)
Eugene "Red" McDaniel, American Defense Institute, Alexandria, VA (p. 194)
*Constantine C. Menges, Hudson Institute, Washington, DC (p. 199)
*F. Andy Messing, Jr., National Defense Council Foundation, Alexandria, VA (p. 200)
*Steven W. Mosher, Population Research Institute, Front Royal, VA (p. 208)
*Ross H. Munro, Center for Security Studies, Washington, DC (p. 209)
Jeremiah O'Keeffe, Plano, TX (p. 217)
William E. Odom, Hudson Institute, Washington, DC (p. 218)
Edward A. Olsen, Naval Postgraduate School, Monterey, CA (p. 219)
Charles M. Perry, Institute for Foreign Policy Analysis, Cambridge, MA (p. 226)
*Robert Pfaltzgraff, Jr., Institute for Foreign Policy Analysis, Cambridge, MA (p. 227)
*Daryl Plunk, The Heritage Foundation, Washington, DC (p. 230)
Barry W. Poulson, University of Colorado, Boulder, CO (p. 232)
*Jim Przystup, Institute for National Strategic Studies, Washington, DC (p. 234)
Hilton Root, Economy Strategy Institute, Washington, DC (p. 243)
David C. Rose, University of Missouri, St. Louis, St. Louis, MO (p. 243)
*Edward L. Rowny, Washington, DC (p. 245)

---

* Has testified before a state or federal legislative committee

NORTHEAST ASIA (Continued)

*Alfred P. Rubin, Tufts University, Medford, MA (p. 246)
*William A. Rusher, Claremont Institute, San Francisco, CA (p. 247)
Al Santoli, American Foreign Policy Council, Washington, DC (p. 250)
Robert A. Scalapino, University of California, Berkeley, Berkeley, CA (p. 251)
Mary Jane Skanderup, Pacific Forum CSIS, Honolulu, HI (p. 261)
*Richard H. Solomon, United States Institute of Peace, Washington, DC (p. 265)
*William J. Taylor, Jr., Taylor Associates, Inc., Bethesda, MD (p. 275)
Roy E. Thoman, West Texas A & M University, Canyon, TX (p. 277)
W. Scott Thompson, Tufts University, Medford, MA (p. 278)
John J. Tkacik, The Heritage Foundation, Washington, DC (p. 279)
*Mead Treadwell, Institute of the North, Anchorage, AK (p. 281)
Arthur Waldron, American Enterprise Institute, Washington, DC (p. 287)
*Richard L. Walker, University of South Carolina, Columbia, SC (p. 287)
Jude Wanniski, Polyconomics, Parsippany, NJ (p. 288)
*Charles Wolf, Jr., RAND, Santa Monica, CA (p. 297)
*Larry Wortzel, The Heritage Foundation, Washington, DC (p. 299)
*Michael K. Young, George Washington University Law School, Washington, DC (p. 300)
George T. Yu, University of Illinois, Champaign, IL (p. 301)

PROMOTING DEMOCRACY/PUBLIC DIPLOMACY

*I. Dean Ahmad, Minaret of Freedom Institute, Bethesda, MD (p. 36)
Ford A. Anderson, State Policy Network, Dallas, TX (p. 38)
*George Ayittey, American University, Washington, DC (p. 42)
Carlos Ball, Agencia Interamericana de Prensa Economica, Boca Raton, FL (p. 44)
*Sandor Balogh, Hudson Valley Community College, East Greenbush, NY (p. 45)
Ilan Berman, American Foreign Policy Council, Washington, DC (p. 51)
Morton Blackwell, Leadership Institute, Arlington, VA (p. 54)
*Mark Blitz, Claremont McKenna College, Claremont, CA (p. 55)
Paul J. Bonicelli, Patrick Henry College, Purcellville, VA (p. 57)
*Peter Brookes, The Heritage Foundation, Washington, DC (p. 61)
Charles Brooks, The Strategy Group, Arlington, VA (p. 62)
*Harold O. J. Brown, Reformed Theological Seminary, Charlotte, NC (p. 63)
Kurt Campbell, Center for Strategic and International Studies, Washington, DC (p. 68)
*John E. Carey, International Defense Consultants, Inc., Arlington, VA (p. 69)
*Ariel Cohen, The Heritage Foundation, Washington, DC (p. 77)
Helle C. Dale, The Heritage Foundation, Washington, DC (p. 88)
*Kenneth E. de Graffenreid, Institute of World Politics, Washington, DC (p. 89)
*Midge Decter, New York, NY (p. 91)
*James S. Denton, Washington, DC (p. 93)
Dana Dillon, The Heritage Foundation, Washington, DC (p. 96)
*Joseph DioGuardi, Albanian American Civic League, Ossining, NY (p. 96)
*Joseph D. Douglass, Jr., The Redwood Institute, Falls Church, VA (p. 98)
Georges Fauriol, International Republican Institute, Washington, DC (p. 110)
Robert Feidler, International Legal Projects Institute, Grand Forks, ND (p. 110)
*George Folsom, International Republican Institute, Washington, DC (p. 114)
Hillel Fradkin, Ethics and Public Policy Center, Washington, DC (p. 115)
*Milton Friedman, Hoover Institution, Stanford, CA (p. 117)
*Frank J. Gaffney, Jr., Center for Security Policy, Washington, DC (p. 119)
*Jeffrey B. Gayner, Americans for Sovereignty, Washington, DC (p. 121)
*Roy Godson, National Strategy Information Center, Washington, DC (p. 125)
Nikolas Gvosdev, *The National Interest*, Washington, DC (p. 131)
Roger Hamburg, Indiana University South Bend, South Bend, IN (p. 133)
Robert Hawkins, Jr., Institute for Contemporary Studies, Oakland, CA (p. 137)
Paul Henze, Washington, VA (p. 140)

PROMOTING DEMOCRACY/PUBLIC DIPLOMACY (Continued)

Bruce Herschensohn, Pepperdine University School of Public Policy, Malibu, CA (p. 141)

Charles Horner, Hudson Institute, Washington, DC (p. 146)

*Michael Horowitz, Hudson Institute, Washington, DC (p. 146)

*Olga S. Hruby, Research Center for Religious and Human Rights, New York, NY (p. 148)

Edward L. Hudgins, The Objectivist Center, Washington, DC (p. 148)

G. Philip Hughes, White House Writer's Group, Washington, DC (p. 149)

*Fred C. Ikle, Center for Strategic and International Studies, Washington, DC (p. 151)

Niger Roy Innis, Congress of Racial Equality, New York, NY (p. 151)

*Harvey M. Jacobs, University of Wisconsin, Madison, WI (p. 153)

*Charles W. Jarvis, United Seniors Association, Fairfax, VA (p. 153)

*Michael Johns, Melville, NY (p. 154)

Steve Johnson, The Heritage Foundation, Washington, DC (p. 155)

*Christopher Joyner, Georgetown University, Washington, DC (p. 156)

Francis X. Kane, Strategy, Technology and Space, Inc., San Antonio, TX (p. 157)

Adrian Karatnycky, Freedom House, New York, NY (p. 158)

*Mark N. Katz, George Mason University, Fairfax, VA (p. 158)

Brian T. Kennedy, Claremont Institute, Claremont, CA (p. 161)

*Charles R. Kesler, Henry Salvatori Center, Claremont, CA (p. 162)

Jeane J. Kirkpatrick, American Enterprise Institute, Washington, DC (p. 164)

*Elie Krakowski, EDK Consulting, Baltimore, MD (p. 168)

*Lawrence Kudlow, Kudlow & Co., LLC, New York, NY (p. 170)

*Ernest W. Lefever, Chevy Chase, MD (p. 177)

*John Lenczowski, Institute of World Politics, Washington, DC (p. 177)

Leonard P. Liggio, Atlas Economic Research Foundation, Fairfax, VA (p. 180)

Hafeez Malik, Villanova University, Villanova, PA (p. 187)

*Yuri N. Maltsev, Carthage College, Kenosha, WI (p. 188)

*Robert Mandel, Lewis and Clark College, Portland, OR (p. 188)

Clifford D. May, The Foundation for the Defense of Democracies, Washington, DC (p. 192)

*Nina May, *Renaissance Connection.com/RCNetwork.net*, Washington, DC (p. 192)

Edward T. McMullen, Jr., South Carolina Policy Council, Columbia, SC (p. 197)

Lawrence J. McQuillan, Pacific Research Institute, San Francisco, CA (p. 197)

Samuel P. Menefee, Regent University, Virginia Beach, VA (p. 199)

*Constantine C. Menges, Hudson Institute, Washington, DC (p. 199)

Andrew A. Michta, Rhodes College, Memphis, TN (p. 201)

*Joseph A. Morris, Lincoln Legal Foundation, Chicago, IL (p. 207)

*Steven W. Mosher, Population Research Institute, Front Royal, VA (p. 208)

*Joshua Muravchik, American Enterprise Institute, Washington, DC (p. 209)

Henry R. Nau, George Washington University, Washington, DC (p. 211)

Richard Alan Nelson, Louisiana State University, Baton Rouge, LA (p. 212)

Michael J. Novak, Jr., American Enterprise Institute, Washington, DC (p. 215)

*Fred O. Oladeinde, The Foundation for Democracy in Africa, Washington, DC (p. 218)

*Richard Olivastro, People Dynamics, Farmington, CT (p. 218)

Juliana Geran Pilon, American University, Washington, DC (p. 228)

*Roger Pilon, Cato Institute, Washington, DC (p. 228)

*Daryl Plunk, The Heritage Foundation, Washington, DC (p. 230)

*Solomon W. Polachek, State University of New York, Binghamton, Binghamton, NY (p. 230)

*Dennis Polhill, Independence Institute, Golden, CO (p. 230)

*Edward Potter, Employment Policy Foundation, Washington, DC (p. 231)

Arch Puddington, Freedom House, New York, NY (p. 234)

*Andrew F. Quinlan, Center for Freedom and Prosperity, Alexandria, VA (p. 234)

Richard W. Rahn, NOVECON, Alexandria, VA (p. 236)

*David B. Rivkin, Jr., Baker & Hostetler, Washington, DC (p. 241)

*James S. Robbins, National Defense University, Washington, DC (p. 241)

Hilton Root, Economy Strategy Institute, Washington, DC (p. 243)

PROMOTING DEMOCRACY/PUBLIC DIPLOMACY (Continued)

*Allen H. Roth, New York State Advisory Council on Privatization, New York, NY (p. 244)
*Edward L. Rowny, Washington, DC (p. 245)
*Frank Ruddy, Ruddy & Muir, Chevy Chase, MD (p. 246)
Al Santoli, American Foreign Policy Council, Washington, DC (p. 250)
Robert A. Schadler, Center for First Principles, Washington, DC (p. 251)
*Peter W. Schramm, John M. Ashbrook Center for Public Affairs, Ashland, OH (p. 254)
Robert Schuettinger, Washington International Studies Council, Washington, DC (p. 254)
Jeffrey Leigh Sedgwick, University of Massachusetts, Amherst, MA (p. 255)
Radek Sikorski, American Enterprise Institute, Washington, DC (p. 260)
*Gregory Simpkins, The Foundation for Democracy in Africa, Washington, DC (p. 260)
*Fred L. Smith, Jr., Competitive Enterprise Institute, Washington, DC (p. 263)
*Richard F. Staar, Hoover Institution, Stanford, CA (p. 267)
*John D. Sullivan, Center for International Private Enterprise, Washington, DC (p. 271)
*John J. Tierney, Jr., Institute of World Politics, Washington, DC (p. 279)
Kenneth R. Timmerman, Maryland Taxpayers Association, Bethesda, MD (p. 279)
Phillip N. Truluck, The Heritage Foundation, Washington, DC (p. 281)
*Robert F. Turner, University of Virginia School of Law, Charlottesville, VA (p. 282)
Jon Basil Utley, Ludwig von Mises Institute, Washington, DC (p. 283)
*Dane Waters, Initiative and Referendum Institute, Leesburg, VA (p. 289)
*W. Bruce Weinrod, International Technology and Trade Associates, Inc.,
    Washington, DC (p. 292)
*Paul Weyrich, Free Congress Foundation, Washington, DC (p. 293)
Dana White, The Heritage Foundation, Washington, DC (p. 293)
*Larry Wortzel, The Heritage Foundation, Washington, DC (p. 299)
*Michael K. Young, George Washington University Law School, Washington, DC (p. 300)
George T. Yu, University of Illinois, Champaign, IL (p. 301)

RUSSIA AND EURASIA

*Leon Aron, American Enterprise Institute, Washington, DC (p. 41)
Ilan Berman, American Foreign Policy Council, Washington, DC (p. 51)
Jonas Bernstein, American Foreign Policy Council, Washington, DC (p. 51)
Morton Blackwell, Leadership Institute, Arlington, VA (p. 54)
*Stephen J. Blank, U. S. Army War College, Carlisle, PA (p. 54)
Peter J. Boettke, James M. Buchanan Center for Political Economy, Fairfax, VA (p. 56)
Charles Brooks, The Strategy Group, Arlington, VA (p. 62)
*Andrzej Brzeski, University of California, Davis, CA (p. 64)
Kurt Campbell, Center for Strategic and International Studies, Washington, DC (p. 68)
*John E. Carey, International Defense Consultants, Inc., Arlington, VA (p. 69)
John Clark, Hudson Institute, Indianapolis, IN (p. 75)
*Ariel Cohen, The Heritage Foundation, Washington, DC (p. 77)
Robert Conquest, Hoover Institution, Stanford, CA (p. 80)
*Ralph A. Cossa, Pacific Forum CSIS, Honolulu, HI (p. 83)
Melvin Croan, University of Wisconsin, Madison, WI (p. 86)
Helle C. Dale, The Heritage Foundation, Washington, DC (p. 88)
*Arnaud de Borchgrave, Center for Strategic and International Studies, Washington, DC (p. 89)
*Midge Decter, New York, NY (p. 91)
*James S. Denton, Washington, DC (p. 93)
*Joseph D. Douglass, Jr., The Redwood Institute, Falls Church, VA (p. 98)
Dennis J. Dunn, Southwest Texas State University, San Marcos, TX (p. 100)
Richard M. Ebeling, Hillsdale College, Hillsdale, MI (p. 102)
*Nicholas Nash Eberstadt, American Enterprise Institute, Washington, DC (p. 103)
Mark Elliott, Samford University, Birmingham, AL (p. 106)
*Barry S. Fagin, United States Air Force Academy, USAF Academy, CO (p. 108)

RUSSIA AND EURASIA (Continued)

*Charles H. Fairbanks, Jr., The Paul H. Nitze School of Advanced International Studies, Washington, DC (p. 108)

*Harvey Feldman, The Heritage Foundation, Washington, DC (p. 110)

*Gloria Taylor Fisher, Interstate Commission on the Potomac River Basin, Alexandria, VA (p. 112)

Mary C. FitzGerald, Hudson Institute, Washington, DC (p. 112)

*George Folsom, International Republican Institute, Washington, DC (p. 114)

*David Forte, Cleveland State University, Cleveland, OH (p. 114)

*Barbara Hackman Franklin, Barbara Franklin Enterprises, Washington, DC (p. 116)

*Robert O. Freedman, Baltimore Hebrew University, Baltimore, MD (p. 116)

George Friedman, Stratfor.com, Austin, TX (p. 117)

*Frank J. Gaffney, Jr., Center for Security Policy, Washington, DC (p. 119)

*Jeffrey B. Gayner, Americans for Sovereignty, Washington, DC (p. 121)

*William Geimer, Jamestown Foundation, Washington, DC (p. 122)

Reuel Marc Gerecht, American Enterprise Institute, Washington, DC (p. 123)

Alexander J. Groth, University of California, Davis, Davis, CA (p. 130)

Nikolas Gvosdev, *The National Interest*, Washington, DC (p. 131)

Roger Hamburg, Indiana University South Bend, South Bend, IN (p. 133)

Steve H. Hanke, Johns Hopkins University, Baltimore, MD (p. 134)

Ronald L. Hatchett, University of St. Thomas, Houston, TX (p. 137)

*Clark C. Havighurst, Duke University School of Law, Durham, NC (p. 137)

William Anthony Hay, Foreign Policy Research Institute, Philadelphia, PA (p. 138)

Paul Henze, Washington, VA (p. 140)

Bruce Herschensohn, Pepperdine University School of Public Policy, Malibu, CA (p. 141)

Charles Horner, Hudson Institute, Washington, DC (p. 146)

*Olga S. Hruby, Research Center for Religious and Human Rights, New York, NY (p. 148)

John C. Hulsman, The Heritage Foundation, Washington, DC (p. 149)

*Laurence Jarvik, Washington, DC (p. 153)

D. Gale Johnson, University of Chicago, Chicago, IL (p. 155)

Shyam J. Kamath, California State University, Hayward, Hayward, CA (p. 157)

Francis X. Kane, Strategy, Technology and Space, Inc., San Antonio, TX (p. 157)

Adrian Karatnycky, Freedom House, New York, NY (p. 158)

*Mark N. Katz, George Mason University, Fairfax, VA (p. 158)

Brian T. Kennedy, Claremont Institute, Claremont, CA (p. 161)

Fred Kiesner, Loyola Marymount University, Los Angeles, CA (p. 163)

Jeane J. Kirkpatrick, American Enterprise Institute, Washington, DC (p. 164)

*Elie Krakowski, EDK Consulting, Baltimore, MD (p. 168)

*Lawrence Kudlow, Kudlow & Co., LLC, New York, NY (p. 170)

*Andrew Langer, National Federation of Independent Business, Washington, DC (p. 174)

Michael A. Ledeen, American Enterprise Institute, Washington, DC (p. 176)

*John Lenczowski, Institute of World Politics, Washington, DC (p. 177)

William S. Lind, Free Congress Foundation, Washington, DC (p. 180)

*Robert J. Loewenberg, Institute for Advanced Strategic and Political Studies, Washington, DC (p. 182)

Edward D. Lozansky, American University in Moscow, Washington, DC (p. 184)

Hafeez Malik, Villanova University, Villanova, PA (p. 187)

*Yuri N. Maltsev, Carthage College, Kenosha, WI (p. 188)

*Robert Mandel, Lewis and Clark College, Portland, OR (p. 188)

Yuri Mantilla, Family Research Council, Washington, DC (p. 189)

Clifford D. May, The Foundation for the Defense of Democracies, Washington, DC (p. 192)

E. Wayne Merry, American Foreign Policy Council, Washington, DC (p. 199)

Paul E. Michelson, Huntington College, Huntington, IN (p. 201)

Andrew A. Michta, Rhodes College, Memphis, TN (p. 201)

*John H. Moore, Grove City College, Grove City, PA (p. 206)

---

* Has testified before a state or federal legislative committee

RUSSIA AND EURASIA (Continued)

Ronald Nash, Reformed Theological Seminary, Oviedo, FL (p. 211)
Thomas M. Nichols, U. S. Naval War College, Newport, RI (p. 213)
Stephen Nix, International Republican Institute, Washington, DC (p. 214)
Jeremiah O'Keeffe, Plano, TX (p. 217)
William E. Odom, Hudson Institute, Washington, DC (p. 218)
*Martha Brill Olcott, Carnegie Endowment for International Peace, Washington, DC (p. 218)
Rocco M. Paone, U. S. Naval Academy, Annapolis, MD (p. 221)
Kyle Parker, American Foreign Policy Council, Washington, DC (p. 222)
Bruce Parrott, The Paul H. Nitze School for Advanced International Studies, Washington, DC (p. 222)
Ellen F. Paul, Bowling Green State University, Bowling Green, OH (p. 223)
*Svetozar Pejovich, Texas A&M University, Dallas, TX (p. 224)
*Robert Pfaltzgraff, Jr., Institute for Foreign Policy Analysis, Cambridge, MA (p. 227)
Juliana Geran Pilon, American University, Washington, DC (p. 228)
*Richard Pipes, Cambridge, MA (p. 229)
Herman Pirchner, Jr., American Foreign Policy Council, Washington, DC (p. 229)
*Dennis Polhill, Independence Institute, Golden, CO (p. 230)
*William C. Potter, Monterey Institute of International Studies, Monterey, CA (p. 231)
Barry W. Poulson, University of Colorado, Boulder, CO (p. 232)
Richard W. Rahn, NOVECON, Alexandria, VA (p. 236)
*Amy Ridenour, National Center for Public Policy Research, Washington, DC (p. 240)
Sandy Rios, Concerned Women for America, Washington, DC (p. 240)
*David B. Rivkin, Jr., Baker & Hostetler, Washington, DC (p. 241)
*James S. Robbins, National Defense University, Washington, DC (p. 241)
Hilton Root, Economy Strategy Institute, Washington, DC (p. 243)
Azade-Ayse Rorlich, University of Southern California, Los Angeles, CA (p. 243)
*Edward L. Rowny, Washington, DC (p. 245)
Edward J. Rozek, University of Northern Colorado, Boulder, CO (p. 245)
Peter Rutland, Wesleyan University, Middletown, CT (p. 248)
Al Santoli, American Foreign Policy Council, Washington, DC (p. 250)
Paul J. Saunders, The Nixon Center, Washington, DC (p. 250)
Robert A. Scalapino, University of California, Berkeley, Berkeley, CA (p. 251)
Harvey Sicherman, Foreign Policy Research Institute, Philadelphia, PA (p. 259)
Radek Sikorski, American Enterprise Institute, Washington, DC (p. 260)
*Dimitri Simes, The Nixon Center, Washington, DC (p. 260)
*Richard F. Staar, Hoover Institution, Stanford, CA (p. 267)
*Lewis A. Tambs, Tempe, AZ (p. 273)
Roy E. Thoman, West Texas A & M University, Canyon, TX (p. 277)
Ewa M. Thompson, Rice University, Houston, TX (p. 277)
*Mead Treadwell, Institute of the North, Anchorage, AK (p. 281)
Jon Basil Utley, Ludwig von Mises Institute, Washington, DC (p. 283)
*William R. Van Cleave, Southwest Missouri State University, Springfield, MO (p. 284)
*Balint Vazsonyi, Center for the American Founding, McLean, VA (p. 284)
Jude Wanniski, Polyconomics, Parsippany, NJ (p. 288)
Michael Y. Warder, Los Angeles Children's Scholarship Fund, Long Beach, CA (p. 289)
*Alan Rufus Waters, California State University, Fresno, Fresno, CA (p. 289)
*Paul Weyrich, Free Congress Foundation, Washington, DC (p. 293)
Anne A. Witkowsky, Center for Strategic and International Studies, Washington, DC (p. 296)
*Charles Wolf, Jr., RAND, Santa Monica, CA (p. 297)

SOUTH ASIA (including India and Pakistan)

Roger Bate, International Policy Network, Washington, DC (p. 47)
*Peter Brookes, The Heritage Foundation, Washington, DC (p. 61)
Charles Brooks, The Strategy Group, Arlington, VA (p. 62)

SOUTH ASIA (Continued)

Mahmood Butt, Eastern Illinois University, Charleston, IL (p. 66)
Daniel Claingaert, International Republican Institute, Washington, DC (p. 68)
*John E. Carey, International Defense Consultants, Inc., Arlington, VA (p. 69)
Ted Galen Carpenter, Cato Institute, Washington, DC (p. 71)
Pradyumna S. Chauhan, Arcadia University, Glenside, PA (p. 73)
*Ralph A. Cossa, Pacific Forum CSIS, Honolulu, HI (p. 83)
*Arnaud de Borchgrave, Center for Strategic and International Studies, Washington, DC (p. 89)
*Midge Decter, New York, NY (p. 91)
Dana Dillon, The Heritage Foundation, Washington, DC (p. 96)
Khalid Duran, *TransIslam Magazine*, Bethesda, MD (p. 100)
Hillel Fradkin, Ethics and Public Policy Center, Washington, DC (p. 115)
George Friedman, Stratfor.com, Austin, TX (p. 117)
*Frank J. Gaffney, Jr., Center for Security Policy, Washington, DC (p. 119)
Phillip D. Grub, Eastern Washington University, Spokane, WA (p. 130)
Steve H. Hanke, Johns Hopkins University, Baltimore, MD (p. 134)
Bruce Herschensohn, Pepperdine University School of Public Policy, Malibu, CA (p. 141)
Shyam J. Kamath, California State University, Hayward, Hayward, CA (p. 157)
*Geoffrey Kemp, The Nixon Center, Washington, DC (p. 161)
Jeane J. Kirkpatrick, American Enterprise Institute, Washington, DC (p. 164)
*Elie Krakowski, EDK Consulting, Baltimore, MD (p. 168)
*Deepak Lal, University of California at Los Angeles, Los Angeles, CA (p. 172)
Hafeez Malik, Villanova University, Villanova, PA (p. 187)
*Robert Mandel, Lewis and Clark College, Portland, OR (p. 188)
Theodore C. Mataxis, American Military University, Denver, CO (p. 191)
Eugene "Red" McDaniel, American Defense Institute, Alexandria, VA (p. 194)
Jerome Anthony McDuffie, University of North Carolina, Pembroke, Lumberton, NC (p. 195)
*F. Andy Messing, Jr., National Defense Council Foundation, Alexandria, VA (p. 200)
Fariborz L. Mokhtari, National Defense University, Washington, DC (p. 204)
*Steven W. Mosher, Population Research Institute, Front Royal, VA (p. 208)
*Ross H. Munro, Center for Security Studies, Washington, DC (p. 209)
Tom Neumann, Jewish Institute for National Security Affairs, Washington, DC (p. 213)
*James H. Noyes, Hoover Institution, Stanford, CA (p. 215)
Jeremiah O'Keeffe, Plano, TX (p. 217)
James P. O'Leary, Catholic University of America, Washington, DC (p. 217)
Edward A. Olsen, Naval Postgraduate School, Monterey, CA (p. 219)
*James Phillips, The Heritage Foundation, Washington, DC (p. 228)
Danielle Pletka, American Enterprise Institute, Washington, DC (p. 229)
Barry W. Poulson, University of Colorado, Boulder, CO (p. 232)
*Amy Ridenour, National Center for Public Policy Research, Washington, DC (p. 240)
Hilton Root, Economy Strategy Institute, Washington, DC (p. 243)
*Edward L. Rowny, Washington, DC (p. 245)
Al Santoli, American Foreign Policy Council, Washington, DC (p. 250)
Robert A. Scalapino, University of California, Berkeley, Berkeley, CA (p. 251)
Timothy Samuel Shah, Ethics and Public Policy Center, Washington, DC (p. 257)
Devinda R. Subasinghe, St. Petersburg, FL (p. 271)
W. Scott Thompson, Tufts University, Medford, MA (p. 278)
Jude Wanniski, Polyconomics, Parsippany, NJ (p. 288)
*Larry Wortzel, The Heritage Foundation, Washington, DC (p. 299)

SOUTHEAST ASIA (including Burma, Cambodia, Laos, Vietnam, Singapore, Malaysia, Indonesia, the Philippines, Australia, and New Zealand)

*M. Gene Aldridge, New Mexico Independence Research Institute, Las Cruces, NM (p. 36)
William Ball, Northern Michigan University, Marquette, MI (p. 44)
*Doug Bandow, Cato Institute, Washington, DC (p. 45)

SOUTHEAST ASIA (Continued)

*Claude E. Barfield, American Enterprise Institute, Washington, DC (p. 45)
 Arnold Beichman, Hoover Institution, Stanford, CA (p. 49)
 Ellen Bork, Project for the New American Century, Washington, DC (p. 57)
*Peter Brookes, The Heritage Foundation, Washington, DC (p. 61)
 T. Patrick Burke, St. Joseph's University, Wynnewood, PA (p. 65)
 Daniel Claingaert, International Republican Institute, Washington, DC (p. 68)
 Kurt Campbell, Center for Strategic and International Studies, Washington, DC (p. 68)
*John E. Carey, International Defense Consultants, Inc., Arlington, VA (p. 69)
 Ted Galen Carpenter, Cato Institute, Washington, DC (p. 71)
 Gregory B. Christainsen, California State University, Hayward, Hayward, CA (p. 74)
 Jonathan Clarke, Cato Institute, Washington, DC (p. 75)
*Ralph A. Cossa, Pacific Forum CSIS, Honolulu, HI (p. 83)
 Dana Dillon, The Heritage Foundation, Washington, DC (p. 96)
 Ivan Eland, Cato Institute, Washington, DC (p. 105)
*Edwin J. Feulner, The Heritage Foundation, Washington, DC (p. 111)
 Sara Fitzgerald, The Heritage Foundation, Washington, DC (p. 113)
*Robert O. Freedman, Baltimore Hebrew University, Baltimore, MD (p. 116)
 George Friedman, Stratfor.com, Austin, TX (p. 117)
*Jeffrey B. Gayner, Americans for Sovereignty, Washington, DC (p. 121)
 Samuel Gregg, Acton Institute for the Study of Religion and Liberty, Grand Rapids, MI (p. 129)
 Phillip D. Grub, Eastern Washington University, Spokane, WA (p. 130)
 Steve H. Hanke, Johns Hopkins University, Baltimore, MD (p. 134)
 Bruce Herschensohn, Pepperdine University School of Public Policy, Malibu, CA (p. 141)
*Chalmers Johnson, Japan Policy Research Institute, Cardiff, CA (p. 155)
 Shyam J. Kamath, California State University, Hayward, Hayward, CA (p. 157)
 Jeane J. Kirkpatrick, American Enterprise Institute, Washington, DC (p. 164)
*Elie Krakowski, EDK Consulting, Baltimore, MD (p. 168)
*James Andrew Lewis, Center for Strategic and International Studies, Washington, DC (p. 179)
*Robert Mandel, Lewis and Clark College, Portland, OR (p. 188)
 Theodore C. Mataxis, American Military University, Denver, CO (p. 191)
 Jerome Anthony McDuffie, University of North Carolina, Pembroke, Lumberton, NC (p. 195)
*Maurice McTigue, Mercatus Center at George Mason University, Arlington, VA (p. 197)
*F. Andy Messing, Jr., National Defense Council Foundation, Alexandria, VA (p. 200)
 Fariborz L. Mokhtari, National Defense University, Washington, DC (p. 204)
*Steven W. Mosher, Population Research Institute, Front Royal, VA (p. 208)
*Ross H. Munro, Center for Security Studies, Washington, DC (p. 209)
 Jeremiah O'Keeffe, Plano, TX (p. 217)
 Edward A. Olsen, Naval Postgraduate School, Monterey, CA (p. 219)
 Paolo Pasicolan, The Heritage Foundation, Washington, DC (p. 222)
 Barry W. Poulson, University of Colorado, Boulder, CO (p. 232)
*Jim Przystup, Institute for National Strategic Studies, Washington, DC (p. 234)
*R. Sean Randolph, Bay Area Economic Forum, San Francisco, CA (p. 236)
*Amy Ridenour, National Center for Public Policy Research, Washington, DC (p. 240)
 Hilton Root, Economy Strategy Institute, Washington, DC (p. 243)
*Edward L. Rowny, Washington, DC (p. 245)
*Alfred P. Rubin, Tufts University, Medford, MA (p. 246)
 Al Santoli, American Foreign Policy Council, Washington, DC (p. 250)
 Robert A. Scalapino, University of California, Berkeley, Berkeley, CA (p. 251)
*Sheldon W. Simon, Arizona State University, Tempe, AZ (p. 260)
*Richard H. Solomon, United States Institute of Peace, Washington, DC (p. 265)
*Robert F. Turner, University of Virginia School of Law, Charlottesville, VA (p. 282)
 Arthur Waldron, American Enterprise Institute, Washington, DC (p. 287)
*Murray Weidenbaum, Weidenbaum Center, St. Louis, MO (p. 291)
*Charles Wolf, Jr., RAND, Santa Monica, CA (p. 297)

SOUTHEAST ASIA (Continued)

*Larry Wortzel, The Heritage Foundation, Washington, DC (p. 299)
George T. Yu, University of Illinois, Champaign, IL (p. 301)

UNITED NATIONS

Ken L. Adelman, TechCentralStation, Washington, DC (p. 35)
*Sandor Balogh, Hudson Valley Community College, East Greenbush, NY (p. 45)
Philip Bom, Regent University, Redmond, WA (p. 56)
Paul J. Bonicelli, Patrick Henry College, Purcellville, VA (p. 57)
Karol Boudreaux, George Mason University School of Law, Arlington, VA (p. 58)
*Allen Buchanan, University of Arizona, Tucson, AZ (p. 64)
Ted Galen Carpenter, Cato Institute, Washington, DC (p. 71)
Pradyumna S. Chauhan, Arcadia University, Glenside, PA (p. 73)
Helle C. Dale, The Heritage Foundation, Washington, DC (p. 88)
Mark De Young, World Youth Alliance, New York, NY (p. 90)
*Midge Decter, New York, NY (p. 91)
*Thomas DeWeese, American Policy Center, Warrenton, VA (p. 94)
Mark Falcoff, American Enterprise Institute, Washington, DC (p. 109)
*Harvey Feldman, The Heritage Foundation, Washington, DC (p. 110)
*David Forte, Cleveland State University, Cleveland, OH (p. 114)
*Wanda Franz, National Right to Life Committee, Washington, DC (p. 116)
*Frank J. Gaffney, Jr., Center for Security Policy, Washington, DC (p. 119)
Giulio Gallarotti, Wesleyan University, Middletown, CT (p. 120)
*Jeffrey B. Gayner, Americans for Sovereignty, Washington, DC (p. 121)
Gidon A. Gottlieb, University of Chicago Law School, Chicago, IL (p. 127)
Samuel Gregg, Acton Institute for the Study of Religion and Liberty, Grand Rapids, MI (p. 129)
Alexander J. Groth, University of California, Davis, Davis, CA (p. 130)
Bruce Herschensohn, Pepperdine University School of Public Policy, Malibu, CA (p. 141)
*John Hillen, Foreign Policy Research Institute, Philadephia, PA (p. 142)
*Fred C. Ikle, Center for Strategic and International Studies, Washington, DC (p. 151)
Niger Roy Innis, Congress of Racial Equality, New York, NY (p. 151)
*Christopher Joyner, Georgetown University, Washington, DC (p. 156)
Francis X. Kane, Strategy, Technology and Space, Inc., San Antonio, TX (p. 157)
Adrian Karatnycky, Freedom House, New York, NY (p. 158)
Robert G. Kaufman, University of Vermont, Burlington, VT (p. 159)
Jeane J. Kirkpatrick, American Enterprise Institute, Washington, DC (p. 164)
*David B. Kopel, Independence Institute, Golden, CO (p. 167)
*Elie Krakowski, EDK Consulting, Baltimore, MD (p. 168)
Daniel Lapin, Toward Tradition, Mercer Island, WA (p. 174)
*Robert Mandel, Lewis and Clark College, Portland, OR (p. 188)
Yuri Mantilla, Family Research Council, Washington, DC (p. 189)
Theodore C. Mataxis, American Military University, Denver, CO (p. 191)
*Nina May, *Renaissance Connection.com/RCNetwork.net*, Washington, DC (p. 192)
Eugene "Red" McDaniel, American Defense Institute, Alexandria, VA (p. 194)
*Joseph A. Morris, Lincoln Legal Foundation, Chicago, IL (p. 207)
*Joshua Muravchik, American Enterprise Institute, Washington, DC (p. 209)
Julie N. Neff, Concerned Women for America, Washington, DC (p. 211)
*Richard Olivastro, People Dynamics, Farmington, CT (p. 218)
*J. A. Parker, Lincoln Institute for Research and Education, Washington, DC (p. 221)
Jordan Paust, University of Houston Law Center, Houston, TX (p. 223)
*Ronald W. Pearson, Pearson & Pipkin, Inc., Washington, DC (p. 224)
Philip Peters, Lexington Institute, Arlington, VA (p. 226)
*Howard Phillips, The Conservative Caucus, Inc., Vienna, VA (p. 227)
Juliana Geran Pilon, American University, Washington, DC (p. 228)
*Edward Potter, Employment Policy Foundation, Washington, DC (p. 231)

---

* Has testified before a state or federal legislative committee

UNITED NATIONS (Continued)

Arch Puddington, Freedom House, New York, NY (p. 234)
Jeremy Rabkin, Cornell University, Ithaca, NY (p. 235)
*Amy Ridenour, National Center for Public Policy Research, Washington, DC (p. 240)
*David B. Rivkin, Jr., Baker & Hostetler, Washington, DC (p. 241)
*J. Milnor Roberts, High Frontier, Arlington, VA (p. 241)
Robert Royal, Faith & Reason Institute, Washington, DC (p. 245)
*Frank Ruddy, Ruddy & Muir, Chevy Chase, MD (p. 246)
William L. Saunders, Family Research Council, Washington, DC (p. 250)
Robert A. Scalapino, University of California, Berkeley, Berkeley, CA (p. 251)
Brett D. Schaefer, The Heritage Foundation, Washington, DC (p. 252)
*Phyllis Schlafly, Eagle Forum, St. Louis, MO (p. 253)
*Nina Shea, Freedom House, Washington, DC (p. 258)
Shaun Small, Empower America, Washington, DC (p. 262)
*Fred L. Smith, Jr., Competitive Enterprise Institute, Washington, DC (p. 263)
*W. Shepherd Smith, Jr., Institute for Youth Development, Washington, DC (p. 264)
Devinda R. Subasinghe, St. Petersburg, FL (p. 271)
Roy E. Thoman, West Texas A & M University, Canyon, TX (p. 277)
W. Scott Thompson, Tufts University, Medford, MA (p. 278)
*John J. Tierney, Jr., Institute of World Politics, Washington, DC (p. 279)
*Herbert W. Titus, Virginia Beach, VA (p. 279)
*Robert F. Turner, University of Virginia School of Law, Charlottesville, VA (p. 282)
*Balint Vazsonyi, Center for the American Founding, McLean, VA (p. 284)
*Edwin D. Williamson, Sullivan & Cromwell, Washington, DC (p. 295)
*John C. Willke, Life Issues Institute, Inc., Cincinnati, OH (p. 295)
*Larry Wortzel, The Heritage Foundation, Washington, DC (p. 299)
*Wendy Wright, Concerned Women for America, Washington, DC (p. 299)
John Yoo, University of California, Berkeley, Berkeley, CA (p. 300)

WESTERN EUROPE

Jefferson Adams, Sarah Lawrence College, Bronxville, NY (p. 34)
*M. Gene Aldridge, New Mexico Independence Research Institute, Las Cruces, NM (p. 36)
Anton Andereggen, Lewis and Clark College, Portland, OR (p. 37)
Nigel Ashford, Institute for Humane Studies at George Mason University,
    Arlington, VA (p. 41)
*Claude E. Barfield, American Enterprise Institute, Washington, DC (p. 45)
Dennis L. Bark, Hoover Institution, Stanford, CA (p. 45)
*Patrick M. Boarman, National University San Diego, San Diego, CA (p. 55)
Paul J. Bonicelli, Patrick Henry College, Purcellville, VA (p. 57)
Charles Brooks, The Strategy Group, Arlington, VA (p. 62)
*John E. Carey, International Defense Consultants, Inc., Arlington, VA (p. 69)
Ted Galen Carpenter, Cato Institute, Washington, DC (p. 71)
Jonathan Clarke, Cato Institute, Washington, DC (p. 75)
Angelo M. Codevilla, Boston University, Boston, MA (p. 77)
*Joseph I. Coffey, Princeton, NJ (p. 77)
*Ariel Cohen, The Heritage Foundation, Washington, DC (p. 77)
Robert Conquest, Hoover Institution, Stanford, CA (p. 80)
Melvin Croan, University of Wisconsin, Madison, WI (p. 86)
Helle C. Dale, The Heritage Foundation, Washington, DC (p. 88)
*Arnaud de Borchgrave, Center for Strategic and International Studies, Washington, DC (p. 89)
Damjan de Krnjevic-Miskovic, The National Interest, Washington, DC (p. 90)
*Midge Decter, New York, NY (p. 91)
*Thomas Duesterberg, Manufacturers Alliance, Arlington, VA (p. 99)
Peter J. Duignan, Hoover Institution, Stanford, CA (p. 99)
Robert Dujarric, Hudson Institute, Washington, DC (p. 99)

WESTERN EUROPE (Continued)

Dennis J. Dunn, Southwest Texas State University, San Marcos, TX (p. 100)

Ivan Eland, Cato Institute, Washington, DC (p. 105)

*Richard Fairbanks, Center for Strategic and International Studies, Washington, DC (p. 109)

*Edwin J. Feulner, The Heritage Foundation, Washington, DC (p. 111)

*Robert Fike, Americans for Tax Reform, Washington, DC (p. 111)

Sara Fitzgerald, The Heritage Foundation, Washington, DC (p. 113)

*George Folsom, International Republican Institute, Washington, DC (p. 114)

Elizabeth Fox-Genovese, Emory University, Atlanta, GA (p. 115)

*Barbara Hackman Franklin, Barbara Franklin Enterprises, Washington, DC (p. 116)

George Friedman, Stratfor.com, Austin, TX (p. 117)

*Frank J. Gaffney, Jr., Center for Security Policy, Washington, DC (p. 119)

Nile Gardiner, The Heritage Foundation, Washington, DC (p. 120)

*Jeffrey B. Gayner, Americans for Sovereignty, Washington, DC (p. 121)

Gary L. Geipel, Hudson Institute, Indianapolis, IN (p. 122)

*James K. Glassman, American Enterprise Institute, Washington, DC (p. 124)

Gidon A. Gottlieb, University of Chicago Law School, Chicago, IL (p. 127)

Paul Y. Hammond, University of Pittsburgh, Pittsburgh, PA (p. 133)

Steve H. Hanke, Johns Hopkins University, Baltimore, MD (p. 134)

Ronald L. Hatchett, University of St. Thomas, Houston, TX (p. 137)

William Anthony Hay, Foreign Policy Research Institute, Philadelphia, PA (p. 138)

*Thomas H. Henriksen, Hoover Institution, Stanford, CA (p. 140)

Bruce Herschensohn, Pepperdine University School of Public Policy, Malibu, CA (p. 141)

Edward L. Hudgins, The Objectivist Center, Washington, DC (p. 148)

John C. Hulsman, The Heritage Foundation, Washington, DC (p. 149)

Niger Roy Innis, Congress of Racial Equality, New York, NY (p. 151)

Francis X. Kane, Strategy, Technology and Space, Inc., San Antonio, TX (p. 157)

*Geoffrey Kemp, The Nixon Center, Washington, DC (p. 161)

Jeane J. Kirkpatrick, American Enterprise Institute, Washington, DC (p. 164)

*Marvin H. Kosters, American Enterprise Institute, Washington, DC (p. 168)

Marie-Josee Kravis, Hudson Institute, Indianapolis, IN (p. 169)

Michael A. Ledeen, American Enterprise Institute, Washington, DC (p. 176)

Kurt R. Leube, Hoover Institution, Stanford, CA (p. 178)

*James Andrew Lewis, Center for Strategic and International Studies, Washington, DC (p. 179)

Leonard P. Liggio, Atlas Economic Research Foundation, Fairfax, VA (p. 180)

*Robert Mandel, Lewis and Clark College, Portland, OR (p. 188)

Eugene "Red" McDaniel, American Defense Institute, Alexandria, VA (p. 194)

Edward T. McMullen, Jr., South Carolina Policy Council, Columbia, SC (p. 197)

Samuel P. Menefee, Regent University, Virginia Beach, VA (p. 199)

*Constantine C. Menges, Hudson Institute, Washington, DC (p. 199)

E. Wayne Merry, American Foreign Policy Council, Washington, DC (p. 199)

Iain Murray, Statistical Assessment Service, Washington, DC (p. 209)

Henry R. Nau, George Washington University, Washington, DC (p. 211)

Mario Navarro da Costa, American Society for the Defense of Tradition, Family and Property, McLean, VA (p. 211)

*Ronald Nehring, Americans for Tax Reform, San Diego, CA (p. 212)

*Stephen R. Norton, Western Policy Center, Washington, DC (p. 215)

Jeremiah O'Keeffe, Plano, TX (p. 217)

William E. Odom, Hudson Institute, Washington, DC (p. 218)

Rocco M. Paone, U. S. Naval Academy, Annapolis, MD (p. 221)

Charles M. Perry, Institute for Foreign Policy Analysis, Cambridge, MA (p. 226)

*Robert Pfaltzgraff, Jr., Institute for Foreign Policy Analysis, Cambridge, MA (p. 227)

Barry W. Poulson, University of Colorado, Boulder, CO (p. 232)

*Ernest Preeg, Manufacturers Alliance, Arlington, VA (p. 232)

*Michael Radu, Foreign Policy Research Institute, Philadelphia, PA (p. 235)

---

* Has testified before a state or federal legislative committee

WESTERN EUROPE (Continued)

Paul A. Rahe, University of Tulsa, Tulsa, OK (p. 236)
*David B. Rivkin, Jr., Baker & Hostetler, Washington, DC (p. 241)
*L. Jacobo Rodriguez, Cato Institute, Washington, DC (p. 242)
*Allen H. Roth, New York State Advisory Council on Privatization, New York, NY (p. 244)
*Edward L. Rowny, Washington, DC (p. 245)
Robert Royal, Faith & Reason Institute, Washington, DC (p. 245)
*Mark E. Rush, Washington and Lee University, Lexington, VA (p. 247)
Gary Schmitt, Project for the New American Century, Washington, DC (p. 253)
Robert Schuettinger, Washington International Studies Council, Washington, DC (p. 254)
*Ralph Segalman, California State University, Northridge, Northridge, CA (p. 256)
Harvey Sicherman, Foreign Policy Research Institute, Philadelphia, PA (p. 259)
Radek Sikorski, American Enterprise Institute, Washington, DC (p. 260)
*John Sitilides, Western Policy Center, Washington, DC (p. 261)
John C. Soper, John Carroll University, University Heights, OH (p. 266)
*James Stergios, Pioneer Institute for Public Policy Research, Boston, MA (p. 268)
Jerry K. Sweeney, South Dakota State University, Brookings, SD (p. 273)
Ewa M. Thompson, Rice University, Houston, TX (p. 277)
*John J. Tierney, Jr., Institute of World Politics, Washington, DC (p. 279)
Vladimir Tismaneanu, University of Maryland, College Park, MD (p. 279)
*Balint Vazsonyi, Center for the American Founding, McLean, VA (p. 284)
Jude Wanniski, Polyconomics, Parsippany, NJ (p. 288)
*Alan Rufus Waters, California State University, Fresno, Fresno, CA (p. 289)
*Murray Weidenbaum, Weidenbaum Center, St. Louis, MO (p. 291)
*Rolf A. Weil, Roosevelt University, Chicago, IL (p. 291)
*W. Bruce Weinrod, International Technology and Trade Associates, Inc., Washington, DC (p. 292)
*Kenneth Weinstein, Hudson Institute, Washington, DC (p. 292)
*John C. Willke, Life Issues Institute, Inc., Cincinnati, OH (p. 295)
Catherine Windels, Pfizer, Inc., New York, NY (p. 296)
Anne A. Witkowsky, Center for Strategic and International Studies, Washington, DC (p. 296)
*Charles Wolf, Jr., RAND, Santa Monica, CA (p. 297)
*Michael K. Young, George Washington University Law School, Washington, DC (p. 300)

Health and Welfare

AGING/ELDER CARE

*M. Gene Aldridge, New Mexico Independence Research Institute, Las Cruces, NM (p. 36)
Eloise Anderson, Claremont Institute, Sacramento, CA (p. 38)
*Julaine K. Appling, Family Research Institute of Wisconsin, Madison, WI (p. 40)
*Naomi Lopez Bauman, Orlando, FL (p. 47)
Douglas Besharov, American Enterprise Institute, Washington, DC (p. 52)
David Brownlee, Family First, Tampa, FL (p. 64)
*Victoria Craig Bunce, Council for Affordable Health Insurance,
    Inver Grove Heights, MN (p. 65)
*Stuart Butler, The Heritage Foundation, Washington, DC (p. 66)
*Michael A. Ciamarra, Alabama Policy Institute, Birmingham, AL (p. 74)
*Richard T. Colgan, Bridgewater State College, Warwick, RI (p. 78)
*Kenneth L. Connor, Family Research Council, Washington, DC (p. 80)
Bob Corkins, Kansas Legislative Education and Research, Inc., Topeka, KS (p. 82)
*Lawrence Cranberg, Austin, TX (p. 85)
Marie Dolan, New York State Federation of Catholic School Parents, Flushing, NY (p. 96)
*Carrie Gordon Earll, Focus on the Family, Colorado Springs, CO (p. 102)
*Louis D. Enoff, Enoff Associates Limited, Sykesville, MD (p. 107)
*James Frogue, American Legislative Exchange Council, Washington, DC (p. 118)
*Robert Goldberg, Manhattan Institute, Springfield, NJ (p. 125)
Scott Gottlieb, American Enterprise Institute, Washington, DC (p. 127)
Steven A. Grossman, HPS Group, LLC, Silver Spring, MD (p. 130)
*Erick Gustafson, Citizens for a Sound Economy, Washington, DC (p. 131)
Eric Hanushek, Hoover Institution, Stanford, CA (p. 135)
*Joel W. Hay, University of Southern California, Los Angeles, CA (p. 137)
*John MacDonald Hood, John Locke Foundation, Raleigh, NC (p. 145)
*Charles W. Jarvis, United Seniors Association, Fairfax, VA (p. 153)
*Michael Johns, Melville, NY (p. 154)
*W. Thomas Kelly, Savers and Investors League, Mirror Lake, NH (p. 161)
John F. Kilner, The Center for Bioethics and Human Dignity, Bannockburn, IL (p. 163)
Laurence Kotlikoff, Boston University, Boston, MA (p. 168)
*Rita P. Maguire, Arizona Center for Public Policy, Phoenix, AZ (p. 186)
Mary P. Mahoney, United Seniors Association, Inc., Washington, DC (p. 187)
*Roger P. Maickel, Purdue University, Lafayette, IN (p. 187)
*Jim Martin, 60 Plus Association, Arlington, VA (p. 190)
Mary Martin, The Seniors Coalition, Springfield, VA (p. 190)
Merrill Matthews, Jr., Institute for Policy Innovation, Lewisville, TX (p. 192)
*Conrad F. Meier, Heartland Institute, Chicago, IL (p. 198)
*Brant S. Mittler, Texas Public Policy Foundation, San Antonio, TX (p. 204)
*Robert Moffit, The Heritage Foundation, Washington, DC (p. 204)
*Michael A. Morrisey, University of Alabama, Birmingham, Birmingham, AL (p. 207)
*Steven W. Mosher, Population Research Institute, Front Royal, VA (p. 208)
Ronald Nash, Reformed Theological Seminary, Oviedo, FL (p. 211)
Nina Owcharenko, The Heritage Foundation, Washington, DC (p. 220)
*J. A. Parker, Lincoln Institute for Research and Education, Washington, DC (p. 221)
*John Powell, The Seniors Coalition, Springfield, VA (p. 232)
*Amy Ridenour, National Center for Public Policy Research, Washington, DC (p. 240)
*Richard O. Rowland, Grassroot Institute of Hawaii, Aiea, HI (p. 245)
Doug Stiegler, Association of Maryland Families, Woodstock, MD (p. 269)
Jeff Stier, American Council on Science and Health, New York, NY (p. 269)
*Richard Teske, Strategic Advocacy, Arlington, VA (p. 275)
Gerald Walpin, Katten Muchin Zavis Rosenman, New York, NY (p. 288)
Nona Wegner, Citizens for Better Medicare, Washington, DC (p. 291)

AGING/ELDER CARE (Continued)

*Gail Wilensky, Project HOPE, Bethesda, MD (p. 294)

GOVERNMENT HEALTH PROGRAMS

Bruce N. Ames, University of California, Berkeley, Berkeley, CA (p. 37)
*Joseph Antos, American Enterprise Institute, Washington, DC (p. 39)
*Naomi Lopez Bauman, Orlando, FL (p. 47)
William C. Binning, Youngstown State University, Youngstown, OH (p. 53)
*Sue A. Blevins, Institute for Health Freedom, Washington, DC (p. 54)
Brian Boyle, O'Melveny & Myers LLP, Washington, DC (p. 58)
*Twila Brase, Citizens' Council on Health Care, St. Paul, MN (p. 60)
James Bruner, New York Family Policy Council, Albany, NY (p. 64)
*Victoria Craig Bunce, Council for Affordable Health Insurance,
    Inver Grove Heights, MN (p. 65)
*Stuart Butler, The Heritage Foundation, Washington, DC (p. 66)
*John Calfee, American Enterprise Institute, Washington, DC (p. 67)
*Robert Cihak, Evergreen Freedom Foundation, Kirkland, WA (p. 74)
John F. Cogan, Hoover Institution, Stanford, CA (p. 77)
Bob Corkins, Kansas Legislative Education and Research, Inc., Topeka, KS (p. 82)
*Jerry Cox, Arkansas Family Council, Little Rock, AR (p. 84)
*Lawrence Cranberg, Austin, TX (p. 85)
*Lisa Dean, Free Congress Foundation, Washington, DC (p. 91)
Bryan Dowd, University of Minnesota, Minneapolis, MN (p. 98)
*Fran Eaton, Eagle Forum of Illinois, Oak Forest, IL (p. 102)
*Evelyn Ebzery, Memorial Hospital of Sheridan County, Sheridan, WY (p. 103)
*Louis D. Enoff, Enoff Associates Limited, Sykesville, MD (p. 107)
*Susan K. Feigenbaum, University of Missouri, St. Louis, St. Louis, MO (p. 110)
*Roger Feldman, University of Minnesota, Minneapolis, MN (p. 110)
Paul J. Feldstein, University of California, Irvine, Irvine, CA (p. 110)
*Robert Fike, Americans for Tax Reform, Washington, DC (p. 111)
*Wanda Franz, National Right to Life Committee, Washington, DC (p. 116)
*H. E. Frech, III, University of California, Santa Barbara, Santa Barbara, CA (p. 116)
*James Frogue, American Legislative Exchange Council, Washington, DC (p. 118)
Dana R. Gache, Alabama Policy Institute, Birmingham, AL (p. 119)
Carrie J. Gavora, Strategic Health Solutions, Washington, DC (p. 121)
*Steven Globerman, Western Washington University, Bellingham, WA (p. 125)
*Robert Goldberg, Manhattan Institute, Springfield, NJ (p. 125)
Tomi Gomory, Florida State University, Tallahassee, FL (p. 126)
John C. Goodman, National Center for Policy Analysis, Dallas, TX (p. 126)
*Linda Gorman, Independence Institute, Golden, CO (p. 127)
Steven A. Grossman, HPS Group, LLC, Silver Spring, MD (p. 130)
*Erick Gustafson, Citizens for a Sound Economy, Washington, DC (p. 131)
*Edmund F. Haislmaier, Strategic Policy Management, Washington, DC (p. 132)
Robin Hanson, George Mason University, Fairfax, VA (p. 134)
Eric Hanushek, Hoover Institution, Stanford, CA (p. 135)
*Joel W. Hay, University of Southern California, Los Angeles, CA (p. 137)
Jay F. Hein, Hudson Institute, Indianapolis, IN (p. 139)
*Robert B. Helms, American Enterprise Institute, Washington, DC (p. 139)
*Roberta Herzberg, Utah State University, Logan, UT (p. 141)
*John MacDonald Hood, John Locke Foundation, Raleigh, NC (p. 145)
*Kerri Houston, American Conservative Union Field Office, Dallas, TX (p. 147)
*Michael Johns, Melville, NY (p. 154)
*Eugene M. Kolassa, University of Mississippi, University, MS (p. 167)
Laurence Kotlikoff, Boston University, Boston, MA (p. 168)
*Andrea S. Lafferty, Traditional Values Coalition, Washington, DC (p. 172)

GOVERNMENT HEALTH PROGRAMS (Continued)

Dianna Lightfoot, National Physicians Center for Family Resources, Birmingham, AL **(p. 180)**
Cotton M. Lindsay, Clemson University, Clemson, SC **(p. 181)**
*****Mike Long,** Complete Abstinence Eduation Program, Durham, NC **(p. 183)**
Mary P. Mahoney, United Seniors Association, Inc., Washington, DC **(p. 187)**
*****Roger P. Maickel,** Purdue University, Lafayette, IN **(p. 187)**
Merrill Matthews, Jr., Institute for Policy Innovation, Lewisville, TX **(p. 192)**
*****John McClaughry,** Ethan Allen Institute, Concord, VT **(p. 193)**
Olivia M. McDonald, Regent University, Virginia Beach, VA **(p. 195)**
*****Marty McGeein,** McGeein Group, Bethesda, MD **(p. 196)**
Lawrence J. McQuillan, Pacific Research Institute, San Francisco, CA **(p. 197)**
*****Conrad F. Meier,** Heartland Institute, Chicago, IL **(p. 198)**
Harry Messenheimer, Rio Grande Foundation, Tijeras, NM **(p. 200)**
Christopher Middleton, Pacific Research Institute, San Francisco, CA **(p. 201)**
*****Thomas P. Miller,** Cato Institute, Washington, DC **(p. 202)**
*****Brant S. Mittler,** Texas Public Policy Foundation, San Antonio, TX **(p. 204)**
*****Robert Moffit,** The Heritage Foundation, Washington, DC **(p. 204)**
E. Haavi Morreim, University of Tennessee, Memphis, Memphis, TN **(p. 206)**
*****Michael A. Morrisey,** University of Alabama, Birmingham, Birmingham, AL **(p. 207)**
*****James Morrison,** Morrison Associates, Scottsdale, AZ **(p. 207)**
Joe Moser, Galen Institute, Alexandria, VA **(p. 207)**
Stephen Moses, Center for Long-Term Care Financing, Seattle, WA **(p. 207)**
*****Steven W. Mosher,** Population Research Institute, Front Royal, VA **(p. 208)**
Ronald Nash, Reformed Theological Seminary, Oviedo, FL **(p. 211)**
George Nesterczuk, Nesterczuk and Associates, Vienna, VA **(p. 212)**
*****Edward Neuschler,** Institute for Health Policy Solutions, Washington, DC **(p. 213)**
*****Michael J. O'Dea,** Christus Medicus Foundation, Bloomfield Hills, MI **(p. 216)**
*****Jane M. Orient,** Association of American Physicians and Surgeons, Tucson, AZ **(p. 219)**
Nina Owcharenko, The Heritage Foundation, Washington, DC **(p. 220)**
*****Mark V. Pauly,** University of Pennsylvania, Philadelphia, PA **(p. 223)**
*****John Powell,** The Seniors Coalition, Springfield, VA **(p. 232)**
Harold Calvin Ray, National Center for Faith-Based Initiatives, West Palm Beach, FL **(p. 237)**
*****William H. Reid,** Horseshoe, TX **(p. 238)**
Dallas L. Salisbury, Employee Benefit Research Institute, Washington, DC **(p. 248)**
*****Susan Sarnoff,** Ohio University, Athens, OH **(p. 250)**
*****Thomas R. Saving,** Texas A&M University, College Station, TX **(p. 251)**
Greg Scandlen, National Center for Policy Analysis, Washington, DC **(p. 251)**
*****Ralph Segalman,** California State University, Northridge, Northridge, CA **(p. 256)**
*****Pete Sepp,** National Taxpayers Union, Alexandria, VA **(p. 257)**
*****E. Donald Shapiro,** New York Law School, Scottsdale, AZ **(p. 258)**
*****W. Shepherd Smith, Jr.,** Institute for Youth Development, Washington, DC **(p. 264)**
Jeff Stier, American Council on Science and Health, New York, NY **(p. 269)**
*****Kathleen M. Sullivan,** Project Reality, Golf, IL **(p. 271)**
*****Michael Tanner,** Cato Institute, Washington, DC **(p. 274)**
Tammy Tengs, University of California, Irvine, Irvine, CA **(p. 275)**
*****Richard Teske,** Strategic Advocacy, Arlington, VA **(p. 275)**
*****Grace-Marie Turner,** Galen Institute, Alexandria, VA **(p. 281)**
Charlotte Twight, Boise State University, Boise, ID **(p. 282)**
*****Gail Wilensky,** Project HOPE, Bethesda, MD **(p. 294)**
Catherine Windels, Pfizer, Inc., New York, NY **(p. 296)**
Gene C. Wunder, Washburn University, Topeka, KS **(p. 299)**

HEALTH CARE REFORM

*****M. Gene Aldridge,** New Mexico Independence Research Institute, Las Cruces, NM **(p. 36)**
*****Joseph Antos,** American Enterprise Institute, Washington, DC **(p. 39)**

HEALTH CARE REFORM (Continued)

*Charles N. Aswad, Medical Society of the State of New York, Lake Success, NY (p. 41)
*Doug Bandow, Cato Institute, Washington, DC (p. 45)
 John Barrett, Beacon Hill Institute, Boston, MA (p. 46)
*Naomi Lopez Bauman, Orlando, FL (p. 47)
 Bill Becker, Maine Policy Center, Portland, ME (p. 48)
*Mark A. Behrens, Shook, Hardy & Bacon, L.L.P., Washington, DC (p. 49)
 Douglas Besharov, American Enterprise Institute, Washington, DC (p. 52)
*Fran Bevan, Eagle Forum of Pennsylvania, North Huntingdon, PA (p. 53)
 William C. Binning, Youngstown State University, Youngstown, OH (p. 53)
 Greg Blankenship, Illinois Policy Institute, Springfield, IL (p. 54)
*Sue A. Blevins, Institute for Health Freedom, Washington, DC (p. 54)
 Walter Block, Loyola University New Orleans, New Orleans, LA (p. 55)
 Brian Boyle, O'Melveny & Myers LLP, Washington, DC (p. 58)
*Twila Brase, Citizens' Council on Health Care, St. Paul, MN (p. 60)
*Harold O. J. Brown, Reformed Theological Seminary, Charlotte, NC (p. 63)
*Allen Buchanan, University of Arizona, Tucson, AZ (p. 64)
 James M. Buchanan, Center for the Study of Public Choice, Fairfax, VA (p. 64)
*Victoria Craig Bunce, Council for Affordable Health Insurance,
    Inver Grove Heights, MN (p. 65)
 T. Patrick Burke, St. Joseph's University, Wynnewood, PA (p. 65)
*Henry N. Butler, Chapman University, Orange, CA (p. 66)
*Stuart Butler, The Heritage Foundation, Washington, DC (p. 66)
*Dominic M. Calabro, Florida TaxWatch Research Institute, Inc., Tallahassee, FL (p. 67)
*Jon Charles Caldara, Independence Institute, Golden, CO (p. 67)
*James B. Cardle, Texas Citizen Action Network, Austin, TX (p. 69)
 John K. Carlisle, Capital Research Center, Washington, DC (p. 70)
*Robert Cihak, Evergreen Freedom Foundation, Kirkland, WA (p. 74)
 Kenneth W. Clarkson, University of Miami, Coral Gables, FL (p. 75)
*Jerome F. Climer, The Congressional Institute, Alexandria, VA (p. 76)
 John F. Cogan, Hoover Institution, Stanford, CA (p. 77)
*Laurence Cohen, Yankee Institute for Public Policy Studies, Glastonbury, CT (p. 78)
*Stephen Cole, State University of New York, Stony Brook, NY (p. 78)
 Kellyanne Conway, the polling company/WomanTrend, Washington, DC (p. 80)
*Louis J. Cordia, Cordia Companies, Alexandria, VA (p. 82)
 Bob Corkins, Kansas Legislative Education and Research, Inc., Topeka, KS (p. 82)
*Al Cors, National Taxpayers Union and Foundation, Alexandria, VA (p. 82)
 Patricia M. Danzon, University of Pennsylvania, Philadelphia, PA (p. 88)
 Robert G. de Posada, The Latino Coalition, Washington, DC (p. 90)
*William J. Dennis, National Federation of Independent Business Research Foundation,
    Washington, DC (p. 93)
 John Desser, Coalition for Affordable Health Coverage, Washington, DC (p. 93)
 Bryan Dowd, University of Minnesota, Minneapolis, MN (p. 98)
*Evelyn Ebzery, Memorial Hospital of Sheridan County, Sheridan, WY (p. 103)
*James R. Edwards, Jr., Hudson Institute, Washington, DC (p. 104)
*Louis D. Enoff, Enoff Associates Limited, Sykesville, MD (p. 107)
 Richard A. Epstein, University of Chicago Law School, Chicago, IL (p. 107)
*Susan K. Feigenbaum, University of Missouri, St. Louis, St. Louis, MO (p. 110)
*Roger Feldman, University of Minnesota, Minneapolis, MN (p. 110)
 Paul J. Feldstein, University of California, Irvine, Irvine, CA (p. 110)
 Peter Ferrara, International Center for Law and Economics, Washington, DC (p. 110)
 Marilyn R. Flowers, Ball State University, Muncie, IN (p. 113)
 William F. Ford, Middle Tennessee State University, Murfreesboro, TN (p. 114)
 Michael Franc, The Heritage Foundation, Washington, DC (p. 115)
*Walton Francis, Fairfax, VA (p. 115)

HEALTH CARE REFORM (Continued)

*Wanda Franz, National Right to Life Committee, Washington, DC **(p. 116)**

*H. E. Frech, III, University of California, Santa Barbara, Santa Barbara, CA **(p. 116)**

*James Frogue, American Legislative Exchange Council, Washington, DC **(p. 118)**

Dana R. Gache, Alabama Policy Institute, Birmingham, AL **(p. 119)**

Carrie J. Gavora, Strategic Health Solutions, Washington, DC **(p. 121)**

*Gary Glenn, American Family Association of Michigan, Midland, MI **(p. 124)**

*Steven Globerman, Western Washington University, Bellingham, WA **(p. 125)**

*Robert Goldberg, Manhattan Institute, Springfield, NJ **(p. 125)**

John C. Goodman, National Center for Policy Analysis, Dallas, TX **(p. 126)**

*Linda Gorman, Independence Institute, Golden, CO **(p. 127)**

Scott Gottlieb, American Enterprise Institute, Washington, DC **(p. 127)**

Steven A. Grossman, HPS Group, LLC, Silver Spring, MD **(p. 130)**

*Paul Guppy, Washington Policy Center, Seattle, WA **(p. 131)**

*Erick Gustafson, Citizens for a Sound Economy, Washington, DC **(p. 131)**

*Edmund F. Haislmaier, Strategic Policy Management, Washington, DC **(p. 132)**

*Ronald Hansen, University of Rochester, Rochester, NY **(p. 134)**

Robin Hanson, George Mason University, Fairfax, VA **(p. 134)**

Eric Hanushek, Hoover Institution, Stanford, CA **(p. 135)**

*Lynn Harsh, Evergreen Freedom Foundation, Olympia, WA **(p. 136)**

*Joel W. Hay, University of Southern California, Los Angeles, CA **(p. 137)**

Jay F. Hein, Hudson Institute, Indianapolis, IN **(p. 139)**

*Frank J. Heller, Maine Policy Ronin Network, Brunswick, ME **(p. 139)**

*Robert B. Helms, American Enterprise Institute, Washington, DC **(p. 139)**

*David R. Henderson, Hoover Institution, Pacific Grove, CA **(p. 139)**

*Roberta Herzberg, Utah State University, Logan, UT **(p. 141)**

Regina E. Herzlinger, Harvard Business School, Boston, MA **(p. 141)**

*Fred Holden, Phoenix Enterprises, Arvada, CO **(p. 144)**

*John MacDonald Hood, John Locke Foundation, Raleigh, NC **(p. 145)**

*Kerri Houston, American Conservative Union Field Office, Dallas, TX **(p. 147)**

*Robert Hughes, The National Association for the Self-Employed, Washington, DC **(p. 149)**

*Charles W. Jarvis, United Seniors Association, Fairfax, VA **(p. 153)**

*Michael Johns, Melville, NY **(p. 154)**

*Daniel H. "Stormy" Johnson, Jr., The Heritage Foundation, Washington, DC **(p. 155)**

*Raymond J. Keating, Small Business Survival Committee, Manorville, NY **(p. 159)**

*W. Thomas Kelly, Savers and Investors League, Mirror Lake, NH **(p. 161)**

Karen Kerrigan, the polling company, Washington, DC **(p. 162)**

John F. Kilner, The Center for Bioethics and Human Dignity, Bannockburn, IL **(p. 163)**

Daniel Klein, Santa Clara University, Santa Clara, CA **(p. 165)**

*Eugene M. Kolassa, University of Mississippi, University, MS **(p. 167)**

Laurence Kotlikoff, Boston University, Boston, MA **(p. 168)**

*Edward J. Larson, University of Georgia School of Law, Athens, GA **(p. 175)**

Dianna Lightfoot, National Physicians Center for Family Resources, Birmingham, AL **(p. 180)**

Loren E. Lomasky, Bowling Green State University, Bowling Green, OH **(p. 182)**

Michael Lynch, *Reason* Magazine, New Haven, CT **(p. 184)**

*Rita P. Maguire, Arizona Center for Public Policy, Phoenix, AZ **(p. 186)**

Mary P. Mahoney, United Seniors Association, Inc., Washington, DC **(p. 187)**

*Yuri N. Maltsev, Carthage College, Kenosha, WI **(p. 188)**

Willard G. Manning, University of Chicago, Chicago, IL **(p. 188)**

Merrill Matthews, Jr., Institute for Policy Innovation, Lewisville, TX **(p. 192)**

*John McClaughry, Ethan Allen Institute, Concord, VT **(p. 193)**

*Marty McGeein, McGeein Group, Bethesda, MD **(p. 196)**

Lawrence J. McQuillan, Pacific Research Institute, San Francisco, CA **(p. 197)**

Thomas Mead, Maine Policy Center, Portland, ME **(p. 198)**

*Daniel Mead Smith, Washington Policy Center, Seattle, WA **(p. 198)**

HEALTH CARE REFORM (Continued)

*Conrad F. Meier, Heartland Institute, Chicago, IL (p. 198)

Harry Messenheimer, Rio Grande Foundation, Tijeras, NM (p. 200)

Christopher Middleton, Pacific Research Institute, San Francisco, CA (p. 201)

*Thomas P. Miller, Cato Institute, Washington, DC (p. 202)

*Brant S. Mittler, Texas Public Policy Foundation, San Antonio, TX (p. 204)

*Robert Moffit, The Heritage Foundation, Washington, DC (p. 204)

Suzanne C. Moore, Delaware Public Policy Institute, Wilmington, DE (p. 206)

E. Haavi Morreim, University of Tennessee, Memphis, Memphis, TN (p. 206)

*Michael A. Morrisey, University of Alabama, Birmingham, Birmingham, AL (p. 207)

*James Morrison, Morrison Associates, Scottsdale, AZ (p. 207)

Joe Moser, Galen Institute, Alexandria, VA (p. 207)

Stephen Moses, Center for Long-Term Care Financing, Seattle, WA (p. 207)

*Steven W. Mosher, Population Research Institute, Front Royal, VA (p. 208)

Phyllis Berry Myers, Centre for New Black Leadership, Washington, DC (p. 210)

George Nesterczuk, Nesterczuk and Associates, Vienna, VA (p. 212)

*Edward Neuschler, Institute for Health Policy Solutions, Washington, DC (p. 213)

*Michael J. O'Dea, Christus Medicus Foundation, Bloomfield Hills, MI (p. 216)

*Richard Olivastro, People Dynamics, Farmington, CT (p. 218)

Glenn Oppel, Rocky Mountain Enterprise Institute, Billings, MT (p. 219)

*Jane M. Orient, Association of American Physicians and Surgeons, Tucson, AZ (p. 219)

Nina Owcharenko, The Heritage Foundation, Washington, DC (p. 220)

*J. A. Parker, Lincoln Institute for Research and Education, Washington, DC (p. 221)

*Mark V. Pauly, University of Pennsylvania, Philadelphia, PA (p. 223)

Laura Pemberton, National Federation of Independent Business, Washington, DC (p. 225)

*Lovett C. Peters, Pioneer Institute for Public Policy Research, Boston, MA (p. 226)

*Bruce Phillips, National Federation of Independent Business, Washington, DC (p. 227)

*David R. Pinkus, Small Business United of Texas, Austin, TX (p. 229)

*Sally C. Pipes, Pacific Research Institute, San Francisco, CA (p. 229)

*Solomon W. Polachek, State University of New York, Binghamton, Binghamton, NY (p. 230)

*Edward Potter, Employment Policy Foundation, Washington, DC (p. 231)

*John Powell, The Seniors Coalition, Springfield, VA (p. 232)

Rob Raffety, Mercatus Center at George Mason University, Arlington, VA (p. 235)

*William H. Reid, Horseshoe, TX (p. 238)

*Rita Ricardo-Campbell, Hoover Institution, Stanford, CA (p. 239)

*Amy Ridenour, National Center for Public Policy Research, Washington, DC (p. 240)

*Gary Robbins, Fiscal Associates, Arlington, VA (p. 241)

J. Patrick Rooney, Golden Rule Insurance Company, Indianapolis, IN (p. 243)

Peter H. Rossi, University of Massachusetts, Amherst, MA (p. 244)

*Richard O. Rowland, Grassroot Institute of Hawaii, Aiea, HI (p. 245)

Dallas L. Salisbury, Employee Benefit Research Institute, Washington, DC (p. 248)

*Susan Sarnoff, Ohio University, Athens, OH (p. 250)

*Sally Satel, American Enterprise Institute, Washington, DC (p. 250)

*Thomas R. Saving, Texas A&M University, College Station, TX (p. 251)

Greg Scandlen, National Center for Policy Analysis, Washington, DC (p. 251)

*Thomas A. Schatz, Citizens Against Government Waste, Washington, DC (p. 252)

*Bill Schilling, Wyoming Business Alliance / Wyoming Heritage Foundation, Casper, WY (p. 253)

*Phyllis Schlafly, Eagle Forum, St. Louis, MO (p. 253)

*Ralph Segalman, California State University, Northridge, Northridge, CA (p. 256)

*Donald J. Senese, 60 Plus Association, Arlington, VA (p. 257)

*E. Donald Shapiro, New York Law School, Scottsdale, AZ (p. 258)

Tracie Sharp, State Policy Network, Richmond, CA (p. 258)

*Fred L. Smith, Jr., Competitive Enterprise Institute, Washington, DC (p. 263)

*Harvey A. Smith, Arizona State University, Tempe, AZ (p. 263)

HEALTH CARE REFORM (Continued)

Brad Snavely, Michigan Family Forum, Lansing, MI (p. 264)
*C. Eugene Steuerle, Urban Institute, Washington, DC (p. 268)
*William Craig Stubblebine, Claremont McKenna College, Claremont, CA (p. 271)
 Christopher B. Summers, Maryland Public Policy Institute, Germantown, MD (p. 272)
 David G. Surdam, University of Chicago, Chicago, IL (p. 272)
*Alexander Tabarrok, Mercatus Center at George Mason University, Arlington, VA (p. 273)
*Michael Tanner, Cato Institute, Washington, DC (p. 274)
 Tammy Tengs, University of California, Irvine, Irvine, CA (p. 275)
*Richard Teske, Strategic Advocacy, Arlington, VA (p. 275)
*David J. Theroux, The Independent Institute, Oakland, CA (p. 276)
*Forest M. Thigpen, Mississippi Family Council, Jackson, MS (p. 277)
 Kenneth R. Timmerman, Maryland Taxpayers Association, Bethesda, MD (p. 279)
*Grace-Marie Turner, Galen Institute, Alexandria, VA (p. 281)
 Charlotte Twight, Boise State University, Boise, ID (p. 282)
*Peggy Venable, Texas Citizens for a Sound Economy, Austin, TX (p. 284)
*Kevin Vigilante, Rumford, RI (p. 285)
 William Waller, Venable, Baetjer, Howard & Civiletti, LLP, Washington, DC (p. 287)
*Malcolm Wallop, Frontiers of Freedom Institute, Fairfax, VA (p. 288)
 Jude Wanniski, Polyconomics, Parsippany, NJ (p. 288)
*Kurt T. Weber, Cascade Policy Institute, Portland, OR (p. 290)
 Nona Wegner, Citizens for Better Medicare, Washington, DC (p. 291)
*Gail Wilensky, Project HOPE, Bethesda, MD (p. 294)
*Bob Williams, Evergreen Freedom Foundation, Olympia, WA (p. 295)
 Catherine Windels, Pfizer, Inc., New York, NY (p. 296)
*Robert O. C. Worcester, Maryland Business for Responsive Government,
    Baltimore, MD (p. 298)
 Gene C. Wunder, Washburn University, Topeka, KS (p. 299)
 Richard Zeckhauser, Harvard University, Cambridge, MA (p. 302)

HOUSING AND HOMELESSNESS

*Naomi Lopez Bauman, Orlando, FL (p. 47)
 Cecil E. Bohanon, Ball State University, Muncie, IN (p. 56)
 Bernard J. Frieden, Massachusetts Institute of Technology, Cambridge, MA (p. 117)
*Stephen Goldsmith, Manhattan Institute for Policy Research, New York, NY (p. 126)
 Tomi Gomory, Florida State University, Tallahassee, FL (p. 126)
*Erick Gustafson, Citizens for a Sound Economy, Washington, DC (p. 131)
 Eric Hanushek, Hoover Institution, Stanford, CA (p. 135)
 Howard Husock, Manhattan Institute for Policy Research, New York, NY (p. 150)
 Niger Roy Innis, Congress of Racial Equality, New York, NY (p. 151)
*Jack Kemp, Empower America, Washington, DC (p. 161)
*Heather MacDonald, Manhattan Institute for Policy Research, New York, NY (p. 185)
 Olivia M. McDonald, Regent University, Virginia Beach, VA (p. 195)
*Edgar O. Olsen, University of Virginia, Charlottesville, VA (p. 219)
*J. A. Parker, Lincoln Institute for Research and Education, Washington, DC (p. 221)
*Star Parker, Coalition on Urban Renewal and Education, Washington, DC (p. 222)
 Harold Calvin Ray, National Center for Faith-Based Initiatives, West Palm Beach, FL (p. 237)
 Peter H. Rossi, University of Massachusetts, Amherst, MA (p. 244)
 Peter D. Salins, Manhattan Institute for Policy Research, New York, NY (p. 248)
*Sally Satel, American Enterprise Institute, Washington, DC (p. 250)
*James Stergios, Pioneer Institute for Public Policy Research, Boston, MA (p. 268)
*Rebecca Swartz, Hudson Institute, Madison, WI (p. 272)
*E. Fuller Torrey, Bethesda, MD (p. 280)
*Jason Turner, Center for Self-Sufficiency, Shorewood, WI (p. 281)

HOUSING AND HOMELESSNESS (Continued)

*Robert L. Woodson, Sr., National Center for Neighborhood Enterprise, Washington, DC (p. 298)

MEDICAID

*Naomi Lopez Bauman, Orlando, FL (p. 47)
*William W. Beach, The Heritage Foundation, Washington, DC (p. 48)
 Douglas Besharov, American Enterprise Institute, Washington, DC (p. 52)
*Kenneth Brown, Rio Grande Foundation, Albuquerque, NM (p. 63)
*Michael Carozza, Bristol-Myers Squibb, Washington, DC (p. 70)
*Michael A. Ciamarra, Alabama Policy Institute, Birmingham, AL (p. 74)
*Robert Cihak, Evergreen Freedom Foundation, Kirkland, WA (p. 74)
 John F. Cogan, Hoover Institution, Stanford, CA (p. 77)
*Robert J. Cynkar, Cooper & Kirk, PLLC, Washington, DC (p. 87)
*Gerry Dickinson, South Carolina Policy Council, Columbia, SC (p. 95)
*James Frogue, American Legislative Exchange Council, Washington, DC (p. 118)
 Dana R. Gache, Alabama Policy Institute, Birmingham, AL (p. 119)
*Robert Goldberg, Manhattan Institute, Springfield, NJ (p. 125)
 Steven A. Grossman, HPS Group, LLC, Silver Spring, MD (p. 130)
*Erick Gustafson, Citizens for a Sound Economy, Washington, DC (p. 131)
*Edmund F. Haislmaier, Strategic Policy Management, Washington, DC (p. 132)
 Eric Hanushek, Hoover Institution, Stanford, CA (p. 135)
*Joel W. Hay, University of Southern California, Los Angeles, CA (p. 137)
 Regina E. Herzlinger, Harvard Business School, Boston, MA (p. 141)
*John MacDonald Hood, John Locke Foundation, Raleigh, NC (p. 145)
*Charles W. Jarvis, United Seniors Association, Fairfax, VA (p. 153)
*Michael Johns, Melville, NY (p. 154)
*Eugene M. Kolassa, University of Mississippi, University, MS (p. 167)
 Laurence Kotlikoff, Boston University, Boston, MA (p. 168)
 Merrill Matthews, Jr., Institute for Policy Innovation, Lewisville, TX (p. 192)
*John McClaughry, Ethan Allen Institute, Concord, VT (p. 193)
*Marty McGeein, McGeein Group, Bethesda, MD (p. 196)
*Conrad F. Meier, Heartland Institute, Chicago, IL (p. 198)
 Harry Messenheimer, Rio Grande Foundation, Tijeras, NM (p. 200)
 Christopher Middleton, Pacific Research Institute, San Francisco, CA (p. 201)
*Thomas P. Miller, Cato Institute, Washington, DC (p. 202)
*Brant S. Mittler, Texas Public Policy Foundation, San Antonio, TX (p. 204)
*Michael A. Morrisey, University of Alabama, Birmingham, Birmingham, AL (p. 207)
 Joe Moser, Galen Institute, Alexandria, VA (p. 207)
 Stephen Moses, Center for Long-Term Care Financing, Seattle, WA (p. 207)
*Edward Neuschler, Institute for Health Policy Solutions, Washington, DC (p. 213)
*Michael J. O'Dea, Christus Medicus Foundation, Bloomfield Hills, MI (p. 216)
 Nina Owcharenko, The Heritage Foundation, Washington, DC (p. 220)
*Duane Parde, American Legislative Exchange Council, Washington, DC (p. 221)
*J. A. Parker, Lincoln Institute for Research and Education, Washington, DC (p. 221)
*Sally C. Pipes, Pacific Research Institute, San Francisco, CA (p. 229)
*John Powell, The Seniors Coalition, Springfield, VA (p. 232)
*Scott Pullins, Ohio Taxpayers Association and OTA Foundation, Columbus, OH (p. 234)
 Dallas L. Salisbury, Employee Benefit Research Institute, Washington, DC (p. 248)
*Susan Sarnoff, Ohio University, Athens, OH (p. 250)
 Greg Scandlen, National Center for Policy Analysis, Washington, DC (p. 251)
*Richard Teske, Strategic Advocacy, Arlington, VA (p. 275)
*Grace-Marie Turner, Galen Institute, Alexandria, VA (p. 281)
*Gail Wilensky, Project HOPE, Bethesda, MD (p. 294)
*Bob Williams, Evergreen Freedom Foundation, Olympia, WA (p. 295)

---

* Has testified before a state or federal legislative committee

MEDICARE

*Joseph Antos, American Enterprise Institute, Washington, DC (p. 39)
*Naomi Lopez Bauman, Orlando, FL (p. 47)
 Douglas Besharov, American Enterprise Institute, Washington, DC (p. 52)
*Sue A. Blevins, Institute for Health Freedom, Washington, DC (p. 54)
*Victoria Craig Bunce, Council for Affordable Health Insurance,
   Inver Grove Heights, MN (p. 65)
*Stuart Butler, The Heritage Foundation, Washington, DC (p. 66)
*John Calfee, American Enterprise Institute, Washington, DC (p. 67)
*Michael Carozza, Bristol-Myers Squibb, Washington, DC (p. 70)
*Robert Cihak, Evergreen Freedom Foundation, Kirkland, WA (p. 74)
 John F. Cogan, Hoover Institution, Stanford, CA (p. 77)
 Lois J. Copeland, Hillsdale, NJ (p. 81)
 Neil S. Crispo, Florida State University, Tallahassee, FL (p. 86)
*Robert J. Cynkar, Cooper & Kirk, PLLC, Washington, DC (p. 87)
 Bryan Dowd, University of Minnesota, Minneapolis, MN (p. 98)
*Evelyn Ebzery, Memorial Hospital of Sheridan County, Sheridan, WY (p. 103)
*Ryan Ellis, Council for Government Reform, Arlington, VA (p. 106)
*Stephen Entin, Institute for Research on the Economics of Taxation, Washington, DC (p. 107)
*Susan K. Feigenbaum, University of Missouri, St. Louis, St. Louis, MO (p. 110)
*Roger Feldman, University of Minnesota, Minneapolis, MN (p. 110)
 Peter Ferrara, International Center for Law and Economics, Washington, DC (p. 110)
*Walton Francis, Fairfax, VA (p. 115)
*H. E. Frech, III, University of California, Santa Barbara, Santa Barbara, CA (p. 116)
*James Frogue, American Legislative Exchange Council, Washington, DC (p. 118)
 Dana R. Gache, Alabama Policy Institute, Birmingham, AL (p. 119)
 Carrie J. Gavora, Strategic Health Solutions, Washington, DC (p. 121)
*Robert Goldberg, Manhattan Institute, Springfield, NJ (p. 125)
 John C. Goodman, National Center for Policy Analysis, Dallas, TX (p. 126)
 Steven A. Grossman, HPS Group, LLC, Silver Spring, MD (p. 130)
*Erick Gustafson, Citizens for a Sound Economy, Washington, DC (p. 131)
*Edmund F. Haislmaier, Strategic Policy Management, Washington, DC (p. 132)
 Eric Hanushek, Hoover Institution, Stanford, CA (p. 135)
*Joel W. Hay, University of Southern California, Los Angeles, CA (p. 137)
*Robert B. Helms, American Enterprise Institute, Washington, DC (p. 139)
 Regina E. Herzlinger, Harvard Business School, Boston, MA (p. 141)
*John MacDonald Hood, John Locke Foundation, Raleigh, NC (p. 145)
*Charles W. Jarvis, United Seniors Association, Fairfax, VA (p. 153)
*Michael Johns, Melville, NY (p. 154)
*Eugene M. Kolassa, University of Mississippi, University, MS (p. 167)
 Laurence Kotlikoff, Boston University, Boston, MA (p. 168)
 Mary P. Mahoney, United Seniors Association, Inc., Washington, DC (p. 187)
*Roger P. Maickel, Purdue University, Lafayette, IN (p. 187)
*Jim Martin, 60 Plus Association, Arlington, VA (p. 190)
 Mary Martin, The Seniors Coalition, Springfield, VA (p. 190)
 John N. Mathys, DePaul University, Elmhurst, IL (p. 191)
 Merrill Matthews, Jr., Institute for Policy Innovation, Lewisville, TX (p. 192)
*Conrad F. Meier, Heartland Institute, Chicago, IL (p. 198)
 Harry Messenheimer, Rio Grande Foundation, Tijeras, NM (p. 200)
 Christopher Middleton, Pacific Research Institute, San Francisco, CA (p. 201)
*Thomas P. Miller, Cato Institute, Washington, DC (p. 202)
*Brant S. Mittler, Texas Public Policy Foundation, San Antonio, TX (p. 204)
*Robert Moffit, The Heritage Foundation, Washington, DC (p. 204)
*Michael A. Morrisey, University of Alabama, Birmingham, Birmingham, AL (p. 207)
 Joe Moser, Galen Institute, Alexandria, VA (p. 207)

MEDICARE (Continued)

Ronald Nash, Reformed Theological Seminary, Oviedo, FL (p. 211)
Glenn Oppel, Rocky Mountain Enterprise Institute, Billings, MT (p. 219)
*Jane M. Orient, Association of American Physicians and Surgeons, Tucson, AZ (p. 219)
Nina Owcharenko, The Heritage Foundation, Washington, DC (p. 220)
*J. A. Parker, Lincoln Institute for Research and Education, Washington, DC (p. 221)
*Mark V. Pauly, University of Pennsylvania, Philadelphia, PA (p. 223)
*Sally C. Pipes, Pacific Research Institute, San Francisco, CA (p. 229)
*John Powell, The Seniors Coalition, Springfield, VA (p. 232)
*Andrew Rettenmaier, Texas A&M University, College Station, TX (p. 239)
*Amy Ridenour, National Center for Public Policy Research, Washington, DC (p. 240)
*Aldona Robbins, Fiscal Associates, Arlington, VA (p. 241)
Dallas L. Salisbury, Employee Benefit Research Institute, Washington, DC (p. 248)
*Susan Sarnoff, Ohio University, Athens, OH (p. 250)
*Thomas R. Saving, Texas A&M University, College Station, TX (p. 251)
Greg Scandlen, National Center for Policy Analysis, Washington, DC (p. 251)
*Thomas A. Schatz, Citizens Against Government Waste, Washington, DC (p. 252)
*Donald J. Senese, 60 Plus Association, Arlington, VA (p. 257)
*Alexander Tabarrok, Mercatus Center at George Mason University, Arlington, VA (p. 273)
*Michael Tanner, Cato Institute, Washington, DC (p. 274)
*Richard Teske, Strategic Advocacy, Arlington, VA (p. 275)
*Grace-Marie Turner, Galen Institute, Alexandria, VA (p. 281)
Charlotte Twight, Boise State University, Boise, ID (p. 282)
Nona Wegner, Citizens for Better Medicare, Washington, DC (p. 291)
*Gail Wilensky, Project HOPE, Bethesda, MD (p. 294)
Gene C. Wunder, Washburn University, Topeka, KS (p. 299)

POVERTY AND DEPENDENCY

Theodore David Abram, American Institute for Full Employment, Klamath Falls, OR (p. 34)
Eloise Anderson, Claremont Institute, Sacramento, CA (p. 38)
Michael B. Barkey, Center for the Study of Compassionate Conservatism,
    Grand Rapids, MI (p. 46)
*Naomi Lopez Bauman, Orlando, FL (p. 47)
David Beito, University of Alabama, Tuscaloosa, AL (p. 49)
Douglas Besharov, American Enterprise Institute, Washington, DC (p. 52)
Anthony Bradley, Acton Institute for the Study of Religion and Liberty,
    Grand Rapids, MI (p. 59)
*Martin D. Brown, Richmond, VA (p. 63)
James M. Buchanan, Center for the Study of Public Choice, Fairfax, VA (p. 64)
*David Caprara, The Empowerment Network, Fredericksburg, VA (p. 69)
*James B. Cardle, Texas Citizen Action Network, Austin, TX (p. 69)
*J. R. Clark, University of Tennessee, Chattanooga, Chattanooga, TN (p. 75)
Kenneth W. Clarkson, University of Miami, Coral Gables, FL (p. 75)
John F. Cogan, Hoover Institution, Stanford, CA (p. 77)
*John E. Coons, University of California at Berkeley, Berkeley, CA (p. 81)
Richard S. Davis, Washington Research Council, Seattle, WA (p. 89)
*Paul Dunn, University of Louisiana, Monroe, Monroe, LA (p. 100)
*Nicholas Nash Eberstadt, American Enterprise Institute, Washington, DC (p. 103)
Barbara Elliott, Center for Renewal, Houston, TX (p. 105)
Peter Ferrara, International Center for Law and Economics, Washington, DC (p. 110)
Richard B. Freeman, National Bureau of Economic Research, Cambridge, MA (p. 116)
Lowell E. Gallaway, Ohio University, Athens, OH (p. 120)
*Stephen Goldsmith, Manhattan Institute for Policy Research, New York, NY (p. 126)
Tomi Gomory, Florida State University, Tallahassee, FL (p. 126)
Virgil Gulker, Kids Hope USA, Holland, MI (p. 130)

POVERTY AND DEPENDENCY (Continued)

Eric Hanushek, Hoover Institution, Stanford, CA (p. 135)

Rea Hederman, Jr., The Heritage Foundation, Washington, DC (p. 139)

Jay F. Hein, Hudson Institute, Indianapolis, IN (p. 139)

Regina E. Herzlinger, Harvard Business School, Boston, MA (p. 141)

*John MacDonald Hood, John Locke Foundation, Raleigh, NC (p. 145)

*Alan Inman, Institute for Responsible Fatherhood and Family Revitalization, Largo, MD (p. 151)

Niger Roy Innis, Congress of Racial Equality, New York, NY (p. 151)

Earl W. Jackson, Sr., Samaritan Project, Chesapeake, VA (p. 152)

Kirk A. Johnson, Mackinac Center for Public Policy, Midland, MI (p. 155)

Darlene A. Kennedy, Centre for New Black Leadership, Baltimore, MD (p. 162)

Phil Kent, Southeastern Legal Foundation, Atlanta, GA (p. 162)

*Marvin H. Kosters, American Enterprise Institute, Washington, DC (p. 168)

Arthur B. Laffer, A. B. Laffer Associates, San Diego, CA (p. 172)

*Stephen Lazarus, Center for Public Justice, Annapolis, MD (p. 176)

*Heather MacDonald, Manhattan Institute for Policy Research, New York, NY (p. 185)

Mary P. Mahoney, United Seniors Association, Inc., Washington, DC (p. 187)

*Yuri N. Maltsev, Carthage College, Kenosha, WI (p. 188)

Olivia M. McDonald, Regent University, Virginia Beach, VA (p. 195)

*Michael J. McManus, Marriage Savers, Potomac, MD (p. 197)

*Maurice McTigue, Mercatus Center at George Mason University, Arlington, VA (p. 197)

*Lawrence Mead, New York University, New York, NY (p. 198)

Paul T. Mero, The Sutherland Institute, Salt Lake City, UT (p. 199)

*Steven W. Mosher, Population Research Institute, Front Royal, VA (p. 208)

Charles Murray, American Enterprise Institute, Washington, DC (p. 209)

*Richard John Neuhaus, Institute on Religion and Public Life, New York, NY (p. 213)

Seth W. Norton, Wheaton College, Wheaton, IL (p. 215)

Michael J. Novak, Jr., American Enterprise Institute, Washington, DC (p. 215)

Kate O'Beirne, *National Review*, Washington, DC (p. 216)

*Marvin Olasky, University of Texas, Austin, TX (p. 218)

*Star Parker, Coalition on Urban Renewal and Education, Washington, DC (p. 222)

John Raisian, Hoover Institution, Stanford, CA (p. 236)

Harold Calvin Ray, National Center for Faith-Based Initiatives, West Palm Beach, FL (p. 237)

Robert Rector, The Heritage Foundation, Washington, DC (p. 237)

*Brian Riedl, The Heritage Foundation, Washington, DC (p. 240)

Russell Roberts, Weidenbaum Center, St. Louis, MO (p. 242)

*Susan Sarnoff, Ohio University, Athens, OH (p. 250)

*D. Eric Schansberg, Indiana University Southeast, New Albany, IN (p. 252)

*Bradley R. Schiller, American University, Washington, DC (p. 253)

David Schmidtz, University of Arizona, Tucson, AZ (p. 253)

*Ralph Segalman, California State University, Northridge, Northridge, CA (p. 256)

*Rebecca Swartz, Hudson Institute, Madison, WI (p. 272)

*Michael Tanner, Cato Institute, Washington, DC (p. 274)

*Forest M. Thigpen, Mississippi Family Council, Jackson, MS (p. 277)

*Jason Turner, Center for Self-Sufficiency, Shorewood, WI (p. 281)

R. Emmett Tyrrell, The American Alternative Foundation, Alexandria, VA (p. 282)

*Lee H. Walker, New Coalition for Economic and Social Change, Chicago, IL (p. 287)

Jude Wanniski, Polyconomics, Parsippany, NJ (p. 288)

Ben J. Wattenberg, American Enterprise Institute, Washington, DC (p. 290)

Thomas G. West, University of Dallas, Irving, TX (p. 293)

*Robert L. Woodson, Sr., National Center for Neighborhood Enterprise, Washington, DC (p. 298)

*Nicholas Zill, Westat Inc., Rockville, MD (p. 302)

SOCIAL SECURITY AND RETIREMENT

Theodore David Abram, American Institute for Full Employment, Klamath Falls, OR **(p. 34)**
*****Naomi Lopez Bauman,** Orlando, FL **(p. 47)**
*****William W. Beach,** The Heritage Foundation, Washington, DC **(p. 48)**
 Douglas Besharov, American Enterprise Institute, Washington, DC **(p. 52)**
 Andrew Biggs, Cato Institute, Washington, DC **(p. 53)**
 Walter Block, Loyola University New Orleans, New Orleans, LA **(p. 55)**
 Thomas E. Borcherding, Claremont Graduate University, Claremont, CA **(p. 57)**
 James M. Buchanan, Center for the Study of Public Choice, Fairfax, VA **(p. 64)**
*****Steve Buckstein,** Cascade Policy Institute, Portland, OR **(p. 65)**
*****Stuart Butler,** The Heritage Foundation, Washington, DC **(p. 66)**
*****Dominic M. Calabro,** Florida TaxWatch Research Institute, Inc., Tallahassee, FL **(p. 67)**
 Jameson Campaigne, Jr., Jameson Books, Inc., Ottawa, IL **(p. 68)**
*****James B. Cardle,** Texas Citizen Action Network, Austin, TX **(p. 69)**
*****Michael Carozza,** Bristol-Myers Squibb, Washington, DC **(p. 70)**
*****J. R. Clark,** University of Tennessee, Chattanooga, Chattanooga, TN **(p. 75)**
 Kenneth W. Clarkson, University of Miami, Coral Gables, FL **(p. 75)**
*****Jerome F. Climer,** The Congressional Institute, Alexandria, VA **(p. 76)**
 John F. Cogan, Hoover Institution, Stanford, CA **(p. 77)**
 John Colyandro, Texas Conservative Coalition, Austin, TX **(p. 79)**
 Kellyanne Conway, the polling company/WomanTrend, Washington, DC **(p. 80)**
*****Louis J. Cordia,** Cordia Companies, Alexandria, VA **(p. 82)**
 Bob Corkins, Kansas Legislative Education and Research, Inc., Topeka, KS **(p. 82)**
 Robert Costello, Social Security Choice.org, Washington, DC **(p. 83)**
 Edward H. Crane, Cato Institute, Washington, DC **(p. 85)**
 Neil S. Crispo, Florida State University, Tallahassee, FL **(p. 86)**
 Robert G. de Posada, The Latino Coalition, Washington, DC **(p. 90)**
 Pete du Pont, National Center for Policy Analysis, Wilmington, DE **(p. 98)**
 Gerald P. Dwyer, Jr., Federal Reserve Bank of Atlanta, Atlanta, GA **(p. 101)**
 Isaac Ehrlich, State University of New York, Buffalo, Buffalo, NY **(p. 105)**
*****Ryan Ellis,** Council for Government Reform, Arlington, VA **(p. 106)**
*****Eric M. Engen,** American Enterprise Institute, Washington, DC **(p. 107)**
*****Louis D. Enoff,** Enoff Associates Limited, Sykesville, MD **(p. 107)**
*****Stephen Entin,** Institute for Research on the Economics of Taxation, Washington, DC **(p. 107)**
 Martin Feldstein, National Bureau of Economic Research, Cambridge, MA **(p. 110)**
 Peter Ferrara, International Center for Law and Economics, Washington, DC **(p. 110)**
*****Robert Fike,** Americans for Tax Reform, Washington, DC **(p. 111)**
 Marilyn R. Flowers, Ball State University, Muncie, IN **(p. 113)**
 William F. Ford, Middle Tennessee State University, Murfreesboro, TN **(p. 114)**
*****Tom Giovanetti,** Institute for Policy Innovation, Lewisville, TX **(p. 124)**
 John C. Goodman, National Center for Policy Analysis, Dallas, TX **(p. 126)**
 Alfredo Goyburu, The Heritage Foundation, Washington, DC **(p. 127)**
*****Erick Gustafson,** Citizens for a Sound Economy, Washington, DC **(p. 131)**
 James M. Hamilton, For Our Grandchildren, Fairfax, VA **(p. 133)**
 Eric Hanushek, Hoover Institution, Stanford, CA **(p. 135)**
 Paul V. Harberger, Foundation Francisco Marroquin, Santa Monica, CA **(p. 135)**
 Charles G. Hardin, Council for Government Reform, Arlington, VA **(p. 135)**
 Regina E. Herzlinger, Harvard Business School, Boston, MA **(p. 141)**
*****John MacDonald Hood,** John Locke Foundation, Raleigh, NC **(p. 145)**
*****Kerri Houston,** American Conservative Union Field Office, Dallas, TX **(p. 147)**
 Dennis S. Ippolito, Southern Methodist University, Dallas, TX **(p. 152)**
 Thomas Ivancie, America's Future Foundation, Washington, DC **(p. 152)**
*****Charles W. Jarvis,** United Seniors Association, Fairfax, VA **(p. 153)**
*****David John,** The Heritage Foundation, Washington, DC **(p. 154)**
*****W. Thomas Kelly,** Savers and Investors League, Mirror Lake, NH **(p. 161)**

***** Has testified before a state or federal legislative committee**

SOCIAL SECURITY AND RETIREMENT (Continued)

Darlene A. Kennedy, Centre for New Black Leadership, Baltimore, MD **(p. 162)**
Kent King, Missouri State Teachers Association, Columbia, MO **(p. 164)**
Laurence Kotlikoff, Boston University, Boston, MA **(p. 168)**
Arthur B. Laffer, A. B. Laffer Associates, San Diego, CA **(p. 172)**
*****John H. Langbein,** Yale Law School, New Haven, CT **(p. 173)**
Edward J. Lopez, University of North Texas, Denton, TX **(p. 183)**
Telly L. Lovelace, Coalition on Urban Renewal and Education, Washington, DC **(p. 183)**
*****Rita P. Maguire,** Arizona Center for Public Policy, Phoenix, AZ **(p. 186)**
Mary P. Mahoney, United Seniors Association, Inc., Washington, DC **(p. 187)**
*****Jim Martin,** 60 Plus Association, Arlington, VA **(p. 190)**
Mary Martin, The Seniors Coalition, Springfield, VA **(p. 190)**
John N. Mathys, DePaul University, Elmhurst, IL **(p. 191)**
Merrill Matthews, Jr., Institute for Policy Innovation, Lewisville, TX **(p. 192)**
Derrick A. Max, Alliance for Worker Retirement Security, Washington, DC **(p. 192)**
J. Huston McCulloch, Ohio State University, Columbus, OH **(p. 194)**
Norbert Michel, The Heritage Foundation, Washington, DC **(p. 201)**
*****Thomas P. Miller,** Cato Institute, Washington, DC **(p. 202)**
*****Robert Moffit,** The Heritage Foundation, Washington, DC **(p. 204)**
Matt Moore, National Center for Policy Analysis, Dallas, TX **(p. 206)**
*****Steven W. Mosher,** Population Research Institute, Front Royal, VA **(p. 208)**
*****Deroy Murdock,** Atlas Economic Research Foundation, New York, NY **(p. 209)**
Chuck Muth, American Conservative Union, Alexandria, VA **(p. 210)**
Ronald Nash, Reformed Theological Seminary, Oviedo, FL **(p. 211)**
*****Richard Olivastro,** People Dynamics, Farmington, CT **(p. 218)**
Glenn Oppel, Rocky Mountain Enterprise Institute, Billings, MT **(p. 219)**
*****J. A. Parker,** Lincoln Institute for Research and Education, Washington, DC **(p. 221)**
*****Star Parker,** Coalition on Urban Renewal and Education, Washington, DC **(p. 222)**
Laura Pemberton, National Federation of Independent Business, Washington, DC **(p. 225)**
*****Lovett C. Peters,** Pioneer Institute for Public Policy Research, Boston, MA **(p. 226)**
*****Nancy M. Pfotenhauer,** Independent Women's Forum, Arlington, VA **(p. 227)**
Jose Pinera, Cato Institute, Washington, DC **(p. 228)**
*****Edward Potter,** Employment Policy Foundation, Washington, DC **(p. 231)**
*****John Powell,** The Seniors Coalition, Springfield, VA **(p. 232)**
Ralph Rector, The Heritage Foundation, Washington, DC **(p. 237)**
George Reisman, Pepperdine University, Laguna Hills, CA **(p. 238)**
*****Andrew Rettenmaier,** Texas A&M University, College Station, TX **(p. 239)**
Alan Reynolds, Cato Institute, Washington, DC **(p. 239)**
*****Rita Ricardo-Campbell,** Hoover Institution, Stanford, CA **(p. 239)**
*****Amy Ridenour,** National Center for Public Policy Research, Washington, DC **(p. 240)**
Michael Riley, Taxpayers Network, Inc., Cedarburg, WI **(p. 240)**
*****Aldona Robbins,** Fiscal Associates, Arlington, VA **(p. 241)**
Russell Roberts, Weidenbaum Center, St. Louis, MO **(p. 242)**
Dallas L. Salisbury, Employee Benefit Research Institute, Washington, DC **(p. 248)**
*****Thomas R. Saving,** Texas A&M University, College Station, TX **(p. 251)**
*****Thomas A. Schatz,** Citizens Against Government Waste, Washington, DC **(p. 252)**
*****Bradley R. Schiller,** American University, Washington, DC **(p. 253)**
*****Ralph Segalman,** California State University, Northridge, Northridge, CA **(p. 256)**
*****Donald J. Senese,** 60 Plus Association, Arlington, VA **(p. 257)**
*****Hans F. Sennholz,** Grove City College, Grove City, PA **(p. 257)**
Shaun Small, Empower America, Washington, DC **(p. 262)**
Denison E. Smith, For Our Grandchildren, Washington, DC **(p. 263)**
*****Fred L. Smith, Jr.,** Competitive Enterprise Institute, Washington, DC **(p. 263)**
*****C. Eugene Steuerle,** Urban Institute, Washington, DC **(p. 268)**
Charles Stuart, University of California, Santa Barbara, Santa Barbara, CA **(p. 271)**

SOCIAL SECURITY AND RETIREMENT (Continued)

David G. Surdam, University of Chicago, Chicago, IL (p. 272)
*Alexander Tabarrok, Mercatus Center at George Mason University, Arlington, VA (p. 273)
*Michael Tanner, Cato Institute, Washington, DC (p. 274)
James R. "J.T." Taylor, Empower America, Washington, DC (p. 274)
Edwin R. Thompson, Personal Retirement Alliance, Ltd., New York, NY (p. 277)
Charlotte Twight, Boise State University, Boise, ID (p. 282)
*Peggy Venable, Texas Citizens for a Sound Economy, Austin, TX (p. 284)
Russ Walker, Citizens for a Sound Economy, Keizer, OR (p. 287)
*Malcolm Wallop, Frontiers of Freedom Institute, Fairfax, VA (p. 288)
Jude Wanniski, Polyconomics, Parsippany, NJ (p. 288)
Tom Washburne, Home School Legal Defense Association, Purcellville, VA (p. 289)
*Murray Weidenbaum, Weidenbaum Center, St. Louis, MO (p. 291)
*Rolf A. Weil, Roosevelt University, Chicago, IL (p. 291)
Alvin Williams, Black America's PAC, Washington, DC (p. 294)
*Robert L. Woodson, Sr., National Center for Neighborhood Enterprise, Washington, DC (p. 298)

SUBSTANCE ABUSE

Eloise Anderson, Claremont Institute, Sacramento, CA (p. 38)
*David J. Armor, George Mason University, Fairfax, VA (p. 40)
*Bela A. Balogh, University of Mary, Bismarck, ND (p. 45)
Douglas Besharov, American Enterprise Institute, Washington, DC (p. 52)
*David Boaz, Cato Institute, Washington, DC (p. 55)
*John Calfee, American Enterprise Institute, Washington, DC (p. 67)
*Len Deo, New Jersey Family Policy Council, Parsippany, NJ (p. 93)
*Joseph D. Douglass, Jr., The Redwood Institute, Falls Church, VA (p. 98)
Nick Gillespie, Reason Foundation, Los Angeles, CA (p. 123)
Steven A. Grossman, HPS Group, LLC, Silver Spring, MD (p. 130)
Eric Hanushek, Hoover Institution, Stanford, CA (p. 135)
*Joel W. Hay, University of Southern California, Los Angeles, CA (p. 137)
*Alfred N. Himelson, Woodland Hills, CA (p. 143)
*John A. Howard, Howard Center for Family, Religion and Society, Rockford, IL (p. 147)
*David B. Kopel, Independence Institute, Golden, CO (p. 167)
*Eli Lehrer, *The American Enterprise*, Washington, DC (p. 177)
*George Liebmann, Calvert Institute for Policy Research, Baltimore, MD (p. 180)
*Mike Long, Complete Abstinence Eduation Program, Durham, NC (p. 183)
*Heather MacDonald, Manhattan Institute for Policy Research, New York, NY (p. 185)
*Roger P. Maickel, Purdue University, Lafayette, IN (p. 187)
Edmund McGarrell, Hudson Institute, Indianapolis, IN (p. 195)
*Michael J. McManus, Marriage Savers, Potomac, MD (p. 197)
Harold Calvin Ray, National Center for Faith-Based Initiatives, West Palm Beach, FL (p. 237)
*William H. Reid, Horseshoe, TX (p. 238)
*James A. Roumasset, University of Hawaii, Honolulu, HI (p. 245)
*Susan Sarnoff, Ohio University, Athens, OH (p. 250)
*Sally Satel, American Enterprise Institute, Washington, DC (p. 250)
*W. Shepherd Smith, Jr., Institute for Youth Development, Washington, DC (p. 264)
Jeff Stier, American Council on Science and Health, New York, NY (p. 269)
Jacob Sullum, *Reason* Magazine, Fairfax, VA (p. 272)
Tammy Tengs, University of California, Irvine, Irvine, CA (p. 275)
*Mark Thornton, Columbus State University, Columbus, GA (p. 278)
*Jason Turner, Center for Self-Sufficiency, Shorewood, WI (p. 281)
*Kevin Vigilante, Rumford, RI (p. 285)
*Robert L. Woodson, Sr., National Center for Neighborhood Enterprise, Washington, DC (p. 298)

WEALTH CREATION/FINANCIAL EMPOWERMENT

Damon Ansell, Americans for Tax Reform, Washington, DC (p. 39)

*Naomi Lopez Bauman, Orlando, FL (p. 47)

*William W. Beach, The Heritage Foundation, Washington, DC (p. 48)

Anthony Bradley, Acton Institute for the Study of Religion and Liberty, Grand Rapids, MI (p. 59)

James M. Buchanan, Center for the Study of Public Choice, Fairfax, VA (p. 64)

*Stuart Butler, The Heritage Foundation, Washington, DC (p. 66)

*David Caprara, The Empowerment Network, Fredericksburg, VA (p. 69)

*Louis J. Cordia, Cordia Companies, Alexandria, VA (p. 82)

Robert Costello, Social Security Choice.org, Washington, DC (p. 83)

*Paul K. Driessen, Committee for a Constructive Tomorrow, Fairfax, VA (p. 98)

*Paul Dunn, University of Louisiana, Monroe, Monroe, LA (p. 100)

*Tom Giovanetti, Institute for Policy Innovation, Lewisville, TX (p. 124)

*Stephen Goldsmith, Manhattan Institute for Policy Research, New York, NY (p. 126)

Eric Hanushek, Hoover Institution, Stanford, CA (p. 135)

Jay F. Hein, Hudson Institute, Indianapolis, IN (p. 139)

*Fred Holden, Phoenix Enterprises, Arvada, CO (p. 144)

*John MacDonald Hood, John Locke Foundation, Raleigh, NC (p. 145)

*Alan Inman, Institute for Responsible Fatherhood and Family Revitalization, Largo, MD (p. 151)

Niger Roy Innis, Congress of Racial Equality, New York, NY (p. 151)

*Charles W. Jarvis, United Seniors Association, Fairfax, VA (p. 153)

*David John, The Heritage Foundation, Washington, DC (p. 154)

*Bruce Alan Johnson, Bruce Alan Johnson Associates, Indianapolis, IN (p. 155)

*W. Thomas Kelly, Savers and Investors League, Mirror Lake, NH (p. 161)

Darlene A. Kennedy, Centre for New Black Leadership, Baltimore, MD (p. 162)

Daniel Lapin, Toward Tradition, Mercer Island, WA (p. 174)

*Jim Martin, 60 Plus Association, Arlington, VA (p. 190)

*John McClaughry, Ethan Allen Institute, Concord, VT (p. 193)

Lawrence J. McQuillan, Pacific Research Institute, San Francisco, CA (p. 197)

*Steven W. Mosher, Population Research Institute, Front Royal, VA (p. 208)

*Deroy Murdock, Atlas Economic Research Foundation, New York, NY (p. 209)

Phyllis Berry Myers, Centre for New Black Leadership, Washington, DC (p. 210)

Michael J. Novak, Jr., American Enterprise Institute, Washington, DC (p. 215)

*Fred O. Oladeinde, The Foundation for Democracy in Africa, Washington, DC (p. 218)

*Star Parker, Coalition on Urban Renewal and Education, Washington, DC (p. 222)

Harold Calvin Ray, National Center for Faith-Based Initiatives, West Palm Beach, FL (p. 237)

Ralph Rector, The Heritage Foundation, Washington, DC (p. 237)

Robert E. Russell, Jr., The Heritage Foundation, Geneva, IL (p. 247)

*Thomas R. Saving, Texas A&M University, College Station, TX (p. 251)

*Fred L. Smith, Jr., Competitive Enterprise Institute, Washington, DC (p. 263)

*David Strom, Taxpayers League of Minnesota, Plymouth, MN (p. 270)

*Rebecca Swartz, Hudson Institute, Madison, WI (p. 272)

*Michael Tanner, Cato Institute, Washington, DC (p. 274)

James R. "J.T." Taylor, Empower America, Washington, DC (p. 274)

*Grace-Marie Turner, Galen Institute, Alexandria, VA (p. 281)

*Terry W. Van Allen, Kemah, TX (p. 283)

*Peggy Venable, Texas Citizens for a Sound Economy, Austin, TX (p. 284)

Alvin Williams, Black America's PAC, Washington, DC (p. 294)

*Robert L. Woodson, Sr., National Center for Neighborhood Enterprise, Washington, DC (p. 298)

WELFARE/WELFARE REFORM

Theodore David Abram, American Institute for Full Employment, Klamath Falls, OR (p. 34)

WELFARE/WELFARE REFORM (Continued)

Eloise Anderson, Claremont Institute, Sacramento, CA **(p. 38)**

Martin Anderson, Hoover Institution, Stanford, CA **(p. 38)**

Brian Backstrom, Empire Foundation for Policy Research, Clifton Park, NY **(p. 42)**

Hunter Baker, Georgia Family Council, Norcross, GA **(p. 43)**

*****Charles A. Ballard,** Institute for Responsible Fatherhood and Family Revitalization, Largo, MD **(p. 45)**

Michael B. Barkey, Center for the Study of Compassionate Conservatism, Grand Rapids, MI **(p. 46)**

*****Naomi Lopez Bauman,** Orlando, FL **(p. 47)**

Douglas Besharov, American Enterprise Institute, Washington, DC **(p. 52)**

Walter Block, Loyola University New Orleans, New Orleans, LA **(p. 55)**

Anthony Bradley, Acton Institute for the Study of Religion and Liberty, Grand Rapids, MI **(p. 59)**

*****Martin D. Brown,** Richmond, VA **(p. 63)**

James M. Buchanan, Center for the Study of Public Choice, Fairfax, VA **(p. 64)**

*****Dominic M. Calabro,** Florida TaxWatch Research Institute, Inc., Tallahassee, FL **(p. 67)**

Leslie Carbone, Fairfax, VA **(p. 69)**

*****Robert Carleson,** American Civil Rights Union, Alexandria, VA **(p. 70)**

*****Allan C. Carlson,** Howard Center for Family, Religion and Society, Rockford, IL **(p. 70)**

*****Michael A. Ciamarra,** Alabama Policy Institute, Birmingham, AL **(p. 74)**

John Clark, Hudson Institute, Indianapolis, IN **(p. 75)**

John F. Cogan, Hoover Institution, Stanford, CA **(p. 77)**

Neil S. Crispo, Florida State University, Tallahassee, FL **(p. 86)**

*****Janice Shaw Crouse,** Concerned Women for America, Washington, DC **(p. 87)**

Richard S. Davis, Washington Research Council, Seattle, WA **(p. 89)**

*****Len Deo,** New Jersey Family Policy Council, Parsippany, NJ **(p. 93)**

*****Donald J. Devine,** Center for American Values, Shady Side, MD **(p. 94)**

*****Phillip DeVous,** Acton Institute for the Study of Religion and Liberty, Grand Rapids, MI **(p. 94)**

Barbara Elliott, Center for Renewal, Houston, TX **(p. 105)**

*****Louis D. Enoff,** Enoff Associates Limited, Sykesville, MD **(p. 107)**

Peter Ferrara, International Center for Law and Economics, Washington, DC **(p. 110)**

John Findley, Pacific Legal Foundation, Sacramento, CA **(p. 111)**

Jennifer Garrett, The Heritage Foundation, Washington, DC **(p. 120)**

*****Tom Giovanetti,** Institute for Policy Innovation, Lewisville, TX **(p. 124)**

*****Stephen Goldsmith,** Manhattan Institute for Policy Research, New York, NY **(p. 126)**

Tomi Gomory, Florida State University, Tallahassee, FL **(p. 126)**

Leonard M. Greene, Institute for SocioEconomic Studies, White Plains, NY **(p. 129)**

Virgil Gulker, Kids Hope USA, Holland, MI **(p. 130)**

Eric Hanushek, Hoover Institution, Stanford, CA **(p. 135)**

*****Lynn Harsh,** Evergreen Freedom Foundation, Olympia, WA **(p. 136)**

David Hartman, The Lone Star Foundation, Austin, TX **(p. 136)**

Rea Hederman, Jr., The Heritage Foundation, Washington, DC **(p. 139)**

Jay F. Hein, Hudson Institute, Indianapolis, IN **(p. 139)**

Regina E. Herzlinger, Harvard Business School, Boston, MA **(p. 141)**

*****Randy Hicks,** Georgia Family Council, Norcross, GA **(p. 141)**

David Hogberg, Public Interest Institute, Mount Pleasant, IA **(p. 144)**

*****John MacDonald Hood,** John Locke Foundation, Raleigh, NC **(p. 145)**

*****Charles D. Hurley,** Iowa Family Policy Center, Pleasant Hill, IA **(p. 150)**

*****Alan Inman,** Institute for Responsible Fatherhood and Family Revitalization, Largo, MD **(p. 151)**

Niger Roy Innis, Congress of Racial Equality, New York, NY **(p. 151)**

Kirk A. Johnson, Mackinac Center for Public Policy, Midland, MI **(p. 155)**

Darlene A. Kennedy, Centre for New Black Leadership, Baltimore, MD **(p. 162)**

Phil Kent, Southeastern Legal Foundation, Atlanta, GA **(p. 162)**

WELFARE/WELFARE REFORM (Continued)

*David B. Kopel, Independence Institute, Golden, CO (p. 167)
*Marvin H. Kosters, American Enterprise Institute, Washington, DC (p. 168)
 Laurence Kotlikoff, Boston University, Boston, MA (p. 168)
*Jill Cunningham Lacey, Capital Research Center, Damascus, MD (p. 171)
 Arthur B. Laffer, A. B. Laffer Associates, San Diego, CA (p. 172)
*Andrea S. Lafferty, Traditional Values Coalition, Washington, DC (p. 172)
*Mark R. Levin, Landmark Legal Foundation, Herndon, VA (p. 178)
 Dianna Lightfoot, National Physicians Center for Family Resources, Birmingham, AL (p. 180)
*Mike Long, Complete Abstinence Eduation Program, Durham, NC (p. 183)
 Telly L. Lovelace, Coalition on Urban Renewal and Education, Washington, DC (p. 183)
*Heather MacDonald, Manhattan Institute for Policy Research, New York, NY (p. 185)
 Myron Magnet, Manhattan Institute for Policy Research, New York, NY (p. 186)
*Rita P. Maguire, Arizona Center for Public Policy, Phoenix, AZ (p. 186)
 Merrill Matthews, Jr., Institute for Policy Innovation, Lewisville, TX (p. 192)
*John McClaughry, Ethan Allen Institute, Concord, VT (p. 193)
*Michael J. McManus, Marriage Savers, Potomac, MD (p. 197)
 Lawrence J. McQuillan, Pacific Research Institute, San Francisco, CA (p. 197)
*Lawrence Mead, New York University, New York, NY (p. 198)
 Harry Messenheimer, Rio Grande Foundation, Tijeras, NM (p. 200)
*James H. Miller, Wisconsin Policy Research Institute, Mequon, WI (p. 202)
 Stephen Monsma, Pepperdine University, Malibu, CA (p. 205)
*Steven W. Mosher, Population Research Institute, Front Royal, VA (p. 208)
 Charles Murray, American Enterprise Institute, Washington, DC (p. 209)
 Lauren Noyes, The Heritage Foundation, Washington, DC (p. 216)
 Kate O'Beirne, *National Review*, Washington, DC (p. 216)
*Marvin Olasky, University of Texas, Austin, TX (p. 218)
*Gary J. Palmer, Alabama Policy Institute, Birmingham, AL (p. 221)
*Star Parker, Coalition on Urban Renewal and Education, Washington, DC (p. 222)
*Darryl Paulson, University of South Florida, St. Petersburg, FL (p. 223)
*Nancy M. Pfotenhauer, Independent Women's Forum, Arlington, VA (p. 227)
*Edward Potter, Employment Policy Foundation, Washington, DC (p. 231)
*Scott Pullins, Ohio Taxpayers Association and OTA Foundation, Columbus, OH (p. 234)
 Harold Calvin Ray, National Center for Faith-Based Initiatives, West Palm Beach, FL (p. 237)
 Robert Rector, The Heritage Foundation, Washington, DC (p. 237)
*W. Robert Reed, University of Oklahoma, Norman, OK (p. 238)
*Brian Riedl, The Heritage Foundation, Washington, DC (p. 240)
 Russell Roberts, Weidenbaum Center, St. Louis, MO (p. 242)
*Richard O. Rowland, Grassroot Institute of Hawaii, Aiea, HI (p. 245)
*Susan Sarnoff, Ohio University, Athens, OH (p. 250)
*Bradley R. Schiller, American University, Washington, DC (p. 253)
*Geoffrey F. Segal, Reason Public Policy Institute, Los Angeles, CA (p. 256)
*Ralph Segalman, California State University, Northridge, Northridge, CA (p. 256)
*Jamie Self, Georgia Family Council, Norcross, GA (p. 256)
*Amy L. Sherman, Hudson Institute, Charlottesville, VA (p. 259)
*Robert A. Sirico, Acton Institute for the Study of Religion and Liberty, Grand Rapids, MI (p. 261)
*James Skillen, Center for Public Justice, Annapolis, MD (p. 261)
*W. Shepherd Smith, Jr., Institute for Youth Development, Washington, DC (p. 264)
*Lisa Snell, Reason Foundation, Los Angeles, CA (p. 265)
*David Strom, Taxpayers League of Minnesota, Plymouth, MN (p. 270)
 Charles Stuart, University of California, Santa Barbara, Santa Barbara, CA (p. 271)
*Kathleen M. Sullivan, Project Reality, Golf, IL (p. 271)
*Rebecca Swartz, Hudson Institute, Madison, WI (p. 272)
*Michael Tanner, Cato Institute, Washington, DC (p. 274)

WELFARE/WELFARE REFORM (Continued)

Tammy Tengs, University of California, Irvine, Irvine, CA (p. 275)
*Forest M. Thigpen, Mississippi Family Council, Jackson, MS (p. 277)
*Jason Turner, Center for Self-Sufficiency, Shorewood, WI (p. 281)
 R. Emmett Tyrrell, The American Alternative Foundation, Alexandria, VA (p. 282)
*Malcolm Wallop, Frontiers of Freedom Institute, Fairfax, VA (p. 288)
 Thomas G. West, University of Dallas, Irving, TX (p. 293)
*Robert L. Woodson, Sr., National Center for Neighborhood Enterprise,
    Washington, DC (p. 298)
*Charmaine Crouse Yoest, University of Virginia, Charlottesville, VA (p. 300)
*Nicholas Zill, Westat Inc., Rockville, MD (p. 302)
 Ronald A. Zumbrun, The Zumbrun Law Firm, Sacramento, CA (p. 303)

Information Technology

INTELLECTUAL PROPERTY

William F. Adkinson, Progress & Freedom Foundation, Washington, DC **(p. 35)**
David L. Applegate, Olson & Hierl, LTD, Chicago, IL **(p. 39)**
*****Sonia Arrison,** Pacific Research Institute, San Francisco, CA **(p. 41)**
*****Claude E. Barfield,** American Enterprise Institute, Washington, DC **(p. 45)**
*****Naomi Lopez Bauman,** Orlando, FL **(p. 47)**
*****Tom W. Bell,** Chapman University, Orange, CA **(p. 50)**
John J. Bethune, Barton College, Wilson, NC **(p. 53)**
*****Lillian BeVier,** University of Virginia, Charlottesville, VA **(p. 53)**
Walter Block, Loyola University New Orleans, New Orleans, LA **(p. 55)**
Jameson Campaigne, Jr., Jameson Books, Inc., Ottawa, IL **(p. 68)**
Robert Chitester, Palmer R. Chitester Fund, Erie, PA **(p. 73)**
*****Michael A. Ciamarra,** Alabama Policy Institute, Birmingham, AL **(p. 74)**
*****Bartlett D. Cleland,** Institute for Policy Innovation, Lewisville, TX **(p. 76)**
Andrew I. Cohen, University of Oklahoma, Norman, OK **(p. 77)**
*****Clyde Wayne Crews, Jr.,** Cato Institute, Washington, DC **(p. 86)**
*****James DeLong,** Progress & Freedom Foundation, Washington, DC **(p. 92)**
Gerald P. Dwyer, Jr., Federal Reserve Bank of Atlanta, Atlanta, GA **(p. 101)**
*****James R. Edwards, Jr.,** Hudson Institute, Washington, DC **(p. 104)**
*****Jeffrey A. Eisenach,** Progress & Freedom Foundation, Washington, DC **(p. 105)**
Richard A. Epstein, University of Chicago Law School, Chicago, IL **(p. 107)**
*****Barry S. Fagin,** United States Air Force Academy, USAF Academy, CO **(p. 108)**
*****Barbara Hackman Franklin,** Barbara Franklin Enterprises, Washington, DC **(p. 116)**
Michael Friedland, Knobbe, Martens, Olson & Bear, LLP, Irvine, CA **(p. 117)**
Raymond L. Gifford, Progress & Freedom Foundation, Washington, DC **(p. 123)**
*****Tom Giovanetti,** Institute for Policy Innovation, Lewisville, TX **(p. 124)**
*****Steven Globerman,** Western Washington University, Bellingham, WA **(p. 125)**
Samuel Gregg, Acton Institute for the Study of Religion and Liberty, Grand Rapids, MI **(p. 129)**
*****Erick Gustafson,** Citizens for a Sound Economy, Washington, DC **(p. 131)**
*****Robert Hahn,** American Enterprise Institute, Washington, DC **(p. 132)**
*****Ronald Hansen,** University of Rochester, Rochester, NY **(p. 134)**
Mark Y. Herring, Winthrop University, Rock Hill, SC **(p. 140)**
*****Greg Kaza,** Arkansas Policy Foundation, Little Rock, AR **(p. 159)**
F. Scott Kieff, Washington University, St. Louis, MO **(p. 163)**
*****George Landrith,** Frontiers of Freedom Institute, Fairfax, VA **(p. 173)**
*****Richard Langlois,** University of Connecticut, Storrs, CT **(p. 174)**
*****Kent Lassman,** Progress & Freedom Foundation, Raleigh, NC **(p. 175)**
*****James Andrew Lewis,** Center for Strategic and International Studies, Washington, DC **(p. 179)**
Stanley J. Liebowitz, University of Texas, Dallas, Richardson, TX **(p. 180)**
James Lucier, Prudential Securities, Arlington, VA **(p. 184)**
*****Jim Martin,** 60 Plus Association, Arlington, VA **(p. 190)**
*****Nancie G. Marzulla,** Defenders of Property Rights, Washington, DC **(p. 191)**
*****Roger J. Marzulla,** Defenders of Property Rights, Washington, DC **(p. 191)**
Merrill Matthews, Jr., Institute for Policy Innovation, Lewisville, TX **(p. 192)**
*****Randolph J. May,** Progress & Freedom Foundation, Washington, DC **(p. 193)**
*****David N. Mayer,** Capital University Law School, Columbus, OH **(p. 193)**
*****Roger E. Meiners,** University of Texas, Arlington, Arlington, TX **(p. 198)**
Norbert Michel, The Heritage Foundation, Washington, DC **(p. 201)**
*****Joseph A. Morris,** Lincoln Legal Foundation, Chicago, IL **(p. 207)**
*****Milton L. Mueller,** Syracuse University, Syracuse, NY **(p. 208)**
Edward J. Ohlert, JAYCOR, McLean, VA **(p. 218)**
*****J. A. Parker,** Lincoln Institute for Research and Education, Washington, DC **(p. 221)**
Laura Bennett Peterson, Washington, DC **(p. 226)**

INTELLECTUAL PROPERTY (Continued)

*Daniel J. Popeo, Washington Legal Foundation, Washington, DC (p. 231)
*David G. Post, Temple University School of Law, Philadelphia, PA (p. 231)
*James Prendergast, Americans for Technology Leadership, Washington, DC (p. 232)
*Scott Pullins, Ohio Taxpayers Association and OTA Foundation, Columbus, OH (p. 234)
*Alan C. Raul, Sidley & Austin Brown & Wood, LLP, Washington, DC (p. 237)
*Charles F. Rule, Fried, Frank, Harris, Shriver & Jacobson, Washington, DC (p. 246)
*Thomas A. Schatz, Citizens Against Government Waste, Washington, DC (p. 252)
*Phyllis Schlafly, Eagle Forum, St. Louis, MO (p. 253)
*John W. Schlicher, Gray, Cary, Ware & Freidenrich, Palo Alto, CA (p. 253)
 Robert Haney Scott, California State University, Chico, Chico, CA (p. 255)
 Kannon K. Shanmugam, Kirkland & Ellis, Washington, DC (p. 258)
 J. Gregory Sidak, American Enterprise Institute, Washington, DC (p. 259)
*Solveig Singleton, Competitive Enterprise Institute, Washington, DC (p. 261)
*Fred L. Smith, Jr., Competitive Enterprise Institute, Washington, DC (p. 263)
*Alexander Tabarrok, Mercatus Center at George Mason University, Arlington, VA (p. 273)
 James R. "J.T." Taylor, Empower America, Washington, DC (p. 274)
*Adam D. Thierer, Cato Institute, Washington, DC (p. 276)
*Jason M. Thomas, Citizens for a Sound Economy, Washington, DC (p. 277)
 Frank J. Tipler, Tulane University, New Orleans, LA (p. 279)
*Eugene Volokh, University of California at Los Angeles, Los Angeles, CA (p. 285)
*Malcolm Wallop, Frontiers of Freedom Institute, Fairfax, VA (p. 288)
*Paul Weyrich, Free Congress Foundation, Washington, DC (p. 293)
 Jason Wright, Frontiers of Freedom Institute, Fairfax, VA (p. 299)

PRIVACY

 David L. Applegate, Olson & Hierl, LTD, Chicago, IL (p. 39)
*Julaine K. Appling, Family Research Institute of Wisconsin, Madison, WI (p. 40)
*Sonia Arrison, Pacific Research Institute, San Francisco, CA (p. 41)
*Tom W. Bell, Chapman University, Orange, CA (p. 50)
*Lillian BeVier, University of Virginia, Charlottesville, VA (p. 53)
*Sue A. Blevins, Institute for Health Freedom, Washington, DC (p. 54)
*Twila Brase, Citizens' Council on Health Care, St. Paul, MN (p. 60)
*Scott Bullock, Institute for Justice, Washington, DC (p. 65)
*Victoria Craig Bunce, Council for Affordable Health Insurance,
    Inver Grove Heights, MN (p. 65)
*David Burton, Argus Group, Alexandria, VA (p. 66)
*Michael A. Ciamarra, Alabama Policy Institute, Birmingham, AL (p. 74)
*Bartlett D. Cleland, Institute for Policy Innovation, Lewisville, TX (p. 76)
 Andrew I. Cohen, University of Oklahoma, Norman, OK (p. 77)
*Clyde Wayne Crews, Jr., Cato Institute, Washington, DC (p. 86)
*Lisa Dean, Free Congress Foundation, Washington, DC (p. 91)
*Robert Destro, Catholic University of America, Washington, DC (p. 94)
*Thomas DeWeese, American Policy Center, Warrenton, VA (p. 94)
 Gerald P. Dwyer, Jr., Federal Reserve Bank of Atlanta, Atlanta, GA (p. 101)
*William Eggers, Deloitte Research-Public Sector, Washington, DC (p. 104)
*Jeffrey A. Eisenach, Progress & Freedom Foundation, Washington, DC (p. 105)
*Barry S. Fagin, United States Air Force Academy, USAF Academy, CO (p. 108)
*David Forte, Cleveland State University, Cleveland, OH (p. 114)
 Raymond L. Gifford, Progress & Freedom Foundation, Washington, DC (p. 123)
*Tom Giovanetti, Institute for Policy Innovation, Lewisville, TX (p. 124)
 Andrew Grainger, New England Legal Foundation, Boston, MA (p. 128)
*Erick Gustafson, Citizens for a Sound Economy, Washington, DC (p. 131)
 Mark Y. Herring, Winthrop University, Rock Hill, SC (p. 140)
*Robert L. Hershey, Robert L. Hershey, P.E., Washington, DC (p. 141)

PRIVACY (Continued)

Daniel Klein, Santa Clara University, Santa Clara, CA **(p. 165)**
*****David B. Kopel,** Independence Institute, Golden, CO **(p. 167)**
Montgomery N. Kosma, Jones, Day, Reavis & Pogue, Washington, DC **(p. 167)**
Gary Kreep, United States Justice Foundation, Escondido, CA **(p. 169)**
*****Kent Lassman,** Progress & Freedom Foundation, Raleigh, NC **(p. 175)**
Tom Lenard, Progress & Freedom Foundation, Washington, DC **(p. 177)**
*****James Andrew Lewis,** Center for Strategic and International Studies, Washington, DC **(p. 179)**
*****Morgan Long,** American Legislative Exchange Council, Washington, DC **(p. 183)**
James Lucier, Prudential Securities, Arlington, VA **(p. 184)**
Mary P. Mahoney, United Seniors Association, Inc., Washington, DC **(p. 187)**
*****Randolph J. May,** Progress & Freedom Foundation, Washington, DC **(p. 193)**
*****Thomas P. Miller,** Cato Institute, Washington, DC **(p. 202)**
*****Joseph A. Morris,** Lincoln Legal Foundation, Chicago, IL **(p. 207)**
Erie J. Novotny, Fairfax Station, VA **(p. 215)**
*****Jane M. Orient,** Association of American Physicians and Surgeons, Tucson, AZ **(p. 219)**
Laura Pemberton, National Federation of Independent Business, Washington, DC **(p. 225)**
*****William H. Peterson,** Washington, DC **(p. 227)**
*****James Prendergast,** Americans for Technology Leadership, Washington, DC **(p. 232)**
*****Scott Pullins,** Ohio Taxpayers Association and OTA Foundation, Columbus, OH **(p. 234)**
*****Andrew F. Quinlan,** Center for Freedom and Prosperity, Alexandria, VA **(p. 234)**
*****Alan C. Raul,** Sidley & Austin Brown & Wood, LLP, Washington, DC **(p. 237)**
*****Charles E. Rice,** Notre Dame Law School, Notre Dame, IN **(p. 239)**
*****Paul Rubin,** Emory University, Atlanta, GA **(p. 246)**
*****Thomas A. Schatz,** Citizens Against Government Waste, Washington, DC **(p. 252)**
*****Phyllis Schlafly,** Eagle Forum, St. Louis, MO **(p. 253)**
*****Solveig Singleton,** Competitive Enterprise Institute, Washington, DC **(p. 261)**
*****Frances B. Smith,** Consumer Alert, Washington, DC **(p. 263)**
*****Fred L. Smith, Jr.,** Competitive Enterprise Institute, Washington, DC **(p. 263)**
*****Paul Schott Stevens,** Dechert, Price & Rhoads, Washington, DC **(p. 269)**
Jacob Sullum, *Reason* Magazine, Fairfax, VA **(p. 272)**
*****Alexander Tabarrok,** Mercatus Center at George Mason University, Arlington, VA **(p. 273)**
Charlotte Twight, Boise State University, Boise, ID **(p. 282)**
*****Eugene Volokh,** University of California at Los Angeles, Los Angeles, CA **(p. 285)**
Tom Washburne, Home School Legal Defense Association, Purcellville, VA **(p. 289)**
*****Lori L. Waters,** Eagle Forum, Washington, DC **(p. 289)**
*****Paul Weyrich,** Free Congress Foundation, Washington, DC **(p. 293)**
*****Natalie Williams,** Robinson, DiLando and Whitaker, Sacramento, CA **(p. 295)**

TELECOMMUNICATIONS AND THE INTERNET

Donald L. Alexander, Western Michigan University, Kalamazoo, MI **(p. 36)**
David L. Applegate, Olson & Hierl, LTD, Chicago, IL **(p. 39)**
*****Sonia Arrison,** Pacific Research Institute, San Francisco, CA **(p. 41)**
Brent Baker, Media Research Center, Alexandria, VA **(p. 43)**
*****Keith G. Baker,** Florida TaxWatch Research Institute, Inc., Tallahassee, FL **(p. 43)**
Dennis L. Bark, Hoover Institution, Stanford, CA **(p. 45)**
*****William W. Beach,** The Heritage Foundation, Washington, DC **(p. 48)**
*****Tom W. Bell,** Chapman University, Orange, CA **(p. 50)**
Greg Blankenship, Illinois Policy Institute, Springfield, IL **(p. 54)**
Gordon L. Brady, Center for the Study of Public Choice, Fairfax, VA **(p. 60)**
Arthur C. Brooks, Syracuse University, Syracuse, NY **(p. 61)**
*****Samuel Casey Carter,** Acade Metrics, LLC, Washington, DC **(p. 71)**
Robert Chitester, Palmer R. Chitester Fund, Erie, PA **(p. 73)**
*****Michael A. Ciamarra,** Alabama Policy Institute, Birmingham, AL **(p. 74)**
Kenneth W. Clarkson, University of Miami, Coral Gables, FL **(p. 75)**

TELECOMMUNICATIONS AND THE INTERNET (Continued)

*Bartlett D. Cleland, Institute for Policy Innovation, Lewisville, TX (p. 76)
John Colyandro, Texas Conservative Coalition, Austin, TX (p. 79)
*Louis J. Cordia, Cordia Companies, Alexandria, VA (p. 82)
*Christine G. Crafton, Motorola, Inc., Washington, DC (p. 84)
Robert Crandall, Brookings Institution, Washington, DC (p. 85)
*Michael A. Crew, Rutgers University, Newark, NJ (p. 85)
*Clyde Wayne Crews, Jr., Cato Institute, Washington, DC (p. 86)
*Lisa Dean, Free Congress Foundation, Washington, DC (p. 91)
*James DeLong, Progress & Freedom Foundation, Washington, DC (p. 92)
Arthur M. Diamond, Jr., University of Nebraska, Omaha, Omaha, NE (p. 95)
*Thomas Duesterberg, Manufacturers Alliance, Arlington, VA (p. 99)
*William Eggers, Deloitte Research-Public Sector, Washington, DC (p. 104)
*Jeffrey A. Eisenach, Progress & Freedom Foundation, Washington, DC (p. 105)
Joyce Elam, Florida International University, Miami, FL (p. 105)
*Barry S. Fagin, United States Air Force Academy, USAF Academy, CO (p. 108)
Howard Fienberg, Statistical Assessment Service, Washington, DC (p. 111)
Neal B. Freeman, Blackwell Corporation, Vienna, VA (p. 116)
David D. Friedman, Santa Clara University, San Jose, CA (p. 117)
Harold Furchtgott-Roth, American Enterprise Institute, Washington, DC (p. 119)
Jonathan Garthwaite, The Heritage Foundation, Washington, DC (p. 120)
*James Gattuso, The Heritage Foundation, Washington, DC (p. 121)
Raymond L. Gifford, Progress & Freedom Foundation, Washington, DC (p. 123)
James S. Gilmore, The Heritage Foundation, Washington, DC (p. 123)
*Tom Giovanetti, Institute for Policy Innovation, Lewisville, TX (p. 124)
*James K. Glassman, American Enterprise Institute, Washington, DC (p. 124)
*Steven Globerman, Western Washington University, Bellingham, WA (p. 125)
Thomas Golab, Competitive Enterprise Institute, Washington, DC (p. 125)
*Stephen Goldsmith, Manhattan Institute for Policy Research, New York, NY (p. 126)
Frank Gregorsky, Exacting Editorial Services, Vienna, VA (p. 129)
*Erick Gustafson, Citizens for a Sound Economy, Washington, DC (p. 131)
Rebecca Hagelin, The Heritage Foundation, Washington, DC (p. 131)
Thomas Hazlett, Manhattan Institute for Policy Research, Washington, DC (p. 138)
*David R. Henderson, Hoover Institution, Pacific Grove, CA (p. 139)
*Robert L. Hershey, Robert L. Hershey, P.E., Washington, DC (p. 141)
Peter Huber, Manhattan Institute for Policy Research, New York, NY (p. 148)
Donna Rice Hughes, Enough Is Enough, Great Falls, VA (p. 149)
Louis James, Henry Hazlitt Foundation and Free-Market.Net, Chicago, IL (p. 153)
*Laurence Jarvik, Washington, DC (p. 153)
Milton Kafoglis, Emory University, Decatur, GA (p. 156)
Richard T. Kaplar, Media Institute, Washington, DC (p. 157)
Diane S. Katz, Mackinac Center for Public Policy, Midland, MI (p. 158)
*Greg Kaza, Arkansas Policy Foundation, Little Rock, AR (p. 159)
Barry P. Keating, University of Notre Dame, Notre Dame, IN (p. 159)
*Lisa Graham Keegan, Education Leaders Council, Washington, DC (p. 160)
Karen Kerrigan, the polling company, Washington, DC (p. 162)
George A. Keyworth, Progress & Freedom Foundation, Washington, DC (p. 163)
*Lynne Kiesling, Reason Public Policy Institute, Los Angeles, CA (p. 163)
*David B. Kopel, Independence Institute, Golden, CO (p. 167)
Montgomery N. Kosma, Jones, Day, Reavis & Pogue, Washington, DC (p. 167)
Joel Kotkin, Pepperdine University, Malibu, CA (p. 168)
*George Landrith, Frontiers of Freedom Institute, Fairfax, VA (p. 173)
*Richard Langlois, University of Connecticut, Storrs, CT (p. 174)
Daniel Lapin, Toward Tradition, Mercer Island, WA (p. 174)
*Kent Lassman, Progress & Freedom Foundation, Raleigh, NC (p. 175)

TELECOMMUNICATIONS AND THE INTERNET (Continued)

Tom Lenard, Progress & Freedom Foundation, Washington, DC **(p. 177)**

Leonard A. Leo, The Federalist Society for Law and Public Policy Studies, Washington, DC **(p. 178)**

*****James Andrew Lewis,** Center for Strategic and International Studies, Washington, DC **(p. 179)**

Stanley J. Liebowitz, University of Texas, Dallas, Richardson, TX **(p. 180)**

*****Morgan Long,** American Legislative Exchange Council, Washington, DC **(p. 183)**

James Lucier, Prudential Securities, Arlington, VA **(p. 184)**

*****Rita P. Maguire,** Arizona Center for Public Policy, Phoenix, AZ **(p. 186)**

*****Dennis Mansfield,** Boise, ID **(p. 189)**

Merrill Matthews, Jr., Institute for Policy Innovation, Lewisville, TX **(p. 192)**

*****Randolph J. May,** Progress & Freedom Foundation, Washington, DC **(p. 193)**

*****Bobby McCormick,** Clemson University, Clemson, SC **(p. 194)**

Darrell McKigney, Small Business Survival Committee, Washington, DC **(p. 196)**

Ted Morgan, The Heritage Foundation, Washington, DC **(p. 206)**

*****Milton L. Mueller,** Syracuse University, Syracuse, NY **(p. 208)**

Richard Alan Nelson, Louisiana State University, Baton Rouge, LA **(p. 212)**

George R. Neumann, University of Iowa, Iowa City, IA **(p. 213)**

Stuart W. Nolan, Jr., Springfield, VA **(p. 214)**

Seth W. Norton, Wheaton College, Wheaton, IL **(p. 215)**

Erie J. Novotny, Fairfax Station, VA **(p. 215)**

*****J. A. Parker,** Lincoln Institute for Research and Education, Washington, DC **(p. 221)**

Laura Pemberton, National Federation of Independent Business, Washington, DC **(p. 225)**

Laura Bennett Peterson, Washington, DC **(p. 226)**

*****Bruce Phillips,** National Federation of Independent Business, Washington, DC **(p. 227)**

*****David G. Post,** Temple University School of Law, Philadelphia, PA **(p. 231)**

*****James Prendergast,** Americans for Technology Leadership, Washington, DC **(p. 232)**

*****Scott Pullins,** Ohio Taxpayers Association and OTA Foundation, Columbus, OH **(p. 234)**

*****Alan C. Raul,** Sidley & Austin Brown & Wood, LLP, Washington, DC **(p. 237)**

*****Amy Ridenour,** National Center for Public Policy Research, Washington, DC **(p. 240)**

Russell Roberts, Weidenbaum Center, St. Louis, MO **(p. 242)**

*****Charles F. Rule,** Fried, Frank, Harris, Shriver & Jacobson, Washington, DC **(p. 246)**

*****Thomas A. Schatz,** Citizens Against Government Waste, Washington, DC **(p. 252)**

*****Bill Schilling,** Wyoming Business Alliance / Wyoming Heritage Foundation, Casper, WY **(p. 253)**

*****Howard Segermark,** Segermark Associates, Inc., Washington, DC **(p. 256)**

J. Gregory Sidak, American Enterprise Institute, Washington, DC **(p. 259)**

Betsy Page Sigman, Georgetown University, Washington, DC **(p. 259)**

*****Solveig Singleton,** Competitive Enterprise Institute, Washington, DC **(p. 261)**

Michael Spiller, The Heritage Foundation, Washington, DC **(p. 267)**

Irwin Stelzer, Hudson Institute, Washington, DC **(p. 268)**

Charles Stuart, University of California, Santa Barbara, Santa Barbara, CA **(p. 271)**

Christopher B. Summers, Maryland Public Policy Institute, Germantown, MD **(p. 272)**

*****Alexander Tabarrok,** Mercatus Center at George Mason University, Arlington, VA **(p. 273)**

*****Bruce Taylor,** National Law Center for Children and Families, Fairfax, VA **(p. 274)**

James R. "J.T." Taylor, Empower America, Washington, DC **(p. 274)**

*****Adam D. Thierer,** Cato Institute, Washington, DC **(p. 276)**

*****Jason M. Thomas,** Citizens for a Sound Economy, Washington, DC **(p. 277)**

R. Emmett Tyrrell, The American Alternative Foundation, Alexandria, VA **(p. 282)**

*****Peggy Venable,** Texas Citizens for a Sound Economy, Austin, TX **(p. 284)**

*****Eugene Volokh,** University of California at Los Angeles, Los Angeles, CA **(p. 285)**

Russ Walker, Citizens for a Sound Economy, Keizer, OR **(p. 287)**

*****Malcolm Wallop,** Frontiers of Freedom Institute, Fairfax, VA **(p. 288)**

John Wohlstetter, Discovery Institute, Washington, DC **(p. 297)**

Jason Wright, Frontiers of Freedom Institute, Fairfax, VA **(p. 299)**

Labor

DAVIS-BACON ACT

*William T. Alpert, University of Connecticut, Stamford, CT (p. 37)
*Charles W. Baird, California State University, Hayward, Hayward, CA (p. 43)
*Naomi Lopez Bauman, Orlando, FL (p. 47)
  Walter Block, Loyola University New Orleans, New Orleans, LA (p. 55)
*David Denholm, Public Service Research Foundation, Vienna, VA (p. 92)
*Susan Eckerly, National Federation of Independent Business, Washington, DC (p. 103)
  Lowell E. Gallaway, Ohio University, Athens, OH (p. 120)
*Stephen O. Goodrick, National Right to Work Committee, Springfield, VA (p. 126)
*Robert Hunter, Mackinac Center for Public Policy, Midland, MI (p. 150)
  Karen Kerrigan, the polling company, Washington, DC (p. 162)
*William A. Keyes, The Institute on Political Journalism, Washington, DC (p. 162)
*Marvin H. Kosters, American Enterprise Institute, Washington, DC (p. 168)
  John E. Kramer, Institute for Justice, Washington, DC (p. 168)
*Adrian T. Moore, Reason Foundation, Los Angeles, CA (p. 205)
  Suzanne C. Moore, Delaware Public Policy Institute, Wilmington, DE (p. 206)
*Ronald Nehring, Americans for Tax Reform, San Diego, CA (p. 212)
*Herbert R. Northrup, University of Pennsylvania, Haverford, PA (p. 215)
  Ivan G. Osorio, Capital Research Center, Washington, DC (p. 220)
*Star Parker, Coalition on Urban Renewal and Education, Washington, DC (p. 222)
*Edward Potter, Employment Policy Foundation, Washington, DC (p. 231)
*Geoffrey F. Segal, Reason Public Policy Institute, Los Angeles, CA (p. 256)
*Richard Vedder, Ohio University, Athens, OH (p. 284)
*Murray Weidenbaum, Weidenbaum Center, St. Louis, MO (p. 291)
*Bob Williams, Evergreen Freedom Foundation, Olympia, WA (p. 295)
  Walter E. Williams, George Mason University, Fairfax, VA (p. 295)
*Robert L. Woodson, Sr., National Center for Neighborhood Enterprise,
    Washington, DC (p. 298)
*Robert O. C. Worcester, Maryland Business for Responsive Government,
    Baltimore, MD (p. 298)

FAMILY AND MEDICAL LEAVE

*William T. Alpert, University of Connecticut, Stamford, CT (p. 37)
*Naomi Lopez Bauman, Orlando, FL (p. 47)
*William Conerly, Conerly Consulting, Portland, OR (p. 79)
*Len Deo, New Jersey Family Policy Council, Parsippany, NJ (p. 93)
*Susan Eckerly, National Federation of Independent Business, Washington, DC (p. 103)
*Deanna R. Gelak, Family and Medical Leave Act Technical Corrections Coalition,
    Springfield, VA (p. 122)
  Thomas R. Ireland, University of Missouri, St. Louis, St. Louis, MO (p. 152)
  Karen Kerrigan, the polling company, Washington, DC (p. 162)
*Marvin H. Kosters, American Enterprise Institute, Washington, DC (p. 168)
*Andrew Langer, National Federation of Independent Business, Washington, DC (p. 174)
  Suzanne C. Moore, Delaware Public Policy Institute, Wilmington, DE (p. 206)
*Herbert R. Northrup, University of Pennsylvania, Haverford, PA (p. 215)
*Nancy M. Pfotenhauer, Independent Women's Forum, Arlington, VA (p. 227)
*Bruce Phillips, National Federation of Independent Business, Washington, DC (p. 227)
*Edward Potter, Employment Policy Foundation, Washington, DC (p. 231)
  Harold Calvin Ray, National Center for Faith-Based Initiatives, West Palm Beach, FL (p. 237)
  John F. Scalia, Greenberg Traurig, LLP, McLean, VA (p. 251)
  Jason Wright, Frontiers of Freedom Institute, Fairfax, VA (p. 299)

JOB TRAINING/WELFARE TO WORK

Theodore David Abram, American Institute for Full Employment, Klamath Falls, OR **(p. 34)**
*****Stephen Adams,** Pioneer Institute for Public Policy Research, Boston, MA **(p. 34)**
John T. Addison, University of South Carolina, Columbia, SC **(p. 34)**
Eloise Anderson, Claremont Institute, Sacramento, CA **(p. 38)**
Douglas Besharov, American Enterprise Institute, Washington, DC **(p. 52)**
Anthony Bradley, Acton Institute for the Study of Religion and Liberty,
    Grand Rapids, MI **(p. 59)**
*****James B. Cardle,** Texas Citizen Action Network, Austin, TX **(p. 69)**
*****Robert Carleson,** American Civil Rights Union, Alexandria, VA **(p. 70)**
*****Stephen M. Colarelli,** Central Michigan University, Mount Pleasant, MI **(p. 78)**
*****John W. Courtney,** American Institute for Full Employment, Klamath Falls, OR **(p. 83)**
*****Susan Eckerly,** National Federation of Independent Business, Washington, DC **(p. 103)**
Barbara Elliott, Center for Renewal, Houston, TX **(p. 105)**
*****Stephen Goldsmith,** Manhattan Institute for Policy Research, New York, NY **(p. 126)**
Roger Hamburg, Indiana University South Bend, South Bend, IN **(p. 133)**
Jay F. Hein, Hudson Institute, Indianapolis, IN **(p. 139)**
*****Robert Hunter,** Mackinac Center for Public Policy, Midland, MI **(p. 150)**
Niger Roy Innis, Congress of Racial Equality, New York, NY **(p. 151)**
*****Marvin H. Kosters,** American Enterprise Institute, Washington, DC **(p. 168)**
Edward T. McMullen, Jr., South Carolina Policy Council, Columbia, SC **(p. 197)**
*****Lawrence Mead,** New York University, New York, NY **(p. 198)**
Suzanne C. Moore, Delaware Public Policy Institute, Wilmington, DE **(p. 206)**
*****David B. Muhlhausen,** The Heritage Foundation, Washington, DC **(p. 208)**
*****Herbert R. Northrup,** University of Pennsylvania, Haverford, PA **(p. 215)**
*****Nancy M. Pfotenhauer,** Independent Women's Forum, Arlington, VA **(p. 227)**
*****Solomon W. Polachek,** State University of New York, Binghamton, Binghamton, NY **(p. 230)**
*****Edward Potter,** Employment Policy Foundation, Washington, DC **(p. 231)**
Harold Calvin Ray, National Center for Faith-Based Initiatives, West Palm Beach, FL **(p. 237)**
Robert Rector, The Heritage Foundation, Washington, DC **(p. 237)**
*****Brian Riedl,** The Heritage Foundation, Washington, DC **(p. 240)**
*****Bradley R. Schiller,** American University, Washington, DC **(p. 253)**
*****Ralph Segalman,** California State University, Northridge, Northridge, CA **(p. 256)**
*****Lawrence Wohl,** Gustavus Adolphus College, St. Peter, MN **(p. 297)**
*****Robert L. Woodson, Sr.,** National Center for Neighborhood Enterprise,
    Washington, DC **(p. 298)**

LABOR AND EMPLOYMENT

John T. Addison, University of South Carolina, Columbia, SC **(p. 34)**
Eloise Anderson, Claremont Institute, Sacramento, CA **(p. 38)**
*****Naomi Lopez Bauman,** Orlando, FL **(p. 47)**
Gary Becker, University of Chicago, Chicago, IL **(p. 48)**
Donald Bellante, University of South Florida, Tampa, FL **(p. 50)**
Walter Block, Loyola University New Orleans, New Orleans, LA **(p. 55)**
Jennifer C. Braceras, Independent Women's Forum, Arlington, VA **(p. 59)**
*****Matthew J. Brouillette,** The Commonwealth Foundation, Harrisburg, PA **(p. 62)**
*****Milton L. Chappell,** National Right to Work Legal Defense Foundation, Springfield, VA **(p. 72)**
*****Linda Chavez,** Center for Equal Opportunity, Sterling, VA **(p. 73)**
*****Barry R. Chiswick,** University of Illinois, Chicago, Chicago, IL **(p. 73)**
*****Roger Clegg,** Center for Equal Opportunity, Sterling, VA **(p. 76)**
*****William Conerly,** Conerly Consulting, Portland, OR **(p. 79)**
*****Wendell Cox,** Wendell Cox Consultancy, Belleville, IL **(p. 84)**
*****Carl DeMaio,** Reason Foundation, Los Angeles, CA **(p. 92)**
*****David Denholm,** Public Service Research Foundation, Vienna, VA **(p. 92)**
Helene Denney, Nevada Policy Research Insitute, Las Vegas, NV **(p. 92)**

***** Has testified before a state or federal legislative committee

LABOR AND EMPLOYMENT (Continued)

*William J. Dennis, National Federation of Independent Business Research Foundation, Washington, DC (p. 93)

*Phillip DeVous, Acton Institute for the Study of Religion and Liberty, Grand Rapids, MI (p. 94)

*Thomas J. DiLorenzo, Loyola College, Clarksville, MD (p. 96)

*Susan Eckerly, National Federation of Independent Business, Washington, DC (p. 103)

Richard B. Freeman, National Bureau of Economic Research, Cambridge, MA (p. 116)

Lowell E. Gallaway, Ohio University, Athens, OH (p. 120)

*Deanna R. Gelak, Family and Medical Leave Act Technical Corrections Coalition, Springfield, VA (p. 122)

Stefan Gleason, National Right to Work Legal Defense Foundation, Springfield, VA (p. 124)

*Stephen O. Goodrick, National Right to Work Committee, Springfield, VA (p. 126)

Andrew Grainger, New England Legal Foundation, Boston, MA (p. 128)

*Charlene Haar, Education Policy Institute, Washington, DC (p. 131)

Thomas R. Haggard, University of South Carolina, Columbia, SC (p. 132)

Justin Heet, Hudson Institute, Indianapolis, IN (p. 139)

*Robert Hughes, The National Association for the Self-Employed, Washington, DC (p. 149)

*Robert Hunter, Mackinac Center for Public Policy, Midland, MI (p. 150)

*Harry G. Hutchison, Wayne State University, Detroit, MI (p. 150)

David Kendrick, National Legal and Policy Center, Falls Church, VA (p. 161)

Kent King, Missouri State Teachers Association, Columbia, MO (p. 164)

*Marvin H. Kosters, American Enterprise Institute, Washington, DC (p. 168)

*Raymond J. LaJeunesse, Jr., National Right to Work Legal Defense Foundation, Springfield, VA (p. 172)

*John H. Langbein, Yale Law School, New Haven, CT (p. 173)

Reed Larson, National Right to Work Committee, Springfield, VA (p. 175)

Dwight R. Lee, University of Georgia, Athens, GA (p. 176)

*Mark R. Levin, Landmark Legal Foundation, Herndon, VA (p. 178)

Cotton M. Lindsay, Clemson University, Clemson, SC (p. 181)

Frederick R. Lynch, Claremont McKenna College, Claremont, CA (p. 184)

Joseph P. McHugh, Reed Smith LLP, Pittsburgh, PA (p. 196)

Richard B. McKenzie, University of California, Irvine, Irvine, CA (p. 196)

Lawrence J. McQuillan, Pacific Research Institute, San Francisco, CA (p. 197)

*Maurice McTigue, Mercatus Center at George Mason University, Arlington, VA (p. 197)

*Mark A. Mix, National Right to Work Committee, Springfield, VA (p. 204)

Suzanne C. Moore, Delaware Public Policy Institute, Wilmington, DE (p. 206)

*Michael A. Morrisey, University of Alabama, Birmingham, Birmingham, AL (p. 207)

Chuck Muth, American Conservative Union, Alexandria, VA (p. 210)

*Ronald Nehring, Americans for Tax Reform, San Diego, CA (p. 212)

George R. Neumann, University of Iowa, Iowa City, IA (p. 213)

*Herbert R. Northrup, University of Pennsylvania, Haverford, PA (p. 215)

Ronald L. Oaxaca, University of Arizona, Tucson, AZ (p. 218)

Ivan G. Osorio, Capital Research Center, Washington, DC (p. 220)

*J. A. Parker, Lincoln Institute for Research and Education, Washington, DC (p. 221)

*David R. Pinkus, Small Business United of Texas, Austin, TX (p. 229)

*Solomon W. Polachek, State University of New York, Binghamton, Binghamton, NY (p. 230)

*Edward Potter, Employment Policy Foundation, Washington, DC (p. 231)

*Mark S. Pulliam, Latham & Watkins, San Diego, CA (p. 234)

John Raisian, Hoover Institution, Stanford, CA (p. 236)

Peter Rutland, Wesleyan University, Middletown, CT (p. 248)

Dallas L. Salisbury, Employee Benefit Research Institute, Washington, DC (p. 248)

John F. Scalia, Greenberg Traurig, LLP, McLean, VA (p. 251)

*Hans F. Sennholz, Grove City College, Grove City, PA (p. 257)

*Robert A. Sirico, Acton Institute for the Study of Religion and Liberty, Grand Rapids, MI (p. 261)

LABOR AND EMPLOYMENT (Continued)

Clifford W. Smith, University of Rochester, Rochester, NY (p. 262)
Alan C. Stockman, University of Rochester, Rochester, NY (p. 269)
*David J. Theroux, The Independent Institute, Oakland, CA (p. 276)
Graham S. Toft, Hudson Institute, Indianapolis, IN (p. 280)
Jude Wanniski, Polyconomics, Parsippany, NJ (p. 288)
John T. Warner, Clemson University, Clemson, SC (p. 289)
*Murray Weidenbaum, Weidenbaum Center, St. Louis, MO (p. 291)
Walter E. Williams, George Mason University, Fairfax, VA (p. 295)
*Lawrence Wohl, Gustavus Adolphus College, St. Peter, MN (p. 297)
*W. James Young, National Right to Work Legal Defense Foundation, Springfield, VA (p. 301)
Edward W. Younkins, Wheeling Jesuit University, Wheeling, WV (p. 301)

MINIMUM WAGE

John T. Addison, University of South Carolina, Columbia, SC (p. 34)
*Douglas K. Adie, Ohio University, Athens, OH (p. 35)
*William T. Alpert, University of Connecticut, Stamford, CT (p. 37)
*Charles W. Baird, California State University, Hayward, Hayward, CA (p. 43)
Donald Bellante, University of South Florida, Tampa, FL (p. 50)
Walter Block, Loyola University New Orleans, New Orleans, LA (p. 55)
*Matthew J. Brouillette, The Commonwealth Foundation, Harrisburg, PA (p. 62)
*Linda Chavez, Center for Equal Opportunity, Sterling, VA (p. 73)
*Barry R. Chiswick, University of Illinois, Chicago, Chicago, IL (p. 73)
Boyd D. Collier, Tarleton State University, Stephenville, TX (p. 78)
*David Denholm, Public Service Research Foundation, Vienna, VA (p. 92)
*Susan Eckerly, National Federation of Independent Business, Washington, DC (p. 103)
Lowell E. Gallaway, Ohio University, Athens, OH (p. 120)
*Tom Giovanetti, Institute for Policy Innovation, Lewisville, TX (p. 124)
*Linda Gorman, Independence Institute, Golden, CO (p. 127)
*Grant R. Gulibon, The Commonwealth Foundation, Harrisburg, PA (p. 130)
*Paul Guppy, Washington Policy Center, Seattle, WA (p. 131)
*Jake Haulk, Allegheny Institute for Public Policy, Pittsburgh, PA (p. 137)
*David R. Henderson, Hoover Institution, Pacific Grove, CA (p. 139)
*Joseph Horton, University of Central Arkansas, Conway, AR (p. 146)
*Robert Hunter, Mackinac Center for Public Policy, Midland, MI (p. 150)
Niger Roy Innis, Congress of Racial Equality, New York, NY (p. 151)
*Raymond J. Keating, Small Business Survival Committee, Manorville, NY (p. 159)
Darlene A. Kennedy, Centre for New Black Leadership, Baltimore, MD (p. 162)
Karen Kerrigan, the polling company, Washington, DC (p. 162)
*William A. Keyes, The Institute on Political Journalism, Washington, DC (p. 162)
*Marvin H. Kosters, American Enterprise Institute, Washington, DC (p. 168)
Arthur B. Laffer, A. B. Laffer Associates, San Diego, CA (p. 172)
*George Landrith, Frontiers of Freedom Institute, Fairfax, VA (p. 173)
Dwight R. Lee, University of Georgia, Athens, GA (p. 176)
*Rita P. Maguire, Arizona Center for Public Policy, Phoenix, AZ (p. 186)
Suzanne C. Moore, Delaware Public Policy Institute, Wilmington, DE (p. 206)
Chuck Muth, American Conservative Union, Alexandria, VA (p. 210)
Ronald Nash, Reformed Theological Seminary, Oviedo, FL (p. 211)
George R. Neumann, University of Iowa, Iowa City, IA (p. 213)
*Herbert R. Northrup, University of Pennsylvania, Haverford, PA (p. 215)
*Jim Panyard, Pennsylvania Manufacturer's Association, Harrisburg, PA (p. 221)
*Bruce Phillips, National Federation of Independent Business, Washington, DC (p. 227)
*David R. Pinkus, Small Business United of Texas, Austin, TX (p. 229)
*Solomon W. Polachek, State University of New York, Binghamton, Binghamton, NY (p. 230)
*Edward Potter, Employment Policy Foundation, Washington, DC (p. 231)

MINIMUM WAGE (Continued)

George Reisman, Pepperdine University, Laguna Hills, CA (p. 238)
Russell Roberts, Weidenbaum Center, St. Louis, MO (p. 242)
*Richard O. Rowland, Grassroot Institute of Hawaii, Aiea, HI (p. 245)
*Paul Rubin, Emory University, Atlanta, GA (p. 246)
*D. Eric Schansberg, Indiana University Southeast, New Albany, IN (p. 252)
*Bradley R. Schiller, American University, Washington, DC (p. 253)
*Hans F. Sennholz, Grove City College, Grove City, PA (p. 257)
*Mark Thornton, Columbus State University, Columbus, GA (p. 278)
*Richard Vedder, Ohio University, Athens, OH (p. 284)
*Murray Weidenbaum, Weidenbaum Center, St. Louis, MO (p. 291)
Walter J. Wessels, North Carolina State University, Raleigh, NC (p. 292)
Walter E. Williams, George Mason University, Fairfax, VA (p. 295)
*Lawrence Wohl, Gustavus Adolphus College, St. Peter, MN (p. 297)
Jason Wright, Frontiers of Freedom Institute, Fairfax, VA (p. 299)

OSHA

*Richard B. Belzer, Regulatory Checkbook, Washington, DC (p. 50)
Walter Block, Loyola University New Orleans, New Orleans, LA (p. 55)
*Susan E. Dudley, Mercatus Center at George Mason University, Arlington, VA (p. 99)
*Susan Eckerly, National Federation of Independent Business, Washington, DC (p. 103)
Price V. Fishback, University of Arizona, Tucson, AZ (p. 112)
Karen Kerrigan, the polling company, Washington, DC (p. 162)
*Andrew Langer, National Federation of Independent Business, Washington, DC (p. 174)
*Herbert R. Northrup, University of Pennsylvania, Haverford, PA (p. 215)
Ivan G. Osorio, Capital Research Center, Washington, DC (p. 220)
*Daniel J. Popeo, Washington Legal Foundation, Washington, DC (p. 231)
*Edward Potter, Employment Policy Foundation, Washington, DC (p. 231)
*Susan Sarnoff, Ohio University, Athens, OH (p. 250)
Miro M. Todorovich, Scientists and Engineers for Secure Energy, New York, NY (p. 280)
*Richard Vedder, Ohio University, Athens, OH (p. 284)
*Murray Weidenbaum, Weidenbaum Center, St. Louis, MO (p. 291)
Ronald A. Zumbrun, The Zumbrun Law Firm, Sacramento, CA (p. 303)

RIGHT TO WORK

David W. Almasi, National Center for Public Policy Research, Washington, DC (p. 37)
*Charles W. Baird, California State University, Hayward, Hayward, CA (p. 43)
*Pat Bradburn, Virginians for Property Rights, Catharpin, VA (p. 59)
*Matthew J. Brouillette, The Commonwealth Foundation, Harrisburg, PA (p. 62)
Bruce N. Cameron, National Right to Work Legal Defense Foundation, Springfield, VA (p. 68)
*Anthony T. Caso, Pacific Legal Foundation, Sacramento, CA (p. 72)
*Milton L. Chappell, National Right to Work Legal Defense Foundation, Springfield, VA (p. 72)
Richard J. Clair, National Right to Work Legal Defense Foundation, Springfield, VA (p. 74)
*Charles H. Cunningham, National Rifle Association, Washington, DC (p. 87)
*Brad W. Dacus, Pacific Justice Institute, Citrus Heights, CA (p. 87)
*David Denholm, Public Service Research Foundation, Vienna, VA (p. 92)
*Phillip DeVous, Acton Institute for the Study of Religion and Liberty, Grand Rapids, MI (p. 94)
*Gerry Dickinson, South Carolina Policy Council, Columbia, SC (p. 95)
*Susan Eckerly, National Federation of Independent Business, Washington, DC (p. 103)
*Robert Fike, Americans for Tax Reform, Washington, DC (p. 111)
Stefan Gleason, National Right to Work Legal Defense Foundation, Springfield, VA (p. 124)
*Gary Glenn, American Family Association of Michigan, Midland, MI (p. 124)
*Stephen O. Goodrick, National Right to Work Committee, Springfield, VA (p. 126)
*Robert Hunter, Mackinac Center for Public Policy, Midland, MI (p. 150)
Niger Roy Innis, Congress of Racial Equality, New York, NY (p. 151)

RIGHT TO WORK (Continued)

David Kendrick, National Legal and Policy Center, Falls Church, VA **(p. 161)**
Phil Kent, Southeastern Legal Foundation, Atlanta, GA **(p. 162)**
Kent King, Missouri State Teachers Association, Columbia, MO **(p. 164)**
*****Raymond J. LaJeunesse, Jr.,** National Right to Work Legal Defense Foundation, Springfield, VA **(p. 172)**
Reed Larson, National Right to Work Committee, Springfield, VA **(p. 175)**
Joseph G. Lehman, Mackinac Center for Public Policy, Midland, MI **(p. 177)**
*****Myron Lieberman,** Education Policy Institute, Washington, DC **(p. 180)**
Michael Lynch, *Reason* Magazine, New Haven, CT **(p. 184)**
Brett A. Magbee, Oklahoma Council of Public Affairs, Oklahoma City, OK **(p. 186)**
J. J. Mahoney, Diversified Consultants, Mount Pleasant, SC **(p. 187)**
*****Mark A. Mix,** National Right to Work Committee, Springfield, VA **(p. 204)**
Chuck Muth, American Conservative Union, Alexandria, VA **(p. 210)**
*****Ronald Nehring,** Americans for Tax Reform, San Diego, CA **(p. 212)**
George R. Neumann, University of Iowa, Iowa City, IA **(p. 213)**
*****Herbert R. Northrup,** University of Pennsylvania, Haverford, PA **(p. 215)**
R. Marc Nuttle, Norman, OK **(p. 216)**
Ivan G. Osorio, Capital Research Center, Washington, DC **(p. 220)**
*****Joseph P. Overton,** Mackinac Center for Public Policy, Midland, MI **(p. 220)**
*****Jim Panyard,** Pennsylvania Manufacturer's Association, Harrisburg, PA **(p. 221)**
*****J. A. Parker,** Lincoln Institute for Research and Education, Washington, DC **(p. 221)**
*****John Paulton,** Focus on the Family, Colorado Springs, CO **(p. 223)**
*****Edward Potter,** Employment Policy Foundation, Washington, DC **(p. 231)**
*****Don Racheter,** Public Interest Institute, Mount Pleasant, IA **(p. 235)**
*****Lawrence W. Reed,** Mackinac Center for Public Policy, Midland, MI **(p. 237)**
*****Hans F. Sennholz,** Grove City College, Grove City, PA **(p. 257)**
*****Forrest L. Turpen,** Christian Educators Association International, Pasadena, CA **(p. 282)**
Walter J. Wessels, North Carolina State University, Raleigh, NC **(p. 292)**
*****Bob Williams,** Evergreen Freedom Foundation, Olympia, WA **(p. 295)**
*****Robert O. C. Worcester,** Maryland Business for Responsive Government, Baltimore, MD **(p. 298)**
Jason Wright, Frontiers of Freedom Institute, Fairfax, VA **(p. 299)**
*****W. James Young,** National Right to Work Legal Defense Foundation, Springfield, VA **(p. 301)**
Edward W. Younkins, Wheeling Jesuit University, Wheeling, WV **(p. 301)**
Ronald A. Zumbrun, The Zumbrun Law Firm, Sacramento, CA **(p. 303)**

UNEMPLOYMENT INSURANCE

Theodore David Abram, American Institute for Full Employment, Klamath Falls, OR **(p. 34)**
John T. Addison, University of South Carolina, Columbia, SC **(p. 34)**
*****Naomi Lopez Bauman,** Orlando, FL **(p. 47)**
Don Carrington, John Locke Foundation, Raleigh, NC **(p. 71)**
*****William Conerly,** Conerly Consulting, Portland, OR **(p. 79)**
*****John W. Courtney,** American Institute for Full Employment, Klamath Falls, OR **(p. 83)**
*****Susan Eckerly,** National Federation of Independent Business, Washington, DC **(p. 103)**
*****Louis D. Enoff,** Enoff Associates Limited, Sykesville, MD **(p. 107)**
*****Deanna R. Gelak,** Family and Medical Leave Act Technical Corrections Coalition, Springfield, VA **(p. 122)**
*****John MacDonald Hood,** John Locke Foundation, Raleigh, NC **(p. 145)**
*****Robert Hunter,** Mackinac Center for Public Policy, Midland, MI **(p. 150)**
*****Marvin H. Kosters,** American Enterprise Institute, Washington, DC **(p. 168)**
George R. Neumann, University of Iowa, Iowa City, IA **(p. 213)**
*****Herbert R. Northrup,** University of Pennsylvania, Haverford, PA **(p. 215)**
Ronald L. Oaxaca, University of Arizona, Tucson, AZ **(p. 218)**
*****Edward Potter,** Employment Policy Foundation, Washington, DC **(p. 231)**

UNEMPLOYMENT INSURANCE (Continued)

Dallas L. Salisbury, Employee Benefit Research Institute, Washington, DC **(p. 248)**
*****Bob Williams,** Evergreen Freedom Foundation, Olympia, WA **(p. 295)**
*****Lawrence Wohl,** Gustavus Adolphus College, St. Peter, MN **(p. 297)**

UNIONS

John T. Addison, University of South Carolina, Columbia, SC **(p. 34)**
*****William T. Alpert,** University of Connecticut, Stamford, CT **(p. 37)**
*****Charles W. Baird,** California State University, Hayward, Hayward, CA **(p. 43)**
*****Gary Beckner,** Association of American Educators, Laguna Hills, CA **(p. 48)**
Donald Bellante, University of South Florida, Tampa, FL **(p. 50)**
Walter Block, Loyola University New Orleans, New Orleans, LA **(p. 55)**
*****Kenneth Boehm,** National Legal and Policy Center, Falls Church, VA **(p. 56)**
*****Matthew J. Brouillette,** The Commonwealth Foundation, Harrisburg, PA **(p. 62)**
*****Jon Charles Caldara,** Independence Institute, Golden, CO **(p. 67)**
*****Milton L. Chappell,** National Right to Work Legal Defense Foundation, Springfield, VA **(p. 72)**
*****Linda Chavez,** Center for Equal Opportunity, Sterling, VA **(p. 73)**
Richard J. Clair, National Right to Work Legal Defense Foundation, Springfield, VA **(p. 74)**
Peter Cleary, American Conservative Union, Alexandria, VA **(p. 75)**
*****Brad W. Dacus,** Pacific Justice Institute, Citrus Heights, CA **(p. 87)**
*****David Denholm,** Public Service Research Foundation, Vienna, VA **(p. 92)**
*****Phillip DeVous,** Acton Institute for the Study of Religion and Liberty, Grand Rapids, MI **(p. 94)**
Timothy R. Dzierba, Medaille College, Buffalo, NY **(p. 101)**
*****Susan Eckerly,** National Federation of Independent Business, Washington, DC **(p. 103)**
*****Robert Fike,** Americans for Tax Reform, Washington, DC **(p. 111)**
*****Peter Flaherty,** National Legal and Policy Center, Falls Church, VA **(p. 113)**
Stefan Gleason, National Right to Work Legal Defense Foundation, Springfield, VA **(p. 124)**
*****Stephen O. Goodrick,** National Right to Work Committee, Springfield, VA **(p. 126)**
Clint W. Green, Acton Institute for the Study of Religion and Liberty,
    Grand Rapids, MI **(p. 128)**
*****Charlene Haar,** Education Policy Institute, Washington, DC **(p. 131)**
*****Lynn Harsh,** Evergreen Freedom Foundation, Olympia, WA **(p. 136)**
*****Robert Hunter,** Mackinac Center for Public Policy, Midland, MI **(p. 150)**
David Kendrick, National Legal and Policy Center, Falls Church, VA **(p. 161)**
Karen Kerrigan, the polling company, Washington, DC **(p. 162)**
Kent King, Missouri State Teachers Association, Columbia, MO **(p. 164)**
*****David W. Kirkpatrick,** Citizens for Educational Freedom, Douglassville, PA **(p. 164)**
*****Marvin H. Kosters,** American Enterprise Institute, Washington, DC **(p. 168)**
*****Raymond J. LaJeunesse, Jr.,** National Right to Work Legal Defense Foundation,
    Springfield, VA **(p. 172)**
*****George Landrith,** Frontiers of Freedom Institute, Fairfax, VA **(p. 173)**
Reed Larson, National Right to Work Committee, Springfield, VA **(p. 175)**
Dwight R. Lee, University of Georgia, Athens, GA **(p. 176)**
Joseph G. Lehman, Mackinac Center for Public Policy, Midland, MI **(p. 177)**
*****Mark R. Levin,** Landmark Legal Foundation, Herndon, VA **(p. 178)**
*****Myron Lieberman,** Education Policy Institute, Washington, DC **(p. 180)**
Wendell H. McCulloch, Jr., California State University, Long Beach, Long Beach, CA **(p. 194)**
Lawrence J. McQuillan, Pacific Research Institute, San Francisco, CA **(p. 197)**
*****Mark A. Mix,** National Right to Work Committee, Springfield, VA **(p. 204)**
*****Adrian T. Moore,** Reason Foundation, Los Angeles, CA **(p. 205)**
Chuck Muth, American Conservative Union, Alexandria, VA **(p. 210)**
*****Ronald Nehring,** Americans for Tax Reform, San Diego, CA **(p. 212)**
George Nesterczuk, Nesterczuk and Associates, Vienna, VA **(p. 212)**
George R. Neumann, University of Iowa, Iowa City, IA **(p. 213)**
*****Herbert R. Northrup,** University of Pennsylvania, Haverford, PA **(p. 215)**

UNIONS (Continued)

Mike O'Neill, Landmark Legal Foundation, Herndon, VA (p. 217)

Ivan G. Osorio, Capital Research Center, Washington, DC (p. 220)

*Joseph P. Overton, Mackinac Center for Public Policy, Midland, MI (p. 220)

*J. A. Parker, Lincoln Institute for Research and Education, Washington, DC (p. 221)

*Edward Potter, Employment Policy Foundation, Washington, DC (p. 231)

Arch Puddington, Freedom House, New York, NY (p. 234)

Joseph D. Reid, Jr., George Mason University, Fairfax, VA (p. 238)

George Reisman, Pepperdine University, Laguna Hills, CA (p. 238)

*Terrence M. Scanlon, Capital Research Center, Washington, DC (p. 251)

*D. Eric Schansberg, Indiana University Southeast, New Albany, IN (p. 252)

*Geoffrey F. Segal, Reason Public Policy Institute, Los Angeles, CA (p. 256)

*Lou Sheldon, Traditional Values Coalition, Washington, DC (p. 258)

*Robert A. Sirico, Acton Institute for the Study of Religion and Liberty, Grand Rapids, MI (p. 261)

*Forrest L. Turpen, Christian Educators Association International, Pasadena, CA (p. 282)

*Richard Vedder, Ohio University, Athens, OH (p. 284)

*Murray Weidenbaum, Weidenbaum Center, St. Louis, MO (p. 291)

*Kenneth Weinstein, Hudson Institute, Washington, DC (p. 292)

Walter J. Wessels, North Carolina State University, Raleigh, NC (p. 292)

*Bob Williams, Evergreen Freedom Foundation, Olympia, WA (p. 295)

*W. James Young, National Right to Work Legal Defense Foundation, Springfield, VA (p. 301)

Edward W. Younkins, Wheeling Jesuit University, Wheeling, WV (p. 301)

National Security

ARMS CONTROL

Ken L. Adelman, TechCentralStation, Washington, DC **(p. 35)**
*Naomi Lopez Bauman, Orlando, FL **(p. 47)**
Ilan Berman, American Foreign Policy Council, Washington, DC **(p. 51)**
*Stephen J. Blank, U. S. Army War College, Carlisle, PA **(p. 54)**
*Peter Brookes, The Heritage Foundation, Washington, DC **(p. 61)**
Kurt Campbell, Center for Strategic and International Studies, Washington, DC **(p. 68)**
*John E. Carey, International Defense Consultants, Inc., Arlington, VA **(p. 69)**
Angelo M. Codevilla, Boston University, Boston, MA **(p. 77)**
*Joseph I. Coffey, Princeton, NJ **(p. 77)**
Henry F. Cooper, High Frontier, Arlington, VA **(p. 81)**
*Ralph A. Cossa, Pacific Forum CSIS, Honolulu, HI **(p. 83)**
*Midge Decter, New York, NY **(p. 91)**
*Joseph D. Douglass, Jr., The Redwood Institute, Falls Church, VA **(p. 98)**
*Alan Dowty, University of Notre Dame, Notre Dame, IN **(p. 98)**
Ivan Eland, Cato Institute, Washington, DC **(p. 105)**
Fritz W. Ermarth, The Nixon Center, Washington, DC **(p. 108)**
Howard Fienberg, Statistical Assessment Service, Washington, DC **(p. 111)**
*David Forte, Cleveland State University, Cleveland, OH **(p. 114)**
George Friedman, Stratfor.com, Austin, TX **(p. 117)**
*Frank J. Gaffney, Jr., Center for Security Policy, Washington, DC **(p. 119)**
Philip Gold, Discovery Institute, Seattle, WA **(p. 125)**
James T. Hackett, Carlsbad, CA **(p. 131)**
John C. Hulsman, The Heritage Foundation, Washington, DC **(p. 149)**
Paul Kapur, Claremont McKenna College, Claremont, CA **(p. 158)**
Robert G. Kaufman, University of Vermont, Burlington, VT **(p. 159)**
*Geoffrey Kemp, The Nixon Center, Washington, DC **(p. 161)**
*George Landrith, Frontiers of Freedom Institute, Fairfax, VA **(p. 173)**
*Ernest W. Lefever, Chevy Chase, MD **(p. 177)**
Hafeez Malik, Villanova University, Villanova, PA **(p. 187)**
*Robert Mandel, Lewis and Clark College, Portland, OR **(p. 188)**
Eugene "Red" McDaniel, American Defense Institute, Alexandria, VA **(p. 194)**
Thomas M. Nichols, U. S. Naval War College, Newport, RI **(p. 213)**
Edward J. Ohlert, JAYCOR, McLean, VA **(p. 218)**
*Mackubin T. Owens, U. S. Naval War College, Newport, RI **(p. 220)**
Charles V. Pena, Cato Institute, Washington, DC **(p. 225)**
*Richard Perle, American Enterprise Institute, Washington, DC **(p. 225)**
Charles M. Perry, Institute for Foreign Policy Analysis, Cambridge, MA **(p. 226)**
*Robert Pfaltzgraff, Jr., Institute for Foreign Policy Analysis, Cambridge, MA **(p. 227)**
*William C. Potter, Monterey Institute of International Studies, Monterey, CA **(p. 231)**
*Amy Ridenour, National Center for Public Policy Research, Washington, DC **(p. 240)**
*David B. Rivkin, Jr., Baker & Hostetler, Washington, DC **(p. 241)**
*Edward L. Rowny, Washington, DC **(p. 245)**
*Phyllis Schlafly, Eagle Forum, St. Louis, MO **(p. 253)**
*Dimitri Simes, The Nixon Center, Washington, DC **(p. 260)**
*Sheldon W. Simon, Arizona State University, Tempe, AZ **(p. 260)**
*Harvey A. Smith, Arizona State University, Tempe, AZ **(p. 263)**
*Henry Sokolski, Non-Proliferation Policy Education Center, Washington, DC **(p. 265)**
*Richard H. Solomon, United States Institute of Peace, Washington, DC **(p. 265)**
Jack Spencer, The Heritage Foundation, Washington, DC **(p. 267)**
*H. Baker Spring, The Heritage Foundation, Washington, DC **(p. 267)**
*Richard F. Staar, Hoover Institution, Stanford, CA **(p. 267)**
*Edward Teller, Hoover Institution, Stanford, CA **(p. 275)**

ARMS CONTROL (Continued)

*David J. Theroux, The Independent Institute, Oakland, CA (p. 276)
*John J. Tierney, Jr., Institute of World Politics, Washington, DC (p. 279)
*Robert F. Turner, University of Virginia School of Law, Charlottesville, VA (p. 282)
*William R. Van Cleave, Southwest Missouri State University, Springfield, MO (p. 284)
*W. Bruce Weinrod, International Technology and Trade Associates, Inc.,
   Washington, DC (p. 292)
 Anne A. Witkowsky, Center for Strategic and International Studies, Washington, DC (p. 296)
*Larry Wortzel, The Heritage Foundation, Washington, DC (p. 299)
 John Yoo, University of California, Berkeley, Berkeley, CA (p. 300)

DEFENSE BUDGET

*Doug Bandow, Cato Institute, Washington, DC (p. 45)
*Saul Z. Barr, University of Tennessee, Gulf Shores, AL (p. 46)
*John E. Berthoud, National Taxpayers Union, Alexandria, VA (p. 52)
*Peter Brookes, The Heritage Foundation, Washington, DC (p. 61)
*John E. Carey, International Defense Consultants, Inc., Arlington, VA (p. 69)
 Merrick Carey, Lexington Institute, Arlington, VA (p. 70)
 Chris Carr, Georgia Public Policy Foundation, Atlanta, GA (p. 71)
 Eliot A. Cohen, The Paul H. Nitze School of Advanced International Studies,
   Washington, DC (p. 78)
 Milton R. Copulos, National Defense Council Foundation, Alexandria, VA (p. 82)
 James Courter, Lexington Institute, Arlington, VA (p. 83)
*C. W. Cowles, Central Michigan University, Midlothian, VA (p. 84)
*Arnaud de Borchgrave, Center for Strategic and International Studies, Washington, DC (p. 89)
 Thomas Donnelly, American Enterprise Institute, Washington, DC (p. 97)
 Peter J. Duignan, Hoover Institution, Stanford, CA (p. 99)
 Ivan Eland, Cato Institute, Washington, DC (p. 105)
 George Friedman, Stratfor.com, Austin, TX (p. 117)
*Frank J. Gaffney, Jr., Center for Security Policy, Washington, DC (p. 119)
 Philip Gold, Discovery Institute, Seattle, WA (p. 125)
 Roger Hamburg, Indiana University South Bend, South Bend, IN (p. 133)
 Robert Higgs, The Independent Institute, Covington, LA (p. 142)
*John Hillen, Foreign Policy Research Institute, Philadephia, PA (p. 142)
 Dennis S. Ippolito, Southern Methodist University, Dallas, TX (p. 152)
 Robert Jastrow, George C. Marshall Institute, Washington, DC (p. 153)
*Chalmers Johnson, Japan Policy Research Institute, Cardiff, CA (p. 155)
 Paul Kapur, Claremont McKenna College, Claremont, CA (p. 158)
*Lawrence Kudlow, Kudlow & Co., LLC, New York, NY (p. 170)
 William S. Lind, Free Congress Foundation, Washington, DC (p. 180)
*Edward N. Luttwak, Center for Strategic and International Studies, Washington, DC (p. 184)
*H. Joachim Maitre, Center for Defense Journalism, Boston, MA (p. 187)
 Eugene "Red" McDaniel, American Defense Institute, Alexandria, VA (p. 194)
 Lawrence J. McQuillan, Pacific Research Institute, San Francisco, CA (p. 197)
 William E. Odom, Hudson Institute, Washington, DC (p. 218)
 Edward J. Ohlert, JAYCOR, McLean, VA (p. 218)
*Mackubin T. Owens, U. S. Naval War College, Newport, RI (p. 220)
 Charles V. Pena, Cato Institute, Washington, DC (p. 225)
*Richard Perle, American Enterprise Institute, Washington, DC (p. 225)
 Charles M. Perry, Institute for Foreign Policy Analysis, Cambridge, MA (p. 226)
 Paul A. Rahe, University of Tulsa, Tulsa, OK (p. 236)
*Robert C. Richardson, High Frontier, Arlington, VA (p. 239)
*Amy Ridenour, National Center for Public Policy Research, Washington, DC (p. 240)
*Edward L. Rowny, Washington, DC (p. 245)
 Sam C. Sarkesian, Loyola University Chicago, Chicago, IL (p. 250)

---

* Has testified before a state or federal legislative committee

DEFENSE BUDGET (Continued)

*Thomas A. Schatz, Citizens Against Government Waste, Washington, DC (p. 252)
 Gary Schmitt, Project for the New American Century, Washington, DC (p. 253)
*Sheldon W. Simon, Arizona State University, Tempe, AZ (p. 260)
 Jack Spencer, The Heritage Foundation, Washington, DC (p. 267)
*H. Baker Spring, The Heritage Foundation, Washington, DC (p. 267)
 Michael D. Stroup, Stephen F. Austin State University, Nacogdoches, TX (p. 270)
 Gordon Sumner, Jr., Sumner Association, Santa Fe, NM (p. 272)
*Loren B. Thompson, Lexington Institute, Arlington, VA (p. 278)
*T. Rogers Wade, Georgia Public Policy Foundation, Atlanta, GA (p. 286)
*Murray Weidenbaum, Weidenbaum Center, St. Louis, MO (p. 291)
*Clinton H. Whitehurst, Jr., Clemson University, Clemson, SC (p. 294)
*J. D. Williams, Williams Associates International, Inc., Arlington, VA (p. 295)
*Charles Wolf, Jr., RAND, Santa Monica, CA (p. 297)
*Larry Wortzel, The Heritage Foundation, Washington, DC (p. 299)
 Jason Wright, Frontiers of Freedom Institute, Fairfax, VA (p. 299)

EMERGING THREATS/THREAT ASSESSMENT

*Doug Bandow, Cato Institute, Washington, DC (p. 45)
 Ilan Berman, American Foreign Policy Council, Washington, DC (p. 51)
*Stephen J. Blank, U. S. Army War College, Carlisle, PA (p. 54)
*Peter Brookes, The Heritage Foundation, Washington, DC (p. 61)
 Charles Brooks, The Strategy Group, Arlington, VA (p. 62)
 Kurt Campbell, Center for Strategic and International Studies, Washington, DC (p. 68)
*John E. Carey, International Defense Consultants, Inc., Arlington, VA (p. 69)
 Merrick Carey, Lexington Institute, Arlington, VA (p. 70)
*Joseph I. Coffey, Princeton, NJ (p. 77)
 Henry F. Cooper, High Frontier, Arlington, VA (p. 81)
*John F. Copper, Rhodes College, Memphis, TN (p. 82)
*Ralph A. Cossa, Pacific Forum CSIS, Honolulu, HI (p. 83)
 James Courter, Lexington Institute, Arlington, VA (p. 83)
 Helle C. Dale, The Heritage Foundation, Washington, DC (p. 88)
*Arnaud de Borchgrave, Center for Strategic and International Studies, Washington, DC (p. 89)
*Kenneth E. de Graffenreid, Institute of World Politics, Washington, DC (p. 89)
*Midge Decter, New York, NY (p. 91)
 Dana Dillon, The Heritage Foundation, Washington, DC (p. 96)
*Joseph D. Douglass, Jr., The Redwood Institute, Falls Church, VA (p. 98)
 Peter J. Duignan, Hoover Institution, Stanford, CA (p. 99)
 Robert Dujarric, Hudson Institute, Washington, DC (p. 99)
 Khalid Duran, *TransIslam Magazine*, Bethesda, MD (p. 100)
 Georges Fauriol, International Republican Institute, Washington, DC (p. 110)
*Harvey Feldman, The Heritage Foundation, Washington, DC (p. 110)
 Mary C. FitzGerald, Hudson Institute, Washington, DC (p. 112)
*George Folsom, International Republican Institute, Washington, DC (p. 114)
 Hillel Fradkin, Ethics and Public Policy Center, Washington, DC (p. 115)
*Robert O. Freedman, Baltimore Hebrew University, Baltimore, MD (p. 116)
 George Friedman, Stratfor.com, Austin, TX (p. 117)
*Frank J. Gaffney, Jr., Center for Security Policy, Washington, DC (p. 119)
 Gary L. Geipel, Hudson Institute, Indianapolis, IN (p. 122)
*Roy Godson, National Strategy Information Center, Washington, DC (p. 125)
 Philip Gold, Discovery Institute, Seattle, WA (p. 125)
 Gidon A. Gottlieb, University of Chicago Law School, Chicago, IL (p. 127)
 James T. Hackett, Carlsbad, CA (p. 131)
 Roger Hamburg, Indiana University South Bend, South Bend, IN (p. 133)
 William Anthony Hay, Foreign Policy Research Institute, Philadelphia, PA (p. 138)

EMERGING THREATS/THREAT ASSESSMENT (Continued)

*John Hillen, Foreign Policy Research Institute, Philadephia, PA (p. 142)

John C. Hulsman, The Heritage Foundation, Washington, DC (p. 149)

*Fred C. Ikle, Center for Strategic and International Studies, Washington, DC (p. 151)

*Chalmers Johnson, Japan Policy Research Institute, Cardiff, CA (p. 155)

Paul Kapur, Claremont McKenna College, Claremont, CA (p. 158)

*Mark N. Katz, George Mason University, Fairfax, VA (p. 158)

Robert G. Kaufman, University of Vermont, Burlington, VT (p. 159)

*Geoffrey Kemp, The Nixon Center, Washington, DC (p. 161)

Brian T. Kennedy, Claremont Institute, Claremont, CA (p. 161)

Jeane J. Kirkpatrick, American Enterprise Institute, Washington, DC (p. 164)

*Elie Krakowski, EDK Consulting, Baltimore, MD (p. 168)

*Lawrence Kudlow, Kudlow & Co., LLC, New York, NY (p. 170)

William S. Lind, Free Congress Foundation, Washington, DC (p. 180)

*Robert J. Loewenberg, Institute for Advanced Strategic and Political Studies, Washington, DC (p. 182)

*Edward N. Luttwak, Center for Strategic and International Studies, Washington, DC (p. 184)

Hafeez Malik, Villanova University, Villanova, PA (p. 187)

*Robert Mandel, Lewis and Clark College, Portland, OR (p. 188)

Eugene "Red" McDaniel, American Defense Institute, Alexandria, VA (p. 194)

Olivia M. McDonald, Regent University, Virginia Beach, VA (p. 195)

Dave McIntyre, ANSER Institute for Homeland Security, Arlington, VA (p. 196)

*Steven Metz, U. S. Army War College Strategic Studies Institute, Carlisle Barracks, PA (p. 200)

James Arnold Miller, Interaction Systems Incorporated, Vienna, VA (p. 202)

*Steven W. Mosher, Population Research Institute, Front Royal, VA (p. 208)

*Ross H. Munro, Center for Security Studies, Washington, DC (p. 209)

Tom Neumann, Jewish Institute for National Security Affairs, Washington, DC (p. 213)

C. Preston Noell, III, Tradition, Family, Property, Inc., McLean, VA (p. 214)

Michael Noonan, Foreign Policy Research Institute, Philadelphia, PA (p. 214)

*William O'Keefe, George C. Marshall Institute, Washington, DC (p. 216)

Jeremiah O'Keeffe, Plano, TX (p. 217)

William E. Odom, Hudson Institute, Washington, DC (p. 218)

Edward J. Ohlert, JAYCOR, McLean, VA (p. 218)

*Richard Olivastro, People Dynamics, Farmington, CT (p. 218)

Rocco M. Paone, U. S. Naval Academy, Annapolis, MD (p. 221)

Patrick J. Parker, Hollister, CA (p. 222)

*Richard Perle, American Enterprise Institute, Washington, DC (p. 225)

Charles M. Perry, Institute for Foreign Policy Analysis, Cambridge, MA (p. 226)

*Robert Pfaltzgraff, Jr., Institute for Foreign Policy Analysis, Cambridge, MA (p. 227)

*James Phillips, The Heritage Foundation, Washington, DC (p. 228)

*Richard Pipes, Cambridge, MA (p. 229)

*Daryl Plunk, The Heritage Foundation, Washington, DC (p. 230)

Paul A. Rahe, University of Tulsa, Tulsa, OK (p. 236)

*William H. Reid, Horseshoe, TX (p. 238)

*Robert C. Richardson, High Frontier, Arlington, VA (p. 239)

*Amy Ridenour, National Center for Public Policy Research, Washington, DC (p. 240)

*David B. Rivkin, Jr., Baker & Hostetler, Washington, DC (p. 241)

*James S. Robbins, National Defense University, Washington, DC (p. 241)

*J. Milnor Roberts, High Frontier, Arlington, VA (p. 241)

*Edward L. Rowny, Washington, DC (p. 245)

Al Santoli, American Foreign Policy Council, Washington, DC (p. 250)

Harvey Sicherman, Foreign Policy Research Institute, Philadelphia, PA (p. 259)

*Dimitri Simes, The Nixon Center, Washington, DC (p. 260)

*Sheldon W. Simon, Arizona State University, Tempe, AZ (p. 260)

*S. Fred Singer, Science and Environmental Policy Project, Arlington, VA (p. 260)

---

* Has testified before a state or federal legislative committee

EMERGING THREATS/THREAT ASSESSMENT (Continued)

*Richard H. Solomon, United States Institute of Peace, Washington, DC (p. 265)
Jack Spencer, The Heritage Foundation, Washington, DC (p. 267)
*H. Baker Spring, The Heritage Foundation, Washington, DC (p. 267)
*Richard F. Staar, Hoover Institution, Stanford, CA (p. 267)
Gordon Sumner, Jr., Sumner Association, Santa Fe, NM (p. 272)
*Loren B. Thompson, Lexington Institute, Arlington, VA (p. 278)
*John J. Tierney, Jr., Institute of World Politics, Washington, DC (p. 279)
Miro M. Todorovich, Scientists and Engineers for Secure Energy, New York, NY (p. 280)
Jon Basil Utley, Ludwig von Mises Institute, Washington, DC (p. 283)
*William R. Van Cleave, Southwest Missouri State University, Springfield, MO (p. 284)
Lloyd R. Vasey, Pacific Forum CSIS, Honolulu, HI (p. 284)
*Jeffrey D. Wallin, American Academy for Liberal Education, Washington, DC (p. 287)
*J. D. Williams, Williams Associates International, Inc., Arlington, VA (p. 295)
*Charles Wolf, Jr., RAND, Santa Monica, CA (p. 297)
*Larry Wortzel, The Heritage Foundation, Washington, DC (p. 299)

EXPORT CONTROLS/MILITARY TRANSFERS

*Stephen J. Blank, U. S. Army War College, Carlisle, PA (p. 54)
*Peter Brookes, The Heritage Foundation, Washington, DC (p. 61)
Charles Brooks, The Strategy Group, Arlington, VA (p. 62)
*John E. Carey, International Defense Consultants, Inc., Arlington, VA (p. 69)
Henry F. Cooper, High Frontier, Arlington, VA (p. 81)
*Kenneth E. de Graffenreid, Institute of World Politics, Washington, DC (p. 89)
George Friedman, Stratfor.com, Austin, TX (p. 117)
*Frank J. Gaffney, Jr., Center for Security Policy, Washington, DC (p. 119)
G. Philip Hughes, White House Writer's Group, Washington, DC (p. 149)
Paul Kapur, Claremont McKenna College, Claremont, CA (p. 158)
Michael A. Ledeen, American Enterprise Institute, Washington, DC (p. 176)
*James Andrew Lewis, Center for Strategic and International Studies, Washington, DC (p. 179)
Hafeez Malik, Villanova University, Villanova, PA (p. 187)
*Robert Mandel, Lewis and Clark College, Portland, OR (p. 188)
Wendell H. McCulloch, Jr., California State University, Long Beach, Long Beach, CA (p. 194)
Eugene "Red" McDaniel, American Defense Institute, Alexandria, VA (p. 194)
Tom Neumann, Jewish Institute for National Security Affairs, Washington, DC (p. 213)
Erie J. Novotny, Fairfax Station, VA (p. 215)
Edward J. Ohlert, JAYCOR, McLean, VA (p. 218)
*Richard Perle, American Enterprise Institute, Washington, DC (p. 225)
Charles M. Perry, Institute for Foreign Policy Analysis, Cambridge, MA (p. 226)
*William C. Potter, Monterey Institute of International Studies, Monterey, CA (p. 231)
*Henry Sokolski, Non-Proliferation Policy Education Center, Washington, DC (p. 265)
*H. Baker Spring, The Heritage Foundation, Washington, DC (p. 267)
*Edward Teller, Hoover Institution, Stanford, CA (p. 275)
*Murray Weidenbaum, Weidenbaum Center, St. Louis, MO (p. 291)
*Larry Wortzel, The Heritage Foundation, Washington, DC (p. 299)

HOMELAND SECURITY/CIVIL DEFENSE

*M. Gene Aldridge, New Mexico Independence Research Institute, Las Cruces, NM (p. 36)
*John S. Baker, Jr., Louisiana State University, Baton Rouge, LA (p. 43)
*M. Miller Baker, McDermott, Will & Emery, Washington, DC (p. 44)
*Saul Z. Barr, University of Tennessee, Gulf Shores, AL (p. 46)
*Sandy Liddy Bourne, American Legislative Exchange Council, Washington, DC (p. 58)
*Marshall J. Breger, Catholic University of America, Washington, DC (p. 60)
*Peter Brookes, The Heritage Foundation, Washington, DC (p. 61)
Charles Brooks, The Strategy Group, Arlington, VA (p. 62)

HOMELAND SECURITY/CIVIL DEFENSE (Continued)

*Harry Bruno, Thomas University, Thomasville, GA (p. 64)
 Kurt Campbell, Center for Strategic and International Studies, Washington, DC (p. 68)
*John E. Carey, International Defense Consultants, Inc., Arlington, VA (p. 69)
 Merrick Carey, Lexington Institute, Arlington, VA (p. 70)
*Jerome F. Climer, The Congressional Institute, Alexandria, VA (p. 76)
*Louis J. Cordia, Cordia Companies, Alexandria, VA (p. 82)
 Helle C. Dale, The Heritage Foundation, Washington, DC (p. 88)
*Midge Decter, New York, NY (p. 91)
 Dana Dillon, The Heritage Foundation, Washington, DC (p. 96)
 Peter J. Duignan, Hoover Institution, Stanford, CA (p. 99)
*James R. Edwards, Jr., Hudson Institute, Washington, DC (p. 104)
*Jean Bethke Elshtain, University of Chicago, Chicago, IL (p. 106)
 Richard E. Friedman, National Strategy Forum, Chicago, IL (p. 118)
*Frank J. Gaffney, Jr., Center for Security Policy, Washington, DC (p. 119)
 James S. Gilmore, The Heritage Foundation, Washington, DC (p. 123)
 Philip Gold, Discovery Institute, Seattle, WA (p. 125)
 Gina Marie Hatheway, The Heritage Foundation, Washington, DC (p. 137)
*Robert L. Hershey, Robert L. Hershey, P.E., Washington, DC (p. 141)
*John Hillen, Foreign Policy Research Institute, Philadephia, PA (p. 142)
*Fred C. Ikle, Center for Strategic and International Studies, Washington, DC (p. 151)
 Jeane J. Kirkpatrick, American Enterprise Institute, Washington, DC (p. 164)
 Glenn G. Lammi, Washington Legal Foundation, Washington, DC (p. 173)
*George Landrith, Frontiers of Freedom Institute, Fairfax, VA (p. 173)
*Randy Larsen, ANSER Institute for Homeland Security, Arlington, VA (p. 174)
*James Andrew Lewis, Center for Strategic and International Studies, Washington, DC (p. 179)
 William S. Lind, Free Congress Foundation, Washington, DC (p. 180)
*Edward N. Luttwak, Center for Strategic and International Studies, Washington, DC (p. 184)
*Heather MacDonald, Manhattan Institute for Policy Research, New York, NY (p. 185)
 Mary P. Mahoney, United Seniors Association, Inc., Washington, DC (p. 187)
 Clifford D. May, The Foundation for the Defense of Democracies, Washington, DC (p. 192)
*Nina May, *Renaissance Connection.com/RCNetwork.net*, Washington, DC (p. 192)
*Tom McClusky, National Taxpayers Union Foundation, Alexandria, VA (p. 193)
 Olivia M. McDonald, Regent University, Virginia Beach, VA (p. 195)
 Dave McIntyre, ANSER Institute for Homeland Security, Arlington, VA (p. 196)
*Edwin Meese III, The Heritage Foundation, Washington, DC (p. 198)
 James Arnold Miller, Interaction Systems Incorporated, Vienna, VA (p. 202)
 Fariborz L. Mokhtari, National Defense University, Washington, DC (p. 204)
*Joseph A. Morris, Lincoln Legal Foundation, Chicago, IL (p. 207)
 Ronald Nash, Reformed Theological Seminary, Oviedo, FL (p. 211)
 George Nesterczuk, Nesterczuk and Associates, Vienna, VA (p. 212)
 Tom Neumann, Jewish Institute for National Security Affairs, Washington, DC (p. 213)
 Michael Noonan, Foreign Policy Research Institute, Philadelphia, PA (p. 214)
*William O'Keefe, George C. Marshall Institute, Washington, DC (p. 216)
 Jeremiah O'Keeffe, Plano, TX (p. 217)
 William E. Odom, Hudson Institute, Washington, DC (p. 218)
 Edward J. Ohlert, JAYCOR, McLean, VA (p. 218)
*Richard Olivastro, People Dynamics, Farmington, CT (p. 218)
 Rocco M. Paone, U. S. Naval Academy, Annapolis, MD (p. 221)
*J. A. Parker, Lincoln Institute for Research and Education, Washington, DC (p. 221)
 Charles M. Perry, Institute for Foreign Policy Analysis, Cambridge, MA (p. 226)
*Robert Pfaltzgraff, Jr., Institute for Foreign Policy Analysis, Cambridge, MA (p. 227)
*Daniel Pipes, Middle East Forum, Philadelphia, PA (p. 229)
*Daniel J. Popeo, Washington Legal Foundation, Washington, DC (p. 231)
*Stephen Presser, Northwestern University School of Law, Chicago, IL (p. 233)

---

* Has testified before a state or federal legislative committee

HOMELAND SECURITY/CIVIL DEFENSE (Continued)

*Janos Radvanyi, Mississippi State University, Mississippi State, MS (p. 235)
*Robert C. Richardson, High Frontier, Arlington, VA (p. 239)
*Amy Ridenour, National Center for Public Policy Research, Washington, DC (p. 240)
*David B. Rivkin, Jr., Baker & Hostetler, Washington, DC (p. 241)
*James S. Robbins, National Defense University, Washington, DC (p. 241)
*Edward L. Rowny, Washington, DC (p. 245)
 Michael Scardaville, The Heritage Foundation, Washington, DC (p. 251)
*Phyllis Schlafly, Eagle Forum, St. Louis, MO (p. 253)
*Peter W. Schramm, John M. Ashbrook Center for Public Affairs, Ashland, OH (p. 254)
*Jay Sekulow, American Center for Law and Justice, Virginia Beach, VA (p. 256)
*Harvey A. Smith, Arizona State University, Tempe, AZ (p. 263)
 Jack Spencer, The Heritage Foundation, Washington, DC (p. 267)
*Paul Schott Stevens, Dechert, Price & Rhoads, Washington, DC (p. 269)
 Margaret D. Stock, United States Military Academy, West Point, NY (p. 269)
 James R. "J.T." Taylor, Empower America, Washington, DC (p. 274)
*David J. Theroux, The Independent Institute, Oakland, CA (p. 276)
*Loren B. Thompson, Lexington Institute, Arlington, VA (p. 278)
*Terry W. Van Allen, Kemah, TX (p. 283)
*Malcolm Wallop, Frontiers of Freedom Institute, Fairfax, VA (p. 288)
*Murray Weidenbaum, Weidenbaum Center, St. Louis, MO (p. 291)
*John W. Whitehead, The Rutherford Institute, Charlottesville, VA (p. 293)
*Clinton H. Whitehurst, Jr., Clemson University, Clemson, SC (p. 294)
*J. D. Williams, Williams Associates International, Inc., Arlington, VA (p. 295)
 Anne A. Witkowsky, Center for Strategic and International Studies, Washington, DC (p. 296)
*Larry Wortzel, The Heritage Foundation, Washington, DC (p. 299)
 Jason Wright, Frontiers of Freedom Institute, Fairfax, VA (p. 299)

INTELLIGENCE GATHERING AND COVERT OPERATIONS

 Jefferson Adams, Sarah Lawrence College, Bronxville, NY (p. 34)
 Ken L. Adelman, TechCentralStation, Washington, DC (p. 35)
 Arnold Beichman, Hoover Institution, Stanford, CA (p. 49)
*Peter Brookes, The Heritage Foundation, Washington, DC (p. 61)
*Kenneth Brown, Rio Grande Foundation, Albuquerque, NM (p. 63)
*Harry Bruno, Thomas University, Thomasville, GA (p. 64)
 Jameson Campaigne, Jr., Jameson Books, Inc., Ottawa, IL (p. 68)
*John E. Carey, International Defense Consultants, Inc., Arlington, VA (p. 69)
 Angelo M. Codevilla, Boston University, Boston, MA (p. 77)
 Henry F. Cooper, High Frontier, Arlington, VA (p. 81)
*Arnaud de Borchgrave, Center for Strategic and International Studies, Washington, DC (p. 89)
*Kenneth E. de Graffenreid, Institute of World Politics, Washington, DC (p. 89)
*Midge Decter, New York, NY (p. 91)
*Joseph D. Douglass, Jr., The Redwood Institute, Falls Church, VA (p. 98)
 Peter J. Duignan, Hoover Institution, Stanford, CA (p. 99)
 Ivan Eland, Cato Institute, Washington, DC (p. 105)
 Fritz W. Ermarth, The Nixon Center, Washington, DC (p. 108)
*George Folsom, International Republican Institute, Washington, DC (p. 114)
 Janice J. Gabbert, Wright State University, Dayton, OH (p. 119)
*Frank J. Gaffney, Jr., Center for Security Policy, Washington, DC (p. 119)
 Reuel Marc Gerecht, American Enterprise Institute, Washington, DC (p. 123)
*Roy Godson, National Strategy Information Center, Washington, DC (p. 125)
 Roger Hamburg, Indiana University South Bend, South Bend, IN (p. 133)
 Gina Marie Hatheway, The Heritage Foundation, Washington, DC (p. 137)
 Paul Henze, Washington, VA (p. 140)
*John Hillen, Foreign Policy Research Institute, Philadephia, PA (p. 142)

INTELLIGENCE GATHERING AND COVERT OPERATIONS (Continued)

John C. Hulsman, The Heritage Foundation, Washington, DC (p. 149)

*Chalmers Johnson, Japan Policy Research Institute, Cardiff, CA (p. 155)

Paul Kapur, Claremont McKenna College, Claremont, CA (p. 158)

*Elie Krakowski, EDK Consulting, Baltimore, MD (p. 168)

*Lawrence Kudlow, Kudlow & Co., LLC, New York, NY (p. 170)

Michael A. Ledeen, American Enterprise Institute, Washington, DC (p. 176)

*Ernest W. Lefever, Chevy Chase, MD (p. 177)

*James Andrew Lewis, Center for Strategic and International Studies, Washington, DC (p. 179)

*Heather MacDonald, Manhattan Institute for Policy Research, New York, NY (p. 185)

*Robert Mandel, Lewis and Clark College, Portland, OR (p. 188)

Clifford D. May, The Foundation for the Defense of Democracies, Washington, DC (p. 192)

Wendell H. McCulloch, Jr., California State University, Long Beach, Long Beach, CA (p. 194)

Samuel P. Menefee, Regent University, Virginia Beach, VA (p. 199)

*Constantine C. Menges, Hudson Institute, Washington, DC (p. 199)

Herbert E. Meyer, Real-World Intelligence, Inc., Friday Harbor, WA (p. 200)

*Abraham H. Miller, Walnut Creek, CA (p. 201)

James Arnold Miller, Interaction Systems Incorporated, Vienna, VA (p. 202)

*Steven W. Mosher, Population Research Institute, Front Royal, VA (p. 208)

*Ross H. Munro, Center for Security Studies, Washington, DC (p. 209)

Richard Alan Nelson, Louisiana State University, Baton Rouge, LA (p. 212)

*Stephen R. Norton, Western Policy Center, Washington, DC (p. 215)

Erie J. Novotny, Fairfax Station, VA (p. 215)

Jeremiah O'Keeffe, Plano, TX (p. 217)

William E. Odom, Hudson Institute, Washington, DC (p. 218)

Edward J. Ohlert, JAYCOR, McLean, VA (p. 218)

*Richard Perle, American Enterprise Institute, Washington, DC (p. 225)

*James Phillips, The Heritage Foundation, Washington, DC (p. 228)

*Richard Pipes, Cambridge, MA (p. 229)

Rorin Morse Platt, Campbell University, Buies Creek, NC (p. 229)

*James S. Robbins, National Defense University, Washington, DC (p. 241)

*Edward L. Rowny, Washington, DC (p. 245)

Robert E. Russell, Jr., The Heritage Foundation, Geneva, IL (p. 247)

Al Santoli, American Foreign Policy Council, Washington, DC (p. 250)

Sam C. Sarkesian, Loyola University Chicago, Chicago, IL (p. 250)

Gary Schmitt, Project for the New American Century, Washington, DC (p. 253)

*Solveig Singleton, Competitive Enterprise Institute, Washington, DC (p. 261)

*Stephen Sloan, University of Oklahoma, Norman, OK (p. 262)

*Richard F. Staar, Hoover Institution, Stanford, CA (p. 267)

*Lawrence B. Sulc, Nathan Hale Institute, St. Helena Island, SC (p. 271)

Gordon Sumner, Jr., Sumner Association, Santa Fe, NM (p. 272)

*John J. Tierney, Jr., Institute of World Politics, Washington, DC (p. 279)

John J. Tkacik, The Heritage Foundation, Washington, DC (p. 279)

Vladislav Todorov, University of Pennsylvania, Philadelphia, PA (p. 279)

*Robert F. Turner, University of Virginia School of Law, Charlottesville, VA (p. 282)

*T. Rogers Wade, Georgia Public Policy Foundation, Atlanta, GA (p. 286)

*Richard L. Walker, University of South Carolina, Columbia, SC (p. 287)

*Jeffrey D. Wallin, American Academy for Liberal Education, Washington, DC (p. 287)

*Malcolm Wallop, Frontiers of Freedom Institute, Fairfax, VA (p. 288)

*John W. Whitehead, The Rutherford Institute, Charlottesville, VA (p. 293)

*J. D. Williams, Williams Associates International, Inc., Arlington, VA (p. 295)

*Larry Wortzel, The Heritage Foundation, Washington, DC (p. 299)

MILITARY STRATEGY

Andrew J. Bacevich, Boston University, Boston, MA (p. 42)

MILITARY STRATEGY (Continued)

*Doug Bandow, Cato Institute, Washington, DC **(p. 45)**

*Saul Z. Barr, University of Tennessee, Gulf Shores, AL **(p. 46)**

Ilan Berman, American Foreign Policy Council, Washington, DC **(p. 51)**

*Stephen J. Blank, U. S. Army War College, Carlisle, PA **(p. 54)**

*Peter Brookes, The Heritage Foundation, Washington, DC **(p. 61)**

Arthur C. Brooks, Syracuse University, Syracuse, NY **(p. 61)**

Charles Brooks, The Strategy Group, Arlington, VA **(p. 62)**

Kurt Campbell, Center for Strategic and International Studies, Washington, DC **(p. 68)**

*John E. Carey, International Defense Consultants, Inc., Arlington, VA **(p. 69)**

Merrick Carey, Lexington Institute, Arlington, VA **(p. 70)**

Chris Carr, Georgia Public Policy Foundation, Atlanta, GA **(p. 71)**

Angelo M. Codevilla, Boston University, Boston, MA **(p. 77)**

*Joseph I. Coffey, Princeton, NJ **(p. 77)**

Henry F. Cooper, High Frontier, Arlington, VA **(p. 81)**

Milton R. Copulos, National Defense Council Foundation, Alexandria, VA **(p. 82)**

*Ralph A. Cossa, Pacific Forum CSIS, Honolulu, HI **(p. 83)**

James Courter, Lexington Institute, Arlington, VA **(p. 83)**

Melvin Croan, University of Wisconsin, Madison, WI **(p. 86)**

*Arnaud de Borchgrave, Center for Strategic and International Studies, Washington, DC **(p. 89)**

*Kenneth E. de Graffenreid, Institute of World Politics, Washington, DC **(p. 89)**

*Midge Decter, New York, NY **(p. 91)**

Dana Dillon, The Heritage Foundation, Washington, DC **(p. 96)**

Thomas Donnelly, American Enterprise Institute, Washington, DC **(p. 97)**

*Joseph D. Douglass, Jr., The Redwood Institute, Falls Church, VA **(p. 98)**

Peter J. Duignan, Hoover Institution, Stanford, CA **(p. 99)**

Fritz W. Ermarth, The Nixon Center, Washington, DC **(p. 108)**

Howard Fienberg, Statistical Assessment Service, Washington, DC **(p. 111)**

Mary C. FitzGerald, Hudson Institute, Washington, DC **(p. 112)**

George Friedman, Stratfor.com, Austin, TX **(p. 117)**

Janice J. Gabbert, Wright State University, Dayton, OH **(p. 119)**

*Frank J. Gaffney, Jr., Center for Security Policy, Washington, DC **(p. 119)**

Philip Gold, Discovery Institute, Seattle, WA **(p. 125)**

Roger Hamburg, Indiana University South Bend, South Bend, IN **(p. 133)**

Paul Henze, Washington, VA **(p. 140)**

*John Hillen, Foreign Policy Research Institute, Philadephia, PA **(p. 142)**

John C. Hulsman, The Heritage Foundation, Washington, DC **(p. 149)**

*Chalmers Johnson, Japan Policy Research Institute, Cardiff, CA **(p. 155)**

Paul Kapur, Claremont McKenna College, Claremont, CA **(p. 158)**

Robert G. Kaufman, University of Vermont, Burlington, VT **(p. 159)**

Brian T. Kennedy, Claremont Institute, Claremont, CA **(p. 161)**

Jeane J. Kirkpatrick, American Enterprise Institute, Washington, DC **(p. 164)**

*Lawrence Kudlow, Kudlow & Co., LLC, New York, NY **(p. 170)**

*Randy Larsen, ANSER Institute for Homeland Security, Arlington, VA **(p. 174)**

Richard Lessner, American Renewal, Washington, DC **(p. 178)**

William S. Lind, Free Congress Foundation, Washington, DC **(p. 180)**

Herbert L. London, Hudson Institute, Indianapolis, IN **(p. 182)**

*Edward N. Luttwak, Center for Strategic and International Studies, Washington, DC **(p. 184)**

*H. Joachim Maitre, Center for Defense Journalism, Boston, MA **(p. 187)**

Eugene "Red" McDaniel, American Defense Institute, Alexandria, VA **(p. 194)**

Dave McIntyre, ANSER Institute for Homeland Security, Arlington, VA **(p. 196)**

*Edwin Meese III, The Heritage Foundation, Washington, DC **(p. 198)**

*Steven Metz, U. S. Army War College Strategic Studies Institute, Carlisle Barracks, PA **(p. 200)**

*Ross H. Munro, Center for Security Studies, Washington, DC **(p. 209)**

Ronald Nash, Reformed Theological Seminary, Oviedo, FL **(p. 211)**

MILITARY STRATEGY (Continued)

Thomas M. Nichols, U. S. Naval War College, Newport, RI (p. 213)
Michael Noonan, Foreign Policy Research Institute, Philadelphia, PA (p. 214)
*Stephen R. Norton, Western Policy Center, Washington, DC (p. 215)
*William O'Keefe, George C. Marshall Institute, Washington, DC (p. 216)
Jeremiah O'Keeffe, Plano, TX (p. 217)
William E. Odom, Hudson Institute, Washington, DC (p. 218)
Edward J. Ohlert, JAYCOR, McLean, VA (p. 218)
Edward A. Olsen, Naval Postgraduate School, Monterey, CA (p. 219)
*Mackubin T. Owens, U. S. Naval War College, Newport, RI (p. 220)
Rocco M. Paone, U. S. Naval Academy, Annapolis, MD (p. 221)
Patrick J. Parker, Hollister, CA (p. 222)
*Richard Perle, American Enterprise Institute, Washington, DC (p. 225)
Charles M. Perry, Institute for Foreign Policy Analysis, Cambridge, MA (p. 226)
*Robert Pfaltzgraff, Jr., Institute for Foreign Policy Analysis, Cambridge, MA (p. 227)
Paul A. Rahe, University of Tulsa, Tulsa, OK (p. 236)
*Robert C. Richardson, High Frontier, Arlington, VA (p. 239)
*Amy Ridenour, National Center for Public Policy Research, Washington, DC (p. 240)
*David B. Rivkin, Jr., Baker & Hostetler, Washington, DC (p. 241)
*James S. Robbins, National Defense University, Washington, DC (p. 241)
*J. Milnor Roberts, High Frontier, Arlington, VA (p. 241)
*Edward L. Rowny, Washington, DC (p. 245)
Gregory W. Sand, Saint Louis College of Pharmacy, St. Louis, MO (p. 249)
Al Santoli, American Foreign Policy Council, Washington, DC (p. 250)
Sam C. Sarkesian, Loyola University Chicago, Chicago, IL (p. 250)
*Phyllis Schlafly, Eagle Forum, St. Louis, MO (p. 253)
Gary Schmitt, Project for the New American Century, Washington, DC (p. 253)
Harvey Sicherman, Foreign Policy Research Institute, Philadelphia, PA (p. 259)
Radek Sikorski, American Enterprise Institute, Washington, DC (p. 260)
*Harvey A. Smith, Arizona State University, Tempe, AZ (p. 263)
Jack Spencer, The Heritage Foundation, Washington, DC (p. 267)
*H. Baker Spring, The Heritage Foundation, Washington, DC (p. 267)
Gordon Sumner, Jr., Sumner Association, Santa Fe, NM (p. 272)
*Lewis A. Tambs, Tempe, AZ (p. 273)
*William J. Taylor, Jr., Taylor Associates, Inc., Bethesda, MD (p. 275)
*Loren B. Thompson, Lexington Institute, Arlington, VA (p. 278)
Miro M. Todorovich, Scientists and Engineers for Secure Energy, New York, NY (p. 280)
*Robert F. Turner, University of Virginia School of Law, Charlottesville, VA (p. 282)
*William R. Van Cleave, Southwest Missouri State University, Springfield, MO (p. 284)
*T. Rogers Wade, Georgia Public Policy Foundation, Atlanta, GA (p. 286)
*Malcolm Wallop, Frontiers of Freedom Institute, Fairfax, VA (p. 288)
*J. D. Williams, Williams Associates International, Inc., Arlington, VA (p. 295)
*Charles Wolf, Jr., RAND, Santa Monica, CA (p. 297)
*Larry Wortzel, The Heritage Foundation, Washington, DC (p. 299)

MISSILE DEFENSE

Ken L. Adelman, TechCentralStation, Washington, DC (p. 35)
Martin Anderson, Hoover Institution, Stanford, CA (p. 38)
Ilan Berman, American Foreign Policy Council, Washington, DC (p. 51)
*Stephen J. Blank, U. S. Army War College, Carlisle, PA (p. 54)
*Peter Brookes, The Heritage Foundation, Washington, DC (p. 61)
*John E. Carey, International Defense Consultants, Inc., Arlington, VA (p. 69)
Merrick Carey, Lexington Institute, Arlington, VA (p. 70)
Angelo M. Codevilla, Boston University, Boston, MA (p. 77)
*Joseph I. Coffey, Princeton, NJ (p. 77)

---

* Has testified before a state or federal legislative committee

MISSILE DEFENSE (Continued)

Henry F. Cooper, High Frontier, Arlington, VA (p. 81)
*Louis J. Cordia, Cordia Companies, Alexandria, VA (p. 82)
*Ralph A. Cossa, Pacific Forum CSIS, Honolulu, HI (p. 83)
James Courter, Lexington Institute, Arlington, VA (p. 83)
*Arnaud de Borchgrave, Center for Strategic and International Studies, Washington, DC (p. 89)
*Kenneth E. de Graffenreid, Institute of World Politics, Washington, DC (p. 89)
*Midge Decter, New York, NY (p. 91)
*Joseph D. Douglass, Jr., The Redwood Institute, Falls Church, VA (p. 98)
Ivan Eland, Cato Institute, Washington, DC (p. 105)
George Friedman, Stratfor.com, Austin, TX (p. 117)
Janice J. Gabbert, Wright State University, Dayton, OH (p. 119)
*Frank J. Gaffney, Jr., Center for Security Policy, Washington, DC (p. 119)
*Jeffrey B. Gayner, Americans for Sovereignty, Washington, DC (p. 121)
James T. Hackett, Carlsbad, CA (p. 131)
Gina Marie Hatheway, The Heritage Foundation, Washington, DC (p. 137)
Robert Jastrow, George C. Marshall Institute, Washington, DC (p. 153)
*Chalmers Johnson, Japan Policy Research Institute, Cardiff, CA (p. 155)
Paul Kapur, Claremont McKenna College, Claremont, CA (p. 158)
Brian T. Kennedy, Claremont Institute, Claremont, CA (p. 161)
Jeane J. Kirkpatrick, American Enterprise Institute, Washington, DC (p. 164)
*Lawrence Kudlow, Kudlow & Co., LLC, New York, NY (p. 170)
*George Landrith, Frontiers of Freedom Institute, Fairfax, VA (p. 173)
Richard Lessner, American Renewal, Washington, DC (p. 178)
*Robert J. Loewenberg, Institute for Advanced Strategic and Political Studies,
    Washington, DC (p. 182)
Edward D. Lozansky, American University in Moscow, Washington, DC (p. 184)
*Robert Mandel, Lewis and Clark College, Portland, OR (p. 188)
*Jim Martin, 60 Plus Association, Arlington, VA (p. 190)
*Nina May, *Renaissance Connection.com/RCNetwork.net*, Washington, DC (p. 192)
Eugene "Red" McDaniel, American Defense Institute, Alexandria, VA (p. 194)
Thomas Mead, Maine Policy Center, Portland, ME (p. 198)
Fariborz L. Mokhtari, National Defense University, Washington, DC (p. 204)
*Steven W. Mosher, Population Research Institute, Front Royal, VA (p. 208)
Tom Neumann, Jewish Institute for National Security Affairs, Washington, DC (p. 213)
C. Preston Noell, III, Tradition, Family, Property, Inc., McLean, VA (p. 214)
*William O'Keefe, George C. Marshall Institute, Washington, DC (p. 216)
William E. Odom, Hudson Institute, Washington, DC (p. 218)
Edward J. Ohlert, JAYCOR, McLean, VA (p. 218)
Edward A. Olsen, Naval Postgraduate School, Monterey, CA (p. 219)
Charles V. Pena, Cato Institute, Washington, DC (p. 225)
*Richard Perle, American Enterprise Institute, Washington, DC (p. 225)
Charles M. Perry, Institute for Foreign Policy Analysis, Cambridge, MA (p. 226)
*Robert Pfaltzgraff, Jr., Institute for Foreign Policy Analysis, Cambridge, MA (p. 227)
*Robert C. Richardson, High Frontier, Arlington, VA (p. 239)
*Amy Ridenour, National Center for Public Policy Research, Washington, DC (p. 240)
*David B. Rivkin, Jr., Baker & Hostetler, Washington, DC (p. 241)
*J. Milnor Roberts, High Frontier, Arlington, VA (p. 241)
*Allen H. Roth, New York State Advisory Council on Privatization, New York, NY (p. 244)
*Edward L. Rowny, Washington, DC (p. 245)
*Phyllis Schlafly, Eagle Forum, St. Louis, MO (p. 253)
*S. Fred Singer, Science and Environmental Policy Project, Arlington, VA (p. 260)
*Harvey A. Smith, Arizona State University, Tempe, AZ (p. 263)
*Henry Sokolski, Non-Proliferation Policy Education Center, Washington, DC (p. 265)
*Richard H. Solomon, United States Institute of Peace, Washington, DC (p. 265)

MISSILE DEFENSE (Continued)

Jack Spencer, The Heritage Foundation, Washington, DC (**p. 267**)
*H. Baker Spring, The Heritage Foundation, Washington, DC (**p. 267**)
 Gordon Sumner, Jr., Sumner Association, Santa Fe, NM (**p. 272**)
 James R. "J.T." Taylor, Empower America, Washington, DC (**p. 274**)
*Edward Teller, Hoover Institution, Stanford, CA (**p. 275**)
 Roy E. Thoman, West Texas A & M University, Canyon, TX (**p. 277**)
*Loren B. Thompson, Lexington Institute, Arlington, VA (**p. 278**)
 Miro M. Todorovich, Scientists and Engineers for Secure Energy, New York, NY (**p. 280**)
*Mead Treadwell, Institute of the North, Anchorage, AK (**p. 281**)
*Robert F. Turner, University of Virginia School of Law, Charlottesville, VA (**p. 282**)
*William R. Van Cleave, Southwest Missouri State University, Springfield, MO (**p. 284**)
*Jeffrey D. Wallin, American Academy for Liberal Education, Washington, DC (**p. 287**)
*Malcolm Wallop, Frontiers of Freedom Institute, Fairfax, VA (**p. 288**)
 Michael Y. Warder, Los Angeles Children's Scholarship Fund, Long Beach, CA (**p. 289**)
*W. Bruce Weinrod, International Technology and Trade Associates, Inc.,
    Washington, DC (**p. 292**)
 Robert Whitelaw, Virginia Polytechnic Institute and State University, Blacksburg, VA (**p. 294**)
*J. D. Williams, Williams Associates International, Inc., Arlington, VA (**p. 295**)
*Larry Wortzel, The Heritage Foundation, Washington, DC (**p. 299**)
 Jason Wright, Frontiers of Freedom Institute, Fairfax, VA (**p. 299**)

NATO AND OTHER ALLIANCES

*Doug Bandow, Cato Institute, Washington, DC (**p. 45**)
 Dennis L. Bark, Hoover Institution, Stanford, CA (**p. 45**)
*Saul Z. Barr, University of Tennessee, Gulf Shores, AL (**p. 46**)
 Eric A. Belgrad, Towson State University, Towson, MD (**p. 49**)
 Ilan Berman, American Foreign Policy Council, Washington, DC (**p. 51**)
*Stephen J. Blank, U. S. Army War College, Carlisle, PA (**p. 54**)
 Paul J. Bonicelli, Patrick Henry College, Purcellville, VA (**p. 57**)
*Peter Brookes, The Heritage Foundation, Washington, DC (**p. 61**)
*John E. Carey, International Defense Consultants, Inc., Arlington, VA (**p. 69**)
 Ted Galen Carpenter, Cato Institute, Washington, DC (**p. 71**)
 John Clark, Hudson Institute, Indianapolis, IN (**p. 75**)
 Craig T. Cobane, Culver-Stockton College, Canton, MO (**p. 76**)
 Angelo M. Codevilla, Boston University, Boston, MA (**p. 77**)
*Joseph I. Coffey, Princeton, NJ (**p. 77**)
 Eliot A. Cohen, The Paul H. Nitze School of Advanced International Studies,
    Washington, DC (**p. 78**)
 James Courter, Lexington Institute, Arlington, VA (**p. 83**)
 Melvin Croan, University of Wisconsin, Madison, WI (**p. 86**)
 Helle C. Dale, The Heritage Foundation, Washington, DC (**p. 88**)
*Arnaud de Borchgrave, Center for Strategic and International Studies, Washington, DC (**p. 89**)
 Damjan de Krnjevic-Miskovic, The National Interest, Washington, DC (**p. 90**)
*Midge Decter, New York, NY (**p. 91**)
*Joseph D. Douglass, Jr., The Redwood Institute, Falls Church, VA (**p. 98**)
 Peter J. Duignan, Hoover Institution, Stanford, CA (**p. 99**)
 Ivan Eland, Cato Institute, Washington, DC (**p. 105**)
*George Folsom, International Republican Institute, Washington, DC (**p. 114**)
*David Forte, Cleveland State University, Cleveland, OH (**p. 114**)
 George Friedman, Stratfor.com, Austin, TX (**p. 117**)
*Frank J. Gaffney, Jr., Center for Security Policy, Washington, DC (**p. 119**)
 Nile Gardiner, The Heritage Foundation, Washington, DC (**p. 120**)
*Jeffrey B. Gayner, Americans for Sovereignty, Washington, DC (**p. 121**)
 Gary L. Geipel, Hudson Institute, Indianapolis, IN (**p. 122**)

---

* Has testified before a state or federal legislative committee

NATO AND OTHER ALLIANCES (Continued)

Philip Gold, Discovery Institute, Seattle, WA **(p. 125)**
Gidon A. Gottlieb, University of Chicago Law School, Chicago, IL **(p. 127)**
Nikolas Gvosdev, *The National Interest,* Washington, DC **(p. 131)**
Paul Y. Hammond, University of Pittsburgh, Pittsburgh, PA **(p. 133)**
Jerzy Hauptmann, Park University, Kansas City, MO **(p. 137)**
William Anthony Hay, Foreign Policy Research Institute, Philadelphia, PA **(p. 138)**
*****John Hillen,** Foreign Policy Research Institute, Philadephia, PA **(p. 142)**
John C. Hulsman, The Heritage Foundation, Washington, DC **(p. 149)**
Paul Kapur, Claremont McKenna College, Claremont, CA **(p. 158)**
Adrian Karatnycky, Freedom House, New York, NY **(p. 158)**
Robert G. Kaufman, University of Vermont, Burlington, VT **(p. 159)**
Jeane J. Kirkpatrick, American Enterprise Institute, Washington, DC **(p. 164)**
Leonard P. Liggio, Atlas Economic Research Foundation, Fairfax, VA **(p. 180)**
William S. Lind, Free Congress Foundation, Washington, DC **(p. 180)**
Edward D. Lozansky, American University in Moscow, Washington, DC **(p. 184)**
*****Edward N. Luttwak,** Center for Strategic and International Studies, Washington, DC **(p. 184)**
Mary P. Mahoney, United Seniors Association, Inc., Washington, DC **(p. 187)**
*****H. Joachim Maitre,** Center for Defense Journalism, Boston, MA **(p. 187)**
Hafeez Malik, Villanova University, Villanova, PA **(p. 187)**
*****Robert Mandel,** Lewis and Clark College, Portland, OR **(p. 188)**
Eugene "Red" McDaniel, American Defense Institute, Alexandria, VA **(p. 194)**
Paul E. Michelson, Huntington College, Huntington, IN **(p. 201)**
Andrew A. Michta, Rhodes College, Memphis, TN **(p. 201)**
*****Joshua Muravchik,** American Enterprise Institute, Washington, DC **(p. 209)**
Henry Myers, James Madison University, Harrisonburg, VA **(p. 210)**
Tom Neumann, Jewish Institute for National Security Affairs, Washington, DC **(p. 213)**
Thomas M. Nichols, U. S. Naval War College, Newport, RI **(p. 213)**
*****Stephen R. Norton,** Western Policy Center, Washington, DC **(p. 215)**
William E. Odom, Hudson Institute, Washington, DC **(p. 218)**
Edward J. Ohlert, JAYCOR, McLean, VA **(p. 218)**
Rocco M. Paone, U. S. Naval Academy, Annapolis, MD **(p. 221)**
*****Richard Perle,** American Enterprise Institute, Washington, DC **(p. 225)**
Charles M. Perry, Institute for Foreign Policy Analysis, Cambridge, MA **(p. 226)**
*****Robert Pfaltzgraff, Jr.,** Institute for Foreign Policy Analysis, Cambridge, MA **(p. 227)**
*****Howard Phillips,** The Conservative Caucus, Inc., Vienna, VA **(p. 227)**
*****Robert C. Richardson,** High Frontier, Arlington, VA **(p. 239)**
*****J. Milnor Roberts,** High Frontier, Arlington, VA **(p. 241)**
*****Edward L. Rowny,** Washington, DC **(p. 245)**
Gary Schmitt, Project for the New American Century, Washington, DC **(p. 253)**
Radek Sikorski, American Enterprise Institute, Washington, DC **(p. 260)**
*****Dimitri Simes,** The Nixon Center, Washington, DC **(p. 260)**
*****John Sitilides,** Western Policy Center, Washington, DC **(p. 261)**
*****Richard F. Staar,** Hoover Institution, Stanford, CA **(p. 267)**
*****William J. Taylor, Jr.,** Taylor Associates, Inc., Bethesda, MD **(p. 275)**
*****Robert F. Turner,** University of Virginia School of Law, Charlottesville, VA **(p. 282)**
Lawrence A. Uzzell, Keston Institute, Waxahachie, TX **(p. 283)**
*****Balint Vazsonyi,** Center for the American Founding, McLean, VA **(p. 284)**
*****T. Rogers Wade,** Georgia Public Policy Foundation, Atlanta, GA **(p. 286)**
*****W. Bruce Weinrod,** International Technology and Trade Associates, Inc., Washington, DC **(p. 292)**
*****Clinton H. Whitehurst, Jr.,** Clemson University, Clemson, SC **(p. 294)**
*****Larry Wortzel,** The Heritage Foundation, Washington, DC **(p. 299)**
John Yoo, University of California, Berkeley, Berkeley, CA **(p. 300)**

PEACEKEEPING

*Doug Bandow, Cato Institute, Washington, DC (p. 45)
Dennis L. Bark, Hoover Institution, Stanford, CA (p. 45)
Eric A. Belgrad, Towson State University, Towson, MD (p. 49)
Paul J. Bonicelli, Patrick Henry College, Purcellville, VA (p. 57)
*Peter Brookes, The Heritage Foundation, Washington, DC (p. 61)
*Hungdah Chiu, University of Maryland School of Law, Baltimore, MD (p. 74)
*Joseph I. Coffey, Princeton, NJ (p. 77)
Melvin Croan, University of Wisconsin, Madison, WI (p. 86)
Helle C. Dale, The Heritage Foundation, Washington, DC (p. 88)
*Arnaud de Borchgrave, Center for Strategic and International Studies, Washington, DC (p. 89)
Damjan de Krnjevic-Miskovic, The National Interest, Washington, DC (p. 90)
Peter J. Duignan, Hoover Institution, Stanford, CA (p. 99)
*Jean Bethke Elshtain, University of Chicago, Chicago, IL (p. 106)
*Charles H. Fairbanks, Jr., The Paul H. Nitze School of Advanced International Studies, Washington, DC (p. 108)
Georges Fauriol, International Republican Institute, Washington, DC (p. 110)
*George Folsom, International Republican Institute, Washington, DC (p. 114)
*Frank J. Gaffney, Jr., Center for Security Policy, Washington, DC (p. 119)
*Jeffrey B. Gayner, Americans for Sovereignty, Washington, DC (p. 121)
Paul Y. Hammond, University of Pittsburgh, Pittsburgh, PA (p. 133)
Paul Henze, Washington, VA (p. 140)
*John Hillen, Foreign Policy Research Institute, Philadephia, PA (p. 142)
John C. Hulsman, The Heritage Foundation, Washington, DC (p. 149)
*Christopher Joyner, Georgetown University, Washington, DC (p. 156)
Jeane J. Kirkpatrick, American Enterprise Institute, Washington, DC (p. 164)
*Elie Krakowski, EDK Consulting, Baltimore, MD (p. 168)
Olivia M. McDonald, Regent University, Virginia Beach, VA (p. 195)
*Constantine C. Menges, Hudson Institute, Washington, DC (p. 199)
Andrew A. Michta, Rhodes College, Memphis, TN (p. 201)
Fariborz L. Mokhtari, National Defense University, Washington, DC (p. 204)
*Joshua Muravchik, American Enterprise Institute, Washington, DC (p. 209)
*Stephen R. Norton, Western Policy Center, Washington, DC (p. 215)
Edward J. Ohlert, JAYCOR, McLean, VA (p. 218)
*Richard Perle, American Enterprise Institute, Washington, DC (p. 225)
Charles M. Perry, Institute for Foreign Policy Analysis, Cambridge, MA (p. 226)
*Robert Pfaltzgraff, Jr., Institute for Foreign Policy Analysis, Cambridge, MA (p. 227)
*David B. Rivkin, Jr., Baker & Hostetler, Washington, DC (p. 241)
*James S. Robbins, National Defense University, Washington, DC (p. 241)
*Edward L. Rowny, Washington, DC (p. 245)
*Frank Ruddy, Ruddy & Muir, Chevy Chase, MD (p. 246)
Al Santoli, American Foreign Policy Council, Washington, DC (p. 250)
Sam C. Sarkesian, Loyola University Chicago, Chicago, IL (p. 250)
Brett D. Schaefer, The Heritage Foundation, Washington, DC (p. 252)
*Phyllis Schlafly, Eagle Forum, St. Louis, MO (p. 253)
*Stephen Sloan, University of Oklahoma, Norman, OK (p. 262)
*Richard H. Solomon, United States Institute of Peace, Washington, DC (p. 265)
Jack Spencer, The Heritage Foundation, Washington, DC (p. 267)
*Richard F. Staar, Hoover Institution, Stanford, CA (p. 267)
*William J. Taylor, Jr., Taylor Associates, Inc., Bethesda, MD (p. 275)
*David J. Theroux, The Independent Institute, Oakland, CA (p. 276)
Roy E. Thoman, West Texas A & M University, Canyon, TX (p. 277)
Miro M. Todorovich, Scientists and Engineers for Secure Energy, New York, NY (p. 280)
*Robert F. Turner, University of Virginia School of Law, Charlottesville, VA (p. 282)
*Larry Wortzel, The Heritage Foundation, Washington, DC (p. 299)

---

* Has testified before a state or federal legislative committee

PEACEKEEPING (Continued)

John Yoo, University of California, Berkeley, Berkeley, CA (p. 300)

READINESS AND MANPOWER

Ken L. Adelman, TechCentralStation, Washington, DC (p. 35)
*David J. Armor, George Mason University, Fairfax, VA (p. 40)
Andrew J. Bacevich, Boston University, Boston, MA (p. 42)
*Saul Z. Barr, University of Tennessee, Gulf Shores, AL (p. 46)
*Peter Brookes, The Heritage Foundation, Washington, DC (p. 61)
Merrick Carey, Lexington Institute, Arlington, VA (p. 70)
Angelo M. Codevilla, Boston University, Boston, MA (p. 77)
Eliot A. Cohen, The Paul H. Nitze School of Advanced International Studies, Washington, DC (p. 78)
Milton R. Copulos, National Defense Council Foundation, Alexandria, VA (p. 82)
James Courter, Lexington Institute, Arlington, VA (p. 83)
*Donald J. Devine, Center for American Values, Shady Side, MD (p. 94)
*Elaine Donnelly, Center for Military Readiness, Livonia, MI (p. 97)
Robert Dujarric, Hudson Institute, Washington, DC (p. 99)
Ivan Eland, Cato Institute, Washington, DC (p. 105)
Mary C. FitzGerald, Hudson Institute, Washington, DC (p. 112)
George Friedman, Stratfor.com, Austin, TX (p. 117)
*Frank J. Gaffney, Jr., Center for Security Policy, Washington, DC (p. 119)
Paul Y. Hammond, University of Pittsburgh, Pittsburgh, PA (p. 133)
*John Hillen, Foreign Policy Research Institute, Philadephia, PA (p. 142)
Paul Kapur, Claremont McKenna College, Claremont, CA (p. 158)
Robert G. Kaufman, University of Vermont, Burlington, VT (p. 159)
Jeane J. Kirkpatrick, American Enterprise Institute, Washington, DC (p. 164)
William S. Lind, Free Congress Foundation, Washington, DC (p. 180)
Eugene "Red" McDaniel, American Defense Institute, Alexandria, VA (p. 194)
Olivia M. McDonald, Regent University, Virginia Beach, VA (p. 195)
Tom Neumann, Jewish Institute for National Security Affairs, Washington, DC (p. 213)
Michael Noonan, Foreign Policy Research Institute, Philadelphia, PA (p. 214)
William E. Odom, Hudson Institute, Washington, DC (p. 218)
*Richard Olivastro, People Dynamics, Farmington, CT (p. 218)
*Jane M. Orient, Association of American Physicians and Surgeons, Tucson, AZ (p. 219)
*J. A. Parker, Lincoln Institute for Research and Education, Washington, DC (p. 221)
Patrick J. Parker, Hollister, CA (p. 222)
Charles V. Pena, Cato Institute, Washington, DC (p. 225)
*Richard Perle, American Enterprise Institute, Washington, DC (p. 225)
*Edward L. Rowny, Washington, DC (p. 245)
Jack Spencer, The Heritage Foundation, Washington, DC (p. 267)
*William J. Taylor, Jr., Taylor Associates, Inc., Bethesda, MD (p. 275)
*Richard L. Walker, University of South Carolina, Columbia, SC (p. 287)
John T. Warner, Clemson University, Clemson, SC (p. 289)
*Charmaine Crouse Yoest, University of Virginia, Charlottesville, VA (p. 300)

TERRORISM AND INTERNATIONAL CRIME

Ken L. Adelman, TechCentralStation, Washington, DC (p. 35)
*I. Dean Ahmad, Minaret of Freedom Institute, Bethesda, MD (p. 36)
*M. Gene Aldridge, New Mexico Independence Research Institute, Las Cruces, NM (p. 36)
*Doug Bandow, Cato Institute, Washington, DC (p. 45)
Arnold Beichman, Hoover Institution, Stanford, CA (p. 49)
Ilan Berman, American Foreign Policy Council, Washington, DC (p. 51)
Paul J. Bonicelli, Patrick Henry College, Purcellville, VA (p. 57)
*Marshall J. Breger, Catholic University of America, Washington, DC (p. 60)

TERRORISM AND INTERNATIONAL CRIME (Continued)

*Peter Brookes, The Heritage Foundation, Washington, DC (p. 61)
 Charles Brooks, The Strategy Group, Arlington, VA (p. 62)
*Harry Bruno, Thomas University, Thomasville, GA (p. 64)
*John E. Carey, International Defense Consultants, Inc., Arlington, VA (p. 69)
 Merrick Carey, Lexington Institute, Arlington, VA (p. 70)
*Hungdah Chiu, University of Maryland School of Law, Baltimore, MD (p. 74)
 Craig T. Cobane, Culver-Stockton College, Canton, MO (p. 76)
*Ralph A. Cossa, Pacific Forum CSIS, Honolulu, HI (p. 83)
 Helle C. Dale, The Heritage Foundation, Washington, DC (p. 88)
*Arnaud de Borchgrave, Center for Strategic and International Studies, Washington, DC (p. 89)
*Kenneth E. de Graffenreid, Institute of World Politics, Washington, DC (p. 89)
 Damjan de Krnjevic-Miskovic, The National Interest, Washington, DC (p. 90)
*Midge Decter, New York, NY (p. 91)
 Dana Dillon, The Heritage Foundation, Washington, DC (p. 96)
*Joseph D. Douglass, Jr., The Redwood Institute, Falls Church, VA (p. 98)
 Peter J. Duignan, Hoover Institution, Stanford, CA (p. 99)
 Khalid Duran, *TransIslam Magazine*, Bethesda, MD (p. 100)
*James R. Edwards, Jr., Hudson Institute, Washington, DC (p. 104)
 Ivan Eland, Cato Institute, Washington, DC (p. 105)
*Jean Bethke Elshtain, University of Chicago, Chicago, IL (p. 106)
*Charles H. Fairbanks, Jr., The Paul H. Nitze School of Advanced International Studies,
    Washington, DC (p. 108)
*Harvey Feldman, The Heritage Foundation, Washington, DC (p. 110)
 Hillel Fradkin, Ethics and Public Policy Center, Washington, DC (p. 115)
 Richard E. Friedman, National Strategy Forum, Chicago, IL (p. 118)
 Adam Fuller, Toward Tradition, Mercer Island, WA (p. 118)
*Frank J. Gaffney, Jr., Center for Security Policy, Washington, DC (p. 119)
*Jeffrey B. Gayner, Americans for Sovereignty, Washington, DC (p. 121)
 Reuel Marc Gerecht, American Enterprise Institute, Washington, DC (p. 123)
*Roy Godson, National Strategy Information Center, Washington, DC (p. 125)
 Thomas Golab, Competitive Enterprise Institute, Washington, DC (p. 125)
 Nikolas Gvosdev, *The National Interest*, Washington, DC (p. 131)
 Roger Hamburg, Indiana University South Bend, South Bend, IN (p. 133)
*Christopher C. Harmon, Marine Corps University, Quantico, VA (p. 135)
 Paul Henze, Washington, VA (p. 140)
*John Hillen, Foreign Policy Research Institute, Philadephia, PA (p. 142)
 John C. Hulsman, The Heritage Foundation, Washington, DC (p. 149)
 Steve Johnson, The Heritage Foundation, Washington, DC (p. 155)
*Christopher Joyner, Georgetown University, Washington, DC (p. 156)
*Paul Kamenar, Washington Legal Foundation, Washington, DC (p. 157)
 Paul Kapur, Claremont McKenna College, Claremont, CA (p. 158)
*Geoffrey Kemp, The Nixon Center, Washington, DC (p. 161)
 Paul Kengor, Grove City College, Grove City, PA (p. 161)
 Phil Kent, Southeastern Legal Foundation, Atlanta, GA (p. 162)
 Jeane J. Kirkpatrick, American Enterprise Institute, Washington, DC (p. 164)
*Douglas W. Kmiec, The Catholic University of America, Washington, DC (p. 166)
*David B. Kopel, Independence Institute, Golden, CO (p. 167)
*Elie Krakowski, EDK Consulting, Baltimore, MD (p. 168)
*Lawrence Kudlow, Kudlow & Co., LLC, New York, NY (p. 170)
 Glenn G. Lammi, Washington Legal Foundation, Washington, DC (p. 173)
*George Landrith, Frontiers of Freedom Institute, Fairfax, VA (p. 173)
*Randy Larsen, ANSER Institute for Homeland Security, Arlington, VA (p. 174)
*Ernest W. Lefever, Chevy Chase, MD (p. 177)
 William S. Lind, Free Congress Foundation, Washington, DC (p. 180)

TERRORISM AND INTERNATIONAL CRIME (Continued)

*Edward N. Luttwak, Center for Strategic and International Studies, Washington, DC (p. 184)
*H. Joachim Maitre, Center for Defense Journalism, Boston, MA (p. 187)
 Hafeez Malik, Villanova University, Villanova, PA (p. 187)
 Clifford D. May, The Foundation for the Defense of Democracies, Washington, DC (p. 192)
 Olivia M. McDonald, Regent University, Virginia Beach, VA (p. 195)
 Dave McIntyre, ANSER Institute for Homeland Security, Arlington, VA (p. 196)
 Lawrence J. McQuillan, Pacific Research Institute, San Francisco, CA (p. 197)
*Edwin Meese III, The Heritage Foundation, Washington, DC (p. 198)
 Samuel P. Menefee, Regent University, Virginia Beach, VA (p. 199)
*Constantine C. Menges, Hudson Institute, Washington, DC (p. 199)
*Abraham H. Miller, Walnut Creek, CA (p. 201)
*Henry I. Miller, Hoover Institution, Stanford, CA (p. 202)
 James Arnold Miller, Interaction Systems Incorporated, Vienna, VA (p. 202)
 Fariborz L. Mokhtari, National Defense University, Washington, DC (p. 204)
*Joseph A. Morris, Lincoln Legal Foundation, Chicago, IL (p. 207)
*Steven W. Mosher, Population Research Institute, Front Royal, VA (p. 208)
 Richard Alan Nelson, Louisiana State University, Baton Rouge, LA (p. 212)
 Tom Neumann, Jewish Institute for National Security Affairs, Washington, DC (p. 213)
 Michael Noonan, Foreign Policy Research Institute, Philadelphia, PA (p. 214)
 Erie J. Novotny, Fairfax Station, VA (p. 215)
*William O'Keefe, George C. Marshall Institute, Washington, DC (p. 216)
 Jeremiah O'Keeffe, Plano, TX (p. 217)
 Edward J. Ohlert, JAYCOR, McLean, VA (p. 218)
 Paolo Pasicolan, The Heritage Foundation, Washington, DC (p. 222)
 Charles V. Pena, Cato Institute, Washington, DC (p. 225)
*Richard Perle, American Enterprise Institute, Washington, DC (p. 225)
*James Phillips, The Heritage Foundation, Washington, DC (p. 228)
*Daniel Pipes, Middle East Forum, Philadelphia, PA (p. 229)
 Danielle Pletka, American Enterprise Institute, Washington, DC (p. 229)
*Daniel J. Popeo, Washington Legal Foundation, Washington, DC (p. 231)
*William C. Potter, Monterey Institute of International Studies, Monterey, CA (p. 231)
*Michael Radu, Foreign Policy Research Institute, Philadelphia, PA (p. 235)
 Robert J. Rafalko, University of New Haven, West Haven, CT (p. 235)
 Paul A. Rahe, University of Tulsa, Tulsa, OK (p. 236)
*William Ratliff, Hoover Institution, Stanford, CA (p. 236)
*William H. Reid, Horseshoe, TX (p. 238)
*Amy Ridenour, National Center for Public Policy Research, Washington, DC (p. 240)
*David B. Rivkin, Jr., Baker & Hostetler, Washington, DC (p. 241)
*James S. Robbins, National Defense University, Washington, DC (p. 241)
*Allen H. Roth, New York State Advisory Council on Privatization, New York, NY (p. 244)
*Edward L. Rowny, Washington, DC (p. 245)
*Alfred P. Rubin, Tufts University, Medford, MA (p. 246)
*William A. Rusher, Claremont Institute, San Francisco, CA (p. 247)
 Gregory W. Sand, Saint Louis College of Pharmacy, St. Louis, MO (p. 249)
 Al Santoli, American Foreign Policy Council, Washington, DC (p. 250)
*Peter W. Schramm, John M. Ashbrook Center for Public Affairs, Ashland, OH (p. 254)
*Jay Sekulow, American Center for Law and Justice, Virginia Beach, VA (p. 256)
*Dimitri Simes, The Nixon Center, Washington, DC (p. 260)
*Sheldon W. Simon, Arizona State University, Tempe, AZ (p. 260)
*Solveig Singleton, Competitive Enterprise Institute, Washington, DC (p. 261)
*Stephen Sloan, University of Oklahoma, Norman, OK (p. 262)
*Harvey A. Smith, Arizona State University, Tempe, AZ (p. 263)
*Richard H. Solomon, United States Institute of Peace, Washington, DC (p. 265)
*Paul Schott Stevens, Dechert, Price & Rhoads, Washington, DC (p. 269)

TERRORISM AND INTERNATIONAL CRIME (Continued)

Margaret D. Stock, United States Military Academy, West Point, NY (p. 269)
*Lawrence B. Sulc, Nathan Hale Institute, St. Helena Island, SC (p. 271)
James R. "J.T." Taylor, Empower America, Washington, DC (p. 274)
*David J. Theroux, The Independent Institute, Oakland, CA (p. 276)
*Mark Thornton, Columbus State University, Columbus, GA (p. 278)
*John J. Tierney, Jr., Institute of World Politics, Washington, DC (p. 279)
Vladislav Todorov, University of Pennsylvania, Philadelphia, PA (p. 279)
Miro M. Todorovich, Scientists and Engineers for Secure Energy, New York, NY (p. 280)
*Robert F. Turner, University of Virginia School of Law, Charlottesville, VA (p. 282)
Jon Basil Utley, Ludwig von Mises Institute, Washington, DC (p. 283)
*Malcolm Wallop, Frontiers of Freedom Institute, Fairfax, VA (p. 288)
*Murray Weidenbaum, Weidenbaum Center, St. Louis, MO (p. 291)
*Edwin D. Williamson, Sullivan & Cromwell, Washington, DC (p. 295)
*Larry Wortzel, The Heritage Foundation, Washington, DC (p. 299)
*Michael K. Young, George Washington University Law School, Washington, DC (p. 300)

Natural Resources and Environment

AIR

*Jonathan H. Adler, Case Western Reserve University, Cleveland, OH (p. 35)

Bruce N. Ames, University of California, Berkeley, Berkeley, CA (p. 37)

Ron Arnold, Center for the Defense of Free Enterprise, Bellevue, WA (p. 40)

Alex A. Beehler, Charles G. Koch Charitable Foundation, Washington, DC (p. 49)

*Richard B. Belzer, Regulatory Checkbook, Washington, DC (p. 50)

*Sandy Liddy Bourne, American Legislative Exchange Council, Washington, DC (p. 58)

David F. Bradford, Princeton University, Princeton, NJ (p. 59)

Gordon L. Brady, Center for the Study of Public Choice, Fairfax, VA (p. 60)

*Wayne T. Brough, Citizens for a Sound Economy, Washington, DC (p. 62)

*Kenneth W. Chilton, Institute for Study of Economics and the Environment, St. Charles, MO (p. 73)

Charli Coon, The Heritage Foundation, Washington, DC (p. 81)

Roy E. Cordato, John Locke Foundation, Raleigh, NC (p. 82)

Robert Crandall, Brookings Institution, Washington, DC (p. 85)

*Michael De Alessi, Reason Foundation, Los Angeles, CA (p. 89)

*Kathleen B. de Bettencourt, Environmental Literacy Council, Washington, DC (p. 89)

*Susan E. Dudley, Mercatus Center at George Mason University, Arlington, VA (p. 99)

*Becky Norton Dunlop, The Heritage Foundation, Washington, DC (p. 100)

*Ward Elliott, Claremont McKenna College, Claremont, CA (p. 106)

Michael Fumento, Hudson Institute, Washington, DC (p. 118)

*Dana Joel Gattuso, Competitive Enterprise Institute, Alexandria, VA (p. 121)

*Erick Gustafson, Citizens for a Sound Economy, Washington, DC (p. 131)

*Steven Hayward, American Enterprise Institute, Washington, DC (p. 138)

*Robert L. Hershey, Robert L. Hershey, P.E., Washington, DC (p. 141)

*John R. Hill, Alabama Policy Institute, Birmingham, AL (p. 142)

Jim Johnston, Heartland Institute, Wilmette, IL (p. 156)

Diane S. Katz, Mackinac Center for Public Policy, Midland, MI (p. 158)

*Andrew Langer, National Federation of Independent Business, Washington, DC (p. 174)

*Jay H. Lehr, Environmental Education Enterprises, Ostrander, OH (p. 177)

Gary Libecap, University of Arizona, Tucson, AZ (p. 179)

*Ben Lieberman, Competitive Enterprise Institute, Washington, DC (p. 179)

Richard S. Lindzen, Massachusetts Institute of Technology, Cambridge, MA (p. 181)

Randall Lutter, American Enterprise Institute, Washington, DC (p. 184)

*Roger P. Maickel, Purdue University, Lafayette, IN (p. 187)

*Brian Mannix, Mercatus Center at George Mason University, Arlington, VA (p. 188)

*Jeff Marks, National Association of Manufacturers, Washington, DC (p. 189)

*Nancie G. Marzulla, Defenders of Property Rights, Washington, DC (p. 191)

*Roger J. Marzulla, Defenders of Property Rights, Washington, DC (p. 191)

*Bobby McCormick, Clemson University, Clemson, SC (p. 194)

*John Merrifield, University of Texas, San Antonio, San Antonio, TX (p. 199)

*Patrick Michaels, University of Virginia, Charlottesville, VA (p. 200)

*A. Alan Moghissi, Institute for Regulatory Science, Alexandria, VA (p. 204)

Suzanne C. Moore, Delaware Public Policy Institute, Wilmington, DE (p. 206)

*William Perry Pendley, Mountain States Legal Foundation, Lakewood, CO (p. 225)

Bruce Piasecki, AHC Group, Saratoga Springs, NY (p. 228)

Paul Portney, Resources for the Future, Washington, DC (p. 231)

*David Ridenour, National Center for Public Policy Research, Washington, DC (p. 240)

*David B. Rivkin, Jr., Baker & Hostetler, Washington, DC (p. 241)

*David Rothbard, Committee for a Constructive Tomorrow, Washington, DC (p. 244)

*James A. Roumasset, University of Hawaii, Honolulu, HI (p. 245)

*Craig Rucker, Committee for a Constructive Tomorrow, Washington, DC (p. 246)

AIR (Continued)

*Bill Schilling, Wyoming Business Alliance / Wyoming Heritage Foundation, Casper, WY (p. 253)

*John Shanahan, National Mining Association, Washington, DC (p. 258)

*S. Fred Singer, Science and Environmental Policy Project, Arlington, VA (p. 260)

Jeff Stier, American Council on Science and Health, New York, NY (p. 269)

*Jerry Taylor, Cato Institute, Washington, DC (p. 274)

*Mead Treadwell, Institute of the North, Anchorage, AK (p. 281)

*Malcolm Wallop, Frontiers of Freedom Institute, Fairfax, VA (p. 288)

*Murray Weidenbaum, Weidenbaum Center, St. Louis, MO (p. 291)

Robert Whitelaw, Virginia Polytechnic Institute and State University, Blacksburg, VA (p. 294)

Bruce Yandle, Clemson University, Clemson, SC (p. 300)

Ronald A. Zumbrun, The Zumbrun Law Firm, Sacramento, CA (p. 303)

CLIMATE CHANGE

*Jonathan H. Adler, Case Western Reserve University, Cleveland, OH (p. 35)

Alex Avery, Hudson Institute, Staunton, VA (p. 41)

*Dennis T. Avery, Hudson Institute, Churchville, VA (p. 42)

*Sallie Baliunas, Harvard University, Cambridge, MA (p. 44)

*Robert C. Balling, Arizona State University, Tempe, AZ (p. 45)

Roger Bate, International Policy Network, Washington, DC (p. 47)

Alex A. Beehler, Charles G. Koch Charitable Foundation, Washington, DC (p. 49)

*Mark A. Bloomfield, American Council for Capital Formation, Washington, DC (p. 55)

*Sandy Liddy Bourne, American Legislative Exchange Council, Washington, DC (p. 58)

David F. Bradford, Princeton University, Princeton, NJ (p. 59)

*Robert L. Bradley, Jr., Institute for Energy Research, Houston, TX (p. 59)

*Wayne T. Brough, Citizens for a Sound Economy, Washington, DC (p. 62)

*H. Sterling Burnett, National Center for Policy Analysis, Dallas, TX (p. 65)

John K. Carlisle, Capital Research Center, Washington, DC (p. 70)

Charli Coon, The Heritage Foundation, Washington, DC (p. 81)

Roy E. Cordato, John Locke Foundation, Raleigh, NC (p. 82)

*Michael De Alessi, Reason Foundation, Los Angeles, CA (p. 89)

*Kathleen B. de Bettencourt, Environmental Literacy Council, Washington, DC (p. 89)

*Fred W. Decker, Mount Hood Society, Corvallis, OR (p. 91)

*Paul K. Driessen, Committee for a Constructive Tomorrow, Fairfax, VA (p. 98)

*Becky Norton Dunlop, The Heritage Foundation, Washington, DC (p. 100)

*Myron Ebell, Competitive Enterprise Institute, Washington, DC (p. 103)

*Stephen Entin, Institute for Research on the Economics of Taxation, Washington, DC (p. 107)

Howard Fienberg, Statistical Assessment Service, Washington, DC (p. 111)

Michael Fumento, Hudson Institute, Washington, DC (p. 118)

Paul Georgia, Competitive Enterprise Institute, Washington, DC (p. 122)

*James K. Glassman, American Enterprise Institute, Washington, DC (p. 124)

*Erick Gustafson, Citizens for a Sound Economy, Washington, DC (p. 131)

Larry Hart, Hartco Strategies, Washington, DC (p. 136)

*Robert L. Hershey, Robert L. Hershey, P.E., Washington, DC (p. 141)

*John R. Hill, Alabama Policy Institute, Birmingham, AL (p. 142)

*Chris Horner, Competitive Enterprise Institute, Washington, DC (p. 146)

Robert Jastrow, George C. Marshall Institute, Washington, DC (p. 153)

*Christopher Joyner, Georgetown University, Washington, DC (p. 156)

Diane S. Katz, Mackinac Center for Public Policy, Midland, MI (p. 158)

Karen Kerrigan, the polling company, Washington, DC (p. 162)

*George Landrith, Frontiers of Freedom Institute, Fairfax, VA (p. 173)

*Andrew Langer, National Federation of Independent Business, Washington, DC (p. 174)

*Stephen Lazarus, Center for Public Justice, Annapolis, MD (p. 176)

*Jay H. Lehr, Environmental Education Enterprises, Ostrander, OH (p. 177)

---

* Has testified before a state or federal legislative committee

CLIMATE CHANGE (Continued)

Gary Libecap, University of Arizona, Tucson, AZ **(p. 179)**
Richard S. Lindzen, Massachusetts Institute of Technology, Cambridge, MA **(p. 181)**
*Stephen B. Lovejoy, Purdue University, West Lafayette, IN **(p. 183)**
Randall Lutter, American Enterprise Institute, Washington, DC **(p. 184)**
Lisa MacLellan, Pacific Research Institute, San Francisco, CA **(p. 185)**
*Rita P. Maguire, Arizona Center for Public Policy, Phoenix, AZ **(p. 186)**
*Brian Mannix, Mercatus Center at George Mason University, Arlington, VA **(p. 188)**
*Nancie G. Marzulla, Defenders of Property Rights, Washington, DC **(p. 191)**
*Roger J. Marzulla, Defenders of Property Rights, Washington, DC **(p. 191)**
*Bobby McCormick, Clemson University, Clemson, SC **(p. 194)**
*Patrick Michaels, University of Virginia, Charlottesville, VA **(p. 200)**
*A. Alan Moghissi, Institute for Regulatory Science, Alexandria, VA **(p. 204)**
*Thomas Gale Moore, Hoover Institution, Stanford, CA **(p. 206)**
*Deroy Murdock, Atlas Economic Research Foundation, New York, NY **(p. 209)**
Iain Murray, Statistical Assessment Service, Washington, DC **(p. 209)**
Robert H. Nelson, University of Maryland, College Park, MD **(p. 212)**
Bruce Piasecki, AHC Group, Saratoga Springs, NY **(p. 228)**
George Reisman, Pepperdine University, Laguna Hills, CA **(p. 238)**
*David Ridenour, National Center for Public Policy Research, Washington, DC **(p. 240)**
*David B. Rivkin, Jr., Baker & Hostetler, Washington, DC **(p. 241)**
*David Rothbard, Committee for a Constructive Tomorrow, Washington, DC **(p. 244)**
*James A. Roumasset, University of Hawaii, Honolulu, HI **(p. 245)**
Charles Rubin, Duquesne University, Pittsburgh, PA **(p. 246)**
*Craig Rucker, Committee for a Constructive Tomorrow, Washington, DC **(p. 246)**
*Frank Ruddy, Ruddy & Muir, Chevy Chase, MD **(p. 246)**
*Bill Schilling, Wyoming Business Alliance / Wyoming Heritage Foundation, Casper, WY **(p. 253)**
*Donald J. Senese, 60 Plus Association, Arlington, VA **(p. 257)**
*S. Fred Singer, Science and Environmental Policy Project, Arlington, VA **(p. 260)**
*Frances B. Smith, Consumer Alert, Washington, DC **(p. 263)**
*Robert Stavins, Harvard University, Cambridge, MA **(p. 268)**
Irwin Stelzer, Hudson Institute, Washington, DC **(p. 268)**
James L. Sweeney, Stanford University, Stanford, CA **(p. 272)**
*Jerry Taylor, Cato Institute, Washington, DC **(p. 274)**
*Margo Thorning, American Council for Capital Formation, Washington, DC **(p. 278)**
Richard H. Timberlake, Jr., Bogart, GA **(p. 279)**
Miro M. Todorovich, Scientists and Engineers for Secure Energy, New York, NY **(p. 280)**
*Mead Treadwell, Institute of the North, Anchorage, AK **(p. 281)**
*Murray Weidenbaum, Weidenbaum Center, St. Louis, MO **(p. 291)**

ENERGY

*Stephen Adams, Pioneer Institute for Public Policy Research, Boston, MA **(p. 34)**
Ron Arnold, Center for the Defense of Free Enterprise, Bellevue, WA **(p. 40)**
*Sallie Baliunas, Harvard University, Cambridge, MA **(p. 44)**
*William W. Beach, The Heritage Foundation, Washington, DC **(p. 48)**
Alex A. Beehler, Charles G. Koch Charitable Foundation, Washington, DC **(p. 49)**
Cecil E. Bohanon, Ball State University, Muncie, IN **(p. 56)**
*Sandy Liddy Bourne, American Legislative Exchange Council, Washington, DC **(p. 58)**
*Robert L. Bradley, Jr., Institute for Energy Research, Houston, TX **(p. 59)**
*Wayne T. Brough, Citizens for a Sound Economy, Washington, DC **(p. 62)**
*H. Sterling Burnett, National Center for Policy Analysis, Dallas, TX **(p. 65)**
*Kenneth W. Chilton, Institute for Study of Economics and the Environment, St. Charles, MO **(p. 73)**
*Bernard L. Cohen, University of Pittsburgh, Pittsburgh, PA **(p. 77)**

ENERGY (Continued)

Charli Coon, The Heritage Foundation, Washington, DC (p. 81)

Milton R. Copulos, National Defense Council Foundation, Alexandria, VA (p. 82)

*Louis J. Cordia, Cordia Companies, Alexandria, VA (p. 82)

*Lawrence Cranberg, Austin, TX (p. 85)

*Michael A. Crew, Rutgers University, Newark, NJ (p. 85)

*Michael De Alessi, Reason Foundation, Los Angeles, CA (p. 89)

*Kathleen B. de Bettencourt, Environmental Literacy Council, Washington, DC (p. 89)

*Paul K. Driessen, Committee for a Constructive Tomorrow, Fairfax, VA (p. 98)

*Susan E. Dudley, Mercatus Center at George Mason University, Arlington, VA (p. 99)

*Becky Norton Dunlop, The Heritage Foundation, Washington, DC (p. 100)

*Paula Easley, Resource Development Council for Alaska, Anchorage, AK (p. 102)

*Myron Ebell, Competitive Enterprise Institute, Washington, DC (p. 103)

Jefferson G. Edgens, Morehead State University – Jackson Center, Jackson, KY (p. 103)

*Stephen Entin, Institute for Research on the Economics of Taxation, Washington, DC (p. 107)

*Edward W. Erickson, North Carolina State University, Raleigh, NC (p. 107)

*Richard Fairbanks, Center for Strategic and International Studies, Washington, DC (p. 109)

Howard Fienberg, Statistical Assessment Service, Washington, DC (p. 111)

*Robert Fike, Americans for Tax Reform, Washington, DC (p. 111)

*Allan Fitzsimmons, Balanced Resource Solutions, Woodbridge, VA (p. 113)

*Robert Franciosi, Goldwater Institute, Phoenix, AZ (p. 115)

David D. Friedman, Santa Clara University, San Jose, CA (p. 117)

Michael Fumento, Hudson Institute, Washington, DC (p. 118)

Steven Garrison, Public Interest Institute, Mount Pleasant, IA (p. 120)

Paul Georgia, Competitive Enterprise Institute, Washington, DC (p. 122)

*Erick Gustafson, Citizens for a Sound Economy, Washington, DC (p. 131)

Alam E. Hammad, Alexandria, VA (p. 133)

Steve H. Hanke, Johns Hopkins University, Baltimore, MD (p. 134)

*Mike Hardiman, Hardiman Consulting, Washington, DC (p. 135)

Larry Hart, Hartco Strategies, Washington, DC (p. 136)

*Steven Hayward, American Enterprise Institute, Washington, DC (p. 138)

*Robert L. Hershey, Robert L. Hershey, P.E., Washington, DC (p. 141)

*Don Hodel, Silverthorne, CO (p. 143)

*Chris Horner, Competitive Enterprise Institute, Washington, DC (p. 146)

Douglas A. Houston, University of Kansas, Lawrence, KS (p. 147)

Jim Johnston, Heartland Institute, Wilmette, IL (p. 156)

Dale W. Jorgenson, Harvard University, Cambridge, MA (p. 156)

Diane S. Katz, Mackinac Center for Public Policy, Midland, MI (p. 158)

*Geoffrey Kemp, The Nixon Center, Washington, DC (p. 161)

Phil Kent, Southeastern Legal Foundation, Atlanta, GA (p. 162)

*Lynne Kiesling, Reason Public Policy Institute, Los Angeles, CA (p. 163)

*George Landrith, Frontiers of Freedom Institute, Fairfax, VA (p. 173)

*Andrew Langer, National Federation of Independent Business, Washington, DC (p. 174)

Lawrence J. Lau, Stanford University, Stanford, CA (p. 175)

*Jay H. Lehr, Environmental Education Enterprises, Ostrander, OH (p. 177)

*Ben Lieberman, Competitive Enterprise Institute, Washington, DC (p. 179)

*Rita P. Maguire, Arizona Center for Public Policy, Phoenix, AZ (p. 186)

*Ken Malloy, Center for the Advancement of Energy Markets, Washington, DC (p. 188)

*Brian Mannix, Mercatus Center at George Mason University, Arlington, VA (p. 188)

*Nancie G. Marzulla, Defenders of Property Rights, Washington, DC (p. 191)

*Roger J. Marzulla, Defenders of Property Rights, Washington, DC (p. 191)

*John McClaughry, Ethan Allen Institute, Concord, VT (p. 193)

*Bobby McCormick, Clemson University, Clemson, SC (p. 194)

Walter J. Mead, University of California, Santa Barbara, Santa Barbara, CA (p. 198)

*Patrick Michaels, University of Virginia, Charlottesville, VA (p. 200)

---

* Has testified before a state or federal legislative committee

ENERGY (Continued)

*Robert J. Michaels, California State University, Fullerton, Fullerton, CA (p. 201)
 Dennis D. Miller, Baldwin-Wallace College, Berea, OH (p. 201)
*Ross H. Munro, Center for Security Studies, Washington, DC (p. 209)
 Robert H. Nelson, University of Maryland, College Park, MD (p. 212)
*Richard Olivastro, People Dynamics, Farmington, CT (p. 218)
 Sean Paige, Competitive Enterprise Institute, Washington, DC (p. 220)
*Gary J. Palmer, Alabama Policy Institute, Birmingham, AL (p. 221)
*William S. Peirce, Case Western Reserve University, Cleveland, OH (p. 224)
*William Perry Pendley, Mountain States Legal Foundation, Lakewood, CO (p. 225)
*Nancy M. Pfotenhauer, Independent Women's Forum, Arlington, VA (p. 227)
*James Phillips, The Heritage Foundation, Washington, DC (p. 228)
 Bruce Piasecki, AHC Group, Saratoga Springs, NY (p. 228)
 Paul Portney, Resources for the Future, Washington, DC (p. 231)
*Scott Pullins, Ohio Taxpayers Association and OTA Foundation, Columbus, OH (p. 234)
 George Reisman, Pepperdine University, Laguna Hills, CA (p. 238)
*Amy Ridenour, National Center for Public Policy Research, Washington, DC (p. 240)
*David Ridenour, National Center for Public Policy Research, Washington, DC (p. 240)
*David B. Rivkin, Jr., Baker & Hostetler, Washington, DC (p. 241)
*David Rothbard, Committee for a Constructive Tomorrow, Washington, DC (p. 244)
*James A. Roumasset, University of Hawaii, Honolulu, HI (p. 245)
*Craig Rucker, Committee for a Constructive Tomorrow, Washington, DC (p. 246)
*Bill Schilling, Wyoming Business Alliance / Wyoming Heritage Foundation,
     Casper, WY (p. 253)
*John Shanahan, National Mining Association, Washington, DC (p. 258)
*S. Fred Singer, Science and Environmental Policy Project, Arlington, VA (p. 260)
*Fred L. Smith, Jr., Competitive Enterprise Institute, Washington, DC (p. 263)
*Harvey A. Smith, Arizona State University, Tempe, AZ (p. 263)
*Robert J. Smith, Center for Private Conservation, Washington, DC (p. 264)
*Robert Stavins, Harvard University, Cambridge, MA (p. 268)
 Irwin Stelzer, Hudson Institute, Washington, DC (p. 268)
 James L. Sweeney, Stanford University, Stanford, CA (p. 272)
*Jerry Taylor, Cato Institute, Washington, DC (p. 274)
*Edward Teller, Hoover Institution, Stanford, CA (p. 275)
*Margo Thorning, American Council for Capital Formation, Washington, DC (p. 278)
 Richard H. Timberlake, Jr., Bogart, GA (p. 279)
 Frank J. Tipler, Tulane University, New Orleans, LA (p. 279)
 Miro M. Todorovich, Scientists and Engineers for Secure Energy, New York, NY (p. 280)
*Mead Treadwell, Institute of the North, Anchorage, AK (p. 281)
 Peter M. VanDoren, Cato Institute, Washington, DC (p. 284)
*Peggy Venable, Texas Citizens for a Sound Economy, Austin, TX (p. 284)
*Malcolm Wallop, Frontiers of Freedom Institute, Fairfax, VA (p. 288)
*Murray Weidenbaum, Weidenbaum Center, St. Louis, MO (p. 291)
 Robert Whitelaw, Virginia Polytechnic Institute and State University, Blacksburg, VA (p. 294)
*Ron F. Williamson, Great Plains Public Policy Institute, Sioux Falls, SD (p. 295)
 James Q. Wilson, Pepperdine University, Malibu, CA (p. 296)
 Jason Wright, Frontiers of Freedom Institute, Fairfax, VA (p. 299)
 Ronald A. Zumbrun, The Zumbrun Law Firm, Sacramento, CA (p. 303)

ENVIRONMENTAL EDUCATION

*Jonathan H. Adler, Case Western Reserve University, Cleveland, OH (p. 35)
 David W. Almasi, National Center for Public Policy Research, Washington, DC (p. 37)
*Dennis T. Avery, Hudson Institute, Churchville, VA (p. 42)
 Richard A. Baer, Jr., Cornell University, Ithaca, NY (p. 42)
*Sallie Baliunas, Harvard University, Cambridge, MA (p. 44)

ENVIRONMENTAL EDUCATION (Continued)

Alex A. Beehler, Charles G. Koch Charitable Foundation, Washington, DC **(p. 49)**

John M. Beers, Annecy Institute for the Study of Virtue and Liberty, Washington, DC **(p. 49)**

Walter Block, Loyola University New Orleans, New Orleans, LA **(p. 55)**

Daniel B. Botkin, Center for the Study of the Environment, Santa Barbara, CA **(p. 58)**

*****Sandy Liddy Bourne,** American Legislative Exchange Council, Washington, DC **(p. 58)**

*****Jim L. Bowyer,** University of Minnesota, St. Paul, MN **(p. 58)**

Gordon L. Brady, Center for the Study of Public Choice, Fairfax, VA **(p. 60)**

*****Wayne T. Brough,** Citizens for a Sound Economy, Washington, DC **(p. 62)**

*****J. R. Clark,** University of Tennessee, Chattanooga, Chattanooga, TN **(p. 75)**

Charli Coon, The Heritage Foundation, Washington, DC **(p. 81)**

Roy E. Cordato, John Locke Foundation, Raleigh, NC **(p. 82)**

*****Michael De Alessi,** Reason Foundation, Los Angeles, CA **(p. 89)**

*****Kathleen B. de Bettencourt,** Environmental Literacy Council, Washington, DC **(p. 89)**

*****Fred W. Decker,** Mount Hood Society, Corvallis, OR **(p. 91)**

*****Phillip DeVous,** Acton Institute for the Study of Religion and Liberty, Grand Rapids, MI **(p. 94)**

*****Thomas DeWeese,** American Policy Center, Warrenton, VA **(p. 94)**

Douglas S. Doudney, Coalition for Property Rights, Orlando, FL **(p. 97)**

*****Susan E. Dudley,** Mercatus Center at George Mason University, Arlington, VA **(p. 99)**

*****Becky Norton Dunlop,** The Heritage Foundation, Washington, DC **(p. 100)**

*****Gloria Taylor Fisher,** Interstate Commission on the Potomac River Basin, Alexandria, VA **(p. 112)**

*****Allan Fitzsimmons,** Balanced Resource Solutions, Woodbridge, VA **(p. 113)**

Michael Fumento, Hudson Institute, Washington, DC **(p. 118)**

John Galandak, Foundation for Free Enterprise, Paramus, NJ **(p. 119)**

*****Erick Gustafson,** Citizens for a Sound Economy, Washington, DC **(p. 131)**

Larry Hart, Hartco Strategies, Washington, DC **(p. 136)**

*****Donna H. Hearne,** Constitutional Coalition, St. Louis, MO **(p. 138)**

*****Robert L. Hershey,** Robert L. Hershey, P.E., Washington, DC **(p. 141)**

*****Karl Hess,** The Land Center, Las Cruces, NM **(p. 141)**

*****Charles W. Jarvis,** United Seniors Association, Fairfax, VA **(p. 153)**

Robert Jastrow, George C. Marshall Institute, Washington, DC **(p. 153)**

Diane S. Katz, Mackinac Center for Public Policy, Midland, MI **(p. 158)**

Michael Kellman, University of Oregon, Eugene, OR **(p. 160)**

David N. Laband, Auburn University, Auburn, AL **(p. 171)**

*****Andrew Langer,** National Federation of Independent Business, Washington, DC **(p. 174)**

Dwight R. Lee, University of Georgia, Athens, GA **(p. 176)**

*****Jay H. Lehr,** Environmental Education Enterprises, Ostrander, OH **(p. 177)**

*****Mark R. Levin,** Landmark Legal Foundation, Herndon, VA **(p. 178)**

*****Stephen B. Lovejoy,** Purdue University, West Lafayette, IN **(p. 183)**

*****Roger P. Maickel,** Purdue University, Lafayette, IN **(p. 187)**

*****Nancie G. Marzulla,** Defenders of Property Rights, Washington, DC **(p. 191)**

*****Roger J. Marzulla,** Defenders of Property Rights, Washington, DC **(p. 191)**

Jack McVaugh, Arizona School Choice Trust, Scottsdale, AZ **(p. 198)**

*****Patrick Michaels,** University of Virginia, Charlottesville, VA **(p. 200)**

*****A. Alan Moghissi,** Institute for Regulatory Science, Alexandria, VA **(p. 204)**

Suzanne C. Moore, Delaware Public Policy Institute, Wilmington, DE **(p. 206)**

David Nutter, Mercatus Center at George Mason University, Arlington, VA **(p. 216)**

*****Richard Olivastro,** People Dynamics, Farmington, CT **(p. 218)**

Sean Paige, Competitive Enterprise Institute, Washington, DC **(p. 220)**

*****Christine Patterson,** Texas Public Policy Foundation, San Antonio, TX **(p. 223)**

*****William Perry Pendley,** Mountain States Legal Foundation, Lakewood, CO **(p. 225)**

Gale L. Pooley, Star, ID **(p. 230)**

Victor Porlier, Center for Civic Renewal, Inc., Delmar, NY **(p. 231)**

Russell Roberts, Weidenbaum Center, St. Louis, MO **(p. 242)**

---

* Has testified before a state or federal legislative committee

ENVIRONMENTAL EDUCATION (Continued)

*David Rothbard, Committee for a Constructive Tomorrow, Washington, DC (p. 244)
 Robert Royal, Faith & Reason Institute, Washington, DC (p. 245)
 Charles Rubin, Duquesne University, Pittsburgh, PA (p. 246)
*Craig Rucker, Committee for a Constructive Tomorrow, Washington, DC (p. 246)
*Michael Sanera, Basis Charter High School, Tucson, AZ (p. 249)
*Bill Schilling, Wyoming Business Alliance / Wyoming Heritage Foundation,
   Casper, WY (p. 253)
*John Semmens, Laissez-Faire Institute, Chandler, AZ (p. 256)
*S. Fred Singer, Science and Environmental Policy Project, Arlington, VA (p. 260)
*Robert A. Sirico, Acton Institute for the Study of Religion and Liberty,
   Grand Rapids, MI (p. 261)
*Fred L. Smith, Jr., Competitive Enterprise Institute, Washington, DC (p. 263)
 John C. Soper, John Carroll University, University Heights, OH (p. 266)
*Robert Stavins, Harvard University, Cambridge, MA (p. 268)
 Jeff Stier, American Council on Science and Health, New York, NY (p. 269)
*James Streeter, National Wilderness Institute, Washington, DC (p. 270)
 Jane Shaw Stroup, PERC – The Center for Free Market Environmentalism,
   Bozeman, MT (p. 270)
 Michael W. Thompson, Thomas Jefferson Institute for Public Policy, Springfield, VA (p. 278)
 Miro M. Todorovich, Scientists and Engineers for Secure Energy, New York, NY (p. 280)
*Elizabeth M. Whelan, American Council on Science and Health, New York, NY (p. 293)
 Robert Whitelaw, Virginia Polytechnic Institute and State University, Blacksburg, VA (p. 294)
*Michael K. Young, George Washington University Law School, Washington, DC (p. 300)

ENVIRONMENTAL REGULATION

*Jonathan H. Adler, Case Western Reserve University, Cleveland, OH (p. 35)
 David W. Almasi, National Center for Public Policy Research, Washington, DC (p. 37)
 Terry L. Anderson, PERC – The Center for Free Market Environmentalism,
   Bozeman, MT (p. 38)
*Dennis T. Avery, Hudson Institute, Churchville, VA (p. 42)
 Alex A. Beehler, Charles G. Koch Charitable Foundation, Washington, DC (p. 49)
*Richard B. Belzer, Regulatory Checkbook, Washington, DC (p. 50)
*Patrick M. Boarman, National University San Diego, San Diego, CA (p. 55)
 Daniel B. Botkin, Center for the Study of the Environment, Santa Barbara, CA (p. 58)
*Sandy Liddy Bourne, American Legislative Exchange Council, Washington, DC (p. 58)
*Jim L. Bowyer, University of Minnesota, St. Paul, MN (p. 58)
 Gordon L. Brady, Center for the Study of Public Choice, Fairfax, VA (p. 60)
*Wayne T. Brough, Citizens for a Sound Economy, Washington, DC (p. 62)
*F. Patricia Callahan, American Association of Small Property Owners, Washington, DC (p. 68)
 Merrick Carey, Lexington Institute, Arlington, VA (p. 70)
 John K. Carlisle, Capital Research Center, Washington, DC (p. 70)
*Kenneth W. Chilton, Institute for Study of Economics and the Environment,
   St. Charles, MO (p. 73)
 Bonner R. Cohen, Lexington Institute, Arlington, VA (p. 77)
*Stephen Cole, State University of New York, Stony Brook, NY (p. 78)
 Charli Coon, The Heritage Foundation, Washington, DC (p. 81)
 Roy E. Cordato, John Locke Foundation, Raleigh, NC (p. 82)
 Dennis Coyle, Catholic University of America, Washington, DC (p. 84)
*Michael A. Crew, Rutgers University, Newark, NJ (p. 85)
*Charles Cushman, American Land Rights Association, Battle Ground, WA (p. 87)
*Michael De Alessi, Reason Foundation, Los Angeles, CA (p. 89)
*Kathleen B. de Bettencourt, Environmental Literacy Council, Washington, DC (p. 89)
 Christopher DeMuth, American Enterprise Institute, Washington, DC (p. 92)
*Phillip DeVous, Acton Institute for the Study of Religion and Liberty, Grand Rapids, MI (p. 94)

ENVIRONMENTAL REGULATION (Continued)

*Susan E. Dudley, Mercatus Center at George Mason University, Arlington, VA (p. 99)

*Becky Norton Dunlop, The Heritage Foundation, Washington, DC (p. 100)

*Steven J. Eagle, George Mason University School of Law, Arlington, VA (p. 101)

*Paula Easley, Resource Development Council for Alaska, Anchorage, AK (p. 102)

*Evelyn Ebzery, Memorial Hospital of Sheridan County, Sheridan, WY (p. 103)

Jefferson G. Edgens, Morehead State University – Jackson Center, Jackson, KY (p. 103)

*Stephen Entin, Institute for Research on the Economics of Taxation, Washington, DC (p. 107)

*Gloria Taylor Fisher, Interstate Commission on the Potomac River Basin, Alexandria, VA (p. 112)

*Allan Fitzsimmons, Balanced Resource Solutions, Woodbridge, VA (p. 113)

*Robert Franciosi, Goldwater Institute, Phoenix, AZ (p. 115)

Bernard J. Frieden, Massachusetts Institute of Technology, Cambridge, MA (p. 117)

Michael Fumento, Hudson Institute, Washington, DC (p. 118)

*Dana Joel Gattuso, Competitive Enterprise Institute, Alexandria, VA (p. 121)

Paul Georgia, Competitive Enterprise Institute, Washington, DC (p. 122)

*Erick Gustafson, Citizens for a Sound Economy, Washington, DC (p. 131)

*Robert Hale, Northwest Legal Foundation, Minot, ND (p. 132)

*Mike Hardiman, Hardiman Consulting, Washington, DC (p. 135)

Robert C. Harrison, Defenders of Property Rights, Washington, DC (p. 136)

Larry Hart, Hartco Strategies, Washington, DC (p. 136)

*Steven Hayward, American Enterprise Institute, Washington, DC (p. 138)

*Robert L. Hershey, Robert L. Hershey, P.E., Washington, DC (p. 141)

*Karl Hess, The Land Center, Las Cruces, NM (p. 141)

*Chris Horner, Competitive Enterprise Institute, Washington, DC (p. 146)

Peter Huber, Manhattan Institute for Policy Research, New York, NY (p. 148)

*James Huffman, Lewis and Clark Law School, Portland, OR (p. 148)

Jim Johnston, Heartland Institute, Wilmette, IL (p. 156)

Dale W. Jorgenson, Harvard University, Cambridge, MA (p. 156)

*Paul Kamenar, Washington Legal Foundation, Washington, DC (p. 157)

Diane S. Katz, Mackinac Center for Public Policy, Midland, MI (p. 158)

Martin S. Kaufman, Atlantic Legal Foundation, New York, NY (p. 159)

*Sam Kazman, Competitive Enterprise Institute, Washington, DC (p. 159)

Phil Kent, Southeastern Legal Foundation, Atlanta, GA (p. 162)

Karen Kerrigan, the polling company, Washington, DC (p. 162)

*David B. Kopel, Independence Institute, Golden, CO (p. 167)

David N. Laband, Auburn University, Auburn, AL (p. 171)

*Carol W. LaGrasse, Property Rights Foundation of America, Inc., Stony Creek, NY (p. 172)

Glenn G. Lammi, Washington Legal Foundation, Washington, DC (p. 173)

*Andrew Langer, National Federation of Independent Business, Washington, DC (p. 174)

*Jay H. Lehr, Environmental Education Enterprises, Ostrander, OH (p. 177)

*Mark R. Levin, Landmark Legal Foundation, Herndon, VA (p. 178)

Marlo Lewis, Competitive Enterprise Institute, Washington, DC (p. 179)

Gary Libecap, University of Arizona, Tucson, AZ (p. 179)

*Ben Lieberman, Competitive Enterprise Institute, Washington, DC (p. 179)

Angela Logomasini, Competitive Enterprise Institute, Washington, DC (p. 182)

*Stephen B. Lovejoy, Purdue University, West Lafayette, IN (p. 183)

James Lucier, Prudential Securities, Arlington, VA (p. 184)

Randall Lutter, American Enterprise Institute, Washington, DC (p. 184)

*Rita P. Maguire, Arizona Center for Public Policy, Phoenix, AZ (p. 186)

*Roger P. Maickel, Purdue University, Lafayette, IN (p. 187)

*Brian Mannix, Mercatus Center at George Mason University, Arlington, VA (p. 188)

*Nancie G. Marzulla, Defenders of Property Rights, Washington, DC (p. 191)

*Roger J. Marzulla, Defenders of Property Rights, Washington, DC (p. 191)

John N. Mathys, DePaul University, Elmhurst, IL (p. 191)

ENVIRONMENTAL REGULATION (Continued)

*John McClaughry, Ethan Allen Institute, Concord, VT (p. 193)
Lawrence J. McQuillan, Pacific Research Institute, San Francisco, CA (p. 197)
*Patrick Michaels, University of Virginia, Charlottesville, VA (p. 200)
*Henry I. Miller, Hoover Institution, Stanford, CA (p. 202)
*A. Alan Moghissi, Institute for Regulatory Science, Alexandria, VA (p. 204)
Suzanne C. Moore, Delaware Public Policy Institute, Wilmington, DE (p. 206)
Robert H. Nelson, University of Maryland, College Park, MD (p. 212)
Sean Paige, Competitive Enterprise Institute, Washington, DC (p. 220)
E. C. Pasour, Jr., North Carolina State University, Raleigh, NC (p. 222)
*Sam Peltzman, University of Chicago Graduate School of Business, Chicago, IL (p. 225)
*William Perry Pendley, Mountain States Legal Foundation, Lakewood, CO (p. 225)
*Nancy M. Pfotenhauer, Independent Women's Forum, Arlington, VA (p. 227)
*Daniel J. Popeo, Washington Legal Foundation, Washington, DC (p. 231)
*Alan C. Raul, Sidley & Austin Brown & Wood, LLP, Washington, DC (p. 237)
Patricia Reed, Independent Women's Forum, Arlington, VA (p. 237)
George Reisman, Pepperdine University, Laguna Hills, CA (p. 238)
*David Ridenour, National Center for Public Policy Research, Washington, DC (p. 240)
*David W. Riggs, Capital Research Center, Washington, DC (p. 240)
*Robin Rivett, Pacific Legal Foundation, Sacramento, CA (p. 241)
*David B. Rivkin, Jr., Baker & Hostetler, Washington, DC (p. 241)
*Paul Rosenzweig, The Heritage Foundation, Washington, DC (p. 243)
*David Rothbard, Committee for a Constructive Tomorrow, Washington, DC (p. 244)
*Craig Rucker, Committee for a Constructive Tomorrow, Washington, DC (p. 246)
*Bill Schilling, Wyoming Business Alliance / Wyoming Heritage Foundation,
    Casper, WY (p. 253)
*John Shanahan, National Mining Association, Washington, DC (p. 258)
*S. Fred Singer, Science and Environmental Policy Project, Arlington, VA (p. 260)
*Robert A. Sirico, Acton Institute for the Study of Religion and Liberty,
    Grand Rapids, MI (p. 261)
*Fred L. Smith, Jr., Competitive Enterprise Institute, Washington, DC (p. 263)
*Robert J. Smith, Center for Private Conservation, Washington, DC (p. 264)
*Robert Stavins, Harvard University, Cambridge, MA (p. 268)
Irwin Stelzer, Hudson Institute, Washington, DC (p. 268)
Jeff Stier, American Council on Science and Health, New York, NY (p. 269)
*James Streeter, National Wilderness Institute, Washington, DC (p. 270)
*Richard L. Stroup, PERC – The Center for Free Market Environmentalism,
    Bozeman, MT (p. 271)
James L. Sweeney, Stanford University, Stanford, CA (p. 272)
*Jerry Taylor, Cato Institute, Washington, DC (p. 274)
Michael W. Thompson, Thomas Jefferson Institute for Public Policy, Springfield, VA (p. 278)
Miro M. Todorovich, Scientists and Engineers for Secure Energy, New York, NY (p. 280)
*Mead Treadwell, Institute of the North, Anchorage, AK (p. 281)
Peter M. VanDoren, Cato Institute, Washington, DC (p. 284)
*W. Kip Viscusi, Harvard Law School, Cambridge, MA (p. 285)
Russ Walker, Citizens for a Sound Economy, Keizer, OR (p. 287)
*Murray Weidenbaum, Weidenbaum Center, St. Louis, MO (p. 291)
*Elizabeth M. Whelan, American Council on Science and Health, New York, NY (p. 293)
Jennifer Zambone, Mercatus Center at George Mason University, Arlington, VA (p. 301)
Ronald A. Zumbrun, The Zumbrun Law Firm, Sacramento, CA (p. 303)

FORESTRY AND NATIONAL PARKS

*Frank H. Armstrong, University of Vermont, Burlington, VT (p. 40)
Ron Arnold, Center for the Defense of Free Enterprise, Bellevue, WA (p. 40)
Alex Avery, Hudson Institute, Staunton, VA (p. 41)

FORESTRY AND NATIONAL PARKS (Continued)

*Dennis T. Avery, Hudson Institute, Churchville, VA (p. 42)

John Baden, Foundation for Research on Economics and the Environment, Bozeman, MT (p. 42)

Alex A. Beehler, Charles G. Koch Charitable Foundation, Washington, DC (p. 49)

*Lillian BeVier, University of Virginia, Charlottesville, VA (p. 53)

Daniel B. Botkin, Center for the Study of the Environment, Santa Barbara, CA (p. 58)

*Sandy Liddy Bourne, American Legislative Exchange Council, Washington, DC (p. 58)

*Jim L. Bowyer, University of Minnesota, St. Paul, MN (p. 58)

*H. Sterling Burnett, National Center for Policy Analysis, Dallas, TX (p. 65)

Robert Chitester, Palmer R. Chitester Fund, Erie, PA (p. 73)

Bonner R. Cohen, Lexington Institute, Arlington, VA (p. 77)

Charli Coon, The Heritage Foundation, Washington, DC (p. 81)

*Charles Cushman, American Land Rights Association, Battle Ground, WA (p. 87)

*Michael De Alessi, Reason Foundation, Los Angeles, CA (p. 89)

*Kathleen B. de Bettencourt, Environmental Literacy Council, Washington, DC (p. 89)

*Paul K. Driessen, Committee for a Constructive Tomorrow, Fairfax, VA (p. 98)

*Susan E. Dudley, Mercatus Center at George Mason University, Arlington, VA (p. 99)

*Becky Norton Dunlop, The Heritage Foundation, Washington, DC (p. 100)

*Paula Easley, Resource Development Council for Alaska, Anchorage, AK (p. 102)

*Myron Ebell, Competitive Enterprise Institute, Washington, DC (p. 103)

*Evelyn Ebzery, Memorial Hospital of Sheridan County, Sheridan, WY (p. 103)

Jefferson G. Edgens, Morehead State University – Jackson Center, Jackson, KY (p. 103)

*Allan Fitzsimmons, Balanced Resource Solutions, Woodbridge, VA (p. 113)

*Erick Gustafson, Citizens for a Sound Economy, Washington, DC (p. 131)

Steve H. Hanke, Johns Hopkins University, Baltimore, MD (p. 134)

*Mike Hardiman, Hardiman Consulting, Washington, DC (p. 135)

Robert C. Harrison, Defenders of Property Rights, Washington, DC (p. 136)

*Donna H. Hearne, Constitutional Coalition, St. Louis, MO (p. 138)

*Karl Hess, The Land Center, Las Cruces, NM (p. 141)

*Don Hodel, Silverthorne, CO (p. 143)

*James Huffman, Lewis and Clark Law School, Portland, OR (p. 148)

David N. Laband, Auburn University, Auburn, AL (p. 171)

*Andrew Langer, National Federation of Independent Business, Washington, DC (p. 174)

*Donald R. Leal, PERC – The Center for Free Market Environmentalism, Bozeman, MT (p. 176)

Robert G. Lee, University of Washington, Seattle, WA (p. 176)

*Rita P. Maguire, Arizona Center for Public Policy, Phoenix, AZ (p. 186)

*Nancie G. Marzulla, Defenders of Property Rights, Washington, DC (p. 191)

*Roger J. Marzulla, Defenders of Property Rights, Washington, DC (p. 191)

*Bobby McCormick, Clemson University, Clemson, SC (p. 194)

Walter J. Mead, University of California, Santa Barbara, Santa Barbara, CA (p. 198)

Robert H. Nelson, University of Maryland, College Park, MD (p. 212)

*Frank Nims, Oregonians in Action, Tigard, OR (p. 214)

Randal O'Toole, Thoreau Institute, Bandon, OR (p. 217)

Sean Paige, Competitive Enterprise Institute, Washington, DC (p. 220)

*William Perry Pendley, Mountain States Legal Foundation, Lakewood, CO (p. 225)

Paul Portney, Resources for the Future, Washington, DC (p. 231)

*David Ridenour, National Center for Public Policy Research, Washington, DC (p. 240)

*David W. Riggs, Capital Research Center, Washington, DC (p. 240)

*Robin Rivett, Pacific Legal Foundation, Sacramento, CA (p. 241)

*Bill Schilling, Wyoming Business Alliance / Wyoming Heritage Foundation, Casper, WY (p. 253)

*Randy T. Simmons, Utah State University, Logan, UT (p. 260)

*Robert J. Smith, Center for Private Conservation, Washington, DC (p. 264)

---

* Has testified before a state or federal legislative committee

FORESTRY AND NATIONAL PARKS (Continued)

*Robert Stavins, Harvard University, Cambridge, MA (p. 268)
*James Streeter, National Wilderness Institute, Washington, DC (p. 270)
 Gordon Sumner, Jr., Sumner Association, Santa Fe, NM (p. 272)
*Jerry Taylor, Cato Institute, Washington, DC (p. 274)
*Mead Treadwell, Institute of the North, Anchorage, AK (p. 281)
*Malcolm Wallop, Frontiers of Freedom Institute, Fairfax, VA (p. 288)
*Ron F. Williamson, Great Plains Public Policy Institute, Sioux Falls, SD (p. 295)
 Ronald A. Zumbrun, The Zumbrun Law Firm, Sacramento, CA (p. 303)

FREE-MARKET ENVIRONMENTALISM

*Jonathan H. Adler, Case Western Reserve University, Cleveland, OH (p. 35)
*I. Dean Ahmad, Minaret of Freedom Institute, Bethesda, MD (p. 36)
 David W. Almasi, National Center for Public Policy Research, Washington, DC (p. 37)
 Terry L. Anderson, PERC – The Center for Free Market Environmentalism,
    Bozeman, MT (p. 38)
*Lewis Andrews, Yankee Institute for Public Policy Studies, Hartford, CT (p. 39)
*Doug Bandow, Cato Institute, Washington, DC (p. 45)
*Joseph L. Bast, Heartland Institute, Chicago, IL (p. 47)
 Roger Bate, International Policy Network, Washington, DC (p. 47)
 Alex A. Beehler, Charles G. Koch Charitable Foundation, Washington, DC (p. 49)
 John M. Beers, Annecy Institute for the Study of Virtue and Liberty, Washington, DC (p. 49)
*Kathy Benedetto, National Wilderness Institute, Washington, DC (p. 50)
 Walter Block, Loyola University New Orleans, New Orleans, LA (p. 55)
 Karol Boudreaux, George Mason University School of Law, Arlington, VA (p. 58)
*Sandy Liddy Bourne, American Legislative Exchange Council, Washington, DC (p. 58)
*Matthew J. Brouillette, The Commonwealth Foundation, Harrisburg, PA (p. 62)
*H. Sterling Burnett, National Center for Policy Analysis, Dallas, TX (p. 65)
*John A. Charles, Cascade Policy Institute, Portland, OR (p. 72)
 Gregory B. Christainsen, California State University, Hayward, Hayward, CA (p. 74)
*J. R. Clark, University of Tennessee, Chattanooga, Chattanooga, TN (p. 75)
 Andrew I. Cohen, University of Oklahoma, Norman, OK (p. 77)
 Bonner R. Cohen, Lexington Institute, Arlington, VA (p. 77)
 Boyd D. Collier, Tarleton State University, Stephenville, TX (p. 78)
 Charli Coon, The Heritage Foundation, Washington, DC (p. 81)
 Roy E. Cordato, John Locke Foundation, Raleigh, NC (p. 82)
*Louis J. Cordia, Cordia Companies, Alexandria, VA (p. 82)
 Dennis Coyle, Catholic University of America, Washington, DC (p. 84)
*Michael De Alessi, Reason Foundation, Los Angeles, CA (p. 89)
 Christopher DeMuth, American Enterprise Institute, Washington, DC (p. 92)
 William C. Dennis, Dennis Consulting, MacLean, VA (p. 93)
*Phillip DeVous, Acton Institute for the Study of Religion and Liberty, Grand Rapids, MI (p. 94)
*Thomas DeWeese, American Policy Center, Warrenton, VA (p. 94)
*Gerry Dickinson, South Carolina Policy Council, Columbia, SC (p. 95)
*Susan E. Dudley, Mercatus Center at George Mason University, Arlington, VA (p. 99)
*Becky Norton Dunlop, The Heritage Foundation, Washington, DC (p. 100)
*Paul Dunn, University of Louisiana, Monroe, Monroe, LA (p. 100)
*Paula Easley, Resource Development Council for Alaska, Anchorage, AK (p. 102)
*Evelyn Ebzery, Memorial Hospital of Sheridan County, Sheridan, WY (p. 103)
 Jefferson G. Edgens, Morehead State University – Jackson Center, Jackson, KY (p. 103)
*Stephen Entin, Institute for Research on the Economics of Taxation, Washington, DC (p. 107)
*Gloria Taylor Fisher, Interstate Commission on the Potomac River Basin,
    Alexandria, VA (p. 112)
*Allan Fitzsimmons, Balanced Resource Solutions, Woodbridge, VA (p. 113)
 Giulio Gallarotti, Wesleyan University, Middletown, CT (p. 120)

FREE-MARKET ENVIRONMENTALISM (Continued)

*Dana Joel Gattuso, Competitive Enterprise Institute, Alexandria, VA (p. 121)

Paul Georgia, Competitive Enterprise Institute, Washington, DC (p. 122)

*Robert E. Gordon, Jr., National Wilderness Institute, Washington, DC (p. 127)

*Erick Gustafson, Citizens for a Sound Economy, Washington, DC (p. 131)

*Mike Hardiman, Hardiman Consulting, Washington, DC (p. 135)

Robert C. Harrison, Defenders of Property Rights, Washington, DC (p. 136)

*Steven Hayward, American Enterprise Institute, Washington, DC (p. 138)

*Robert L. Hershey, Robert L. Hershey, P.E., Washington, DC (p. 141)

*Karl Hess, The Land Center, Las Cruces, NM (p. 141)

*Chris Horner, Competitive Enterprise Institute, Washington, DC (p. 146)

Peter Huber, Manhattan Institute for Policy Research, New York, NY (p. 148)

*James Huffman, Lewis and Clark Law School, Portland, OR (p. 148)

*Charles W. Jarvis, United Seniors Association, Fairfax, VA (p. 153)

Jim Johnston, Heartland Institute, Wilmette, IL (p. 156)

Diane S. Katz, Mackinac Center for Public Policy, Midland, MI (p. 158)

*Lynne Kiesling, Reason Public Policy Institute, Los Angeles, CA (p. 163)

Jo Kwong, Atlas Economic Research Foundation, Fairfax, VA (p. 171)

Arthur B. Laffer, A. B. Laffer Associates, San Diego, CA (p. 172)

*Deepak Lal, University of California at Los Angeles, Los Angeles, CA (p. 172)

*Andrew Langer, National Federation of Independent Business, Washington, DC (p. 174)

Daniel Lapin, Toward Tradition, Mercer Island, WA (p. 174)

*Donald R. Leal, PERC – The Center for Free Market Environmentalism, Bozeman, MT (p. 176)

Dwight R. Lee, University of Georgia, Athens, GA (p. 176)

*Jay H. Lehr, Environmental Education Enterprises, Ostrander, OH (p. 177)

Kurt R. Leube, Hoover Institution, Stanford, CA (p. 178)

*Mark R. Levin, Landmark Legal Foundation, Herndon, VA (p. 178)

Marlo Lewis, Competitive Enterprise Institute, Washington, DC (p. 179)

Angela Logomasini, Competitive Enterprise Institute, Washington, DC (p. 182)

*Stephen B. Lovejoy, Purdue University, West Lafayette, IN (p. 183)

*Brian Mannix, Mercatus Center at George Mason University, Arlington, VA (p. 188)

*Nancie G. Marzulla, Defenders of Property Rights, Washington, DC (p. 191)

*Roger J. Marzulla, Defenders of Property Rights, Washington, DC (p. 191)

John N. Mathys, DePaul University, Elmhurst, IL (p. 191)

*John McClaughry, Ethan Allen Institute, Concord, VT (p. 193)

*Bobby McCormick, Clemson University, Clemson, SC (p. 194)

*Kelly McCutchen, Georgia Public Policy Foundation, Atlanta, GA (p. 194)

Lawrence J. McQuillan, Pacific Research Institute, San Francisco, CA (p. 197)

*John Merrifield, University of Texas, San Antonio, San Antonio, TX (p. 199)

*Patrick Michaels, University of Virginia, Charlottesville, VA (p. 200)

Paul E. Michelson, Huntington College, Huntington, IN (p. 201)

Dennis D. Miller, Baldwin-Wallace College, Berea, OH (p. 201)

*A. Alan Moghissi, Institute for Regulatory Science, Alexandria, VA (p. 204)

*James Elliott Moore, II, University of Southern California, Los Angeles, CA (p. 205)

*Deroy Murdock, Atlas Economic Research Foundation, New York, NY (p. 209)

Robert H. Nelson, University of Maryland, College Park, MD (p. 212)

Randal O'Toole, Thoreau Institute, Bandon, OR (p. 217)

Sean Paige, Competitive Enterprise Institute, Washington, DC (p. 220)

E. C. Pasour, Jr., North Carolina State University, Raleigh, NC (p. 222)

*Sam Peltzman, University of Chicago Graduate School of Business, Chicago, IL (p. 225)

Bruce Piasecki, AHC Group, Saratoga Springs, NY (p. 228)

*Amy Ridenour, National Center for Public Policy Research, Washington, DC (p. 240)

*David Ridenour, National Center for Public Policy Research, Washington, DC (p. 240)

*David W. Riggs, Capital Research Center, Washington, DC (p. 240)

FREE-MARKET ENVIRONMENTALISM (Continued)

Russell Roberts, Weidenbaum Center, St. Louis, MO (p. 242)
*David Rothbard, Committee for a Constructive Tomorrow, Washington, DC (p. 244)
*James A. Roumasset, University of Hawaii, Honolulu, HI (p. 245)
*Richard O. Rowland, Grassroot Institute of Hawaii, Aiea, HI (p. 245)
*Craig Rucker, Committee for a Constructive Tomorrow, Washington, DC (p. 246)
*John Shanahan, National Mining Association, Washington, DC (p. 258)
*Randy T. Simmons, Utah State University, Logan, UT (p. 260)
*Robert A. Sirico, Acton Institute for the Study of Religion and Liberty, Grand Rapids, MI (p. 261)
*Fred L. Smith, Jr., Competitive Enterprise Institute, Washington, DC (p. 263)
*Robert J. Smith, Center for Private Conservation, Washington, DC (p. 264)
Vernon L. Smith, George Mason University, Arlington, VA (p. 264)
John C. Soper, John Carroll University, University Heights, OH (p. 266)
Irwin Stelzer, Hudson Institute, Washington, DC (p. 268)
Jeff Stier, American Council on Science and Health, New York, NY (p. 269)
*James Streeter, National Wilderness Institute, Washington, DC (p. 270)
Jane Shaw Stroup, PERC – The Center for Free Market Environmentalism, Bozeman, MT (p. 270)
Michael D. Stroup, Stephen F. Austin State University, Nacogdoches, TX (p. 270)
*Richard L. Stroup, PERC – The Center for Free Market Environmentalism, Bozeman, MT (p. 271)
James L. Sweeney, Stanford University, Stanford, CA (p. 272)
*Alexander Tabarrok, Mercatus Center at George Mason University, Arlington, VA (p. 273)
*Jerry Taylor, Cato Institute, Washington, DC (p. 274)
*David J. Theroux, The Independent Institute, Oakland, CA (p. 276)
*Peggy Venable, Texas Citizens for a Sound Economy, Austin, TX (p. 284)
Russ Walker, Citizens for a Sound Economy, Keizer, OR (p. 287)
*Malcolm Wallop, Frontiers of Freedom Institute, Fairfax, VA (p. 288)
*Elizabeth M. Whelan, American Council on Science and Health, New York, NY (p. 293)
Jason Wright, Frontiers of Freedom Institute, Fairfax, VA (p. 299)
Edward W. Younkins, Wheeling Jesuit University, Wheeling, WV (p. 301)
Ronald A. Zumbrun, The Zumbrun Law Firm, Sacramento, CA (p. 303)

LAND USE

*Jonathan H. Adler, Case Western Reserve University, Cleveland, OH (p. 35)
*I. Dean Ahmad, Minaret of Freedom Institute, Bethesda, MD (p. 36)
John Baden, Foundation for Research on Economics and the Environment, Bozeman, MT (p. 42)
Richard A. Baer, Jr., Cornell University, Ithaca, NY (p. 42)
Alex A. Beehler, Charles G. Koch Charitable Foundation, Washington, DC (p. 49)
*Kathy Benedetto, National Wilderness Institute, Washington, DC (p. 50)
*Robert K. Best, Pacific Legal Foundation, Sacramento, CA (p. 52)
Richard Bjornseth, Valdosta State University, Valdosta, GA (p. 54)
Daniel B. Botkin, Center for the Study of the Environment, Santa Barbara, CA (p. 58)
*Sandy Liddy Bourne, American Legislative Exchange Council, Washington, DC (p. 58)
*Pat Bradburn, Virginians for Property Rights, Catharpin, VA (p. 59)
*James Burling, Pacific Legal Foundation, Sacramento, CA (p. 65)
*H. Sterling Burnett, National Center for Policy Analysis, Dallas, TX (p. 65)
*Dan Byfield, American Land Foundation, Taylor, TX (p. 67)
*F. Patricia Callahan, American Association of Small Property Owners, Washington, DC (p. 68)
*Robert Carleson, American Civil Rights Union, Alexandria, VA (p. 70)
John K. Carlisle, Capital Research Center, Washington, DC (p. 70)
*John A. Charles, Cascade Policy Institute, Portland, OR (p. 72)
John Cobin, Montauk Financial Group, Greenville, SC (p. 76)

LAND USE (Continued)

Bonner R. Cohen, Lexington Institute, Arlington, VA (p. 77)
Peter F. Colwell, University of Illinois, Urbana, IL (p. 79)
*Ward Connerly, American Civil Rights Institute, Sacramento, CA (p. 80)
Dennis Coyle, Catholic University of America, Washington, DC (p. 84)
*Charles Cushman, American Land Rights Association, Battle Ground, WA (p. 87)
*Michael De Alessi, Reason Foundation, Los Angeles, CA (p. 89)
*Gerry Dickinson, South Carolina Policy Council, Columbia, SC (p. 95)
Douglas S. Doudney, Coalition for Property Rights, Orlando, FL (p. 97)
*Becky Norton Dunlop, The Heritage Foundation, Washington, DC (p. 100)
*Steven J. Eagle, George Mason University School of Law, Arlington, VA (p. 101)
*Paula Easley, Resource Development Council for Alaska, Anchorage, AK (p. 102)
*John C. Eastman, Chapman University School of Law, Orange, CA (p. 102)
*Myron Ebell, Competitive Enterprise Institute, Washington, DC (p. 103)
*Evelyn Ebzery, Memorial Hospital of Sheridan County, Sheridan, WY (p. 103)
Jefferson G. Edgens, Morehead State University – Jackson Center, Jackson, KY (p. 103)
*Robert Ernst, Banbury Fund, Salmas, CA (p. 108)
William A. Fischel, Dartmouth College, Hanover, NH (p. 112)
*Gloria Taylor Fisher, Interstate Commission on the Potomac River Basin,
    Alexandria, VA (p. 112)
*Allan Fitzsimmons, Balanced Resource Solutions, Woodbridge, VA (p. 113)
Bernard J. Frieden, Massachusetts Institute of Technology, Cambridge, MA (p. 117)
Leonard Gilroy, Reason Foundation, Los Angeles, CA (p. 123)
*Gary Glenn, American Family Association of Michigan, Midland, MI (p. 124)
*Peter Gordon, University of Southern California, Los Angeles, CA (p. 126)
*Grant R. Gulibon, The Commonwealth Foundation, Harrisburg, PA (p. 130)
*Paul Guppy, Washington Policy Center, Seattle, WA (p. 131)
*Erick Gustafson, Citizens for a Sound Economy, Washington, DC (p. 131)
*Robert Hale, Northwest Legal Foundation, Minot, ND (p. 132)
*Mike Hardiman, Hardiman Consulting, Washington, DC (p. 135)
Robert C. Harrison, Defenders of Property Rights, Washington, DC (p. 136)
*Steven Hayward, American Enterprise Institute, Washington, DC (p. 138)
*Donna H. Hearne, Constitutional Coalition, St. Louis, MO (p. 138)
*Karl Hess, The Land Center, Las Cruces, NM (p. 141)
*Randall G. Holcombe, Florida State University, Tallahassee, FL (p. 144)
*James Huffman, Lewis and Clark Law School, Portland, OR (p. 148)
*Harvey M. Jacobs, University of Wisconsin, Madison, WI (p. 153)
*Paul Kamenar, Washington Legal Foundation, Washington, DC (p. 157)
Diane S. Katz, Mackinac Center for Public Policy, Midland, MI (p. 158)
*Douglas W. Kmiec, The Catholic University of America, Washington, DC (p. 166)
David N. Laband, Auburn University, Auburn, AL (p. 171)
*Carol W. LaGrasse, Property Rights Foundation of America, Inc., Stony Creek, NY (p. 172)
Glenn G. Lammi, Washington Legal Foundation, Washington, DC (p. 173)
*George Landrith, Frontiers of Freedom Institute, Fairfax, VA (p. 173)
*Andrew Langer, National Federation of Independent Business, Washington, DC (p. 174)
*Jay H. Lehr, Environmental Education Enterprises, Ostrander, OH (p. 177)
Gary Libecap, University of Arizona, Tucson, AZ (p. 179)
*George Liebmann, Calvert Institute for Policy Research, Baltimore, MD (p. 180)
*Stephen B. Lovejoy, Purdue University, West Lafayette, IN (p. 183)
*Rita P. Maguire, Arizona Center for Public Policy, Phoenix, AZ (p. 186)
*Dennis Mansfield, Boise, ID (p. 189)
*Nancie G. Marzulla, Defenders of Property Rights, Washington, DC (p. 191)
*Roger J. Marzulla, Defenders of Property Rights, Washington, DC (p. 191)
*John McClaughry, Ethan Allen Institute, Concord, VT (p. 193)
*Edwin S. Mills, Northwestern University, Evanston, IL (p. 202)

---

* Has testified before a state or federal legislative committee

LAND USE (Continued)

*James Elliott Moore, II, University of Southern California, Los Angeles, CA (p. 205)

Suzanne C. Moore, Delaware Public Policy Institute, Wilmington, DE (p. 206)

*William Moshofsky, Oregonians in Action Legal Center, Tigard, OR (p. 208)

*Laurence S. Moss, Babson College, Babson Park, MA (p. 208)

Robert H. Nelson, University of Maryland, College Park, MD (p. 212)

*Frank Nims, Oregonians in Action, Tigard, OR (p. 214)

Randal O'Toole, Thoreau Institute, Bandon, OR (p. 217)

Sean Paige, Competitive Enterprise Institute, Washington, DC (p. 220)

E. C. Pasour, Jr., North Carolina State University, Raleigh, NC (p. 222)

Ellen F. Paul, Bowling Green State University, Bowling Green, OH (p. 223)

*William Perry Pendley, Mountain States Legal Foundation, Lakewood, CO (p. 225)

*Roger Pilon, Cato Institute, Washington, DC (p. 228)

*Daniel J. Popeo, Washington Legal Foundation, Washington, DC (p. 231)

R. S. Radford, Pacific Legal Foundation, Sacramento, CA (p. 235)

*David Ridenour, National Center for Public Policy Research, Washington, DC (p. 240)

*David W. Riggs, Capital Research Center, Washington, DC (p. 240)

*Robin Rivett, Pacific Legal Foundation, Sacramento, CA (p. 241)

Ron Robinson, Young America's Foundation, Herndon, VA (p. 242)

*Craig Rucker, Committee for a Constructive Tomorrow, Washington, DC (p. 246)

*Anthony Rufolo, Portland State University, Portland, OR (p. 246)

*Bill Schilling, Wyoming Business Alliance / Wyoming Heritage Foundation, Casper, WY (p. 253)

*Randy T. Simmons, Utah State University, Logan, UT (p. 260)

*Robert J. Smith, Center for Private Conservation, Washington, DC (p. 264)

*Samuel R. Staley, Buckeye Institute for Public Policy Solutions, Columbus, OH (p. 268)

*Robert Stavins, Harvard University, Cambridge, MA (p. 268)

*James Streeter, National Wilderness Institute, Washington, DC (p. 270)

*Jerry Taylor, Cato Institute, Washington, DC (p. 274)

Miro M. Todorovich, Scientists and Engineers for Secure Energy, New York, NY (p. 280)

*Ronald Utt, The Heritage Foundation, Washington, DC (p. 283)

Peter M. VanDoren, Cato Institute, Washington, DC (p. 284)

Russ Walker, Citizens for a Sound Economy, Keizer, OR (p. 287)

*Ben A. Wallis, Jr., Institute for Human Rights, San Antonio, TX (p. 287)

Ronald A. Zumbrun, The Zumbrun Law Firm, Sacramento, CA (p. 303)

PROPERTY RIGHTS

*Jonathan H. Adler, Case Western Reserve University, Cleveland, OH (p. 35)

*I. Dean Ahmad, Minaret of Freedom Institute, Bethesda, MD (p. 36)

David W. Almasi, National Center for Public Policy Research, Washington, DC (p. 37)

Lee J. Alston, University of Colorado-Boulder, Boulder, CO (p. 37)

Robert V. Andelson, American Institute for Economic Research, Auburn, AL (p. 37)

Terry L. Anderson, PERC – The Center for Free Market Environmentalism, Bozeman, MT (p. 38)

Ron Arnold, Center for the Defense of Free Enterprise, Bellevue, WA (p. 40)

John Baden, Foundation for Research on Economics and the Environment, Bozeman, MT (p. 42)

Sammy Basu, Willamette University, Salem, OR (p. 47)

Roger Bate, International Policy Network, Washington, DC (p. 47)

Alex A. Beehler, Charles G. Koch Charitable Foundation, Washington, DC (p. 49)

*Kathy Benedetto, National Wilderness Institute, Washington, DC (p. 50)

*Robert K. Best, Pacific Legal Foundation, Sacramento, CA (p. 52)

*Lillian BeVier, University of Virginia, Charlottesville, VA (p. 53)

Walter Block, Loyola University New Orleans, New Orleans, LA (p. 55)

Cecil E. Bohanon, Ball State University, Muncie, IN (p. 56)

PROPERTY RIGHTS (Continued)

Karol Boudreaux, George Mason University School of Law, Arlington, VA (p. 58)

*Sandy Liddy Bourne, American Legislative Exchange Council, Washington, DC (p. 58)

*Pat Bradburn, Virginians for Property Rights, Catharpin, VA (p. 59)

Gordon L. Brady, Center for the Study of Public Choice, Fairfax, VA (p. 60)

*Matthew J. Brouillette, The Commonwealth Foundation, Harrisburg, PA (p. 62)

*Scott Bullock, Institute for Justice, Washington, DC (p. 65)

*James Burling, Pacific Legal Foundation, Sacramento, CA (p. 65)

*H. Sterling Burnett, National Center for Policy Analysis, Dallas, TX (p. 65)

*Dan Byfield, American Land Foundation, Taylor, TX (p. 67)

*F. Patricia Callahan, American Association of Small Property Owners, Washington, DC (p. 68)

Jameson Campaigne, Jr., Jameson Books, Inc., Ottawa, IL (p. 68)

*James B. Cardle, Texas Citizen Action Network, Austin, TX (p. 69)

*Robert Carleson, American Civil Rights Union, Alexandria, VA (p. 70)

John K. Carlisle, Capital Research Center, Washington, DC (p. 70)

Alejandro A. Chafuen, Atlas Economic Research Foundation, Fairfax, VA (p. 72)

*John A. Charles, Cascade Policy Institute, Portland, OR (p. 72)

Robert Chitester, Palmer R. Chitester Fund, Erie, PA (p. 73)

Kenneth W. Clarkson, University of Miami, Coral Gables, FL (p. 75)

John Cobin, Montauk Financial Group, Greenville, SC (p. 76)

Andrew I. Cohen, University of Oklahoma, Norman, OK (p. 77)

Bonner R. Cohen, Lexington Institute, Arlington, VA (p. 77)

Peter F. Colwell, University of Illinois, Urbana, IL (p. 79)

Kellyanne Conway, the polling company/WomanTrend, Washington, DC (p. 80)

Charli Coon, The Heritage Foundation, Washington, DC (p. 81)

*Louis J. Cordia, Cordia Companies, Alexandria, VA (p. 82)

*Wendell Cox, Wendell Cox Consultancy, Belleville, IL (p. 84)

Dennis Coyle, Catholic University of America, Washington, DC (p. 84)

*Charles Cushman, American Land Rights Association, Battle Ground, WA (p. 87)

*Robert J. Cynkar, Cooper & Kirk, PLLC, Washington, DC (p. 87)

*Michael De Alessi, Reason Foundation, Los Angeles, CA (p. 89)

*James DeLong, Progress & Freedom Foundation, Washington, DC (p. 92)

*Phillip DeVous, Acton Institute for the Study of Religion and Liberty, Grand Rapids, MI (p. 94)

*Thomas DeWeese, American Policy Center, Warrenton, VA (p. 94)

*Gerry Dickinson, South Carolina Policy Council, Columbia, SC (p. 95)

Douglas S. Doudney, Coalition for Property Rights, Orlando, FL (p. 97)

*Susan E. Dudley, Mercatus Center at George Mason University, Arlington, VA (p. 99)

*Becky Norton Dunlop, The Heritage Foundation, Washington, DC (p. 100)

*Paul Dunn, University of Louisiana, Monroe, Monroe, LA (p. 100)

*Steven J. Eagle, George Mason University School of Law, Arlington, VA (p. 101)

*Paula Easley, Resource Development Council for Alaska, Anchorage, AK (p. 102)

*John C. Eastman, Chapman University School of Law, Orange, CA (p. 102)

*Myron Ebell, Competitive Enterprise Institute, Washington, DC (p. 103)

*Evelyn Ebzery, Memorial Hospital of Sheridan County, Sheridan, WY (p. 103)

Jefferson G. Edgens, Morehead State University – Jackson Center, Jackson, KY (p. 103)

Richard A. Epstein, University of Chicago Law School, Chicago, IL (p. 107)

*Robert Ernst, Banbury Fund, Salmas, CA (p. 108)

*Robert Fike, Americans for Tax Reform, Washington, DC (p. 111)

William A. Fischel, Dartmouth College, Hanover, NH (p. 112)

*Gloria Taylor Fisher, Interstate Commission on the Potomac River Basin, Alexandria, VA (p. 112)

*Allan Fitzsimmons, Balanced Resource Solutions, Woodbridge, VA (p. 113)

David E. R. Gay, University of Arkansas, Fayetteville, AR (p. 121)

*Todd Gaziano, The Heritage Foundation, Washington, DC (p. 121)

Paul Georgia, Competitive Enterprise Institute, Washington, DC (p. 122)

---

* Has testified before a state or federal legislative committee

PROPERTY RIGHTS (Continued)

Leonard Gilroy, Reason Foundation, Los Angeles, CA (p. 123)

*Gary Glenn, American Family Association of Michigan, Midland, MI (p. 124)

*Robert E. Gordon, Jr., National Wilderness Institute, Washington, DC (p. 127)

Andrew Grainger, New England Legal Foundation, Boston, MA (p. 128)

Samuel Gregg, Acton Institute for the Study of Religion and Liberty, Grand Rapids, MI (p. 129)

*Erick Gustafson, Citizens for a Sound Economy, Washington, DC (p. 131)

*Robert Hale, Northwest Legal Foundation, Minot, ND (p. 132)

Steve H. Hanke, Johns Hopkins University, Baltimore, MD (p. 134)

*Mike Hardiman, Hardiman Consulting, Washington, DC (p. 135)

Robert C. Harrison, Defenders of Property Rights, Washington, DC (p. 136)

Thomas Hazlett, Manhattan Institute for Policy Research, Washington, DC (p. 138)

*Donna H. Hearne, Constitutional Coalition, St. Louis, MO (p. 138)

*Karl Hess, The Land Center, Las Cruces, NM (p. 141)

Peter J. Hill, Wheaton College, Wheaton, IL (p. 142)

*Don Hodel, Silverthorne, CO (p. 143)

*Chris Horner, Competitive Enterprise Institute, Washington, DC (p. 146)

*James Huffman, Lewis and Clark Law School, Portland, OR (p. 148)

*Harvey M. Jacobs, University of Wisconsin, Madison, WI (p. 153)

Jim Johnston, Heartland Institute, Wilmette, IL (p. 156)

*Paul Kamenar, Washington Legal Foundation, Washington, DC (p. 157)

Diane S. Katz, Mackinac Center for Public Policy, Midland, MI (p. 158)

Martin S. Kaufman, Atlantic Legal Foundation, New York, NY (p. 159)

*Sam Kazman, Competitive Enterprise Institute, Washington, DC (p. 159)

*W. Thomas Kelly, Savers and Investors League, Mirror Lake, NH (p. 161)

Phil Kent, Southeastern Legal Foundation, Atlanta, GA (p. 162)

F. Scott Kieff, Washington University, St. Louis, MO (p. 163)

*Douglas W. Kmiec, The Catholic University of America, Washington, DC (p. 166)

Gary Kreep, United States Justice Foundation, Escondido, CA (p. 169)

Jo Kwong, Atlas Economic Research Foundation, Fairfax, VA (p. 171)

*Carol W. LaGrasse, Property Rights Foundation of America, Inc., Stony Creek, NY (p. 172)

Glenn G. Lammi, Washington Legal Foundation, Washington, DC (p. 173)

*George Landrith, Frontiers of Freedom Institute, Fairfax, VA (p. 173)

*Andrew Langer, National Federation of Independent Business, Washington, DC (p. 174)

Daniel Lapin, Toward Tradition, Mercer Island, WA (p. 174)

*Donald R. Leal, PERC – The Center for Free Market Environmentalism, Bozeman, MT (p. 176)

Dwight R. Lee, University of Georgia, Athens, GA (p. 176)

*Jay H. Lehr, Environmental Education Enterprises, Ostrander, OH (p. 177)

*Mark R. Levin, Landmark Legal Foundation, Herndon, VA (p. 178)

Gary Libecap, University of Arizona, Tucson, AZ (p. 179)

*Stephen B. Lovejoy, Purdue University, West Lafayette, IN (p. 183)

Lisa MacLellan, Pacific Research Institute, San Francisco, CA (p. 185)

Brett A. Magbee, Oklahoma Council of Public Affairs, Oklahoma City, OK (p. 186)

*Rita P. Maguire, Arizona Center for Public Policy, Phoenix, AZ (p. 186)

*Dennis Mansfield, Boise, ID (p. 189)

*Nancie G. Marzulla, Defenders of Property Rights, Washington, DC (p. 191)

*Roger J. Marzulla, Defenders of Property Rights, Washington, DC (p. 191)

*Nina May, *Renaissance Connection.com/RCNetwork.net*, Washington, DC (p. 192)

*John McClaughry, Ethan Allen Institute, Concord, VT (p. 193)

*Bobby McCormick, Clemson University, Clemson, SC (p. 194)

Lawrence J. McQuillan, Pacific Research Institute, San Francisco, CA (p. 197)

Jack McVaugh, Arizona School Choice Trust, Scottsdale, AZ (p. 198)

*Edwin Meese III, The Heritage Foundation, Washington, DC (p. 198)

*William H. Mellor, Institute for Justice, Washington, DC (p. 199)

PROPERTY RIGHTS (Continued)

Harry Messenheimer, Rio Grande Foundation, Tijeras, NM (p. 200)

Norbert Michel, The Heritage Foundation, Washington, DC (p. 201)

*Edwin S. Mills, Northwestern University, Evanston, IL (p. 202)

*James Elliott Moore, II, University of Southern California, Los Angeles, CA (p. 205)

*William Moshofsky, Oregonians in Action Legal Center, Tigard, OR (p. 208)

Robert G. Natelson, Missoula, MT (p. 211)

Mario Navarro da Costa, American Society for the Defense of Tradition, Family and Property, McLean, VA (p. 211)

*Frank Nims, Oregonians in Action, Tigard, OR (p. 214)

*Richard Olivastro, People Dynamics, Farmington, CT (p. 218)

Sean Paige, Competitive Enterprise Institute, Washington, DC (p. 220)

*J. A. Parker, Lincoln Institute for Research and Education, Washington, DC (p. 221)

Ellen F. Paul, Bowling Green State University, Bowling Green, OH (p. 223)

*Valery J. Pech, Colorado Springs, CO (p. 224)

*William Perry Pendley, Mountain States Legal Foundation, Lakewood, CO (p. 225)

Bruce Piasecki, AHC Group, Saratoga Springs, NY (p. 228)

*Roger Pilon, Cato Institute, Washington, DC (p. 228)

Gale L. Pooley, Star, ID (p. 230)

*Daniel J. Popeo, Washington Legal Foundation, Washington, DC (p. 231)

*Scott Pullins, Ohio Taxpayers Association and OTA Foundation, Columbus, OH (p. 234)

R. S. Radford, Pacific Legal Foundation, Sacramento, CA (p. 235)

*Amy Ridenour, National Center for Public Policy Research, Washington, DC (p. 240)

*David Ridenour, National Center for Public Policy Research, Washington, DC (p. 240)

*David W. Riggs, Capital Research Center, Washington, DC (p. 240)

*Robin Rivett, Pacific Legal Foundation, Sacramento, CA (p. 241)

Ron Robinson, Young America's Foundation, Herndon, VA (p. 242)

*David Rothbard, Committee for a Constructive Tomorrow, Washington, DC (p. 244)

*James A. Roumasset, University of Hawaii, Honolulu, HI (p. 245)

*Paul Rubin, Emory University, Atlanta, GA (p. 246)

*Craig Rucker, Committee for a Constructive Tomorrow, Washington, DC (p. 246)

*Richard A. Samp, Washington Legal Foundation, Washington, DC (p. 248)

David Schmidtz, University of Arizona, Tucson, AZ (p. 253)

Robert Haney Scott, California State University, Chico, Chico, CA (p. 255)

*John Shanahan, National Mining Association, Washington, DC (p. 258)

Frank A. Shepherd, Pacific Legal Foundation, Coral Gables, FL (p. 259)

*Jack Shockey, Citizens for Property Rights, Hamilton, VA (p. 259)

*Randy T. Simmons, Utah State University, Logan, UT (p. 260)

*Robert A. Sirico, Acton Institute for the Study of Religion and Liberty, Grand Rapids, MI (p. 261)

*Fred L. Smith, Jr., Competitive Enterprise Institute, Washington, DC (p. 263)

*Robert J. Smith, Center for Private Conservation, Washington, DC (p. 264)

*John A. Sparks, Grove City College, Grove City, PA (p. 266)

*James Streeter, National Wilderness Institute, Washington, DC (p. 270)

Michael D. Stroup, Stephen F. Austin State University, Nacogdoches, TX (p. 270)

*Richard L. Stroup, PERC – The Center for Free Market Environmentalism, Bozeman, MT (p. 271)

*William Craig Stubblebine, Claremont McKenna College, Claremont, CA (p. 271)

*Alexander Tabarrok, Mercatus Center at George Mason University, Arlington, VA (p. 273)

*John Taylor, Virginia Institute for Public Policy, Potomac Falls, VA (p. 274)

*David J. Theroux, The Independent Institute, Oakland, CA (p. 276)

*Mark Thornton, Columbus State University, Columbus, GA (p. 278)

*Balint Vazsonyi, Center for the American Founding, McLean, VA (p. 284)

*Peggy Venable, Texas Citizens for a Sound Economy, Austin, TX (p. 284)

Dane vonBreichenruchardt, U. S. Bill of Rights Foundation, Washington, DC (p. 286)

---

* Has testified before a state or federal legislative committee

PROPERTY RIGHTS (Continued)

Russ Walker, Citizens for a Sound Economy, Keizer, OR **(p. 287)**
*****Ben A. Wallis, Jr.,** Institute for Human Rights, San Antonio, TX **(p. 287)**
*****Malcolm Wallop,** Frontiers of Freedom Institute, Fairfax, VA **(p. 288)**
Jason Wright, Frontiers of Freedom Institute, Fairfax, VA **(p. 299)**
Bruce Yandle, Clemson University, Clemson, SC **(p. 300)**
Edward W. Younkins, Wheeling Jesuit University, Wheeling, WV **(p. 301)**
Jerry Zandstra, Acton Institute for the Study of Religion and Liberty, Grand Rapids, MI **(p. 301)**
Ronald A. Zumbrun, The Zumbrun Law Firm, Sacramento, CA **(p. 303)**

RESEARCH FUNDING

*****Sallie Baliunas,** Harvard University, Cambridge, MA **(p. 44)**
Alex A. Beehler, Charles G. Koch Charitable Foundation, Washington, DC **(p. 49)**
*****Sandy Liddy Bourne,** American Legislative Exchange Council, Washington, DC **(p. 58)**
Gordon L. Brady, Center for the Study of Public Choice, Fairfax, VA **(p. 60)**
*****Kenneth Brown,** Rio Grande Foundation, Albuquerque, NM **(p. 63)**
*****Stephen Cole,** State University of New York, Stony Brook, NY **(p. 78)**
Kellyanne Conway, the polling company/WomanTrend, Washington, DC **(p. 80)**
*****Michael R. Darby,** University of California at Los Angeles, Los Angeles, CA **(p. 89)**
Arthur M. Diamond, Jr., University of Nebraska, Omaha, Omaha, NE **(p. 95)**
*****Becky Norton Dunlop,** The Heritage Foundation, Washington, DC **(p. 100)**
Howard Fienberg, Statistical Assessment Service, Washington, DC **(p. 111)**
Michael Fumento, Hudson Institute, Washington, DC **(p. 118)**
Robin Hanson, George Mason University, Fairfax, VA **(p. 134)**
Charles L. Harper, John Templeton Foundation, Radnor, PA **(p. 135)**
*****Robert L. Hershey,** Robert L. Hershey, P.E., Washington, DC **(p. 141)**
*****Karl Hess,** The Land Center, Las Cruces, NM **(p. 141)**
*****Jacqueline Kasun,** Humboldt State University, Arcata, CA **(p. 158)**
Michael Kellman, University of Oregon, Eugene, OR **(p. 160)**
F. Scott Kieff, Washington University, St. Louis, MO **(p. 163)**
*****Jay H. Lehr,** Environmental Education Enterprises, Ostrander, OH **(p. 177)**
Lawrence J. McQuillan, Pacific Research Institute, San Francisco, CA **(p. 197)**
*****Patrick Michaels,** University of Virginia, Charlottesville, VA **(p. 200)**
*****John H. Moore,** Grove City College, Grove City, PA **(p. 206)**
E. C. Pasour, Jr., North Carolina State University, Raleigh, NC **(p. 222)**
*****David W. Riggs,** Capital Research Center, Washington, DC **(p. 240)**
*****Terrence M. Scanlon,** Capital Research Center, Washington, DC **(p. 251)**
*****Stuart Schlossman,** Harvard Medical School, Boston, MA **(p. 253)**
*****Pete Sepp,** National Taxpayers Union, Alexandria, VA **(p. 257)**
*****S. Fred Singer,** Science and Environmental Policy Project, Arlington, VA **(p. 260)**
*****Jack Sommer,** Political Economy Research Institute, Charlotte, NC **(p. 266)**
John E. R. Staddon, Duke University, Durham, NC **(p. 267)**
Jeff Stier, American Council on Science and Health, New York, NY **(p. 269)**
Miklos N. Szilagyi, University of Arizona, Tucson, AZ **(p. 273)**
*****Mead Treadwell,** Institute of the North, Anchorage, AK **(p. 281)**
*****Terry W. Van Allen,** Kemah, TX **(p. 283)**

SOUND SCIENCE

Bruce N. Ames, University of California, Berkeley, Berkeley, CA **(p. 37)**
Alex Avery, Hudson Institute, Staunton, VA **(p. 41)**
*****Dennis T. Avery,** Hudson Institute, Churchville, VA **(p. 42)**
John Baden, Foundation for Research on Economics and the Environment, Bozeman, MT **(p. 42)**
*****Sallie Baliunas,** Harvard University, Cambridge, MA **(p. 44)**

SOUND SCIENCE (Continued)

Alex A. Beehler, Charles G. Koch Charitable Foundation, Washington, DC (p. 49)

*Robert K. Best, Pacific Legal Foundation, Sacramento, CA (p. 52)

*Fran Bevan, Eagle Forum of Pennsylvania, North Huntingdon, PA (p. 53)

Daniel B. Botkin, Center for the Study of the Environment, Santa Barbara, CA (p. 58)

*Sandy Liddy Bourne, American Legislative Exchange Council, Washington, DC (p. 58)

Nigel M. de S. Cameron, Institute for Humane Studies at George Mason University, Arlington, VA (p. 68)

*Kenneth W. Chilton, Institute for Study of Economics and the Environment, St. Charles, MO (p. 73)

*Bernard L. Cohen, University of Pittsburgh, Pittsburgh, PA (p. 77)

Bonner R. Cohen, Lexington Institute, Arlington, VA (p. 77)

Gregory Conko, Competitive Enterprise Institute, Washington, DC (p. 79)

Kellyanne Conway, the polling company/WomanTrend, Washington, DC (p. 80)

Charli Coon, The Heritage Foundation, Washington, DC (p. 81)

Milton R. Copulos, National Defense Council Foundation, Alexandria, VA (p. 82)

*Michael De Alessi, Reason Foundation, Los Angeles, CA (p. 89)

*Thomas DeWeese, American Policy Center, Warrenton, VA (p. 94)

Eric Dezenhall, Nichols Dezenhall Management Group, Washington, DC (p. 94)

Arthur M. Diamond, Jr., University of Nebraska, Omaha, Omaha, NE (p. 95)

*Paul K. Driessen, Committee for a Constructive Tomorrow, Fairfax, VA (p. 98)

*Susan E. Dudley, Mercatus Center at George Mason University, Arlington, VA (p. 99)

*Becky Norton Dunlop, The Heritage Foundation, Washington, DC (p. 100)

Howard Fienberg, Statistical Assessment Service, Washington, DC (p. 111)

*Gloria Taylor Fisher, Interstate Commission on the Potomac River Basin, Alexandria, VA (p. 112)

*Allan Fitzsimmons, Balanced Resource Solutions, Woodbridge, VA (p. 113)

Michael Fumento, Hudson Institute, Washington, DC (p. 118)

*Dana Joel Gattuso, Competitive Enterprise Institute, Alexandria, VA (p. 121)

Paul Georgia, Competitive Enterprise Institute, Washington, DC (p. 122)

Tomi Gomory, Florida State University, Tallahassee, FL (p. 126)

*Erick Gustafson, Citizens for a Sound Economy, Washington, DC (p. 131)

*Mike Hardiman, Hardiman Consulting, Washington, DC (p. 135)

Charles L. Harper, John Templeton Foundation, Radnor, PA (p. 135)

Larry Hart, Hartco Strategies, Washington, DC (p. 136)

*Robert L. Hershey, Robert L. Hershey, P.E., Washington, DC (p. 141)

*Karl Hess, The Land Center, Las Cruces, NM (p. 141)

Peter Huber, Manhattan Institute for Policy Research, New York, NY (p. 148)

Jonathan Imber, Wellesley College, Wellesley, MA (p. 151)

Robert Jastrow, George C. Marshall Institute, Washington, DC (p. 153)

*Bruce Alan Johnson, Bruce Alan Johnson Associates, Indianapolis, IN (p. 155)

Diane S. Katz, Mackinac Center for Public Policy, Midland, MI (p. 158)

Michael Kellman, University of Oregon, Eugene, OR (p. 160)

Phil Kent, Southeastern Legal Foundation, Atlanta, GA (p. 162)

Karen Kerrigan, the polling company, Washington, DC (p. 162)

F. Scott Kieff, Washington University, St. Louis, MO (p. 163)

Raymond J. Krizek, Northwestern University, Evanston, IL (p. 169)

*George Landrith, Frontiers of Freedom Institute, Fairfax, VA (p. 173)

*Andrew Langer, National Federation of Independent Business, Washington, DC (p. 174)

*Jay H. Lehr, Environmental Education Enterprises, Ostrander, OH (p. 177)

Richard S. Lindzen, Massachusetts Institute of Technology, Cambridge, MA (p. 181)

Angela Logomasini, Competitive Enterprise Institute, Washington, DC (p. 182)

*Stephen B. Lovejoy, Purdue University, West Lafayette, IN (p. 183)

*Nancie G. Marzulla, Defenders of Property Rights, Washington, DC (p. 191)

*Roger J. Marzulla, Defenders of Property Rights, Washington, DC (p. 191)

SOUND SCIENCE (Continued)

Lawrence J. McQuillan, Pacific Research Institute, San Francisco, CA (p. 197)

*Patrick Michaels, University of Virginia, Charlottesville, VA (p. 200)

*Henry I. Miller, Hoover Institution, Stanford, CA (p. 202)

Steven J. Milloy, *junkscience.com*, Washington, DC (p. 202)

*A. Alan Moghissi, Institute for Regulatory Science, Alexandria, VA (p. 204)

Iain Murray, Statistical Assessment Service, Washington, DC (p. 209)

Robert H. Nelson, University of Maryland, College Park, MD (p. 212)

*Jane M. Orient, Association of American Physicians and Surgeons, Tucson, AZ (p. 219)

Sean Paige, Competitive Enterprise Institute, Washington, DC (p. 220)

*William Perry Pendley, Mountain States Legal Foundation, Lakewood, CO (p. 225)

*Alan C. Raul, Sidley & Austin Brown & Wood, LLP, Washington, DC (p. 237)

*David W. Riggs, Capital Research Center, Washington, DC (p. 240)

*Robin Rivett, Pacific Legal Foundation, Sacramento, CA (p. 241)

*David Rothbard, Committee for a Constructive Tomorrow, Washington, DC (p. 244)

Charles Rubin, Duquesne University, Pittsburgh, PA (p. 246)

*Craig Rucker, Committee for a Constructive Tomorrow, Washington, DC (p. 246)

*Michael Sanera, Basis Charter High School, Tucson, AZ (p. 249)

*Stuart Schlossman, Harvard Medical School, Boston, MA (p. 253)

*John Shanahan, National Mining Association, Washington, DC (p. 258)

Frank A. Shepherd, Pacific Legal Foundation, Coral Gables, FL (p. 259)

*S. Fred Singer, Science and Environmental Policy Project, Arlington, VA (p. 260)

*Robert A. Sirico, Acton Institute for the Study of Religion and Liberty, Grand Rapids, MI (p. 261)

*Frances B. Smith, Consumer Alert, Washington, DC (p. 263)

Ted J. Smith, III, Virginia Commonwealth University, Richmond, VA (p. 264)

*Jack Sommer, Political Economy Research Institute, Charlotte, NC (p. 266)

Jeff Stier, American Council on Science and Health, New York, NY (p. 269)

*Jerry Taylor, Cato Institute, Washington, DC (p. 274)

*Edward Teller, Hoover Institution, Stanford, CA (p. 275)

Frank J. Tipler, Tulane University, New Orleans, LA (p. 279)

Miro M. Todorovich, Scientists and Engineers for Secure Energy, New York, NY (p. 280)

*Mead Treadwell, Institute of the North, Anchorage, AK (p. 281)

Russ Walker, Citizens for a Sound Economy, Keizer, OR (p. 287)

John G. West, Discovery Institute, Seattle, WA (p. 292)

*Elizabeth M. Whelan, American Council on Science and Health, New York, NY (p. 293)

Anne A. Witkowsky, Center for Strategic and International Studies, Washington, DC (p. 296)

Jason Wright, Frontiers of Freedom Institute, Fairfax, VA (p. 299)

Jennifer Zambone, Mercatus Center at George Mason University, Arlington, VA (p. 301)

Richard Zeckhauser, Harvard University, Cambridge, MA (p. 302)

STEWARDSHIP

*Jonathan H. Adler, Case Western Reserve University, Cleveland, OH (p. 35)

Terry L. Anderson, PERC – The Center for Free Market Environmentalism, Bozeman, MT (p. 38)

Michael B. Barkey, Center for the Study of Compassionate Conservatism, Grand Rapids, MI (p. 46)

Alex A. Beehler, Charles G. Koch Charitable Foundation, Washington, DC (p. 49)

John M. Beers, Annecy Institute for the Study of Virtue and Liberty, Washington, DC (p. 49)

*Sandy Liddy Bourne, American Legislative Exchange Council, Washington, DC (p. 58)

*H. Sterling Burnett, National Center for Policy Analysis, Dallas, TX (p. 65)

Alejandro A. Chafuen, Atlas Economic Research Foundation, Fairfax, VA (p. 72)

Peter F. Colwell, University of Illinois, Urbana, IL (p. 79)

Charli Coon, The Heritage Foundation, Washington, DC (p. 81)

*Michael De Alessi, Reason Foundation, Los Angeles, CA (p. 89)

STEWARDSHIP (Continued)

William C. Dennis, Dennis Consulting, MacLean, VA (p. 93)
*Phillip DeVous, Acton Institute for the Study of Religion and Liberty, Grand Rapids, MI (p. 94)
*Paul K. Driessen, Committee for a Constructive Tomorrow, Fairfax, VA (p. 98)
*Becky Norton Dunlop, The Heritage Foundation, Washington, DC (p. 100)
*Evelyn Ebzery, Memorial Hospital of Sheridan County, Sheridan, WY (p. 103)
*Gloria Taylor Fisher, Interstate Commission on the Potomac River Basin, Alexandria, VA (p. 112)
*Allan Fitzsimmons, Balanced Resource Solutions, Woodbridge, VA (p. 113)
*Mike Hardiman, Hardiman Consulting, Washington, DC (p. 135)
*Donna H. Hearne, Constitutional Coalition, St. Louis, MO (p. 138)
*Karl Hess, The Land Center, Las Cruces, NM (p. 141)
*Don Hodel, Silverthorne, CO (p. 143)
Diane S. Katz, Mackinac Center for Public Policy, Midland, MI (p. 158)
*Andrew Langer, National Federation of Independent Business, Washington, DC (p. 174)
*Donald R. Leal, PERC – The Center for Free Market Environmentalism, Bozeman, MT (p. 176)
*Stephen B. Lovejoy, Purdue University, West Lafayette, IN (p. 183)
*Rita P. Maguire, Arizona Center for Public Policy, Phoenix, AZ (p. 186)
*Nancie G. Marzulla, Defenders of Property Rights, Washington, DC (p. 191)
*Roger J. Marzulla, Defenders of Property Rights, Washington, DC (p. 191)
Lawrence J. McQuillan, Pacific Research Institute, San Francisco, CA (p. 197)
David Nutter, Mercatus Center at George Mason University, Arlington, VA (p. 216)
*Richard Olivastro, People Dynamics, Farmington, CT (p. 218)
Sean Paige, Competitive Enterprise Institute, Washington, DC (p. 220)
*William Perry Pendley, Mountain States Legal Foundation, Lakewood, CO (p. 225)
Bruce Piasecki, AHC Group, Saratoga Springs, NY (p. 228)
*Daniel J. Popeo, Washington Legal Foundation, Washington, DC (p. 231)
*David W. Riggs, Capital Research Center, Washington, DC (p. 240)
*David Rothbard, Committee for a Constructive Tomorrow, Washington, DC (p. 244)
*James A. Roumasset, University of Hawaii, Honolulu, HI (p. 245)
*Craig Rucker, Committee for a Constructive Tomorrow, Washington, DC (p. 246)
*Robert A. Sirico, Acton Institute for the Study of Religion and Liberty, Grand Rapids, MI (p. 261)
*Fred L. Smith, Jr., Competitive Enterprise Institute, Washington, DC (p. 263)
*Robert J. Smith, Center for Private Conservation, Washington, DC (p. 264)
*James Streeter, National Wilderness Institute, Washington, DC (p. 270)
Miro M. Todorovich, Scientists and Engineers for Secure Energy, New York, NY (p. 280)
Edward W. Younkins, Wheeling Jesuit University, Wheeling, WV (p. 301)
Ronald A. Zumbrun, The Zumbrun Law Firm, Sacramento, CA (p. 303)

URBAN SPRAWL/LIVABLE CITIES

*Stephen Adams, Pioneer Institute for Public Policy Research, Boston, MA (p. 34)
*Jonathan H. Adler, Case Western Reserve University, Cleveland, OH (p. 35)
David W. Almasi, National Center for Public Policy Research, Washington, DC (p. 37)
Robert V. Andelson, American Institute for Economic Research, Auburn, AL (p. 37)
*Lewis Andrews, Yankee Institute for Public Policy Studies, Hartford, CT (p. 39)
Alex A. Beehler, Charles G. Koch Charitable Foundation, Washington, DC (p. 49)
*Robert K. Best, Pacific Legal Foundation, Sacramento, CA (p. 52)
Richard Bjornseth, Valdosta State University, Valdosta, GA (p. 54)
Walter Block, Loyola University New Orleans, New Orleans, LA (p. 55)
Daniel B. Botkin, Center for the Study of the Environment, Santa Barbara, CA (p. 58)
*Sandy Liddy Bourne, American Legislative Exchange Council, Washington, DC (p. 58)
*Pat Bradburn, Virginians for Property Rights, Catharpin, VA (p. 59)
*Matthew J. Brouillette, The Commonwealth Foundation, Harrisburg, PA (p. 62)

URBAN SPRAWL/LIVABLE CITIES (Continued)

*William P. Browne, Central Michigan University, Mount Pleasant, MI (p. 64)
 Shane Burkhardt, Hudson Institute, Indianapolis, IN (p. 65)
*H. Sterling Burnett, National Center for Policy Analysis, Dallas, TX (p. 65)
*Dan Byfield, American Land Foundation, Taylor, TX (p. 67)
*F. Patricia Callahan, American Association of Small Property Owners, Washington, DC (p. 68)
 John K. Carlisle, Capital Research Center, Washington, DC (p. 70)
*John A. Charles, Cascade Policy Institute, Portland, OR (p. 72)
 Peter Cleary, American Conservative Union, Alexandria, VA (p. 75)
*Laurence Cohen, Yankee Institute for Public Policy Studies, Glastonbury, CT (p. 78)
 Peter F. Colwell, University of Illinois, Urbana, IL (p. 79)
*Louis J. Cordia, Cordia Companies, Alexandria, VA (p. 82)
*Wendell Cox, Wendell Cox Consultancy, Belleville, IL (p. 84)
*Michael De Alessi, Reason Foundation, Los Angeles, CA (p. 89)
*Thomas DeWeese, American Policy Center, Warrenton, VA (p. 94)
 Douglas S. Doudney, Coalition for Property Rights, Orlando, FL (p. 97)
*Becky Norton Dunlop, The Heritage Foundation, Washington, DC (p. 100)
*Paul Dunn, University of Louisiana, Monroe, Monroe, LA (p. 100)
*Steven J. Eagle, George Mason University School of Law, Arlington, VA (p. 101)
*Paula Easley, Resource Development Council for Alaska, Anchorage, AK (p. 102)
 Jefferson G. Edgens, Morehead State University – Jackson Center, Jackson, KY (p. 103)
*Stephen Entin, Institute for Research on the Economics of Taxation, Washington, DC (p. 107)
*Robert Fike, Americans for Tax Reform, Washington, DC (p. 111)
*Gloria Taylor Fisher, Interstate Commission on the Potomac River Basin,
   Alexandria, VA (p. 112)
 Fred E. Foldvary, Santa Clara University, Santa Clara, CA (p. 114)
*Robert Franciosi, Goldwater Institute, Phoenix, AZ (p. 115)
 Bernard J. Frieden, Massachusetts Institute of Technology, Cambridge, MA (p. 117)
 Leonard Gilroy, Reason Foundation, Los Angeles, CA (p. 123)
*Peter Gordon, University of Southern California, Los Angeles, CA (p. 126)
*Grant R. Gulibon, The Commonwealth Foundation, Harrisburg, PA (p. 130)
*Erick Gustafson, Citizens for a Sound Economy, Washington, DC (p. 131)
*Randy H. Hamilton, University of California, Berkeley, Berkeley, CA (p. 133)
*Mike Hardiman, Hardiman Consulting, Washington, DC (p. 135)
 Robert C. Harrison, Defenders of Property Rights, Washington, DC (p. 136)
 David T. Hartgen, University of North Carolina, Charlotte, Charlotte, NC (p. 136)
 Robert Hawkins, Jr., Institute for Contemporary Studies, Oakland, CA (p. 137)
*Steven Hayward, American Enterprise Institute, Washington, DC (p. 138)
*Donna H. Hearne, Constitutional Coalition, St. Louis, MO (p. 138)
*Karl Hess, The Land Center, Las Cruces, NM (p. 141)
*Randall G. Holcombe, Florida State University, Tallahassee, FL (p. 144)
*John MacDonald Hood, John Locke Foundation, Raleigh, NC (p. 145)
*James Huffman, Lewis and Clark Law School, Portland, OR (p. 148)
 Howard Husock, Manhattan Institute for Policy Research, New York, NY (p. 150)
 Sanford Ikeda, State University of New York, Purchase, NY (p. 151)
 Niger Roy Innis, Congress of Racial Equality, New York, NY (p. 151)
*Harvey M. Jacobs, University of Wisconsin, Madison, WI (p. 153)
 Diane S. Katz, Mackinac Center for Public Policy, Midland, MI (p. 158)
*Jack Kemp, Empower America, Washington, DC (p. 161)
*Douglas W. Kmiec, The Catholic University of America, Washington, DC (p. 166)
 Jo Kwong, Atlas Economic Research Foundation, Fairfax, VA (p. 171)
*George Landrith, Frontiers of Freedom Institute, Fairfax, VA (p. 173)
*Andrew Langer, National Federation of Independent Business, Washington, DC (p. 174)
*Jay H. Lehr, Environmental Education Enterprises, Ostrander, OH (p. 177)
*Eli Lehrer, *The American Enterprise*, Washington, DC (p. 177)

URBAN SPRAWL/LIVABLE CITIES (Continued)

Martin A. Levin, Brandeis University, Waltham, MA (p. 178)

*George Liebmann, Calvert Institute for Policy Research, Baltimore, MD (p. 180)

*Peter Linneman, University of Pennsylvania, Philadelphia, PA (p. 181)

*Rita P. Maguire, Arizona Center for Public Policy, Phoenix, AZ (p. 186)

Steve Mariotti, National Foundation for Teaching Entrepreneurship, New York, NY (p. 189)

*Nancie G. Marzulla, Defenders of Property Rights, Washington, DC (p. 191)

*Roger J. Marzulla, Defenders of Property Rights, Washington, DC (p. 191)

*Kelly McCutchen, Georgia Public Policy Foundation, Atlanta, GA (p. 194)

*Edwin S. Mills, Northwestern University, Evanston, IL (p. 202)

*James Elliott Moore, II, University of Southern California, Los Angeles, CA (p. 205)

Suzanne C. Moore, Delaware Public Policy Institute, Wilmington, DE (p. 206)

*William Moshofsky, Oregonians in Action Legal Center, Tigard, OR (p. 208)

Richard F. Muth, Emory University, Atlanta, GA (p. 210)

*Frank Nims, Oregonians in Action, Tigard, OR (p. 214)

Randal O'Toole, Thoreau Institute, Bandon, OR (p. 217)

Sean Paige, Competitive Enterprise Institute, Washington, DC (p. 220)

*Darryl Paulson, University of South Florida, St. Petersburg, FL (p. 223)

*Edward Potter, Employment Policy Foundation, Washington, DC (p. 231)

R. S. Radford, Pacific Legal Foundation, Sacramento, CA (p. 235)

*Amy Ridenour, National Center for Public Policy Research, Washington, DC (p. 240)

*David Ridenour, National Center for Public Policy Research, Washington, DC (p. 240)

*David W. Riggs, Capital Research Center, Washington, DC (p. 240)

*Richard O. Rowland, Grassroot Institute of Hawaii, Aiea, HI (p. 245)

Charles Rubin, Duquesne University, Pittsburgh, PA (p. 246)

*Anthony Rufolo, Portland State University, Portland, OR (p. 246)

Peter D. Salins, Manhattan Institute for Policy Research, New York, NY (p. 248)

Peter Samuel, *Toll Roads Newsletter*, Frederick, MD (p. 249)

*Randy T. Simmons, Utah State University, Logan, UT (p. 260)

*Fred L. Smith, Jr., Competitive Enterprise Institute, Washington, DC (p. 263)

*Robert J. Smith, Center for Private Conservation, Washington, DC (p. 264)

*Jack Sommer, Political Economy Research Institute, Charlotte, NC (p. 266)

*Samuel R. Staley, Buckeye Institute for Public Policy Solutions, Columbus, OH (p. 268)

*Alexander Tabarrok, Mercatus Center at George Mason University, Arlington, VA (p. 273)

*Jerry Taylor, Cato Institute, Washington, DC (p. 274)

*John Taylor, Virginia Institute for Public Policy, Potomac Falls, VA (p. 274)

*David J. Theroux, The Independent Institute, Oakland, CA (p. 276)

Miro M. Todorovich, Scientists and Engineers for Secure Energy, New York, NY (p. 280)

*Ronald Utt, The Heritage Foundation, Washington, DC (p. 283)

*Terry W. Van Allen, Kemah, TX (p. 283)

*Peggy Venable, Texas Citizens for a Sound Economy, Austin, TX (p. 284)

Jude Wanniski, Polyconomics, Parsippany, NJ (p. 288)

Jason Wright, Frontiers of Freedom Institute, Fairfax, VA (p. 299)

Ronald A. Zumbrun, The Zumbrun Law Firm, Sacramento, CA (p. 303)

WASTE MANAGEMENT

*Jonathan H. Adler, Case Western Reserve University, Cleveland, OH (p. 35)

Bruce N. Ames, University of California, Berkeley, Berkeley, CA (p. 37)

Ron Arnold, Center for the Defense of Free Enterprise, Bellevue, WA (p. 40)

Alex Avery, Hudson Institute, Staunton, VA (p. 41)

' Alex A. Beehler, Charles G. Koch Charitable Foundation, Washington, DC (p. 49)

*Richard B. Belzer, Regulatory Checkbook, Washington, DC (p. 50)

*Sandy Liddy Bourne, American Legislative Exchange Council, Washington, DC (p. 58)

*Kenneth W. Chilton, Institute for Study of Economics and the Environment,
St. Charles, MO (p. 73)

WASTE MANAGEMENT (Continued)

*Bernard L. Cohen, University of Pittsburgh, Pittsburgh, PA (p. 77)

*Michael A. Crew, Rutgers University, Newark, NJ (p. 85)

*Michael De Alessi, Reason Foundation, Los Angeles, CA (p. 89)

*Paul K. Driessen, Committee for a Constructive Tomorrow, Fairfax, VA (p. 98)

*Susan E. Dudley, Mercatus Center at George Mason University, Arlington, VA (p. 99)

*Becky Norton Dunlop, The Heritage Foundation, Washington, DC (p. 100)

*Paul Dunn, University of Louisiana, Monroe, Monroe, LA (p. 100)

 Andrew W. Foshee, McNeese State University, Lake Charles, LA (p. 115)

 Steven B. Frates, Claremont McKenna College, Claremont, CA (p. 116)

*Dana Joel Gattuso, Competitive Enterprise Institute, Alexandria, VA (p. 121)

*Robert L. Hershey, Robert L. Hershey, P.E., Washington, DC (p. 141)

 Diane S. Katz, Mackinac Center for Public Policy, Midland, MI (p. 158)

*David B. Kopel, Independence Institute, Golden, CO (p. 167)

 Raymond J. Krizek, Northwestern University, Evanston, IL (p. 169)

 Howard Kunreuther, University of Pennsylvania, Philadelphia, PA (p. 170)

*Andrew Langer, National Federation of Independent Business, Washington, DC (p. 174)

 Angela Logomasini, Competitive Enterprise Institute, Washington, DC (p. 182)

*A. Alan Moghissi, Institute for Regulatory Science, Alexandria, VA (p. 204)

*Adrian T. Moore, Reason Foundation, Los Angeles, CA (p. 205)

 Bruce Piasecki, AHC Group, Saratoga Springs, NY (p. 228)

 Paul Portney, Resources for the Future, Washington, DC (p. 231)

 Patricia Reed, Independent Women's Forum, Arlington, VA (p. 237)

*David W. Riggs, Capital Research Center, Washington, DC (p. 240)

*Craig Rucker, Committee for a Constructive Tomorrow, Washington, DC (p. 246)

*Geoffrey F. Segal, Reason Public Policy Institute, Los Angeles, CA (p. 256)

*Robert Stavins, Harvard University, Cambridge, MA (p. 268)

*Richard L. Stroup, PERC – The Center for Free Market Environmentalism, Bozeman, MT (p. 271)

*Jerry Taylor, Cato Institute, Washington, DC (p. 274)

 Miro M. Todorovich, Scientists and Engineers for Secure Energy, New York, NY (p. 280)

WATER

*Jonathan H. Adler, Case Western Reserve University, Cleveland, OH (p. 35)

 Bruce N. Ames, University of California, Berkeley, Berkeley, CA (p. 37)

 Ron Arnold, Center for the Defense of Free Enterprise, Bellevue, WA (p. 40)

 Alex Avery, Hudson Institute, Staunton, VA (p. 41)

 Roger Bate, International Policy Network, Washington, DC (p. 47)

 Alex A. Beehler, Charles G. Koch Charitable Foundation, Washington, DC (p. 49)

*Robert K. Best, Pacific Legal Foundation, Sacramento, CA (p. 52)

*Sandy Liddy Bourne, American Legislative Exchange Council, Washington, DC (p. 58)

*Dan Byfield, American Land Foundation, Taylor, TX (p. 67)

 Boyd D. Collier, Tarleton State University, Stephenville, TX (p. 78)

 Charli Coon, The Heritage Foundation, Washington, DC (p. 81)

*Michael A. Crew, Rutgers University, Newark, NJ (p. 85)

*Michael De Alessi, Reason Foundation, Los Angeles, CA (p. 89)

 Douglas S. Doudney, Coalition for Property Rights, Orlando, FL (p. 97)

*Susan E. Dudley, Mercatus Center at George Mason University, Arlington, VA (p. 99)

*Becky Norton Dunlop, The Heritage Foundation, Washington, DC (p. 100)

*Paul Dunn, University of Louisiana, Monroe, Monroe, LA (p. 100)

 Jefferson G. Edgens, Morehead State University – Jackson Center, Jackson, KY (p. 103)

*Robert Ernst, Banbury Fund, Salmas, CA (p. 108)

*Gloria Taylor Fisher, Interstate Commission on the Potomac River Basin, Alexandria, VA (p. 112)

 Steven B. Frates, Claremont McKenna College, Claremont, CA (p. 116)

WATER (Continued)

Steve H. Hanke, Johns Hopkins University, Baltimore, MD (p. 134)
Robert C. Harrison, Defenders of Property Rights, Washington, DC (p. 136)
*Donna H. Hearne, Constitutional Coalition, St. Louis, MO (p. 138)
*Karl Hess, The Land Center, Las Cruces, NM (p. 141)
*James Huffman, Lewis and Clark Law School, Portland, OR (p. 148)
Diane S. Katz, Mackinac Center for Public Policy, Midland, MI (p. 158)
*Andrew Langer, National Federation of Independent Business, Washington, DC (p. 174)
*Donald R. Leal, PERC – The Center for Free Market Environmentalism, Bozeman, MT (p. 176)
*Jay H. Lehr, Environmental Education Enterprises, Ostrander, OH (p. 177)
Gary Libecap, University of Arizona, Tucson, AZ (p. 179)
Angela Logomasini, Competitive Enterprise Institute, Washington, DC (p. 182)
*Stephen B. Lovejoy, Purdue University, West Lafayette, IN (p. 183)
*Rita P. Maguire, Arizona Center for Public Policy, Phoenix, AZ (p. 186)
*Roger P. Maickel, Purdue University, Lafayette, IN (p. 187)
*Brian Mannix, Mercatus Center at George Mason University, Arlington, VA (p. 188)
*Nancie G. Marzulla, Defenders of Property Rights, Washington, DC (p. 191)
*Roger J. Marzulla, Defenders of Property Rights, Washington, DC (p. 191)
*John Merrifield, University of Texas, San Antonio, San Antonio, TX (p. 199)
*Adrian T. Moore, Reason Foundation, Los Angeles, CA (p. 205)
*William Perry Pendley, Mountain States Legal Foundation, Lakewood, CO (p. 225)
Bruce Piasecki, AHC Group, Saratoga Springs, NY (p. 228)
Paul Portney, Resources for the Future, Washington, DC (p. 231)
*David W. Riggs, Capital Research Center, Washington, DC (p. 240)
*Robin Rivett, Pacific Legal Foundation, Sacramento, CA (p. 241)
*S. Fred Singer, Science and Environmental Policy Project, Arlington, VA (p. 260)
*Robert J. Smith, Center for Private Conservation, Washington, DC (p. 264)
*Robert Stavins, Harvard University, Cambridge, MA (p. 268)
Jeff Stier, American Council on Science and Health, New York, NY (p. 269)
*James Streeter, National Wilderness Institute, Washington, DC (p. 270)
*Jerry Taylor, Cato Institute, Washington, DC (p. 274)
Miro M. Todorovich, Scientists and Engineers for Secure Energy, New York, NY (p. 280)
*Peggy Venable, Texas Citizens for a Sound Economy, Austin, TX (p. 284)
*Ben A. Wallis, Jr., Institute for Human Rights, San Antonio, TX (p. 287)
Bruce Yandle, Clemson University, Clemson, SC (p. 300)
Ronald A. Zumbrun, The Zumbrun Law Firm, Sacramento, CA (p. 303)

WILDLIFE MANAGEMENT/ENDANGERED SPECIES

*Jonathan H. Adler, Case Western Reserve University, Cleveland, OH (p. 35)
Terry L. Anderson, PERC – The Center for Free Market Environmentalism, Bozeman, MT (p. 38)
Ron Arnold, Center for the Defense of Free Enterprise, Bellevue, WA (p. 40)
Alex Avery, Hudson Institute, Staunton, VA (p. 41)
*Dennis T. Avery, Hudson Institute, Churchville, VA (p. 42)
John Baden, Foundation for Research on Economics and the Environment, Bozeman, MT (p. 42)
Alex A. Beehler, Charles G. Koch Charitable Foundation, Washington, DC (p. 49)
Daniel B. Botkin, Center for the Study of the Environment, Santa Barbara, CA (p. 58)
Karol Boudreaux, George Mason University School of Law, Arlington, VA (p. 58)
*Sandy Liddy Bourne, American Legislative Exchange Council, Washington, DC (p. 58)
Gordon L. Brady, Center for the Study of Public Choice, Fairfax, VA (p. 60)
*H. Sterling Burnett, National Center for Policy Analysis, Dallas, TX (p. 65)
*Dan Byfield, American Land Foundation, Taylor, TX (p. 67)
Jameson Campaigne, Jr., Jameson Books, Inc., Ottawa, IL (p. 68)

WILDLIFE MANAGEMENT/ENDANGERED SPECIES (Continued)

Bonner R. Cohen, Lexington Institute, Arlington, VA (p. 77)
Charli Coon, The Heritage Foundation, Washington, DC (p. 81)
*Charles H. Cunningham, National Rifle Association, Washington, DC (p. 87)
*Charles Cushman, American Land Rights Association, Battle Ground, WA (p. 87)
*Michael De Alessi, Reason Foundation, Los Angeles, CA (p. 89)
Douglas S. Doudney, Coalition for Property Rights, Orlando, FL (p. 97)
*Becky Norton Dunlop, The Heritage Foundation, Washington, DC (p. 100)
*Paula Easley, Resource Development Council for Alaska, Anchorage, AK (p. 102)
*Myron Ebell, Competitive Enterprise Institute, Washington, DC (p. 103)
*Evelyn Ebzery, Memorial Hospital of Sheridan County, Sheridan, WY (p. 103)
Jefferson G. Edgens, Morehead State University – Jackson Center, Jackson, KY (p. 103)
*Robert Ernst, Banbury Fund, Salmas, CA (p. 108)
*Allan Fitzsimmons, Balanced Resource Solutions, Woodbridge, VA (p. 113)
*Robert E. Gordon, Jr., National Wilderness Institute, Washington, DC (p. 127)
*Mike Hardiman, Hardiman Consulting, Washington, DC (p. 135)
Robert C. Harrison, Defenders of Property Rights, Washington, DC (p. 136)
*Donna H. Hearne, Constitutional Coalition, St. Louis, MO (p. 138)
*Karl Hess, The Land Center, Las Cruces, NM (p. 141)
*James Huffman, Lewis and Clark Law School, Portland, OR (p. 148)
Diane S. Katz, Mackinac Center for Public Policy, Midland, MI (p. 158)
*Andrew Langer, National Federation of Independent Business, Washington, DC (p. 174)
*Donald R. Leal, PERC – The Center for Free Market Environmentalism,
    Bozeman, MT (p. 176)
Lisa MacLellan, Pacific Research Institute, San Francisco, CA (p. 185)
*Rita P. Maguire, Arizona Center for Public Policy, Phoenix, AZ (p. 186)
*Nancie G. Marzulla, Defenders of Property Rights, Washington, DC (p. 191)
*Roger J. Marzulla, Defenders of Property Rights, Washington, DC (p. 191)
Samuel P. Menefee, Regent University, Virginia Beach, VA (p. 199)
*John Merrifield, University of Texas, San Antonio, San Antonio, TX (p. 199)
*William Moshofsky, Oregonians in Action Legal Center, Tigard, OR (p. 208)
*Frank Nims, Oregonians in Action, Tigard, OR (p. 214)
Randal O'Toole, Thoreau Institute, Bandon, OR (p. 217)
Sean Paige, Competitive Enterprise Institute, Washington, DC (p. 220)
*William Perry Pendley, Mountain States Legal Foundation, Lakewood, CO (p. 225)
*Daniel J. Popeo, Washington Legal Foundation, Washington, DC (p. 231)
*David Ridenour, National Center for Public Policy Research, Washington, DC (p. 240)
*David W. Riggs, Capital Research Center, Washington, DC (p. 240)
*Robin Rivett, Pacific Legal Foundation, Sacramento, CA (p. 241)
Russell Roberts, Weidenbaum Center, St. Louis, MO (p. 242)
*James A. Roumasset, University of Hawaii, Honolulu, HI (p. 245)
*Craig Rucker, Committee for a Constructive Tomorrow, Washington, DC (p. 246)
David Schmidtz, University of Arizona, Tucson, AZ (p. 253)
*Randy T. Simmons, Utah State University, Logan, UT (p. 260)
*Robert J. Smith, Center for Private Conservation, Washington, DC (p. 264)
*James Streeter, National Wilderness Institute, Washington, DC (p. 270)
*Jerry Taylor, Cato Institute, Washington, DC (p. 274)
Miro M. Todorovich, Scientists and Engineers for Secure Energy, New York, NY (p. 280)
*Ben A. Wallis, Jr., Institute for Human Rights, San Antonio, TX (p. 287)
*Malcolm Wallop, Frontiers of Freedom Institute, Fairfax, VA (p. 288)
Jason Wright, Frontiers of Freedom Institute, Fairfax, VA (p. 299)
Ronald A. Zumbrun, The Zumbrun Law Firm, Sacramento, CA (p. 303)

Regulation and Deregulation

COSTS AND BENEFITS OF REGULATION

*Jonathan H. Adler, Case Western Reserve University, Cleveland, OH (p. 35)
 Donald L. Alexander, Western Michigan University, Kalamazoo, MI (p. 36)
 David W. Almasi, National Center for Public Policy Research, Washington, DC (p. 37)
*Keith G. Baker, Florida TaxWatch Research Institute, Inc., Tallahassee, FL (p. 43)
*Naomi Lopez Bauman, Orlando, FL (p. 47)
*William W. Beach, The Heritage Foundation, Washington, DC (p. 48)
 Paul Beckner, Citizens for a Sound Economy, Washington, DC (p. 48)
*Richard B. Belzer, Regulatory Checkbook, Washington, DC (p. 50)
 Lisa E. Bernstein, University of Chicago Law School, Chicago, IL (p. 51)
*Patrick M. Boarman, National University San Diego, San Diego, CA (p. 55)
 Michael J. Boskin, Hoover Institution, Stanford, CA (p. 57)
*Marshall J. Breger, Catholic University of America, Washington, DC (p. 60)
*Wayne T. Brough, Citizens for a Sound Economy, Washington, DC (p. 62)
*Victoria Craig Bunce, Council for Affordable Health Insurance,
    Inver Grove Heights, MN (p. 65)
*H. Sterling Burnett, National Center for Policy Analysis, Dallas, TX (p. 65)
 Charles Calomiris, American Enterprise Institute, Washington, DC (p. 68)
*Kenneth W. Chilton, Institute for Study of Economics and the Environment,
    St. Charles, MO (p. 73)
 Paul A. Cleveland, Birmingham Southern College, Birmingham, AL (p. 76)
 John Cobin, Montauk Financial Group, Greenville, SC (p. 76)
 Gregory Conko, Competitive Enterprise Institute, Washington, DC (p. 79)
*C. W. Cowles, Central Michigan University, Midlothian, VA (p. 84)
*Christine G. Crafton, Motorola, Inc., Washington, DC (p. 84)
 Robert Crandall, Brookings Institution, Washington, DC (p. 85)
*Michael A. Crew, Rutgers University, Newark, NJ (p. 85)
*Clyde Wayne Crews, Jr., Cato Institute, Washington, DC (p. 86)
 Neil S. Crispo, Florida State University, Tallahassee, FL (p. 86)
*Ward S. Curran, Trinity College, Hartford, CT (p. 87)
*Robert J. Cynkar, Cooper & Kirk, PLLC, Washington, DC (p. 87)
*Michael De Alessi, Reason Foundation, Los Angeles, CA (p. 89)
*William J. Dennis, National Federation of Independent Business Research Foundation,
    Washington, DC (p. 93)
*Thomas J. DiLorenzo, Loyola College, Clarksville, MD (p. 96)
*Susan E. Dudley, Mercatus Center at George Mason University, Arlington, VA (p. 99)
*William C. Dunkelberg, National Federation of Independent Business,
    Wynnewood, PA (p. 100)
*Myron Ebell, Competitive Enterprise Institute, Washington, DC (p. 103)
*Susan Eckerly, National Federation of Independent Business, Washington, DC (p. 103)
 Jefferson G. Edgens, Morehead State University – Jackson Center, Jackson, KY (p. 103)
 Ana Eiras, The Heritage Foundation, Washington, DC (p. 105)
*Jeffrey A. Eisenach, Progress & Freedom Foundation, Washington, DC (p. 105)
 Robert B. Ekelund, Auburn University, Auburn, AL (p. 105)
*Roger Feldman, University of Minnesota, Minneapolis, MN (p. 110)
*Robert Fike, Americans for Tax Reform, Washington, DC (p. 111)
*Edward H. Fleischman, Linklaters, New York, NY (p. 113)
*Walton Francis, Fairfax, VA (p. 115)
*Barbara Hackman Franklin, Barbara Franklin Enterprises, Washington, DC (p. 116)
 Harold Furchtgott-Roth, American Enterprise Institute, Washington, DC (p. 119)
*James Gattuso, The Heritage Foundation, Washington, DC (p. 121)
*Deanna R. Gelak, Family and Medical Leave Act Technical Corrections Coalition,
    Springfield, VA (p. 122)

COSTS AND BENEFITS OF REGULATION (Continued)

*Ernest Gellhorn, George Mason University School of Law, Washington, DC (p. 122)

 Paul Georgia, Competitive Enterprise Institute, Washington, DC (p. 122)

 Raymond L. Gifford, Progress & Freedom Foundation, Washington, DC (p. 123)

 Leonard Gilroy, Reason Foundation, Los Angeles, CA (p. 123)

*Steven Globerman, Western Washington University, Bellingham, WA (p. 125)

*Robert Goldberg, Manhattan Institute, Springfield, NJ (p. 125)

*Wendy Lee Gramm, Mercatus Center at George Mason University, Arlington, VA (p. 128)

*Erick Gustafson, Citizens for a Sound Economy, Washington, DC (p. 131)

*James D. Gwartney, Florida State University, Tallahassee, FL (p. 131)

*Robert Hahn, American Enterprise Institute, Washington, DC (p. 132)

 Steve H. Hanke, Johns Hopkins University, Baltimore, MD (p. 134)

*Ronald Hansen, University of Rochester, Rochester, NY (p. 134)

 Karen R. Harned, National Federation of Independent Business Legal Foundation, Washington, DC (p. 135)

 Scott E. Harrington, University of South Carolina, Columbia, SC (p. 135)

*Steven Hayward, American Enterprise Institute, Washington, DC (p. 138)

 Thomas Hazlett, Manhattan Institute for Policy Research, Washington, DC (p. 138)

*David R. Henderson, Hoover Institution, Pacific Grove, CA (p. 139)

*Robert L. Hershey, Robert L. Hershey, P.E., Washington, DC (p. 141)

 Robert Higgs, The Independent Institute, Covington, LA (p. 142)

*Thomas D. Hopkins, Rochester Institute of Technology, Rochester, NY (p. 145)

*Joseph Horton, University of Central Arkansas, Conway, AR (p. 146)

 Douglas A. Houston, University of Kansas, Lawrence, KS (p. 147)

 Sanford Ikeda, State University of New York, Purchase, NY (p. 151)

 Jim Johnston, Heartland Institute, Wilmette, IL (p. 156)

 Dale W. Jorgenson, Harvard University, Cambridge, MA (p. 156)

 Shyam J. Kamath, California State University, Hayward, Hayward, CA (p. 157)

*Paul Kamenar, Washington Legal Foundation, Washington, DC (p. 157)

*Edward J. Kane, Boston College, Chestnut Hill, MA (p. 157)

 Shawn Kantor, University of Arizona, Tucson, AZ (p. 157)

 Diane S. Katz, Mackinac Center for Public Policy, Midland, MI (p. 158)

 Martin S. Kaufman, Atlantic Legal Foundation, New York, NY (p. 159)

*Sam Kazman, Competitive Enterprise Institute, Washington, DC (p. 159)

*Raymond J. Keating, Small Business Survival Committee, Manorville, NY (p. 159)

*W. Thomas Kelly, Savers and Investors League, Mirror Lake, NH (p. 161)

 Phil Kent, Southeastern Legal Foundation, Atlanta, GA (p. 162)

 Karen Kerrigan, the polling company, Washington, DC (p. 162)

*Lynne Kiesling, Reason Public Policy Institute, Los Angeles, CA (p. 163)

 Daniel Klein, Santa Clara University, Santa Clara, CA (p. 165)

*Marvin H. Kosters, American Enterprise Institute, Washington, DC (p. 168)

*Randall Kroszner, University of Chicago, Chicago, IL (p. 170)

*Deepak Lal, University of California at Los Angeles, Los Angeles, CA (p. 172)

*George Landrith, Frontiers of Freedom Institute, Fairfax, VA (p. 173)

*Andrew Langer, National Federation of Independent Business, Washington, DC (p. 174)

*Kent Lassman, Progress & Freedom Foundation, Raleigh, NC (p. 175)

 Tom Lenard, Progress & Freedom Foundation, Washington, DC (p. 177)

*Mark R. Levin, Landmark Legal Foundation, Herndon, VA (p. 178)

 Gary Libecap, University of Arizona, Tucson, AZ (p. 179)

 James Lucier, Prudential Securities, Arlington, VA (p. 184)

 Randall Lutter, American Enterprise Institute, Washington, DC (p. 184)

 Paul W. MacAvoy, Yale School of Management, New Haven, CT (p. 185)

 Tibor R. Machan, Chapman University, Silverado Canyon, CA (p. 185)

*Ken Malloy, Center for the Advancement of Energy Markets, Washington, DC (p. 188)

 Henry G. Manne, University of Chicago Law School, Chicago, IL (p. 188)

---

* Has testified before a state or federal legislative committee

COSTS AND BENEFITS OF REGULATION (Continued)

*Brian Mannix, Mercatus Center at George Mason University, Arlington, VA (p. 188)
 Michael Marlow, California Polytechnic State University, San Luis Obispo, CA (p. 189)
*Roger J. Marzulla, Defenders of Property Rights, Washington, DC (p. 191)
*Randolph J. May, Progress & Freedom Foundation, Washington, DC (p. 193)
*Bobby McCormick, Clemson University, Clemson, SC (p. 194)
 John O. McGinnis, Cardozo School of Law, New York, NY (p. 196)
 Lawrence J. McQuillan, Pacific Research Institute, San Francisco, CA (p. 197)
*Daniel Mead Smith, Washington Policy Center, Seattle, WA (p. 198)
*Conrad F. Meier, Heartland Institute, Chicago, IL (p. 198)
*Henry I. Miller, Hoover Institution, Stanford, CA (p. 202)
*Edwin S. Mills, Northwestern University, Evanston, IL (p. 202)
*Adrian T. Moore, Reason Foundation, Los Angeles, CA (p. 205)
 Cassandra Chrones Moore, Cato Institute, Washington, DC (p. 205)
*James Elliott Moore, II, University of Southern California, Los Angeles, CA (p. 205)
 Suzanne C. Moore, Delaware Public Policy Institute, Wilmington, DE (p. 206)
*Thomas Gale Moore, Hoover Institution, Stanford, CA (p. 206)
*Michael A. Morrisey, University of Alabama, Birmingham, Birmingham, AL (p. 207)
 Chuck Muth, American Conservative Union, Alexandria, VA (p. 210)
 George R. Neumann, University of Iowa, Iowa City, IA (p. 213)
 David C. Nott, Reason Foundation, Los Angeles, CA (p. 215)
 Sean Paige, Competitive Enterprise Institute, Washington, DC (p. 220)
*J. A. Parker, Lincoln Institute for Research and Education, Washington, DC (p. 221)
 E. C. Pasour, Jr., North Carolina State University, Raleigh, NC (p. 222)
*Svetozar Pejovich, Texas A&M University, Dallas, TX (p. 224)
*Sam Peltzman, University of Chicago Graduate School of Business, Chicago, IL (p. 225)
 Laura Bennett Peterson, Washington, DC (p. 226)
*Nancy M. Pfotenhauer, Independent Women's Forum, Arlington, VA (p. 227)
*Bruce Phillips, National Federation of Independent Business, Washington, DC (p. 227)
 Bruce Piasecki, AHC Group, Saratoga Springs, NY (p. 228)
*Michael Podgursky, University of Missouri, Columbia, MO (p. 230)
*Daniel J. Popeo, Washington Legal Foundation, Washington, DC (p. 231)
 Paul Portney, Resources for the Future, Washington, DC (p. 231)
*Edward Potter, Employment Policy Foundation, Washington, DC (p. 231)
*Stephen Presser, Northwestern University School of Law, Chicago, IL (p. 233)
*Andrew F. Quinlan, Center for Freedom and Prosperity, Alexandria, VA (p. 234)
*Don Racheter, Public Interest Institute, Mount Pleasant, IA (p. 235)
*David B. Rivkin, Jr., Baker & Hostetler, Washington, DC (p. 241)
*Paul Rubin, Emory University, Atlanta, GA (p. 246)
*Linda Runbeck, Taxpayers League of Minnesota, Plymouth, MN (p. 247)
*Susan Sarnoff, Ohio University, Athens, OH (p. 250)
*Thomas R. Saving, Texas A&M University, College Station, TX (p. 251)
*Terrence M. Scanlon, Capital Research Center, Washington, DC (p. 251)
 G. W. Schwert, University of Rochester, Rochester, NY (p. 255)
*Geoffrey F. Segal, Reason Public Policy Institute, Los Angeles, CA (p. 256)
*Pete Sepp, National Taxpayers Union, Alexandria, VA (p. 257)
*S. Fred Singer, Science and Environmental Policy Project, Arlington, VA (p. 260)
*Solveig Singleton, Competitive Enterprise Institute, Washington, DC (p. 261)
*Robert A. Sirico, Acton Institute for the Study of Religion and Liberty,
    Grand Rapids, MI (p. 261)
*Fred L. Smith, Jr., Competitive Enterprise Institute, Washington, DC (p. 263)
*Samuel R. Staley, Buckeye Institute for Public Policy Solutions, Columbus, OH (p. 268)
 Irwin Stelzer, Hudson Institute, Washington, DC (p. 268)
 Jeff Stier, American Council on Science and Health, New York, NY (p. 269)
*David Strom, Taxpayers League of Minnesota, Plymouth, MN (p. 270)

COSTS AND BENEFITS OF REGULATION (Continued)

Michael D. Stroup, Stephen F. Austin State University, Nacogdoches, TX (p. 270)

*Alexander Tabarrok, Mercatus Center at George Mason University, Arlington, VA (p. 273)

Tammy Tengs, University of California, Irvine, Irvine, CA (p. 275)

*Jason M. Thomas, Citizens for a Sound Economy, Washington, DC (p. 277)

*Mark Thornton, Columbus State University, Columbus, GA (p. 278)

Miro M. Todorovich, Scientists and Engineers for Secure Energy, New York, NY (p. 280)

*Robert D. Tollison, University of Mississippi, University, MS (p. 280)

*Grace-Marie Turner, Galen Institute, Alexandria, VA (p. 281)

Peter M. VanDoren, Cato Institute, Washington, DC (p. 284)

*Peggy Venable, Texas Citizens for a Sound Economy, Austin, TX (p. 284)

Dane vonBreichenruchardt, U. S. Bill of Rights Foundation, Washington, DC (p. 286)

*Malcolm Wallop, Frontiers of Freedom Institute, Fairfax, VA (p. 288)

*Stephen J. K. Walters, Loyola College, Baltimore, MD (p. 288)

*Murray Weidenbaum, Weidenbaum Center, St. Louis, MO (p. 291)

Walter E. Williams, George Mason University, Fairfax, VA (p. 295)

Bruce Yandle, Clemson University, Clemson, SC (p. 300)

Edward W. Younkins, Wheeling Jesuit University, Wheeling, WV (p. 301)

Richard Zeckhauser, Harvard University, Cambridge, MA (p. 302)

Ronald A. Zumbrun, The Zumbrun Law Firm, Sacramento, CA (p. 303)

ELECTRICITY DEREGULATION

Michael K. Block, University of Arizona, Tucson, AZ (p. 55)

*Sandy Liddy Bourne, American Legislative Exchange Council, Washington, DC (p. 58)

*Wayne T. Brough, Citizens for a Sound Economy, Washington, DC (p. 62)

*H. Sterling Burnett, National Center for Policy Analysis, Dallas, TX (p. 65)

*James B. Cardle, Texas Citizen Action Network, Austin, TX (p. 69)

*Michael A. Carvin, Jones, Day, Reavis & Pogue, Washington, DC (p. 71)

Charli Coon, The Heritage Foundation, Washington, DC (p. 81)

*Clyde Wayne Crews, Jr., Cato Institute, Washington, DC (p. 86)

*Ward S. Curran, Trinity College, Hartford, CT (p. 87)

*Robert J. Cynkar, Cooper & Kirk, PLLC, Washington, DC (p. 87)

*Phillip DeVous, Acton Institute for the Study of Religion and Liberty, Grand Rapids, MI (p. 94)

*Susan E. Dudley, Mercatus Center at George Mason University, Arlington, VA (p. 99)

*Susan Eckerly, National Federation of Independent Business, Washington, DC (p. 103)

*Jeffrey A. Eisenach, Progress & Freedom Foundation, Washington, DC (p. 105)

Robert B. Ekelund, Auburn University, Auburn, AL (p. 105)

*Edward W. Erickson, North Carolina State University, Raleigh, NC (p. 107)

Paul Georgia, Competitive Enterprise Institute, Washington, DC (p. 122)

Raymond L. Gifford, Progress & Freedom Foundation, Washington, DC (p. 123)

*Robert Hahn, American Enterprise Institute, Washington, DC (p. 132)

*Robert L. Hershey, Robert L. Hershey, P.E., Washington, DC (p. 141)

*Don Hodel, Silverthorne, CO (p. 143)

Douglas A. Houston, University of Kansas, Lawrence, KS (p. 147)

Jim Johnston, Heartland Institute, Wilmette, IL (p. 156)

Diane S. Katz, Mackinac Center for Public Policy, Midland, MI (p. 158)

*David Keating, National Taxpayers Union, Alexandria, VA (p. 159)

*David A. Keene, American Conservative Union, Washington, DC (p. 160)

Phil Kent, Southeastern Legal Foundation, Atlanta, GA (p. 162)

*Lynne Kiesling, Reason Public Policy Institute, Los Angeles, CA (p. 163)

*Deepak Lal, University of California at Los Angeles, Los Angeles, CA (p. 172)

Tom Lenard, Progress & Freedom Foundation, Washington, DC (p. 177)

James Lucier, Prudential Securities, Arlington, VA (p. 184)

Paul W. MacAvoy, Yale School of Management, New Haven, CT (p. 185)

*Rita P. Maguire, Arizona Center for Public Policy, Phoenix, AZ (p. 186)

ELECTRICITY DEREGULATION (Continued)

*Ken Malloy, Center for the Advancement of Energy Markets, Washington, DC **(p. 188)**
*Jim Martin, 60 Plus Association, Arlington, VA **(p. 190)**
*Roger J. Marzulla, Defenders of Property Rights, Washington, DC **(p. 191)**
*Bobby McCormick, Clemson University, Clemson, SC **(p. 194)**
*Robert J. Michaels, California State University, Fullerton, Fullerton, CA **(p. 201)**
*Adrian T. Moore, Reason Foundation, Los Angeles, CA **(p. 205)**
 Jeremiah O'Keeffe, Plano, TX **(p. 217)**
*Sam Peltzman, University of Chicago Graduate School of Business, Chicago, IL **(p. 225)**
*William H. Peterson, Washington, DC **(p. 227)**
*Dennis Polhill, Independence Institute, Golden, CO **(p. 230)**
*Scott Pullins, Ohio Taxpayers Association and OTA Foundation, Columbus, OH **(p. 234)**
*R. Sean Randolph, Bay Area Economic Forum, San Francisco, CA **(p. 236)**
 George Reisman, Pepperdine University, Laguna Hills, CA **(p. 238)**
*David B. Rivkin, Jr., Baker & Hostetler, Washington, DC **(p. 241)**
*Thomas R. Saving, Texas A&M University, College Station, TX **(p. 251)**
 J. Gregory Sidak, American Enterprise Institute, Washington, DC **(p. 259)**
 Vernon L. Smith, George Mason University, Arlington, VA **(p. 264)**
 Irwin Stelzer, Hudson Institute, Washington, DC **(p. 268)**
*William Craig Stubblebine, Claremont McKenna College, Claremont, CA **(p. 271)**
 James L. Sweeney, Stanford University, Stanford, CA **(p. 272)**
*Jerry Taylor, Cato Institute, Washington, DC **(p. 274)**
 Lester G. Telser, University of Chicago, Chicago, IL **(p. 275)**
*Mark Thornton, Columbus State University, Columbus, GA **(p. 278)**
 Miro M. Todorovich, Scientists and Engineers for Secure Energy, New York, NY **(p. 280)**
 Peter M. VanDoren, Cato Institute, Washington, DC **(p. 284)**
*Murray Weidenbaum, Weidenbaum Center, St. Louis, MO **(p. 291)**

REGULATION THROUGH LITIGATION

 Damon Ansell, Americans for Tax Reform, Washington, DC **(p. 39)**
*Robert K. Best, Pacific Legal Foundation, Sacramento, CA **(p. 52)**
 Brian Boyle, O'Melveny & Myers LLP, Washington, DC **(p. 58)**
*Marshall J. Breger, Catholic University of America, Washington, DC **(p. 60)**
 Brian P. Brooks, O'Melveny & Myers LLP, Washington, DC **(p. 62)**
*H. Sterling Burnett, National Center for Policy Analysis, Dallas, TX **(p. 65)**
*Henry N. Butler, Chapman University, Orange, CA **(p. 66)**
*John Calfee, American Enterprise Institute, Washington, DC **(p. 67)**
 Charli Coon, The Heritage Foundation, Washington, DC **(p. 81)**
*C. W. Cowles, Central Michigan University, Midlothian, VA **(p. 84)**
*Roger C. Cramton, Cornell Law School, Ithaca, NY **(p. 85)**
*Ward S. Curran, Trinity College, Hartford, CT **(p. 87)**
*Robert J. Cynkar, Cooper & Kirk, PLLC, Washington, DC **(p. 87)**
 Michael E. DeBow, Samford University, Birmingham, AL **(p. 91)**
*James DeLong, Progress & Freedom Foundation, Washington, DC **(p. 92)**
*Thomas J. DiLorenzo, Loyola College, Clarksville, MD **(p. 96)**
*Susan Eckerly, National Federation of Independent Business, Washington, DC **(p. 103)**
 Jack Faris, National Federation of Independent Business, Washington, DC **(p. 109)**
 Peter Ferrara, International Center for Law and Economics, Washington, DC **(p. 110)**
*Edward H. Fleischman, Linklaters, New York, NY **(p. 113)**
*Michael Flynn, American Legislative Exchange Council, Washington, DC **(p. 113)**
*James Gattuso, The Heritage Foundation, Washington, DC **(p. 121)**
*Todd Gaziano, The Heritage Foundation, Washington, DC **(p. 121)**
 Andrew Grainger, New England Legal Foundation, Boston, MA **(p. 128)**
*Wendy Lee Gramm, Mercatus Center at George Mason University, Arlington, VA **(p. 128)**
*Michael S. Greve, American Enterprise Institute, Washington, DC **(p. 129)**

REGULATION THROUGH LITIGATION (Continued)

*Erick Gustafson, Citizens for a Sound Economy, Washington, DC (p. 131)
*Robert Hahn, American Enterprise Institute, Washington, DC (p. 132)
 Scott E. Harrington, University of South Carolina, Columbia, SC (p. 135)
*Steven Hayward, American Enterprise Institute, Washington, DC (p. 138)
*Michael Horowitz, Hudson Institute, Washington, DC (p. 146)
 Diane S. Katz, Mackinac Center for Public Policy, Midland, MI (p. 158)
 Martin S. Kaufman, Atlantic Legal Foundation, New York, NY (p. 159)
 Phil Kent, Southeastern Legal Foundation, Atlanta, GA (p. 162)
 Karen Kerrigan, the polling company, Washington, DC (p. 162)
 F. Scott Kieff, Washington University, St. Louis, MO (p. 163)
*Lynne Kiesling, Reason Public Policy Institute, Los Angeles, CA (p. 163)
*David B. Kopel, Independence Institute, Golden, CO (p. 167)
 Glenn G. Lammi, Washington Legal Foundation, Washington, DC (p. 173)
*George Landrith, Frontiers of Freedom Institute, Fairfax, VA (p. 173)
*Andrew Langer, National Federation of Independent Business, Washington, DC (p. 174)
 Leonard A. Leo, The Federalist Society for Law and Public Policy Studies,
    Washington, DC (p. 178)
*Robert A. Levy, Cato Institute, Washington, DC (p. 179)
 Margaret A. Little, Law Office of Margaret Little, Stratford, CT (p. 181)
*Dennis E. Logue, University of Oklahoma, Norman, OK (p. 182)
 Paul W. MacAvoy, Yale School of Management, New Haven, CT (p. 185)
*Nancie G. Marzulla, Defenders of Property Rights, Washington, DC (p. 191)
*Roger J. Marzulla, Defenders of Property Rights, Washington, DC (p. 191)
 Lawrence J. McQuillan, Pacific Research Institute, San Francisco, CA (p. 197)
*Edwin S. Mills, Northwestern University, Evanston, IL (p. 202)
 Cassandra Chrones Moore, Cato Institute, Washington, DC (p. 205)
*Joseph A. Morris, Lincoln Legal Foundation, Chicago, IL (p. 207)
 Chuck Muth, American Conservative Union, Alexandria, VA (p. 210)
*Walter K. Olson, Manhattan Institute for Policy Research, Chappaqua, NY (p. 219)
 Sean Paige, Competitive Enterprise Institute, Washington, DC (p. 220)
 Terence J. Pell, Center for Individual Rights, Washington, DC (p. 224)
*Sam Peltzman, University of Chicago Graduate School of Business, Chicago, IL (p. 225)
 Laura Bennett Peterson, Washington, DC (p. 226)
*Bruce Phillips, National Federation of Independent Business, Washington, DC (p. 227)
*Daniel J. Popeo, Washington Legal Foundation, Washington, DC (p. 231)
*Stephen Presser, Northwestern University School of Law, Chicago, IL (p. 233)
*Scott Pullins, Ohio Taxpayers Association and OTA Foundation, Columbus, OH (p. 234)
*Alan C. Raul, Sidley & Austin Brown & Wood, LLP, Washington, DC (p. 237)
*David B. Rivkin, Jr., Baker & Hostetler, Washington, DC (p. 241)
*Paul Rubin, Emory University, Atlanta, GA (p. 246)
*Charles F. Rule, Fried, Frank, Harris, Shriver & Jacobson, Washington, DC (p. 246)
*Richard A. Samp, Washington Legal Foundation, Washington, DC (p. 248)
*Susan Sarnoff, Ohio University, Athens, OH (p. 250)
*Thomas A. Schatz, Citizens Against Government Waste, Washington, DC (p. 252)
*Pete Sepp, National Taxpayers Union, Alexandria, VA (p. 257)
*John Shanahan, National Mining Association, Washington, DC (p. 258)
*Solveig Singleton, Competitive Enterprise Institute, Washington, DC (p. 261)
 William H. Slattery, Atlantic Legal Foundation, New York, NY (p. 262)
*Fred L. Smith, Jr., Competitive Enterprise Institute, Washington, DC (p. 263)
 Jeff Stier, American Council on Science and Health, New York, NY (p. 269)
*David Strom, Taxpayers League of Minnesota, Plymouth, MN (p. 270)
 Miro M. Todorovich, Scientists and Engineers for Secure Energy, New York, NY (p. 280)
 Dane vonBreichenruchardt, U. S. Bill of Rights Foundation, Washington, DC (p. 286)
*Malcolm Wallop, Frontiers of Freedom Institute, Fairfax, VA (p. 288)

---

* Has testified before a state or federal legislative committee

REGULATION THROUGH LITIGATION (Continued)

*Stephen J. K. Walters, Loyola College, Baltimore, MD (p. 288)
*Bob Williams, Evergreen Freedom Foundation, Olympia, WA (p. 295)
Jason Wright, Frontiers of Freedom Institute, Fairfax, VA (p. 299)
Jennifer Zambone, Mercatus Center at George Mason University, Arlington, VA (p. 301)
Ronald A. Zumbrun, The Zumbrun Law Firm, Sacramento, CA (p. 303)

REGULATORY BUDGETING

*Jonathan H. Adler, Case Western Reserve University, Cleveland, OH (p. 35)
*Richard B. Belzer, Regulatory Checkbook, Washington, DC (p. 50)
Thomas E. Borcherding, Claremont Graduate University, Claremont, CA (p. 57)
*Marshall J. Breger, Catholic University of America, Washington, DC (p. 60)
*C. W. Cowles, Central Michigan University, Midlothian, VA (p. 84)
*Clyde Wayne Crews, Jr., Cato Institute, Washington, DC (p. 86)
*Ward S. Curran, Trinity College, Hartford, CT (p. 87)
*Carl DeMaio, Reason Foundation, Los Angeles, CA (p. 92)
*Susan E. Dudley, Mercatus Center at George Mason University, Arlington, VA (p. 99)
*Susan Eckerly, National Federation of Independent Business, Washington, DC (p. 103)
Jack Faris, National Federation of Independent Business, Washington, DC (p. 109)
*Walton Francis, Fairfax, VA (p. 115)
*James Gattuso, The Heritage Foundation, Washington, DC (p. 121)
*Todd Gaziano, The Heritage Foundation, Washington, DC (p. 121)
*Wendy Lee Gramm, Mercatus Center at George Mason University, Arlington, VA (p. 128)
*Thomas D. Hopkins, Rochester Institute of Technology, Rochester, NY (p. 145)
Karen Kerrigan, the polling company, Washington, DC (p. 162)
*Lynne Kiesling, Reason Public Policy Institute, Los Angeles, CA (p. 163)
*Marvin H. Kosters, American Enterprise Institute, Washington, DC (p. 168)
Tom Lenard, Progress & Freedom Foundation, Washington, DC (p. 177)
Paul W. MacAvoy, Yale School of Management, New Haven, CT (p. 185)
*Roger J. Marzulla, Defenders of Property Rights, Washington, DC (p. 191)
John O. McGinnis, Cardozo School of Law, New York, NY (p. 196)
*Adrian T. Moore, Reason Foundation, Los Angeles, CA (p. 205)
David C. Nott, Reason Foundation, Los Angeles, CA (p. 215)
*Alan C. Raul, Sidley & Austin Brown & Wood, LLP, Washington, DC (p. 237)
Miro M. Todorovich, Scientists and Engineers for Secure Energy, New York, NY (p. 280)

REGULATORY REFORM

*Douglas K. Adie, Ohio University, Athens, OH (p. 35)
William F. Adkinson, Progress & Freedom Foundation, Washington, DC (p. 35)
*Jonathan H. Adler, Case Western Reserve University, Cleveland, OH (p. 35)
Bruce N. Ames, University of California, Berkeley, Berkeley, CA (p. 37)
Martin Anderson, Hoover Institution, Stanford, CA (p. 38)
*Robert A. Anthony, George Mason University School of Law, Arlington, VA (p. 39)
*Claude E. Barfield, American Enterprise Institute, Washington, DC (p. 45)
Robert J. Barro, Harvard University, Cambridge, MA (p. 46)
Paul Beckner, Citizens for a Sound Economy, Washington, DC (p. 48)
*Richard B. Belzer, Regulatory Checkbook, Washington, DC (p. 50)
*Robert K. Best, Pacific Legal Foundation, Sacramento, CA (p. 52)
Michael K. Block, University of Arizona, Tucson, AZ (p. 55)
*Patrick M. Boarman, National University San Diego, San Diego, CA (p. 55)
Michael J. Boskin, Hoover Institution, Stanford, CA (p. 57)
*Sandy Liddy Bourne, American Legislative Exchange Council, Washington, DC (p. 58)
*Marshall J. Breger, Catholic University of America, Washington, DC (p. 60)
William Breit, Trinity University, San Antonio, TX (p. 60)
*Wayne T. Brough, Citizens for a Sound Economy, Washington, DC (p. 62)

REGULATORY REFORM (Continued)

*Robert Carleson, American Civil Rights Union, Alexandria, VA (p. 70)
*Kenneth W. Chilton, Institute for Study of Economics and the Environment, St. Charles, MO (p. 73)
Bonner R. Cohen, Lexington Institute, Arlington, VA (p. 77)
*Louis J. Cordia, Cordia Companies, Alexandria, VA (p. 82)
*C. W. Cowles, Central Michigan University, Midlothian, VA (p. 84)
*Douglas Cox, Gibson, Dunn & Crutcher LLP, Washington, DC (p. 84)
James K. Coyne, National Air Transportation Association, Alexandria, VA (p. 84)
*Christine G. Crafton, Motorola, Inc., Washington, DC (p. 84)
*Roger C. Cramton, Cornell Law School, Ithaca, NY (p. 85)
Robert Crandall, Brookings Institution, Washington, DC (p. 85)
*Michael A. Crew, Rutgers University, Newark, NJ (p. 85)
*Clyde Wayne Crews, Jr., Cato Institute, Washington, DC (p. 86)
Neil S. Crispo, Florida State University, Tallahassee, FL (p. 86)
*Ward S. Curran, Trinity College, Hartford, CT (p. 87)
*Robert J. Cynkar, Cooper & Kirk, PLLC, Washington, DC (p. 87)
*Michael De Alessi, Reason Foundation, Los Angeles, CA (p. 89)
*James DeLong, Progress & Freedom Foundation, Washington, DC (p. 92)
*Carl DeMaio, Reason Foundation, Los Angeles, CA (p. 92)
Christopher DeMuth, American Enterprise Institute, Washington, DC (p. 92)
*Susan E. Dudley, Mercatus Center at George Mason University, Arlington, VA (p. 99)
*Paula Easley, Resource Development Council for Alaska, Anchorage, AK (p. 102)
*Susan Eckerly, National Federation of Independent Business, Washington, DC (p. 103)
Jefferson G. Edgens, Morehead State University – Jackson Center, Jackson, KY (p. 103)
*Jeffrey A. Eisenach, Progress & Freedom Foundation, Washington, DC (p. 105)
Robert B. Ekelund, Auburn University, Auburn, AL (p. 105)
*Bert Ely, Ely & Company, Inc., Alexandria, VA (p. 106)
Richard A. Epstein, University of Chicago Law School, Chicago, IL (p. 107)
*Susan K. Feigenbaum, University of Missouri, St. Louis, St. Louis, MO (p. 110)
*Edward H. Fleischman, Linklaters, New York, NY (p. 113)
William F. Ford, Middle Tennessee State University, Murfreesboro, TN (p. 114)
*Walton Francis, Fairfax, VA (p. 115)
*Barbara Hackman Franklin, Barbara Franklin Enterprises, Washington, DC (p. 116)
Amy Frantz, Public Interest Institute, Mount Pleasant, IA (p. 116)
*H. E. Frech, III, University of California, Santa Barbara, Santa Barbara, CA (p. 116)
David D. Friedman, Santa Clara University, San Jose, CA (p. 117)
Harold Furchtgott-Roth, American Enterprise Institute, Washington, DC (p. 119)
*James Gattuso, The Heritage Foundation, Washington, DC (p. 121)
*Todd Gaziano, The Heritage Foundation, Washington, DC (p. 121)
*Ernest Gellhorn, George Mason University School of Law, Washington, DC (p. 122)
Paul Georgia, Competitive Enterprise Institute, Washington, DC (p. 122)
Raymond L. Gifford, Progress & Freedom Foundation, Washington, DC (p. 123)
Leonard Gilroy, Reason Foundation, Los Angeles, CA (p. 123)
*Steven Globerman, Western Washington University, Bellingham, WA (p. 125)
*Wendy Lee Gramm, Mercatus Center at George Mason University, Arlington, VA (p. 128)
*Erick Gustafson, Citizens for a Sound Economy, Washington, DC (p. 131)
*Robert Hahn, American Enterprise Institute, Washington, DC (p. 132)
*Robert Hale, Northwest Legal Foundation, Minot, ND (p. 132)
Steve H. Hanke, Johns Hopkins University, Baltimore, MD (p. 134)
*Ronald Hansen, University of Rochester, Rochester, NY (p. 134)
Robin Hanson, George Mason University, Fairfax, VA (p. 134)
Scott E. Harrington, University of South Carolina, Columbia, SC (p. 135)
*Robert L. Hershey, Robert L. Hershey, P.E., Washington, DC (p. 141)
James E. Hinish, Jr., Regent University, Williamsburg, VA (p. 143)

REGULATORY REFORM (Continued)

*Thomas D. Hopkins, Rochester Institute of Technology, Rochester, NY (p. 145)
 Douglas A. Houston, University of Kansas, Lawrence, KS (p. 147)
 Edward L. Hudgins, The Objectivist Center, Washington, DC (p. 148)
*David John, The Heritage Foundation, Washington, DC (p. 154)
 Jim Johnston, Heartland Institute, Wilmette, IL (p. 156)
 Milton Kafoglis, Emory University, Decatur, GA (p. 156)
*Edward J. Kane, Boston College, Chestnut Hill, MA (p. 157)
 Richard T. Kaplar, Media Institute, Washington, DC (p. 157)
 Diane S. Katz, Mackinac Center for Public Policy, Midland, MI (p. 158)
 Martin S. Kaufman, Atlantic Legal Foundation, New York, NY (p. 159)
*W. Thomas Kelly, Savers and Investors League, Mirror Lake, NH (p. 161)
 Karen Kerrigan, the polling company, Washington, DC (p. 162)
*Lynne Kiesling, Reason Public Policy Institute, Los Angeles, CA (p. 163)
 Daniel Klein, Santa Clara University, Santa Clara, CA (p. 165)
 Montgomery N. Kosma, Jones, Day, Reavis & Pogue, Washington, DC (p. 167)
*Marvin H. Kosters, American Enterprise Institute, Washington, DC (p. 168)
 Robert Krol, California State University, Northridge, Northridge, CA (p. 169)
*Randall Kroszner, University of Chicago, Chicago, IL (p. 170)
*Andrew Langer, National Federation of Independent Business, Washington, DC (p. 174)
 Patricia H. Lee, Institute for Justice, Washington, DC (p. 176)
 Tom Lenard, Progress & Freedom Foundation, Washington, DC (p. 177)
 Leonard A. Leo, The Federalist Society for Law and Public Policy Studies,
   Washington, DC (p. 178)
*Mark R. Levin, Landmark Legal Foundation, Herndon, VA (p. 178)
*James Andrew Lewis, Center for Strategic and International Studies, Washington, DC (p. 179)
 Marlo Lewis, Competitive Enterprise Institute, Washington, DC (p. 179)
 Gary Libecap, University of Arizona, Tucson, AZ (p. 179)
 Randall Lutter, American Enterprise Institute, Washington, DC (p. 184)
 Paul W. MacAvoy, Yale School of Management, New Haven, CT (p. 185)
*Johnathon R. Macey, Cornell University, Ithaca, NY (p. 185)
 Tibor R. Machan, Chapman University, Silverado Canyon, CA (p. 185)
*Brian Mannix, Mercatus Center at George Mason University, Arlington, VA (p. 188)
 Mary Martin, The Seniors Coalition, Springfield, VA (p. 190)
*Nancie G. Marzulla, Defenders of Property Rights, Washington, DC (p. 191)
*Roger J. Marzulla, Defenders of Property Rights, Washington, DC (p. 191)
*Randolph J. May, Progress & Freedom Foundation, Washington, DC (p. 193)
 John O. McGinnis, Cardozo School of Law, New York, NY (p. 196)
 Darrell McKigney, Small Business Survival Committee, Washington, DC (p. 196)
 Lawrence J. McQuillan, Pacific Research Institute, San Francisco, CA (p. 197)
*Daniel Mead Smith, Washington Policy Center, Seattle, WA (p. 198)
*Conrad F. Meier, Heartland Institute, Chicago, IL (p. 198)
*Robert J. Michaels, California State University, Fullerton, Fullerton, CA (p. 201)
*Edwin S. Mills, Northwestern University, Evanston, IL (p. 202)
*Adrian T. Moore, Reason Foundation, Los Angeles, CA (p. 205)
 Cassandra Chrones Moore, Cato Institute, Washington, DC (p. 205)
*Thomas Gale Moore, Hoover Institution, Stanford, CA (p. 206)
*Michael A. Morrisey, University of Alabama, Birmingham, Birmingham, AL (p. 207)
 Chuck Muth, American Conservative Union, Alexandria, VA (p. 210)
*William A. Niskanen, Cato Institute, Washington, DC (p. 214)
 David C. Nott, Reason Foundation, Los Angeles, CA (p. 215)
*Sam Peltzman, University of Chicago Graduate School of Business, Chicago, IL (p. 225)
 Laura Bennett Peterson, Washington, DC (p. 226)
*William H. Peterson, Washington, DC (p. 227)
*Nancy M. Pfotenhauer, Independent Women's Forum, Arlington, VA (p. 227)

REGULATORY REFORM (Continued)

Bruce Piasecki, AHC Group, Saratoga Springs, NY (p. 228)
*Daniel J. Popeo, Washington Legal Foundation, Washington, DC (p. 231)
Paul Portney, Resources for the Future, Washington, DC (p. 231)
*Edward Potter, Employment Policy Foundation, Washington, DC (p. 231)
*Stephen Presser, Northwestern University School of Law, Chicago, IL (p. 233)
*Scott Pullins, Ohio Taxpayers Association and OTA Foundation, Columbus, OH (p. 234)
*Don Racheter, Public Interest Institute, Mount Pleasant, IA (p. 235)
*Alan C. Raul, Sidley & Austin Brown & Wood, LLP, Washington, DC (p. 237)
*David Ridenour, National Center for Public Policy Research, Washington, DC (p. 240)
*David B. Rivkin, Jr., Baker & Hostetler, Washington, DC (p. 241)
Llewellyn Rockwell, Jr., Ludwig von Mises Institute, Auburn, AL (p. 242)
*L. Jacobo Rodriguez, Cato Institute, Washington, DC (p. 242)
Jonathan Rose, Arizona State University, Tempe, AZ (p. 243)
*David Rothbard, Committee for a Constructive Tomorrow, Washington, DC (p. 244)
*Craig Rucker, Committee for a Constructive Tomorrow, Washington, DC (p. 246)
*Charles F. Rule, Fried, Frank, Harris, Shriver & Jacobson, Washington, DC (p. 246)
*Terrence M. Scanlon, Capital Research Center, Washington, DC (p. 251)
*Geoffrey F. Segal, Reason Public Policy Institute, Los Angeles, CA (p. 256)
*John Shanahan, National Mining Association, Washington, DC (p. 258)
J. Gregory Sidak, American Enterprise Institute, Washington, DC (p. 259)
*Randy T. Simmons, Utah State University, Logan, UT (p. 260)
*S. Fred Singer, Science and Environmental Policy Project, Arlington, VA (p. 260)
*Solveig Singleton, Competitive Enterprise Institute, Washington, DC (p. 261)
*Fred L. Smith, Jr., Competitive Enterprise Institute, Washington, DC (p. 263)
Brad Snavely, Michigan Family Forum, Lansing, MI (p. 264)
Irwin Stelzer, Hudson Institute, Washington, DC (p. 268)
Jeff Stier, American Council on Science and Health, New York, NY (p. 269)
*Alexander Tabarrok, Mercatus Center at George Mason University, Arlington, VA (p. 273)
*Jerry Taylor, Cato Institute, Washington, DC (p. 274)
*David J. Theroux, The Independent Institute, Oakland, CA (p. 276)
*Jason M. Thomas, Citizens for a Sound Economy, Washington, DC (p. 277)
*Robert D. Tollison, University of Mississippi, University, MS (p. 280)
Peter M. VanDoren, Cato Institute, Washington, DC (p. 284)
*Peggy Venable, Texas Citizens for a Sound Economy, Austin, TX (p. 284)
*W. Kip Viscusi, Harvard Law School, Cambridge, MA (p. 285)
Dane vonBreichenruchardt, U. S. Bill of Rights Foundation, Washington, DC (p. 286)
William Waller, Venable, Baetjer, Howard & Civiletti, LLP, Washington, DC (p. 287)
Peter J. Wallison, American Enterprise Institute, Washington, DC (p. 288)
William K. S. Wang, Hastings College of Law, San Francisco, CA (p. 288)
Jude Wanniski, Polyconomics, Parsippany, NJ (p. 288)
*Murray Weidenbaum, Weidenbaum Center, St. Louis, MO (p. 291)
*Bob Williams, Evergreen Freedom Foundation, Olympia, WA (p. 295)
*Gary Wolfram, Hillsdale College, Hillsdale, MI (p. 297)
*Robert L. Woodson, Sr., National Center for Neighborhood Enterprise, Washington, DC (p. 298)
Bruce Yandle, Clemson University, Clemson, SC (p. 300)
Jennifer Zambone, Mercatus Center at George Mason University, Arlington, VA (p. 301)
Ronald A. Zumbrun, The Zumbrun Law Firm, Sacramento, CA (p. 303)

RISK ASSESSMENT

*Richard B. Belzer, Regulatory Checkbook, Washington, DC (p. 50)
*Sandy Liddy Bourne, American Legislative Exchange Council, Washington, DC (p. 58)
*Marshall J. Breger, Catholic University of America, Washington, DC (p. 60)
*Wayne T. Brough, Citizens for a Sound Economy, Washington, DC (p. 62)

* Has testified before a state or federal legislative committee

RISK ASSESSMENT (Continued)

*H. Sterling Burnett, National Center for Policy Analysis, Dallas, TX (p. 65)

*John Calfee, American Enterprise Institute, Washington, DC (p. 67)

Charles Calomiris, American Enterprise Institute, Washington, DC (p. 68)

*Kenneth W. Chilton, Institute for Study of Economics and the Environment, St. Charles, MO (p. 73)

Bonner R. Cohen, Lexington Institute, Arlington, VA (p. 77)

*Ward S. Curran, Trinity College, Hartford, CT (p. 87)

*Michael De Alessi, Reason Foundation, Los Angeles, CA (p. 89)

*Paul K. Driessen, Committee for a Constructive Tomorrow, Fairfax, VA (p. 98)

*Susan E. Dudley, Mercatus Center at George Mason University, Arlington, VA (p. 99)

*Susan Eckerly, National Federation of Independent Business, Washington, DC (p. 103)

Howard Fienberg, Statistical Assessment Service, Washington, DC (p. 111)

*Ernest Gellhorn, George Mason University School of Law, Washington, DC (p. 122)

Paul Georgia, Competitive Enterprise Institute, Washington, DC (p. 122)

*Wendy Lee Gramm, Mercatus Center at George Mason University, Arlington, VA (p. 128)

Steve H. Hanke, Johns Hopkins University, Baltimore, MD (p. 134)

*Ronald Hansen, University of Rochester, Rochester, NY (p. 134)

Robin Hanson, George Mason University, Fairfax, VA (p. 134)

Larry Hart, Hartco Strategies, Washington, DC (p. 136)

*Robert L. Hershey, Robert L. Hershey, P.E., Washington, DC (p. 141)

Thomas R. Ireland, University of Missouri, St. Louis, St. Louis, MO (p. 152)

Jim Johnston, Heartland Institute, Wilmette, IL (p. 156)

*Edward J. Kane, Boston College, Chestnut Hill, MA (p. 157)

Shawn Kantor, University of Arizona, Tucson, AZ (p. 157)

Martin S. Kaufman, Atlantic Legal Foundation, New York, NY (p. 159)

Karen Kerrigan, the polling company, Washington, DC (p. 162)

Howard Kunreuther, University of Pennsylvania, Philadelphia, PA (p. 170)

*Andrew Langer, National Federation of Independent Business, Washington, DC (p. 174)

James W. Lark, III, University of Virginia, Charlottesville, VA (p. 174)

Tom Lenard, Progress & Freedom Foundation, Washington, DC (p. 177)

Paul W. MacAvoy, Yale School of Management, New Haven, CT (p. 185)

*Rita P. Maguire, Arizona Center for Public Policy, Phoenix, AZ (p. 186)

*Brian Mannix, Mercatus Center at George Mason University, Arlington, VA (p. 188)

*Roger J. Marzulla, Defenders of Property Rights, Washington, DC (p. 191)

John O. McGinnis, Cardozo School of Law, New York, NY (p. 196)

*Henry I. Miller, Hoover Institution, Stanford, CA (p. 202)

Steven J. Milloy, junkscience.com, Washington, DC (p. 202)

*A. Alan Moghissi, Institute for Regulatory Science, Alexandria, VA (p. 204)

Cassandra Chrones Moore, Cato Institute, Washington, DC (p. 205)

Jeremiah O'Keeffe, Plano, TX (p. 217)

*Jane M. Orient, Association of American Physicians and Surgeons, Tucson, AZ (p. 219)

*Nancy M. Pfotenhauer, Independent Women's Forum, Arlington, VA (p. 227)

*Daniel J. Popeo, Washington Legal Foundation, Washington, DC (p. 231)

Paul Portney, Resources for the Future, Washington, DC (p. 231)

*Alan C. Raul, Sidley & Austin Brown & Wood, LLP, Washington, DC (p. 237)

*David Rothbard, Committee for a Constructive Tomorrow, Washington, DC (p. 244)

*Paul Rubin, Emory University, Atlanta, GA (p. 246)

*Craig Rucker, Committee for a Constructive Tomorrow, Washington, DC (p. 246)

*Linda Runbeck, Taxpayers League of Minnesota, Plymouth, MN (p. 247)

*John Shanahan, National Mining Association, Washington, DC (p. 258)

*S. Fred Singer, Science and Environmental Policy Project, Arlington, VA (p. 260)

Jeff Stier, American Council on Science and Health, New York, NY (p. 269)

*Richard L. Stroup, PERC – The Center for Free Market Environmentalism, Bozeman, MT (p. 271)

RISK ASSESSMENT (Continued)

*Jerry Taylor, Cato Institute, Washington, DC (p. 274)
 Tammy Tengs, University of California, Irvine, Irvine, CA (p. 275)
 Miro M. Todorovich, Scientists and Engineers for Secure Energy, New York, NY (p. 280)
*W. Kip Viscusi, Harvard Law School, Cambridge, MA (p. 285)
*Murray Weidenbaum, Weidenbaum Center, St. Louis, MO (p. 291)
 Bruce Yandle, Clemson University, Clemson, SC (p. 300)
 Jennifer Zambone, Mercatus Center at George Mason University, Arlington, VA (p. 301)
 Richard Zeckhauser, Harvard University, Cambridge, MA (p. 302)

TRANSPORTATION DEREGULATION

 Damon Ansell, Americans for Tax Reform, Washington, DC (p. 39)
*Dana Berliner, Institute for Justice, Washington, DC (p. 51)
 Lisa E. Bernstein, University of Chicago Law School, Chicago, IL (p. 51)
 Walter Block, Loyola University New Orleans, New Orleans, LA (p. 55)
*Jon Charles Caldara, Independence Institute, Golden, CO (p. 67)
*John A. Charles, Cascade Policy Institute, Portland, OR (p. 72)
 John Cobin, Montauk Financial Group, Greenville, SC (p. 76)
*Wendell Cox, Wendell Cox Consultancy, Belleville, IL (p. 84)
*Susan Eckerly, National Federation of Independent Business, Washington, DC (p. 103)
 Robert B. Ekelund, Auburn University, Auburn, AL (p. 105)
*James Gattuso, The Heritage Foundation, Washington, DC (p. 121)
*Robert Hahn, American Enterprise Institute, Washington, DC (p. 132)
 David T. Hartgen, University of North Carolina, Charlotte, Charlotte, NC (p. 136)
 John E. Kramer, Institute for Justice, Washington, DC (p. 168)
 James Lucier, Prudential Securities, Arlington, VA (p. 184)
 Paul W. MacAvoy, Yale School of Management, New Haven, CT (p. 185)
*Bobby McCormick, Clemson University, Clemson, SC (p. 194)
*Adrian T. Moore, Reason Foundation, Los Angeles, CA (p. 205)
 Cassandra Chrones Moore, Cato Institute, Washington, DC (p. 205)
*James Elliott Moore, II, University of Southern California, Los Angeles, CA (p. 205)
*Thomas Gale Moore, Hoover Institution, Stanford, CA (p. 206)
 Iain Murray, Statistical Assessment Service, Washington, DC (p. 209)
*Herbert R. Northrup, University of Pennsylvania, Haverford, PA (p. 215)
 Randal O'Toole, Thoreau Institute, Bandon, OR (p. 217)
*Sam Peltzman, University of Chicago Graduate School of Business, Chicago, IL (p. 225)
 Penn Pfiffner, Independence Institute, Golden, CO (p. 227)
*Dennis Polhill, Independence Institute, Golden, CO (p. 230)
*Robert W. Poole, Jr., Reason Foundation, Los Angeles, CA (p. 230)
 Gabriel Roth, Chevy Chase, MD (p. 244)
*Richard O. Rowland, Grassroot Institute of Hawaii, Aiea, HI (p. 245)
*Charles F. Rule, Fried, Frank, Harris, Shriver & Jacobson, Washington, DC (p. 246)
*John Semmens, Laissez-Faire Institute, Chandler, AZ (p. 256)
*Pete Sepp, National Taxpayers Union, Alexandria, VA (p. 257)
 Thomas L. Tacker, Embry-Riddle Aeronautical University, Daytona Beach, FL (p. 273)
*David J. Theroux, The Independent Institute, Oakland, CA (p. 276)
*Jason M. Thomas, Citizens for a Sound Economy, Washington, DC (p. 277)
 Peter M. VanDoren, Cato Institute, Washington, DC (p. 284)
*Murray Weidenbaum, Weidenbaum Center, St. Louis, MO (p. 291)
*Clinton H. Whitehurst, Jr., Clemson University, Clemson, SC (p. 294)

---

* Has testified before a state or federal legislative committee

U.S. Organizations

60 PLUS ASSOCIATION

Jim Martin, President
1600 Wilson Boulevard, Suite 960, Arlington, VA 22209
703-807-2070   fax 703-807-2073   jmartin@60plus.org   *www.60plus.org*

The 60 Plus Association is a non-partisan, non-profit organization supporting a free-enterprise, less-government, and less-taxes approach to seniors issues. 60 Plus publishes a newsletter, *Senior Voice*, produces a Congressional Scorecard, and presents the Guardian of Senior Rights Award to legislators in the U. S. Congress who vote to support seniors. Called a conservative alternative to the American Association of Retired Persons (AARP), 60 Plus endorses the personalization of Social Security and works actively for the repeal of the estate (death) tax. *Tax Status:* 501(c)(4).

Issues: Repeal of the estate (death) tax; Personalization of Social Security; Balanced budget constitutional amendment; Electricity deregulation; Opposition to judicial usurpation; Eliminating federal funding of advocacy organizations.

ACCURACY IN MEDIA

Reed Irvine, Chairman
4455 Connecticut Avenue, N.W., Suite 330, Washington, DC 20008
202-364-4401   fax 202-364-4098   ar1@aim.org   *www.aim.org*

Accuracy in Media is a news media watchdog group, launched in 1969 to challenge and correct the biased reporting of the American press. AIM publishes a twice-monthly newsletter, the *AIM Report*, syndicates a weekly newspaper column, and broadcasts a daily radio commentary called *Media Monitor*. AIM representatives attend annual shareholder meetings of top media companies and engage reporters, editors, and producers in ongoing debates about particular stories. *Tax Status:* 501(c)(3).

Issues: Media manipulation of public opinion; Media misreporting of important issues; Journalistic arrogance and cavalier attitude toward facts; The greatest stories never told.

ACTON INSTITUTE FOR THE STUDY OF RELIGION AND LIBERTY

Rev. Robert A. Sirico, President
161 Ottawa Avenue, N.W., Suite 301, Grand Rapids, MI 49503
616-454-3080   fax 616-454-9454   rsirico@acton.org   *www.acton.org*

The mission of the Acton Institute is to educate the religious and business communities on the moral virtues of a society with limited government and a free-market economy. The Acton Institute conducts a series of conferences and seminars for seminarians, religious studies students, business leaders, and religious and lay leaders to study the relationship between ethics, liberty, and the free market economy. The Institute also sponsors public lectures, publishes a series of monographs, and produces a bimonthly journal. Senior staff members are active participants in radio, TV, and print editorial outreach. *Tax Status:* 501(c)(3).

Issues: Welfare reform; Environmental stewardship; Free trade; Religion and public life.

ALABAMA POLICY INSTITUTE

Gary J. Palmer, President
402 Office Park Drive, Suite 300, Birmingham, AL 35223
205-870-9900   fax 205-870-4407   garyp@alabamapolicy.org
www.alabamapolicyinstitute.org

The Alabama Policy Institute is a research and education organization that embraces and promotes the principles of free markets and limited constitutional government as envisioned by the Founding Fathers. API's guiding philosophy is that public policy is family policy and that strong families are indispensable to the preservation of a free and prosperous society. It is the Institute's mission to enter the public square of policy development with ideas for the revitalization of American institutions in economics, government and the culture. *Tax Status:* 501(c)(3).

Issues: Tax reform; Tort reform; Environmental education; Education; Social issues; Gambling.

ALLEGHENY INSTITUTE FOR PUBLIC POLICY

Dr. Jake Haulk, President
305 Mt. Lebanon Boulevard, Suite 305, Pittsburgh, PA 15234
412-440-0079   fax 412-440-0085   aipp@alleghenyinstitute.org
www.alleghenyinstitute.org

The Allegheny Institute is a non-profit research and education organization. Its mission is to defend the interests of taxpayers, citizens and businesses against an increasingly burdensome and intrusive government. To that end, the Allegheny Institute formulates and advocates public policies that roll back the size and scope of local government as well as create a more accountable government. Its efforts are guided by the principles of free enterprise, property rights, civil society and individual freedom that are the bedrock upon which this nation was founded. *Tax Status:* 501(c)(3).

Issues: Allegheny County Row Office elimination; Transportation: surface, water and air; Economic freedom and regulations; Free market driven economic development; Education reform modeled on The Heritage Foundation "No Excuses" campaign.

ETHAN ALLEN INSTITUTE

John McClaughry, President
4836 Kirby Mountain Road, Concord, VT 05824
802-695-1448   fax 802-695-1436   eai@ethanallen.org   *www.ethanallen.org*

The mission of the Ethan Allen Institute is to influence public policy in Vermont by helping its people to better understand and put into practice the fundamentals of a free society – individual liberty, private property, competitive free enterprise, limited and frugal government, strong local communities, personal responsibility, and expanded opportunity for human endeavor. *Tax Status:* 501(c)(3).

Issues: Fiscal policy; Education; Environment; Health care.

ALLIANCE DEFENSE FUND

Alan Sears, President
15333 North Pima Road, Suite 165, Scottsdale, AZ 85260
480-444-0020   fax 480-444-0025   asears@alliancedefensefund.org
www.alliancedefensefund.org

The Alliance Defense Fund is a national organization that supports the legal defense and advocacy of religious freedom, the sanctity of life, and family values through funding, training, and strategic planning. *Tax Status:* 501(c)(3).

Issues: Restoring religious freedom; Definition of the family; Employment and religious freedom; Parents' rights; Abolishing partial-birth abortion; Litigation training.

ALLIANCE FOR AMERICA

Rosanne Corriera, President
P. O. Box 449, Caroga Park, NY 12032
518-835-6702   afa@allianceforamerican.org   *www.allianceforamerica.org*

The Alliance for America is a coalition of grassroots organizations dedicated to protecting the Constitution, property rights, human beings, and the environment. The Alliance operates a broadcast fax network to provide legislative updates on emerging congressional action on property rights and the environment. *Tax Status:* 501(c)(4).

Issues: Property rights; Free-market environmentalism.

ALLIANCE FOR AMERICA FOUNDATION

Rosanne Corriera, President
P. O. Box 449, Caroga Lake, NY 12032
518-835-6702   afa@allianceforamerica.org   *www.allianceforamerica.org*

The Alliance for America is a non-profit, grassroots organization of conservationists dedicated to finally bringing human concerns into environmental decision-making. As an umbrella organization, the Alliance for America represents over 500 diverse groups – ranchers, teachers, shrimpers, homemakers, recreationists, loggers, nurses, and citizens – in 50 states. It is dedicated to achieving balance in environmental issues and serves as a clearinghouse dedicated to public education and outreach. *Tax Status:* 501(c)(3).

Issues: Property rights; Free-market environmentalism.

ALLIANCE FOR MARRIAGE

Matt Daniels, President
P. O. Box 1305, Springfield, VA 22151-0305
703-425-9060   fax 703-425-9061   afm1@allianceformarriage.org
www.allianceformarriage.org

The Alliance for Marriage is a non-partisan research and education organization dedicated to promoting marriage and addressing the epidemic of fatherless families in the United States. AFM exists to educate the public, the media, elected officials, and civil society leaders on the benefits of marriage for children, adults and society. AFM also exists to promote reforms designed to strengthen the institution of marriage and restore a culture of married fatherhood in American society. *Tax Status:* 501(c)(3).

Issues: Marriage and family policy; Education; Tax reform; Media coverage of marriage and families; Judicial reform; Marriage building programs.

ALLIANCE FOR THE SEPARATION OF SCHOOL & STATE

Marshall Fritz, President
4546 East Ashlan, Number 3282, Fresno, CA 93726
559-292-1776   fax 559-292-7582   marshall@sepschool.org   *www.sepschool.org*

The mission of the Alliance for Separation of School & State is to inform Americans how education can be improved – especially for the poor – by ending state, local, and federal government involvement in school attendance, content, teacher and institutional approval, and financing. *Tax Status:* 501(c)(3).

Issues: Separation of school and state; Parental rights and obligations in education; Full parental school choice; Repeal school content and standards mandates; Return school attendance decisions to parents.

ALLIANCE FOR WORKER RETIREMENT SECURITY

Derrick A. Max, Executive Director
1331 Pennsylvania Avenue, N.W., Suite 600, Washington, DC 20004-1290
202-637-3453   fax 202-637-3182   *www.retiresecure.org*

The Alliance for Worker Retirement Security is a broad-based coalition of organizations dedicated to reforming the Social Security system to ensure an adequate retirement income and an opportunity for workers to create personal economic wealth.

Issues: Social Security reform.

AMERICA'S FUTURE FOUNDATION

Thomas Ivancie, President and CEO
1508 21st Street, N.W., Washington, DC 20036
202-544-7707   fax 202-530-1084   tom@americasfuture.org   *www.americasfuture.org*

America's Future Foundation educates and mobilizes today's young Americans and tomorrow's leaders in support of limited government, free markets, personal responsibility, moral virtue, world leadership, and technological progress. Through its educational and outreach programs, the Foundation provides the mechanism to harness the political and social energy of like-minded young professionals, broadcasting its positive message nationwide. *Tax Status:* 501(c)(3).

AMERICAN ACADEMY FOR LIBERAL EDUCATION

Jeffery Wallin, President
1710 Rhode Island Avenue, N.W., 4th Floor, Washington, DC 20036
202-452-8611   fax 202-452-8620   info@aale.org   *www.aale.org*

The American Academy for Liberal Education is a national association of colleges, universities, and schools dedicated to strengthening and promoting liberal arts education through institutional and programmatic accreditation. The essential component of AALE's measures is a set of curricular requirements, the Education Standards, which emphasize the importance of good teaching. The Academy is a non-profit, non-sectarian organization recognized by the Department of Education as a national agency for the accreditation of institutions of higher learning. *Tax Status:* 501(c)(3).

Issues: Educational effectiveness assessment (postsecondary); Charter schools (secondary); Distance learning (postsecondary); Higher education.

AMERICAN ALLIANCE FOR TAX EQUITY

Robert J. Lagomarsino, Chairman
1600 Broadway, Suite 2500, Denver, CO 80202
303-831-5000   fax 303-831-5032

AATE is a non-profit educational organization established to promote tax reform and tax reduction in America. AATE seeks to inform the American public about existing and proposed tax policies that are unfair to taxpayers, support a system that wastes revenues, and support tax practices that do not serve the U.S. national interest. AATE advocates repeal of tax laws that benefit special interests without sound economic or policy purposes that serve the nation as a whole. *Tax Status:* 501(c)(3).

Issues: Small business and farm tax relief; Two income and middle income families tax relief; Reducing the precentage of income and net worth for taxes and regulation compliance.

AMERICAN ASSOCIATION OF CHRISTIAN SCHOOLS

Carl Herbster, President
P. O. Box 1097, Independence, MO 64051-0597
816-252-9900   fax 816-252-6700   national@aacs.org   *www.aacs.org*

Founded in 1972, the American Association of Christian Schools serves over 200,000 students and teachers in member schools throughout the United States. The general purpose and objectives of AACS are to aid in promoting, establishing, advancing, and developing Christian schools in America. AACS provides practical assistance to members, academically, legally and legislatively through a number of services and publications. *Tax Status:* 501(c)(3).

Issues: School choice; Tuition tax credits; Restoring religious freedom.

AMERICAN ASSOCIATION OF SMALL PROPERTY OWNERS

F. Patricia Callahan, President
4200 Cathedral Avenue, N.W., Suite 515, Washington, DC 20016
202-244-6277   fax 202-363-3669   president@aaspo.org   *www.aaspo.org*

AASPO works for the right of small property owners to prosper freely and fairly – to make possible the American dream of building wealth with real estate. Its mission and goals are threefold: To create public understanding of the vital and growing role small property owners play in our nation's economy; to create a lively network for small property owners through which they may exchange shared concerns and problems as well as ideas and experiences that my solve them; and to create a better and more informed and realistic public policy environment on the local, state and national levels. *Tax Status:* 501(c)(3).

Issues: Tax policy; Lead-based paint; Rent control; Land use and zoning; Environmental regulation/economic development; Judicial reform.

AMERICAN CENTER FOR LAW AND JUSTICE

Jay Sekulow, Chief Counsel
1000 Regent University Drive, P. O. Box 64429, Virginia Beach, VA 23467
757-226-2489   fax 757-226-2836   aclj@aclj.org   *www.aclj.org*

The ACLJ engages in litigation, provides legal services, renders advice and counsels clients, and supports attorneys who are involved in defending the religious and civil liberties of Americans. The American Center has a national network of attorneys who are committed to the defense of Judeo-Christian values. It cooperates with other organizations that are committed to a similar mission, and serves the public through educational efforts regarding First Amendment and religious freedom issues as well as pro-family and pro-life concerns. *Tax Status:* 501(c)(3).

Issues: Protection of private religious speech; Protection of religious freedom in the workplace; Supporting government decisions that acknowledge the importance of religion; Protection of religious parental rights in the raising of their children; Protecting the unborn, elderly and infirm.

AMERICAN CIVIL RIGHTS COALITION

Ward Connerly, Chairman
P. O. Box 188350, Sacramento, CA 95818
916-444-2278   fax 916-444-2279   feedback@acri.org   *www.acrc1.org*

The American Civil Rights Coalition is a grassroots advocacy organization focused on the elimination of racial and gender preferences. Working with activists in different states and in Washington, DC, ACRC seeks to duplicate the California Civil Rights Initiative's success in other states and at the federal level. ACRC focuses on providing assistance and guidance to individuals and groups in other states who are interested in pursuing anti-preference legislation or ballot initiatives; advocating the elimination of racial and gender preferences in federal programs and policies; and monitoring California's Proposition 209 lawsuits and future implementation efforts. *Tax Status:* 501(c)(4).

Issues: Racial privacy initiative; Legislation concerning racial preferences and classifications.

AMERICAN CIVIL RIGHTS INSTITUTE

Ward Connerly, Chairman
P. O. Box 188350, Sacramento, CA 95818
916-444-2278   fax 916-444-2279   feedback@acri.org   *www.acri.org*

The American Civil Rights Institute is a national, non-profit organization dedicated to educating the American public about the problems created by racial and gender preferences in government programs and policies. ACRI members believe that civil rights are individual rights, and that government policies should not advocate group rights over individual rights. *Tax Status:* 501(c)(3).

Issues: Racial preferences, quotas, and set-asides; Race relations; Educational reform; Racial classification on government forms.

AMERICAN CIVIL RIGHTS UNION

Robert Carleson, Chairman and CEO
3213 Duke Street, Number 625, Alexandria, VA 22314
703-566-2696   fax 703-566-2322   rcarleson@aol.com   *www.civilrightsunion.org*

The mission of the American Civil Rights Union is to uphold the Constitution and the Bill of Rights as written. It is committed to defending all the rights enumerated therein unlike the American Civil Liberties Union which defends some, opposes some, and is silent on others. The American Civil Rights Union's priority as a new organization is to concentrate initially on those rights opposed by the ACLU. *Tax Status:* 501(c)(3).

Issues: The Scouting Legal Defense Fund/freedom of association; Freedom of religion/San Diego cross case; Property rights; Right to keep and bear arms; The 10th Amendment rights of states; Separation of powers.

AMERICAN CONSERVATIVE UNION

Chuck Muth, Executive Director
1007 Cameron Street, Alexandria, VA 22314
703-836-8602   fax 703-836-8606   acu@conservative.org   *www.conservative.org*

The ACU is a conservative lobbying organization. ACU's purpose is to communicate and advance the goals and principles of conservatism through one multi-issue, umbrella organization. ACU's statement of principles details its support of capitalism, belief in the doctrine of original intent of the Framers of the Constitution, confidence in traditional moral values, and commitment to a strong national defense. Annually since 1971, ACU has published ratings of Congress. Based on actual votes cast on a wide range of issues, each member of the House and Senate is rated on a 0 to 100 scale, designed to indicate the strength of their adherence to conservative principles. *Tax Status:* 501(c)(4).

Issues: Defense and national security; Tax reform; Campaign finance reform; Education reform; National sovereignty; Protecting Medicare and Social Security.

AMERICAN COUNCIL FOR CAPITAL FORMATION

Mark A. Bloomfield, President
1750 K Street, N.W., Suite 400, Washington, DC 20006
202-293-5811   fax 202-785-8165

The American Council for Capital Formation and its public policy affiliate, the ACCF Center for Policy Research, are unique in their focus on the role of public policies to promote the saving and investment essential to economic growth, job creation, and international competitiveness. For more than a quarter of a century, the ACCF and its research affiliate have brought the message to U.S. and international policymakers, the media, and the public that a nation's economic strength and stability depend upon well reasoned economic and environmental policies to promote capital formation.

Issues: Tax reform; Free enterprise/entrepreneurship; Environmental education.

AMERICAN COUNCIL OF TRUSTEES AND ALUMNI

Jerry L. Martin, President
1726 M Street, N.W., Suite 800, Washington, DC 20036-4525
202-467-6787   fax 202-467-6784   info@goacta.org   *www.goacta.org*

The American Council of Trustees and Alumni is a tax-exempt, non-profit, educational organization committed to academic freedom, excellence and accountability at America's colleges and universities. Founded in 1995, and formerly known as the National Alumni Forum, ACTA is the only national organization that is dedicated to working with alumni, donors, trustees and education leaders across the country to support liberal arts education, uphold high academic standards, safeguard the free exchange of ideas on campus, and ensure that the next generation receives a philosophically-balanced, open-minded, high-quality education at an affordable price. *Tax Status:* 501(c)(3).

Issues: Political correctness; Academic standards; Teacher education; Core curricula; Higher education; Responsible trusteeship and academic philanthropy.

AMERICAN COUNCIL ON SCIENCE AND HEALTH

Dr. Elizabeth M. Whelan, President
1995 Broadway, Second Floor, New York, NY 10023-5860
212-362-7044   fax 212-362-4919   acsh@acsh.org   *www.acsh.org*

The American Council on Science and Health is a national consumer-education organization concerned with issues related to food, chemicals, pharmaceuticals, life-style, the environment, and human health. ACSH is an independent, non-profit, tax-exempt organization founded in 1978. *Tax Status:* 501(c)(3).

Issues: Chemicals and the environment; Nutrition and the elderly; Pesticides and food safety; Smoking and health; Biotechnology and pharmaceuticals; Global warming and health.

AMERICAN DEFENSE INSTITUTE

Capt. Eugene B. "Red" McDaniel, USN (Ret.), President
1055 North Fairfax Street, Suite 200, Alexandria, VA 22314
703-519-7000   fax 703-519-8627   emb1@americandefinst.org   *www.ojc.org/adi*

The American Defense Institute is a non-profit, non-partisan organization that seeks to educate the public, especially the young, concerning the importance of a strong national defense to protect freedom and democracy. ADI believes that providing young Americans with the necessary training and incentive now is an investment in strong leadership for the future of the nation. ADI was founded on the belief that American moral and military strength are essential for peace. *Tax Status:* 501(c)(3).

Issues: Defense; National security; Prisoners of war; Foreign policy.

THE AMERICAN EDUCATION REFORM FOUNDATION

Susan Mitchell, President
2025 North Summit Avenue, Suite 103, Milwaukee, WI 53202
414-319-9160   fax 414-765-0220   mitchell@parentchoice.org

The American Education Reform Foundation works to advance public policy that empowers parents to choose the best schools for their children. *Tax Status:* 501(c)(4).

Issues: Education choice.

AMERICAN ENTERPRISE INSTITUTE

Christopher DeMuth, President
1150 17th Street, N.W., Washington, DC 20036
202-862-5800   fax 202-862-7177   info@aei.org   *www.aei.org*

The American Enterprise Institute, founded in 1943, sponsors original research on government policy, the American economy, and American politics. AEI research aims to preserve and to strengthen the foundations of a free society – limited government, competitive private enterprise, vital cultural and political institutions, and vigilant defense – through rigorous inquiry, debate, and writing. The Institute is home to many accomplished economists, legal scholars, political scientists, and foreign policy specialists. The American Enterprise Institute is an independent, non-partisan organization financed by tax-deductible contributions from corporations, foundations, and individuals. *Tax Status:* 501(c)(3).

Issues: Economic policy; Foreign and defense policy; Social and political studies.

AMERICAN FAMILY ASSOCIATION

Rev. Donald Wildmon, Executive Director
P. O. Drawer 2440, 107 Parkgate Drive, Tupelo, MS 38803
662-844-5036   fax 662-844-9176   buddy@afa.net   *www.afa.net*

The American Family Association exists to motivate and equip citizens to change the culture to reflect biblical truth. The Association believes that God has communicated absolute truth to man through the Bible, and that all men everywhere at all times are subject to the authority of God's Word. Therefore, a culture based on Biblical truth best serves the well-being of our country, in accordance with the vision of our founding fathers. *Tax Status:* 501(c)(3).

Issues: Preservation of the marriage and family; Decency and morality; Sanctity of human life; Stewardship; Media integrity.

AMERICAN FAMILY ASSOCIATION FOUNDATION

Rev. Donald Wildmon, Executive Director
P. O. Drawer 2440, 107 Parkgate Drive, Tupelo, MS 38803
662-844-5036   fax 662-844-9176   buddy@afa.net   *www.afa.net*

The American Family Association Foundation is a Christian organization dedicated to promoting the biblical ethic of decency in American society with primary emphasis on television and other media. *Tax Status:* 501(c)(4).

Issues: Culture; Entertainment; The Family; Gambling; Pornography.

AMERICAN FOREIGN POLICY COUNCIL

Herman Pirchner, Jr., President
1521 16th Street, N.W., Washington, DC 20036
202-462-6055   fax 202-462-6045   afpc@afpc.org   *www.afpc.org*

The American Foreign Policy Council's mission is to bring information to those who make or influence the foreign policy of the United States and to assist leaders in the former USSR and other parts of the world in building democracies and market economies. *Tax Status:* 501(c)(3).

Issues: Russia; Foreign aid; China; Missile defense; Central Asia; Middel East.

AMERICAN INSTITUTE FOR FULL EMPLOYMENT

Theodore David Abram, Executive Director
2636 Biehn Street, Klamath Falls, OR 97601
800-562-7752   fax 541-273-6796   teda@jeld-wen.com   *www.fullemployment.org*

The mission of the American Institute for Full Employment is to develop the concepts needed to achieve full employment in America and to do so in a fashion that will utilize and enhance free enterprise and minimize or eliminate governmental involvement or influence. "Full employment" means universal access to jobs with career potential, and adequate retirement benefits, for all who can work, especially those who are receiving public assistance as a substitute for the opportunities and rewards of paid work. *Tax Status:* 501(c)(3).

Issues: Welfare; Unemployment; Social Security; Food stamps; High school economic textbooks.

AMERICAN LAND RIGHTS ASSOCIATION

Chuck Cushman, Executive Director
P. O. Box 400, Battle Ground, WA 98604
360-687-3087   fax 360-687-2973   alra@pacifier.com   *www.landrights.org*

Dedicated to the wise use of America's resources, the ALRA is a national clearinghouse and support coalition, encouraging private property ownership, family recreation, multiple use of federal lands, commodity production, and access to federally controlled lands. Its purpose is to oppose selfish, single-use restrictive land designations that damage local economies, schools, and roads in rural America. ALRA maintains a fax/e-mail communication network; organizes coalitions to fight property rights threats; sponsors special events, rallies, and conferences; carries out grassroots training and campaigns in teamwork with allied groups; and has a speakers bureau.

Issues: Oppose land aquisition trust funds that permit eminent domain; No net loss of private property; Private property rights; Oppose land acquisition; Access to federal land and resources; Endangered Species Act reform.

AMERICAN LEGISLATIVE EXCHANGE COUNCIL

Duane Parde, Executive Director
1129 20th Street, N.W., Suite 500, Washington, DC 20036
202-466-3800   fax 202-466-3801   Info@alec.org   *www.alec.org*

The American Legislative Exchange Council's mission is to advance the Jeffersonian principles of free markets, limited government, federalism, and individual liberty through a non-partisan partnership among America's state legislators and concerned members of the private sector, the federal government, and the general public. *Tax Status:* 501(c)(3).

Issues: Education reform; Tax reduction and fiscal discipline; Privatization of public services; Federal balanced budget amendment; Tort reform; Free-market health care solutions.

AMERICAN POLICY CENTER

Thomas DeWeese, President
98 Alexandria Pike, Suite 43, Warrenton, VA 20186-2849
540-341-8911   fax 540-341-8917

The American Policy Center, located in suburban Washington, D.C., is a privately funded, non-profit, tax-exempt grassroots action and education foundation dedicated to the promotion of free enterprise and limited government regulations over commerce and individuals. *Tax Status:* 501(c)(4).

Issues: Education; Property rights; Privacy rights; United Nations.

AMERICAN RENEWAL

Dr. Richard Lessner, Executive Director
801 G Street, N.W., Washington, DC 20001
202-624-3011   fax 202-303-2134   rel@frc.org   *www.american-renewal.org*

American Renewal was created in 1992 to educate the general public and cultural leaders about traditional American values, to promote the philosophy of America's Founding Fathers concerning the nature of ordered liberty, and to assist other non-profit organizations in meeting the same objectives. American Renewal has underwritten the costs of video campaigns on public policy issues, supported the drafting and placement of policy advocacy advertising, and undertaken efforts to provide the nation's political parties with information regarding traditional American values. American Renewal also lobbies Congress on such issues as abortion, religious persecution, and the defense of marriage. *Tax Status:* 501(c)(4).

Issues: Partial-birth abortion; U.S.-China policy; Religious persecution.

AMERICAN SOCIETY FOR THE DEFENSE OF TRADITION, FAMILY AND PROPERTY

Mario Navarro da Costa, Director, Washington Bureau
1344 Merrie Ridge Road, McLean, VA 22101
703-243-2104   fax 703-243-2105   american.tfp@pobox.com   *www.tfp.org*

The American TFP is a civic, cultural, and non-partisan organization which, inspired by the traditional teachings of the Roman Catholic Church, works to defend and promote the principles of private ownership, family, and Christian values. TFP does this by studying both the foundations of America's traditions, to invigorate them, and the components of disintegration, to counteract them. *Crusade*, its bimonthly magazine, analyzes and comments on national and international events, culture, history, and Catholic social doctrine, among other topics. *Tax Status:* 501(c)(3).

Issues: Judicial activism; Euthanasia; Religious persecution of Christians; Abortion; Blasphemy in the culture; Ballistic missile defense.

AMERICAN STUDIES CENTER–RADIO AMERICA

James Roberts, President
1030 15th Street, N.W., Suite 700, Washington, DC 20005
202-408-0944   fax 202-408-1087   gcorombos@radioamerica.org   *www.radioamerica.org*

A project of the American Studies Center, Radio America produces and distributes programs reflecting a commitment to traditional American values, limited government, and the free market. *Tax Status:* 501(c)(3).

Issues: Media; War on Terrorism; Defense and intelligence; Taxation; American government; Government spending.

AMERICAN TEXTBOOK COUNCIL

Gilbert T. Sewall, Director
475 Riverside Drive, Suite 448, New York, NY 10115
212-870-2760   fax 212-870-2720   atc@columbia.edu

The American Textbook Council was established to advance the quality of history textbooks. The Council endorses the production of textbooks that embody vivid narrative style, stress significant people and events, and promote better understanding of all cultures, including America's, on the principle that improved textbooks will advance the curriculum, stimulate student learning, and encourage educational achievement for children of all backgrounds. It also provides a forum for educators and others interested in improving the educational materials and maintains a clearinghouse of information about social studies textbooks consulted by educators and policymakers at all levels. *Tax Status:* 501(c)(3).

Issues: History and social studies curriculum and textbooks; Development of improved history and social studies instructional materials; Civic and character education.

AMERICAN TORT REFORM ASSOCIATION

Sherman Joyce, President
1101 Connecticut Avenue, N.W., Suite 400, Washington, DC 20036
202-682-1163   fax 202-682-1022   sjoyce@atra.org   *www.atra.org*

The American Tort Reform Association's mission is to bring greater fairness, predictability, and efficiency to the civil justice system through public education and legislative reform. It pursues its mission by coordinating and supporting the activities of state tort reform coalitions; by keeping its members informed of tort reform developments; by serving as a national voice of the tort reform movement; and by attempting to change public attitudes toward civil litigation. *Tax Status:* 501(c)(6).

Issues: Product liability reform; Punitive damages reform; Joint and several liability reform; Medical liability reform; Collateral source reform.

AMERICANS FOR COMMUNITY AND FAITH CENTERED ENTERPRISE

Dr. Michael S. Joyce, President
1201 Pennsylvania Avenue, N.W., Suite 300, Washington, DC 20036
202-661-4740

The mission of ACFE is to revitalize civil society in America, particularly through the community and faith-centered organizations that are working to help their neighbors in need. Such organizations understand that many contemporary social pathologies cannot be explained as the result of financial poverty alone, but rather, are in part symptomatic of widespread moral and spiritual impoverishment. ACFE is committed to energizing the private sector in order to build support for organizations serving on the frontlines in communities throughout America – the groups, projects, works, and individuals that make up the "armies of compassion."

Issues: Citizenship and civil society; Religion and public life; Philanthropy.

AMERICANS FOR TAX REFORM

Grover Norquist, President
1920 L Street, Suite 200, Washington, DC 20036
202-785-0266   fax 202-785-0261   jzysk@atr-dc.org   *www.atr.org*

Americans for Tax Reform is a coalition of taxpayer groups opposing any and all tax increases at the state, federal, and local levels. ATR works with state tax groups to ask all candidates for office to sign the Taxpayer Protection Pledge committing officeholders to oppose tax increases. ATR publicizes the Cost of Government Day each year – the day until which Americans must work to pay the cost of taxes and regulations. ATR also coordinates the Reagan Legacy Project urging Congress and state legislatures to name memorials after President Reagan. *Tax Status:* 501(c)(4).

Issues: Opposing all tax increases; Supporting moves toward a flat tax; Reforming state pensions; Paycheck protection legislation; Constitutional amendment to require a 2/3 vote for tax increases; Electronic commerce – opposing taxes on the Internet.

AMERICANS FOR TAX REFORM FOUNDATION

Grover Norquist, President
1920 L Street, Suite 200, Washington, DC 20036
202-785-0266   fax 202-785-0261   jzysk@atr-dc.org   *www.atr.org*

Americans for Tax Reform Foundation serves as a national information clearinghouse for the grassroots taxpayers' movement working with state and county-level groups. ATRF is a non-profit research and education organization and works to highlight the true cost of high taxes, oversight and government spending. *Tax Status:* 501(c)(3).

Issues: Taxpayer Protection Pledge; Social Security privatization; 2/3 supermajority to raise taxes; State-level taxpayer legislation; Cost of Government Day.

AMERICANS FOR TECHNOLOGY LEADERSHIP

James Prendergast, Executive Director
1413 K Street, N.W., 12th Floor, Washington, DC 20005
202-835-2030   fax 202-318-7803

Americans for Technology Leadership is a broad-based coalition of technology professionals, consumers and organizations dedicated to limiting government regulation of technology and fostering competitive market solutions to public policy issues affecting the technology industry. ATL believes that this approach will ensure that all Americans are able to take advantage of the benefits of the technologies that are shaping the new economy.

Issues: Internet technology; Regulations.

AMERICANS UNITED FOR LIFE

Clarke D. Forsythe, President
310 South Peoria, Suite 300, Chicago, IL 60607
312-492-7234   fax 312-492-7235   information@unitedforlife.org   *www.unitedforlife.org*

The mission of Americans United for Life is to protect every person in America from abortion and euthanasia through law and education. AUL is a non-sectarian, non-partisan, public-interest, non-profit group that specializes in legislation, litigation, and education. Founded in 1971, AUL focuses on initiatives that will change public policy and opinion on sanctity of human life issues in the short term, while laying the groundwork for comprehensive protection of human life over the long term. AUL serves pro-life legislators, lobbyists, and leaders at the state and national levels. *Tax Status:* 501(c)(3).

Issues: Preventing legalized assisted suicide; The abortion-breast cancer link; Fetal-homicide legislation; Defending pro-life legislation in the courts; Dispelling the myth that abortion is a necessary evil; Educating state legislators.

ANNECY INSTITUTE FOR THE STUDY OF VIRTUE AND LIBERTY

Rev. John M. Beers
429 N Street, S.W., Suite 109 South, Washington, DC 20024
202-863-0756   fax 202-863-0756   jmbeers@earthlink.com

The Annecy Institute asserts that public policy discussions should be informed by an appreciation of the health and dignity of the human person, and how these values are upheld by a system of free enterprise, limited government and strong civil society.

ANSER INSTITUTE FOR HOMELAND SECURITY

Randy Larsen, Director
2900 South Quincy Street, Suite 800, Arlington, VA 22206
703-416-2000

ANSER Institute for Homeland Security is a non-profit public service research institute. It is their belief that the 21st Century will present the Maerican people with far different national security challenges than the 20th Century. Preparing for these new challenges will require a determined, integrated effort at every stage of the process: deterrence, prevention, preemption, crisis management, consequence management, attribution and retaliation. America needs a clear national strategy and a partnership that includes federal, state, local and private sector support. The Institute's *Journal of Homeland Security*, weekly email Newsletter, and website – *www.homelandsecurity.org* – offer many useful resources.

SUSAN B. ANTHONY LIST

Jane Abraham, President
1800 Diagonal Road, Suite 285, Alexandria, VA 22314
703-683-5558   fax 703-549-5588   info@sba-list.org   *www.sba-list.org*

Susan B. Anthony List, Inc. is a not-for-profit membership organization with a connected political action committee (SBA List Candidate Fund) dedicated to training pro-life activists and candidates, advocating the passage of pro-life legislation in Congress, and increasing the percentage of pro-life women in Congress. *Tax Status:* 501(c)(4).

Issues: All abortion related issues.

ARKANSAS FAMILY COUNCIL

Jerry Cox, Executive Director
414 South Pulaski, Suite 2, Little Rock, AR 72201
501-375-7000   fax 501-375 7040   info@familycouncil.org   *www.familycouncil.org*

The Arkansas Family Council was established in 1989 in association with Focus on the Family and Dr. James Dobson. AFC is a conservative research and education organization dedicated to upholding traditional values. *Tax Status:* 501(c)(3).

Issues: Sanctity of life; Parental rights; Voter education; Home schooling; Abstinence and out-of-wedlock births; Traditional values in schools.

ARKANSAS POLICY FOUNDATION

Hon. Greg Kaza, Executive Director
111 Center Street, Suite 1610, Little Rock, AR 72202
501-537-0825   fax 501-375-4171   kaza@reformarkansas.org   *www.reformarkansas.org*

Founded in 1995, the Arkansas Policy Foundation is an independent, non-partisan public policy think tank committed to the goals of economic growth, individual opportunity, and education reform. *Tax Status:* 501(c)(3).

Issues: Education reform; Tax policy; Business cycle research.

JOHN M. ASHBROOK CENTER FOR PUBLIC AFFAIRS

Peter W. Schramm, Executive Director
Ashland University, 401 College Avenue, Ashland, OH 44805
419-289-5411   fax 419-289-5425   ashbrook@ashland.edu   *www.ashbrook.org*

The John M. Ashbrook Center for Public Affairs at Ashland University is an academic forum for the study, research, and discussion of the principles and practices of American constitutional government and politics. The Ashbrook Center's programs are directed to the scholarly defense of individual liberty, limited constitutional government, and civic morality, which together constitute American's democratic way of life. It sponsors the Ashbrook Scholar program, publishes scholarly monographs and books, hosts a series of campus lectures and conferences, and provides internship opportunities for students interested in careers related to public affairs. *Tax Status:* 501(c)(3).

Issues: Foreign policy; Race and ethnicity; Future of conservatism; Education.

ASSOCIATION OF AMERICAN EDUCATORS

Gary Beckner, Executive Director
25201 Paseo de Alicia, Suite 104, Laguna Hills, CA 92653
949-595-7979   fax 949-595-7970   info@aaeteachers.org   *www.aaeteachers.org*

The Association of American Educators serves as a national, professional alternative to teacher unions, offering many of the same benefits of the unions – without the politics. AAE encourages and empowers educators who subscribe to the idea that education should aim to improve a young person's character as well as intellect, and who believe that public schools should be under the control of, and accountable to, the parents, citizens, and taxpayers of the local communities they serve. *Tax Status:* 501(c)(6).

Issues: Promoting character education; Fighting federal intervention in public education; Establishing state affiliates of the AAE; Promoting higher entrance/career professional standards for teachers.

ASSOCIATION OF AMERICAN PHYSICIANS AND SURGEONS

Jane M. Orient, M.D., Director
1601 North Tucson Boulevard, Suite 9, Tucson, AZ 85716
800-635-1196   fax 520-326-3529   *www.aapsonline.org*

Since 1943, AAPS has been the only national association of physicians in all specialties dedicated to preserving and protecting the sanctity of the patient-physician relationship. AAPS believes this patient-physician relationship must be free from all third-party interference – whether from the government, insurance companies, or health care plans. It believes patients' ability to choose their physicians and care that's best for their needs is inviolable.

Issues: Fighting increased government control of the practice of medicine; Opposing increased government power to criminalize medicine and prosecute physicians; Supporting unrestricted private contracting with Medicare patients; Opposing national provider ID and central patient database; Opposing government enforcement of HIPAA regulations; Defending physicians through legal action.

ASSOCIATION OF CHRISTIAN SCHOOLS INTERNATIONAL

Ken Smitherman, President
P. O. Box 35097, Colorado Springs, CO 80935
719-528-6906   fax 719-531-0631   ken_smitherman@acsi.org   *www.acsi.org*

The mission of Association of Christian Schools International is to enable Christian educators and schools worldwide to prepare students for life. ACSI provides an array of services and programs through regional offices and its departments of academic affairs, international ministries, legal/legislative affairs, early education services, and student activities. *Tax Status:* 501(c)(3).

Issues: Develop Urban School Services Department; Strengthen administrative leadership; Develop new Christian textbook series; Strengthen international Christian schools; Achieve national recognition for preschool accreditation; Promote K-12 Christian school accreditation.

ATLANTIC LEGAL FOUNDATION

William H. Slattery, President
150 East 42nd Street, 2nd Floor, New York, NY 10017
212-573-1960   fax 212-857-3653   Atlanticlaw@earthlink.net   *www.atlanticlegal.org*

Atlantic Legal Foundation is a litigating organization that advocates the principles of limited government, the free market system, and the rights of individuals. Atlantic works to hold governments (federal, state, and local) accountable for their actions and challenges burdensome governmental regulations. It also works to keep junk science out of the courtroom. *Tax Status:* 501(c)(3).

Issues: Science and the law; Property rights; Student rights; Illegal government regulations; Affirmative action; Political correctness.

ATLAS ECONOMIC RESEARCH FOUNDATION

Alejandro Chafuen, President
4084 University Drive, Suite 103, Fairfax, VA 22030
703-934-6969   fax 703-352-7530   atlas@atlasusa.org   *www.atlasusa.org*

The mission of the Atlas Economic Research Foundation is to discover, develop, and support intellectual entrepreneurs worldwide who have the potential to create independent public policy institutes and related programs that advance Atlas's vision and to provide ongoing support as such institutes and programs mature. *Tax Status:* 501(c)(3).

Issues: New technologies and public policy; Judicial security/rule of law; Environmental regulation/health; Free trade; Property rights (including intellectual); Ethics of economics.

THE JOSIAH BARTLETT CENTER FOR PUBLIC POLICY

Arthur Mudge, Chairman
7 South State Street, P. O. Box 897, Concord, NH 03302
603-224-4450   fax 603-224-4329   jbartlett@jbartlett.org   *www.jbartlett.org*

The Josiah Bartlett Center for Public Policy is a non-profit, non-partisan, independent think tank focused on state and local public policy issues that affect the quality of life for New Hampshire's citizens. To improve economic prosperity and the general welfare, the Center provides information, research, and analysis to decision makers. The Center has as its core beliefs individual freedom and responsibility, limited and accountable government, and an appreciation of the role of the free enterprise system. *Tax Status:* 501(c)(3).

Issues: Education; State-local fiscal structure; Health; New Hampshire's economy and public policy.

BEACON HILL INSTITUTE FOR PUBLIC POLICY RESEARCH

David G. Tuerck, Executive Director
Suffolk University, 8 Ashburton Place, Boston, MA 02108
617-573-8750   fax 617-720-4272   bhi@beaconhill.org   *www.beaconhill.org*

The Beacon Hill Institute applies economic analysis to public policy issues of importance to Massachusetts, the states, and the nation. BHI employs state-of-the-art econometric and statistical methods to produce technically sound research. The basic analytical tool is the free-market model. Analyses are published in formats ranging from comprehensive policy studies to brief articles and opinion editorials. The Institute promotes discussion of the issues through sponsorship of forums and lectures and through its web site and quarterly newsletter. *Tax Status:* 501(c)(3).

Issues: State tax modeling; Economic competitiveness; Project labor agreements; Education spending; Universal health care in the states; Tax policy in Massachusetts.

THE BECKET FUND FOR RELIGIOUS LIBERTY

Kevin J. Hasson, President
1350 Connecticut Avenue, N.W., Suite 605, Washington, DC 20036
202-955-0095   fax 202-955-0090   mail@becketfund.org   *www.becketfund.org*

The Becket Fund for Religious Liberty is a bipartisan and ecumenical, public interest law firm that protects the free expression of all religious traditions. Three guiding principles of the Fund's mission are: Freedom of religion is a basic human right that no government may lawfully deny; religious expression – from all traditions – is a natural part of life in civilized society, and religious arguments, on all sides of a question, are a normal and healthy element in public debate; and religious people and institutions are entitled to participate in govenrment affairs on an equal basis with everyone else, and should not be excluded for professing their faith. *Tax Status:* 501(c)(3).

Issues: Religious liberty; Church-state relations; Religion and public life.

BELLWETHER FORUM

Robert W. Painter, President
945 McKinney Street, Suite 410, Houston, TX 77002
713-866-6252   fax 713-866-6253   info@bellwetherforum.org   *www.bellwetherforum.org*

Bellwether Forum is a non-profit, non-partisan organization that promotes political, policy, and career leadership and education. The Forum's programs target working young professionals, but are open to everyone. Bellwether Forum is headquartered in Houston, Texas but sponsors programs from coast to coast and even abroad. *Tax Status:* 501(c)(3).

Issues: Expanding number of young professionals involved in the conservative movement; Offering evening classes in various cities through the Bellwether University program; Providing networking opportunities to introduce young professionals to the new face of conservatism; Pairing college student leaders with young professionals to transition from college to community involvement; Teaching base government and civics to disadvantaged young adults; Establishing strategic relationships with conservative organizations abroad.

BEST FRIENDS FOUNDATION

Elayne Bennett, Founder and President
4455 Connecticut Avenue, N.W., Suite 310, Washington, DC 20008
202-237-8156   fax 202-237-2776   webmaster@bestfriendsfoundation.org
www.bestfriendsfoundation.org

The Best Friends Foundation is an educational foundation that operates the Best Friends Program in Washington, D.C. area schools and trains educators to teach its self-respect through self-restraint curriculum throughout the country. As a character-building and youth-development program with a message of abstinence from sex, drugs and alcohol, Best Friends has offered guidance to adolescent girls (5th or 6th grade through high school graduation) since 1987 and to adolescent boys since 2001. College scholarships are provided. Best Friends is a grassroots program currently operating in 102 schools in 14 states and the U.S. Virgin Islands. The Foundation is supported by grants from private foundations, corporations, and individual donors and receives no government funds. *Tax Status:* 501(c)(3).

Issues: Reducing teen pregnancy; Reducing drug and alcohol abuse by adolescents.

THE BILL OF RIGHTS INSTITUTE

Victoria Hughes, President
1001 Connecticut Avenue, N.W., Suite 219, Washington, DC 20036
202-822-4622   fax 202-822-4630   info@billofrights.org   *www.billofrights.org*

Founded in 1999, the Bill of Rights Institute's mission is to educate high school students about the Bill of Rights through classroom material and programs that teach: What the Bill of Rights protects, both explicitly and implicitly; how the Bill of Rights affects our daily lives; and how the Bill of Rights shapes our society. The Institute is dedicated to helping high school Social Studies teachers enhance their students' understanding of their rights and responsibilities as citizens, as well as the historical and intellectual origins of the U.S. Constitution and the Bill of Rights. *Tax Status:* 501(c)(3).

BLACK ALLIANCE FOR EDUCATIONAL OPTIONS

Lawrence C. Patrick, III, President and CEO
501 C Street, N.E., Suite 3, Washington, DC 20002
202-544-9870   fax 202-544-7680   lawrence@baeo.org   *www.baeo.org*

To actively support parental choice to empower families and increase educational options for Black children. BAEO supports charter schools, tax-supported vouchers for low-income families, privately funded scholarships to private schools, tuition tax credits benefiting low-income families, home schooling, public-private partnerships, supplementary education programs, and innovations in existing public schools. *Tax Status:* 501(c)(3).

Issues: To continue to develop strong chapters which will bolster the school choice movement on national, state and local levels.

JAMES M. BUCHANAN CENTER

Tyler Cowen, General Director
George Mason University, MSN 1D3, Fairfax, VA 22030
703-993-2330   fax 703-993-2323   crobert@gmu.edu   *www.gmu.edu/jbc*

The James M. Buchanan Center for Political Economy is a research and education organization at George Mason University. Through the interdisciplinary study of economics, law, and the humanities, the Center's faculty seeks to advance knowledge of how societies achieve freedom, prosperity, and peace. The Center is named in honor of Nobel Prize-winning economist and GMU Professor James M. Buchanan. With a commitment to rigorous, interdisciplinary scholarship, the Buchanan Center bridges academic theory and real-world practice. To foster scholarly inquiry into the nature of the market process, the Center nurtures and supports graduate students. *Tax Status:* 501(c)(3).

Issues: Public choice; Law and economics; Austrian economics; Social change.

BUCKEYE INSTITUTE FOR PUBLIC POLICY SOLUTIONS

Dr. Samuel R. Staley, President
4100 North High Street, Suite 200, Columbus, OH 43214
614-262-1593   fax 614-262-1927   buckeye@buckeyeinstitute.org
www.buckeyeinstitute.org

The Buckeye Institute for Public Policy Solutions is a non-profit research and education institute made up of Ohio professors and scholars as well as a full-time staff in Columbus. The Institute publishes reports and commentaries on pressing Ohio policy issues, in addition to sponsoring educational conferences and seminars. The mission of the Buckeye Institute is to provide market-oriented solutions for state and local problems facing Ohioans. The Institute's work focuses on six primary areas: Education, economic development, taxes and spending, health care, poverty and welfare, and the environment. *Tax Status:* 501(c)(3).

Issues: Education reform; Taxation and fiscal issues; Privatization; Welfare reform; Deregulation; Economic development.

CALIFORNIA PUBLIC POLICY FOUNDATION

John Kurzweil, President
P. O. Box 931, Camarillo, CA 93011
805-445-9183   fax 805-445-7193   calprev@gte.net   *www.cppf.org*

Since its founding in 1986, California Public Policy Foundation, a non-profit, non-partisan, educational organization, has provided California a responsible, articulate, effective voice – primarily through its flagship publication *California Political Review Magazine* – for limited government, individual responsibility, self-reliance, and personal virtue. CPPF's mission is building communications networks that unify and make more effective California's conservative movement. *Tax Status:* 501(c)(3).

Issues: The rule of law and judicial activism; Religious freedom; Freedom of association.

CALVERT INSTITUTE FOR POLICY RESEARCH, INC.

George W. Liebmann, Executive Director
8 West Hamilton Street, Baltimore, MD 21201
410-662-7252   fax 410-539-3973   calvert@attach.net   *www.calvertinstitute.org*

The Calvert Institute for Policy Research is an independent, non-partisan public policy research institution committed to generating new ideas based on the principles of free enterprise, limited government and personal responsibility. The Institute seeks to make Maryland worthy of its fond nickname, "The Free State." The Calvert Institute serves as a clearinghouse for public policy information on the benefit of a society based upon restricted government. All of the Institute's publications are available to the general public upon request. *Tax Status:* 501(c)(3).

Issues: K-12 Education; State and local tax policy; Transportation planning and funding; State/local government management and privatization; Business development, retention and regulation.

CAPITAL RESEARCH CENTER

Terrence Scanlon, President
1513 16th Street, N.W., Washington, DC 20036
202-483-6900   fax 202-483-6902   crc@capitalresearch.org   *www.capitalresearch.org*

Capital Research Center is an education and research institute studying critical issues in philanthropy, with a special focus on non-profit public interest and advocacy groups, their funding sources, their agendas (open and hidden), and their impact on public policy and society. CRC publishes four monthly newsletters – *Organization Trends*; *Foundation Watch*; *Labor Watch*; and *Compassion and Culture* – as well as *Patterns of Corporate Philanthropy*, an annual book-length analysis of the public affairs giving patterns of America's largest publicly held corporations. CRC's web site contains two special databases – green-watch.com, which examines the environmental movement and educationwatch.org, which looks at groups supporting and opposing school choice. *Tax Status:* 501(c)(3).

Issues: Revival of private charity; Charity's role in the post-welfare state; Corporate giving to advocacy groups; Monitoring left-wing advocacy groups; Monitoring education reform groups; Monitoring environmental groups.

CAPITOL RESOURCE INSTITUTE

Michael Mears, Executive Director
1414 K Street, Suite 200, Sacramento, CA 95814
916-498-1940   fax 916-448-2888   capitolres@aol.com   *www.capitolresource.org*

Capitol Resource Institute is a non-profit organization engaged in coalition-building, media outreach, lobbying, and legislative tracking. The organization is dedicated to the principles of traditional families, parental rights, limited government, and citizen responsibility. *Tax Status:* 501(c)(3).

Issues: Marriage; Education; Parental rights; Gambling; Health; Privacy.

CASCADE POLICY INSTITUTE

Steve Buckstein, President
813 S.W. Alder Street, Suite 450, Portland, OR 97205
503-242-0900   fax 503-242-3822   info@cascadepolicy.org   *www.cascadepolicy.org*

Cascade Policy Institute was founded in January 1991 as a non-profit research and educational organization to focus on Oregon state and local issues. The Institute's mission is to explore and advance public policy alternatives that foster individual liberty, personal responsibility, and economic opportunity. *Tax Status:* 501(c)(3).

Issues: Education reform; Urban growth; Transit; Social Security privatization; Health care reform.

CATO INSTITUTE

Edward H. Crane, President
1000 Massachusetts Avenue, N.W., Washington, DC 20001
202-842-0200   fax 202-842-3490   cato@cato.org   *www.cato.org*

Cato Institute is a public policy research organization dedicated to the traditional American principles of individual liberty, limited government, free markets, and peace. The Institute publishes *Regulation* Magazine, *Cato Journal, Cato Policy Report,* and a wide variety of books and policy studies covering the whole range of public policy issues. Cato holds frequent policy conferences in Washington as well as seminars around the United States and in London, Mexico City, Moscow, and Shanghai. In order to maintain its independence, the Institute accepts no government funding, but receives support from foundations, corporations, and more than 12,000 individual sponsors. *Tax Status:* 501(c)(3).

Issues: Social Security privatization; Fundamental tax reform; Limited constitutional government; Free trade; Global warming; Term limits.

CENTER FOR THE AMERICAN FOUNDING

Dr. Balint Vazsonyi, Director
1311 Dolley Madison Boulevard, Suite 2A, McLean, VA 22101
703-556-6595   fax 703-556-6875   info@founding.org   *www.founding.org*

The Center for the American Founding is sponsored by the non-profit Potomac Foundation and advocates and practices discussion of national issues as they relate to America's founding principles. For continued success, the Center believes the Nation should return to the rule of law, individual rights, security of property, and the same American identity for all its citizens. *Tax Status:* 501(c)(3).

Issues: The Constitution; Culture wars; Anti-Americanism; The demographic assault; Western civilization; Rights versus entitlements.

CENTER FOR ARIZONA POLICY

Len Munsil, President and General Counsel
11000 North Scottsdale Road, Suite 120, Scottsdale, AZ 85254
480-922-3101   fax 480-922-9785   info@azpolicy.org   *www.azpolicy.org*

The mission of the Center for Arizona Policy is to strengthen the family by educating Arizonans on public policy issues that impact the family and equipping them to promote traditional values. *Tax Status:* 501(c)(3).

Issues: Marriage; Abortion; Pornography; Education; Homosexuality; Gambling.

THE CENTER FOR BIOETHICS AND HUMAN DIGNITY

Dr. John F. Kilner, President
2065 Half Day Road, Bannockburn, IL 60015
847-317-8180   fax 847-317-8153   cbhd@cbhd.org   *www.cbhd.org*

The Center for Bioethics and Human Dignity exists to help individuals and organizations address the pressing bioethical challenges of our day, including managed care, end-of-life treatment, genetic intervention, euthanasia and suicide, reproductive technologies, and alternative medicine. The Center affirms human dignity through bioethics by providing educational opportunities, renewing health care professionalism, encouraging ethical scientific research, informing public policy, and equipping the world to uphold the God-given dignity of human beings. *Tax Status:* 501(c)(3).

Issues: Biotechnology; Clinical/bedside ethics in health care; Genetics; End-of-life/palliative care; Reproductive technologies; Cloning/stem cell research.

CENTER FOR THE DEFENSE OF FREE ENTERPRISE

Alan Gottlieb, President
12500 N.E. Tenth Place, Bellevue, WA 98005
425-455-5038   fax 425-451-3959   website@cdfe.org   *www.cdfe.org*

The Center for the Defense of Free Enterprise was established so that Americans who understood and valued the free enterprise system could contribute to the defense and promotion of the economic system that made America the most prosperous nation on the planet. *Tax Status:* 501(c)(3).

Issues: Wise use of the environment; Environmental movement accountability; Exposing over-regulation; Lowering the tax burden; Publishing free enterprise materials; Research on economic issues.

CENTER FOR ECONOMIC AND POLICY EDUCATION

Dr. Gary Quinlivan, Executive Director
Saint Vincent College, 300 Fraser Purchase Road, Latrobe, PA 15650-2690
724-537-4597   fax 724-537-4599   cepe@stvincent.edu   *www.stvincent.edu/cepe/*

The mission of the Center for Economic and Policy Education is to explore major public policy issues within the context of a free political economy and American civil tradition and to provide enhanced educational opportunities and policy analysis for students, faculty, and the general public. *Tax Status:* 501(c)(3).

Issues: Free trade; Privatization; Free-market solutions to environmental problems; Founding Fathers; Constitutional issues; Postmodernism and the culture wars.

CENTER FOR EDUCATION REFORM

Jeanne Allen, President
1001 Connecticut Avenue, N.W., Suite 204, Washington, DC 20036
202-822-9000   fax 202-822-5077   cer@edreform.com   *www.edreform.com*

The Center for Education Reform is an independent, national, non-profit educational organization providing support and guidance to individuals nationwide who are working to bring fundamental reforms to their schools. CER's mission is to promote educational excellence and to expand access and accountability in America's schools. *Tax Status:* 501(c)(3).

Issues: School choice; Charter schools; Accountability, standards and testing.

CENTER FOR EQUAL OPPORTUNITY

Linda Chavez, President
1400 Pidgeon Hill Drive, Suite 500, Sterling, VA 20165
703-421-5443   fax 703-421-6401   comment@ceousa.org   *www.ceousa.org*

The Center for Equal Opportunity conducts research and education on issues related to race, ethnicity, and assimilation. *Tax Status:* 501(c)(3).

Issues: Civil rights; Bilingual education; Immigration; Affirmative action.

CENTER FOR FREEDOM AND PROSPERITY

Andrew F. Quinlan, President and CEO
6023 Shaffer Drive, Alexandria, VA 22310
202-285-0244   fax 208-728-9639   quinlan@freedomandprosperity.org

The Center for Freedom and Prosperity seeks to promote economic prosperity by advocating competitive markets and limited government. It strives to: Lower tax burdens and create a more simple and fair tax code; promote economic competition and the entrepreneurial spirit; improve the retirement security of seniors by promoting a fiscally stable system of personal savings accounts; reduce the size of government and return it to the Constitutional limits put forth by the Founding Fathers; protect financial and personal privacy; protect the right to private property; protect the right to free association; encourage free and open trade; advocate global free market principles; and, defend national sovereignty. The Center will accomplish these goals by educating the American people and its elected representatives.

Issues: Tax reform and competition; Free trade and global competition; Rights to privacy, property and free association.

CENTER FOR IMMIGRATION STUDIES

Mark Krikorian, Executive Director
1522 K Street, N.W., Suite 820, Washington, DC 20005
202-466-8185   fax 202-466-8076   center@cis.org   *www.cis.org*

The Center for Immigration Studies is an independent, non-partisan, non-profit research organization founded in 1985. It is the nation's only think tank devoted exclusively to research and policy analysis of the economic, social, demographic, fiscal, and other impacts of immigration on the United States. It is the Center's mission to expand the base of public knowledge and understanding of the need for an immigration policy that gives first concern to the broad national interest. The Center is animated by a pro-immigrant, low-immigration vision which seeks fewer immigrants but a warmer welcome for those admitted. *Tax Status:* 501(c)(3).

CENTER FOR INDIVIDUAL RIGHTS

Terence J. Pell, Chief Executive Officer
1233 20th Street, N.W., Suite 300, Washington, DC 20036
202-833-8400   fax 202-833-8410   cir@mail.wdn.com   *www.cir-usa.org*

The Center for Individual Rights is a non-profit public interest law firm. CIR's mission is to advance a broad, civil libertarian conception of individual rights against intrusive bureaucracies, meddlesome interest groups, and statist ideologues and activists. CIR believes that the principal purpose of the law, and especially of the Constitution, is to restrain these forces. It pursues this mission through the direct litigation of precedent-setting cases, primarily in federal court, concentrating on areas of the law where individual rights are particularly at risk – freedom of speech, civil rights, and sexual harassment law. *Tax Status:* 501(c)(3).

Issues: Ending racial preferences; Free speech; Political correctness in higher education; Disparate treatment of religious groups; Unconstitutionality of hate crime laws; Extending *Hopwood* ruling to other states.

CENTER FOR INTERNATIONAL PRIVATE ENTERPRISE

John Sullivan, Executive Director
1155 15th Street, N.W., Suite 700, Washington, DC 20005
202-721-9200   fax 202-721-9250   cipe@cipe.org   *www.cipe.org*

The Center for International Private Enterprise's mission is the building and strengthening of democracy around the globe through the promotion of private enterprise, market-oriented reform, and legal, regulatory, and business institutions. *Tax Status:* 501(c)(3).

Issues: Legal and regulatory reform; Continuing training initiatives; Institution building; Anti-corruption; Corporate governance and business ethics; Women entrepreneurs.

CENTER FOR INTERNATIONAL RELATIONS

Dr. Lee Edwards, President
1513 16th Street, N.W., Washington, DC 20036
703-971-1490   fax 202-269-9353

The Center for International Relations has a dual mission: To encourage studies, seminars, and other educational projects about communism and the Cold War and to serve as a clearinghouse for information about free-market-oriented think tanks around the world. CIR's number one priority at present is to help the Victims of Communism Memorial Foundation to design, construct, and operate an international memorial in Washington, D.C. to the victims of communism. *Tax Status:* 501(c)(3).

Issues: Victims of Communism Memorial Foundation.

CENTER FOR LAW AND RELIGIOUS FREEDOM

Gregory S. Baylor, Director
4208 Evergreen Lane, Suite 222, Annandale, VA 22003
703-642-1070   fax 703-642-1075   clrf@clsnet.org   *www.clsnet.org*

The Center for Law and Religious Freedom (CLRF) has been a respected voice in the First Amendment arena since 1975. The Center's primary mission is to defend and advance the religious freedom of all Americans. In 1993, the Center expanded its mission to include defending the sanctity of human life from conception to natural death. The Center pursues its mission through legislative advocacy, "test case" litigation, friend-of-the-court briefs, and providing information to CLS members and the general public. *Tax Status:* 501(c)(3).

CENTER FOR LONG-TERM CARE FINANCING

Stephen Moses, President
2212 Queen Anne Avenue North, Suite 110, Seattle, WA 98109
206-283-7036   fax 206-283-6536

The Center for LTC Financing is a charitable, non-profit organization, dedicated to ensuring quality long-term care for all Americans by promoting public policy that targets scarce public resources to the neediest, while encouraging people who are young, healthy and affluent enough, to take responsibility for themselves. *Tax Status:* 501(c)(3).

CENTER FOR MARKET-BASED EDUCATION, INC.

Judy Alger, President
P. O. Box 373, Rumney, NH 03266-0373
603-786-9562   fax 603-786-9463   choiceforchildren@juno.com
www.choiceforchildrennh.org

The Center for Market-Based Education seeks to enable qualified students to attend independent schools selected by their parents. It provides scholarship assistance and serves as a resource center through fundraising from business and community sources. The Center's plan will effect a relationship with selected independent schools in New Hampshire and assist those schools in choosing students for opportunity scholarships based upon financial need. *Tax Status:* 501(c)(3).

Issues: School choice; Business and education partnerships.

CENTER FOR MEDIA AND PUBLIC AFFAIRS

Dr. S. Robert Lichter, President
2100 L Street, N.W., Suite 300, Washington, DC 20037
202-223-2942   fax 202-872-4014   cmpamm@aol.com   *www.cmpa.com*

The Center for Media and Public Affairs is a non-partisan, non-profit research and educational organization which conducts scientific studies of news and entertainment media. CMPA seeks to provide an empirical basis for ongoing debates over media fairness and impact through well-documented, timely, and readable studies of media content. Its primary research tool is content analysis, which is applied both to news coverage and to the information content of entertainment messages. CMPA also conducts surveys to illuminate the media's role in American society. *Tax Status:* 501(c)(3).

Issues: Violence in entertainment media; Coverage of science, health, and technology issues; Politics and elections.

CENTER FOR MILITARY READINESS

Elaine Donnelly, President
P. O. Box 51600, Livonia, MI 48151
734-464-9430   fax 734-464-6678   info@cmrlink.org   *www.cmrlink.org*

The Center for Military Readiness is an independent public policy research and education organization that examines military personnel issues. CMR publishes *CMR Notes* and opinion articles that analyze the consequences of unwise social engineering; provides testimony and research materials to Congress, Executive Branch agencies, and the media; and organizes policy conferences. CMR is a unique alliance of civilian, active duty and retired military people in all 50 states, which promotes high standards and excellence in all forms of military training. CMR supports women in the military, but opposes combat assignments and gender-related policies that erode morale and overall readiness. *Tax Status:* 501(c)(3).

Issues: Co-ed basic training; International agreements affecting U.S. troops; Women in combat: land, sea, and air; Ongoing efforts to accommodate homosexuals in the military; Sexual misconduct and the culture of the military; Family concerns and pregnancy effects on readiness.

CENTER FOR POLICY AND LEGAL STUDIES

Bruce Yandle, Director
Clemson University, 201 Sirrine Hall, Clemson, SC 29634
864-656-1346   fax 864-646-4532   yandle@clemson.edu
http://business.clemson.edu/cpls/

The Center for Policy and Legal Studies applies free-market principles to public policy questions. Bringing together students and faculty in economics, agricultural economics, engineering, and other disciplines, the Center identifies issues, obtains private support, and produces reports and books based on student and faculty research. The Center also sponsors policy conferences and speakers.

Issues: Environmental policy; Education and economic growth; Trade and antitrust policy; Economics of freedom; Analysis of the South Carolina economy.

CENTER FOR POLICY RESEARCH OF NEW JERSEY

Gregg M. Edwards, President
P. O. Box 12, Florham Park, NJ 07932
609-273-6333   fax 973-966-6897   gmedwards@att.net

Established in 2002, the Center for Policy Research of New Jersey is the State's first and only independent research and educational organization dedicated to developing and promoting public policies founded on the principles of free markets, limited government, individual initiative and community engagement. CPRNJ addresses issues facing New Jersey's state and local government, including taxation, public spending, education, economic development, land use, and transportation. CPRNJ furthers its purpose through the production of detailed policy proposals, the aggressive advocacy of those proposals, and the sponsorship of forums and seminars. *Tax Status:* 501(c)(3).

Issues: Taxation; Government spending; Education; Economic growth; Land use; Transportation.

CENTER FOR PUBLIC JUSTICE

Dr. James W. Skillen, President
2444 Solomons Island Road, Suite 201, Annapolis, MD 21401
410-571-6300   fax 410-571-6365   inquiries@cpjustice.org   *www.cpjustice.org*

The Center for Public Justice seeks to advance justice in government and political life. It carries out its mission by: Articulating a Christian political philosophy; providing educational resources for leadership development; conducting political research and developing policy proposals; and building coalitions with other groups for public influence. ***Tax Status:*** 501(c)(3).

Issues: Relation of government to civil society; Welfare reform; School choice; Religious liberty; Electoral reform; International justice.

CENTER FOR RENEWAL

Barbara Elliott, President
9525 Katy Freeway, Suite 303, Houston, TX 77024
713-984-1343   fax 713-984-0409   belliott@centerforrenewal.org
www.centerforrenewal.org

The Center for Renewal is a non-profit organization whose mission is to empower Christ-centered ministries that transform lives by encouraging effective compassion and by connecting resources to needs. Its goals are to: Enhance capacity and competence in life-changing faith-based organizations; educate compassionate leaders in giving wisely, and connect them to social entrepreneurs on the front line of service; and communicate the vision through the success stories of faith-based efforts in speeches, articles, radio and television broadcasts, and on the Internet.

CENTER FOR SECURITY POLICY

Frank J. Gaffney, Jr., Director
1920 L Street, N.W., Suite 210, Washington, DC 20036
202-835-9077   fax 202-835-9066   info@security-policy.org   *www.security-policy.org*

The Center for Security Policy exists to stimulate and inform the national and international debate about all aspects of security policy, notably those bearing on the foreign, defense, economic, financial, and technology interests of the U.S. CSP contributes to this debate by the rapid preparation and real-time dissemination of analyses and policy recommendations via computerized fax, published articles, and electronic media. The Center's principal audience is the U.S. security policy-making community, corresponding organizations in key foreign governments, the press (domestic and foreign), the global business and financial community, and interested individuals in the public at large. ***Tax Status:*** 501(c)(3).

Issues: Homeland security/ballistic missile defense; Arms control and global treaties; Hollowing out of U.S. military; Middle East peace process; NATO expansion; Pacific Rim.

CENTER FOR STRATEGIC AND INTERNATIONAL STUDIES

Dr. John J. Hamre, President and CEO
1800 K Street, N.W., Washington, DC 20006
202-887-0200   fax 202-775-3199   jvondra@csis.org   *www.csis.org*

Founded in 1962, the Center for Strategic and International Studies is a non-partisan public policy research institution dedicated to analysis and policy impact. With a staff of 180, CSIS experts generate strategic analysis in key functional areas, such as international finance and trade, and U.S. domestic, economic, foreign, and national security policies. The Center also convenes government, private-sector, and academic leaders from around the world to examine an array of issues and provide concrete action proposals. ***Tax Status:*** 501(c)(3).

Issues: National and international security; Governance for the global age; Trade, technology and energy.

CENTER FOR THE STUDY OF POPULAR CULTURE

David Horowitz, President
9911 West Pico Boulevard, Suite 1290, Los Angeles, CA 90035
323-556-2550   dhorowitz@cspc.org   *www.cspc.org*

The Center for the Study of Popular Culture is a non-profit organization dedicated to strengthening the foundations of a free society. CSPC's flagship publication is the webzine, FrontPageMagazine.com. *Tax Status:* 501(c)(3).

Issues: Political correctness; The culture war; The welfare state; Bilingualism; Popular culture and Hollywood.

CENTER FOR THE AMERICAN IDEA

W. Winston Elliott, III, President
9525 Katy Freeway, Suite 303, Houston, TX 77024
713-984-1343   fax 713-984-0409   info@americanidea.org   *www.americanidea.org*

The Center for the American Idea is a non-profit educational organization founded in 1976 and supported by foundations, businesses and individuals. The Center's programs assist teachers as they educate their students in the principles of American Civilization, including liberty, private property, the rule of law, constitutionally limited government and an enduring moral order. *Tax Status:* 501(c)(3).

CENTER FOR THE STUDY OF COMPASSIONATE CONSERVATISM

Michael B. Barkey, President
521 Bayberry Point Drive, N.W., Suite A, Grand Rapids, MI 49544
616-453-2019   info@compassionateconservative.cc

The mission of the Center for the Study of Compassionate Conservatism is to advance a coherent, principled conservative governing philosophy that will serve as a true bridge from the era of big government to a new era in which there is a full and healthy trust in people to govern themselves. The compassionate conservative movement must be fully equipped to defend the compassion and morality of government policies that show due respect for the individual, civil society, and the marketplace. To that end, the Center works to promote pro-active, people-centered approaches to public policy by providing a forum for compassionate conservative thinkers who recognize a real, but limited, role for government in furthering the common good.

THE CENTER FOR THE STUDY OF TAXATION

Patricia M. Soldano, President
3090 Bristol Street, Suite 250, Costa Mesa, CA 92626
714-641-8067   fax 714-641-3128   soldano@center4studytax.com
www.center4studytax.com

The Center for the Study of Taxation was formed in 1992 by a group of families and family-owned enterprises concerned with the impact of transfer taxes. It is dedicated to preserving a healthy economic and tax climate that will be beneficial to all Americans. Concentrating on the gift, estate and generation-skipping taxes, CST analyzes and reports on the economic impact of legislative and administrative initiatives, provides information about potentially adverse or beneficial changes in law, and supports research on economic and tax subjects of interest and concern to individuals, families, and family businesses. *Tax Status:* 501(c)(6).

Issues: Estate, gift and generation-skipping taxes.

CENTER FOR THE STUDY OF THE ENVIRONMENT

Dr. Daniel B. Botkin, President and Founder
P. O. Box 30700, Santa Barbara, CA 93130
805-452-3988   fax 805-569-9170   info@naturestudy.org

The Center for the Study of the Environment is a private not-for-profit organization, providing information, identification, analysis and optimal solutions to environmental problems. CSE projects are conducted on global, regional and local scales.

CENTER OF THE AMERICAN EXPERIMENT

Dr. Mitchell Pearlstein, President
12 South 6th Street, Suite 1024, Minneapolis, MN 55402
612-338-3605   fax 612-338-3621   amexp@amexp.org   *www.amexp.org*

Center of the American Experiment opened its doors in 1990 as a non-partisan, tax-exempt public policy and educational institution. CAE brings conservative and alternative ideas to bear on difficult problems facing Minnesota and the nation. *Tax Status:* 501(c)(3).

Issues: Education reform; Government reform; Fatherlessness; Taxes; Marriage.

CENTRE FOR NEW BLACK LEADERSHIP

Phyllis Berry Myers, President and CEO
202 G Street, N.E., Washington, DC 20002
202-546-9505   fax 202-546-9506   cnbl@aol.com   *www.cnbl.org*

The Centre for New Black Leadership exists to encourage the formulation of public policies that enhance the ability of individuals and communities to develop market-oriented, community-based approaches to solving economic and social problems. CNBL is a *thinking* and *doing* center. It is a non-partisan, not-for-profit, public policy research and advocacy organization. Its mission is to develop leaders, shape public policy, and serve people and their communities. *Tax Status:* 501(c)(3).

Issues: Economic development and minority franchising opportunities; Government and faith-based institutions; Emerging leaders in the black community; Health care; Social Security reform; Education, charter schools and publicly financed education vouchers.

CHILDREN FIRST AMERICA

John Kirtley, President and CEO
901 McClain Road, Suite 802, P. O. Box 330, Bentonville, AR 72712
501-273-6957   fax 501-273-9362   info@childrenfirstamerica.org
www.childrenfirstamerica.org

Children First America's mission is to promote parental choice in education through private tuition grants and tax funded options, giving all families the power to choose the K-12 school that best fulfills the hopes and dreams they have for their children. *Tax Status:* 501(c)(3).

Issues: New private voucher programs; Popularizing school choice; Development of citizen grass-roots educational organizations.

CHILDREN FIRST TENNESSEE

Priscilla Caine, President
102 Walnut Street, Chattanooga, TN 37403
423-756-0410   fax 423-756-8250   priscilla@childrenfirsttn.org   *www.childrenfirsttn.org*

Children First Tennessee is an urban education initiative designed to equalize educational opportunities for Hamilton County elementary school students by offering low income families private educational options normally denied them because of costs; recruit "at-risk" children into most appropriate schools; and encourage the start of new, private school initiatives in low-income neighborhoods. Children First Tennessee operates by accumulating private gifts from individuals, corporations, and foundations.

Issues: Education scholarships and school choice.

CHILDREN FIRST UTAH

Carolyn Sharette, Executive Director
455 East South Temple, Salt Lake City, UT 84111
801-363-0946   fax 801-524-2374   info@childrenfirstutah.org   *www.childrenfirstutah.org*

The mission of Children First Utah is to maximize educational opportunity for children by offering tuition assistance for needy families and promoting a diverse and competitive educational environment. CFU believes that all children, regardless of economic circumstances, deserve access to educational opportunities and that parents deserve the right to choose among the broadest possible range of educational alternatives. *Tax Status:* 501(c)(3).

Issues: Private vouchers; School choice.

CHILDREN'S EDUCATION FUND

Richard H. Collins, Founder and Chairman
P. O. Box 225748, Dallas, TX 75222-5718
972-298-1811   fax 972-572-1515   rhcoll@yahoo.com   *www.todayfoundation.org*

The Children's Education Fund offers scholarships to Dallas-area students from low-income families to use toward tuition to the schools of their choice. CEF is part of the Today Foundation, a nonprofit organization committed to raising the public's and policy makers' awareness of education, taxation and criminal justice issues. *Tax Status:* 501(c)(3).

Issues: Educate the public about school choice; Provide scholarships and technology to disadvantaged students.

CHRISTIAN CIVIC LEAGUE OF MAINE

Michael S. Heath, Executive Director
P. O. Box 5459, Augusta, ME 04332
207-622-7634   fax 207-621-0035   email@cclmaine.org   *www.cclmaine.org*

Christian Civic League of Maine exists for the purpose of bringing a Christian influence to the public square through effectively working with public policymakers and members by providing accurate, timely, and persuasive information from a Biblical perspective. *Tax Status:* 501(c)(4).

Issues: Family policy; Educational choice; Human sexuality; Gambling; Sanctity of life issues.

CHRISTIAN COALITION OF AMERICA

Roberta Combs, President
499 South Capitol Street, S.W., Suite 615, Washington, DC 20003
202-479-6900   fax 202-479-4260   coalition@cc.org   *www.cc.org*

The Christian Coalition is a non-profit, grassroots citizen organization. Its mission is to represent the Christian point of view before local councils, state legislatures, and Congress; to proclaim its values in the public arena and in the media; to train leaders for effective social and political action; and to protest religious discrimination and anti-Christian bigotry. *Tax Status:* 501(c)(4).

Issues: Religious persecution; American community renewal; Education reform; Religious freedom amendment; Family tax relief; Banning partial-birth abortion.

CHRISTIAN EDUCATORS ASSOCIATION INTERNATIONAL

Forrest L. Turpen, Executive Director
P. O. Box 41300, Pasadena, CA 91114
626-798-1124   fax 626-798-2346   info@ceai.org   *www.ceai.org*

CEAI's mission is to encourage, equip and empower Christian educators in public and private schools. In pursuit of this mission, CEAI focuses on proclaiming God's Word as true wisdom and knowledge, portraying teaching as a God-given calling, promoting educational excellence, preserving our Judeo-Christian heritage and values, along with providing a forum on educational issues from a Christian world view. *Tax Status:* 501(c)(3).

Issues: Churches adopting public schools; Increasing quality and quantity of teachers; Character education; Rights of religious persons in public education; Parental control of children's education; Rights of teachers vs. unions.

CHRISTIAN LEGAL SOCIETY

Samuel Casey, Executive Director
4208 Evergreen Lane, Suite 222, Annandale, VA 22003
703-642-1070   fax 703-642-1075   clshq@clsnet.org   *www.christianlegalsociety.org*

Christian Legal Society is a national grassroots network of more than 3,500 Christian lawyers and law students. Among its activities, CLS advocates voluntary or low-fee legal assistance for the needy through its Public Ministries; defends religious freedom and the sanctity of innocent human life in judicial and legislative forums through its Center for Law and Religious Freedom; and operates a Law Student Ministry for more than 120,000 law students on more than 175 law school campuses. *Tax Status:* 501(c)(3).

Issues: Religious accommodation in the workplace; Charitable choice in welfare reform; International religious persecution; Promoting stem cell research that does not destroy embryos; Opposing physician-assisted suicide; Ban on partial-birth abortion.

CITIZENS AGAINST GOVERNMENT WASTE

Thomas A. Schatz, President
1900 M Street, N.W., Suite 500, Washington, DC 20036
202-467-5300   fax 202-467-4253   grassroots@cagw.org   *www.cagw.org*

Citizens Against Government Waste educates Americans about waste, mismanagement, and inefficiency in the federal government. *Tax Status:* 501(c)(3).

Issues: Corporate welfare; Agriculture; Internal Revenue Service; Government waste; Medicare; Procurement reform.

CITIZENS AGAINST HIGHER TAXES

James H. Broussard, Chairman
P. O. Box 343, Hershey, PA 17033
717-867-5491   fax 717-867-6124   caht@aol.com

Citizens Against Higher Taxes is a statewide grassroots organization working for taxpayers' rights, limited government, and the market economy in Pennsylvania. It cooperates with some 250 local taxpayer groups to elect pro-taxpayer and pro-reform school boards. *Tax Status:* 501(c)(4).

Issues: Cutting taxes; Limiting government spending; Initiative and Referendum; Controlling the unchecked power of the teachers' union; Electing pro-taxpayer candidates through our state PAC.

CITIZENS FOR A SOUND ECONOMY

Paul Beckner, President
1900 M Street, N.W., Suite 500, Washington, DC 20036
202-783-3870   fax 202-783-4687   cse@cse.org   *www.cse.org*

Citizens for a Sound Economy is a grassroots organization dedicated to free markets and limited government and to the highest level of personal involvement in public policy activism. Through recruitment, training, and political participation, CSE seeks to improve the well-being of American consumers through common-sense economic policies. CSE's army of self-identified activists endeavors to set the agenda on federal, state, and local issues. It continually recruits, educates, and enables new members to participate effectively in public policy debates – all to fight for free-market solutions to public policy issues. *Tax Status:* 501(c)(4).

Issues: Taxation/tax reform; Federal budget; Entitlement reform; Environmental regulation; Health care reform; International trade.

CITIZENS FOR A SOUND ECONOMY FOUNDATION

Paul Beckner, President
1900 M Street, N.W., Suite 500, Washington, DC 20036
202-783-3870   fax 202-783-4687   cse@cse.org   *www.cse.org*

Citizens for a Sound Economy Foundation provides grassroots citizens with clear, concise, and timely information on key economic issues. By making economic issues accessible to interested citizens, CSE Foundation fosters a more active and meaningful dialogue between elected officials and their constituents. *Tax Status:* 501(c)(3).

Issues: Tax reform; Civil justice; Education reform; Technology policy; Environmental reform; Regulatory reform.

CITIZENS FOR LAW AND ORDER

Bob Nicholas, President
P. O. Box 1291, Sonoma, CA 95476
707-938-3778   fax 707-938-8962

Founded in 1970, Citizens for Law and Order is a California-based crime victims organization. Among its activities, the organization analyzes, from a criminal justice perspective, every judicial race and district attorneys race in the state. CLO offers assistance to organizations in other states that are interested in establishing a judicial monitoring project. *Tax Status:* 501(c)(4).

Issues: Criminal justice statistics; Judicial monitoring.

CITIZENS' COUNCIL ON HEALTH CARE

Twila Brase, R.N., President
1954 University Avenue West, Suite 8, St. Paul, MN 55104
651-646-8935   fax 651-646-0100   info@cchconline.org   *www.cchconline.org*

To facilitate public participation in the health care debate by sharing policy analysis, information, and alternatives, CCHC is a citizen's resource for designing the future of health care. CCHC exists to prevent health care rationing by enabling individual control of health care decisions through free-market principles. *Tax Status:* 501(c)(3).

Issues: Impact of managed care; Provider taxes; Medical confidentiality; Growth of government health care; Empowerment of public health departments; Consumer-driven health care.

CLAREMONT INSTITUTE

Brian Kennedy, President
250 West First Street, Suite 330, Claremont, CA 91711
909-621-6825   fax 909-626-8724   info@claremont.org   *www.claremont.org*

The mission of the Claremont Institute is to restore the principles of the American Founding to their rightful, preeminent authority in our national life. The Claremont Institute finds the answers to America's problems in the principles on which our nation was founded. These principles are expressed most eloquently in the Declaration of Independence, which proclaims that "all men are created equal and are endowed by their Creator with certain inalienable rights...." To recover the Founding principles in our political life means recovering a limited and accountable government that respects private property, promotes stable family life and maintains a strong defense. Through its books, policy briefings, conferences and seminars, as well as the World Wide Web, the Institute engages Americans in an informed discussion of the principles and policies necessary to rebuild our civic institutions. *Tax Status:* 501(c)(3).

Issues: Ballistic missile defense; The American Founding; Family and culture; Civil rights/racial preferences.

CNSNEWS.COM

Scott Hogenson, Executive Editor
325 South Patrick Street, Alexandria, VA 22314
877-267-6397   fax 703-683-7045   shogenson@cnsnews.com   *www.cnsnews.com*

CNSNews.com is an online primary news source for citizens, news organizations and broadcasters, who put a higher premium on balance than spin, and serves as an effort to provide an alternative news source which looks for those stories that are too often ignored or under-reported. It endeavors to fairly present all legitimate sides of a story and debunk popular, albeit incorrect, myths about cultural and policy issues. CNSNews.com copy may be used, reproduced, rebroadcast and/or republished by any private or public news organization at no cost, but with appropriate editorial credit assigned as a professional courtesy. *Tax Status:* 501(c)(3).

Issues: Politics; Culture; World Affairs; General interest news.

COALITION ON URBAN RENEWAL & EDUCATION (CURE)

Star Parker, President
126 C Street, N.W., Washington, DC 20001
202-479-2873   fax 202-783-9376   info@urbancure.org   *www.urbancure.org*

The Coalition on Urban Renewal and Education is a non-profit research foundation which seeks a dialogue on how social policies impact America's inner cities and the poor. CURE provides a conservative voice in the national debate on critical social policy issues. Its mission is to strengthen the moral culture of America and to rebuild the black family. Its objective is to build better race relations and enhance moral stability in America. CURE sponsors national workshops for women leaving welfare, a campus lecture series, and media commentary. *Tax Status:* 501(c)(3).

Issues: Welfare; Social Security and retirement; Poverty and dependency.

COALITIONS FOR AMERICA

Eric Licht, President
717 Second Street, N.E., Washington, DC 20002
202-546-3000   fax 202-547-0392

Coalitions for America is a conservative, pro-business lobbying organization that seeks to promote sound fiscal policies, traditional values, and a strong national defense. *Tax Status:* 501(c)(4).

COMMITTEE FOR A CONSTRUCTIVE TOMORROW

David Rothbard, President
P. O. Box 65722, Washington, DC 20035
202-429-2737   fax 301-858-0944   info@cfact.org   *www.cfact.org*

Founded in 1985, the Committee For A Constructive Tomorrow was created to offer a new voice on consumer and environmental issues. The Committee boldly proclaims that the Western values of competition, progress, freedom, and stewardship can and do offer the best hope for protecting not only the earth and its wildlife, but even more importantly, its people. CFACT works to promote free-market and safe technological solutions to such growing concerns as waste-management, food production and processing, electrical generation, air and water quality, wildlife protection and much more. The Committee produces a national radio commentary called ''Just the Facts'' that is heard daily on some 300 stations across the country. *Tax Status:* 501(c)(3).

Issues: Global warming; Property rights; Religion and the environment; Waste management; Population issues; Pesticides and toxins.

COMMITTEE FOR MONETARY RESEARCH AND EDUCATION

Elizabeth Currier, President
10004 Greenwood Court, Charlotte, NC 28215
704-598-3717   fax 704-599-7036   cmre@worldnet.att.net   *www.cmre.org*

The Committee for Monetary Research and Education is engaged in education on currency markets and the principles of sound money. To fulfill its purpose, CMRE conducts meetings and publishes educational materials. Committee meetings cover such issues as prospects for inflation or deflation; direction of the bond, stock, and currency markets; and conditions in the banking industry and markets around the world. *Tax Status:* 501(c)(3).

Issues: Currencies; International credits; Euro development; Role of the dollar in international markets; Markets inflation/deflation; Federal Reserve System/banking.

THE COMMONWEALTH FOUNDATION

Matthew J. Brouillette, President
225 State Street, Suite 302, Harrisburg, PA 17101
717-671-1901   fax 717-671-1905   info@commonwealthfoundation.org
www.commonwealthfoundation.org

The mission of The Commonwealth Foundation is to improve the quality of life for all Pennsylvanians by advancing public policies based on the principles of limited government, economic freedom, and individual responsibility. *Tax Status:* 501(c)(3).

Issues: Tax and fiscal policy; Education policy; Labor policy; Health care policy; Environmental policy; Business climate policy.

COMPETITIVE ENTERPRISE INSTITUTE

Fred L. Smith, Jr., President
1001 Connecticut Avenue, N.W., Suite 1250, Washington, DC 20036
202-331-1010   fax 202-331-0640   info@cei.org   *www.cei.org*

The Competitive Enterprise Institute is a non-profit public policy group committed to advancing the principles of free enterprise and limited government. CEI believes that consumers are best helped not by government regulation but by being allowed to make their own choices in a free marketplace. CEI produces groundbreaking research on regulatory issues, promotes its ideas and solutions to the public and the media, and works with policymakers to ensure an effective and powerful voice for economic freedom. *Tax Status:* 501(c)(3).

Issues: Global warming and energy use; Safety issues: automobile, food and drug; Chemical risk; Internet and e-commerce; Anti-trust; Intellectual property rights.

CONCERNED WOMEN FOR AMERICA

Beverly LaHaye, Chairman
1015 15th Street, N.W., Suite 1100, Washington, DC 20005
202-488-7000   fax 202-488-0806   mail@cwfa.org   *www.cwfa.org*

The mission of Concerned Women for America is to protect and promote Biblical values among all citizens – first through prayer, then education, and finally by influencing our society – thereby reversing the decline in moral values in our nation. *Tax Status:* 501(c)(3).

Issues: Sanctity of life; Religious freedom; Defense of the family; Pornography; Education; National sovereignty.

THE CONGRESSIONAL INSTITUTE

Jerome F. Climer, President
401 Wythe Street, Suite 103, Alexandria, VA 22314
202-547-4600   fax 202-547-3556   change_leader@conginst.org   *www.conginst.org*

Since 1987, the Congressional Institute has been studying the Congress through private- and public-sector conferences, strategic-planning sessions for Members and staff, policy research, and briefings for policymakers about the Government Performance and Results Act (PL 103-62) and other process reform ideas. The Institute's web site provides information on how to manage change in the public sector and other useful information. *Tax Status:* 501(c)(4).

Issues: Governance; Taxes; Health care; Environment; Trade; Technology.

THE CONSERVATIVE CAUCUS, INC.

Howard Phillips, Chairman
450 Maple Avenue East, Vienna, VA 22180
703-938-9626   fax 703-281-4108   corndorf@cais.com   *www.conservativeusa.org*

The Conservative Caucus, Inc. strives to safeguard our God-given rights to life, liberty, and property – by requiring the Federal government to adhere to the limitations and fulfill the obligations specified in the U.S. Constitution. *Tax Status:* 501(c)(4).

Issues: China and MFN; Panama/Panama Canal; Socialized medicine; Revenue tariff in lieu of income tax; Defunding the Left; Withdrawal from WTO, NAFTA, NATO, and UN.

CONSUMER ALERT

Frances Smith, Executive Director
1001 Connecticut Avenue, N.W., Suite 1128, Washington, DC 20036
202-467-5809   fax 202-467-5814   info@consumeralert.org   *www.consumeralert.org*

Consumer Alert's mission is to enhance understanding and appreciation of the consumer benefits of a market economy so that individuals and policymakers rely more on private, rather than government, approaches to consumer concerns. *Tax Status:* 501(c)(3).

Issues: Food safety; Finance/banking/e-commerce; Global climate change proposals; Trade; Agriculture subsidies; Auto safety.

CORNERSTONE POLICY RESEARCH

Karen Testerman, President
Two Eagle Square, Suite 400, Concord, NH 03301
603-672-4735   fax 603-673-4836   nhfamily@earthlink.net   *www.nhcornerstone.org*

The mission of Cornerstone Policy Research is to preserve, protect and promote traditional family values in New Hampshire; to provide resources that honor, support and build families; and to positively influence culture and public policy decision-makers through research, education and communication.

COUNCIL FOR CITIZENS AGAINST GOVERNMENT WASTE

Thomas A. Schatz, President
1301 Connecticut Avenue, N.W., Suite 400, Washington, DC 20036
202-467-5300   fax 202-467-4253   grassroots@cagw.org   *www.cagw.org*

The Council serves as the lobbying arm of the Citizens Against Government Waste and tabulates annual Congressional Ratings, which measure the willingness of each member of Congress to fight government waste and reduce the federal deficit. *Tax Status:* 501(c)(4).

Issues: Corporate welfare; Government waste; Procurement reform.

COUNCIL FOR GOVERNMENT REFORM

Charles G. Hardin, President
3124 North Tenth Street, Arlington, VA 22201
703-243-7400   fax 703-243-7403   chardin@govreform.org   *www.govreform.org*

The Council for Government Reform seeks changes which encourage responsible and limited government. Its purpose is to foster a system of government supported by a lower, smaller and less intrusive tax burden and to assure that government lives up to commitments made to its citizens. *Tax Status:* 501(c)(4).

Issues: Social Security reform.

CRIMINAL JUSTICE LEGAL FOUNDATION

Michael D. Rushford, President
2131 L Street, Sacramento, CA 95816
916-446-0345   fax 916-446-1194   cjlf@cjlf.org   *www.cjlf.org*

The Criminal Justice Legal Foundation is a non-profit public interest law organization representing the interests of law-abiding citizens before California and federal courts. The objective of the Foundation's program of scholarly advocacy is to win precedent-setting Appellate and Supreme Court decisions that restore balance between the rights of criminals and the rights of the victims of crime. The Foundation also encourages the development of responsible criminal justice policy through its publication of studies and articles dealing with crime and criminal law. *Tax Status:* 501(c)(3).

Issues: Crime; Criminal law; Sentencing habitual criminals; Habeas Corpus; Death penalty; Anti-terrorism.

DEFENDERS OF PROPERTY RIGHTS

Nancie G. Marzulla, President
1350 Connecticut Avenue, N.W., Suite 410, Washington, DC 20036
202-822-6770   fax 202-822-6774   mail@yourpropertyrights.org
www.yourpropertyrights.org

The mission of Defenders of Property Rights is to ensure that the Fifth Amendment's guarantee be given the full effect of the law that the framers' intended. *Tax Status:* 501(c)(3).

Issues: State and federal environmental laws; Land use and zoning; Constitutional issues; Regulatory agencies; Intellectual property rights.

DISCOVERY INSTITUTE

Bruce Chapman, President
1402 Third Avenue, Suite 400, Seattle, WA 98101
206-292-0401   fax 206-682-5320   discovery@discovery.org   *www.discovery.org*

The Discovery Institute's mission is to make practical a positive vision of the future. The Institute does this by discovering and promoting ideas that can chart the future in the common-sense tradition of representative government, the free market, and individual liberty. This mission is promoted through books, reports, legislative testimony, articles, public conferences, and debates, plus media coverage and Discovery's own publications and web site. *Tax Status:* 501(c)(3).

Issues: Science and culture; Environment; Defense; Technology; Future of law; Regionalism.

DONORSTRUST

Whitney L. Ball, Executive Director
111 North Henry Street, Aleaxandria, VA 22314
703-535-3563   fax 703-535-3564   moreinfo@donorstrust.org   *www.donorstrust.org*

The mission of the Trust is to help alleviate, through education, research, and private initiative, society's most pervasive and radical needs, including those relating to social welfare, health, the environment, economics, governance, foreign relations, and arts and culture; and to encourage philanthropy and individual giving and responsibility, as opposed to governmental involvement, as an answer to society's needs. *Tax Status:* 501(c)(3).

EAGLE FORUM

Phyllis Schlafly, President
316 Pennsylvania Avenue, S.E., Suite 203, Washington, DC 20003
202-544-0353   fax 202-547-6996   eagle@eagleforum.org   *www.eagleforum.org*

The Eagle Forum's mission is to enable conservative and pro-family men and women to participate in the process of self-government and public policymaking so that America will continue to be a land of individual liberty, respect for family integrity, public and private virtue, national independence, constitutional government, and private enterprise. To this end, it trains citizen volunteers on how to affect government policies in Congress, state legislatures, city councils, and school boards; elect candidates at every level; and articulate conservative, pro-family policies through the media.   Eagle Forum functions through its volunteer leaders in every state. *Tax Status:* 501(c)(4).

Issues: Defeating UN treaties and conference implementation; Curbing an activist judiciary; Across-the-board tax cuts; Reducing federal control of education; Defunding wasteful federal programs; Protecting privacy, such as driver, financial, and medical records.

ECONOMIC FREEDOM INSTITUTE

Dr. Edward W. Ryan, Director
Manhattanville College, 2900 Purchase Street, Purchase, NY 10577
914-694-3372   fax 914-694-2386   ryane@mville.edu

EFI provides a forum for the study, analysis, and discussion of the nature of economic freedom and its implications. It fosters the exchange and development of ideas concerning policies and programs of importance in regional, national, and international arenas. Open to a variety of veiwpoints and philosophies, participants in EFI include scholars, corporate executives, and officials from labor unions, non-profit institutions, and various levels of government. EFI's primary audience is Westchester and Fairfield counties.

EDUCATE GIRLS GLOBALLY

Lawrence A. Chickering, President
P. O. Box 29090, San Francisco, CA 94129-0090
415-561-2260   info@educategirls.org   *www.educategirls.org*

The mission of Educate Girls Globally is to act as a catalyst to promote girls primary education in developing countries through community participation to increase enrollment and retention of girls. Educating girls is the best investment a developing country can make to overcome social ills. When girls remain in school, their earnings increase, and they promote important social reforms. EGG's staff is assisted by a variety of consultants, advisors, and partners who bring a wide variety of skills and experiences to the challenge of promoting girls' education. *Tax Status:* 501(c)(3).

EDUCATION CONSUMERS CONSULTANTS NETWORK

Dr. J. E. Stone, Principal
P. O. Box 4411, Johnson City, TN 37602
423-282-6832   fax 423-282-6832

The Education Consumers Consultants Network is a partnership of scholars and educators dedicated to serving interests of parents, policymakers, and taxpayers. It is affiliated with the Education Consumers ClearingHouse – a grassroots "Consumers Union" for the consumers of public education. Just as some law firms specialize in serving consumer clients, the Education Consumers Consultants Network specializes in serving the needs of parents, officeholders, and other members of the lay public for impartial second opinions regarding education policies, plans, and recommendations.

EDUCATION EXCELLENCE COALITION

Jim and Fawn Spady, Co-Directors
4426 2nd Avenue NE, Seattle, WA 98105-6191
206-634-0589   fax 206-633-3561   jimspady@aol.com   *www.wacharterschools.org*

The mission of the Education Excellence Coalition is to revitalize public education through legislative reforms based on deregulation, competition, and parental choice. The Coalition raised $1,000,000 and gathered 200,000 signatures, qualifying Initiative 177 – Washington State's Charter School Initiative – for the 1996 statewide ballot. Founded in 1994 by dissatisfied public school parents and teachers, the Coalition is an advocate for strong charter school laws. *Tax Status:* 501(c)(4).

Issues: Charter school legislation.

EDUCATION INDUSTRY ASSOCIATION

Chris Yelich, Executive Director
104 West Main Street, Suite 101, Watertown, WI 53094-0348
800-252-3280   fax 920-206-1475   cyelich@aepp.org   *www.aepp.org*

The Education Industry Association is a professional network of education businesses dedicated to delivering and advancing the education of children and youth by promoting education reform through entrepreneurship. *Tax Status:* 501(c)(6).

Issues: Promoting education reform through entrepreneurship.

EDUCATION LEADERS COUNCIL

Hon. Lisa Graham Keegan, Chief Executive Officer
1225 19th Street, N.W., Suite 400, Washington, DC 20036
202-261-2600   fax 202-261-2638   info@educationleaders.org
www.educationleaders.org/index.htm

The Education Leaders Council serves as a network and national voice for state and local officials who believe true education reform centers on the needs and choices of families, empowers parents and teachers to work in concert to chart the course of a child's education, increases accountability in America's schools, and restores local control over school policies and practices. ELC's members include the state education chiefs of Arizona, Michigan, Georgia, Florida, Virginia, and Pennsylvania. *Tax Status:* 501(c)(3).

Issues: Education reform; Charter schools; Local control of education; Child-centered funding of schools; State standards and assessments; Federal regulatory relief.

EDUCATION POLICY INSTITUTE

Myron Lieberman, Chairman
4401-A Connecticut Avenue, N.W., PMB 294, Washington, DC 20008-2322
202-244-7535   fax 202-244-7584   info@educationpolicy.org   *www.educationpolicy.org*

Education Policy Institute seeks to improve education through research, policy analysis, and the development of responsible alternatives to existing policies and practices. In these activities, EPI strives to promote greater parental choice in education, a more competitive education industry, an enlarged role for the for-profit sector, and other policies that address the problems of both public and private schools. *Tax Status:* 501(c)(3).

Issues: Role of teacher unions; Parent/teacher relations; Educational employment relations; School choice; Real cost of education; Education in the media.

EMPIRE FOUNDATION FOR POLICY RESEARCH

Thomas Carroll, President
Four Chelsea Place, Clifton Park, NY 12065
518-383-2877   fax 518-383-2841   empire@capital.net

The Empire Foundation is a non-profit research and education organization focused on New York State public policy. *Tax Status:* 501(c)(3).

Issues: School choice and education reform; Tax/budget policies; Economic development.

EMPLOYMENT POLICY FOUNDATION

Edward Potter, President

1015 15th Street, N.W., Suite 1200, Washington, DC 20005

202-789-8685   fax 202-789-8684   epotter@epf.org   *www.epf.org*

The Employment Policy Foundation provides economic analysis and commentary on U.S. employment policies affecting economic growth, job creation, productivity, standard of living, and business competitiveness. Through a wide-ranging communications program, it seeks to separate economic fact from fiction and to provide a sound basis for assessing the utility of existing employment policies and proposals for reform. *Tax Status:* 501(c)(3).

Issues: Mandated benefits; Trade and employment; Ergonomics; Pay equity; Workforce demographics; Labor and skill shortage.

EMPOWER AMERICA

James R. Taylor, President and CEO

1801 K Street, N.W., Suite 410, Washington, DC 20006

202-452-8200   fax 202-833-0388   jt@empower.org   *www.empower.org*

Empower America is a public policy institute and political advocacy organization that formulates and promotes progressive-conservative policies based on the principles of economic growth, international leadership, and cultural renewal. *Tax Status:* 501(c)(4).

Issues: Internet and technology policy; Education reform; Tax reform; Social Security reform; National security.

THE EMPOWERMENT NETWORK

David Caprara, President

17 Rosewood Drive, Fredericksburg, VA 22408

540-220-8841   fax 540-891-4624   davidcap@aol.com   *www.empowermentnetwork.com*

The mission of The Empowerment Network is to build economic capacity and develop entrepreneurial skill sets among families living within low-income communities. *Tax Status:* 501(c)(4).

Issues: Home ownership; Urban enterprise; Welfare reform; Family preservation; Education; Technology development.

ENOUGH IS ENOUGH

Donna Rice Hughes, President

746 Walker Road, P. O. Box 116, Great Falls, VA 22066

eieca@enough.org   *www.enough.org*

Enough Is Enough's mission is to make the Internet safe for children and families. EIE's approach is to advance solutions which promote equality, fairness and respect for human dignity – with a three pronged approach of shared responsibility between the public, technology, and the law – and to influence public opinion to recognize the inherent harms of pornography and sexual predators. EIE stands for freedom of speech as defined by the Constitution of the United States; a culture where people are respected and valued; childhood with a protected period of innocence; healthy sexuality; and a society free from the sexual exploitation of children and women. *Tax Status:* 501(c)(3).

Issues: Making the Internet safe for children and families; Internet policy in schools and libraries; Enforcement of existing Internet obscenity/child pornography laws; Public education on Internet safety.

ETHICS AND PUBLIC POLICY CENTER

Dr. Hillel Fradkin, President
1015 15th Street, N.W., Suite 900, Washington, DC 20005
202-682-1200   fax 202-408-0632   ethics@eppc.org   *www.eppc.org*

The Ethics and Public Policy Center was established in 1976 to clarify and reinforce the bond between the Judeo-Christian moral tradition and the public debate over domestic and foreign policy issues. Its programs include research, writing, publication, and conferences. The Center affirms the political relevance of the great Western ethical imperatives – respect for the dignity of every person, individual freedom and responsibility, justice, the rule of law, and limited government. It maintains that moral reasoning is an essential complement to empirical calculation in the shaping of public policy. *Tax Status:* 501(c)(3).

Issues: Religion and U.S. foreign policy; Evangelical, Catholic, and Jewish studies; Press coverage of religion; Judicial activism and the rule of law; Law and society; Evangelicals' activity in the public square.

EVERGREEN FREEDOM FOUNDATION

Bob Williams, President
P. O. Box 552, Olympia, WA 98507
360-956-3482   fax 360-352-1874   effwa@effwa.org   *www.effwa.org*

The Evergreen Freedom Foundation's mission is to advance individual liberty, free enterprise, and responsible government. EFF's efforts center on providing public policy research and alternatives in the following areas: state budget and tax policies; welfare reform; health care reform; education; and citizenship and governance issues. Its Governing Principles include: responsible self-governance is the cornerstone of a free society; government must protect the constitutional and inalienable rights of the individual; government's regulatory functions must be minimal and firmly rooted in constitutional authority; and government is to be accountable to the people in all matters. *Tax Status:* 501(c)(3).

Issues: Budget and taxes; Health care reform; Education reform; Citizenship and governance; Welfare reform; Teachers union accountability.

FAITH & REASON INSTITUTE

Robert Royal, President
1513 16th Street, N.W., Washington, DC 20036
202-234-8200   fax 202-234-7702   info@frinstitute.org   *www.frinstitute.org*

The Faith and Reason Institute aims at bringing both faith and reason to bear on all the issues that confront our nation. It is the first Washington think-tank devoted to encouraging both of these essential dimensions of our existence. The Institute seeks to recover the ancient Western understanding of human knowledge and divine revelation as co-ordinate calls upon the human spirit that need to be translated into everyday practice. Unlike other institutions interested in religion, it addresses questions of economics, politics, public policy, science, technology, the environment, and public culture from the perspectives of both faith and reason. The Institute conducts a program of research, conferences, seminars, and publishing aimed at introducing better ideas of faith and reason to the culture as a whole.

Issues: Religion and Western Civilization; Character and culture; Law and religion; Alternatives to public education; Catholicism and the American Public Square; Religion and globalization.

FAMILIES NORTHWEST

Jeff Kemp, Executive Director

P. O. Box 40584, Bellevue, WA 98015

425-869-4001   fax 425-869-4002   info@familiesnorthwest.org   *www.wafamily.org*

Families Northwest exists to encourage the development of communities where families are valued and nurtured. It is an information, research, and communications organization that strives to multiply its efforts on behalf of families by networking with various leaders in state government, the media, churches, and businesses who Families Northwest believes can help change hearts and attitudes about the importance of family on a larger scale. Families Northwest also comments on public policy, informs citizens about community issues, produces public service announcements on family relationships, and promotes civic responsibility, family-friendly business practices, and marriage-strengthening principles. *Tax Status:* 501(c)(3).

Issues: Marriage and divorce; Increasing family time together; Parental rights; Family-friendly business; Abstinence education and healthy relationships; Strengthening roles of both mothers and fathers.

FAMILY FIRST

Jeff Downing, Chairman

645 M Street, Suite 21, Lincoln, NE 68508

402-435-3210   fax 402-435-3280   nebfirst@familyfirst.org   *www.familyfirst.org*

Family First is a non-profit family policy council affiliated with Focus on the Family and is particularly concerned with public policy issues that affect families in Nebraska. *Tax Status:* 501(c)(3).

Issues: Fatherhood; Marriage and divorce; Abstinence; Family tax issues.

FAMILY FIRST

Mark Merrill, President

101 East Kennedy Boulevard, Suite 1070, Tampa, FL 33602

813-222-8300   fax 813-222-8301   info@familyfirst.net   *www.familyfirst.net*

Family First is an independent, non-profit research and communications organization dedicated to raising awareness about the vital importance of families in our society. Established in 1991 and based in Tampa, Florida, Family First promotes ideas, issues and principles that strengthen the family. *Tax Status:* 501(c)(3).

Issues: Marriage; Education; Fatherhood; Juvenile crime; Grandparenting.

THE FAMILY FOUNDATION

John Whitlock, President

6767 Forest Hill Avenue, Suite 270, Richmond, VA 23225

804-330-8331   fax 804-330-8337   vafamily@familyfoundation.org   *www.familyfoundation.org*

Established in 1985, the Family Foundation is Virginia's largest and oldest pro-family organization. It works to promote through state law and citizen action, a safe, prosperous and wholesome Commonwealth. The Foundation's mission is to ensure that the law of the Commonwealth of Virginia: reflects the relevance of faith and heritage; protects human life, from the unborn to those near the end of life; promotes strong and secure families by safeguarding the integrity of marriage as a lifetime covenant between one man and one woman; encourages and empowers parents to exercise authority over the decisions of their minor children; reduces taxes and government intrusion on families, churches and businesses; and encourages and empowers citizens to participate in the electoral process and bring their collective influence to bear on their state and national legislators. *Tax Status:* 501(c)(3).

Issues: Education reform; Child day care; Family issues; Family tax relief; Pro-life issues; State-sponsored gambling.

THE FAMILY FOUNDATION OF KENTUCKY

Kent Ostrander, Executive Director
P. O. Box 22100, Lexington, KY 40522
606-255-5400   fax 606-233-3330   kent@tffky.org   *www.tffky.org*

The Family Foundation is a non-profit educational organization that works in the public policy arena to strengthen families and protect the values that make families strong in Kentucky. *Tax Status:* 501(c)(3).

Issues: Gambling; Gay rights; Abstinence education; Striptease regulation; Hate crimes law.

FAMILY INSTITUTE OF CONNECTICUT

Ken Von Kohorn, Chairman
77 Buckingham Street, Hartford, CT 06106
860 548 0066   fax 860 548 9545   info@ctfamily.org   *www.ctfamily.org*

The Family Institute of Connnecticut's mission is to encourage and strengthen the family as the foundation of society and to promote sound, ethical and moral values in our culture and government. *Tax Status:* 501(c)(3).

Issues: Marriage savers; Fatherhood movement; Educational improvement through school choice and scholarships; Defense of marriage (oppose same-sex marriage).

FAMILY POLICY NETWORK

Joe Glover, Founder and President
P. O. Box 1199, Forest, VA 24551-1199
888-442-7317   fax 804-525-3214   salt@familypolicynetwork.org
www.familypolicynetwork.org

Family Policy Network is a non-profit organization working to promote and preserve traditional values in American life through education, grassroots lobbying and media relations. Nationally, FPN educates individuals and churches on moral public policy issues through email and fax newsletters and with a web site updated daily with pro-family news. FPN also represents the American Family Association as their state affiliate organization in Virginia, working with local volunteers to change the culture to reflect Biblical truth throughout the Commonwealth. *Tax Status:* 501(c)(3).

Issues: Oppose the promotion of homosexuality; Fight distribution of pornographic materials and programs; Defend the sanctity of human life; Parental rights; Religious freedom.

FAMILY RESEARCH COUNCIL

Kenneth L. Connor, President
801 G Street, N.W., Washington, DC 20001
202-393-2100   fax 202-393-2134   corrdept@frc.org   *www.frc.org*

The Family Research Council champions marriage and family as the foundation of civilization, the seedbed of virtue, and the wellspring of society. The Council shapes public debate and formulates public policy that values human life and upholds the institutions of marriage and the family. Believing that God is the author of life, liberty, and the family, FRC promotes the Judeo-Christian worldview as the basis for a just, free, and stable society. *Tax Status:* 501(c)(3).

Issues: Judicial reform; Sanctity of life; Education reform; Parental rights; Marriage and sexuality; Global religious persecution.

FAMILY RESEARCH INSTITUTE OF WISCONSIN

Juliane K. Appling, Executive Director
222 South Hamilton Street, Suite 23, Madison, WI 53701
608-256-3228   fax 608-256-3370   friwimm@aol.com   *www.fri-wi.org*

The Family Research Institute of Wisconsin's mission is to inform, educate, and involve the general public and policymakers in the development of public policy that strengthens the stability of marriage and family. FRIW looks at legislative issues and public policy from a Judeo-Christian, pro-family perspective. *Tax Status:* 501(c)(3).

Issues: Same-sex marriage; No-fault divorce reform; Partial-birth abortion; Renewal of marriage culture; Physician-assisted suicide.

THE FEDERALIST SOCIETY FOR LAW AND PUBLIC POLICY STUDIES

Eugene B. Meyer, Executive Director
1015 18th Street, N.W., Suite 425, Washington, DC 20036
202-822-8138   fax 202-296-8061   fedsoc@radix.net   *www.fed-soc.org*

The Federalist Society is a group of conservatives and libertarians interested in the current state of the legal order. Founded on the principles that the state exists to preserve freedom, that the separation of governmental powers is central to the Constitution, and that it is emphatically the province and duty of the judiciary to say what the law is, not what it should be, the Society seeks both to promote an awareness of these principles and to further their application. This entails reordering priorities within the legal system to place a premium on individual liberty, traditional values, and the rule of law. It also requires restoring the recognition of the importance of these norms among lawyers, judges, law students, and professors. *Tax Status:* 501(c)(3).

Issues: Legal; Constitutional.

THE FLAGSTAFF INSTITUTE

Richard L. Bolin, Director
P. O. Box 986, Flagstaff, AZ 86002-0986
928-779-0052   fax 928-774-8589   instflag@aol.com   *www.wepza.org*

Founded in 1976, The Flagstaff Institute is a non-profit research institution dedicated to improved world trade and business. It specializes in research on trade flows of manufactured goods around the world, especially those from the developing countries to the advanced nations. Since, 1985 it has managed the private non-profit World Economic Processing Zones Association (WEPZA) which has 47 members operating 150 industrial free zone sites in 42 countries. *Tax Status:* 501(c)(3).

Issues: Enhanced communications with Economic Processing Zones and Free Zones; Expanded program seminars worldwide for members and users of Zones; World Economic Processing Zones Association (WEPZA) Research Center; Protection of Free Zone incentives in poor countries; Organize members to coordinate policies to have influence on WTO decisions; Solicit financial assistance from corporate users of EPZs and Free Zones.

FLINT HILLS CENTER FOR PUBLIC POLICY

George Pearson, Acting Director
P. O. Box 782317, Wichita, KS 67278
316-634-0218   fax 316-634-0219   inquiries@flinthills.org   *www.flinthills.org*

The Flint Hills Center for Public Policy, dedicated to the constitutional principles of limited government, open markets, and individual freedom and responsibility, serves as an independent source of information regarding public policy issues in Kansas. *Tax Status:* 501(c)(3).

Issues: Health care reform; Taxes.

FLORIDA TAXWATCH RESEARCH INSTITUTE, INC.

Dominic M. Calabro, President and CEO
106 North Bronough Street, Tallahassee, FL 32302-2209
850-222-5052   fax 850-222-7476   dcalabro@floridataxwatch.org
www.floridataxwatch.org

Florida TaxWatch is the only statewide organization in Florida devoted entirely to protecting and promoting the political and economic freedoms of its citizens as well as the economic prosperity of the state. As a private, non-profit, non-partisan research institute, Florida TaxWatch seeks to make the state competitve, healthy and economically prosperous by supporting credible research efforts which promote productivity enhancements and illuminate and explain the statewide impact of economic and tax-and-spend policies and practices. It endeavors to diligently and effectively build government efficiency and promote responsible, cost-effective improvements in expenditures to the benefit of all taxpayers. *Tax Status:* 501(c)(3).

Issues: Tax policy and tax reforms; Cost-efficient state spending; Cost-effective appropriations.

FOCUS ON THE FAMILY

Dr. James C. Dobson, President
8605 Explorer Drive, Colorado Springs, CO 80920
719-531-3400   fax 719-548-4525   corrdpt@fotf.org   *www.family.org*

Focus on the Family is dedicated to the preservation of the home, the sanctity of human life, and the sacredness and permanence of marriage and the family. Focus publishes *Citizen*, a monthly publication for pro-family activists. *Tax Status:* 501(c)(3).

Issues: Marriage/divorce; Life issues; Education; Gender issues; Sexuality; Gambling.

THOMAS B. FORDHAM FOUNDATION

Chester E. Finn, Jr., President
1627 K Street, N.W., Suite 600, Washington, DC 20006
202-223-5452   fax 202-223-9226   fordham@dunst.com   *www.edexcellence.net*

The Thomas B. Fordham Foundation is empowered to make grants which advance charitable and educational activities both within the city of Dayton, Ohio and elsewhere; to engage in and sponsor research in the field of education and publish the results; and to provide scholarship assistance for students attending elementary, secondary, and college level educational institutions. The Foundation seeks to advance understanding and acceptance of effective reform strategies that incorporate the principles of: dramatically higher standards; an education system designed for and responsive to the needs of its users; verifiable outcomes and accountability; equality of opportunity; a solid core curriculum taught by knowledgeable, expert instructors; and educational diversity, competition, and choice. *Tax Status:* 501(c)(3).

Issues: School choice; School standards and accountability; Teacher quality; Special education.

FOREIGN POLICY RESEARCH INSTITUTE

Dr. Harvey Sicherman, President
1528 Walnut Street, Suite 610, Philadelphia, PA 19102
215-732-3774   fax 215-732-4401   fpri@fpri.org   *www.fpri.org*

Founded in 1955, FPRI is dedicated to bringing the insights of scholarship to bear on the development of policies that advance U.S. national interests abroad. The Institute works in three areas: Research, publication, and education. *Tax Status:* 501(c)(3).

Issues: U.S. foreign policy; U.S. defense posture; Secondary school teacher training in History/ U.S. foreign policy; Terrorism, counter-terrorism and homeland security; Middle East diplomacy; East Asian security.

FOUNDATION FOR COMMUNITY AND FAITH CENTERED ENTERPRISE

Dr. Michael S. Joyce, President
6245 North 24th Parkway, Suite 106, Phoenix, AZ 85016
602-840-9066   fax 602-840-9064   information@fcfe.org

FCFE is a non-profit organization that is committed to strengthening civil society by providing citizens timely access to information, publicizing the efforts of those on the frontlines of the armies of compassion, encouraging effective philanthropy, and advancing the arguments for religion's rightful place in America's public square. It also conducts research that helps to improve the ability of these troops to serve their communities. *Tax Status:* 501(c)(3).

Issues: Civil Society; Faith-based and volunteer initiatives.

FOUNDATION FOR ECONOMIC EDUCATION

Dr. Brooks Colburn, Interim President
30 South Broadway, Irvington, NY 10533
914-591-7230   fax 914-591-8910   fee@fee.org   *www.fee.org*

Foundation for Economic Education is devoted to educating people, especially young people, in the principles of free-market economics and individual liberty. FEE is not concerned directly with policy. Rather, FEE is concerned with ideas – ideas that in the long run will promote policies consistent with free markets and individual liberty. FEE publishes the monthly journal, *Ideas on Liberty*. *Tax Status:* 501(c)(3).

Issues: Economic education.

FOUNDATION FOR FREE ENTERPRISE

John Galandak, President
South 61 Paramus Road, P. O. Box 768, Paramus, NJ 07653-0768
201-368-2100   fax 201-368-3438   jgalandak@fffe.org   *www.fffe.org*

The mission of the Foundation for Free Enterprise is to provide leadership in furthering the understanding and appreciation of the free-market system by educating young people and others who will influence the future concerning free-market economics, limited government, individual self-reliance, and the preservation of the entrepreneurial spirit. *Tax Status:* 501(c)(3).

Issues: Free enterprise education for students and teachers; Development of an educational resource bank; Seminars for business leaders on free-market effectiveness; Video conferencing capability; Student internship program.

THE FOUNDATION FOR INDIVIDUAL RIGHTS IN EDUCATION

Thor L. Halvorssen, Executive Director
210 West Washington Square, Suite 303, Philadelphia, PA 19106
215-717-3473   fax 215-717-3440   info@thefire.org   *www.thefire.org*

The mission of FIRE is to defend and sustain individual rights at America's increasingly repressive and partisan colleges and universities. These rights include freedom of speech, legal equality, due process, religious liberty, and sanctity of conscience – the essential qualities of individual liberty and dignity. FIRE is not merely another voice in "the culture wars." It exists for nothing less than to restore to our institutions of higher education – through accurate exposure of abuses, strategic and tactical efficiency, a media network, and legal assistance to those helpless before the winds of campus orthodoxy – the core values of liberty, dignity, open debate, and respect of private conscience. *Tax Status:* 501(c)(3).

Issues: Legal inequality and double standards in the academy; Equal rights on campus for the politically incorrect; Academic freedom and due process; Rights of private and religious conscience; Freedom of speech on campus; Sensitivity training, thought reform, and indoctrination.

FOUNDATION FOR RESEARCH ON ECONOMICS AND THE ENVIRONMENT

John A. Baden, Chairman
945 Technology Boulevard, Suite 101F, Bozeman, MT 59718
406-585-1776   fax 406-585-3000   jbaden@free-eco.org   *www.free-eco.org*

FREE's mission is to advance conservation and environmental values consistent with individual freedom and responsibility, such as private property rights, market incentives, and voluntary organizations. FREE works with leaders in universities, businesses, environmental groups, government, the media, and think tanks. It also conducts an environmental economics seminar series for federal judges and environmental law professors, and sponsors and writes books and articles. *Tax Status:* 501(c)(3).

Issues: Environmental economics.

FOUNDATION FOR TEACHING ECONOMICS

Gary M. Walton, President
260 Russell Boulevard, Suite B, Davis, CA 95616-3839
530-757-4630   fax 530-757-4636   information@fte.org   *www.fte.org*

The Foundation for Teaching Economics is a non-profit entity organized for the purpose of introducing young individuals, selected for their leadership potential, to an economic way of thinking about national and international issues and to promote excellence in economic education by helping teachers of economics become more effective educators. Through its programs the FTE strives to ensure that teachers and students understand the role that a market-based economy plays in democracy, equality and freedom. *Tax Status:* 501(c)(3).

THE FOUNDATION FOR THE DEFENSE OF DEMOCRACIES

Clifford D. May, Executive Director
1020 19th Street, N.W. Suite 340, Washington, DC 20036
202-207-0190   fax 202-207-0191   *www.defenddemocracy.org*

The Foundation for the Defense of Democracies conducts research and education on international terrorism – the most serious security threat to the United States and other free, democratic nations. FDD produces independent analyses of global terrorist threats, as well as of the historical, cultural, philosophical and ideological factors that drive terrorism, and which threaten democracies and the individual freedoms guaranteed within democratic societies. Non-profit, non-partisan and non-ideological, FDD promotes informed debate about policies and positions that will most effectively abolish the scourge of international terrorism. In addition, FDD works to improve education about democracies, and to help promote democracy in troubled regions around the globe. *Tax Status:* 501(c)(3).

Issues: Terrorism and counter-terrorism; Defending democratic societies; Freedom of religion.

FOUNDATION FRANCISCO MARROQUIN

Paul V. Harberger, President
P. O. Box 1806, Santa Monica, CA 90406-1806
310-395-5047   fax 772-288-0670   pvh@ffmnet.org   *www.ffmnet.org*

The Foundation Francisco Marroquin was established to encourage and support Latin Americans who were, devoting their lives, sometimes at considerable risk, to schools, centers and institutes that emphasized the principles and ethics of a free society. Founded in 1980, the FFM is affiliated with the Universidad Francisco Marroquin, the market-oriented university founded in Guatemala by Manuel Ayau. The FFM continues to promote the principles of individual freedom and free markets in the Latin America and the logic of how societies of free individuals are more productive and peaceful that those directed by a central power. *Tax Status:* 501(c)(3).

FREE CONGRESS FOUNDATION

Paul M. Weyrich, President
717 Second Street, N.E., Washington, DC 20002
202-546-3000   fax 202-543-5605   info@freecongress.org   *www.freecongress.org*

The Free Congress Foundation is dedicated to conservative governance, traditional values, and institutional reform. It is politically conservative – but more than that – it is culturally conservative. The Free Congress Foundation stands firm for our Nation's great, traditional, Judeo-Christian culture against the long slide into cultural and moral decay of political correctness. The Foundation embraces the concept of coalition-building focused on particular issues. *Tax Status:* 501(c)(3).

Issues: Judicial activism; Technology policy; Privacy issues; Voters' rights; Cultural conservatism; Grassroots organizing.

FREE MARKET FOUNDATION

Kelly Shackelford, President
903 East 18th Street, Suite 230, Plano, TX 75074
972-423-8889   fax 972-423-8899   *www.freemarket.org*

The Free Market Foundation's mission is through research and education to strengthen and protect the individual and family by supporting principles that promote responsible citizenship, limited government, free enterprise, private property ownership, limited taxation, and Judeo-Christian values. *Tax Status:* 501(c)(3).

Issues: Pro-family issues; Religious freedom; Parental rights.

FREE SPEECH COALITION, INC.

William J. Olson, Legal Co-Counsel
8180 Greensboro Drive, Suite 1070, McLean, VA 22102-3860
703-356-6912   fax 703-356-5085   freespeechcoalition@mindspring.com
www.freespeechcoalition.org

The Free Speech Coalition, founded in 1993, is a non-partisan group of ideologically diverse non-profit organizations and the for-profit organizations which help them raise funds and implement programs. Our purpose is to protect the First Amendment rights of non-profits and reduce or eliminate the excessive regulatory burdens they face, including the costly and duplicative fund-raising registration requirements now required in almost every state. *Tax Status:* 501(c)(4).

Issues: Attack over-reaching state charitable solicitation laws; Protecting non-profit donor lists; Opposing restrictions on non-profit issue advocacy; Defend Constitutional rights of advocacy organizations; Preserve access of advocacy organizations to non-profit postal rate.

FREEDOM HOUSE

Adrian Karatnycky, President
120 Wall Street, 26th Floor, New York, NY 10005
212-514-8040   fax 212-514-8055   frhouse@freedomhouse.org   *www.freedomhouse.org*

Freedom House is a non-profit, non-partisan organization that promotes democracy and freedom throughout the world. It seeks an engaged U.S. foreign policy; evaluates human rights conditions; sponsors public education campaigns; conducts training and assistance programs; and provides support for the rule of law, an independent media, and effective local governance. Established in 1941, Freedom House is based in Washington, D.C. and New York City and has overseas offices in Bucharest, Budapest, Belgrade, Kiev, and Warsaw. *Tax Status:* 501(c)(3).

Issues: Democracy and democratization; Human rights; Free-market reforms; Independent media; Rule of law; Corruption.

FREEDOMS FOUNDATION AT VALLEY FORGE

Aaron Siegel, President and CEO
1601 Valley Forge Road, P. O. Box 706, Valley Forge, PA 19482
610-933-8825   fax 610-935-0522   ffvf@ffvf.org   *www.ffvf.org*

Freedoms Foundation at Valley Forge is a non-profit, non-partisan educational organization which seeks to educate youth about America's founding principles and the balance of rights and responsibilities of citizens. Annually, students from all 50 states participate in Freedoms Foundation's programs, which include U.S. history, core values, the private enterprise system, and constitutional rights and citizens' responsibilities. To date, more than 100,000 people have been reached through these education and award programs. Additionally, elementary and secondary school educators take part in graduate credit seminars and workshops on effective techniques for teaching citizenship. *Tax Status:* 501(c)(3).

Issues: Citizenship education; Terrorism seminar for teachers; Civics education; Free enterprise education; Leadership education.

MILTON AND ROSE FRIEDMAN FOUNDATION

Gordon St. Angelo, President and CEO
One American Square, P. O. Box 82078, Indianapolis, IN 46282
317-681-0745   fax 317-681-0945   laura@friedmanfoundation.org
www.friedmanfoundation.org

The mission of the Friedman Foundation is to promote public understanding of the need for major reform in K-12 education and of the role that competition through parental choice can play in achieving that reform. Started by Milton and Rose Friedman in 1996, the Foundation conducts public education and research programs. *Tax Status:* 501(c)(3).

Issues: K-12 Education; Parental choice; Teachers unions and teachers; Entrepreneurship in schools.

FRONTIERS OF FREEDOM

Sen. Malcolm Wallop, Chairman
12011 Lee Jackson Memorial Highway, Suite 310, Fairfax, VA 22033
703-246-0110   fax 703-246-0129   info@ff.org   *www.ff.org*

The Frontiers of Freedom Institute is a non-profit research and education organization focused on constitutional rights and limited government issues. *Tax Status:* 501(c)(4).

Issues: Property rights; Energy; Endangered Species Act reform; Global warming/climate change; Missile defense/national security.

FRONTIERS OF FREEDOM INSTITUTE

Sen. Malcolm Wallop, Chairman
12011 Lee Jackson Memorial Highway, Suite 310, Fairfax, VA 22033
703-246-0110   fax 703-246-0129   freedom@ff.org   *www.ff.org*

The Frontiers of Freedom Institute is a non-profit research and education organization focused on constitutional rights and limited government issues. *Tax Status:* 501(c)(3).

Issues: Flat tax; Cuba; Endangered Species Act reform/property rights; FDA reform; Global warming/climate change.

THE FUND FOR AMERICAN STUDIES

Roger Ream, President
1706 New Hampshire Avenue, N.W., Washington, DC 20009
202-986-0384   fax 202-986-0390   rream@tfas.org   *www.tfas.org*

The Fund for American Studies advances the values of freedom, constitutional democracy, and a free-market economy by sponsoring educational programs for students who have demonstrated outstanding leadership potential. These programs include institutes held at Georgetown University that prepare young people for honorable leadership through educational studies in the theory of a free society and practical internships with organizations in the nation's capital (www.dcinternships.org). The Fund also sponsors international programs in Eastern and Central Europe and the Eastern Mediterranean as well as an institute on philanthropy and voluntary service at Indiana University. *Tax Status:* 501(c)(3).

Issues: Journalism; Economics and business; The American Founding; Conflict analysis; Transformation from communism; Philanthropy.

FUTURE OF FREEDOM FOUNDATION

Jacob Hornberger, President
11350 Random Hills Road, Suite 800, Fairfax, VA 22030
703-934-6101   fax 703-352-8678   fff@fff.org   *www.fff.org*

The Future of Freedom Foundation's mission is to advance liberty and the libertarian philosophy by presenting an uncompromising moral, philosophical, and economic case for individual freedom and limited government. *Tax Status:* 501(c)(3).

Issues: General libertarian issues.

GALEN INSTITUTE

Grace-Marie Turner, President
P. O. Box 19080, Alexandria, VA 22320
703-299-8900   fax 703-299-0721   gracemarie@galen.org   *www.galen.org*

The Galen Institute is a not-for-profit public policy organization devoted to research and education on health and tax policy. Galen brings a unique approach to public policy research, serving as a broker of the ideas of the top experts in the market-based policy community. Its goal is to expand public education about free-market ideas to invigorate a consumer-driven market for health services and increase access to affordable, privately-owned medical insurance. *Tax Status:* 501(c)(3).

Issues: Reduction in the number of uninsured through expansion of privately-owned medical coverage; Reform of the tax treatment of health insurance; Health care deregulation; Public policy consensus building; Communication and public education on free-market health reform.

GEORGIA FAMILY COUNCIL

Randy Hicks, President
5380 Peachtree Industrial Boulevard, Suite 100, Norcross, GA 30071
770-242-0001   fax 770-242-0501   randy@gafam.org   *www.gafam.org*

The mission of the Georgia Family Council is to strengthen the family by shaping public policy, informing public opinion, and equipping leaders to be effective advocates for the family. *Tax Status:* 501(c)(3).

Issues: Fatherhood; Marriage; Divorce reform; Internet pornography; Vouchers; Video poker.

GEORGIA PUBLIC POLICY FOUNDATION

T. Rogers Wade, President
6100 Lake Forest Drive, N.W., Suite 110, Atlanta, GA 30328
404-256-4050   fax 404-256-9909   gppf@gppf.org   *www.gppf.org*

The Georgia Public Policy Foundation is an independent, non-partisan organization dedicated to keeping all Georgians informed about their government and to providing practical ideas on key public policy issues. The Foundation believes in and actively supports private enterprise, limited government, a strong national defense, and personal and moral responsibility. A non-profit, member-supported organization, the Georgia Public Policy Foundation acts as a catalyst for public policy debate and action by providing positive, practical research and innovative ideas and initiatives, and sponsors forums that provide direct access to policymakers and lawmakers. *Tax Status:* 501(c)(3).

Issues: Education; Legal reform; Taxes; Growth/Transportation; Strong national defense.

GOLDEN STATE CENTER FOR PUBLIC POLICY STUDIES

Brian Kennedy, President
The Claremont Institute, 1127 11th Street, Suite 206, Sacramento, CA 95814
916-446-7924   fax 916-446-7990   britrav@aol.com   *www.claremont.org/1_goldstctr.cfm*

Located in California's capital city, Sacramento, the Golden State Center for Policy Studies – a project of The Claremont Institute – seeks to draw on the Institute's scholarship and research for practical application to the policies of the nation's largest and most influential state. *Tax Status:* 501(c)(3).

Issues: Education reform; Divorce reform; Welfare reform; Ballistic missile defense of the West; Second Amendment rights.

GOLDWATER INSTITUTE

Darcy A. Olsen, Executive Director
500 East Coronado Road, Phoenix, AZ 85004
602-462-5000   fax 602-256-7045   info@goldwaterinstitute.org
www.goldwaterinstitute.org

The Goldwater Institute is an independent, non-partisan research and educational organization devoted to the study of Arizona public policy. Through its research papers, editorials and policy briefings, the Institute promotes public policy founded on the principles of limited government, economic freedom, and individual responsibility. *Tax Status:* 501(c)(3).

Issues: Privatization; Health/welfare/children's issues; Transportation; Regulatory reform; Urban growth; Education.

GRASSROOT INSTITUTE OF HAWAII

Richard O. Rowland, President
P. O. Box 1046, Aiea, HI 96701
808-487-4959   fax 808-484-0117   grassroot@hawaii.rr.com

The mission of the Grassroot Institute of Hawaii is to identify "people problems," such as barriers to productivity, wealth creation and personal happiness, and then study, analyze, publish and aggressively pursue creative self-government centered solutions. *Tax Status:* 501(c)(3).

GREAT PLAINS PUBLIC POLICY INSTITUTE

Ron Williamson, President
P. O. Box 88138, Sioux Falls, SD 57109
605-332-2641   fax 605-731-0043   rfwmanag@aol.com   *www.greatplainsppi.org*

The mission of the Great Plains Public Policy Institute is to formulate and promote free enterprise solutions to public policy problems based on the principles of individual responsibility, limited government, privatization and traditional American values. *Tax Status:* 501(c)(3).

Issues: Free enterprise; Education; Market's role in environmental issues; Property rights.

GREATER EDUCATIONAL OPPORTUNITIES FOUNDATION

Kevin Teasley, President
302 South Meridian Street, Suite 201, Indianapolis, IN 46225
317-524-3770 fax 317-524-3773 teasleygeo@aol.com *www.geofoundation.org*

The mission of the Greater Educational Opportunities Foundation is to raise the awareness and understanding of school choice across the country. **Tax Status:** 501(c)(3).

Issues: School choice.

A. C. GREEN YOUTH FOUNDATION

A. C. Green, Jr., President
P. O. Box 1709, Phoenix, AZ 85001
602-528-0790 fax 602-528-0783 info@acgreen.com *www.acgreen.com*

The goal of the A. C. Green Youth Foundation is to serve both the youth and the communities in which they live by providing information about sexual abstinence and social issues that concern our young people and educating them to make responsible choices to prepare them for their future. **Tax Status:** 501(c)(3).

Issues: Summer leadership camps; Abstinence education via web site and curriculum.

GREENING EARTH SOCIETY

Chris Paynter, Executive Director
1575 Eye Street, N.W., Suite 300, Washington, DC 20005
202-898-1876 fax 202-289-8450 cpaynter@greeningearthsociety.org
www.greeningearthsociety.org

Greening Earth Society is dedicated to promoting the optimistic scientific viewpoint that mankind is a part of nature, rather than apart from nature. GES stands for the proposition that humankind's industrial evolution is good, not bad, and that humans' utilizing fossil fuels to enable our economic activity is as natural as breathing. Its mission is to share the good news about our adaptable climate: That Nature is growing stronger and greener as human activity causes atmospheric carbon dioxide levels to rise.

Issues: Climate change/Global warming; The carbon dioxide issue; Soil carbon storage; Fossil fuel use.

GUN OWNERS OF AMERICA

Larry Pratt, Executive Director
8001 Forbes Place, Suite 102, Springfield, VA 22151
703-321-8585 fax 703-321-8408 goamail@gunowners.org *www.gunowners.org*

Gun Owners of America believes in applying one of the late Sen. Everett Dirksen's favorite sayings: "When I feel the heat, I see the light." To apply the heat, GOA encourages its members to use the legislative updates regularly provided to them as the basis for contacting their elected officials. GOA takes a no-compromise approach. Efforts to settle on compromise have only led to a steady erosion of our liberties. What is needed is the commitment to the steady retaking of lost ground – resulting in the elimination of all infringements of the Second Amendment. Free e-mail or fax bulletin subscriptions are available. **Tax Status:** 501(c)(4).

Issues: Defunding the FBI's instant check of registering gun buyers; National reciprocity law for the concealed carry of firearms; Elimination of national instant background check; Repeal of the ban on semi-automatic firearms; Repeal of the school zone gun ban; Repeal of the Lautenberg Amendment.

HAWAII FAMILY FORUM

Kelly Rosati, Executive Director
270 Kuulei Road, Suite 205, Kailau, HI 96734
808-230-2100   fax 808-230-2102   info@hawaiifamilyforum.org
www.hawaiifamilyforum.org

Hawaii Family Forum is a non-profit family policy council associated with Focus on the Family and is particularly concerned with preserving and strengthening families in Hawaii. *Tax Status:* 501(c)(3).

Issues: Sanctity of life/abortion; Sanctity of life/physician-assisted suicide; Defeating commercial gambling; Sex industry regulation; Traditional marriage preservation; Protecting minors from adult exploitation by raising the legal age of sexual consent.

HENRY HAZLITT FOUNDATION

Chris Whitten, Founder and Chairman
401 North Franklin Street, Suite 3E, Chicago, IL 60610
312-494-9433   fax 312-494-9441   chris@hazlitt.org   *www.hazlitt.org*

The central program of the Henry Hazlitt Foundation is Free-Market.net the Freedom Network. Free-Market Net's entire purpose is to use the Internet to encourage communication, cooperation, and positive action for freedom. *Tax Status:* 501(c)(3).

Issues: School reform; Free-market environmentalism; Internet freedom.

HEARTLAND INSTITUTE

Joseph Bast, President and CEO
19 South LaSalle, Suite 903, Chicago, IL 60603
312-377-4000   fax 312-377-5000   think@heartland.org   *www.heartland.org*

The Heartland Institute is an 18-year-old, independent, non-profit center for public policy research. Heartland's mission is to be an indispensable source of research and news for journalists and the nation's 8,000 state and federal elected officials. It operates PolicyBot, an online database and search engine giving customers instant access to over 8,000 documents from 300 think tanks and advocacy groups. Heartland also publishes a bimonthly magazine; three monthly newspapers; a monthly members' newsletter; and policy studies, books, videos, and other products. *Tax Status:* 501(c)(3).

Issues: Environment; School reform; Health care.

THE JESSE HELMS CENTER FOUNDATION

John Dodd, President
P. O. Box 247, Wingate, NC 28174
704-233-1776   fax 704-233-1787   ckphifer@jessehelmscenter.org
www.jessehelmscenter.org

The Jesse Helms Center Foundation exists in order to preserve and promote the principles of traditional values, democratic government and free enterprise upon which U.S. Senator Helms has built his life and career. The work of the Center involves education, historical preservation and citizen awareness through a broad range of programs. *Tax Status:* 501(c)(3).

Issues: Protecting and promoting Senator Helm's legacy; Teaching principles of free enterprise to the next generation; Developing character education programs for young people; Promoting public and foreign policy understanding through lecture series; Developing teacher workshops regarding the instruction of our Founding principles.

THE HERITAGE FOUNDATION

Edwin J. Feulner, Ph.D., President
214 Massachusetts Avenue, N.E., Washington, DC 20002
202-546-4400   fax 202-546-8328   info@heritage.org   *www.heritage.org*

Founded in 1973, The Heritage Foundation is a research and educational institute whose mission is to formulate and promote conservative public policies based on the principles of free enterprise, limited government, individual freedom, traditional American values, and a strong national defense. Heritage's staff pursues this mission by performing timely and accurate research addressing key policy issues and effectively marketing these findings to its primary audiences: Members of Congress, key congressional staff, policymakers in the executive branch, the nation's news media, state officials, and the academic and policy communities. Heritage products include publications, articles, lectures, conferences and meetings, and its Town Hall web community of over 90 conservative organizations. The Heritage Foundation is committed to building an America where freedom, opportunity, prosperity, and civil society flourish. *Tax Status:* 501(c)(3).

Issues: Homeland security and ballistic missile defense; Reality-based scoring, budget and tax reform; Health care reform; Education reform; Support for marriage and family and preservation of welfare reform; Free trade.

HIGH FRONTIER

Amb. Henry Cooper, Director
2800 Shirlington Road, Suite 405, Arlington, VA 22206
703-671-4111   fax 703-931-6432   high.frontier@verizon.net   *www.highfrontier.org*

High Frontier was formed to examine the potential for defending America against missile attack. High Frontier played a principal role in developing the basis for President Ronald Reagan's Strategic Defense Initiative – SDI. As a non-profit, non-partisan educational organization, High Frontier continues to inform the public about the clear, present, and growing threat of ballistic missiles and their weapons of mass destruction and to recommend cost-effective defense concepts that can be deployed in the near future. *Tax Status:* 501(c)(3).

Issues: Ballistic missile defense; Terrorism; Defense spending; Proliferation; Military readiness; Weapons of mass destruction.

HISPANIC AMERICAN CENTER FOR ECONOMIC RESEARCH

Eneas A. Biglione
4084 University Drive, Suite 103, Fairfax, VA 22030-6812
703/934-6969

The Hispanic American Center for Economic Research is supported entirely through gifts from individuals, philanthropic foundations, and corporations. Its goal is to promote the study of issues pertinent to the countries of Hispanic America as well as Hispanic Americans living in the United States, especially as they relate to the values of personal and economic liberty, limited government under the rule of law, and individual responsibility. HACER does this by both generating and supporting independent research. *Tax Status:* 501(c)(3).

HISPANIC COUNCIL FOR REFORM AND EDUCATIONAL OPTIONS

Juan Lara, President
8122 Datapoint Drive, Suite 316, San Antonio, TX 78229
877-888-2736   hcrea@hcreo.org   *www.hcreo.org*

The Hispanic Council for Reform and Educational Options (CREO) was founded in the summer of 2001 to improve educational outcomes for Hispanic children by empowering families through parental choice in education. CREO's purpose is to be a national voice for the right of Hispanic families to access all educational options and to be an agent for equity and quality in education. *Tax Status:* 501(c)(3).

Issues: Parental empowerment through school choice.

HOME SCHOOL LEGAL DEFENSE ASSOCIATION

J. Michael Smith, President
P. O. Box 3000, Purcellville, VA 20134
540-338-5600   fax 540-338-7611   mailroom@hslda.org   *www.hslda.org*

The purpose of Home School Legal Defense Association is to protect the freedom of parents to teach their children at home with minimal state interference. HSLDA attorneys serve as advocates of home schooling before the courts, state legislatures, Congress, national and local press, and higher education. HSLDA represents its members in courts throughout the country. *Tax Status:* 501(c)(3).

Issues: Oppose UN convention on the rights of the child; Oppose education vouchers/support education tax credits; Repeal School-to-Work Act; Support the elimination of the federal role in education; Support religious freedom; Support parental literacy.

HOOVER INSTITUTION

John Raisian, Director
Stanford University, Stanford, CA 94305-6010
650-723-1754   fax 650-723-1687   info@hoover.stanford.edu   *www.hoover.org*

The Hoover Institution, a public policy research center devoted to the advanced study of domestic and international affairs, was founded in 1919 by Herbert Hoover, who later became the 31st President of the United States. The principles of indivudal, economic, and political freedom; private enterprise; and representative government were fundamental to the Institution's founder. The Institution's 60 resident scholars – specialists in economics, political science, history, international relations, and law – study, write, and publish on current public policy issues. The specialized collection of documents, which started as a war library, has grown to become one of the most renowned private archives on economic, political, and social change. *Tax Status:* 501(c)(3).

Issues: American public education; National security; Accountability of government to society; Political and economic reform in former communists states; American individualism and values; Property rights, the rule of law, and economic performance.

HOWARD CENTER OF FAMILY, RELIGION AND SOCIETY

Allan C. Carlson, President
934 North Main Street, Rockford, IL 61103
815-964-5819   fax 815-965-1826   allan@profam.org   *www.profam.org*

The Howard Center for Family, Religion and Society emphasizes the bond between religion and family strength. Goals include articulating a scientifically, historically, and morally sound pro-family world view that can serve as a reliable guide to culture, law, and public policy; rallying a broad pro-family community that combines the wholesome elements from all religious faiths that acknowledge a natural order to the creation; providing religiously motivated pro-family activists with scientific research on the family and society; and raising an effective, global pro-family voice to counter the destructive elements within the emerging international modernist culture. *Tax Status:* 501(c)(3).

Issues: Family economics; Religion; Community; Marriage; Child care; Taxation and the family.

HUDSON INSTITUTE

Herbert I. London, President
Herman Kahn Center, 5395 Emerson Way, Indianapolis, IN 46226
317-545-1000   fax 317-545-9639   info@hudson.org   *www.hudson.org*

Hudson Institute scholars develop concrete solutions to perplexing issues facing governments, business and industry, and the public. The scope of the Institute's work covers the spectrum of topics crucial to society: Housing and urban policy, welfare reform, crime control, and the workforce. Hudson provides insight and understanding into other major issues confronting the nation and the world, such as national security, agriculture and the environment, foreign relations, civil justice, telecommunications, and more. *Tax Status:* 501(c)(3).

Issues: Crime control; Welfare reform; Civil society and cultural renewal; Workforce policy; Education; Asian relations.

ILLINOIS FAMILY INSTITUTE

John Koehler, M.D., President
799 West Roosevelt Road, Building 3, Suite 218, Glen Ellyn, IL 60137
630-790-8370   fax 630-790-8390   info@illinoisfamily.org   *www.illinoisfamily.org*

The Illinois Family Institute's mission is to create an environment where families can flourish by equipping churches and influencing public policymakers through leadership, information, and training. IFI's work includes social policy research and publications and educating and mobilizing citizens for social action. *Tax Status:* 501(c)(3).

Issues: Parental rights; Active citizenship; Physicians Resource Council; School choice.

ILLINOIS POLICY INSTITUTE

Greg Blankenship, Director
718 South 7th Street, Suite 305, Springfield, IL 62703
217-544-4759   info@illinoispolicyinstitute.org   *www.illinoispolicyinstitute.org*

Founded in June 2002, the Illinois Policy Institute is a free market oriented think tank dedicated to state public policy issues in Illinois. The Institute is the only free market think tank located in the State Capital of Springfield. Its mission is to preserve and strengthen the societal foundations of the Land of Lincoln. Through the promotion of the benefits of limited government, competitive private enterprise as well as Illinois' critical cultural and political institutions via rigorous inquiry, debate, and writing, the Institute strives to unleash the full potential of the citizens of Illinois to lead good and productive lives. *Tax Status:* 501(c)(3).

Issues: Education funding; Health care; Electoral reform; Technology policy; State budgeting.

INDEPENDENCE INSTITUTE

Jon Charles Caldara, President
14142 Denver West Parkway, Suite 185, Golden, CO 80401
303-279-6536   fax 303-279-4176   webmngr@i2i.org   *www.independenceinstitute.net*

The Independence Institute is a Colorado-based state think tank founded on the principle of individual responsibility and the small-government philosophy of the Declaration of Independence. The Institute publishes issues papers, editorials, and books. It also hosts a public television talk show and Independence staff appear frequently on television and radio. The Institute's Parent Information Center provides families with free report cards on individual public schools at www.parentinfocenter.org. *Tax Status:* 501(c)(3).

Issues: Education reform; Transportation; Local government; Court accountability; Second Amendment; Property rights.

THE INDEPENDENT INSTITUTE

David J. Theroux, Founder and President
100 Swan Way, Oakland, CA 94621-1428
510-632-1366   fax 510-568-6040   info@independent.org   *www.independent.org*

The Independent Institute is a non-partisan, scholarly, public policy research and educational organization that sponsors comprehensive studies of social and economic issues. Institute studies are widely distributed as books – *The Independent Review* (quarterly journal), *Independent Policy Reports, The Lighthouse* (weekly email newsletter), and other publications – and form the basis for numerous conferences and media programs for leaders in academia, business, policymaking, the media as well as the general public. *Tax Status:* 501(c)(3).

Issues: Taxation; Money, banking, and finance; Environment; Employment and unemployment; Criminal justice and liability; Health care.

INDEPENDENT WOMEN'S FORUM

Nancy Mitchell Pfotenhauer, President
4141 North Henderson Street, P. O. Box 3058, Arlington, VA 22203
703-558-4991   fax 703-558-4994   iwf@iwf.org   *www.iwf.org*

The Mission of the Independent Women's Forum is to affirm women's participation in and contributions to a free, self-governing society. IWF speaks for those who: Believe in individual liberty and responsibility for self-governance, the superiority of the market economy, and the imperative of equal opportunity for all; respect and appreciate the differences between, and the complementary nature of, the two sexes; affirm the family as the foundation of society; believe women are capable of defining and asserting their interests and concerns in private and public life, and reject the false view that women are the victims of oppression; believe political differences are best resolved at the ballot box, and therefore oppose court imposition of what the democratic process rejects; and endorse individual recognition and reward based on work and merit, without regard to group membership or classification. *Tax Status:* 501(c)(3).

Issues: Affirmative action; Women and the economy; Title IX in academics; Women in the military; HIV/AIDS prevention; Violence against women.

INDIANA FAMILY INSTITUTE

Curt Smith, President
55 Monument Circle, Suite 322, Indianapolis, IN 46204-5910
317-423-9178   fax 314-423-9421   ifi@hoosierfamily.org   *www.hoosierfamily.org*

The Indiana Family Institute is a research and educational organization dedicated to preserving and restoring the family in the home and public square. *Tax Status:* 501(c)(3).

Issues: Divorce reform; Fatherhood; Statutory rape enforcement; Welfare reform; Parental rights in education.

INDIANA POLICY REVIEW FOUNDATION

T. Craig Ladwig, Editor-in-Chief, *Indiana Policy Review*
P. O. Box 12306, Fort Wayne, IN 46863-2306
260-420-9131   fax 260-424-7104   ipr@iquest.net

Indiana Policy Review's mission is to highlight and provide a forum for debate on public policy issues in Indiana. *Tax Status:* 501(c)(3).

Issues: Private property; Land use; Municipal annexation; Hiring quotas.

INDIVIDUAL RIGHTS FOUNDATION

Patrick Manshardt, Director
Thorpe & Thorpe, 601 West 5th Street, 8th Floor, Los Angeles, CA 90071
213-680-9940   fax 213-617-1314   info@cspc.org   *www.cspc.org/irf/*

The Individual Rights Foundation is a public interest law project that protects constitutional rights from governmental infringement and has created a national network of lawyers which responds to the growing threat to First Amendment rights by college administrators and government officials. Its Civil Rights Project is devoted to establishing race- and gender-neutral standards in public life.

Issues: Constitutional rights; Civil rights/racial preferences; Gender bias; Education unions.

INITIATIVE AND REFERENDUM INSTITUTE

Dane Waters, President
P. O. Box 6306, Leesburg, VA 20178
703-723-9621   fax 703-723-9619

The mission of the Initiative and Referendum Institute is to research and develop clear analysis of the initiative process and its use; to inform and educate the public about the process and its effects; and to provide effective leadership in litigation, defending the initiative process and the right of citizens to reform their government.

INSTITUTE FOR AMERICAN VALUES

David Blankenhorn, President
1841 Broadway, Room 211, New York, NY 10023
212-246-3942   fax 212-541-6665   info@americanvalues.org   *www.americanvalues.org*

The Institute for American Values, founded in 1987, is a private, non-partisan organization devoted to research, publication, and public education on major issues of family well-being and civil society. The Institute's immediate mission is to examine the status and future of the family as a social institution. Its larger mission is to examine the social sources of competence, character, and citizenship. *Tax Status:* 501(c)(3).

Issues: Motherhood; Fatherhood; Marriage; International civil society and the definition of the human person; At-risk youth; Children of divorce.

INSTITUTE FOR CONTEMPORARY STUDIES

Dr. Robert B. Hawkins, Jr., President and CEO
1611 Telegraph Avenue, Suite 406, Oakland, CA 94612
510-238-5010   fax 510-238-8440   icspress.com   *www.icspress.com*

Vast experience and evidence demonstrate that we have the capacity to govern our lives. The information age is ushering in exciting new possibilities for people everywhere to expand their self-governing capabilities. The challenge is to make it happen. ICS believes that men and women who control their lives through self-governing institutions live more productive lives. These possibilities will only be realized when we have the necessary knowledge, practical information and leadership. ICS is committed to promoting self-governing ways of life by working on all three of these important components. *Tax Status:* 501(c)(3).

Issues: Empowerment; Governance and leadership; Educational choice; Civic education; Entrepreneurship; Environment.

INSTITUTE FOR COREAN-AMERICAN STUDIES

Dr. Snyja P. Kim, President and Chairman
965 Clover Court, Blue Bell, PA 19422
610-277-9989   fax 610-277-3289   icas@icasinc.org   *www.icasinc.org*

Institute for Corean-American Studies was established in 1973. It is a non-profit, non-partisan, and private educational and research organization incorporated in the Commonwealth of Pennsylvania. ICAS is non-agent of any government, and solely supported by voluntary contributions. Its purpose is to engage in a wide range of issues and affairs of importance. ICAS promotes pertinent relations and conducts appropriate activities to enhance cooperation and to pursue peace and prosperity in association with people of mutual interests, with a special emphasis on multilateral relations between the United States and Asia-Pacific rim nations. Presently, ICAS maintains a roster of sixty-four Fellows from around the world.

INSTITUTE FOR ENERGY RESEARCH

Dr. Robert L. Bradley, Jr., President
6219 Olympia Drive, Houston, TX 77057
713-974-1918   fax 713-974-1918   *www.iertx.org*

Founded in 1989 from a predecessor non-profit organization, the Institute for Energy Research conducts historical research and evaluates public policies in the oil, gas, coal, orimulsion, and electric markets. Through publications, speeches, and media attention, IER articulates free-market positions that respect private property rights and promote efficient outcomes for energy consumers and producers. Funding for the Institute is entirely through the tax-deductible contributions of individuals, foundations, and corporations. Government funding is neither solicited nor accepted to retain IER's status as a private-sector institution. *Tax Status:* 501(c)(3).

INSTITUTE FOR FOREIGN POLICY ANALYSIS

Dr. Robert L. Pfaltzgraff, Jr., President
675 Massachusetts Avenue, 10th Floor, Cambridge, MA 02139
617-492-2116   fax 617-492-8242   mail@ifpa.org   *www.ifpa.org*

Founded in 1976, the Institute for Foreign Policy Analysis is a research and strategic planning organization, specializing in national security, foreign policy, economic security, and government-industrial relations. IFPA provides programs and services designed to assist senior government policymakers, the military services, industry executives, the media, technology developers, foundations, and the public in assessing the implications of changes in the global and regional security landscape. IFPA conducts major studies, prepares quick-reaction analyses, organizes high-level conferences in the U.S. and abroad, convenes workshops and seminars, provides briefings, and publishes reports on cutting-edge topics. *Tax Status:* 501(c)(3).

Issues: National security strategy and planning; Euro-Atlantic security policies and institutions; Asian-Pacific, Middle East and Persian Gulf security; Counterproliferation policies and strategies; Theater missile defense; Geopolitical energy security.

INSTITUTE FOR HEALTH FREEDOM

Sue Blevins, President
1825 Eye Street, N.W., Suite 400, Washington, DC 20006
202-429-6610   fax 202-861-1973   feedback@forhealthfreedom.org
www.forhealthfreedom.org

The IHF mission is to present the ethical and economic case for strengthening personal health freedom and bringing this issue to the forefront of America's health policy debate. The Institute does not endorse any health care treatment, product, provider, or organization. Through its research, publications, and public policy debates, the IHF provides a forum for exchanging ideas about health freedom and works with scholars and policy experts in the areas of economics, health care, law, philosophy, and the sciences to foster public debate. Research and analyses are published via policy briefings, newspaper editorials, television appearances, professional conferences, public meetings, and the IHF web site. *Tax Status:* 501(c)(3).

Issues: Medical privacy; Medicare; Children's health care; Health insurance; FDA; Medical Savings Accounts.

INSTITUTE FOR HUMANE STUDIES

Marty Zupan, President
3401 North Fairfax Drive, Suite 440, Arlington, VA 22201-4432
703-993-4880   fax 703-993-4890   ihs@gmu.edu   *www.theihs.org*

The mission of IHS is to support the achievement of a freer society by facilitating the development of students, scholars, and other intellectuals who share an interest in liberty and who demonstrate the potential to advance the principles and practice of freedom. IHS awards scholarships to university students from around the world and sponsors the attendance of hundreds of students at its summer seminars and other programs designed to assist students into careers in academia, journalism, policy, and film. IHS hosts a job bank and provides other intellectual and career resources on its web sites, *theihs.org* and *libertyguide.com*. *Tax Status:* 501(c)(3).

INSTITUTE FOR JUSTICE

William Mellor, President and General Counsel
1717 Pennsylvania Avenue, N.W., Suite 200, Washington, DC 20006
202-955-1300   fax 202-955-1329   general@ij.org   *www.ij.org*

The Institute for Justice is a non-profit, public interest law firm that, through strategic litigation, training, communications, and outreach, advances a rule of law under which individuals can control their own destinies as free and responsible members of society. IJ litigates to secure economic liberty, school choice, private property rights, freedom of speech, and other vital individual liberties, and to restore constitutional limits on the power of government. In addition, it trains law students, lawyers and policy activists in the tactics of public interest litigation to advance individual rights. Through these activities, IJ extends the benefits of freedom to those whose full enjoyment of liberty is denied by government. *Tax Status:* 501(c)(3).

Issues: Economic liberty; School choice; Private property; First Amendment.

INSTITUTE FOR POLICY INNOVATION

Tom Giovanetti, President
250 South Stemmons, Suite 215, Lewisville, TX 75067
972-874-5139   fax 972-874-5144   tomg@ipi.org   *www.ipi.org*

Institute for Policy Innovation is a non-profit, non-partisan educational organization. IPI's purposes are to conduct research and develop and promote innovative and non-partisan solutions to today's public policy problems. Its focus is on developing new approaches to governing that harness the strengths of individual choice, limited government, and free markets. *Tax Status:* 501(c)(3).

Issues: Tax reform; Estate tax reform; Privatizing Social Security disability; Social Security reform; Education choice.

INSTITUTE FOR RESEARCH ON THE ECONOMICS OF TAXATION

Stephen Entin, Executive Director and Chief Economist
1710 Rhode Island Avenue, N.W., 11th Floor, Washington, DC 20036
202-463-1400   fax 202-463-6199   sentin@iret.org   *www.iret.org*

IRET is a non-partisan economic research institute dedicated to free-market economic policies. IRET's goal is to promote better understanding of economics among public policy officials, the media, and the public, and to help formulate economic policies that contribute to economic growth, efficiency, and competitiveness. IRET analyzes government tax, budget, monetary, regulatory, retirement and health care policies, and proposals for incremental and fundamental reforms. These policies are judged according to their effects on economic incentives for individuals and businesses, on resource allocation, on the efficient functioning of the market economy, and on personal freedom and property rights. *Tax Status:* 501(c)(3).

Issues: Fundamental tax reform; Taxation of saving and business investment; International and other business tax issues; Social Security privatization/reform; Medicare/health care reform; Environmental regulations, mandates, and social cost issues.

INSTITUTE FOR SOCIOECONOMIC STUDIES

Leonard Greene, President
20 New King Street, White Plains, NY 10604
914-428-7400   fax 914-684-1809   info@socioeconomic.org   *www.socioeconomic.org*

The mission of the non-profit Institute for SocioEconomic Studies is to conduct, educate, research, and promote understanding in areas such as the quality of life, social motivation, poverty, urban regeneration, and the problems of the elderly, primarily as they relate to domestic government policy. Since its founding in 1974, the Institute has explored approaches to comprehensive welfare reform, work incentives, health care reform, and related social policy issues. Through its publications, seminars, and special initiatives, the Institute has been successful in providing a national forum for the dissemination of information and the free exchange of ideas. *Tax Status:* 501(c)(3).

Issues: Welfare reform; Consumer-based health care reform.

INSTITUTE FOR STUDY OF ECONOMICS AND THE ENVIRONMENT

Dr. Kenneth W. Chilton, Director
Lindenwood University, 209 South Kingshighway, St. Charles, MO 63301
636-949-4742   fax 636-949-4992   kchilton@lindenwood.edu
www.lindenwood.edu/isee/isee.htm

The Institute for Study of Economics and the Environment is a planned program of teaching and research at Lindenwood University and a unit of the University's National Center for the Study of American Culture and Values. The Institute's mission is to improve student and public understanding of the basic economic concepts that can be used to guide effective and efficient environmental policymaking. Key economic principles which can be applied to environmental decision-making include: environmental protection is linked to economic well-being; limited resources introduce tradeoffs; market-like mechanisms can improve environmental policy; and incentives motivate behavior.

INSTITUTE FOR THE TRANSFORMATION OF LEARNING

Dr. Howard L. Fuller, Founder and Director
750 North 18th Street, Milwaukee, WI 53233
414-288-5775   fax 414-288-6199   fullerh@marquette.edu   *www.itlmuonline.org*

The Institute for the Transformation of Learning is an education reform organization working across system boundaries to develop a new community of learning infrastructures that builds and maintains learning environments focusing on student achievement. *Tax Status:* 501(c)(3).

Issues: Developing a school development and design center; Providing technical assistance to charter schools; Education reform.

INSTITUTE FOR YOUTH DEVELOPMENT

W. Shepherd Smith, President
P. O. Box 16560, Washington, DC 20041
703-471-8750   fax 703-471-8409   info@youthdevelopment.org
www.youthdevelopment.org

The Institute for Youth Development encourages young people to avoid behaviors that jeopardize their health and well-being by promoting integrated prevention messages and skills. IYD conducts research, promotes messages, and devises comprehensive programs targeting American youth to avoid five interconnected unhealthy risk behaviors: Alcohol, drugs, sex, tobacco, and violence. IYD believes that if parents and adults provide children/teens with consistent risk-avoidance messages, young people are capable of choosing to avoid these behaviors altogether, especially if they are empowered by positive relationships with parents and family. *Tax Status:* 501(c)(3).

Issues: Youth and tobacco, alcohol, illegal drugs, sexual activity, and violence; Risk behavior interconnections; Age of risk behavior debut; Parent/child connections as protective for youth risk behavior; Parent education; Role of the faith community in helping youth avoid harmful behaviors.

INSTITUTE OF THE NORTH

Mead Treadwell, Managing Director
Alaska Pacific University, P. O. Box 101700, Anchorage, AK 99501
907-343-2400   fax 907-343-2211

The mission of the Institute of the North is to research and teach Northern regional, national and international strategy and to help the world fulfill its obligations of common ownership of resources, lands and seas. The Institute provides a home for the Northern Forum, an organization of 22 regional Governors including Japan, Korea, China, Russia, Norway, Sweden, Finland, Canada and Alaska. The institute produces research, publications, and sponsored programs as well as offering degree granting programs.

INSTITUTE OF WORLD POLITICS

Dr. John Lenczowski, Director
1521 16th Street, N.W., Washington, DC 20036
202-462-2101   fax 202-462-7031   johnl@iwp.edu   *www.iwp.edu*

The Institute of World Politics is a graduate school of statecraft and national security, offering courses accredited by Boston University. Its mission is to provide a sound understanding of international realities, methods of statecraft, and the historic principles of American political philosophy to protect and advance American national interests. IWP's specific goals are to meet the educational needs of those with current or future professional interest in foreign affairs; to deepen understanding of statecraft, including defense strategy, diplomacy, intelligence, opinion formation, economic strategy, and leadership; and to increase awareness of political realities that affect the security interests of the United States. *Tax Status:* 501(c)(3).

Issues: National security education; Education in statecraft; International realities/threats; Civic education/American founding principles; Moral leadership; Education reform.

INSTITUTE ON RELIGION AND DEMOCRACY

Diane Knippers, President
1110 Vermont Avenue, N.W., Suite 1180, Washington, DC 20005-3544
202-969-8430   fax 202-969-8429   mail@ird-renew.org   *www.ird-renew.org*

Institute on Religion and Democracy monitors and counters the political influences of the religious left. IRD helps members of mainline churches work to reclaim their denominations from far-left church officials, critiques radical feminist theology, defends orthodox Christianity as a force for societal cohesion and renewal, and works to defend persecuted Christians overseas. *Tax Status:* 501(c)(3).

Issues: International religious liberty; Defending marriage; Radical feminism; War on terror; Religious-left lobbying in Washington; Islam.

INSTITUTE ON RELIGION AND PUBLIC LIFE

Rev. Richard John Neuhaus, President
156 Fifth Avenue, Suite 400, New York, NY 10010
212-627-2288   fax 212-627-2184   ft@firstthings.com   *www.firstthings.com*

An inter-religious, non-partisan research and educational institute, Religion and Public Life's purpose is to advance a religiously informed public philosophy for the ordering of public life. Politics is in large part a function of culture and at the heart of culture are beliefs and practices that are religious in nature. RPL aims to strengthen religion's role in support of a free and just social order, including an appropriate political economy for such an order. Not limited to the American experiment in representative democracy, RPL is international in its concern for the religious dimensions of cultural, political, and economic developments in the modern world. To advance its mission, RPL publishes the monthly journal *First Things. Tax Status:* 501(c)(3).

Issues: Abortion; Judicial usurpation; Christians and Israel; Christian unity; School choice; Urban underclass.

INTERCOLLEGIATE STUDIES INSTITUTE

T. Kenneth Cribb, Jr., President
3901 Centerville Road, P. O. Box 4431, Wilmington, DE 19807
302-652-4600   fax 302-652-1760   isi@isi.org   *www.isi.org*

The Intercollegiate Studies Institute is a non-profit, non-partisan, tax-exempt educational organization whose purpose is to instill in successive generations a better understanding of the values and institutions that sustain a free society. Through its integrated program of lectures, conferences, publications, and fellowships, ISI works to educate for liberty – to identify the best and brightest college students and to nurture in these future leaders an allegiance to the American ideal of ordered liberty. To accomplish this goal, ISI seeks to deepen the next generation's appreciation of the nation's founding principles – limited government, individual liberty, personal responsibility, free enterprise, and moral standards. *Tax Status:* 501(c)(3).

Issues: Western civilization studies; Quality of higher education; Political correctness on campus; Student journalism; America's civic literacy; Donor intent in higher education.

INTERNATIONAL POLICY NETWORK

Roger Bate, Director
1001 Connecticut Avenue, N.W., Suite 1250, Washington, DC 20036
202-431-5635   fax 202-331-0640   info@policynetwork.net   *www.policynetwork.net*

International Policy Network is a non-profit, non-governmental organization whose mission is to "share ideas that free people" and to encourage the sharing of ideas by intellectuals and others interested in public policy issues, especially those having international implications. IPN achieves this mission by helping to facilitate the publication of educational materials and the organization of conferences, seminars and other activities. IPN believes that people around the world would be better off if they were governed not by overbearing autocrats or unaccountable bureaucrats, but by the institutions of the free society – property rights, the rule of law, free markets and free speech.

Issues: Economics and competition; Sustainable development and the environment; Sovereignty and globalization; Technology; Health care issues.

INTERNATIONAL REPUBLICAN INSTITUTE

George Folsom, President
1225 Eye Street, N.W., Suite 700, Washington, DC 20005
202-408-9450   fax 202-408-9462   iri@iri.org   *www.iri.org*

The International Republican Institute promotes democracy, free markets, and the rule of law in more than 35 countries. It plays a valuable role in helping bring greater stability to the world. Stable democracies not only further the cause of peace, but also enhance American opportunities for business investment and trade. IRI is not part of the Republican Party. Its programs are non-partisan and adhere to fundamental principles such as individual liberty, the rule of law, and the entrepreneurial spirit that fosters economic development. *Tax Status:* 501(c)(3).

INTERNET EDUCATION EXCHANGE (IEDX)

Christopher Smith, Executive Director
P. O. Box 61731, Phoenix, AZ 85082
480-385-1221   fax 480-385-1222

The mission of iEdx is to pioneer the improvement of learning, schooling and teaching in the United States via the use of the Internet as a powerful tool to build understanding and support for the two key means of raising the tide in American education: Expanding the array of options for parents and teachers in the education of America's young people and injecting healthy competition into America's school systems.

IOWA FAMILY POLICY CENTER

Charles D. Hurley, President
1100 North Hickory, Suite 105, Des Moines, IA 50327
515-263-3495   fax 515-263-3498   info@iowaprofamily.org   *www.iowaprofamily.org*

The Iowa Family Policy Center endeavors to strengthen Iowa's families. *Tax Status:* 501(c)(3).

Issues: Community marriage agreements; Covenant marriage legislation; Education reform; Gambling repeal; Defense of Marriage Act.

IOWANS FOR TAX RELIEF

Edward D. Failor, Sr., President
2610 Park Avenue, Muscatine, IA 52761
563-264-8080   fax 563-264-2413   *www.taxrelief.org*

Our primary purpose is to limit total government spending and total taxes for the benefit of all the people. Responsible limits on taxes and spending are needed to protect freedom, provide jobs, increase incentives and opportunities, control inflation, reduce interest rates, and achieve a better life for all.

ISLAMIC INSTITUTE

Khalid Saffuri, Chairman
1920 L Street, N.W., Suite 200, Washington, DC 20036
202-955-7174   fax 202-785-0261   *www.islamicinstitute.org*

The Islamic Institute, a membership based, non-profit and non-partisan organization, was established to create a better understanding between the American Muslim community and the political leadership. The Institute provides a platform to promote an Islamic perspective on domestic issues (social and fiscal) to help enhance the Muslim community's input in the decision-making process, works to cultivate and expand American Muslim participation in the electoral prosess, and seeks to educate the American and Muslim communities about the many values and beliefs which they share in common. *Tax Status:* 501(c)(3).

Issues: The free market; Taxes; Education; Human Rights; Civil rights; Promoting democracy.

JAMESTOWN FOUNDATION

William Geimer, President
4516 43rd Street, N.W., Washington, DC 20016
202-483-8888   fax 202-483-8337   host@jamestown.org   *www.jamestown.org*

The mission of the Jamestown Foundation is to monitor the evolution of the republics of the former Soviet Union; to provide information about, and analysis of, trends there that affect the vital interests of the United States and the West; and to encourage the development of democracy and free enterprise in that part of the world. *Tax Status:* 501(c)(3).

Issues: Former Soviet Union.

THOMAS JEFFERSON INSTITUTE FOR PUBLIC POLICY

Michael W. Thompson, President
9035 Golden Sunset Lane, Springfield, VA 22153
703-440-9447   fax 703-455-1531   mikethompson@erols.com
www.thomasjeffersoninst.org

The mission of the Thomas Jefferson Institute for Public Policy is to provide Virginia's political, business, and academic communities with thoughtful, realistic, useful, and non-partisan analysis of public policy issues confronting the Commonwealth. These alternative policy ideas focus on state and local issues and are based on the Institute's belief in free markets, limited government, and individual responsibility. The general areas of interest for the Institute are reforming government, economic development, excellence in education, and improving health and welfare. *Tax Status:* 501(c)(3).

Issues: Taxes; Education; Government downsizing/budget; Transportation; Economic development.

JEWISH INSTITUTE FOR NATIONAL SECURITY AFFAIRS

Tom Neumann, Executive Director
1717 K Street, N.W., Suite 800, Washington, DC 20036
202-833-0020   fax 202-296-6452   info@jinsa.org   *www.jinsa.org*

The Jewish Institute for National Security Affairs is a not-for-profit, non-partisan, educational organization committed to expalining the need for a prudent national security policy for the U.S. and Israel and to strengthening the stragetic cooperative relationship between these two democracies. Having achieved a reputation as a credible and independent resource, JINSA publishes its research in the *Journal of International Security Affairs*, email/fax briefings and other publications. Recent programs include missions to Israel, Taiwan, Uzbekistan, NATO/SHAPE, Turkey and Ramstein AFB. JINSA sponsors conferences around the world and arranges Pentagon interchanges to foster dialogue between military and civilian leaders. *Tax Status:* 501(c)(3).

Issues: American defense and security issues; Middle East security; U.S.-Israel strategic cooperation; Emerging threats/threat assessment; Terrorism and international crime; NATO and other alliances.

JEWISH POLICY CENTER

Matthew Brooks, Executive Director
50 F Street, N.W., Suite 100, Washington, DC 20001
202-638-2411   fax 202-638-6694   london@jewish-policy.org

Four thousand years of Jewish history suggest possible solutions to current issues based on a solid foundation of moral values, respect for the dignity and independence of the individual, and a concern for the building and continuation of healthy communities. The Jewish Policy Center's mission is to create, articulate, continually examine, and advocate conservative approaches to social, economic, and foreign policy issues from the perspective of the Jewish community. *Tax Status:* 501(c)(3).

Issues: School choice; Jewish communal affairs; Affirmative action; Welfare reform; First Amendment; War on terror.

JUDICIAL WATCH, INC.

Larry Klayman, Chairman and General Counsel
501 School Street, S.W., Suite 500, Washington, DC 20024
202-646-5172   fax 202-646-5199   info@judicialwatch.org   *www.judicialwatch.org*

Judicial Watch is a non-partisan, non-profit foundation that serves as an ethical and legal watchdog over America's government and judicial systems to promote political and legal reform. Judicial Watch also undertakes strong affirmative actions on a case-by-case basis to police ethical and legal transgressions by government officials and judges. *Tax Status:* 501(c)(3).

Issues: Abuse of authority by the Executive Branch; Campaign finance reform; Reform of judicial appointment process.

JUNKSCIENCE.COM

Steven Milloy, Founder and Publisher
1155 Connecticut Avenue, N.W., Suite 300, Washington, DC 20036
202-467-8586   fax 202-467-0768   milloy@cais.com   *www.junkscience.com*

Junkscience.com seeks to provide its online community of users with a rich collection of resources for highlighting, exposing and debunking the faulty scientific data, studies and analyses which are used to further special agendas. *Tax Status:* 501(c)(4).

Issues: Junk science; Global warming; Public health priorities; Risk; Health scares.

JUSTICE FELLOWSHIP

Pat Nolan, President
1856 Old Reston Avenue, Reston, VA 20190
703-904-7313   fax 703-478-9679   pnolan@justicefellowship.org
www.justicefellowship.org

Justice Fellowship is a non-profit on-line community of Christians working to reform the criminal justice system to reflect Biblically based principles of restorative justice for America's criminal justice system. *Tax Status:* 501(c)(3).

Issues: Religious Freedom Restoration Act; Criminal justice research; Juvenile justice; Engaging the Church in restorative justice; Victims' rights legislation; Model criminal justice legislation.

KIDS HOPE USA

Virgil Gulker, Executive Director
P. O. Box 2517, Holland, MI 49422-2517
616-546-3580   fax 616-546-3586   vgulker@kidshopeusa.org   *www.kidshopeusa.org*

KIDS HOPE USA gives churches the capacity to recruit, screen, train, supervise, and affirm their own members to develop one-to-one relationships with at-risk children at the neighborhood elementary school level. *Tax Status:* 501(c)(3).

Issues: Replication of KIDS HOPE USA program in other states; Working with school districts/ superintendents to introduce KIDS HOPE USA to a community.

BEVERLY LAHAYE INSTITUTE

Dr. Janice Shaw Crouse, Executive Director and Senior Fellow
1015 15th Street, N.W., Suite 1103, Washington, DC 20005
202-289-4182   fax 202-488-0806   *www.beverlylahayeinstiute.org*

The mission of the LaHaye Institute is to conduct, promote and disseminate research and analysis that: (1) increases understanding of women's concerns and issues, (2) helps preserve and strengthen the family, (3) undergirds the Judeo-Christian foundation of American culture, (4) tracks American cultural and demographic trends, and (5) informs and educates policymakers and opinion leaders, media and the general public.

Issues: Family and Marriage issues; Religion and public life; Welfare reform; Education.

LANDMARK LEGAL FOUNDATION

Mark R. Levin, President
445-B Carlisle Drive, Herndon, VA 20170
703-689-2370   fax 703-689-2373   marklevin@aol.com   *www.landmarklegal.org*

Landmark Legal Foundation promotes and defends the Constitution and individual liberty. The organization litigates cases involving school choice, private property rights, free enterprise, free speech, and tax limitation. Landmark also promotes government accountability and exposes official corruption through litigation and public education. *Tax Status:* 501(c)(3).

Issues: School choice; Property rights; Public integrity; Free speech; Tax limitation; Free enterprise.

LEADERSHIP INSTITUTE

Morton C. Blackwell, President
Steven P.J. Wood Building, 1101 North Highland Street, Arlington, VA 22201
703-247-2000   fax 703-247-2001   lead@leadershipinstitute.org
www.leadershipinstitute.org

The Leadership Institute is a national training organization for preparing future generations of conservative leaders. It is devoted to the task of identifying, recruiting, training, and placing philosophically committed conservatives in positions of influence in the public policy process. Since its founding in 1979, more than 33,000 young adherents of the principles of limited government, free enterprise, a strong national defense, and traditional family values have been given the skills necessary for successful and effective leadership. *Tax Status:* 501(c)(3).

LEAGUE OF PRIVATE PROPERTY VOTERS

Chuck Cushman, Chairman
P. O. Box 423, Battle Ground, WA 98604
360-687-2471   fax 360-687-2973   lppv@pacifier.com   *www.landrights.org*

The League of Private Property Voters is a nationwide non-profit coalition of organizations and individuals organized in 1990. LPPV has developed and publishes the *Private Property Congressional Vote Index,* a congressional vote scorecard designed to let the public know how each U.S. Representative and Senator voted on important private property and federal land-use issues. The *Vote Index* is co-sponsored by over 600 land-use groups across the country. LPPV's mission is to provide citizens with the tools to hold their Senators and Congressmen accountable for their votes.

Issues: Congressional vote ratings; No net loss of private land; Land acquisition; Private property rights; Access to federal land and resources; Endangered Species Act reform.

LEXINGTON INSTITUTE

Merrick Carey, Chief Executive Officer
1600 Wilson Boulevard, Suite 900, Arlington, VA 22209
703-522-5828   fax 703-522-5837   carey@lexingtoninstitute.org
www.lexingtoninstitute.org

It is the Lexington Institute's goal to inform and shape the public debate of national priorities in areas of surpassing importance to the future success of democracy, such as education policy, tax reform, regulatory philosophy, and national defense. The Institute strives to find non-governmental, market-based solutions to public policy challenges from the belief and conviction that a dynamic private sector is the greatest engine for social progress and economic prosperity. By promoting America's ability to project power around the globe, the Institute seeks, not only to defend the homeland of democracy, but also to sustain the international stability in which other free-market democracies may thrive. *Tax Status:* 501(c)(3).

Issues: National security; Education reform; Regulation; International economics and trade; Postal reform.

LIBERTY FUND, INC.

George Martin, President
8335 Allison Pointe Trail, Suite 300, Indianapolis, IN 46250
317-842-0880   fax 317-577-9067   webmaster@libertyfund.org.   *www.libertyfund.org*

The Liberty Fund is a private foundation engaged in the study of the ideal of a society of free and responsible individuals through a program of discussion conferences and book publishing. The Liberty Fund does not make grants, and conference participation is by invitation only. *Tax Status:* 501(c)(3).

LIBERTY MATTERS

Dan Byfield, President
P. O. Box 1207, Taylor, TX 76574
800-847-0227   libertym@libertymatters.org   *www.libertymatters.org*

Liberty Matter's mission is to inform and inspire the individual to preserve liberty, the principles of freedom, our Constitution and private property rights for all generations. *Tax Status:* 501(c)(3).

Issues: Constitutional issues; Property rights.

LINCOLN INSTITUTE FOR RESEARCH AND EDUCATION

J. A. Parker, President
1001 Connecticut Avenue, N.W., Suite 1135, Washington, DC 20036
202-223-5112

The Lincoln Institute for Research and Education was founded in 1978 to study public policy issues that affect the lives of black middle America and to make its findings available to elected officials and the public. The Institute is dedicated to seeking ways to improve the standard of living, quality of life, and freedom for all Americans. Through its research and education program, the Lincoln Institute transmits pro-private enterprise views on public policy issues to policymakers at the local, state, and federal levels. *Tax Status:* 501(c)(3).

Issues: Inflation; Education; National defense; Criminal justice; Health; Culture.

LINCOLN INSTITUTE OF PUBLIC OPINION RESEARCH

Lowman S. Henry, Chairman and CEO
453 Springlake Road, Harrisburg, PA 17112
717-671-0776   fax 717-671-1176   lhenry@lincolninstitute.org   *www.lincolninstitute.org*

The Lincoln Institute is a non-profit, non-partisan educational foundation dedicated to promoting the ideals of free-market economics and individual liberty through the conduct of public opinion research in Pennsylvania. *Tax Status:* 501(c)(3).

Issues: Business/economic climate; Local tax reform; Clean air standards; Education reform; Welfare issues; Nonprofits.

LINCOLN LEGAL FOUNDATION

Joseph A. Morris, President and General Counsel
100 West Monroe Street, Suite 2101, Chicago, IL 60603
312-606-0951   fax 312-606-0879   mdlrchicago@aol.com

The Lincoln Legal Foundation seeks to defend individual liberty, private property and the free market, limited constituional government, the federal system, and American national sovereignty through litigation, legal and public policy research and analysis, and education of the bench, bar, and public. *Tax Status:* 501(c)(3).

Issues: Religious liberty; Free speech, including commercial speech; Property rights; Tort reform; Rights of victims of crime; Terrorism and homeland security.

LINK INSTITUTE

Phil Brach, Board Member
P. O. Box 6821, Libertyville, IL 60048
866-828-5465   *www.linkinstitute.org*

Link Institute, a non-profit organization, is committed to promoting and supporting schools with rigorous academic content and virtue-based character education. Link Institute works with parents, teachers, administrators, and policymakers to further this vision of excellence. Link Institute develops and distributes ideas, materials and tools that foster content and character in the classroom. *Tax Status:* 501(c)(3).

Issues: School curriculum; Character development; Education standards; Education reform.

JOHN LOCKE FOUNDATION

John MacDonald Hood, President
200 West Morgan Street, Suite 200, Raleigh, NC 27601
919-828-3876   fax 919-821-5117   jhood@johnlocke.org   *www.johnlocke.org*

The John Locke Foundation is a non-profit, non-partisan research institute that studies state and local public policy issues from a free-market, limited-government perspective. The Locke Foundation publishes a monthly newspaper, *Carolina Journal,* as well as several weekly and monthly newsletters with targeted audiences (lobbyists, local officials, college administrators). The Foundation holds regular monthly luncheons as well as a weekly discussion club. Research products run the gamut from one-page briefs to 70-page studies. *Tax Status:* 501(c)(3).

Issues: Tax reform/reduction; Local government; Education reform/charter schools; Higher education reform; Medicaid reform; Land use/mass transit issues.

THE LONE STAR FOUNDATION AND REPORT

David Hartman, Chairman
10711 Burnet Road, Suite 333, Austin, TX 78758
512-835-1803   fax 512-832-9905   *www.lonestarreport.org*

To balance progress and prosperity of Texas and its communities, it is necessary to formulate a common vision, common goals, and the policies needed to achieve these ends. The Lone Star Foundation is a Texas-based "think-tank" devoted to providing the resources and research needed for the development of public policy based on traditional Texas values of family, freedom, free enterprise, and the Constitution. *The Lone Star Report*, a weekly newsletter on state affairs and government, is the foundation's principal form of communication, providing independent and non-partisan coverage of the activities of the Texas Legislature, special committees, elections, and state agencies. The Research Division offers the critical analysis required to formulate innovative state policy. *Tax Status:* 501(c)(3).

LOUISIANA FAMILY FORUM

Rev. Gene Mills, Executive Director
655 Saint Ferdinand Street, Baton Rouge, LA 70802
225-344-8533   fax 225-344-9006   info@lafamilyforum.org   *www.lafamilyforum.org*

The Louisiana Family Forum seeks to persuasively present Biblical principles in the centers of influence on issues affecting the family through research, education, communications and networking. *Tax Status:* 501(c)(3).

Issues: Marriage and the traditional family; Sexual abstinence outside of marriage; Community Marriage Agreements; Covenant Marriage; Educational issues; Sanctity of life issues.

CLARE BOOTHE LUCE POLICY INSTITUTE

Michelle Easton, President
112 Elden Street, Suite P, Herndon, VA 20170
703-318-0730   fax 703-318-8867   cblpi@erols.com   *www.cblpolicyinstitute.org*

The Institute's mission is to take conservative ideas to young women and mentor them into effective leaders and to make parents preeminent in the education of their children. The Institute reaches out to women on college campuses to counter the overwhelming dominance in the media and public discussion of liberals and radical feminists falsely claiming to speak for women. It is also committed to improving education by giving parents the flexibility to choose the most appropriate government, private, religious or home-based school for their child. Activities include speaker programs, leadership training, issue conferences, research, publications, and coordination with other organizations. *Tax Status:* 501(c)(3).

Issues: Promoting conservative women as role models; Women's studies programs and gender equity education; Affirmative action; Academic standards, tests, and accountability systems; School choice; Children First private scholarships.

MACKINAC CENTER FOR PUBLIC POLICY

Lawrence W. Reed, President
140 West Main Street, P. O. Box 568, Midland, MI 48640
989-631-0900   fax 989-631-0964   mcpp@mackinac.org   *www.mackinac.org*

The Mackinac Center for Public Policy is a non-partisan research and educational organization devoted to improving the quality of life for all Michigan citizens by promoting sound solutions to state and local policy questions. The Mackinac Center assists policy makers, scholars, business people, the media and the public by providing objective analysis of Michigan issues. The goal of all Center reports, commentaries and educational programs is to equip Michigan citizens and other decision makers to better evaluate policy options. *Tax Status:* 501(c)(3).

Issues: Education and school choice; Labor law; Privatization; Economic development.

THE JAMES MADISON INSTITUTE

J. Stanley Marshall, Founding Chairman
P. O. Box 37460, Tallahassee, FL 32315
850-386-3131   fax 850-386-1807   jmi@jamesmadison.org   *www.jamesmadison.org*

The James Madison Institute is a Florida-based non-partisan, non-profit research and educational organization dedicated to advancing such timeless ideals as economic freedom, limited government, federalism, traditional values, the rule of law, and individual liberty coupled with responsibility. *Tax Status:* 501(c)(3).

Issues: Education reform; Environmental regulation; Property rights; Unfunded mandates; Government growth and expenditures; Tax issues.

MAINE POLICY CENTER

Bill Becker, Executive Director
P. O. Box 7829, Portland, ME 04112
207-831-4674   info@mainepolicy.org   *www.mainepolicy.org*

The Maine Policy Center is an independent, non-profit research and education organization dedicated to the study of state and local public policy issues. Founded in December 2002, the Center seeks to explore and advance policy alternatives that foster individual liberty, personal responsibility, and economic opportunity. *Tax Status:* 501(c)(3).

Issues: Helath care reform; Tax reform; Education issues.

MAINE PUBLIC POLICY INSTITUTE

Betsy Chapman, Board Member
P. O. Box 187, Hampden, ME 04444
207-944-3264   fax 207-862-2433

Founded in July 2001, the Maine Public Policy Institute is a non-profit, non-partisan organization. The Institute's mission is to advance sound policies based on the principles of free enterprise, individual liberty, traditional American values, and limited constitutional government. Institute staff pursues this mission by conducting timely scholarly research on important state and local issues and then disseminating the findings to elected officials, the media, business leaders, community organizations, and individual citizens. The Institute relies solely on voluntary support from individuals, private foundations and businesses, and neither accepts government funding nor conducts contract research. *Tax Status:* 501(c)(3).

Issues: Tax reform; Solutions to health care; Educational reform.

MANA

Alma Morales Riojas, President and CEO
1725 K Street, N.W., Suite 501, Washington, DC 20006
202-833-0060   fax 202-496-0588   manaceo@aol.com   *www.hermana.org*

MANA, A National Latina Organization, is a non-profit, advocacy organization established in 1974. It's mission is to empower Latinas through leadership development, community service, and advocacy. MANA fulfills its mission through programs designed to develop the leadership skills of Latinas, promote community service by Latinas, and provide Latinas with advocacy opportunities. Support for these programs is derived from members, corporations, foundations, and government grants. Founded by Mexican-American women, the membership voted to become MANA, A National Latina Organization in honor of the diversity of its ranks. Today MANA advocates for all Latinas. *Tax Status:* 501(c)(3).

MANHATTAN INSTITUTE FOR POLICY RESEARCH

Lawrence J. Mone, President
52 Vanderbilt Avenue, New York, NY 10017
212-599-7000   fax 212-599-3494   mi@manhattan-institute.org
www.manhattan-institute.org

The Manhattan Institute is a non-partisan, independent research and educational organization supported by tax-deductible gifts from individuals, foundations, and corporations. The Institute's goal is to develop and encourage public policies at all levels of government to allow individuals the greatest scope for achieving their potential, both as participants in a productive economy and as members of a functioning society. *Tax Status:* 501(c)(3).

Issues: Welfare reform; Education; Urban innovation; Legal reform.

THE MARRIAGE LAW PROJECT

William Duncan, Acting Director
Columbus School of Law, 3600 John McCormack Road, N.E., Washington, DC 20064
202-319-6215   fax 202-319-4459   info@marriagewatch.org   *www.marriagewatch.org*

The Marriage Law Project's mission is to reaffirm the legal definition of marriage as the union of one man and one woman through scholarly, legal and educational work. *Tax Status:* 501(c)(3).

Issues: Reaffirm the legal definition of marriage as a man and a woman; Respond to Vermont's civil unions law.

GEORGE C. MARSHALL INSTITUTE

Dr. Robert Jastrow, Chairman
1625 K Street, N.W., Suite 1050, Washington, DC 20006
202-296-9655   fax 202-296-9714   info@marshall.org   *www.marshall.org*

The George C. Marshall Institute is a non-profit institution dedicated to encouraging the use of sound science in making public policy. Decisions and conclusions about many public policy matters are shaped by advances in science and technology. For that reason, unbiased and scientifically accurate assessments of the meaning of these advnaces for policy are critical. *Tax Status:* 501(c)(3).

Issues: Global climate change; National missile defense; Civic environmentalism; Science policymaking.

MARYLAND BUSINESS FOR RESPONSIVE GOVERNMENT

Robert O. C. Worcester, President
10 Light Street, Suite 300-B, Baltimore, MD 21202
410-547-1295   fax 410-539-3126

Maryland Business for Responsive Government is a statewide, non-partisan, political research and education organization that works to improve Maryland's business climate. It informs and educates Maryland's business and political communities and public at large on matters relating to economic development and job growth. MBRG publishes *Roll Call* following each legislative session and rates legislators on business issues from that session. It also produces *For the Record* annually, rating Maryland's congressional members on business issues.

Issues: Health care reform; Economic development.

THE MARYLAND PUBLIC POLICY INSTITUTE

Christopher B. Summers, President
P. O. Box 195, Germantown, MD 20875
240-686-3510   fax 240-686-3511   info@mdpolicy.org   *www.mdpolicy.org*

The Maryland Public Policy Institute is a non-partisan research and educational institute whose mission is to formulate and promote public policies at the state and local government level based on principles of free enterprise, limited government, and a civil society. *Tax Status:* 501(c)(3).

Issues: Criminal justice; Economic and fiscal policy; Education; Health care; Environment.

MARYLAND TAXPAYERS ASSOCIATION

Kenneth R. Timmerman, President
7831 Woodmont Avenue, Suite 396, Bethesda, MD 20814
301-946-2918   president@mdtaxes.org   *www.mdtaxes.org*

The Maryland Taxpayers Association is a statewide, non-partisan organization of Maryland taxpayers and county taxpayer organizations working to promote effective, fiscally efficient government. MTA provides expert testimony before the State legislature on bills of concern and carries out investigations of government waste. MTA hosts lectures and other public events, publishes the MTA Newsletter, advises the press on current issues affecting the Maryland taxpayer, and provides educational resources on tax issues for Maryland's students, teachers, and concerned citizens. *Tax Status:* 501(c)(3).

MASSACHUSETTS CITIZENS FOR MARRIAGE

Sarah McVay Pawlick, President
1277 Main Street, Waltham, MA 02451
781-647-1942   fax 781-647-1950   tom@masscitizens.com   *www.masscitizens.com*

The Massachusetts Citizens for Marriage is a non-partisan grassroots organization concerned with the threat to traditional families and marriage. MCC advocates public policy solutions to these challenges and specifically advocates the passage of the "Protection of Marriage Amendment" to the Masschusetts Constitution in order to protect the status of marriage in Massachusetts from confusion or litigation. *Tax Status:* 501(c)(3).

Issues: Defense of marriage; Preservation of traditional marriage.

MASSACHUSETTS FAMILY INSTITUTE

Ron Crews, President
381 Elliot Street, Suite 130L, Newton Upper Falls, MA 02464-1156
617-928-0800   fax 617-928-1515   mafamily@mafamily.org   *www.mafamily.org*

The Massachusetts Family Institute is a non-profit educational organization dedicated to strengthening two-parent families in Massachusetts and restoring foundational principles to the cultural and legislative arenas. *Tax Status:* 501(c)(3).

Issues: Divorce reform; Education; Adoption reform; Parental rights; Gambling; Fatherhood.

MEDIA RESEARCH CENTER

L. Brent Bozell, III, President
325 South Patrick Street, Alexandria, VA 22314-3580
703-683-9733   fax 703-683-9736   mrc@mediaresearch.org   *www.mediaresearch.org*

The Media Research Center was established as a media watchdog organization in 1987 with a mission to bring political balance and responsibility to the nation's news media. Today, MRC's research and analysis operation exposes and neutralizes liberal bias in the news and entertainment media. MRC publishes newsletters, monographs, and books; produces a nationally syndicated column and regular op-ed pieces; provides research to other conservatives combating media bias; hosts two political Internet web sites – *www.MediaResearch.org* and *www.CNSNews.com*; and provides spokespersons for television, radio, and print interviews. MRC's News Division, CNSNews.com, Free Market Project and Internship Program advance and defend the conservative movement. *Tax Status:* 501(c)(3).

Issues: Media bias; Politics in entertainment; Media bias in economic issues; Political balance in the media; Free enterprise; News and reporting source.

MICHIGAN FAMILY FORUM

Brad Snavely, Executive Director
P. O. Box 15216, Lansing, MI 48901-5216
517-374-1171   fax 517-374-6112   info@michiganfamily.org   *www.michiganfamily.org*

The mission of MFF is quite simple: To stimulate cultural renewal by strengthening Michigan families through public advocacy, education and collaboration. This mission is accomplished by aggressively promoting a positive legislative agenda and providing thoughtful, cutting-edge research focused on four key areas: Protecting our children, strengthening marriage, promoting responsible fatherhood and honoring our elders. *Tax Status:* 501(c)(3).

Issues: Marriage and marriage enrichment; Well-being of children; Fatherhood; Abstinence; Pornography.

MINARET OF FREEDOM INSTITUTE

Dr. I. Dean Ahmad, President
4323 Rosedale Avenue, Bethesda, MD 20814
301-907-0947   fax 301-656-4714

The Minaret of Freedom Institute was founded in 1993 with a dual mission for educating both Muslims and non-Muslims. For non-Muslims its mission is: To counter distortions and misconceptions about Islamic beliefs and practice; to demonstrate the Islamic origins of modern values like the rule of law and sciences like market economics; and to advance the status of Muslim peoples maligned by a hostile environment in the West and oppressed by repressive political regimes in the East. For Muslims, in fulfillment of the obligations laid upon them by the Qur'an and the Sunnah, its mission is: To discover and publish the politico-economic policy implications of Islamic law (shari'ah) and their consequences on the economic well-being of the community; to expose both American and Islamic-world Muslims to free market thought; to educate Islamic religious and community leaders in economics and in the fact that liberty is a necessary, though not sufficient, condition for the achievement of a good society; and to promote the establishment of free trade and justice (an essential common interest of Islam and the West).

MINNESOTA FAMILY COUNCIL

Thomas Prichard, President
2855 Anthony Place South, Suite 150, Minneapolis, MN 55418
612-789-8811   fax 612-789-8858   mail@mfc.org   www.mfc.org

The Minnesota Family Council is a non-profit, non-partisan pro-family organization. MFC is dedicated to strengthening families by grounding public policy in the Judeo-Christian principles upon which American government and society are founded. The Council is building a grassroots network of families and individuals concerned about traditional values; educating and training citizens for political and community involvement; and actively promoting key issues in the Minnesota legislature, the U.S. Congress, and the media. MFC also publishes a monthly newspaper, the *Pro-Family News*. **Tax Status:** 501(c)(4).

Issues: Education reform/school choice; Divorce law reform; Family tax relief/charity tax credit; Parental rights; Abstinence/marriage promotion; Data privacy (medical records).

LUDWIG VON MISES INSTITUTE

Llewellyn H. Rockwell, Jr., President
518 West Magnolia Avenue, Auburn, AL 36832
334-321-2100   fax 334-321-2119   mail@mises.org   www.mises.org

The Ludwig von Mises Institute is an educational and scholarly center of the Austrian School of economics and classical liberalism. The Institute funds graduate students; directs their education; sponsors faculty research; hosts conferences, seminars, and summer schools; and publishes books, journals, and newsletters. **Tax Status:** 501(c)(3).

Issues: Opposing war; Abolishing the central bank; Restoring freedom of association and contract; Eliminating taxes and spending; Establishing laissez-faire; Delegitimizing the central state.

MISSISSIPPI FAMILY COUNCIL

Forest Thigpen, President
P. O. Box 13514, Jackson, MS 39236
601-969-1200   fax 601-969-1600   mail@msfamily.org   www.msfamily.org

The mission of the Mississippi Family Council is to research cultural and public policy issues that affect families and to distribute this information to policymakers, news media, community leaders and the general public in an effort to strengthen the role of the family and reduce the role of government in society. **Tax Status:** 501(c)(3).

Issues: Charter schools; Reducing out-of-wedlock births; Oppose expansion of government-provided day care; Tax relief; Accountability of government agencies, including schools; Improving reading and literacy.

MOUNTAIN STATES LEGAL FOUNDATION

William Perry Pendley, President and Chief Legal Officer
2596 South Lewis Way, Lakewood, CO 80227
303-292-2021   fax 303-292-1980   info@mountainstateslegal.org
www.mountainstateslegal.org

Mountain States Legal Foundation is a non-profit, public interest legal center dedicated to individual liberty, the right to own and use property, limited and ethical government, and the free-enterprise system. Through litigation on behalf of private citizens, associations, and local governments since its creation in 1977, MSLF has developed expertise regarding environmental policy, property rights, and race-based decision making, which it now applies nationwide. *Tax Status:* 501(c)(3).

Issues: Property rights; Environmental policy; Race-based decision-making; Federal land management; Federal government over-reach; Limited and ethical government.

MURRAY HILL INSTITUTE

Kathleen McGarry, President
243 Lexington Avenue, New York, NY 10016
646-742-2845   fax 646-742-2851   kmcgarry@mhplace.org   *www.murrayhillinstitute.org*

Murray Hill Institute is devoted to the study of the distinct contribution that women make to society. The Institute addresses the varied needs of professional women, as well as university students preparing for professional life. Through conferences, lectures, seminars, and publications, the Institute explores and promotes an eminently positive feminism. The programs sponsored by Murray Hill Institute are inspired by the thought and work of Blessed Josemaría Escrivá, the founder of Opus Dei, a personal Prelature of the Catholic Church. The programs offered by the Institute are open to individuals of all races, creeds, and ethnic backgrounds. *Tax Status:* 501(c)(3).

Issues: Professional development seminars; Mentoring program; Networking for junior professional women; Publish an annual journal or quarterly newsletter; Sponsor a 2003 Annual Conference.

NATIONAL ASSOCIATION OF SCHOLARS

Dr. Bradford Wilson, Executive Director
221 Witherspoon Street, 2nd Floor, Princeton, NJ 08542-3215
609-683-7878   fax 609-683-0316   nas@nas.org   *www.nas.org*

The National Association of Scholars is an association of professors, graduate students, and administrators committed to rational discourse as the foundation for academic life in a free society. NAS works to enrich the substance and strengthen the integrity of scholarship and teaching, convinced that only through an informed understanding of the Western intellectual heritage and the realities of the contemporary world can citizen and scholar be equipped to sustain Western civilization's achievements. *Tax Status:* 501(c)(3).

Issues: Academic standards; Politicization of academic life; Curriculum reform; Teacher education.

NATIONAL CENTER FOR FATHERING

Ken R. Canfield, Ph.D., President
P. O. Box 413888, Kansas City, MO 64141
913-384-4661   fax 913-384-4665

The mission of the National Center for Fathering is to inspire and equip men to be better fathers. In response to a dramatic trend towards fatherlessness in America, the Center was founded in 1990 to conduct research on fathers and fathering, and to develop practical resources to prepare dads for nearly every fathering situation.

NATIONAL CENTER FOR NEIGHBORHOOD ENTERPRISE

Robert L. Woodson, Sr., President
1424 16th Street, N.W., Suite 300, Washington, DC 20036
202-518-6500   fax 202-588-0314   info@ncne.com   *www.ncne.com*

The mission of the National Center for Neighborhood Enterprise is to empower neighborhood leaders to promote solutions that reduce crime and violence, restore families, revitalize low-income communities, and create economic enterprise. NCNE's purpose is to support those healing agents that have proven they have solutions to society's problems, but lack resources and technical skills. NCNE identifies and supports effective grassroots service providers through technical assistance and public policy initiatives, and, through its Hands-Across program, helps link them to sources of support. *Tax Status:* 501(c)(3).

Issues: Youth crime and violence; Community revitalization; Welfare reform; Economic development; Family restoration; Leadership development and training.

NATIONAL CENTER FOR POLICY ANALYSIS

John C. Goodman, President
12655 North Central Expressway, Suite 720, Dallas, TX 75243
972-386-6272   fax 972-386-0924   ncpa@ncpa.org   *www.ncpa.org*

The National Center for Policy Analysis seeks innovative private sector solutions to public policy problems. The NCPA's approach to these problems encourages individual rights, free enterprise, and self-government. The NCPA's goal is to develop and promote private alternatives to government regulation and control, solving problems by relying on the strengths of the competitive, entrepreneurial sector. Target audiences include policymakers, business and community leaders, the media and the general public. *Tax Status:* 501(c)(3).

Issues: Taxes; Health policy; Social Security and Medicare; Education; Environment and energy; Welfare.

NATIONAL CENTER FOR PUBLIC POLICY RESEARCH

Amy Ridenour, President
777 North Capitol Street, N.E., Suite 803, Washington, DC 20002
202-371-1400   fax 202-408-7773   info@nationalcenter.org   *www.nationalcenter.org*

The National Center for Public Policy Research provides the media, policy experts, and legislators with a conservative perspective on late-breaking, emerging public policy issues. Ongoing programs include the Environmental Policy Task Force, which promotes private solutions to environmental problems, the use of sound science in environmental policymaking, and reducing regulatory burdens on citizens and businesses. Project 21 is the National Center's program to promote a new generation of conservative African-American leadership. *Tax Status:* 501(c)(3).

Issues: Regulatory reform; Environmental policy; Defense; Issues affecting minority Americans; Social Security and Medicare reform.

NATIONAL CHAMBER FOUNDATION

David Hirschmann, Executive Vice President
1615 H Street, N.W., Washington, DC 20062
202-463-5500   fax 202-463-3129   ncf@uschamber.com   *www.uschamber.com/ncf*

The National Chamber Foundation mission is to drive the policy debate on key issues by formulating arguments, developing options and influencing thinking in an effort to move the American business agenda forward. The Foundation serves policy makers and the business community by providing a forum where leaders can consider and advocate new ideas that benefit American business. *Tax Status:* 501(c)(3).

Issues: Building support for international trade; Defining the rules for the new eCommerce economy; Reforming health care; Reforming Social Security.

NATIONAL COALITION FOR THE PROTECTION OF CHILDREN & FAMILIES

Rick Schatz, President and CEO
800 Compton Road, Suite 9224, Cincinnati, OH 45231
513-521-6227   fax 513-521-6337   ncpcf@eos.net   *www.nationalcoalition.org*

The mission of the National Coalition for the Protection of Children & Families is to help people live better lives free from the influences of pornography and the sexualized messages of the culture. The National Coalition works to raise public awareness, assist communites, respond to victims, link arms with the faith community, network with like-minded organizations, and influence public policy in an effort to reduce sexual exploitation and other effects of pornography. *Tax Status:* 501(c)(3).

Issues: Protecting children from Internet pornography; Advocating enforcement of pornography laws; Assisting victims of sex crimes and pornography-related offenses; Educating the public on the effects of pornography and the sexualized culture; Helping concerned citizens effect change in their communities.

NATIONAL COUNCIL FOR ADOPTION

Thomas C. Atwood, President
225 North Washington Street, Alexandria, VA 22314
703-299-6633   fax 703-299-6004   ncfaclc@ibm.net   *www.ncfa-usa.org*

The National Council for Adoption assures the well-being of adoptable children, birth parents, and adoptive families by promoting professionally sound adoption policy and practice. The goals of the National Council for Adoption are to promote public adoption policy; inform the public about the need and value of adoption; encourage a high standard of professional, ethical adoption practice; and develop a base of support for adoption. *Tax Status:* 501(c)(3).

Issues: Adoption; Foster care; AIDS orphan adoption programs; Child welfare.

NATIONAL DEFENSE COUNCIL FOUNDATION

Major F. Andy Messing, Jr., USAR (Ret.), Executive Director
1220 King Street, Suite 1, Alexandria, VA 22314
703-836-3443   fax 703-836-5402   ndcf@erols.com   *www.ndcf.org*

The National Defense Council Foundation is a non-profit think tank studying defense and foreign affairs issues that face the United States of America today. Specializing in the study of low-intensity conflict, the drug war, and energy concerns, NDCF is a non-governmental organization and receives no federal funding or direction. NDCF staff brief Congress, the media, and its members on salient matters that affect the socioeconomic, political, and military aspects of the Nation. *Tax Status:* 501(c)(3).

Issues: Small wars; Drug wars; China's hostile military; Emerging threats to the U.S.; Energy and environment relating to national security.

NATIONAL FATHERHOOD INITIATIVE

Roland Warren, President
101 Lake Forest Boulevard, Suite 360, Gaithersburg, MD 20877
301-948-0599   fax 301-948-4325   info@fatherhood.org   *www.fatherhood.org*

The National Fatherhood Initiative was founded in 1994 to stimulate a society-wide movement to confront the growing problem of father absence and is dedicated to improving the well-being of children by increasing the proportion of children growing up with involved, responsible, and committed fathers. A non-profit, non-sectarian, and non-partisan organization, the NFI conducts public-awareness campaigns promoting responsible fatherhood, organizes conferences and community fatherhood forums, provides training and resource materials to organizations seeking to establish support programs for fathers, publishes a quarterly newsletter, and distributes resources to men seeking to become more effective fathers. *Tax Status:* 501(c)(3).

Issues: Fatherhood; Marriage; Abstinence promotion; Welfare reform.

NATIONAL FOUNDATION FOR TEACHING ENTREPRENEURSHIP

Steve Mariotti, President
120 Wall Street, 29th Floor, New York, NY 10005
212-232-3333   fax 212-232-2244   info@nfte.com   *www.nfte.com*

The mission of the National Foundation for Teaching Entrepreneurship is to develop products and services that enable teachers and youth workers to inspire self-esteem and self-sufficiency in low-income youth by teaching entrepreneurship. NFTE runs over 200 programs per year around the world, working with at-risk children and teaching them the basics of the free enterprise system. NFTE graduates approximately 4,000 students per year with the requirement that each student start a small business. *Tax Status:* 501(c)(3).

Issues: Teaching entrepreneurship; Attracting top teachers to inner-city teaching.

NATIONAL HUMANITIES INSTITUTE

Joseph Baldacchino, President
P. O. Box 1387, Bowie, MD 20718-1387
301-464-4277   fax 301-464-4277   mail@nhinet.org   *www.nhinet.org*

The National Humanities Institute promotes research, publishing, and teaching in the humanities with emphasis on the importance of culture and society. To elevate society it is necessary to change the basic orientation of the culture. Any real and lasting renewal of Western and American society must start in the humanities – in universities, literature and the arts – and must be based on concrete historical experience. *Tax Status:* 501(c)(3).

Issues: Ethics; Epistemology; Cultural basis of society; Constitutionalism; Civil society; National sovereignty.

NATIONAL INSTITUTE FOR LABOR RELATIONS RESEARCH

Stan Greer, Program Director and Senior Research Associate
5211 Port Royal Road, Suite 500, Springfield, VA 22151
703-321-9606   fax 703-321-7342   research@nilrr.org   *www.nilrr.org*

The Institute's primary function is to act as a research facility for the general public, scholars and students. It provides the supplementary analysis and research necessary to expose the inequities of compulsory unionism. The NILRR publishes monographs, brochures and briefing papers designed to stimulate research and discussion with easy-to-read summaries of current events. The Institute also conducts non-partisan analysis and study for the benefit of the general public. *Tax Status:* 501(c)(3).

NATIONAL INSTITUTE FOR PUBLIC POLICY

Amb. David J. Smith, Chief Operating Officer
3031 Javier Road, Suite 300, Fairfax, VA 22031
703-698-0563   fax 703-698-0566   nippnsr@aol.com   *www.nipp.org*

The National Institute for Public Policy is a non-profit corporation founded in 1981 to promote public education on international issues. The National Institute provides wide-ranging strategic analyses in the public interest, integrating political, military, historical, social, and economic perspectives. National Institute studies extend across the full spectrum of international relations and national security affairs, including geopolitics, U.S. defense policy, arms control, regional developments, weapons proliferation and export controls, space policy, low-intensity conflict, and education in the area of national defense. *Tax Status:* 501(c)(3).

Issues: Proliferation; National missile defense; Information security and warfare; Arms control; Examining the nuclear abolitionist movement; Reforming the U.S. intelligence community.

NATIONAL LAWYERS ASSOCIATION

Mario Mandina, President
17201 East 40 Highway, Suite 207, Independence, MO 64055
800-471-2994   fax 816-471-2995   ceo@nla.org   *www.nla.org*

The Association's mission is to preserve and protect the structures of the U.S. government as established by its Founding Fathers; promote the principles and transcendent truths set forth in the Declaration of Independence, including, but not limited to, the sanctity of life, the rule of law, equality, and justice; improve the image of the legal profession by encouraging members to adopt and maintain the highest ethical and moral standards; provide services, benefits, technology, education, guidance, and professional assistance to its members; and encourage members and the legal community as a whole to earn the respect and trust of the American people by conducting themselves with professionalism and integrity. *Tax Status:* 501(c)(6).

Issues: Educate attorneys and general populace about Declaration of Independence; Provide videos and lesson plans to schools for inclusion in curriculum; Education through the NLA Foundation.

NATIONAL LEGAL AND POLICY CENTER

Kenneth Boehm, Chairman
107 Park Washington Court, Falls Church, VA 22046-4237
703-237-1970   fax 703-237-2090   kboehm@nlpc.org   *www.nlpc.org*

NLPC promotes ethics, openness and accountability in government through research, education and legal action. NLPC distributes the Code of Ethics for Government. NLPC is different because it combines knowledge and action, and conducts credible and high quality research and public education. These knowledge-based activities provide the expertise and credibility to take action through lawsuits, Complaints, Congressional testimony, and even street demonstrations. This integration of knowledge and action provides for maximum impact. *Tax Status:* 501(c)(3).

Issues: Legal Services Corporation; Labor unions; Campaign finance reform.

NATIONAL LEGAL CENTER FOR THE PUBLIC INTEREST

Ernest B. Hueter, President
1600 K Street, N.W., Suite 800, Washington, DC 20006
202-466-9360   fax 202-466-9366   info@nlcpi.org   *www.nlcpi.org*

The National Legal Center for the Public Interest is a law and education foundation. Its mission is to foster knowledge about law and the administration of justice in a society committed to the rights of individuals, free enterprise, private ownership of property, balanced use of private and public resources, limited government, and a fair and efficient judiciary. The Center concentrates on providing the public and private sectors with timely information on legal, legislative, regulatory, and economic issues of national importance and accomplishes this goal through its various publications, briefings, and lectures. *Tax Status:* 501(c)(3).

Issues: The liability explosion; Intellectual property; Environmental regulation; Competition policy and regulated industries; Workplace issues; Legal institutions.

NATIONAL LEGAL FOUNDATION

Steven W. Fitschen, President
2224 Virginia Beach Boulevard, Suite 204, Virginia Beach, VA 23454
757-463-6133   fax 757-463-6055   nlf@nlf.net   *www.nlf.net*

Founded in 1985, the National Legal Foundation is a public interest law firm specializing in constitutional law and dedicated to defending religious liberties, fighting the homosexual agenda, protecting the unborn, and challenging outcome-based education programs. In 1995, the National Legal Foundation formed an in-house think tank, the Minuteman Institute, that concentrates on early American studies, classical liberal studies, constitutional studies, religion and society studies, pro-life studies, family studies, and a judicial monitoring project. Through its Judicial Monitoring Project, the Minuteman Institute has conducted extensive research outlining impeachment as a legitimate remedy for judicial tyranny. *Tax Status:* 501(c)(3).

Issues: Religious liberty; Homosexual agenda; Outcome-based education; Judicial impeachment.

NATIONAL PHYSICIANS CENTER FOR FAMILY RESOURCES

Dianna Lightfoot, President
402 Office Park Drive, Suite 307, Birmingham, AL 35223
205-870-0234   fax 205-870-1890   nphyctr@bellsouth.net   *www.physicianscenter.org*

The National Physicians Center for Family Resources seeks to produce and promote family-friendly educational resources with the assistance of a national network of physicians as project advisors. Our goal is to partner with families by providing objective information designed to be presented within the framework of families' individual moral and religious convictions. *Tax Status:* 501(c)(3).

Issues: Medical/Health Policy; Child welfare; Adolescent health; Abstinence-centered resources.

NATIONAL RESULTS COUNCIL

Bill Niederloh, President and CEO
2885 Country Drive, Suite 100, St. Paul, MN 55117
651-787-0704   fax 651-787-0576   nrc@pclink.com   *www.nationalresultscouncil.org*

The National Results Council's mission is to assist disadvantaged people to become self-sufficient by tracking the performance of employment programs and reporting the results to consumers, service providers, funders and policymakers. *Tax Status:* 501(c)(3).

Issues: Employment and training; Disability issues; Program evaluation and data management.

NATIONAL RIFLE ASSOCIATION

Wayne LaPierre, Executive Vice President
11250 Waples Mill Road, Fairfax, VA 22030
703-267-1000   fax 703-267-3989   nra-contact@nra.org   *www.nra.org*

Founded in 1871, the three-million-member National Rifle Association promotes the shooting sports and protects the right to keep and bear arms. NRA trains thousands of law enforcement members and tens of thousands of law-abiding citizens annually on safe and responsible firearms ownership. NRA houses the National Firearms Museum and related entities include the NRA Foundation and the Firearms Civil Rights Legal Defense Fund. *Tax Status:* 501(c)(4).

Issues: Defending Second Amendment rights; Criminal justice reform.

NATIONAL RIGHT TO LIFE COMMITTEE

Dr. Wanda Franz, President
512 10th Street, N.W., Washington, DC 20004
202-626-8800   fax 202-737-9189   nrlc@nrlc.org   *www.nrlc.org*

The National Right to Life Committee is a grassroots, single-issue, pro-life organization with affiliates in every state and 2,500 chapters nationwide. NRLC emphasizes education, legislation, and political action to work to stop abortion, infanticide, and euthanasia, and to overturn *Roe* v. *Wade*. *Tax Status:* 501(c)(4).

Issues: Abortion; Physician-assisted suicide; Infanticide; Medicare reform; Health care reform; Campaign finance reform.

NATIONAL RIGHT TO READ FOUNDATION

Joy Sweet, Executive Director
P. O. Box 490, The Plains, VA 20198
540-349-1614   fax 540-349-3065   phonicsman@msn.com   *www.nrrf.org*

Responding to students unable to read their own diplomas, the National Right to Read Foundation was founded with the mission of returning scientific research-based, systematic phonics instruction, along with good literature, to each of the nation's elementary schools. To accomplish this, the Foundation utilizes a toll-free help line to counsel parents, teachers, school board members, principals, and legislators about what they can do to help their own children, students, school district, or state return to proven reading teaching practices. The NRRF web site also provides up-to-date information on research, legislation, successful programs, and resources available to promote phonics. *Tax Status:* 501(c)(3).

Issues: Phonics instruction; Reading research.

NATIONAL RIGHT TO WORK COMMITTEE

Reed Larson, President
8001 Braddock Road, Suite 500, Springfield, VA 22160
703-321-9820   fax 703-321-8239   les@nrtw.org   *www.right-to-work.org*

The National Right to Work Committee is dedicated to advancing the principle that every worker must have the right – but no worker should ever be compelled – to join or financially support a labor union. *Tax Status:* 501(c)(4).

Issues: Worker protection laws regarding union dues; Passage of state right-to-work laws; Revocation of unions' immunity to anti-extortion laws.

NATIONAL RIGHT TO WORK LEGAL DEFENSE FOUNDATION

Reed Larson, President
8001 Braddock Road, Suite 500, Springfield, VA 22160
703-321-8510   fax 703-321-9319   info@nrtw.org   *www.nrtw.org*

The National Right to Work Legal Defense Foundation is a non-profit, charitable organization providing free legal aid to employees whose human or civil rights have been violated by compulsory unionism abuses. The Foundation is assisting thousands of employees in nearly 500 cases nationwide. *Tax Status:* 501(c)(3).

Issues: Using U.S. Supreme Court rulings and state Right to Work laws to defend workers suffering the abuses of compulsory unionism; Protecting workers from union violence; Upholding workers' religious and political objections to forced union dues.

NATIONAL STRATEGY FORUM

Richard Friedman, President
53 West Jackson Boulevard, Suite 516, Chicago, IL 60604
312-697-1286   fax 312-697-1296   natstrat@natstratfm.org   *www.nationalstrategy.com*

As a non-partisan organization, the National Strategy Forum espouses no political cause. It is united by the following principles – the goal that the U.S. national strategy should be a genuine and just peace, sought in common cause with the community of free and independent nations; the advancement and preservation of democracy is essential to promote human rights, inspire principled cultural achievement and maximize economic development; and an informed public opinion and enduring non-partisan consensus are fundamental parts of national security in a democratic society. *Tax Status:* 501(c)(3).

Issues: Catastrophic terrorism; Tension and conflict in India and Pakistan; U.S.-Taiwan-mainland China relations; Homeland defense-cyber war; U.S. military force projection-peacemaking; Mass migration.

NATIONAL STRATEGY INFORMATION CENTER

Roy Godson, President
1730 Rhode Island Avenue, N.W., Suite 500, Washington, DC 20036
202-429-0129   fax 202-659-5429   nsic@ix.netcom.com

The National Strategy Information Center seeks to further education on security challenges; encourage innovations in military, intelligence, and geopolitical affairs; and promote cooperation among democratic elements in strategic regions of the world. Leveraging its resources through partnerships with large organizations, the Center has worked closely with U.S. and foreign universities, professional associations (such as the American Bar Association Committee on Law and National Security), and business and labor organizations in the U.S. and abroad. Specializing in intelligence, international organized crime, and ethnic and religious conflict, the Center promotes scholarly research and serves as a resource for the news media. *Tax Status:* 501(c)(3).

Issues: Organized crime; Intelligence reform; Civics education.

NATIONAL TAX LIMITATION COMMITTEE

Lewis K. Uhler, President
151 North Sunrise Avenue, Suite 901, Roseville, CA 95661
916-786-9400   fax 916-786-8163   lkuhler@ns.net   *www.limittaxes.org*

National Tax Limitation Committee's mission is to encourage structural changes in fiscal and governance practices at all levels of government, to limit and control taxes and spending, and to enhance the power and freedom of individuals and their enterprises. **Tax Status:** 501(c)(4).

NATIONAL TAX LIMITATION FOUNDATION

Lewis K. Uhler, President
151 North Sunrise Avenue, Suite 901, Roseville, CA 95661
916-786-9400   fax 916-786-8163   lkuhler@ns.net   *www.limittaxes.org*

The National Tax Limitation Foundation engages in educational and research activities designed to facilitate structural change, reform, and discipline in government at all levels. **Tax Status:** 501(c)(3).

NATIONAL TAXPAYERS UNION

John Berthoud, President
108 North Alfred Street, Alexandria, VA 22314
703-683-5700   fax 703-683-5722   ntu@ntu.org   *www.ntu.org*

The National Taxpayers Union is a 300,000-member, non-profit, non-partisan citizen organization that works for lower taxes, less wasteful spending, taxpayers rights, and accountable government at all levels. Founded in 1969, NTU supports constitutional limitations on taxes and spending as well as replacing the current tax system with a flat-rate income tax or national sales tax. **Tax Status:** 501(c)(4).

Issues: Balanced Budget Amendment; Tax reform; IRS reform; State and local tax limits; Reducing government spending; Tax Limitation Amendment.

NATIONAL TAXPAYERS UNION FOUNDATION

John Berthoud, President
108 North Alfred Street, Alexandria, VA 22314
703-683-5700   fax 703-683-5722   ntuf@ntu.org   *www.ntu.org*

The National Taxpayers Union Foundation, the research and education affiliate of the National Taxpayers Union, disseminates information regarding the effects of fiscal and economic policies on taxpayers. **Tax Status:** 501(c)(3).

Issues: Entitlement reform; Tracking congressional spending; Interest group analysis; Economic analysis; Tax reform.

NATIONAL WILDERNESS INSTITUTE

Robert Gordon, Executive Director
Georgetown Station, P. O. Box 25766, Washington, DC 20007
703-836-7404   fax 703-836-7405   nwi@nwi.org   *www.nwi.org*

The National Wilderness Institute is dedicated to using science to guide the wise management of natural resources for the benefit and enjoyment of people. Recognizing the direct, positive relationship between freedom and progress, and environmental quality, NWI champions private stewardship, which enhances nature's bounty while encouraging economic growth. NWI also recognizes that renewable resources such as wildlife, fish, wetlands, wilderness, forest, range, air, water, and soil are dynamic, resilient, and respond positively to wise management. Therefore, NWI supports site and situation-specific practices that unleash the creative forces of the free market, protect or extend private property rights, and reduce the inefficient and counterproductive effects of government regulations. **Tax Status:** 501(c)(3).

Issues: Endangered species; Wetlands; Biodiversity; Environmental regulation; Federal lands management; Private property rights.

NEBRASKA TAXPAYERS FOR FREEDOM

David Kagan, State Chairman
P. O. Box 6452, Omaha, NE 68106-0452
402-551-0921   ncf@phonet.com

Founded in 1978, Nebraska Taxpayers for Freedom educates and informs the citizens and elected officials of Nebraska about the private sector solutions that exist to solve the political, economic, and social problems in the state and in our nation. NTF analyszes the budgets of city, county, and state governments to identify and address wasteful spending and taxpayer abuse. NTF publishes annual voting records of Nebraska elected officials – federal, state, county and local.

Issues: Local, state, and federal government tax and spending policies; Rate and publish official voting records of elected officials; Educate members to be effective advocates for taxpayer concerns.

NEVADA POLICY RESEARCH INSTITUTE

Helene Denney, Executive Director
2073 East Sahara Avenue, Suite B, Las Vegas, NV 89104
702-222-0642   fax 702-227-0927   info@npri.org   *www.npri.org*

The Nevada Policy Research Institute is a non-partisan, non-profit public policy and education organization founded in 1991. NPRI embraces the principles of limited government, individual responsibility, and a free and competitive market. It conducts research on public policy issues important to Nevada and disseminates the information by means of television, radio, print, and electronic media to elected officials, academicians, business leaders, NPRI members, and interested Nevadans. *Tax Status:* 501(c)(3).

Issues: Taxes; Education; Labor.

NEW COALITION FOR ECONOMIC AND SOCIAL CHANGE

Lee Walker, President and CEO
300 South Wacker Drive, Suite 3020, Chicago, IL 60606
312-427-1290   fax 312-427-1291   lwalker@newcoalition.org   *www.newcoalition.org*

The mission of the New Coalition for Economic and Social Change is to encourage the pursuit of alternative public policies that promote economic independence and strengthen the institutions of the family, school, church, and community. The Coalition describes its dream as economic independence and social advancement for blacks and all other Americans. *Tax Status:* 501(c)(3).

Issues: Affirmative opportunity; Education reform; Affordable housing without subsidies or grants.

NEW ENGLAND LEGAL FOUNDATION

Andrew Grainger, President
150 Lincoln Street, Boston, MA 02111
617-695-3660   fax 617-695-3656   nelf@juno.com   *www.nelfonline.org*

The New England Legal Foundation's mission is to protect the economic rights of persons and organizations and to advance free enterprise principles through the legal system. *Tax Status:* 501(c)(3).

Issues: Employment; Property rights; Taxation; Environment; Corporate/securities regulation; High-tech commerce privacy.

NEW JERSEY FAMILY POLICY COUNCIL

Len Deo, Executive Director
P. O. Box 6011, Parsippany, NJ 07054
973-263-5258   fax 973-263-3772   info@njfpc.org   *www.njfpc.org*

The mission of the NJFPC is to intervene and respond to the breakdown that the traditional family, the cornerstone of a virtuous society, is experiencing. In light of the decline in moral standards, the Council is energized by a strong desire and dedication to puruse justice and righteousness. It articulates its message through experts in law, medicine, education, media, business, government and the church. *Tax Status:* 501(c)(3).

Issues: Marriage Builders Program/Reduction in the divorce rate; Father Builders Program/ Reduction in the number of father-absent homes; Youth Builders Program/Reduction in out of wedlock births and sexually transmitted disease rate/Increase teen chastity pledges; Grassroots education/Increasing citizen involvement and awareness; Advocate for added legal protections for women and children from assault and molestation; Advocate for childhood protection from exposure to Internet pornography in public instituions.

NEW MEXICO INDEPENDENCE RESEARCH INSTITUTE

M. Gene Aldridge, President and CEO
2401 Nieve Lane, Las Cruces, NM 88005
505-523-8700   fax 505-523-8800   gsaldridge@zianet.com   *www.zianet.com/nmiri*

To provide high quality scientifically-based policy research which fosters personal responsibility, limited government, and free market economics. The purpose of the Institute is to advance education, and to further other charitable, educational and scientific purposes, in the field of the promotion of free enterprise, limited government, and the fostering of personal responsibility as pertaining to New Mexico and the United States. *Tax Status:* 501(c)(3).

Issues: Taxation; State government fiscal policy; Economic forecasting; Property rights; U.S.-Mexico border economics; Higher education reward systems.

NEW YORK FAMILY POLICY COUNCIL

Steven J. Kidder, Ph.D., Chairman
Three E-Comm Square, Albany, NY 12207
518-432-8756x3157   fax 518-426-4351   *www.nyfpc.org*

The New York Family Policy Council exists to reaffirm and promote the traditional family unit and the Judeo-Christian value system upon which it is built. *Tax Status:* 501(c)(3).

Issues: Exposing and turning back the homosexual agenda; Partnering with other pro-life groups for an array of pro-life legislative initiatives; Addressing pornography peddled to children; Improving educational choice for parents; Reforming family court; Restricting gambling.

PAUL NITZE SCHOOL OF ADVANCED INTERNATIONAL STUDIES

Jessica P. Einhorn, Dean
1740 Massachusetts Avenue, N.W., Washington, DC 20036
202-663-5600   fax 202-663-5615   *www.sais-jhu.edu*

Founded in 1943, Johns Hopkins University's School for Advanced International Studies has three primary goals: To provide a professional education that adheres to the highest standards of scholarship while taking a practical approach to preparing students for international leadership; to conduct and disseminate scholarly research related to contemporary issues of concern to the United States and other nations; and to offer mid-career educational opportunities for individuals already working in international affairs. *Tax Status:* 501(c)(3).

Issues: American foreign policy; Social change and development; International economics; Regional conflicts; Energy, science, and technology.

THE NIXON CENTER

Dimitri K. Simes, President
1615 L Street, N.W., Suite 1250, Washington, DC 20036
202-887-1000   fax 202-887-5222   mail@nixoncenter.org   *www.nixoncenter.org*

A bipartisan public policy institution formed by former President Richard Nixon in January 1994, The Nixon Center is committed to the analysis of challenges to United States policy through the prism of American national interest. The Center is a programmatically independent division of the Richard Nixon Library and Birthplace Foundation. *Tax Status:* 501(c)(3).

Issues: American national security; U.S.-China relations; U.S.-Russian relations; U.S. policy towards Iran; Caspian Basin energy geopolitics; Immigration.

NONPROLIFERATION POLICY EDUCATION CENTER

Henry Sokolski, Executive Director
1718 M Street, N.W., Suite 244, Washington, DC 20036
202-466-4406   fax 202-659-5429   npec@ix.netcom.com   *www.npec-web.org*

The Nonproliferation Policy Education Center is a non-profit educational organization founded in 1994 to promote a better understanding of strategic weapons proliferation issues among policymakers, journalists, and university professors. NPEC holds faculty teaching seminars nation-wide, as well as nonproliferation policy forums within the executive branch and on Capitol Hill, and commissions and publishes research to help fill key gaps in the existing literature on proliferation issues. *Tax Status:* 501(c)(3).

Issues: Implementation of the Korean nuclear deal; Super-terrorism; Russian strategic weapons proliferation; Proliferation in the Middle East and Southwest Asia; Chinese strategic weapons proliferation.

NORTH CAROLINA FAMILY POLICY COUNCIL

Bill Brooks, President
P. O. Box 20607, Raleigh, NC 27619
919-807-0800   fax 919-807-0900   ncfpc@aol.com   *www.ncfpc.org*

The mission of the North Carolina Family Policy Council is to strengthen the family by educating North Carolinians on public policy issues that impact the family and equipping citizens to be voices of persuasion on behalf of traditional family values in their localities. *Tax Status:* 501(c)(3).

Issues: Fatherhood; Gambling; School-to-Work; Marriage reform; Abstinence education; Education.

NORTH DAKOTA FAMILY ALLIANCE

Christina Kindel, Executive Director
4007 State Street North, Bismarck, ND 58503
701-223-3575   fax 701-223-1133   ndfa@mindspring.com   *www.ndfa.org*

North Dakota Family Alliance is a non-profit organization dedicated to strengthening families in North Dakota by equipping, informing and educating policy leaders, elected officials, institutions and concerned citizens on the issues that impact the family. *Tax Status:* 501(c)(3).

Issues: Education, Goals 2000, and School-to-Work; Gambling; Taxation; Abortion; Health care / mandatory immunizations; Youth Awareness in Government.

THE OBJECTIVIST CENTER

David Kelley, Executive Director
11 Raymond Avenue, Suite 31, Poughkeepsie, NY 12603
845-471-6100   fax 845-471-6195   toc@objectivistcenter.org   *www.objectivistcenter.org*

The goal of The Objectivist Center is to help create a new culture in our society, a culture in tune with the entrepreneurial spirit of the new economy, a culture that affirms the core Objectivist values of reason, individualism, freedom, and achievement. *Tax Status:* 501(c)(3).

OHIO ROUNDTABLE

David Zanotti, President
31005 Solon Road, Solon, OH 44139
440-349-3393   fax 440-349-0154   ohroundtab@aol.com   *www.ohioroundtable.org*

As a non-profit, non-partisan research and education organization dedicated to restoring traditional principles to public policy, the Ohio Roundtable conducts research on local, state, and federal policy issues and then communicates that information through *The Public Square* radio programs and the Ohio Roundtable web site. The Roundtable also maintains ongoing dialogue with business leaders, clergy, lawmakers, and families across Ohio through seminars, publications, and special projects. *Tax Status:* 501(c)(3).

Issues: Education; School choice; Religious liberty; Tax reform; Judicial reform; Term limits.

OHIO TAXPAYERS ASSOCIATION

Scott Pullins, Chairman
P. O. Box 163339, Columbus, OH 43216-3339
614-224-27851   fax 877-471-0273

Ohio Taxpayers Association is a non-profit, non-partisan organization that conducts both direct and grassroots lobbying. In addition, it rates and disseminates candidates' positions on important tax, spending, and regulatory issues. OTA is free to accept unlimited contributions from businesses, corporations, or individuals. Because this organization lobbies, contributions to it are not tax-deductible.

OKLAHOMA COUNCIL OF PUBLIC AFFAIRS, INC.

Brett A. Magbee, Executive Director
100 West Wilshire Boulevard, Suite C-3, Oklahoma City, OK 73116
405-843-9212   fax 405-843-9436   ocpa@ocpathink.org   *www.ocpathink.org*

OCPA's mission is to accumulate, evaluate, and disseminate public policy ideas and information for Oklahoma consistent with the principles of free enterprise, limited government, and individual initiative. *Tax Status:* 501(c)(3).

Issues: Economics; Education; Governance; Justice; Culture.

OKLAHOMA FAMILY POLICY COUNCIL

Michael L. Jestes, Executive Director
3908 North Peniel Avenue, Suite 100, Bethany, OK 73008-3458
405-787-7744   fax 405-787-3900   okfamilypc@aol.com

Oklahoma Family Policy Council's mission is to strengthen families, to educate Oklahomans on public policy as it impacts the family, to encourage responsible citizenship, and to restore traditional, Judeo-Christian principles in American public policy. *Tax Status:* 501(c)(3).

Issues: Governor and First Lady's Marriage Initiative; Abstinence education for your people/ character-based model; Character education for schools, business and government; Education reform; Reducing state tax rates, estate, and inheritance taxes; Parents directing their children education and upbringing.

OREGON CITIZENS FOR A SOUND ECONOMY

Russ Walker, Northwest Director
744 Saddlewood Court, N.E., Keizer, OR 97303-3937
503-463-9457

Oregon Citizens for a Sound Economy is a grassroots orgainzation of Oregonians who support free-market solutions to public policy problems. Oregon CSE's members support less government, fewer regulations, and lower taxes. OCSE is an affiliate of the 250,000-member Citizens for a Sound Economy, which is based in Washington, D.C. *Tax Status:* 501(c)(4).

OREGONIANS IN ACTION

Frank Nims, President
P. O. Box 230637, Tigard, OR 97281
503-620-0258   fax 503-639-6891   oiaec@oia.org   *www.oia.org*

Oregonians In Action is a statewide, non-profit, non-partisan organization fighting for property rights and balanced and realistic land-use regulations through active lobbying in legislative and regulatory arenas, networking with other organizations, and working closely with landowners. OIA works with the Oregonians In Action Legal Center and Oregonians In Action Education Center, which are separate 501(c)(3) organizations with the same concerns on these issues. The Education Center concentrates on educating the public and landowners about property rights and land-use regulatory issues. *Tax Status:* 501(c)(4).

Issues: Compensation for regulatory takings; Requiring notice of proposed regulations; Reforming farm/forest land zoning; Removing oppressive rural dwelling rules; Opposing high-density zoning in urban areas.

OREGONIANS IN ACTION LEGAL CENTER

William Moshofsky, President
P. O. Box 230637, Tigard, OR 97281
503-620-0258   fax 503-639-6891   bill@oia.org   *www.oia.org*

The Oregonians In Action Legal Center is a statewide, non-profit, non-partisan organization dedicated to using litigation to protect private property rights from excessive government land-use regulations. Financed entirely by private donations, the Center provides free legal services in precedent-setting property rights cases at all judicial levels, from local government hearings to the U.S. Supreme Court. The Center is involved as primary counsel in most cases, but also provides friend of the court briefs in cases handled by others. *Tax Status:* 501(c)(3).

Issues: Compensation for partial regulatory takings; Arbitrary minimum parcel size for land divisions; Getting relief from rigid ripeness criteria; Denial of farm dwellings based on income standard; Fighting wildlife overlay regulations on private land; Opposing exactions that violate *Dolan v. City of Tigard.*

OREGONS TAXPAYERS UNITED EDUCATIONAL FOUNDATION

Bill Sizemore, Executive Director
16140 S.E. 82nd Drive, Clackamas, OR 97015
503-655-0600   fax 503-655-7414   mail@out.org   *www.otu.org*

Oregon Taxpayers United Educational Foundation was founded in 1993 to minimize the percentage of the taxpayers' income and property taken from taxation and to place realistic limits on the size and growth of government bureaucracy. The Foundation believes government today is too big, spends too much, and is controlled by powerful public employee unions and other self-serving special interests. The Foundation's goal is to return control of government to its citizens. *Tax Status:* 501(c)(3).

Issues: Educate the public on public policy issues; Reduce government regulation and the tax burden; Unite taxpayers against wasteful government spending; Restore accountability in government; Protect the integrity of the initiative system; Privatizing public services.

OREGONS TAXPAYERS UNITED PAC

Bill Sizemore, Executive Director
16140 S.E. 82nd Drive, Clackamas, OR 97015
503-655-0600   fax 503-655-7414   mail@out.org   *www.otu.org*

Oregon Taxpayers United PAC is the most successful initiative group in the nation. The PAC works through the initiative system to minimize the percentage of the taxpayers' income and property taken by taxation and place realistic limits on the size and growth of government bureaucracy. Oregons Taxpayers United PAC also fights to stop public employee unions and self-serving special interest groups from continuing to expand the size and intrusiveness of government. *Tax Status:* 501(c)(4).

Issues: Reduce government regulation and the tax burden; Unite taxpayers against wasteful government spending; Restore accountability in government; Protect private property rights; Privatize public services; Limit terms for public office-holders.

PACIFIC FORUM CSIS

Rear Adm. Lloyd R. Vasey, USN (Ret.), Founder and Senior Policy Advisor
1001 Bishop Street, Pauahi Tower, Suite 1150, Honolulu, HI 96813
808-521-6745   fax 808-599-8690   pacforum@hawaii.rr.com   *www.csis.org/pacfor/*

Based in Honolulu, Hawaii, the Pacific Forum CSIS is a non-profit, private, public policy research institute which operates as the Asia-Pacific arm of the Center for Strategic and International Studies of Washington, D.C. Founded in 1975, the thrust of the Forum's work is to help stimulate cooperative policies in the Asia-Pacific region through debate and analyses undertaken with the region's leaders in the academic, government, and corporate arenas. Programs encompass current and emerging issues in political, security, economic-business, and ocean policy issues. Pacific Forum CSIS also collaborates with a network of more than 30 research institues around the Pacific Rim. *Tax Status:* 501(c)(3).

Issues: Multilateral security mechanisms; Bilateral relationships in East Asia; Comparative political economics in East Asia; Nuclear energy, non-proliferation and transparency.

PACIFIC JUSTICE INSTITUTE

Brad W. Dacus, Esq., President
P. O. Box 4366, Citrus Heights, CA 95611
916-857-6900   fax 916-857-6902   braddacus@pacificjustice.org   *www.pacificjustice.org*

Today, people find themselves entangled in legal issues, increasingly so in areas of parents' rights, religious freedom, and our civil liberties. Pacific Justice Institute has stepped into this gulf, enabling capable and willing attorneys to effectively serve their clients, and working diligently without charge to provide these attorneys and their clients with experienced legal research support, timely financial resources, client-sensitive media support, access to a thorough bank of briefs and sample briefings, and strategic planning with insight and experience. PJI's focus is to coordinate and oversee large numbers of concurrent court actions, through a network of affiiate attorneys nation-wide. *Tax Status:* 501(c)(3).

Issues: Religious freedom and liberties; Parents' rights; Redirection of union dues to charities; Defending against anti-family, anti-faith legislation.

PACIFIC LEGAL FOUNDATION

Robert K. Best, President
10360 Old Placerville Road, Suite 100, Sacramento, CA 95827
916-362-2833 fax 916-362-2932 plf@pacificlegal.org *www.pacificlegal.org*

Founded in 1973, Pacific Legal Foundation is a public interest, non-profit legal foundation whose mission is to protect the individual and economic freedoms of Americans and promote the concepts of limited government and the free-enterprise system. PLF represents the economic, social, and environmental interests of the public in court while emphasizing private property rights; freedom from excessive government regulation; free-market economics; balanced environmental policy; and non-wasteful, productive, and fiscally sound government. Through its litigation, PLF combats race and gender preferences, quotas, and set-asides in government hiring, education, and contracting. **Tax Status:** 501(c)(3).

Issues: Property rights; Government quotas and preferences; Environmental regulation, including Endangered Species Act reform; Education reform; Enforcing Constitutional limits on federal government powers.

PACIFIC RESEARCH INSTITUTE FOR PUBLIC POLICY

Sally C. Pipes, President and CEO
755 Sansome Street, Suite 450, San Francisco, CA 94111
415-989-0833 fax 415-989-2411 spipes@pacificresearch.org *www.pacificresearch.org*

The Pacific Research Institute for Public Policy promotes the principles of individual freedom and personal responsibility. The Institute believes these principles are best encouraged through policies that emphasize a free economy, private initiative, and limited government. By focusing on public policy issues such as education, the environment, economics, and social welfare, PRI strives to foster a better understanding of the principles of a free society among leaders in government, academia, the media, and the business community. **Tax Status:** 501(c)(3).

Issues: Education reform; Environment and property rights; Health and welfare reform; Technology and freedom; Economic issues; Privatization.

PALMETTO FAMILY COUNCIL

Dr. Oran P. Smith, Executive Director
P. O. Box 11953, Columbia, SC 29211
803-733-5601 fax 803-733-5601 email@palmettofamily.org *www.palmettofamily.org*

The Palmetto Family Council is a non-profit public research and educational organization committed to promoting Judeo-Christian principles on issues affecting the family through research, education, and networking. PFC uses principled persuasion to address cultural issues and promote responsible citizenship. **Tax Status:** 501(c)(3).

Issues: Renewing a marriage culture; Lottery; Father absence; Life issues; Choice in education.

PARENTS TELEVISION COUNCIL

Lara Mahaney, Director of Corporate and Entertainment Affairs
707 Wilshire Boulevard, Suite 2075, Los Angeles, CA 90017
213-629-9255 fax 213-629-9254 ptcmembers@parentstv.org *www.parentstv.org*

Established in 1995, the Hollywood-focused mission of the Parents Television Council is to bring America's demand for values-driven television programming to the entertainment industry. PTC offers private-sector solutions to restore television to its roots as an independent and socially responsible entertainment medium. **Tax Status:** 501(c)(3).

Issues: Restoring the "family hour" to prime time TV; Television ratings; Video games; Music; FCC issues pertaining to indecency.

PENNSYLVANIA FAMILY INSTITUTE
Michael Geer, President
1240 North Mountain Avenue, Harrisburg, PA 17112
717-545-0600   fax 717-545-8107   pafamily@aol.com   *www.pafamily.org*

The Pennsylvania Family Institute's mission is to strengthen families by restoring to public life the traditional, foundational principles and values essential for the well-being of society using a fourfold strategy of raising media awareness of the importance of the family; conducting family-impact analysis, research, and testimony in the state capitol; communicating with the grassroots, informing them of trends in culture and public policy; and encouraging voting and responsible citizenship. *Tax Status:* 501(c)(3).

Issues: School choice; Parental rights in education; Divorce reform; Gambling; Day care; Abortion.

PERC – THE CENTER FOR FREE MARKET ENVIRONMENTALISM
Terry Anderson, Executive Director
502 South 19th Avenue, Suite 211, Bozeman, MT 59718
406-587-9591   fax 406-586-7555   perc@perc.org   *www.perc.org*

PERC seeks to provide market solutions to environmental and natural resource problems. As a proponent of free-market environmentalism, the Center offers alternatives to excessive government control and regulation. Its endeavors are guided by the following principles: Private property rights encourage stewardship of resources; government subsidies often degrade the environment; market incentives spur individuals to conserve resources and protect environmental quality; and polluters should be liable for the harm they cause others. PERC concentrates on three program areas: Research and policy analysis, outreach to opinion leaders, and environmental education in elementary to graduate school levels. *Tax Status:* 501(c)(3).

Issues: Endangered species; Public land management; Water and air pollution; Community management of natural resources; Environmental education; Environmental entrepreneurs.

PERSONAL RETIREMENT ALLIANCE, LTD.
Edwin R. Thompson, President
330 East 38th Street, Suite 55, New York, NY 10163-4353
212-972-9012   fax 212-972-9014   ethompson@iOptOut.org   *www.iOptOut.org*

The Personal Retirement Alliance is a national non-profit organization dedicated to promoting full privatization of the Social Security system in accordance with sound moral and economic principles. The Alliance advocates the implementation of a program that provides all Americans with the option of accumulating retirement savings in individually owned, fully portable and privately managed personal retirement accounts (PRA's) funded with a portion of the FICA taxes. The Alliance also acts as a vehicle for the average citizen to get involved, both through membership and activism. *Tax Status:* 501(c)(3).

Issues: Social Security privatization.

PHILANTHROPY ROUNDTABLE
Adam Meyerson, President
1150 17th Street, N.W., Suite 503, Washington, DC 20036
202-822-8333   fax 202-822-8325   main@philanthropyroundtable.org
www.philanthropyroundtable.org

The Philanthropy Roundtable is a national association of individual donors, foundation trustees and staff, and corporate giving executives. Its mission is to foster excellence in philanthropy and to assist donors in advancing freedom, opportunity, and personal responsibility. *Tax Status:* 501(c)(3).

Issues: Education; Marriage and family; War on terrorism; Environmental stewardship; Character-based social services; Public policy.

PIONEER INSTITUTE FOR PUBLIC POLICY RESEARCH

Stephen Adams, Executive Director
85 Devonshire Street, Eighth Floor, Boston, MA 02109
617-723-2277   fax 617-723-1880   pioneer@pioneerInstitute.org
www.pioneerinstitute.org

The Pioneer Institute is a think tank dedicated to changing the intellectual climate in Massachusetts with programs that develop solutions to real-world social and economic problems. Underlying Pioneer's work is a belief in individual freedom and responsibility, limited and accountable government, and the application of free-market principles to public policy. Pioneer devotes half of its efforts to the reform of K-12 education, with a focus on competition and the expansion of parental choice. In addition, Pioneer examines opportunities for restructuring and reducing the size of Massachusetts' government through competition, privatization, and deregulation. *Tax Status:* 501(c)(3).

Issues: Charter schools; Privatization; Welfare reform; Economic development programs; Health care; Education reform.

POLICY AND TAXATION GROUP

Patricia M. Soldano, President
3941 South Bristol Street, Unit E, PMB 46, Santa Ana, CA 92704
714-641-6913   fax 714-641-3128   pmsoldano@policyandtaxationgroup.com
www.policyandtaxationgroup.com

The Policy and Taxation Group is dedicated to the repeal of the gift, estate and generation-skipping tax and the elimination of the destructive effect that those taxes have on families, family businesses, job creation, the national economy and government revenues.

Issues: Estate, gift and generation-skipping taxes.

POLISH-AMERICAN FOUNDATION FOR ECONOMIC RESEARCH AND EDUCATION

John M. Malek, Founder and President
P. O. Box 1475, Torrance, CA 90505
310-316-6888   fax 310-316-6888   pafere@cs.com   *www.kapitalizm.republika.pl/pafere/*

Founded in 2000, the Polish-American Foundation for Economic Research and Education is a private, non-profit educational and research organization dedicated to helping Polish-Americans and Polish-speaking people of Eastern and Central Europe gain a better understanding of economics. PAFERE operates on the premise that historical experience and basic facts about human nature prove conclusively that a free society based on market order, limited government under the rule of law, and individual responsibility is essential for prosperity and human happiness. *Tax Status:* 501(c)(3).

Issues: Economic education; Economic competition.

POPULATION RESEARCH INSTITUTE

Steven W. Mosher, President
P. O. Box 1559, Front Royal, VA 22630
540-622-5240   fax 540-622-2728   pri@pop.org   *www.pop.org*

The mission and priorities of the Population Research Institute are: To make a case against the widely held, but fundamentally wrongheaded, development paradigm which places economic and population growth in opposition to one another; to articulate the material and social benefits of moderate population growth and promote economic development through models which respect the dignity and rights of the individual human being; and to document abuses of human rights in the name of population control, which have occurred in almost every corner of the developing world, and work for the elimination of such abuses. *Tax Status:* 501(c)(3).

Issues: Population; Human rights abuses; Economic development; Resource availability.

PRISON FELLOWSHIP MINISTRIES

Hon. Mark L. Earley, President and Chief Executive Officer
P. O. Box 17500, Washington, DC 20041
703-478-0100   fax 703-834-3658   tom_pratt@pfm.org   *www.pfm.org*

Prison Fellowship Ministries is a non-profit, volunteer-based organization with a mission to exhort, assist, and equip the Church in its ministry to prisoners, ex-prisoners, victims, and their families and in its advancement of Biblical standards of justice. To accomplish this mission, Prison Fellowship recruits, trains, and mobilizes volunteers from a wide variety of backgrounds and denominations to participate in a broad array of in-prison and community ministries. *Tax Status:* 501(c)(3).

Issues: Religious Freedom Restoration Act; Juvenile crime; Victims' rights; Meaningful work programs in prisons; Victim-offender reconciliation.

PROGRESS & FREEDOM FOUNDATION

Raymond L. Gifford, President
1401 H Street, N.W., Suite 1075, Washington, DC 20005
202-289-8928   fax 202-289-6079   pff@aol.com   *www.pff.org*

The Progress & Freedom Foundation studies technology and its implications for public policy. The Foundation believes the digital revolution is creating changes in society that cause power to migrate away from large, centralized institutions and move closer to the people, and, in that sense, inherently favors personal freedom. PFF's public policy studies examine the implications of this phenomenon for government with an eye toward producing government structures that are smaller, less bureaucratic, and less intrusive in cultural and economic affairs. *Tax Status:* 501(c)(3).

Issues: Telecommunications policy; First Amendment, encryption, and privacy; Market structure of the communications industry; Competition in electric energy; Medical innovation and regulation; Social implications of the digital revolution.

PROJECT 21

David W. Almasi, Director
777 North Capitol Street, N.E., Suite 803, Washington, DC 20002
202-371-1400   fax 202-408-7773   project21@nationalcenter.org
www.nationalcenter.org

Project 21 is an African-American leadership network founded to promote the views of African-Americans whose entrepreneurial spirit, sense of family and commitment to individual responsibility that has not been traditionally echoed by the nation's civil rights establishment. Project 21 acts as a public relations network for moderate and conservative African-Americans, and is interested in promoting those African-Americans who want to discuss their beliefs not only in the privacy of their own homes but in thousands of homes across the nation through media outreach. *Tax Status:* 501(c)(3).

Issues: Civil rights; School choice; Environmental justice; Tax policy; Welfare reform.

PROJECT FOR THE NEW AMERICAN CENTURY

Gary Schmitt, Executive Director
1150 17th Street, N.W., Suite 510, Washington, DC 20036
202-293-4983   fax 202-293-4572   project@newamericancentury.org
www.newamericancentury.org

Established in 1997, the Project for the New American Century is a non-profit educational organization whose goal is to promote American global leadership. Through issue briefs, study groups, and roundtables, the Project supports national security policies which maintain America's role as the world's preeminent power and enhance the country's ability to shape the international order in a way favorable to American principles and interests. *Tax Status:* 501(c)(3).

Issues: U.S. Defense strategy and resources; U.S.-China policy; War on terrorism; U.S.-Iraq policy; Expansion of democracy abroad; Middle East "Peace Process".

PROJECT REALITY

Kathleen Sullivan, Director
P. O. Box 97, Golf, IL 60029-0097
847-729-3298   fax 847-729-9744   info@projectreality.org   *www.projectreality.org*

Since 1985, Project Reality has been at the forefront of the national field of adolescent health education with the promotion of abstinence-centered programs in the public schools. Project Reality's values and character-based curricula emphasize abstinence until marriage as the best choice and the healthiest lifestyle for adolescents. *Tax Status:* 501(c)(3).

Issues: Abstinence-until-marriage education; Expanding the Illinois Abstinence Coalition; Expanding the National Abstinence Clearinghouse Coalition; *Power of Abstinence* seminars for adults; *Reality Check* youth rallies; Media promotion of abstinence until marriage.

PROPERTY RIGHTS FOUNDATION OF AMERICA, INC.

Carol W. LaGrasse, President and Founder
P. O. Box 75, Stoney Creek, NY 12878
518-696-5748   lagrasse@prfamerica.org

The Property Rights Foundation of America is dedicated to the defense and enhancement of the fundamental right to own and use private property as guaranteed in the United States Constitution and to keeping land in private ownership. *Tax Status:* 501(c)(3).

Issues: Zoning; State and federal land acquisition; UNESCO biosphere reserves; New York state wetlands; Heritage rivers and other corridors; Conservation easements/land trusts.

PUBLIC INTEREST INSTITUTE

Don Racheter, President
600 North Jackson Street, Mount Pleasant, IA 52641
319-385-3462   fax 319-385-3799   public.interest.institute@limitedgovernment.org
www.limitedgovernment.org

The Public Interest Institute's goals are to become an information and analysis resource for all Iowans; provide local, state, and national policymakers with a rigorous, objective, and understandable analysis of specific policy initiatives; identify practical alternatives for action on critical state and local issues; and provide a forum for policymakers and individuals to share ideas and concerns. The Institute promotes the importance of a free-enterprise economic system and its relationship to a free and democratic society. PII seeks to support the proper role of a limited government in a society based upon individual freedom and liberty. *Tax Status:* 501(c)(3).

Issues: Limiting government; Tax relief; Spending limits; Government efficiency; Education; Iowa civics.

PUBLIC POLICY INSTITUTE OF NEW YORK STATE

David F. Shaffer, President
152 Washington Avenue, Albany, NY 12210-2289
518-465-7511   fax 518-432-4537   *www.ppinys.org*

Founded in 1981, the Public Policy Institute is a research and educational organization whose purpose is to formulate and promote public policies that will restore New York's economic competitiveness. The Institute accomplishes this mission by conducting timely, in-depth research addressing key state policy issues. These findings are effectively communicated to the Institute's primary audiences: members of the New York State Legislature, key legislative staff members, policymakers in the Executive branch, the state's news media, and the academic and policy communities. The Institute is affiliated with The Business Council of New York State, Inc. *Tax Status:* 501(c)(3).

Issues: State tax reform and budget priorities; Economic competitiveness and growth.

PUBLIC SERVICE RESEARCH COUNCIL

David Y. Denholm, President
320-D Maple Avenue East, Vienna, VA 22180
703-242-3575   fax 703-242-3579   publicsrc@erols.com

Public Service Research Council is a national citizens lobby founded in 1973 to oppose public sector union control of the size, cost, and quality of public services and union special interest influence on public policy. The Council sponsors Americans Against Union Control of Government, monitors legislation at the state and federal level, and mobilizes grassroots action against pro-union bills and support for bills to roll back existing union special privileges and legal immunities. *Tax Status:* 501(c)(4).

Issues: Public-sector union bargaining; Strikes against government; Prevailing wage laws; Project labor agreements; Living wage laws; Union political activity.

PUBLIC SERVICE RESEARCH FOUNDATION

David Y. Denholm, President
320-D Maple Avenue East, Vienna, VA 22180
703-242-3575   fax 703-242-3579   info@psrf.org   *www.psrf.org*

PSRF is an independent research and educational organization studying the impact of unions in government on government and union special interest influence on public policy. It conducts and sponsors research on unionism, publishes *Government Union Review,* a quarterly journal, and distributes information through exhibits at conventions of public officials. The Foundation supports and encourages professional educator groups as an alternative to teacher unionism; provides speakers for meetings of business, civic and political groups; and provides information to news media. *Tax Status:* 501(c)(3).

Issues: Public-sector unionism; Public-sector collective bargaining; Prevailing wage laws; Union influence on public policy; Teacher union influence on education; Compulsory unionism.

REASON FOUNDATION

David C. Nott, President
3415 South Sepulveda Boulevard, Suite 400, Los Angeles, CA 90034
310-391-2245   fax 310-391-4395   gpassantino@reason.org   *www.reason.org*

Reason Foundation is a national research and educational organization that explores and promotes the twin values of rationality and freedom as the basic underpinnings of a good society. Reason provides practical public policy research, analysis, and commentary based upon principles of individual liberty and responsibility, limited government, and market competition. *Reason* is the nation's monthly magazine of "free minds and free markets." Reason Public Policy Institute directly engages the policy process, seeking strategies that emphasize cooperation, flexibility, local knowledge, and results. *Tax Status:* 501(c)(3).

Issues: Aviation security; Surface transportation; Environmental policy; Privatization and government reform; Culture; Education.

RELIGIOUS FREEDOM COALITION

William J. Murray, Founder and Chairman
P. O. Box 77511, Washington, DC 20013
202-543-0300   fax 202-543-8447   webmaster@rfcnet.org   *www.rfcnet.org*

The Religious Freedom Coalition is a social conservative advocacy organization which works to inform the Congress and general public of alternatives to the liberal agenda. The RFC holds the Bible as being the highest standard to which government can be held and maintains that the church, not big government, is the answer to most social problems. *Tax Status:* 501(c)(3).

Issues: Protecting children, born and unborn; Protecting the right of citizens to pray at public events; Protecting religious symbols from secular destruction; Preserving the family as the basic social unit; Saving America's children from the public school system; Stopping the homosexual and feminist agenda from overtaking American families.

RIO GRANDE FOUNDATION

Harry Messenheimer, Ph.D., President
P. O. Box 2015, Tijeras, NM 87059
505-286-2030   fax 505-286-2422   hmessen@nmia.com   *www.riograndefoundation.org*

The Rio Grande Foundation is an independent, non-partisan, tax-exempt research and educational organization dedicated to the study of public policy. Through its research papers, workshops, editorials and policy briefings the Foundation promotes public policy founded upon the principles of limited government, economic freedom and individual responsibility. To promote these principles and to assist New Mexico leaders in developing policies based on a limited government and free market approach, the Rio Grande Foundation neither seeks nor accepts government funding. The Foundation relies solely on contributions from the private sector to fund its activities. *Tax Status:* 501(c)(3).

Issues: Tax policy; Medicaid; School choice; Smart growth; Water; Tax and spending limitations.

ROCKFORD INSTITUTE

Dr. Thomas Fleming, President
928 North Main Street, Rockford, IL 61103
815-964-5053   fax 815-964-9403   info@rockfordinstitute.org
www.chroniclesmagazine.org

The Rockford Institute's chief activity is the publication of the monthly magazine, *Chronicles: A Magazine of American Culture.* In addition, the Institute operates an op-ed service, a summer school, a speakers bureau, and an audiotape lecture series; holds regular conferences throughout the year at home and abroad, including the John Randolph Club; and publishes two or three books annually. *Tax Status:* 501(c)(3).

Issues: Classical education; Authentic federalism; America-first economic and foreign policy; Insurgent Islam; The restoration of Christendom; The primacy of the family.

ROCKY MOUNTAIN FAMILY COUNCIL

Thomas McMillen, President
8704 Yates Drive, Suite 205, Westminster, CO 80030
303-292-1800   fax 303-796-7848   rmfc@aol.com   *www.rmfc.org*

The Rocky Mountain Family Council exists to promote renewal in families, marriages, education, and government throughout the Rocky Mountain region. This is accomplished through communication with the Colorado legislature and through RMFC's Charter School and Marriage projects. *Tax Status:* 501(c)(3).

Issues: Divorce reform; Charter schools; Family tax relief; Parental notice and consent; Same sex marriage; Domestic partner benefit policies.

ROSE INSTITUTE FOR STATE AND LOCAL GOVERNMENT

Dr. Ralph A. Rossum, Director
Claremont McKenna College, 340 East 9th Street, Claremont, CA 91711-6420
909-621-8159   fax 909-607-4288   roseinstitute@claremontmckenna.edu
www.mckenna.edu

Using computer technology, students and faculty, the Rose Institute advances knowledge about politics and helps create services that make the political process more democratic. Through the development of large computerized databases and advanced geographic retrieval systems, students become involved in projects focusing on such topics as redistricting, fiscal analysis, California demographics, survey research, and legal and regulatory analysis and, therefore, contribute to a better understanding of many aspects of California's state and local government.

Issues: State and local government; State fiscal policy; Regulation; Elections.

THE RUTHERFORD INSTITUTE

John Whitehead, President
P. O. Box 7482, Charlottesville, VA 22906
434-978-3888 fax 434-978-1789 tristaff@rutherford.org *www.rutherford.org*

The Rutherford Institute is a non-profit, civil liberties legal and educational organization dedicated to protecting the religious rights of persons in the public arena, aided by a network of hundreds of attorneys willing to represent persons on a *pro-bono* basis. Rutherford also protects the right of parents to determine the religious and educational upbringing of their children when denied by the government. It is dedicated to protecting the constitutional rights of churches and other religious organizations when the government attempts to restrict such organizations by imposing restrictive zoning regulations. *Tax Status:* 501(c)(3).

Issues: Protecting religious expression; Free speech issues; Parental rights; Sanctity of human life; Church rights; International religious persecution.

SCIENCE AND ENVIRONMENTAL POLICY PROJECT

S. Fred. Singer, President
1600 Eads Street Street, Suite 712-S, Arlington, VA 22202-2907
703-920-2744 fax 815-461-7448 sepp@sepp.org *www.sepp.org*

The Science and Environmental Policy Project is a non-profit educational association of scientists concerned with providing a sound scientific base for environmental policies. *Tax Status:* 501(c)(3).

Issues: Global warming; Ozone depletion; Urban air pollution; Chemical and radiation risk.

SECOND AMENDMENT FOUNDATION

Alan Gottlieb, Founder
James Madison Building, 12500 N.E. Tenth Place, Bellevue, WA 98005
425-454-7012 fax 425-451-3959 akagunnut@aol.com *www.saf.org*

The Second Amendment Foundation's mission is to protect and defend the right to keep and bear arms. *Tax Status:* 501(c)(3).

Issues: Public education about the right to keep and bear arms; Legal defense of gun rights; Publishing on gun rights.

THE SENIORS COALITION

Mary Martin, Chairman of the Board and Executive Director
9001 Braddock Road, Suite 200, Springfield, VA 22151
703-239-1960 fax 703-239-1985 tsc@senior.org *www.senior.org*

The Seniors Coalition is a non-profit, non-partisan, education and issue advocacy organization that represents the interests and concerns of America's senior citizens at both the state and federal levels. Its mission is to protect the quality of life and economic well-being that older Americans have earned while supporting common sense solutions to the challenges of the future. The Coalition was founded as a public advocacy group during the fight to repeal the Medicare Catastrophic Coverage Act in 1989. Since then, it has grown rapidly and expanded its advocacy to include a wide range of other important issues. *Tax Status:* 501(c)(4).

Issues: Medicare; Social Security; Long-term care; Pharmaceutical issues; Tax reform; Regulatory reform.

SHENANGO INSTITUTE FOR PUBLIC POLICY

Paul Kengor, President
P. O. Box 245, Grove City, PA 16127
724-458-3394   fax 724-458-2181   sipp@shenangoinstitute.org
www.shenangoinstitute.org

The Shenango Institute for Public Policy's mission is to formulate and promote public policies at the local-government level based on the principles of free enterprise, limited government, individual freedom and responsibility, and a respect for traditional values. Focusing on the central-western Pennsylvania area, including Lawrence, Mercer, Butler and Venango counties, the SIPP supports: Private sector solutions to social and economic problems; competitive market processes in the delivery of government services; requiring governments to prove that benefits outweigh costs before embarking on public works projects; and evaluation of social services on an outcomes rather than inputs basis. *Tax Status:* 501(c)(3).

Issues: Education; Privatization; Trade; Taxes.

SMALL BUSINESS SURVIVAL COMMITTEE

Darrell McKigney, President
1920 L Street, N.W., Suite 200, Washington, DC 20036
202-785-0238   fax 202-822-8118   darrell@sbsc.org   *www.sbsc.org*

The Small Business Survival Committee works to influence legislation and policies that help to create a favorable and productive environment for small businesses and entrepreneurship. By educating policymakers, legislators, the media and the public about the critical role that small businesses play in our economy – and how government actions can positively or negatively affect the small business community – SBSC strives to establish a solid public policy foundation upon which entrepreneurial activity and small businesses can survive and flourish. *Tax Status:* 501(c)(4).

Issues: Taxes and spending; Health care; Trade; Regulation; Energy and environment; Telecommunications and the Internet.

SMALL BUSINESS SURVIVAL FOUNDATION

Darrell McKigney, President
1920 L Street, N.W., Suite 200, Washington, DC 20036
202-785-0238   fax 202-822-8118   darrell@sbsc.org   *www.sbsc.org*

The Small Business Survival Foundation studies and analyzes legislation and government-led initiatives and their impact on the small business/entrepreneurial sector of the U.S. economy and its workforce. The Foundation examines government proposals from a limited government perspective and offers alternatives that put entrepreneurial success and strength at the center of the economy. Foundation studies and analyses are shared with elected officials, the public and the media. *Tax Status:* 501(c)(3).

Issues: Tax reform; Global climate/environmental issues; IRS overhaul; Health care; Workplace/labor issues.

SMITH CENTER FOR PRIVATE ENTERPRISE STUDIES

Charles Baird, Director
California State University, Hayward, 25800 Carlos Bee Boulevard, MB 2597,
Hayward, CA 94542
510-885-3275   fax 510-885-4222   cbaird@csuhayward.edu
www.sbe.csuhayward.edu/sbesc

By sponsoring public speeches, conferences, and publications, the Smith Center promotes understanding of the free-enterprise system. Through its training program for high school teachers and contests for high school students, the Center endeavors to reach out beyond the University with the classical liberal message. *Tax Status:* 501(c)(3).

Issues: Labor relations; Union dues in politics; Affirmative action; Term limits; Tax limitation; School choice.

SOCIAL PHILOSOPHY AND POLICY CENTER

Fred D. Miller, Jr., Executive Director
Bowling Green State University, 225 Troupe Street, Bowling Green, OH 43403
419-372-2536   fax 419-372-8738   sppc@listproc.bgsu.edu   *www.bgsu.edu/offices/sppc*

The Social Philosophy and Policy Center examines public policy issues from an ethical perspective, reflecting the belief that policy questions cannot be addressed adequately by empirical investigation alone. Factual research can reveal the optimal or efficient policy by which certain public ends may be attained, yet the validity of those ends is still open to question from an ethical standpoint. Drawing upon the work of eminent scholars in philosophy, political science, law, economics, history, and other disciplines, the Center disseminates the ideas of these scholars through conferences, research fellowships, books, research papers, and an interdisciplinary journal. *Tax Status:* 501(c)(3).

Issues: Education; Tax policy; American historiography; Property rights; Welfare reform; Economic policy.

SOCIAL SECURITY CHOICE.ORG

Robert Costello, President
1300 Pennsylvania Avenue, N.W., Suite 700, Washington, DC 20004
202-204-3040   fax 202-789-7349   info@socialsecuritychoice.org
www.socialsecuritychoice.org

Social Security Choice.org is a non-partisan, grassroots, issue advocacy group dedicated to the cause of modernizing and reforming the Social Security sytem by giving workers the option to voluntarily place a portion or all of their Social Security taxes in personal retirement accounts. It represents thousands of Americans who want to have more control over their retirement futures and supports local chapters in a variety of educational activities, including speakers' bureaus, activity meetings, newsletters, and distribution of materials to new voters and young families. It also assists in efforts to let Congress know how much support already exists for Social Security Choice. Local chapters can be established on a university campus, in a neighborhood or community, or across an entire Congressional District.

SOUTH CAROLINA POLICY COUNCIL

Edward T. McMullen, Jr., Ph.D., President
1323 Pendleton Street, Columbia, SC 29201
803-779-5022   fax 803-779-4953   etm@scpolicycouncil.com   *www.scpolicycouncil.com*

Established in 1986, the South Carolina Policy Council is a non-partisan, tax-exempt public policy research and education foundation whose mission is to educate its members and all South Carolinians about state and local public policy based on the traditional South Carolina values of individual liberty and responsibility, free enterprise, and limited government. *Tax Status:* 501(c)(3).

Issues: Government reduction; Tax and budget reform; Anti-lottery; Environmental issues; Unionization and right to work; Education reform.

SOUTH DAKOTA FAMILY POLICY COUNCIL

Robert Regier, Executive Director
P. O. Box 88007, Sioux Falls, SD 57109
605-335-8100   fax 605-335-4029   sdfamily@aol.com

The South Dakota Family Policy Council provides research and analysis of family issues through various publications and media efforts, facilitates action by pro-family citizens and grassroots groups, and lobbies for pro-family interests in Pierre, the state capital. *Tax Status:* 501(c)(3).

Issues: Marriage/divorce; Video gambling; School choice; Abstinence; Pornography; Government waste.

SOUTHEASTERN LEGAL FOUNDATION

Phil Kent, President
3340 Peachtree Road, N.E., Suite 2515, Atlanta, GA 30326
404-365-8500   fax 404-365-0017   *www.southeasternlegal.org*

The Southeastern Legal Foundation, founded in 1976, is a conservative public interest law firm that advocates limited government, individual liberties, private property rights, and the free-enterprise system. Guided by the framework of the U.S. Constitution and participating in cases throughout the U.S., SLF seeks to defend the rights of individuals, organized groups, and corporations whose rights are infringed by government power in the local, state, and federal arenas. *Tax Status:* 501(c)(3).

Issues: Affirmative action; Tort reform; Challenge statistical sampling census plan; Judicial review activities; Private property takings cases.

STATE POLICY NETWORK

Tracie Sharp, President
6255 Arlington Boulevard, Richmond, CA 94805-1601
510-965-9700   fax 510-965-9701   spn@spn.org   *www.spn.org*

State Policy Network is the professional service organization for the state-based free market think tank community. It supports the independent, state-based policy research organizations whose work is devoted to individual liberty, free markets, limited government, and supporting America's unique cultural institutions. SPN serves as a clearinghouse and resource for independent state-based think tanks and affiliated organizations. It develops and coordinates programs and projects with its policy institutes that improve the understanding of the economic, cultural, and political foundations that are critical to preserving a free and prosperous society. *Tax Status:* 501(c)(3).

Issues: Education; Internet/technology; Environment; Privatization; Tax/budget; Health care.

STATISTICAL ASSESSMENT SERVICE

S. Robert Lichter, President
2100 L Street, N.W., Suite 300, Washington, DC 20037
202-223-3193   fax 202-872-4014   vital@stats.org   *www.stats.org*

STATS is a research organization dedicated to improving public understanding of scientific and statistical information. STATS monitors and evaluates research information at its source, consults journalists about the methodology and possible controversy behind particular research, matches journalists to appropriate experts, informs the policymaking debate, and educates journalists about sound research practice in preparing for tomorrow's stories. *Tax Status:* 501(c)(3).

Issues: Misrepresentation of scientific data; Health scares; Crime and youth violence; Environment; Biotechnology; Urban myths and legends.

STRONGER FAMILIES FOR OREGON

Mike Howden, Executive Director
P. O. Box 948, Salem, OR 97308
503-585-9383   fax 503-399-1698   michael@oregonfamily.org   *www.strongerfamilies.com*

Stronger Families for Oregon is a non-profit family policy council. Its mission encompasses the production and distribution of resources on issues that affect the family, including research, media contact, decision-maker resources and local issue assistance. Stronger Families promotes ideas and common sense principles that strengthen families and communities. *Tax Status:* 501(c)(3).

Issues: Abstinence education; Marriage enrichment; Fatherlessness; Juvenile crime; Gambling; Pornography/Adult businesses.

SUSQUEHANNA VALLEY CENTER FOR PUBLIC POLICY

Dr. Charles E. Greenawalt, Senior Fellow and Director of Research Projects
P. O. Box 338, Hershey, PA 17033
717-361-8905   fax 717-361-8945   susvalley@aol.com

The Susquehanna Valley Center for Public Policy is an independent, non-partisan, non-profit public policy research organization established to help Pennsylvanians build a brighter future. It's mission is to serve as a source of informed public policy information, discussion, and debate on matters of local government in central Pennsylvania. The Center commissions, distributes, and publishes reports, studies, issue papers, analyses, and articles as well as periodically sponsoring conferences, forums, seminars, and symposia for educational and information dissemination purposes. The SVCPP values are accountability, economy, efficiency, and responsiveness in local government, with an emphasis on free market principles and the role and responsibilities of citizenship that form the foundation of our political structure.

Issues: State and local government.

THE SUTHERLAND INSTITUTE

Paul T. Mero, President
111 East 5600 South, Suite 202, Salt Lake City, UT 84107
801-281-2081   fax 801-281-2414   si@sutherlandinstitute.org
www.sutherlandinstitute.org

The mission of the Sutherland Institute is to improve the state's economic, social, and political climate by disseminating workable ideas to decision makers in Utah – government officials as well as business and education leaders. Sutherland does this by publishing and disseminating policy papers, brochures, books, and newsletters; by holding conferences and seminars for legislators and the general public; and by furnishing speakers, articles, and opinion pieces to the local media. Sutherland's strategy includes touching on today's critical issues as well as setting the agenda for future policy debates. *Tax Status:* 501(c)(3).

Issues: Education reform/school choice; Free-market growth; Tax limitation.

TAX FOUNDATION

Scott Hodge, Executive Director
1900 M Street, N.W., Washington, DC 20005
202-464-6200   fax 202-464-6201   tf@taxfoundation.org   *www.taxfoundation.org*

The Tax Foundation, founded in 1937, is a non-profit, non-partisan educational organization that monitors fiscal issues at all levels of government. Serving as a national clearinghouse for providing citizens with a better understanding of their tax system and the effects of tax policy, the Foundation analyzes data from all levels of government, explores the effect of tax policy on businesses and individuals alike, and channels this information to the general public. *Tax Status:* 501(c)(3).

Issues: Corporate and individual income taxes; Excise taxes; Federal tax and budget reform/cuts/compliance; International taxation; State taxes and state allocation of federal taxes; Tax Freedom Day.

TAXPAYERS NETWORK, INC.

Michael Riley, President and Founder
W67 N222 Evergreen Boulevard, Suite 200, Cedarburg, WI 53012-2645
262-375-4190   fax 262-375-3732

TNI is a non-profit organization educating America's citizens about a common sense, free enterprise system with economic opportunity and limited government. Founded in 1992 with the intent to bring selected public policy ideas from the east coast think-tanks to the Midwest, TNI is now a nationwide organization with some 90,000 members in 47 states. TNI works to educate its members, citizen groups, the general public and elected officials about pressing issues in public policy and solutions to public policy problems.

TEACH AMERICA

Patrick J. Keleher, Jr., President
Georgetown Square, 522 4th Street, Wilmette, IL 60091
847-256-8476   fax 847-256-8482   teach522@aol.com

In 1990, TEACH America was created as a non-profit organization to implement consumer-driven, family-centered solutions to chronic education problems. TEACH America develops and leads public policy initiatives on issues such as private school scholarships, through its FOCUS Fund (Family Options for Children Urban Scholarships Fund) division; parental choice; parental rights; charter schools; privatization; alternative teacher certification; teacher formation and development; teacher private practice; and applied education ethics. TEACH America is a national coalition, bipartisan and multi-ethnic, of parents, community and business leaders, educators, and general taxpayers. *Tax Status:* 501(c)(3).

Issues: School choice; School finance and taxes; Privately funded scholarships; Issues in higher education; Teacher private practice.

TEEN-AID, INC.

LeAnna Benn, National Director
723 East Jackson, Spokane, WA 99207
509-482-2868   fax 509-482-7994   teenaid@teen-aid.org   *www.teen-aid.org*

The mission of Teen-aid is to create awareness in teens regarding the consequences of premarital sexual activity; promote the benefits of postponing sexual activity while encouraging abstinence as a premarital lifestyle; provide materials and resources for character-based family life education; and increase parent-teen communication regarding character, responsibility, sexuality, substance abuse, and self-sufficiency. *Tax Status:* 501(c)(3).

Issues: Distributing directive materials; Accessing federal abstinence funding; Training educators.

TEXAS CITIZENS FOR A SOUND ECONOMY

Peggy Venable, Director
1005 Congress Avenue, Suite 910, Austin, TX 78701
512-476-5905   fax 512-476-5906   pvenable@cse.org   *www.cse.org/cse*

Texas Citizens for a Sound Economy is a grassroots organization of Texans who support free-market solutions to public policy problems. Texas CSE's members support less government, fewer regulations, and lower taxes. Texas CSE is a 48,000 member state affiliate of the 250,000-member Citizens for a Sound Economy, which is based in Washington, D.C. *Tax Status:* 501(c)(4).

Issues: Tax and budget (state and federal); Environmental policy; Health care policy; Regulatory issues; Education.

TEXAS CONSERVATIVE COALITION

John Colyandro, Executive Director
P. O. Box 2659, Austin, TX 78768
512-474-1798   fax 512-482-8355   john.colyandro@txcc.org   *www.txcc.org*

The Texas Conservative Coalition is an organization of and for Texas state legislators committed to shaping public policy for the good of all Texans through the promotion of conservative principles – limited government, free enterprise, individual liberties, and traditional family values. *Tax Status:* 501(c)(4).

Issues: Family; Health care policy; Education; State finance issues; Agency oversight; Environmental issues.

TEXAS CONSERVATIVE COALITION RESEARCH INSTITUTE

John Colyandro, Executive Director
910 Congress Avenue, Austin, TX 78701
512-474-6042   fax 512-482-8355   john.colyandro@txccri.org   *www.txccri.org*

The Texas Conservative Coalition Research Institute was founded in 1996 on the principles of limited government, individual liberties, free enterprise and traditional family values. It is committed to shaping public policy through a principled approach to government by educating the general public and elected officials at all levels of government in the positive benefits of the application of those principles. *Tax Status:* 501(c)(3).

Issues: A principled approach to government; Education; Health care policy; Media bias.

TEXAS JUSTICE FOUNDATION

Allan Parker, Jr., President
8122 Datapoint Drive, Suite 812, San Antonio, TX 78229
210-614-7157   fax 210-614-6656   info@txjf.org   *www.txjf.org*

The Texas Justice Foundation is a non-profit, public interest litigation foundation that represents clients at no charge in landmark cases promoting limited government, free markets, private property rights, and parental rights. *Tax Status:* 501(c)(3).

Issues: Parental rights in education; School violence/safety; Property rights; Religious liberty; School choice; Women's health issues.

TEXAS PUBLIC POLICY FOUNDATION

Brooke Rollins, President
8122 Datapoint Drive, Suite 816, San Antonio, TX 78229
210-614-0080   fax 210-614-2649   tppf@tppf.org   *www.tppf.org*

The Texas Public Policy Foundation is a non-partisan research institute guided by the core principles of limited government, free enterprise, private property rights, and individual responsibility. The Foundation's mission is to improve Texas government by generating academically sound research and data on major issues and by recommending the findings to opinion leaders, policymakers, the media, and the public. *Tax Status:* 501(c)(3).

Issues: Limited government/government efficiency; Tort reform; Education reform; Tax/fiscal policy; Health care; Transportation.

THOREAU INSTITUTE

Randal O'Toole, Senior Economist
P. O. Box 1590, Bandon, OR 97411
541-347-1517   fax 305-422-0379   web@ti.org   *www.ti.org*

Inspired both by Henry David Thoreau's love of the natural world and his dislike of big government, the Thoreau Institute seeks ways to protect the environment without regulation, bureaucracy, or central control.

Issues: Wildlife conservation; Urban transportation and growth; Public lands.

TOWARD TRADITION

Rabbi Daniel Lapin, President
P. O. Box 58, Mercer Island, WA 98040
206-236-3046   fax 206-236-3288   rabbilapin@towardtradition.org
www.towardtradition.org

The mission of Toward Tradition is to create and expand a national alliance of Jewish and Christian conservatives that will contribute to an economic, cultural, and political restoration of American greatness. *Tax Status:* 501(c)(3).

Issues: Taxation; Crime; Education; Economics; Privatization.

TRADITION, FAMILY, PROPERTY, INC.

C. Preston Noell, III, President
1344 Merrie Ridge Road, McLean, VA 22101
703-243-2104   fax 703-243-2105   tfp.inc@pobox.com   *www.tfp.org*

Tradition, Family, Property, Inc. is a civic, cultural, and non-partisan organization which, inspired by the traditional teachings of the Roman Catholic Church, works to defend and promote the principles of private ownership, family, and Christian values. TFP does this by studying both the foundations of America's traditions, to invigorate them, and the components of disintegration, to counteract them. *Tax Status:* 501(c)(4).

Issues: Judicial activism; Euthanasia; Religious persecution of Christians; Abortion; Ballistic missile defense; Narco-Guerilla Crisis in Colombia.

TRADITIONAL VALUES COALITION

Rev. Lou Sheldon, Chairman
139 C Street, S.E., Washington, DC 20003
202-547-8570   fax 202-546-6403   tvcwashdc@traditionalvalues.org
www.traditionalvalues.org

Traditional Values Coalition comprises 43,000 member churches of various Christian denominations. The organization serves as a lobbying and education group advocating a return to our nation's traditional cultural values. TVC stays in regular contact with elected government leaders in an effort to uphold our religious freedoms and articulate the Judeo-Christian principles on which America was founded. *Tax Status:* 501(c)(3).

Issues: Religious freedom; Homosexual activism; Abortion; Pornography; Education; Family issues.

U. S. BILL OF RIGHTS FOUNDATION

Dane vonBreichenruchardt, President
263 Kentucky Avenue, S.E., Washington, DC 20003
202-546-7079   fax 202-546-7079   usbor@aol.com

The Bill of Rights Foundation is a non-partisan public interest advocacy organization seeking remedies at law on targeted legal issues that contravene the Bill of Rights and related constitutional law. The Foundation offers legal counsel and representation to effected public and private entities and supplemental expert legal consulting to principal counselors including research, strategy development, brief preparations, oral arguments, or filings of *amicus curiae* briefs. *Tax Status:* 501(c)(3).

Issues: Second Amendment; Civil asset forfeiture; Property rights; First Amendment; Non-profit charitable solicitation regulation; Regulatory reform.

UNITED SENIORS ASSOCIATION

Charles Jarvis, President
3900 Jermantown Road, Suite 450, Fairfax, VA 22030
703-359-6500   fax 703-359-6510   usa@unitedseniors.org   *www.unitedseniors.org*

The United Seniors Association is dedicated to protecting the retirement security of all Americans and fights to protect the interests and values of members and others concerned about the health, security, and dignity of America's seniors. Working in Washington, D.C. and at the grassroots level around the country, USA educates and mobilizes seniors who share the philosophy that individual freedom, personal responsibility, a vibrant free enterprise system, traditional values, and a strong national defense are the hallmarks of American liberty and a just society. USA believes that well-informed seniors ultimately are their own best representatives. *Tax Status:* 501(c)(4).

Issues: Ending the raid on the Social Security Trust Fund; Repealing Social Security tax increase; Medicare reform; Social Security reform; Protecting private pensions; Election year scare tactics aimed at seniors.

U. S. ENGLISH FOUNDATION

Mauro E. Mujica, Chairman and CEO
1747 Pennsylvania Avenue, N.W., Suite 1050, Washington, DC 20006
202-833-0100   fax 202-833-0108   info@us-english.org   *www.us-english.org/foundation/*

The U.S. English Foundation is a tax-exempt non-profit organization. The Foundation has several missions: Helping improve the teaching of English to immigrants, to allow them to enjoy the economic opportunities available in this country; studying language policy and its effects around the world, so we can apply the lessons learned through the experiences of other countries to the United States; and raising public awareness through the media about the importance of our common language. *Tax Status:* 501(c)(3).

U. S. ENGLISH, INC.

Mauro E. Mujica, Chairman and CEO
1747 Pennsylvania Avenue, N.W., Suite 1050, Washington, DC 20006
202-833-0100   fax 202-833-0108   tschultz@us-english.org   *www.us-english.org*

Founded in 1983 by the late Sen. S.I. Hayakawa of California, U.S. English is the largest national, non-partisan, non-profit citizens' action group dedicated to preserving the unifying role of the English language in the United States. Its efforts support making English the official language of government at all levels and encourage immigrants to learn English, allowing them to enjoy the economic opportunities available in this country. *Tax Status:* 501(c)(4).

Issues: Official English (state and federal); Bilingual education reform; Tax credits for teaching English; Puerto Rico statehood and language concerns; Hispanic vote in 2000.

UNITED STATES INSTITUTE OF PEACE

Richard H. Solomon, President
1200 17th Street, N.W., Suite 200, Washington, DC 20036
202-457-1700   fax 202-429-6063   usip_requests@usip.org   *www.usip.org*

The United States Institute of Peace is an independent, non-partisan federal institution created and funded by Congress to strengthen the nation's capacity to promote the peaceful resolution of international conflict. Established in 1984, the Institute meets its congressional mandate through an array of programs, including grants, fellowships, conferences and workshops, library services, publications, and other educational activities. The Institute's board of directors is appointed by the President of the United States and confirmed by the Senate. *Tax Status:* 501(c)(3).

UNITED STATES JUSTICE FOUNDATION

Gary Kreep, Executive Director
2091 East Valley Parkway, Suite 1-C, Escondido, CA 92027
760-741-8086   fax 760-741-9548   usjf@usjf.org   *www.usjf.net*

The United States Justice Foundation is a non-profit public interest, legal action organization dedicated to instruct, inform and educate the public on, and to litigate, significant legal issues confronting America. *Tax Status:* 501(c)(3).

Issues: Education; Parental rights; Property rights; First Amendment rights of pro-life picketers; Privacy rights; Government harassment of government critics.

U. S. TERM LIMITS

Stacie Rumenap, Executive Director
10 G Street, N.E., Suite 410, Washington, DC 20002
202-379-3000   fax 202-379-3010   admin@ustermlimits.org   *www.termlimits.org*

Focusing on Congress and state legislatures, U. S. Term Limits is an issue advocacy organization that provides information to the public on officeholders' and candidates' positions on term limits and their willingness to limit their own terms. *Tax Status:* 501(c)(3).

Issues: Term Limits.

URBAN FAMILY COUNCIL

Betty Jean Wolfe, President
P. O. Box 11415, Philadelphia, PA 19111
215-663-9494   fax 215-663-9444   bjwolfe@urbanfamily.org   *www.urbanfamily.org*

The Urban Family Council is an inter-racial, urban-based progressive pro-family/pro-child organization dedicated to the City, its children and families and to influencing the public square and the marketplace of ideas with the Judeo-Christian ethic. *Tax Status:* 501(c)(3).

Issues: Developing leaders from the minority community; Urban father absence; Abortion, marriage, family, children; School choice; Influencing urban network media outlets; Racial unity on the issues of the day.

VICTIMS OF COMMUNISM MEMORIAL FOUNDATION

Dr. Lee Edwards, President
1513 16th Street, N.W., Washington, DC 20036
202-387-7015   fax 202-387-7017   vocmemorial@aol.com

The Victims of Communism Memorial Foundation was established to commemorate the more than 100 million victims of Communism, to honor those who successfully resisted Communist tyranny, to educate current and future generations about the winning of the Cold War, and to document Communism's continuing crimes against humanity. The ultimate goal of the Foundation is to build a Victims of Communism Memorial Museum in the Nation's capital regarding this epic struggle of the 20th Century.

VIRGINIA INSTITUTE FOR PUBLIC POLICY

John Taylor, President
20461 Tappahannock Place, Potomac Falls, VA 20165-4791
703-421-8635   fax 703-421-8631   jtaylor@virginiainstitute.org
www.virginiainstitute.org

The Virginia Institute for Public Policy is an independent, non-partisan research organization committed to the goals of individual opportunity and economic growth. Through research, policy recommendations, and symposia, the Institute works ahead of the political process to lay the intellectual foundation for a society dedicated to individual liberty, free enterprise, private property, the rule of law, and constitutionally limited government. *Tax Status:* 501(c)(3).

Issues: Devolution of power and federalism; Economic policy; Education reform; Environmental policy/property rights; Privatization; Tax reform.

WALLBUILDERS

David Barton, President and Founder
P. O. Box 397, Aledo, TX 76008
817-441-6044   fax 817-441-6866   info@wallbuilders.com   *www.wallbuilders.com*

WallBuilder's goal is to exert direct and positive influence in government, education, and the family by educating the nation concerning the Godly foundation of the country; providing information to federal, state, and local officials as they develop public policies which reflect Biblical values; and encouraging Christians to be involved in the civic arena. *Tax Status:* 501(c)(3).

Issues: Religious liberty; Judicial restraint; Family; Education.

WASHINGTON EVANGELICALS FOR RESPONSIBLE GOVERNMENT

Bob Higley, Lobbyist and Director
P. O. Box 86, Olympia, WA 98507-0086
360-705-0840   info@werg.org   *www.werg.org*

Washington Evangelicals for Responsible Government provides an evangelical Christian lobbyist for the Washington State Legislature and to State Government Agencies. Legislation and Rulings are evaluated from a Biblical perspective, and testimony is presented at hearings held on issues affecting the Christian community. *Tax Status:* 501(c)(4).

WASHINGTON LEGAL FOUNDATION

Daniel Popeo, Chairman and General Counsel
2009 Massachusetts Avenue, N.W., Washington, DC 20036
202-588-0302   fax 202-588-0386   administration@wlf.org   *www.wlf.org*

The Washington Legal Foundation is a non-profit, free enterprise public interest law and policy center. Founded 25 years ago, WLF advocates free enterprise principles, responsible government, property rights, strong national security and defense, and a balanced civil and criminal justice system. Using a unique three-pronged approach: litigating precedent-setting issues in the courts and before government agencies, publishing and marketing timely and relevant legal studies, and ensuring maximum exposure for its work with policymakers and the media, the Washington Legal Foundation is able to shape public policy and work with allies in government and our legal system to strengthen America's free enterprise system. *Tax Status:* 501(c)(3).

Issues: Civil justice reform; Strong national security and defense; Trial lawyers' tactics' impact on the economy; Government accountability; Regulatory reform; Environmental regulation and enforcement.

WASHINGTON POLICY CENTER

Daniel Mead Smith, President
4025 Delridge Way, S.W., Suite 210, Seattle, WA 98106
206-937-9691   fax 206-938-6313   wpc@washingtonpolicy.org
www.washingtonpolicy.org

The Washington Policy Center is a statewide, non-profit, research and education organization based in Seattle. As a non-partisan, free-market think tank, it publishes studies on a variety of issues, sponsors events and conferences and educates citizens on public policy issues facing Washington state. The Washington Policy Center is rapidly becoming recognized as Washington state's source for independent, public policy analysis providing high quality research for the benefit of the state's citizens, policymakers and media. Ideas developed through its research provide a basis of debate and formation of sound public policy on key issues facing the state of Washington. *Tax Status:* 501(c)(3).

Issues: Competitve bidding for government services; Government regulations; Tax and budget policy; Small business and entrepreneurial issues; Free-market environmental solutions; Labor policy.

WASHINGTON RESEARCH COUNCIL

Richard S. Davis, President
108 South Washington Street, Suite 406, Seattle, WA 98104
206-467-7088   fax 206-467-6957   wrc@researchcouncil.org   *www.researchcouncil.org*

The mission of the Washington Research Council is to serve its members and the public by promoting effective public policy and efficient government through independent and objective fiscal analyses of important policy questions and through broad communication of its findings. *Tax Status:* 501(c)(3).

WASHINGTON SCHOLARSHIP FUND

Daniel La Bry, President and Executive Director
1133 15th Street, N.W., Suite 550, Washington, DC 20005
202-293-5560   fax 202-293-7893   dlabry@wsf-dc.org   *www.wsf-dc.org*

The Washington Scholarship Fund is a not-for-profit organization dedicated to providing hope, opportunity and access to low-income families in our Nation's Capital. Through privately funded scholarships, it enables families to place their K-12 students in the educational environment they believe is best suited to help their children reach their fullest potential. WSF assists more than 1,200 scholarship recipients enrolled in 130-plus schools as well as homeschool environments. Over 23,000 applications have been submitted for scholarship assistance since 1997-98, and WSF still receives about 8-10 applications for every scholarship it awards. Applicants are chosen by lottery and allowed to choose any school environment a family desires. *Tax Status:* 501(c)(3).

Issues: Private K-12 scholarship funding; Maintaining and expanding K-12 scholarship availability; Analysis of effects of program on scholarship students; Low-income family motivations for exercising school choice; Low-income family needs for successful private school experiences.

WEB WISE KIDS, INC.

Monigue Nelson, President
P. O. Box 27203, Santa Ana, CA 92799
714-435-2885   fax 714-435-0523   *www.webwisekids.org*

Web Wise Kids takes a pro-active approach against predators through preventative measures by teaching children online safety awareness. Children who are aware, educated and prepared are less likely to be victims of any sort of crime, including Internet crime. WWK offers a youth program targeting middle school-aged children.

Issues: Internet obscenity; Internet education.

WEIDENBAUM CENTER

Dr. Steven S. Smith, Director
Washington University, Campus Box 1027, St. Louis, MO 63130
314-935-5662   fax 314-935-5688   smith@wc.wustl.edu   *http://csab.wustl.edu/*

The mission of the Weidenbaum Center is to improve public understanding of the private-enterprise system in a global context, thereby fostering a policy environment within which the U.S. market economy can prosper. This mission is accomplished by providing relevant, timely, and credible research on American business and the private-enterprise system. Weidenbaum's research efforts are focused on four primary program areas: Regulation, environment, global marketplace, and management issues. *Tax Status:* 501(c)(3).

Issues: Climate change; Environmental federalism; Reform of environmental regulation; Regulatory budgeting/accounting; Regulatory reform; Effects of trade side agreements.

WESTERN POLICY CENTER

John Sitilides, Executive Director
1990 M Street, N.W, Suite 610, Washington, DC 20036
202-530-1425   fax 202-530-0261   info@westernpolicy.org   *www.westernpolicy.org*

The Western Policy Center is a public policy organziation promoting U.S. geostrategic interests and Western values and institutions throughout southeastern Europe, with special emphasis on Greece, Turkey, and Balkans issues. Its Washington, D.C. office opened in 1998 to help focus the U.S. government on constructive, pro-active policies concerning the eastern Mediterranean and the Balkans, on bilateral and regional levels; improving relations among Greece, Turkey, and Cyprus, especially within NATO and EU frameworks; and promoting creative approaches to resolving Aegean differences, the Cyprus problem and Balkan instability. To achieve its objectives, the WPC undertakes regular policy analysis and development, national and international public affairs programming, and Internet publications and communications. *Tax Status:* 501(c)(3).

Issues: Greek-Turkish relations; EU-Turkey relations; U.S.-NATO relations; Balkan stability; War on terrorism; European human rights.

WISCONSIN POLICY RESEARCH INSTITUTE

James H. Miller, President
P. O. Box 487, Thiensville, WI 53092
262-241-0514   fax 262-241-0774   wpri@execpc.com   *www.wpri.org*

The Wisconsin Policy Research Institute is a non-profit organization established to study public policy issues affecting the state of Wisconsin. WPRI's goal is to provide non-partisan research on key issues that affect citizens living in Wisconsin so that their elected representatives are able to make informed decisions to improve the quality of life and future of the state. The Institute's major priority is to improve the accountability of Wisconsin's government, based on the belief that the views of the citizens of Wisconsin should guide the decisions of government officials. *Tax Status:* 501(c)(3).

Issues: Education; Crime; Taxes; Welfare; Privatization; Public opinion polls.

YANKEE INSTITUTE FOR PUBLIC POLICY STUDIES

Lewis Andrews, Executive Director
Trinity College, P. O. Box 260660, Hartford, CT 06126
860-297-4271   fax 860-987-6218   info@yankeeinstitute.org   *www.yankeeinstitute.org*

The Yankee Institute for Public Policy Studies produces public policy studies, white papers, seminars, and news media communications on issues affecting the future of Connecticut and the nation. *Tax Status:* 501(c)(3).

Issues: Education reform; Analysis of state budget; Analysis of state income tax.

YOUNG AMERICA'S FOUNDATION

Ron Robinson, President
110 Elden Street, Herndon, VA 20170
800-292-9231   fax 703-318-9122   yaf@yaf.org   *www.yaf.org*

Young America's Foundation is committed to ensuring that increasing numbers of young Americans understand and are inspired by the ideas of individual freedom, limited government, a strong national defense, free enterprise, and traditional values. YAF operates Ronald Reagan's Western White House, Rancho del Cielo, in Santa Barbara as the centerpiece of its Presidential Leadership Program. *Tax Status:* 501(c)(3).

Issues: Conservative conferences and lectures; Political correctness; Abolishing racial preferences; Reagan legacy; Students' ability to defend faith and freedom; Liberal bias in schools.

International Experts

Ahmad, Nizam
Director, Making Our Economy Right
NEG 2-A, Road 84, Gulshan-2, Dhaka 1212,
BANGLADESH
011-880-2-8829070
fax 011-880-2-8829070
nizam@bdmail.net   *www.moer.org*
Issues: Democratic institutions and elections;
Economics of development; Environment;
Government; Health care; International trade
and financial institutions; Privatization and
deregulation

Alexeyeva, Ludmilla
Chairman, Moscow Helsinki Group
22 Bolshoy Golovin Pereulok, Block 1,
103045 Moscow, RUSSIA
011-7-095-207-6069
fax 011-7-095-207-6069
Issues: Democratic institutions and elections;
Education; Fiscal policy and taxation;
Government; International relations and
organizations; Labor; Terrorism and drugs

Allen, Murray, M.D.
Senior Fellow in Health Studies, The Fraser
Institute
1770 Burrard Street, 4th Floor, Vancouver,
BC V6J 3G7, CANADA
604-688-0221   fax 604-688-8539
murraya@fraserinstitute.ca
www.fraserinstitute.ca
Issues: Health care

Anderson, Dr. Digby
The Social Affairs Unit
Regent Street, Suite 5/6, First Floor, Morley
House, London W1R 5AB, UNITED
KINGDOM
011-44-207-637-4356
fax 011-44-207-436-8530
digbyanderson@compuserve.com
www.socialaffairsunit.org.uk
Issues: Culture and the humanities; Religion
and philosophy

Anton, Dr. Ion
President, International Center for
Entrepreneurial Studies
University of Bucharest, Blvd. Mihail
Kogalniceanu 64, Sala 220, Bucharest 5,
ROMANIA
011-40-1-313-3340   fax 011-40-1-313-3340
Issues: Economics of development; Fiscal policy
and taxation; International relations and
organizations; Privatization and deregulation

Ariff, Dr. Mohamed
Executive Director, Malaysian Institute of
Economic Research
9th Floor Menara Dayabumi, Julan Sultan
Hishamuddin, P. O. Box 12160, 50768 Kuala
Lumpur, MALAYSIA
011-603-22725897
fax 011-603-22730197
ariff@mier.po.my   *www.mier.org.my*
Issues: Economics of development;
International trade and financial institutions

Aruj, Daniela
Conferences and Seminars, Fundación
Global
Roca 1654, Mar del Plata 7600, ARGENTINA
011-54-223-486-3400
fax 011-54-223-535-6245
daruj@fglobal.org   *www.fglobal.org*
Issues: Economics of development;
International trade and financial institutions

Arvanitopoulos, Constantine
Executive Director, Constantinos
Karamanlis Institute for Democracy
12 Vas. Sofias Street, Athens 106 74, GREECE
011-30-1-725-7495
fax 011-30-1-725-7510
Info@idkaramanlis.gr
www.idkaramanlis.gr
Issues: Democratic institutions and elections;
International relations and organizations

Ayau Cordon, Dr. Manuel F.
6 Ave. 7-58, Zona 9, Guatemala City 1009,
GUATEMALA
011-502-362-1864
fax 011-502-334-3035   muso@ufm.edu.gt
Issues: Economics of development; Fiscal policy
and taxation; International trade and financial
institutions

Ayodele, Thompson
Coordinator, Institute of Public Policy
Analysis
6 Majolate Street, P.O. Box 6434, Shomolu-
Lagos, NIGERIA
011-234-1-823093
fax 011-234-1-288-2876
thompsondele@onebox.com
www.ippanigeria.org
Issues: Economics of development;
Environment; International trade and financial
institutions

Baquerizo Alvarado, Ivan
Director, Fundacion Libertad
Av. 9 de Octubre #1911 y Esmeraldes, Ed.
Finansur, piso 21, Guayaquil, ECUADOR
011-593-4-2372531
fax 011-593-4-2372532
info@fundacionlibertad.org
www.fundacionlibertad.org
Issues: International trade and financial
institutions

Baron, Maria
Director of Transparency Policies, Center for
the Implementation of Public Policies
Promoting Equity and Growth
Av. Callao 25, 1B, C1022AAA Buenos Aires,
ARGENTINA
011-54-11-4384-9009
fax 011-54-11-4371-1221
mbaron@cippec.org   *www.cippec.org*
Issues: Democratic institutions and elections;
Government; International relations and
organizations

Begovic, Dr. Boris
Vice President, Center for Liberal-
Democratic Studies
Ulica 29 Novembra 10, 5th Floor, 11000
Belgrade, YUGOSLAVIA
011-381-11-322-5024
fax 011-381-11-322-5517
boris.begovich@clds.org.yu
www.clds.org.yu
Issues: Privatization and deregulation

Bengtsson, Mattias
President, Timbro
Grev Turegatan 19, P. O. Box 5234, S-102 45
Stockholm, SWEDEN
011-46-587-898-10
fax 011-46-587-898-50
mattiasb@timbro.se   *www.timbro.se*
Issues: Culture and the humanities;
Environment; Fiscal policy and taxation

Benson, Iain T.
Executive Director, Centre for Cultural
Renewal
503-39 Robertson Road, Ottawa, ON K2H
8R2, CANADA
613-567-9010   fax 613-567-6061
info@culturalrenewal.ca
www.culturalrenewal.ca
Issues: Culture and the humanities;
Government; Religion and philosophy

Berggren, Dr. Niclas
Vice President, The Ratio Institute
P. O. Box 5095, SE-102 42 Stockholm,
SWEDEN
011-46-8-587-054-04
fax 011-64-8-587-898-56
niclas.berggren@ratioinstitutet.nu
www.ratioinstitutet.nu
Issues: Democratic institutions and elections;
Economics of development; Fiscal policy and
taxation; Government; International trade and
financial institutions; Privatization and
deregulation; Religion and philosophy

Bernholz, Dr. Peter
Professor Emeritus, Universitaet Basel
Postfach, CH-4003 Basel, SWITZERLAND
011-44-79-321-701
peter.bernholz@unibas.ch
Issues: Democratic institutions and elections;
Economics of development; Government;
International relations and organizations;
International trade and financial institutions;
Terrorism and drugs

Biggs-Davison, Lisl
Centre for Research into Post-Communist
Economics
57 Tufton Street, London SW1P 3QL,
UNITED KINGDOM
011-44-20-72331050
fax 011-44-20-72331050
crce@freewire.co.uk
Issues: Economics of development

Biletskyy, Volodymyr S.
Director of Technical Science, Ukrainian
Center for Cultural Studies
45, Artema str., 83086 Donetsk, UKRAINE
011-380-62-337-04-80
fax 011-380-62-337-04-80
shid@uvika.dn.ua
Issues: Culture and the humanities; Democratic
institutions and elections; Education;
Environment

bin Zabri, Adlin Murtadza
Fellow, Institute of Policy Research
48-2, Jalan Telawi, Bangsar Baru, 59100
Kuala Lampur, MALAYSIA
011-603-2283-2788
fax 011-603-2283-2615
adlinmz@pc.jaring.my
Issues: Government; International relations and
organizations; International trade and
financial institutions; Privatization and
deregulation

Bish, Dr. Robert L.
Professor Emeritus, Local Government
Institute
University of Victoria, 104-65 Songhees
Road, Victoria BC V9A 6T3, CANADA
250-360-0390   fax 250-388-6147
rbish@uvic.ca   *www.hsd.uvic.ca/lgi/*
Issues: Democratic institutions and elections;
Government; Privatization and deregulation

Blundell, John
General Director, Institute of Economic
Affairs
2 Lord North Street, Westminster, London
SW1P 3LB, UNITED KINGDOM
011-44-20-7799-8900
fax 011-44-20-7799-2137
jblundell@iea.org.uk   *www.iea.org.uk*
Issues: Privatization and deregulation

Bobel, Dr. Ingo
Professor of Economics and Strategy,
International University of Monaco
2, Avenue Prince Héréditaire Albert, Entrée
B, Stade Louis II, MC-98000 Monaco,
MONACO
011-37-797-986-986
fax 011-37-797-9205-2830
ibobel@univmonaco.edu
www.univmonaco.edu
Issues: Economics of development; Fiscal policy
and taxation; Government; International
relations and organizations; Privatization and
deregulation

Boceta Alvarez, Vicente
Secretary General, Circulo De Empresarios
Serrano, 1-4°, 28001 Madrid, SPAIN
011-34-91-578-1472
fax 011-34-91-577-4871
sgral@circulodeempresarios.org
Issues: Economics of development

Bogdanov, Latchezar
Economist, Institute for Market Economics
P. O. Box 803, 82A, Dondukov Boulevard,
Floor 3, 1000 Sofia, BULGARIA
011-359-2-943-36-48
fax 011-359-2-943-33-52
bogdanov@ime.bg   *www.ime-bg.org*
Issues: Economics of development; Education;
Fiscal policy and taxation; Government;
International trade and financial institutions;
Privatization and deregulation

Bogdanovicius, Andrius
Policy Analyst, Lithuanian Free Market
Institute
56 Birutes Street, LT-2004 Vilnius,
LITHUANIA
011-370-5-272-73-73
fax 011-370-5-272-72-79
andrius@freema.org   *www.freema.org*
Issues: International trade and financial
institutions; Privatization and deregulation

Bongiovanni, Gerardo
Director General, Fundacion Libertad
Mitre 170, 2000 Rosario, Santa Fe,
ARGENTINA
011-54-341-424-5000
fax 011-54-341-424-5111
gbongiovanni@libertad.org.ar
www.libertad.org.ar
Issues: Democratic institutions and elections;
Fiscal policy and taxation

Bouckaert, Dr. Boudewijn
Professor, University of Ghent
Law School, Department of Legal Theory,
Baliestraat 99, 9000 Ghent, BELGIUM
011-32-9-264-6806
fax 011-32-9-264-6983
boudewijn.bouckaert@rug.ac.be
www.novacivilas.org
Issues: Democratic institutions and elections;
Environment; Privatization and deregulation;
Religion and philosophy

Bouillon, Dr. Hardy
Head of Academic Affairs, Centre for the
New Europe
Christophstrasse 9, D-54290 Trier,
GERMANY
011-49-651-9940-918
fax 011-49-651-9940-919
hardy.bouillon@cne-network.org
www.centrefortheneweurope.org
Issues: Culture and the humanities; Education;
Privatization and deregulation; Religion and
philosophy

Brantingham, Paul
Senior Fellow, The Fraser Institute
1770 Burrard Street, 4th Floor, Vancouver,
BC V6J 3G7, CANADA
604-688-0221   fax 604-688-8539
www.fraserinstitute.ca
Issues: Justice and crime

Braun, Miguel
Director of Fiscal Policy, Center for the
Implementation of Public Policies
Promoting Equity and Growth
Av. Callao 25, 1B, C1022AAA Buenos Aires,
ARGENTINA
011-54-114-384-9009
fax 011-54-114-371-1221
mbraun@cippec.org   *www.cippec.org*
Issues: Economics of development; Fiscal policy
and taxation

Brennan, Dr. H. Geoffrey
Professor, Australian National University
Research School of Social Sciences, Social
and Political Theory Group, Canberra ACT
200, AUSTRALIA
011-61-02-6125-3411
fax 011-61-02-6125-0599
geoffrey.brennan@anu.edu.au
www.anu.edu.au
Issues: Democratic institutions and elections;
Fiscal policy and taxation; Government;
Religion and philosophy

Buckingham, Jennifer
Policy Analyst, The Centre for Independent
Studies
P. O. Box 92, St. Leonards, NSW 1590,
AUSTRALIA
011-61-2-9438-4377
fax 011-61-2-9439-7310
jbuckingham@cis.org.au   *www.cis.org.au*
Issues: Education

Butler, Dr. Eamonn
Director, Adam Smith Institute
23 Great Smith Street, London SW1P 3BL,
UNITED KINGDOM
011-44-20-7222-4995
fax 011-44-20-7222-7544
eamonn@adamsmith.org.uk
www.adamsmith.org.uk
Issues: Education; Health care; Privatization
and deregulation

Caceres, Carlos
President of the Board, Libertad y Desarrollo
Los Conquistodores 1700, p. 18-B,
Providencia, Santiago, CHILE
011-56-2-333-8089
fax 011-56-2-333-9442
carlosfcaceres@123.cl   *www.lyd.com*
Issues: Economics of development

Cavanaro, Rodolfo
Research, Fundacion Alberdif
Colon 90, Mendoza 1035, ARGENTINA
011-54-261-423-0630
fax 011-54-61-257-103
Issues: Economics of development;
Government

Chelminski, Vladimir
Executive Director, Caracas Chamber of
Commerce
Apartado 3958, Caracas 1010A,
VENEZUELA
011-58-2-571-3222
fax 011-58-2-571-0050
vladche1467@cantv.net   *www.ccc.com.ve*
Issues: Economics of development; Fiscal policy
and taxation; Government; Privatization and
deregulation

Chu, Dr. Yun-han
Senior Advisor, Institute for National Policy
Research
5F, 238, Sungjiang Road, Taipei, TAIWAN
011-886-2-2511-5009
fax 011-886-2-2560-5536
inprpd@ms8.hinet.net
www.inpr.org.tw/inpre.htm
Issues: Democratic institutions and elections;
Economics of development; Fiscal policy and
taxation; Government; International trade and
financial institutions

Clemens, Jason
Director of Fiscal Studies and Non-Profit
Studies, The Fraser Institute
1770 Burrard Street, 4th Floor, Vancouver,
BC V6J 3G7, CANADA
604-714-4544   fax 604-688-8539
jasonc@fraserinstitute.ca
www.fraserinstitute.ca
Issues: Fiscal policy and taxation; Government;
Privatization and deregulation

Collacott, Martin
Senior Fellow, The Fraser Institute
1770 Burrard Street, 4th Floor, Vancouver,
BC V6J 3G7, CANADA
604-688-0221   fax 604-688-8539
martinc@fraserinstitute.ca
www.fraserinstitute.ca
Issues: Military and defense policy; National
security and alliance relations; Terrorism and
drugs

Collins, Philip
Director, Social Market Foundation
11 Tufton Street, Westminster, London
SW1P 3QB, UNITED KINGDOM
011-44-207-222-7060
fax 011-44-207-222-3010   *www.smf.co.uk*
Issues: Democratic institutions and elections;
Education

Colombatto, Dr. Enrico
Professor of Economics, University of Torino
Corso Unione Sovietica 218-bis, Torino
10134, ITALY
011-39-011-670-6068
fax 011-39-011-670-6062
enrico.colombatto@unito.it
Issues: Culture and the humanities; Economics
of development; Environment

Comanescu, Dan Cristian
President, Mises Institute-Romania
Str. Valeriu Braniste, nr 56, Bloc. A, Sc.B, Et.
3, Bucharest 74136, ROMANIA
011-40-1-326-76-62
contact@misesromania.org
www.misesromania.org
Issues: Economics of development

Cooper, Dr. Barry
Director, Alberta Policy Research Centre,
The Fraser Institute
815 First Street, S.W., Number 301, Calgary,
AB T2P 1N3, CANADA
403-216-7175   fax 403-234-9010
barryc@fraserinstitute.ca
www.fraserinstitute.ca
Issues: Environment; Fiscal policy and taxation;
Government; Military and defense policy;
Terrorism and drugs

Cowley, Peter
Director of School Performance Studies,
The Fraser Institute
1770 Burrard Street, 4th Floor, Vancouver,
BC V6J 3G7, CANADA
604-714-4556   fax 604-688-8539
peterc@fraserinstitute.ca
www.fraserinstitute.ca
Issues: Education

Crowley, Brian Lee
President, Atlantic Institute for Market
Studies
2000 Barrington Street, Suite 1006, Cogswell
Tower, Halifax, N.S. B3J 3K1, CANADA
902-429-1143   fax 902-425-1393
aims@aims.ca   *www.aims.ca*
Issues: Economics of development; Education;
Energy; Environment; Fiscal policy and
taxation; Government; Health care; Labor;
Privatization and deregulation

Dahlmanns, Dr. Gert
Vorstand, Frankfurter Institut - Stiftung
Marktwirtschaft und Politik
Am Jaegerwaeldchen 12, 35041 Marburg,
GERMANY
011-49-6172-6647-0
fax 011-49-6172-22292
institut@frankfurter-institut.de
www.frankfurter-institut.de
Issues: Democratic institutions and elections;
Economics of development; Education;
Environment; Fiscal policy and taxation;
Government; Health care; International trade
and financial institutions; Labor; Privatization
and deregulation

de Ampuero, Dora
Executive Director, Instituto Ecuatoriano de
Economia Politica
Higueras 106 y Costanera, Urdesa Central,
Guayaquil, ECUADOR
011-593-4-2881011
fax 011-593-4-2885991
dampuero@ecua.net.ec   *www.his.com/ieep*
Issues: Agriculture; Democratic institutions and
elections; Economics of development;
Environment; Fiscal policy and taxation;
International trade and financial institutions;
Privatization and deregulation

de Bolivar, Dr. Carolina
President, Instituto Cultural Ludwig von
Mises, A.C.
Avenida del Olmo 2-201, Col. Álamos 2da.
Sección, Querétaro, 76160, MEXICO
011-52-442-2126375
fax 011-52-442-2126446
icumi@mpsnet.com.mx
www.icumi.org.mx
Issues: Culture and the humanities; Education;
Justice and crime

de Mattei, Roberto
Professor, Centro Culturale Lepanto
Via Giuseppe Sacconi, 4/b, 00196 Roma,
ITALY
011-39-06-3233307
fax 011-39-06-32110310
rdemattei@libero.it   *www.lepanto.org*
Issues: Culture and the humanities;
International relations and organizations;
Religion and philosophy

de Nicola, Alessandro, Esq.
President, Adam Smith Society
Via Cornaggia 10, 20123 Milano, ITALY
011-39-02-8514-830
fax 011-39-02-8514-825
alessandro.de-nicola@it.eyi.com
www.adamsmith.it
Issues: Justice and crime; Privatization and
deregulation

de Santibañes, Fernando
Fundacion Libertad
Maipu 1232, Piso 12, Buenos Aires, 1006,
ARGENTINA
011-54-11-4314-6799
fax 011-54-11-4314-6955
fdsanti@hotmail.com
Issues: International trade and financial
institutions

de Soto, Dr. Hernando
Institute for Liberty and Democracy
Av. Del Parque Norte 829, San Isidro, Lima
27, PERU
011-51-1-225-4131
fax 011-51-1-475-9559
postmaster@ild.org.pe   *www.ild.org.pe*
Issues: Economics of development; Fiscal policy
and taxation; Government

Debroy, Bibek
Centre for Civil Society
B-12 Kailash Colony, New Delhi 110048,
INDIA
011-91-11-646-8282
fax 011-91-11-646-2453
http://www.ccsindia.org
Issues: Economics of development; Fiscal policy
and taxation

Desrochers, Pierre
Research Director, Montreal Economic
Institute
6418, rue Saint-Hubert Street, 2e, Montreal,
QC H2S 2M2, CANADA
514-273-0969   fax 514-273-0967
pdesrochers@iedm.org   *www.iedm.org*
Issues: Economics of development;
Environment

Dezsériné, Dr. Maria Major
Executive Director, Foundation for Market
Economy
Dombovari ut 17/19, H-1117 Budapest,
HUNGARY
011-361-204-2951
fax 011-361-204-2953
ipargazd@matavnet.hu
www.elender.hu/fme
Issues: Economics of development

Diniz, Arthur Chagas
President, Instituto Liberal
Rua Professor Alfredo Gomes 28 - Botafogo,
22251-080 Rio de Janeiro, BRAZIL
011-55-21-2539-1115
fax 011-55-21-2537-7206
ilrj@gbl.com.br   *www.institutoliberal.org.br*
Issues: Privatization and deregulation

Doron, Daniel
Director, Israel Center for Social and
Economic Progress
P. O. Box 84124, Mevasseret Zion 90805,
ISRAEL
011-972-2-5346463
fax 011-972-2-5330122
mail@icsep.org.il   *www.icsep.org.il*
Issues: Culture and the humanities; Economics
of development; Government; International
relations and organizations

Ducote, Nicolas J.
Executive Director, Center for the
Implementation of Public Policies
Promoting Equity and Growth
Av. Callao 25, 1B, C1022AAA Buenos Aires,
ARGENTINA
011-54-11-4384-9009
fax 011-54-11-4371-1221
nducote@cippec.org   *www.cippec.org*
Issues: Democratic institutions and elections;
Government; International relations and
organizations

Durston, Kirk
National Director, New Scholars Society
R.R. 2, Wallenstein, ON N0B 2S0, CANADA
519-698-2561   fax 519-698-2551
kirk@newscholars.com
Issues: Religion and philosophy

Easton, Prof. Steve
Senior Visiting Fellow and Adjunct Scholar,
The Fraser Institute
1770 Burrard Street, 4th Floor, Vancouver,
BC V6J 3G7, CANADA
604-688-0221   fax 604-688-8539
stevee@fraserinstitute.ca
www.fraserinstitute.ca
Issues: Education; Fiscal policy and taxation

Egan, Patrick
Director, Freedom House
1054 Bp. Falk Miksa u. 30. 4/2, H-1118
Budapest, HUNGARY
011-36-1-354-1230
fax 011-36-1-354-1233
fh@freedomhouse.hu   *www.ngonet.org*
Issues: Democratic institutions and elections;
Government

Esmail, Nadeem
Health Policy Analyst, The Fraser Institute
1770 Burrard Street, 4th Floor, Vancouver,
BC V6J 3G7, CANADA
604-688-0221   fax 604-688-8539
nadeeme@fraserinstitute.ca
www.fraserinstitute.ca
Issues: Health care

Espinosa, J. Rolando
Director, Centro de Estudios en Educacion
y Econmia
15 de Mayo 1531 Pte., Monterrey CP NL
64040, MEXICO
011-52-83-44-4824
fax 011-52-34-2743-3
ceeejrer@nll.telmex.net.mx
Issues: Culture and the humanities; Economics
of development; Education; Government;
Religion and philosophy

Evans, Alexander
Research Director, Policy Exchange
Clutha House, 10 Storey's Gate, London
SW1P 3AY, UNITED KINGDOM
011-44-20-7340-2655
fax 011-44-20-7222-5859
alexander.evans@policyexchange.org.uk
www.policyexchange.org
Issues: Economics of development;
International relations and organizations;
International trade and financial institutions

Evans, Dr. Tim
President and Director General, Centre for
the New Europe
Rue du Luxembourg 23, 1000 Brussels,
BELGIUM
011-32-2-506-40-00
fax 011-32-2-506-40-09
tim.evans@cne-network.org
www.centrefortheneweurope.org
Issues: Economics of development;
Environment; Fiscal policy and taxation;
Health care; International relations and
organizations; International trade and
financial institutions; Labor; Privatization and
deregulation

Falque, Max
International Consultant for Environmental
Policy, Max Falque Conseil
La Tuiliere, 84330 Le Barroux, FRANCE
011-33-4-9062-4852
fax 011-33-4-9062-4896
max.falque@wanadoo.fr
Issues: Environment

Felice, Dr. Flavio
General Secretary, Instituto Acton
Via Delle Plaje 1, TE 64100 Teramo, ITALY
011-39-861-410-808
fax 011-39-338-176-6148
info@actonitalia.org   *www.actonitalia.org*
Issues: Culture and the humanities; Religion
and philosophy

Flanagan, Tom
Senior Fellow, Alberta Policy Research
Centre, The Fraser Institute
815 First Street, S.W., Number 301, Calgary
AB T2P 1N3, CANADA
604-688-0221   fax 604-688-8539
www.fraserinstitute.ca
Issues: Government

Fleming, Greg
Managing Director, The Maxim Institute
49 Cape Horn Road, Hillsborough,
Auckland, NEW ZEALAND
011-64-9-627-3261
fax 011-64-9-627-3264
mail@maxim.org.nz   *www.maxim.org.nz*
Issues: Culture and the humanities; Education

Flores, Tomas
Director of the Economic Program, Libertad
y Desarrollo
Alcantara 498, Las Condes, Santiago, CHILE
011-56-2234-1894
fax 011-56-2234-1893   lyd@lyd.com
www.lyd.com
Issues: Fiscal policy and taxation

Gaidar, Dr. Yegor
Director, Institute of Economy in Transition
5, Gazetny pereulok, strojenije 3, 5 Moscow
103918, RUSSIA
011-7-095-229-6413
fax 011-7-095-203-8816   lena@iet.ru
www.iet.ru/index2.htm
Issues: Fiscal policy and taxation; Government;
International trade and financial institutions

Garces, Francisco
Chinquihue 6618, Vitacura, Santiago,
CHILE
011-562-2426-718   fax 011-562-234-1893
Issues: International trade and financial
institutions

Garello, Jacques
Universite Aix Marseille 3
3, avenue Robert Schuman, Aix en Provence
13100, FRANCE
011-33-442-17-2992
fax 011-33-442-59-3887
jacques.garello@univ.u-3mrs.fr
www.univ.u-3mrs.fr
Issues: Economics of development; Fiscal policy
and taxation; International relations and
organizations; International trade and
financial institutions

Garello, Pierre
Professor of Economics, Centre d'Analyse
Economique
Universite Aix-Marseille 3, 3, avenue Robert
Schuman, 13100 Aix-en-Provence, FRANCE
011-33-442-17-2992
fax 011-33-442-59-3887
pierre.garello@univ.u-3mrs.fr
www.u-3mrs.fr
Issues: Economics of development; Fiscal policy
and taxation; Justice and crime; Religion and
philosophy

Gergils, Hakan
Director, Ecofin Invest
Surbrunnsgatan 42, S-113 48 Stockholm,
SWEDEN
011-46-8-612-0195
fax 011-46-8-612-0196
gergils@ecofin.se   *www.ecofin.se*
Issues: Economics of development; Fiscal policy
and taxation; Government; International trade
and financial institutions; Privatization and
deregulation

Ghersi, Dr. Enrique
Director, Centro de Investigacion y Estudios
Legales (CITEL)
Libertadores 350, San Isidro, Lima 27, PERU
011-51-1-441-3424
fax 011-51-1-442-6161
eghersi@gcgvascd.com.pe
Issues: Economics of development; Justice and
crime; Privatization and deregulation;
Terrorism and drugs

Gibson, Gordon
Senior Fellow in Canadian Studies
The Fraser Institute
1770 Burrard Street, 4th Floor, Vancouver,
BC V6J 3G7, CANADA
604-737-7878   fax 604-737-7877
gordong@fraserinstitute.ca
www.fraserinstitute.ca
Issues: Democratic institutions and elections;
Government

Giersch, Dr. Herbert
Preusserstrasse 17-19, D-24105 Kiel,
GERMANY
011-49-431-8814-489
fax 011-49-431-8814-500
Issues: Economics of development;
International trade and financial institutions;
Privatization and deregulation

Gissurarsen, Hannes H.
Professor of Politics, University of Iceland
101 Reykjavik, ICELAND
011-354-562-0224
fax 011354-552-6806   hannesgi@rhi.hi.is
Issues: Environment; Religion and philosophy

Godart-Van der Kroon, Annette
President, Ludwig von Mises Institute
Europe
Herendreef 20, 3001 Leuven, BELGIUM
011-32-16-295-833
fax 011-32-16-584-568
annette.godart@vonmises-europe.org
www.vonmisesinstitute-europe.org
Issues: Democratic institutions and elections;
Government; International relations and
organizations

Graham, John R.
Director of Pharmaceutical Policy Research,
The Fraser Institute
1770 Burrard Street, 4th Floor, Vancouver,
BC V6J 3G7, CANADA
604-714-4557   fax 604-688-8539
johng@fraserinstitute.ca
www.fraserinstitute.ca
Issues: Health care

Green, Dr. David G.
Director, CIVITAS: The Institute for the
Study of Civil Society
The Mezzanine, Elizabeth House, 39 York
Road, London SE1 7NQ, UNITED
KINGDOM
011-44-20-7401-5470
fax 011-44-20-7401-5471
david.green@civitas.org.uk
www.civitas.org.uk
Issues: Health care

Green, Dr. Kenneth
Director, Centre for Risk and Regulation
Studies, The Fraser Institute
1770 Burrard Street, 4th Floor, Vancouver,
BC V6J 3G7, CANADA
604-688-0221   fax 604-688-8539
keng@fraserinstitute.ca
www.fraserinstitute.ca
Issues: Environment; Privatization and
deregulation

Grubel, Dr. Herbert
David Somerville Chair in Taxation and
Finance, The Fraser Institute
1770 Burrard Street, 4th Floor, Vancouver,
BC V6J 3G7, CANADA
604-688-0221   fax 604-688-8539
herbg@fraserinstitute.ca
www.fraserinstitute.ca
Issues: Fiscal policy and taxation; International
trade and financial institutions; Privatization
and deregulation

Guijarro, Sr. Rocio
General Manager, Centro de Divulgacion del
Conocimiento Economico (CEDICE)
Avda. Andres Eloy Blanco (Este 2), Edificio
Camara de Comercio de Caracas, Los
Caobos, Caracus, VENEZUELA
011-58-212-571-3357
fax 011-58-212-576-0512
cedice@cedice.net.ve   *www.cedice.org.ve*
Issues: Economics of development; Fiscal policy
and taxation; Privatization and deregulation

Guzman, Eugenio
Director of the Political Program, Libertad
y Desarrollo
Alcantara 498, Las Condes, Santiago, CHILE
011-56-2234-1894
fax 011-56-2234-1893
eguzman@lyd.com   *www.lyd.com*
Issues: Democratic institutions and elections;
Justice and crime

Harries, Owen
Senior Fellow, The Centre for Independent
Studies
P. O. Box 92, St. Leonards, NSW 1590,
AUSTRALIA
011-61-2-9438-4377
fax 011-61-2-9439-7310
oharries@cis.org.au   *www.cis.org.au*
Issues: Economics of development;
International relations and organizations

Heath, Allister
Economics Correspondent, The Business
Newspaper
PA News Centre, 292 Vauxhall Bridge Road,
London SW1V 1SS, UNITED KINGDOM
011-44-7958-722-877
allister_heath@yahoo.co.uk
Issues: International relations and
organizations

Henderson, Paul
Researcher, The Maxim Institute
49 Cape Horn Road, Hillsborough,
Auckland, NEW ZEALAND
011-64-9-627-3261
fax 011-64-9-627-3264
mail@maxim.org.nz   *www.maxim.org.nz*
Issues: Democratic institutions and elections;
Religion and philosophy

Hepburn, Claudia R.
Director of Education Policy, The Fraser
Institute
47 Rosedale Road, Toronto, ON M4W 2P5,
CANADA
416-967-2923   fax 416-967-2916
claudiah@fraserinstitute.ca
www.fraserinstitute.ca
Issues: Education

Holle, Peter
President, Frontier Centre for Public Policy
201-63 Albert Street, Winnepeg, MB R3J
2M9, CANADA
204-957-1567   fax 204-957-1570
hollcp@fcpp.org   *www.fcpp.org*
Issues: Economics of development; Fiscal policy
and taxation; Government; Privatization and
deregulation

Hough, Dr. Michael
Director, Institute for Strategic Studies
University of Pretoria, Pretoria 0002,
SOUTH AFRICA
011-27-12-420-2407
fax 011-27-12-420-2693
wmartin@postino.up.ac.za
Issues: Military and defense policy; National
security and alliance relations; Terrorism and
drugs

Jaime, Edna
General Director, Centro de Investigacion
para el Desarrollo, A.C.
Jaime Balmes No. 11 Edif. D-2o. Piso, Col.
Los Morales Polanco, 11510 Mexico, D.F.,
MEXICO
011-52-55-5985-1010
fax 011-52-55-5985-1030
info@cidac.org.mx   *www.cidac.org*
Issues: Economics of development; Education;
Fiscal policy and taxation

Joch, Dr. Roman
Civic Institute
Vysehradska 49, 128 00 Prague 2, CZECH
REPUBLIC
011-420-22492-3563
fax 011-420-22492-3563
obcinst@mbox.vol.cz   *www.obcinst.cz*
Issues: Democratic institutions and elections;
Government; International relations and
organizations; Justice and crime; Military and
defense policy; National security and alliance
relations; Religion and philosophy

Johansson, Dr. Dan
The Ratio Institute
P. O. Box 5095, SE 102-42 Stockholm,
SWEDEN
011-46-8-587-054-02
fax 011-46-8-587-898-56
dan.johansson@ratioinstitutet.nu
www.ratioinstitutet.nu
Issues: Fiscal policy and taxation; Government

Johansson, Mats
Editor-in-Chief, Svenska Dagbladet
105 17 Stockholm, SWEDEN
011-46-8-13-5228
fax 011-46-8-13-5225
mats.johansson@svd.se   *www.svd.se*
Issues: Culture and the humanities

Jones, Laura
Adjunct Scholar, The Fraser Institute
1770 Burrard Street, 4th Floor, Vancouver,
BC V6J 3G7, CANADA
604-688-0221   fax 604-688-8539
www.fraserinstitute.ca
Issues: Environment

Jovanovic, Aleksandra, Ph.D.
President, Free Market Center
Francuska 59, 11000 Belgrade, Serbia,
YUGOSLAVIA
011-381-11-187-245   fmc@yubc.net
www.fmc.org.yu
Issues: Economics of development;
Government

Kaji, Motoo
Chairman, The International House of
Japan, Inc.
5-11-6 Roppongi, Minato-ku, Tokyo 106-
0032, JAPAN
011-813-3470-3212
fax 011-813-3470-3170
kaji@i-house.or.jp   *www.i-house.or.jp*
Issues: Economics of development; Education;
Fiscal policy and taxation; International
relations and organizations; International
trade and financial institutions; Privatization
and deregulation

Karlson, Nils
President, The Ratio Institute
P. O. Box 5095, SE-102 42 Stockholm,
SWEDEN
011-46-8-587-054-00
fax 011-46-8-587-054-05
nils.karlson@ratioinstitutet.nu
www.ratioinstitutet.nu
Issues: Democratic institutions and elections;
Economics of development

Kasper, Prof. Wolfgang
The Centre for Independent Studies
7, The Point, Tura Beach 2548, AUSTRALIA
011-61-2-6495-0390
fax 011-61-2-9439-7310
wkasper@cis.org.au   *www.cis.org.au*
Issues: Economics of development;
International trade and financial institutions;
Labor; Privatization and deregulation

Kaziyeva, Dr. Raissa
President, SIFE Kazakhstan
12, Lisa Chaikina Street, Almty 480020,
KAZAKHSTAN
Issues: Economics of development

Kelly-Gagnon, Mon. Michael
Executive Director, Montreal Economic
Institute
6418, rue Saint-Hubert Street, 2e, Montreal,
QC H2S 2M2, CANADA
514-273-0969   fax 514-273-0967
mkellygagnon@iedm.org   *www.iedm.org*
Issues: Democratic institutions and elections;
Education; Fiscal policy and taxation;
Government; Health care; Privatization and
deregulation

Kerr, Roger
Executive Director, New Zealand Business
Roundtable
P. O. Box 10-147, Wellington, NEW
ZEALAND
011-64-4-4990790
fax 011-64-4-471-1304
rkerr@nzbr.org.nz   *www.nzbr.org.nz*
Issues: Fiscal policy and taxation; Labor;
Privatization and deregulation

Koffsmon, Ms. Ariana L.
Coordinator of the Health Care Policy Area,
Center for the Implementation of Public
Policies Promoting Equity and Growth
Av. Callao 25, 1B, C1022AAA Buenos Aires,
ARGENTINA
011-54-11-4384-9009
fax 011-54-11-4371-1221
akoffsmon@cippec.org   *www.cippec.org*
Issues: Health care

Kondratowicz, Dr. Andrzej
General Director, Adam Smith Research
Centre
ul. Bednarska 16, 00-321 Warsaw, POLAND
011-48-22-828-4707
fax 011-48-22-828-0614
kondratowicz@adam-smith.pl
www.adam-smith.pl
Issues: Economics of development; Fiscal policy
and taxation; Government; Privatization and
deregulation

Kozhaya, Norma
Economist, Montreal Economic Institute
6418, rue Saint-Hubert Street, 2e, Montreal,
QC H2S 2M2, CANADA
514-273-0969   fax 514-273-0967
nkozhaya@iedm.org   *www.iedm.org*
Issues: Fiscal policy and taxation; Government

Krastev, Ivan
Program Director, Political Research, Centre
for Liberal Strategies
4, Alexander Battenberg Street, 1000 Sofia,
BULGARIA
011-359-2-981-8126
fax 011-359-2-981-8125
mail@cls-sofia.org   *www.cls-sofia.org*
Issues: Economics of development;
Government; International relations and
organizations

Krause, Dr. Martin
Dean, ESEADE Graduate School
Uriarte 2472, Buenos Aires 1425,
ARGENTINA
011-54-11-4773-5825
fax 011-54-11-4772-7243
martin@eseade.edu.ar   *www.eseade.edu.ar*
Issues: Democratic institutions and elections;
Environment; Fiscal policy and taxation;
Government; Privatization and deregulation

Kurrild-Klitgaard, Dr. Peter
Associate Professor, University of Southern
Denmark
Department of Political Science and Public
Management, Campusvej 55, DK 5230
Odense M, DENMARK
011-45-6550-1000
fax 011-45-6619-2577
kurrild@sam.sdu.dk   *www.sdu.dk*
Issues: Democratic institutions and elections;
Fiscal policy and taxation; Government

Laarman, Frank
Founder, French Taxpayers Association
42, rue des Jeuneurs, Cedex 2, F-75077 Paris,
FRANCE
011-33-1-42-21-16-24
fax 011-33-1-42-33-29-35
lekieffre@contribuables.net
Issues: Fiscal policy and taxation

Lamprechter, Dr. Barbara
Secretary General, Friedrich A. v. Hayek
Institut
Wipplingerstrasse 25, A-1010 Wien,
AUSTRIA
011-43-1-534-51-376
fax 011-43-1-534-51-233
barbara.lamprechter@hayek-institut.at
www.hayek-institut.at

Larrain A., Luis
Deputy Director, Libertad y Desarrollo
Alcantara 498, Las Condes, Santiago, CHILE
011-56-2-3774800
fax 011-56-2-2341893
llarrain@lyd.com   *www.lyd.com*
Issues: Labor; Privatization and deregulation

Larroulet, Cristian
Executive Director, Libertad y Desarrollo
Alcantara 498, Las Condes, Santiago, CHILE
011-56-2-3774800
fax 011-56-2-2077723
clarroulet@lyd.com   *www.lyd.com*
Issues: Economics of development;
Government; Privatization and deregulation

Lee, Dr. Jane
Chief Executive, Hong Kong Policy Research
Institute
5/F, China Hong Kong Tower, 8-12
Hennessy Road, Wanchai, HONG KONG
011-852-2686-1905
fax 011-852-2648-4303
janelee@hkrpi.org.hk   *www.hkpri.org.hk*
Issues: Democratic institutions and elections;
Government; International relations and
organizations; Privatization and deregulation

Leme, Dr. Og F.
Instituto Liberal
Rus Professor Alfredo Gomes 28, Rio de
Janeiro 22251-080, BRAZIL
011-55-21-2539-1115
fax 011-55-21-2537-7206
ilrj@gbl.com.br   *www.institutoliberal.org.br*
Issues: Education; Fiscal policy and taxation;
Government; Health care; Privatization and
deregulation

Lemennicier, Dr. Bertrand
Director of Academic Affairs, Institute for
Economic Studies
Universite de Paris, 35 Avenue Mac-Mahon,
Paris 75017, FRANCE
011-33-1-43-808517
fax 011-33-1-48-88-9757
ies.europe@ieseurope.asso.fr
www.ieseurope.asso.fr
Issues: Economics of development; Fiscal policy
and taxation; International relations and
organizations; Privatization and deregulation

Lemieux, Dr. Pierre
Professor, Universite du Quebec en
Outaouais
C. P. 725 Tour de la Bourse, Montreal H4Z
1J0, CANADA
819-585-4480   fax 819-585-4423
pl@pierrelemieux.org
www.pierrelemieux.org
Issues: Fiscal policy and taxation; Government;
Health care; International trade and financial
institutions; Privatization and deregulation

Leontjeva, Elena
Founder and Chairman of the Board,
Lithuanian Free Market Institute
56 Birutes Street, LT-2004 Vilnius,
LITHUANIA
011-370-5-272-25-84
fax 011-370-5-272-12-79
lelena@freema.org   www.freema.org
Issues: Agriculture; Economics of development;
Education; Fiscal policy and taxation;
Government; Labor; Privatization and
deregulation

Lepage, Henri
Executive Director, Institut Euro 92
35 avenue Mac-Mahon, Paris 75017,
FRANCE
011-33-1-4380-6232
fax 011-33-1-4888-9757
lepageh@cybercable.fr   www.euro92.org
Issues: Agriculture; Economics of development;
Energy; Environment; Fiscal policy and
taxation

LeRoy, Sylvia
Policy Analyst, The Fraser Institute
815 First Street, S.W., Number 301, Calgary,
AB T2P 1N3, CANADA
403-216-7175   fax 403-234-9010
sylvial@fraserinstitute.ca
www.fraserinstitute.ca
Issues: Environment

Lindsay, Greg
Executive Director, The Centre for
Independent Studies
P. O. Box 92, St. Leonards, NSW 1590,
AUSTRALIA
011-61-2-9438-4377
fax 011-61-2-9439-7310
glindsay@cis.org.au   www.cis.org.au
Issues: Culture and the humanities; Democratic
institutions and elections; Economics of
development; Education; Government;
International trade and financial institutions;
Labor; Privatization and deregulation; Religion
and philosophy

Lippert, Dr. Owen
Fellow, International Policy Network
Room 145, 180 Wellington Street, Ottawa,
Ontario K1A 0A6, CANADA
613-290-7532   owenlippert@yahoo.ca
Issues: International trade and financial
institutions; Justice and crime

Livestro, Joshua
Director, Edmund Burke Foundation
Noordeinde 10D, P. O. Box 10498, 2501 HL,
The Hague, NETHERLANDS
011-31-060-3925180
livestro@burkestichting.nl
www.burkerstichting.nl
Issues: Education; Government; International
relations and organizations; Justice and crime;
Religion and philosophy; Terrorism and drugs

Logan, Bruce
Director, The Maxim Institute
49 Cape Horn Road, Hillsborough,
Auckland, NEW ZEALAND
011-64-9-627-3261
fax 011-64-9-627-3264
mail@maxim.org.nz   www.maxim.org.nz
Issues: Education; Religion and philosophy

Louw, Leon M.
Free Market Foundation
P. O. Box 785121, Sandton 2146, SOUTH
AFRICA
011-27-11-88-4-0270
fax 011-27-11-88-4-5672
fmf@mweb.co.za
www.freemarketfoundation.com
Issues: Agriculture; Democratic institutions and
elections; Economics of development;
Education; Environment; Fiscal policy and
taxation; Government; Health care;
International relations and organizations;
International trade and financial institutions;
Justice and crime; Labor; Privatization and
deregulation; Religion and philosophy

Lowenberg, Dr. Robert
President, Institute for Advanced Strategic
and Political Studies
16 Bilu Street, Jerusalem 93221, ISRAEL
011-972-2-563-8171
fax 011-972-2-563-8176   www.iasps.org
Issues: Democratic institutions and elections;
Fiscal policy and taxation; Government;
International relations and organizations;
Military and defense policy; National security
and alliance relations; Privatization and
deregulation; Religion and philosophy

Maggiolo, Daniel
International Affairs, Fundacion Libertad
Mitre 170, 2000 Rosario, Santa Fe,
ARGENTINA
011-54-341-424-5000
fax 011-54-341-424-5111
dmaggiolo@citynet.net.ar
www.libertad.org.ar
Issues: International relations and
organizations; International trade and
financial institutions

Main, Dr. Brian G.M.
Director, David Hume Institute
25 Buccleuch Place, Edinburgh EH8 9LN,
Scotland, UNITED KINGDOM
011-44-131-667-9609
fax 011-44-131-667-9609
hume.instiitute@ed.ae.uk
www.ed.ac.uk/dhi/
Issues: Culture and the humanities; Fiscal policy
and taxation; Government

Maley, Barry R.
Senior Fellow, The Centre for Independent
Studies
P. O. Box 92, St. Leonards, NSW 1590,
AUSTRALIA
011-61-2-9438-4377
fax 011-61-2-9439-7310
bmaley@cis.org.au   *www.cis.org.au*
Issues: Culture and the humanities; Education

Manaev, Dr. Oleg
Chairman, Independent Institute of Socio-
Economic and Political Studies
P. O. Box 219, Minsk 220030, BELARUS
011-375-172-22-80-49
fax 011-375-172-52-32-10
liseps@user.unibel.by
www.cacedu.unibel.by/iisep
Issues: Economics of development;
Government

Mancke, Dr. Richard B.
DtA Professor of Enterpreneurship,
Associate Dean & Director of the MBA
Program, Handleshochchule Leipzig
Jahn Allee 59, 04109 Leipzig, GERMANY
011-49-341-9851-732
fax 011-49-341-9851-731
mancke@mba.hhl.de   *www.hhl.de/mba*
Issues: Education; Energy; International
relations and organizations; International
trade and financial institutions

Manliev, Prof. George
Executive Director, Institute of Public
Administration and European Integration
18, Vitosha Boulevard, 1000 Sofia,
BULGARIA
011-3592-980-9747
fax 011-3592-980-9679
g.manliev@government.bg
www.ipaei.government.bg
Issues: Government; Privatization and
deregulation

Manners, Ronald B.
Chairman, Mannkal Economic Education
Foundation
19 Richardson Street, West Perth, Western
Australia 6005, AUSTRALIA
011-61-8-9322-6777
fax 011-61-8-9322-6788
mannwest@mannkal.org
www.mannkal.org
Issues: Economics of development

Manning, Preston
Senior Fellow, The Fraser Institute
815 First Street, S.W., Number 301, Calgary,
AB T2P 1N3, CANADA
403-216-7175   fax 403-234-9010
prestonm@fraserinstitute.ca
www.fraserinstitute.ca
Issues: Democratic institutions and elections;
Government

Marsland, Dr. David
Professor, Centre for Epidemiological
Research, Brunel University
Osterley Campus, Isleworth, Middlesex TW7
5DU, UNITED KINGDOM
011-44-020-8891-0121
Issues: Education; Government; Health care;
Privatization and deregulation

Marty, Eduardo
President, Junior Achievement of Argentina
Maipu 859, Ciudad de Buenos Aires, Buenos
Aires C1006ACK, ARGENTINA
011-54-11-4-312-5022
fax 011-54-11-4-312-5022
emarty@junior.org.ar   *www.junior.org.ar*
Issues: Economics of development; Education

Mayora Alvarado, Dr. Eduardo
Professor of Law, Universidad Francisco
Marroquin
6a. calle Final, Zona 10, Guatemala 01010,
GUATEMALA
011-502-366-2531
fax 011-502-366-2540
mayorae@intelnet.net.gt   *www.ufm.edu.gt*
Issues: Environment; Fiscal policy and taxation;
Justice and crime; Privatization and
deregulation

McDowell, Dr. Gary L.
Director, Institute of United States Studies
Senate House, Malet Street, London WC1E
7HU, UNITED KINGDOM
011-44-207-862-8693
fax 011-44-207-862-8696
gary.mcdowel@sas.ac.uk
www.sas.ac.uk/iuss
Issues: Culture and the humanities;
Government; Justice and crime

McMahon, Fred
Director of the Centre for Globalization
Studies, The Fraser Institute
1770 Burrard Street, 4th Floor, Vancouver,
BC V6J 3G7, CANADA
604-688-0221   fax 604-688-8539
fredm@fraserinstitute.ca
www.fraserinstitute.ca
Issues: Economics of development;
Government; International relations and
organizations; International trade and
financial institutions

Mejia-Vergnaud, Andres
Fundacion DL
Calle 25 Norte # 5A 43 of 202, Cali,
COLOMBIA
011-572-683-7237
fax 011-572-653-0260
fdl@fundaciondl.org
http://www.fundaciondl.org
Issues: Economics of development;
Government

Mellar, Dr. Tamas
President, Hungarian Central Statistical
Office
Keleti Karoly u. 5-7, P. O. Box 51, H-1024
Budapest, HUNGARY
011-36-1-201-9246
fax 011-36-1-202-0739
tamas.mellar@ksh.gov.hu
Issues: Economics of development; Fiscal policy
and taxation

Mensa, Charles
President, Institute of Economic Affairs -
Ghana
P. O. Box 01936, Christianborg, Accra,
GHANA
011-233-21-244-716
fax 011-233-21-222-313
cmensa@africaonline.com.gh
Issues: Democratic institutions and elections;
Economics of development; Fiscal policy and
taxation; Privatization and deregulation

Migue, Jean-Luc
Senior Fellow, The Fraser Institute
3181 Galais Street, St. Foy, Quebec, G1@
2Z7, CANADA
418-651-1968   fax 418-651-7937
jlmigue@sympatico.ca   *www.iedm.org*
Issues: Democratic institutions and elections;
Fiscal policy and taxation; Health care

Miller, Charles
Edmund Burke Institute
Crookhaven, Coleen, Skibereen, IRELAND
011-35-3137-8-5043
fax 011-35-3166-1-8721
edmundburke@eircom.net
www.edmundburke-institute.org
Issues: Government; International trade and
financial institutions

Min, Byuong-Kyun
President, Korean Center for Free
Enterprise
Do-Won Building, 292-20, Dowha-dong
Mapo-ku, Seoul 121-728, KOREA
011-82-2-6730-3030
fax 011-82-2-6730-3001
bkmin@cfe.org   *www.cfe.org*
Issues: Economics of development; Fiscal policy
and taxation; Privatization and deregulation

Miniter, Richard
Senior Fellow, Centre for the New Europe
Rue du Luxembourg 23, 1000 Brussels,
BELGIUM
011-32-2-506-40-00
fax 011-32-2-506-40-09
cne-brussels@cne-network.org
http://www.cne-network.org
Issues: International trade and financial
institutions; Military and defense policy

Minogue, Dr. Kenneth Robert

Emeritus Professor of Political Science,
University of London
43 Perrymead Street, London SW6 3SN,
UNITED KINGDOM
011-020-7731-0421
fax 011-020-7371-9135
k.minogue@lse.ac.uk
Issues: Culture and the humanities; Democratic
institutions and elections; Education; Religion
and philosophy

Mitra, Barun S.

Liberty Institute
J-259, Saket (2nd Floor), New Delhi 110 017,
INDIA
011-91-11-652-8244
fax 011-91-11-653-2345
liberty@nda.vsnl.net.in
www.libertyindia.org
Issues: Agriculture; Economics of development;
Energy; Environment; International trade and
financial institutions; Privatization and
deregulation

Monterroso, Fernando

President, Universidad Francisco Marroquin
6 Calle Final, Zona 10, Guatemala City 01010,
GUATEMALA
011-502-338-7813
fax 011-502-334-6896
fmonterroso@ufm.cdu.gt
www.ufm.edu.gt
Issues: Education

Morris, Julian

Director, International Policy Network
2 Lord North Street, P. O. Box 38525,
London SW1P 3YB, UNITED KINGDOM
011-44-20-7799-8922
fax 011-44-20-7233-1070
julian@policynetwork.net
www.policynetwork.net
Issues: Economics of development;
Environment; Health care; International trade
and financial institutions

Muchnik, Alexander

President, Institute of Municipal Democracy
and Human Rights
68, Pushkinskaya Street, Odessa 65023,
UKRAINE
011-380-482-226746
fax 011-380-482-346208
Issues: Democratic institutions and elections;
Government

Murashev, Arkady

Krieble Institute
44, Bolshaya Nikitskaya St., strojenije 2,
121069 Moscow, RUSSIA
011-7-095-290-2309
fax 011-7-095-291-1595
admin@clcp.ru   *www.clcp.ru*
Issues: Fiscal policy and taxation; Government;
International relations and organizations;
International trade and financial institutions;
Privatization and deregulation; Terrorism
and drugs

Mykhailychenko, Kostyantyn

Executive Director, Ukrainian Center for
Independent Political Research
Suite 20, 4/26 Pyrogova Street, 01030 Kiev,
UKRAINE
011-380-44-235-6505
fax 011-380-44-235-6505
ucipr@ucipr.kiev.ua   *www.ucipr.kiev.ua*
Issues: Democratic institutions and elections;
Economics of development; Government;
Justice and crime; National security and
alliance relations

Nahan, Dr. Mike

Executive Director, Institute of Public Affairs
Limited
Level 2, 410 Collins Street, Melbourne, VIC
3000, AUSTRALIA
011-61-3-9600-4744
fax 011-61-3-9602-4989
mdnahan@ipa.org.au   *www.ipa.org.au*
Issues: Economics of development; Fiscal policy
and taxation; Government

Naishul, Dr. Vitaly

Director, Institute for the Study of Russian
Economy
Bolshaia Nikitskaya st. 44-2, Room 26, 121854
Moscow, RUSSIA
011-7-095-290-5108
fax 011-7-095-291-1595
economic@clcp.ru
http://www.libertarium.ru/eng/organiz/e-isre.html
Issues: Culture and the humanities; Fiscal policy
and taxation; Government; Privatization and
deregulation

Narayan, Dr. Jayaprakash
Campaign Coordinator, Lok Satta
401, Nirmal Towers, Dwarakapuri Colony,
Punjagutta, Hyderabad 500 082, INDIA
011-91-40-3350778
fax 011-91-40-3350783
loksatta@satyam.net.in   *www.loksatta.org*
Issues: Democratic institutions and elections;
Energy; Government; Health care; Justice
and crime

Narino, Juan Camilo
Director, Instituto de Ciencia Politica
Transversal 6 No. 27-10: Oficina 103 Edificio
Antares, Bogota, COLOMBIA
011-571-3429-419   fax 011-571-2433-361
Issues: Democratic institutions and elections;
Government; International trade and financial
institutions; Privatization and deregulation

Nasr, Dr. Salim
General Director, Lebanese Center for
Policy Studies
Tayyar Center Sin al-Fin, Box 55215, Beirut,
LEBANON
011-961-1-490-561
fax 011-961-1-490-375
psalem@lcps.org.lb   *www.lcps-lebanon.org*
Issues: Democratic institutions and elections;
Education; Environment; Fiscal policy and
taxation; Government; International relations
and organizations

Nicholls, Gerry
Vice President, National Citizens Coalition
600 6th Avenue, S.W., Suite 240, Calgary, AB
T2P 0S5, CANADA
403-269-3545   fax 403-269-4696
national@citizenscoalition.org
www.citizenscoalition.org
Issues: Democratic institutions and elections;
Fiscal policy and taxation; Privatization and
deregulation

Noffke, Carl
Professor, Almard Corporation
P. O. Box 2928, Northcliff, Johannesburg
2115, SOUTH AFRICA
011-27-11-476-4344
fax 011-27-11-476-4344
cnoffke@worldonline.co.za
Issues: Democratic institutions and elections;
Economics of development; Government;
International relations and organizations;
International trade and financial institutions;
Military and defense policy

Norton, Andrew
Director of Liberalising Learning
The Centre for Independent Studies
P. O. Box 92, St. Leonards, NSW 1590,
AUSTRALIA
011-61-2-9438-4377
fax 011-61-2-9439-7310
anorton@cis.org.au   *www.cis.org.au*
Issues: Education

O'Connor, Michael
Executive Director, Australia Defence
Association
P. O. Box 1131, Doncaster East, Victoria
3109, AUSTRALIA
011-61-3-9842-6203
fax 011-61-3-9841-8413
ada@netcore.com.au   *www.ada.asn.au*
Issues: Military and defense policy; National
security and alliance relations

Oravec, Dr. Jan
President, F. A. Hayek Foundation Bratislava
Drienova 24, 826 03 Bratislava, SLOVAKIA
011-421-2-4341-0148
fax 011-421-2-4341-0146
hayek@changenet.sk   *www.hayek.sk*
Issues: Economics of development; Fiscal policy
and taxation; Privatization and deregulation

Owens, Dennis
Senior Policy Analyst, Frontier Centre for
Public Policy
201-63 Albert Street, Winnepeg, MB R3J
2M9, CANADA
204-957-1567   fax 204-957-1570
owensd@fcpp.org   *www.fcpp.org*
Issues: Culture and the humanities; Education;
Energy; Health care

Palda, Filip
Senior Fellow, The Fraser Institute
1770 Burrard Street, 4th Floor, Vancouver,
BC V6J 3G7, CANADA
604-688-0221   fax 604-688-8539
www.fraserinstitute.ca
Issues: Democratic institutions and elections;
Fiscal policy and taxation

Papasotiriou, Harry

Director, Society for Social and Economic
Studies
P. O. Box 78, 19003 Markopoulo Attikis,
Mesogeia, GREECE
011-30-2990-40208
fax 011-30-2990-40208
hpapasot@ekome.gr   *www.ekome.gr*
Issues: Democratic institutions and elections;
Economics of development; Fiscal policy and
taxation; International relations and
organizations; International trade and
financial institutions; Military and defense
policy; National security and alliance relations;
Privatization and deregulation

Parkinson, Sid

Executive Director, St. Lawrence Institute
P. O. Box 307, NDG Station, Montreal, QC
H4A 3P6, CANADA
514-233-8321   fax 514-489-0312
sid@stlawrenceinstitute.org
www.stlawrenceinstitute.org
Issues: Culture and the humanities; Military and
defense policy; National security and alliance
relations

Pazos de la Torre, Dr. Luis A.

General Director, Centro de Investigaciones
Sobre la Libre Empresa
Camelia 329, Col. Florida, 01030 Mexico,
D.F., MEXICO
011-52-5662-4500
fax 011-52-5661-5410
ceninves@infolatina.com.mx
www.cisle.org.mx
Issues: Democratic institutions and elections;
Economics of development; Fiscal policy and
taxation; Government; Privatization and
deregulation

Petroni, Angelo M.

Professor of Philosophy of Social Science-
University of Bologna, Centro di Ricerca e
Documentazione Luigi Einaudi
Via Ponza 4, 10121 Torino, ITALY
011-39-011-5591611
fax 011-39-011-5591691
segreteria@centroeinaudi.it
www.centroeinaudi.it
Issues: Culture and the humanities; Democratic
institutions and elections; Government;
Religion and philosophy

Piasecka, Aneta

Senior Policy Analyst, Lithuanian Free
Market Institute
56 Birutes Street, LT-2004 Vilnius,
LITHUANIA
011-370-5-272-27-88
fax 011-370-5-272-72-79
aneta@freema.org   *www.freema.org*
Issues: Fiscal policy and taxation; Privatization
and deregulation

Pidluska, Inna

Head, Department of Economic and Social
Analysis, Ukrainian Center for Independent
Political Research
15 Khreshchatyk Street, Suite 1, Kyiv 01001,
UKRAINE
011-380-44-234-9315
fax 011-380-44-234-9315
kam@political.kiev.ua
www.ucipr.webjump.com
Issues: Economics of development;
Government; National security and alliance
relations; Privatization and deregulation

Pirie, Dr. Madsen

President, Adam Smith Institute
23 Great Smith Street, London SW1P 3BL,
UNITED KINGDOM
011-44-207-222-4995
fax 011-44-207-222-7544
madsen@adamsmith.org.uk
www.adamsmith.org.uk
Issues: Education; Government; Health care;
International trade and financial institutions;
Labor; Privatization and deregulation

Plunier, Guy

International Relations & Public and Press
Relations, Sauvegarde Retraites
110 Boulevard Saint German, Paris 75006,
FRANCE
011-33-1-4329-1441
fax 011-33-1-4329-1464
guy.plunier@wanadoo.fr
www.sauvegarde-retraites.org
Issues: Fiscal policy and taxation; Health care;
International relations and organizations

Pollard, Stephen
Senior Fellow, Centre for the New Europe
Rue du Luxembourg 23, 1000 Brussels,
BELGIUM
011-32-2-506-40-00
fax 011-32-2-506-40-09
cne-brussels@cne-network.org
www.cne-network.org
Issues: Culture and the humanities; Democratic
institutions and elections; Government

Prohasky, George
Co-Chairman of the Board of Trustees,
Center for Economic Development
Balsha 1, bl. 9, j.k. Ivan Vazov, 1408 Sofia,
BULGARIA
011-359-2-953-4204
fax 011-359-2-953-3644   ced@ced.bg
www.ced.bg
Issues: Economics of development; Fiscal policy
and taxation; Government; Privatization and
deregulation

Prokopijevic, Dr. Miro
Professor, Institute for European Studies
Trg Nikole Pasica 11, 11000 Belgrade,
SERBIA
011-381-11-3298-797
mprokop@eunet.yu   *www.fmc.org.yu*
Issues: Democratic institutions and elections;
Economics of development; Fiscal policy and
taxation; Privatization and deregulation

Raguonis, Audronis
Senior Fellow, Lithuanian Free Market
Institute
56 Birutes Street, LT-2004 Vilnius,
LITHUANIA
011-370-5-272-25-84
fax 011-370-5-272-12-79
raguonis@freema.org   *www.freema.org*
Issues: Economics of development;
International trade and financial institutions

Raiman, Laura Elizabeth
Managing Director, Raiman & Associates
Montevideo 666, 9th Floor # 908, 1019
Buenos Aires, ARGENTINA
011-54-11-4373-3932/7045
fax 011-54-11-4373-3932/7045
lraiman@ba.net
Issues: International relations and
organizations

Raju, S. V.
Editor, *Freedom First,*
3rd Floor, Army and Navy Building, 148
Mahatma Gandhi Road, Mumbai 400 001,
INDIA
011-91-22-284-3416
fax 011-91-22-284-3416
freedom@vsnl.com
Issues: Agriculture; Democratic institutions and
elections; Economics of development;
Education; Fiscal policy and taxation;
International relations and organizations;
Justice and crime; Privatization and
deregulation; Terrorism and drugs

Ranzolin, Sr. Ricardo Borges
President, Instituto Liberal-RS
Rua Santa Teresinha, 59, Bairro Farroupilha,
CEP 90040-180 Porte Alegre, BRAZIL
011-55-51-332-2376
fax 011-55-51-332-2376
il-rs@vanet.com.br   *www.il-rs.com.br*
Issues: Culture and the humanities; Economics
of development; Education; Environment;
Fiscal policy and taxation; Government;
International relations and organizations;
International trade and financial institutions;
Labor; Privatization and deregulation; Religion
and philosophy

Ratnapala, Prof. Suri
University of Queensland
T.C. Beirne School of Law, Room W344,
Queensland, 4072, AUSTRALIA
011-61-7-3365-2460
fax 011-61-7-3365-1454
s.ratnapala@laco.uq.edu.au
www.uq.edu.au
Issues: Democratic institutions and elections;
Government; Justice and crime

Ravina, Dr. Luis
Dean, Universidad de Navarra
Facultad de Economicas y Empresariales,
31080 Pamplona, SPAIN
011-34-948-425-625
fax 011-34-948-425-626
lravina@unav.es   *www.unav.es/econom*
Issues: Economics of development;
International trade and financial institutions;
Religion and philosophy

Redwood, Rt. Hon. John

Professor, Middlesex University Business
School
House of Commons, London SW1A 0AA,
UNITED KINGDOM
011-44-07711-486555
fax 011-44-0207-219-6191
redwoodj@parliament.uk
Issues: Democratic institutions and elections;
Economics of development; Fiscal policy and
taxation; Government; International relations
and organizations; National security and
alliance relations; Privatization and
deregulation

Reid, Michael

Senior Researcher, The Maxim Institute
49 Cape Horn Road, Hillsborough,
Auckland, NEW ZEALAND
011-64-9-627-3261
fax 011-64-9-627-3264
mail@maxim.org.nz   *www.maxim.org.nz*
Issues: Education

Rivas, Axel

Coordinator of the Education Policy Area,
Center for the Implementation of Public
Policies Promoting Equity and Growth
Av. Callao 25, 1B, C1022AAA Buenos Aires,
ARGENTINA
011-54-11-4384-9009
fax 011-54-11-4371-1221
arivas@cippec.org   *www.cippec.org*
Issues: Education

Rivas, Hugo Maul

Director, Economic Area, CIEN - Center for
Research on the National Economy
12 Calle 1-25, Zona 10, Edificio Germinis,
Torre Norte, Oficina 1702, Guatemala City,
GUATEMALA
011-502-335-3415
fax 011-502-335-3416
curizarh@cien.org.gt   *www.cien.org.gt*
Issues: Economics of development;
Privatization and deregulation

Robinson, Dr. Colin

Professor, University of Surrey
1A Gunnersbury Avenue, Ealing, London
W5 3NH, UNITED KINGDOM
011-20-8993-9886
fax 011-20-8993-9927
colin@gunnersbury.freeserve.co.uk
Issues: Energy; Government; Privatization and
deregulation

Runde, Sonia Cavallo

Senior Fellow, Center for the
Implementation of Public Policies
Promoting Equity and Growth
Av. Callao 25, 1B, C1022AAA Buenos Aires,
ARGENTINA
011-54-11-4384-9009
fax 011-54-11-4371-1221
scavallo@cippec.org   *www.cippec.org*
Issues: Economics of development; Health care

Sabino, Dr. Carlos A.

Centro de Divulgacion del Conocimiento
Economico (CEDICE)
Avda. Isla de Margarita, Ed. 677, 1-A
Cumbres de Curumo, Caracas 1080,
VENEZUELA
011-58-212-976-0909
fax 011-58212-977-2426
sabino@telcel.net.ve
Issues: Democratic institutions and elections;
Economics of development; Government;
Privatization and deregulation

Salin, Pascal

Professor of Economics, Universite Paris-
Dauphine
89 Boulevard Saint Michel, Paris 75005,
FRANCE
011-33-1-43-54-3911
fax 011-33-1-44-07-1065
salin@club-internet.fr   *www.dauphine.fr*
Issues: Economics of development; Fiscal policy
and taxation; Privatization and deregulation

Salinas-Leon, Dr. Roberto

Director of Policy Analysis, TV Azteca
Periferico sur 4121, Col. Fuentes del
Pedregal, Mexico, D.F. 14141, MEXICO
011-52-55-3090-1313
fax 011-52-55-3099-9181
rmsalinas@tvazteca.com.mx
www.toditoeconomico.com.mx
Issues: Economics of development;
International trade and financial institutions;
Privatization and deregulation; Religion and
philosophy

Sally, Dr. Razeen
Senior Lecturer, London School of
Economics and Political Science
Houghton Street, London WC2A 2AE,
UNITED KINGDOM
011-44-207-955-6788
fax 011-44-207-955-7446
r.sally@lse.ac.uk   *www.lse.ac.uk*
Issues: Economics of development;
International relations and organizations;
International trade and financial institutions

Salvia, Gabriel
Executive Director, Fundacion Atlas Para
Una Sociedad Libre
Av. R. S. Peña 628 8 T1, Buenos Aires 1425,
ARGENTINA
011-54-11-4343-3886
fax 011-54-11-4343-3886   *www.atlas.org.ar*
Issues: Economics of development; Fiscal policy
and taxation

Samardzija, Dr. Visnja
Head of the European Integration
Department, Institute for International
Relations
ul. Ljudevita Farkasa Vukotinovica 2, P. O.
Box 303, 100 00 Zagreb, CROATIA
011-385-1-48-26-522
fax 011-385-1-48-28-361
visnja@mairmo.irmo.hr   *www.imo.hr*
Issues: Economics of development;
International relations and organizations

Samayoa B., Estuardo
President, Centro de Estudios Economico-
Sociales
Apartado 652, Guatamala City 1901,
GUATEMALA
011-502-332-2402
fax 011-502-332-2420
cees@cees.org.gt   *www.cees.org.gt*
Issues: Education; Energy; International trade
and financial institutions; Terrorism and drugs

Sarlo, Christopher
Senior Fellow, The Fraser Institute, and
Professor of Economics, Nipissing University
Box 5002, North Bay ON P1B 8L7, CANADA
604-688-0221   fax 604-688-8539
www.fraserinstitute.ca
Issues: Fiscal policy and taxation

Saunders, Professor Peter
Director of Social Policy Research
The Centre for Independent Studies
P. O. Box 92, St. Leonards, NSW 1590,
AUSTRALIA
011-61-2-9438-4377   fax 011-
61-2-9439-7310
psaunders@cis.org.au   *www.cis.org.au*
Issues: Culture and the humanities;
Privatization and deregulation

Schmidt, Dieter A.
Institute for Foreign Relations of the Hanns
Seidel Foundation
Lazarettstr. 33, D-80636 Munich, GERMANY
011-49-89-12-58-200
fax 011-49-89-12-58-368
schmidt@hss.de   *www.hss.de*
Issues: International relations and
organizations; Military and defense policy

Schwarz, Dr. Jiri
President, Liberalni Institut
Spalena 51, 110 00 Prague 1, CZECH
REPUBLIC
011-420-2-249122199
fax 011-420-2-24930203
jiri.schwarz@libirist.cz   *www.libinst.cz*
Issues: Fiscal policy and taxation; Government;
Privatization and deregulation

Schwarz, Dr. Jurgen
University of the German Armed Forces
Angerst 9, 82515 Wolfrasthausen,
GERMANY
011-49-089-6004-2044
fax 011-49-089-6004-4460
ifip@unibw-muenchen.de
www.unibw-muenchen.de
Issues: Government; International relations and
organizations; Military and defense policy;
National security and alliance relations

Seeman, Neil
Director of CANSTATS, The Fraser Institute
260 Heath Street West, Number 605,
Toronto, ON M5P 3L6, CANADA
416-489-0532
neils@fraserinstitute.ca
www.fraserinstitute.ca
Issues: Culture and the humanities

Semin, Michal

Executive Director, Civic Institute
Vysehradska 49, 120 00 Prague 2, CZECH
REPUBLIC
011-42-2-298-791
fax 011-42-2-298-791
obcinst@mbox.vol.cz   *www.obcinst.cz*
Issues: Culture and the humanities; Education;
Religion and philosophy

Shah, Parth

President, Centre for Civil Society
B-12 Kailash Colony, New Delhi 110 048,
INDIA
011-91-11-646-8282
fax 011-91-11-646-2453
parth@ccsindia.org   *www.ccsindia.org*
Issues: Culture and the humanities; Economics
of development; Fiscal policy and taxation

Shaw, Mr. Enrique

Director, Public Sector Reform, Center for
the Implementation of Public Policies
Promoting Equity and Growth
Av. Callao 25, 1B, C1022AAA Buenos Aires,
ARGENTINA
011-54-11-4384-9009
fax 011-54-11-4371-1221
eshaw@cippec.org   *www.cippec.org*
Issues: Privatization and deregulation

Sheffer, Kenneth

Counsellor to the President, The Heritage
Foundation
Baskerville House, 13 Duddell Street, Suite
401, Central, SAR, HONG KONG
011-852-2522-2555
fax 011-852-2524-6644
ken@kensheffer.com
Issues: International relations and
organizations; International trade and
financial institutions

Shikwati, James S.

Director, Inter Region Economic Network
[IREN]
Box 135, GPO Code 00100, Nairobi, KENYA
011-254-2-2723258
fax 011-254-2-2723258
info@irenkenya.org   *www.irenkenya.org*
Issues: Agriculture; Democratic institutions and
elections; Economics of development;
Education; Environment; Health care;
International relations and organizations;
International trade and financial institutions;
Privatization and deregulation

Sima, Dr. Josef

Research Fellow, Liberalni Institut
Spalena 51, Prague 110 00, CZECH
REPUBLIC
011-420-2-249-30796
fax 011-420-2-249-30203
josef@sima@libinst.cz   *www.libinst.cz*
Issues: Economics of development; Fiscal policy
and taxation; International trade and financial
institutions

Simasius, Dr. Remigijus

Senior Policy Analyst, Lithuanian Free
Market Institute
56 Birutes Street, LT-2004 Vilnius,
LITHUANIA
011-370-5-272-25-84
fax 011-370-5-272112-79
remigijus@freema.org   *www.freema.org*
Issues: Education; Energy; Health care; Justice
and crime; Labor; Privatization and
deregulation

Sirc, Ljubo, CBE

Director, Centre for Research into Post-
Communist Economics
57 Tufton Street, London SW1P 3QL,
UNITED KINGDOM
011-020-7233-1050
fax 011-020-7233-1050
Issues: Fiscal policy and taxation; Government;
International trade and financial institutions;
Privatization and deregulation

Snoen, Jan Arild

Bygdoy alle 61, N-0265 Oslo, NORWAY
011-47-2255-6327   snosians@online.no
Issues: Education; Energy; Environment;
International trade and financial institutions

Snow, Adrienne DeLong

Managing Director, Centre for the Study of
Civic Renewal
P. O. Box 19045, 360 A Bloor Street West,
Toronto, ON M5S 1X1, CANADA
416-580-4885   fax 416-588-9580
asnow@civicrenewalonline.org
www.civicrenewalonline.org
Issues: Culture and the humanities; Education

Soipee, Dr. Noordin
Chairman and CEO, Institute of Strategic
and International Studies
No. 1 Pesiaran Sultan Salahuddin, P. O. Box
14124, 50778 Kuala Lumpur, MALAYSIA
011-603-2693-9366
fax 011-60-3-2693-9430
webmaster@isis.po.my   *www.jaring.my/isis*
Issues: Economics of development;
International relations and organizations

Sopuck, Robert
Director, Rural Renaissance Project,
Frontier Centre for Public Policy
201-63 Albert Street, Winnepeg, Manitoba
R3J 2M9, CANADA
204-957-1567   fax 204-957-1570
sopuckr@fcpp.org   *www.fcpp.org*
Issues: Agriculture; Economics of development;
Environment; Government

Spinanger, Dr. Dean
Senior Research Associate, Kiel Institute of
World Economics
Deesternbrooker Weg 120, D-24105 Kiel,
GERMANY
011-49-431-8814207
fax 011-49-431-8814500
dspinanger@ifw.uni-kiel.de
www.uni-kiel.de/IfW/homeeng.htm
Issues: Economics of development;
International trade and financial institutions;
Labor

Stanchev, Dr. Krassen
Executive Director, Institute for Market
Economics
P. O. Box 803, 82A, Dondukov Boulevard,
Floor 3, Sofia 1000, BULGARIA
011-359-2-943-36-48
fax 011-359-2-943-33-52
stanchev@ime.bg   *www.ime-bg.org*
Issues: Democratic institutions and elections;
Economics of development; Fiscal policy and
taxation; Government; International trade and
financial institutions; Privatization and
deregulation; Religion and philosophy

Stein, Peter
Economist, Stein Brothers AB
Kommendorsgatan 14, 114 48 Stockholm,
SWEDEN
011-46-8-662-6980
fax 011-46-8-663-3305
pst_brs@algonet.se
Issues: Fiscal policy and taxation; Government;
Health care; Privatization and deregulation

Steponaviciene, Guoda
Vice President, Lithuanian Free Market
Institute
56 Birutes Street, LT-2004 Vilnius,
LITHUANIA
011-370-5-272-73-73
fax 011-370-5-272-72-79
guoda@freema.org   *www.freema.org*
Issues: Health care

Steverlynck, Maria
Program Officer, Fundacion Republica para
una Nueva Generacion
Reconquista 609, 8 piso, Buenos Aires 1003,
ARGENTINA
011-54-11-4312-1903
fax 011-54-11-4311-1834
ams@interar.com.ar
Issues: Democratic institutions and elections;
Education; Environment; Justice and crime

Stewart, Rigoberto, Ph.D.
Executive Director, Institute for Liberty and
Policy Analysis
Apartado 329-4050, Alajuela, COSTA RICA
011-506-438-2464
fax 011-506-438-2444
riggo@inlap.com   *www.inlap.com*
Issues: Economics of development;
International trade and financial institutions

Svedaite, Rita
Policy Analyst, Lithuanian Free Market
Institute
56 Birutes Street, LT-2004 Vilnius,
LITHUANIA
011-370-5-272-23-54
fax 011-370-5-272-72-79
rita@freema.org   *www.freema.org*
Issues: Environment; International trade and
financial institutions; Labor

Svejna, Ivan
Director, F. A. Hayek Foundation Bratislava
Drienova 24, 826 03 Bratislava, SLOVAKIA
011-421-2-4341-0148
fax 011-421-2-4341-0146
ivan.svejna@hayek.sk   *www.hayek.sk*
Issues: Fiscal policy and taxation; Privatization
and deregulation

Taffin, Benoite
President, French Taxpayers Association
42, rue des Jeuneurs, Cedex 02, Paris 75077,
FRANCE
011-33-42-21-16-24
fax 011-33-42-33-29-35
durrieu@contribuables.net
www.contribuables.com
Issues: Fiscal policy and taxation; Government;
Privatization and deregulation

Tapia, Jose Luis
President and CEO, Instituto de Libre
Empresa
Calle Barajas 522, Lima 41, PERU
011-51-1-475-9752
fax 011-51-1-475-9752   *www.ileperu.org*
Issues: Democratic institutions and elections;
Government; International trade and financial
institutions; Privatization and deregulation

Tarras-Wahlberg, Bjorn
President, World Taxpayers Associations
Torsvikssv 28, Stockholm SE-18134,
SWEDEN
011-46-70-325-00-11
fax 011-46-8-765-82-80
btw@worldtaxpayers.org
www.worldtaxpayers.org
Issues: Democratic institutions and elections;
Economics of development; Fiscal policy and
taxation; Government; International relations
and organizations; Privatization and
deregulation

Tashan, Seyfi
Director, Turkish Foreign Policy Institute
Bilkent University – East Campus, 06533
Ankara, TURKEY
011-90-312-266-2869
fax 011-90-312-266-2871
tashan@foreignpolicy.org.tr
www.foreignpolicy.org.tr
Issues: International relations and
organizations; Military and defense policy;
National security and alliance relations;
Terrorism and drugs

Thompson, John C.
President, The Mackenzie Institute
P. O. Box 338, Adelaide Station, Toronto,
ON M5C 2J4, CANADA
416-686-4063
mackenzieinstitute@compuserve.com
www.mackenzieinstitute.com
Issues: Military and defense policy; National
security and alliance relations; Terrorism and
drugs

Tien, Dr. Hung-Mao
Chairman of the Board, Institute for
National Policy Research
5F, 238, Sungjiang Road, Taipei, TAIWAN
011-886-2-2511-5009
fax 011-886-2-2560-5536
inprpd@ms8.hinet.net
www.inpr.org.tw/inpre.htm
Issues: Democratic institutions and elections;
Economics of development; Fiscal policy and
taxation; Government

Tooley, James, Ph.D.
Professor of Education Policy and Director,
E. G. West Centre
University of Newcastle Upon Tyne,
Newcastle Upon Tyne NE1 7RU, UNITED
KINGDOM
011-44-191-222-6374
fax 011-44-191-222-8170
j.n.tooley@ncl.ac.uk   *www.ncl.ac.uk/egwest*
Issues: Economics of development; Education;
Privatization and deregulation

Trumpa, Ugnius
President, Lithuanian Free Market Institute
56 Birutes Street, LT-2004 Vilnius,
LITHUANIA
011-370-5-272-25-84
fax 011-370-5-272-12-79
ugnius@freema.org   *www.freema.org*
Issues: Economics of development; Fiscal policy
and taxation; Government; International
relations and organizations; Privatization and
deregulation; Religion and philosophy

Tsumori, Dr. Kayoko
Policy Analyst, The Centre for Independent Studies
P. O. Box 92, St. Leonards, NSW 1590, AUSTRALIA
011-61-2-9438-4377
fax 011-61-2-9439-7310
ktsumori@cis.org.au   *www.cis.org.au*
Issues: Democratic institutions and elections; Government; Labor; Privatization and deregulation

Vacic, Dr. Zoran
President, Center for Liberal-Democratic Studies
Ulica 29 Novembra 10, 5th Floor, 11000 Belgrade, Serbia, YUGOSLAVIA
011-381-11-322-50-24
fax 011-381-11-322-55-71
zoran.vacic@clds.org.yu   *www.clds.org.yu*
Issues: Health care

Vainiene, Ruta
Vice President, Lithuanian Free Market Institute
56 Birutes Street, LT-2004 Vilnius, LITHUANIA
011-370-5-272-23-54
fax 011-370-5-272-72-79
ruta@freema.org   *www.freema.org*
Issues: Fiscal policy and taxation

Vanberg, Dr. Viktor
Professor, Department of Economics, Wirtschaftspolitik, University of Freiburg
Abteilung fur Wirtschaftspolitik, Platz der Alten Synagoge, D-79085 Freiburg im Breisgau, GERMANY
011-49-761-203-2319
fax 011-49-761-203-2322
vvanberg@vwl.uni-freiburg.de
www.vwl.uni-freiburg.de
Issues: Democratic institutions and elections

Vancura, Petr
Director, Prague Institute for National Security
Vysehradska 49, 128 00 Prague 2, CZECH REPUBLIC
011-420-2-2272-4820
fax 011-420-2-2271-2439
petr.van@volny.cz
Issues: Democratic institutions and elections; International relations and organizations; Military and defense policy; National security and alliance relations

Vander Elst, Philip
Author and Journalist,
11 High Street, Ascott-under-Wychwood, Oxfordshire OX7 6AW, UNITED KINGDOM
011-44-1993-830-693
fax 011-44-1993-830-062
pvandere@aol.com
Issues: Culture and the humanities; Democratic institutions and elections; Government; International relations and organizations; Religion and philosophy

Vilpisauskas, Ramunas
Senior Policy Analyst, Lithuanian Free Market Institute
56 Birutes Street, LT-2004 Vilnius, LITHUANIA
011-370-5-272-73-73
fax 011-370-5-272-72-79
ramunas@freema.org   *www.freema.org*
Issues: Agriculture; Government; International relations and organizations; National security and alliance relations

Volk, Yevgeny
Coordinator, Moscow Office, The Heritage Foundation
44, block 2, Bolshaya Nikitskaya Street, GSP-5 Moscow 123995, RUSSIA
011-7-095-290-6107
fax 011-7-095-291-1595
heritage@clcp.ru   *www.heritage.org*
Issues: Democratic institutions and elections; Government; International relations and organizations; International trade and financial institutions; Military and defense policy; National security and alliance relations; Privatization and deregulation

Vukotic, Dr. Veselin
Professor, Faculty of Economics, University of Montenegro
Jovana Tomasevica 37, Podgorica 81000, MONTENEGRO
011-381-81-241-504
fax 011-381-81-243-544   vukotic@cg.yu
Issues: Economics of development; Privatization and deregulation

Wadhwa, Rakesh
Executive Director, Nepal Recreation Centre Pvt. Ltd.
Casino Everest, c/o The Everest Hotel, P. O. Box 659, New Baneshwor, Kathmandu, NEPAL
011-977-1-780100
fax 011-977-1-782284
everest@mos.com.np
Issues: Energy; Environment; Fiscal policy and taxation; Government; Health care

Wadhwa, Shalini
Chairperson, Great Savers
C-4/23, Safdarjung Devp. Area, New Delhi 110-016, INDIA
652-2881   fax 652-2883
swads@mos.com.np
Issues: Economics of development; Fiscal policy and taxation; Privatization and deregulation

Walker, Dr. Michael A.
Executive Director, The Fraser Institute
1770 Burrard Street, 4th Floor, Vancouver, BC V6J 3G7, CANADA
604-688-0221   fax 604-688-8539
michaelw@fraserinstitute.ca
www.fraserinstitute.ca
Issues: Economics of development; Fiscal policy and taxation; Government; Health care; International trade and financial institutions; Privatization and deregulation

Watrin, Dr. Christian
Professor, Institute of Economic Policy Research
University of Koeln, WiSo-Hochhaus, 7th Floor, Room 762, D-50923 Koeln, GERMANY
011-49-221-935-24-47
fax 011-49-221-935-24-46
chwatrin@aol.com
Issues: Economics of development; International trade and financial institutions

Wei, Dr. Yung
President, Vanguard Institute for Policy Studies
2F, 15 Chi-Nan Road, Sec.1, Taipei 100, TAIWAN
011-886-2-2395-2045
fax 011-886-2-2395-2052
ywei@cc.nctu.edu.tw
Issues: Democratic institutions and elections; Government; International relations and organizations; National security and alliance relations

Westholm, Dr. Carl-Johan
S Rudbecksg 5, SE-752 36 Uppsala, SWEDEN
011-46-706-97-15-23
fax 011-46-18-55-59-16
carl-johan@westholm.biz
Issues: Democratic institutions and elections; International trade and financial institutions

Whetstone, Linda
Chairman, International Policy Network
Bassetts Manor, Hartfield, East Sussex TN7 4LA, UNITED KINGDOM
011-44-1892-770304
fax 011-44-1892-777873
linda@policynetwork.net
Issues: Agriculture

Williams, Alan Lee
Director, Atlantic Council of the United Kingdom
185 Tower Bridge Road, London SE1 2UF, UNITED KINGDOM
011-44-207-403-0640
fax 011-44-207-403-0901
acuk@atlantic-council.org.uk
Issues: Democratic institutions and elections; Education; International relations and organizations; Military and defense policy; Terrorism and drugs

Wong, Professor Richard
Director, Hong Kong Centre for Economic Research
c/o School of Economics and Finance, The University of Hong Kong, Pokfulam Road, HONG KONG
011-852-2548-9300
fax 011-852-2548-3223
hkcer@econ.hku.hk   *www.hku.hk/hkcer/*
Issues: Economics of development; International trade and financial institutions

Yayla, Dr. Atilla
President, Association for Liberal Thinking
GMK Bulvari No: 108/17, Maltepe, 06570 Ankara, TURKEY
011-90-312-230-8703
fax 011-90-312-230-8003
liberal@ada.net.tr   *www.liberal-dt.org.tr*
Issues: Culture and the humanities; Democratic institutions and elections; Government; International relations and organizations; Justice and crime; Religion and philosophy; Terrorism and drugs

Yonkova-Hristova, Assenka
Research Director, Institute for Market
Economics
P. O. Box 803, 82A, Dondukov Boulevard,
Floor 3, 1000 Sofia, BULGARIA
011-359-2-943-36-48
fax 011-359-2-943-33-52
assia@ime.bg   *www.ime-bg.org*
Issues: Economics of development; Fiscal policy
and taxation; Government; Privatization and
deregulation

Zagorski, Dr. Andrei
Senior Vice President, East-West Institute
78/2000 Rasínovo nabrezi, 120 00 Prague 2,
CZECH REPUBLIC
011-420-2-2198-4222
fax 011-420-2-2491-7854
andrei.zagorski@iews.cz
Issues: Government; International relations and
organizations; Military and defense policy;
National security and alliance relations

Zakhazchenko, Olga
International Centre for Policy Studies
13-A Pymonenka Street, 04050 Kiev,
UKRAINE
011-380-44-236-4477
fax 011-380-44-236-4668
office@icps.kiev.ua   *www.icps.kiev.ua*
Issues: Democratic institutions and elections;
Government

Zemanovicova, Dr. Daniela
Reader in Economy, Transparency
International Slovakia
Bajkalska 25, 82718 Bratislava 212,
SLOVAKIA
011-4212-5341-1020
fax 011-4212-5823-3304
danielaz@transparency.sk
www.transparency.sk
Issues: Government; Privatization and
deregulation

Zylberberg, Dr. Meir
Doctor en Cienoias Economicas,
Fundacion Libre
Avda. Santa Fe 3353-12a, Buenos Aires 1425,
ARGENTINA
011-541-1-4823-3680
fax 011-541-1-4823-3680
meirzylb@cvtci.com.ar
Issues: Economics of development; Fiscal policy
and taxation; Privatization and deregulation

International Organizations

ADAM SMITH INSTITUTE
23 Great Smith Street
London SW1P 3BL, UNITED KINGDOM
011-44-207-222-4995
fax 011-44-207-222-7544
www.adamsmith.org.uk

ADAM SMITH RESEARCH CENTRE
ul. Bednarska 16
00-321 Warsaw, POLAND
011-48-22-828-4707
fax 011-48-22-828-0614
www.adam-smith.pl

ADAM SMITH SOCIETY
Via Cornaggia 10
20123 Milano, ITALY
011-39-02-8514-830
fax 011-39-02-8514-825
www.adamsmith.it

ASSOCIATION FOR LIBERAL THINKING
GMK Bulvari No: 108/17
Maltepe, 06570 Ankara, TURKEY
011-90-312-230-8703
fax 011-90-312-230-8003
www.liberal-dt.org.tr

ATLANTIC COUNCIL OF THE UNITED KINGDOM
185 Tower Bridge Road
London SE1 2UF, UNITED KINGDOM
011-44-207-403-0640
fax 011-44-207-403-0901

ATLANTIC INSTITUTE FOR MARKET STUDIES
2000 Barrington Street, Suite 1006,
Cogswell Tower
Halifax, N.S. B3J 3K1, CANADA
902-429-1143   fax 902-425-1393
www.aims.ca

AUSTRALIA DEFENCE ASSOCIATION
P. O. Box 1131
Doncaster East, Victoria 3109,
AUSTRALIA
011-61-3-9842-6203
fax 011-61-3-9841-8413
www.ada.asn.au

AUSTRALIAN NATIONAL UNIVERSITY
Research School of Social Sciences, Social
and Political Theory Group
Canberra ACT 200, AUSTRALIA
011-61-02-6125-3411
fax 011-61-02-6125-0599
www.anu.edu.au

CENTER FOR ECONOMIC DEVELOPMENT
Balsha 1, bl. 9, j.k. Ivan Vazov
1408 Sofia, BULGARIA
011-359-2-953-4204
fax 011-359-2-953-3644
www.ced.bg

CENTER FOR LIBERAL-DEMOCRATIC STUDIES
Ulica 29 Novembra 10, 5th Floor
11000 Belgrade, Serbia, YUGOSLAVIA
011-381-11-322-50-24
fax 011-381-11-322-55-71
www.clds.org.yu

CENTER FOR STRATEGIC AND INTERNATIONAL STUDIES
Jl. Tanah Abang III No. 23-27
Jakarta 10160, INDONESIA
011-62-21-386-5532
fax 011-62-21-380-9641
www.csis.or.id

CENTER FOR THE IMPLEMENTATION OF PUBLIC POLICIES PROMOTING EQUITY AND GROWTH
Av. Callao 25, 1B
C1022AAA Buenos Aires, ARGENTINA
011-54-11-4384-9009
fax 011-54-11-4371-1221
www.cippec.org

CENTRE D'ANALYSE ECONOMIQUE
Universite Aix-Marseille 3, 3, avenue
Robert Schuman
13100 Aix-en-Provence, FRANCE
011-33-442-17-2992
fax 011-33-442-59-3887
www.u-3mrs.fr

CENTRE FOR CIVIL SOCIETY
B-12 Kailash Colony
New Delhi 110 048, INDIA
011-91-11-646-8282
fax 011-91-11-646-2453
www.ccsindia.org

CENTRE FOR CULTURAL RENEWAL
503-39 Robertson Road
Ottawa, ON K2H 8R2, CANADA
613-567-9010   fax 613-567-6061
www.culturalrenewal.ca

CENTRE FOR LIBERAL STRATEGIES
4, Alexander Battenberg Street
1000 Sofia, BULGARIA
011-359-2-981-8126
fax 011-359-2-981-8125
www.cls-sofia.org

CENTRE FOR RESEARCH INTO POST-COMMUNIST ECONOMICS
57 Tufton Street
London SW1P 3QL, UNITED KINGDOM
011-020-7233-1050
fax 011-020-7233-1050

CENTRE FOR THE NEW EUROPE
Rue du Luxembourg 23
1000 Brussels, BELGIUM
011-32-2-506-40-00
fax 011-32-2-506-40-09
www.centrefortheneweurope.org

CENTRE FOR THE STUDY OF CIVIC RENEWAL
P. O. Box 19045, 360 A Bloor Street West
Toronto, ON M5S 1X1, CANADA
416-580-4885   fax 416-588-9580
www.civicrenewalonline.org

CENTRO CULTURALE LEPANTO
Via Giuseppe Sacconi, 4/b
00196 Roma, ITALY
011-39-06-3233307
fax 011-39-06-32110310
www.lepanto.org

CENTRO DE DIVULGACION DEL CONOCIMIENTO ECONOMICO (CEDICE)
Avda. Andres Eloy Blanco (Este 2), Edificio
Camara de Comercio de Caracas
Los Caobos, Caracus, VENEZUELA
011-58-212-571-3357
fax 011-58-212-576-0512
www.cedice.org.ve

CENTRO DE ESTUDIOS ECONOMICO-SOCIALES
Apartado 652
Guatamala City 1901, GUATEMALA
011-502-332-2402
fax 011-502-332-2420
www.cees.org.gt

CENTRO DE ESTUDIOS EN EDUCACION Y ECONMIA
15 de Mayo 1531 Pte.
Monterrey CP NL 64040, MEXICO
011-52-83-44-4824   fax 011-52-34-2743-3

CENTRO DE INVESTIGACION PARA EL DESARROLLO, A.C.
Jaime Balmes No. 11 Edif. D-2o. Piso, Col.
Los Morales Polanco
11510 Mexico, D.F., MEXICO
011-52-55-5985-1010
fax 011-52-55-5985-1030
www.cidac.org

CENTRO DE INVESTIGACION Y ESTUDIOS LEGALES (CITEL)
Libertadores 350, San Isidro
Lima 27, PERU
011-51-1-441-3424
fax 011-51-1-442-6161

CENTRO DE INVESTIGACIONES SOBRE LA LIBRE EMPRESA
Camelia 329, Col. Florida
01030 Mexico, D.F., MEXICO
011-52-5662-4500
fax 011-52-5661-5410
www.cisle.org.mx

CENTRO DI RICERCA E DOCUMENTAZIONE LUIGI EINAUDI
Via Ponza 4
10121 Torino, ITALY
011-39-011-5591611
fax 011-39-011-5591691
www.centroeinaudi.it

CIEN - CENTER FOR RESEARCH ON THE NATIONAL ECONOMY
12 Calle 1-25, Zona 10, Edificio Germinis,
Torre Norte, Oficina 1702
Guatemala City, GUATEMALA
011-502-335-3415
fax 011-502-335-3416
www.cien.org.gt

CIRCULO DE EMPRESARIOS
Serrano, 1-4°
28001 Madrid, SPAIN
011-34-91-578-1472
fax 011-34-91-577-4871

CIVIC INSTITUTE
Vysehradska 49
120 00 Prague 2, CZECH REPUBLIC
011-42-2-298-791
fax 011-42-2-298-791
www.obcinst.cz

CIVITAS: THE INSTITUTE FOR THE STUDY OF CIVIL SOCIETY
The Mezzanine, Elizabeth House, 39 York Road
London SE1 7NQ, UNITED KINGDOM
011-44-20-7401-5470
fax 011-44-20-7401-5471
www.civitas.org.uk

CONSTANTINOS KARAMANLIS INSTITUTE FOR DEMOCRACY
12 Vas. Sofias Street
Athens 106 74, GREECE
011-30-1-725-7495
fax 011-30-1-725-7510
www.idkaramanlis.gr

DAVID HUME INSTITUTE
25 Buccleuch Place
Edinburgh EH8 9LN, Scotland, UNITED KINGDOM
011-44-131-667-9609
fax 011-44-131-667-9609
www.ed.ac.uk/dhi/

E. G. WEST CENTRE
University of Newcastle Upon Tyne
Newcastle Upon Tyne NE1 7RU, UNITED KINGDOM
011-44-191-222-6374
fax 011-44-191-222-8170
www.ncl.ac.uk/egwest

EAST-WEST INSTITUTE
78/2000 Rasínovo nabrezi
120 00 Prague 2, CZECH REPUBLIC
011-420-2-2198-4222
fax 011-420-2-2491-7854

EDMUND BURKE FOUNDATION
Noordeinde 10D, P. O. Box 10498
2501 HL, The Hague, NETHERLANDS
011-31-060-3925180
www.burkerstichting.nl

EDMUND BURKE INSTITUTE
Crookhaven
Coleen, Skibereen, IRELAND
011-35-3137-8-5043
fax 011-35-3166-1-8721
www.edmundburke-institute.org

F. A. HAYEK FOUNDATION BRATISLAVA
Drienova 24
826 03 Bratislava, SLOVAKIA
011-421-2-4341-0148
fax 011-421-2-4341-0146
www.hayek.sk

FOUNDATION FOR MARKET ECONOMY
Dombóvári út 17/19
H-1117 Budapest, HUNGARY
011-361-204-2951
fax 011-361-204-2953
www.elender.hu/fme

FRANKFURTER INSTITUT - STIFTUNG MARKTWIRTSCHAFT UND POLITIK
Am Jaegerwaeldchen 12
35041 Marburg, GERMANY
011-49-6172-6647-0
fax 011-49-6172-22292
www.frankfurter-institut.de

FREE MARKET CENTER
Francuska 59
11000 Belgrade, Serbia, YUGOSLAVIA
011-381-11-187-245
www.fmc.org.yu

FREE MARKET FOUNDATION
P. O. Box 785121
Sandton 2146, SOUTH AFRICA
011-27-11-88-4-0270
fax 011-27-11-88-4-5672
www.freemarketfoundation.com

FREEDOM HOUSE
1054 Bp. Falk Miksa u. 30. 4/2
H-1118 Budapest, HUNGARY
011-36-1-354-1230
fax 011-36-1-354-1233
www.ngonet.org

FRENCH TAXPAYERS ASSOCIATION
42, rue des Jeuneurs, Cedex 02
Paris 75077, FRANCE
011-33-42-21-16-24
fax 011-33-42-33-29-35
www.contribuables.com

FRIEDRICH A. V. HAYEK INSTITUT
Wipplingerstrasse 25
A-1010 Wien, AUSTRIA
011-43-1-534-51-376
fax 011-43-1-534-51-233
www.hayek-institut.at

FRONTIER CENTRE FOR PUBLIC POLICY
201-63 Albert Street
Winnepeg, MB R3J 2M9, CANADA
204-957-1567   fax 204-957-1570
www.fcpp.org

FUNDACION ALBERDIF
Colon 90
Mendoza 1035, ARGENTINA
011-54-261-423-0630
fax 011-54-61-257-103

FUNDACION ATLAS PARA UNA SOCIEDAD LIBRE
Av. R. S. Pena 628 8 T1
Buenos Aires 1425, ARGENTINA
011-54-11-4343-3886
fax 011-54-11-4343-3886
www.atlas.org.ar

FUNDACION DL
Calle 25 Norte # 5A 43 of 202
Cali, COLOMBIA
011-572-683-7237
fax 011-572-653-0260
http://www.fundaciondl.org

FUNDACIÓN GLOBAL
Roca 1654
Mar del Plata 7600, ARGENTINA
011-54-223-486-3400
fax 011-54-223-535-6245
www.fglobal.org

FUNDACION INICIATIVA
Bolivar 553, 5 piso of C
Cordoba 5000, ARGENTINA
011-54-351-424-2912
fax 011-54-351-424-2912

FUNDACION LIBERTAD
Av. 9 de Octubre #1911 y Esmeraldes, Ed.
Finansur, piso 21
Guayaquil, ECUADOR
011-593-4-2372531
fax 011-593-4-2372532
www.fundacionlibertad.org

FUNDACION LIBERTAD
Mitre 170
2000 Rosario, Santa Fe, ARGENTINA
011-54-341-424-5000
fax 011-54-341-424-5111
www.libertad.org.ar

FUNDACION LIBRE
Avda. Santa Fe 3353-12a
Buenos Aires 1425, ARGENTINA
011-541-1-4823-3680
fax 011-541-1-4823-3680

FUNDACION REPUBLICA PARA UNA NUEVA GENERACION
Reconquista 609, 8 piso
Buenos Aires 1003, ARGENTINA
011-54-11-4312-1903
fax 011-54-11-4311-1834

GLASNOST PUBLIC POLICY FOUNDATION
15/6, 1st Kolobovsky pereulok
103051 Moscow, RUSSIA
011-7-095-299-8538
fax 011-7-095-299-8538
www.glasnostonline.org

HONG KONG CENTRE FOR ECONOMIC RESEARCH
c/o School of Economics and Finance,
The University of Hong Kong, Pokfulam
Road
HONG KONG
011-852-2548-9300
fax 011-852-2548-3223
www.hku.hk/hkcer/

HONG KONG POLICY RESEARCH INSTITUTE
5/F., China Hong Kong Tower, 8-12
Hennessy Road
Wanchai, HONG KONG
011-852-2686-1905
fax 011-852-2648-4303
www.hkpri.org.hk

INDEPENDENT INSTITUTE OF SOCIO-ECONOMIC AND POLITICAL STUDIES
P. O. Box 219
Minsk 220030, BELARUS
011-375-172-22-80-49
fax 011-375-172-52-32-10
www.cacedu.unibel.by/iisep

INSTITUT D'HISTOIRE SOCIALE
4 Avenue Benoit Frachon
Nanterre 92023, FRANCE
011-33-1-4614-0929
fax 011-33-1-4614-0925
www.iisg.nl/instfr.html

INSTITUT EURO 92
35 avenue Mac-Mahon
Paris 75017, FRANCE
011-33-1-4380-6232
fax 011-33-1-4888-9757
www.euro92.org

INSTITUT HERACLITE
73, rue de la Faisanderie
75116 Paris, FRANCE
011-33-01-45-03-04-95
fax 011-33-01-45-03-04-95
www.institutheraclite.org

INSTITUTE FOR ADVANCED STRATEGIC AND POLITICAL STUDIES
16 Bilu Street
Jerusalem 93221, ISRAEL
011-972-2-563-8171
fax 011-972-2-563-8176
www.iasps.org

INSTITUTE FOR ECONOMIC STUDIES
Universite de Paris, 35 Avenue Mac-Mahon
Paris 75017, FRANCE
011-33-1-43-808517
fax 011-33-1-48-88-9757
www.ieseurope.asso.fr

INSTITUTE FOR EUROPEAN STUDIES
Trg Nikole Pasica 11
11000 Belgrade, SERBIA
011-381-11-3298-797
www.fmc.org.yu

INSTITUTE FOR FOREIGN RELATIONS OF THE HANNS SEIDEL FOUNDATION
Lazarettstr. 33
D-80636 Munich, GERMANY
011-49-89-12-58-200
fax 011-49-89-12-58-368
www.hss.de

INSTITUTE FOR INTERNATIONAL RELATIONS
ul. Ljudevita Farkasa Vukotinovica 2, P. O. Box 303
100 00 Zagreb, CROATIA
011-385-1-48-26-522
fax 011-385-1-48-28-361
www.imo.hr

INSTITUTE FOR LIBERTY AND DEMOCRACY
Av. Del Parque Norte 829, San Isidro
Lima 27, PERU
011-51-1-225-4131
fax 011-51-1-475-9559
www.ild.org.pe

INSTITUTE FOR LIBERTY AND POLICY ANALYSIS
Apartado 329-4050
Alajuela, COSTA RICA
011-506-438-2464
fax 011-506-438-2444
www.inlap.com

INSTITUTE FOR MARKET ECONOMICS
P. O. Box 803, 82A, Dondukov Boulevard, Floor 3
Sofia 1000, BULGARIA
011-359-2-943-36-48
fax 011-359-2-943-33-52
www.ime-bg.org

INSTITUTE FOR NATIONAL POLICY RESEARCH
5F, 238, Sungjiang Road
Taipei, TAIWAN
011-886-2-2511-5009
fax 011-886-2-2560-5536
www.inpr.org.tw/inpre.htm

INSTITUTE FOR PRIVATE ENTERPRISE AND DEMOCRACY
4, Trebacka ul.
00-074 Warszawa, POLAND
011-48-22-630-9705
fax 011-48-22-826-2596

INSTITUTE FOR SMALL BUSINESS DEVELOPMENT
1364 Budapest Pf. 279
H-1024 Budapest, HUNGARY
011-36-1-355-6737
fax 011-36-1-266-2308
www.kfi.matav.hu

INSTITUTE FOR STRATEGIC STUDIES
University of Pretoria
Pretoria 0002, SOUTH AFRICA
011-27-12-420-2407
fax 011-27-12-420-2693

INSTITUTE FOR THE STUDY OF RUSSIAN ECONOMY
Bolshaia Nikitskaya st. 44-2, Room 26
121854 Moscow, RUSSIA
011-7-095-290-5108
fax 011-7-095-291-1595
http://www.libertarium.ru/eng/organiz/e-isre.html

INSTITUTE OF ASIAN STUDIES
Prajadhipok-Rambhaibarni Blgd, 7th
Floor, Chulalongkorn University
Bangkok 10330, THAILAND
011-66-2-218-7464
fax 011-66-2-255-1124
www.ias.culla.ac.th

INSTITUTE OF ECONOMIC AFFAIRS
2 Lord North Street, Westminster
London SW1P 3LB, UNITED KINGDOM
011-44-20-7799-8900
fax 011-44-20-7799-2137
www.iea.org.uk

INSTITUTE OF ECONOMIC AFFAIRS - GHANA
P. O. Box 01936
Christianborg, Accra, GHANA
011-233-21-244-716
fax 011-233-21-222-313

INSTITUTE OF ECONOMIC POLICY RESEARCH
University of Koeln, WiSo-Hochhaus, 7th
Floor, Room 762
D-50923 Koeln, GERMANY
011-49-221-935-24-47
fax 011-49-221-935-24-46

INSTITUTE OF ECONOMY IN TRANSITION
5, Gazetny pereulok, strojenije 3
5 Moscow 103918, RUSSIA
011-7-095-229-6413
fax 011-7-095-203-8816
www.iet.ru/index2.htm

INSTITUTE OF MUNICIPAL DEMOCRACY AND HUMAN RIGHTS
68, Pushkinskaya Street
Odessa 65023, UKRAINE
011-380-482-226746
fax 011-380-482-346208

INSTITUTE OF POLICY RESEARCH
48-2, Jalan Telawi, Bangsar Baru
59100 Kuala Lampur, MALAYSIA
011-603-2283-2788
fax 011-603-2283-2615

INSTITUTE OF PUBLIC ADMINISTRATION AND EUROPEAN INTEGRATION
18, Vitosha Boulevard
1000 Sofia, BULGARIA
011-3592-980-9747
fax 011-3592-980-9679
www.ipaei.government.bg

INSTITUTE OF PUBLIC AFFAIRS LIMITED
Level 2, 410 Collins Street
Melbourne, VIC 3000, AUSTRALIA
011-61-3-9600-4744
fax 011-61-3-9602-4989
www.ipa.org.au

INSTITUTE OF PUBLIC POLICY ANALYSIS
6 Majolate Street, P.O. Box 6434
Shomolu- Lagos, NIGERIA
011-234-1-823093
fax 011-234-1-288-2876
www.ippanigeria.org

INSTITUTE OF SOUTHEAST ASIAN STUDIES
30 Heng Mui Keng Terrace
Pasir Panjang 119614, SINGAPORE
011-65-6778-0955
fax 011-65-6778-1735
www.iseas.edu.sg

INSTITUTE OF STRATEGIC AND INTERNATIONAL STUDIES
No. 1 Pesiaran Sultan Salahuddin, P. O.
Box 14124
50778 Kuala Lumpur, MALAYSIA
011-603-2693-9366
fax 011-60-3-2693-9430
www.jaring.my/isis

INSTITUTE OF UNITED STATES STUDIES

Senate House, Malet Street
London WC1E 7HU, UNITED KINGDOM
011-44-207-862-8693
fax 011-44-207-862-8696
www.sas.ac.uk/iuss

INSTITUTO CULTURAL LUDWIG VON MISES, A.C.

Avenida del Olmo 2-201, Col. Álamos 2da.
Sección
Querétaro, 76160, MEXICO
011-52-442-2126375
fax 011-52-442-2126446
www.icumi.org.mx

INSTITUTO DE CIENCIA POLITICA

Transversal 6 No. 27-10: Oficina 103
Edificio Antares
Bogota, COLOMBIA
011-571-3429-419   fax 011-571-2433-361

INSTITUTO DE LIBRE EMPRESA

Calle Barajas 522
Lima 41, PERU
011-51-1-475-9752
fax 011-51-1-475-9752
www.ileperu.org

INSTITUTO ECUATORIANO DE ECONOMIA POLITICA

Higueras 106 y Costanera, Urdesa Central
Guayaquil, ECUADOR
011-593-4-2881011
fax 011-593-4-2885991
www.his.com/ieep

INSTITUTO LIBERAL

Rua Professor Alfredo Gomes 28 -
Botafogo
22251-080 Rio de Janeiro, BRAZIL
011-55-21-2539-1115
fax 011-55-21-2537-7206
www.institutoliberal.org.br

INSTITUTO LIBERAL-RS

Rua Santa Teresinha, 59, Bairro
Farroupilha
CEP 90040-180 Porte Alegre, BRAZIL
011-55-51-332-2376
fax 011-55-51-332-2376
www.il-rs.com.br

INTER REGION ECONOMIC NETWORK [IREN]

Box 135, GPO Code 00100
Nairobi, KENYA
011-254-2-2723258
fax 011-254-2-2723258
www.irenkenya.org

INTERNATIONAL CENTER FOR ENTREPRENEURIAL STUDIES

University of Bucharest, Blvd. Mihail
Kogalniceanu 64, Sala 220
Bucharest 5, ROMANIA
011-40-1-313-3340
fax 011-40-1-313-3340

INTERNATIONAL POLICY NETWORK

2 Lord North Street, P. O. Box 38525
London SW1P 3YB, UNITED KINGDOM
011-44-20-7799-8922
fax 011-44-20-7233-1070
www.policynetwork.net

ISLAMABAD POLICY RESEARCH INSTITUTE

20-A College Road, F-7/2
Islamabad, PAKISTAN
011-92-51-922-2813
fax 011-92-51-920-1204

ISRAEL CENTER FOR SOCIAL AND ECONOMIC PROGRESS

P. O. Box 84124
Mevasseret Zion 90805, ISRAEL
011-972-2-5346463
fax 011-972-2-5330122
www.icsep.org.il

KIEL INSTITUTE OF WORLD ECONOMICS

Deesternbrooker Weg 120
D-24105 Kiel, GERMANY
011-49-431-8814207
fax 011-49-431-8814500
www.uni-kiel.de/IfW/homeeng.htm

KONRAD ADENAUER FOUNDATION

Rathausallee 12
D-53757 Sankt Augustin, GERMANY
011-49-2241-24-6230
fax 011-49-2241-24-6547
www.kas.de

KOREAN CENTER FOR FREE ENTERPRISE
Do-Won Building, 292-20, Dowha-dong
Mapo-ku
Seoul 121-728, KOREA
011-82-2-6730-3030
fax 011-82-2-6730-3001
www.cfe.org

KRIEBLE INSTITUTE
44, Bolshaya Nikitskaya St., strojenije 2
121069 Moscow, RUSSIA
011-7-095-290-2309
fax 011-7-095-291-1595
www.clcp.ru

LAJOS BATTHYANY FOUNDATION
Eotvos Utca 24 I emelet 16
H-1067 Budapest, HUNGARY
011-36-1-332-5305
fax 011-36-1-269-4099
www.hungary.com/bla/

LEBANESE CENTER FOR POLICY STUDIES
Tayyar Center Sin al-Fin, Box 55215
Beirut, LEBANON
011-961-1-490-561
fax 011-961-1-490-375
www.lcps-lebanon.org

LIBERALNI INSTITUT
Spalena 51
110 00 Prague 1, CZECH REPUBLIC
011-420-2-249122199
fax 011-420-2-24930203
www.libinst.cz

LIBERTAD Y DESARROLLO
Alcantara 498, Las Condes
Santiago, CHILE
011-56-2-3774800
fax 011-56-2-2077723
www.lyd.com

LIBERTY INSTITUTE
J-259, Saket (2nd Floor)
New Delhi 110 017, INDIA
011-91-11-652-8244
fax 011-91-11-653-2345
www.libertyindia.org

LITHUANIAN FREE MARKET INSTITUTE
56 Birutes Street
LT-2004 Vilnius, LITHUANIA
011-370-5-272-25-84
fax 011-370-5-272-12-79
www.freema.org

LOCAL GOVERNMENT INSTITUTE
University of Victoria, 104-65 Songhees Road
Victoria BC V9A 6T3, CANADA
250-360-0390   fax 250-388-6147
www.hsd.uvic.ca/lgi/

LOK SATTA
401, Nirmal Towers, Dwarakapuri Colony
Punjagutta, Hyderabad 500 082, INDIA
011-91-40-3350778
fax 011-91-40-3350783
www.loksatta.org

LUDWIG VON MISES INSTITUTE EUROPE
Herendreef 20
3001 Leuven, BELGIUM
011-32-16-295-833
fax 011-32-16-584-568
www.vonmisesinstitute-europe.org

MAKING OUR ECONOMY RIGHT
NEG 2-A, Road 84, Gulshan-2
Dhaka 1212, BANGLADESH
011-880-2-8829070
fax 011-880-2-8829070
www.moer.org

MALAYSIAN INSTITUTE OF ECONOMIC RESEARCH
9th Floor Menara Dayabumi, Julan Sultan
Hishamuddin, P. O. Box 12160
50768 Kuala Lumpur, MALAYSIA
011-603-22725897
fax 011-603-22730197
www.mier.org.my

MANNKAL ECONOMIC EDUCATION FOUNDATION
19 Richardson Street, West Perth
Western Australia 6005, AUSTRALIA
011-61-8-9322-6777
fax 011-61-8-9322-6788
www.mannkal.org

MAX FALQUE CONSEIL
La Tuiliere
84330 Le Barroux, FRANCE
011-33-4-9062-4852
fax 011-33-4-9062-4896

MISES INSTITUTE-ROMANIA
Str. Valeriu Braniste, nr 56, Bloc. A, Sc.B,
Et. 3
Bucharest 74136, ROMANIA
011-40-1-326-76-62
www.misesromania.org

MONTREAL ECONOMIC INSTITUTE
6418, rue Saint-Hubert Street, 2e
Montreal, QC H2S 2M2, CANADA
514-273-0969   fax 514-273-0967
www.iedm.org

MOSCOW HELSINKI GROUP
22 Bolshoy Golovin Pereulok, Block 1
103045 Moscow, RUSSIA
011-7-095-207-6069
fax 011-7-095-207-6069

NATIONAL CITIZENS COALITION
600 6th Avenue, S.W., Suite 240
Calgary, AB T2P 0S5, CANADA
403-269-3545   fax 403-269-4696
www.citizenscoalition.org

NEW SCHOLARS SOCIETY
R.R. 2
Wallenstein, ON N0B 2S0, CANADA
519-698-2561   fax 519-698-2551

**NEW ZEALAND BUSINESS
ROUNDTABLE**
P. O. Box 10-147
Wellington, NEW ZEALAND
011-64-4-4990790
fax 011-64-4-471-1304
www.nzbr.org.nz

PARADIGMES
1 rue de la Treille
60300 Senlis, FRANCE
011-33-1-53-77-61-41
fax 011-33-1-45-63-35-48
www.paradigmes.com

POLICY EXCHANGE
Clutha House, 10 Storey's Gate
London SW1P 3AY, UNITED KINGDOM
011-44-20-7340-2655
fax 011-44-20-7222-5859
www.policyexchange.org

**PRAGUE INSTITUTE FOR NATIONAL
SECURITY**
Vysehradska 49
128 00 Prague 2, CZECH REPUBLIC
011-420-2-2272-4820
fax 011-420-2-2271-2439

PRIVATE SECTOR ORGANIZATION
3rd Floor, Suite 316, South Tower,
Sandton Square
Sandton City, SOUTH AFRICA
011-27-83-429-37231
fax 011-27-11-883-9320
www.pso.org.za

PUBLIC POLICY INSTITUTE
Visegradi u. 4 fszt. 4
H-1132 Budapest, HUNGARY
011-36-1-239-1199
fax 011-36-1-239-1951

SHALEM CENTER
22A Hatzfira Street, P. O. Box 8787
Jerusalem, ISRAEL
011-972-2-566-2202
fax 011-972-2-566-1171
www.shalem.org.il

SIFE KAZAKHSTAN
12, Lisa Chaikina Street
Almty 480020, KAZAKHSTAN

**SINGAPORE INTERNATIONAL
FOUNDATION**
9 Penang Road #12-01, Park Mall
238459, SINGAPORE
011-65-6837-8700
fax 011-65-6837-8710
www.sif.org.sg

SOCIAL MARKET FOUNDATION
11 Tufton Street
Westminster, London SW1P 3QB,
UNITED KINGDOM
011-44-207-222-7060
fax 011-44-207-222-3010
www.smf.co.uk

**SOCIETY FOR SOCIAL AND ECONOMIC
STUDIES**
P. O. Box 78
19003 Markopoulo Attikis, Mesogeia,
GREECE
011-30-2990-40208
fax 011-30-2990-40208
www.ekome.gr

SOUTH AFRICAN INSTITUTE OF RACE RELATIONS

Dumbarton House, 1 Church Street, Suite 6
Cape Town 8001, SOUTH AFRICA
011-27-82-424-5456
fax 011-27-21-424-3678
www.sairr.org.za

ST. LAWRENCE INSTITUTE

P. O. Box 307, NDG Station
Montreal, QC H4A 3P6, CANADA
514-233-8321   fax 514-489-0312
www.stlawrenceinstitute.org

THE CENTRE FOR INDEPENDENT STUDIES

P. O. Box 92
St. Leonards, NSW 1590, AUSTRALIA
011-61-2-9438-4377
fax 011-61-2-9439-7310
www.cis.org.au

THE FRASER INSTITUTE

1770 Burrard Street, 4th Floor
Vancouver, BC V6J 3G7, CANADA
604-688-0221   fax 604-688-8539
www.fraserinstitute.ca

THE HERITAGE FOUNDATION

44, block 2, Bolshaya Nikitskaya Street
GSP-5 Moscow 123995, RUSSIA
011-7-095-290-6107
fax 011-7-095-291-1595
www.heritage.org

THE HERITAGE FOUNDATION

Baskerville House, 13 Duddell Street
Suite 401
Central, SAR, HONG KONG
011-852-2522-2555
fax 011-852-2524-6644

THE INTERNATIONAL HOUSE OF JAPAN, INC.

5-11-6 Roppongi, Minato-ku
Tokyo 106-0032, JAPAN
011-813-3470-3212
fax 011-813-3470-3170
www.i-house.or.jp

THE MACKENZIE INSTITUTE

P. O. Box 338, Adelaide Station
Toronto, ON M5C 2J4, CANADA
416-686-4063
www.mackenzieinstitute.com

THE MAXIM INSTITUTE

49 Cape Horn Road
Hillsborough, Auckland, NEW ZEALAND
011-64-9-627-3261
fax 011-64-9-627-3264
www.maxim.org.nz

THE RATIO INSTITUTE

P. O. Box 5095
SE-102 42 Stockholm, SWEDEN
011-46-8-587-054-00
fax 011-46-8-587-054-05
www.ratioinstitutet.nu

THE SOCIAL AFFAIRS UNIT

Regent Street, Suite 5/6, First Floor, Morley House
London W1R 5AB, UNITED KINGDOM
011-44-207-637-4356
fax 011-44-207-436-8530
www.socialaffairsunit.org.uk

TIMBRO

Grev Turegatan 19, P. O. Box 5234
S-102 45 Stockholm, SWEDEN
011-46-587-898-10
fax 011-46-587-898-50
www.timbro.se

TRANSPARENCY INTERNATIONAL SLOVAKIA

Bajkalska 25
82718 Bratislava 212, SLOVAKIA
011-4212-5341-1020
fax 011-4212-5823-3304
www.transparency.sk

TURKISH FOREIGN POLICY INSTITUTE

Bilkent University – East Campus
06533 Ankara, TURKEY
011-90-312-266-2869
fax 011-90-312-266-2871
www.foreignpolicy.org.tr

TV AZTECA

Periferico sur 4121, Col. Fuentes del Pedregal
Mexico, D.F. 14141, MEXICO
011-52-55-3090-1313
fax 011-52-55-3099-9181
www.toditoeconomico.com.mx

U.S.-UKRAINE FOUNDATION
40-A Moscovska St.
044 Kyiv, UKRAINE
011-380-44-290-65-63
fax 011-380-44-290-6464
www.usukraine.org

UKRAINIAN CENTER FOR CULTURAL STUDIES
45, Artema str.
83086 Donetsk, UKRAINE
011-380-62-337-04-80
fax 011-380-62-337-04-80

UKRAINIAN CENTER FOR INDEPENDENT POLITICAL RESEARCH
Suite 20, 4/26 Pyrogova Street
01030 Kiev, UKRAINE
011-380-44-235-6505
fax 011-380-44-235-6505
www.ucipr.kiev.ua

VANGUARD INSTITUTE FOR POLICY STUDIES
2F, 15 Chi-Nan Road, Sec.1
Taipei 100, TAIWAN
011-886-2-2395-2045
fax 011-886-2-2395-2052

WORLD TAXPAYERS ASSOCIATIONS
Torsvikssv 28
Stockholm SE-18134, SWEDEN
011-46-70-325-00-11
fax 011-46-8-765-82-80
www.worldtaxpayers.org

Indexes

State Index of U.S. Experts and Organizations

ALABAMA

EXPERTS

Robert V. Andelson, American Institute for Economic Research, Auburn, AL. **(p. 37)**
N. Scott Arnold, University of Alabama, Birmingham, Birmingham, AL. **(p. 40)**
Saul Z. Barr, University of Tennessee, Gulf Shores, AL. **(p. 46)**
David Beito, University of Alabama, Tuscaloosa, AL. **(p. 49)**
Michael A. Ciamarra, Alabama Policy Institute, Birmingham, AL. **(p. 74)**
Paul A. Cleveland, Birmingham Southern College, Birmingham, AL. **(p. 76)**
Jim F. Couch, University of North Alabama, Florence, AL. **(p. 83)**
Michael E. DeBow, Samford University, Birmingham, AL. **(p. 91)**
Robert B. Ekelund, Auburn University, Auburn, AL. **(p. 105)**
Mark Elliott, Samford University, Birmingham, AL. **(p. 106)**
Dana R. Gache, Alabama Policy Institute, Birmingham, AL. **(p. 119)**
John R. Hill, Alabama Policy Institute, Birmingham, AL. **(p. 142)**
David N. Laband, Auburn University, Auburn, AL. **(p. 171)**
Kristin D. Landers, Alabama Policy Institute, Birmingham, AL. **(p. 173)**
Dianna Lightfoot, National Physicians Center for Family Resources, Birmingham, AL. **(p. 180)**
Forrest McDonald, University of Alabama, Coker, AL. **(p. 195)**
Michael A. Morrisey, University of Alabama, Birmingham, Birmingham, AL. **(p. 207)**
Gary J. Palmer, Alabama Policy Institute, Birmingham, AL. **(p. 221)**
Llewellyn Rockwell, Jr., Ludwig von Mises Institute, Auburn, AL. **(p. 242)**
Stephen J. Ware, Samford University, Birmingham, AL. **(p. 289)**
Leland Yeager, Auburn University, Auburn, AL. **(p. 300)**

ORGANIZATIONS

Alabama Policy Institute, Birmingham, AL. **(p. 628)**
Ludwig von Mises Institute, Auburn, AL. **(p. 695)**
National Physicians Center for Family Resources, Birmingham, AL. **(p. 701)**

ALASKA

EXPERTS

Paula Easley, Resource Development Council for Alaska, Anchorage, AK. **(p. 102)**
James W. Muller, University of Alaska, Anchorage, AK. **(p. 208)**
Mead Treadwell, Institute of the North, Anchorage, AK. **(p. 281)**

ORGANIZATIONS

Institute of the North, Anchorage, AK. **(p. 683)**

ARIZONA

EXPERTS

Barry Asmus, National Center for Policy Analysis, Scottsdale, AZ. **(p. 41)**
Robert C. Balling, Arizona State University, Tempe, AZ. **(p. 45)**
Michael K. Block, University of Arizona, Tucson, AZ. **(p. 55)**

Clint Bolick, Institute for Justice, Phoenix, AZ. **(p. 56)**
Richard L. Bolin, The Flagstaff Institute, Flagstaff, AZ. **(p. 56)**
Allen Buchanan, University of Arizona, Tucson, AZ. **(p. 64)**
Price V. Fishback, University of Arizona, Tucson, AZ. **(p. 112)**
Robert Franciosi, Goldwater Institute, Phoenix, AZ. **(p. 115)**
Mary F. Gifford, Field, Sarvas, King and Coleman, Phoenix, AZ. **(p. 123)**
A. C. Green, Jr., A. C. Green Youth Foundation, Phoenix, AZ. **(p. 128)**
Marianne Jennings, Arizona State University, Tempe, AZ. **(p. 154)**
Michael S. Joyce, Foundation for Community and Faith Centered Enterprise, Phoenix, AZ. **(p. 156)**
Shawn Kantor, University of Arizona, Tucson, AZ. **(p. 157)**
Gary Libecap, University of Arizona, Tucson, AZ. **(p. 179)**
Nelson Llumiquinga, Arizona School Choice Trust, Phoenix, AZ. **(p. 182)**
Jordan Lorence, Alliance Defense Fund, Scottsdale, AZ. **(p. 183)**
Rita P. Maguire, Arizona Center for Public Policy, Phoenix, AZ. **(p. 186)**
Jack McVaugh, Arizona School Choice Trust, Scottsdale, AZ. **(p. 198)**
James Morrison, Morrison Associates, Scottsdale, AZ. **(p. 207)**
Len Munsil, Center for Arizona Policy, Scottsdale, AZ. **(p. 209)**
Ronald L. Oaxaca, University of Arizona, Tucson, AZ. **(p. 218)**
Darcy A. Olsen, Goldwater Institute, Phoenix, AZ. **(p. 219)**
Jane M. Orient, Association of American Physicians and Surgeons, Tucson, AZ. **(p. 219)**
Jan S. Prybyla, Pennsylvania State University, Tucson, AZ. **(p. 234)**
Jonathan Rose, Arizona State University, Tempe, AZ. **(p. 243)**
Michael Sanera, Basis Charter High School, Tucson, AZ. **(p. 249)**
David Schmidtz, University of Arizona, Tucson, AZ. **(p. 253)**
Alan E. Sears, Alliance Defense Fund, Scottsdale, AZ. **(p. 255)**
John Semmens, Laissez-Faire Institute, Chandler, AZ. **(p. 256)**
E. Donald Shapiro, New York Law School, Scottsdale, AZ. **(p. 258)**
Sheldon W. Simon, Arizona State University, Tempe, AZ. **(p. 260)**
Stephen Slivinski, Goldwater Institute, Phoenix, AZ. **(p. 262)**
Christopher Smith, Internet Education Exchange (iEdx), Scottsdale, AZ. **(p. 262)**
Harvey A. Smith, Arizona State University, Tempe, AZ. **(p. 263)**
Miklos N. Szilagyi, University of Arizona, Tucson, AZ. **(p. 273)**
Lewis A. Tambs, Tempe, AZ. **(p. 273)**
Bob Walpole, The Flagstaff Institute, Flagstaff, AZ. **(p. 288)**

ORGANIZATIONS

Alliance Defense Fund, Scottsdale, AZ. **(p. 629)**
Association of American Physicians and Surgeons, Tucson, AZ. **(p. 640)**
Center for Arizona Policy, Scottsdale, AZ. **(p. 645)**
The Flagstaff Institute, Flagstaff, AZ. **(p. 666)**
Foundation for Community and Faith Centered Enterprise, Phoenix, AZ. **(p. 668)**
Goldwater Institute, Phoenix, AZ. **(p. 673)**
A. C. Green Youth Foundation, Phoenix, AZ. **(p. 674)**
Internet Education Exchange (iEdx), Phoenix, AZ. **(p. 685)**

ARKANSAS

EXPERTS

Jerry Cox, Arkansas Family Council, Little Rock, AR. **(p. 84)**
D. P. Diffine, Harding University, Searcy, AR. **(p. 95)**
David E. R. Gay, University of Arkansas, Fayetteville, AR. **(p. 121)**

Lawrence Gunnells, CSF Arkansas, Little Rock, AR. (p. 130)
Joseph Horton, University of Central Arkansas, Conway, AR. (p. 146)
Greg Kaza, Arkansas Policy Foundation, Little Rock, AR. (p. 159)
John Kirtley, Children First America, Bentonville, AR. (p. 165)
Oscar Stilley, Arkansans for School Choice, Fort Smith, AR. (p. 269)

ORGANIZATIONS

Arkansas Family Council, Little Rock, AR. (p. 639)
Arkansas Policy Foundation, Little Rock, AR. (p. 640)
Children First America, Bentonville, AR. (p. 652)

CALIFORNIA

EXPERTS

James C. W. Ahiakpor, California State University, Hayward, Hayward, CA. (p. 35)
Lawrence Alexander, University of San Diego School of Law, San Diego, CA. (p. 36)
Bruce N. Ames, University of California, Berkeley, Berkeley, CA. (p. 37)
Annelise Anderson, Hoover Institution, Stanford, CA. (p. 38)
Eloise Anderson, Claremont Institute, Sacramento, CA. (p. 38)
Martin Anderson, Hoover Institution, Stanford, CA. (p. 38)
Michael Antonucci, Education Intelligence Agency, Elk Grove, CA. (p. 39)
Sonia Arrison, Pacific Research Institute, San Francisco, CA. (p. 41)
Stephen M. Bainbridge, University of California at Los Angeles, Los Angeles, CA. (p. 43)
Charles W. Baird, California State University, Hayward, Hayward, CA. (p. 43)
Dennis L. Bark, Hoover Institution, Stanford, CA. (p. 45)
Gary Beckner, Association of American Educators, Laguna Hills, CA. (p. 48)
Gary D. Becks, Rescue Task Force, El Cajon, CA. (p. 48)
Arnold Beichman, Hoover Institution, Stanford, CA. (p. 49)
Charles H. Bell, Jr., Bell, McAndrews, Hiltachk & Davidian, Sacramento, CA. (p. 49)
Tom W. Bell, Chapman University, Orange, CA. (p. 50)
Joseph Bessette, Claremont McKenna College, Claremont, CA. (p. 52)
Robert K. Best, Pacific Legal Foundation, Sacramento, CA. (p. 52)
Mark Blitz, Claremont McKenna College, Claremont, CA. (p. 55)
Patrick M. Boarman, National University San Diego, San Diego, CA. (p. 55)
Donald R. Booth, Chapman University, Orange, CA. (p. 57)
Thomas E. Borcherding, Claremont Graduate University, Claremont, CA. (p. 57)
Michael J. Boskin, Hoover Institution, Stanford, CA. (p. 57)
Daniel B. Botkin, Center for the Study of the Environment, Santa Barbara, CA. (p. 58)
Floyd G. Brown, Young America's Foundation Reagan Ranch Project, Santa Barbara, CA. (p. 63)
Sharon Browne, Pacific Legal Foundation, Sacramento, CA. (p. 63)
Andrzej Brzeski, University of California, Davis, CA. (p. 64)
James Burling, Pacific Legal Foundation, Sacramento, CA. (p. 65)
Henry N. Butler, Chapman University, Orange, CA. (p. 66)
Anthony T. Caso, Pacific Legal Foundation, Sacramento, CA. (p. 72)
Lawrence A. Chickering, Educate Girls Globally, San Francisco, CA. (p. 73)
Gregory B. Christainsen, California State University, Hayward, Hayward, CA. (p. 74)
John F. Cogan, Hoover Institution, Stanford, CA. (p. 77)
Peter Collier, Center for the Study of Popular Culture, Los Angeles, CA. (p. 78)
Ward Connerly, American Civil Rights Institute, Sacramento, CA. (p. 80)
Robert Conquest, Hoover Institution, Stanford, CA. (p. 80)
John E. Coons, University of California at Berkeley, Berkeley, CA. (p. 81)

Harry V. Jaffa, Claremont Institute, Claremont, CA. **(p. 153)**
Chalmers Johnson, Japan Policy Research Institute, Cardiff, CA. **(p. 155)**
Robin Johnson, Reason Public Policy Institute, Los Angeles, CA. **(p. 155)**
Shyam J. Kamath, California State University, Hayward, Hayward, CA. **(p. 157)**
Paul Kapur, Claremont McKenna College, Claremont, CA. **(p. 158)**
Jacqueline Kasun, Humboldt State University, Arcata, CA. **(p. 158)**
Brian T. Kennedy, Claremont Institute, Claremont, CA. **(p. 161)**
Charles R. Kesler, Henry Salvatori Center, Claremont, CA. **(p. 162)**
Lynne Kiesling, Reason Public Policy Institute, Los Angeles, CA. **(p. 163)**
Fred Kiesner, Loyola Marymount University, Los Angeles, CA. **(p. 163)**
Manuel Klausner, Individual Rights Foundation, Los Angeles, CA. **(p. 165)**
Daniel Klein, Santa Clara University, Santa Clara, CA. **(p. 165)**
Joel Kotkin, Pepperdine University, Malibu, CA. **(p. 168)**
Thomas L. Krannawitter, Claremont Institute, Claremont, CA. **(p. 168)**
Gary Kreep, United States Justice Foundation, Escondido, CA. **(p. 169)**
Robert Krol, California State University, Northridge, Northridge, CA. **(p. 169)**
John Kurzweil, California Public Policy Foundation, Camarillo, CA. **(p. 171)**
Deborah J. LaFetra, Pacific Legal Foundation, Sacramento, CA. **(p. 171)**
Arthur B. Laffer, A. B. Laffer Associates, San Diego, CA. **(p. 172)**
Deepak Lal, University of California at Los Angeles, Los Angeles, CA. **(p. 172)**
Lawrence J. Lau, Stanford University, Stanford, CA. **(p. 175)**
Kurt R. Leube, Hoover Institution, Stanford, CA. **(p. 178)**
Carlos Lopez, Menlo College, Atherton, CA. **(p. 183)**
Frederick R. Lynch, Claremont McKenna College, Claremont, CA. **(p. 184)**
Tibor R. Machan, Chapman University, Silverado Canyon, CA. **(p. 185)**
Lisa MacLellan, Pacific Research Institute, San Francisco, CA. **(p. 185)**
Lara Mahaney, Parents Television Council, Los Angeles, CA. **(p. 186)**
John M. Malek, Polish-American Foundation for Economic Research and Education, Torrance, CA. **(p. 187)**
Michael Marlow, California Polytechnic State University, San Luis Obispo, CA. **(p. 189)**
Ken Masugi, Claremont Institute, Claremont, CA. **(p. 191)**
Wendell H. McCulloch, Jr., California State University, Long Beach, Long Beach, CA. **(p. 194)**
Richard B. McKenzie, University of California, Irvine, Irvine, CA. **(p. 196)**
Lawrence J. McQuillan, Pacific Research Institute, San Francisco, CA. **(p. 197)**
Walter J. Mead, University of California, Santa Barbara, Santa Barbara, CA. **(p. 198)**
Robert J. Michaels, California State University, Fullerton, Fullerton, CA. **(p. 201)**
Christopher Middleton, Pacific Research Institute, San Francisco, CA. **(p. 201)**
Abraham H. Miller, Walnut Creek, CA. **(p. 201)**
Henry I. Miller, Hoover Institution, Stanford, CA. **(p. 202)**
Terry M. Moe, Hoover Institution, Stanford, CA. **(p. 204)**
Stephen Monsma, Pepperdine University, Malibu, CA. **(p. 205)**
Adrian T. Moore, Reason Foundation, Los Angeles, CA. **(p. 205)**
James Elliott Moore, II, University of Southern California, Los Angeles, CA. **(p. 205)**
Thomas Gale Moore, Hoover Institution, Stanford, CA. **(p. 206)**
Jennifer Roback Morse, Hoover Institution, Vista, CA. **(p. 207)**
Ramon H. Myers, Hoover Institution, Stanford, CA. **(p. 210)**
Ronald Nehring, Americans for Tax Reform, San Diego, CA. **(p. 212)**
David C. Nott, Reason Foundation, Los Angeles, CA. **(p. 215)**
James H. Noyes, Hoover Institution, Stanford, CA. **(p. 215)**
M. Lester O'Shea, Walnut Creek, CA. **(p. 217)**
Edward A. Olsen, Naval Postgraduate School, Monterey, CA. **(p. 219)**
Daniel Palm, Azusa Pacific University, Azusa, CA. **(p. 220)**

Patrick J. Parker, Hollister, CA. **(p. 222)**
William Perry, William Perry & Associates, Agua Dulce, CA. **(p. 226)**
Sally C. Pipes, Pacific Research Institute, San Francisco, CA. **(p. 229)**
John J. Pitney, Jr., Claremont McKenna College, Claremont, CA. **(p. 229)**
Robert W. Poole, Jr., Reason Foundation, Los Angeles, CA. **(p. 230)**
William C. Potter, Monterey Institute of International Studies, Monterey, CA. **(p. 231)**
Dennis Prager, The Prager Perspective, Van Nuys, CA. **(p. 232)**
Eric Premack, California State University Institute for Education Reform, Sacramento, CA. **(p. 232)**
Mark S. Pulliam, Latham & Watkins, San Diego, CA. **(p. 234)**
Alvin Rabushka, Hoover Institution, Stanford, CA. **(p. 235)**
R. S. Radford, Pacific Legal Foundation, Sacramento, CA. **(p. 235)**
John Raisian, Hoover Institution, Stanford, CA. **(p. 236)**
R. Sean Randolph, Bay Area Economic Forum, San Francisco, CA. **(p. 236)**
William Ratliff, Hoover Institution, Stanford, CA. **(p. 236)**
George Reisman, Pepperdine University, Laguna Hills, CA. **(p. 238)**
Rita Ricardo-Campbell, Hoover Institution, Stanford, CA. **(p. 239)**
Robin Rivett, Pacific Legal Foundation, Sacramento, CA. **(p. 241)**
Azade-Ayse Rorlich, University of Southern California, Los Angeles, CA. **(p. 243)**
Ralph A. Rossum, Claremont McKenna College, Claremont, CA. **(p. 244)**
William A. Rusher, Claremont Institute, San Francisco, CA. **(p. 247)**
Michael D. Rushford, Criminal Justice Legal Foundation, Sacramento, CA. **(p. 247)**
Robert A. Scalapino, University of California, Berkeley, Berkeley, CA. **(p. 251)**
Kent Scheidegger, Criminal Justice Legal Foundation, Sacramento, CA. **(p. 252)**
John W. Schlicher, Gray, Cary, Ware & Freidenrich, Palo Alto, CA. **(p. 253)**
Robert Haney Scott, California State University, Chico, Chico, CA. **(p. 255)**
Gerald W. Scully, San Juan Capistrano, CA. **(p. 255)**
Geoffrey F. Segal, Reason Public Policy Institute, Los Angeles, CA. **(p. 256)**
Ralph Segalman, California State University, Northridge, Northridge, CA. **(p. 256)**
Tracie Sharp, State Policy Network, Richmond, CA. **(p. 258)**
Steven M. Sheffrin, University of California, Davis, Davis, CA. **(p. 258)**
Bernard Siegan, University of San Diego School of Law, San Diego, CA. **(p. 259)**
Peter Skerry, Claremont McKenna College, Claremont, CA. **(p. 261)**
Lisa Snell, Reason Foundation, Los Angeles, CA. **(p. 265)**
Patricia M. Soldano, Policy and Taxation Group, Santa Ana, CA. **(p. 265)**
Thomas Sowell, Hoover Institution, Stanford, CA. **(p. 266)**
Nancy Z. Spillman, Economic Education Enterprises, Canoga Park, CA. **(p. 267)**
Richard F. Staar, Hoover Institution, Stanford, CA. **(p. 267)**
Charles Stuart, University of California, Santa Barbara, Santa Barbara, CA. **(p. 271)**
William Craig Stubblebine, Claremont McKenna College, Claremont, CA. **(p. 271)**
James L. Sweeney, Stanford University, Stanford, CA. **(p. 272)**
Edward Teller, Hoover Institution, Stanford, CA. **(p. 275)**
Tammy Tengs, University of California, Irvine, Irvine, CA. **(p. 275)**
David J. Theroux, The Independent Institute, Oakland, CA. **(p. 276)**
Mary L. G. Theroux, The Independent Institute, Oakland, CA. **(p. 276)**
Randy Thomasson, Campaign for California Families, Sacramento, CA. **(p. 277)**
Jay L. Tontz, California State University, Hayward, Hayward, CA. **(p. 280)**
Brian S. Tracy, Brian Tracy International, Solana Beach, CA. **(p. 280)**
Forrest L. Turpen, Christian Educators Association International, Pasadena, CA. **(p. 282)**
Lewis Uhler, National Tax Limitation Committee, Roseville, CA. **(p. 283)**
Michael M. Uhlmann, Claremont Graduate University, Claremont, CA. **(p. 283)**
Eugene Volokh, University of California at Los Angeles, Los Angeles, CA. **(p. 285)**
Gary M. Walton, Foundation for Teaching Economics, Davis, CA. **(p. 288)**

William K. S. Wang, Hastings College of Law, San Francisco, CA. (p. 288)
Michael Y. Warder, Los Angeles Children's Scholarship Fund, Long Beach, CA. (p. 289)
Alan Rufus Waters, California State University, Fresno, Fresno, CA. (p. 289)
David L. Weeks, Azusa Pacific University, Azusa, CA. (p. 291)
Natalie Williams, Robinson, DiLando and Whitaker, Sacramento, CA. (p. 295)
Russell Williams, Jefferson Center for Character Education, Mission Viejo, CA. (p. 295)
James Q. Wilson, Pepperdine University, Malibu, CA. (p. 296)
Charles Wolf, Jr., RAND, Santa Monica, CA. (p. 297)
Thomas Wood, Americans Against Discrimination and Preferences, Berkley, CA. (p. 298)
John Yoo, University of California, Berkeley, Berkeley, CA. (p. 300)
Ronald A. Zumbrun, The Zumbrun Law Firm, Sacramento, CA. (p. 303)

ORGANIZATIONS

Alliance for the Separation of School & State, Fresno, CA. (p. 630)
American Civil Rights Coalition, Sacramento, CA. (p. 632)
American Civil Rights Institute, Sacramento, CA. (p. 632)
Association of American Educators, Laguna Hills, CA. (p. 640)
California Public Policy Foundation, Camarillo, CA. (p. 644)
Capitol Resource Institute, Sacramento, CA. (p. 644)
Center for the Study of Popular Culture, Los Angeles, CA. (p. 651)
The Center for the Study of Taxation, Costa Mesa, CA. (p. 651)
Center for the Study of the Environment, Santa Barbara, CA. (p. 651)
Christian Educators Association International, Pasadena, CA. (p. 653)
Citizens for Law and Order, Sonoma, CA. (p. 655)
Claremont Institute, Claremont, CA. (p. 655)
Criminal Justice Legal Foundation, Sacramento, CA. (p. 659)
Educate Girls Globally, San Francisco, CA. (p. 660)
Foundation for Teaching Economics, Davis, CA. (p. 669)
Foundation Francisco Marroquin, Santa Monica, CA. (p. 669)
Golden State Center for Public Policy Studies, Sacramento, CA. (p. 673)
Hoover Institution, Stanford, CA. (p. 677)
The Independent Institute, Oakland, CA. (p. 678)
Individual Rights Foundation, Los Angeles, CA. (p. 679)
Institute for Contemporary Studies, Oakland, CA. (p. 680)
National Tax Limitation Committee, Roseville, CA. (p. 703)
National Tax Limitation Foundation, Roseville, CA. (p. 703)
Pacific Justice Institute, Citrus Heights, CA. (p. 709)
Pacific Legal Foundation, Sacramento, CA. (p. 710)
Pacific Research Institute for Public Policy, San Francisco, CA. (p. 710)
Parents Television Council, Los Angeles, CA. (p. 710)
Policy and Taxation Group, Santa Ana, CA. (p. 712)
Polish-American Foundation for Economic Research and Education, Torrance, CA. (p. 712)
Reason Foundation, Los Angeles, CA. (p. 715)
Rose Institute for State and Local Government, Claremont, CA. (p. 716)
Smith Center for Private Enterprise Studies, Hayward, CA. (p. 718)
State Policy Network, Richmond, CA. (p. 720)
United States Justice Foundation, Escondido, CA. (p. 725)
Web Wise Kids, Inc., Santa Ana, CA. (p. 728)

Lewis Andrews, Yankee Institute for Public Policy Studies, Hartford, CT. **(p. 39)**
Dominick T. Armentano, University of Hartford, West Hartford, CT. **(p. 40)**
Brian Brown, Family Institute of Connecticut, Hartford, CT. **(p. 63)**
Laurence Cohen, Yankee Institute for Public Policy Studies, Glastonbury, CT. **(p. 78)**
Ward S. Curran, Trinity College, Hartford, CT. **(p. 87)**
Giulio Gallarotti, Wesleyan University, Middletown, CT. **(p. 120)**
Gerald A. Gunderson, Trinity College, Hartford, CT. **(p. 130)**
John H. Langbein, Yale Law School, New Haven, CT. **(p. 173)**
Richard Langlois, University of Connecticut, Storrs, CT. **(p. 174)**
Margaret A. Little, Law Office of Margaret Little, Stratford, CT. **(p. 181)**
Charles H. Logan, University of Connecticut, Storrs, CT. **(p. 182)**
Michael Lynch, *Reason* Magazine, New Haven, CT. **(p. 184)**
Paul W. MacAvoy, Yale School of Management, New Haven, CT. **(p. 185)**
Richard Olivastro, People Dynamics, Farmington, CT. **(p. 218)**
Judyth Pendell, Bloomfield, CT. **(p. 225)**
George Priest, Yale Law School, New Haven, CT. **(p. 233)**
Robert J. Rafalko, University of New Haven, West Haven, CT. **(p. 235)**
Peter Rutland, Wesleyan University, Middletown, CT. **(p. 248)**
Charles P. Stetson, U. S. Fund for Leadership Training, Southport, CT. **(p. 268)**
Ken Von Kohorn, Family Institute of Connecticut, Hartford, CT. **(p. 285)**

ORGANIZATIONS

Family Institute of Connecticut, Hartford, CT. **(p. 665)**
Yankee Institute for Public Policy Studies, Hartford, CT. **(p. 729)**

DELAWARE

EXPERTS

Bryan Auchterlonie, Intercollegiate Studies Institute, Wilmington, DE. **(p. 41)**
T. Kenneth Cribb, Jr., Intercollegiate Studies Institute, Wilmington, DE. **(p. 86)**
Pete du Pont, National Center for Policy Analysis, Wilmington, DE. **(p. 98)**
Charles M. Elson, University of Delaware, Newark, DE. **(p. 106)**
Linda S. Gottfredson, University of Delaware, Newark, DE. **(p. 127)**
Suzanne C. Moore, Delaware Public Policy Institute, Wilmington, DE. **(p. 206)**
Jeff Nelson, Intercollegiate Studies Institute, Wilmington, DE. **(p. 212)**
Phyllis H. Witcher, Protecting Marriage, Inc., Wilmington, DE. **(p. 296)**

ORGANIZATIONS

Intercollegiate Studies Institute, Wilmington, DE. **(p. 684)**

DISTRICT OF COLUMBIA

EXPERTS

Carol Adelman, Hudson Institute, Washington, DC. **(p. 34)**
Ken L. Adelman, TechCentralStation, Washington, DC. **(p. 35)**
William F. Adkinson, Progress & Freedom Foundation, Washington, DC. **(p. 35)**
Jeanne Allen, Center for Education Reform, Washington, DC. **(p. 36)**
Richard V. Allen, Washington, DC. **(p. 36)**
David W. Almasi, National Center for Public Policy Research, Washington, DC. **(p. 37)**
Damon Ansell, Americans for Tax Reform, Washington, DC. **(p. 39)**

F. Patricia Callahan, American Association of Small Property Owners, Washington, DC. (p. 68)

Charles Calomiris, American Enterprise Institute, Washington, DC. (p. 68)

Kurt Campbell, Center for Strategic and International Studies, Washington, DC. (p. 68)

John K. Carlisle, Capital Research Center, Washington, DC. (p. 70)

Michael Carozza, Bristol-Myers Squibb, Washington, DC. (p. 70)

Ted Galen Carpenter, Cato Institute, Washington, DC. (p. 71)

Samuel Casey Carter, Acade Metrics, LLC, Washington, DC. (p. 71)

Michael A. Carvin, Jones, Day, Reavis & Pogue, Washington, DC. (p. 71)

Ralph L. Casale, Center for Individual Rights, Washington, DC. (p. 71)

Lynne V. Cheney, American Enterprise Institute, Washington, DC. (p. 73)

Michele A. Clark, Johns Hopkins University School of Advanced International Studies, Washington, DC. (p. 75)

Jody Manley Clarke, Competitive Enterprise Institute, Washington, DC. (p. 75)

Jonathan Clarke, Cato Institute, Washington, DC. (p. 75)

Ariel Cohen, The Heritage Foundation, Washington, DC. (p. 77)

Eliot A. Cohen, The Paul H. Nitze School of Advanced International Studies, Washington, DC. (p. 78)

Eric Cohen, Ethics and Public Policy Center, Washington, DC. (p. 78)

Charles Colson, Prison Fellowship Ministries, Washington, DC. (p. 79)

Roberta Combs, Christian Coalition of America, Washington, DC. (p. 79)

Gregory Conko, Competitive Enterprise Institute, Washington, DC. (p. 79)

Kenneth L. Connor, Family Research Council, Washington, DC. (p. 80)

Kellyanne Conway, the polling company/WomanTrend, Washington, DC. (p. 80)

Charli Coon, The Heritage Foundation, Washington, DC. (p. 81)

Charles J. Cooper, Cooper & Kirk, PLLC, Washington, DC. (p. 81)

Robert Costello, Social Security Choice.org, Washington, DC. (p. 83)

Douglas Cox, Gibson, Dunn & Crutcher LLP, Washington, DC. (p. 84)

Dennis Coyle, Catholic University of America, Washington, DC. (p. 84)

Christine G. Crafton, Motorola, Inc., Washington, DC. (p. 84)

Robert Crandall, Brookings Institution, Washington, DC. (p. 85)

Edward H. Crane, Cato Institute, Washington, DC. (p. 85)

Clyde Wayne Crews, Jr., Cato Institute, Washington, DC. (p. 86)

Alan R. Crippen, II, Family Research Council, Washington, DC. (p. 86)

Michael Cromartie, Ethics and Public Policy Center, Washington, DC. (p. 86)

Janice Shaw Crouse, Concerned Women for America, Washington, DC. (p. 87)

Charles H. Cunningham, National Rifle Association, Washington, DC. (p. 87)

Robert J. Cynkar, Cooper & Kirk, PLLC, Washington, DC. (p. 87)

Timothy J. Dailey, Family Research Council, Washington, DC. (p. 88)

Helle C. Dale, The Heritage Foundation, Washington, DC. (p. 88)

Kathleen B. de Bettencourt, Environmental Literacy Council, Washington, DC. (p. 89)

Arnaud de Borchgrave, Center for Strategic and International Studies, Washington, DC. (p. 89)

Kenneth E. de Graffenreid, Institute of World Politics, Washington, DC. (p. 89)

Damjan de Krnjevic-Miskovic, The National Interest, Washington, DC. (p. 90)

Robert G. de Posada, The Latino Coalition, Washington, DC. (p. 90)

Veronique de Rugy, Cato Institute, Washington, DC. (p. 90)

Pia de Solenni, Family Research Council, Washington, DC. (p. 90)

Brian Dean, International Republican Institute, Washington, DC. (p. 90)

Lisa Dean, Free Congress Foundation, Washington, DC. (p. 91)

Buffy DeBreaux-Watts, American Board for Certification of Teacher Excellence, Washington, DC. (p. 91)

James DeLong, Progress & Freedom Foundation, Washington, DC. (p. 92)

Sara Fitzgerald, The Heritage Foundation, Washington, DC. **(p. 113)**
Michael Flynn, American Legislative Exchange Council, Washington, DC. **(p. 113)**
George Folsom, International Republican Institute, Washington, DC. **(p. 114)**
John Fonte, Hudson Institute, Washington, DC. **(p. 114)**
Hillel Fradkin, Ethics and Public Policy Center, Washington, DC. **(p. 115)**
Michael Franc, The Heritage Foundation, Washington, DC. **(p. 115)**
Barbara Hackman Franklin, Barbara Franklin Enterprises, Washington, DC. **(p. 116)**
Wanda Franz, National Right to Life Committee, Washington, DC. **(p. 116)**
Robert Freedman, Institute for Justice, Washington, DC. **(p. 116)**
James Frogue, American Legislative Exchange Council, Washington, DC. **(p. 118)**
John Frydenlund, Citizens Against Government Waste, Washington, DC. **(p. 118)**
Francis Fukuyama, The Paul H. Nitze School of Advanced International Studies,
    Washington, DC. **(p. 118)**
Michael Fumento, Hudson Institute, Washington, DC. **(p. 118)**
Harold Furchtgott-Roth, American Enterprise Institute, Washington, DC. **(p. 119)**
Frank J. Gaffney, Jr., Center for Security Policy, Washington, DC. **(p. 119)**
Nile Gardiner, The Heritage Foundation, Washington, DC. **(p. 120)**
Jennifer Garrett, The Heritage Foundation, Washington, DC. **(p. 120)**
Jonathan Garthwaite, The Heritage Foundation, Washington, DC. **(p. 120)**
James Gattuso, The Heritage Foundation, Washington, DC. **(p. 121)**
Carrie J. Gavora, Strategic Health Solutions, Washington, DC. **(p. 121)**
Jeffrey B. Gayner, Americans for Sovereignty, Washington, DC. **(p. 121)**
Todd Gaziano, The Heritage Foundation, Washington, DC. **(p. 121)**
William Geimer, Jamestown Foundation, Washington, DC. **(p. 122)**
Ernest Gellhorn, George Mason University School of Law, Washington, DC. **(p. 122)**
Paul Georgia, Competitive Enterprise Institute, Washington, DC. **(p. 122)**
Reuel Marc Gerecht, American Enterprise Institute, Washington, DC. **(p. 123)**
Raymond L. Gifford, Progress & Freedom Foundation, Washington, DC. **(p. 123)**
James S. Gilmore, The Heritage Foundation, Washington, DC. **(p. 123)**
James K. Glassman, American Enterprise Institute, Washington, DC. **(p. 124)**
Paul Glastris, Western Policy Center, Washington, DC. **(p. 124)**
Roy Godson, National Strategy Information Center, Washington, DC. **(p. 125)**
Thomas Golab, Competitive Enterprise Institute, Washington, DC. **(p. 125)**
Robert A. Goldwin, American Enterprise Institute, Washington, DC. **(p. 126)**
Robert E. Gordon, Jr., National Wilderness Institute, Washington, DC. **(p. 127)**
Scott Gottlieb, American Enterprise Institute, Washington, DC. **(p. 127)**
Alfredo Goyburu, The Heritage Foundation, Washington, DC. **(p. 127)**
Michael S. Greve, American Enterprise Institute, Washington, DC. **(p. 129)**
Daniel T. Griswold, Cato Institute, Washington, DC. **(p. 129)**
Marie Gryphon, Cato Institute, Washington, DC. **(p. 130)**
Erick Gustafson, Citizens for a Sound Economy, Washington, DC. **(p. 131)**
Nikolas Gvosdev, *The National Interest*, Washington, DC. **(p. 131)**
Charlene Haar, Education Policy Institute, Washington, DC. **(p. 131)**
Rebecca Hagelin, The Heritage Foundation, Washington, DC. **(p. 131)**
Robert Hahn, American Enterprise Institute, Washington, DC. **(p. 132)**
Edmund F. Haislmaier, Strategic Policy Management, Washington, DC. **(p. 132)**
Jerome J. Hanus, American University, Washington, DC. **(p. 134)**
Mike Hardiman, Hardiman Consulting, Washington, DC. **(p. 135)**
Karen R. Harned, National Federation of Independent Business Legal Foundation,
    Washington, DC. **(p. 135)**
Robert C. Harrison, Defenders of Property Rights, Washington, DC. **(p. 136)**
Larry Hart, Hartco Strategies, Washington, DC. **(p. 136)**
Kevin A. Hassett, American Enterprise Institute, Washington, DC. **(p. 137)**

Karen Kerrigan, the polling company, Washington, DC. **(p. 162)**
Dimitri Kesari, Family Research Council, Washington, DC. **(p. 162)**
William A. Keyes, The Institute on Political Journalism, Washington, DC. **(p. 162)**
George A. Keyworth, Progress & Freedom Foundation, Washington, DC. **(p. 163)**
Matthew Kibbe, Citizens for a Sound Economy, Washington, DC. **(p. 163)**
Owen Kirby, International Republican Institute, Washington, DC. **(p. 164)**
Jeane J. Kirkpatrick, American Enterprise Institute, Washington, DC. **(p. 164)**
Larry Klayman, Judicial Watch, Washington, DC. **(p. 165)**
Ann C. Klucsarits, The Heritage Foundation, Washington, DC. **(p. 165)**
Douglas W. Kmiec, The Catholic University of America, Washington, DC. **(p. 166)**
Robert H. Knight, Concerned Women for America, Washington, DC. **(p. 166)**
Diane Knippers, Institute on Religion and Democracy, Washington, DC. **(p. 166)**
Richard D. Komer, Institute for Justice, Washington, DC. **(p. 167)**
Patrick Korten, The Becket Fund for Religious Liberty, Washington, DC. **(p. 167)**
Montgomery N. Kosma, Jones, Day, Reavis & Pogue, Washington, DC. **(p. 167)**
Marvin H. Kosters, American Enterprise Institute, Washington, DC. **(p. 168)**
John E. Kramer, Institute for Justice, Washington, DC. **(p. 168)**
Mark Krikorian, Center for Immigration Studies, Washington, DC. **(p. 169)**
Jeffrey Krilla, International Republican Institute, Washington, DC. **(p. 169)**
Irving Kristol, The Public Interest, Washington, DC. **(p. 169)**
William Kristol, *The Weekly Standard*, Washington, DC. **(p. 169)**
George Krumbhaar, USBUDGET.COM, Washington, DC. **(p. 170)**
Peter J. LaBarbera, Concerned Women for America, Washington, DC. **(p. 171)**
Andrea S. Lafferty, Traditional Values Coalition, Washington, DC. **(p. 172)**
Beverly LaHaye, Concerned Women for America, Washington, DC. **(p. 172)**
Glenn G. Lammi, Washington Legal Foundation, Washington, DC. **(p. 173)**
David M. Lampton, The Nixon Center, Washington, DC. **(p. 173)**
Andrew Langer, National Federation of Independent Business, Washington, DC. **(p. 174)**
Casey Lartigue, Jr., Cato Institute, Washington, DC. **(p. 175)**
Janet LaRue, Concerned Women for America, Washington, DC. **(p. 175)**
Michael A. Ledeen, American Enterprise Institute, Washington, DC. **(p. 176)**
Patricia H. Lee, Institute for Justice, Washington, DC. **(p. 176)**
Andrew T. LeFevre, American Legislative Exchange Council, Washington, DC. **(p. 177)**
Eli Lehrer, *The American Enterprise*, Washington, DC. **(p. 177)**
Seth Leibsohn, Empower America, Washington, DC. **(p. 177)**
Tom Lenard, Progress & Freedom Foundation, Washington, DC. **(p. 177)**
John Lenczowski, Institute of World Politics, Washington, DC. **(p. 177)**
Leonard A. Leo, The Federalist Society for Law and Public Policy Studies, Washington, DC. **(p. 178)**
Richard Lessner, American Renewal, Washington, DC. **(p. 178)**
Curt A. Levey, Center for Individual Rights, Washington, DC. **(p. 178)**
Robert A. Levy, Cato Institute, Washington, DC. **(p. 179)**
James Andrew Lewis, Center for Strategic and International Studies, Washington, DC. **(p. 179)**
Marlo Lewis, Competitive Enterprise Institute, Washington, DC. **(p. 179)**
Eric Licht, Coalitions for America, Washington, DC. **(p. 179)**
Linda Lichter, Center for Media and Public Affairs, Washington, DC. **(p. 179)**
S. Robert Lichter, Center for Media and Public Affairs, Washington, DC. **(p. 179)**
Ben Lieberman, Competitive Enterprise Institute, Washington, DC. **(p. 179)**
Myron Lieberman, Education Policy Institute, Washington, DC. **(p. 180)**
James R. Lilley, American Enterprise Institute, Washington, DC. **(p. 180)**
William S. Lind, Free Congress Foundation, Washington, DC. **(p. 180)**
Brink Lindsey, Cato Institute, Washington, DC. **(p. 181)**

Christopher Morris, Capital Research Center, Washington, DC. (**p. 207**)
David B. Muhlhausen, The Heritage Foundation, Washington, DC. (**p. 208**)
Mauro E. Mujica, U. S. English, Inc., Washington, DC. (**p. 208**)
Ross H. Munro, Center for Security Studies, Washington, DC. (**p. 209**)
Joshua Muravchik, American Enterprise Institute, Washington, DC. (**p. 209**)
Charles Murray, American Enterprise Institute, Washington, DC. (**p. 209**)
Iain Murray, Statistical Assessment Service, Washington, DC. (**p. 209**)
William J. Murray, Religious Freedom Coalition, Washington, DC. (**p. 209**)
Phyllis Berry Myers, Centre for New Black Leadership, Washington, DC. (**p. 210**)
Henry R. Nau, George Washington University, Washington, DC. (**p. 211**)
Anne D. Neal, American Council of Trustees and Alumni, Washington, DC. (**p. 211**)
Julie N. Neff, Concerned Women for America, Washington, DC. (**p. 211**)
Clark Neily, Institute for Justice, Washington, DC. (**p. 212**)
Tom Neumann, Jewish Institute for National Security Affairs, Washington, DC. (**p. 213**)
Edward Neuschler, Institute for Health Policy Solutions, Washington, DC. (**p. 213**)
William A. Niskanen, Cato Institute, Washington, DC. (**p. 214**)
Stephen Nix, International Republican Institute, Washington, DC. (**p. 214**)
Grover Norquist, Americans for Tax Reform, Washington, DC. (**p. 214**)
Stephen R. Norton, Western Policy Center, Washington, DC. (**p. 215**)
Michael J. Novak, Jr., American Enterprise Institute, Washington, DC. (**p. 215**)
John Nowacki, Free Congress Foundation, Washington, DC. (**p. 215**)
Lauren Noyes, The Heritage Foundation, Washington, DC. (**p. 216**)
Kate O'Beirne, *National Review*, Washington, DC. (**p. 216**)
Scott O'Connell, The Heritage Foundation, Washington, DC. (**p. 216**)
William O'Keefe, George C. Marshall Institute, Washington, DC. (**p. 216**)
James P. O'Leary, Catholic University of America, Washington, DC. (**p. 217**)
William E. Odom, Hudson Institute, Washington, DC. (**p. 218**)
Fred O. Oladeinde, The Foundation for Democracy in Africa, Washington, DC. (**p. 218**)
Martha Brill Olcott, Carnegie Endowment for International Peace, Washington, DC.
 (**p. 218**)
Daniel Oliver, Pacific Research Institute, Washington, DC. (**p. 219**)
Norman J. Ornstein, American Enterprise Institute, Washington, DC. (**p. 219**)
Ivan G. Osorio, Capital Research Center, Washington, DC. (**p. 220**)
Nina Owcharenko, The Heritage Foundation, Washington, DC. (**p. 220**)
Sean Paige, Competitive Enterprise Institute, Washington, DC. (**p. 220**)
Tom G. Palmer, Cato Institute, Washington, DC. (**p. 221**)
Duane Parde, American Legislative Exchange Council, Washington, DC. (**p. 221**)
J. A. Parker, Lincoln Institute for Research and Education, Washington, DC. (**p. 221**)
Kyle Parker, American Foreign Policy Council, Washington, DC. (**p. 222**)
Star Parker, Coalition on Urban Renewal and Education, Washington, DC. (**p. 222**)
Bruce Parrott, The Paul H. Nitze School for Advanced International Studies, Washington,
 DC. (**p. 222**)
Paolo Pasicolan, The Heritage Foundation, Washington, DC. (**p. 222**)
Lawrence C. Patrick, III, Black Alliance for Educational Options, Washington, DC. (**p. 222**)
Ronald W. Pearson, Pearson & Pipkin, Inc., Washington, DC. (**p. 224**)
Terence J. Pell, Center for Individual Rights, Washington, DC. (**p. 224**)
Laura Pemberton, National Federation of Independent Business, Washington, DC.
 (**p. 225**)
Charles V. Pena, Cato Institute, Washington, DC. (**p. 225**)
Richard Perle, American Enterprise Institute, Washington, DC. (**p. 225**)
Roland I. Perusse, Inter-American Institute, Washington, DC. (**p. 226**)
Laura Bennett Peterson, Washington, DC. (**p. 226**)
William H. Peterson, Washington, DC. (**p. 227**)

William L. Saunders, Family Research Council, Washington, DC. **(p. 250)**
Greg Scandlen, National Center for Policy Analysis, Washington, DC. **(p. 251)**
Terrence M. Scanlon, Capital Research Center, Washington, DC. **(p. 251)**
Michael Scardaville, The Heritage Foundation, Washington, DC. **(p. 251)**
Robert A. Schadler, Center for First Principles, Washington, DC. **(p. 251)**
Brett D. Schaefer, The Heritage Foundation, Washington, DC. **(p. 252)**
Thomas A. Schatz, Citizens Against Government Waste, Washington, DC. **(p. 252)**
Bradley R. Schiller, American University, Washington, DC. **(p. 253)**
Gary Schmitt, Project for the New American Century, Washington, DC. **(p. 253)**
William Schneider, American Enterprise Institute, Washington, DC. **(p. 254)**
Robert Schuettinger, Washington International Studies Council, Washington, DC. **(p. 254)**
Michael A. Schuyler, Institute for Research on the Economics of Taxation, Washington, DC. **(p. 254)**
Michael Schwartz, Concerned Women for America, Washington, DC. **(p. 254)**
Victor E. Schwartz, American Tort Reform Association, Washington, DC. **(p. 254)**
Howard Segermark, Segermark Associates, Inc., Washington, DC. **(p. 256)**
Timothy Samuel Shah, Ethics and Public Policy Center, Washington, DC. **(p. 257)**
John Shanahan, National Mining Association, Washington, DC. **(p. 258)**
Kannon K. Shanmugam, Kirkland & Ellis, Washington, DC. **(p. 258)**
Nina Shea, Freedom House, Washington, DC. **(p. 258)**
Lou Sheldon, Traditional Values Coalition, Washington, DC. **(p. 258)**
J. Gregory Sidak, American Enterprise Institute, Washington, DC. **(p. 259)**
Betsy Page Sigman, Georgetown University, Washington, DC. **(p. 259)**
Radek Sikorski, American Enterprise Institute, Washington, DC. **(p. 260)**
Dimitri Simes, The Nixon Center, Washington, DC. **(p. 260)**
Rita Simon, American University, Washington, DC. **(p. 260)**
Gregory Simpkins, The Foundation for Democracy in Africa, Washington, DC. **(p. 260)**
Solveig Singleton, Competitive Enterprise Institute, Washington, DC. **(p. 261)**
John Sitilides, Western Policy Center, Washington, DC. **(p. 261)**
Shaun Small, Empower America, Washington, DC. **(p. 262)**
Anita Smith, Institute for Youth Development, Washington, DC. **(p. 262)**
Denison E. Smith, For Our Grandchildren, Washington, DC. **(p. 263)**
Frances B. Smith, Consumer Alert, Washington, DC. **(p. 263)**
Fred L. Smith, Jr., Competitive Enterprise Institute, Washington, DC. **(p. 263)**
Robert J. Smith, Center for Private Conservation, Washington, DC. **(p. 264)**
W. Shepherd Smith, Jr., Institute for Youth Development, Washington, DC. **(p. 264)**
John Michael Snyder, Citizens Committee for the Right to Keep and Bear Arms, Washington, DC. **(p. 265)**
Henry Sokolski, Non-Proliferation Policy Education Center, Washington, DC. **(p. 265)**
Diane Sollee, Coalition for Marriage, Family and Couples Education, Washington, DC. **(p. 265)**
Richard H. Solomon, United States Institute of Peace, Washington, DC. **(p. 265)**
Christina Hoff Sommers, American Enterprise Institute, Washington, DC. **(p. 266)**
Matthew Spalding, The Heritage Foundation, Washington, DC. **(p. 266)**
Jack Spencer, The Heritage Foundation, Washington, DC. **(p. 267)**
Michael Spiller, The Heritage Foundation, Washington, DC. **(p. 267)**
Peter S. Sprigg, Family Research Council, Washington, DC. **(p. 267)**
H. Baker Spring, The Heritage Foundation, Washington, DC. **(p. 267)**
Irwin Stelzer, Hudson Institute, Washington, DC. **(p. 268)**
C. Eugene Steuerle, Urban Institute, Washington, DC. **(p. 268)**
Paul Schott Stevens, Dechert, Price & Rhoads, Washington, DC. **(p. 269)**
Christine Stolba, Ethics and Public Policy Center, Washington, DC. **(p. 269)**
James Streeter, National Wilderness Institute, Washington, DC. **(p. 270)**

ORGANIZATIONS

Statistical Assessment Service, Washington, DC. **(p. 720)**
Tax Foundation, Washington, DC. **(p. 721)**
Traditional Values Coalition, Washington, DC. **(p. 724)**
U. S. Bill of Rights Foundation, Washington, DC. **(p. 724)**
U. S. English Foundation, Washington, DC. **(p. 725)**
U. S. English, Inc., Washington, DC. **(p. 725)**
United States Institute of Peace, Washington, DC. **(p. 725)**
U. S. Term Limits, Washington, DC. **(p. 725)**
Victims of Communism Memorial Foundation, Washington, DC. **(p. 726)**
Washington Legal Foundation, Washington, DC. **(p. 727)**
Washington Scholarship Fund, Washington, DC. **(p. 728)**
Western Policy Center, Washington, DC. **(p. 728)**

FLORIDA

EXPERTS

Keith G. Baker, Florida TaxWatch Research Institute, Inc., Tallahassee, FL. **(p. 43)**
Carlos Ball, Agencia Interamericana de Prensa Economica, Boca Raton, FL. **(p. 44)**
Naomi Lopez Bauman, Orlando, FL. **(p. 47)**
Donald Bellante, University of South Florida, Tampa, FL. **(p. 50)**
Thomas A. Breslint, Florida International University, Miami, FL. **(p. 61)**
David Brownlee, Family First, Tampa, FL. **(p. 64)**
Dominic M. Calabro, Florida TaxWatch Research Institute, Inc., Tallahassee, FL. **(p. 67)**
Kenneth W. Clarkson, University of Miami, Coral Gables, FL. **(p. 75)**
Neil S. Crispo, Florida State University, Tallahassee, FL. **(p. 86)**
Marshall L. De Rosa, Florida Atlantic University, Davie, FL. **(p. 90)**
Douglas S. Doudney, Coalition for Property Rights, Orlando, FL. **(p. 97)**
June Teufel Dreyer, University of Miami, Coral Gables, FL. **(p. 98)**
Thomas R. Dye, Florida State University, Tallahassee, FL. **(p. 101)**
Joyce Elam, Florida International University, Miami, FL. **(p. 105)**
Tomi Gomory, Florida State University, Tallahassee, FL. **(p. 126)**
Jay P. Greene, Manhattan Institute for Policy Research, Davie, FL. **(p. 128)**
James D. Gwartney, Florida State University, Tallahassee, FL. **(p. 131)**
Randall G. Holcombe, Florida State University, Tallahassee, FL. **(p. 144)**
J. Stanley Marshall, The James Madison Institute, Tallahassee, FL. **(p. 190)**
Robert W. McGee, Barry University, Miami Shores, FL. **(p. 195)**
Mark Merrill, Family First, Tampa, FL. **(p. 199)**
Ronald Nash, Reformed Theological Seminary, Oviedo, FL. **(p. 211)**
Darryl Paulson, University of South Florida, St. Petersburg, FL. **(p. 223)**
Philip K. Porter, University of South Florida, Tampa, FL. **(p. 231)**
William L. Proctor, Flagler College, St. Augustine, FL. **(p. 233)**
Harold Calvin Ray, National Center for Faith-Based Initiatives, West Palm Beach, FL. **(p. 237)**
Paul Craig Roberts, Institute for Political Economy, Panama City Beach, FL. **(p. 242)**
Frank A. Shepherd, Pacific Legal Foundation, Coral Gables, FL. **(p. 259)**
Devinda R. Subasinghe, St. Petersburg, FL. **(p. 271)**
Thomas L. Tacker, Embry-Riddle Aeronautical University, Daytona Beach, FL. **(p. 273)**
Chris R. Thomas, University of South Florida, Tampa, FL. **(p. 277)**
James W. Witt, University of West Florida, Pensacola, FL. **(p. 296)**
Thomas W. Zimmerer, Saint Leo University, Saint Leo, FL. **(p. 302)**

ORGANIZATIONS

Family First, Tampa, FL. **(p. 664)**
Florida TaxWatch Research Institute, Inc., Tallahassee, FL. **(p. 667)**
The James Madison Institute, Tallahassee, FL. **(p. 691)**

GEORGIA

EXPERTS

Craig E. Aronoff, Kennesaw State College, Kennesaw, GA. **(p. 41)**
Hunter Baker, Georgia Family Council, Norcross, GA. **(p. 43)**
George J. Benston, Emory University, Atlanta, GA. **(p. 51)**
Richard Bjornseth, Valdosta State University, Valdosta, GA. **(p. 54)**
Harry Bruno, Thomas University, Thomasville, GA. **(p. 64)**
Chris Carr, Georgia Public Policy Foundation, Atlanta, GA. **(p. 71)**
Barbara Christmas, Professional Association of Georgia Educators, Chamblee, GA. **(p. 74)**
Glenn Delk, Georgia Charter Schools, Atlanta, GA. **(p. 92)**
Charles Delorme, Jr., University of Georgia, Athens, GA. **(p. 92)**
John Douglas, Alston & Bird, Atlanta, GA. **(p. 97)**
Valle Simms Dutcher, Southeastern Legal Foundation, Atlanta, GA. **(p. 101)**
Gerald P. Dwyer, Jr., Federal Reserve Bank of Atlanta, Atlanta, GA. **(p. 101)**
Tim G. Echols, TeenPact Teen Leadership School, Jefferson, GA. **(p. 103)**
Elizabeth Fox-Genovese, Emory University, Atlanta, GA. **(p. 115)**
Randy Hicks, Georgia Family Council, Norcross, GA. **(p. 141)**
Milton Kafoglis, Emory University, Decatur, GA. **(p. 156)**
James B. Kau, University of Georgia, Athens, GA. **(p. 158)**
Phil Kent, Southeastern Legal Foundation, Atlanta, GA. **(p. 162)**
Joseph M. Knippenberg, Oglethorpe University, Atlanta, GA. **(p. 166)**
Edward J. Larson, University of Georgia School of Law, Athens, GA. **(p. 175)**
Peter Augustine Lawler, Berry College, Mount Berry, GA. **(p. 175)**
Dwight R. Lee, University of Georgia, Athens, GA. **(p. 176)**
Kelly McCutchen, Georgia Public Policy Foundation, Atlanta, GA. **(p. 194)**
Mark E. Mitchell, Thomas University, Thomasville, GA. **(p. 203)**
Richard F. Muth, Emory University, Atlanta, GA. **(p. 210)**
Holly Robinson, Georgia Public Policy Foundation, Atlanta, GA. **(p. 242)**
Paul Rubin, Emory University, Atlanta, GA. **(p. 246)**
Jamie Self, Georgia Family Council, Norcross, GA. **(p. 256)**
Baker Smith, U. S. Constitutional Rights Legal Defense Fund, Inc., Marietta, GA. **(p. 262)**
Mark Thornton, Columbus State University, Columbus, GA. **(p. 278)**
Richard H. Timberlake, Jr., Bogart, GA. **(p. 279)**
T. Rogers Wade, Georgia Public Policy Foundation, Atlanta, GA. **(p. 286)**
Christopher Heath Wellman, Georgia State University, Atlanta, GA. **(p. 292)**
Joe D. Whitley, Alston & Bird LLP, Atlanta, GA. **(p. 294)**
Todd G. Young, Southeastern Legal Foundation, Atlanta, GA. **(p. 301)**

ORGANIZATIONS

Georgia Family Council, Norcross, GA. **(p. 672)**
Georgia Public Policy Foundation, Atlanta, GA. **(p. 673)**
Southeastern Legal Foundation, Atlanta, GA. **(p. 720)**

HAWAII

EXPERTS

Ralph A. Cossa, Pacific Forum CSIS, Honolulu, HI. **(p. 83)**
Kelly Rosati, Hawaii Family Forum, Kaneohe, HI. **(p. 243)**
James A. Roumasset, University of Hawaii, Honolulu, HI. **(p. 245)**
Richard O. Rowland, Grassroot Institute of Hawaii, Aiea, HI. **(p. 245)**
Mary Jane Skanderup, Pacific Forum CSIS, Honolulu, HI. **(p. 261)**
Lloyd R. Vasey, Pacific Forum CSIS, Honolulu, HI. **(p. 284)**
Kate Xiao Zhou, University of Hawaii, Honolulu, HI. **(p. 302)**
Malia Zimmerman, Grassroot Institute of Hawaii, Kailua, HI. **(p. 302)**

ORGANIZATIONS

Grassroot Institute of Hawaii, Aiea, HI. **(p. 673)**
Hawaii Family Forum, Kailau, HI. **(p. 675)**
Pacific Forum CSIS, Honolulu, HI. **(p. 709)**

IDAHO

EXPERTS

Derrick Allen Dalton, Boise State University, Boise, ID. **(p. 88)**
Dennis Mansfield, Boise, ID. **(p. 189)**
Gale L. Pooley, Star, ID. **(p. 230)**
Charlotte Twight, Boise State University, Boise, ID. **(p. 282)**

ILLINOIS

EXPERTS

David L. Applegate, Olson & Hierl, LTD, Chicago, IL. **(p. 39)**
Joseph L. Bast, Heartland Institute, Chicago, IL. **(p. 47)**
Jonathan James Bean, Southern Illinois University, Carbondale, IL. **(p. 48)**
Gary Becker, University of Chicago, Chicago, IL. **(p. 48)**
Lisa E. Bernstein, University of Chicago Law School, Chicago, IL. **(p. 51)**
Amy E. Black, Wheaton College, Wheaton, IL. **(p. 54)**
Greg Blankenship, Illinois Policy Institute, Springfield, IL. **(p. 54)**
Philip L. Brach, Midtown Educational Foundation, Chicago, IL. **(p. 59)**
S. Jan Brakel, Isaac Ray Center, Inc., Chicago, IL. **(p. 60)**
Adrian Brigham, Citizens for Educational Freedom of Illinois, Streamwood, IL. **(p. 61)**
Don S. Browning, University of Chicago, Chicago, IL. **(p. 64)**
Mahmood Butt, Eastern Illinois University, Charleston, IL. **(p. 66)**
Steven Calabresi, Northwestern University School of Law, Chicago, IL. **(p. 67)**
Jameson Campaigne, Jr., Jameson Books, Inc., Ottawa, IL. **(p. 68)**
Allan C. Carlson, Howard Center for Family, Religion and Society, Rockford, IL. **(p. 70)**
Barry R. Chiswick, University of Illinois, Chicago, Chicago, IL. **(p. 73)**
Robert L. Clinton, Southern Illinois University, Carbondale, IL. **(p. 76)**
George Clowes, Heartland Institute, Chicago, IL. **(p. 76)**
Peter F. Colwell, University of Illinois, Urbana, IL. **(p. 79)**
Wendell Cox, Wendell Cox Consultancy, Belleville, IL. **(p. 84)**
John W. Danford, Loyola University Chicago, Chicago, IL. **(p. 88)**
Fran Eaton, Eagle Forum of Illinois, Oak Forest, IL. **(p. 102)**
Jean Bethke Elshtain, University of Chicago, Chicago, IL. **(p. 106)**

ORGANIZATIONS

Americans United for Life, Chicago, IL. **(p. 639)**
The Center for Bioethics and Human Dignity, Bannockburn, IL. **(p. 646)**
Henry Hazlitt Foundation, Chicago, IL. **(p. 675)**
Heartland Institute, Chicago, IL. **(p. 675)**
Howard Center of Family, Religion and Society, Rockford, IL. **(p. 677)**
Illinois Family Institute, Glen Ellyn, IL. **(p. 678)**
Illinois Policy Institute, Springfield, IL. **(p. 678)**
Lincoln Legal Foundation, Chicago, IL. **(p. 690)**
Link Institute, Libertyville, IL. **(p. 690)**
National Strategy Forum, Chicago, IL. **(p. 702)**
New Coalition for Economic and Social Change, Chicago, IL. **(p. 704)**
Project Reality, Golf, IL. **(p. 714)**
Rockford Institute, Rockford, IL. **(p. 716)**
TEACH America, Wilmette, IL. **(p. 722)**

INDIANA

EXPERTS

Cecil E. Bohanon, Ball State University, Muncie, IN. **(p. 56)**
Gerard V. Bradley, Notre Dame Law School, Notre Dame, IN. **(p. 59)**
Gregory Paul Brinker, Marion County Justice Agency, Indianapolis, IN. **(p. 61)**
Shane Burkhardt, Hudson Institute, Indianapolis, IN. **(p. 65)**
J. Daryl Charles, Taylor University, Upland, IN. **(p. 72)**
John Clark, Hudson Institute, Indianapolis, IN. **(p. 75)**
Micah Clark, American Family Association, Indianapolis, IN. **(p. 75)**
John L. Conant, Indiana State University, Terre Haute, IN. **(p. 79)**
Aurelian Craiutu, Indiana University, Bloomington, IN. **(p. 85)**
Kay Crawford, Hudson Institute, Indianapolis, IN. **(p. 85)**
Alan Dowty, University of Notre Dame, Notre Dame, IN. **(p. 98)**
Lenore T. Ealy, Emergent Enterprises, Carmel, IN. **(p. 101)**
Steven D. Ealy, Liberty Fund, Inc., Indianapolis, IN. **(p. 101)**
Robert C. Enlow, Milton and Rose Friedman Foundation, Indianapolis, IN. **(p. 107)**
Marilyn R. Flowers, Ball State University, Muncie, IN. **(p. 113)**
Richard W. Garnett, Notre Dame Law School, Notre Dame, IN. **(p. 120)**
Gary L. Geipel, Hudson Institute, Indianapolis, IN. **(p. 122)**
Roger Hamburg, Indiana University South Bend, South Bend, IN. **(p. 133)**
Justin Heet, Hudson Institute, Indianapolis, IN. **(p. 139)**
Jay F. Hein, Hudson Institute, Indianapolis, IN. **(p. 139)**
Natalie K. Hipple, Hudson Institute, Indianapolis, IN. **(p. 143)**
Robert L. Hoy, Educational CHOICE Charitable Trust, Indianapolis, IN. **(p. 147)**
Eve Jackson, The PEERS Project, Indianapolis, IN. **(p. 152)**
Bruce Alan Johnson, Bruce Alan Johnson Associates, Indianapolis, IN. **(p. 155)**
Barry P. Keating, University of Notre Dame, Notre Dame, IN. **(p. 159)**
Marie-Josee Kravis, Hudson Institute, Indianapolis, IN. **(p. 169)**
T. Craig Ladwig, Indiana Policy Review Foundation, Fort Wayne, IN. **(p. 171)**
Byron S. Lamm, State Policy Network, Fort Wayne, IN. **(p. 173)**
Herbert L. London, Hudson Institute, Indianapolis, IN. **(p. 182)**
Stephen B. Lovejoy, Purdue University, West Lafayette, IN. **(p. 183)**
Roger P. Maickel, Purdue University, Lafayette, IN. **(p. 187)**
Edmund McGarrell, Hudson Institute, Indianapolis, IN. **(p. 195)**
Paul E. Michelson, Huntington College, Huntington, IN. **(p. 201)**

Charles E. Rice, Notre Dame Law School, Notre Dame, IN. **(p. 239)**
J. Patrick Rooney, Golden Rule Insurance Company, Indianapolis, IN. **(p. 243)**
D. Eric Schansberg, Indiana University Southeast, New Albany, IN. **(p. 252)**
Curt Smith, Indiana Family Institute, Indianapolis, IN. **(p. 263)**
Gordon St. Angelo, Milton and Rose Friedman Foundation, Indianapolis, IN. **(p. 267)**
Richard Stith, Valpariso University School of Law, Valpariso, IN. **(p. 269)**
Kevin Teasley, Greater Educational Opportunities Foundation, Indianapolis, IN. **(p. 275)**
Graham S. Toft, Hudson Institute, Indianapolis, IN. **(p. 280)**
Catherine Zuckert, University of Notre Dame, Notre Dame, IN. **(p. 302)**
Michael Zuckert, University of Notre Dame, Notre Dame, IN. **(p. 302)**

ORGANIZATIONS

Milton and Rose Friedman Foundation, Indianapolis, IN. **(p. 671)**
Greater Educational Opportunities Foundation, Indianapolis, IN. **(p. 674)**
Hudson Institute, Indianapolis, IN. **(p. 677)**
Indiana Family Institute, Indianapolis, IN. **(p. 679)**
Indiana Policy Review Foundation, Fort Wayne, IN. **(p. 679)**
Liberty Fund, Inc., Indianapolis, IN. **(p. 689)**

IOWA

EXPERTS

Jeffrey R. Boeyink, Iowans for Tax Relief, Muscatine, IA. **(p. 56)**
Edward D. Failor, Sr., Iowans for Tax Relief, Muscatine, IA. **(p. 108)**
Amy Frantz, Public Interest Institute, Mount Pleasant, IA. **(p. 116)**
Steven Garrison, Public Interest Institute, Mount Pleasant, IA. **(p. 120)**
David Hogberg, Public Interest Institute, Mount Pleasant, IA. **(p. 144)**
Charles D. Hurley, Iowa Family Policy Center, Pleasant Hill, IA. **(p. 150)**
Dean Kleckner, Truth About Trade and Technology, Des Moines, IA. **(p. 165)**
George R. Neumann, University of Iowa, Iowa City, IA. **(p. 213)**
Don Racheter, Public Interest Institute, Mount Pleasant, IA. **(p. 235)**
David Stanley, National Taxpayers Union, Muscatine, IA. **(p. 268)**
Robert Sutherland, Cornell College, Mount Vernon, IA. **(p. 272)**

ORGANIZATIONS

Iowa Family Policy Center, Des Moines, IA. **(p. 685)**
Iowans for Tax Relief, Muscatine, IA. **(p. 685)**
Public Interest Institute, Mount Pleasant, IA. **(p. 714)**

KANSAS

EXPERTS

Bob Corkins, Kansas Legislative Education and Research, Inc., Topeka, KS. **(p. 82)**
Douglas A. Houston, University of Kansas, Lawrence, KS. **(p. 147)**
Karl Peterjohn, Kansas Taxpayers Network, Wichita, KS. **(p. 226)**
Gene C. Wunder, Washburn University, Topeka, KS. **(p. 299)**

ORGANIZATIONS

Flint Hills Center for Public Policy, Wichita, KS. **(p. 666)**

KENTUCKY

EXPERTS

Harry Borders, Kentucky League for Educational Alternatives, Frankfort, KY. **(p. 57)**
Jefferson G. Edgens, Morehead State University – Jackson Center, Jackson, KY. **(p. 103)**
R. Albert Mohler, Jr., The Southern Baptist Theological Seminary, Louisville, KY. **(p. 204)**
Thomas Patrick Monaghan, American Center for Law and Justice, New Hope, KY. **(p. 204)**
Kent Ostrander, The Family Foundation of Kentucky, Lexington, KY. **(p. 220)**
Eugenia Froedge Toma, University of Kentucky, Lexington, KY. **(p. 280)**

ORGANIZATIONS

The Family Foundation of Kentucky, Lexington, KY. **(p. 665)**

LOUISIANA

EXPERTS

John S. Baker, Jr., Louisiana State University, Baton Rouge, LA. **(p. 43)**
Walter Block, Loyola University New Orleans, New Orleans, LA. **(p. 55)**
William F. Campbell, The Philadelphia Society, Baton Rouge, LA. **(p. 68)**
Nicholas Capaldi, Loyola University New Orleans, New Orleans, LA. **(p. 69)**
Kevin L. Cope, Louisiana State University, Baton Rouge, LA. **(p. 81)**
Paul Dunn, University of Louisiana, Monroe, Monroe, LA. **(p. 100)**
Andrew W. Foshee, McNeese State University, Lake Charles, LA. **(p. 115)**
Robert Higgs, The Independent Institute, Covington, LA. **(p. 142)**
Eric Mack, Tulane University, New Orleans, LA. **(p. 185)**
Gene Mills, Louisiana Family Forum, Baton Rouge, LA. **(p. 202)**
Richard Alan Nelson, Louisiana State University, Baton Rouge, LA. **(p. 212)**
Ellis Sandoz, Eric Voegelin Institute, Baton Rouge, LA. **(p. 249)**
James R. Stoner, Louisiana State University, Baton Rouge, LA. **(p. 270)**
Frank J. Tipler, Tulane University, New Orleans, LA. **(p. 279)**

ORGANIZATIONS

Louisiana Family Forum, Baton Rouge, LA. **(p. 691)**

MAINE

EXPERTS

Bill Becker, Maine Policy Center, Portland, ME. **(p. 48)**
Michael S. Heath, Christian Civic League of Maine, Augusta, ME. **(p. 138)**
Frank J. Heller, Maine Policy Ronin Network, Brunswick, ME. **(p. 139)**
Thomas Mead, Maine Policy Center, Portland, ME. **(p. 198)**
Richard E. Morgan, Bowdoin College, Brunswick, ME. **(p. 206)**
Ron Trowbridge, Maine Policy Center, Durham, ME. **(p. 281)**

ORGANIZATIONS

Christian Civic League of Maine, Augusta, ME. **(p. 653)**
Maine Policy Center, Portland, ME. **(p. 692)**
Maine Public Policy Institute, Hampden, ME. **(p. 692)**

MARYLAND

EXPERTS

I. Dean Ahmad, Minaret of Freedom Institute, Bethesda, MD. **(p. 36)**
Joseph Baldacchino, National Humanities Institute, Bowie, MD. **(p. 44)**
Charles A. Ballard, Institute for Responsible Fatherhood and Family Revitalization, Largo, MD. **(p. 45)**
Eric A. Belgrad, Towson State University, Towson, MD. **(p. 49)**
Herman Belz, University of Maryland, College Park, MD. **(p. 50)**
James Bovard, Rockville, MD. **(p. 58)**
Frank A. Burd, Baltimore Council on Foreign Affairs, Baltimore, MD. **(p. 65)**
Charles E. Butterworth, University of Maryland, College Park, MD. **(p. 67)**
Kaleem Caire, American Education Reform Council, Bowie, MD. **(p. 67)**
Hungdah Chiu, University of Maryland School of Law, Baltimore, MD. **(p. 74)**
Donald J. Devine, Center for American Values, Shady Side, MD. **(p. 94)**
Thomas J. DiLorenzo, Loyola College, Clarksville, MD. **(p. 96)**
Denis Doyle, Doyle Associates, Chevy Chase, MD. **(p. 98)**
Khalid Duran, *TransIslam Magazine*, Bethesda, MD. **(p. 100)**
Louis D. Enoff, Enoff Associates Limited, Sykesville, MD. **(p. 107)**
Robert O. Freedman, Baltimore Hebrew University, Baltimore, MD. **(p. 116)**
Bruce L. Gardner, University of Maryland, College Park, MD. **(p. 120)**
Doris Gordon, Libertarians for Life, Wheaton, MD. **(p. 126)**
Steven A. Grossman, HPS Group, LLC, Silver Spring, MD. **(p. 130)**
Paige Holland Hamp, Maryland Public Policy Institute, Germantown, MD. **(p. 133)**
Steve H. Hanke, Johns Hopkins University, Baltimore, MD. **(p. 134)**
Claudia B. Horn, The Alliance Group, LLC, North Potomac, MD. **(p. 145)**
Alan Inman, Institute for Responsible Fatherhood and Family Revitalization, Largo, MD. **(p. 151)**
Darlene A. Kennedy, Centre for New Black Leadership, Baltimore, MD. **(p. 162)**
Malcolm Kovacs, Montgomery College, Rockville, MD. **(p. 168)**
Elie Krakowski, EDK Consulting, Baltimore, MD. **(p. 168)**
Jill Cunningham Lacey, Capital Research Center, Damascus, MD. **(p. 171)**
Stephen Lazarus, Center for Public Justice, Annapolis, MD. **(p. 176)**
Ernest W. Lefever, Chevy Chase, MD. **(p. 177)**
George Liebmann, Calvert Institute for Policy Research, Baltimore, MD. **(p. 180)**
Bruno V. Manno, The Annie E. Casey Foundation, Baltimore, MD. **(p. 188)**
Marty McGeein, McGeein Group, Bethesda, MD. **(p. 196)**
Daniel McGroarty, White House Writer's Group, Chevy Chase, MD. **(p. 196)**
Michael J. McManus, Marriage Savers, Potomac, MD. **(p. 197)**
Robert H. Nelson, University of Maryland, College Park, MD. **(p. 212)**
Charles J. O'Malley, Charles J. O'Malley & Associates, Inc., Annapolis, MD. **(p. 217)**
Rocco M. Paone, U. S. Naval Academy, Annapolis, MD. **(p. 221)**
Gabriel Roth, Chevy Chase, MD. **(p. 244)**
Frank Ruddy, Ruddy & Muir, Chevy Chase, MD. **(p. 246)**
Peter Samuel, *Toll Roads Newsletter*, Frederick, MD. **(p. 249)**
Diana J. Schaub, Loyola College, Baltimore, MD. **(p. 252)**
James Skillen, Center for Public Justice, Annapolis, MD. **(p. 261)**

Doug Stiegler, Association of Maryland Families, Woodstock, MD. **(p. 269)**
Christopher B. Summers, Maryland Public Policy Institute, Germantown, MD. **(p. 272)**
William J. Taylor, Jr., Taylor Associates, Inc., Bethesda, MD. **(p. 275)**
Kenneth R. Timmerman, Maryland Taxpayers Association, Bethesda, MD. **(p. 279)**
Vladimir Tismaneanu, University of Maryland, College Park, MD. **(p. 279)**
E. Fuller Torrey, Bethesda, MD. **(p. 280)**
Stephen J. K. Walters, Loyola College, Baltimore, MD. **(p. 288)**
Roland Warren, National Fatherhood Initiative, Gaithersburg, MD. **(p. 289)**
Gail Wilensky, Project HOPE, Bethesda, MD. **(p. 294)**
Martin Morse Wooster, Northfeld Assocaties, Silver Spring, MD. **(p. 298)**
Robert O. C. Worcester, Maryland Business for Responsive Government, Baltimore, MD. **(p. 298)**
Nicholas Zill, Westat Inc., Rockville, MD. **(p. 302)**

ORGANIZATIONS

Calvert Institute for Policy Research, Inc., Baltimore, MD. **(p. 644)**
Center for Public Justice, Annapolis, MD. **(p. 650)**
Maryland Business for Responsive Government, Baltimore, MD. **(p. 693)**
The Maryland Public Policy Institute, Germantown, MD. **(p. 693)**
Maryland Taxpayers Association, Bethesda, MD. **(p. 693)**
Minaret of Freedom Institute, Bethesda, MD. **(p. 695)**
National Fatherhood Initiative, Gaithersburg, MD. **(p. 698)**
National Humanities Institute, Bowie, MD. **(p. 699)**

MASSACHUSETTS

EXPERTS

Stephen Adams, Pioneer Institute for Public Policy Research, Boston, MA. **(p. 34)**
Barbara Anderson, Citizens for Limited Taxation and Government, Peabody, MA. **(p. 38)**
Hadley Arkes, Amherst College, Amherst, MA. **(p. 40)**
Andrew J. Bacevich, Boston University, Boston, MA. **(p. 42)**
Sallie Baliunas, Harvard University, Cambridge, MA. **(p. 44)**
Dale Ballou, University of Massachusetts, Amherst, MA. **(p. 45)**
Randy Barnett, Boston University School of Law, Boston, MA. **(p. 46)**
John Barrett, Beacon Hill Institute, Boston, MA. **(p. 46)**
Robert J. Barro, Harvard University, Cambridge, MA. **(p. 46)**
Linda Brown, Pioneer Institute for Public Policy Research, Boston, MA. **(p. 63)**
Ronald Cass, Boston University School of Law, Boston, MA. **(p. 72)**
Charles Chieppo, Pioneer Institute for Public Policy Research, Boston, MA. **(p. 73)**
Angelo M. Codevilla, Boston University, Boston, MA. **(p. 77)**
Ron Crews, Massachusetts Family Institute, Newton Upper Falls, MA. **(p. 86)**
Edwin J. Delattre, Boston University, Boston, MA. **(p. 91)**
John R. Diggs, Jr., South Hadley, MA. **(p. 95)**
Thomas Doherty, Brandeis University, Waltham, MA. **(p. 96)**
Mickey Edwards, Harvard University, Cambridge, MA. **(p. 104)**
Chip Faulkner, Citizens for Limited Taxation and Government, Wentham, MA. **(p. 109)**
Martin Feldstein, National Bureau of Economic Research, Cambridge, MA. **(p. 110)**
Richard B. Freeman, National Bureau of Economic Research, Cambridge, MA. **(p. 116)**
Bernard J. Frieden, Massachusetts Institute of Technology, Cambridge, MA. **(p. 117)**
Mary Ann Glendon, Harvard Law School, Cambridge, MA. **(p. 124)**
Charles L. Glenn, Boston University, Boston, MA. **(p. 124)**
Andrew Grainger, New England Legal Foundation, Boston, MA. **(p. 128)**

ORGANIZATIONS

New England Legal Foundation, Boston, MA. (p. 704)
Pioneer Institute for Public Policy Research, Boston, MA. (p. 712)

MICHIGAN

EXPERTS

Charles M. Achilles, Eastern Michigan University, Ypsilanti, MI. (p. 34)
Donald L. Alexander, Western Michigan University, Kalamazoo, MI. (p. 36)
William Allen, Michigan State University, East Lansing, MI. (p. 37)
Dominic A. Aquila, Ave Maria University, Ypsilanti, MI. (p. 40)
Larry P. Arnn, Hillsdale College, Hillsdale, MI. (p. 40)
William Ball, Northern Michigan University, Marquette, MI. (p. 44)
Michael B. Barkey, Center for the Study of Compassionate Conservatism, Grand Rapids, MI. (p. 46)
Christopher Beiting, Ave Maria College, Ypsilanti, MI. (p. 49)
David J. Bobb, Hillsdale College, Hillsdale, MI. (p. 56)
Anthony Bradley, Acton Institute for the Study of Religion and Liberty, Grand Rapids, MI. (p. 59)
William P. Browne, Central Michigan University, Mount Pleasant, MI. (p. 64)
Brian Carpenter, Mackinac Center for Public Policy, Midland, MI. (p. 70)
Stephen M. Colarelli, Central Michigan University, Mount Pleasant, MI. (p. 78)
John Coonradt, Mackinac Center for Public Policy, Midland, MI. (p. 81)
Mickey Craig, Hillsdale College, Hillsdale, MI. (p. 85)
Werner J. Dannhauser, Michigan State University, East Lansing, MI. (p. 88)
Phillip DeVous, Acton Institute for the Study of Religion and Liberty, Grand Rapids, MI. (p. 94)
Elaine Donnelly, Center for Military Readiness, Livonia, MI. (p. 97)
Clark Durant, New Common School Foundation, Detroit, MI. (p. 101)
Richard M. Ebeling, Hillsdale College, Hillsdale, MI. (p. 102)
Robert Eden, Hillsdale College, Hillsdale, MI. (p. 103)
Gary Glenn, American Family Association of Michigan, Midland, MI. (p. 124)
Clint W. Green, Acton Institute for the Study of Religion and Liberty, Grand Rapids, MI. (p. 128)
Samuel Gregg, Acton Institute for the Study of Religion and Liberty, Grand Rapids, MI. (p. 129)
Virgil Gulker, Kids Hope USA, Holland, MI. (p. 130)
Robert Hunter, Mackinac Center for Public Policy, Midland, MI. (p. 150)
Harry G. Hutchison, Wayne State University, Detroit, MI. (p. 150)
Douglas A. Jeffrey, Hillsdale College, Hillsdale, MI. (p. 154)
Kirk A. Johnson, Mackinac Center for Public Policy, Midland, MI. (p. 155)
Diane S. Katz, Mackinac Center for Public Policy, Midland, MI. (p. 158)
Maurice Kelman, Wayne State University Law School, Troy, MI. (p. 161)
Annette Kirk, Russell Kirk Center, Mecosta, MI. (p. 164)
James E. Kostrava, Funding Freedom, Stanford, MI. (p. 168)
Michael D. LaFaive, Mackinac Center for Public Policy, Midland, MI. (p. 171)
Joseph G. Lehman, Mackinac Center for Public Policy, Midland, MI. (p. 177)
Kris Alan Mauren, Acton Institute for the Study of Religion and Liberty, Grand Rapids, MI. (p. 192)
Paul W. McCracken, University of Michigan Business School, Ann Arbor, MI. (p. 194)
Ingrid Merikoski, Earhart Foundation, Ann Arbor, MI. (p. 199)
Michael J. O'Dea, Christus Medicus Foundation, Bloomfield Hills, MI. (p. 216)
Joseph P. Overton, Mackinac Center for Public Policy, Midland, MI. (p. 220)
Mark J. Perry, University of Michigan, Flint, Flint, MI. (p. 226)

ORGANIZATIONS

MINNESOTA

EXPERTS

ORGANIZATIONS

MISSISSIPPI

EXPERTS

Eugene M. Kolassa, University of Mississippi, University, MS. **(p. 167)**
Janos Radvanyi, Mississippi State University, Mississippi State, MS. **(p. 235)**
Forest M. Thigpen, Mississippi Family Council, Jackson, MS. **(p. 277)**
Robert D. Tollison, University of Mississippi, University, MS. **(p. 280)**
Scott J. Vitell, University of Mississippi, University, MS. **(p. 285)**
Donald Wildmon, American Family Association, Tupelo, MS. **(p. 294)**

ORGANIZATIONS

American Family Association, Tupelo, MS. **(p. 635)**
American Family Association Foundation, Tupelo, MS. **(p. 635)**
Mississippi Family Council, Jackson, MS. **(p. 695)**

MISSOURI

EXPERTS

David L. Adams, Concordia Seminary, St. Louis, MO. **(p. 34)**
Ken R. Canfield, National Center for Fathering, Kansas City, MO. **(p. 69)**
Kenneth W. Chilton, Institute for Study of Economics and the Environment, St. Charles, MO. **(p. 73)**
Craig T. Cobane, Culver-Stockton College, Canton, MO. **(p. 76)**
Mae Duggan, Citizens for Educational Freedom, St. Louis, MO. **(p. 99)**
Martin Duggan, Educational Freedom Foundation, St. Louis, MO. **(p. 99)**
Susan K. Feigenbaum, University of Missouri, St. Louis, St. Louis, MO. **(p. 110)**
Jules B. Gerard, Washington University, St. Louis, MO. **(p. 122)**
Jerzy Hauptmann, Park University, Kansas City, MO. **(p. 137)**
Donna H. Hearne, Constitutional Coalition, St. Louis, MO. **(p. 138)**
Carl Herbster, American Association of Christian Schools, Independence, MO. **(p. 140)**
James Hitchcock, St. Louis University, St. Louis, MO. **(p. 143)**
Richard P. Hutchison, Landmark Legal Foundation, Kansas City, MO. **(p. 150)**
Thomas R. Ireland, University of Missouri, St. Louis, St. Louis, MO. **(p. 152)**
Theodore "Sylvester" John, Students In Free Enterprise, Springfield, MO. **(p. 154)**
F. Scott Kieff, Washington University, St. Louis, MO. **(p. 163)**
Kent King, Missouri State Teachers Association, Columbia, MO. **(p. 164)**
Joy Kiviat, Citizens for Educational Freedom, St. Louis, MO. **(p. 165)**
Timothy Lamer, *World Magazine*, Ellisville, MO. **(p. 173)**
Glenn M. MacDonald, Washington University, St. Louis, MO. **(p. 185)**
Mario Mandina, National Lawyers Association, Independence, MO. **(p. 188)**
Bruce A. Nasby, Students In Free Enterprise, Springfield, MO. **(p. 210)**
Timothy G. O'Rourke, University of Missouri, St. Louis, St. Louis, MO. **(p. 217)**
Michael Podgursky, University of Missouri, Columbia, MO. **(p. 230)**
Russell Roberts, Weidenbaum Center, St. Louis, MO. **(p. 242)**
David C. Rose, University of Missouri, St. Louis, St. Louis, MO. **(p. 243)**
Gregory W. Sand, Saint Louis College of Pharmacy, St. Louis, MO. **(p. 249)**
Phyllis Schlafly, Eagle Forum, St. Louis, MO. **(p. 253)**
Steven S. Smith, Weidenbaum Center, St. Louis, MO. **(p. 264)**
William R. Van Cleave, Southwest Missouri State University, Springfield, MO. **(p. 284)**
Murray Weidenbaum, Weidenbaum Center, St. Louis, MO. **(p. 291)**
Lawrence H. White, University of Missouri, St. Louis, St. Louis, MO. **(p. 293)**

NEVADA

EXPERTS

Helene Denney, Nevada Policy Research Insitute, Las Vegas, NV. **(p. 92)**

ORGANIZATIONS

Nevada Policy Research Institute, Las Vegas, NV. **(p. 704)**

NEW HAMPSHIRE

EXPERTS

Judy Alger, Center for Market-Based Education, Inc., Rumney, NH. **(p. 36)**
William A. Fischel, Dartmouth College, Hanover, NH. **(p. 112)**
Kathy Getchell, Center for Market-Based Education, Inc., Londonderry, NH. **(p. 123)**
Susan D. Hollins, The Josiah Bartlett Center for Public Policy, Concord, NH. **(p. 145)**
W. Thomas Kelly, Savers and Investors League, Mirror Lake, NH. **(p. 161)**
Mary Beth Klee, Link Institute, Portsmouth, NH. **(p. 165)**
John T. Scott, Dartmouth College, Hanover, NH. **(p. 255)**
Karen Testerman, Cornerstone Policy Research, Concord, NH. **(p. 275)**

ORGANIZATIONS

The Josiah Bartlett Center for Public Policy, Concord, NH. **(p. 641)**
Center for Market-Based Education, Inc., Rumney, NH. **(p. 648)**
Cornerstone Policy Research, Concord, NH. **(p. 658)**

NEW JERSEY

EXPERTS

Stephen H. Balch, National Association of Scholars, Princeton, NJ. **(p. 44)**
Janet Beales, Kids One, East Brunswick, NJ. **(p. 48)**
David F. Bradford, Princeton University, Princeton, NJ. **(p. 59)**
Gary Crosby Brasor, National Association of Scholars, Princeton, NJ. **(p. 60)**
Joseph I. Coffey, Princeton, NJ. **(p. 77)**
Lois J. Copeland, Hillsdale, NJ. **(p. 81)**
Michael A. Crew, Rutgers University, Newark, NJ. **(p. 85)**
Len Deo, New Jersey Family Policy Council, Parsippany, NJ. **(p. 93)**
Jeffrey M. Friedman, *Critical Review*, Princeton, NJ. **(p. 117)**
John Galandak, Foundation for Free Enterprise, Paramus, NJ. **(p. 119)**
Robert P. George, Princeton University, Princeton, NJ. **(p. 122)**
Robert Goldberg, Manhattan Institute, Springfield, NJ. **(p. 125)**
George Kelling, Rutgers University, Newark, NJ. **(p. 160)**
Dorothy Knauer, Protestant Community Centers, Inc., Newark, NJ. **(p. 166)**
Jack W. Lavery, Lavery Consulting Group, LLC, Washington Crossing, NJ. **(p. 175)**
Kevin P. Moriarty, Scholarship Fund for Inner-City Children, Newark, NJ. **(p. 206)**
Sam Perelli, United Taxpayers of New Jersey, Cedar Grove, NJ. **(p. 225)**
David Popenoe, Rutgers University, New Brunswick, NJ. **(p. 230)**
Glenn M. Ricketts, National Association of Scholars, Princeton, NJ. **(p. 239)**
Cecilia E. Rouse, Princeton University, Princeton, NJ. **(p. 245)**
Jude Wanniski, Polyconomics, Parsippany, NJ. **(p. 288)**

Keith E. Whittington, Princeton University, Princeton, NJ. (p. 294)
Bradford P. Wilson, National Association of Scholars, Princeton, NJ. (p. 296)

ORGANIZATIONS

Center for Policy Research of New Jersey, Florham Park, NJ. (p. 649)
Foundation for Free Enterprise, Paramus, NJ. (p. 668)
National Association of Scholars, Princeton, NJ. (p. 696)
New Jersey Family Policy Council, Parsippany, NJ. (p. 705)

NEW MEXICO

EXPERTS

John Agresto, John Agresto and Associates, Santa Fe, NM. (p. 35)
M. Gene Aldridge, New Mexico Independence Research Institute, Las Cruces, NM. (p. 36)
Kenneth Brown, Rio Grande Foundation, Albuquerque, NM. (p. 63)
Karl Hess, The Land Center, Las Cruces, NM. (p. 141)
Harry Messenheimer, Rio Grande Foundation, Tijeras, NM. (p. 200)
Roger Michener, Placitas, NM. (p. 201)
Gordon Sumner, Jr., Sumner Association, Santa Fe, NM. (p. 272)

ORGANIZATIONS

New Mexico Independence Research Institute, Las Cruces, NM. (p. 705)
Rio Grande Foundation, Tijeras, NM. (p. 716)

NEW YORK

EXPERTS

Jefferson Adams, Sarah Lawrence College, Bronxville, NY. (p. 34)
Brian C. Anderson, Manhattan Institute for Policy Research, New York, NY. (p. 38)
Frank Annunziata, Rochester Institute of Technology, Rochester, NY. (p. 39)
Charles N. Aswad, Medical Society of the State of New York, Lake Success, NY. (p. 41)
Iwan Azis, Cornell University, Ithaca, NY. (p. 42)
Brian Backstrom, Empire Foundation for Policy Research, Clifton Park, NY. (p. 42)
Richard A. Baer, Jr., Cornell University, Ithaca, NY. (p. 42)
Sandor Balogh, Hudson Valley Community College, East Greenbush, NY. (p. 45)
Robert J. Batemarco, Peekskill, NY. (p. 47)
David J. BenDaniel, Cornell University, Ithaca, NY. (p. 50)
Judith A. Best, State University of New York, Cortland, Cortland, NY. (p. 52)
David Blankenhorn, Institute for American Values, New York, NY. (p. 54)
Lester Brickman, Cardozo School of Law, New York, NY. (p. 61)
Arthur C. Brooks, Syracuse University, Syracuse, NY. (p. 61)
B. Jason Brooks, Empire Foundation for Policy Research, Clifton Park, NY. (p. 62)
James Bruner, New York Family Policy Council, Albany, NY. (p. 64)
Thomas Carroll, Empire Foundation for Policy Research, Clifton Park, NY. (p. 71)
Michael John Caslin, III, National Foundation for Teaching Entrepreneurship, New York, NY. (p. 71)
Cecilia Chang, St. John's University, Jamaica, NY. (p. 72)
John Chubb, Edison Schools, Inc., New York, NY. (p. 74)
Henry C. Clark, III, Canisius College, Buffalo, NY. (p. 74)
Brooks Colburn, Foundation for Economic Education, Irvington-on-Hudson, NY. (p. 78)

Stephen Cole, State University of New York, Stony Brook, NY. **(p. 78)**
Roger C. Cramton, Cornell Law School, Ithaca, NY. **(p. 85)**
Candace de Russy, State University of New York, Bronxville, NY. **(p. 90)**
Mark De Young, World Youth Alliance, New York, NY. **(p. 90)**
Midge Decter, New York, NY. **(p. 91)**
Douglas Dean Dewey, Children's Scholarship Fund, New York, NY. **(p. 94)**
Joseph DioGuardi, Albanian American Civic League, Ossining, NY. **(p. 96)**
Marie Dolan, New York State Federation of Catholic School Parents, Flushing, NY. **(p. 96)**
William A. Donohue, Catholic League for Religious and Civil Rights, New York, NY. **(p. 97)**
Diallo Dphrepaulezz, New York, NY. **(p. 98)**
Timothy R. Dzierba, Medaille College, Buffalo, NY. **(p. 101)**
Isaac Ehrlich, State University of New York, Buffalo, Buffalo, NY. **(p. 105)**
Edward H. Fleischman, Linklaters, New York, NY. **(p. 113)**
Seymour Fliegel, Center for Educational Innovation – Public Education Association, New York, NY. **(p. 113)**
John H. Fund, *OpinionJournal.com*, New York, NY. **(p. 119)**
Maggie Gallagher, Offining, NY. **(p. 119)**
John Taylor Gatto, Odysseus Group Inc., New York, NY. **(p. 121)**
Steven Goldberg, City College, New York, NY. **(p. 125)**
Stephen Goldsmith, Manhattan Institute for Policy Research, New York, NY. **(p. 126)**
Leonard M. Greene, Institute for SocioEconomic Studies, White Plains, NY. **(p. 129)**
Ronald Hansen, University of Rochester, Rochester, NY. **(p. 134)**
C. Lowell Harriss, Columbia University, Bronxville, NY. **(p. 136)**
Eugene Heath, State University of New York, New Platz, New Paltz, NY. **(p. 138)**
Robert A. Heineman, Alfred University, Alfred, NY. **(p. 139)**
Carl Helstrom, JM Foundation, New York, NY. **(p. 139)**
Heather Higgins, Independent Women's Forum, New York, NY. **(p. 142)**
Thomas D. Hopkins, Rochester Institute of Technology, Rochester, NY. **(p. 145)**
Steven Horwitz, St. Lawrence University, Canton, NY. **(p. 147)**
Richard R. Hough, III, Children's Scholarship Fund, New York, NY. **(p. 147)**
Olga S. Hruby, Research Center for Religious and Human Rights, New York, NY. **(p. 148)**
Peter Huber, Manhattan Institute for Policy Research, New York, NY. **(p. 148)**
Howard Husock, Manhattan Institute for Policy Research, New York, NY. **(p. 150)**
Carol Iannone, New York, NY. **(p. 150)**
Sanford Ikeda, State University of New York, Purchase, NY. **(p. 151)**
Niger Roy Innis, Congress of Racial Equality, New York, NY. **(p. 151)**
Tamar Jacoby, Manhattan Institute for Policy Research, New York, NY. **(p. 153)**
Michael Johns, Melville, NY. **(p. 154)**
Adrian Karatnycky, Freedom House, New York, NY. **(p. 158)**
Martin S. Kaufman, Atlantic Legal Foundation, New York, NY. **(p. 159)**
Raymond J. Keating, Small Business Survival Committee, Manorville, NY. **(p. 159)**
John Kekes, Charlton, NY. **(p. 160)**
David Kelley, The Objectivist Center, Poughkeepsie, NY. **(p. 160)**
Steven J. Kidder, New York Family Policy Council, Albany, NY. **(p. 163)**
Wendy Kopp, Teach for America, New York, NY. **(p. 167)**
Lawrence Kudlow, Kudlow & Co., LLC, New York, NY. **(p. 170)**
Carol W. LaGrasse, Property Rights Foundation of America, Inc., Stony Creek, NY. **(p. 172)**
Heather MacDonald, Manhattan Institute for Policy Research, New York, NY. **(p. 185)**
Johnathon R. Macey, Cornell University, Ithaca, NY. **(p. 185)**
Myron Magnet, Manhattan Institute for Policy Research, New York, NY. **(p. 186)**
Steve Mariotti, National Foundation for Teaching Entrepreneurship, New York, NY. **(p. 189)**
Elizabeth Marquardt, Institute for American Values, New York, NY. **(p. 189)**

Jerold L. Zimmerman, University of Rochester, Rochester, NY. (p. 302)
Karl Zinsmeister, American Enterprise Institute, Cazenovia, NY. (p. 302)

ORGANIZATIONS

Alliance for America, Caroga Park, NY. (p. 629)
Alliance for America Foundation, Caroga Lake, NY. (p. 630)
American Council on Science and Health, New York, NY. (p. 634)
American Textbook Council, New York, NY. (p. 637)
Atlantic Legal Foundation, New York, NY. (p. 641)
Economic Freedom Institute, Purchase, NY. (p. 660)
Empire Foundation for Policy Research, Clifton Park, NY. (p. 661)
Foundation for Economic Education, Irvington, NY. (p. 668)
Freedom House, New York, NY. (p. 670)
Institute for American Values, New York, NY. (p. 680)
Institute for SocioEconomic Studies, White Plains, NY. (p. 682)
Institute on Religion and Public Life, New York, NY. (p. 684)
Manhattan Institute for Policy Research, New York, NY. (p. 692)
Murray Hill Institute, New York, NY. (p. 696)
National Foundation for Teaching Entrepreneurship, New York, NY. (p. 699)
New York Family Policy Council, Albany, NY. (p. 705)
The Objectivist Center, Poughkeepsie, NY. (p. 706)
Personal Retirement Alliance, Ltd., New York, NY. (p. 711)
Property Rights Foundation of America, Inc., Stoney Creek, NY. (p. 714)
Public Policy Institute of New York State, Albany, NY. (p. 714)

NORTH CAROLINA

EXPERTS

David S. Ball, North Carolina State University, Raleigh, NC. (p. 44)
Joel Belz, *World Magazine*, Asheville, NC. (p. 50)
Herbert B. Berkowitz, The Heritage Foundation, Wilimington, NC. (p. 51)
John J. Bethune, Barton College, Wilson, NC. (p. 53)
Bill Brooks, North Carolina Family Policy Council, Raleigh, NC. (p. 62)
Harold O. J. Brown, Reformed Theological Seminary, Charlotte, NC. (p. 63)
Don Carrington, John Locke Foundation, Raleigh, NC. (p. 71)
J. Paul Combs, Appalachian Regional Development Institute, Boone, NC. (p. 79)
Roy E. Cordato, John Locke Foundation, Raleigh, NC. (p. 82)
Elizabeth Currier, Committee for Monetary Research and Education, Inc., Charlotte, NC.
(p. 87)
John Dodd, Jesse Helms Center, Wingate, NC. (p. 96)
Edward W. Erickson, North Carolina State University, Raleigh, NC. (p. 107)
David T. Hartgen, University of North Carolina, Charlotte, Charlotte, NC. (p. 136)
Clark C. Havighurst, Duke University School of Law, Durham, NC. (p. 137)
Jonathan Hill, North Carolina Citizens for a Sound Economy, Raleigh, NC. (p. 142)
John MacDonald Hood, John Locke Foundation, Raleigh, NC. (p. 145)
Dale M. Hoover, North Carolina State University, Raleigh, NC. (p. 145)
Thomas Hyde, Pfeiffer University, Misenheimer, NC. (p. 150)
Lindalyn Kakadelis, North Carolina Education Alliance, Pineville, NC. (p. 157)
Charles R. Knoeber, North Carolina State University, Raleigh, NC. (p. 166)
Kent Lassman, Progress & Freedom Foundation, Raleigh, NC. (p. 175)
Bernard T. Lomas, The Heritage Foundation, Chapel Hill, NC. (p. 182)
Mike Long, Complete Abstinence Eduation Program, Durham, NC. (p. 183)

Jerome Anthony McDuffie, University of North Carolina, Pembroke, Lumberton, NC. (p. 195)
Thomas Nechyba, Duke University, Durham, NC. (p. 211)
Anthony I. Negbenebor, Gardner-Webb University, Boiling Springs, NC. (p. 212)
E. C. Pasour, Jr., North Carolina State University, Raleigh, NC. (p. 222)
Rorin Morse Platt, Campbell University, Buies Creek, NC. (p. 229)
Jack Sommer, Political Economy Research Institute, Charlotte, NC. (p. 266)
John E. R. Staddon, Duke University, Durham, NC. (p. 267)
Richard Wagner, *Carolina Journal*/John Locke Foundation, Raleigh, NC. (p. 286)
Walter J. Wessels, North Carolina State University, Raleigh, NC. (p. 292)

ORGANIZATIONS

Committee for Monetary Research and Education, Charlotte, NC. (p. 657)
The Jesse Helms Center Foundation, Wingate, NC. (p. 675)
John Locke Foundation, Raleigh, NC. (p. 690)
North Carolina Family Policy Council, Raleigh, NC. (p. 706)

NORTH DAKOTA

EXPERTS

Bela A. Balogh, University of Mary, Bismarck, ND. (p. 45)
Robert Feidler, International Legal Projects Institute, Grand Forks, ND. (p. 110)
Robert Hale, Northwest Legal Foundation, Minot, ND. (p. 132)
Robert Stanley Herren, North Dakota State University, Fargo, ND. (p. 140)
Christina Kindel, North Dakota Family Alliance, Bismarck, ND. (p. 164)

ORGANIZATIONS

North Dakota Family Alliance, Bismarck, ND. (p. 706)

OHIO

EXPERTS

Douglas K. Adie, Ohio University, Athens, OH. (p. 35)
Jonathan H. Adler, Case Western Reserve University, Cleveland, OH. (p. 35)
Benjamin Alexander, Franciscan University of Steubenville, Steubenville, OH. (p. 36)
Saundra Berry, Cleveland Scholarship and Tutoring Program, Cleveland, OH. (p. 52)
William C. Binning, Youngstown State University, Youngstown, OH. (p. 53)
David Brennan, White Hat Management, Akron, OH. (p. 61)
Deborah Burstion-Donbraye, American Multimedia Inc. of Nigeria, Cleveland, OH. (p. 66)
Harry M. Clor, Kenyon College, Gambier, OH. (p. 76)
Bruce L. Edwards, Jr., Bowling Green State University, Bowling Green, OH. (p. 104)
David Forte, Cleveland State University, Cleveland, OH. (p. 114)
Janice J. Gabbert, Wright State University, Dayton, OH. (p. 119)
Lowell E. Gallaway, Ohio University, Athens, OH. (p. 120)
James R. Gaston, Franciscan University of Steubenville, Steubenville, OH. (p. 120)
John Green, University of Akron, Akron, OH. (p. 128)
Joshua Hall, Buckeye Institute for Public Policy Solutions, Columbus, OH. (p. 132)
Robert D. Hisrich, Case Western Reserve University, Cleveland, OH. (p. 143)
Candice Hoke, Cleveland State University, Cleveland, OH. (p. 144)
William B. Irvine, III, Wright State University, Dayton, OH. (p. 152)

Stephen Krason, Franciscan University of Steubenville, Steubenville, OH. **(p. 169)**
Robert A. Lawson, Capital University, Columbus, OH. **(p. 176)**
Jay H. Lehr, Environmental Education Enterprises, Ostrander, OH. **(p. 177)**
Loren E. Lomasky, Bowling Green State University, Bowling Green, OH. **(p. 182)**
David N. Mayer, Capital University Law School, Columbus, OH. **(p. 193)**
J. Huston McCulloch, Ohio State University, Columbus, OH. **(p. 194)**
Dennis D. Miller, Baldwin-Wallace College, Berea, OH. **(p. 201)**
Fred D. Miller, Jr., Bowling Green State University, Bowling Green, OH. **(p. 201)**
Michael A. Nelson, University of Akron, Akron, OH. **(p. 212)**
Ellen F. Paul, Bowling Green State University, Bowling Green, OH. **(p. 223)**
Jeffrey E. Paul, Bowling Green State University, Bowling Green, OH. **(p. 223)**
William S. Peirce, Case Western Reserve University, Cleveland, OH. **(p. 224)**
Scott Pullins, Ohio Taxpayers Association and OTA Foundation, Columbus, OH. **(p. 234)**
Susan Sarnoff, Ohio University, Athens, OH. **(p. 250)**
Rick Schatz, National Coalition for the Protection of Children and Families, Cincinnati, OH. **(p. 252)**
Peter W. Schramm, John M. Ashbrook Center for Public Affairs, Ashland, OH. **(p. 254)**
Larry Schweikart, University of Dayton, Dayton, OH. **(p. 255)**
John C. Soper, John Carroll University, University Heights, OH. **(p. 266)**
Samuel R. Staley, Buckeye Institute for Public Policy Solutions, Columbus, OH. **(p. 268)**
James A. Stever, University of Cincinnati, Hamilton, OH. **(p. 269)**
Rebecca A. Thacker, Ohio University, Athens, OH. **(p. 276)**
Richard Vedder, Ohio University, Athens, OH. **(p. 284)**
John C. Willke, Life Issues Institute, Inc., Cincinnati, OH. **(p. 295)**
David Zanotti, Ohio Roundtable, Strongsville, OH. **(p. 301)**

ORGANIZATIONS

John M. Ashbrook Center for Public Affairs, Ashland, OH. **(p. 640)**
Buckeye Institute for Public Policy Solutions, Columbus, OH. **(p. 643)**
National Coalition for the Protection of Children & Families, Cincinnati, OH. **(p. 698)**
Ohio Roundtable, Solon, OH. **(p. 707)**
Ohio Taxpayers Association, Columbus, OH. **(p. 707)**
Social Philosophy and Policy Center, Bowling Green, OH. **(p. 719)**

OKLAHOMA

EXPERTS

Andrew I. Cohen, University of Oklahoma, Norman, OK. **(p. 77)**
David Dunn, Oklahoma Family Policy Council, Bethany, OK. **(p. 100)**
Brandon Dutcher, Oklahoma Council of Public Affairs, Oklahoma City, OK. **(p. 101)**
Bertil L. Hanson, Oklahoma State University, Stillwater, OK. **(p. 134)**
Michael L. Jestes, Oklahoma Family Policy Council, Bethany, OK. **(p. 154)**
Dennis E. Logue, University of Oklahoma, Norman, OK. **(p. 182)**
Brett A. Magbee, Oklahoma Council of Public Affairs, Oklahoma City, OK. **(p. 186)**
R. Marc Nuttle, Norman, OK. **(p. 216)**
Paul A. Rahe, University of Tulsa, Tulsa, OK. **(p. 236)**
W. Robert Reed, University of Oklahoma, Norman, OK. **(p. 238)**
Stephen Sloan, University of Oklahoma, Norman, OK. **(p. 262)**
Kenneth Wood, The Oklahoma Christian Coalition, Oklahoma City, OK. **(p. 298)**

ORGANIZATIONS

Oklahoma Council of Public Affairs, Inc., Oklahoma City, OK. **(p. 707)**
Oklahoma Family Policy Council, Bethany, OK. **(p. 707)**

OREGON

EXPERTS

Theodore David Abram, American Institute for Full Employment, Klamath Falls, OR. **(p. 34)**
Anton Andereggen, Lewis and Clark College, Portland, OR. **(p. 37)**
Sammy Basu, Willamette University, Salem, OR. **(p. 47)**
Steve Buckstein, Cascade Policy Institute, Portland, OR. **(p. 65)**
John A. Charles, Cascade Policy Institute, Portland, OR. **(p. 72)**
William Conerly, Conerly Consulting, Portland, OR. **(p. 79)**
John W. Courtney, American Institute for Full Employment, Klamath Falls, OR. **(p. 83)**
Fred W. Decker, Mount Hood Society, Corvallis, OR. **(p. 91)**
Thompson Mason Faller, University of Portland, Portland, OR. **(p. 109)**
Michael Howden, Stronger Families for Oregon, Salem, OR. **(p. 147)**
James Huffman, Lewis and Clark Law School, Portland, OR. **(p. 148)**
Michael Kellman, University of Oregon, Eugene, OR. **(p. 160)**
Robert Mandel, Lewis and Clark College, Portland, OR. **(p. 188)**
William Moshofsky, Oregonians in Action Legal Center, Tigard, OR. **(p. 208)**
Frank Nims, Oregonians in Action, Tigard, OR. **(p. 214)**
Randal O'Toole, Thoreau Institute, Bandon, OR. **(p. 217)**
Anthony Rufolo, Portland State University, Portland, OR. **(p. 246)**
Russ Walker, Citizens for a Sound Economy, Keizer, OR. **(p. 287)**
Kurt T. Weber, Cascade Policy Institute, Portland, OR. **(p. 290)**
Nick Weller, Cascade Policy Institute, Portland, OR. **(p. 292)**

ORGANIZATIONS

American Institute for Full Employment, Klamath Falls, OR. **(p. 635)**
Cascade Policy Institute, Portland, OR. **(p. 645)**
Oregon Citizens for a Sound Economy, Keizer, OR. **(p. 707)**
Oregonians In Action, Tigard, OR. **(p. 708)**
Oregonians In Action Legal Center, Tigard, OR. **(p. 708)**
Oregons Taxpayers United Educational Foundation, Clackamas, OR. **(p. 708)**
Oregons Taxpayers United PAC, Clackamas, OR. **(p. 709)**
Stronger Families for Oregon, Salem, OR. **(p. 720)**
Thoreau Institute, Bandon, OR. **(p. 723)**

PENNSYLVANIA

EXPERTS

Fran Bevan, Eagle Forum of Pennsylvania, North Huntingdon, PA. **(p. 53)**
Stephen J. Blank, U. S. Army War College, Carlisle, PA. **(p. 54)**
Matthew J. Brouillette, The Commonwealth Foundation, Harrisburg, PA. **(p. 62)**
James H. Broussard, Citizens Against Higher Taxes, Hershey, PA. **(p. 63)**
T. Patrick Burke, St. Joseph's University, Wynnewood, PA. **(p. 65)**
James B. Burnham, Duquesne University, Pittsburgh, PA. **(p. 66)**
George F. Cahill, The "Pride in America" Company, Pittsburgh, PA. **(p. 67)**
Pradyumna S. Chauhan, Arcadia University, Glenside, PA. **(p. 73)**

Robert Chitester, Palmer R. Chitester Fund, Erie, PA. **(p. 73)**
Bernard L. Cohen, University of Pittsburgh, Pittsburgh, PA. **(p. 77)**
Patricia M. Danzon, University of Pennsylvania, Philadelphia, PA. **(p. 88)**
William T. Devlin, Urban Family Council, Philadelphia, PA. **(p. 94)**
John J. DiIulio, Jr., University of Pennsylvania, Philadelphia, PA. **(p. 95)**
Daniel J. Dougherty, Pennsylvania Federation-Citizens for Educational Freedom, Philadelphia, PA. **(p. 97)**
William C. Dunkelberg, National Federation of Independent Business, Wynnewood, PA. **(p. 100)**
Murray Friedman, American Jewish Committee, Philadelphia, PA. **(p. 117)**
James Fyfe, Temple University, Philadelphia, PA. **(p. 119)**
Michael Geer, Pennsylvania Family Institute, Harrisburg, PA. **(p. 122)**
Charlie Gerow, Quantum Communications, Harrisburg, PA. **(p. 123)**
Dennis A. Giorno, REACH Alliance, Harrisburg, PA. **(p. 124)**
Paul Gottfried, Elizabethtown College, Elizabethtown, PA. **(p. 127)**
Charles Greenwalt, II, Susquehanna Valley Center for Public Policy, Hershey, PA. **(p. 129)**
Grant R. Gulibon, The Commonwealth Foundation, Harrisburg, PA. **(p. 130)**
Thor L. Halvorssen, The Foundation for Individual Rights in Education, Philadelphia, PA. **(p. 132)**
Paul Y. Hammond, University of Pittsburgh, Pittsburgh, PA. **(p. 133)**
Charles L. Harper, John Templeton Foundation, Radnor, PA. **(p. 135)**
Jake Haulk, Allegheny Institute for Public Policy, Pittsburgh, PA. **(p. 137)**
William Anthony Hay, Foreign Policy Research Institute, Philadelphia, PA. **(p. 138)**
Lowman Henry, Lincoln Institute of Public Opinion Research, Inc., Harrisburg, PA. **(p. 140)**
John Hillen, Foreign Policy Research Institute, Philadephia, PA. **(p. 142)**
Byron Johnson, University of Pennsylvania, Philadelphia, PA. **(p. 155)**
Paul Kengor, Grove City College, Grove City, PA. **(p. 161)**
Synja P. Kim, Institute for Corean-American Studies, Blue Bell, PA. **(p. 163)**
John Kincaid, Lafayette College, Easton, PA. **(p. 163)**
David W. Kirkpatrick, Citizens for Educational Freedom, Douglassville, PA. **(p. 164)**
James J. Kirschke, Villanova University, Villanova, PA. **(p. 164)**
Alan Charles Kors, The Foundation for Individual Rights in Education, Philadelphia, PA. **(p. 167)**
Melvin A. Kulbicki, York College of Pennsylvania, York, PA. **(p. 170)**
Howard Kunreuther, University of Pennsylvania, Philadelphia, PA. **(p. 170)**
Peter Linneman, University of Pennsylvania, Philadelphia, PA. **(p. 181)**
Hsien-Tung Liu, Bloomsburg University, Bloomsburg, PA. **(p. 181)**
Alan Luxemberg, Foreign Policy Research Institute, Philadelphia, PA. **(p. 184)**
Hafeez Malik, Villanova University, Villanova, PA. **(p. 187)**
Anthony M. Matteo, Elizabethtown College, Elizabethtown, PA. **(p. 191)**
W. Wesley McDonald, Elizabethtown College, Elizabethtown, PA. **(p. 195)**
Joseph P. McHugh, Reed Smith LLP, Pittsburgh, PA. **(p. 196)**
Allan H. Meltzer, Carnegie Mellon University, Pittsburgh, PA. **(p. 199)**
Steven Metz, U. S. Army War College Strategic Studies Institute, Carlisle Barracks, PA. **(p. 200)**
John H. Moore, Grove City College, Grove City, PA. **(p. 206)**
Michael Noonan, Foreign Policy Research Institute, Philadelphia, PA. **(p. 214)**
Herbert R. Northrup, University of Pennsylvania, Haverford, PA. **(p. 215)**
Jim Panyard, Pennsylvania Manufacturer's Association, Harrisburg, PA. **(p. 221)**
Mark V. Pauly, University of Pennsylvania, Philadelphia, PA. **(p. 223)**
Sanford Pinsker, Franklin and Marshall College, Lancaster, PA. **(p. 229)**
Daniel Pipes, Middle East Forum, Philadelphia, PA. **(p. 229)**

David G. Post, Temple University School of Law, Philadelphia, PA. **(p. 231)**
Gary M. Quinlivan, Center for Economic and Policy Education, Latrobe, PA. **(p. 234)**
Michael Radu, Foreign Policy Research Institute, Philadelphia, PA. **(p. 235)**
Charles Rubin, Duquesne University, Pittsburgh, PA. **(p. 246)**
David W. Saxe, Pennsylvania State University, University Park, PA. **(p. 251)**
Arthur J. Schwartz, John Templeton Foundation, Radnor, PA. **(p. 254)**
Hans F. Sennholz, Grove City College, Grove City, PA. **(p. 257)**
Colleen Sheehan, Villanova University, Villanova, PA. **(p. 258)**
Lawrence Sherman, University of Pennsylvania, Philadelphia, PA. **(p. 259)**
Harvey Sicherman, Foreign Policy Research Institute, Philadelphia, PA. **(p. 259)**
Aaron Siegel, Freedoms Foundation at Valley Forge, Valley Forge, PA. **(p. 259)**
John A. Sparks, Grove City College, Grove City, PA. **(p. 266)**
Ann C. Thomson, The Commonwealth Foundation, Harrisburg, PA. **(p. 278)**
Vladislav Todorov, University of Pennsylvania, Philadelphia, PA. **(p. 279)**
Bradley C. S. Watson, Saint Vincent College, Latrobe, PA. **(p. 290)**
Betty Jean Wolfe, Urban Family Council, Philadephia, PA. **(p. 297)**

ORGANIZATIONS

Allegheny Institute for Public Policy, Pittsburgh, PA. **(p. 629)**
Center for Economic and Policy Education, Latrobe, PA. **(p. 646)**
Citizens Against Higher Taxes, Hershey, PA. **(p. 654)**
The Commonwealth Foundation, Harrisburg, PA. **(p. 657)**
Foreign Policy Research Institute, Philadelphia, PA. **(p. 667)**
The Foundation for Individual Rights in Education, Philadelphia, PA. **(p. 668)**
Freedoms Foundation at Valley Forge, Valley Forge, PA. **(p. 671)**
Institute for Corean-American Studies, Blue Bell, PA. **(p. 680)**
Lincoln Institute of Public Opinion Research, Harrisburg, PA. **(p. 689)**
Pennsylvania Family Institute, Harrisburg, PA. **(p. 711)**
Shenango Institute for Public Policy, Grove City, PA. **(p. 718)**
Susquehanna Valley Center for Public Policy, Hershey, PA. **(p. 721)**
Urban Family Council, Philadelphia, PA. **(p. 726)**

RHODE ISLAND

EXPERTS

Richard T. Colgan, Bridgewater State College, Warwick, RI. **(p. 78)**
Thomas M. Nichols, U. S. Naval War College, Newport, RI. **(p. 213)**
Mackubin T. Owens, U. S. Naval War College, Newport, RI. **(p. 220)**
Kevin Vigilante, Rumford, RI. **(p. 285)**

SOUTH CAROLINA

EXPERTS

John T. Addison, University of South Carolina, Columbia, SC. **(p. 34)**
John Cobin, Montauk Financial Group, Greenville, SC. **(p. 76)**
Gerry Dickinson, South Carolina Policy Council, Columbia, SC. **(p. 95)**
Reuben Greenberg, Charleston Police Department, Charleston, SC. **(p. 128)**
Steven E. Grosby, Clemson University, Clemson, SC. **(p. 129)**
Thomas R. Haggard, University of South Carolina, Columbia, SC. **(p. 132)**
Scott E. Harrington, University of South Carolina, Columbia, SC. **(p. 135)**
Mark Y. Herring, Winthrop University, Rock Hill, SC. **(p. 140)**

Cotton M. Lindsay, Clemson University, Clemson, SC. **(p. 181)**
J. J. Mahoney, Diversified Consultants, Mount Pleasant, SC. **(p. 187)**
Bobby McCormick, Clemson University, Clemson, SC. **(p. 194)**
Edward T. McMullen, Jr., South Carolina Policy Council, Columbia, SC. **(p. 197)**
Paul C. Peterson, Coastal Carolina University, Conway, SC. **(p. 227)**
Oran P. Smith, Palmetto Family Council, Columbia, SC. **(p. 264)**
Lawrence B. Sulc, Nathan Hale Institute, St. Helena Island, SC. **(p. 271)**
David Swindell, Clemson University, Clemson, SC. **(p. 273)**
Richard L. Walker, University of South Carolina, Columbia, SC. **(p. 287)**
John T. Warner, Clemson University, Clemson, SC. **(p. 289)**
Donald V. Weatherman, Erskine College, Due West, SC. **(p. 290)**
Clinton H. Whitehurst, Jr., Clemson University, Clemson, SC. **(p. 294)**
Clyde N. Wilson, University of South Carolina, Columbia, SC. **(p. 296)**
Bruce Yandle, Clemson University, Clemson, SC. **(p. 300)**

ORGANIZATIONS

Center for Policy and Legal Studies, Clemson, SC. **(p. 649)**
Palmetto Family Council, Columbia, SC. **(p. 710)**
South Carolina Policy Council, Columbia, SC. **(p. 719)**

SOUTH DAKOTA

EXPERTS

Kay Glover, Citizens for Choice in Education, Sturgis, SD. **(p. 125)**
William D. Richardson, University of South Dakota, Vermillion, SD. **(p. 239)**
Jerry K. Sweeney, South Dakota State University, Brookings, SD. **(p. 273)**
Ron F. Williamson, Great Plains Public Policy Institute, Sioux Falls, SD. **(p. 295)**

ORGANIZATIONS

Great Plains Public Policy Institute, Sioux Falls, SD. **(p. 673)**
South Dakota Family Policy Council, Sioux Falls, SD. **(p. 719)**

TENNESSEE

EXPERTS

Dedrick Briggs, Charter School Resource Center of Tennessee, Memphis, TN. **(p. 61)**
Kay Brooks, TnHomeEd.com, Nashville, TN. **(p. 62)**
Priscilla Caine, Children First Tennessee, Chattanooga, TN. **(p. 67)**
J. R. Clark, University of Tennessee, Chattanooga, Chattanooga, TN. **(p. 75)**
Howard Cochran, Jr., Belmont University, Nashville, TN. **(p. 77)**
John F. Copper, Rhodes College, Memphis, TN. **(p. 82)**
William F. Ford, Middle Tennessee State University, Murfreesboro, TN. **(p. 114)**
Kenneth M. Holland, University of Memphis, Memphis, TN. **(p. 144)**
Walter Jewell, Professional Educators of Tennessee, Franklin, TN. **(p. 154)**
Richard D. Land, Ethics and Religious Liberty Commission, Nashville, TN. **(p. 173)**
Deryl W. Martin, Tennessee Technological University, Cookeville, TN. **(p. 190)**
William R. Marty, University of Memphis, Memphis, TN. **(p. 190)**
Wilfred M. McClay, University of Tennessee, Chattanooga, Chattanooga, TN. **(p. 193)**
Andrew A. Michta, Rhodes College, Memphis, TN. **(p. 201)**
E. Haavi Morreim, University of Tennessee, Memphis, Memphis, TN. **(p. 206)**

Michael J. Neth, Middle Tennessee State University, Murfreesboro, TN. **(p. 213)**
Bobbie Patray, Eagle Forum of Tennessee, Nashville, TN. **(p. 222)**
David A. Patterson, University of Memphis, Memphis, TN. **(p. 223)**
Claude Pressnell, Tennessee Independent Colleges and Universities, Nashville, TN. **(p. 233)**
John W. Robbins, Trinity Foundation, Unicoi, TN. **(p. 241)**
T. Alexander Smith, University of Tennessee, Knoxville, Knoxville, TN. **(p. 264)**
J. E. Stone, East Tennessee State University, Johnson City, TN. **(p. 270)**

ORGANIZATIONS

Children First Tennessee, Chattanooga, TN. **(p. 652)**
Education Consumers Consultants Network, Johnson City, TN. **(p. 660)**

TEXAS

EXPERTS

Robert Aguirre, San Antonio, TX. **(p. 35)**
Ryan C. Amacher, University of Texas, Arlington, Arlington, TX. **(p. 37)**
Ford A. Anderson, State Policy Network, Dallas, TX. **(p. 38)**
Martin Angell, A Choice for Every Child Foundation, Dallas, TX. **(p. 39)**
David Barton, WallBuilders, Inc., Aledo, TX. **(p. 46)**
Samuel Bostaph, University of Dallas, Irving, TX. **(p. 57)**
Robert L. Bradley, Jr., Institute for Energy Research, Houston, TX. **(p. 59)**
William Breit, Trinity University, San Antonio, TX. **(p. 60)**
H. Sterling Burnett, National Center for Policy Analysis, Dallas, TX. **(p. 65)**
John S. Butler, University of Texas, Austin, TX. **(p. 66)**
Dan Byfield, American Land Foundation, Taylor, TX. **(p. 67)**
James B. Cardle, Texas Citizen Action Network, Austin, TX. **(p. 69)**
Bartlett D. Cleland, Institute for Policy Innovation, Lewisville, TX. **(p. 76)**
Boyd D. Collier, Tarleton State University, Stephenville, TX. **(p. 78)**
Richard H. Collins, Children's Education Fund, Dallas, TX. **(p. 78)**
John Colyandro, Texas Conservative Coalition, Austin, TX. **(p. 79)**
Lawrence Cranberg, Austin, TX. **(p. 85)**
Leo Paul S. de Alvarez, University of Dallas, Irving, TX. **(p. 89)**
Richard J. Dougherty, University of Dallas, Irving, TX. **(p. 97)**
John Jay Douglass, University of Houston Law Center, Houston, TX. **(p. 97)**
Dennis J. Dunn, Southwest Texas State University, San Marcos, TX. **(p. 100)**
Barbara Elliott, Center for Renewal, Houston, TX. **(p. 105)**
W. Winston Elliott, III, Center for the American Idea, Houston, TX. **(p. 106)**
Burton W. Folsom, Jr., Center for the American Idea, Houston, TX. **(p. 114)**
George Friedman, Stratfor.com, Austin, TX. **(p. 117)**
Eirik Furubotn, Texas A&M University, College Station, TX. **(p. 119)**
Tom Giovanetti, Institute for Policy Innovation, Lewisville, TX. **(p. 124)**
Norval D. Glenn, University of Texas, Austin, TX. **(p. 125)**
John C. Goodman, National Center for Policy Analysis, Dallas, TX. **(p. 126)**
Lino A. Graglia, University of Texas, Austin, TX. **(p. 128)**
John R. Hanson, II, Texas A&M University, College Station, TX. **(p. 134)**
Edward J. Harpham, University of Texas, Dallas, Richardson, TX. **(p. 135)**
David Hartman, The Lone Star Foundation, Austin, TX. **(p. 136)**
Ronald L. Hatchett, University of St. Thomas, Houston, TX. **(p. 137)**
Joseph Horn, University of Texas, Austin, TX. **(p. 146)**
Kerri Houston, American Conservative Union Field Office, Dallas, TX. **(p. 147)**

Dennis S. Ippolito, Southern Methodist University, Dallas, TX. **(p. 152)**
John Kain, University of Texas, Dallas, Richardson, TX. **(p. 157)**
Francis X. Kane, Strategy, Technology and Space, Inc., San Antonio, TX. **(p. 157)**
Jane Kilgore, Austin CEO Foundation, Austin, TX. **(p. 163)**
Anthony K. Knopp, University of Texas, Brownsville, Brownsville, TX. **(p. 166)**
Robert C. Koons, University of Texas, Austin, TX. **(p. 167)**
Stacey Ladd, Worth the Wait, Pampa, TX. **(p. 171)**
Matthew Ladner, Children First America, Austin, TX. **(p. 171)**
Juan Lara, Hispanic Council for Reform and Educational Options, San Antonio, TX. **(p. 174)**
Stanley J. Liebowitz, University of Texas, Dallas, Richardson, TX. **(p. 180)**
Thomas K. Lindsay, University of Dallas, Irving, TX. **(p. 181)**
Edward J. Lopez, University of North Texas, Denton, TX. **(p. 183)**
Merrill Matthews, Jr., Institute for Policy Innovation, Lewisville, TX. **(p. 192)**
Joe S. McIlheney, Jr., Medical Institute for Sexual Health, Austin, TX. **(p. 196)**
Roger E. Meiners, University of Texas, Arlington, Arlington, TX. **(p. 198)**
John Merrifield, University of Texas, San Antonio, San Antonio, TX. **(p. 199)**
Brant S. Mittler, Texas Public Policy Foundation, San Antonio, TX. **(p. 204)**
Matt Moore, National Center for Policy Analysis, Dallas, TX. **(p. 206)**
William Murchison, Baylor University, Waco, TX. **(p. 209)**
Jeremiah O'Keeffe, Plano, TX. **(p. 217)**
Patsy O'Neill, Charter School Resource Center of Texas, San Antonio, TX. **(p. 217)**
Marvin Olasky, University of Texas, Austin, TX. **(p. 218)**
Allan E. Parker, Jr., Texas Justice Foundation, San Antonio, TX. **(p. 221)**
Christine Patterson, Texas Public Policy Foundation, San Antonio, TX. **(p. 223)**
Jordan Paust, University of Houston Law Center, Houston, TX. **(p. 223)**
Svetozar Pejovich, Texas A&M University, Dallas, TX. **(p. 224)**
David R. Pinkus, Small Business United of Texas, Austin, TX. **(p. 229)**
William H. Reid, Horseshoe, TX. **(p. 238)**
Andrew Rettenmaier, Texas A&M University, College Station, TX. **(p. 239)**
John E. Rocha, Sr., Center for the American Idea, Houston, TX. **(p. 242)**
Doug Rogers, Association of Texas Professional Educators, Austin, TX. **(p. 243)**
Timothy P. Roth, University of Texas, El Paso, El Paso, TX. **(p. 244)**
John Ruszkiewicz, University of Texas, Austin, TX. **(p. 247)**
Thomas R. Saving, Texas A&M University, College Station, TX. **(p. 251)**
Larry J. Sechrest, Sul Ross State University, Alpine, TX. **(p. 255)**
Kelly Shackelford, Free Market Foundation, Plano, TX. **(p. 257)**
Michael D. Stroup, Stephen F. Austin State University, Nacogdoches, TX. **(p. 270)**
Michael Sullivan, Texas Public Policy Foundation, Austin, TX. **(p. 272)**
Roy E. Thoman, West Texas A & M University, Canyon, TX. **(p. 277)**
Ewa M. Thompson, Rice University, Houston, TX. **(p. 277)**
Glen E. Thurow, University of Dallas, Irving, TX. **(p. 279)**
Lawrence A. Uzzell, Keston Institute, Waxahachie, TX. **(p. 283)**
Terry W. Van Allen, Kemah, TX. **(p. 283)**
Peggy Venable, Texas Citizens for a Sound Economy, Austin, TX. **(p. 284)**
Ben A. Wallis, Jr., Institute for Human Rights, San Antonio, TX. **(p. 287)**
Donna Watson, Children First America, Austin, TX. **(p. 290)**
Michael W. Watson, Children First America, Austin, TX. **(p. 290)**
Thomas G. West, University of Dallas, Irving, TX. **(p. 293)**

ORGANIZATIONS

Bellwether Forum, Houston, TX. **(p. 642)**
Center for Renewal, Houston, TX. **(p. 650)**
Center for the American Idea, Houston, TX. **(p. 651)**
Children's Education Fund, Dallas, TX. **(p. 653)**
Free Market Foundation, Plano, TX. **(p. 670)**
Hispanic Council for Reform and Educational Options, San Antonio, TX. **(p. 676)**
Institute for Energy Research, Houston, TX. **(p. 680)**
Institute for Policy Innovation, Lewisville, TX. **(p. 682)**
Liberty Matters, Taylor, TX. **(p. 689)**
The Lone Star Foundation and Report, Austin, TX. **(p. 690)**
National Center for Policy Analysis, Dallas, TX. **(p. 697)**
Texas Citizens for a Sound Economy, Austin, TX. **(p. 722)**
Texas Conservative Coalition, Austin, TX. **(p. 722)**
Texas Conservative Coalition Research Institute, Austin, TX. **(p. 723)**
Texas Justice Foundation, San Antonio, TX. **(p. 723)**
Texas Public Policy Foundation, San Antonio, TX. **(p. 723)**
WallBuilders, Aledo, TX. **(p. 726)**

UTAH

EXPERTS

Paul Cassell, University of Utah, Salt Lake City, UT. **(p. 72)**
Bryce J. Christensen, Southern Utah University, Cedar City, UT. **(p. 74)**
Elisa Clements, Education Excellence Utah, Salt Lake City, UT. **(p. 76)**
Ralph C. Hancock, Brigham Young University, Provo, UT. **(p. 133)**
Roberta Herzberg, Utah State University, Logan, UT. **(p. 141)**
Mike Jerman, Utah Taxpayers Association, Salt Lake City, UT. **(p. 154)**
Michael W. McConnell, University of Utah, Salt Lake City, UT. **(p. 194)**
Paul T. Mero, The Sutherland Institute, Salt Lake City, UT. **(p. 199)**
Anthony A. Peacock, Utah State University, Logan, UT. **(p. 224)**
Carolyn Sharette, Children First Utah, Salt Lake City, UT. **(p. 258)**
Richard Sherlock, Utah State University, Logan, UT. **(p. 259)**
Randy T. Simmons, Utah State University, Logan, UT. **(p. 260)**
Richard B. Wirthlin, Wirthlin Worldwide, South Jordan, UT. **(p. 296)**

ORGANIZATIONS

Children First Utah, Salt Lake City, UT. **(p. 653)**
The Sutherland Institute, Salt Lake City, UT. **(p. 721)**

VERMONT

EXPERTS

Frank H. Armstrong, University of Vermont, Burlington, VT. **(p. 40)**
Robert G. Kaufman, University of Vermont, Burlington, VT. **(p. 159)**
John McClaughry, Ethan Allen Institute, Concord, VT. **(p. 193)**
Laurie Morrow, Montpelier, VT. **(p. 207)**

ORGANIZATIONS

Ethan Allen Institute, Concord, VT. **(p. 629)**

VIRGINIA

EXPERTS

Henry J. Abraham, Charlottesville, VA. **(p. 34)**
Jane Abraham, Susan B. Anthony List, Alexandria, VA. **(p. 34)**
Robert A. Anthony, George Mason University School of Law, Arlington, VA. **(p. 39)**
David J. Armor, George Mason University, Fairfax, VA. **(p. 40)**
Nigel Ashford, Institute for Humane Studies at George Mason University, Arlington, VA. **(p. 41)**
Thomas C. Atwood, National Council For Adoption, Alexandria, VA. **(p. 41)**
Alex Avery, Hudson Institute, Staunton, VA. **(p. 41)**
Dennis T. Avery, Hudson Institute, Churchville, VA. **(p. 42)**
Lawson R. Bader, Mercatus Center at George Mason University, Arlington, VA. **(p. 42)**
Brent Baker, Media Research Center, Alexandria, VA. **(p. 43)**
Steve Baldwin, Fairfax, VA. **(p. 44)**
Whitney L. Ball, DonorsTrust, Alexandria, VA. **(p. 44)**
Bruce R. Bartlett, National Center for Policy Analysis, Great Falls, VA. **(p. 46)**
Gary L. Bauer, Campaign for Working Families, Arlington, VA. **(p. 47)**
Gregory S. Baylor, Center for Law and Religious Freedom, Annandale, VA. **(p. 47)**
James T. Bennett, George Mason University, Fairfax, VA. **(p. 51)**
John E. Berthoud, National Taxpayers Union, Alexandria, VA. **(p. 52)**
Lillian BeVier, University of Virginia, Charlottesville, VA. **(p. 53)**
Dick Bishirjian, YorktownUniversity.com, Norfolk, VA. **(p. 53)**
Wayman R. Bishop, The Family Foundation of Virginia, Richmond, VA. **(p. 53)**
Paul H. Blackman, NRA Institute for Legislative Action, Fairfax, VA. **(p. 54)**
Morton Blackwell, Leadership Institute, Arlington, VA. **(p. 54)**
Kenneth Boehm, National Legal and Policy Center, Falls Church, VA. **(p. 56)**
Peter J. Boettke, James M. Buchanan Center for Political Economy, Fairfax, VA. **(p. 56)**
Paul J. Bonicelli, Patrick Henry College, Purcellville, VA. **(p. 57)**
Donald J. Boudreaux, George Mason University, Fairfax, VA. **(p. 58)**
Karol Boudreaux, George Mason University School of Law, Arlington, VA. **(p. 58)**
L. Brent Bozell, III, Media Research Center, Alexandria, VA. **(p. 59)**
Jennifer C. Braceras, Independent Women's Forum, Arlington, VA. **(p. 59)**
Pat Bradburn, Virginians for Property Rights, Catharpin, VA. **(p. 59)**
Demian Brady, National Taxpayers Union Foundation, Alexandria, VA. **(p. 59)**
Gordon L. Brady, Center for the Study of Public Choice, Fairfax, VA. **(p. 60)**
Christian N. Braunlich, Thomas Jefferson Institute for Public Policy, Alexandria, VA. **(p. 60)**
Mychele Brickner, Clare Boothe Luce Policy Institute, Herndon, VA. **(p. 61)**
Charles Brooks, The Strategy Group, Arlington, VA. **(p. 62)**
Martin D. Brown, Richmond, VA. **(p. 63)**
James M. Buchanan, Center for the Study of Public Choice, Fairfax, VA. **(p. 64)**
Francis H. Buckley, George Mason University School of Law, Arlington, VA. **(p. 64)**
David Burton, Argus Group, Alexandria, VA. **(p. 66)**
Bruce N. Cameron, National Right to Work Legal Defense Foundation, Springfield, VA. **(p. 68)**
Nigel M. de S. Cameron, Institute for Humane Studies at George Mason University, Arlington, VA. **(p. 68)**
David Caprara, The Empowerment Network, Fredericksburg, VA. **(p. 69)**

Walton Francis, Fairfax, VA. **(p. 115)**
Matthew J. Franck, Radford University, Radford, VA. **(p. 115)**
Neal B. Freeman, Blackwell Corporation, Vienna, VA. **(p. 116)**
Chris Freund, The Family Foundation of Virginia, Richmond, VA. **(p. 117)**
Dana Joel Gattuso, Competitive Enterprise Institute, Alexandria, VA. **(p. 121)**
Deanna R. Gelak, Family and Medical Leave Act Technical Corrections Coalition,
    Springfield, VA. **(p. 122)**
David Gersten, Center for Equal Opportunity, Sterling, VA. **(p. 123)**
Roberta M. Gilbert, Center for the Study of Human Systems, Falls Church, VA. **(p. 123)**
Stefan Gleason, National Right to Work Legal Defense Foundation, Springfield, VA.
    (p. 124)
Stephen O. Goodrick, National Right to Work Committee, Springfield, VA. **(p. 126)**
Wendy Lee Gramm, Mercatus Center at George Mason University, Arlington, VA. **(p. 128)**
Frank Gregorsky, Exacting Editorial Services, Vienna, VA. **(p. 129)**
Os Guinness, Trinity Forum, McLean, VA. **(p. 130)**
James M. Hamilton, For Our Grandchildren, Fairfax, VA. **(p. 133)**
Alam E. Hammad, Alexandria, VA. **(p. 133)**
Robin Hanson, George Mason University, Fairfax, VA. **(p. 134)**
Charles G. Hardin, Council for Government Reform, Arlington, VA. **(p. 135)**
Christopher C. Harmon, Marine Corps University, Quantico, VA. **(p. 135)**
John C. Harrison, University of Virginia, Charlottesville, VA. **(p. 136)**
Louis W. Hensler III, Regent University, Virginia Beach, VA. **(p. 140)**
Paul Henze, Washington, VA. **(p. 140)**
Jack High, George Mason University, Arlington, VA. **(p. 142)**
James E. Hinish, Jr., Regent University, Williamsburg, VA. **(p. 143)**
E. D. Hirsch, Jr., Core Knowledge Foundation, Charlottesville, VA. **(p. 143)**
Scott Hogenson, *CNSNews.com*, Alexandria, VA. **(p. 144)**
Robert Holland, Lexington Institute, Arlington, VA. **(p. 144)**
Jacob G. Hornberger, Future of Freedom Foundation, Fairfax, VA. **(p. 146)**
Donna Rice Hughes, Enough Is Enough, Great Falls, VA. **(p. 149)**
James D. Hunter, University of Virginia, Charlottesville, VA. **(p. 149)**
Earl W. Jackson, Sr., Samaritan Project, Chesapeake, VA. **(p. 152)**
Bradley P. Jacob, Regent University, Virginia Beach, VA. **(p. 152)**
Paul Jacob, Citizens in Charge and Citizens in Charge Foundation, Woodbridge, VA.
    (p. 153)
Charles W. Jarvis, United Seniors Association, Fairfax, VA. **(p. 153)**
Mark N. Katz, George Mason University, Fairfax, VA. **(p. 158)**
David Keating, National Taxpayers Union, Alexandria, VA. **(p. 159)**
David Kendrick, National Legal and Policy Center, Falls Church, VA. **(p. 161)**
Kate Kennedy, Independent Women's Forum, Arlington, VA. **(p. 162)**
Christopher J. Klicka, Home School Legal Defense Association, Purcellville, VA. **(p. 165)**
Lisa M. Korsak, Mercatus Center at George Mason University, Arlington, VA. **(p. 167)**
Michael Krauss, George Mason University School of Law, Arlington, VA. **(p. 169)**
Jo Kwong, Atlas Economic Research Foundation, Fairfax, VA. **(p. 171)**
Raymond J. LaJeunesse, Jr., National Right to Work Legal Defense Foundation,
    Springfield, VA. **(p. 172)**
George Landrith, Frontiers of Freedom Institute, Fairfax, VA. **(p. 173)**
Wayne LaPierre, National Rifle Association, Fairfax, VA. **(p. 174)**
James W. Lark, III, University of Virginia, Charlottesville, VA. **(p. 174)**
Randy Larsen, ANSER Institute for Homeland Security, Arlington, VA. **(p. 174)**
Reed Larson, National Right to Work Committee, Springfield, VA. **(p. 175)**
Mark R. Levin, Landmark Legal Foundation, Herndon, VA. **(p. 178)**
Leonard P. Liggio, Atlas Economic Research Foundation, Fairfax, VA. **(p. 180)**

Andrew F. Quinlan, Center for Freedom and Prosperity, Alexandria, VA. **(p. 234)**
Rob Raffety, Mercatus Center at George Mason University, Arlington, VA. **(p. 235)**
Richard W. Rahn, NOVECON, Alexandria, VA. **(p. 236)**
Patricia Reed, Independent Women's Forum, Arlington, VA. **(p. 237)**
Joseph D. Reid, Jr., George Mason University, Fairfax, VA. **(p. 238)**
Patrick Reilly, Cardinal Newman Society, Falls Church, VA. **(p. 238)**
Steven Rhoads, University of Virginia, Charlottesville, VA. **(p. 239)**
Robert C. Richardson, High Frontier, Arlington, VA. **(p. 239)**
Aldona Robbins, Fiscal Associates, Arlington, VA. **(p. 241)**
Gary Robbins, Fiscal Associates, Arlington, VA. **(p. 241)**
J. Milnor Roberts, High Frontier, Arlington, VA. **(p. 241)**
Ron Robinson, Young America's Foundation, Herndon, VA. **(p. 242)**
Kathy Rothschild, The Leadership Institute, Arlington, VA. **(p. 244)**
Ronald D. Rotunda, George Mason University School of Law, Arlington, VA. **(p. 244)**
Mark E. Rush, Washington and Lee University, Lexington, VA. **(p. 247)**
Steven Alan Samson, Liberty University, Lynchburg, VA. **(p. 249)**
John F. Scalia, Greenberg Traurig, LLP, McLean, VA. **(p. 251)**
Suzanne Scholte, Defense Forum Foundation, Falls Church, VA. **(p. 254)**
Kurt Schuler, Arlington, VA. **(p. 254)**
Jay Sekulow, American Center for Law and Justice, Virginia Beach, VA. **(p. 256)**
Donald J. Senese, 60 Plus Association, Arlington, VA. **(p. 257)**
Pete Sepp, National Taxpayers Union, Alexandria, VA. **(p. 257)**
Amy L. Sherman, Hudson Institute, Charlottesville, VA. **(p. 259)**
Jack Shockey, Citizens for Property Rights, Hamilton, VA. **(p. 259)**
S. Fred Singer, Science and Environmental Policy Project, Arlington, VA. **(p. 260)**
J. Michael Smith, Home School Legal Defense Association, Purcellville, VA. **(p. 263)**
Ted J. Smith, III, Virginia Commonwealth University, Richmond, VA. **(p. 264)**
Vernon L. Smith, George Mason University, Arlington, VA. **(p. 264)**
Neil H. Snyder, University of Virginia, Charlottesville, VA. **(p. 265)**
Don Soifer, Lexington Institute, Arlington, VA. **(p. 265)**
Jacob Sullum, *Reason* Magazine, Fairfax, VA. **(p. 272)**
Joy Sweet, National Right to Read Foundation, The Plains, VA. **(p. 273)**
Alexander Tabarrok, Mercatus Center at George Mason University, Arlington, VA. **(p. 273)**
Bruce Taylor, National Law Center for Children and Families, Fairfax, VA. **(p. 274)**
John Taylor, Virginia Institute for Public Policy, Potomac Falls, VA. **(p. 274)**
Richard Teske, Strategic Advocacy, Arlington, VA. **(p. 275)**
Stephen Thayer, American Conservative Union, Alexandria, VA. **(p. 276)**
Loren B. Thompson, Lexington Institute, Arlington, VA. **(p. 278)**
Michael W. Thompson, Thomas Jefferson Institute for Public Policy, Springfield, VA. **(p. 278)**
Herbert W. Titus, Virginia Beach, VA. **(p. 279)**
Gordon Tullock, George Mason University School of Law, Arlington, VA. **(p. 281)**
Grace-Marie Turner, Galen Institute, Alexandria, VA. **(p. 281)**
Robert F. Turner, University of Virginia School of Law, Charlottesville, VA. **(p. 282)**
John Tuskey, Regent University, Virginia Beach, VA. **(p. 282)**
Lil Tuttle, Clare Boothe Luce Policy Institute, Herndon, VA. **(p. 282)**
R. Emmett Tyrrell, The American Alternative Foundation, Alexandria, VA. **(p. 282)**
Karen I. Vaughn, George Mason University, Fairfax, VA. **(p. 284)**
Balint Vazsonyi, Center for the American Founding, McLean, VA. **(p. 284)**
Melara Zyla Vickers, Independent Women's Forum, Arlington, VA. **(p. 285)**
Richard E. Wagner, George Mason University, Fairfax, VA. **(p. 286)**
Malcolm Wallop, Frontiers of Freedom Institute, Fairfax, VA. **(p. 288)**
Tom Washburne, Home School Legal Defense Association, Purcellville, VA. **(p. 289)**

ORGANIZATIONS

High Frontier, Arlington, VA. **(p. 676)**
Hispanic American Center for Economic Research, Fairfax, VA. **(p. 676)**
Home School Legal Defense Association, Purcellville, VA. **(p. 677)**
Independent Women's Forum, Arlington, VA. **(p. 679)**
Initiative and Referendum Institute, Leesburg, VA. **(p. 679)**
Institute for Humane Studies, Arlington, VA. **(p. 681)**
Thomas Jefferson Institute for Public Policy, Springfield, VA. **(p. 686)**
Justice Fellowship, Reston, VA. **(p. 687)**
Landmark Legal Foundation, Herndon, VA. **(p. 688)**
Leadership Institute, Arlington, VA. **(p. 688)**
Lexington Institute, Arlington, VA. **(p. 689)**
Clare Boothe Luce Policy Institute, Herndon, VA. **(p. 691)**
Media Research Center, Alexandria, VA **(p. 694)**
National Council for Adoption, Alexandria, VA. **(p. 698)**
National Defense Council Foundation, Alexandria, VA. **(p. 698)**
National Institute for Labor Relations Research, Springfield, VA. **(p. 699)**
National Institute for Public Policy, Fairfax, VA. **(p. 699)**
National Legal and Policy Center, Falls Church, VA. **(p. 700)**
National Legal Foundation, Virginia Beach, VA. **(p. 700)**
National Rifle Association, Fairfax, VA. **(p. 701)**
National Right to Read Foundation, The Plains, VA. **(p. 701)**
National Right to Work Committee, Springfield, VA. **(p. 702)**
National Right to Work Legal Defense Foundation, Springfield, VA. **(p. 702)**
National Taxpayers Union, Alexandria, VA. **(p. 703)**
National Taxpayers Union Foundation, Alexandria, VA. **(p. 703)**
Population Research Institute, Front Royal, VA. **(p. 712)**
Public Service Research Council, Vienna, VA. **(p. 715)**
Public Service Research Foundation, Vienna, VA. **(p. 715)**
The Rutherford Institute, Charlottesville, VA. **(p. 717)**
Science and Environmental Policy Project, Arlington, VA. **(p. 717)**
The Seniors Coalition, Springfield, VA. **(p. 717)**
Tradition, Family, Property, Inc., McLean, VA. **(p. 724)**
United Seniors Association, Fairfax, VA. **(p. 724)**
Virginia Institute for Public Policy, Potomac Falls, VA. **(p. 726)**
Young America's Foundation, Herndon, VA. **(p. 729)**

WASHINGTON

EXPERTS

Mary Cunningham Agee, The Nurturing Network, White Salmon, WA. **(p. 35)**
Ron Arnold, Center for the Defense of Free Enterprise, Bellevue, WA. **(p. 40)**
John H. Beck, Gonzaga University, Spokane, WA. **(p. 48)**
LeAnna Benn, Teen Aid, Spokane, WA. **(p. 50)**
Philip Bom, Regent University, Redmond, WA. **(p. 56)**
James E. Bond, Seattle University, Seattle, WA. **(p. 56)**
Gary Bullert, Columbia Basin College, Pasco, WA. **(p. 65)**
John Carlson, Washington Policy Center, Seattle, WA. **(p. 70)**
Bruce K. Chapman, Discovery Institute, Seattle, WA. **(p. 72)**
Robert Cihak, Evergreen Freedom Foundation, Kirkland, WA. **(p. 74)**
Andrew Coulson, Mackinac Center for Public Policy, Poulsbo, WA. **(p. 83)**
Charles Cushman, American Land Rights Association, Battle Ground, WA. **(p. 87)**
Richard S. Davis, Washington Research Council, Seattle, WA. **(p. 89)**
Richard Derham, Washington Policy Center, Seattle, WA. **(p. 93)**

Adam Fuller, Toward Tradition, Mercer Island, WA. **(p. 118)**
Steven Globerman, Western Washington University, Bellingham, WA. **(p. 125)**
Philip Gold, Discovery Institute, Seattle, WA. **(p. 125)**
Daniel J. Goldhaber, University of Washington, Seattle, WA. **(p. 125)**
Alan Gottlieb, Citizens Committee for the Right to Keep and Bear Arms, Bellevue, WA. **(p. 127)**
Phillip D. Grub, Eastern Washington University, Spokane, WA. **(p. 130)**
Paul Guppy, Washington Policy Center, Seattle, WA. **(p. 131)**
Lynn Harsh, Evergreen Freedom Foundation, Olympia, WA. **(p. 136)**
Paul T. Hill, University of Washington, Seattle, WA. **(p. 142)**
Jeff Kemp, Families Northwest, Bellevue, WA. **(p. 161)**
Daniel Lapin, Toward Tradition, Mercer Island, WA. **(p. 174)**
Robert G. Lee, University of Washington, Seattle, WA. **(p. 176)**
David W. Madsen, Seattle University, Seattle, WA. **(p. 186)**
Daniel Mead Smith, Washington Policy Center, Seattle, WA. **(p. 198)**
Herbert E. Meyer, Real-World Intelligence, Inc., Friday Harbor, WA. **(p. 200)**
Stephen Moses, Center for Long-Term Care Financing, Seattle, WA. **(p. 207)**
David Charles Nice, Washington State University, Pullman, WA. **(p. 213)**
Peter J. Saunders, Central Washington University, Ellensburg, WA. **(p. 250)**
Fawn Spady, Education Excellence Coalition, Seattle, WA. **(p. 266)**
Jim Spady, Education Excellence Coalition, Seattle, WA. **(p. 266)**
John G. West, Discovery Institute, Seattle, WA. **(p. 292)**
Bob Williams, Evergreen Freedom Foundation, Olympia, WA. **(p. 295)**

ORGANIZATIONS

American Land Rights Association, Battle Ground, WA. **(p. 636)**
Center for the Defense of Free Enterprise, Bellevue, WA. **(p. 646)**
Center for Long-Term Care Financing, Seattle, WA. **(p. 648)**
Discovery Institute, Seattle, WA. **(p. 659)**
Education Excellence Coalition, Seattle, WA. **(p. 661)**
Evergreen Freedom Foundation, Olympia, WA. **(p. 663)**
Families Northwest, Bellevue, WA. **(p. 664)**
League of Private Property Voters, Battle Ground, WA. **(p. 688)**
Second Amendment Foundation, Bellevue, WA. **(p. 717)**
Teen-aid, Inc., Spokane, WA. **(p. 722)**
Toward Tradition, Mercer Island, WA. **(p. 723)**
Washington Evangelicals for Responsible Government, Olympia, WA. **(p. 726)**
Washington Policy Center, Seattle, WA. **(p. 727)**
Washington Research Council, Seattle, WA. **(p. 727)**

WEST VIRGINIA

EXPERTS

Russell S. Sobel, West Virginia University, Morgantown, WV. **(p. 265)**
James Biser Whisker, West Virginia University, Morgantown, WV. **(p. 293)**
Edward W. Younkins, Wheeling Jesuit University, Wheeling, WV. **(p. 301)**

WISCONSIN

EXPERTS

Julaine K. Appling, Family Research Institute of Wisconsin, Madison, WI. **(p. 40)**
John F. Bibby, University of Wisconsin, Milwaukee, Milwaukee, WI. **(p. 53)**
Charles H. Breeden, Marquette University, Milwaukee, WI. **(p. 60)**
Melvin Croan, University of Wisconsin, Madison, WI. **(p. 86)**
Howard Fuller, Marquette University, Milwaukee, WI. **(p. 118)**
Harvey M. Jacobs, University of Wisconsin, Madison, WI. **(p. 153)**
Yuri N. Maltsev, Carthage College, Kenosha, WI. **(p. 188)**
James H. Miller, Wisconsin Policy Research Institute, Mequon, WI. **(p. 202)**
Susan Mitchell, The American Education Reform Foundation, Milwaukee, WI. **(p. 203)**
J. Marshall Osborn, University of Wisconsin, Madison, WI. **(p. 220)**
Arthur Pontynen, University of Wisconsin, Oshkosh, WI. **(p. 230)**
Michael Riley, Taxpayers Network, Inc., Cedarburg, WI. **(p. 240)**
Rebecca Swartz, Hudson Institute, Madison, WI. **(p. 272)**
Charles Sykes, Wisconsin Policy Research Institute, Mequon, WI. **(p. 273)**
Jason Turner, Center for Self-Sufficiency, Shorewood, WI. **(p. 281)**
Christopher Wolfe, Marquette University, Milwaukee, WI. **(p. 297)**
Chris Yelich, Education Industry Association, Watertown, WI. **(p. 300)**

ORGANIZATIONS

The American Education Reform Foundation, Milwaukee, WI. **(p. 634)**
Education Industry Association, Watertown, WI. **(p. 661)**
Family Research Institute of Wisconsin, Madison, WI. **(p. 666)**
Institute for the Transformation of Learning, Milwaukee, WI. **(p. 683)**
Taxpayers Network, Inc., Cedarburg, WI. **(p. 721)**
Wisconsin Policy Research Institute, Thiensville, WI. **(p. 729)**

WYOMING

EXPERTS

Evelyn Ebzery, Memorial Hospital of Sheridan County, Sheridan, WY. **(p. 103)**
Bill Schilling, Wyoming Business Alliance / Wyoming Heritage Foundation, Casper, WY. **(p. 253)**

National Research Organizations

Organizations conducting research and analysis of national issues.

American Enterprise Institute, Washington, DC. **(p. 634)**
Americans for Tax Reform Foundation, Washington, DC. **(p. 638)**
Black Alliance for Educational Options, Washington, DC. **(p. 643)**
James M. Buchanan Center, Fairfax, VA. **(p. 643)**
Capital Research Center, Washington, DC. **(p. 644)**
Cato Institute, Washington, DC. **(p. 645)**
Center for Education Reform, Washington, DC. **(p. 646)**
Center for Security Policy, Washington, DC. **(p. 650)**
Center for Strategic and International Studies, Washington, DC. **(p. 650)**
Center for the Study of Popular Culture, Los Angeles, CA. **(p. 651)**
Citizens for a Sound Economy Foundation, Washington, DC. **(p. 655)**
Claremont Institute, Claremont, CA. **(p. 655)**
Competitive Enterprise Institute, Washington, DC. **(p. 657)**
Discovery Institute, Seattle, WA. **(p. 659)**
Ethics and Public Policy Center, Washington, DC. **(p. 663)**
Family Research Council, Washington, DC. **(p. 665)**
The Federalist Society for Law and Public Policy Studies, Washington, DC. **(p. 666)**
Thomas B. Fordham Foundation, Washington, DC. **(p. 667)**
Foreign Policy Research Institute, Philadelphia, PA. **(p. 667)**
Free Congress Foundation, Washington, DC. **(p. 670)**
Frontiers of Freedom Institute, Fairfax, VA. **(p. 671)**
Galen Institute, Alexandria, VA. **(p. 672)**
Heartland Institute, Chicago, IL. **(p. 675)**
The Heritage Foundation, Washington, DC. **(p. 676)**
Hispanic Council for Reform and Educational Options, San Antonio, TX. **(p. 676)**
Hoover Institution, Stanford, CA. **(p. 677)**
Hudson Institute, Indianapolis, IN. **(p. 677)**
The Independent Institute, Oakland, CA. **(p. 678)**
Institute for American Values, New York, NY. **(p. 680)**
Institute for Contemporary Studies, Oakland, CA. **(p. 680)**
Institute for Foreign Policy Analysis, Cambridge, MA. **(p. 681)**
Institute for Health Freedom, Washington, DC. **(p. 681)**
Institute for Policy Innovation, Lewisville, TX. **(p. 682)**
Institute for Research on the Economics of Taxation, Washington, DC. **(p. 682)**
Lexington Institute, Arlington, VA. **(p. 689)**
Clare Boothe Luce Policy Institute, Herndon, VA. **(p. 691)**
Manhattan Institute for Policy Research, New York, NY. **(p. 692)**
Ludwig von Mises Institute, Auburn, AL. **(p. 695)**
National Center for Neighborhood Enterprise, Washington, DC. **(p. 697)**
National Center for Policy Analysis, Dallas, TX. **(p. 697)**
National Center for Public Policy Research, Washington, DC. **(p. 697)**
National Chamber Foundation, Washington, DC. **(p. 697)**
National Fatherhood Initiative, Gaithersburg, MD. **(p. 698)**
National Legal Center for the Public Interest, Washington, DC. **(p. 700)**
Paul Nitze School of Advanced International Studies, Washington, DC. **(p. 705)**
Pacific Research Institute for Public Policy, San Francisco, CA. **(p. 710)**
PERC – The Center for Free Market Environmentalism, Bozeman, MT. **(p. 711)**
Progress & Freedom Foundation, Washington, DC. **(p. 713)**
Reason Foundation, Los Angeles, CA. **(p. 715)**
Social Philosophy and Policy Center, Bowling Green, OH. **(p. 719)**
WallBuilders, Aledo, TX. **(p. 726)**
Weidenbaum Center, St. Louis, MO. **(p. 728)**

National Organizations with State Networks

Organizations having one or more of the following systems:
state or local chapters or directors; extensive, national database and communications systems;
national membership organizational structure; outreach to campuses around the country; or other
extensive, informal associations throughout the nation.

60 Plus Association, Arlington, VA. **(p. 628)**
Alliance for America, Caroga Park, NY. **(p. 629)**
American Association of Christian Schools, Independence, MO. **(p. 631)**
American Association of Small Property Owners, Washington, DC. **(p. 632)**
American Conservative Union, Alexandria, VA. **(p. 633)**
American Council of Trustees and Alumni, Washington, DC. **(p. 633)**
American Legislative Exchange Council, Washington, DC. **(p. 636)**
Americans for Tax Reform, Washington, DC. **(p. 638)**
Association of American Educators, Laguna Hills, CA. **(p. 640)**
Association of Christian Schools International, Colorado Springs, CO. **(p. 641)**
Best Friends Foundation, Washington, DC. **(p. 642)**
Black Alliance for Educational Options, Washington, DC. **(p. 643)**
Children First America, Bentonville, AR. **(p. 652)**
Christian Coalition of America, Washington, DC. **(p. 653)**
Citizens Against Government Waste, Washington, DC. **(p. 654)**
Citizens for a Sound Economy, Washington, DC. **(p. 654)**
Coalitions for America, Washington, DC. **(p. 656)**
Concerned Women for America, Washington, DC. **(p. 657)**
Eagle Forum, Washington, DC. **(p. 660)**
Education Leaders Council, Washington, DC. **(p. 661)**
Family Research Council, Washington, DC. **(p. 665)**
The Federalist Society for Law and Public Policy Studies, Washington, DC. **(p. 666)**
Focus on the Family, Colorado Springs, CO. **(p. 667)**
Freedoms Foundation at Valley Forge, Valley Forge, PA. **(p. 671)**
Intercollegiate Studies Institute, Wilmington, DE. **(p. 684)**
Leadership Institute, Arlington, VA. **(p. 688)**
Liberty Matters, Taylor, TX. **(p. 689)**
National Association of Scholars, Princeton, NJ. **(p. 696)**
National Physicians Center for Family Resources, Birmingham, AL. **(p. 701)**
National Rifle Association, Fairfax, VA. **(p. 701)**
National Right to Life Committee, Washington, DC. **(p. 701)**
National Right to Work Committee, Springfield, VA. **(p. 702)**
National Taxpayers Union, Alexandria, VA. **(p. 703)**
State Policy Network, Richmond, CA. **(p. 720)**
Traditional Values Coalition, Washington, DC. **(p. 724)**
United Seniors Association, Fairfax, VA. **(p. 724)**

State Policy Research Organizations

Organizations conducting research and analysis of state policy issues in their respective states.

Alabama Policy Institute, Birmingham, AL. **(p. 628)**
Allegheny Institute for Public Policy, Pittsburgh, PA. **(p. 629)**
Ethan Allen Institute, Concord, VT. **(p. 629)**
Arkansas Policy Foundation, Little Rock, AR. **(p. 640)**
The Josiah Bartlett Center for Public Policy, Concord, NH. **(p. 641)**
Beacon Hill Institute for Public Policy Research, Boston, MA. **(p. 642)**
Buckeye Institute for Public Policy Solutions, Columbus, OH. **(p. 643)**
California Public Policy Foundation, Camarillo, CA. **(p. 644)**
Calvert Institute for Policy Research, Inc., Baltimore, MD. **(p. 644)**
Cascade Policy Institute, Portland, OR. **(p. 645)**
Center for Policy Research of New Jersey, Florham Park, NJ. **(p. 649)**
Center of the American Experiment, Minneapolis, MN. **(p. 652)**
The Commonwealth Foundation, Harrisburg, PA. **(p. 657)**
Empire Foundation for Policy Research, Clifton Park, NY. **(p. 661)**
Evergreen Freedom Foundation, Olympia, WA. **(p. 663)**
Flint Hills Center for Public Policy, Wichita, KS. **(p. 666)**
Georgia Public Policy Foundation, Atlanta, GA. **(p. 673)**
Golden State Center for Public Policy Studies, Sacramento, CA. **(p. 673)**
Goldwater Institute, Phoenix, AZ. **(p. 673)**
Grassroot Institute of Hawaii, Aiea, HI. **(p. 673)**
Great Plains Public Policy Institute, Sioux Falls, SD. **(p. 673)**
Illinois Policy Institute, Springfield, IL. **(p. 678)**
Independence Institute, Golden, CO. **(p. 678)**
Indiana Policy Review Foundation, Fort Wayne, IN. **(p. 679)**
Thomas Jefferson Institute for Public Policy, Springfield, VA. **(p. 686)**
John Locke Foundation, Raleigh, NC. **(p. 690)**
Mackinac Center for Public Policy, Midland, MI. **(p. 691)**
The James Madison Institute, Tallahassee, FL. **(p. 691)**
Maine Policy Center, Portland, ME. **(p. 692)**
Maine Public Policy Institute, Hampden, ME. **(p. 692)**
Maryland Business for Responsive Government, Baltimore, MD. **(p. 693)**
The Maryland Public Policy Institute, Germantown, MD. **(p. 693)**
Nevada Policy Research Institute, Las Vegas, NV. **(p. 704)**
New Mexico Independence Research Institute, Las Cruces, NM. **(p. 705)**
New York Family Policy Council, Albany, NY. **(p. 705)**
Ohio Roundtable, Solon, OH. **(p. 707)**
Ohio Taxpayers Association, Columbus, OH. **(p. 707)**
Oklahoma Council of Public Affairs, Inc., Oklahoma City, OK. **(p. 707)**
Oregonians In Action, Tigard, OR. **(p. 708)**
Pioneer Institute for Public Policy Research, Boston, MA. **(p. 712)**
Public Interest Institute, Mount Pleasant, IA. **(p. 714)**
Public Policy Institute of New York State, Albany, NY. **(p. 714)**
Rio Grande Foundation, Tijeras, NM. **(p. 716)**
Rose Institute for State and Local Government, Claremont, CA. **(p. 716)**
Shenango Institute for Public Policy, Grove City, PA. **(p. 718)**
South Carolina Policy Council, Columbia, SC. **(p. 719)**
Susquehanna Valley Center for Public Policy, Hershey, PA. **(p. 721)**
The Sutherland Institute, Salt Lake City, UT. **(p. 721)**
Texas Citizens for a Sound Economy, Austin, TX. **(p. 722)**
Texas Conservative Coalition Research Institute, Austin, TX. **(p. 723)**
Texas Public Policy Foundation, San Antonio, TX. **(p. 723)**
Virginia Institute for Public Policy, Potomac Falls, VA. **(p. 726)**
Washington Policy Center, Seattle, WA. **(p. 727)**
Washington Research Council, Seattle, WA. **(p. 727)**
Wisconsin Policy Research Institute, Thiensville, WI. **(p. 729)**
Yankee Institute for Public Policy Studies, Hartford, CT. **(p. 729)**

Family Policy Councils

Organizations conducting research and analysis of policy issues and their impact on families.

Arkansas Family Council, Little Rock, AR. **(p. 639)**
Capitol Resource Institute, Sacramento, CA. **(p. 644)**
Center for Arizona Policy, Scottsdale, AZ. **(p. 645)**
Christian Civic League of Maine, Augusta, ME. **(p. 653)**
Cornerstone Policy Research, Concord, NH. **(p. 658)**
Families Northwest, Bellevue, WA. **(p. 664)**
Family First, Lincoln, NE. **(p. 664)**
Family First, Tampa, FL. **(p. 664)**
The Family Foundation, Richmond, VA. **(p. 664)**
The Family Foundation of Kentucky, Lexington, KY. **(p. 665)**
Family Institute of Connecticut, Hartford, CT. **(p. 665)**
Family Policy Network, Forest, VA. **(p. 665)**
Family Research Council, Washington, DC. **(p. 665)**
Family Research Institute of Wisconsin, Madison, WI. **(p. 666)**
Focus on the Family, Colorado Springs, CO. **(p. 667)**
Free Market Foundation, Plano, TX. **(p. 670)**
Georgia Family Council, Norcross, GA. **(p. 672)**
Hawaii Family Forum, Kailau, HI. **(p. 675)**
Illinois Family Institute, Glen Ellyn, IL. **(p. 678)**
Indiana Family Institute, Indianapolis, IN. **(p. 679)**
Iowa Family Policy Center, Des Moines, IA. **(p. 685)**
Louisiana Family Forum, Baton Rouge, LA. **(p. 691)**
Massachusetts Citizens for Marriage, Waltham, MA. **(p. 694)**
Massachusetts Family Institute, Newton Upper Falls, MA. **(p. 694)**
Michigan Family Forum, Lansing, MI. **(p. 694)**
Minnesota Family Council, Minneapolis, MN. **(p. 695)**
Mississippi Family Council, Jackson, MS. **(p. 695)**
New Jersey Family Policy Council, Parsippany, NJ. **(p. 705)**
New York Family Policy Council, Albany, NY. **(p. 705)**
North Carolina Family Policy Council, Raleigh, NC. **(p. 706)**
North Dakota Family Alliance, Bismarck, ND. **(p. 706)**
Oklahoma Family Policy Council, Bethany, OK. **(p. 707)**
Palmetto Family Council, Columbia, SC. **(p. 710)**
Pennsylvania Family Institute, Harrisburg, PA. **(p. 711)**
Project 21, Washington, DC. **(p. 713)**
Rocky Mountain Family Council, Westminster, CO. **(p. 716)**
South Dakota Family Policy Council, Sioux Falls, SD. **(p. 719)**
Stronger Families for Oregon, Salem, OR. **(p. 720)**
Urban Family Council, Philadelphia, PA. **(p. 726)**

Litigating Organizations

Organizations conducting and/or funding litigation.

Alliance Defense Fund, Scottsdale, AZ. **(p. 629)**
American Center for Law and Justice, Virginia Beach, VA. **(p. 632)**
American Civil Rights Union, Alexandria, VA. **(p. 633)**
Americans United for Life, Chicago, IL. **(p. 639)**
Atlantic Legal Foundation, New York, NY. **(p. 641)**
The Becket Fund for Religious Liberty, Washington, DC. **(p. 642)**
Center for Equal Opportunity, Sterling, VA. **(p. 646)**
Center for Individual Rights, Washington, DC. **(p. 647)**
Center for Law and Religious Freedom, Annandale, VA. **(p. 648)**
Christian Legal Society, Annandale, VA. **(p. 654)**
Criminal Justice Legal Foundation, Sacramento, CA. **(p. 659)**
Defenders of Property Rights, Washington, DC. **(p. 659)**
The Federalist Society for Law and Public Policy Studies, Washington, DC. **(p. 666)**
Home School Legal Defense Association, Purcellville, VA. **(p. 677)**
Individual Rights Foundation, Los Angeles, CA. **(p. 679)**
Institute for Justice, Washington, DC. **(p. 682)**
Judicial Watch, Inc., Washington, DC. **(p. 687)**
Landmark Legal Foundation, Herndon, VA. **(p. 688)**
Lincoln Legal Foundation, Chicago, IL. **(p. 690)**
The Marriage Law Project, Washington, DC. **(p. 693)**
Mountain States Legal Foundation, Lakewood, CO. **(p. 696)**
National Legal and Policy Center, Falls Church, VA. **(p. 700)**
National Legal Foundation, Virginia Beach, VA. **(p. 700)**
National Right to Work Legal Defense Foundation, Springfield, VA. **(p. 702)**
New England Legal Foundation, Boston, MA. **(p. 704)**
Oregonians In Action Legal Center, Tigard, OR. **(p. 708)**
Pacific Justice Institute, Citrus Heights, CA. **(p. 709)**
Pacific Legal Foundation, Sacramento, CA. **(p. 710)**
The Rutherford Institute, Charlottesville, VA. **(p. 717)**
Southeastern Legal Foundation, Atlanta, GA. **(p. 720)**
Texas Justice Foundation, San Antonio, TX. **(p. 723)**
U. S. Bill of Rights Foundation, Washington, DC. **(p. 724)**
United States Justice Foundation, Escondido, CA. **(p. 725)**
Washington Legal Foundation, Washington, DC. **(p. 727)**

501(c)(4) Organizations

60 Plus Association, Arlington, VA. **(p. 628)**
Alliance for America, Caroga Park, NY. **(p. 629)**
American Civil Rights Coalition, Sacramento, CA. **(p. 632)**
American Conservative Union, Alexandria, VA. **(p. 633)**
The American Education Reform Foundation, Milwaukee, WI. **(p. 634)**
American Family Association Foundation, Tupelo, MS. **(p. 635)**
American Policy Center, Warrenton, VA. **(p. 636)**
American Renewal, Washington, DC. **(p. 636)**
Americans for Tax Reform, Washington, DC. **(p. 638)**
Susan B. Anthony List, Alexandria, VA. **(p. 639)**
Christian Civic League of Maine, Augusta, ME. **(p. 653)**
Christian Coalition of America, Washington, DC. **(p. 653)**
Citizens Against Higher Taxes, Hershey, PA. **(p. 654)**
Citizens for a Sound Economy, Washington, DC. **(p. 654)**
Citizens for Law and Order, Sonoma, CA. **(p. 655)**
Coalitions for America, Washington, DC. **(p. 656)**
The Congressional Institute, Alexandria, VA. **(p. 658)**
The Conservative Caucus, Inc., Vienna, VA. **(p. 658)**
Council for Citizens Against Government Waste, Washington, DC. **(p. 658)**
Council for Government Reform, Arlington, VA. **(p. 659)**
Eagle Forum, Washington, DC. **(p. 660)**
Education Excellence Coalition, Seattle, WA. **(p. 661)**
Empower America, Washington, DC. **(p. 662)**
The Empowerment Network, Fredericksburg, VA. **(p. 662)**
Free Speech Coalition, Inc., McLean, VA. **(p. 670)**
Frontiers of Freedom, Fairfax, VA. **(p. 671)**
Gun Owners of America, Springfield, VA. **(p. 674)**
Junkscience.com, Washington, DC. **(p. 687)**
Minnesota Family Council, Minneapolis, MN. **(p. 695)**
National Rifle Association, Fairfax, VA. **(p. 701)**
National Right to Life Committee, Washington, DC. **(p. 701)**
National Right to Work Committee, Springfield, VA. **(p. 702)**
National Tax Limitation Committee, Roseville, CA. **(p. 703)**
National Taxpayers Union, Alexandria, VA. **(p. 703)**
Oregon Citizens for a Sound Economy, Keizer, OR. **(p. 707)**
Oregonians In Action, Tigard, OR. **(p. 708)**
Oregons Taxpayers United PAC, Clackamas, OR. **(p. 709)**
Public Service Research Council, Vienna, VA. **(p. 715)**
The Seniors Coalition, Springfield, VA. **(p. 717)**
Small Business Survival Committee, Washington, DC. **(p. 718)**
Texas Citizens for a Sound Economy, Austin, TX. **(p. 722)**
Texas Conservative Coalition, Austin, TX. **(p. 722)**
Tradition, Family, Property, Inc., McLean, VA. **(p. 724)**
United Seniors Association, Fairfax, VA. **(p. 724)**
U. S. English, Inc., Washington, DC. **(p. 725)**
Washington Evangelicals for Responsible Government, Olympia, WA. **(p. 726)**

Country Index of International Experts and Organizations

ARGENTINA

EXPERTS

Daniela Aruj, Fundación Global. **(p. 732)**
Maria Baron, Center for the Implementation of Public Policies Promoting Equity and Growth. **(p. 733)**
Gerardo Bongiovanni, Fundacion Libertad. **(p. 734)**
Miguel Braun, Center for the Implementation of Public Policies Promoting Equity and Growth. **(p. 735)**
Rodolfo Cavanaro, Fundacion Alberdif. **(p. 735)**
Fernando de Santibañes, Fundacion Libertad. **(p. 737)**
Nicolas J. Ducote, Center for the Implementation of Public Policies Promoting Equity and Growth. **(p. 737)**
Ariana L. Koffsmon, Center for the Implementation of Public Policies Promoting Equity and Growth. **(p. 742)**
Martin Krause, ESEADE Graduate School. **(p. 743)**
Daniel Maggiolo, Fundacion Libertad. **(p. 745)**
Eduardo Marty, Junior Achievement of Argentina. **(p. 745)**
Laura Elizabeth Raiman, Raiman & Associates. **(p. 750)**
Axel Riva, Center for the Implementation of Public Policies Promoting Equity and Growth. **(p. 751)**
Sonia Cavallo Runde, Center for the Implementation of Public Policies Promoting Equity and Growth. **(p. 751)**
Gabriel Salvia, Fundacion Atlas Para Una Sociedad Libre. **(p. 752)**
Enrique Shaw, Center for the Implementation of Public Policies Promoting Equity and Growth. **(p. 753)**
Maria Steverlynck, Fundacion Republica para una Nueva Generacion. **(p. 754)**
Meir Zylberberg, Fundacion Libre. **(p. 758)**

ORGANIZATIONS

Center for the Implementation of Public Policies Promoting Equity and Growth. (p. 760)
Fundacion Alberdif. (p. 763)
Fundacion Atlas Para Una Sociedad Libre. (p. 763)
Fundación Global. (p. 763)
Fundacion Iniciativa. (p. 763)
Fundacion Libertad. (p. 763)
Fundacion Libre. (p. 763)
Fundacion Republica para una Nueva Generacion. (p. 763)

AUSTRALIA

EXPERTS

H. Geoffrey Brennan, Australian National University. **(p. 735)**
Jennifer Buckingham, The Centre for Independent Studies. **(p. 735)**
Owen Harries, The Centre for Independent Studies. **(p. 740)**
Wolfgang Kasper, The Centre for Independent Studies. **(p. 742)**
Greg Lindsay, The Centre for Independent Studies. **(p. 744)**
Barry R. Maley, The Centre for Independent Studies. **(p. 745)**
Ronald B. Manners, Mannkal Economic Education Foundation. **(p. 745)**
Mike Nahan, Institute of Public Affairs Limited. **(p. 747)**
Andrew Norton, The Centre for Independent Studies. **(p. 748)**
Michael O'Connor, Australia Defence Association. **(p. 748)**
Suri Ratnapala, University of Queensland. **(p. 750)**

BRAZIL

EXPERTS

Arthur Chagas Diniz, Instituto Liberal. **(p. 737)**
Og F. Leme, Instituto Liberal. **(p. 743)**
Ricardo Borges Ranzolin, Instituto Liberal-RS. **(p. 750)**

ORGANIZATIONS

Instituto Liberal. (p. 766)
Instituto Liberal-RS. (p. 766)

BULGARIA

EXPERTS

Latchezar Bogdanov, Institute for Market Economics. **(p. 734)**
Ivan Krastev, Centre for Liberal Strategies. **(p. 742)**
Goerge Manliev, Institute of Public Administration and European Integration. **(p. 745)**
George Prohasky, Center for Economic Development. **(p. 750)**
Krassen Stanchev, Institute for Market Economics. **(p. 754)**
Assenka Yonkova-Hristova, Institute for Market Economics. **(p. 758)**

ORGANIZATIONS

Center for Economic Development. (p. 760)
Centre for Liberal Strategies. (p. 761)
Institute for Market Economics. (p. 764)
Institute of Public Administration and European Integration. (p. 765)

CANADA

EXPERTS

Murray Allen, The Fraser Institute. **(p. 732)**
Iain T. Benson, Centre for Cultural Renewal. **(p. 733)**
Robert L. Bish, Local Government Institute. **(p. 734)**
Paul Brantingham, The Fraser Institute. **(p. 734)**
Jason Clemens, The Fraser Institute. **(p. 735)**
Martin Collacott, The Fraser Institute. **(p. 735)**
Barry Cooper, The Fraser Institute. **(p. 736)**
Peter Cowley, The Fraser Institute. **(p. 736)**
Brian Lee Crowley, Atlantic Institute for Market Studies. **(p. 736)**
Pierre Desrochers, Montreal Economic Institute. **(p. 737)**
Kirk Durston, New Scholars Society. **(p. 738)**
Steve Easton, The Fraser Institute. **(p. 738)**
Nadeem Esmail, The Fraser Institute. **(p. 738)**
Tom Flanagan, The Fraser Institute. **(p. 738)**
Gordon Gibson, The Fraser Institute. **(p. 739)**
John R. Graham, The Fraser Institute. **(p. 740)**
Kenneth Green, The Fraser Institute. **(p. 740)**
Herbert Grubel, The Fraser Institute. **(p. 740)**
Claudia R. Hepburn, The Fraser Institute. **(p. 741)**
Peter Holle, Frontier Centre for Public Policy. **(p. 741)**
Laura Jones, The Fraser Institute. **(p. 741)**
Michael Kelly-Gagnon, Montreal Economic Institute. **(p. 742)**
Norma Kozhaya, Montreal Economic Institute. **(p. 742)**
Pierre Lemieux, Universite du Quebec en Outaouais. **(p. 743)**
Sylvia LeRoy, The Fraser Institute. **(p. 744)**

Owen Lippert, International Policy Network. **(p. 744)**
Preston Manning, The Fraser Institute. **(p. 745)**
Fred McMahon, The Fraser Institute. **(p. 746)**
Jean-Luc Migue, The Fraser Institute. **(p. 746)**
Gerry Nicholls, National Citizens Coalition. **(p. 748)**
Dennis Owens, Frontier Centre for Public Policy. **(p. 748)**
Filip Palda, The Fraser Institute. **(p. 748)**
Sid Parkinson, St. Lawrence Institute. **(p. 749)**
Christopher Sarlo, Nipissing University. **(p. 752)**
Neil Seeman, The Fraser Institute. **(p. 752)**
Adrienne DeLong Snow, Centre for the Study of Civic Renewal. **(p. 753)**
Robert Sopuck, Frontier Centre for Public Policy. **(p. 754)**
John C. Thompson, The Mackenzie Institute. **(p. 755)**
Michael A. Walker, The Fraser Institute. **(p. 757)**

ORGANIZATIONS

Atlantic Institute for Market Studies. **(p. 760)**
Centre for Cultural Renewal. **(p. 761)**
Centre for the Study of Civic Renewal. **(p. 761)**
Frontier Centre for Public Policy. **(p. 763)**
Local Government Institute. **(p. 767)**
Montreal Economic Institute. **(p. 768)**
National Citizens Coalition. **(p. 768)**
New Scholars Society. **(p. 768)**
St. Lawrence Institute. **(p. 769)**
The Fraser Institute. **(p. 769)**
The Mackenzie Institute. **(p. 769)**

CHILE

EXPERTS

Carlos Caceres, Libertad y Desarrollo. **(p. 735)**
Tomas Flores, Libertad y Desarrollo. **(p. 739)**
Francisco Garces. **(p. 739)**
Eugenio Guzman, Libertad y Desarrollo. **(p. 740)**
Luis Larrain A., Libertad y Desarrollo. **(p. 743)**
Cristian Larroulet, Libertad y Desarrollo. **(p. 743)**

ORGANIZATIONS

Libertad y Desarrollo. **(p. 767)**

COLOMBIA

EXPERTS

Andres Mejia-Vergnaud, Fundacion DL. **(p. 746)**
Juan Camilo Narino, Instituto de Ciencia Politica. **(p. 748)**

ORGANIZATIONS

Fundacion DL. **(p. 763)**
Instituto de Ciencia Politica. **(p. 766)**

COSTA RICA

EXPERTS

Rigoberto Stewart, Institute for Liberty and Policy Analysis. **(p. 754)**

ORGANIZATIONS

Institute for Liberty and Policy Analysis. (p. 764)

CROATIA

EXPERTS

Visnja Samardzija, Institute for International Relations. **(p. 752)**

ORGANIZATIONS

Institute for International Relations. (p. 764)

CZECH REPUBLIC

EXPERTS

Roman Joch, Civic Institute. **(p. 741)**
Jiri Schwarz, Liberalni Institut. **(p. 752)**
Michal Semin, Civic Institute. **(p. 753)**
Josef Sima, Liberalni Institut. **(p. 753)**
Petr Vancura, Prague Institute for National Security. **(p. 756)**
Andrei Zagorski, East-West Institute. **(p. 758)**

ORGANIZATIONS

Civic Institute. (p. 762)
East-West Institute. (p. 762)
Liberalni Institut. (p. 767)
Prague Institute for National Security. (p. 768)

DENMARK

EXPERTS

Peter Kurrild-Klitgaard, University of Southern Denmark. **(p. 743)**

ECUADOR

EXPERTS

Ivan Baquerizo Alvarado, Fundacion Libertad. **(p. 733)**
Dora de Ampuero, Instituto Ecuatoriano de Economia Politica. **(p. 736)**

ORGANIZATIONS

Fundacion Libertad. (p. 763)
Instituto Ecuatoriano de Economia Politica. (p. 766)

Roberto de Mattei, Centro Culturale Lepanto. (p. 737)
Alessandro de Nicola, Adam Smith Society. (p. 737)
Flavio Felice, Instituto Acton. (p. 738)
Angelo M. Petroni, Centro di Ricerca e Documentazione Luigi Einaudi. (p. 749)

ORGANIZATIONS

Adam Smith Society. (p. 760)
Centro Culturale Lepanto. (p. 761)
Centro di Ricerca e Documentazione Luigi Einaudi. (p. 761)

JAPAN

EXPERTS

Motoo Kaji, The International House of Japan, Inc.. (p. 742)

ORGANIZATIONS

The International House of Japan, Inc.. (p. 769)

KAZAKHSTAN

EXPERTS

Raissa Kaziyeva, SIFE Kazakhstan. (p. 742)

ORGANIZATIONS

SIFE Kazakhstan. (p. 768)

KENYA

EXPERTS

James S. Shikwati, Inter Region Economic Network [IREN]. (p. 753)

ORGANIZATIONS

Inter Region Economic Network [IREN]. (p. 766)

KOREA

EXPERTS

Byuong-Kyun Min, Korean Center for Free Enterprise. (p. 746)

ORGANIZATIONS

Korean Center for Free Enterprise. (p. 767)

Instituto Cultural Ludwig von Mises, A.C.. **(p. 766)**
TV Azteca. **(p. 769)**

MONACO

EXPERTS

Ingo Bobel, International University of Monaco. **(p. 734)**

MONTENEGRO

EXPERTS

Veselin Vukotic, University of Montenegro. **(p. 756)**

NEPAL

EXPERTS

Rakesh Wadhwa, Nepal Recreation Centre Pvt. Ltd.. **(p. 757)**

NETHERLANDS

EXPERTS

Joshua Livestro, Edmund Burke Foundation. **(p. 744)**

ORGANIZATIONS

Edmund Burke Foundation. (p. 762)

NEW ZEALAND

EXPERTS

Greg Fleming, The Maxim Institute. **(p. 739)**
Paul Henderson, The Maxim Institute. **(p. 741)**
Roger Kerr, New Zealand Business Roundtable. **(p. 742)**
Bruce Logan, The Maxim Institute. **(p. 744)**
Michael Reid, The Maxim Institute. **(p. 751)**

ORGANIZATIONS

New Zealand Business Roundtable. (p. 768)
The Maxim Institute. (p. 769)

NIGERIA

EXPERTS

Thompson Ayodele, Institute of Public Policy Analysis. **(p. 732)**

ORGANIZATIONS

Institute of Public Policy Analysis. (p. 765)

ORGANIZATIONS

Glasnost Public Policy Foundation. (p. 763)
Institute for the Study of Russian Economy. (p. 765)
Institute of Economy in Transition. (p. 765)
Krieble Institute. (p. 767)
Moscow Helsinki Group. (p. 768)
The Heritage Foundation. (p. 769)

SERBIA

EXPERTS

Miro Prokopijevic, Institute for European Studies. (p. 750)

ORGANIZATIONS

Institute for European Studies. (p. 764)

SINGAPORE

ORGANIZATIONS

Institute of Southeast Asian Studies. (p. 765)
Singapore International Foundation. (p. 768)

SLOVAKIA

EXPERTS

Jan Oravec, F. A. Hayek Foundation Bratislava. (p. 748)
Ivan Svejna, F. A. Hayek Foundation Bratislava. (p. 754)
Daniel Zemanovicova, Transparency International Slovakia. (p. 758)

ORGANIZATIONS

F. A. Hayek Foundation Bratislava. (p. 762)
Transparency International Slovakia. (p. 769)

SOUTH AFRICA

EXPERTS

Michael Hough, Institute for Strategic Studies. (p. 741)
Leon M. Louw, Free Market Foundation. (p. 744)
Carl Noffke, Almard Corporation. (p. 748)

ORGANIZATIONS

Free Market Foundation. (p. 762)
Institute for Strategic Studies. (p. 765)
Private Sector Organization. (p. 768)
South African Institute of Race Relations. (p. 769)

SPAIN

EXPERTS

Vicente Boceta Alvarez, Circulo De Empresarios. **(p. 734)**
Luis Ravina, Universidad de Navarra. **(p. 750)**

ORGANIZATIONS

Circulo De Empresarios. **(p. 762)**

SWEDEN

EXPERTS

Mattias Bengtsson, Timbro. **(p. 733)**
Niclas Berggren, The Ratio Institute. **(p. 733)**
Hakan Gergils, Ecofin Invest. **(p. 739)**
Dan Johansson, The Ratio Institute. **(p. 741)**
Mats Johansson, Svenska Dagbladet. **(p. 741)**
Nils Karlson, The Ratio Institute. **(p. 742)**
Peter Stein, Stein Brothers AB. **(p. 754)**
Bjorn Tarras-Wahlberg, World Taxpayers Associations. **(p. 755)**
Carl-Johan Westholm. **(p. 757)**

ORGANIZATIONS

The Ratio Institute. **(p. 769)**
Timbro. **(p. 769)**
World Taxpayers Associations. **(p. 770)**

SWITZERLAND

EXPERTS

Peter Bernholz, Universitaet Basel. **(p. 733)**

TAIWAN

EXPERTS

Yun-han Chu, Institute for National Policy Research. **(p. 735)**
Hung-Mao Tien, Institute for National Policy Research. **(p. 755)**
Yung Wei, Vanguard Institute for Policy Studies. **(p. 757)**

ORGANIZATIONS

Institute for National Policy Research. **(p. 764)**
Vanguard Institute for Policy Studies. **(p. 770)**

THAILAND

ORGANIZATIONS

Institute of Asian Studies. **(p. 765)**

TURKEY

EXPERTS

Seyfi Tashan, Turkish Foreign Policy Institute. **(p. 755)**
Atilla Yayla, Association for Liberal Thinking. **(p. 757)**

ORGANIZATIONS

Association for Liberal Thinking. (p. 760)
Turkish Foreign Policy Institute. (p. 769)

UKRAINE

EXPERTS

Volodymyr S. Biletskyy, Ukrainian Center for Cultural Studies. **(p. 733)**
Alexander Muchnik, Institute of Municipal Democracy and Human Rights. **(p. 747)**
Kostyantyn Mykhailychenko, Ukrainian Center for Independent Political Research. **(p. 747)**
Inna Pidluska, Ukrainian Center for Independent Political Research. **(p. 749)**
Olga Zakhazchenko, International Centre for Policy Studies. **(p. 758)**

ORGANIZATIONS

Institute of Municipal Democracy and Human Rights. (p. 765)
U.S.-Ukraine Foundation. (p. 770)
Ukrainian Center for Cultural Studies. (p. 770)
Ukrainian Center for Independent Political Research. (p. 770)

UNITED KINGDOM

EXPERTS

Digby Anderson, The Social Affairs Unit. **(p. 732)**
Lisl Biggs-Davison, Centre for Research into Post-Communist Economics. **(p. 733)**
John Blundell, Institute of Economic Affairs. **(p. 734)**
Eamonn Butler, Adam Smith Institute. **(p. 735)**
Philip Collins, Social Market Foundation. **(p. 736)**
Alexander Evans, Policy Exchange. **(p. 738)**
David G. Green, CIVITAS: The Institute for the Study of Civil Society. **(p. 740)**
Allister Heath, The Business Newspaper. **(p. 740)**
Brian G.M. Main, David Hume Institute. **(p. 745)**
David Marsland, Brunel University. **(p. 745)**
Gary L. McDowell, Institute of United States Studies. **(p. 746)**
Kenneth Robert Minogue, University of London. **(p. 747)**
Julian Morris, International Policy Network. **(p. 747)**
Madsen Pirie, Adam Smith Institute. **(p. 749)**
John Redwood, Middlesex University Business School. **(p. 751)**
Colin Robinson, University of Surrey. **(p. 751)**
Razeen Sally, London School of Economics and Political Science. **(p. 752)**
Ljubo Sirc, CBE, Centre for Research into Post-Communist Economics. **(p. 753)**
James Tooley, E. G. West Centre. **(p. 755)**
Philip Vander Elst. (p. 756)
Linda Whetstone, International Policy Network. **(p. 757)**
Alan Lee Williams, Atlantic Council of the United Kingdom. **(p. 757)**

ORGANIZATIONS

Adam Smith Institute. (p. 760)
Atlantic Council of the United Kingdom. (p. 760)
Centre for Research into Post-Communist Economics. (p. 761)
CIVITAS: The Institute for the Study of Civil Society. (p. 762)
David Hume Institute. (p. 762)
E. G. West Centre. (p. 762)
Institute of Economic Affairs. (p. 765)
Institute of United States Studies. (p. 766)
International Policy Network. (p. 766)
Policy Exchange. (p. 768)
Social Market Foundation. (p. 768)
The Social Affairs Unit. (p. 769)

VENEZUELA

EXPERTS

Vladimir Chelminski, Caracas Chamber of Commerce. **(p. 735)**
Rocio Guijarro, Centro de Divulgacion del Conocimiento Economico (CEDICE). **(p. 740)**
Carlos Sabino, Centro de Divulgacion del Conocimiento Economico (CEDICE). **(p. 751)**

ORGANIZATIONS

Centro de Divulgacion del Conocimiento Economico (CEDICE). (p. 761)

YUGOSLAVIA

EXPERTS

Boris Begovic, Center for Liberal-Democratic Studies. **(p. 733)**
Aleksandra Jovanovic, Free Market Center. **(p. 741)**
Zoran Vacic, Center for Liberal-Democratic Studies. **(p. 756)**

ORGANIZATIONS

Center for Liberal-Democratic Studies. (p. 760)
Free Market Center. (p. 762)

Periodicals

ABA Watch: The Federalist Society for Law and Public Policy Studies, 1015 18th Street, N.W., Suite 425, Washington, DC 20036, 202/822-8138, Editors – Jennifer E. Lakin and Jessica King. published semiannually. www.fed-soc.org

Academic Questions: National Association of Scholars, 221 Witherspoon Street, Second Floor, Princeton, NJ 08542-3215, 609/683-7878, Editor – Bradford Wilson, quarterly. www.nas.org

Adolescent & Family Health: Institute for Youth Development, P. O. Box 16560, Washington, DC 20041, 703/471-8750, Editor in Chief – Alma L. Golden, quarterly. www.youthdevelopment.org

ALEC Policy Forum: American Legislative Exchange Council, 1129 20th Street, N.W., Suite 500, Washington, DC 20006, 202/466-3800, Director of Public Affairs – David Wargin, quarterly. www.alec.org

The American Enterprise: American Enterprise Institute, 1150 17th Street, N.W., Washington, DC 20036, 202/862-5800, Editor-in-Chief – Karl Zinsmeister, bimonthly. www.aei.org

American Experiment Quarterly: Center of the American Experiment, 1024 Plymouth Building, 12 South 6th Street, Minneapolis, MN 55402, 612/338-3605, Editor – Mitchell B. Pearlstein, quarterly. www.amexp.org

American Outlook: Hudson Institute, 5395 Emerson Way, Indianapolis, IN 46226, 317/545-9639, Editor-in-Chief – S. T. Karnick, quarterly. www.hudson.org

The American Spectator: Gilder Publishing, 291A Main Street, Great Barrington, MA 01230, 800/524-3469, Editor – R. Emmett Tyrrell, Jr., bimonthly. www.spectator.org

Brainstorm: Politics, Policy & Culture in the Northwest, 6490 Horton Road, West Linn, OR 97068, 503/557-8622, Managing Editors – Bridget Barton and Jim Pasero, monthly. www.brainstorm.com

BreakPoint WorldView: Prison Fellowship Ministries, P. O. Box 1550, Merrifield, VA 22166-1550, 703/478-0100, Editor – Chuck Colson, monthly. www.pfm.org

California Political Review: California Public Policy Foundation, 4656 Saloma Avenue Sherman Oaks, CA 91403, 805/445-9183, Editor – John Kurzweil, bimonthly. www.cppf.org

Campus: America's Student Magazine: Intercollegiate Studies Institute, 3901 Centerville Road, P. O. Box 4431, Wilmington, DE 19807-0431, 302/652-4600, Editor – Stanley K. Ridgley, two issues during the academic year. www.isi.org

Campus newspapers (over 100 of them): Intercollegiate Studies Institute, 3901 Centerville Road, P. O. Box 4431, Wilmington, DE 19807-0431, 302/652-4600. www.isi.org

Carolina Journal: John Locke Foundation, 200 West Morgan Street, Suite 200, Raleigh, NC 27601, 919/828-3876, Editor – Richard Wagner, monthly. www.johnlocke.org

The Cato Journal: Cato Institute, 1000 Massachusetts Avenue, N.W., Washington, DC 20001, 202/842-0200, Editor – James A. Dorn, three issues per year. www.cato.org

Cato Policy Report: Cato Institute, 1000 Massachusetts Avenue, N.W., Washington, DC 20001, 202/842-0200, Editor – David Boaz, bimonthly. www.cato.org

Chechnya Weekly: The Jamestown Foundation, 4516 43rd Street, N.W., Washington, DC 20016, 202/483-8888, weekly. www.jamestown.org

China Brief: The Jamestown Foundation, 4516 43rd Street, N.W., Washington, DC 20016, 202/483-8888, bimonthly. www.jamestown.org

The China Leadership Monitor: The Hoover Institution, Stanford University, 94305-6010, General Editor – H. Lyman Miller, quarterly. clm@hoover.stanford.edu

Chronicles: The Rockford Institute, 928 North Main Street, Rockford, IL 61103, 815/964-5054, Editor – Dr. Thomas Fleming, monthly. www.chroniclesmagazine.org

Citizen: Focus on the Family, 8605 Explorer Drive, Colorado Springs, CO 80995-7450, 800/232-6459, Editor – Tom Hess, monthly. www.family.org

City Journal: Manhattan Institute, 52 Vanderbilt Avenue, New York, NY 10017, 212/599-7000, Editor – Myron Magnet, quarterly. www.manhattan-institute.org

Claremont Review of Books: The Claremont Institute, 250 West First Street, Suite 330, Claremont, CA 91711, 909/621-6825, Editor – Charles R. Kesler, quarterly. www.claremont.org

CMR Notes: Center for Military Readiness, P. O. Box 51600, Livonia, MI 48151, 734/464-9430, Editor – Elaine Donnelly, ten issues per year. www.cmrlink.org

Commentary: American Jewish Committee, 165 East 56th Street, New York, NY 10022, 212/891-1400, Editor – Neal Kozodoy, eleven issues per year. www.commentarymagazine.com

Compassion and Culture: Capital Research Center, 1513 16th Street, N.W., Washington, DC 20036-1480, 202/483-6900, Editor – Jill Cunningham Lacey, monthly. www.capitalresearch.org

Conservative Chronicle: Hampton Publishing Company, 9 Second Street, N.W., P. O. Box 317, Hampton, IA 50441, 800/888-3039, weekly. www.conservativechronicle.com

Consumers' Research: Consumers' Research, Inc., 800 Maryland Avenue N.E., Washington, DC 20002, 202/546-1713, Editor – Alex Adrianson, monthly.

CRISIS Magazine: CRISIS Magazine, 1814½ N Street, N.W., Washington, DC 20036, 202/861-7790, Editor – Deal W. Hudson, monthly. www.crisismagazine.com

Doublethink: America's Future Foundation, 1508 21st Street, N.W., Washington, DC 20036, 202/544-7707, Editor – Justin Torres, quarterly. www.americasfuture.org

Economic Affairs: The Institute of Economic Affairs, 2 Lord North Street, Westminster, London SW1P 3LB, United Kingdom, 011-020-7799-8900, Editor – Colin Robinson, quarterly. www.iea.org.uk

Education Next: The Hoover Institution, Stanford University, Stanford, CA 94305-6010, 650/723-3373, Editor-in-Chief – Paul E. Peterson, quarterly. www.educationnext.org

Environment & Climate News: The Heartland Institute, 19 South LaSalle, Suite 903, Chicago, IL 60603, 312/377-4000, Editor – Diane Carol Bast, monthly. www.heartland.org

Family Policy: Family Research Council, 801 G Street, N.W., Washington, DC 20001, 202/393-2100, Editor – Greg Di Napoli, bimonthly. www.frc.org

Family Voice: Concerned Women for America, 1015 15th Street N.W., Suite 1100, Washington, DC 20005, 202/488-7000, Editor – Pamela Pearson Wong, bimonthly. www.cwfa.org

The Family in America: The Howard Center for Family, Religion & Society, 934 North Main Street, Rockford, IL 61103, 800/461-3113, Editor – Allan Carlson, monthly. www.profam.org

First Things: The Institute on Religion and Public Life, 156 5th Avenue, Suite 400, New York, NY 10010, 212/627-1985, Editor – James Nuechterlein, ten issues per year. www.firstthings.com

Focus on the Family: Focus on the Family, 8605 Explorer Drive, Colorado Springs, CO 80920-1051, 800/232-6459, Editor – Tom Neven, monthly. www.family.org

Fraser Forum: The Fraser Institute, 1770 Burrard Street, 4th Floor, Vancouver, B.C., Canada V6J 3G7, 604/688-0221, Chief Editor – Michael Walker, monthly. www.fraserinstitute.ca

The Free Market: Ludwig von Mises Institute, 518 West Magnolia Avenue, Auburn, AL 36832-4528, 334/321-2100, Editorial Vice President – Jeffrey Tucker, monthly. www.mises.org

Foundation Watch: Capital Research Center, 1513 16ᵗʰ Street, N.W., Washington, DC 20036-1480, 202/483-6900, Editor – John K. Carlisle, monthly. www.capitalresearch.org

Government Union Review: Public Service Research Foundation, 320-D Maple Avenue East, Vienna, VA 22180, 703/242-3575, Editor – Thomas W. Jacobson, quarterly. www.psrf.org

Government WasteWatch: Citizens Against Government Waste, 1301 Connecticut Avenue, N.W., Suite 400, Washington, DC 20036, 202/467-5300, Editor – Sean Rushton, quarterly. www.cagw.org

Health Care News: The Heartland Institute, 19 South LaSalle, Suite 903, Chicago, IL 60603, 312/377-4000, Editor – Diane Carol Bast, monthly. www.heartland.org

Heritage Today: The Heritage Foundation, 214 Massachusetts Avenue, N.E., Washington, DC 20002, 202/546-4400, Editor – Andrew Blasko, quarterly. www.heritage.org

Hoover Digest: Hoover Institution, Hoover Press, Stanford University, Stanford, CA 94305-6010, 800/935-2882, Editor – Peter Robinson, quarterly. www.hoover.org

Human Events: Human Events Publishing, LLC, One Massachusetts Avenue, N.W., Washington, DC 20001, 202/216-0600, Editor – Terence P. Jeffrey, weekly.

Human Life Review: Human Life Foundation, Inc., 215 Lexington Avenue, New York, NY 10016, 212/685-5210, Editor – Maria McFadden, quarterly. www.humanlifereview.com

Ideas on Liberty: Foundation for Economic Education, Inc., 30 South Broadway, Irvington, NY 10533, 914/591-7230, Editor – Sheldon Richman, monthly. www.fee.org

Imprimis: Hillsdale College, 33 East College Street, Hillsdale, MI 49242, 800/437-2268, Editor – Douglas A. Jeffery, monthly. www.hillsdale.edu

The Independent Review: The Independent Institute, 100 Swan Way, Oakland, CA 94621-1428, 510/632-1366, Editor – Robert Higgs, quarterly. www.independent.org

Indiana Policy Review: Indiana Policy Review Foundation, P. O. Box 12306, Fort Wayne, IN 46863, 317/236-7360, Editor – Thomas D. Hession, quarterly.

The Insider: The Heritage Foundation, 214 Massachusetts Avenue, N.E., Washington, DC 20002, 202/546-4400, Editor – Andrew Walker, monthly. www.heritage.org

Insight: The Washington Times Corporation, 3600 New York Avenue, N.E., Washington, DC 20002, 800/356-3588, Managing Editor – Paul M. Rodriguez, weekly. www.insightmag.com

IPI Insights: The Institute for Policy Innovation, 250 South Stemmons, Suite 215, Lewisville, TX 75067, 972/874-5139, Editor – Betty Medlock, bimonthly. www.ipi.org

Intellectual Ammunition: The Heartland Institute, 19 South LaSalle, Suite 903, Chicago, IL 60603, 312/377-4000, Editor – Diane Carol Bast, bimonthly. www.heartland.org

The Intercollegiate Review: Intercollegiate Studies Institute, 3901 Centerville Road, P. O. Box 4431, Wilmington, DE 19807-0431, 302/652-4600, Editors – Jeffrey O. Nelson and Mark C. Henrie, biannually. www.isi.org

Issues & Views: Issues & Views, P. O. Box 467, New York, NY 10025, Editor – Elizabeth Wright, quarterly. www.issues-views.com

The Journal of International Security Affairs: Jewish Institute for National Security Affairs, 1717 K Street N.W., Suite 800, Washington, DC 20036, 202/833-0020, quarterly. www.jinsa.org

Journal of Markets & Morality: Center for Economic Personalism at the Acton Institute for the Study of Religion and Liberty, 161 Ottawa Avenue, N.W., Suite 301, Grand Rapids, MI 49503, 616/454-3080, Executive Editor – Stephen J. Grabill, semiannually. www.acton.org

Journal of the Flagstaff Institute: The Flagstaff Institute, P. O. Box 986, Flagstaff, AZ 86002, 928/779-0052, Editor – Richard L. Bolin, semiannually. www.wepza.org

The Journal of the James Madison Institute: The James Madison Institute, P. O. Box 37460, Tallahassee, FL 32315, 850/376-1119, Editor – Rosemary Dupras, quarterly. www.jamesmadison.org

Jubilee: Prison Fellowship Ministries, P. O. Box 1550, Merrifield, VA 22116-1550, 703/478-0100, Editor – David Carlson, nine issues per year. www.pfm.org

Labor Watch: Capital Research Center, 1513 16th Street, N.W., Washington, DC 20036-1480, 202/483-6900, Editor – Ivan Osorio, monthly. www.capitalresearch.org

The Limbaugh Letter: The Limbaugh Letter, P. O. Box 420058, Palm Coast, FL 43142-0058, 800/935-8558, Editor-in-Chief – Rush Limbaugh, monthly.

Limits: Public Interest Institute at Iowa Wesleyan College, 600 North Jackson Street, Mt. Pleasant, IA 52641, Editor – Don Racheter, quarterly. www.limitedgovernment.org

Lincoln Review: Lincoln Institute for Research and Education, 1001 Connecticut Avenue, N.W., Suite 1135, Washington, DC 20036, 202/223-5112, Editor – J. A. Parker, bimonthly.

Media Monitor: Center for Media and Public Affairs, 2100 L Street, N.W., Suite 300, Washington, DC 20037, 202/223-2942, Editor – S. Robert Lichter, bimonthly. www.cmpa.org

Media Reality Check: Media Research Center, 325 South Patrick Street, Alexandria, VA 22314, 703/683-9733, Editors – Brent Baker and Rich Noyes, weekly. www.mediaresearch.org

Michigan Education Report: Mackinac Center for Public Policy, 140 West Main Street, P. O. Box 568, Midland, MI 48640, 989-631-0900, Editor – Samuel A. Walker, quarterly. www.mackinac.org

Michigan Privatization Report: Mackinac Center for Public Policy, 140 West Main Street, P. O. Box 568, Midland, MI 48640, 989/631-0900, Editor – David Bardallis, quarterly. www.mackinac.org

Middle East Quarterly: Middle East Forum, 1500 Walnut Street, Suite 1050, Philadelphia, PA 19102, 215/546-5406, Editor – Martin Kramer, quarterly. http://www.meforum.org/meq/

The Mises Review: Ludwig von Mises Institute, 518 West Magnolia Avenue, Auburn, AL 36832-4528, 334/321-2100, Editor – David Gordon, quarterly. www.mises.org

Modern Age: Intercollegiate Studies Institute, 3901 Centerville Road, P. O. Box 4431, Wilmington, DE 19807, 302/652-4600, Editor – George A. Panichas, quarterly. www.isi.org

The National Interest: The National Interest, 1615 L Street, N.W., Suite 1230, Washington, DC 20036, 202/467-4884, Editor – Adam Garfinkle, quarterly. www.nationalinterest.org

National Review: National Review, Inc., 215 Lexington Avenue, New York, NY 10016, 212/679-7330, Editor – Richard Lowery, biweekly. www.nationalreview.com

Navigator: The Objectivist Center, 11 Raymond Avenue, Suite 31, Poughkeepsie, NY 12569, 845/471-6100, Editor – Roger Donway, eleven issues per year. www.objectivistcenter.org

The New Criterion: The New Criterion, 850 7th Avenue, Suite 400, New York, NY 10019, 212/247-6980, Editor – Hilton Kramer, ten issues per year. www.newcriterion.com

Organization Trends: Capital Research Center, 1513 16th Street, N.W., Washington, DC 20036-1480, 202/483-6900, Editor – John K. Carlisle, monthly. www.capitalresearch.org

Opportunity: Education Leaders Council, 1001 Connecticut Avenue, N.W., Suite 204, Washington, DC 20036, 202/822-9000, Editor – Gary Huggins, quarterly. www.edreform.com/elc

Orbis: Foreign Policy Research Institute, 1528 Walnut Street, Suite 610, Philadelphia, PA 19102-3684, 215/732-3774, Editor – David Eisenhower, quarterly. www.fpri.org

Pennsylvania Families & Schools: Pennsylvania Family Institute, 1240 North Mountain Road, Harrisburg, PA 17112, 717/545-0600, Editor – Thomas J. Shaheen, quarterly. www.pafamily.org

PERC Reports: PERC – The Center for Free Market Environmentalism, 502 South 19th Avenue, Suite 211, Bozeman, MT 59718-6821, 406/587-9591, Editor – Jane S. Shaw, quarterly. www.perc.org

Perspective: Oklahoma Council of Public Affairs, 100 West Wilshire, Suite C-3, Oklahoma City, OK 73116, 405/843-9212, Editor – Brandon Dutcher, monthly. www.ocpathink.org

Philanthropy: The Philanthropy Roundtable, 1150 17th Street, NW, Suite 503, Washington, DC 20036, 202/822-8333, Editor – Scott Walter, bimonthly. www.philanthropyroundtable.org

Phyllis Schlafly Report: Eagle Forum, P. O. Box 618, Alton, IL 62002, 618/462-5415, Editor – Phyllis Schlafly, monthly. www.eagleforum.org

Pioneering Spirit: Pioneer Institute for Public Policy Research, 85 Devonshire Street, 8th Floor, Boston, MA 02109, 617/723-2277, Editor – Stephen J. Adams, quarterly. www.pioneerinstitute.org

Policy: The Centre for Independent Studies, P. O. Box 9, St. Leonards, NSW 1590 Australia, 011-61-2-9438-4377, Editor – Susan Windybank, quarterly. www.cis.org.au

Policy Review: Policy Review, 818 Connecticut Avenue, N.W., Suite 601, Washington, DC 20006, 202/466-6730, Editor – Tod Lindberg, bimonthly. www.policyreview.org

Political Science Reviewer: Intercollegiate Studies Institute, 3901 Centerville Road, P. O. Box 4431, Wilmington, DE 19807, 302/652-4600, Editor – George W. Carey, annual. www.isi.org

Priorities for Health: American Council on Science and Health, 1995 Broadway, 2nd Floor, New York, NY 10023, 212/362-7044, Editor-in-Chief – Jack Raso, quarterly. www.acsh.org

Privatization Watch: Reason Foundation, 3415 South Sepulveda Boulevard, Suite 400, Los Angeles, CA 90034, 310/391-2245, Editor – Geoffrey F. Segal, monthly. www.reason.org

Property Rights Reporter: Defenders of Property Rights, 1350 Connecticut Avenue, N.W., Suite 410, Washington, DC 20036, 202/822-6770, Editor – Nancie G. Marzulla, quarterly. www.defendersproprights.org

The Public Interest: National Affairs, Inc., 1112 16th Street, N.W., Suite 140, Washington, DC 20036, 202/785-8555, Editors – Irving Kristol and Nathan Glazer, quarterly. www.thepublicinterest.com

Quarterly Journal of Austrian Economics: Ludwig von Mises Institute, 518 West Magnolia Avenue, Auburn, AL 36832-4528, 334/321-2100, Editorial Vice President – Jeffrey Tucker, quarterly. www.mises.org

Reason: Reason Foundation, 3415 South Sepulveda Boulevard, Suite 400, Los Angeles, CA 90034-6064, 310/391-2245, Editor in Chief – Nick Gillespie, eleven issues per year. www.reason.org

Regulation: Cato Institute, 1000 Massachusetts Avenue, N.W., Washington, DC 20001, 202/842-0200, Editor – Peter VanDoren, quarterly. www.cato.org

Religion & Liberty: The Acton Institute for the Study of Religion and Liberty, 161 Ottawa Avenue, N.W., Suite 301, Grand Rapids, MI 49503, 616/454-3080, Editor – Greg Dunn bimonthly. www.acton.org

Russia and Eurasia Review: The Jamestown Foundation, 4516 43rd Street, NW Washington, DC 20016, 202/483-8888, Executive Editor – Harry Kopp, bimonthly. www.jamestown.org

Rutherford: The Rutherford Institute, P. O. Box 7482, Charlottesville, VA 22906-7482, 434/978-3888 quarterly. www.rutherford.org

School Reform News: The Heartland Institute, 19 South LaSalle, Suite 903, Chicago, IL 60603, 312/377-4000, Editor – Diane Carol Bast, monthly. www.heartland.org

Toward Tradition: Toward Tradition, P. O. Box 58, Mercer Island, WA 98040, 206/236-3046, Editorial Director – David Klinghoffer, quarterly. www.towardtradition.org

Tax Features: Tax Foundation, 1250 H Street, N.W., Suite 750, Washington, DC 20005, 202/783-2760, Editor – Bill Ahern, bimonthly. www.taxfoundation.org

The University Bookman: The Russell Kirk Center for Cultural Renewal, P. O. Box 4, Mecosta, MI 49332, 231/972-7655, Editor – Jeffery O. Nelson, quarterly. www.kirkcenter.org

Veritas: Texas Public Policy Foundation, P. O. Box 40519, San Antonio, TX 78229, 210/614-0080, President – Jeff M. Judson, quarterly. www.tppf.org

The Washington Quarterly: Center for Strategic and International Studies, 1800 K Street, NW, Suite 400, Washington DC 20006, 202/887-0200, Editor – Alexander T. J. Lennon, quarterly. www.csis.org

Washington Watch: Family Research Council, 801 G Street, N.W., Washington, DC 20001, 202/393-2100, Senior Editor – Karl Day, ten issues per year. www.frc.org

Washington Times National Weekly Edition: The Washington Times Corporation, 3600 New York Avenue, N.E., Washington, DC 20002, 202/636-3318, Managing Editor – Robert J. Morton, weekly. www.americasnewspaper.com

The Weekly Standard: News America Publishing, Inc., 1150 17th Street, N.W., Suite 505, Washington, DC 20036-4617, Editor – William Kristol, weekly. www.weeklystandard.com

Wisconsin Interest: Wisconsin Policy Research Institute, P. O. Box 487, Thiensville, WI 53092, 262/241-0514, Editor – Charles J. Sykes, published three times per year. www.wpri.org

World: World Magazine, Inc. (no mail), 85 Tunnel Road, Suite 12, Asheville, NC 28805, 828/232-5260, Editor-in-Chief – Marvin Olasky, weekly.

The Women's Quarterly: Independent Women's Forum, P. O. Box 3058, Arlington, VA 22203-0058, 703/558-4991, Editor – Charlotte Hays, quarterly. www.iwf.org

NOTES

NOTES

NOTES

EXPERTISE ONLINE

POLICY EXPERTS

A web version of this directory is updated regularly at:

www.policyexperts.org

Address data changes to policyexperts@heritage.org.

THE INSIDER

The *Insider*—a monthly newsletter published by Heritage's
Coalition Relations Department—features articles on current
issues, noteworthy excerpts from the public discourse, strategies for
media outreach and effectiveness, and other special items of
interest. Additionally, the *Insider* provides an annotated
bibliography of current articles, newsletters, books, and
publications by the the public policy community; the latest
developments on public-interest legal actions as well as inside the
conservative movement.

The Insider is available in its searchable database format at:

www.heritage.org/insider

THE HERITAGE FOUNDATION

To learn more about The Heritage Foundation and its programs, or to
access online versions of all Heritage publications, visit:

www.heritage.org